The American Constitution and the Judicial Process

The Dorsey Series in Political Science

Consulting Editor   SAMUEL C. PATTERSON   *The University of Iowa*

The American Constitution and the Judicial Process

WALLACE MENDELSON

Professor of Political Science
The University of Texas at Austin

 1980

The Dorsey Press
Homewood, Illinois 60430

IRWIN-DORSEY LIMITED
Georgetown, Ontario L7G 4B3

ISBN 0-256-02361-1
Library of Congress Catalog Card No. 79–54417

Printed in the United States of America

1 2 3 4 5 6 7 8 9 0 MP 7 6 5 4 3 2 1 0

M. J. M.

Though inland far we be,
Thou dost hear the boundless sea.
Thy heart is always doing lovely things.

Preface

This book differs in several ways from other "political science" casebooks on constitutional law. It generally avoids editorial "explanations" of the leading cases. Too many students read them rather than the opinions—and too many others, instead of analyzing the opinions for themselves, accept the editor's analysis at face value. This defeats the purpose of a casebook: student exposure to the challenge of the primary source material with all its subtleties and cross currents. Indeed in my view the material is so rich and so subject to differing interpretations, that any editor's "explanations"—attempting to simplify—are bound to be misleading.

Another difficulty in editorial predigestion of the cases is that it may—innocently no doubt—taint the material with the editor's biases and possible misunderstandings. Thus the instructor becomes something of a captive in his own classroom. For with many students the printed word is apt to carry more weight than the oral. In sum, I have tried to present the raw material with minimal interference in other people's classrooms. I have, however, presented numerous quaeres—in the hope of stimulating scholarly thought and discussion. This entails some risk. Authors may slant questions of course—so too straightforward questions may seem slanted to a biased reader. The rewards of the socratic method, one hopes, will justify these risks. The ultimate safeguard is the good sense of our students.

Unlike some case collections this one presents not only majority, but concurring and dissenting opinions. This, of course, is crucial for minority views often clarify or delineate the scope of the majority position. They sometimes indicate what lies beyond the legal horizon.

Finally, I have not skimped quantitatively. Not all of the cases are apt to be covered in a one-semester course. Yet this surely is a bonus. It gives the instructor room for choice (and experimentation from semester to semester). Above all, it serves the needs of specially gifted students, those who crave more than the average class can handle. Surely we owe them something extra. Even instructors who offer two-semester courses may find at least some leeway for choice—and a bit extra for students who want it.

For those who are not acquainted with the recording of Supreme Court decisions a few words of guidance may be useful. Prior to 1875, the Court's work was published by "authorized" reporters, as follows: Dallas (Dall.) 1789–1800; Cranch (Cr.) 1801–1815; Wheaton (Wheat.) 1816–1827; Peters (Pet.) 1828–1842; Howard (How.) 1843–1860; Black (Bl.) 1861–1862; Wallace (Wall.) 1863–1874. The famous case of *Marbury* v. *Madison,* for example, is found in 1 Cr. 137 (1803). This reference, or citation, means that the case was decided in 1803 and is included in Vol. 1 of the Cranch reports at page 137. Since 1874 the work of the Supreme Court has been set out in the official *Supreme Court Reports* (U.S. Government Printing Office). In this series a case is cited, or referred to, by a volume number; the abbreviation, U.S.; a page number; and the date of the decision. Thus *Gitlow* v. *New York,* 268 U.S. 652 (1925), was decided in 1925 and will be found in vol. 268 of the *Supreme Court Reports* at page 652. The foregoing citation systems are used in this book. There are, however, two rival private reporting systems; namely, *The Supreme Court Reporter* (West Publishing Company) and *United States Supreme Court Reports, Lawyers Edition* (Lawyer's Cooperative Publishing Company). The former is identified by the abbreviation, S. Ct., the latter by the abbreviation, L. Ed. Volume and page numbers and decision dates are used with these identifying symbols just as they are used as indicated above with respect to the official *Supreme Court Reports.* Thus the *Gitlow* case will be found in 268 U.S. 652 (1925) and also in 45 S. Ct. 625 (1925) and 69 L.Ed. 1138 (1925). At the beginning of each volume of the two private reporter systems there is a conversion table which translates the official into the private citation and vice versa.

Cases referred to in the text without citation have been cited earlier, or are reproduced with citations following the text material in which they are mentioned. Footnotes have been eliminated from virtually all of the opinions represented herein. Those that remain have been renumbered.

I gratefully acknowledge help from Henry Abraham, Robert Dixon, David Fellman, Tinsley Yarbrough, and several anonymous "readers".

Above all I am indebted to Kelly McWhirter, who worked so hard and pleasantly on the manuscript.

December 1979   **Wallace Mendelson**

Summary of Contents

Table of Contents

Note: An asterisk preceding a case title indicates that the case has been listed earlier, and is being used again to make a
different point in a different context.

part

I

DIFFUSION OF GOVERNMENTAL POWER AS A SHIELD FOR FREEDOM

1

Judicial Review: Adjudication vis-à-vis Legislation in the Making of Public Policy

JUDICIAL POWER

Marbury v. *Madison*
1 Cranch 137 (1803)

Near the end of the first Adams administration Congress authorized the President to appoint several justices of the peace for the District of Columbia. This was the occasion of the famous "midnight appointments" and the failure of Adams's Secretary of State to deliver the commissions of appointment. When the new administration took office, Secretary of State Madison, by direction of President Jefferson, refused delivery. Thereupon Marbury, one of the midnight appointees, went directly ("originally") to the Supreme Court requesting a judicial order (a writ of mandamus) to compel Madison to deliver his commission.

Article III, Section 2, of the Constitution gives the Supreme Court original jurisdiction only in cases "affecting Ambassadors, other public Ministers and Consuls, and those in which a State shall be a Party. . . ." Plainly Marbury's case did not fall in this category. Yet Marbury went originally to the Supreme Court, because in his view an act of Congress (Section 13 of the Judiciary Act of 1789) authorized him to do so. It was this apparent clash between the Constitution and the act of Congress which became the crux of the Court's decision.

Mr. Chief Justice Marshall delivered the opinion of the Court. [First he observed that Marbury had a vested right to the office in question, and that a writ of mandamus was the proper remedy for securing such a right. Then he turned to the problem of whether that remedy "can issue from this Court."]

The act to establish the judicial courts of the United States authorizes the Supreme Court "to issue writs of mandamus, in cases warranted by the principles and usages of law, to any courts appointed, or persons holding office, under the authority of the United States." . . . The Constitution vests the whole judicial power of

3

the United States in one Supreme Court, and such inferior courts as Congress shall, from time to time, ordain and establish. . . . In the distribution of this power, it is declared, that "the Supreme Court shall have original Jurisdiction, in all Cases affecting Ambassadors, other public Ministers and Consuls, and those in which a State shall be a Party. In all other cases, the Supreme Court shall have appellate jurisdiction." . . . If it had been intended to leave it in the discretion of the legislature, to apportion the judicial power between the Supreme and inferior courts, according to the will of that body, it would certainly have been useless to have proceeded further than to have defined the judicial power, and the tribunals in which it should be vested. The subsequent part of the section is mere surplusage—is entirely without meaning if such is to be the construction. . . . To enable this Court, then, to issue a mandamus, it must be shown to be an exercise of appellate jurisdiction, or to be necessary to enable them to exercise appellate jurisdiction. . . . It is the essential criterion of appellate jurisdiction, that it revises and corrects the proceedings in a cause already instituted, and does not create that cause. Although, therefore, a mandamus may be directed to courts, yet to issue such a writ to an officer, for the delivery of a paper, is, in effect, the same as to sustain an original action for that paper, and therefore, seems not to belong to appellate, but to original jurisdiction. Neither is it necessary in such a case as this, to enable the Court to exercise its appellate jurisdiction. The authority, therefore, given to the Supreme Court, by the act establishing the judicial courts of the United States, to issue writs of mandamus to public officers, appears not to be warranted by the Constitution; and it becomes necessary to inquire whether a jurisdiction so conferred can be exercised.

The question whether an act repugnant to the Constitution can become the law of the land, is a question deeply interesting to the United States; but, happily, not of an intricacy proportioned to its interest. It seems only necessary to recognize certain principles, supposed to have been long and well established, to decide it.

That the people have an original right to establish, for their future government, such principles as, in their opinion, shall most conduce to their own happiness, is the basis on which the whole American fabric has been erected. The exercise of this original right is a very great exertion; nor can it nor ought it to be frequently repeated. The principles, therefore, so established, are deemed fundamental. And as the authority from which they proceed is supreme, and can seldom act, they are designed to be permanent.

This original and supreme will organizes the government, and assigns to different departments their respective powers. It may either stop here, or establish certain limits not to be transcended by those departments.

The government of the United States is of the latter description. The powers of the legislature are defined and limited; and that those limits may not be mistaken, or forgotten, the Constitution is written. To what purpose are powers limited, and to what purpose is that limitation committed to writing, if these limits may, at any time, be passed by those intended to be restrained? The distinction between a government with limited and unlimited powers is abolished, if those limits do not confine the persons on whom they are imposed, and if acts prohibited and acts allowed are of equal obligation. It is a proposition too plain to be contested, that the Constitution controls any legislative act repugnant to it; or, that the legislation may alter the Constitution by an ordinary act.

Between these alternatives there is no middle ground. The Constitution is either a superior paramount law, unchangeable by ordinary means, or it is on a level with ordinary legislative acts, and, like other acts, is alterable when the legislature shall please to alter it.

If the former part of the alternative be true, then a legislative act contrary to the Constitution is not law; if the latter part be true, then written constitutions are absurd attempts, on the part of the people, to limit a power in its own nature illimitable.

Certainly all those who have framed written constitutions contemplate them as forming the fundamental and paramount law of the nation, and, consequently, the theory of every such government must be, than an act of the legislature, repugnant to the constitution, is void.

This theory is essentially attached to a written constitution, and is consequently to be considered, by this Court, as one of the fundamental principles of our society. It is not, therefore, to be lost sight of in the further consideration of this subject.

If an act of the legislature, repugnant to the Constitution, is void, does it, notwithstanding its invalidity, bind the courts, and oblige them to give it effect? Or, in other words, though it be not law, does it constitute a rule as operative as if it was a law? This would be to overthrow in fact what was established in theory; and would seem, at first view, an absurdity too gross to be insisted on. It shall, however, receive a more attentive consideration.

It is emphatically the province and duty of the judicial department to say what the law is. Those who apply the rule to particular cases, must of necessity expound and interpret that rule. If two laws conflict with each other, the courts must decide on the operation of each.

So if a law be in opposition to the Constitution; if both the law and the Constitution apply to a particular case, so that the court must either decide that case conformably to the law, disregarding the Constitution, or conformably to the Constitution, disregarding the law, the court must determine which of these conflicting rules governs the case. This is of the very essence of judicial duty.

If, then, the courts are to regard the Constitution, and the Constitution is superior to any ordinary act of the legislature, the Constitution, and not such ordinary act, must govern the case to which they both apply.

Those, then, who controvert the principle that the Constitution is to be considered, in court, as a paramount law, are reduced to the necessity of maintaining that court must close their eyes on the Constitution, and see only the law.

This doctrine would subvert the very foundation of all written constitutions. It would declare than an act which, according to the principles and theory of our government, is entirely void, is yet, in practice, completely obligatory. It would declare that if the legislature shall do what is expressly forbidden, such act, notwithstanding the express prohibition, is in reality effectual. It would be giving to the legislature a practical and real omnipotence, with the same breath which professes to restrict their powers within narrow limits. It is prescribing limits, and declaring that those limits may be passed at pleasure.

That it thus reduces to nothing what we have deemed the greatest improvement on political institutions, a written constitution, would of itself be sufficient, in America, where written constitutions have been viewed with so much reverence, for rejecting the construction. But the peculiar expressions of the Constitution of the United States furnish additional arguments in favor of its rejection.

The judicial power of the United States is extended to all cases arising under the Constitution.

Could it be the intention of those who gave this power, to say that in using it the Constitution should not be looked into? That a case arising under the Constitution should be decided without examining the instrument under which it arises?

This is too extravagant to be maintained.

In some cases, then, the Constitution must be looked into by the judges. And if they can open it at all, what part of it are they forbidden to read or to obey?

There are many other parts of the Constitution which serve to illustrate this subject.

It is declared that "No Tax or Duty shall be

laid on Articles exported from any State." Suppose a duty on the export of cotton, of tobacco, or of flour; and a suit instituted to recover it. Ought judgment to be rendered in such a case? Ought the judges to close their eyes on the Constitution, and only see the law?

The Constitution declares that "No Bill of Attainder or ex post facto Law shall be passed."

If, however, such a bill should be passed, and a person should be prosecuted under it, must the court condemn to death those victims whom the Constitution endeavors to preserve?

"No Person," says the Constitution, "shall be convicted of Treason unless on the Testimony of two Witnesses to the same overt Act, or on Confession in open Court."

Here the language of the Constitution is addressed especially to the courts. It prescribes, directly for them, a rule of evidence not to be departed from. If the legislature should change that rule, and declare one witness, or a confession out of court, sufficient for conviction, must the constitutional principle yield to the legislative act?

From these, and many other selections which might be made, it is apparent that the framers of the Constitution contemplated that instrument as a rule for the government of courts, as well as of the legislature.

Why otherwise does it direct the judges to take an oath to support it? This oath certainly applies in an especial manner to their conduct in their official character. How immoral to impose it on them, if they were to be used as the instruments, and the knowing instruments, for violating what they swear to support!

The oath of office, too, imposed by the legislative opinion on this subject. It is in these words: "I do solemnly swear that I will administer justice without respect to persons, and do equal right to the poor and to the rich; and that I will faithfully and impartially discharge all the duties incumbent on me as _____, according to the best of my abilities and understanding, agreeably to the Constitution and laws of the United States."

Why does a judge swear to discharge his duties agreeably to the Constitution of the United States, if that Constitution forms no rule for his government? if it is closed upon him, and cannot be inspected by him?

If such be the real state of things, this is worse than solemn mockery. To prescribe, or to take this oath, becomes equally a crime.

It is also not entirely unworthy of observation, that in declaring what shall be the supreme law of the land, the Constitution itself is first mentioned; and not the laws of the United States generally, but those only which shall be made in pursuance of the Constitution, have that rank.

Thus, the particular phraseology of the Constitution of the United States confirms and strengthens the principle, supposed to be essential to all written constitutions, that a law repugnant to the Constitution is void; and that courts, as well as other departments, are bound by that instrument.

Dred Scott v. *Sandford*
19 Howard 393 (1857)

Marbury was the first case in which the Supreme Court held an act of Congress unconstitutional; *Dred Scott* was the second. While the first involved only a narrow technical matter of no great significance to the nation, the second involved a major—perhaps *the* major—issue of national policy in antebellum America. The problem was this. Many Americans were at the very least skeptical of slavery and did not want it to spread into the new territories. Others insisted on freedom for Southerners to carry their institutions—their way of life—wherever they chose. This conflict of views was resolved with respect to the Louisiana Purchase by the Missouri Compromise in 1820. It provided that slavery could be introduced into the southern, but not into the northern, part of the Louisiana territory. The dividing line was 36°30' north latitude.

The problem arose again in the 1840s with the acquisition of the Mexican and Oregon territories. The Wilmot Proviso, supported by all but one Northern state legislature, would have outlawed slavery in *all* of the new domain. After its adoption by the United States House of Representatives in 1847, Southern leaders abandoned their willingness to extend the Missouri Compromise and insisted that Congress had no power to exclude slavery from any territory. Inevitably, then, the Wilmot Proviso died in the United States Senate, where the South was dominant (there states, not people, are represented equally).

The result was that for years the new territories had to do without government, because Congress was deadlocked on the issue of slavery extension. The Compromise of 1850 and the Kansas-Nebraska Act of 1854 left the issue open—*the Senate and House being hopelessly divided.* After years of congressional indecision the Supreme Court undertook in *Dred Scott* to settle the issue by killing both the Missouri Compromise approach and, implicitly, the Wilmot Proviso in favor of constitutional freedom for slavery in all of the territories. This, it has been said, was a major step toward the Civil War.

Dred Scott—plainly a test case—arose as follows. Scott, a slave in Missouri, was taken by his master to live in free territory, that is, where the Missouri Compromise purported to outlaw slavery. Thereafter Scott returned to Missouri and sued his new master for his freedom, on the basis that residence in free territory had made him free. The suit began in a federal court, which, per Article III of the Constitution, had jurisdiction of cases between *citizens* of different states. Scott claimed to be a Missouri citizen, while his "master" was a citizen of New York.

Mr. Chief Justice Taney delivered the opinion of the court. . . .

[The Court observed first that persons of African descent "were not intended to be included" as citizens of the United States but were considered by the Founding Fathers "as a subordinate and inferior class of beings, who . . . had no rights or privileges but such as those who held the power and the government might choose to grant them."]

Now if the removal [to free territory] did not give [Scott and his family] their freedom, then by his own admission he is still a slave; and whatever opinions may be entertained in favor of a free person of the African race, no one supposes that a slave is a citizen of the State or of the United States. If, therefore, the acts done by his owner did not make them free persons, he is still a slave, and certainly incapable of suing in the character of a citizen. . . .

The Act of Congress, upon which the plaintiff relies [the Missouri compromise], declares that slavery and involuntary servitude, except as a punishment for crime, shall be forever prohibited in all that part of the territory ceded by France, under the name of Louisiana, which lies north of thirty-six degrees thirty minutes north latitude, and not included within the limits of Missouri. And the difficulty which meets us at the threshold of this part of the inquiry is, whether Congress was authorized to pass this law under any of the powers granted to it by the Constitution; for if the authority is not given by that instrument, it is the duty of this court to declare it void and inoperative, and incapable of conferring freedom upon any one who is held as a slave under the laws of any one of the States. . . . The Territory being a part of the United States, the Government and the citizen both enter it under the authority of the Constitution, with their respective rights defined and marked out; and the Federal Government can exercise no power over his person or property, beyond what the instrument confers, nor lawfully deny any right which it has reserved.

A reference to a few of the provisions of the Constitution will illustrate this proposition.

For example, no one, we presume, will contend that Congress can make any law in a Territory respecting the establishment of religion, or the free exercise thereof, or abridging the freedom of speech or of the press, or the right of the people of the Territory peaceably to assemble, and to petition the Government for the redress of grievances.

Nor can Congress deny to the people the right to keep and bear arms, nor the right to trial by jury, nor compel any one to be a witness against himself in a criminal proceeding.

These powers, and others, in relation to rights of person, which it is not necessary here to enumerate, are, in express and positive terms, denied to the General Government; and the rights of private property have been guarded with equal care. Thus the rights of property are united with the rights of person, and placed on the same ground by the fifth amendment to the Constitution. . . . An Act of Congress which deprives a person of the United States of his liberty or property merely because he came himself or brought his property into a particular Territory of the United States, and who had committed no offense against the laws, could hardly be dignified with the name of due process of law. . . .

And this prohibition is not confined to the States, but the words are general, and extend to the whole territory over which the Constitution gives it power to legislate, including those portions of it remaining under territorial government, as well as that covered by States. It is a total absence of power everywhere within the dominion of the United States, and places the citizens of a territory, so far as these rights are concerned, on the same footing with citizens of the States, and guards them as firmly and plainly against any inroads which the general government might attempt, under the plea of implied or incidental powers. And if Congress itself cannot do this—if it is beyond the powers conferred on the Federal Government—it will be admitted, we presume, that it could not authorize a territorial government to exercise them. It could confer no power on any local government, established by its authority, to violate the provisions of the Constitution.

It seems, however, to be supposed, that there is a difference between property in a slave and other property, and that different rules may be applied to it in expounding the Constitution of the United States. And the laws and usages of nations, and the writings of eminent jurists upon the relation of master and slave and their mutual rights and duties, and the powers which governments may exercise over it, have been dwelt upon in the argument.

But . . . if the Constitution recognizes the right of property of the master in a slave, and makes no distinction between that description of property and other property owned by a citizen, no tribunal, acting under the authority of the United States, whether it be legislative, executive, or judicial, has a right to draw such a distinction, or deny to it the benefit of the provisions and guarantees which have been provided for the protection of private property against the encroachments of the Government.

Now . . . the right of property in a slave is distinctly and expressly affirmed in the Constitution. The right to traffic in it, like an ordinary article of merchandise and property, was guaranteed to the citizens of the United States, in every State that might desire it, for twenty years. And the Government in express terms is pledged to protect it in all future time, if the slave escapes from his owner. . . . And no word can be found in the Constitution which gives Congress a greater power over slave property, or which entitles property of that kind to less protection than property of any other description. The only power conferred is the power coupled with the duty of guarding and protecting the owner in his rights.

Upon these considerations, it is the opinion of the court that the Act of Congress [the Missouri Compromise] which prohibited a citizen from holding and owning property of this kind in the territory of the United States north of the line therein mentioned, is not warranted by the Constitution, and is therefore void; and that neither Dred Scott himself, nor any of his family, were made free by being carried into this territory; even if they had been carried there by the owner, with the intention of becoming a permanent resident. . . .

Upon the whole, therefore, it is the judgment of this court, that it appears by the record before us that the plaintiff in error is not a citizen of Missouri, in the sense in which that word is used in the Constitution; and that the Circuit Court of the United States, for that reason, had no jurisdiction in the case, and could give no judgment in it.

Its judgment for the defendant must, consequently, be reversed, and a mandate issued directing the suit to be dismissed for want of jurisdiction.

[Justices Wayne, Nelson, Daniel, Campbell, and Catron delivered concurring opinions. Mr. Justice Grier concurred in the opinions of Chief Justice Taney and Mr. Justice Nelson.]

Mr. Justice McLean dissenting. . . .

In the argument, it was said that a colored citizen would not be an agreeable member of society. This is more a matter of taste than of law. Several of the States have admitted persons of color to the right of suffrage, and in this view have recognised them as citizens; and this has been done in the slave as well as the free States. On the question of citizenship, it must be admitted that we have not been very fastidious. Under the late treaty with Mexico, we have made citizens of all grades, combinations, and colors. The same was done in the admission of Louisiana and Florida. No one ever doubted,

and no court ever held, that the people of these Territories did not become citizens under the treaty. They have exercised all the rights of citizens, without being naturalized under the acts of Congress. . . .

We need not refer to the mercenary spirit which introduced the infamous traffic in slaves, to show the degradation of negro slavery in our country. This system was imposed upon our colonial settlements by the mother country, and it is due to truth to say that the commercial colonies and States were chiefly engaged in the traffic. But we know as a historical fact, that James Madison, that great and good man, a leading member in the Federal Convention, was solicitous to guard the language of that instrument so as not to convey the idea that there could be property in man.

I prefer the lights of Madison, Hamilton, and Jay, as a means of construing the Constitution in all its bearings, rather than to look behind that period, into a traffic which is now declared to be piracy, and punished with death by Christian nations. I do not like to draw the sources of our domestic relations from so dark a ground. Our independence was a great epoch in the history of freedom; and while I admit the Government was not made especially for the colored race, yet many of them were citizens of the New England States, and exercised the rights of suffrage when the Constitution was adopted, and it was not doubted by any intelligent person that its tendencies would greatly ameliorate their condition.

Many of the States, on the adoption of the Constitution, or shortly afterward, took measures to abolish slavery within their respective jurisdictions; and it is a well-known fact that a belief was cherished by the leading men, South as well as North, that the institution of slavery would gradually decline, until it would become extinct. The increased value of slave labor, in the culture of cotton and sugar, prevented the realization of this expectation. Like all other communities and States, the South were influenced by what they considered to be their own interests. . . .

Mr. Justice Curtis dissenting. . . .

The conclusions at which I have arrived on this part of the case are:

First. That the free native-born citizens of each State are citizens of the United States.

Second. That as free colored persons born within some of the States are citizens of those States, such persons are also citizens of the United States.

Third. That every such citizen, residing in any State, has the right to sue and is liable to be sued in the federal courts, as a citizen of that State in which he resides.

Fourth. That as the plea to the jurisdiction in this case shows no facts, except that the plaintiff was of African descent, and his ancestors were sold as slaves, and as these facts are not inconsistent with his citizenship of the United States, and his residence in the State of Missouri, the plea to the jurisdiction was bad, and the judgment of the Circuit Court overruling it, was correct.

I dissent, therefore, from that part of the opinion of the majority of the court, in which it is held that a person of African descent cannot be a citizen of the United States; . . .

Nor, in my judgment, will the position, that a prohibition to bring slaves into a Territory deprives any one of his property without due process of law, bear examination.

It must be remembered that this restriction on the legislative power is not peculiar to the Constitution of the United States; it was borrowed from Magna Charta; was brought to America by our ancestors, as part of their inherited liberties, and has existed in all the States, usually in the very words of the great charter. It existed in every political community in America in 1787, when the ordinance prohibiting slavery north and west of the Ohio was passed.

And if a prohibition of slavery in a Territory in 1820 violated this principle of Magna Charta, the ordinance of 1787 also violated it; and what power had, I do not say the Congress of the Confederation alone, but the Legislature of Virginia, or the Legislature of any or all the States of the Confederacy, to consent to such a violation? The people of the States had conferred no such power. I think I may at least say, if the Congress did then violate Magna Charta by the ordinance, no one discovered that violation. Besides, if the prohibition upon all persons, citizens as well as others, to bring slaves into a Territory, and a declaration that if brought they shall be free, deprives citizens of their property without due process of law, what shall we say of the legislation of many of the slaveholding States which have enacted the same prohibition? As early as October, 1778, a law was passed in Virginia, that thereafter no slave should be imported into that Commonwealth by sea or by land, and that every slave who should be imported should become free. . . . I am not aware that such laws, though they exist in many States, were ever supposed to be in conflict with the principle of Magna Charta incorporated into the State Constitution. It was certainly understood by the Convention which framed the Constitution, and has been so understood ever since, that, under the power to regulate commerce, Congress could prohibit the importation of slaves; and the exercise of the power was restrained till 1808. A citizen of the United States owns slaves in Cuba, and brings them to the United States, where they are set free by the legislation of Congress. Does this legislation deprive him of his property without due process of law? If so, what becomes of the laws prohibiting the slave trade? If not, how can a similar regulation respecting a Territory violate the fifth amendment of the Constitution? . . .

Note and quaere: The implications of *Marbury* with respect to judicial policymaking became clear in *Dred Scott*—if they had not already been made clear in *Fletcher v. Peck, 6 Cranch 87 (1810), the first case in which the Court found a state law unconstitutional. It is crucial that the power of judicial review—whether used aggressively as in Dred Scott and Fletcher or with restraint—applies* not only to federal and state legislation but to acts of the President; the federal administrative agencies; the lower federal courts; the state governors; the state administrative agencies; the state courts; all counties, cities, and towns; and school and other special districts—in sum, all agencies of government in the United States.

Might a foreign observer find this concentration of power confusing, in view of our outspoken commitment to the diffusion of governmental power? In view of our dedication to the ideal of democracy and the rule of law, might such an observer be further confused by the fact that the ultimate holders of such power are not elected by the people, nor are their acts subject to judicial inquiry (i.e., the rule of law), as are the acts of all others who wield governmental power in this country? Are these seeming paradoxes more apparent than real? Could we be confident of explaining them satisfactorily to intelligent outside observers? Does the awsome scope of judicial review explain (or justify) the principle of "judicial restraint" or antiactivisim, which some judges insist on (or at least profess)?

The Judiciary Act of 1789, Section 25

This measure, adopted by the first Congress, authorized Supreme Court review of final state court decisions which *reject* claims (or rights) based on the federal Constitution, treaties, or laws. All such cases, according to this legislation, "may be reexamined and reversed or affirmed in the Supreme Court." Obviously the first Congress (some 19 members of which had been members of the Constitutional Convention) believed that state courts would have the power of judicial review, and that in such matters the Supreme Court should have the last judicial word. Otherwise national law—including the Constitution—could be interpreted *with finality* to mean different things by the courts of different states. Congress and President Washington (who approved the Judiciary Act of 1789) apparently recognized well in advance of *Marbury* v. *Madison* that judicial review was to be a basic part of our governmental system.

Section 25 was challenged and upheld in *Martin* v. *Hunter's Lessee,* 1 Wheaton 304 (1816), as well as in *Cohens* v. *Virginia* (below).

Cohens v. Virginia
6 Wheaton 264 (1821)

Cohens had been convicted in a state court for violating a Virginia antilottery statute. Having exhausted all state appeals, he sought review by the Supreme Court of the United States on "federal question" grounds; that is, because of an alleged conflict between the state law and a federal law authorizing lotteries. Section 25 of the Judiciary Act of 1789 gave the Supreme Court reviewing authority in such cases. In exercising it, Marshall's Court let stand Cohens's conviction on the ground that the congressional lottery act applied only in the District of Columbia. The decision is important not for that holding, but because of the Supreme Court's repudiation of Virginia's argument that the federal tribunal had no authority to review the judgment of a state court in a case involving federal law.

Mr. Chief Justice Marshall delivered the opinion of the Court: . . .

The questions presented to the court by the first two points made at the bar are of great magnitude, and may truly be said vitally to affect the Union. They exclude the inquiry whether the Constitution and laws of the United States have been violated by the judgment which the plaintiffs in error seek to review; and maintain that, admitting such violation, it is not in the power of the government to apply a corrective. They maintain that the nation does not possess a department capable of restraining, peaceably, and by authority of law, any attempts which may be made, by a part, against the legitimate powers of the whole; and that the government is reduced to the alternative of submitting to such attempts, or of resisting them by force. They maintain that the Constitution of the United States has provided no tribunal for the final construction of itself, or of the laws or treaties of the nation; but that this power may be exercised in the last resort by the courts of every state of the Union. That the Constitution, laws, and treaties may receive as many constructions as there are states; and that this is not a mischief, or, if a mischief is irremediable. . . .

1st. The first question to be considered is, whether the jurisdiction of this court is excluded by the character of the parties, one of them being a state, and the other a citizen of that state?

The 2d section of the third article of the Constitution defines the extent of the judicial power of the United States. Jurisdiction is given to the courts of the Union in two classes of cases. In the first, their jurisdiction depends on the character of the cause, whoever may be the parties. This class comprehends "all cases in law and equity arising under this Constitution, the laws of the United States, and treaties made, or which shall be made, under their authority." This clause extends the jurisdiction of the court to all the cases described, without making in its terms any exception whatever, and without any regard to the condition of the party. If there be any exception, it is to be implied against the express words of the article.

In the second class, the jurisdiction depends entirely on the character of the parties. In this are comprehended "controversies between two or more States, between a State and citizens of another State," "and between a State and foreign states, citizens, or subjects." If these be the parties, it is entirely unimportant what may be the subject of controversy. Be it what it may, these parties have a constitutional right to come into the courts of the Union. . . .

If . . . a case arising under the Constitution, or a law, must be one in which a party comes into court to demand something conferred on him by the Constitution or a law, we think the construction too narrow. A case in law or equity consists of the right of the one part, as well as of the other, and may truly be said to arise under the Constitution or a law of the United States, whenever its correct decision depends on the construction of either. . . .

The jurisdiction of the court, then, being extended by the letter of the Constitution to all cases arising under it, or under the laws of the United States, it follows that those who would withdraw any case of this description from that jurisdiction, must sustain the exemption they claim, on the spirit and true meaning of the Constitution, which spirit and true meaning must be so apparent as to overrule the words which its framers have employed. The counsel for the defendant in error have undertaken to do this; and have laid down the general proposition, that a sovereign independent state is not suable, except by its own consent.

This general proposition will not be controverted. But its consent is not requisite in each particular case. It may be given in a general law. And if a state has surrendered any portion of its sovereignty, the question whether a liability to suit be a part of this portion, depends on the instrument by which the surrender is made. If upon a just construction of that instrument, it shall appear that the state has submitted to be sued, then it has parted with this sovereign right of judging in every case on the justice of its own pretensions, and has entrusted that power to a tribunal in whose impartiality it confides.

The American states, as well as the American people, have believed a close and firm Union to be essential to their liberty and to their happiness. They have been taught by experience, that this Union cannot exist without a government for the whole; and they have been taught by the same experience that this government would be a mere shadow, that must disappoint all their hopes, unless invested with large portions of that sovereignty which belongs to independent states. Under the influence of this opinion, and thus instructed by experience, the American people, in the conventions of their respective states, adopted the present Constitution.

If it could be doubted whether, from its nature, it were not supreme in all cases where it is empowered to act, that doubt would be removed by the declaration that "this Constitution, and the laws of the United States which shall be made in pursuance thereof and all treaties made, or which shall be made, under the authority of the United States, shall be the supreme law of the land; and the judges in every state shall be bound thereby, anything in the Constitution or laws of any state to the contrary notwithstanding."

This is the authoritative language of the American people; and, if gentlemen please, of the American states. It marks with lines too strong to be mistaken, the characteristic distinc-

tion between the government of the Union and those of the states. The general government, though limited as to its objects, is supreme with respect to those objects. This principle is a part of the Constitution; and if there by any who deny its necessity, none can deny its authority.

To this supreme government ample powers are confided; and if it were possible to doubt the great purposes for which they were so confided, the people of the United States have declared that they are given "in order to form a more perfect union, establish justice, insure domestic tranquillity, provide for the common defense, promote the general welfare, and secure the blessings of liberty to themselves and their posterity."

With the ample powers confided to this supreme government, for these interesting purposes, are connected many express and important limitations on the sovereignty of the states, which are made for the same purposes. The powers of the Union on the great subjects of war, peace, and commerce, and on many others, are in themselves limitations of the sovereignty of the states; but in addition to these, the sovereignty of the states is surrendered in many instances where the surrender can only operate to the benefit of the people, and where, perhaps, no other power is conferred on congress than a conservative power to maintain the principles established in the Constitution. The maintenance of these principles in their purity is certainly among the great duties of the government. One of the instruments by which this duty may be peaceably performed is the judicial department. It is authorized to decide all cases, of every description, arising under the Constitution or laws of the United States. From this general grant of jurisdiction, no exception is made of those cases in which a state may be a party. When we consider the situation of the government of the Union and of a state, in relation to each other; the nature of our Constitution; the subordination of the state governments to that Constitution; the great purpose for which jurisdiction over all cases arising under the Constitution and laws of the United States, is confided to the judicial department; are we at liberty to insert in this general grant, an exception of those cases in which a state may be a party? Will the spirit of the Constitution justify this attempt to control its words? We think it will not. We think a case arising under the Constitution or laws of the United States, is cognizable in the courts of the Union, whoever may be the parties to that case. . . .

. . . If jurisdiction depended entirely on the character of the parties, and was not given where the parties have not an original right to come into court, that part of the 2d section of the 3rd article, which extends the judicial power to all cases arising under the Constitution and laws of the United States, would be surplusage. It is to give jurisdiction where the character of the parties would not give it, that this very important part of the clause was inserted. It may be true, that the partiality of the state tribunals, in ordinary controversies between a state and its citizens, was not apprehended, and therefore the judicial power of the Union was not extended to such cases; but this was not the sole nor the greatest object for which this department was created. A more important, a much more interesting object, was the preservation of the Constitution and laws of the United States, so far as they can be preserved by judicial authority; and therefore the jurisdiction of the courts of the Union was expressly extended to all cases arising under that Constitution and those laws. If the Constitution or laws may be violated by proceedings instituted by a state against its own citizens, and if that violation may be such as essentially to affect the Constitution and the laws, such as to arrest the progress of government in its constitutional course, why should these cases be excepted from that provision which expressly extends the judicial power of the Union to *all* cases arising under the Constitution and laws? . . .

2d. The second objection to the jurisdiction of the court is, that its appellate power cannot be exercised, in any case, over the judgment of a state court.

This objection is sustained chiefly by arguments drawn from the supposed total separation of the judiciary of a state from that of the Union, and their entire independence of each other. The argument considers the federal judiciary as completely foreign to that of a state; and as being no more connected with it, in any respect whatever, than the court of a foreign state. If this hypothesis be just, the argument founded on it is equally so; but if the hypothesis be not supported by the Constitution, the argument fails with it.

This hypothesis is not found on any words in the Constitution, which might seem to countenance it, but on the unreasonableness of giving a contrary construction to words which seem to require it; and on the incompatibility of the application of the appellate jurisdiction to the judgments of state courts, with that constitutional relation which subsists between the government of the Union and the governments of those states which compose it.

Let this unreasonableness, this total incompatibility, be examined.

That the United States form, for many, and for most important purposes, a single nation, has not yet been denied. In war, we are one people. In making peace, we are one people. In all commercial regulations, we are one and the same people. In many other respects, the American people are one; and the government which is alone capable of controlling and managing their interests in all these respects, is the government of the Union. It is their government, and in that character, they have no other. America has chosen to be, in many respects, and to many purposes, a nation; and for all these purposes, her government is complete; to all these objects it is competent. The people have declared, that in the exercise of all powers given for these objects, it is supreme. It can, then, in effecting these objects, legitimately control all individuals or governments within the American territory. The constitution and laws of a state, so far as they are repugnant to the Constitution and laws of the United States, are absolutely void. These states are constituent parts of the United States; they are members of one great empire—for some purposes sovereign, for some purposes subordinate.

In a government so constituted, is it unreasonable, that the judicial power should be competent to give efficacy to the constitutional laws of the legislature? That department can decide on the validity of the constitution or law of a state, if it be repugnant to the Constitution or to a law of the United States. Is it unreasonable, that it should also be empowered to decide on the judgment of a state tribunal enforcing such unconstitutional law? Is it so very unreasonable, as to furnish a justification for controlling the words of the constitution?

We think it is not. We think that in a government acknowledgedly supreme, with respect to objects of vital interest to the nation, there is nothing inconsistent with sound reason, nothing incompatible with the nature of government, in making all its departments supreme, so far as respects those objects, and so far as is necessary to their attainment. The exercise of the appellate power over those judgments of the state tribunals which may contravene the Constitution or laws of the United States, is, we believe, essential to the attainment of those objects.

The propriety of entrusting the construction of the Constitution, and laws made in pursuance thereof, to the judiciary of the Union has not, we believe, as yet, been drawn into question. It seems to be a corollary from this political axiom, that the federal courts should either possess exclusive jurisdiction in such cases, or a power to revise the judgment rendered in them, by the state tribunals. If the federal and state courts have concurrent jurisdiction in all cases arising under the Constitution, laws, and treaties of the United States; and if a case of this description brought in a state court cannot be removed before judgment, nor revised after judgment, then the construction of the

Constitution, laws, and treaties of the United States is not confided particularly to their judicial department, but is confided equally to that department and to the state courts, however they may be constituted. "Thirteen independent courts," says a very celebrated statesman (and we have now more than twenty such courts), "of final jurisdiction over the same causes, arising upon the same laws, is a hydra in government, from which nothing but contradiction and confusion can proceed."

. . . Let the nature and objects of our Union be considered; let the great fundamental principles, on which the fabric stands, be examined; and we think, the result must be, that there is nothing so extravagantly absurd, in giving to the court of the nation the power of revising the decisions of local tribunals, on questions which affect the nation, as to require that words which import this power should be restricted by a forced construction. . . .

Judgment affirmed.

Madison on Section 25

James Madison, in a letter to J. C. Cabell, dated April 1, 1833, said:

. . . The jurisdiction claimed for the federal judiciary [under Section 25] is truly the only defensive armour of the federal government, or, rather, for the Constitution and laws of the United States. Strip it of that armour, and the door is wide open for nullification, anarchy, and convulsion. . . .

LIMITATIONS ON JUDICIAL POWER—JUSTICIABILITY

Introduction

Sheldon v. Sill (excerpt)
8 Howard 440 (1850)

It must be admitted, that if the Constitution had ordained and established the inferior courts, and distributed to them their respective powers, they could not be restricted or divested by Congress. But as it has made no such distribution, one of two consequences must result,—either that each inferior court created by Congress must exercise all the judicial powers not given to the Supreme Court, or that Congress, having the power to establish the courts, must define their respective jurisdictions. The first of these inferences has never been asserted, and could not be defended with any show of reason, and if not, the latter would seem to follow as a necessary consequence. And it would seem to follow, also, that, having a right to prescribe, Congress may withhold from any court of its creation jurisdiction of any of the enumerated controversies. Courts created by statute can have no jurisdiction but such as the statute confers. No one of them can assert a just claim to jurisdiction exclusively conferred on another, or withheld from all.

Note: The Norris-La Guardia Act of 1932 provided that yellow-dog contracts (see the *Adair* and *Coppage* cases, mentioned in notes below, Chapter 6) "shall not be enforceable in any court of the United States." This measure was upheld in *Lauf* v. *E. G. Skinner & Co.,* 303 U.S. 323 (1938).

Ex parte McCardle, 7 Wallace 506 (1869), involved a civilian held by the army for trial before a military tribunal because he had published subversive newspaper articles. He petitioned for a writ of habeas corpus, as authorized by an 1867 act of Congress. Having lost his case at the trial level, he appealed to the Supreme Court, also as authorized by the 1867 legislation. After the Supreme Court had heard the *appeal,* but before decision, Congress repealed that part of the 1867 act which authorized appeal to the Supreme Court in such cases. This was part of a congressional effort to "protect" Reconstruction from interference by the Supreme Court. The repeal act was upheld in *McCardle* even with respect to that case already pending in the Court.

Ashwander v. *TVA* (excerpt)
297 U.S. 288, 346–348 (1836)

Mr. Justice Brandeis, concurring . . . .

The Court developed, for its own governance in the cases confessedly within its jurisdiction, a series of rules under which it has avoided passing upon a large part of all the constitutional questions pressed upon it for decision. They are:

1. The Court will not pass upon the constitutionality of legislation in a friendly, non-adversary, proceeding, declining because to decide such questions "is legitimate only in the last resort, and as a necessity in the determination of real, earnest and vital controversy between individuals. It never was the thought that, by means of a friendly suit, a party beaten in the legislature could transfer to the courts an inquiry as to the constitutionality of the legislative act." *Chicago & Grand Trunk Ry.* v. *Wellman,* 143 U.S. 339, 345. . . .

2. The Court will not "anticipate a question of constitutional law in advance of the necessity of deciding it." *Liverpool, N. Y. & P. S. S. Co.* v. *Emigration Commissioners,* 113 U.S. 33, 39; . . . "It is not the habit of the Court to decide questions of a constitutional nature unless absolutely necessary to a decision of the case." *Burton* v. *United States,* 196 U.S. 283, 295.

3. The Court will not "formulate a rule of constitutional law broader than is required by the precise facts to which it is to be applied." *Liverpool, N. Y. & P. S. S. Co.* v. *Emigration Commissioners, supra.* . . .

4. The Court will not pass upon a constitutional question although properly presented by the record, if there is also present some other ground upon which the case may be disposed of. This rule has found most varied application. Thus, if a case can be decided on either of two grounds, one involving a constitutional question, the other a question of statutory construction or general law, the Court will decide only the latter. *Siler* v. *Louisville & Nashville R. Co.,*

213 U.S. 175, 191; *Light* v. *United States*, 220 U.S. 523, 538. Appeals from the highest court of a state challenging its decision of a question under the Federal Constitution are frequently dismissed because the judgment can be sustained on an independent state ground. *Berea College* v. *Kentucky*, 211 U.S. 45, 53.

5. The Court will not pass upon the validity of a statute upon complaint of one who fails to show that he is injured by its operation. *Tyler* v. *The Judges*, 179 U.S. 405; *Hendrick* v. *Maryland*, 235 U.S. 610, 621. Among the many applications of this rule, none is more striking than the denial of the right of challenge to one who lacks a personal or property right. Thus, the challenege by a public official interested only in the performance of his official duty will not be entertained. . . . In *Fairchild* v. *Hughes*, 258 U.S. 126, the Court affirmed the dismissal of a suit brought by a citizen who sought to have the Nineteenth Amendment declared unconstitutional. In *Massachusetts* v. *Mellon*, 262 U.S. 447, the challenge of the federal Maternity Act was not entertained although made by the Commonwealth on behalf of all its citizens.

6. The Court will not pass upon the constitutionality of a statute at the instance of one who has availed himself of its benefits. *Great Falls Mfg. Co.* v. *Attorney General*, 124 U.S. 581. . . .

7. "When the validity of an act of the Congress is drawn in question, and even if a serious doubt of constitutionality is raised, it is a cardinal principle that this Court will first ascertain whether a construction of the statute is fairly possible by which the question may be avoided." *Cromwell* v. *Benson*, 285 U.S. 22, 62."

Wallace Mendelson, "Mr. Justice Douglas . . . ," 38 *The Journal of Politics* 918 (1976) (excerpt)

Not so long ago it was sound liberal doctrine that judges should avoid as much as possible adjudication of constitutional issues. This view found classic expression in the Brandeis minor-

ity opinion in *Ashwander*. As the Justice put it off the bench, "The most important thing we do is not doing." The thought of course was that the fewer social issues preempted by courts, the more that are left for resolution via the democratic process. With the advant of the Roosevelt Court the Brandeis view become majority doctrine in *Rescue Army* v. *Municipal Court* [331 U.S. 549 (1947)]. Old-fashioned liberalism had won a major victory.

Deeply skeptical with respect to our political processes, today's "activists"—the new liberals?—seem markedly inclined to put their policy eggs in the judicial basket. Indeed their great victories have been won in court. And so it is not strange that a major element of modern activism is an effort to open more widely the gateway to the federal judiciary. Indeed it seems no more than caricature to suggest that the "neo-liberal" goal is to shunt as many policy issues as possible from the political processes to the federal courts, especially the Supreme Court.

Flast v. *Cohen* (excerpt)
392 U.S. 83, 84–97 (1968)

Mr. Chief Justice Warren delivered the opinion of the Court. . . .

The jurisdiction of federal courts is defined and limited by Article III of the Constitution. In terms relevant to the question for decision in this case, the judicial power of federal courts is constitutionally restricted to "cases" and "controversies." As is so often the situation in constitutional adjudication, those two words have an iceberg quality, containing beneath their surface simplicity submerged complexities which go to the very heart of our constitutional form of government. Embodied in the words "cases" and "controversies" are two complementary but somewhat different limitations. In part those words limit the business of federal courts to questions presented in an adversary context and in a form historically viewed as capable of resolution through the judicial process. And in part those words define the role assigned to the judiciary in a tripartite allocation of power to assure that the federal courts will not intrude into areas committed to the other branches of government. Justiciability is the term of art employed to give expression to this dual limitation placed upon federal courts by the case and controversy doctrine.

Justiciability is itself a concept of uncertain meaning and scope. Its reach is illustrated by the various grounds upon which questions sought to be adjudicated in federal courts have been held not to be justiciable. Thus, no justiciable controversy is presented when the parties seek adjudication of only a political question,[1] when the parties are asking for an advisory opinion,[2] when the question sought to be adjudicated has been mooted by subsequent developments,[3] and when there is no standing to maintain the action.[4] Yet it remains true that "[j]usticiability is . . . not a legal concept with a fixed content of susceptible or scientific verification. Its utilization is the resultant of many subtle pressures. . . ." *Poe* v. *Ullman*, 367 U.S. 497, 508 (1961).

Part of the difficulty in giving precise meaning and form to the concept of justiciability stems from the uncertain historical antecedents of the case and controversy doctrine. For example, Mr. Justice Frankfurter twice suggested that historical meaning could be imparted to the concepts of justiciability and case and controversy by reference to the practices of the courts of Westminster when the Constitution was adopted. *Joint Anti-Fascist Committee* v. *McGrath*, 341 U.S. 123, 150 (1951) (concurring opinion); *Coleman* v. *Miller*, 307 U.S. 433, 460

(1939) (concurring opinion). However, the power of English judges to deliver advisory opinions was well-established at the time the Constitution was drafted. 3 Davis, *Administrative Law Treatise* 127–128 (1958). And it is quite clear that "the oldest and most consistent thread in the federal law of justiciability is that federal courts will not give advisory opinions." Wright, *Federal Courts* 34 (1963).[5] Thus, the implicit policies embodied in Article III, and not history alone, impose the rule against advisory opinions on federal courts. When the federal judicial power is invoked to pass upon the validity of actions by the Legislative and Executive Branches of the Government, the rule against advisory opinions implements the separation of powers prescribed by the Constitution and confines federal courts to the role assigned them by Article III. See *Muskrat* v. *United States*, 219 U.S. 346 (1911); 3 Johnston, *Correspondence and Public Papers of John Jay* 486–489 (1893) (correspondence between Secretary of State Jefferson and Chief Justice Jay). However, the rule against advisory opinions also recognizes that such suits often "are not pressed before the Court with that clear concreteness provided when a question emerges precisely framed and necessary for decision from a clash of adversary argument exploring every aspect of a multifaced situation embracing conflicting and demanding interests." *United States* v. *Fruehauf*, 365 U.S. 146, 157 (1961). Consequently, the Article III prohibition against advisory opinions reflects the complementary constitutional considerations expressed by the justiciability doctrine: Federal judicial power is limited to those disputes which confine federal courts to a role consistent with a system of separated powers and which are traditionally thought to be capable of resolution through the judicial process.

Additional uncertainty exists in the doctrine of justiciability because that doctrine has become a blend of constitutional requirements

---

[1] See, *e.g.*, Commercial Trust Co. v. Miller, 262 U.S. 51 (1923); Luther v. Borden, 7 How. 1 (1849).

[2] See, *e.g.*, United States v. Fruehauf, 365 U.S. 146 (1961); Muskrat v. United States, 219 U.S. 346 (1911).

[3] See, *e.g.*, California v. San Pablo & T. R. Co., 149 U.S. 308 (1893).

[4] See, *e.g.*, Tileston v. Ullman, 318 U.S. 44 (1943); Frothingham v. Mellon, 262 U.S. 447 (1923).

[5] The rule against advisory opinions was established as early as 1793, see 3 Johnston, Correspondence and Public Papers of John Jay 486–489 (1893). . . .

and policy considerations. And a policy limitation is "not always clearly distinguished from the constitutional limitation." *Barrows* v. *Jackson*, 346 U.S. 249, 255 (1953). For example, in his concurring opinion in *Ashwander* v. *Tennessee Valley Authority*, 297 U.S. 288, 345–348 (1936), Mr. Justice Brandeis listed seven rules developed by this Court "for its own governance" to avoid passing prematurely on constitutional questions. Because the rules operate in "cases confessedly within [the Court's] jurisdiction," *id.*, at 346, they find their source in policy, rather than purely constitutional, considerations. However, several of the cases cited by Mr. Justice Brandeis in illustrating the rules of self-governance articulated purely constitutional grounds for decision. See, *e.g.*, *Massachusetts* v. *Mellon*, 262 U.S. 447 (1923); *Fairchild* v. *Hughes*, 258 U.S. 126 (1922); *Chicago & Grand Trunk R. Co.* v. *Wellman*, 143 U.S. 339 (1892). The "many subtle pressures" which cause policy considerations to blend into the constitutional limitations of Article III make the justiciability doctrine one of uncertain and shifting contours.

Standing to Litigate

THE PRE-WARREN ERA

Tileston v. *Ullman*
318 U.S. 44 (1943)

Per Curiam.

This case comes here on appeal to review a declaratory judgment of the Supreme Court of Errors of Connecticut that §§ 6246 and 6562 of the General Statutes of Connecticut of 1930—prohibiting the use of drugs or instruments to prevent conception, and the giving of assistance or counsel in their use—are applicable to appellant, a registered physician, and as applied to him are constitutional. 129 Conn. 84, 26 A.2d 582, 588.

The suit was tried and judgment rendered on the allegations of the complaint which are stipulated to be true. Appellant alleged that the statute, if applicable to him, would prevent his giving professional advice concerning the use of contraceptives to three patients whose condition of health was such that their lives would be endangered by child-bearing, and that appellees, law enforcement officers of the state, intend to prosecute any offense against the statute and "claim or may claim" that the proposed professional advice would constitute such an offense. The complaint set out in detail the danger to the lives of appellant's patients in the event that they should bear children, but contained no allegations asserting any claim under the Fourteenth Amendment of infringement of appellant's liberty or his property rights. The relief prayed was a declaratory judgment as to whether the statutes are applicable to appellant and if so whether they constitute a valid exercise of constitutional power "within the meaning and intent of Amendment XIV of the Constitution of the United States prohibiting a state from depriving any person of life without due process of law." On stipulation of the parties the state superior court ordered these questions of law reserved for the consideration and advice of the Supreme Court of Errors. That court, which assumed without deciding that the case was an appropriate one for a declaratory judgment, ruled that the statutes "prohibit the action proposed to be done" appellant and "are constitutional."

We are of the opinion that the proceeding in the state courts presents no constitutional question which appellant has standing to assert. The sole constitutional attack upon the statutes under the Fourteenth Amendment is confined to their deprivation of life—obviously not appellant's but his patients'. There is no allegation or proof that appellant's life is in danger. His patients are not parties to this proceeding and there is no basis on which we can say that he has standing to secure an adjudication of his patients' constitutional right to life, which they do not assert in their own behalf. . . . No question is raised in the record with respect to the deprivation of appellant's liberty or property in contravention of the Fourteenth Amendment nor is there anything in the opinion or judgment of the Supreme Court of Errors which indicates or would support a decision of any question other than those raised in the superior court and reserved by it for decision of the Supreme Court of Errors. That court's practice is to decline to answer questions not reserved. General Statutes § 5652; *Loomis Institute* v. *Healy*, 98 Conn. 102, 129, 119 A. 31; *John J. McCarthy Co.* v. *Alsop*, 122 Conn. 288, 298–99, 189 A. 464.

Since the appeal must be dismissed on the ground that appellant has no standing to litigate the constitutional question which the record presents, it is unnecessary to consider whether the record shows the existence of a genuine case or controversy essential to the exercise of the jurisdiction of this Court. *Cf. Nashville, C. & St. L. Ry. Co.* v. *Wallace*, 288 U.S. 249, 259.

Dismissed.

Note: In *Poe* v. *Ullman*, 367 U.S. 497 (1961), the plaintiffs asked the Court to declare unconstitutional Connecticut laws prohibiting the use of contraceptives. The action was dismissed on the ground that there was no justiciable *case or controversy* (see Constitution, Article III, Section 2) because the state had never tried to enforce them since their adoption in 1879:

> . . . federal judicial power is to be exercised to strike down legislation . . . only at the instance of one who is himself immediately harmed, or immediately threatened with harm, by the challenged action. . . . This court cannot be umpire to debates concerning harmless, empty shadows. To find it necessary to pass on these statutes now, in order to protect appellants from the hazards of prosecution, would be to close our eyes to reality.

Justices Black, Douglas, Harlan, and Stewart dissented. The crux of the dissenting position perhaps is found in the Harlan opinion:

> . . . the most substantial claim which these married persons press is their right to enjoy the privacy of their marital relations free of the enquiry of the criminal law. . . . And I cannot agree that their enjoyment of this privacy is not substantially impinged upon, when they are told that if they use contraceptives . . . the only thing that stands between them and being forced to render criminal account of their marital privacy is the whim of the prosecutor. . . .

Frothingham v. *Mellon*
262 U.S. 447 (1923)

This case was initiated by a federal taxpayer *as such*. She sought to enjoin enforcement of the federal Maternity Act of 1921—an early welfare measure authorizing grants-in-aid "to reduce maternal and infant mortality." She charged the act "is a usurpation of power not granted to Congress," and thus a violation of the Tenth Amendment. The case was dismissed "for want of jurisdiction."

Mr. Justice Sutherland delivered the opinion of the Court. . . .

[T]his . . . plaintiff alleges . . . that she is a taxpayer of the United States; and her contention, though not clear, seems to be that the effect of the appropriations complained of will be to increase the burden of future taxation and thereby take her property without due process of law. The right of a taxpayer to enjoin the execution of a federal appropriation act, on the ground that it is invalid and will result in taxation for illegal purposes, has never been passed upon by this Court. In cases where it was presented, the question has either been allowed to pass sub silentio or the determination of it expressly withheld. *Millard* v. *Roberts,* 202 U.S. 429, 438; *Wilson* v. *Shaw,* 204 U.S. 24, 31; *Bradfield* v. *Roberts,* 175 U.S. 291, 295. The case last cited came here from the Court of Appeals of the District of Columbia, and that court sustained the right of the plaintiff to sue by treating the case as one directed against the District of Columbia, and therefore subject to the rule frequently stated by this Court, that resident taxpayers may sue to enjoin an illegal use of the moneys of a municipal corporation. *Roberts* v. *Bradfield,* 12 App.D.C. 453, 459–460. The interest of a taxpayer of a municipality in the application of its moneys is direct and immediate and the remedy by injunction to prevent their misuse is not inappropriate. It is upheld by a large number of state cases and is the rule of this Court. *Crampton* v. *Zabriskie,* 101 U.S. 601, 609. Nevertheless, there are decisions to the contrary. See, for example, *Miller* v. *Grandy,* 13 Mich. 540, 550. The reasons which support the extension of the equitable remedy to a single taxpayer in such cases are based upon the peculiar relation of the corporate taxpayer to the corporation, which is not without some resemblance to that subsisting between stockholder and private corporation. IV *Dillon Municipal Corporations,* 5th Ed., § 1580 et seq. But the relation of a taxpayer of the United States to the Federal Government is very different. His interest in the moneys of the Treasury—partly realized from taxation and partly from other sources—is shared with millions of others; is comparatively minute and indeterminable; and the effect upon future taxation, of any payment out of the funds, so remote, fluctuating and uncertain, that no basis is afforded for an appeal to the preventive powers of a court of equity.

The administration of any statute, likely to produce additional taxation to be imposed upon a vast number of taxpayers, the extent of whose several liability is indefinite and constantly changing, is essentially a matter of public and not of individual concern. If one taxpayer may champion and litigate such a cause, then every other taxpayer may do the same, not only in respect of the statute here under review but also in respect of every other appropriation act and statute whose administration requires the outlay of public money, and whose validity may be questioned. The bare suggestion of such a result, with its attendant inconveniences, goes far to sustain the conclusion which we have reached, that a suit of this character cannot be maintained. It is of much significance that no precedent sustaining the right to maintain suits like this has been called to our attention, although, since the formation of the government, as an examination of the acts of Congress will disclose, a large number of statutes appropriating or involving the expenditure of moneys for non-federal purposes have been enacted and carried into effect.

The functions of government under our system are apportioned. To the legislative department has been committed the duty of making laws; to the executive the duty of executing them; and to the judiciary the duty of interpreting and applying them in cases properly brought before the courts. The general rule is that neither department may invade the province of the other and neither may control, direct or restrain the action of the other. We are not now speaking of the merely ministerial duties of officials. *Gaines* v. *Thompson,* 7 Wall. 347. We have no power per se to review and annul acts of Congress on the ground that they are unconstitutional. That question may be considered only when the justification for some direct injury suffered or threatened, presenting a justiciable issue, is made to rest upon such an act. Then the power exercised is that of ascertaining and declaring the law applicable to the controversy. It amounts to little more than the negative power to disregard an unconstitutional enactment, which otherwise would stand in the way of the enforcement of a legal right. The party who invokes the power must be able to show not only that the statute is invalid but that he has sustained or is immediately in danger of sustaining some direct injury as the result of its enforcement, and not merely that he suffers in some indefinite way in common with people generally. If a case for preventive relief be presented the court enjoins, in effect, not the execution of the statute, but the acts of the official, the statute notwithstanding. Here the . . . plaintiff [has] no such case. Looking through forms of words to the substance of [the] complaint, it is merely that officials of the executive department of the government are executing and will execute an act of Congress asserted to be unconstitutional; and this we are asked to prevent. To do so would be not to decide a judicial controversy, but to assume a position of authority over the governmental acts of another and coequal department, an authority which plainly we do not possess.

THE WARREN ERA

Flast v. *Cohen*
392 U.S. 83 (1968)

Mr. Chief Justice Warren delivered the opinion of the Court.

In *Frothingham* v. *Mellon,* 262 U.S. 447 (1923), this Court ruled that a federal taxpayer is without standing to challenge the constitutionality of a federal statute. That ruling has stood for 45 years as an impenetrable barrier to suits against acts of Congress brought by individuals who can assert only the interest of federal taxpayers. In this case, we must decide whether the *Frothingham* barrier should be lowered when a taxpayer attacks a federal statute on the ground that it violates the Establishment and Free Exercise Clauses of the First Amendment.

Appellants filed suit in the United States District Court for the Southern District of New York

to enjoin the allegedly unconstitutional expenditure of federal funds under Titles I and II of the Elementary and Secondary Education Act of 1965, 79 Stat. 27, 20 U.S.C. § 241a et seq., 821 et seq. (Supp. 1966). The complaint alleged that the seven appellants had as common attribute that "each pay income taxes of the United States," and it is clear from the complaint that the appellants were resting their standing to maintain the action solely on their status as federal taxpayers. The appellees, who are charged by Congress with administering the Elementary and Secondary Education Act of 1965, were sued in their official capacities.

The gravamen of the appellants' complaint was that federal funds appropriated under the Act were being used to finance instruction in reading, arithmetic, and other subjects in religious schools, and to purchase textbooks and other instructional materials for use in such schools. Such expenditures were alleged to be in contravention of the Establishment and Free Exercise Clauses of the First Amendment. . . .

[A three-judge court ruled] on the authority of *Frothingham* that appellants lacked standing. . . . For reasons explained at length below, we hold that appellants do have standing as federal taxpayers to maintain this action, and the judgment below must be reversed. . . .

II.

This Court first faced squarely the question whether a litigant asserting only his status as a taxpayer has standing to maintain a suit in a federal court in *Frothingham* v. *Mellon, supra,* and that decision must be the starting point for analysis in this case. . . .

Although the barrier *Frothingham* erected against federal taxpayer suits has never been breached, the decision has been the source of some confusion and the object of considerable criticism. The confusion has developed as commentators have tried to determine whether *Frothingham* establishes a constitutional bar to taxpayer suits or whether the Court was simply imposing a rule of self-restraint which was not constitutionally compelled. . . . The opinion delivered in *Frothingham* can be read to support either position. . . . Whatever the merits of the current debate over *Frothingham*, its very existence suggests that we should undertake a fresh examination of the limitations upon standing to sue in a federal court and the application of those limitations to taxpayer suits.

III.

. . . Standing is an aspect of justiciability and, as such, the problem of standing is surrounded by the same complexities and vagaries that inhere in justiciability. Standing has been called one of "the most amorphous [concepts] in the entire domain of public law." Some of the complexities peculiar to standing problems result because standing "serves, on occasion, as a shorthand expression for all the various elements of justiciability." In addition, there are at work in the standing doctrine the many subtle pressures which tend to cause policy considerations to blend into constitutional limitations.

Despite the complexities and uncertainties, some meaningful form can be given to the jurisdictional limitations placed on federal court power by the concept of standing. The fundamental aspect of standing is that it focuses on the party seeking to get his complaint before a federal court and not on the issues he wishes to have adjudicated. The "gist of the question of standing" is whether the party seeking relief has "alleged such a personal stake in the outcome of the controversy as to assure that concrete adverseness which sharpens the presentation of issues upon which the court so largely depends for illumination of difficult constitutional questions." *Baker* v. *Carr*, 369 U.S. 186, 204 (1962). In other words, when standing is placed in issue in a case, the question is whether the person whose standing is challenged is a proper party to request an adjudication of a particular issue and not whether the issue itself is justiciable. Thus, a party may have standing in a particular case, but the federal court may nevertheless decline to pass on the

merits of the case because, for example, it presents a political question. A proper party is demanded so that federal courts will not be asked to decide "ill-defined controversies over constitutional issues," *United Public Workers* v. *Mitchell*, 330 U.S. 75, 90 (1947), or a case which is of "a hypothetical or abstract character," *Aetna Life Insurance Co.* v. *Haworth*, 300 U.S. 227, 240 (1937): So stated, the standing requirement is closely related to, although more general than, the rule that federal courts will not entertain friendly suits, *Chicago & Grand Trunk R. Co.* v. *Wellman, supra,* 143 U.S. 339 (1892), or those which are feigned or collusive in nature, *United States* v. *Johnson,* 319 U.S. 302 (1943); *Lord* v. *Veazie,* 8 How. 251 (1850). . . .

[T]he emphasis in standing problems is on whether the party invoking federal court jurisdiction has "a personal stake in the outcome of the controversy," *Baker* v. *Carr, supra,* 369 U.S. at 204, and whether the dispute touches upon "the legal relations of parties having adverse legal interests." *Aetna Life Insurance Co.* v. *Haworth, supra,* at 300 U.S. 241. A taxpayer may or may not have the requisite personal stake in the outcome, depending upon the circumstances of the particular case. Therefore, we find no absolute bar in Article III to suits by federal taxpayers challenging allegedly unconstitutional federal taxing and spending programs. There remains, however, the problem of determining the circumstances under which a federal taxpayer will be deemed to have the personal stake and interest that imparts the necessary concrete adverseness to such litigation so that standing can be conferred on the taxpayer *qua* taxpayer consistent with the constitutional limitations of Article III.

IV.

. . .

The nexus demanded of federal taxpayers has two aspects to it. First, the taxpayer must establish a logical link between the status and the type of legislative enactment attacked. Thus, a taxpayer will be a proper party to allege the unconstitutionality only of exercises of congressional power under the taxing and spending clause of Art. I, § 8, of the Constitution. It will not be sufficient to allege an incidental expenditure of tax funds in the administration of an essentially regulatory statute. This requirement is consistent with the limitation imposed upon state taxpayer standing in federal courts in *Doremus* v. *Board of Education*, 342 U.S. 429 (1952). Secondly the taxpayer must establish a nexus between that status and the precise nature of the constitutional infringement alleged. Under this requirement, the taxpayer must show that the challenged enactment exceeds specific constitutional limitations imposed upon the exercise of the congressional taxing and spending power and not simply that the enactment is generally beyond the powers delegated to Congress by Art. I, § 8. When both nexuses are established, the litigant will have shown a taxpayer's stake in the outcome of the controversy and will be a proper and appropriate party to invoke a federal court's jurisdiction.

The taxpayer-appellants in this case have satisfied both nexuses to support their claim of standing under the test we announce today. Their constitutional challenge is made to an exercise by Congress of its power under Art. I, § 8, to spend for the general welfare, and the challenged program involves a substantial expenditure of federal tax funds. In addition, appellants have alleged that the challenged expenditures violate the Establishment and Free Exercise Clauses of the First Amendment. . . .

The allegations of the taxpayer in *Frothingham* v. *Mellon, supra,* were quite different from those made in this case, and the result in *Frothingham* is consistent with the test of taxpayer standing announced today. The taxpayer in *Frothingham* attacked a federal spending program and she, therefore, established the first nexus required. However, she lacked standing because her constitutional attack was not based on an allegation that Congress, in enacting the Maternity Act of 1921, had breached a specific limitation upon its taxing and spending power.

The taxpayer in *Frothingham* alleged essentially that Congress, by enacting the challenged statute, had exceeded the general powers delegated to it by Art. I, § 8, and that Congress had thereby invaded the legislative province reserved to the States by the Tenth Amendment. . . .

We have noted that the Establishment Clause of the First Amendment does specifically limit the taxing and spending power conferred by Art. I, § 8. Whether the Constitution contains other specific limitations can be determined only in the context of future cases. However, whenever such specific limitations are found, we believe a taxpayer will have a clear stake as a taxpayer in assuring that they are not breached by Congress. Consequently, we hold that a taxpayer will have standing consistent with Article III to invoke federal judicial power when he alleges that congressional action under the taxing and spending clause is in derogation of those constitutional provisions which operate to restrict the exercise of the taxing and spending power. The taxpayer's allegation in such cases would be that his tax money is being extracted and spent in violation of specific constitutional protections against such abuses of legislative power. Such an injury is appropriate for judicial redress, and the taxpayer has established the necessary nexus between his status and the nature of the allegedly unconstitutional action to support his claim of standing to secure judicial review. Under such circumstances, we feel confident that the questions will be framed with the necessary specificity, that the issues will be contested with the necessary adverseness and that the litigation will be pursued with the necessary vigor to assure that the constitutional challenge will be made in a form traditionally thought to be capable of judicial resolution. We lack that confidence in cases such as *Frothingham* where a taxpayer seeks to employ a federal court as a forum in which to air his generalized grievances about the conduct of government or the allocation of power in the Federal System.

While we express no view at all on the merits

of appellants' claims in this case, their complaint contains sufficient allegations under the criteria we have outlined to give them standing to invoke a federal court's jurisdiction for an adjudication on the merits.

Mr. Justice Douglas, concurring.

While I have joined the opinion of the Court, I do not think that the test it lays down is a durable one for the reasons stated by my Brother Harlan. I think, therefore, that it will suffer erosion and in time result in the demise of *Frothingham* v. *Mellon*, 262 U.S. 447. It would therefore be the part of wisdom, as I see the problem, to be rid of *Frothingham* here and now.

I do not view with alarm, as does my Brother Harlan, the consequences of that course. *Frothingham*, decided in 1923, was in the heyday of substantive due process, when courts were sitting in judgment on the wisdom or reasonableness of legislation. The claim in *Frothingham* was that a federal regulatory Act dealing with maternity deprived the plaintiff of property without due process of law. When the Court used substantive due process to determine the wisdom or reasonableness of legislation, it was indeed transforming itself into the Court of Revision which was rejected by the Constitutional Convention. It was that judicial attitude, not the theory of standing to sue rejected in *Frothingham*, that involved "important hazards for the continued effectiveness of the federal judiciary," to borrow a phrase from my Brother Harlan. A contrary result in *Frothingham* in that setting might well have accentuated an ominous trend to judicial supremacy.

But we no longer undertake to exercise that kind of power. Today's problem is in a different setting.

Most laws passed by Congress do not contain even a ghost of a constitutional question. The "political" decisions, as distinguished from the "justiciable" ones, occupy most of the spectrum of congressional action. The case or controversy requirement comes into play only when the Federal Government does something that affects a person's life, his liberty, or his property. . . .

Taxpayers can be vigilant private attorney generals. Their stake in the outcome of litigation may be *de minimis* by financial standards, yet very great when measured by a particular constitutional mandate. . . .

I would not be niggardly therefore in giving private attorneys general standing to sue. I would certainly not wait for Congress to give its blessing to our deciding cases clearly within our Article III jurisdiction. To wait for a sign from Congress is to allow important Constitutional questions to go undecided and personal liberty unprotected. . . .

Mr. Justice Stewart, concurring.

I join the judgment and opinion of the Court, which I understand to hold only that a federal taxpayer has standing to assert that a specific expenditure of federal funds violates the Establishment Clause of the First Amendment. Because that clause plainly prohibits taxing and spending in aid of religion, every taxpayer can claim a personal constitutional right not to be taxed for the support of a religious institution. The present case is thus readily distinguishable from *Frothingham* v. *Mellon*, 262 U.S. 447, where the taxpayer relied not on an explicit constitutional prohibition but questioned instead the scope of the powers delegated to the national legislature by Article I of the Constitution. . . .

Mr. Justice Fortas, concurring.

I would confine the ruling in this case to the proposition that a taxpayer may maintain a suit to challenge the validity of a federal expenditure on the ground that the expenditure violates the Establishment Clause. As the Court's opinion recites, there is enough in the constitutional history of the Establishment Clause to support the thesis that this Clause includes a *specific* prohibition upon the use of the power to tax to support an establishment of religion. There is no reason to suggest, and no basis in the logic of this decision for implying, that there may be other types of congressional expenditures which may be attacked by a litigant solely on the basis of his status as a taxpayer. . . .

Mr. Justice Harlan, dissenting [summary].

[The essence of this dissent was that the majority's test was "not in any sense a measurement of any plaintiff's interest in the outcome of any suit. [The] Court's standard for the determination of standing and its criteria for the satisfaction of that standard are entirely unrelated." Excluding expenditures "incidental" to an "essentially regulatory program" has nothing to do with a plaintiff's interest in the outcome of a suit. Is the Establishment Clause really "a more 'specific' limitation upon Congress' powers than are the various other constitutional commands"?

[The basic difficulty, per Mr. Justice Harlan, was that the Court was trying to retain a theoretical "personal interest" requirement while in fact recognizing the rights of "private attorneys general" to sue. Such "public action" suits, he thought, "involve important hazards for the continued effectiveness of the federal judiciary." The majority seems aware of this, but its limitations are "wholly untenable." Congress has authority, he felt, to permit plaintiffs without economic or other personal interest to bring public actions. The Court should wait for Congress to do so, if it should find them desirable.]

> *Note:* For comment on the lowering of justiciability barriers during the Warren era, see opinion of Mr. Justice Powell in *Richardson,* below.

THE POST-WARREN ERA

United States v. *Richardson*
418 U.S. 166 (1974)

Mr. Chief Justice Burger delivered the opinion of the Court.

We granted certiorari in this case to determine whether the respondent has standing to bring an action as a federal taxpayer alleging that certain provisions concerning public reporting of expenditures under the certain provisions concerning public reporting of expenditures under the Central Intelligence Agency Act of 1949 violate Art. I, § 9, cl. 7, of the Constitution which provides:

> "No Money shall be drawn from the Treasury, but in Consequence of Appropriations made by Law; and a regular Statement and Account of the Receipts and Expenditures of all public Money shall be published from time to time."

Respondent brought this suit in the United States District Court on a complaint in which he recites attempts to obtain from the Government information concerning detailed expenditures of the Central Intelligence Agency. . . . In essence, the respondent asked the federal court to declare unconstitutional that provision of the Central Intelligence Agency Act which permits the Agency to account for its expenditures "solely on the certificate of the Director." The only injury alleged by respondent was that he "cannot obtain a document that sets out the expenditures and receipts" of the CIA but on the contrary was "asked to accept a fraudulent document." The District Court granted a motion for dismissal on the ground respondent lacked standing under [*Flast*], and that the subject matter raised political questions not suited for judicial disposition.

The Court of Appeals sitting en banc, with three judges dissenting, reversed, holding that the respondent had standing to bring this action. The majority relied chiefly on [the "two-tier test" of *Flast*]. . . . We conclude that respondent lacks standing to maintain a suit for the relief sought and we reverse.

I. . . . Recently in *Association of Data Processing Service Organizations, Inc.* v. *Camp,* 397 U.S. 150 (1970), the Court, while noting that "[g]eneralizations about standing to sue are largely worthless as such," emphasized that "[o]ne generalization is, however, necessary and that is that the question of standing in the federal courts is to be considered in the framework of Article III which restricts judicial power to 'cases' and 'controversies.'" Although the recent holding of the Court in [*Flast*] is a starting point in an examination of respondent's claim to prosecute this suit as a taxpayer, that case must be read with reference to its principal predecessor, [*Frothingham*]. . . . While the "impenetrable barrier to suits against Acts of Congress brought by individuals who can assert only the interest of federal taxpayers," had been slightly lowered [in *Flast*], the Court made clear it was reaffirming the principle of Forthingham precluding a taxpayer's use of "a federal court as a forum in which to air his generalized grievances." . . .

II.   Although the Court made it very explicit in *Flast* that a "fundamental aspect of standing" is that it focuses primarily on the *party* seeking to get his complaint before the federal court rather than "on the issues he wishes to have adjudicated," it made equally clear that

> "in ruling on [taxpayer] standing, it is both appropriate and necessary to look to the substantive issues for another purpose, namely, to determine whether there is a logical nexus between the status asserted and the claim sought to be adjudicated."

We therefore turn to an examination of the issues sought to be raised by respondent's complaint to determine whether he is "a proper and appropriate party to invoke federal judicial power" with respect to those issues.

We need not and do not reach the merits of the constitutional attack on the statue; our inquiry into the "substantive issues" is for the limited purpose indicated above. The mere recital of the respondent's claims and an examination of the statute under attack demonstrate how far he falls short of the standing criteria of *Flast* and how neatly he falls within the *Frothingham* holding left undisturbed. Although the

status he rests on is that he is a taxpayer, his challenge is not addressed to the taxing or spending power, but to the statutes regulating the CIA, specifically 50 U.S.C. § 403J(b). That section provides different accounting and reporting requirements and procedures for the CIA, as is also done with respect to other governmental agencies dealing in confidential areas.

Respondent makes no claim that appropriated funds are being spent in violation of a "specific constitutional limitation upon the [taxing and spending power]." Rather, he asks the courts to compel the Government to give him information on precisely how the CIA spends its funds. Thus there is no "logical nexus" between the asserted status of taxpayer and the claimed failure of the Congress to require the Executive to supply a more detailed report of the expenditures of that agency.

The question presented thus is simply and narrowly whether these claims meet the standards for taxpayer standing set forth in *Flast*; we hold they do not. Respondent is seeking "to employ a federal court as a forum in which to air his generalized grievances about the conduct of government." Both *Frothingham* and *Flast* reject that basis for standing.

III.   The Court of Appeals held that the basis of taxpayer standing "need not always be the appropriation and the spending of [taxpayer's] money for an invalid purpose. The personal stake may come from an injury in fact even if it is not directly economic in nature."

The respondent's claim is that without detailed information on CIA expenditures—and hence its activities—he cannot intelligently follow the actions of Congress or the Executive, nor can he properly fulfill his obligations as a member of the electorate in voting for candidates seeking national office.

This is surely the kind of a generalized grievance described in both *Frothingham* and *Flast* since the impact on him is plainly undifferentiated and "common to all members of the public." *Ex parte Lévitt*, 302 U.S. 633, 634 (1937); *Laird* v. *Tatum*, 408 U.S. 1, 13 (1972). While we can hardly dispute that this respondent has a genuine interest in the use of funds and that his interest may be prompted by his status as a taxpayer, he has not alleged that, as a taxpayer, he is in danger of suffering any particular concrete injury as a result of the operation of this statute. As the Court noted in *Sierra Club* v. *Morton*, 405 U.S. 727 (1972), "a mere 'interest in a problem,' no matter how longstanding the interest and no matter how qualified the organization is in evaluating the problem, is not sufficient by itself to render the organization 'adversely affected' or 'aggrieved' within the meaning of the APA."

Ex parte Lévitt, supra, is especially instructive. There Lévitt sought to challenge the validity of the commission of a Supreme Court Justice who had been nominated and confirmed as such while he was a member of the Senate. Lévitt alleged that the appointee had voted for an increase in the emoluments provided by Congress for Justices of the Supreme Court during the term for which he was last elected to the United States Senate. The claim was that the appointment violated the explicit prohibition of Art. I, § 6, cl. 2, of the Constitution. The Court disposed of Lévitt's claim, stating: "It is an established principle that to entitle a private individual to invoke the judicial power to determine the validity of executive or legislative action he must show that he *has sustained or is immediately in danger of sustaining a direct injury* as the result of that action and it is not sufficient that he has merely a general interest common to all members of the public." (Emphasis supplied.)

Of course, if Lévitt's allegations were true, they made out an arguable violation of an explicit prohibition of the Constitution. Yet even this was held insufficient to support standing because, whatever Lévitt's injury, it was one he shared with "all members of the public." Respondent here, like the petitioner in *Lévitt*, also fails to clear the threshold hurdle of [*Baker* v. *Carr* and *Flast*].

It can be argued that if respondent is not permitted to litigate this issue, no one can do so. In a very real sense, the absence of any particular individual or class to litigate these claims gives support to the argument that the subject matter is committed to the surveillance of Congress, and ultimately to the political process. Any other conclusion would mean that the Founding Fathers intended to set up something in the nature of an Athenian democracy or a New England town meeting to oversee the conduct of the National Government by means of lawsuits in federal courts. The Constitution created a *representative* Government with the representatives directly responsible to their constituents at stated periods of two, four, and six years; that the Constitution does not afford a judicial remedy does not, of course, completely disable the citizen who is not satisfied with the "ground rules" established by the Congress for reporting expenditures of the Executive Branch. Lack of standing within the narrow confines of Art. III jurisdiction does not impair the right to assert his views in the political forum or at the polls. Slow, cumbersome, and unresponsive though the traditional electoral process may be thought at times, our system provides for changing members of the political branches when dissatisfied citizens convince a sufficient number of their fellow electors that elected representatives are delinquent in performing duties committed to them.

As our society has become more complex, our numbers more vast, our lives more varied, and our resources more strained, citizens increasingly request the intervention of the courts on a greater variety of issues that at any period of our national development. The acceptance of new categories of judicially cognizable injury has not eliminated the basic principle that to invoke judicial power the claimant must have a "personal stake in the outcome" [*Baker* v. *Carr*], or a "particular, concrete injury" [*Sierra Club*], or "a direct injury" [*Lévitt*], in short, something more than "generalized grievances" [*Flast*]. Respondent has failed to meet these fundamental tests. . . .

Reversed.

Mr. Justice Powell, concurring.

I join the opinion of the Court because I am in accord with most of its analysis, particularly insofar as it relies on traditional barriers against federal taxpayer or citizen standing. And I agree that [*Flast*], which set the boundaries for the arguments of the parties before us, is the most directly relevant precedent and quite correctly absorbs a major portion of the Court's attention. I write solely to indicate that I would go further than the Court and would lay to rest the approach undertaken in *Flast*. I would not overrule *Flast* on its facts, because it is now settled that federal taxpayer standing exists in Establishment Clause cases. I would not, however, perpetuate the doctrinal confusion inherent in the *Flast* two-part "nexus" test. That test is not a reliable indicator of when a federal taxpayer has standing, and it has no sound relationship to the question whether such a plaintiff, with no other interest at stake, should be allowed to bring suit against one of the branches of the Federal Government. In my opinion, it should be abandoned.

I.   My difficulties with *Flast* are several. The opinion purports to separate the question of standing from the merits, yet it abruptly returns to the substantive issues raised by a plaintiff for the purpose of determining "whether there is a logical nexus between the status asserted and the claim sought to be adjudicated." Similarly, the opinion distinguishes between constitutional and prudential limits on standing. I find it impossible, however, to determine whether the two-part "nexus" test created in *Flast* amounts to a constitutional or a prudential limitation, because it has no meaningful connection with the Court's statement of the bare-minimum constitutional requirements for standing.

Drawing upon [*Baker* v. *Carr*], the Court in *Flast* stated the "'gist of the question of standing'" as "whether the party seeking relief has 'alleged such a personal stake in the outcome of the controversy as to assure that concrete ad-

verseness which sharpens the presentation of issues upon which the court so largely depends for illumination of difficult constitutional questions.'" [T]his is now the controlling definition of the irreducible Art. III case-or-controversy requirements for standing. But, as Mr. Justice Harlan pointed out in his dissent in *Flast*, it is impossible to see how an inquiry about the existence of "concrete adverseness" is furthered by an application of the *Flast* test. . . .

In my opinion, Mr. Justice Harlan's critique of the *Flast* "nexus" test is unanswerable. As he pointed out, "the Court's standard for the determination of standing [i.e., concrete adverseness] and its criteria for the satisfaction of that standard are entirely unrelated." . . .

The ambiguities inherent in the *Flast* "nexus" limitations on federal taxpayer standing are illustrated by this case. There can be little doubt about respondent's fervor in pursuing his case. [T]he intensity of his interest appears to bear no relationship to the fact that, literally speaking, he is not challenging directly a congressional exercise of the taxing and spending power. On the other hand, if the involvement of the taxing and spending power has some relevance, it requires no great leap in reasoning to conclude that the Statement and Account Clause, Art. I, § 9, cl. 7, on which respondent relies, is inextricably linked to that power. And that clause might well be seen as a "specific" limitation on congressional spending. Indeed, it could be viewed as the most democratic of limitations. Thus, although the Court's application of *Flast* to the instant case is probably literally correct, adherence to the *Flast* test in this instance suggests, as does *Flast* itself, that the test is not a sound or logical limitation on standing.

The lack of real meaning and of principled content in the *Flast* "nexus" test renders it likely that it will in time collapse of its own weight, as Mr. Justice Douglas predicted in his concurring opinion in that case. This will present several options for the Court. It may either reaffirm pre-*Flast* prudential limitations on federal and citizen taxpayer standing; attempt new doctrinal departures in this area, as would Mr. Justice Stewart; or simply drop standing barriers altogether, as, judging by his concurring opinion in *Flast* and his dissenting opinion today, would Mr. Justice Douglas. I believe the first option to be the appropriate course, for reasons which may be emphasized by noting the difficulties I see with the other two. And, while I do not disagree at this late date with the *Baker* v. *Carr* statement of the constitutional indicia of standing, I further believe that constitutional limitations are not the only pertinent considerations.

II.   Mr. Justice Stewart, joined by Mr. Justice Marshall, would grant citizen or taxpayer standing under those clauses of the Constitution that impose on the Federal Government "an affirmative duty" to do something on behalf of its citizens and taxpayers. Although he distinguishes between an affirmative constitutional duty and a "constitutional prohibition" for purposes of this case, it does not follow that Mr. Justice Stewart would deny federal taxpayer standing in all cases involving a constitutional prohibition, as his concurring opinion in *Flast* makes clear. Rather, he would find federal taxpayer standing, and perhaps citizen standing, in all cases based on constitutional clauses setting forth an affirmative duty and in unspecified cases where the constitutional clause at issue may be seen as a plain or explicit prohibition.

For purposes of determining whether a taxpayer or citizen has standing to challenge the actions of the Federal Government, I fail to perceive a meaningful distinction between constitutional clauses that set forth duties and those that set forth prohibitions. In either instance, the relevant inquiry is the same—may a plaintiff, relying on nothing other than citizen or taxpayer status, bring suit to adjudicate whether an entity of the Federal Government is carrying out its responsibilities in conformance with the requirements of the Constitution? A taxpayer's or citizen's interest in and willingness to pursue with vigor such a suit would not

turn on whether the constitutional clause at issue imposed a duty on the Government to do something for him or prohibited the Government from doing something to him. Prohibitions and duties in this context are opposite sides of the same coin. Thus, I do not believe that the inquiry whether federal courts should entertain public actions is advanced by line drawing between affirmative duties and prohibitions.

In short, in my opinion my Brother Stewart's view fails to provide a meaningful stopping point between an all-or-nothing position with regard to federal taxpayer or citizen standing. In this respect, it shares certain of the deficiencies of *Flast*. I suspect that this may also be true of any intermediate position in this area. Mr. Justice Douglas correctly discerns, I think, that the alternatives here as a matter of doctrine are essentially bipolar. His preference is clear: "I would be as liberal in allowing taxpayers standing to object to . . . violations of the First Amendment as I would in granting standing to people to complain of any invasion of their rights under the Fourth Amendment or the Fourteenth or under any other guarantee in the Constitution itself or in the Bill of Rights." [*Flast.*] My view is to the contrary.

III.   Relaxation of standing requirements is directly related to the expansion of judicial power. It seems to me inescapable that allowing unrestricted taxpayer or citizen standing would significantly alter the allocation of power at the national level, with a shift away from a democratic form of government. I also believe that repeated and essentially head-on confrontations between the life-tenured branch and the representative branches of government will not, in the long run, be beneficial to either. The public confidence essential to the former and the vitality critical to the latter may well erode if we do not exercise self-restraint in the utilization of our power to negative the actions of the other branches. We should be ever mindful of the contradictions that would arise if a democracy were to permit general oversight of the elected branches of government by a nonrepresentative, and in large measure insulated, judicial branch. Moreover, the argument that the Court should allow unrestricted taxpayer or citizen standing underestimates the ability of the representative branches of the Federal Government to respond to the citizen pressure that has been responsible in large measure for the current drift toward expanded standing. Indeed, taxpayer or citizen advocacy, given its potentially broad base, is precisely the type of leverage that in a democracy ought to be employed against the branches that were intended to be responsive to public attitudes about the appropriate operation of government. . . .

Unrestrained standing in federal taxpayer or citizen suits would create a remarkably illogical system of judicial supervision of the coordinate branches of the Federal Government. Randolph's proposed Council of Revision, which was repeatedly rejected by the Framers, at least had the virtue of being systematic; every law passed by the legislature automatically would have been previewed by the Judiciary before the law could take effect. On the other hand, since the Judiciary cannot select the taxpayers or citizens who bring suit or the nature of the suits, the allowance of public actions would produce uneven and sporadic review, the quality of which would be influenced by the resources and skill of the particular plaintiff. And issues would be presented in abstract form. . . .

The power recognized in *Marbury* v. *Madison*, is a potent one. Its prudent use seems to me incompatible with unlimited notions of taxpayer and citizen standing. Were we to utilize this power as indiscriminately as is now being urged, we may witness efforts by the representative branches drastically to curb its use. Due to what many have regarded as the unresponsiveness of the Federal Government to recognized needs or serious inequities in our society, recourse to the federal courts has attained an unprecedented popularity in recent decades. Those courts have often acted as a major

instrument of social reform. But this has not always been the case, as experiences under the New Deal illustrate. The public reaction to the substantive due process holdings of the federal courts during that period requires no elaboration, and it is not unusual for history to repeat itself.

Quite apart from this possibility, we risk a progressive impairment of the effectiveness of the federal courts if their limited resources are diverted increasingly from their historic role to the resolution of public-interest suits brought by litigants who cannot distinguish themselves from all taxpayers or all citizens. The irreplaceable value of the power articulated by Chief Justice Marshall lies in the protection it has afforded the constitutional rights and liberties of individual citizens and minority groups against oppressive or discriminatory government action. It is this role, not some amorphous general supervision of the operations of government, that has maintained public esteem for the federal courts and has permitted the peaceful coexistence of the countermajoritarian implications of judicial review and the democratic principles upon which our Federal Government in the final analysis rests.

The considerations outlined above underlie, I believe, the traditional hostility of the Court to federal taxpayer or citizen standing where the plaintiff has nothing at stake other than his interest as a taxpayer or citizen. . . .

To be sure standing barriers have been substantially lowered in the last three decades. The Court has confirmed the power of Congress to open the federal courts to representatives of the public interest through specific statutory grants of standing. E.g., [FCC v. *Sanders Bros. Radio Station*, 309 U.S. 470 (1940); *Scripps-Howard Radio, Inc.* v. FCC, 316 U.S. 4 (1942).] Even in the absence of specific statutory grants of standing, economic interests that at one time would not have conferred standing have been reexamined and found sufficient. . . . Noneconomic interests have been recognized. E.g., *Baker* v. *Carr*; *Sierra Club* v. *Morton*. A

stringently limited exception for federal taxpayer standing has been created. *Flast* v. *Cohen,*
supra. The concept of particularized injury has
been dramatically diluted. E.g., *United States* v.
SCRAP, 412 U.S. 669 (1973).

The revolution in standing doctrine that has
occurred, particularly in the 12 years since *Baker*
v. *Carr,* has not meant, however, that standing
barriers have disappeared altogether. . . . Indeed, despite the diminution of standing
requirements in the last decade, the Court has
not broken with the traditional requirement
that, in the absence of a specific statutory grant
of the right of review, a plaintiff must allege
some particularized injury that sets him apart
from the man on the street.

I recognize that the Court's allegiance to a
requirement of particularized injury has on occasion required a reading of the concept that
threatens to transform it beyond recognition.
E.g., *Baker* v. *Carr; Flast* v. *Cohen, supra.*[1] But
despite such occasional digressions, the
requirement remains, and I think it does so for
the reasons outlined above. In recognition of
those considerations, we should refuse to go the
last mile towards abolition of standing
requirements that is implicit in broadening the
"precarious opening" for federal taxpayers
created by *Flast* or in allowing a citizen *qua* citizen to invoke the power of the federal courts to
negative unconstitutional acts of the Federal
Government.

In sum, I believe we should limit the expansion of federal taxpayer and citizen standing in the absence of specific statutory authorization to an outer boundary drawn by the
results in *Flast* and *Baker* v. *Carr.* I think we
should face up to the fact that *all* such suits are

an effort "to employ a federal court as a forum in
which to air . . . generalized grievances about
the conduct of government or the allocation of
power in the Federal System." . . . The Court
should explicitly reaffirm traditional prudential
barriers against such public actions. My reasons
for this view are rooted in respect for democratic processes and in the conviction that "[t]he
powers of the federal judiciary will be adequate
for the great burdens placed upon them only if
they are employed prudently, with recognition
of the strengths as well as the hazards that go
with our kind of representative government."
[*Flast* v. *Cohen*] (Harlan, J., dissenting).

Mr. Justice Douglas, dissenting.

I would affirm the judgment of the Court of
Appeals on the "standing" issue. . . .
Whatever may be the merits of the underlying
claim, it seems clear that the taxpayer in the
present case is not making a generalized complaint about the operation of Government. He
does not even challenge the constitutionality of
the Central Intelligence Agency Act. He only
wants to know the amount of tax money exacted
from him that goes into CIA activities. Secrecy of the Government acquires new sanctity
when his claim is denied. . . .

From the history of [Art. I, § 9, cl. 7] it is
apparent that the Framers inserted it in the
Constitution to give the public knowledge of
the way public funds are expended. No one has
a greater "personal stake" in policing this
protective measure than a taxpayer. Indeed, if a
taxpayer may not raise the question, who may
do so? . . .

Mr. Justice Stewart, with whom Mr. Justice
Marshall joins, dissenting.

The Court's decisions in [*Flast* and *Frothingham*] throw very little light on the question at
issue in this case. For, unlike the plaintiffs in
those cases, Richardson did not bring this action
asking a court to invalidate a federal statute on
the ground that it was beyond the delegated

---

[1] Baker v. Carr may have a special claim to sui generis
status. It was perhaps a necessary response to the manifest
distortion of democratic principles practiced by malapportioned legislatures and to abuses of the political system so
pervasive as to undermine democratic processes. Flast v.
Cohen may also have been a reaction to what appeared at the
time as an immutable political logjam that included unsuc-
cessful efforts to confer specific statutory grants of standing.

power of Congress to enact or that it contravened some constitutional prohibition. Richardson's claim is of an entirely different order. It is that Art. I, § 9, cl. 7, of the Constitution, the Statement and Account Clause, gives him a right to receive, and imposes on the Government a corresponding affirmative duty to supply, a periodic report of the receipts and expenditures "of all public Money." In support of his standing to litigate this claim, he has asserted his status both as a taxpayer and as a citizen-voter. Whether the Statement and Account Clause imposes upon the Government an affirmative duty to supply the information requested and whether that duty runs to every taxpayer or citizen are questions that go to the substantive merits of this litigation. Those questions are not now before us, but I think that the Court is quite wrong in holding that the respondent was without standing to raise them in the trial court. . . .

When the duty relates to a very particularized and explicit performance by the asserted obligor, such as the payment of money or the rendition of specific items of information, there is no necessity to resort to any extended analysis, such as the Flast nexus tests, in order to find standing in the obligee. Under such circumstances, the duty itself, running as it does from the defendant to the plaintiff, provides fully adequate assurance that the plaintiff is not seeking to "employ a federal court as a forum in which to air his generalized grievances about the conduct of government or the allocation of power in the Federal System." [Flast.] If such a duty arose in the context of a contract between private parties, no one would suggest that the obligee should be barred from the courts. It seems to me that when the asserted duty is, as here, as particularized, palpable, and explicit as those which courts regularly recognize in private contexts, it should make no difference that the obligor is the government and the duty is embodied in our organic law. Certainly after *United States* v. *SCRAP*, 412 U.S. 669 (1973), it does not matter that those to whom the duty is

owed may be many. "[S]tanding is not to be denied simply because many people suffer the same injury." Id. . . .

Mr. Justice Brennan, dissenting

The "standing" of a plaintiff to be heard on a claim of invasion of his alleged legally protected right is established, in my view, by his good-faith allegation that " 'the challenged action has caused him injury in fact.' " *Barlow* v. *Collins*, 397 U.S. 159, 167 (1970) . . . . Richardson plainly alleged injury in fact. My Brother Stewart demonstrates this in his analysis of Richardson's claimed right to have the budget of the Central Intelligence Agency published. . . . Moreover, his complaint, properly construed, alleged that the violations caused him injury not only in respect of his right as a citizen to know how Congress was spending the public fisc, but also in respect of his right as a voter to receive information to aid his decision how and for whom to vote. These claims may ultimately fail on the merits, but Richardson has "standing" to assert them. . . . The two-pronged test fashioned by *Flast* was not a qualification upon these general principles but was fashioned solely as a determinant of standing of plaintiffs alleging only injury as taxpayers who challenge alleged violations of the [religion clauses] of the First Amendment. The extension of that test to the very different challenges here only produces the confusion evidenced by the differing views of the *Flast* test expressed in the several opinions filed today in these cases. Outside its proper sphere, as my Brother Powell soundly observes, that test is not "a reliable indicator of when a federal taxpayer has standing." We avoid that confusion if, we recognize that "alleged injury in fact, reviewability, and the merits pose questions that are largely distinct from one another, each governed by its own considerations. To fail to isolate and treat each inquiry independently of the other two, so far as possible, is to risk obscuring what is at issue in a given case, and thus to risk uninformed, poorly reasoned decisions that may result in injustice. . . . The risk of ambiguity and injustice can be minimized by cleanly severing, so far as possible, the inquiries into reviewability and the merits from the determination of standing."

Warth v. *Seldin* (excerpt)
442 U.S. 490 (1975)

Penfield, New York (a suburb of Rochester), adopted a zoning ordinance in 1962 which allocated 98 percent of the town's vacant land to single-family detached housing. By imposing unreasonable requirements relating to lot size, setback, floor area, and habitable space, it was alleged, this ordinance excluded from the town persons of low and middle income (including minorities). This, it was charged, violates the First, Ninth, and Fourteenth Amendments, as well as congressional legislation. Mr. Justice Powell, for the Court, upheld dismissal of the complaint, finding "that none of the plaintiffs (including low- and moderate-income persons, a housing action group, residents of the neighboring city, a builders association, and a housing development association) had alleged "specific concrete facts demonstrating that the challenged [exclusionary zoning] practices [harmed them] and that [they] personally would benefit in a tangible way from the Court's intervention." One of the plaintiffs, for example, worked in Penfield but resided some 42 miles away. Others claimed the ordinance "forced them . . . to reside in less attractive environments." Still others claimed its effect was to "force" Rochester to impose higher taxes upon them than "would otherwise have been necessary." The builder plaintiffs argued it arbitrarily "deprived them of potential profits."

Mr. Justice Douglas, dissenting, observed that:

Standing has become a barrier to access to the federal courts, just as "the political question" was in earlier decades. The mounting caseload of federal courts is well known. But cases such as this one reflect festering sores in our society; and the American dream teaches that if one reaches high enough and persists there is a forum where justice is dispensed. I would lower the technical barriers and let the courts serve that ancient need. They can in time be curbed by legislative or constitutional restraints if an emergency arises.

Mr. Justice Brennan, with whom Mr. Justice White and Mr. Justice Marshall join, dissenting.

In this case, a wide range of plaintiffs, alleging various kinds of injuries, claimed to have been affected by the Penfield zoning ordinance, on its face and as applied, and by other practices of the defendant officials of Penfield. Alleging that as a result of these laws and practices low- and moderate-income and minority people have been excluded from Penfield, and that this exclusion is unconstitutional, plaintiffs sought injunctive, declaratory, and monetary relief. The Court today, in an opinion that purports to be a "standing" opinion but that actually, I believe, has overtones of outmoded notions of pleading and of justiciability, refuses to find that any of the variously situated plaintiffs can clear numerous hurdles, some constructed here for the first time, necessary to establish "standing." While the Court gives lip-service to the principle, oft-repeated in recent years, that "standing in no way depends on the plaintiff's contention that particular conduct is illegal," . . . in fact the opinion, which tosses out of court almost every conceivable kind of plaintiff who could be injured by the activity claimed to be unconstitutional, can be explained only by an indefensible hostility to the claim on the merits. I can appreciate the Court's reluctance to adjudicate the complex and difficult legal questions involved in determining the constitutionality of practices which assertedly limit residence in a particular municipality to those who are white and relatively well-off, and I also understand that the merits of this case could involve grave sociological and political ramifications. But courts cannot refuse to hear a case on the merits merely because they would prefer not to, and it is quite clear, when the record is viewed with dispassion, that at least three of the groups of plaintiffs have made allegations, and supported them with affidavits and documentary evidence, sufficient to survive a motion to dismiss for lack of standing. . . .

Political Questions

THE PRE-WARREN ERA

Coleman v. *Miller*
307 U.S. 433 (1939)

Following the *Child Labor Cases* (see Chapter 3), Congress in 1924 proposed a child labor amendment to the Constitution. In 1925 the Kansas legislature rejected and later, in 1937, approved this proposal. The validity of the approval was challenged in the state courts on the grounds (among others) that: (1) the prior rejection of the amendment was final, that is, precluded any subsequent action by Kansas on the same proposal; and (2) not having been approved by the prescribed number of states within a reasonable period, the proposed amendment had expired prior to 1937. These contentions were rejected by the state court. On review the Supreme Court disposed of some preliminary matters and then considered these two issues.

Mr. Chief Justice Hughes delivered the opinion of the Court: . . .

The effect of the previous rejection of the amendment and of the lapse of time since its submission.

1. The state court adopted the view expressed by text-writers that a state legislature which has rejected an amendment proposed by the Congress may later ratify. The argument in support of that view is that Article V says nothing of rejection but speaks only of ratification and provides that a proposed amendment shall be valid as part of the Constitution when ratified by three-fourths of the states; that the power to ratify is thus conferred upon the state by the Constitution and, as a ratifying power, persists despite a previous rejection. The opposing view proceeds on an assumption that if ratification by "conventions" were prescribed by the Congress, a convention could not reject and, having adjourned sine die, be reassembled and ratify. It is also premised, in accordance with views expressed by text-writers, that ratification if once given cannot afterwards be rescinded and the amendment rejected, and it is urged that the same effect in the exhaustion of the state's power to act should be ascribed to rejection; that a state can act "but once, either by convention or through its legislature."

Historic instances are cited. In 1865, the Thirteenth Amendment was rejected by the legislature of New Jersey which subsequently ratified it, but the question did not become important as ratification by the requisite number of states had already been proclaimed. The question did arise in connection with the adoption of the Fourteenth Amendment. The legislatures of Georgia, North Carolina and South Carolina had rejected the amendment in November and December, 1866. New governments were erected in those states (and in others) under the direction of Congress. The new legislatures ratified the amendment, that of North Carolina on July 4, 1868, that of South Carolina on July 9, 1868, and that of Georgia on July 21, 1868. Ohio and New Jersey first ratified and then passed resolutions withdrawing their consent. As there were then thirty-seven states, twenty-eight were needed to constitute the requisite three-fourths. On July 9, 1868, the Congress adopted a resolution requesting the Secretary of State to communicate "a list of the states of the Union whose legislatures have ratified the fourteenth article of amendment," and in Secretary Seward's report attention was called to the action of Ohio and New Jersey. On July 20 Secretary Seward issued a proclamation reciting the ratification by twenty-eight states, including North Carolina, South Carolina, Ohio and New Jersey, and stating that it appeared that Ohio and New Jersey had since passed resolutions withdrawing their consent and that "it is deemed a matter of doubt and uncertainty whether such resolutions are not irregular, invalid and therefore ineffectual." The Secretary certified that if the ratifying resolutions of Ohio and New Jersey were still in full force and effect, notwithstanding the attempted withdrawal, the amendment had become a part of the Constitution. On the following day the Congress adopted a concurrent resolution which, reciting that three-fourths of the states having ratified (the list including North Carolina, South Carolina, Ohio and New Jersey), declared the Fourteenth Amendment to be a part of the Constitution and that it should be duly promulgated as such by the Secretary of State. Accord-

ingly, Secretary Seward, on July 28th, issued his proclamation embracing the states mentioned in the congressional resolution and adding Georgia.

Thus the political departments of the government dealt with the effect both of previous rejection and of attempted withdrawal and determined that both were ineffectual in the presence of an actual ratification. . . . This decision by the political departments of the government as to the validity of the adoption of the Fourteenth Amendment has been accepted.

We think that in accordance with this historic precedent the question of the efficacy of ratifications by state legislatures, in the light of previous rejection or attempted withdrawal, should be regarded as a political question pertaining to the political departments, with the ultimate authority in the Congress in the exercise of its control over the promulgation of the adoption of the amendment. . . .

2. The more serious question is whether the proposal by the Congress of the amendment had lost its vitality through lapse of time and hence it could not be ratified by the Kansas legislature in 1937. The argument of petitioners stresses the fact that nearly thirteen years elapsed between the proposal in 1924 and the ratification in question. It is said that when the amendment was proposed there was a definitely adverse popular sentiment and that at the end of 1925 there had been rejection by both houses of the legislatures of sixteen states and ratification by only four states, and that it was not until about 1933 that an aggressive campaign was started in favor of the amendment. In reply, it is urged that Congress did not fix a limit of time for ratification and that an unreasonably long time had not elapsed since the submission; that the conditions which gave rise to the amendment had not been eliminated; that the prevalence of child labor, the diversity of state laws and the disparity in their administration, with the resulting competitive inequalities, continued to exist. Reference is also made to the fact that a number of the states have treated the

amendment as still pending and that in the proceedings of the national government there have been indications of the same view. It is said that there were fourteen ratifications in 1933, four in 1935, one in 1936, and three in 1937.

We have held that the Congress in proposing an amendment may fix a reasonable time for ratification. *Dillon* v. *Gloss*, 256 U.S. 368. There we sustained the action of the Congress in providing in the proposed Eighteenth Amendment that it should be inoperative unless ratified within seven years. No limitation of time for ratification is provided in the instant case either in the proposed amendment or in the resolution of submission. But petitioners contend that, in the absence of a limitation by the Congress, the Court can and should decide what is a reasonable period within which ratification may be had. We are unable to agree with that contention.

It is true that in *Dillon* v. *Gloss* the Court said that nothing was found in Article V which suggested that an amendment once proposed was to be open to ratification for all time, or that ratification in some states might be separated from that in others by many years and yet be effective; that there was a strong suggestion to the contrary in that proposal and ratification were but succeeding steps in a single endeavor; that as amendments were deemed to be prompted by necessity, they should be considered and disposed of presently; and that there is a fair implication that ratification must be sufficiently contemporaneous in the required number of states to reflect the will of the people in all sections at relatively the same period; and hence that ratification must be within some reasonable time after the proposal. These considerations were cogent reasons for the decision in *Dillon* v. *Gloss*, that the Congress had the power to fix a reasonable time for ratification. But it does not follow that, whenever Congress has not exercised that power, the Court should take upon itself the responsibility of deciding what constitutes a reasonable time and determine accordingly the validity of ratifications. That question was not involved in *Dillon* v. *Gloss* and, in accordance with familiar principle, what was there said must be read in the light of the point decided.

Where are to be found the criteria for such a judicial determination? None are to be found in Constitution or statute. In their endeavor to answer this question petitioners' counsel have suggested that at least two years should be allowed; that six years would not seem to be unreasonably long; that seven years had been used by the Congress as a reasonable period; that one year, six months and thirteen days was the average time used in passing upon amendments which have been ratified since the first ten amendments; that three years, six months and twenty-five days has been the longest time used in ratifying. To this list of variables, counsel add that "the nature and extent of publicity and the activity of the public and of the legislatures of the several states in relation to any particular proposal should be taken into consideration." That statement is pertinent, but there are additional matters to be examined and weighed. When a proposed amendment springs from a conception of economic needs, it would be necessary, in determining whether a reasonable time had elapsed since its submission, to consider the economic conditions prevailing in the country, whether these had so far changed since the submission as to make the proposal no longer responsive to the conception which inspired it or whether conditions were such as to intensify the feeling of need and the appropriateness of the proposed remedial action. In short, the question of a reasonable time in many cases would involve, as in this case it does involve, an appraisal of a great variety of relevant conditions, political, social and economic, which can hardly be said to be within the appropriate range of evidence receivable in a court of justice and as to which it would be an extravagant extension of judicial authority to assert judicial notice as the basis of deciding a controversy with respect to the validity of an amendment actually ratified. On the other hand, these conditions are appropriate for the consideration of the political departments of the government. The questions they involve are essentially political and not justiciable. They can be decided by the Congress with the full knowledge and appreciation ascribed to the national legislature of the political, social and economic conditions which have prevailed during the period since the submission of the amendment.

Our decision that the Congress has the power under Article V to fix a reasonable limit of time for ratification in proposing an amendment proceeds upon the assumption that the question, what is a reasonable time, lies within the congressional province. If it be deemed that such a question is an open one when the limit has not been fixed in advance, we think that it should also be regarded as an open one for the consideration of the Congress when, in the presence of certified ratifications by three-fourths of the states, the time arrives for the promulgation of the adoption of the amendment. The decision by the Congress, in its control of the action of the Secretary of State, of the question whether the amendment had been adopted within a reasonable time would not be subject to review by the courts. . . .

For the reasons we have stated . . . we think that the Congress in controlling the promulgation of the adoption of a constitutional amendment has the final determination of the question whether by lapse of time its proposal of the amendment had lost its vitality prior to the required ratifications. The state officials should not be restrained from certifying to the Secretary of State the adoption by the legislature of Kansas of the resolution of ratification.

As we find no reason for disturbing the decision of the Supreme Court of Kansas in denying the mandamus sought by petitioners, its judgment is affirmed but upon the grounds stated in this opinion.

[Justices Black, Frankfurter, Douglas, and Roberts thought the case should be dismissed on jurisdictional grounds. But since a majority held otherwise and had brought the case before the Court, the four Justices concurred in the result reached, but for these different reasons:]

Congress, possessing exclusive power over the amending process, cannot be bound by and is under no duty to accept the pronouncements upon that exclusive power by this Court or by the Kansas courts. Neither state nor federal courts can review that power. Therefore, any judicial expression amounting to more than mere acknowledgment of exclusive Congressional power over the political process of amendment is a mere admonition to the Congress in the nature of an advisory opinion, given wholly without constitutional authority.

[Justices Butler and McReynolds dissented on the ground that because more than a reasonable time had elapsed since the proposal of the amendment, it was no longer subject to approval by the states. That is, the dissenters considered this a legal, not a political, question.]

Note and quaere: Though it has been urged to do so many times, the Court has never interfered with the process of constitutional amendment. That is, no effort to have an amendment invalidated has been successful. Thus *Hollingsworth* v. *Virginia*, 3 Dallas 378 (1798), rejected the argument that a proposed amendment, like legislation, must be presented to the President for his approval or rejection. *Hawke* v. *Smith*, 253 U.S. 221 (1920), held that when a state legislature approves a proposed amendment pursuant to Article V of the federal Constitution, it acts in a federal capacity. Hence an amendment, otherwise properly adopted, is not invalid though not submitted to popular referendum as "required" by some state constitutions. *United States* v. *Sprague*, 282 U.S. 716 (1919), found no merit in the argument that since the Eighteenth Amendment restricted basic liberties and states' rights it should have been submitted to state conventions for ratification "by the people," rather than to the state legislatures. In *Leser* v. *Garnet*, 258 U.S. 130 (1922), the Court refused to look into the propriety of state ratifying resolutions on the ground that they had been accepted by the Secretary of State and that his promulgation of the amendment was not subject to question by the judiciary.

Is this holding relevant to the argument, sometimes urged, that the Civil War amendments are invalid because their ratification was obtained in part as least by military force during the Reconstruction? Is the Court's apparent reluctance to block the amending process a corollary of the principle of judicial review? Does it follow, in other words, that if the Court is to have the "last" word as to the meaning of the Constitution, it should leave maximum freedom for the political processes of amendment?

Colegrove v. *Green*
328 U.S. 549 (1946)

Colegrove, a professor and political scientist, challenged Illinois congressional districts for violating both the Constitution and an act of Congress in that (due to demographic shifts) they had become grossly unequal in population. Only seven judges participated in the decision of this case.

Mr. Justice Frankfurther announced the judgment of the Court and an opinion in which Mr. Justice Reed and Mr. Justice Burton concur.

We are of opinion that the petitioners ask of this Court what is beyond its competence to grant. This is one of those demands on judicial power which cannot be met by verbal fencing about "jurisdiction." It must be resolved by considerations on the basis of which this Court, from time to time, has refused to intervene in controversies. It has refused to do so because due regard for the effective working of our Government revealed this issue to be of a peculiarly political nature and therefore not meet for judicial determination.

This is not an action to recover for damage because of the discriminatory exclusion of a plaintiff from rights enjoyed by other citizens. The basis for the suit is not a private wrong, but a wrong suffered by Illinois as a polity. . . . In effect this is an appeal to the federal courts to reconstruct the electoral process of Illinois in order that it may be adequately represented in the councils of the Nation. Because the Illinois Legislature has failed to revise its Congressional Representative districts in order to reflect great changes, during more than a generation, in the distribution of its population, we are asked to do this, as it were, for Illinois.

Of course, no court can affirmatively remap the Illinois districts so as to bring them more in conformity with the standards of fairness for a representative system. At best we could only declare the existing electoral system invalid. The result would be to leave Illinois undistricted and to bring into operation, if the Illinois legislature chose not to act, the choice of members for the House of Representatives on a state-wide ticket. The last stage may be worse than the first. The upshot of judicial action may defeat the vital political principle which led Congress, more than a hundred years ago, to require districting. This requirement, in the language of Chancellor Kent, "was recommended by the wisdom and justice of giving, as far as possible, to the local subdivisions of the people of each state, a due influence in the choice of representatives, so as not to leave the aggregate minority of the people in a state, though approaching perhaps to a majority, to be wholly overpowered by the combined action of the numerical majority, without any voice whatever in the national councils." . . . Assuming acquiescence on the part of the authorities of Illinois in the selection of its Representatives by a mode that defies the direction of Congress for selection by districts, the House of Representatives may not acquiesce. In the exercise of its power to judge the qualifications of its own members, the House may reject a delegation of Representatives-at-large. Article I, sec. 5, c. 1. . . . Nothing is clearer than that this controversy concerns matters that bring courts into immediate and active relations with party contests. From the determination of such issues this Court has traditionally held aloof. It is hostile to a democratic system to involve the judiciary in politics of the people. And it is not less pernicious if such judicial intervention in an essentially political contest be dressed up in the abstract phrases of the law.

The petitioners urge with great zeal that the conditions of which they complain are grave evils and offend public morality. The Constitution of the United States gives ample power to provide against these evils. But due regard for the Constitution as a viable system precludes judicial correction. Authority for dealing with such problems resides elsewhere. Article I, section 4 of the Constitution provides that "The Times, Places and Manner of holding Elections for . . . Representatives, shall be prescribed in each State by the Legislature thereof; but the Congress may at any time by Law make or alter such Regulations, . . ." The short of it is that the Constitution has conferred upon Congress exclusive authority to secure fair representation by the States in the popular House and left to that House determination whether States have fulfilled their responsibility. If Congress failed in exercising its powers, whereby standards of fairness are offended, the remedy ultimately lies with the people. Whether Congress faithfully discharges its duty or not, the subject has been committed to the exclusive control of Congress. An aspect of government from which the judiciary, in view of what is involved, has been excluded by the clear intention of the Constitution cannot be entered by the federal courts because Congress may have been in default in exacting from States obedience to its mandate. . . .

To sustain this action would cut very deep into the very being of Congress. Courts ought not to enter this political thicket. The remedy for unfairness in districting is to secure State legislatures that will apportion properly, or to invoke the ample powers of Congress. The Constitution has many commands that are not enforceable by courts because they clearly fall outside the conditions and purposes that circumscribe judicial action. Thus, "on Demand of the executive Authority," Art. IV. sec. 2, of a State it is the duty of a sister State to deliver up a fugitive from justice. But the fulfillment of this duty cannot be judicially enforced. *Kentucky* v. *Dennison*, 24 How. 66 (1861). The duty to see to it that the laws are faithfully executed cannot be brought under legal compulsion. *Mississippi* v. *Johnson*, 4 Wall. 475 (1867),. Violation of the great guaranty of a republican form of government in States cannot be challenged in the courts. *Pacific Teleph. & Teleg. Co.* v. *Oregon*, 223 U.S. 118 (1912). The Constitution has left the performance, of many duties in our governmental scheme to depend on the fidelity of the executive and legislative action and, ultimately, on the vigilance of the people in exercising their political rights.

[Mr. Justice Rutledge thought the issue was justiciable, but voted to dismiss the case as a matter of equitable discretion in view of the immediacy of the next election and the difficulties of an at-large election.

[Justices Black, Douglas, and Murphy in dissent found the case justiciable.]

THE WARREN ERA

Baker v. *Carr*
369 U.S. 186 (1962)

Like the Illinois congressional districts involved in *Colegrove*, Tennessee's state legislative districts were grossly unequal in population. Plaintiff charged this inequality violated the Equal Protection Clause of the Fourteenth Amendment. Relying on *Colegrove*, a federal district court dismissed the case as nonjusticiable. The Supreme Court reversed, with these comments on the political question doctrine.

Mr. Justice Brennan delivered the opinion of the Court. . . .

JUSTICIABILITY

In holding that the subject matter of this suit was not justiciable, the District Court relied on *Colegrove* v. *Green* and subsequent *per curiam* cases. . . . We understand the District Court to have read the cited cases as compelling the conclusion that since the appellants sought to have a legislative apportionment held unconstitutional, their suit presented a "political question" and was therefore nonjusticiable. We hold that this challenge to an apportionment presents no nonjusticiable "political question." The cited cases do not hold the contrary.

Of course the mere fact that the suit seeks protection of a political right does not mean it presents a political question. . . . Rather, it is argued that apportionment cases, whatever the actual wording of the complaint, can involve no federal constitutional right except one resting on the guaranty of a republican form of government, and that complaints based on that clause have been held to present political questions which are nonjusticiable.

We hold that the claim pleaded here neither rests upon nor implicates the Guaranty Clause and that its justiciability is therefore not foreclosed by our decisions of cases involving that clause. . . .

. . . [I]n the Guaranty Clause cases and in the other "political question" cases, it is the relationship between the judiciary and the coordinate branches of the Federal Government, and not the federal judiciary's relationship to the States, which gives rise to the "political question."

We have said that "in determining whether a question falls within [the political question] category, the appropriateness under our system of government of attributing finality to the action of the political departments and also the

lack of satisfactory criteria for a judicial determination are dominant consideration." *Coleman*
v. *Miller*, 307 U.S. 433, 454-455. The nonjusticiability of a political question is primarily a
function of the separation of powers. Much confusion results from the capacity of the "political
question" label to obscure the need for case-
by-case inquiry. Deciding whether a matter has
in any measure been committed by the
Constitution to another branch of government,
or whether the action of that branch exceeds
whatever authority has been committed, is itself
a delicate exercise in constitutional interpretation, and is a responsibility of this Court as ultimate interpreter of the Constitution. To demonstrate this requires no less than to analyze
representative cases and to infer from them the
analytical threads that make up the political
question doctrine. We shall then show that
none of those threads catches this case.

Foreign Relations.   There are sweeping statements to the effect that all questions touching
foreign relations are political questions. Not
only does resolution of such issues frequently
turn on standards that defy judicial application,
or involve the exercise of a discretion demonstrably committed to the executive or legislature;
but many such questions uniquely demand
single-voiced statement of the Government's
views. Yet it is error to suppose that every case
or controversy which touches foreign relations
lies beyond judicial cognizance. . . . For example, though a court will not ordinarily inquire
whether a treaty has been terminated, since on
that question "governmental action . . . must
be regarded as of controlling importance," if
there has been no conclusive "governmental action" then a court can construe a treaty and may
find it provides the answer. . . .

Dates of Duration of Hostilities.   Though it has
been stated broadly that "the power which declared the necessity is the power to declare its
cessation, and what the cessation requires,"
here too analysis reveals isolable reasons for the
presence of political questions, underlying this
Court's refusal to review the political depart-

ment's determination of when or whether a war
has ended. Dominant is the need for finality in
the political determination, for emergency's nature demands "a prompt and unhesitating
obedience," . . . .

Validity of Enactments.   In *Coleman* v. *Miller*
this Court held that the questions of how long a
proposed amendment to the Federal Constitution remained open to ratification, and what effect a prior rejection had on a subsequent ratification, were committed to congressional resolution and involved criteria of decision that
necessarily escaped the judicial grasp. Similar
considerations apply to the enacting process:
"The respect due to coequal and independent
departments," and the need for finality and certainty about the status of a statute contribute to
judicial reluctance to inquire whether, as
passed, it complied with all requisite for-
malities. But it is not true that courts will never
delve into a legislature's records upon such a
quest: If the enrolled statute lacks an effective
date, a court will not hesitate to seek it in the
legislative journals in order to preserve the
enactment. The political question doctrine, a
tool for maintenance of governmental order,
will not be so applied as to promote only disorder. . . .

It is apparent that several formulations which
vary slightly according to the settings in which
the questions arise may describe a political
question, although each has one or more elements which identifies it as essentially a function of the separation of powers. Prominent on
the surface of any case held to involve a political
question is found a textually demonstrable
constitutional commitment of the issue to a
coordinate political department; or a lack of judicially discoverable and manageable standards
for resolving it; or the impossibility of deciding
without an initial policy determination of a
kind clearly for nonjudicial discretion; or the
impossibility of a court's undertaking independent resolution without expressing lack of the
respect due coordinate branches of government;
or an unusual need for unquestioning adher-

ence to a political decision already made; or the potentiality of embarrassment from multifarious pronouncements by various departments on one question.

Unless one of these formulations is inextricable from the case at bar, there should be no dismissal for non-justiciability on the ground of a political question's presence. The doctrine of which we treat is one of "political question," not one of "political cases." The courts cannot reject as "no law suit" a bona fide controversy as to whether some action denominated "political" exceeds constitutional authority. The cases we have reviewed show the necessity for discriminating inquiry into the precise facts and posture of the particular case, and the impossibility of resolution by any semantic cataloguing.

But it is argued that this case shares the characteristics of decisions that constitute a category not yet considered, cases concerning the Constitution's guaranty, in Art. IV, § 4, of a republican form of government. . . . We shall discover that Guaranty Clause claims involve those elements which define a "political question," and for that reason and no other, they are nonjusticiable. In particular, we shall discover that the nonjusticiability of such claims has nothing to do with their touching upon matters of state governmental organization.

Republican Form of Government. . . . Just as the Court has consistently held that a challenge to state action based on the Guaranty Clause presents no justiciable question so has it held, and for the same reasons, that challenges to congressional action on the ground of inconsistency with that clause present no justiciable question. . . .

We come, finally, to the ultimate inquiry whether our precedents as to what constitutes a nonjusticiable "political question" bring the case before us under the umbrella of that doctrine. A natural beginning is to note whether any of the common characteristics which we have been able to identify and label descriptively are present. We find none: The question

here is the consistency of state action with the Federal Constitution. We have no question decided, or to be decided, by a political branch of government coequal with this Court. Nor do we risk embarrassment of our government abroad, or grave disturbance at home if we take issue with Tennessee as to the constitutionality of her action here challenged. Nor need the appellants, in order to succeed in this action, ask the Court to enter upon policy determinations for which judicially manageable standards are lacking. Judicial standards under the Equal Protection Clause are well developed and familiar, and it has been open to courts since the enactment of the Fourteenth Amendment to determine, if on the particular facts they must, that a discrimination reflects *no* policy, but simply arbitrary and capricious action.

. . . [B]ecause any reliance on the Guaranty Clause could not have succeeded it does not follow that appellants may not be heard on the equal protection claim which in fact they tender. True, it must be clear that the Fourteenth Amendment claim is not so enmeshed with those political question elements which render Guaranty Clause claims nonjusticiable as actually to present a political question itself. But we have found that not to be the case here. . . .

We conclude then that the nonjusticiability of claims resting on the Guaranty Clause which arises from their embodiment of questions that were thought "political," can have no bearing upon the justiciability of the equal protection claim presented in this case. Finally, we emphasize that it is the involvement in Guaranty Clause claims of the elements thought to define "political questions," and no other feature, which could render them nonjusticiable. Specifically, we have said that such claims are not held nonjusticiable because they touch matters of state governmental organization. . . .

. . . [O]nly last Term, in *Gomillion* v. *Lightfoot*, 364 U.S. 339, we applied the Fifteenth Amendment to strike down a redrafting of municipal boundaries which effected a discriminatory impairment of voting rights, in the face of what a majority of the Court of Appeals thought to be a sweeping commitment to state legislatures of the power to draw and redraw such boundaries. . . .

We conclude that the complaint's allegations of a denial of equal protection present a justiciable constitutional cause of action upon which appellants are entitled to a trial and a decision. The right asserted is within the reach of judicial protection under the Fourteenth Amendment. . . .

Reversed and remanded.

Mr. Justice Whittaker did not participate in the decision of this case.

Mr. Justice Douglas, concurring.

. . . We have here a phase of the recurring problem of the relation of the federal courts to state agencies. More particularly, the question is the extent to which a State may weight one person's vote more heavily than it does another's. . . .

The traditional test under the Equal Protection Clause has been whether a State has made "an invidious discrimination," as it does when it selects "a particular race or nationality for oppressive treatment." See *Skinner* v. *Oklahoma*, 316 U.S. 535, 541. Universal equality is not the test; there is room for weighting. As we stated in *Williamson* v. *Lee Optical Co.*, 348 U.S. 483, 489, "The prohibition of the Equal Protection Clause goes no further than the invidious discrimination."

Mr. Justice Clark, concurring. . . .

The controlling facts cannot be disputed. It appears from the record that 37% of the voters of Tennessee elect 20 of the 33 Senators while 40% of the voters elect 63 of the 99 members of the House. But this might not on its face be an "invidious discrimination," . . . for a "statutory discrimination will not be set aside if any state of facts reasonably may be conceived to justify it." *McGowan* v. *Maryland*, 366 U.S. 420, 426 (1961).

. . . The apportionment picture in Tennessee is a topsy-turvical of gigantic proportions. . . . Tennessee's apportionment is a crazy quilt without rational basis. . . .

No one contends that mathematical equality among voters is required by the Equal Protection Clause. But certainly there must be some rational design to a State's districting. The discrimination here does not fit any pattern. . . .

Mr. Justice Stewart, concurring. . . .

Contrary to the suggestion of my brother Harlan, the Court does not say or imply that "state legislatures must be so structured as to reflect with approximate equality the voice of every voter." . . . The Court does not say or imply that there is anything in the Federal Constitution "to prevent a State, acting not irrationally, from choosing any electoral legislative structure it thinks best suited to the interests, temper, and customs of its people." . . .

I repeat, the Court today decides only: (1) that the District Court possessed jurisdiction of the subject matter; (2) that the complaint presents a justiciable controversy; (3) that the appellants have standing. My Brother Clark has made a convincing prima facie showing that Tennessee's system of apportionment is in fact utterly arbitrary—without any possible justification in rationality. My Brother Harlan has, with imagination and ingenuity, hypothesized possibly rational bases for Tennessee's system. But the merits of this case are not before us now. The defendants have not yet had an opportunity to be heard in defense of the State's system of apportionment; indeed, they have not yet even filed an answer to the complaint. As in other cases, the proper place for the trial is in the trial court, not here.

Mr. Justice Frankfurter, whom Mr. Justice Harlan joins, dissenting.

The Court today reverses a uniform course of decision established by a dozen cases, including one by which the very claim now sustained was unanimously rejected only five years ago. The impressive body of rulings thus cast aside reflected the equally uniform course of our political history regarding the relationship between population and legislative representation—a wholly different matter from denial of the franchise to individuals because of race, color, religion or sex. Such a massive repudiation of the experience of our whole past in asserting destructively novel judicial power demands a detailed analysis of the role of this Court in our constitutional scheme. Disregard of inherent limits in the effective exercise of the Court's "judicial Power" not only presages the futility of judicial intervention in the essentially political conflict of forces by which the relation between population and representation has time out of mind been and now is determined. It may well impair the Court's position as the ultimate organ of "the supreme Law of the Land" in that vast range of legal problems, often strongly entangled in popular feeling, on which this Court must pronounce. The Court's authority—possessed of neither of the purse nor the sword—ultimately rests on sustained public confidence in its moral sanction. Such feeling must be nourished by the Court's complete detachment, in fact and in appearance, from political entanglements and by abstention from injecting itself into the clash of political forces in political settlements.

. . . For this Court to direct the District Court to enforce a claim to which the Court has over the years consistently found itself required to deny legal enforcement and at the same time to find it necessary to withhold any guidance to the lower court how to enforce this turnabout, new legal claim, manifests an odd—indeed an esoteric—conception of judicial propriety. . . . To charge courts with the task of accommodating the incommensurable factors of policy that underlie these mathematical puzzles is to attribute, however flatteringly, omnicompetence to judges. . . .

We were soothingly told at the bar of this Court that we need not worry about the kind of remedy a court could effectively fashion once the abstract constitutional right to have courts pass on a state-wide system of electoral districting is recognized as a matter of judicial rhetoric, because legislatures would heed the Court's admonition. This is not only an euphoric hope. It implies a sorry confession of judicial impotence in place of a frank acknowledgment that there is not under our Constitution a judicial remedy for every political mischief, for every undesirable exercise of legislative power. The Framers carefully and with deliberate forethought refused so to enthrone the judiciary. In this situation, as in others of like nature, appeal for relief does not belong here. Appeal must be to an informed, civically militant electorate. In a democratic society like ours, relief must come through an aroused popular conscience that sears the conscience of the people's representatives. In any event there is nothing judicially more unseemly nor more self-defeating than for this Court to make *in terrorem* pronouncements, to indulge in merely empty rhetoric, sounding a word of promise to the ear, sure to be disappointing to the hope
. . . .

. . . The "political question" principle as applied in *Colegrove* has found wide application commensurate with its function as "one of the rules basic to the federal system and this Court's appropriate place within that structure." *Rescue Army* v. *Municipal Court*, 331 U.S. 549, 570. . . .

The *Colegrove* doctrine, in the form in which repeated decisions have settled it, was not an innovation. It represents long judicial thought and experience. From its earliest opinions this Court has consistently recognized a class of controversies which do not lend themselves to judicial standards and judicial remedies. To classify the various instances as "political questions" is rather a form of stating this conclusion than revealing of analysis. . . .

The influence of these converging considerations—the caution not to undertake decision where standards meet for judicial judgment are lacking, the reluctance to interfere with matters of state government in the absence of an unquestionable and effectively enforceable mandate, the unwillingness to make courts arbiters of the broad issues of political organization historically committed to other institutions and for whose adjustment the judicial process is ill-adapted—has been decisive of the settled lines of cases, reaching back more than a century, which holds that Art. IV, § 4, of the Constitution, guaranteeing to the States "a Republican Form of Government," is not enforceable through the courts. . . .

The present case involves all of the elements that have made the Guarantee Clause cases non-justiciable. It is, in effect, a Guarantee Clause claim masquerading under a different label. But it cannot make the case more fit for judicial action that appellants invoke the Fourteenth Amendment rather than Art. IV, § 4, where, in fact, the gist of their complaint is the same—unless it can be found that the Fourteenth Amendment speaks with greater particularity to their situation. We have been admonished to avoid "the tyranny of labels." . . .

. . . Appellants appear as representatives of a class that is prejudiced as a class, in contradistinction to the polity in its entirety. However, the discrimination relied on is the deprivation of what appellants conceive to be their proportionate share of political influence. This, of course, is the practical effect of any allocation of power within the institutions of government. Hardly any distribution of political authority that could be assailed as rendering government nonrepublican would fail similarly to operate to the prejudice of some groups, and to the advantage of others, within the body politic. . . .

What, then, is this question of legislative apportionment? Appellants invoke the right to vote and to have their votes counted. But they are permitted to vote and their votes are counted. They go to the polls, they cast their ballots, they send their representatives to the state councils. Their complaint is simply that the representatives are not sufficiently numerous or powerful—in short, that Tennessee has adopted a basis of representation with which they are dissatisfied. Talk of "debasement" or "dilution" is circular talk. One cannot speak of "debasement" or "dilution" of the value of a vote until there is first defined a standard of reference as to what a vote should be worth. What is actually asked of the Court in this case is to choose among competing bases of representation—ultimately, really, among competing theories of political philosophy—in order to establish an appropriate frame of government for the State of Tennessee and thereby for all of the States of the Union.

In such a matter, abstract analogies which ignore the facts of history deal in unrealities; they betray reason. This is not a case in which a State has, through a device however oblique and sophisticated, denied Negroes or Jews or redheaded persons a vote, or given them only a third or a sixth of a vote. That was *Gomillion* v. *Lightfoot*. What Tennessee illustrates is an old and still widespread method of representation—representation by local geographical division, only in part respective of population—in preference to others, others, forsooth, more appealing. Appellants contest this choice and seek to make this Court the arbiter of the disagreement. They would make the Equal Protection Clause the charter of adjudication, asserting that the equality which it guarantees comports, if not the assurance of equal weight to every voter's vote, at least the basic conception that representation ought to be proportionate to population, a standard by reference to which the reasonableness of apportionment plans may be judged.

To find such a political conception legally enforceable in the broad and unspecific guarantee of equal protection is to rewrite the Constitution. Certainly, "equal protection" is no more secure a foundation for judicial judgment of the permissibility of varying forms of representative government than is "Republican Form." Indeed since "equal protection of the laws" can only mean an equality of persons standing in the same relation to whatever governmental action is challenged, the determination whether treatment is equal presupposes a determination concerning the nature of the relationship. This, with respect to apportionment, means an inquiry into the theoretic base of representation in an acceptably republican state. For a court could not determine the equal-protection issue without in fact first determining the Republican-Form issue, simply because what is reasonable for equal protection purposes will depend upon what frame of government, basically, is allowed. To divorce "equal protection" from "Republican Form" is to talk about half a question.

The notion that representation proportioned to the geographic spread of population is so universally accepted as a necessary element of equality between man and man that it must be taken to be the standard of a political equality preserved by the Fourteenth Amendment—that it is, in appellants' words "the basic principle of representative government"—is, to put it bluntly, not true. However desirable and however desired by some among the great political thinkers and framers of our government, it has never been generally practiced, today or in the past. It was not the English system, it was not the colonial system, it was not the system chosen for the national government by the Constitution, it was not the system exclusively or even predominantly practiced by the States at the time of adoption of the Fourteenth Amendment, it is not predominantly practiced by the States today. Unless judges, the judges of this Court, are to make their private views of political wisdom the measure of the Constitution— views which in all honesty cannot but give the appearance, if not reflect the reality, of involvement with the business of partisan politics so inescapably a part of apportionment controversies—the Fourteenth Amendment

provides no guide for judicial oversight of the representation problem. . . .

Manifestly, the Equal Protection Clause supplies no clearer guide for judicial examination of apportionment methods than would the Guarantee Clause itself. Apportionment, by its character, is a subject of extraordinary complexity, involving—even after the fundamental theoretical issues concerning what is to be represented in a representative legislature have been fought out or compromised—considerations of geography, demography, electoral convenience, economic and social cohesions or divergencies among particular local groups, communications, the practical effects of political institutions like the lobby and the city machine, ancient traditions and ties of settled usage, respect for proven incumbents of long experience and senior status, mathematical mechanics, censuses compiling relevant data, and a host of others. Legislative responses throughout the country to the reapportionment demands of the 1960 Census have glaringly confirmed that these are not factors that lend themselves to evaluations of a nature that are the staple of judicial determinations or for which judges are equipped to adjudicate by legal training or experience or native wit. And this is the more so true because in every strand of this complicated, intricate web of values meet the contending forces of partisan politics. The practical significance of apportionment is that the next election results may differ because of it. Apportionment battles are overwhelmingly party or intra-party contests. It will add a virulent source of friction and tension in federal-state relations to embroil the federal judiciary in them. . . .

Although the District Court had jurisdiction in the very restricted sense of power to determine whether it could adjudicate the claim, the case is of that class of political controversy which, by the nature of its subject, is unfit for federal judicial action. The judgment of the District Court, in dismissing the complaint for failure to state a claim on which relief can be granted, should therefore be affirmed.

Dissenting opinion of Mr. Justice Harlan, whom Mr. Justice Frankfurter joins. . . .

Note: Baker is crucial because it treats the political question doctrine as no (or very little) more than a function of the federal separation of powers. This, of course, substantially restricts the doctrine—and expands the scope of the judicial reviewing power. See K. Scott, "Standing in the Supreme Court: A Functional Analysis", 86 *Harvard Law Review* 645 (1973).

Powell v. *McCormack*
395 U.S. 486 (1969)

Chief Justice Warren delivered the opinion of the Court.

In November 1966, Petitioner Adam Clayton Powell, Jr., was duly elected from the 18th Congressional District of New York to serve in the United States House of Representatives for the 90th Congress. However, pursuant to a House resolution, he was not permitted to take his seat. Powell (and some of the voters of his district) then filed suit in Federal District Court, claiming that the House could exclude him only if it found he failed to meet the standing requirements of age, citizenship, and residence contained in Art. I, § 2, of the Constitution—requirements the House specifically found Powell met—and thus had excluded him unconstitutionally. The District Court dismissed petitioners' complaint "for want of jurisdiction of the subject matter." A panel of the Court of Appeals affirmed the dismissal, although on somewhat different grounds, each judge filing a separate opinion. We have determined that it was error to dismiss the complaint and that petitioner Powell is entitled to a declaratory judgment that he was unlawfully excluded from the 90th Congress. . . .

POLITICAL QUESTION DOCTRINE

1. Textually Demonstrable Constitutional Commitment

Respondents maintain that even if this case is otherwise justiciable, it presents only a political question. It is well established that the federal courts will not adjudicate political questions. . . .

Respondents' first contention is that this case presents a political question because under Art. I, § 5, there has been a "textually demonstrable constitutional commitment" to the House of the "adjudicatory power" to determine Powell's qualifications. Thus it is argued that the House, and the House alone, has power to determine who is qualified to be a member. . . .

. . . [W]hether there is a "textually demonstrable constitutional commitment of the issue to a coordinate political department of government" and what is the scope of such commitment are questions we must resolve for the first time in this case. For, as we pointed out in *Baker* v. *Carr*, "[d]eciding whether a matter has in any measure been committed by the Constitution to another branch of government, or whether the action of that branch exceeds whatever authority has been committed, is itself a delicate exercise in constitutional interpretation and is the responsibility of this Court as ultimate interpreter of the Constitution."

In order to determine the scope of any "textual commitment" under Art. I, § 5, we necessarily must determine the meaning of the phrase to "Be the Judge of the Qualifications of its Own Members." Petitioners argue that the records of the debates during the Constitutional Convention; available commentary from the post-Convention, pre-ratification period; and early congressional applications of Art. I, § 5, support their construction of the section. Respondents insist, however, that a careful examination of the pre-Convention practices of the English Parliament and American colonial assemblies demonstrates that by 1787, a legislature's power to judge the qualifications of its members was generally understood to encompass exclusion or expulsion on the ground that an individual's character or past conduct rendered him unfit to serve. When the Constitution and the debates over its adoption are thus viewed in historical perspective, argue respondents, it becomes clear that the "qualifications" expressly set forth in the Constitution were not meant to limit the long-recognized legislative power to exclude or expel at will, but merely to establish "standing incapacities," which could be altered only by a constitutional amendment. Our examination of the relevant historical materials leads us to the conclusion that petitioners are correct and that the Constitution leaves the House without authority to *exclude* any person, duly elected by his constituents, who meets all the requirements for membership expressly prescribed in the Constitution. . . .

. . . Unquestionably, Congress has an interest in preserving its institutional integrity, but in most cases that interest can be sufficiently safeguarded by the exercise of its power to punish its members for disorderly behavior and, in extreme cases, to expel a member with the concurrence of two-thirds. In short, both the intention of the Framers, to the extent it can be determined, and an examination of the basic principles of our democratic system persuade us that the Constitution does not vest in the Congress a discretionary power to deny membership by a majority vote.

For these reasons, we have concluded that Art. I, § 5, is at most a "textually demonstrable commitment" to Congress to judge only the qualifications expressly set forth in the Constitution. Therefore, the "textual commitment" formulation of the political question doctrine does not bar federal courts from adjudicating petitioners' claims.

2. Other Considerations

Respondents' alternate contention is that the case presents a political question because judicial resolution of petitioners' claim would produce a "potentially embarrassing confrontation between coordinate branches" of the Federal Government. But, as our interpretation of Art. I, § 5, discloses, a determination of petitioner Powell's right to sit would require no more than an interpretation of the Constitution. Such a determination falls within the traditional role accorded courts to interpret the law, and does not involve a "lack of respect due [a] coordinate [branch] of government," nor does it involve an "initial policy determination of a kind clearly for nonjudicial discretion." *Baker* v. *Carr*. Our system of government requires that federal courts on occasion interpret the Constitution in a manner at variance with the construction given the document by another branch. The alleged conflict that such an adjudication may cause cannot justify the courts' avoiding their constitutional responsibility.

Nor are any of the other formulations of a political question "inextricable from the case at bar." *Baker* v. *Carr*. Petitioners seek a determination that the House was without power to exclude Powell from the 90th Congress, which, we have seen, requires an interpretation of the Constitution—a determination for which clearly there are "judicially . . . manageable standards." Finally, a judicial resolution of petitioners' claim will not result in "multifarious pronouncements by various departments on one question." For, as we noted in *Baker* v. *Carr*, it is the responsibility of this Court to act as the ultimate interpreter of the Constitution. *Marbury* v. *Madison*, 1 Cranch 137 (1803). Thus, we conclude that petitioners' claim is not barred by the political question doctrine, and, having determined that the claim is otherwise generally justiciable, we hold that the case is justiciable. . . .

Note: As some observers saw it, *Powell* v. *McCormack* makes the political question doctrine meaningless. See, for example, "The Supreme Court: 1968 Term," 83 *Harvard Law Review* 62–68 (1969):

All Constitutional questions turn on whether some organ of government exceeded its specified powers. Normally, the Court decides whether these powers were exceeded and rules accordingly. The political question doctrine supposedly interrupts that process by declaring a case nonjusticiable. But by the logic of *Powell,* the doctrine can be invoked only if the Constitution committed the power to an organ to act as it did. Thus a court must first inquire whether that organ exceeded its constitutional powers, and can dismiss the suit only if it did not. The same issues then will have been determined as if there were no political question doctrine at all, and the outcome will be the same for the parties.

THE POST-WARREN ERA

O'Brien v. *Brown*
409 U.S. 1 (1972)

This case involved a dispute as to the seating of delegates to the Democratic National Convention of 1972. The Credentials Committee had excluded certain McGovern delegates because of California's winner-take-all rule, and Mayor Daley's Illinois delegation because it was deemed unrepresentative. The court of appeals overruled the Credentials Committee with respect to the McGovern delegates but upheld it with respect to the Daley delegates. The case reached the Supreme Court three days before the opening of the convention.

Per Curiam

. . . [N]o holding of this Court up to now gives support for judicial intervention in the circumstances presented here, involving as they do, relationships of great delicacy and essentially political in nature. Cf. *Luther* v. *Borden,* 7 How. 1 (1849).

It has been understood since our national political parties first came into being as voluntary associations of individuals that the convention itself is the proper forum for determining intra-party disputes as to which delegates shall be seated. . . . we conclude the judgments of the Court of Appeals must be stayed.

Mr. Justice Brennan is of the view that in the limited time available the Court cannot give these difficult and important questions consideration adequate for their proper resolution. . . .

[Justices Marshall and Douglas, dissenting, observed that] The doctrine of "political questions" was fashioned to deal with a very different problem, which has nothing to do with this case. As the Court said in *Baker* v. *Carr* . . . the basic characteristic of a political question is that its resolution would lead a court into conflict with one or more of the coordinate branches of government; courts decline to decide political questions out of deference to the separation of powers . . . . See *Powell* v. *McCormack* . . . . Neither the Executive nor the Legislative Branch . . . purports to have jurisdiction over the claims asserted in these cases. Apart from the judicial forum, only one other forum has been suggested—the full convention of the National

Democratic Party—and that is most assuredlly not a coordinate branch of government. . . .

Gilligan v. *Morgan*
413 U.S. 1 (1973)

Following the National Guard shooting of students at Kent State University, several students requested a federal court order establishing standards for the training, weapons, and operations of the Ohio National Guard and for continuing judicial surveillance of the guard to insure compliance.

Mr. Chief Justice Burger delivered the opinion of the Court.

[After referring to Article I, Section 8, Clause 16 of the Constitution, which vests in Congress the power to provide for a militia and reserves to the states the training thereof "according to the discipline prescribed by Congress," the Chief Justice observed:]

It would be difficult to think of a clearer example of the type of governmental action that was intended by the Constitution to be left to the political branches, directly responsible—as the Judicial Branch is not—to the elective process. Moreover, it is difficult to conceive of an area of governmental activity in which the courts have less competence. The complex subtle, and professional decisions as to the composition, training, equipping, and control of a military force are essentially professional military judgments, subject *always* to civilian control of the Legislative and Executive Branches. The ultimate responsibility for these decisions are appropriately vested in branches of the government which are periodically subject to electoral accountability. It is this power of oversight and control of military force by elected representatives and officials which underlies our entire

constitutional system; the majority opinion of the Court of Appeals failed to give appropriate weight to this separation of powers. . . .

In concluding that no justiciable controversy is presented, it should be clear that we neither hold nor imply that the conduct of the National Guard is always beyond judicial review or that there may not be accountability in a judicial forum for violations of law or for specific unlawful conduct by military personnel, whether by way of damages or injunctive relief. We hold only that no such questions are presented in this case. We decline to require a United States district court to involve itself so directly and so intimately in the task assigned that court by the Court of Appeals.

[Justices Douglas, Brennan, Stewart, and Marshall dissented on the ground that the entire matter had become moot. As one Justice put it, "The Ohio use-of-force rules have now been changed, and are identical to the Army use-of-force rules. Counsel for [the students] stated at oral argument that the . . . rules now in effect provide satisfactory safeguards against unwarranted use of lethal force by the Ohio National Guard. . . . And, as of 1971, special civilian-disturbance-control training has been provided . . . ." .]

Note: In *Atlee* v. *Laird,* 347 F. Supp. 689 (E.D. Pa. 1972), a three-judge federal district court dismissed as a political question a challenge to the constitutionality of the Vietnam conflict. The Supreme Court summarily *affirmed* in *Atlee* v. *Richardson,* 411 U.S. 911 (1973), over the dissent of Justice Douglas, Brennan, and Stewart. This seems to be the only case in which the Supreme Court indicated its view that the propriety of the Vietnam conflict was a political issue.

The Warren Court—despite its substantial easing of justiciability barriers—had steadfastly refused to pass upon the validity of the Vietnam conflict without clearly specifying why it was non-justiciable.

JUDICIAL ROLES

R. Bork, "Neutral Principles and Some First Amendment Problems," 47 *Indiana Law Journal* 1 (1971) (excerpt)

. . . If the judiciary really is supreme, able to rule when and as it sees fit, the society is not democratic. The anomaly is dissipated, however, by the model of government embodied in the structure of the Constitution, a model . . . we may for convenience, though perhaps not with total accuracy, call "Madisonian."

A Madisonian system is not completely democratic, if by "democratic" we man completely majoritarian. It assumes that in wide areas of life majorities are entitled to rule for no better reason than they are majorities. . . . The model has also a counter-majoritarian premise, however, for it assumes there are some areas of life a majority should not control. . . . These are areas properly left to individual freedom, and coercion by the majority in these aspects of life is tyranny.

. . . Minority tyranny occurs if the majority is prevented from ruling where its power is legitimate. Yet, quite obviously, neither the majority nor the minority can be trusted to define the freedom of the other. This dilemma is resolved in constitutional theory, and in popular understanding, by the Supreme Court's power to define both majority and minority freedom through the interpretation of the Constitution. Society consents to be ruled undemocratically within defined areas by certain enduring principles believed to be stated in, and placed beyond the reach of majorities by, the Constitution.

But this resolution of the dilemma imposes severe requirements upon the Court. For it follows that the Court's power is legitimate only if it has, and can demonstrate in reasoned opinions that it has, a valid theory, derived from the Constitution, of the respective spheres of majority and minority freedom. If it does not have such a theory but merely imposes its own value choices, or worse if it pretends to have a theory but actually follows its own predilections, the Court violates the postulates of the Madisonian model that alone justifies its power. It then necessarily abets the tyranny either of the majority or of the minority.

H. Wechsler, "Toward Neutral Principles of Constitutional Law," 73 *Harvard Law Review* 1 (1959) (excerpt)*

Let me repeat what I have thus far tried to say. The courts have both the title and the duty when a case is properly before them to review the actions of the other branches in the light of constitutional provisions, even though the action involves value choices, as invariably action does. In doing so, however, they are bound to function otherwise than as a naked power organ; they participate as courts of law. This calls for facing how determinations of this kind can

_____

* Reprinted by permission of the author.

be asserted to have any legal quality. The answer, I suggest, inheres primarily in that they are—or are obliged to be—entirely principled. A principled decision, in the sense I have in mind, is one that rests on reasons with respect to all the issues in the case, reasons that in their generality and their neutrality transcend any immediate result that is involved. When no sufficient reasons of this kind can be assigned for overturning value choices of the other branches of the Government or of a state, those choices must, of course, survive. Otherwise, as Holmes said in his first opinion for the Court, "a constitution, instead of embodying only relatively fundamental rules of right, as generally understood by all English-speaking communities, would become the partisan of a particular set of ethical or economical opinions. . . .

A. Miller and R. Howell, "The Myth of Neutrality in Constitutional Adjudication," 29 *University of Chicago Law Review* 661 (1960) (excerpt)*

The position taken by . . . Wechsler is based on a view of life and the social process in which litigants (and others) are in agreement on the basic essentials—the goal values—and all that remains is the settlement of preferred ways to reach those ends. Put another way, his position is bottomed on a theory of a fundamental harmony of interests of all members of the American community. But that is precisely what may *not* be present in most important constitutional litigation, such as racial relations, where disagreement is over ends or goals and not the means or tactics to attain them; the administration of the criminal law, where an anti-social being is jousting with something called society; and in many of the civil liberty cases, where again the disagreement is over fundamentals.

To posit a society with a harmony of interests is to rearticulate a fundamental tenet of the American democracy; to speak otherwise is to question, at least in part, one of the underpinnings of the constitutional order. Nevertheless that, in essence, is what is present here, and serves to explain, at least partially, the counting of votes—as Hart says—of "one up (or down) for civil rights" and so on. To put it in other terms, it is the difference between a Hobbesian view of the social process and that of, say, Burke, Locke or Rousseau. . . .

. . . [The] Court *is* a power organ, which aids in the shaping of community values, whether avowedly so as in the hands of a Douglas or whether abashedly so when Frankfurter seeks to convince us that he is an apostle of "self-restraint." Whatever its decision—even a denial of certiorari or taking refuge within the doughy contours of "political questions"—the Court is institutionally a part of a government with affirmative orientation: In a welfare state, it is also concerned with "welfare." The only question is not whether it should be so but whether it should be *outwardly* so, and whether it should try to be systematically, rather than in a helter-skelter manner.

The role, then, of the Supreme Court in an age of positive government must be that of an active participant in government, assisting in furthering the democratic ideal. Acting at least in part as a "national conscience," the Court should help articulate in broad principle the goals of American society.

Learned Hand, *The Spirit of Liberty* 218 (1960) (excerpt)†

There are those who insist that detachment [and neutrality] is an illusion; that our conclusions, when their bases are sifted, always reveal

---

* Source: © 1960 by the University of Chicago.

† Irving Dillard, ed., *The Spirit of Liberty: Papers and Addresses of Learned Hand.* © 1960 by Alfred A. Knopf, Inc.

a passional foundation. Even so, though they be throughout the creatures of past emotional experience, it does not follow that that experience can never predispose us to impartiality. A bias against bias may be as likely a result of some buried crisis, as any other bias. Be that as it may, we know that men do differ widely in this capacity; and the incredulity which seeks to discredit that knowledge is a part of the crusade against reason from which we have already so bitterly suffered. We may deny—and, if we are competent observers, we will deny—that no one can be aware of the danger and in large measure provide against it.

Note and quaere: Is Wechsler's position based (as Miller and Howell insist) on "a theory of fundamental harmony of [social] interests"? Or is it rather that Wechsler (as aware as the rest of us of social conflict) insists that in a polity striving for a more perfect democracy conflicts should be resolved by the democratic processes—with minimal (i.e., only principled and nonpartisan) intervention by judges? Miller and Howell argue that judicial neutrality is impossible; therefore judges should be partisans in "furthering the democratic ideal" and in helping to "articulate . . . the goals of American society." Is it not likely that *both* the majority and dissenting judges in the abortion, obscenity, and school-prayer cases, for example, thought they were doing just that? Is it likely that any judge ever supposed his judgment violated the "democratic ideal" or the proper "goals of American society"? Do these vague but sounding precepts leave judges free—indeed invite them—to impose their own subjective "ideals" and "goals" upon the rest of us?

Does Wechsler's appeal for neutral principles in adjudication offer any greater protection against subjectivity? A neutral principle presumably is one the Court is prepared to apply across the board evenly and equally—not just when it feels like doing so (perhaps out of sympathy or disdain for this or that litigant—or the class he or she "represents"). Short of such nonpartisan principles, according to Wechsler, courts should not interfere with "value choices" of the elected (i.e., politically accountable), agencies of government.

Mr. Justice Holmes emphasized a somewhat similar approach: when the mandate of the Constitution leaves room for doubt in the circumstances of a particular case (at least when First Amendment problems are not involved) that doubt should be resolved in favor of the view adopted by the politically accountable agencies of government. See the Holmes dissents in *Adkins* and in *Lochner* (below, Chapter 6).

Would it be fair to suggest that Miller and Howell lean to "the rule of men," while Wechsler urges "the rule of law"—and that Holmes (not unlike Wechsler) in doubtful cases would leave policy *choices* to those who are elected by, and accountable to, the people?

ORGANIZATION AND JURISDICTION OF THE FEDERAL COURTS

Article III of the Constitution provides for a Supreme Court and authorizes such lower federal courts as Congress may from time to time establish. Pursuant to this grant there are now from one to four federal trial courts (United States district courts) in each state and the District of Columbia. Above them are 11 intermediate appellate tribunals (United States courts of appeals), each having jurisdiction to review decisions from district courts within a specified area of "circuit" and from various federal administrative agencies, such as the Federal Trade Commission. Most federal litigation gets no higher than this second judicial level. Only the very special case can go to the Supreme Court, as we shall see. It is crucial that the sole authority that tribunal gets directly from the Constitution is a very limited original jurisdiction involving states, ambassadors, ministers, and consuls. All other federal court authority is to be distributed in such manner and among such courts as Congress may provide. The appellate authority of the Supreme Court with respect to "inferior" federal courts (and to state courts) is also subject to full congressional control.

Finally, the Constitution (Article III, Section 2, Paragraph 1) provides that federal courts shall have jurisdiction (power to decide) in only two categories of cases. One embraces those arising under the Constitution, federal statutes, and treaties. The reason for this is plain. If national law is to have uniform meaning throughout the nation, it cannot be left to the mutually independent judicial systems of the several states. However, the Constitution does not give this "federal question" jurisdiction, as it is called, exclusively to federal judges. Nor has Congress made it exclusive, except in a very limited field, such as federal bankruptcy. Thus cases involving federal law may arise and be decided in state courts. Beginning with Section 25 of the Judiciary Act of 1789 Congress has always provided for review of such cases by the Supreme Court of the United States, lest federal law have as many meanings as there are states. Madison, we have noted, argued in support of such jurisdiction. Nevertheless, it offended some in the early days that the decision of the highest court of a "sovereign state" should be reversible by an "outside" court. "The great Chief Justice" and his colleagues had something to say on this matter in *Cohens* v. *Virginia*. Since then the constitutional issue has been settled.

The other category of cases which federal courts may decide is that involving certain special parties *regardless of what law is involved*. For example, the ambassador of a foreign country may have his case involving a mere grocery bill tried in a federal court even though no federal law (Constitution, treaty, or act of Congress) is applicable. Obviously in such a case the federal court acts in effect as a special state tribunal. Recognizing this, Congress from the beginning has provided that in litigation of this type the federal courts shall apply state "laws."

Obviously one Supreme Court of nine judges cannot review all cases decided in state and lower federal courts. That some system of selection is necessary finds expression in the constitutional provision giving Congress the power to regulate the Court's appellate jurisdiction (Article III, Section 2, Paragraph 2). Congress has exercised this power by giving a "right" to appeal in a very limited category of cases and by granting the Court discretionary authority to review or not in other situations. One whose claim under federal law is rejected by the highest state court in which the issue can be raised has a "right" of appeal to the Supreme Court of the nation. Such a rejection occurs when a litigant invokes federal law and its validity is denied, or when a litigant challenges a state law as being in violation of the federal Constitution and its validity is upheld. Conversely, when a lower federal court holds a state law in conflict with the federal Constitution, and in certain circumstances when such a court finds an act of Congress invalid, appeal is a matter of "right." Generally speaking, other cases get to the Supreme Court only as a matter of grace. That is to say, the Court may grant or deny review in its discretion by granting or refusing applications for the writ of certiorari. The thought is that since the Justices obviously cannot review all cases, they can by this method spend their limited time and energy where, in their opinion, it will do the most *public* good. For let us be clear, it is the appellate responsibility of

FIGURE 1
Diagram Showing the Reviewing Authority of the Supreme Court

* Direct appeals from district courts are allowed only in very special circumstances.
† A court of appeals, like the court of claims, may certify to the Supreme Court "any question of law . . . as to which instructions are desired." This device is now seldom used because certified questions tend to raise hypothetical, rather than real, issues. These the Supreme Court shuns for the same reasons which have impelled it to avoid giving advisory opinions. *NLRB* v. *Swan Co.*, 313 U.S. 23, 27 (1941).

state supreme courts and the United States courts of appeals to protect the merely private rights of litigants. The Supreme Court's responsibility is larger. Chief Justice Vinson expressed the orthodox view in the following terms:

> The Supreme Court is not, and never has been, primarily concerned with the correction of errors in lower court decisions. . . . If we took every case in which an interesting legal question is raised, or our *prima facie* impression is that the decision below is erroneous, we could not fulfill the constitutional and statutory responsibilities placed upon the Court. To remain effective the Supreme Court must continue to decide only those cases which present questions whose resolution will have immediate importance far beyond the particular facts and parties involved.[1]

For example, a classic case for the exercise of the discretionary power to review is one which will permit the Supreme Court to settle the matter on which two United States courts of appeal are in disagreement. Here the desideratum is not the private interest of any of the litigants, but the public interest in uniformity in the law throughout the nation.

In fact, the distinction between appeals as of right and review via certiorari is somewhat illusory. For over the years there has developed a practice whereby the Court rejects the former when they present what the judges consider only "insubstan-

---

[1] 69 S. Ct. VI (1949). Address before American Bar Association, September 7, 1949.

tial federal questions." See Mr. Justice Frankfurther's remarks in *Daniels* v. *Allen*, 344 U.S. 433, 491 (1953), and "The Insubstantial Federal Question," 62 *Harvard Law Review* 488 (1949).

Commission on Revision of the Federal Court Appellate System, *Structure and Internal Procedures: Recommendations for Change*, 5–9 (1975) (excerpt)*

The United States Supreme Court is today the only court with the power to hand down judgments which constitute binding precedents in all state and federal courts. It is charged with maintaining a harmonious body of national law through its power of review of the judgments in cases brought before it by way of certiorari and appeal. As the number of cases brought to the Supreme Court for review has burgeoned, the number disposed of on the merits after argument has remained relatively constant. Obviously, the major variable has been in the number of cases not accorded plenary review.

The figures are dramatic. In 1951 about 1,200 cases were filed in the Court. Twenty years later the number had tripled to about 3,600. The volume continues to rise: in the most recent complete term over 4,000 cases were filed. By contrast, as Erwin N. Griswold observes, the Court was "hearing about 150 cases on the merits in 1925; it was hearing about 150 cases on the merits twenty five years ago. It hears about 150 cases on the merits today." Elaborating on the same point, he continues: "The number of cases argued orally in 1951 was 128. The number of cases argued orally at the 1973 Term was 170. But there were a considerable number of occasions when two or more cases were heard at a single argument. Thus, there were approximately 150 oral arguments, and this number has been more or less constant for a number of years. It is, in fact, the maximum number that

the Court can be expected to hear on the merits."

The significance of these figures is summarized by Griswold as follows: ". . . Putting it another way, about eighteen percent of paid cases (appeals and certiorari) were heard on the merits twenty years ago, while about six percent of paid cases were heard on the merits during the 1973 Term. What became of the other twelve percent of paid cases? . . . they were lost in the 1973 Term simply because of inadequate appellate capacity to hear cases on a national basis."

The figures discussed above do not include summary dispositions of cases within the Court's appeal docket. . . .

Supreme Court filings may already be an inadequate measure of the real needs of the country for definitive adjudication of national issues. As the needs increase and the proportion of cases accorded review decreases, the number of filings becomes even less likely to reflect the real need accurately. Fewer litigants will seek review, not necessarily because their cause is unimportant by traditional criteria, but rather because there is so little chance of persuading the Court to hear the case. Professors Casper and Posner make the point effectively in their recently-published *Study of the Supreme Court's Caseload:* "[T]he value of filing an application for review with the Supreme Court," they write, "is a function of the probability that review will be granted, and as that probability declines over time due to increases in the number of cases filed coupled with the Court's inability to increase significantly the number of cases it accepts for review, the value of seeking review will fall, and, other things being equal, the number of cases should decline."

The implication of this analysis is clear. In the words of the authors: "[S]hould the Court's

---

* Source: Government Printing Office, Washington, D.C.

caseload level off or even decline in the coming years, this would *not* refute the existence of a serious workload problem—the caseload might simply have become so large in relation to the Court's ability to decide cases that litigants were discouraged from seeking review by the low probability of obtaining it."

There is evidence that this phenomenon has already had its impact and that the data we have discussed may in fact understate the problem today. We know that in cases which the Solicitor General considered 'cert-worthy,' he has refused to request review because of a sensitivity to the Court's workload and a concern that review would be jeopardized in cases of even greater importance. Similarly, private practitioners refer to what has been termed the "hidden docket," those cases in which counsel chose not to seek review only because the probability of a decision on the merits is too low to warrant the expense.

The pressure of this increased competition for the attention of the Supreme Court is not distributed equally in all categories of cases. Understandably, an increasing proportion of the Court's decisions have involved constitutional issues. Since the total number of decisions has remained constant, the result is that the number of those dealing with non-constitutional issues has been decreasing. Prior to 1960, the *Harvard Law Review* reported in 1971, nonconstitutional holdings "almost uniformly" made up two-thirds to three-quarters of the Court's decisions. In more recent years, the proportions have almost been reversed: constitutional cases have comprised between one-half and two-thirds of the Court's plenary decisions. Congressional enactments have imposed federal standards in such areas as occupational health and safety, protection of the environment, product safety, and economic stabilization, to name but a few. Thus, while the scope of federal regulatory legislation—typically including provisions for judicial review—has been steadily broadening, the number of defini-

tive decisions interpreting that legislation has been diminishing. What this means, in absolute figures, is that in each term the Supreme Court can be expected to hand down no more than 80, and perhaps as few as 55, plenary decisions in all areas of federal non-constitutional law. The question is whether this number of decisions is adequate to meet the country's needs for authoritative exposition of recurring issues of national law. . . .

. . . [W]e cannot recommend any solution which would increase the Court's burden. There is ample evidence that the workload of the Justices is such that they are already subject, in the words of Mr. Justice Blackmun, to "greater and more constant pressure" than busy practitioners or hard-working appellate judges, pressure which "relents little even during the summer months." The issue is not whether the Justices find it possible to keep abreast of present work. The evidence is that more than one does so by giving up the "normal extracurricular enjoyments of life"; six or seven days of work a week are not unknown as a regular pattern. Whether or not such burdens should be viewed as an appropriate norm, it hardly seems a desirable solution to increase the number of cases which the Court should be expected to decide. On the contrary, given the complexity and significance of the issues which only the Supreme Court can decide, it may be appropriate to reduce the number of cases which the Court must decide. Both Mr. Justice White and Mr. Justice Rehnquist have invited consideration of this alternative.

Note: At least five of the current justices—Burger, White, Blackmun, Powell, and Rehnquist—agree "on the need for some relief [from its workload] if this Court is to achieve and maintain the optimum level of quality in its work": *Brown Transport Corp.* v. *Atcon, Inc.,* 99 S. Ct. 626, 633, 635 (1978).

2

The Separation of Powers: The President vis-à-vis Congress and the Courts in the Making of Public Policy

INTRODUCTION

Mr. Justice Brandeis in *Myers* v. *United States*, 272 U.S. 52 (1926) (excerpt)

The doctrine of the separation of powers was adopted by the convention of 1787 not to promote efficiency but to preclude the exercise of arbitrary power. The purpose was not to avoid friction but by means of the inevitable friction incident to the distribution of the governmental powers among three departments, to save the people from autocracy.

Mr. Justice Jackson in *The Steel Seizure Case*, 343 U.S. 579 (1952) (excerpt)

While the Constitution diffuses power the better to secure liberty, it also contemplates that practice will integrate the dispersed powers into a workable government. It enjoins upon its branches separateness but interdependence, autonomy but reciprocity. Presidential powers are not fixed but fluctuate, depending upon their disjunction or conjunction with those of Congress.

EXECUTIVE POLICYMAKING: DOMESTIC AFFAIRS

Youngstown Sheet & Tube Co. v. *Sawyer* (*The Steel Seizure Case*)
343 U.S. 579 (1952)

Mr. Justice Black delivered the opinion of the Court.

We are asked to decide whether the President was acting within his constitutional power when he issued an order directing the Secretary of Commerce to take possession of and operate most of the Nation's steel mills. The mill owners argue that the President's order amounts to lawmaking, a legislative function which the Constitution has expressly confided to the Congress and not to the President. The Government's position is that the order was made on findings of the President that his action was necessary to avert a national catastrophe which would inevitably result from a stoppage of steel production, and that in meeting this grave emergency the President was acting within the aggregate of his constitutional powers as the Nation's Chief Executive and the Commander in Chief of the Armed Forces of the United States. . . .

. . . [T]he District Court on April 30 issued a preliminary injunction restraining the Secretary from "continuing the seizure and possession of the plants . . . and from acting under the purported authority of Executive Order No. 10340." On the same day the Court of Appeals stayed the District Court's injunction. Deeming it best that the issues raised be promptly decided by this Court, we granted certiorari on May 3 and set the cause for argument on May 12. . . .

The President's power, if any, to issue the order must stem either from an act of Congress or from the Constitution itself. There is no statute that expressly authorized the President to take possession of property as he did here. Nor is there any act of Congress to which our attention has been directed from which such a power can fairly be implied. Indeed, we do not understand the Government to rely on statutory authorization for this seizure. . . .

. . . [T]he use of the seizure technique to solve labor disputes in order to prevent work stoppages was not only unauthorized by any congressional enactment; prior to this controversy, Congress had refused to adopt that method of settling labor disputes. When the Taft-Hartley Act was under consideration in 1947, Congress rejected an amendment which would have authorized such governmental seizures in cases of emergency. . . . Instead, the plan sought to bring about settlements by use of the customary devices of mediation, conciliation, investigation by boards of inquiry, and public reports. In some instances temporary injunctions were authorized to provide cooling-off periods. All this failing, the unions were left free to strike after a secret vote by employees as to whether they wished to accept their employers' final settlement offer.

It is clear that if the President had authority to issue the order he did, it must be found in some provisions of the Constitution. And it is not claimed that express constitutional language grants this power to the President. The conten-

tion is that presidential power should be implied from the aggregate of his powers under the Constitution. Particular reliance is place on provisions in Article II which say that "The executive Power shall be vested in a President . . ." ; that "he shall take Care that the Laws be faithfully executed"; and that he "shall be Commander in Chief of the Army and Navy of the United States."

The order cannot properly be sustained as an exercise of the President's military power as Commander in Chief of the Armed Forces. The Government attempts to do so by citing a number of cases upholding broad powers in military commanders engaged in day-to-day fighting in a theater of war. Such cases need not concern us here. Even though "theater of war" be an expanding concept, we cannot with faithfulness to our constitutional system hold that the Commander in Chief of the Armed Forces has the ultimate power as such to take possession of private property in order to keep labor disputes from stopping production. This is a job for the Nation's lawmakers, not for its military authorities.

Nor can the seizure order be sustained because of the several constitutional provisions that grant executive power to the President. In the framework of our Constitution, the President's power to see that the laws are faithfully executed refutes the idea that he is to be a lawmaker. The Constitution limits his functions in the lawmaking process to the recommending of laws he thinks wise and the vetoing of laws he thinks bad. And the Constitution is neither silent nor equivocal about who shall make laws which the President is to execute. . . .

The President's order does not direct that a congressional policy be executed in a manner prescribed by Congress—it directs that a presidential policy be executed in a manner prescribed by the President. . . . The power of Congress to adopt such public policies as those proclaimed by the order is beyond question. It can authorize the taking of private property for public use. It can make laws regulating the relationships between employers and employees, prescribing rules designed to settle labor disputes, and fixing wages and working conditions in certain fields of our economy. The Constitution did not subject this lawmaking power of Congress to presidential or military supervision or control.

It is said that other Presidents without congressional authority have taken possession of private business enterprises in order to settle labor disputes. But even if this be true, Congress has not thereby lost its exclusive constitutional authority to make laws necessary and proper to carry out the powers vested by the Constitution "in the Government of the United States, or any Department or Officer thereof."

The Founders of this Nation entrusted the law-making power to the Congress alone in both good and bad times. It would do no good to recall the historical events, the fears of power and the hopes for freedom that lay behind their choice. Such a review would but confirm our holding that this seizure order cannot stand.

Mr. Justice Frankfurter, concurring. . . .

The issue before us can be met, and therefore should be, without attempting to define the President's powers comprehensively. I shall not attempt to delineate what belongs to him by virtue of his office beyond the power even of Congress to contract; what authority belongs to him until Congress acts; what kind of problems may be dealt with either by the Congress or by the President or by both . . . ; what power must be exercised by the Congress and cannot be delegated to the President. . . .

We must therefore put to one side consideration of what powers the President would have had if there had been no legislation whatever bearing on the authority asserted by the seizure, or if the seizure had been only for a short, explicitly temporary period, to be determined automatically unless Congressional approval were given. These and other questions, like or unlike, are not now here. I would exceed

my authority were I to say anything about them.

The question before the Court comes in this setting. Congress has frequently—at least 16 times since 1916—specifically provided for executive seizure of production, transportation, communications, or storage facilities. In every case it has qualified this grant of power with limitations and safeguards. This body of enactments—summarized in tabular form in Appendix I [the Appendix is omitted]—demonstrates that Congress deemed seizure so drastic a power as to require that it be carefully circumscribed whenever the President was vested with this extraordinary authority. The power to seize has uniformly been given only for a limited period or for a defined emergency, or has been repealed after a short period. Its exercise has been restricted to particular circumstances such as "time of war or when war is imminent," the needs of "public safety" or of "national security or defense," or "urgent and impending need." The period of governmental operation has been limited . . . . Seizure statutes usually make executive action dependent on detailed conditions . . . .

Congress in 1947 was again called upon to consider whether governmental seizure should be used to avoid serious industrial shutdowns. Congress decided against conferring such power generally and in advance, without special congressional enactment to meet each particular need. . . . No room for doubt remains that the proponents as well as the opponents of the bill which became the Labor Management Relations Act of 1947 clearly understood that as a result of that legislation the only recourse for preventing a shutdown in any basic industry, after failure of mediation, was Congress. Authorization for seizure as an available remedy for potential dangers was unequivocally put aside. . . .

In adopting the provisions [of the] Labor Management Relations Act of 1947, for dealing with a "national emergency" arising out of a breakdown in peaceful industrial relations,

Congress was very familiar with Government seizure as a protective measure. On a balance of considerations Congress chose not to lodge this power in the President. It chose not to make available in advance a remedy to which both industry and labor were fiercely hostile. In deciding that authority to seize should be given to the President only after full consideration of the particular situation should show such legislation to be necessary, Congress presumably acted on experience with similar industrial conflicts in the past. It evidently assumed that industrial shutdowns in basic industries are not instances of spontaneous generation, and that danger warnings are sufficiently plain before the event to give ample opportunity to start the legislative process into action.

In any event, nothing can be plainer than that Congress made a conscious choice of policy in a field full of perplexity and peculiarly within legislative responsibility for choice. . . .

It cannot be contended that the President would have had power to issue this order had Congress explicitly negated such authority in formal legislation. Congress has expressed its will to withhold this power from the President as though it had said so in so many words. The authoritatively expressed purpose of Congress to disallow such power to the President and to require him, when in his mind the occasion arose for such a seizure, to put the matter to Congress and ask for specific authority from it, could not be more decisive if it had been written into §§ 206–210 of the Labor Management Relations Act of 1947. . . .

. . . But it is now claimed that the President has seizure power by virtue of the Defense Production Act of 1950 and its Amendments. . . . The legislative history of the Defense Production Act . . . cannot possibly be vouched for more than Congressional awareness and tacit approval that the President had charged the Wage Stabilization Board with authority to seek voluntary settlement of labor disputes. . . .

. . . It is an inadmissibly narrow conception of American constitutional law to confine it to the words of the Constitution and to disregard the gloss which life has written upon them. In short, a systematic, unbroken, executive practice, long pursued to the knowledge of the Congress and never before questioned, engaged in by Presidents who have also sworn to uphold the Constitution, making as it were such exercise of power part of the structure of our government, may be treated as a gloss on "executive Power" vested in the President by §§ 1 of Art. II. . . .

Down to the World War II period . . . the record is barren of instances comparable to the one before us. Of twelve seizures by President Roosevelt prior to the enactment of the War Labor Disputes Act in June, 1943, three were sanctioned by existing law, and six others were effected after Congress, on December 8, 1941, had declared the existence of a state of war. In this case, reliance on the powers that flow from declared war has been commendably disclaimed by the Solicitor General. Thus the list of executive assertions of the power of seizure in circumstances comparable to the present reduces to three in the six-month period from June to December of 1941. We need not split hairs in comparing those actions to the one before us, though much might be said by way of differentiation. Without passing on their validity, as we are not called upon to do, it suffices to say that these three isolated instances do not add up, either in number, scope, duration or contemporaneous legal justification, to the kind of executive construction of the Constitution revealed in the *Midwest Oil* case. Nor do they come to us sanctioned by long-continued acquiescence of Congress giving decisive weight to a construction by the Executive of its powers. . . .

Mr. Justice Douglas, concurring. . . .

. . . The branch of government that has the power to pay compensation for a seizure is the only one able to authorize a seizure or make lawful one that the President has effected. That seems to me to be the necessary result of the condemnation provision in the Fifth Amendment. It squares with the theory of checks and balances expounded by Mr. Justice Black in the opinion of the Court in which I join. . . .

Mr. Justice Jackson, concurring in the judgment and opinion of the Court. . . .

The actual art of governing under our Constitution does not and cannot conform to judicial definitions of the power of any of its branches based on isolated clauses or even single Articles torn from context. While the Constitution diffuses power the better to secure liberty, it also contemplates that practice will integrate the dispersed powers into a workable government. It enjoins upon its branches separateness but interdependence, autonomy but reciprocity. Presidential powers are not fixed but fluctuate, depending upon their disjunction or conjunction with those of Congress. We may well begin by a somewhat oversimplified grouping of practical situations in which a President may doubt, or others may challenge, his powers, and by distinguishing roughly the legal consequences of this factor of relativity.

1. When the President acts pursuant to an express or implied authorization of Congress, his authority is at its maximum, for it includes all that he possesses in his own right plus all that Congress can delegate. In these circumstances, and in these only, may he be said (for what it may be worth) to personify the federal sovereignty. If his act is held unconstitutional under these circumstances, it usually means that the Federal Government as an undivided whole lacks power. A seizure executed by the President pursuant to an Act of Congress would be supported by the strongest of presumptions and the widest latitude of judicial interpretation, and the burden of persuasion would rest heavily upon any who might attack it.

2. When the President acts in absence of either a congressional grant or denial of authority, he can only rely upon his own independent powers, but there is a zone of twilight in which he and Congress may have concurrent authority, or in which its distribution is uncertain. Therefore, congressional inertia, indifference or quiescence may sometimes, at least as a practical matter, enable, if not invite, measures on independent presidential responsibility. In this area, any actual test of power is likely to depend on the imperatives of events and contemporary imponderables rather than on abstract theories of law.

3. When the President takes measures incompatible with the expressed or implied will of Congress, his power is at its lowest ebb, for then he can rely only upon his own constitutional powers minus any constitutional powers of Congress over the matter. Courts can sustain exclusive presidential control in such a case only by disabling the Congress from acting upon the subject. Presidential claim to a power at once so conclusive and preclusive must be scrutinized with caution, for what is at stake is the equilibrium established by our constitutional system.

Into which of these classifications does this executive seizure of the steel industry fit? It is eliminated from the first by admission, for it is conceded that no congressional authorization exists for this seizure. . . .

Can it then be defended under flexible tests available to the second category? It seems clearly eliminated from that class because Congress has not left seizure of private property an open field but has covered it by three statutory policies inconsistent with this seizure. . . . None of these were invoked. . . .

This leaves the current seizure to be justified only by the severe tests under the third grouping, where it can be supported only by any remainder of executive power after subtraction of such powers as Congress may have over the subject. In short, we can sustain the President only by holding that seizure of such strike-bound industries is within his domain and beyond control by Congress. Thus, this Court's first review of such seizures occurs under circumstances which leave presidential power most vulnerable to attack and in the least favorable of possible constitutional postures.

I did not suppose, and I am not persuaded, that history leaves it open to question, at least in the courts, that the executive branch, like the Federal Government as a whole, possesses only delegated powers. The purpose of the Constitution was not only to grant power, but to keep it from getting out of hand. However, because the President does not enjoy unmentioned powers does not mean that the mentioned ones should be narrowed by a niggardly construction. Some clauses could be made almost unworkable, as well as immutable, by refusal to indulge some latitude of interpretation for changing times. . . .

The Solicitor General seeks the power of seizure in three clauses of the Executive Article, the first reading, "The executive Power shall be vested in a President of the United States of America." . . .

. . . I cannot accept the view that this clause is a grant in bulk of all conceivable executive power but regard it as an allocation to the presidential office of the generic powers thereafter stated.

The clause on which the Government next relies is that "The President shall be Commander in Chief of the Army and Navy of the United States. . . ."

. . . [The] argument tendered at our bar [is] that the President having, on his own responsibility, sent American troops abroad derives from that act "affirmative power" to seize the means of producing a supply of steel for them. . . .

I cannot foresee all that it might entail if the Court should indorse this argument. Nothing in our Constitution is plainer than that declaration of a war is entrusted only to Congress. Of course, a state of war may in fact exist without a formal declaration. But no doctrine that the Court could promulgate would seem to me more sinister and alarming than that a President whose conduct of foreign affairs is so largely un-

controlled, and often even is unknown, can vastly enlarge his mastery over the internal affairs of the country by his own commitment of the Nation's armed forces to some foreign venture. . . .

The third clause in which the Solicitor General finds seizure powers is that "he shall take Care that the Laws be faithfully executed. . . ." That authority must be matched against words of the Fifth Amendment that "No person shall be . . . deprived of life, liberty or property, without due process of law. . . ." One gives a governmental authority that reaches so far as there is law, the other gives a private right that authority shall go no farther. . . .

The Solicitor General lastly grounds support of the seizure upon nebulous, inherent powers never expressly granted but said to have accrued to the office from the customs and claims of preceding administrations. The plea is for a resulting power to deal with a crisis or an emergency according to the necessities of the case, the unarticulated assumption being that necessity knows no law. . . .

In view of the ease, expedition and safety with which Congress can grant and has granted large emergency powers, certainly ample to embrace this crisis, I am quite unimpressed with the argument that we should affirm possession of them without statute. Such power either has no beginning or it has no end. If it exists, it need submit to no legal restraint. I am not alarmed that it would plunge us straightway into dictatorship, but it is at least a step in that wrong direction. . . .

Mr. Justice Burton, concurring in both the opinion and judgment of the Court. . . .

The controlling fact here is that Congress, within its constitutionally delegated power, has prescribed for the President specific procedures, exclusive of seizure, for his use in meeting the present type of emergency. . . . Under these circumstances, the President's order of April 8 invaded the jurisdiction of Congress. It violated the essence of the principle of the separation of governmental powers. . . .

Mr. Justice Clark, concurring in the judgment of the Court. . . .

I conclude that where Congress has laid down specific procedures to deal with the type of crisis confronting the President, he must follow those procedures in meeting the crisis; but that in the absence of such action by Congress, the President's independent power to act depends upon the gravity of the situation confronting the nation. I cannot sustain the seizure in question because here, . . . , Congress had prescribed methods to be followed by the President in meeting the emergency at hand.

Mr. Chief Justice Vinson, with whom Mr. Justice Reed and Mr. Justice Minton join, dissenting. . . .

A review of executive action demonstrates that our Presidents have on many occasions exhibited the leadership contemplated by the Framers when they made the President Commander in Chief, and imposed upon him the trust to "take Care that the Laws be faithfully executed." With or without explicit statutory authorization, Presidents have at such times dealt with national emergencies by acting promptly and resolutely to enforce legislative programs, at least to save those programs until Congress could act. Congress and the courts have responded to such executive initiative with consistent approval.

Our first President displayed at once the leadership contemplated by the Framers. When the national revenue laws were openly flouted in some sections of Pennsylvania, President Washington, without waiting for a call from the state government, summoned the militia and took decisive steps to secure the faithful execution of the laws. When international disputes engendered by the French revolution threatened to involve this country in war, and while congressional policy remained uncertain, Washington issued his Proclamation of Neutrality. . . .

Jefferson's initiative in the Louisiana Purchase, the Monroe Doctrine, and Jackson's removal of Government deposits from the Bank of the United States further serve to demonstrate by deed what the Framers described by word when they vested the whole of the executive power in the President.

Without declaration of war, President Lincoln took energetic action with the outbreak of the Civil War. He summoned troops and paid them out of the Treasury without appropriation therefor. He proclaimed a naval blockade of the Confederacy and seized ships violating that blockade. Congress, far from denying the validity of these acts, gave them express approval. The most striking action of President Lincoln was the Emancipation Proclamation, issued in aid of the successful prosecution of the Civil War, but wholly without statutory authority.

In an action furnishing a most apt precedent for this case, President Lincoln directed the seizure of rail and telegraph lines leading to Washington without statutory authority. Many months later, Congress recognized and confirmed the power of the President to seize railroads and telegraph lines and provided criminal penalties for interference with Government operation. This Act did not confer on the President any additional powers of seizure. Congress plainly rejected the view that the President's acts had been without legal sanction until ratified by the legislature. . . .

President Hayes authorized the wide-spread use of federal troops during the Railroad Strike of 1877. President Cleveland also used the troops in the Pullman Strike of 1895 and his action is of special significance. No statute authorized this action. No call for help had issued from the Governor of Illinois; indeed Governor Altgeld disclaimed the need for supplemental forces. But the President's concern was that federal laws relating to the free flow of interstate commerce and the mails be continuously and faithfully executed without interruption. To further this aim his agents sought and obtained the injunction upheld by this Court in *In re Debs*, 158 U.S. 564 (1895). The Court scrutinized each of the steps taken by the President to insure execution of the "mass of legislation" dealing with commerce and the mails and gave his conduct full approval. Congress likewise took note of this use of Presidential power to forestall apparent obstacles to the faithful execution of the laws. By separate resolutions, both the Senate and the House commended the Executive's action. . . .

In 1909, President Taft was informed that government owned oil lands were being patented by private parties at such a rate that public oil lands would be depleted in a matter of months. Although Congress had explicitly provided that these lands were open to purchase by United States citizens, 29 Stat. 526 (1897), the President nevertheless ordered the lands withdrawn from sale "[i]n aid of proposed legislation." In *United States* v. *Midwest Oil Co.*, 236 U.S. 459 (1915), the President's action was sustained as consistent with executive practice throughout our history. . . .

During World War I, President Wilson established a War Labor Board without awaiting specific direction by Congress. . . . Effectiveness of War Labor Board decision was accomplished by Presidential action, including seizure of industrial plants. Seizure of the Nation's railroads was also ordered by President Wilson.

Beginning with the Bank Holiday Proclamation and continuing through World War II, executive leadership and initiative were characteristic of President Franklin D. Roosevelt's administration. In 1939, upon the outbreak of war in Europe, the President proclaimed a limited national emergency for the purpose of strengthening our national defense. By May of 1941, the danger from the Axis belligerents having become clear, the President proclaimed "an unlimited national emergency" calling for mobilization of the Nation's defenses to repel aggression. The President took the initiative in strengthening our defenses by acquiring rights from the British Government to establish air bases in exchange for overage destroyers.

In 1941, President Roosevelt acted to protect Iceland from attack by Axis powers when British forces were withdrawn by sending our forces to occupy Iceland. Congress was informed of this action on the same day that our forces reached Iceland. The occupation of Iceland was but one of "at least 125 incidents" in our history in which Presidents, "without Congressional authorization, and in the absence of a declaration of war, [have] ordered the Armed Forces to take action or maintain positions abroad."

Some six months before Pearl Harbor, a dispute at a single aviation plant at Inglewood, California, interrupted a segment of the production of military aircraft. . . . President Roosevelt ordered the seizure of the plant "pursuant to the powers vested in [him] by the Constitution and laws of the United States, as President of the United States of American and Commander in Chief of the Army and Navy of the United States." The Attorney General (Jackson) vigorously proclaimed that the President had the moral duty to keep this Nation's defense effort a "going concern." His ringing moral justification was coupled with a legal justification equally well stated:

"The Presidential proclamation rests upon the aggregate of the Presidential powers derived from the Constitution itself and from statutes enacted by the Congress." . . .

Following passage of the Smith-Connally Act [1943], seizures to assure continued production on the basis of terms recommended by the War Labor Board were based upon that Act as well as upon the President's power under the Constitution and the laws generally. A question did arise as to whether the statutory language relating to "any plant, mine, or facility equipped for the manufacture, production, or mining of any articles or materials" authorized the seizure of properties of Montgomery Ward & Co., a retail department store and mail order concern. The Attorney General (Biddle) issued an opinion that the President possessed the power to seize Montgomery Ward properties to prevent a work stoppage whether or not the terms of the Smith-Connally Act authorized such a seizure. . . . Accordingly, the President ordered seizure of the Chicago properties of Montgomery Ward in April, 1944, when that company refused to obey a War Labor Board order concerning the bargaining representative of its employees in Chicago. In Congress, a Select Committee to Investigate Seizure of the Property of Montgomery Ward & Co., assuming that the terms of the Smith-Connally Act did not cover this seizure, concluded that the seizure "was not only within the Constitutional power but was the plain duty of the President."

More recently, President Truman acted to repel aggression by employing our armed forces in Korea. Upon the intervention of the Chinese Communists, the President proclaimed the existence of an unlimited national emergency requiring the speedy build-up of our defense establishment. Congress responded by providing for increased manpower and weapons for our own armed forces, by increasing military aid under the Mutual Security Program and by enacting economic stabilization measures . . . .

This is but a cursory summary of executive leadership. But it amply demonstrates that Presidents have taken prompt action to enforce the laws and protect the country whether or not Congress happened to provide in advance for the particular method of execution. At the minimum, the executive actions reviewed herein sustain the action of the President in this case.
. . .

History bears out the genius of the Founding Fathers, who created a Government subject to law but not left subject to inertia when vigor and initiative are required. . . .

Schick v. *Reed*
419 U.S. 256 (1974)

Schick, a soldier, was convicted by court martial and sentenced to death for murder in 1954. In 1960 President Eisenhower commuted the sentence to life imprisonment, on condition that Schick never be eligible for parole. Later, arguing that *Furman* v. *Georgia* (mentioned below) invalidated death sentences, Schick sought parole for which he would have been eligible if he had originally received a life rather than a death sentence. This case began as a suit to compel the parole board to consider him for release. The Court upheld presidential power to grant a conditional pardon in these circumstances.

Mr. Chief Justice Burger delivered the opinion of the Court. . . .

A fair reading of the history of the English pardoning power, from which our Art. II, § 2, derives, of the language of that section itself, and of the unbroken practice since 1790 compels the conclusion that the power flows from the Constitution alone, not from any legislative enactments, and that it cannot be modified, abridged, or diminished by the Congress. Additionally, considerations of public policy and humanitarian impulses support an interpretation of that power so as to permit the attachment of any condition which does not otherwise offend the Constitution. The plain purpose of the broad power conferred by § 2 was to allow plenary authority in the President to "forgive" the convicted person in part or entirely, to reduce a penalty in terms of a specified number of years, or to alter it with conditions which are in themselves constitutionally unobjectionable. If we were to accept petitioner's contentions, a commutation of his death sentence to 25 or 30 years would be subject to the same challenge as is now made, *i.e.*, that parole must be available to petitioner because it is to others. That such an interpretation of § 2 would in all probability tend to inhibit the exercise of the pardoning power and reduce the frequency of commutations is hardly open to doubt. We therefore hold that the pardoning power is an enumerated power of the Constitution and its limitations, if any, must be found in the Constitution itself. It would be a curious logic to allow a convicted person who petitions for mercy to retain the full benefit of a lesser punishment with conditions, yet escape burdens readily assumed in accepting the commutation which he sought.

Petitioner's claim must therefore fail. The no-parole condition attached to the commutation of his death sentence is similar to sanctions imposed by legislatures such as mandatory minimum sentences or statutes otherwise precluding parole; it does not offend the Constitution. Similarly the President's action derived solely from his Art. II powers; it did not depend upon Art. 118 of the UCMJ or any other statute fixing a death penalty for murder. It is not correct to say that the condition upon petitioner's commutation was "made possible only through courtmartial's imposition of the death sentence." . . . Of course, the President may not aggravate punishment; the sentence imposed by statute is therefore relevant to a limited extent. But, as shown, the President has constitutional power to attach conditions to his commutation of any sentence. Thus, even if *Furman* v. *Georgia* [408 U.S. 238 (1972)] applies to the military, a matter which we need not and do not decide, it could not effect a conditional commutation which was granted 12 years earlier.

We are not moved by petitioner's argument that it is somehow "unfair" that he be treated differently from persons whose death sentences were pending at the time that *Furman* was decided. Individual acts of clemency inherently call for discriminating choices because no two cases are the same. Indeed, as noted earlier petitioner's life was undoubtedly spared by President Eisenhower's commutation order of March 25, 1960. Nor is petitioner without further remedies since he may, of course, apply to the present or future Presidents for a complete pardon, commutation to time served, or relief from the no-parole condition. We hold only that the conditional commutation of his death sentence was lawful when made and that intervening events have not altered its validity.

Mr. Justice Marshall [with whom Justices Douglas and Brennan join] dissenting. . . .

Since *Furman* is fully retroactive petitioner's case should be simple to resolve. The terms of Art. 118 of the UCMJ provide that a person convicted of premeditated murder "shall suffer death or imprisonment for life as a court-martial may direct." A death sentence was imposed by the court-martial and affirmed by the Board of Review and the United States Court of Military Appeals, 7 U.S.M.C.M.A. 419 (1956). The death sentence so imposed was declared unconstitutional by *Furman* and is therefore null and void as a matter of law. The only legal alternative—simple life imprisonment—must be substituted. Concomitantly, the adverse consequence of the death sentence—the no-parole condition of petitioner's 1960 commutation—must also be voided, as it exceeds the lawful alternative punishment that should have been imposed. Petitioner should now be subject to treatment as a person sentenced to life imprisonment on the date of his original sentence and eligible for parole. . . .

The congressionally prescribed parameters of punishment mark the boundaries within which the Executive must exercise his authority. By virtue of the pardon power the Executive may abstain from enforcing a judgment by judicial authorities; he may not, under the aegis of that power, engage in lawmaking or adjudication. . . .

While the clemency function of the Executive in the federal criminal justice system is consistent with the separation of powers, the attachment of punitive conditions to grants of clemency is not. Prescribing punishment is a prerogative reserved for the lawmaking branch of government, the legislature. As a consequence, President Eisenhower's addition to Schick's commutation of a condition that did not coincide with punishment prescribed by the legislature for *any* military crime, much less this specific offense, was a usurpation of a legislative function. While the exercise of the pardon

power was proper, the imposition of this penal condition was not embraced by that power.

The Court today advances the antecedent English pardon power and prior holdings of this Court in support of the legality of the no-parole condition. Neither body of law has established Executive right to define extra-legislative punishments. Nor does the historical status of the pardon power in England or analysis of prior non-penal conditions supply any relevance here.

Executive Impoundment of Appropriated Funds

Does the "executive power" granted in Article II of the Constitution include presidential authority to impound funds mandatorily appropriated by Congress? Does *Youngstown* (including precedents cited by the dissenters) support such authority? The Supreme Court has not answered these questions, but the Joint Hearings on Impoundment [93d. Cong., 1st. Sess. 839 (1973)] provides some relevant testimony:

> . . . just as Congress has implied power . . . , so does the President have implicit authority—under the executive power clause—in carrying out his constitutional obligations. Impounding funds is one of the most effective means that the President has to maintain fiscal control and to coordinate fiscal policy . . . .

> [The President is confronted with many laws which are not always fully compatible with one another, for example] appropriation acts, . . . the 1946 Full Employment Act, laws consisting of the debt ceilings [and] the Economic Stabilization Act. Above and beyond that, he is looked to by Congress and certainly by the public as one having a very profound responsibility for price stability. Now, when we put all that together, the problem is how best to faithfully execute the laws. (Ibid., p. 372)

> Such a power clearly is prohibited by the Constitution, which empowers the President to veto entire bills only. By impounding appropriated funds, the President is able to modify, reshape, or nullify completely laws passed by the legislative branch, thereby making legislative policy—a power reserved exclusively to Congress. (Ibid., p. 3)

Does Congress have power to limit or forbid presidential impoundment?

> [Recognizing] the functional deficiencies of Congress in adequately checking inflationary pressures [and] reading the Constitution as a living document—not a suicide pact—the President's "executive power" must be deemed to encompass substantial authority to impound in order to check inflation. [Thus it is doubtful] whether Congress can legislate against impoundment . . . when to do so results in substantially increasing the rate of inflation. (Ibid., pp. 363, 838).

Congress rejected this view by adopting the Congressional Budget and Impoundment Control Act of 1974. It provides the President may withhold funds permanently or beyond the fiscal year only with approval of both houses of Congress. Some expenditures may be postponed during the fiscal year in question, provided neither house objects.

Lichter v. *United States*
334 U.S. 742 (1948)

Obviously it would violate the separation of powers for Congress to authorize the President to perform its functions. While Congress is not apt to do that, it is often confronted with situations in which it wants to legislate but is unable to do so in full detail. For example, Congress wanted a tarrif, but it wanted one flexible enough to move up and down in response to changing costs of production both in this country and abroad. To meet that problem Congress adopted a specific tarrif rate and then authorized an executive agency to adjust it within prescribed limits, and only to accommodate the shifting-costs problem. Such a delegation of power was upheld in *Hampton & Co.* v. *United States,* 276 U.S. 394 (1928).

In the present case Congress authorized the executive to "renegotiate" government contracts with suppliers of military equipment for the purpose of reducing "excess profits" on earlier contracts. There was no definition of excess profits in the original act, but the War Department issued a reasonably clear definition of its understanding of the term. Later Congress produced a highly circular definition: "the term 'excess profits' means any amount of a contract . . . price which is found as a result of renegotiation to represent excess profits." The whole measure was challenged on the ground (among others) that the act's definition (i.e., standard for executive action) was so broad and vague as to constitute an invalid delegation of legislative power.

Mr. Justice Burton delivered the opinion of the Court. . . .

On the basis of (*a*) the nature of the particular constitutional powers being employed, (*b*) the current administrative practice later incorporated into the Act and (*c*) the adequacy of the statutory term "excessive profits" as used in this context, we hold that the authority granted was a lawful delegation of administrative authority and not an unconstitutional delegation of legislative power.

(*a*) A constitutional power implies a power of delegation of authority under it sufficient to effect its purposes. This power is especially significant in connection with constitutional war powers under which the exercise of broad discretion as to methods to be employed may be essential to an effective use of its war powers by Congress. The degree to which Congress must specify its policies and standards in order that the administrative authority granted may not be an unconstitutional delegation of its own legislative power is not capable of precise definition. In peace or in war it is essential that the Constitution be scrupulously obeyed, and particularly that the respective branches of the Government keep within the powers assigned to each by the Constitution. On the other hand, it is of the highest importance that the fundamental purposes of the Constitution be kept in mind and given effect in order that, through the Constitution, the people of the United States may in time of war as in peace bring to the support of those purposes the full force of their united action.

In 1942, in the early stages of total global warfare, the exercise of a war power such as the power "To raise and support Armies . . ." and "To provide and maintain a Navy . . ." called for the production by us of war goods in unprecedented volume with the utmost speed, combined with flexibility of control over the product and with a high degree of initiative on the part of the producers. Faced with the need to exercise that power, the question was whether it was beyond the constitutional power of Congress to delegate to the high officials named therein the discretion contained in the original Renegotiation Act of April 28, 1942, and the amendments of October 21, 1942. We believe that the administrative authority there granted was well within the constitutional war powers then being put to their predestined uses.

(*b*) The administrative practices developed under the Renegotiation Act demonstrated the definitive adequacy of the term "excessive profits" as used in the Act. The administrative practices currently developed under the Act in interpreting the term "excessive profits" appear to have come well within the scope of the congressional policy. We have referred above to the War Department Directive of August 10, 1942, and to the Joint Departmental Statement of March 31, 1943, both of which were placed before appropriate Congressional Committees. These clearly stated practices are evidence of a current correct understanding of the congressional intent. This appears from the fact that the congressional action of October 21, 1942, made effective as of April 28, 1942, was taken in the light of the above-mentioned directive and without restricting its effect.

(*c*) The statutory term "excessive profits" in its context, was a sufficient expression of legislative policy and standards to render it constitutional. The fact that this term later was further defined both by administrative action and by statutory amendment indicates the probable desirability of such added definition, but it does not demonstrate that such further definition was a constitutional necessity essential to the validity of the original exercise by Congress of its war powers in initiating a new solution of

an unprecedented problem. The fact that the congressional definition confirmed the administrative practice which already was in effect under the original statutory language tends to show that a statutory definition was not necessary in order to give effect to the congressional intent.

It is not necessary that Congress supply administrative officials with a specific formula for their guidance in a field where flexibility and the adaptation of the congressional policy to infinitely variable conditions constitute the essence of the program. "If Congress shall lay down by legislative act an intelligible principle . . . such legislative action is not a forbidden delegation of legislative power." *Hampton Co.* v. *United States,* 276 U.S. 394. Standards prescribed by Congress are to be read in the light of the conditions to which they are to be applied. "They derive much meaningful content from the purpose of the Act, its factual background and the statutory context in which they appear." *American Power & Light Co.* v. *S.E.C.,* 329 U.S. 90. The purpose of the Renegotiation Act and its factual background establish a sufficient meaning for "excessive profits" as those words are used in practice. The word "excessive" appears twice in the Eighth Amendment to the Constitution: "Excessive bail shall not be required, nor excessive fines imposed. . . ." In the original Renegotiation Act, § 403 (d), there were expressly disallowed to the contractor in determining his profits "compensation paid by a contractor to its officers or employees in excess of a reasonable amount . . ." and "any costs incurred by the contractor which are excessive and unreasonable." "Excessive profits are those in excess of reasonable profits." *Spaulding* v. *Douglas Aircraft Co.,* 154 F.2d 419.

The following, somewhat comparable, legislative specifications are among those which have been held to state a sufficiently definite standard for administrative action:

"Just and reasonable" rates for sales of natural gas, *Federal Power Commission* v. *Hope Gas Co.,* 320 U.S. 591; "public interest, convenience, or necessity" in establishing rules and regulations under the Federal Communications Act, *National Broadcasting Co.* v. *United States*, 319 U.S. 190; prices yielding a "fair return" on the "fair value" of property, *Sunshine Coal Co.* v. *Adkins*, 310 U.S. 381; "unfair methods of competition" distinct from offenses defined under the common law, *Federal Trade Commission* v. *Keppel & Bros.*, 291 U.S. 304; "just and reasonable" rates for the services of commission men, *Tagg Bros. & Moorhead* v. *United States*, 280 U.S. 420; and "fair and reasonable" rent for premises, with final determination in the courts, *Levy Leasing Co.* v. *Siegel*, 258 U.S. 242.

[Mr. Justice Douglas dissented on grounds unrelated to the delegation problem. Mr. Justice Jackson dissented without opinion.]

EXECUTIVE POLICYMAKING: FOREIGN AFFAIRS

United States v. *Curtiss-Wright Export Corp.*
299 U.S. 304 (1936)

By joint resolution Congress authorized the President, if he found it conducive to peace, to impose an embargo on the shipment of arms to the countries at war in the Chaco. Under the terms of this resolution an embargo was proclaimed. Curtiss-Wright was prosecuted for shipping machine guns in violation of the proclamation.

Mr. Justice Sutherland delivered the opinion of the Court: . . .

Whether, if the Joint Resolution had related solely to internal affairs it would be open to the challenge that it constituted an unlawful delegation of legislative power to the Executive, we find it unnecessary to determine. The whole aim of the resolution is to affect a situation entirely external to the United States, and falling within the category of foreign affairs. The determination which we are called to make, therefore, is whether the Joint Resolution, as applied to that situation, is vulnerable to attack under the rule that forbids a delegation of the law-making power. In other words, assuming (but not deciding) that the challenged delegation, if it were confined to internal affairs, would be invalid, may it nevertheless be sustained on the ground that its exclusive aim is to afford a remedy for a hurtful condition within foreign territory?

It will contribute to the elucidation of the question if we first consider the differences between the powers of the federal government in respect of foreign or external affairs and those in respect of domestic or internal affairs. That there are differences between them, and that these differences are fundamental may not be doubted.

The two classes of powers are different, both in respect of their origin and their nature. The broad statement that the federal government can exercise no powers except those specifically enumerated in the Constitution, and such implied powers as are necessary and proper to carry into effect the enumerated powers, is categorically true only in respect of our internal affairs. In that field, the primary purpose of the Constitution was to carve from the general mass of legislative powers *then possessed by the states* such portions as it was thought desirable to vest in the federal government, leaving those not included in the enumeration still in the states. *Carter* v. *Carter Coal Co.*, 298 U.S. 238, 294. That this doctrine applies only to powers which the states had, is self evident. And since the states severally never possessed international powers, such powers could not have been carved from the mass of state powers but obviously were transmitted to the United States from some other source. During the colonial period, those powers were possessed exclusively by and were entirely under the control of the Crown. By the Declaration of Independence, "the Representatives of the United States of America" declared the United [not the several] Colonies to be free and independent states, and as such to have "full Power to levy War, conclude Peace, contract Alliances, establish Commerce and to do all other Acts and Things which Independent States may of right do."

As a result of the separation from Great Britain by the colonies acting as a unit, the powers of external sovereignty passed from the Crown not to the colonies severally, but to the colonies in their collective and corporate capacity as the United States of America. Even before the Declaration, the colonies were a unit in foreign affairs, acting through a common agency—namely the Continental Congress, composed of delegates from the thirteen colonies. That agency exercised the powers of war and peace, raised an army, created a navy, and finally adopted the Declaration of Independence. Rulers come and go; governments end and forms of government change; but sovereignty survives. A political society cannot endure without a supreme will somewhere. Sovereignty is never held in suspense. When, therefore, the external sovereignty of Great Britain in respect of the colonies ceased, it immediately passed to the Union. See *Penhallow* v. *Doane*, 3 Dall. 54, 80–81. That fact was given practical application almost at once. The treaty of peace, made on September 23, 1783, was concluded between his Brittanic Majesty and the "United States of America." 8 Stat.—European Treaties—80.

The Union existed before the Constitution, which was ordained and established among other things to form "a more perfect Union." Prior to that event, it is clear that the Union,

declared by the Articles of Confederation to be "perpetual," was the sole possessor of external sovereignty and in the Union it remained without change save in so far as the Constitution in express terms qualified its exercise. The Framers' Convention was called and exerted its power upon the irrefutable postulate that though the states were several their people in respect of foreign affairs were one. Compare *The Chinese Exclusion Case*, 130 U.S. 581, 604, 606. In that convention, the entire absence of state power to deal with those affairs was thus forcefully stated by Rufus King:

"The states were not 'sovereigns' in the sense contended for by some. They did not possess the peculiar features of sovereignty,—they could not make war, nor peace, nor alliances, nor treaties. Considering them as political beings, they were dumb, for they could not speak to any foreign sovereign whatever. They were deaf, for they could not hear any propositions from such sovereign. They had not even the organs or faculties of defence or offence, for they could not of themselves raise troops, or equip vessels, for war. 5 Elliott's *Debates* 212."

It results that the investment of the federal government with the powers of external sovereignty did not depend upon the affirmative grants of the Constitution. The powers to declare and wage war, to conclude peace, to make treaties, to maintain diplomatic relations with other sovereignties, if they had never been mentioned in the Constitution, would have vested in the federal government as necessary concomitants of nationality. Neither the Constitution nor the laws passed in pursuance or it have any force in foreign territory unless in respect of our own citizens (see *American Banana Co.* v. *United Fruit Co.*, 213 U.S. 347, 356); and operations of the nation in such territory must be governed by treaties, international understandings and compacts, and the principles of international law. As a member of the family of nations, the right and power of the United States in that field are equal to the right and power of the other members of the international family. Otherwise, the United States is not completely sovereign. The power to acquire territory by discovery and occupation (*Jones* v. *United States*, 137 U.S. 202, 212), the power to expel undesirable aliens (*Fong Yue Ting* v. *United States*, 149 U.S. 698, 705 et seq.), the power to make such international agreements as do not constitute treaties in the constitutional sense (*Altman & Co.* v. *United States*, 224 U.S. 583, 600–601; Crandall, *Treaties, Their Making and Enforcement*, 2d ed., p. 102 and note 1), none of which is expressly affirmed by the Constitution, nevertheless exist as inherently inseparable from the conception of nationality. This the court recognized, and in each of the cases cited found the warrant for its conclusions not in the provisions of the Constitution, but in the law of nations.

In *Burnet* v. *Brooks*, 288 U.S. 378, 396, we said, "As a nation with all the attributes of sovereignty, the United States is vested with all the powers of government necessary to maintain an effective control of international relations." Cf. *Carter* v. *Carter Coal Co., supra*, p. 295.

Not only, as we have shown, is the federal power over external affairs in origin and essential character different from that over internal affairs, but participation in the exercise of the power is significantly limited. In this vast external realm, with its important, complicated, delicate and manifold problems, the President alone has the power to speak or listen as a representative of the nation. He *makes* treaties with the advice and consent of the Senate; but he alone negotiates. Into the field of negotiation the Senate cannot intrude; and Congress itself is powerless to invade it. As Marshall said in his great argument of March 7, 1800, in the House of Representatives, "The President is the sole organ of the nation in its external relations, and its sole representative with foreign nations." Annals, 6th Cong., col. 613. . . .

It is important to bear in mind that we are here dealing not alone with an authority vested in the President by an exertion of legislative

power, but with such an authority plus the very delicate, plenary and exclusive power of the President as the sole organ of the federal government in the field of international relations—a power which does not require as a basis for its exercise an act of Congress, but which, of course, like every other governmental power, must be exercised in subordination to the applicable provisions of the Constitution. It is quite apparent that if, in the maintenance of our international relations, embarrassment—perhaps serious embarrassment—is to be avoided and success for our aims achieved, congressional legislation which is to be made effective through negotiation and inquiry within the international field must often accord to the President a degree of discretion and freedom from statutory restriction which would not be admissible were domestic affairs along involved. Moreover, he, not Congress, has the better opportunity of knowing the conditions which prevail in foreign countries, and especially is this true in time of war. He has his confidential sources of information. He has his agents in the form of diplomatic, consular and other officials. Secrecy in respect of information gathered by them may be highly necessary, and the premature disclosure of it productive of harmful results. Indeed, so clearly is this true that the first President refused to accede to a request to lay before the House of Representatives the instructions, correspondence and documents relating to the negotiation of the Jay Treaty—a refusal the wisdom of which was recognized by the House itself and has never since been doubted. In his reply to the request, President Washington said:

"The nature of foreign negotiations requires caution, and their success must often depend on secrecy; and even when brought to a conclusion a full disclosure of all the measures, demands, or eventual concessions which may have been proposed or contemplated would be extremely impolitic; for this might have a pernicious influence on future negotiations, or produce immediate inconveniences, perhaps danger and mischief, in relation to other powers. The necessity of such caution and secrecy was one cogent reason for vesting the power of making treaties in the President, with the advice and consent of the Senate, the principle on which that body was formed confining it to a small number of members. To admit, then, a right in the House of Representatives to demand and to have as a matter of course all the papers respecting a negotiation with a foreign power would be to establish a dangerous precedent. 1 *Messages and Papers of the Presidents*, p. 194. . . ."

In the light of the foregoing observations, it is evident that this court should not be in haste to apply a general rule which will have the effect of condemning legislation like that under review as constituting an unlawful delegation of legis-

lative power. The principles which justify such legislation find overwhelming support in the unbroken legislative practice which has prevailed almost from the inception of the national government to the present day. . . .

The judgment of the court below must be reversed and the cause remanded for further proceedings in accordance with the foregoing opinion.

Mr. Justice McReynolds does not agree. He is of the opinion that the court below reached the right conclusion and its judgment ought to be affirmed.

Mr. Justice Stone took no part in the consideration or decision of this case.

Executive Agreements

Soviet Russia nationalized the assets of a Russian insurance company. The New York judiciary held the act of nationalization, insofar as it related to property in New York, invalid under state law. Meanwhile, by *executive agreement,* the President of the United States in effect acknowledged the validity of the nationalization by agreeing to accept the property in question in partial discharge of Soviety debts to the United States. This executive (Litvinov) agreement was part of a general settlement between the Soviet Union and the United States as a prelude to resumption of diplomatic relations between the two nations. *United States* v. *Pink,* 315 U.S. 203 (1942), held that the agreement superseded state law.

> The powers of the President in the conduct of foreign relations include the power, without the consent of the Senate, to determine the public policy of the United States with respect to the Russian nationalization decrees. . . . A treaty is a 'Law of the Land' under the supremacy clause . . . of the Constitution. Such international compacts and agreements as the Litvinov Assignment have a similar dignity. If the President had the power to determine the policy which was to govern the question of recognition [of Russia], then the Fifth Amendment does not stand in the way of giving full force and effect to the Litvinov Assignment.

Obviously, so-called "isolationist" circles found no comfort in *Pink* and *Curtiss-Wright.* Under Senator Bricker's leadership the following proposed constitutional amendment was offered to the Senate in June, 1953:

> *Section 1.* A provision of a treaty which conflicts with this Constitution shall not be of any force or effect.
> *Section 2.* A treaty shall become effective as internal law in the United States only through legislation which would be valid in the absence of treaty.

Section 3. Congress shall have power to regulate all executive and other agreements with any foreign power or international organization. All such agreements shall be subject to the limitations imposed on treaties by this article.

Section 4. The Congress shall have power to enforce this article by appropriate legislation.

Section 5. This article shall be inoperative unless it shall have been ratified as an amendment to the Constitution by the legislatures of three-fourths of the several States within seven years from the date of its submission.

After debate early in 1954 the Senate voted to substitute the so-called George compromise, which provided:

Section 1. A provision of a treaty or other international agreement which conflicts with this Constitution shall not be of any force or effect.

Section 2. An international agreement other than a treaty shall become effective as internal law in the United States only by an act of Congress.

This was rejected by a vote of one less than the required two-thirds majority in the Senate on February 26, 1954.

The Prize Cases
67 U.S. 635 (1863)

In the absence of a state of war a blockade is illegal in international law. In 1861 President Lincoln declared a blockade of Southern ports—without a formal declaration of war by Congress. This case considers the validity of the blockade and thus of the seizure of certain foreign and Southern vessels when they tried to run it.

Mr. Justice Grier delivered the opinion of the Court. . . .

By the Constitution, Congress alone has the power to declare a national or foreign war. It cannot declare war against a State, or any number of States, by virtue of any clause in the Constitution. The Constitution confers on the President the whole Executive power. He is bound to take care that the laws be faithfully executed. He is Commander-in-chief of the Army and Navy of the United States, and of the militia of the several States when called into the actual service of the United States. He has no power to initiate or declare a war either against a foreign nation or a domestic State. But by the Acts of Congress of February 28th, 1795, and 3d of March, 1807, he is authorized to call out the

militia and use the military and naval forces of the United States in case of invasion by foreign nations, and to suppress insurrection against the government of a State or of the United States.

If a war be made by invasion of a foreign nation, the President is not only authorized but bound to resist force by force. He does not initiate the war, but is bound to accept the challenge without waiting for any special legislative authority. And whether the hostile party be a foreign invader, or States organized in rebellion, it is none the less a war, although the declaration of it be *"unilateral."* Lord Stowell (1 Dodson, 247) observes, "It is not the less a war on *that account,* for war may exist without a declaration on either side. It is so laid down by the best writers on the law of nations. A declaration of war by one country only, is not a mere challenge to be accepted or refused at pleasure by the other."

The battles of Palo Alto and Resaca de la Palma had been fought before the passage of the Act of Congress of May 13th, 1846, which recognized *"a state of war as existing by the act of the Republic of Mexico."* This act not only provided for the future prosecution of the war, but was itself a vindication and ratification of the Act of the President in accepting the challenge without a previous formal declaration of war by Congress.

This greatest of civil wars was not gradually developed by popular commotion, tumultuous assemblies, or local unorganized insurrections. However long may have been its previous conception, it nevertheless sprung forth suddenly from the parent brain, a Minerva in the full panoply of *war*. The President was bound to meet it in the shape it presented itself, without waiting for Congress to baptize it with a name; and no name given to it by him or them could change the fact. . . .

Whether the President in fulfilling his duties, as Commander-in-chief, in suppressing an insurrection, has met with such armed hostile resistance, and a civil war of such alarming proportions as will compel him to accord to them the character of belligerents, is a question to be decided *by him*, and his Court must be governed by the decisions and acts of the political department of the Government to which this power was entrusted. "He must determine what degree of force the crisis demands." The proclamation of blockade is itself official and conclusive evidence to the Court that a state of war existed which demanded and authorized a recourse to such a measure, under the circumstances peculiar to the case. . . .

Without admitting that such an act was necessary under the circumstances, it is plain that if the President had in any manner assumed powers which it was necessary should have the authority or sanction of Congress, that on the well known principle of law, *"omnis ratihabitio*

retrotrahitur et mandato equiparatur," this ratification has operated to perfectly cure the defect. In the case of *Brown* v. *United States* (8 Cr., 131, 132, 133) Mr. Justice Story treats of this subject, and cites numerous authorities to which we may refer to prove this position, and concludes, "I am perfectly satisfied that no subject can commence hostilities or capture property of an enemy, when the sovereign has prohibited it. But suppose he did, I would ask if the sovereign may not ratify his proceedings, and thus by a retroactive operation give validity to them?"

Although Mr. Justice Story dissented from the majority of the Court on the whole case, the doctrine stated by him on this point is correct and fully substantiated by authority.

The objection made to this act of ratification, that it is *ex post facto*, and therefore unconstitutional and void, might possibly have some weight on the trial of an indictment in a criminal Court. But precedents from that source cannot be received as authoritative in a tribunal administering public and international law.

On this first question therefore we are of the opinion that the President had a right, *jure belli*, to institute a blockade of ports in possession of the States in rebellion, which neutrals are bound to regard. . . .

Mr. Justice Nelson, dissenting . . . .

An idea seemed to be entertained that all that was necessary to constitute a war was organized hostility in the district or country in a state of rebellion—that conflicts on land and on sea— the taking of towns and capture of fleets—in fine, the magnitude and dimensions of the resistance against the Government—constituted war with all the belligerent rights belonging to civil war. With a view to enforce this idea, we had, during the argument, an imposing historical detail of the several measures adopted by the Confederate States to enable them to resist the authority of the general Government, and of many bold and daring acts of resistance and of conflict. It was said that war was to be ascertained by looking at the armies and navies or public force of the contending parties, and the battles lost and won—that in the language of one of the learned counsel, "Whenever the situation of opposing hostilities has assumed the proportions and pursued the methods of war, then peace is driven out, the ordinary authority and administration of law are suspended, and war in fact and by necessity is the *status* of the nation until peace is restored and the laws resumed their dominion."

Now, in one sense, no doubt this is war, and may be a war of the most extensive and threatening dimensions and effects, but it is a statement simply of its existence in a material sense, and has no relevancy or weight when the question is what constitutes war in a legal sense, in the sense of the law of nations, and of the Constitution of the United States? For it must be a war in this sense to attach to it all the conse-

quences that belong to belligerent rights. Instead, therefore, of inquiring after armies and navies, and victories lost and won, or organized rebellion against the general Government, the inquiry should be into the law of nations and into the municipal fundamental laws of the Government. For we find there that to constitute a civil war in the sense in which we are speaking, before it can exist, in contemplation of law, it must be recognized or declared by the sovereign power of the State, and which sovereign power by our Constitution is lodged in the Congress of the United States—civil war, therefore, under our system of government, can exist only by an act of Congress, which requires the assent of two of the great departments of the Government, the Executive and Legislative.

[Chief Justice Taney and Justices Catron and Clifford joined in this dissent.]

United States v. *Sisson*
294 F. Supp. 511 (D. Mass. 1968)

This is one of many lower court cases declining to hold the Vietnam conflict or the draft unconstitutional. Most of these cases were dismissed as nonjusticiable. This is not one of the few in which a court—surmounting the justiciability problem—reached the merits of the controversy. Sisson, refusing to submit to induction, contended there was no constitutional authority to conscript him to serve in a war not declared by Congress.

Wyzanski, Chief Judge . . . .

Faced with a defendant who has standing to raise the issue, this Court must inquire as to whether an order requiring service in the armed forces with a strong probability of ultimate service in Vietnam violates any provision of the United States Constitution so as to entitle the person so ordered to disregard the induction order. Put thus, the issue is somewhat deceptive. The court has a procedural, as well as a substantive, problem. It must decide whether the question sought to be raised is in that category of political questions which are not within

a court's jurisdiction and, if the issue falls within the court's jurisdiction, whether, as a matter of substance the defendant is right in his contention that the order is repugnant to the Constitution. Again, while those two aspects are technically separate, they are so close as often to overlap.

Four different types of cases may be noticed.

(1) A person may be required to give military service in connection with a war declared by Congress. *Selective Draft Law Cases* [245 U.S. 366 (1917)].

(2) A person may be required to give military service in order to be ready to serve in a war that

might later be declared by Congress. *Hamilton v. Regents of University of California*, 293 U.S. 245, 260; *United States* v. *O'Brien*, 391 U.S. 367, 377.

(3) There is no Supreme Court case deciding whether a person who has been conscripted in time of peace may be required during his service to respond to an order to fight abroad pursuant to a direction of the President either as Chief Executive or as Commander-in-Chief, wholly unsupported by any Congressional authority but evoked by an emergency. It is important to note that the third hypothetical case is not the present case. The third case, for which, as shown in the June 1968 *Harvard Law Review* Note on Congress, The President, and The Power to Commit Forces to Combat, 81 *Harv. L. Rev.* 1771, there are many Caribbean and other precedents, has as its central characteristic that the President has to act quickly and in an emergency assigns to battle in foreign areas men in the armed forces whether they are volunteers or conscriptees.

Without in any way deciding the point, it may be assumed that to meet the emergency the President need not wait for an Act of Congress and need not segregate those who were conscripted from others who volunteered. Indeed, one may further assume, for the sake of argument, that if the power rests upon emergency and the necessities thereby created, it is within the judicial power to scrutinize the length of time that the emergency may be permitted to serve as a constitutional rationalization for the action. See for possibly comparable cases Justice Holmes's opinion in *Chastleton Corp.* v. *Sinclair*, 264 U.S. 543, his opinion in *Moyer* v. *Peabody*, 212 U.S. 78, and Chief Justice Hughes's opinion in *Sterling* v. *Constantin*, 287 U.S. 378.

Making such assumptions does not imply that the assumptions are correct. Caution is invited by *Ex parte Milligan*, 71 U.S. (4 Wall.) 2 (holding invalid Presidential emergency action, see particularly p. 108) and *The Steel Seizure Case, Youngstown Sheet & Tube Co.* v. *Sawyer*, 343 U.S. 579, in President Truman's Administration (holding that executive action in an emergency even when closely connected with a foreign war was unconstitutional, perhaps partly because it seemed to circumvent a specific statute).

Moreover, as already observed, assumptions with respect to this third type of case are made merely for argument's sake, but do not purport to resolve authoritatively the highly debatable problem whether the issues as to whether emergency creates, or as *Home Bldg. & Loan Ass'n* v. *Blaisdell*, 290 U.S. 398, phrases it, furnishes the occasion for the exercise of power and if so, and whether the emergency may last indefinitely, raise the sort of political questions not appropriate for judicial determination.

(4) The fourth case is the instant controversy before this Court. It presents the question whether a conscript can secure from a court a determination that a war carried on for a long time without a declaration of war but as a result of combined legislative and executive action is a war in which, against his will, he can be required to serve.

A central characteristic of this fourth case, that is the case at bar, is that there has been no declaration of war. But it is an equally central characteristic that in the military steps, including the drafting and assigning of soldiers, the President has not acted alone.

Congress in 1967 extended the Selective Service Act, Pub. L. No. 90-40, 81 Stat. 100. Congress acted with full knowledge that persons called for duty under the Act had been, and are likely to be, sent to Vietnam. Indeed, in 1965 Congress had amended the same Act with the hardly concealed object of punishing persons who tore up their draft cards out of protest at the Vietnam war. See *United States* v. *O'Brien*, 391 U.S. 367.

Moreover, Congress has again and again appropriated money for the draft act, for the Vietnam war, and for cognate activities. Congress has also enacted what is called the Tonkin Gulf Resolution, which some have viewed as advance authorization for the expansion of the Vietnam war.

What the court thus faces is a situation in which there has been joint action by the President and Congress, even if the joint action has not taken the form of a declaration of war.

The absence of the formal declaration of war is not to be regarded as a trivial omission. A declaration of war has more than ritualistic or symbolic significance. What something is called has much to do with how authorities act and also with how those subject to authority respond. . . .

But the fact that a declaration of war is a far more important act than an appropriation act or than an extension of a Selective Service Act does not go the whole way to show that in every situation of foreign military action, a declaration of war is a necessary prerequisite to conscription for that military engagement.

We are reminded by *McCulloch* v. *Maryland*, 17 U.S. (4 Wheat.) 316, and its progeny, that the national government has powers beyond those clearly stipulated in the Constitution. That the Constitution expresses one way of achieving a result does not inevitably carry a negative pregnant. Other ways may be employed by Congress as necessary and proper. Indeed, the implied powers may be not only Congressional but sometimes Presidential. *In re Debs,* 158 U.S. 564. And this implication may be most justifiable in foreign affairs. *United States* v. *Curtiss-Wright Export Corp.,* 299 U.S. 304. What may be involved in the present case is a choice between a limited undeclared war approved by the President and Congress and an unlimited declaration of war through an Act of Congress. The two choices may find support in different, related, but not inconsistent Constitutional powers.

If the national government does have two or more choices there are readily imagined reasons not to elect to exercise the expressly granted power to declare war.

A declaration of war expresses in the most formidable and unlimited terms a belligerent posture against an enemy. In Vietnam it is at least plausibly contended by some in authority that our troops are not engaged in fighting any enemy of the United States but are participating in the defense of what is said to be one country from the aggression of what is said to be another country. It is inappropriate for this court in any way to intimate whether South Vietnam and North Vietnam are separate countries, or whether there is a civil war, or whether there is a failure on the part of the people in Vietnam and elsewhere to abide by agreements made in Geneva. It is sufficient to say that the present situation is one in which the State Department and the other branches of the executive treat our action in Vietnam as though it were different from an unlimited war against an enemy.

Moreover, in the Vietnam situation a declaration of war would produce consequences which no court can fully anticipate. A declaration of war affects treaties of the United States, obligations of the United States under international organizations, and many public and private arrangements. A determination not to declare war is more than an avoidance of a domestic constitutional procedure. It has international implications of vast dimensions. Indeed, it is said that since 1945 no country has declared war on any other country. Whether this is true or not, it shows that not only in the United States but generally, there is a reluctance to take a step which symbolically and practically entails multiple unforeseeable consequences.

From the foregoing this Court concludes that the distinction between a declaration of war and a cooperative action by the legislative and executive with respect to military activities in foreign countries is the very essence of what is meant by a political question. It involves just the sort of evidence, policy considerations, and constitutional principles which elude the normal processes of the judiciary and which are far more suitable for determination by coordinate branches of the government. It is not an act of abdication when a court says that political questions of this sort are not within its jurisdiction. It is a recognition that the tools with which a court can work, the data which it can fairly appraise, the conclusions which it can reach as a basis for entering judgments, have limits.

Because defendant Sisson seeks an adjudication of what is a political question, his motion to dismiss the indictment is denied.

The War Powers Resolution

The War Powers Resolution was adopted by Congress in November 1972, over President Nixon's veto. It begins with a statement that it was the "intent of the framers of the Constitution" that "the collective judgment of both the Congress and the President" will apply to the introduction of armed forces into hostilities or situations where involvement in hostilities is imminent, and that the President may so introduce forces only pursuant to a declaration of war, specific statutory authorization, or "a national emergency created by attack upon the United States, its territories or possessions, or its armed forces." In this context the resolution requires continuing consultation between Congress and the President. Next it provides that when in the absence of a declaration of war armed forces are sent to other countries, the President must submit to Congress within 48 hours a report in writing explaining the circumstances, the legal authority for the action, and its estimated duration.

Finally, the resolution requires that within 60 days after the President submits a report of the use of the armed forces he shall terminate the use of such forces, unless Congress has declared war or enacted a specific authorization for the use of the troops, or has extended the 60-day period, or has been physically unable to meet because of an armed attack on the United States. Under certain circumstances the President may extend the time for an additional 30 days. Provision is also made that authority to use troops shall not be inferred from appropriation resolutions or the ratification of treaties, in the absence of a specific statutory authorization for the use of troops.

For comment on the War Powers Resolution in the context of the Mayaguez incident, see Emerson, "The War Powers Resolutions Tested . . . .," 51 *Notre Dame Law Review* 187 (1975); M. J. Glennon, "Strengthening the War Powers Resolution. . . . .," 60 *Minnesota Law Review* 1 (1975); T. Wicker, "Raising Some Mayaguez Questions," *New York Times*, May 16, 1975, p. 35.

EXECUTIVE APPOINTING AND REMOVAL POWERS

Buckley v. *Valeo* (excerpt)
424 U.S. 1 (1976)

Congress created an eight-member Federal Election Commission to administer the Federal Election Campaign Act of 1971. Two if its members were to be appointed by the President, two by the Senate, two by the House. The Secretary of the Senate and the Clerk of the House served ex officio. Our concern here is whether these provisions are compatible with the presidential appointing power prescribed in Article II, Section 2, Clause 2, of the Constitution (other aspects of the case are presented below, in Chapters 3 and 8).

Per Curiam. . . .

1. Separation of Powers

. . .

This Court has not hesitated to enforce the principles of separation of powers embodied in the Constitution when their application has proved necessary for the decisions of cases and controversies properly before it. The Court has held that executive or administrative duties of a nonjudicial nature may not be imposed on judges holding office under Art. III of the Constitution. *United States* v. *Ferreira,* 54 U.S. 40 (1851); *Hayburn's Case,* 2 U.S. 409, 2 Dall. 409 (1792). The Court has held that the President may not execute and exercise legislative authority belonging only to Congress. *Youngstown Co.* v. *Sawyer, supra.*

More closely in point to the facts of the present case is this Court's decision in *Springer* v. *Philippine Islands* [277 U.S. 189 (1928)] where the Court held that the legislature of the Philippine Islands could not provide for legislative appointment to executive agencies.

2. The Appointments Clause

. . .

The Appointments Clause could, of course, be read as merely dealing with etiquette or protocol in describing "Officers of the United States," but the drafters had a less frivolous purpose in mind. This conclusion is supported by language from *United States* v. *Germaine,* 99 U.S. 508, 509–510 (1878):

> "The Constitution for purposes of appointment very clearly divides all its officers into two classes. The primary class requires a nomination by the President and confirmation by the Senate. But

foreseeing that when offices became numerous, and sudden removals necessary, this mode might be inconvenient, it was provided that, in regard to officers inferior to those specially mentioned, Congress might by law vest their appointment in the President alone, in the courts of law, or in the heads of departments. *That all persons who can be said to hold an office under the government about to be established under the Constitution were intended to be included within one or the other of these modes of appointment there can be little doubt.*" (Emphasis supplied.)

We think that the term "Officers of the United States" as used in Art. II, defined to include "all persons who can be said to hold an office under the government" in *United States* v. *Germaine, supra,* is a term intended to have substantive meaning. We think its fair import is that any appointee exercising significant authority pursuant to the laws of the United States is an Officer of the United States, and must, therefore, be appointed in the manner prescribed by § 2, cl. 2 of that Article.

If "all persons who can be said to hold an office under the government about to be established under the Constitution were intended to be included within one or the other of these modes of appointment," *United States* v. *Germaine, supra,* it is difficult to see how the members of the Commission may escape inclusion. If a Postmaster first class, *Myers* v. *United States,* 272 U.S. 52 (1926), and the Clerk of a District Court, *Matter of Hennen,* 38 U.S. 225 (1839), are inferior officers of the United States within the meaning of the Appointments Clause, as they are, surely the Commissioners before us are at the very least such "inferior Officers" within the meaning of that Clause. . . .

Appellee Commission and amici finally contend, and the majority of the Court of Appeals agreed with them, that whatever shortcomings the provisions for the appointment of members of the Commission might have under Art. II, Congress had ample authority under the Necessary and Proper Clause of Art. I to effectuate this result. We do not agree. . . .

. . . Congress could not, merely because it concluded that such a measure was "necessary and proper" to the discharge of its substantive legislative authority, pass a bill of attainder or ex post facto law contrary to the prohibitions contained in § 9 of Art. I. No more may it vest in itself, or in its officers, the authority to appoint officers of the United States when the Appointments Clause by clear implication prohibits it from doing so.

The trilogy of cases from this Court dealing with the constitutional authority of Congress to circumscribe the President's power to *remove* Officers of the United States is entirely consistent with this conclusion. In *Myers* v. *United States*, 272 U.S. 52 (1926), the Court held that Congress could not by statute divest the President of the power to remove an officer in the Executive Branch whom he was initially authorized to appoint. In explaining its reasoning in that case, the Court said:

"The vesting of the executive power in the President was essentially a grant of the power to execute the laws. But the President alone and unaided could not execute the laws. He must execute them by the system of subordinates. . . . As he is charged specifically to take care that they be faithfully executed, the reasonable implication, even in the absence of express words, was that as part of his executive power he should select those who were to act for him under his direction in the execution of the laws. . . .

"Our conclusion on the merits, sustained by the arguments before stated, is that article 2 grants to the President the executive power of the government—i.e.,

the general administrative control of those executing the laws, including the power of appointment and removal of executive officers—a conclusion confirmed by his obligation to take care that the laws be faithfully executed . . . ." 272 U.S., at 117, 163–164.

In the later case of *Humphrey's Executor*, where it was held that Congress could circumscribe the President's power to remove members of independent regulatory agencies, the Court was careful to note that it was dealing with an agency intended to be independent of executive authority *"except in its selection."* 295 U.S., at 625 (emphasis in original). *Weiner* v. *United States*, 357 U.S. 349 (1958), which applied the holding in *Humphrey's Executor* to a member of the War Crimes Commission, did not question in any respect that members of independent agencies are not independent of the executive with respect to their appointments. . . .

3. The Commission's Powers

. . .

Insofar as the powers confided in the Commission are essentially of an investigative and informative nature, falling in the same general category as those powers which Congress might delegate to one of its own committees, there can be no question that the Commission as presently constituted may exercise them. . . .

But when we go beyond this type of authority to the more substantial powers exercised by the Commission, we reach a different result. The Commission's enforcement power, exemplified by its discretionary power to seek judicial relief, is authority that cannot possibly be regarded as merely in aid of the legislative function of Congress. A law suit is the ultimate remedy for a breach of the law, and it is to the President, and not to the Congress that the Constitution entrusts the responsibility to "take Care that the Laws be faithfully executed." Art. II, § 3. . . . All aspects of the Act are brought within the Commission's broad administrative powers: rule-making, advisory opinions, and determinations of eligibility for funds and even for federal elective office itself. These functions, exercised free from day-to-day supervision of either Congress or the Executive Branch, are more legislative and judicial in nature than are the Commission's enforcement powers, and are of kinds usually performed by independent regulatory agencies or by some department in the Executive Branch under the direction of an Act of Congress. Congress viewed these broad powers as essential to effective and impartial administration of the entire substantive frame-work of the Act. Yet each of these functions also represents the performance of a significant governmental duty exercised pursuant to a public law. While the President may not insist that such functions be delegated to an appointee of his removable at will, *Humphrey's Executor* v. *United States, supra*, none of them operates merely in aid of congressional authority to legislate or is sufficiently removed from the administration and enforcement of public law to allow it to be performed by the present Commission. These administrative functions may therefore be exercised only by persons who are "Officers of the United States." . . .

Wiener v. *United States*
357 U.S. 349 (1958)

This is the last of the trilogy of cases mentioned in *Buckley*. It arose when President Eisenhower undertook to remove a member of the War Claims Commission—a temporary federal agency authorized to pass upon claims by Americans against funds obtained by our government from certain foreign nations in conjunction with World War II. By act of Congress, commission members were appointed by the President with consent of the Senate. Building on the two earlier trilogy cases, the Court was unanimous as to the scope of the President's removal power.

Mr. Justice Frankfurter delivered the opinion of the Court. . . .

Controversy pertaining to the scope and limits of the President's power of removal fills a thick chapter of our political and judicial history. The long stretches of its history, beginning with the very first Congress, with early echoes in the Reports of this Court, were laboriously traversed in *Myers* v. *United States*, 272 U.S. 52, and need not be retraced. President Roosevelt's reliance upon the pronouncements of the Court in that case in removing a member of the Federal Trade Commission on the ground that "the aims and purposes of the Administration with respect to the work of the Commission can be carried out most effectively with personnel of my own selection" reflected contemporaneous professional opinion regarding the significance of the *Myers* decision. Speaking through a Chief Justice who himself had been President, the Court did not restrict itself to the immediate issue before it, the President's inherent power to remove a postmaster, obviously an executive official. As of set purpose and not by way of parenthetic casualness, the Court announced that the President had inherent constitutional power of removal also of officials who have "duties of a quasi-judicial character . . . whose decisions after hearing affect interests of individuals, the discharge of which the President can not in a particular case properly influence or control." *Myers* v. *United States, supra*, at 135. This view of presidential power was deemed to flow from his "constitutional duty of seeing that the laws be faithfully executed." *Ibid.*

The assumption was short-lived that the *Myers* case recognized the President's inherent constitutional power to remove officials, no matter what the relation of the executive to the discharge of their duties and no matter what restrictions Congress may have imposed regarding the nature of their tenure. The versatility of circumstances often mocks a natural desire for definitiveness. Within less than ten years a unanimous Court, in *Humphrey's Executor* v. *United States*, 295 U.S. 602, narrowly confined the scope of the *Myers* decision to include only "all purely executive officers." 295 U.S., at 628. The Court explicitly "disapproved" the expressions in *Myers* supporting the President's inherent constitutional power to remove members of quasi-judicial bodies. 295 U.S., at 626–627. Congress had given members of the Federal Trade Commission a seven-year term and also provided for the removal of a Commissioner by the President for inefficiency, neglect of duty or malfeasance in office. In the present case, Congress provided for a tenure defined by the relatively short period of time during which the War Claims Commission was to operate—that is, it was to wind up not later than three years after the expiration of the time for filing of claims. But nothing was said in the Act about removal. . . .

Humphrey's case was a *cause célèbre*—and not least in the halls of Congress. And what is the essence of the decision in Humphrey's case? It drew a sharp line of cleavage between officials who were part of the Executive establishment and were thus removable by virtue of the President's constitutional powers, and those who are members of a body "to exercise its judgment without the leave or hindrance of any other official or any department of the government," 295 U.S., at 625–626, as to whom a power of removal exists only if Congress may fairly be said to have conferred it. This sharp differentiation derives from the difference in functions between those who are part of the Executive establishment and those whose tasks require absolute freedom from Executive interference. "For it is quite evident," again to quote *Humphrey's Executor*, "that one who holds his office only during the pleasure of another, cannot be depended upon to maintain an attitude of independence against the latter's will." 295 U.S., at 629.

Thus, the most reliable factor for drawing an inference regarding the President's power of removal in our case is the nature of the function that Congress vested in the War Claims Commission. What were the duties that Congress confided to this Commission? And can the inference fairly be drawn from the failure of Congress to provide for removal that these Commissioners were to remain in office at the will of the President? For such is the assertion of power on which petitioner's removal must rest. The ground of President Eisenhower's removal of petitioner was precisely the same as President Roosevelt's removal of Humphrey. Both Presidents desired to have Commissioners, one on the Federal Trade Commission, the other on the War Claims Commission, "of my own selection." They wanted these Commissioners to be their men. The terms of removal in the two cases are identical and express the assumption that the agencies of which the two Commissioners were members were subject in the discharge of their duties to the control of the Executive. An analysis of the Federal Trade Commission Act left this Court in no doubt that such was not the conception of Congress in creating the Federal Trade Commission. The terms of the War Claims Act of 1948 leave no doubt that such was not the conception of Congress regarding the War Claims Commission.

. . . Congress could, of course, have given jurisdiction over these claims to the District Courts or to the Court of Claims. The fact that it chose to establish a Commission to "adjudicate according to law" the classes of claims defined in the statute did not alter the intrinsic judicial character of the task with which the Commission was charged. The claims were to be "adjudicated according to law," that is, on the merits of each claim, supported by evidence and governing legal considerations, by a body that was "entirely free from the control or coercive influence, direct or indirect," *Humphrey's Executor* v. *United States, supra*, 295 U.S., at 629, of either the Executive or the Congress. If, as one must take for granted, the War Claims Act precluded the President from influencing the Commission in passing on a particular claim, *a fortiori* must it be inferred that Congress did not wish to have hang over the Commission the Damocles' sword of removal by the President for no reason other than that he preferred to have on that Commission men of his own choosing.

For such is this case. We have not a removal for cause involving the rectitude of a member of an adjudicatory body, nor even a suspensory removal until the Senate could act upon it by confirming the appointment of a new Commissioner or otherwise dealing with the matter. Judging the matter in all the nakedness in which it is presented, namely, the claim that the President could remove a member of an adjudicatory body like the War Claims Commission merely because he wanted his own appointees on such a Commission, we are compelled to conclude that no such power is given to the President directly by the Constitution, and none is impliedly conferred upon him by statute simply because Congress said nothing about it. The philosophy of *Humphrey's Executor*, in its explicit language as well as its implications, precludes such a claim.

EXECUTIVE PRIVILEGE

United States v. *Nixon*
418 U.S. 683 (1974)

In March 1974, seven staff and other presidential supporters were indicted for Watergate offense: *United States* v. *Mitchell*. President Nixon was named as an unindicted conspirator. On April 18 the trial court in *Mitchell* issued a subpoena *duces tecum* directing the President to deliver up certain tapes and documents relating to specified conversations between him and his aides and advisors. On April 30, the President made public edited transcripts of some conversations, including portions of some of the subpoenaed material. His counsel then moved to quash the subpoena on executive-privilege grounds. This motion was denied, and the issue went directly to the Supreme Court. The case was heard in July. The decision was announced on July 24—the day on which the House Judiciary Committee began its final public debate on impeachment. Within six days the committee adopted three articles of impeachment.

Mr. Chief Justice Burger delivered the opinion of the Court. . . .

. . . [W]e turn to the claim that the subpoena should be quashed because it demands "confidential conversations between a President and his close advisors that it would be inconsistent with the public interest to produce." The first contention is a broad claim that the separation of powers doctrine precludes judicial review of a President's claim of privilege. The second contention is that if he does not prevail on the claim of absolute privilege, the court should hold as a matter of constitutional law that the privilege prevails over the subpoena *duces tecum*.

In the performance of assigned constitutional

duties each branch of the Government must initially interpret the Constitution, and the interpretation of its powers by any branch is due great respect from the others. The President's counsel, as we have noted, reads the Constitution as providing an absolute privilege of confidentiality for all presidential communications. Many decisions of this Court, however, have unequivocally reaffirmed the holding of *Marbury* v. *Madison*, 1 Cranch 137 (1803), that "it is emphatically the province and duty of the judicial department to say what the law is."

No holding of the Court has defined the scope of judicial power specifically relating to the enforcement of a subpoena for confidential presidential communications for use in a criminal prosecution, but other exercises of powers by the Executive Branch and the Legislative Branch have been found invalid as in conflict with the Constitution. . . . Since this Court has consistently exercised the power to construe and delineate claims arising under express powers, it must follow that the Court has authority to interpret claims with respect to powers alleged to derive from enumerated powers.

Our system of government "requires that federal courts on occasion interpret the Constitution in a manner at variance with the construction given the document by another branch." *Powell* v. *McCormack*. . . . Notwithstanding the deference each branch must accord the others, the "judicial power of the United States" vested in the federal courts by Art. III, § 1 of the Constitution can no more be shared with the Executive Branch than the Chief Executive, for example, can share with the Judiciary the veto power, or the Congress share with the Judiciary the power to override a presidential veto. Any other conclusion would be contrary to the basic concept of separation of powers and the checks and balances that flow from the scheme of a tripartite government. We therefore reaffirm that it is "emphatically the province and the duty" of this Court "to say what the law is" with respect to the claim of privilege presented in this case. *Marbury* v. *Madison*.

In support of his claim of absolute privilege, the President's counsel urges two grounds one of which is common to all governments and one of which is peculiar to our system of separation of powers. The first ground is the valid need for protection of communications between high government officials and those who advise and assist them in the performance of their manifold duties; the importance of this confidentiality is too plain to require further discussion. Human experience teaches that those who expect public dissemination of their remarks may well temper candor with a concern for appearances and for their own interests to the detriment of the decisionmaking process. Whatever the nature of the privilege of confidentiality of presidential communications in the exercise of Art. II powers the privilege can be said to derive from the supremacy of each branch within its own assigned area of constitutional duties. Certain powers and privileges flow from the nature of enumerated powers; the protection of the confidentiality of presidential communications has similar constitutional underpinnings.

The second ground asserted by the President's counsel in support of the claim of absolute privilege rests on the doctrine of separation of powers. Here it is argued that the independence of the Executive Branch within its own sphere, insulates a president from a judicial subpoena in an ongoing criminal prosecution, and thereby protects confidential presidential communications.

However, neither the doctrine of separation of powers, nor the need for confidentiality of high level communications, without more, can sustain an absolute, unqualified presidential privilege of immunity from judicial process under all circumstances. The President's need for complete candor and objectivity from advisers calls for great deference from the courts. However, when the privilege depends solely on the broad, undifferentiated claims of public interest in the confidentiality of such conversations, a confrontation with other values arises.

Absent a claim of need to protect military, diplomatic or sensitive national security secrets, we find it difficult to accept the argument that even the very important interest in confidentiality of presidential communications is significantly diminished by production of such material for *in camera* inspection with all the protection that a district court will be obliged to provide.

The impediment that an absolute, unqualified privilege would place in the way of the primary constitutional duty of the Judicial Branch to do justice in criminal prosecutions would plainly conflict with the function of the courts under Art. III. In designing the structure of our Government and dividing and allocating the sovereign power among three co-equal branches, the Framers of the Constitution sought to provide a comprehensive system, but the separate powers were not intended to operate with absolute independence. . . . To read the Art. II powers of the President as providing an absolute privilege as against a subpoena essential to enforcement of criminal statutes on no more than a generalized claim of the public interest in confidentiality of nonmilitary and nondiplomatic discussions would upset the constitutional balance of "a workable government" and gravely impair the role of the courts under Art. III.

Since we conclude that the legitimate needs of the judicial process may outweigh presidential privilege, it is necessary to resolve those competing interests in a manner that preserves the essential functions of each branch. The right and indeed the duty to resolve that question does not free the judiciary from according high respect to the representations made on behalf of the President.

The expectation of a President to the confidentiality of his conversations and correspondence, like the claim of confidentiality of judicial deliberations, for example, has all the values to which we accord deference for the privacy of all citizens and added to those values the necessity for protection of the public interest in candid, objective, and even blunt or harsh opinions in presidential decisionmaking. A President and those who assist him must be free to explore alternatives in the process of shaping policies and making decisions and to do so in a way many would be unwilling to express except privately. These are the considerations justifying a presumptive privilege for presidential communications. The privilege is fundamental to the operation of government and inextricably rooted in the separation of powers under the Constitution. In *Nixon* v. *Sirica*, 487 F. 2d 700 (1973), the Court of Appeals held that such presidential communications are "presumptively privileged," and this position is accepted by both parties in the present litigation. We agree with Mr. Chief Justice Marshall's observation, therefore, that "in no case of this kind would a court be required to proceed against the President as against an ordinary individual." *United States* v. *Burr*, 25 Fed. Cas. 187, 191 (No. 14,694) (CCD Va. 1807).

But this presumptive privilege must be considered in light of our historic commitment to the rule of law. This is nowhere more profoundly manifest than in our view that "the twofold aim [of criminal justice] is that guilt shall not escape or innocence suffer." We have elected to employ an adversary system of criminal justice in which the parties contest all issues before a court of law. The need to develop all relevant facts in the adversary system is both fundamental and comprehensive. The ends of criminal justice would be defeated if judgments were to be founded on a partial or speculative presentation of the facts. The very integrity of the judicial system and public confidence in the system depend on full disclosure of all the facts, within the framework of the rules of evidence. To ensure that justice is done, it is imperative to the function of courts that compulsory process be available for the production of evidence needed either by the prosecution or by the defense.

Only recently the Court restated the ancient proposition of law, albeit in the context of a grand jury inquiry rather than a trial, " 'that the public . . . has a right to every man's evidence' except for those persons protected by a constitutional, common law, or statutory privilege." The privileges referred to by the Court are designed to protect weighty and legitimate competing interests. . . .

In this case the President challenges a subpoena served on him as a third party requiring the production of materials for use in a criminal prosecution on the claim that he has a privilege against disclosure of confidential communications. He does not place his claim of privilege on the ground they are military or diplomatic secrets. As to these areas of Art. II duties the courts have traditionally shown the utmost deference to presidential responsibilities. . . . No case of the Court, however, has extended this high degree of deference to a President's generalized interest in confidentiality. Nowhere in the Constitution as we have noted earlier, is there any explicit reference to a privilege of confidentiality yet to the extent this interest relates to the effective discharge of a President's powers, it is constitutionally based.

The right to the production of all evidence at a criminal trial similarly has constitutional dimensions. . . . It is the manifest duty of the courts to vindicate those guarantees and to accomplish that it is essential that all relevant and admissible evidence be produced.

In this case we must weigh the importance of the general privilege of confidentiality of presidential communications in performance of his responsibilities against the inroads of such a privilege on the fair administration of criminal justice. The interest in preserving confidentiality is weighty indeed and entitled to great respect. However we cannot conclude that advisers will be moved to temper the candor of their remarks by the infrequent occasions of disclosure because of the possibility that such conversations will be called for in the context of a criminal prosecution.

On the other hand, the allowance of the privilege to withhold evidence that is demonstrably relevant in a criminal trial would cut deeply into the guarantee of due process of law and gravely impair the basic function of the courts. A President's acknowledged need for confidentiality in the communications of his office is general in nature, whereas the constitutional need for production of relevant evidence in a criminal proceeding is specific and central to the fair adjudication of a particular criminal case in the administration of justice. Without access to specific facts a criminal prosecution may be totally frustrated. The President's broad interest in confidentiality of communications will not be vitiated by disclosure of a limited number of conversations preliminarily shown to have some bearing on the pending criminal cases.

We conclude that when the ground for asserting privilege as to subpoenaed materials sought for use in a criminal trial is based only on the generalized interest in confidentiality, it cannot prevail over the fundamental demands of due process of law in the fair administration of criminal justice. The generalized assertion of privilege must yield to the demonstrated, specific need for evidence in a pending criminal trial.

. . . Here the District Court treated the material as presumptively privileged, proceeded to find that the Special Prosecutor had made a sufficient showing to rebut the presumption and ordered an *in camera* examination of the subpoenaed material. On the basis of our examination of the record we are unable to conclude that the District Court erred in ordering the inspection. Accordingly we affirm the order of the District Court that subpoenaed materials be transmitted to that court. We now turn to the important question of the District Court's responsibilities in conducting the *in camera* examination of presidential materials or communications delivered under the compulsion of the subpoena *duces tecum*.

Enforcement of the subpoena *duces tecum* was stayed pending this Court's resolution of the issues raised by the petitions for certiorari. Those issues now having been disposed of, the matter of implementation will rest with the District Court. "[T]he guard, furnished to

[President] to protect him from being harassed by vexatious and unnecessary subpoenas, is to be looked for in the conduct of the [district] court after the subpoenas have issued; not in any circumstances which is to precede their being issued." *United States* v. *Burr.* Statements that meet the test of admissibility and relevance must be isolated; all other material must be excised. At this stage the District Court is not limited to representations of the Special Prosecutor as to the evidence sought by the subpoena; the material will be available to the District Court. It is elementary that *in camera* inspection of evidence is always a procedure calling for scrupulous protection against any release or publication of material not found by the court, at that stage, probably admissible in evidence and relevant to the issues of the trial for which it is sought. That being true of an ordinary situation, it is obvious that the District Court has a very heavy responsibility to see to it that presidential conversations, which are either not relevant or not admissible, are accorded that high degree of respect due the President of the United States. Mr. Chief Justice Marshall sitting as a trial judge in the *Burr* case was extraordinarily careful to point out that: "[I]n no case of this kind would a Court be required to proceed against the President as against an ordinary individual." Marshall's statement cannot be read to mean in any sense that a President is above the law, but relates to the singularly unique role under Art. II of a President's communications and activities, related to the performance of duties under that Article. Moreover, a President's communications and activities encompass a vastly wider range of sensitive material than would be true of any "ordinary individual." It is therefore necessary in the public interest to afford presidential confidentiality the greatest protection consistent with the fair administration of justice. The need for confidentiality even as to idle conversations with associates in which casual reference might be made concerning political leaders within the country or foreign statesmen is too obvious to call for

further treatment. We have no doubt that the District Judge will at all times accord to presidential records that high degree of deference suggested in *United States* v. *Burr,* and will discharge his responsibility to see to it that until released to the Special Prosecutor no *in camera* material is revealed to anyone. This burden applies with even greater force to excised material; once the decision is made to excise, the material is restored to its privileged status and should be returned under seal to its lawful custodian.

Since this matter came before the Court during the pendency of a criminal prosecution, and on representations that time is of the essence, the mandate shall issue forthwith.

Mr. Justice Rehnquist took no part in the consideration or decision of these cases.

L. Henkin, *Foreign Affairs and the Constitution* 112 (1975) (excerpt)*

EXECUTIVE PRIVILEGE

Presidents are frequently charged with failure to cooperate when they deny to Congress or its committees information or documents, whether to preserve "confidentiality" of operations within the Executive Branch, or because the Executive believes that they should be "classified" and concealed in the national interest. In regard to foreign relations, in particular, Presidents often claim that disclosure would jeopardize national policies, offend some friendly nation, or otherwise embarrass the United States in its relations with other nations. "Executive privilege" was asserted by President Washington to withhold from the House of Representatives paper relating to the negotiation of the Jay Treaty, but while he justified that in part because the House had no constitutional

* Source: From *Foreign Affairs and the Constitution* by L. Henkin, p. 112. Copyright 1975 by The Foundation Press.

function in the making of treaties, later Presidents refused documents and information which were indisputably relevant to legitimate Congressional concerns.

This issue, too, has not been resolved in principle, but in fact Presidents have prevailed. Congress has never sought to enforce its demands by threat of criminal sanction or citation for contempt against executive officials. In foreign affairs, in particular, Congress has itself recognized limitations, for while it has long demanded reports of all executive departments, it has requested them of the State Department only "if not incompatible with the public interest." But Presidents have been careful not to deny Congress lightly, or too often.

3

Federalism: The Nation and the States in the Making of Public Policy (National Authority)

INTRODUCTION

R. Pound, *Law and Federal Government* 23 (excerpt)*

. . . No domain of continental extent has been ruled otherwise than as an autocracy or as a federal state. Confederacies have fallen apart. Consolidations of independent states, unless in a limited domain, have developed into autocracies. In antiquity the consolidation achieved by Alexander and the almost world-wide consolidation achieved by the Romans resulted in autocratically ruled empires. In the modern world the German-Roman empire of the Middle Ages fell apart. It was neither autocratic nor federal. The British commonwealth of nations has fallen apart politically. Russia has only changed its type of autocrat. But the United States and Canada and Australia show us what we may well call continental domains held together politically, sometimes under great stress, by a federal polity. . . .

* Source: From *Federalism as a Democratic Process* by Pound, McIlwain, and Nichols. Copyright © 1942 by the Trustees of Rutgers College in New Jersey. Reprinted by permission of Rutgers University Press.

H. Wechsler, in A. W. Macmahon (ed.), *Federalism Mature and Emergent* 97 (excerpt)†

. . . In a far flung, free society, the federalist values are enduring. They call upon a people to achieve a unity sufficient to resist their common perils and advance their common welfare, without undue sacrifice of their diversities and the creative energies to which diversity gives rise. They call for government responsive to the will of the full national constituency, without loss of responsiveness to lesser voices, reflecting smaller bodies of opinion, in areas that constitute their own legitimate concern.

Mr. Justice Brandeis, dissenting in *New State Ice Co.* v. *Liebman*, 285 U.S. 262, 310–11 (1932) (excerpt)

The discoveries in physical science, the triumphs in invention, attest the value of the process of trial and error. In large measure, these advances have been due to experimenta-

† New York: Doubleday (1955), p. 97.

tion. . . . There must be power in the States and the Nation to remould, through experimentation, our economic practices and institutions to meet changing social and economic needs. . . .

To stay experimentation in things social and economic is a grave responsibility. Denial of the right to experiment may be fraught with serious consequences to the Nation. It is one of the happy incidents of the federal system that a single courageous State may, if its citizens choose, serve as a laboratory; and try novel social and economic experiments without risk to the rest of the country. This Court has the power to prevent an experiment. We may strike down the statute which embodies it on the ground that, in our opinion, the measure is arbitrary, capricious or unreasonable. We have power to do this, because the due process clause has been held by the Court applicable to matters of substantive law as well as to matters of procedure. But in the exercise of this high power, we must be ever on our guard, lest we erect our prejudices into legal principles. If we would guide by the light of reason, we must let our minds be bold.

NATIONAL AUTHORITY

The National Commerce Power

Gibbons v. *Ogden*
9 Wheaton 1 (1824)

To encourage development of steam navigation, New York granted Robert Fulton (the inventor of the steamboat) exclusive steamboat rights on the Hudson River *in New York* for a limited period of years. Thanks to this grant, Fulton was able to get financial backing and to build successful steamboats, one of which was operated for him under the New York grant by Ogden. Gibbons intruded by running a steamboat from New York to New Jersey in violation of the Fulton "patent." This case began as an action by the Fulton interests to stop the infringement.

Mr. Chief Justice Marshall delivered the opinion of the Court: . . .

The appellant contends that this decree [of the court below] is erroneous, because the laws which purport to give the exclusive privilege it sustains are repugnant to the constitution and laws of the United States.

They are said to be repugnant—

1. To that clause in the constitution which authorizes Congress to regulate commerce.

2. To that which authorizes Congress to promote the progress of science and useful arts. . . .

As preliminary to the very able discussions of the constitution, which we have heard from the bar, and as having some influence on its construction, reference has been made to the political situation of these States, anterior to its formation. It has been said that they were sovereign, were completely independent, and were connected with each other only by a league. This is true. But when these allied sovereigns converted their league into a government, when they converted their Congress of Ambassadors, deputed to deliberate on their common concerns, and to recommend measures of general utility, into a Legislature, empowered to enact laws on the most interesting subjects, the whole character in which the States appear, underwent a change, the extent of which must be determined by a fair consideration of the instrument by which that change was effected.

This instrument contains an enumeration of powers expressly granted by the people to their government. It has been said that these powers ought to be construed strictly. But why ought they to be so construed? Is there one sentence in the constitution which gives countenance to this rule? In the last of the enumerated powers, that which grants, expressly, the means of carrying all others into execution, Congress is authorized "to make all laws which shall be necessary and proper" for the purpose. But this limitation on the means which may be used, is not extended to the powers which are conferred; nor is there one sentence in the constitution which has been pointed out by the gentlemen of the bar, or which we have been able to discern, that prescribes this rule. We do not, therefore, think ourselves justified in adopting it. . . . If, from the imperfection of human language, there should be serious doubts respecting the extent of any given power, it is a well-settled rule that the objects for which it was given, especially when those objects are expressed in the instrument itself, should have great influence in the construction. We know of no reason for excluding this rule from the present case. . . .

The words are: "Congress shall have power to regulate commerce with foreign nations, and among the several States, and with the Indian tribes."

The subject to be regulated is commerce; and our constitution being, as was aptly said at the bar, one of enumeration, and not of definition, to ascertain the extent of the power it becomes necessary to settle the meaning of the word. The counsel for the appellee would limit it to traffic, to buying and selling, or the interchange of commodities, and do not admit that it comprehends navigation. This would restrict a general term, applicable to many objects, to one of its significations. Commerce, undoubtedly, is traffic, but it is something more: it is intercourse. It describes the commercial intercourse between nations, and parts of nations, in all its branches, and is regulated by prescribing rules for carrying on that intercourse. The mind can scarcely conceive a system for regulating commerce between nations, which shall exclude all laws concerning navigation, which shall be silent on the admission of the vessels of the one nation into the ports of the other, and be confined to prescribing rules for the conduct of individuals, in the actual employment of buying and selling, or of barter.

If commerce does not include navigation, the government of the Union has no direct power over that subject, and can make no law prescribing what shall constitute American vessels, or requiring that they shall be navigated by American seamen. Yet this power has been exercised from the commencement of the government, has been exercised with the consent of all, and has been understood by all to be a commercial regulation. All America understands, and has uniformly understood, the word "commerce" to comprehend navigation. It was so understood, and must have been so understood, when the constitution was framed. The power over commerce, including navigation, was one of the primary objects for which the people of America adopted their government, and must have been contemplated in forming it. The convention must have used the word in that sense; because all have understood it in that sense, and the attempt to restrict it comes too late. . . .

The word used in the constitution, then, comprehends, and has been always understood to comprehend, navigation within its meaning; and a power to regulate navigation is as expressly granted as if that term had been added to the word "commerce."

To what commerce does this power extend? The constitution informs us, to commerce "with foreign nations, and among the several States, and with the Indian tribes."

It has, we believe, been universally admitted

that these words comprehend every species of commercial intercourse between the United States and foreign nations. No sort of trade can be carried on between this country and any other, to which this power does not extend. It has been truly said, that commerce, as the word is used in the constitution, is a unit, every part of which is indicated by the term.

If this be the admitted meaning of the word, in its application to foreign nations, it must carry the same meaning throughout the sentence, and remain a unit, unless there be some plain intelligible cause which alters it.

The subject to which the power is next applied, is to commerce "among the several States." The word "among" means intermingled with. A thing which is among others, is intermingled with them. Commerce among the States cannot stop at the external boundary line of each State, but may be introduced into the interior.

It is not intended to say that these words comprehend that commerce which is completely internal, which is carried on between man and man in a State, or between different parts of the same State, and which does not extend to our affect other States. Such a power would be inconvenient, and is certainly unnecessary.

Comprehensive as the word "among" is, it may very properly be restricted to that commerce which concerns more States than one. The phrase is not one which would probably have been selected to indicate the completely interior traffic of a State, because it is not an apt phrase for that purpose; and the enumeration of the particular classes of commerce to which the power was to be extended, would not have been made had the intention been to extend the power to every description. The enumeration presupposes something not enumerated; and that something, if we regard the language or the subject of the sentence, must be the exclusively internal commerce of a State. The genius and character of the whole government seem to be, that its action is to be applied to all the external

concerns of the nation, and to those internal concerns which affect the States generally; but not to those which are completely within a particular State, which do not affect other States, and with which it is not necessary to interfere, for the purpose of executing some of the general powers of the government. The completely internal commerce of a State, then, may be considered as reserved for the State itself.

But, in regulating commerce with foreign nations, the power of Congress does not stop at the jurisdictional lines of the several States. It would be a very useless power if it could not pass those lines. The commerce of the United States with foreign nations, is that of the whole United States. Every district has a right to participate in it. The deep streams which penetrate our country in every direction, pass through the interior of almost every State in the Union, and furnish the means of exercising this right. If Congress has the power to regulate it, that power must be exercised whenever the subject exists. If it exists within the States, if a foreign voyage may commence or terminate at a port within a State, then the power of Congress may be exercised within a state. . . .

We are now arrived at the inquiry—What is this power?

It is the power to regulate; that is, to prescribe the rule by which commerce is to be governed. This power, like all others vested in Congress, is complete in itself, may be exercised to its utmost extent, and acknowledges no limitations, other than are prescribed in the constitution. These are expressed in plain terms, and do not affect the questions which arise in this case, or which have been discussed at the bar. If, as has always been understood, the sovereignty of Congress, though limited to specified objects, is plenary as to those objects, the power over commerce with foreign nations, and among the several States, is vested in Congress as absolutely as it would be in a single government, having in its constitution the same restrictions on the exercise of the power as are found in the constitution of the United States.

The wisdom and the discretion of Congress, their identity with the people, and the influence which their constituents possess at elections, are, in this, as in many other instances, as that, for example, of declaring war, the sole restraints on which they have relied to secure them from its abuse. They are the restraints on which the people must often rely solely, in all representative governments.

The power of Congress, then, comprehends navigation, within the limits of every State in the Union; so far as that navigation may be, in any manner, connected with "commerce with foreign nations, or among the several States, or with the Indian tribes." It may, of consequence, pass the jurisdictional line of New York, and act upon the very waters to which the prohibition now under consideration applies.

But it has been urged with great earnestness, that although the power of Congress to regulate commerce with foreign nations, and among the several States, be co-extensive with the subject itself, and have no other limits than are prescribed in the constitution, yet the States may severally exercise the same power within their respective jurisdictions. In support of this argument, it is said that they possessed it as an inseparable attribute of sovereignty, before the formation of the constitution, and still retain it, except so far as they have surrendered it by that instrument; that this principle results from the nature of the government, and is secured by the tenth amendment; that an affirmative grant of power is not exclusive, unless in its own nature it be such that the continued exercise of it by the former possessor is inconsistent with the grant, and that this is not of that description. . . .

It has been contended by the counsel for the appellant, that, as the word "to regulate" implies in its nature, full power over the thing to be regulated, it excludes, necessarily, the action of all others that would perform the same operation on the same thing. That regulation is designed for the entire result, applying in those parts which remain as they were, as well as to

those which are altered. It produces a uniform whole, which is as much disturbed and deranged by changing what the regulating power designs to leave untouched, as that on which it has operated.

There is great force in this argument, and the Court is not satisfied that it has been refuted.

Since, however, in exercising the power of regulating their own purely internal affairs, whether of trading or police, the States may sometimes enact laws, the validity of which depends on their interfering with and being contrary to, an act of Congress passed in pursuance of the constitution, the court will enter upon the inquiry, whether the laws of New York, as expounded by the highest tribunal of that State, have, in their application to this case, come into collision with an act of Congress, and deprived a citizen of a right to which that act entitles him. Should this collision exist, it will be immaterial whether those laws were passed in virtue of a concurrent power "to regulate commerce with foreign nations and among the several States," or in virtue of a power to regulate their domestic trade and police. In one case and the other, the acts of New York must yield to the law of Congress; and the decision sustaining the privilege they confer, against a right given by a law of the Union, must be erroneous.

[The New York steamboat law was held to be in conflict with federal *legislation* and so invalid under the Supremacy Clause in Article VI of the Constitution. Ogden's claim was thus dismissed.]

[Mr. Justice Johnson, concurring, found the interstate commerce power exclusively national. Thus for him the New York law was invalid, regardless of the act of Congress. In the course of his opinion he observed: "If there was any one object riding over every other in the adoption of the Constitution, it was to keep the commercial intercourse among the States free from all invidious and partial restraints."]

Madison on the Commerce Power

James Madison's view on the commerce power was expressed in his notes on the Constitutional Convention, in which he always referred to himself in the third person. His note for September 15, 1787, said:

> Whether the states are now restrained from laying tonnage duties depends on the extent of the power [of Congress] "to regulate commerce." These terms are vague, but they seem to exclude the power of the states. They may certainly be restrained by treaty. . . . He was more and more convinced that the regulation of commerce was in its nature individible and ought to be wholly under one authority.

Pensacola Telegraph Co. v. Western Union
96 U.S. 1 (1878)

In 1866 Congress provided for a national telegraph system. A Florida law gave exclusive telegraph rights within certain of its counties to a local company, in a manner that would frustrate the congressional program. This is an appeal from a decision upholding the act of Congress.

Mr. Chief Justice Waite delivered the opinion of the court. . . .

Since the case of *Gibbons* v. *Ogden* (9 Wheat. 1), it has never been doubted that commercial intercourse is an element of commerce which comes within the regulating power of Congress. Post-offices and post-roads are established to facilitate the transmission of intelligence. Both commerce and the postal service are placed within the power of Congress, because, being national in their operation, they should be under the protecting care of the national government.

The powers thus granted are not confined to the instrumentalities of commerce, or the postal system known or in use when the Constitution was adopted, but they keep pace with the progress of the country, and adapt themselves to the new developments of times and circumstances. They extend from the horse with its rider to the stage-coach, from the sailing-vessel to the steamboat, from the coach and the steamboat to the railroad, and from the railroad to the telegraph, as these new agencies are successively brought into use to meet the demands of increasing population and wealth. They were intended for the government of the business to which they relate, at all times and under all circumstances. As they were entrusted to the general government for the good of the nation, it is not only the right, but the duty, of Congress to see to it that intercourse among the States and the transmission of intelligence are not obstructed or unnecessarily encumbered by State legislation.

The electric telegraph marks an epoch in the progress of time. In a little more than a quarter of a century it has changed the habits of business, and become one of the necessities of commerce. It is indispensable as a means of inter-communication, but especially is it so in commercial transactions. The statistics of the business before the recent reduction in rates show that more than eighty per cent of all the messages sent by telegraph related to commerce. Goods are sold and money paid upon telegraphic orders. Contracts are made by telegraphic correspondence, cargoes secured, and the movement of ships directed. The telegraphic announcement of the markets abroad regulates prices at home, and a prudent merchant rarely enters upon an important transaction without using the telegraph freely to secure information.

It is not only important to the people, but to the government. . . .

The government of the United States, within the scope of its powers, operates upon every foot of territory under its jurisdiction. It legislates for the whole nation, and is not embarrassed by State lines. Its peculiar duty is to protect one part of the country from encroachments by another upon the national rights which belong to all.

The State of Florida has attempted to confer upon a single corporation the exclusive right of transmitting intelligence by telegraph over a certain portion of its territory. . . . The legislation of Florida, if sustained, excludes all commercial intercourse by telegraph between the citizens of the other States and those residing upon this territory, except by the employment of this corporation. The United States cannot communicate with their own officers by telegraph except in the same way. The State, therefore, clearly has attempted to regulate commercial intercourse between its citizens and those of other States, and to control the transmission of all telegraphic correspondence within its own jurisdiction.

It is unnecessary to decide how far this might have been done if Congress had not acted upon the same subject, for it has acted. The statute of July 24, 1866, in effect, amounts to a prohibition of all State monopolies in this particular. It substantially declares, in the interest of commerce and the convenient transmission of intelligence from place to place by the government of the United States and its citizens, that the erection of telegraph lines shall, so far as State interference is concerned, be free to all who will submit to the conditions imposed by Congress, and that corporations organized under the laws of one State for constructing and operating telegraph lines shall not be excluded by another from prosecuting their business within its jurisdiction, if they accept the terms proposed by the national government for this national privilege. . . .

Decree affirmed.

Mr. Justice Field and Mr. Justice Hunt dissent. . . .

Mr. Justice Harlan did not sit in this case, nor take any part in deciding it.

States' Rights and Laissez-Faire

It will be seen that in the foregoing cases (as late as 1878) the commerce power of Congress was generously construed in the spirit of the Virginia Plan to escape the anarchical conditions that had prevailed under the Articles of Confederation. Then beginning in the 1890s (and continuing until 1937) laissez-faire set in (see the *Knight, Dagenhart, Schechter,* and *Carter* cases, below). Of course, laissez-faire is an economic, not a constitutional, doctrine, but it found expression (as a restriction on national power) in states' rights and the Tenth Amendment.

Even in the laissez-faire era, however, the broad Virginia Plan conception of national power prevailed in cases not involving laissez-faire interests. This double standard is an aspect of what has been called "dual federalism." It meant that states' rights somehow limited even the *expressly delegated* national powers *for some, but not for all, purposes.* Thus dual federalism protected "reputable" business in its more modern transgressions (e.g., trusts and child labor), but not in such old-fashioned immoralities as prostitution, gambling, impure foods, liquor, narcotics, or "fraudulent" margarine (see cases referred to in *Hammer* v. *Dagenhart* and *Bailey* v. *Drexel Furniture Co.,* below).

It would be erroneous to suppose that the sudden new concern for states' rights in the 1890s brought the states new freedom to manage their own affairs. Quite the contrary! States' rights in this context was merely a device to hamstring national government. Contemporaneously with dual federalism, as we shall see, the courts developed the doctrine of "substantive due process" to save "reputable" business interests from the "sovereign states." Thus did laissez-faire economic doctrine find expression in the Constitution—for a time.

United States v. *E. C. Knight*
156 U.S. 1 (1895)

Mr. Chief Justice Fuller . . . delivered the opinion of the court.

By the purchase of the stock of the four Philadelphia refineries, with shares of its own stock, the American Sugar Refining Company acquired nearly complete control of the manufacture of refined sugar within the United States. The bill charged that the contracts under which these purchases were made constituted combinations in restraint of trade, and that in entering into them the defendants combined and conspired to restrain the trade and commerce in refined sugar among the several States and with foreign nations, contrary to the act of Congress of July 2, 1890. . . .

The fundamental question is, whether conceding that the existence of a monopoly in manufacture is established by the evidence, that monopoly can be directly suppressed under the act of Congress in the mode attempted by this bill.

It cannot be denied that the power of the State to protect the lives, health, and property of its citizens, and to preserve good order and the public morals, "the power to govern men and things within the limits of its dominion," is a power originally and always belonging to the States, not surrendered by them to the general government, nor directly restrained by the Constitution of the United States, and essentially exclusive. The relief of the citizens of each

State from the burden of monopoly and the evils resulting from the restraint of trade among such citizens was left with the states to deal with, and this court has recognized their possession of that power even to the extent of holding that an employment or business carried on by private individuals, when it becomes a matter of such public interest and importance as to create a common charge or burden upon the citizen; in other words, when it becomes a practical monopoly, to which the citizen is compelled to resort and by means of which a tribute can be exacted from the community, is subject to regulation by state legislative power. On the other hand, the power of Congress to regulate commerce among the several States is also exclusive. The Constitution does not provide that interstate commerce shall be free, but, by the grant of this exclusive power to regulate it, it was left free except as Congress might impose restraints. Therefore it has been determined that the failure of Congress to exercise this exclusive power in any case is an expression of its will that the subject shall be free from restrictions or impositions upon it by the several States, and if a law passed by a State in the exercise of its acknowledged powers comes into conflict with that will, the Congress and the State cannot occupy the position of equal opposing sovereignties, because the Constitution declares its supremacy and that the laws passed in pursuance thereof; and that which is not supreme must yield to that which is supreme. "Commerce, undoubtedly, is traffic," said Chief Justice Marshall, "but it is something more; it is intercourse. It describes the commercial intercourse between nations and parts of nations in all its branches, and is regulated by prescribing rules for carrying on that intercourse." That which belongs to commerce is within the jurisdiction of the United States, but that which does not belong to commerce is within the jurisdiction of the police power of the State. . . .

The argument is that the power to control the manufacture of refined sugar is a monopoly over a necessary of life, to the enjoyment of which by a large part of the population of the United States interstate commerce is indispensable, and that, therefore, the general government in the exercise of the power to regulate commerce may repress such monopoly directly and set aside the instruments which have created it. But this argument cannot be confined to necessaries of life merely, and must include all articles of general consumption. Doubtless the power to control the manufacture of a given thing involves in a certain sense the control of its disposition, but this is a secondary and not the primary sense; and although the exercise of that power may result in bringing the operation of commerce into play, it does not control it, and affects it only incidentally and indirectly. Commerce succeeds to manufacture, and is not a part of it. The power to regulate commerce is the power to prescribe the rule by which commerce shall be governed, and is a power independent of the power to suppress monopoly. But it may operate in repression of monopoly whenever that comes within the rules by which commerce is governed or whenever the transaction is itself a monopoly of commerce. . . .

It is vital that the independence of the commercial power and of the police power, and the delimitation between them, however sometimes perplexing, should always be recognized and observed, for while the one furnishes the strongest bond of union, the other is essential the preservation of the autonomy of the States as required by our dual form of government; and acknowledged evils, however grave and urgent they may appear to be, had better be borne, than the risk be run, in the effort to suppress them, of more serious consequences by resort to expedients of even doubtful constitutionality. . . .

Contracts, combinations, or conspiracies to control domestic enterprise in manufacture, agriculture, mining, production in all its forms, or to raise or lower prices or wages, might unquestionably tend to restrain external as well as domestic trade, but the restraint would be an indirect result, however inevitable and whatever its extent, and such result would not necessarily determine the object of the contract, combination, or conspiracy.

Again, all the authorities agree that in order to vitiate a contract or combination it is not essential that its result should be a complete monopoly; it is sufficient if it really tends to that end and to deprive the public of the advantages which flow from free competition. Slight reflection will show that if the national power extends to all contracts and combinations in manufacture, agriculture, mining, and other productive industries, whose ultimate result may affect external commerce, comparatively little of business operations and affairs would be left for state control.

It was in the light of well-settled principles that the act of July 2, 1890, was framed. Congress did not attempt thereby to assert the power to deal with monopoly directly as such; or to limit and restrict the rights of corporations created by the States or the citizens of the States in the acquisition, control, or disposition of property; or to regulate or prescribe the price or prices at which such property or the products thereof should be sold; or to make criminal the acts of persons in the acquisition and control of property which the States of their residence or creation sanctioned or permitted. Aside from the provisions applicable where Congress might exercise municipal power, what the law struck at was combinations, contracts, and conspiracies to monopolize trade and commerce among the several States or with foreign nations; but the contracts and acts of the defendants related exclusively to the acquisition of the Philadelphia refineries and the business of sugar refining in Pennsylvania, and bore no direct relation to commerce between the States or with foreign nations. . . . There was nothing in the proofs to indicate any intention to put a restraint upon trade or commerce, and the fact, as we have seen, that trade or commerce might be indirectly affected was not enough to entitle complainants to a decree. . . .

Decree affirmed.

Mr. Justice Harlan, dissenting. . . .

What is commerce among the States? The decisions of this court fully answer the question. "Commerce, undoubtedly, is traffic, but it is something more: it is intercourse." It does not embrace the completely interior traffic of the respective States—that which is "carried on between man and man in a State, or between different parts of the same State and which does not extend to or affect other States"—but it does embrace "every species of commercial intercourse" between the United States and foreign nations and among the States, and, therefore, it includes such traffic or trade, buying, selling, and interchange of commodities, as directly affects or necessarily involves the interests of the People of the United States. "Commerce, as the word is used in the Constitution, is a unit," and "cannot stop at the external boundary line of each State, but may be introduced into the interior." "The genius and character of the whole government seem to be, that its action is to be applied to all the external concerns of the nation, *and to those internal concerns which affect the States generally*."

These principles were announced in *Gibbons v. Ogden,* and have often been approved. . . .

In the light of these principles, determining as well the scope of the power to regulate commerce among the States as the nature of such commerce, we are to inquire whether the act of Congress of July 2, 1890 . . . entitled "An act to protect trade and commerce against unlawful restraints and monopolies" . . . is repugnant to the Constitution. . . .

It would seem to be indisputable that no *combination* of corporations or individuals can, *of right*, impose unlawful restraints upon *interstate* trade, whether upon transportation or upon such interstate intercourse and traffic as precede transportation, any more than it can, *of right*, impose unreasonable restraints upon the completely internal traffic of a State. The supposition cannot be indulged that this general proposition will be disputed. If it be true that a *combination* of corporations or individuals may, so far as the power of Congress is concerned, subject interstate trade, in any of its stages, to unlawful restraints, the conclusion is inevitable that the Constitution has failed to accomplish one primary object of the Union, which was to place commerce *among the States* under the control of the common government of all the people, and thereby relieve or protect it against burdens or restrictions imposed, by whatever authority, for the benefit of particular localities or special interests. . . .

The Shreveport Case
234 U.S. 342 (1914)

Mr. Justice Hughes delivered the opinion of the court. . . .

These suits were brought in the Commerce Court . . . to set aside an order of the Interstate Commerce Commission, dated March 11, 1912, upon the ground that it exceeded the Commission's authority. . . .

The gravamen of the complaint, said the Interstate Commerce Commission, was that the carriers made rates out of Dallas and other Texas points into eastern Texas which were much lower than those which they extended into Texas from Shreveport. The situation may be briefly described: Shreveport, Louisiana, is about 40 miles from the Texas state line, and 231 miles from Houston, Texas, on the line of the Houston, East & West Texas and Houston and Shreveport Companies . . . ; it is 189 miles from Dallas, Texas, on the line of the Texas & Pacific. Shreveport competes with both cities for the trade of the intervening territory. The rates on these lines from Dallas and Houston, respectively, eastward to intermediate points, in Texas, were much less, according to distance, than from Shreveport westward to the same points. It is undisputed that the difference was substantial, and injuriously affected the commerce of Shreveport. . . .

The Interstate Commerce Commission [in effect ordered an equalizing increase in the Texas local rates].

The point of the objection to the order is that, as the discrimination found by the Commission to be unjust arises out of the relation of intrastate rates, maintained under state authority, to interstate rates that have been upheld as reasonable, its correction was beyond the Commission's power. . . .

Congress is empowered to regulate,—that is, to provide the law for the government of interstate commerce, to enact "all appropriate legislation" for its "protection and advancement." . . . As it is competent for Congress to legislate to these ends, unquestionably it may seek their attainment by requiring that the agencies of interstate commerce shall not be used in such manner as to cripple, retard, or destroy it. The fact that carriers are instruments of intrastate commerce, as well as of interstate commerce, does not derogate from the complete and paramount authority of Congress over the latter, or preclude the Federal power from being exerted to prevent the intrastate operations of such carriers from being made a means of injury to that which has been confided to Federal care. Wherever the interstate and intrastate transactions of carriers are so related that the government of the one involves the control of the other, it is Congress, and not the state, that is entitled to prescribe the final and dominant rule, for otherwise Congress would be denied the exercise of its constitutional authority, and the state, and not the nation, would be supreme within the national field. . . .

It is for Congress to supply the needed correction where the relation between intrastate and interstate rates presents the evil to be corrected, and this it may do completely by reason of its control over the interstate carrier in all matters having such a close and substantial relation to interstate commerce that it is necessary or appropriate to exercise the control for the effective government of that commerce.

It is also clear that, in removing the injurious discriminations against interstate traffic arising from the relation of intrastate to interstate rates, Congress is not bound to reduce the latter below what it may deem to be a proper standard fair to the carrier and to the public. Otherwise, it could prevent the injury to interstate commerce only by the sacrifice of its judgment as to interstate rates. Congress is entitled to maintain its own standard as to these rates, and to forbid any discriminatory action by interstate carriers which will obstruct the freedom of movement of interstate traffic over their lines in accordance with the terms it establishes.

Having this power, Congress could provide for its execution through the aid of a subordinate body; and we conclude that the order of the Commission now in question cannot be held invalid upon the ground that it exceeded the authority which Congress could lawfully confer. . . .

Mr. Justice Lurton and Mr. Justice Pitney dissent.

Hammer v. *Dagenhart*
247 U.S. 251 (1918)

To discourage child labor, Congress in 1916 prohibited the shipment in interstate and foreign commerce of any product of mines or factories which employed children below specified ages or employed other children in excess of specified hours.

Mr. Justice Day delivered the opinion of the court: . . .

The attack upon the act rests upon three propositions: First: It is not a regulation of interstate and foreign commerce; second: It contravenes the Tenth Amendment to the Constitution; third: It conflicts with the Fifth Amendment to the Constitution.

The controlling question for decision is: Is it within the authority of Congress in regulating commerce among the states to prohibit the transportation in interstate commerce of manufactured goods, the product of a factory in which, within thirty days prior to their removal therefrom, children under the age of fourteen have been employed or permitted to work, or children between the ages of fourteen and sixteen years have been employed or permitted to work more than eight hours in any day, or more than six days in any week, or after the hour of seven o'clock p.m., or before the hour of 6 o'clock a.m.? . . . But it is insisted that adjudged cases in this court establish the doctrine that the power to regulate given to Congress incidentally includes the authority to prohibit the movement of ordinary commodities and therefore that the subject is not open for discussion. The cases demonstrate the contrary. They rest upon the character of the particular subjects dealt with and the fact that the scope of governmental authority, state or national, possessed over them is such that the authority to prohibit is as to them but the exertion of the power to regulate.

The first of these cases is *Champion* v. *Ames*, 188 U.S. 321, the so-called *Lottery Case*, in which it was held that Congress might pass a law having the effect to keep the channels of commerce free from use in the transportation of tickets used in the promotion of lottery schemes. In *Hipolite Egg Co.* v. *United States*, 220 U.S. 45, this court sustained the power of Congress to pass the Pure Food and Drug Act which prohibited the introduction into the States by means of interstate commerce of impure foods and drugs. In *Hoke* v. *United States*, 227 U.S. 308, this court sustained the constitutionality of the so-called "White Slave Traffic Act" whereby the transportation of a woman in interstate commerce for the purpose of prostitution was forbidden. In that case we said, having reference to the authority of Congress, under the regulatory power, to protect the channels of interstate commerce: "If the facility of interstate transportation can be taken away from the demoralization of lotteries, the debasement of obscene literature, the contagion of diseased cattle or persons, the impurity of food and drugs, the like facility can be taken away from the systematic enticement to, and the enslavement in prostitution and debauchery of women, and, more insistently, of girls."

In *Caminetti* v. *United States*, 242 U.S. 470, we held that Congress might prohibit the transportation of women in interstate commerce for the purposes of debauchery and kindred purposes. In *Clark Distilling Co.* v. *Western Maryland Railway Co.*, 242 U.S. 311, the power of Congress over the transportation of intoxicating liquors was sustained. . . .

In each of these instances the use of interstate transportation was necessary to the accomplishment of harmful results. In other words, although the power over interstate transportation was to regulate, that could only be accomplished by prohibiting the use of the facilities of interstate commerce to effect the evil intended.

This element is wanting in the present case. The thing intended to be accomplished by this statute is the denial of the facilities of interstate commerce to those manufacturers in the States who employ children within the prohibited ages. The act in its effect does not regulate transportation among the states, but aims to standardize the ages at which children may be employed in mining and manufacturing within the states. The goods shipped are of themselves harmless. The act permits them to be freely shipped after thirty days from the time of their removal from the factory. When offered for shipment, and before transportation begins, the labor of their production is over, and the mere fact that they were intended for interstate com-

merce transportation does not make their production subject to federal control under the
commerce power.

Commerce "consists of intercourse and traffic
. . . and includes the transportation of persons
and property, as well as the purchase, sale and
exchange of commodities." The making of
goods and the mining of coal are not commerce,
nor does the fact that these things are to be afterwards shipped, or used in interstate commerce, make their production a part thereof.
Delaware, Lackawanna & Western R.R. Co. v.
Yurkonis, 238 U.S. 439.

Over interstate transportation, or its incidents, the regulatory power of Congress is ample, but the production of articles, intended for
interstate commerce, is a matter of local regulation.

"When the commerce begins is determined,
not by the character of the commodity, nor by
the intention of the owner to transfer it to another state for sale, nor by his preparation of it
for transportation, but by its actual delivery to a
common carrier for transportation, or the actual
commencement of its transfer to another state."
(Mr. Justice Jackson in *In re Greene*, 52 F. 113).
This principle has been recognized often in this
court. *Coe* v. *Errol*, 116 U.S. 517; *Bacon* v. *Illinois*,
227 U.S. 504, and cases cited. If it were otherwise, all manufacture intended for interstate
shipment would be brought under federal control to the practical exclusion of the authority of
the States, a result certainly not contemplated
by the framers of the Constitution when they
vested in Congress the authority to regulate
commerce among the States. *Kidd* v. *Pearson*,
128 U.S. 1, 21.

It is further contended that the authority of
Congress may be exerted to control interstate
commerce in the shipment of child-made goods
because of the effect of the circulation of such
goods in other states where the evil of this class
of labor has been recognized by local legislation, and the right to thus employ child labor
has been more rigorously restrained than in the
State of production. In other words, that the un-

fair competition, thus engendered, may be controlled by closing the channels of interstate
commerce to manufacturers in those States
where the local laws do not meet what Congress
deems to be the more just standard of other
States.

There is no power vested in Congress to
require the States to exercise their police power
so as to prevent possible unfair competition.
Many causes may co-operate to give one State,
by reason of local laws or conditions, an economic advantage over others. The commerce
clause was not intended to give to Congress a
general authority to equalize such conditions.
In some of the States laws have been passed
fixing minimum wages for women, in others
the local law regulates the hours of labor of
women in various employments. Business done
in such States may be at an economic disadvantage when compared with States which have no
such regulations; surely, this fact does not give
Congress the power to deny transportation in
interstate commerce to those who carry on business where the hours of labor and the rate of
compensation for women have not been fixed
by a standard in use in other States and approved by Congress . . .

That there should be limitations upon the
right to employ children in mines and factories
in the interest of their own and the public welfare, all will admit. That such employment is
generally deemed to require regulation is
shown by the fact that the brief of counsel states
that every State in the Union has a law upon the
subject, limiting the right to thus employ children. In North Carolina, the State wherein is
located the factory in which the employment
was had in the present case, no child under
twelve years of age is permitted to work.

It may be desirable that such laws be uniform, but our Federal Government is one of
enumerated powers; "this principle," declared
Chief Justice Marshall in *McCulloch* v. *Maryland*, 4 Wheat. 316, "is universally admitted."

A statute must be judged by its natural and
reasonable effect. *Collins* v. *New Hampshire*, 171

U.S. 30, 33, 34. The control by Congress over interstate commerce cannot authorize the exercise of authority not entrusted to it by the Constitution. *Pipe Line Case*, 234 U.S. 548, 560. The maintenance of the authority of the States over matters purely local is as essential to the preservation of our institutions as is the conservation of the supremacy of the federal power in all matters entrusted to the Nation by the Federal Constitution.

In interpreting the Constitution it must never be forgotten that the nation is made up of States to which are entrusted the powers of local government. . . . To sustain this statute would not be in our judgment a recognition of the lawful exertion of congressional authority over interstate commerce, but would sanction an invasion by the federal power of the control of a matter purely local in its character, and over which no authority has been delegated to Congress in conferring the power to regulate commerce among the States.

We have neither authority nor disposition to question the motives of Congress in enacting this legislation. The purposes intended must be attained consistently with constitutional limitations and not by an invasion of the powers of the States. This court has no more important function than that which devolves upon it the obligation to preserve inviolate the constitutional limitations upon the exercise of authority federal and state to the end that each may continue to discharge, harmoniously with the other, the duties entrusted to it by the Constitution.

In our view the necessary effect of this act is, by means of a prohibition against the movement in interstate commerce of ordinary commercial commodities to regulate the hours of labor of children in factories and mines within the States, a purely state authority. Thus the act in a two-fold sense is repugnant to the Constitution. It not only transcends the authority delegated to Congress over commerce but also exerts a power as to a purely local matter to which the federal authority does not extend. The far reaching result of upholding the act cannot be more plainly indicated than by pointing out that if Congress can thus regulate matters entrusted to local authority by prohibition of the movement of commodities in interstate commerce, all freedom of commerce will be at an end, and the power of the States over local matters may be eliminated, and thus our system of government be practically destroyed.

For these reasons we hold that this law exceeds the constitutional authority of Congress. It follows that the decree of the District Court must be affirmed.

Mr. Justice Holmes, dissenting: . . .

The first step in my argument is to make plain what no one is likely to dispute—that the statute in question is within the power expressly given to Congress if considered only as to its immediate effects and that if invalid it is so only upon some collateral ground. The statute confines itself to prohibiting the carriage of certain goods in interstate or foreign commerce. Congress is given power to regulate such commerce in unqualified terms. It would not be argued today that the power to regulate does not include the power to prohibit. Regulation means the prohibition of something, and when interstate commerce is the matter to be regulated I cannot doubt that the regulation may prohibit any part of such commerce that Congress sees fit to forbid. At all events it is established by the *Lottery Case* and others that have followed it that a law is not beyond the regulative power of Congress merely because it prohibits certain transportation out and out. *Champion* v. *Ames*, 188 U.S. 321, 355, 359, et seq. So I repeat that this statute in its immediate operation is clearly within the Congress's constitutional power.

The question then is narrowed to whether the exercise of its otherwise constitutional power by Congress can be pronounced unconstitutional because of its possible reaction upon the conduct of the States in a matter upon which I have admitted that they are free from direct control. I should have thought that that matter had been disposed of so fully as to leave no room for doubt. I should have thought that the most conspicuous decisions of this Court had made it clear that the power to regulate commerce and other constitutional powers could not be cut down or qualified by the fact that it might interfere with the carrying out of the domestic policy of any State. . . .

The Pure Food and Drug Act which was sustained in *Hipolite Egg Co.* v. *United States,* 220 U.S. 45, with the intimation that "no trade can be carried on between the States to which it [the power of Congress to regulate commerce] does not extend," 57, applies not merely to articles that the changing opinions of the time condemn as intrinsically harmful but to others innocent in themselves, simply on the ground that the order for them was induced by a preliminary fraud. *Weeks* v. *United States,* 245 U.S. 618. It does not matter whether the supposed evil precedes or follows the transportation. It is enough that in the opinion of Congress the transportation encourages the evil. . . .

The act does not meddle with anything belonging to the States. They may regulate their internal affairs and their domestic commerce as they like. But when they seek to send their products across the state line they are no longer within their rights. If there were no Constitution and no Congress their power to cross the line would depend upon their neighbors. Under the Constitution such commerce belongs not to the States but to Congress to regulate. It may carry out its views of public policy whatever indirect effect they may have upon the activities of the States. Instead of being encountered by a prohibitive tariff at her boundaries the State encounters the public policy of the United States which it is for Congress to express. The public policy of the United States is shaped with a view to the benefit of the nation as a whole. . . . The national welfare as understood by Congress may require a different attitude within its sphere from that of some self-seeking State. It seems to me entirely constitutional for Congress to enforce its understanding by all the means at its command.

Mr. Justice McKenna, Mr. Justice Brandeis, and Mr. Justice Clarke concur in this opinion.

Note: Schechter v. *United States,* 295 U.S. 495 (1935), and *Carter* v. *Carter Coal Co.,* 298 U.S. 238 (1936), struck down respectively the National Industrial Recovery Act (1933) and the Bituminous Coal Act (1935). The one had been designed to control cutthroat competitive business practices and improve working conditions; the other to stabilize prices and improve labor standards in the especially hard-pressed soft coal industry. In both cases, the Court found the "flow" or "stream of commerce" concept inapplicable; that is, the wholesaling of chickens in New York (*Schechter*) and coal mining (*Carter*) occured in the one case after, in the other before, the flow of interstate commerce. Here the Court drew upon the old *E. C. Knight* case principle that "manufacturing is not commerce." But if mining and local wholesaling, like manufacturing, are not in themselves commerce, do they not affect commercial affairs in "more states than one"? Compare *Gibbons* v. *Ogden.* Recognizing of necessity that they did, the Court found that such affectation was merely "indirect," however extensive; whereas only "direct" effects could bring such matters within the authority of Congress. In short, affection was considered a qualitative, not a quantitative, principle. As Mr. Justice Sutherland expressed it for the Court in *Carter's* case:

> The distinction between a direct and an indirect effect turns, not upon the magnitude of either the cause or the effect, but entirely upon the manner in which the effect has been brought about. If the production by one man of a single ton of coal intended for interstate sale and shipment, and actually so sold and shipped, affects interstate commerce [only] indirectly, the effect does not become direct by multiplying the tonnage, or increasing the number of men employed.
> . . .

Of course, a major part of the coal produced in the coal-mining states is exported for use in other states. Ninety-six percent of the poultry marketed in New York City came from outside the state. Only a few months before *Schechter's* case the same New York City wholesale poultry industry had been found to be within the national commerce power for antitrust purposes: *Local 167* v. *United States,* 291 U.S. 293 (1934).

The Great Depression, the New Deal, and the Court Reorganization Plan

When the stock market crashed in the fall of 1929, the Great Depression was upon us. Within three years there were some 13 million unemployed out of a labor force of 52 million. This meant that one out of four wage earners could not support their families. The employed in many cases were not much better off. In a wide variety of industries, from steel and iron to textiles, earnings ranged from 20 to 30 cents an hour—and many workers had only part-time employment. One-fourth of the working women in Chicago were getting less than 10 cents an hour.

In 1932, total wages paid were 60 percent less than those paid in 1929. Dividends were 57 percent less, while American business as a whole operated at a net loss of over $5 billion. General Motors common stock fell from 72¾ to 7⅝; Radio Corporation from 101 to 2½; United States Steel from 261¾ to 21¼. The rate of business failures was staggering.

Farmers suffered even more, because for them the depression had begun soon after World War I. As A. N. Schlesinger, Jr., wrote in *The Crisis of the Old Order:*

> The shadow fell over the cities and towns; it fell as heavily over the countryside. Farmers had already drawn extensively on their savings before 1929. The Wall Street explosion only made their situation worse by diminishing even more the demand for

farm products. And, where industry could protect its price structure by meeting reduced demand with reduced output, farmers, unable to control output, saw no way to maintain income except to increase planting. Total crop acreage actually rose in 1930 and showed no significant decline in 1931.

The burden of agricultural adjustment thus fell not on production but on price. The figures were dramatic. Between 1929 and 1934 agricultural production declined 15 percent in volume, 40 percent in price; industrial production 42 percent in volume, 15 percent in price. The relative stability of industrial prices worsened the farmers' terms of trade; the ratio of the prices the farmer received to the prices he paid plunged from 109 in 1919 (in terms of 1910–14 prices) and 89 in 1929 to 64 in 1931. Corn slid down to 15 cents, cotton and wool to 5 cents, hogs and sugar to 3 cents, and beef to 2.5 cents. A farmer who chewed one thick plug of Drummond a day required almost a bushel of wheat a day to keep him in chewing tobacco. It took 16 bushels of wheat—more than the average yield of a whole acre—to buy one of his children a pair of $4 shoes. Net farm income in 1932 was $1.8 billion—less than one-third what it had been three years earlier. So appalling a slump left many farm families with little income, and many with no income at all.

The farmer's obligations—his taxes and his debts—had been calculated in terms of the much higher price levels of the twenties. A cotton farmer who borrowed $800 when cotton was 16 cents a pound, borrowed the equivalent of 5,000 pounds of cotton; now, with cotton moving toward 5 cents, he must pay back the debt with over 15,000 pounds of cotton. And, while the farmer's income fell by 64 percent, his burden of indebtedness fell a mere 7 percent. In the meantime, fences were standing in disrepair, crops were rotting, livestock was not worth the freight to market, farm machinery was wearing out. Some found it cheaper to burn their corn than to sell it and buy coal. On every side, notices of mortgage foreclosures and tax sales were going up on gate posts and in country courthouses. William Allen White summed it up: "Every farmer, whether his farm is under mortgage or not, knows that with farm products priced as they are today, sooner or later he must go down."[1]

In the face of such economic disaster, no government responsive to the wishes of its people could be quiescent. Congress and the executive responded with a "New Deal" immediately after the election of President Roosevelt in 1932. But what of laissez-faire and the Supreme Court?

The judicial age that began in 1895 with the emasculation of the Sherman Anti-Trust Act and the destruction of the income tax closed in 1936 with the invalidation of the first New Deal effort to solve the farm problem (see *United States* v. *Butler*, below). That decision was but one of seven (including *Schechter* and *Carter*) which together destroyed a major portion of the New Deal effort to alleviate the Great Depression. Then came the crucial election of 1936. Would the people support the New Deal, or would they repudiate it as a flagrant violator of the Constitution? As it turned out, President Roosevelt carried all but two states. After this unmatched vindication at the polls he announced a court reorganization plan in February 1937. It was essentially a device to pack, or unpack, the Supreme Court (according to one's bias). A few weeks later, without any change in its membership, the Court rendered opinions in the *Jones & Laughlin* and *Steward Machine Co.* cases (below). Note the

---

[1] Arthur N. Schlesinger, Jr., *The Crisis of the Old Order*, pp. 175–176. Copyright © 1957 by Arthur M. Schlesinger, Jr. Reprinted by permission of Houghton Mifflin Company.

position of each Justice in these two cases and compare his position in *United States* v. *Butler*. Doubtless this "switch in time" helped defeat the reorganization plan by making it unnecessary. In short, the Court responded to the deeply felt needs and wishes of the American people. Or to put it differently, we returned to a broad view of national power—after some 42 years (1895–1936) of laissez-faire.

NLRB v. *Jones & Laughlin Steel Corp.*
301 U.S. 1 (1973)

To improve the purchasing power of labor, Congress in 1935 passed the Wagner (National Labor Relations) Act. It outlawed employer "unfair labor practices"— that is, management efforts to prevent unionization and collective bargaining. Finding that Jones & Laughlin had violated the act, the National Labor Relations Board issued a cease and desist order. This case arose when, pursuant to the statute, the board sought judicial enforcement of its order.

Mr. Chief Justice Hughes delivered the opinion of the Court: . . .

Contesting the ruling of the Board, the respondent argues (1) that the Act is in reality a regulation of labor relations and not of interstate commerce; (2) that the Act can have no application to the respondent's relations with its production employees because they are not subject to regulation by the federal government; and (3) that the provisions of the Act violate section 2 of Article III and the Fifth and Seventh Amendments of the Constitution of the United States.

The facts as to the nature and scope of the business of the Jones & Laughlin Steel Corporation have been found by the Labor Board, and, so far as they are essential to the determination of this controversy, they are not in dispute. . . . .

Summarizing these operations, the Labor Board concluded that the works in Pittsburgh and Aliquippa "might be likened to the heart of a self-contained, highly integrated body. They draw in the raw materials from Michigan, Minnesota, West Virginia, Pennsylvania in part through arteries and by means controlled by the respondent; they transform the materials and then pump them out to all parts of the nation

through the vast mechanism which the respondent has elaborated."

To carry on the activities of the entire steel industry, 33,000 men mine ore, 44,000 men mine coal, 4,000 men quarry limestone, 16,000 men manufacture coke, 343,000 men manufacture steel, and 83,000 men transport its product. Respondent has about 10,000 employees in its Aliquippa plant, which is located in a community of about 30,000 persons. . . .

First. *The scope of the Act.*—. . . The grant of authority to the Board does not purport to extend to the relationship between all industrial employees and employers. Its terms do not impose collective bargaining upon all industry regardless of effects upon interstate or foreign commerce. It purports to reach only what may be deemed to burden or obstruct that commerce and, thus qualified, it must be construed as contemplating the exercise of control within constitutional bounds. It is a familiar principle that acts which directly burden or obstruct interstate or foreign commerce, or its free flow, are within the reach of the congressional power. Acts having that effect are not rendered immune because they grow out of labor disputes. It is the effect upon commerce, not the source of the injury, which is the criterion. Whether or not particular action does affect commerce in such a close and intimate fashion as to be subject to federal control, and hence to lie within the authority conferred upon the Board, is left by the statute to be determined as individual cases arise. We are thus to inquire whether in the instant case the constitutional boundary has been passed.

Second. *The unfair labor practices in question.*—The unfair labor practices found by the Board are those defined in section 8, subdivisions (1) and (3). These provide:

> "Sec. 8. It shall be an unfair labor practice for an employer—
>
> "(1) To interfere with, restrain, or coerce employees in the exercise of the rights guaranteed in section 7." . . .
>
> "(3) By discrimination in regard to hire or tenure of employment or any term or condition of employment to encourage or discourage membership in any labor organization: . . ."

Section 8, subdivision (1), refers to section 7, which is as follows:

> "Sec. 7. Employees shall have the right to self-organization, to form, join, or assist labor organizations, to bargain collectively through representatives of their own choosing, and to engage in concerted activities, for the purpose of collective bargaining or other mutual aid or protection."

Thus, in its present application, the statute goes no further than to safeguard the right of employees to self-organization and to select representatives of their own choosing for collective bargaining or other mutual protection without restraint or coercion by their employer.

That is a fundamental right. Employees have as clear a right to organize and select their representatives for lawful purposes as the respondent has to organize its business and select its own officers and agents. Discrimination and coercion to prevent the free exercise of the right of employees to self-organization and represen-

tation is a proper subject for condemnation by competent legislative authority. Long ago we stated the reason for labor organizations. We said that they were organized out of the necessities of the situation; that a single employee was helpless in dealing with an employer; that he was dependent ordinarily on his daily wage for the maintenance of himself and family; that if the employer refused to pay him the wages that he thought fair, he was nevertheless unable to leave the employ and resist arbitrary and unfair treatment; that union was essential to give laborers opportunity to deal on an equality with their employer. . . .

Third. *The application of the Act to employees engaged in production.—The principle involved.*—Respondent says that whatever may be said of employees engaged in interstate commerce, the industrial relations and activities in the manufacturing department of respondent's enterprise are not subject to federal regulation. The argument rests upon the proposition that manufacturing in itself is not commerce. [Citing cases.].

The fundamental principle is that the power to regulate commerce is the power to enact "all appropriate legislation" for "its protection and advancement" . . . ; to adopt measures "to promote its growth and insure its safety" . . . ; "to foster, protect, control and restrain." . . . That power is plenary and may be exerted to protect interstate commerce "no matter what the source of the dangers which threaten it." . . . Although activities may be intrastate in character when separately considered, if they have such a close and substantial relation to interstate commerce that their control is essential or appropriate to protect that commerce from burdens and obstructions, Congress cannot be denied the power to exercise that control. Undoubtedly the scope of this power must be considered in the light of our dual system of government and may not be extended so as to embrace effects upon interstate commerce so indirect and remote that to embrace them, in view of our complex society, would effectually obliterate the distinction between what is national and what is local and create a completely centralized government. The question is necessarily one of degree. . . .

That intrastate activities, by reason of close and intimate relation to interstate commerce, may fall within federal control is demonstrated in the case of carriers who are engaged in both interstate and intrastate transportation. There federal control has been found essential to secure the freedom of interstate traffic from interference or unjust discrimination and to promote the efficiency of the interstate service. *Shreveport Case* (*Houston, E. & W. T. R. Co.* v. *United States*), 234 U.S. 342; *Railroad Commission* v. *Chicago, B. & Q. R. Co.*, 257 U.S. 563. It is manifest that intrastate rates deal *primarily* with a local activity. But in rate-making they bear such a close relation to interstate rates that effective control of the one must embrace some control over the other. Under the Transportation Act, 1920, Congress went so far as to authorize the Interstate Commerce Commission to establish a state-wide level of intrastate rates in order to prevent an unjust discrimination against interstate commerce. . . .

The close and intimate effect which brings the subject within the reach of federal power may be due to activities in relation to productive industry although the industry when separately viewed is local. This has been abundantly illustrated in the application of the Federal Anti-Trust Act. In the *Standard Oil Co. Case,* 221 U.S. 1, and *American Tobacco Co. Case,* 221 U.S. 106, that statute was applied to combinations of employers engaged in productive industry. . . .

Upon the same principle, the Anti-Trust Act has been applied to the conduct of employees engaged in production. . . .

It is thus apparent that the fact that the employees here concerned were engaged in production is not determinative. The question remains as to the effect upon interstate commerce of the labor practice involved. In the *Schechter Case* we found that the effect there was so re-mote as to be beyond the federal power. To find "immediacy or directness" there was to find it "almost everywhere," a result inconsistent with the maintenance of our federal system. In the *Carter Case,* 298 U.S. 238 [in which the Bituminous Coal Conservation Act of 1935 was struck down], the Court was of the opinion that the provisions of the statute relating to production were invalid upon several grounds,—that there was improper delegation of legislative power, and that the requirements not only went beyond any sustainable measure of protection of interstate commerce but were also inconsistent with due process. These cases are not controlling here.

Fourth. *Effects of the unfair labor practice in respondent's enterprise.*—Giving full weight to respondent's contention with respect to a break in the complete continuity of the "stream of commerce" by reason of respondent's manufacturing operations, the fact remains that the stoppage of those operations by industrial strife would have a most serious effect upon interstate commerce. In view of respondent's far-flung activities, it is idle to say that the effect would be indirect or remote. It is obvious that it would be immediate and might be catastrophic. We are asked to shut our eyes to the plainest facts of our national life and to deal with the question of direct and indirect effects in an intellectual vacuum. Because there may be but indirect and remote effects upon interstate commerce in connection with a host of local enterprises throughout the country, it does not follow that other industrial activities do not have such a close and intimate relation to interstate commerce as to make the presence of industrial strife a matter of the most urgent national concern. When industries organize themselves on a national scale, making their relation to interstate commerce the dominant factor in their activities, how can it be maintained that their industrial labor relations constitute a forbidden field into which Congress may not enter when it is necessary to protect interstate commerce from the paralyzing consequences of industrial war?

We have often said that interstate commerce itself is a practical conception. It is equally true that interferences with that commerce must be appraised by a judgment that does not ignore actual experience.

Experience has abundantly demonstrated that the recognition of the right of employees to self-organization and to have representatives of their own choosing for the purpose of collective bargaining is often an essential condition of industrial peace. Refusal to confer and negotiate has been one of the most prolific causes of strife. This is such an outstanding fact in the history of labor disturbances that it is a proper subject of judicial notice and requires no citation of instances.

[Mr. Justice McReynolds (Mr. Justice Van Devanter, Mr. Justice Sutherland, and Mr. Justice Butler concurring with him) dissented.]

United States v. *Darby Lumber Co.*
312 U.S. 100 (1941)

The Fair Labor Standards Act of 1938 provided for minimum wages for 40-hour standard work week and overtime pay for work in excess of 40 hours per week in certain "interstate" businesses. This case began as a criminal prosecution for violation of the act.

Mr. Justice Stone delivered the opinion of the Court:

The two principal questions raised by the record in this case are, first, whether Congress has constitutional power to prohibit the shipment in interstate commerce of lumber manufactured by employees whose wages are less than a prescribed minimum or whose weekly hours of labor at that wage are greater than a prescribed maximum, and, second, whether it has power to prohibit the employment of workmen in the production of goods "for interstate commerce" at other than prescribed wages and hours. A subsidiary question is whether in connection with such prohibitions Congress can require the employer subject to them to keep records showing the hours worked each day and week by each of his employees including those engaged "in the production and manufacture of goods to wit, lumber for "interstate commerce.'" . . .

The Prohibition of Shipment of the Proscribed Goods in Interstate Commerce. Section 15(*a*) (1) prohibits, and the indictment charges, the shipment in interstate commerce, of goods produced for interstate commerce by employees whose wages and hours of employment do not conform to the requirements of the Act. Since this section is not violated unless the commodity shipped has been produced under labor conditions prohibited by section 6 and section 7, the only question arising under the commerce clause with respect to such shipments is whether Congress has the constitutional power to prohibit them.

While manufacture is not of itself interstate commerce, the shipment of manufactured goods interstate is such commerce and the prohibition of such shipment by Congress is indubitably a regulation of the commerce. The power to regulate commerce is the power "to prescribe the rule by which commerce is to be governed." *Gibbons* v. *Ogden,* 9 Wheat. 1, 196. It extends not only to those regulations which aid, foster, and protect the commerce, but embraces those which prohibit it. It is conceded that the power of Congress to prohibit transportation in interstate commerce includes noxious articles, *Lottery Case,* 188 U.S. 321; stolen articles, *Brooks* v. *United States,* 267 U.S. 432; kidnapped persons, *Gooch* v. *United States,* 297 U.S. 124; and articles such as intoxicating liquor or convict made goods, traffic in which is forbidden or restricted by the laws of the state of destination. *Kentucky Whip & Collar Co.* v. *Illinois Central R. Co.*, 299 U.S. 334.

But it is said that the present prohibition falls within the scope of none of these categories; that while the prohibition is nominally a regulation of the commerce its motive or purpose is regulation of wages and hours of persons engaged in manufacture, the control of which has been reserved to the states and upon which Georgia and some of the states of destination have placed no restriction; that the effect of the present statute is not to exclude the prescribed articles from interstate commerce in aid of state regulations as in *Kentucky Whip & Collar Co.* v. *Illinois Central R. Co., supra,* but instead under the guise of a regulation of interstate commerce, it undertakes to regulate wages and hours within the state contrary to the policy of the state which has elected to leave them unregulated.

The power of Congress over interstate commerce "is complete in itself, may be exercised to its utmost extent, and acknowledges no limitations other than are prescribed in the Constitution." *Gibbons* v. *Ogden, supra.* That power can neither be enlarged nor diminished by the exercise or non-exercise of state power. *Kentucky Whip & Collar Co.* v. *Illinois Central R. Co. supra.* Congress, following its own conception of public policy concerning the restrictions which may appropriately be imposed on interstate commerce, is free to exclude from the commerce articles whose use in the states for which they are destined it may conceive to be injurious to the public health, morals or welfare, even though the state has not sought to regulate their use.

Such regulation is not forbidden invasion of state power merely because either its motive or its consequence is to restrict the use of articles of commerce within the states of destination; and is not prohibited unless by other constitutional provisions. It is no objection to the assertion of the power to regulate interstate commerce that its exercise is attended by the same incidents which attend the exercise of the police power of the states.

The motive and purpose of the present regulation are plainly to make effective the congressional conception of public policy that interstate commerce should not be made the instrument of competition in the distribution of goods produced under substandard labor conditions, which competition is injurious to the commerce and to the states from and to which the commerce flows. The motive and purpose of a regulation of interstate commerce are matters for the legislative judgment upon the exercise of which the Constitution places no restriction and over which the Courts are given no control. *McCray* v. *United States*, 195 U.S. 27; *Sonzinsky* v. *United States*, 300 U.S. 506, 513. "The judicial cannot prescribe to the legislative department of the government limitations upon the exercise of its acknowledged power." *Veazie Bank* v. *Fenno*, 8 Wall. 533, 548. Whatever their motive and purpose, regulations of commerce which do not infringe some constitutional prohibition are within the plenary power conferred on Congress by the commerce clause. Subject only to that limitation, presently to be considered, we conclude that the prohibition of the shipment interstate of goods produced under the forbidden substandard labor conditions is within the constitutional authority of Congress.

In the more than a century which has elapsed since the decision of *Gibbons* v. *Ogden*, these principles of constitutional interpretation have been so long and repeatedly recognized by this Court as applicable to the commerce clause, that there would be little occasion for repeating them now were it not for the decision of this Court 22 years ago in *Hammer* v. *Dagenhart*, 247 U.S. 251. In that case it was held by a bare majority of the Court over the powerful and now classic dissent of Mr. Justice Holmes setting forth the fundamental issues involved, that Congress was without power to exclude the products of child labor from interstate commerce. The reasoning and conclusion of the Court's opinion there cannot be reconciled with the conclusion which we have reached, that the power of Congress under the commerce clause is plenary to exclude any article from interstate commerce subject only to the specific prohibitions of the Constitution.

Hammer v. *Dagenhart* has not been followed. The distinction on which the decision was rested that congressional power to prohibit interstate commerce is limited to articles with in themselves have some harmful or deleterious property—a distinction which was novel when made and unsupported by any provision of the Constitution—has long since been abandoned. *Brooks* v. *United States,* 267 U.S. 432; *Kentucky Whip & Collar Co.* v. *Illinois C. R. Co.,* 299 U.S. 334; *Mulford* v. *Smith,* 307 U.S. 38. The thesis of the opinion that the motive of the prohibition or its effect to control in some measure the use or production within the states of the article thus excluded from the commerce can operate to deprive the regulation of its constitutional authority has long since ceased to have force. And finally we have declared "The authority of the federal government over interstate commerce does not differ in extent or character from that retained by the states over intrastate commerce." *United States* v. *Rock Royal Co-operative,* 307 U.S. 533, 569.

The conclusion is inescapable that *Hammer* v. *Dagenhart* was a departure from the principles which have prevailed in the interpretation of the commerce clause both before and since the decision and that such vitality, as a precedent, as it then had has long since been exhausted. It should be and now is overruled.

Validity of the Wage and Hour Requirements. Section 15(*a*) (2) and sections 6 and 7 require employers to conform to the wage and hour provisions with respect to all employees engaged in the production of goods for interstate commerce. . . .

The recognized need of drafting a workable statute and the well-known circumstances in which it was to be applied are persuasive of the conclusion, which the legislative history supports, that the "production for commerce" intended includes at least production of goods, which, at the time of production, the employer, according to the normal course of his business, intends or expects to move in interstate commerce although, through the exigencies of the business, all of the goods may not thereafter actually enter interstate commerce.

There remains the question whether such restriction on the production of goods for commerce is a permissible exercise of the commerce power. The power of Congress over interstate commerce is not confined to the regulation of commerce among the states. It extends to those activities intrastate which so affect interstate commerce or the exercise of the power of Congress over it as to make regulation of them appropriate means to the attainment of a legitimate end, the exercise of the granted power of Congress to regulate interstate commerce. See *McCulloch* v. *Maryland,* 4 Wheat. 316, 421. . . .

Congress, having by the present Act adopted the policy of excluding from interstate commerce all goods produced for the commerce which do not conform to the specified labor standards, it may choose the means reasonably adapted to the attainment of the permitted end, even though they involve control of intrastate activities. . . . A familiar like exercise of power is the regulation of intrastate transactions which are so commingled with or related to interstate commerce that all must be regulated if the interstate commerce is to be effectively controlled. *Shreveport Case,* 234 U.S. 342. Similarly Congress may require inspection and preventive treatment of all cattle in a disease-infected area in order to prevent shipment in interstate commerce of some of the cattle without the treatment. *Thornton* v. *United States,* 271 U.S. 414. It may prohibit the removal, at destination, of labels required by the Pure Food & Drugs Act to be affixed to articles transported in interstate commerce. *McDermott* v. *Wisconsin,* 228 U.S. 115. And we have recently held that Congress in the exercise of its power to require inspection and grading of tobacco shipped in interstate commerce may compel such inspection and grading of all tobacco sold at local auction rooms from which a substantial part but not all of the tobacco sold is shipped in interstate commerce. *Currin* v. *Wallace,* 306 U.S. 11. . . .

The Sherman Act and the National Labor Relations Act are familiar examples of the exertion of the commerce power to prohibit or control activities wholly intrastate because of their effect on interstate commerce. . . .

The means adopted by section 15(*a*) (2) for the protection of interstate commerce by the suppression of the production of the condemned goods for interstate commerce is so related to the commerce and so affects it as to be within the reach of the commerce power. Congress, to attain its objective in the suppression of nation-wide competition in interstate commerce by goods produced under substandard labor conditions, has made no distinction as to the volume or amount of shipments in the commerce or of production for commerce by any particular shipper or producer. It recognized that in present day industry, competition by a small part may affect the whole and that the total effect of the competition of many small producers may be great. See H. Rept. No. 2182, 75th Cong. 1st Sess., p. 7. The legislation aimed at a whole embraces all its parts. Cf. *National Labor Relations Board* v. *Fainblatt,* 306 U.S. 601, 606. . . .

Our conclusion is unaffected by the Tenth Amendment which provides: "The powers not delegated to the United States by the Constitution, nor prohibited by it to the States, are reserved the States respectively, or to the people." The Amendment states but a truism that all is retained which has not been surrendered. There is nothing in the history of its adoption to suggest that it was more than declaratory of the relationship between the national and state governments as it had been established by the Constitution before the Amendment or that its purpose was other than to allay fears that the new national government might seek to exercise powers not granted, and that the states might not be able to exercise fully their reserved powers.

From the beginning and for many years the Amendment has been construed as not depriving the national government of authority to resort to all means for the exercise of a granted power which are appropriate and plainly adapted to the permitted end. Whatever doubts may have arisen of the soundness of that conclusion they have been put at rest by the decisions under the Sherman Act and the National Labor Relations Act which we have cited.

Validity of the Requirement of Records of Wages and Hours. Section 15(*a*) (5) and section 11(*c*). These requirements are incidental to those for the prescribed wages and hours, and hence validity of the former turns on validity of the latter. Since, as we have held, Congress may require production for interstate commerce to conform to those conditions, it may require the employer, as a means of enforcing the valid law, to keep a record showing whether he has in fact complied with it. The requirement for records even of the intrastate transaction is an appropriate means to the legitimate end. . . .

Wickard v. *Filburn*
317 U.S. 111 (1942)

The second Agricultural Adjustment Act (i.e., the act of 1938), as amended, sought to stabilize the price of farm goods and adjust supply to market needs by establishing a marketing quota for each participating farm. Penalties were prescribed for violation of assigned quotas. The issue in this case was whether wheat grown by Filburn and consumed on his own farm could be counted in determining whether he had exceeded his quota. The contention, of course, was that such wheat, never shipped or intended for shipment in interstate commerce, was not within the regulatory power of Congress.

Mr. Justice Jackson delivered the opinion of the Court: . . .

In July of 1940, pursuant to the Agricultural Adjustment Act of 1938, as then amended, there was established for the appellee's 1941 crop a wheat acreage allotment of 11.1 acres and a normal yield of 20.1 bushels of wheat an acre. He was given notice of such allotment in July of 1940 before the Fall planting of his 1941 crop of wheat, and again in July of 1941, before it was harvested. He sowed, however, 23 acres, and harvested from his 11.9 acres of excess acreage 239 bushels, which under the terms of the Act as amended on May 26, 1941, constituted farm marketing excess, subject to a penalty of 49 cents a bushel, or $117.11 in all. The appellee has not paid the penalty and he has not postponed or avoided it by storing the excess under regulations of the Secretary of Agriculture, or by delivering it up to the Secretary. The Committee, therefore, refused him a marketing card, which was, under the terms of regulations promulgated by the Secretary, necessary to protect a buyer from liability to the penalty and upon its protecting lien.

The general scheme of the Agricultural Adjustment Act of 1938 as related to wheat is to control the volume moving in interstate and foreign commerce in order to avoid surpluses and shortages and the consequent abnormally low or high wheat prices and obstructions to commerce. Within prescribed limits and by prescribed standards the Secretary of Agriculture is directed to ascertain and proclaim each year a national acreage allotment for the next crop of wheat, which is then apportioned to the states and their counties, and is eventually broken up into allotments for individual farms. Loans and payments to wheat farmers are authorized in stated circumstances.

The Act provides further that whenever it appears that the total supply of wheat as of the beginning of any marketing year, beginning July 1, will exceed a normal year's domestic consumption and export by more than 35 percent, the Secretary shall so proclaim not later than May 15 prior to the beginning of such marketing year; and that during the marketing year a compulsory national marketing quota shall be in effect with respect to the marketing of wheat. Between the issuance of the proclamation and June 10, the Secretary must, however, conduct a referendum of farmers who will be subject to the quota to determine whether they favor or oppose it; and if more than one third of the farmers voting in the referendum do oppose, the Secretary must prior to the effective date of the quota by proclamation suspend its operation. . . .

It is urged that under the commerce clause of the Constitution, Article I, section 8, clause 3, Congress does not possess the power it has in this instance sought to exercise. The question would merit little consideration since our decision in *United States* v. *Darby*, 312 U.S. 100, sustaining the federal power to regulate production of goods for commerce except for the fact that this Act extends federal regulation to production not intended in any part for commerce, but wholly for consumption on the farm. The Act includes a definition of "market" and its derivatives so that as related to wheat in addition to its conventional meaning it also means to dispose of "by feeding (in any form) to poultry or livestock which, or the products of which, are sold, bartered, or exchanged, or to be so disposed of." Hence, marketing quotas not only embrace all that may be sold without penalty but also what may be consumed on the premises. Wheat produced on excess acreage is designated as "available for marketing" as so defined and the penalty is imposed thereon. Penalties do not depend upon whether any part of the wheat either within or without the quota is sold or intended to be sold. The sum of this is that the federal government fixes a quota including all that the farmer may harvest for sale or for his own farm needs, and declares that wheat produced on excess acreage may neither be disposed of nor used except upon payment of the penalty or except it is stored as required by the Act or delivered to the Secretary of Agriculture.

Appellee says that this is a regulation of production and consumption of wheat. Such activities are, he urges, beyond the reach of congressional power under the commerce clause, since they are local in character, and their effects upon interstate commerce are at most "indirect." In answer the government argues that the statute regulates neither production nor consumption, but only marketing; and, in the alternative, that if the Act does go beyond the regulation of marketing it is sustainable as a "necessary and proper" implementation of the power of Congress over interstate commerce.

The government's concern lest the Act be held to be a regulation of production or consumption rather than of marketing is attributable to a few dicta and decisions of this Court which might be understood to lay it down that activities such as "production," "manufacturing," and "mining" are strictly "local" and, except in special circumstances which are not present here, cannot be regulated under the commerce power because their effects upon interstate commerce are, as matter of law, only "indirect." Even today, when this power has been held to have great latitude, there is no decision of this Court that such activities may be regulated where no part of the product is intended for interstate commerce or intermingled with the subjects thereof. We believe that a review of the course of decision under the commerce clause will make plain, however, that questions of the power of Congress are not to be decided by reference to any formula which would give controlling force to nomenclature such as "production" and "indirect" and foreclose consid-

eration of the actual effects of the activity in question upon interstate commerce.

At the beginning Chief Justice Marshall described the federal commerce power with a breadth never yet exceeded. *Gibbons* v. *Ogden*, 9 Wheat. 1, 194, 195. He made emphatic the embracing and penetrating nature of this power by warning that effective restraints on its exercise must proceed from political rather than from judicial processes. 9 Wheat. at page 197.

For nearly a century, however, decisions of this Court under the commerce clause dealt rarely with questions of what Congress might do in the exercise of its granted power under the clause and almost entirely with the permissibility of state activity which it was claimed discriminated against or burdened interstate commerce. During this period there was perhaps little occasion for the affirmative exercise of the commerce power, and the influence of the clause on American life and law was a negative one, resulting almost wholly from its operation as a restraint upon the powers of the states. In discussion and decision the point of reference instead of being what was "necessary and proper" to the exercise by Congress of its granted power, was often some concept of sovereignty thought to be implicit in the status of statehood. Certain activities such as "production," "manufacturing," and "mining" were occasionally said to be within the province of state governments and beyond the power of Congress under the commerce clause.

It was not until 1887 with the enactment of the Interstate Commerce Act that the interstate commerce power began to exert positive influence in American law and life. This first important federal resort to the commerce power was followed in 1890 by the Sherman Anti-Trust Act and, thereafter, mainly after 1903, by many others. These statutes ushered in new phases of adjudication, which required the Court to approach the interpretation of the commerce clause in the light of an actual exercise by Congress of its power thereunder.

When it first dealt with this new legislation,

the Court adhered to its earlier pronouncements, and allowed but little scope to the power of Congress. *United States* v. *E. C. Knight Co.,* 156 U.S. 1. These earlier pronouncements also played an important part in several of the five cases in which this Court later held that acts of Congress under the commerce clause were in excess of its power.

Even while important opinions in this line of restrictive authority were being written, however, other cases called forth broader interpretations of the commerce clause destined to supersede the earlier ones, and to bring about a return to the principles first enunciated by Chief Justice Marshall in *Gibbons* v. *Ogden, supra.*

Not long after the decision of *United States* v. *E. C. Knight Co., supra,* Mr. Justice Holmes, in sustaining the exercise of national power over intrastate activity, stated for the Court that "commerce among the states is not a technical legal conception, but a practical one, drawn from the course of business." *Swift & Co.* v. *United States,* 196 U.S. 375, 398. It was soon demonstrated that the effects of many kinds of intrastate activity upon interstate commerce were such as to make them a proper subject of federal regulation. In some cases sustaining the exercise of federal power over intrastate matters the term "direct" was used for the purpose of stating, rather than of reaching, a result; in others it was treated as synonymous with "substantial" or "material"; and in others it was not used at all. Of late its use has been abandoned in cases dealing with questions of federal power under the commerce clause.

In the *Shreveport Rate Cases (Houston, E. & W. T. R. Co.* v. *United States),* 234 U.S. 342, the Court held that railroad rates of an admittedly intrastate character and fixed by authority of the state might, nevertheless, be revised by the federal government because of the economic effects which they had upon interstate commerce. The opinion of Mr. Justice Hughes found federal intervention constitutionally authorized because of "matters having such a close and substantial relation to interstate traffic that the control is essential or appropriate to the security of that traffic, to the efficiency of the interstate service, and to the maintenance of the conditions under which interstate commerce may be conducted upon fair terms and without molestation or hindrance." 234 U.S. at page 351.

The Court's recognition of the relevance of the economic effects in the application of the commerce clause exemplified by this statement has made the mechanical application of legal formulas no longer feasible. Once an economic measure of the reach of the power granted to Congress in the commerce clause is accepted, questions of federal power cannot be decided simply by finding the activity in question to be "production" nor can consideration of its economic effects be foreclosed by calling them "indirect." The present Chief Justice has said in summary of the present state of the law: "The commerce power is not confined in its exercise to the regulation of commerce among the states. It extends to those activities intrastate which so affect interstate commerce, or the exertion of the power of Congress over it, as to make regulation of them appropriate means to the attainment of a legitimate end, the effective execution of the granted power to regulate interstate commerce. . . . The power of Congress over interstate commerce is plenary and complete in itself, may be exercised to its utmost extent, and acknowledges no limitations other than are prescribed in the Constitution. . . . It follows that no form of state activity can constitutionally thwart the regulatory power granted by the commerce clause to Congress. Hence the reach of that power extends to those intrastate activities which in a substantial way interfere with or obstruct the exercise of the granted power." *United States* v. *Wrightwood Dairy Co.,* 315 U.S. 110, 119.

Whether the subject of the regulation in question was "production," "consumption," or "marketing" is, therefore, not material for purposes of deciding the question of federal power before us. That an activity is of local character may help in a doubtful case to determine whether Congress intended to reach it. The same consideration might help in determining whether in the absence of congressional action it would be permissible for the state to exert its power on the subject matter, even though in so doing it to some degree affected interstate commerce. But even if appellant's activity be local and though it may not be regarded as commerce, it may still, whatever its nature, be reached by Congress if it exerts a substantial economic effect on interstate commerce and this irrespective of whether such effect is what might at some earlier time have been defined as "direct" or "indirect."

The parties have stipulated a summary of the economics of the wheat industry. Commerce among the states in wheat is large and important. Although wheat is raised in every state but one, production in most states is not equal to consumption. Sixteen states on average have had a surplus of wheat above their own requirements for feed, seed, and food. Thirty-two states and the District of Columbia, where production has been below consumption, have looked to these surplus-producing states for their supply as well as for wheat for export and carryover.

The wheat industry has been a problem industry for some years. Largely as a result of increased foreign production and import restrictions, annual exports of wheat and flour from the United States during the ten-year period ending in 1940 averaged less than 10 percent of total production, while during the 1920's they averaged more than 25 percent. The decline in the export trade has left a large surplus in production which in connection with an abnormally large supply of wheat and other grains in recent years caused congestion in a number of markets; tied up railroad cars; and caused elevators in some instances to turn away grains, and railroads to institute embargoes to prevent further congestion.

Many countries, both importing and exporting, have sought to modify the impact of the

world market conditions on their own economy. Importing countries have taken measures to stimulate production and self-sufficiency. The four large exporting countries of Argentina, Australia, Canada, and the United States have all undertaken various programs for the relief of growers. Such measures have been designed in part at least to protect the domestic price received by producers. Such plans have generally evolved towards control by the central government.

In the absence of regulation the price of wheat in the United States would be much affected by world conditions. During 1941 producers who cooperated with the Agricultural Adjustment program received an average price on the farm of about $1.16 a bushel as compared with the world market price of 40 cents a bushel.

Differences in farming conditions, however, make these benefits mean different things to different wheat growers. There are several large areas of specialization in wheat, and the concentration on this crop reaches 27 percent of the crop land, and the average harvest runs as high as 155 acres. Except for some use of wheat as stock feed and for seed, the practice is to sell the crop for cash. Wheat from such areas constitutes the bulk of the interstate commerce therein.

On the other hand, in some New England states less than 1 percent of the crop land is devoted to wheat, and the average harvest is less than five acres per farm. In 1940 the average percentage of the total wheat production that was sold in each state as measured by value ranged from 29 percent thereof in Wisconsin to 90 percent in Washington. Except in regions of large-scale production, wheat is usually grown in rotation with other crops; for a nurse crop for grass seeding; and as a cover crop to prevent soil erosion and leaching. Some is sold, some kept for seed, and a percentage of the total production much larger than in areas of specialization is consumed on the farm and grown for such purpose. Such farmers, while growing some wheat, may even find the balance of their interest on the consumer's side.

The effect of consumption of home-grown wheat on interstate commerce is due to the fact that it constitutes the most variable factor in the disappearance of the wheat crop. Consumption on the farm where grown appears to vary in an amount greater than 20 percent of average production. The total amount of wheat consumed as food varies but relatively little, and use as seed is relatively constant.

The maintenance by government regulation of a price for wheat undoubtedly can be accomplished as effectively by sustaining or increasing the demand as by limiting the supply. The effect of the statute before us is to restrict the amount which may be produced for market and the extent as well to which one may forestall resort to the market by producing to meet his own needs. That appellee's own contribution to the demand for wheat may be trivial by itself is not enough to remove him from the scope of federal regulation where, as here, his contribution, taken together with that of many others similarly situated, is far from trivial. *National Labor Relations Board* v. *Fainblatt*, 306 U.S. 601, 606, *et seq.*, 307 U.S. 609; *United States* v. *Darby*, *supra*, 312 U.S. at page 123.

It is well established by decisions of this Court that the power to regulate commerce includes the power to regulate the prices at which commodities in that commerce are dealt in and practices affecting such prices. One of the primary purposes of the Act in question was to increase the market price of wheat and to that end to limit the volume thereof that could affect the market. It can hardly be denied that a factor of such volume and variability as home-consumed wheat would have a substantial influence on price and market conditions. This may arise because being in marketable condition such wheat overhangs the market and, if induced by rising prices, tends to flow into the market and check price increases. But if we assume that it is never marketed, it supplies a need of the man who grew it which would oth-

erwise be reflected by purchases in the open market. Home-grown wheat in this sense competes with wheat in commerce. The stimulation of commerce is a use of the regulatory function quite as definitely as prohibitions or restrictions thereon. This record leaves us in doubt that Congress may properly have considered that wheat consumed on the farm where grown if wholly outside the scheme of regulation would have a substantial effect in defeating and obstructing its purpose to stimulate trade therein at increased prices. . . .

Heart of Atlanta Motel v. United States
379 U.S. 241 (1964)

Mr. Justice Clark delivered the opinion of the Court:

This is a declaratory judgment action attacking the constitutionality of Title II of the Civil Rights Act of 1964. . . . Appellant owns and operates the Heart of Atlanta Motel which has 216 rooms available to transient guests. The motel is located on Courtland Street, two blocks from downtown Peachtree Street. It is readily accessible to interstate highways 75 and 85 and state highways 23 and 41. Appellant solicits patronage from outside the State of Georgia through various national advertising media, including magazines of national circulation; it maintains over fifty billboards and highway signs within the State, soliciting patronage for the motel; it accepts convention trade from outside Georgia and approximately 75 percent of its registered guests are from out of State. Prior to passage of the Act the motel had followed a practice of refusing to rent rooms to Negroes, and it alleged that it intended to continue to do so. In an effort to perpetuate that policy this suit was filed.

The appellant contends that Congress in passing this Act exceeds its power to regulate commerce under Article I, Section 8, clause 3, of the Constitution of the United States. . . .

Title II of the Act

This Title is divided into seven sections beginning with § 201(a) which provides that:

> "All persons shall be entitled to the full and equal enjoyment of the goods, services, facilities, privileges, advantages, and accommodations of any place of public accommodation, as defined in this section, without discrimination or segregation on the ground of race, color, religion, or national origin."

There are listed in § 201(b) four classes of business establishments, each of which "serves the public" and "is a place of public accommodation" within the meaning of § 201(a) "if its operations affect commerce, or if discrimination or segregation by it is supported by State action." The covered establishments are:

> "(1) any inn, hotel, motel, or other establishment which provides lodging to transient guests, other than an establishment located within a building which contains not more than five rooms for rent or hire and which is actually occupied by the proprietor of such establishment as his residence; . . . ."

Section 201(c) defines the phrase "affect commerce" as applied to the above establishments. It first declares that "any inn, hotel, motel, or other establishment which provides lodging to transient guests" affects commerce *per se*. . . .

Application of Title II to Heart of Atlanta Motel

It is admitted that the operation of the motel brings it within the provisions of § 201(a) of the Act and that appellant refused to provide lodging for transient Negroes because of their race or color and that it intends to continue that policy unless restrained.

The sole question posed is, therefore, the constitutionality of the Civil Rights Act of 1964 as applied to these facts. The legislative history of the Act indicates that Congress based the Act on § 5 and the Equal Protection Clause of the Fourteenth Amendment as well as its power to regulate interstate commerce . . . .

The Senate Commerce Committee made it quite clear that the fundamental object of Title II was to vindicate "the deprivation of personal dignity that surely accompanies denials of equal access to public establishments." At the same time, however, it noted that such an objective has been and could be readily achieved "by congressional action based on the commerce power of the Constitution." S.Rep.No.872, *supra*, at 16–17. Our study of the legislative record, made in the light of prior cases, has brought us to the conclusion that Congress possessed ample power in this regard, and we have therefore not considered the other grounds relied upon. . . .

The Basis of Congressional Action

While the Act as adopted carried no congressional findings the record of its passage through each house is replete with evidence of the burdens that discrimination by race or color places upon interstate commerce. . . . This testimony included the fact that our people have become increasingly mobile with millions of people of all races traveling from State to State; that Negroes in particular have been the subject of discrimination in transient accommodations, having to travel great distances to secure the same; that often they have been unable to obtain accommodations and have had to call upon friends to put them up overnight, . . . ; and that these conditions had become so acute as to require the listing of available lodging for Negroes in a special guidebook which was itself "dramatic testimony to the difficulties" Negroes encounter in travel. . . . We shall not burden this opinion with further details since the voluminous testimony presents overwhelming evidence that discrimination by hotels and motels impedes interstate travel.

The Power of Congress over Interstate Travel . . .

[T]he determinative test of the exercise of power by the Congress under the Commerce Clause is simply whether the activity sought to be regulated is "commerce which concerns more States than one" and has a real and substantial relation to the national interest. Let us now turn to this facet of the problem.

That the "intercourse" of which Chief Justice [Marshall] spoke included the movement of persons through more States than one was settled as early as 1849. . . . Nor does it make any difference whether the transportation is commercial in character. . . .

The same interest in protecting interstate commerce which led Congress to deal with segregation in interstate carriers and the white-slave traffic has prompted it to extend the exercise of its power to gambling, *Lottery Case*, 188 U.S. 321 (1903) . . . and to racial discrimination by owners and managers of terminal restaurants, *Boynton* v. *Virginia*, 364 U.S. 454 (1960).

That Congress was legislating against moral wrongs in many of these areas rendered its enactments no less valid. In framing Title II of this Act Congress was also dealing with what it considered a moral problem. But that fact does not detract from the overwhelming evidence of the disruptive effect that racial discrimination has had on commercial intercourse. It was this burden which empowered Congress to enact appropriate legislation, and, given this basis for the exercise of its power, Congress was not restricted by the fact that the particular obstruction to interstate commerce with which it was dealing was also deemed a moral and social wrong.

It is said that the operation of the motel here is of a purely local character. But, assuming this to be true, "[i]f it is interstate commerce that feels the pinch, it does not matter how local the operation which applies the squeeze." *United States* v. *Women's Sportswear Mfrs. Assn.*, 336 U.S. 460, 464 (1949). . . .

We, therefore, conclude that the action of the Congress in the adoption of the Act as applied here to a motel which concededly serves interstate travelers is within the power granted it by the Commerce Clause of the Constitution, as interpreted by this Court for 140 years. . . .

[Justices Black, Douglas, and Goldberg wrote concurring opinions—the latter judges holding that Title II, as applied in this case, could also be justified by virtue of Section 5 of the Fourteenth Amendment.]

National League of Cities v. *Usery*
426 U.S. 833 (1976)

In *Fry* v. *United States*, 421 U.S. 542 (1975), the Court upheld congressional power under the Commerce Clause to limit wage increases for state employees (among others) for anti-inflation purposes. The decision rested in part on *Maryland* v. *Wirtz*, 392 U.S. 183 (1968), which upheld the 1966 extension of the Fair Labor Standards Act (FLSA) to state schools and hospitals. *Wirtz* in turn rested on the rationale of *Darby* and *Jones & Laughlin*, above.

On this basis a federal district court upheld a 1974 congressional extension of FLSA to cover all state and local employees (except executives, administrative, and professional personnel). The Supreme Court reversed that decision.

Mr. Justice Rehnquist delivered the opinion of the Court. . . .

It is established beyond peradventure that the Commerce Clause of Art. I of the Constitution is a grant of plenary authority to Congress. . . .

Appellants in no way challenge these decisions establishing the breadth of authority granted Congress under the commerce power. Their contention, on the contrary, is that when Congress seeks to regulate directly the activities of States as public employers, it transgresses an affirmative limitation on the exercise of its power akin to other commerce power affirmative limitations contained in the Constitution. Congressional enactments which may be fully within the grant of legislative authority contained in the Commerce Clause may nonetheless be invalid because found to offend against the right to trial by jury contained in the Sixth Amendment, or the Due Process Clause of the Fifth Amendment. Appellants' essential contention is that the 1974 amendments to the Act, while undoubtedly within the scope of the Commerce Clause, encounter a similar constitutional barrier because they are to be applied directly to the States and subdivisions of States as employers.

This Court has never doubted that there are limits upon the power of Congress to override state sovereignty, even when exercising its otherwise plenary powers to tax or to regulate commerce which are conferred by Art. I of the Constitution. . . .

Appellee Secretary argues that the cases in which this Court has upheld sweeping exercises of authority by Congress, even though those exercises pre-empted state regulation of the private sector, have already curtailed the sovereignty of the States quite as much as the 1974 amendments to the Fair Labor Standards Act. We do not agree. It is one thing to recognize the authority of Congress to enact laws regulating individual business necessarily subject to the dual sovereignty of the government of the Nation and of the State in which they reside. It is quite another to uphold a similar exercise of congressional authority directed not to private citizens, but to the States as States. We have repeatedly recognized that there are attributes of sovereignty attaching to every state government which may not be impaired by Congress, not because Congress may lack an affirmative grant of legislative authority to reach the matter, but because the Constitution prohibits it from exercising the authority in that manner. . . .

One undoubted attribute to state sovereignty is the States' power to determine the wages which shall be paid to those whom they employ in order to carry out their governmental functions, what hours those persons will work, and what compensation will be provided where these employees may be called upon to work overtime. The question we must resolve in this case, then, is whether these determinations are "functions essential to separate and independent existence," so that Congress may not abrogate the States' otherwise plenary authority to make them.

In their complaint appellants advanced estimates of substantial costs which will be imposed upon them by the 1974 amendments. . . .

Judged solely in terms of increased costs in dollars, these allegations show a significant impact on the functioning of the governmental bodies involved. . . . The State of California, which must devote significant portions of its budget to fire suppression endeavors, estimated that application of the Act to its employment practices will necessitate an increase in its budget of between $8 million and $16 million.

Increased costs are not, of course, the only adverse effects which compliance with the Act will visit upon state and local governments, and in turn upon the citizens who depend upon those governments. In its complaint in intervention, for example, California asserted that it could not comply with the overtime costs (approximately $750,000 per year) which the Act required to be paid to California Highway Patrol cadets during their academy training program. California reported that it had thus been forced to reduce its academy training program from 2,080 hours to only 960 hours, a compromise undoubtedly of substantial importance to those whose safety and welfare may depend upon the preparedness of the California Highway Patrol. . . .

Quite apart from the substantial costs imposed upon the States and their political subdivisions, the Act displaces state policies regarding the manner in which they will structure delivery of those governmental services which their citizens require. The Act, speaking directly to the States *qua* States, requires that they shall pay all but an extremely limited minority of their employees the minimum wage rates currently chosen by Congress. It may well be that as a matter of economic policy it would be desirable that States, just as private employers, comply with these minimum wage requirements. But it cannot be gainsaid that the federal requirement directly supplants the considered policy choices of the States' elected officials and administrators as to how they wish to structure pay scales in state employment. . . .

This dilemma presented by the minimum wage restrictions may seem not immediately different from that faced by private employers, who have long been covered by the Act and who must find ways to increase their gross income if they are to pay higher wages while maintaining current earnings. The difference, however, is that a State is not merely a factor in the "shifting economic arrangements" of the private sector of the economy, *Kovacs* v. *Cooper*, 336 U.S. 77, 95 (1949) (Frankfurter, J., concurring), but is itself a coordinate element in the system established by the framers for governing our federal union. . . .

. . . [B]oth the minimum wage and the maximum hour provisions will impermissibly interfere with the integral government functions of [States and their political subdivisions]. We earlier noted some disagreement between the parties regarding the precise effect the amendments will have in application. We do not believe particularized assessments of actual impact are crucial to resolution of the issue presented, however. For even if we accept appellee's assessments concerning the impact of the amendments, their application will nonetheless significantly alter or displace the States' abilities to structure employer-employee relationships in such areas as fire prevention, police protection, sanitation, public health, and parks and recreation. . . . If Congress may withdraw from the States the authority to make those fundamental employment decisions upon which their systems for performance of these functions must rest, we think there would be little left of the States' "separate and independent existence." Thus, even if appellants may have overestimated the effect which the Act will have upon their current levels and patterns of governmental activity, the dispositive factor is that Congress has attempted to exercise its Commerce Clause authority to prescribe minimum wages and maximum hours to be paid by the States in their capacities as sovereign governments. In so doing, Congress has sought to wield its power in a fashion that would impair the States' "ability to function effectively within a federal system." This exercise of congressional authority does not comport with the federal system of government embodied in the Constitution. We hold that insofar as the challenged amendments operate to directly displace the States' freedom to structure integral operations in areas of traditional governmental functions, they are not within the authority granted Congress by Art. I, § 8, cl. 3.

One final matter requires our attention. Appellee has vigorously urged that we cannot, consistently with the Court's decisions in *Wirtz*, and *Fry*, rule against him here. It is important to examine this contention so that it will be clear what we hold today, and what we do not. . . .

We think our holding today quite consistent with *Fry*. The enactment at issue there was occasioned by an extremely serious problem which endangered the well-being of all the component parts of our federal system and which only collective action by the National Government might forestall. The means selected were carefully drafted so as not to interfere with the States' freedom beyond a very limited, specific period of time. The effect of the across-the-board freeze authorized by that Act, moreover, displaced no state choices as to how governmental operations should be structured nor did it force the States to remake such choices themselves. Instead, it merely required that the wage scales and employment relationships which the States themselves had chosen be maintained during the period of the emergency. Finally, the Economic Stabilization Act operated to reduce the pressures upon state budgets rather than increase them. These factors distinguish the statute in *Fry* from the provisions at issue here. The limits imposed upon the commerce power when Congress seeks to apply it to the States are not so inflexible as to preclude temporary enactments tailored to combat a national emergency. . . .

With respect to the Court's decision in *Wirtz*, we reach a different conclusion. . . . There are undoubtedly factual distinctions between the two situations, but in view of the conclusions expressed earlier in this opinion we do not believe the reasoning in *Wirtz* may any longer be regarded as authoritative. . . .

. . . [W]e have reaffirmed today that the States as States stand on a quite different footing than an individual or a corporation when challenging the exercise of Congress' power to regulate commerce. . . . Congress may not exercise that power so as to force directly upon the States its choices as to how essential decisions regarding the conduct of integral governmental functions are to be made. . . . While there are obvious differences between the schools and hospitals involved in *Wirtz*, and the fire and police departments affected here, each provides an integral portion of those governmental services which the States and their political subdivisions have traditionally afforded their citizens. We are therefore persuaded that *Wirtz* must be overruled.

The judgment of the District Court is accord-ingly reversed and the case is remanded for further proceedings consistent with this opinion.

Mr. Justice Blackmun, concurring.

. . . I may misinterpret the Court's opinion, but it seems to me that it adopts a balancing approach, and does not outlaw federal power in areas such as environmental protection, where the federal interest is demonstrably greater and where state facility compliance with imposed federal standards would be essential. With this understanding on my part of the Court's opinion, I join it.

Mr. Justice Brennan, with whom Mr. Justice White and Mr. Justice Marshall join, dissenting:

. . . [L]aws within the commerce power may not infringe individual liberties. . . . But there is no restraint based on state sovereignty requiring or permitting judicial enforcement anywhere expressed in the Constitution; our decisions over the last century and a half have explicitly rejected the existence of any such restraint on the commerce power. . . .

The reliance of my Brethren upon the Tenth Amendment as "an express declaration of [a state sovereignty] limitation," not only suggests that they overrule governing decisions of this Court that address this question but must astound scholars of the Constitution. . . . [A]lthough my Brethren by fiat strike down the 1974 amendments without analysis of countervailing national considerations, *Fry* by contrary logic remains undisturbed because, on balance, countervailing national considerations override the interference with the State's freedom. Moreover, it is sophistry to say the Economic Stabilization Act "displaced no state choices," but that the 1974 amendments do. Obviously the Stabilization Act—no less than every exercise of a national power delegated to Congress by the Constitution—displaced the State's freedom. It is absurd to suggest that there is a constitutionally significant distinction between curbs against increasing wages and curbs against paying wages lower than the federal minimum.

Today's holding patently is in derogation of the sovereign power of the Nation to regulate interstate commerce. Can the States engage in businesses competing with the private sector and then come to the courts arguing that withdrawing the employees of those businesses from the private sector evades the power of the Federal Government to regulate commerce? No principle given meaningful content by my Brethren today precludes the States from doing just that. Our historic decisions rejecting all suggestions that the States stand in a different position from affected private parties when challenging congressional exercise of the commerce power reflect that very concern.

Also devoid of meaningful content is my Brethren's argument that the 1974 amendments "displace State policies." The amendments neither impose policy objectives on the States nor deny the States complete freedom to fix their own objectives. My Brethren boldly assert that the decision as to wages and hours is an "undoubted attribute of state sovereignty," and then never say why. Indeed, they disclaim any reliance on the costs of compliance with the amendments in reaching today's result. This would enable my Brethren to conclude that, however insignificant that cost, any federal regulation under the commerce power "will nonetheless significantly alter or displace the States' abilities to structure employer-employee relationships." This then would mean that, whether or not state wages are paid for the performance of an "essential" state function (whatever that may mean), the newly discovered state sovereignty constraint could operate as a flat and absolute prohibition against congressional regulation of the wages and hours of state employees under the Commerce Clause. The portent of such a sweeping holding is so ominous for our constitutional jurisprudence as to leave one incredulous. . . .

Judicial restraint in this area merely recognizes that the political branches of our Government are structures to protect the interests of the States, as well as the Nation as a whole, and that the States are fully able to protect their own interests in the premises. Congress is constituted of representatives in both Senate and House *elected from the States.* Decisions upon the extent of federal intervention under the Commerce Clause into the affairs of the States are in that sense decisions of the States themselves. Judicial redistribution of powers granted the National Government by the terms of the Constitution violates the fundamental tenet of our federalism that the extent of federal intervention into the State's affairs in the exercise of delegated powers shall be determined by the States' exercise of political power through their representatives in Congress. See Wechsler, The Political Safeguards of Federalism: The Role of the States in the Composition and Selection of the National Government, 54 *Col. L. Rev.* (1954). . . .

. . . Are state and federal interests being silently balanced, as in the discussion of *Fry?* The best I can make of it is that the 1966 FLSA amendments are struck down and *Wirtz* is overruled on the basis of the conceptually unworkable essential function test; and that the test is unworkable is demonstrated by my Brethren's inability to articulate any meaningful distinctions among state-operated railroads, state-operated schools and hospitals, and state-operated police and fire departments.

We are left then with a catastrophic judicial body blow at Congress' power under the Commerce Clause. Even if Congress may nevertheless accomplish its objectives—for example by conditioning grants of federal funds upon compliance with federal minimum wage and overtime standards—there is an ominous portent of disruption of our constitutional structure implicit in today's mischievous decision. I dissent.

Mr. Justice Stevens, dissenting.

The Court holds that the Federal Government may not interfere with a sovereign state's inherent right to pay a substandard wage to the janitor at the state capitol. The principle on which the holding rests is difficult to perceive.

The Federal Government may, I believe, require the State to act impartially when it hires or fires the janitor, to withhold taxes from his pay check, to observe safety regulations when he is performing his job, to forbid him from burning too much soft coal in the capitol furnace, from dumping untreated refuse in an adjacent waterway, from overloading a state-owned garbage truck or from driving either the truck or the governor's limousine over 55 miles an hour. Even though these and many other activities of the capitol janitor are activities of the state *qua* state, I have no doubt that they are subject to federal regulation. . . .

. . . Since I am unable to identify a limitation on that federal power that would not also invalidate federal regulation of state activities that I consider unquestionably permissible, I am persuaded that this statute is valid. Accordingly, with respect and a great deal of sympathy for the views expressed by the Court, I dissent from its constitutional holding.

The National Power to Tax

Pollock v. *Farmers' Loan & Trust Co.*
158 U.S. 601 (1895)

In 1894, Congress imposed a tax of 2 percent on incomes over $4,000 a year. It was challenged as a violation of Article I, Section 9 of the Constitution, which requires that "No Capitation, or other direct, Tax shall be laid, unless in Proportion to the Census . . . ." What is a "direct tax"? In *Hylton* v. *United States,* 3 Dallas 171 (1796), Mr. Justice Paterson—who had been a member of the Constitutional Convention—said he had no doubt

> the principal . . . objects, that the framers contemplated as falling within the rule of apportionment, were a capitation tax and a tax on land . . . . The provision was made in favor of the southern States. They possessed a large number of slaves; they had extensive tracts of territory, thinly settled, and not very productive. A majority of the states had but few slaves, and several of them a limited territory, well settled, and in a high state of cultivation.

In these circumstances a capitation tax on slaves and others, like a tax on real estate, would be particularly burdensome for the South. To forestall this, Mr. Justice Paterson said, the apportionment rule was included in the Constitution. In sum, along with the three-fifths rule, it was part of the slavery compromise. (To impose a "direct tax" Congress must indicate a specified sum to be raised, and then allocate according to the census the share to be collected in each state. Since the population of the North was substantially greater than that of the South, apportionment would protect Southerners from what they believed would otherwise be an undue tax burden.)

Springer v. *United States,* 102 U.S. 586 (1881)—citing *Hylton*—had upheld a temporary income tax (to finance the Civil War) in the face of charges that it was a direct tax, and therefore invalid because not apportioned.

Mr. Justice Fuller delivered the opinion of the Court. . . .

A tax upon one's whole income is a tax upon the annual receipts [e.g., rent] from his whole property, and as such falls within the same class as a tax upon that property, and is a direct tax, in the meaning of the Constitution. . . . We find it impossible to hold that a [constitutional requirement] can be refined away by forced distinctions between that which gives value to property [its earning power] and the property itself. . . . [The income tax accordingly was held to be unconstitutional.]

Mr. Justice Harlan dissenting. . . .

In determining whether a tax on income from rents is a direct tax, within the meaning of the Constitution, the inquiry is not whether it may in some way indirectly affect the land or the land owner, but whether it is a *direct* tax *on the thing taxed, the land.* The circumstance that such a tax may possibly have the effect to diminish the value of the use of the land is neither decisive of the question nor important. While a tax *on the land* itself, whether at a fixed rate applicable to all lands without regard to their value, or by the acre or according to their market value, might be deemed a direct tax within the meaning of the Constitution as interpreted in the *Hylton* case, a duty on rents is a duty on something distinct and entirely separate from, although issuing out of, the land. . . .

In my judgment—to say nothing of the disregard of the former adjudications of this court,

and of the settled practice of the government—this decision may well excite the gravest apprehensions. It strikes at the very foundations of national authority, in that it denies to the general government a power which is, or may become, vital to the very existence and preservation of the Union in a national emergency, such as that of war with a great commercial nation, during which the collection of all duties upon imports will cease or be materially diminished. It tends to reestablish that condition of helplessness in which Congress found itself during the period of the Articles of Confederation, when it was without authority by laws operating directly upon individuals, to lay and collect, through its own agents, taxes sufficient to pay the debts and defray the expenses of government, but was dependent, in all such matters, upon the good will of the States, and their promptness in meeting requisitions made upon them by Congress. . . .

I dissent from the opinion and judgment of the court.

[The separate dissenting opinions of Justices Brown, Jackson, and White have been omitted here.]

> *Note:* Pollock was circumvented by the Sixteenth Amendment in 1913. In *Graves* v. *New York ex rel. O'Keefe,* 306 U.S. 466 (1939), the Court observed, "The theory, which once won a qualified approval, that a tax on income is legally or economically a tax on its source, is no longer tenable . . . ."

Bailey v. *Drexel Furniture Co.*
259 U.S. 20 (1922)

After the *Dagenhart* case Congress tried to discourage child labor by a special tax on the net income of mines, quarries, factories, and mills employing children under specified ages. Earlier the Court had sustained federal levies on state bank notes, *Veazie Bank* v. *Fenno,* 8 Wallace 533 (1869), and yellow oleomargarine, *McCray* v. *United States,* 145 U.S. 27 (1904). The levy on state bank notes was designed to (and did) drive out state currency in favor of a single monetary system for the entire country. The yellow margarine tax, 40 times higher than the corresponding tax on white margarine, was obviously intended not for revenue but to protect butter from competition—one rationalization for this purpose being that it was somehow fraudulent to make margarine look like butter. The narcotics tax in *United States* v. *Doremus*, 249 U.S. 86 (1919), on the other hand, was so low (a dollar a year on narcotics dealers) that it could not possibly have been calculated to raise revenue. Indeed, it probably was not high enough to pay the costs of collection. Congress's obvious purpose, as disclosed in the elaborate system of records required for narcotics transactions, was to police the drug traffic.

In upholding the bank note, margarine, and narcotics taxes the Court had emphasized that since Congress was exercising an acknowledged power, it was not for judges to examine the legislative motive. In such matters, said the *Veazie* opinion, "the responsibility of the legislature is not to the Courts, but to the people by whom its members are elected." On the basis of these cases Congress thought it could tax child labor out of existence.

Mr. Chief Justice Taft delivered the opinion of the court:

This case presents the question of the constitutional validity of the Child Labor Tax Law. . . .

The law is attacked on the ground that it is a regulation of the employment of child labor in the States—an exclusively state function under the Federal Constitution and within the reservations of the Tenth Amendment. It is defended on the ground that it is a mere excise tax levied by the Congress of the United States under its broad power of taxation conferred by § 8, Article I, of the Federal Constitution. We must construe the law and interpret the intent and meaning of Congress from the language of the act. The words are to be given their ordinary meaning unless the context shows that they are differently used. Does this law impose a tax with only that incidental restraint and regulation which a tax must inevitably involve? Or does it regulate by the use of the so-called tax as a penalty? If a tax, it is clearly an excise. If it were an excise on a commodity or other thing of value we might not be permitted under previous decisions of this court to infer solely from its heavy burden that the act intends a prohibition instead of a tax. But this act is more. It provides a heavy exaction for a departure from a detailed and specified course of conduct in business. That course of business is that employers shall employ in mines and quarries, children of an age greater than sixteen years; in mills and factories, children of an age greater than fourteen years, and shall prevent children of less than sixteen years in mills and factories from working more than eight hours a day or six days in the week. If an employer departs from this prescribed course of business, he is to pay the Government one-tenth of his entire net income in the business for a full year. The amount is not to be proportioned in any degree to the extent or frequency of the departures, but is to be paid by the employer in full measure whether he employs five hundred children for a year, or employs only one for a day. Moreover, if he does not know the child is within the named age limit, he is not to pay; that is to say, it is only where he knowingly departs from the prescribed course that payment is to be exacted. Scienter is associated with penalties not with taxes. The employer's factory is to be subject to inspection at any time not only by the taxing officers of the Treasury, the Department normally charged with the collection of taxes, but also by the Secretary of Labor and his subordinates whose normal function is the advancement and protection of the welfare of the workers. In the light of these features of the act, a court must be blind not to see that the so-called tax is imposed to stop the employment of children within the age limits prescribed. Its prohibitory and regulatory effect and purpose are palpable. All others can see and understand this. How can we properly shut our minds to it?

It is the high duty and function of this court in cases regularly brought to its bar to decline to recognize or enforce seeming laws of Congress, dealing with subjects not entrusted to Congress but left or committed by the supreme law of the land to the control of the States. We can not avoid the duty even though it requires us to refuse to give effect to legislation designed to promote the highest good. The good sought in unconstitutional legislation is an insidious feature because it leads citizens and legislators of good purpose to promote it without thought of the serious breach it will make in the ark of our covenant or the harm which will come from breaking down recognized standards. In the maintenance of local self government, on the one hand, and the national power, on the other, our country has been able to endure and prosper for near a century and a half.

Out of a proper respect for the acts of a coordinate branch of the Government, this court has gone far to sustain taxing acts as such, even though there has been ground for suspecting from the weight of the tax it was intended to destroy its subject. But, in the act before us, the presumption of validity cannot prevail, because the proof of the contrary is found on the very face of its provisions. Grant the validity of this law, and all that Congress would need to do, hereafter, in seeking to take over to its control any one of the great number of subjects of public interest, jurisdiction of which the States have never parted with, and which are reserved to them by the Tenth Amendment, would be to enact a detailed measure of complete regulation of the subject and enforce it by a so-called tax upon departures from it. To give such magic to the word "tax" would be to break down all

constitutional limitation of the powers of Congress and completely wipe out the sovereignty of the States.

The difference between a tax and a penalty is sometimes difficult to define and yet the consequences of the distinction in the required method of their collection often are important. Where the sovereign enacting the law has power to impose both tax and penalty the difference between revenue production and mere regulation may be immaterial, but not so when one sovereign can impose a tax only, and the power of regulation rests in another. Taxes are occasionally imposed in the discretion of the legislature on proper subjects with the primary motive of obtaining revenue from them and with the incidental motive of discouraging them by making their continuance onerous. They do not lose their character as taxes because of the incidental motive. But there comes a time in the extension of the penalizing features of the so-called tax when it loses its character as such and becomes a mere penalty with the characteristics of regulation and punishment. Such is the case in the law before us. Although Congress does not invalidate the contract of employment or expressly declare that the employment within the mentioned ages is illegal, it does exhibit its intent practically to achieve the latter result by adopting the criteria of wrongdoing and imposing its principal consequence on those who transgress its standard.

The case before us can not be distinguished from that of *Hammer* v. *Dagenhart*. . . . Congress there enacted a law to prohibit transportation in interstate commerce of goods made at a factory in which there was employment of children with the same ages and for the same number of hours a day and days in a week as are penalized by the act in this case. This court held the law in that case to be void. It said:

"In our view the necessary effect of this act is, by means of prohibition against the movement in interstate commerce of ordinary commercial commodities, to regulate hours of labor of children in factories and mines within the States, a purely state authority."

In the case at the bar, Congress in the name of a tax which on the face of the act is a penalty seeks to do the same thing, and the effort must be equally futile. . . .

But it is pressed upon us that this court has gone so far in sustaining taxing measures the effect or tendency of which was to accomplish purposes not directly within congressional power that we are bound by authority to maintain this law.

The first of these is *Veazie Bank* v. *Fenno*. . . .

The next case is that of *McCray* v. *United States*. . . . In neither of these cases did the law objected to show on its face as does the law before us the detailed specifications of a regulation of a state concern and business with a heavy exaction to promote the efficacy of such regulation. . . .

United States v. *Doremus* . . . involved the validity of the Narcotic Drug Act, 38 Stat. 785, which imposed a special tax on the manufacture, importation and sale or gift of opium or coca leaves or their compounds or derivatives. . . .

The court said that the act could not be declared invalid just because another motive than taxation, not shown on the face of the act, might have contributed to its passage. This case does not militate against the conclusion we have reached in respect of the law now before us. The court, there, made manifest its view that the provisions of the so-called taxing act must be naturally and reasonably adapted to the collection of the tax and not solely to the achievement of some other purpose plainly within state power. . . .

For the reasons given, we must hold the Child Labor Tax Law invalid and the judgment of the District Court is affirmed.

[Mr. Justice Clarke dissented.]

Note: On August 13, 1787, the Constitutional Convention considered the relation between taxation and regulation. Here is James Madison's view:

The word revenue [is] ambiguous. In many acts, particularly in the regulation of trade, the object would be twofold. The raising of revenue would be one of them. How could it be determined which was the primary or predominant one. . . . When the contest was first opened with Great Britain their power to regulate trade was admitted. Their power to raise revenue rejected. An accurate investigation of the subject afterward proved that no line could be drawn between the two cases.

No one questioned the accuracy of this observation.

Shortly thereafter, on May 13, 1789, in the House of Representatives, Madison argued in favor of a tax on the slave trade. "It is to be hoped," he said, "that by expressing a national disapprobation of this trade, *we may destroy it*, and save ourselves from reproaches, and our posterity the imbecility ever attendant on a country filled with slaves." In short, Madison wanted to destroy the slave trade by taxation, just as later Congressmen wanted to destroy child labor by the same approach.

United States v. *Kahriger*
345 U.S. 22 (1953)

Mr. Justice Reed delivered the opinion of the Court:

The issue raised by this appeal is the constitutionality of the occupational tax provisions of the Revenue Act of 1951, which levy a tax on persons engaged in the business of accepting wagers, and require such persons to register with the Collector of Internal Revenue. The unconstitutionality of the tax is asserted on two grounds. First, it is said that Congress, under the pretense of exercising its power to tax has attempted to penalize illegal intrastate gambling through the regulatory features of the Act (26 U.S.C. [Supp. V] § 3291) and has thus infringed the police power which is reserved to the States. Secondly, it is urged that the registration provisions of the tax violate the privilege against self-incrimination and are arbitrary and vague, contrary to the guarantees of the Fifth Amendment.

The case comes here on appeal, in accordance with 18 U.S.C. § 3731, from the United States District Court for the Eastern District of Pennsylvania, where an information was filed against appellee alleging that he was in the business of accepting wagers and that he willfully failed to register for and pay the occupational tax in question. Appellee moved to dismiss on the ground that the sections upon which the indictment was based were unconstitutional. The District Court sustained the motion on the authority of our opinion in *United States* v. *Constantine*, 296 U.S. 287. The court reasoned that "while the subject matter of this legislation so far as revenue purposes is concerned is within the scope of Federal authority," the tax was unconstitutional in that the information called for by the registrition provisions was "peculiarly applicable to the applicant from the standpoint of law enforcement and vice control," and therefore the whole of the legislation was an infringement by the Federal Government on the police power reserved to the states by the Tenth Amendment. *United States* v. *Kahriger*, 105 F. Supp. 322, 323.

The result below is at odds with the position of the seven other district courts which have considered the matter, and, in our opinion, is erroneous.

In the term following the *Constantine* opinion, this Court pointed out in *Sonzinsky* v. *United States*, 300 U.S. 506, at 513 (a case involving a tax on a "limited class" of objectionable firearms alleged to be prohibitory in effect and "to disclose unmistakably the legislative purpose to regulate rather than to tax"), that the subject of the tax in *Constantine* was "described

or treated as criminal by the taxing statute." The tax in the *Constantine* case was a special additional excise tax of $1,000, placed only on persons who carried on a liquor business in violation of state law. The wagering tax with which we are here concerned applied to all persons engaged in the business of receiving wagers regardless of whether such activity violates state law.

The substance of respondent's position with respect to the Tenth Amendment is that Congress has chosen to tax a specified business which is not within its power to regulate. The precedents are many upholding taxes similar to this wagering tax as a proper exercise of the federal taxing power. In the *License Tax Cases*, 5 Wall. 462, the controversy arose out of indictments for selling lottery tickets and retailing liquor in various states without having first obtained and paid for a license under the Internal Revenue Act of Congress. The objecting taxpayers urged that Congress could not constitutionally tax or regulate activities carried on within a state. P. 470. The Court pointed out that Congress had "no power of regulation nor any direct control" (5 Wall., at 471, 472) over the business there involved. The Court said if the licenses were to be regarded as by themselves giving authority to carry on the licensed business it might be impossible to reconcile the granting of them with the constitution. P. 471.

"But it is not necessary to regard these laws as giving such authority. So far as they relate to trade within State limits, they give none, and can give none. They simply express the purpose of the government not to interfere by penal proceedings with the trade nominally licensed, if the required taxes are paid. The power to tax is not questioned, nor the power to impose penalties for nonpayment of taxes. The granting of a license, therefore, must be regarded as nothing more than a mere form of imposing a tax, and of implying nothing except that the licensee shall be subject to no penalties under national law, if he pays it." *Id.*, at 471.

Appellee would have us say that because there is legislative history indicating a congressional motive to suppress wagering, this tax is not a proper exercise of such taxing power. In the *License Cases, supra,* it was admitted that the federal license "discouraged" the activities. The intent to curtail and hinder, as well as tax, was also manifest in the following cases, and in each of them the tax was upheld: *Veazie Bank* v. *Fenno,* 8 Wall. 533 (tax on paper money issued by state banks); *McCray* v. *United States,* 195 U.S. 27, 59 (tax on colored oleomargarine); *United States* v. *Doremus,* 249 U.S. 86, and *Nigro* v. *United States,* 276 U.S. 332 (tax on narcotics); *Sonzinsky* v. *United States,* 300 U.S. 506 (tax on firearms); *United States* v. *Sanchez,* 340 U.S. 42 (tax on marijuana).

It is conceded that a federal excise tax does not cease to be valid merely because it discourages or deters the activities taxed. Nor is the tax invalid because the revenue obtained is negligible. Appellee, however, argues that the sole purpose of the statute is to penalize only illegal gambling in the states through the guise of a tax measure. As with the above excise taxes which we have held to be valid, the instant tax has a regulatory effect. But regardless of its regulatory effect, the wagering tax produces revenue. As such it surpasses both the narcotics and firearms taxes which we have found valid. . . .

Penalty provisions in tax statutes added for breach of a regulation concerning activities in themselves subject only to state regulation have caused this Court to declare the enactments invalid. Unless there are provisions, extraneous to any tax need, courts are without authority to limit the exercise of the taxing power. All the provisions of this excise are adapted to the collection of a valid tax.

Nor do we find the registration requirements of the wagering tax offensive. All that is required is the filing of names, addresses, and places of business. This is quite general in tax returns. Such data are directly and intimately related to the collection of the tax and are "obviously supportable as in aid of a revenue purpose." *Sonzinsky* v. *United States,* 300 U.S. 506, at 513. The registration provisions made the tax simpler to collect.

Appellee's second assertion is that the wagering tax is unconstitutional because it is a denial of the privilege against self-incrimination as guaranteed by the Fifth Amendment.

Since appellee failed to register for the wagering tax, it is difficult to see how he can now claim the privilege even assuming that the disclosure of violations of law are called for. In *United States* v. *Sullivan,* 274 U.S. 259, defendant was convicted of refusing to file an income tax return. It was assumed that his income "was derived from business in violation of the National Prohibition Act." *Id.*, at 263.

> "As the defendant's income was taxed, the statute, of course, required a return. See *United States* v. *Sischo,* 262 U.S. 165. In the decision that this was contrary to the Constitution, we are of the opinion that the protection of the Fifth Amendment was pressed too far. If the form of return provided called for answers that the defendant was privileged from making he could have raised the objection in the return, but could not on that account refuse to make any return at all." (274 U.S., at 263.)

Assuming that respondent can raise the self-incrimination issue, that privilege has relation only to past acts, not to future acts that may or may not be committed. 8 Wigmore (3d ed., 1940) § 2259(c). If respondent wishes to take wagers subject to excise taxes under § 3285, *supra,* he must pay an occupation tax and register. Under the registration provisions of the wagering tax, appellee is not compelled to confess to acts already committed, he is merely informed by the statute that in order to engage in the business of wagering in the future he must fulfill certain conditions.

Finally, we consider respondent's contention that the order of dismissal was correct because a conviction under the sections in question would violate the due process clause because the classification in arbitrary and the statutory definitions are vague. The applicable definitions are 26 U.S.C. (Supp. V) § 3285(b), (d) and (e). The arbitrariness is said to arise from discrimination because some wagering activities are excluded. The Constitution does not require that a tax statute cover all phases of a taxed or licensed business. Respondent predicates vagueness of the statute upon the use, in defining the subject of the tax, of the description "engaged in the business" of wagering and "usually" in § 3285(b) (2). We have no doubt the definitions make clear the activities covered and excluded.

Reversed.

Mr. Justice Jackson, concurring:

I concur in the judgment and opinion of the Court, but with such doubt that if the minority agreed upon an opinion which did not impair legitimate use of the taxing power I probably would join it. But we deal here with important and contrasting values in our scheme of government, and it is important that neither be allowed to destroy the other. . . .

Mr. Justice Frankfurter, dissenting:

The Court's opinion manifests a natural difficulty in reaching its conclusion. Constitutional issues are likely to arise whenever Congress draws on the taxing power not to raise revenue but to regulate conduct. This is so, of course, because of the distribution of legislative power as between the Congress and the State Legislatures in the regulation of conduct.

To review in detail the decisions of this Court, beginning with *Veazie Bank* v. *Fenno,* 8 Wall. 533, dealing with this ambivalent type of revenue enactment, would be to rehash the familiar. Two generalizations may, however, safely be drawn from this series of cases. Con-

gress may make an oblique use of the taxing power in relation to activities with which Congress may deal directly, as for instance, commerce between the States. Thus, if the dissenting views of Mr. Justice Holmes in *Hammer* v. *Dagenhart,* 247, U.S. 251, 277, had been the decision of the Court, as they became in *United States* v. *Darby,* 312 U.S. 100, the effort to deal with the problem of child labor through an assertion of the taxing power in the statute considered in *Child Labor Tax Case,* 259 U.S. 20, would by the latter case have been sustained. However, when oblique use is made of the taxing power as to matters which substantively are not within the powers delegated to Congress, the Court cannot shut its eyes to what is obviously, because designedly, an attempt to control conduct which the Constitution left to the responsibility of the States, merely because Congress wrapped the legislation in the verbal cellophane of a revenue measure.

Concededly the constitutional questions presented by such legislation are difficult. On the one hand, courts should scrupulously abstain from hobbling congressional choice of policies, particularly when the vast reach of the taxing power is concerned. On the other hand, to allow what otherwise is excluded from congressional authority to be brought within it by casting legislation in the form of a revenue measure could, as so significantly expounded in the *Child Labor Tax Case, supra,* offer an easy way for the legislative imagination to control "any one of the great number of subjects of public interest, jurisdiction of which the States have never parted with. . . ." *Child Labor Tax Case,* at 38. I say "significantly" because Mr. Justice Holmes and two of the Justices who had joined his dissent in *Hammer* v. *Dagenhart,* McKenna and Brandeis, J. J., agreed with the opinion in the *Child Labor Tax Case.* Issues of such gravity affecting the balance of powers within our federal system are not susceptible of comprehensive statement by smooth formulas such as that a tax is nonetheless a tax although it discourages the activities taxed, or, that a tax may be imposed although it may effect ulterior ends. No such phrase, however fine and well-worn, enables one to decide the concrete case.

What is relevant to judgment here is that, even if the history of this legislation as it went through Congress did not give one the libretto to the song, the context of the circumstances which brought forth this enactment—sensationally exploited disclosures regarding gambling in big cities and small, the relation of this gambling to corrupt politics, the impatient public response to these disclosures, the feeling of ineptitude or paralysis on the part of local law-enforcing agencies—emphatically supports what was revealed on the floor of Congress, namely, that what was formally a means of raising revenue for the Federal Government was essentially an effort to check if not to stamp out professional gambling.

A nominal taxing measure must be found an inadmissible intrusion into a domain of legislation reserved for the States not merely when Congress requires that such a measure is to be enforced through a detailed scheme of administration beyond the obvious fiscal needs, as in the *Child Labor Tax Case, supra.* That is one ground for holding that Congress was constitutionally disrespectful of what is reserved to the States. Another basis for deeming such a formal revenue measure inadmissible is presented by this case. In addition to the fact that Congress was concerned with activity beyond the authority of the Federal Government to deal with, the enforcing provision of this enactment is designed for the systematic confession of crimes with a view to prosecution for such crimes under State law.

It is one thing to hold that the exception, which the Fifth Amendment makes to the duty of a witness to give his testimony when relevant to a proceeding in a federal court, does not include the potential danger to that witness of possible prosecution in a State court, *Brown* v. *Walker,* 161 U.S. 591, 606, and, conversely, that the Fifth Amendment does not enable States to give immunity from use in federal courts of testimony given in a State court. *Feldman* v. *United States,* 322 U.S. 487. It is a wholly different thing to hold that Congress, which cannot constitutionally grapple directly with gambling in the States, may compel self-incriminating disclosures for the enforcement of State gambling laws, merely because it does so under the guise of a revenue measure obviously passed not for revenue purposes. The motive of congressional legislation is not for our scrutiny, provided only that the ulterior purpose is not expressed in ways which negate what the revenue words on their face express and, as in this case, which do not seek enforcement of the formal revenue purpose through means that offend those standards of decency in our civilization against which due process is a barrier.

I would affirm this judgment.

Mr. Justice Douglas, while not joining in the entire opinion, agrees with the views expressed herein that this tax is an attempt by the Congress to control conduct which the Constitution has left to the responsibility of the States.

Mr. Justice Black, with whom Mr. Justice Douglas concurs, dissenting:

The Fifth Amendment declares that no person "shall be compelled in any criminal case to be a witness against himself." The Court nevertheless here sustains an Act which requires a man to register and confess that he is engaged in the business of gambling. I think this confession can provide a basis to convict him of a federal crime for having gambled before registration without paying a federal tax. 26 U.S.C. (Supp. V) §§ 3285, 3290, 3291, 3294. Whether or not the Act has this effect, I am sure that it creates a squeezing device contrived to put a man in federal prison if he refuses to confess himself into a state prison as a violator of state gambling laws. The coercion of confessions is a common but justly criticized practice of many countries that do not have or live up to a Bill of Rights. But we have a Bill of Rights that condemns coerced confessions, however refined or legalistic may be the technique of extortion. I would hold that this Act violates the Fifth Amendment. See my dissent in *Feldman* v. *United States*, 322 U.S. 487, 494–503.

Note: Marchetti v. *United States,* 390 U.S. 39 (1968), overruled *Kahriger* solely on self-incrimination—not on tax power—grounds.

New York v. United States
326 U.S. 572 (1946)

A lower court held that the State of New York, like others engaged in the bottling and sale of mineral water, was subject to the federal tax on such operations. New York claimed exemption on the ground that this was a "usual, traditional and essential governmental function." The Supreme Court granted certiorari.

Mr. Justice Frankfurter announced the judgment of the Court and delivered an opinion in which Mr. Justice Rutledge joined. . . .

On the basis of authority the case is quickly disposed of. When States sought to control the liquor traffic by going into the liquor business, they were denied immunity from federal taxes upon the liquor business. *South Carolina* v. *United States*, 199 U.S. 437; *Ohio* v. *Helvering*, 292 U.S. 360. And in rejecting a claim of immunity from federal taxation when Massachusetts took over the street railways of Boston, this Court a decade ago said: "We see no reason for putting the operation of a street railway [by a State] in a different category from the sale of liquors." *Helvering* v. *Powers*, 293 U.S. 214, 227. We certainly see no reason for putting soft drinks in a different constitutional category from hard drinks. See also *Allen* v. *Regents*, 304 U.S. 439.

But the fear that one government may cripple or obstruct the operations of the other early led to the assumption that there was a reciprocal immunity of the instrumentalities of each from taxation by the other. It was assumed that there was an equivalence in the implications of taxation by a State of the governmental activities of the National Government and the taxation by the National Government of State instrumen-

talities. The considerations bearing upon taxation by the States of activities or agencies of the federal government are not correlative with the considerations bearing upon federal taxation of State agencies or activities. The federal government is the government of all the States, and all the States share in the legislative process by which a tax of general applicability is laid.

In the older cases, the emphasis was on immunity from taxation. The whole tendency of recent cases reveals a shift in emphasis to that of limitation upon immunity. They also indicate an awareness of the limited role of courts in assessing the relative weight of the factors upon which immunity is based. Any implied limitation upon the supremacy of the federal power to levy a tax like that now before us, in the absence of discrimination against State activities, brings fiscal and political factors into play. The problem cannot escape issues that do not lend themselves to judgment by criteria and methods of reasoning that are within the professional training and special competence of judges. Indeed the claim of implied immunity by States from federal taxation raises questions not wholly unlike provisions of the Constitution, such as that of Art. IV, § 4, guaranteeing States a republican form of government, see *Pacific States Tel & Tel. Co.* v. *Oregon*, 223 U.S. 118, which this Court has deemed not within its duty to adjudicate.

We have already held that by engaging in the railroad business a State cannot withdraw the railroad from the power of the federal government to regulate commerce. *United States* v. *California*, 297 U.S. 175. See also *University of Illinois* v. *United States*, 289 U.S. 48. Surely the power of Congress to lay taxes has impliedly no less a reach than the power of Congress to regulate commerce. There are, of course, State activities and State-owned property that partake of uniqueness from the point of view of intergovernmental relations. These inherently constitute a class by themselves. Only a State can own a State house; only a State can get income by taxing. These could not be included for purposes of federal taxation in any abstract category of taxpayers without taxing the State as a State. But so long as Congress generally taps a source of revenue by whomsoever earned and not uniquely capable of being earned only by a State, the Constitution of the United States does not forbid it merely because its incidence falls also on a State. . . .

The process of constitutional adjudication does not thrive on conjuring up horrible possibilities that never happen in the real world and devising doctrines sufficiently comprehensive in detail to cover the remotest contingency. Nor need we go beyond what is required for a reasoned disposition of the kind of controversy now before the Court. The restriction upon states not to make laws that discriminate against interstate commerce is a vital constitutional principle, even though "discrimination" is not a code of specifics but a continuous process of application. So we decide enough when we reject limitations upon the taxing power of Congress derived from such untenable criteria as "proprietary" against "governmental" activities of the States, or historically sanctioned activities of Government or activities conducted merely for profit, and find no restriction upon Congress to include the States in levying a tax exacted equally from private persons upon the same subject matter.

Judgment affirmed.

Mr. Justice Jackson took no part in the consideration or decision of this case.

[The concurring opinion of Mr. Justice Rutledge is omitted.]

Mr. Chief Justice Stone concurring:

Mr. Justice Reed, Mr. Justice Murphy, Mr. Justice Burton, and I concur in the result. We are of the opinion that the tax here involved should be sustained and the judgment below affirmed.

In view of our decisions in *South Carolina* v. *United States*, 199 U.S. 437; *Ohio* v. *Helvering*, 292 U.S. 360; *Helvering* v. *Powers*, 293 U.S. 214; and *Allen* v. *Regents*, 304 U.S. 439, we would find it difficult not to sustain the tax in this case, even though we regard as untenable the distinction between "governmental" and "proprietary" interests on which those cases rest to some extent. But we are not prepared to say that the national government may constitutionally lay a nondiscriminatory tax on every class of property and activities of States and individuals alike.

Concededly a federal tax discriminating against a State would be an unconstitutional exertion of power over a coexisting sovereignty within the same framework of government. But our difficulty with the formula, now first suggested as offering a new solution for an old problem, is that a federal tax which is not discriminatory as to the subject matter may nevertheless so affect the State, merely because it is a State that is being taxed, as to interfere unduly with the State's performance of its sovereign functions of government. The counterpart of such undue interference has been recognized since Marshall's day as the implied immunity of each of the dual sovereignties of our constitutional system from taxation by the other. *McCulloch* v. *Maryland*, 4 Wheat. 316. We add nothing to this formula by saying, in a new form of words, that a tax which Congress applies generally to the property and activities of private citizens may not be in some instances constitutionally extended to the States merely because the States are included among those who pay taxes on a like subject of taxation.

If the phrase "non-discriminatory tax" is to be taken in its long accepted meaning as referring to a tax laid on a like subject matter, without regard to the personality of the taxpayer, whether a State, a corporation or a private individual, it is plain that there may be nondiscriminatory taxes which, when laid on a State, would nevertheless impair the sovereign status of the State quite as much as a like tax imposed by a State on property or activities of the national government. *Mayo* v. *United States*, 319 U.S. 441, 447, 448. This is not because the tax can be regarded as discriminatory but because a sovereign government is the taxpayer, and the tax, even though non-discriminatory, may be regarded as infringing its sovereignty.

It is enough for present purposes that the immunity of the State from federal taxation would, in this case, accomplish a withdrawal from the taxing power of the nation a subject of taxation of a nature which has been traditionally within that power from the beginning. Its exercise now, by a non-discriminatory tax, does not curtail the business of the state government more than it does the like business of the citizen. It gives merely an accustomed and reasonable scope to the federal taxing power. Such a withdrawal from a non-discriminatory federal tax, and one which does not bear on the State any differently than on the citizen, is itself an impairment of the taxing power of the national government, and the activity taxed is such that its taxation does not unduly impair the State's functions of government. . . .

The problem is not one to be solved by a formula, but we may look to the structure of the Constitution as our guide to decision. "In a broad sense, the taxing power of either government, even when exercised in a manner admittedly necessary and proper, unavoidably has some effect upon the other. The burden of federal taxation necessarily sets an economic limit to the practical operation of the taxing power of the states, and vice versa. Taxation by either the state or the federal government affects in some measure the cost of operation of the other.

"But neither government may destroy the other nor curtail in any substantial manner the exercise of its powers. Hence the limitation upon the taxing power of each, so far as it affects the other, must receive a practical construction which permits both to function with the minimum of interference each with the other; and that limitation cannot be so varied or extended as seriously to impair either the taxing power of the government imposing the tax . . . or the appropriate exercise of the functions of the government affected by it." *Metcalf & Eddy* v. *Mitchell*, [269 U.S. 514] 523–524. . . .

Mr. Justice Douglas, with whom Mr. Justice Black concurs, dissenting: . . .

I do not believe *South Carolina* v. *United States* states the correct rule. A State's project is as much a legitimate governmental activity whether it is traditional, or akin to private enterprise, or conducted for profit. Cf. *Helvering* v. *Gerhardt*, 304 U.S. 405, 426, 427. A State may deem it as essential to its economy that it own and operate a railroad, a mill, or an irrigation system as it does to own and operate bridges, street lights, or a sewage disposal plant. What might have been viewed in an earlier day as an improvident or even dangerous extension of state activities may today be deemed indispensable. But as Mr. Justice White said in his dissent in *South Carolina* v. *United States,* any activity in which a State engages within the limits of its police power is a legitimate governmental activity. Here a State is disposing of some of its natural resources. Tomorrow it may issue securities, sell power from its public power project, or manufacture fertilizer. Each is an exercise of its power of sovereignty. Must it pay the federal government for the privilege of exercising that inherent power? . . .

. . . To say the present tax will be sustained

because it does not impair the State's functions of government is to conclude either that the sale by the State of its mineral water is not a function of government or that the present tax is so slight as to be no burden. The former obviously is not true. The latter overlooks the fact that the power to tax lightly is the power to tax severely. The power to tax is indeed one of the most effective forms of regulations. And no more powerful instrument for centralization of government could be devised. For with the federal government immune and the States subject to tax, the economic ability of the federal government to expand its activities at the expense of the States is at once apparent. That is the result whether the rule of *South Carolina* v. *United States* be perpetuated or a new rule of discrimination be adopted. . . .

The National Spending Power

United States v. *Butler*
297 U.S. 1 (1936)

To raise farm income and relieve the pressure of unmarketable "surplus" crops, Congress sought to restrict farm production by the Agricultural Adjustment Act of 1933. This was to be accomplished by "benefit payments" to those farmers who would follow an acreage reduction program. The scheme was financed by a special tax on the processing of farm goods. In this case a cotton processor refused to pay the processing tax. The United States brought an action to collect it.

Mr. Justice Roberts delivered the opinion of the Court: . . .

First. At the outset the United States contends that the respondents have no standing to question the validity of the tax. The position is that the act is merely a revenue measure levying an excise upon the activity of processing cotton—a proper subject for the imposition of such a tax—the proceeds of which go into the federal treasury and thus become available for appropriation for any purpose. It is said that what the respondents are endeavoring to do is to challenge the intended use of the money pursuant to Congressional appropriation when, by confession, that money will have become the property of the government and the taxpayer will no longer have any interest in it. *Massachusetts* v. *Mellon*, 262 U.S. 447, is claimed to foreclose litigation by the respondents or other taxpayers, as such, looking to restraint of the expenditure of government funds. That case might be an authority in the petitioners' favor if we were here concerned merely with a suit by a taxpayer to restrain the expenditure of the public moneys. . . . But here the respondents who are called upon to pay moneys as taxes, resist the exaction as a step in an unauthorized plan. This circumstance clearly distinguishes the case. The government in substance and effect asks us to separate the Agricultural Adjustment Act into two statutes, the one levying an excise on processors of certain commodities; the other appropriating the public moneys independently of the first. Passing the novel suggestion that two statutes enacted as parts of a single scheme should be tested as if they were distinct and unrelated, we think the legislation now before us is not susceptible of such separation and treatment.

The tax can only be sustained by ignoring the avowed purpose and operation of the act, and holding it a measure merely laying an excise upon processors to raise revenue for the support of government. Beyond cavil the sole object of the legislation is to restore the purchasing power of agricultural products to a parity with that prevailing in an earlier day; to take money from the processor and bestow it upon farmers who will reduce their acreage for the accomplishment of the proposed end, and, meanwhile, to aid these farmers during the period required to bring the prices of their crops to the desired level. . . .

Second. The Government asserts that even if the respondents may question the propriety of the appropriation embodied in the statute, their attack must fail because Article I, § 8 of the Constitution, authorizes the contemplated expenditure of the funds raised by the tax. This contention presents the great and the controlling question in the case. . . .

The clause thought to authorize the legislation—the first—confers upon the Congress power "to lay and collect Taxes, Duties, Imposts and Excises, to pay the Debts and provide for the common Defence and general Welfare of the United States. . . ." It is not contended that this provision grants power to regulate agricultural production upon the theory that such legislation would promote the general welfare. The government concedes that the phrase "to provide for the general welfare" qualifies the power "to lay and collect taxes." The view that the clause grants power to provide for the general welfare, independently of the taxing power, has never been authoritatively accepted. Mr. Justice Story points out that, if it were adopted, "it is obvious that under color of the generality of the words, to 'provide for the common defence and general welfare,' the government of the United States is, in reality, a government of general and unlimited powers, notwithstanding the subsequent enumeration of specific powers." The true construction undoubtedly is that the only thing granted is the power to tax for the purpose of providing funds for payment of the nation's

debts and making provision for the general welfare.

Nevertheless, the Government asserts that warrant is found in this clause for the adoption of the Agricultural Adjustment Act. The argument is that Congress may appropriate and authorize the spending of moneys for the "general welfare"; that the phrase should be liberally construed to cover anything conducive to national welfare; that decision as to what will promote such welfare rests with Congress alone, and the courts may not review its determination; and, finally, that the appropriation under attack was in fact for the general welfare of the United States.

The Congress is expressly empowered to lay taxes to provide for the general welfare. Funds in the Treasury as a result of taxation may be expended only through appropriation. (Article I, § 9, cl. 7.) They can never accomplish the objects for which they were collected, unless the power to appropriate is as broad as the power to tax. The necessary implication from the terms of the grant is that the public funds may be appropriated "to provide for the general welfare of the United States." These words cannot be meaningless, else they would not have been used. The conclusion must be that they were intended to limit and define the granted power to raise and to expend money. How shall they be construed to effectuate the intent of the instrument?

Since the foundation of the nation, sharp differences of opinion have persisted as to the true interpretation of the phrase. Madison asserted it amounted to no more than a reference to the other powers enumerated in the subsequent clauses of the same section; that, as the United States is a government of limited and enumerated powers, the grant of power to tax and spend for the general national welfare must be confined to the enumerated legislative fields committed to the Congress. In this view the phrase is mere tautology, for taxation and appropriation are or may be necessary incidents of the exercise of any of the enumerated legislative powers. Hamilton, on the other hand, maintained the clause confers a power separate and distinct from those later enumerated, is not restricted in meaning by the grant of them, and Congress consequently has a substantive power to tax and to appropriate, limited only by the requirement that it shall be exercised to provide for the general welfare of the United States. Each contention has had the support of those whose views are entitled to weight. This court has noticed the question, but has never found it necessary to decide which is the true construction. Mr. Justice Story, in his Commentaries, espouses the Hamiltonian position. We shall not review the writings of public men and commentators or discuss the legislative practice. Study of all these leads us to conclude that the reading advocated by Mr. Justice Story is the correct one. While, therefore, the power to tax is not unlimited, its confines are set in the clause which confers it, and not in those of section 8 which bestow and define the legislative powers of the Congress. . . .

We are not now required to ascertain the scope of the phrase "general welfare of the United States" or to determine whether an appropriation in aid of agriculture falls within it. Wholly apart from that question, another principle embedded in our Constitution prohibits the enforcement of the Agricultural Adjustment Act. The act invades the reserved rights of the states. It is a statutory plan to regulate and control agricultural production, a matter beyond the powers delegated to the federal government. The tax, the appropriation of the funds raised, and the direction for their disbursement, are but parts of the plan. They are but means to an unconstitutional end. . . .

The power of taxation, which is expressly granted, may, of course, be adopted as a means to carry into operation another power also expressly granted. But resort to the taxing power to effectuate an end which is not legitimate, not within the scope of the Constitution, is obviously inadmissible. . . .

In the *Child Labor Tax Case*, 259 U.S. 20, and in *Hill* v. *Wallace*, 259 U.S. 44, this court had before it statutes which purported to be taxing measures. But their purpose was found to be to regulate the conduct of manufacturing and trading, not in interstate commerce, but in the states—matters not within any power conferred upon Congress by the Constitution—and the levy of the tax a means to force compliance. The court held this was not a constitutional use, but an unconstitutional abuse of the power to tax. In *Linder* v. *United States*, 268 U.S. 5, we held that the power to tax could not justify the regulation of the practice of a profession, under the pretext of raising revenue. In *United States* v. *Constantine*, 296 U.S. 287, we declared that Congress could not, in the guise of a tax, impose sanctions for violation of state law respecting the local sale of liquor. These decisions demonstrate that Congress could not, under the pretext of raising revenue, lay a tax on processors who refuse to pay a certain price for cotton and exempt those who agree so to do, with the purpose of benefiting producers.

Third. If the taxing power may not be used as the instrument to enforce a regulation of matters of state concern with respect to which the Congress has no authority to interfere, may it, as in the present case, be employed to raise the money necessary to purchase a compliance which the Congress is powerless to command? The Government asserts that whatever might be said against the validity of the plan, if compulsory, it is constitutionally sound because the end is accomplished by voluntary co-operation. There are two sufficient answers to the contention. The regulation is not in fact voluntary. The farmer, of course, may refuse to comply, but the price of such refusal is the loss of benefits. The amount offered is intended to be sufficient to exert pressure on him to agree to the proposed regulation. The power to confer or withhold unlimited benefits is the power to coerce or destroy. If the cotton grower elects not to accept the benefits, he will receive less for his crops; those who receive payments will be able to undersell him. The result may well be financial ruin. . . .

But if the plan were one for purely voluntary co-operation it would stand no better so far as federal power is concerned. At best, it is a scheme for purchasing with federal funds submission to federal regulation of a subject reserved to the states. . . .

Mr. Justice Stone, dissenting:

. . . [The] pivot on which the decision of the Court is made to turn . . . is that a levy unquestionably within the taxing power of Congress may be treated as invalid because it is a step in a plan to regulate agricultural production and is thus a forbidden infringement of state power. The levy is not any the less an exercise of taxing power because it is intended to defray an expenditure for the general welfare rather than for some other support of government. Nor is the levy and collection of the tax pointed to as affecting the regulation. While all federal taxes inevitably have some influence on the internal economy of the states, it is not contended that the levy of a processing tax upon manufacturers using agricultural products as raw material has any perceptible regulatory effect upon either their production or manufacture. The tax is unlike the penalties which were held invalid in the *Child Labor Tax Case*, 259 U.S. 20, in *Hill* v. *Wallace*, 259 U.S. 44, in *Linder* v. *United States*, 268 U.S. 5, 17, and in *United States* v. *Constantine*, 296 U.S. 287, because they were themselves the instruments of regulation by virtue of their coercive effect on matters left to the control of the states. Here regulation, if any there be, is accomplished not by the tax, but by the method by which its proceeds are expended, and would equally be accomplished by any like use of public funds, regardless of their source.

The method may be simply stated. Out of the available fund payments are made to such farmers as are willing to curtail their productive acreage, who in fact do so and who in advance have filed their written undertaking to do so with the Secretary of Agriculture. In saying that this method of spending public moneys is an invasion of the reserved powers of the states, the Court does not assert that the expenditure of public funds to promote the general welfare is not a substantive power specifically delegated to the national government, as Hamilton and Story pronounced it to be. It does not deny that the expenditure of funds for the benefit of farmers and in aid of a program of curtailment of production of agricultural products, and thus of a supposedly better ordered national economy, is within the specifically granted power. But it is declared that state power is nevertheless infringed by the expenditure of the proceeds of the tax to compensate farmers for the curtailment of their cotton acreage. Although the farmer is placed under no legal compulsion to reduce acreage, it is said that the mere offer of compensation for so doing is a species of economic coercion which operates with the same legal force and effect as though the curtailment were made mandatory by act of Congress. In any event it is insisted that even though not coercive the expenditure of public funds to induce the recipients to curtail production is itself an infringement of state power, since the federal government cannot invade the domain of the states by the "purchase" of performance of acts which it has no power to compel.

Of the assertion that the payments to farmers are coercive, it is enough to say that no such contention is pressed by the taxpayer, and no such consequences were to be anticipated or appear to have resulted from the administration of the act. The suggestion of coercion finds no support in the record or in any data showing the actual operation of the act. Threat of loss, not hope of gain, is the essence of economic coercion. . . . The presumption of constitutionality of a statute is not to be overturned by an assertion of its coercive effect which rests on nothing more substantial than groundless speculation.

It is upon the contention that state power is infringed by purchased regulation of agricultural production that chief reliance is placed. It is insisted that, while the Constitution gives to Congress, in specific and unambiguous terms, the power to tax and spend, the power is subject to limitations which do not find their origin in any express provision of the Constitution and to which other expressly delegated powers are not subject.

The Constitution requires that public funds shall be spent for defined purpose, the promotion of the general welfare. Their expenditure usually involves payment on terms which will insure use by the selected recipients within the limits of the constitutional purpose. Expenditures would fail of their purpose and thus lose their constitutional sanction if the terms of payment were not such that by their influence on the action of the recipients the permitted end would be attained. The power of Congress to spend is inseparable from persuasion to action over which Congress has no legislative control. Congress may not command that the science of agriculture be taught in state universities. But if it would aid the teaching of that science by grants to state institutions, it is appropriate, if not necessary, that the grant be on the condition, incorporated in the Morrill Act, 12 Stat. 503, 26 Stat. 417, that it be used for the intended purpose. Similarly it would seem to be compliance with the Constitution, not violation of it, for the government to take and the university to give a contract that the grant would be so used. It makes no difference that there is a promise to do an act which the condition is calculated to induce. Condition and promise are alike valid since both are in furtherance of the national purpose for which the money is appropriated.

These effects upon individual action, which are but incidents of the authorized expenditure of government money, are pronounced to be themselves a limitation upon the granted power. . . .

Such a limitation is contradictory and destructive of the power to appropriate for the public welfare, and is incapable of practical application. The spending power of Congress is in addition to the legislative power and not subordinate to it. This independent grant of the power

of the purse, and its very nature, involving in its exercise the duty to insure expenditure within the granted power, presuppose freedom of selection among divers ends and aims, and the capacity to impose such conditions as will render the choice effective. It is a contradiction in terms to say that there is power to spend for the national welfare, while rejecting any power to impose conditions reasonably adapted to the attainment of the end which alone would justify the expenditure.

The limitation now sanctioned must lead to absurd consequences. The government may give seeds to farmers, but may not condition the gift upon their being planted in places where they are most needed or even planted at all. The government may give money to the unemployed, but may not ask that those who get it shall give labor in return, or even use it to support their families. It may give money to sufferers from earthquake, fire, tornado, pestilence, or flood, but may not impose conditions, health precautions designed to prevent the spread of disease, or induce the movement of population to safer or more sanitary areas. All that, because it is purchased regulation infringing state powers, must be left for the states, who are unable or unwilling to supply the necessary relief. . . .

That the governmental power of the purse is a great one is not now for the first time announced. Every student of the history of government and economics is aware of its magnitude and of its existence in every civilized government. Both were well understood by the framers of the Constitution when they sanctioned the grant of the spending power to the federal government, and both were recognized by Hamilton and Story, whose views of the spending power as standing on a parity with the other powers specifically granted, have hitherto been generally accepted. . . . The power to tax and spend is not without constitutional restraints. One restriction is that the purpose must be truly national. Another is that it may not be used to coerce action left to state control. Another is the conscience and patriotism of Congress and the Executive. . . . Courts are not the only agency of government that must be assumed to have capacity to govern. Congress and the courts both unhappily may falter or be mistaken in the performance of their constitutional duty. But interpretation of our great charter of government which proceeds on any assumption that the responsibility for the preservation of our institutions is the exclusive concern of any one of the three branches of government, or that it alone can save them from destruction is far more likely, in the long run, "to obliterate the constituent members" of "an indestructible union of indestructible states" than the frank recognition that language, even of a constitution, may mean what it says: that the power to tax and spend includes the power to relieve a nationwide economic maladjustment by conditional gifts of money.

Mr. Justice Brandeis and Mr. Justice Cardozo join in this opinion.

Steward Machine Co. v. *Davis*
301 U.S. 548 (1937)

The unemployment aspect of the Social Security Act involves a federal excise (payroll) tax on employers of eight or more workers. The taxpayers are allowed a credit against this tax (to the extent of 90 percent thereof) for any amount paid into a federally approved state unemployment compensation system. The purpose of the credit plainly was to encourage state unemployment insurance legislation. After paying the tax, the company here sued for a full refund.

Mr. Justice Cardozo delivered the opinion of the Court. . . .

The proceeds of the excise when collected are paid into the Treasury at Washington, and thereafter are subject to appropriation like public moneys generally. No presumption can be indulged that they will be misapplied or wasted. Even if they were collected in the hope or expectation that some other and collateral good would be furthered as an incident, that without more would not make the Act invalid. This indeed is hardly questioned. The case for the petitioner is built on the contention that here an ulterior aim is wrought into the very structure of the Act, and what is even more important that the aim is not only ulterior, but essentially unlawful. In particular, the 90 percent credit is relied upon as supporting that conclusion. But before the statute succumbs to an assault upon these lines, two propositions must be made out by the assailant. There must be a showing in the first place that separated from the credit the revenue provisions are incapable of standing by themselves. There must be a showing in the second place that the tax and the credit in combination are weapons of coercion, destroying or impairing the autonomy of the states. The truth of each proposition being essential to the success of the assault, we pass for convenience to a consideration of the second, without pausing to inquire whether there has been a demonstration of the first.

To draw the line intelligently between duress and inducement there is need to remind ourselves of facts as to the problem of unemployment that are now matters of common knowledge. The relevant statistics are gathered in the brief of counsel for the government. Of the many available figures a few only will be mentioned. During the years 1929 to 1936, when the country was passing through a cyclical depression, the number of the unemployed mounted to unprecedented heights. Often the average was more than 10 million; at times a peak was attained of 16 million or more. Disaster to the breadwinner meant disaster to dependents. Accordingly the roll of the unemployed, itself formidable enough, was only a partial roll of the destitute or needy. The fact developed quickly that the states were unable to give the requisite relief. The problem had become national in area and dimensions. There was need of help from the nation if the people were not to starve. It is too late today for the argument to be heard with tolerance that in a crisis so extreme the use of the moneys of the nation to relieve the unemployed and their dependents is a use for any purpose narrower than the promotion of the general welfare. The nation responded to the call of the distressed. Between January 1, 1933, and July 1, 1936, the states (according to statistics submitted by the government) incurred obligations of $689,291,802 for emergency relief; local subdivisions an additional $775,675,366. In the same period the obligations for emergency relief incurred by the national government were $2,929,307,125, or twice the obligations of states and local agencies combined. According to the President's budget message for the fiscal year 1938, the national government expended for public works and unemployment relief for the three fiscal years 1934, 1935, and 1936, the stupendous total of $8,681,000,000. The parens patriae has many reasons—fiscal and economic as well as social and moral—for planning to mitigate disasters that bring these burdens in their train.

In the presence of this urgent need for some remedial expedient, the question is to be answered whether the expedient adopted has overleapt the bounds of power. The assailants of the statute say that its dominant end and aim is to drive the state legislatures under the whip of economic pressure into the enactment of unemployment compensation laws at the bidding of the central government. Supporters of the statute say that its operation is not constraint, but the creation of a larger freedom, the states and the nation joining in a cooperative endeavor to avert a common evil. Before Congress acted, unemployment compensation insurance was still, for the most part, a project and no more. Wisconsin was the pioneer. Her statute was adopted in 1931. At times bills for such insurance were introduced elsewhere, but they did not reach the stage of law. In 1935, four states (California, Massachusetts, New Hampshire, and New York) passed unemployment laws on the eve of the adoption of the Social Security Act, and two others did likewise after the federal act and later in the year. The statutes differed to some extent in type, but were directed to a common end. In 1936, 28 other states fell in line, and eight more the present year. But if states had been holding back before the passage of the federal law, inaction was not owing, for the most part, to the lack of sympathetic interest. Many held back through alarm lest in laying such a toll upon their industries, they would place themselves in a position of economic disadvantage as compared with neighbors or competitors. See House Report, No. 615, 74th Congress, 1st session, p. 8; Senate Report No. 628, 74th Congress, 1st session, p. 11. Two consequences ensued. One was that the freedom of a state to contribute its fair share to the solution of a national problem was paralyzed by fear. The other was that in so far as there was failure by the states to contribute relief according to the measure of their capacity, a disproportionate burden, and a mountainous one, was laid upon the resources of the government of the nation.

The Social Security Act is an attempt to find a method by which all these public agencies may work together to a common end. Every dollar of the new taxes will continue in all likelihood to be used and needed by the nation as long as states are unwilling, whether through timidity or for other motives, to do what can be done at home. At least the inference is permissible that Congress so believed, though retaining undiminished freedom to spend the money as it pleased. On the other hand fulfillment of the home duty will be lightened and encouraged by crediting the taxpayer upon his account with the Treasury of the nation to the extent that his contributions under the laws of the locality have simplified or diminished the problem of relief and the probable demand upon the resources of the fisc. Duplicated taxes, or burdens that approach them, are recognized hardships that government, state or national, may properly avoid. If Congress believed that the general welfare would better be promoted by relief through local units than by the system then in vogue, the cooperating localities ought not in all fairness to pay a second time.

Who then is coerced through the operation of this statute? Not the taxpayer. He pays in fulfillment of the mandate of the local legislature. Not the state. Even now she does not offer a suggestion that in passing the unemployment law she was affected by duress. For all that appears she is satisfied with her choice, and would be sorely disappointed if it were now to be annulled. The difficulty with the petitioner's contention is that it confuses motive with coercion. "Every tax is in some measure regulatory. To some extent it interposes an economic impediment to the activity taxed as compared with others not taxed." In like manner every rebate from a tax when conditioned upon conduct is in some measure a temptation. But to hold that motive or temptation is equivalent to coercion is to plunge the law in endless difficulties. The outcome of such a doctrine is the acceptance of a philosophical determinism by which choice becomes impossible. Till now the law has been guided by a robust common sense which assumes the freedom of the will as a working hypothesis in the solution of its problems. The wisdom of the hypothesis has illustration in this case. Nothing in the case suggests the exertion of a power akin to undue influence, if we assume that such a concept can ever be applied with fitness to the relations between state and nation. Even on that assumption the location of the point at which pressure turns into compulsion, and ceases to be inducement, would be a question of degree,—at times, perhaps, of fact. The point had not been reached when Alabama made her choice. We cannot say that she was acting, not of her unfettered will, but under the strain of a persuasion equivalent to undue influence, when she chose to have relief administered under laws of her own making, by agents of her own selection, instead of under federal laws, administered by federal officers, with all the ensuing evils, at least to many minds, of federal patronage and power. There would be a strange irony, indeed, if her choice were now to be annulled on the basis of an assumed duress in the enactment of a statute which her courts have accepted as a true expression of her will. We think the choice must stand.

[Justices McReynolds, Sutherland, Van Deventer, and Butler dissented.]

Buckley v. *Valeo* (excerpt)
424 U.S. 1 (1976)

The Federal Election Campaign Act, Subtitle H, provides for a Presidential Campaign Fund financed from general revenues. The amount available is determined by taxpayers, who may authorize $1 on their income tax returns ($2 on joint returns) for the fund. Following is the Court's response to a charge that Subtitle H violates the congressional spending power:

Appellants' "general welfare" contention erroneously treats the General Welfare Clause as a limitation upon congressional power. It is rather a grant of power, the scope of which is quite expansive, particularly in view of the enlargement of power by the Necessary and

Proper Clause. *McCulloch* v. *Maryland,* 4 Wheat. 316, 420 (1819). Congress has power to regulate Presidential elections and primaries, *United States* v. *Classic,* 313 U.S. 299 (1941); *Burroughs* v. *United States,* 290 U.S. 534 (1934); and public financing of Presidential elections as a means to reform the electoral process was clearly a choice within the granted power. It is for Congress to decide which expenditures will promote the general welfare: "[T]he power of Congress to authorize expenditure of public moneys for public purposes is not limited by the direct grants of legislative power found in the Constitution." *United States* v. *Butler,* 297 U.S. 1, 66 (1936). See *Helvering* v. *Davis,* 301 U.S. 619, 640–641 (1937). Any limitations upon the exercise of that granted power must be found elsewhere in the Constitution. In this case, Congress was legislating for the "general welfare"—to reduce the deleterious influence of large contributions on our political process, to facilitate communication by candidates with the electorate, and to free candidates from the rigors of fundraising. See S.Rep.No.93–689, pp.

1–10 (1974). Whether the chosen means appear "bad," "unwise," or "unworkable" to us is irrelevant; Congress has concluded that the means are "necessary and proper" to promote the general welfare and we thus decline to find this legislation without the grant of power in Art. I, § 8.

Appellants' challenge to the dollar check-off provision (§ 6096) fails for the same reason. They maintain that Congress is required to permit taxpayers to designate particular candidates or parties as recipients of their money. But the appropriation to the Fund in § 9006 is like any other appropriation from the general revenue except that its amount is determined by reference to the aggregate on the one- and two-dollar authorization on taxpayers' income tax returns. This detail does not constitute the appropriation any less an appropriation by Congress. The fallacy of appellants' argument is therefore apparent; every appropriation made by Congress uses public money in a manner to which some taxpayers object.

Oklahoma v. *United States Civil Service Commission* (excerpt)
330 U.S 127 (1947)

The federal Hatch Act provides that no state official employed in activities "financed in whole or in part" by federal funds shall "take any active part" in political activities. When a state highway commissioner violated this provision, the federal authorities ordered his removal from office. The penalty for noncompliance was the cutting off of highway grants "in an amount equal to two years [of the commissioner's] compensation." Following is the Court's response when Oklahoma challenged the removal order:

While the United States is not concerned with, and has no power to regulate, local political activities as such of state officials, it does have power to fix the terms upon which its money allotments to states shall be disbursed. . . . The end sought by Congress through the Hatch Act is better public service by requiring

those who administer funds for national needs to abstain from active political partisanship. So even though the action taken by Congress does have effect upon certain activities within the state, it has never been thought that such effect made the federal act invalid. . . . Oklahoma adopted the "simple expedient" of not yielding to what she urges is federal coercion. . . . The offer of benefits to a state by the United States dependent upon cooperation by the state with federal plans, assumedly for the general welfare, is not unusual.

> *Note:* The Hatch Act was challenged on First Amendment grounds and upheld in *United Public Workers* v. *Mitchell,* 330 U.S. 75 (1947) and in *Civil Service Commission* v. *Letter Carriers,* below.

Implied and Necessary and Proper Powers

Madison on Implied Powers

In subsequent debate on the [proposed] tenth amendment, Madison successfully resisted an attempt to insert one word, to make it say that powers not *expressly* delegated to the United States are reserved to the states or to the people. No government, he contended, could be limited to express powers: "There must necessarily be admitted powers by implication."

(I. Brant "The Madison Heritage," in E. Cahn (ed.), *The Great Rights* 34 (New York: Macmillan, 1963).

McCulloch v. Maryland
4 Wheaton 316 (1819)

Jeffersonian hostility toward the National Bank found expression in state legislation. Maryland, for example, imposed a special tax on the issuance of notes in Maryland by institutions not chartered in that state. In the context of the times the tax could fall only on the Maryland branch of the National Bank. This case began as an action against the cashier of that bank to collect a penalty of $100 for issuing a note on which the tax had not been paid.

Mr. Chief Justice Marshall delivered the opinion of the Court. . . .

The first question made in the cause is, has Congress power to incorporate a bank? . . .

The power now contested was exercised by the first Congress elected under the present constitution. The bill for incorporating the Bank of the United States did not steal upon an unsuspecting legislature, and pass unobserved. Its principle was completely understood, and was opposed with equal zeal and ability. After being resisted, first in the fair and open field of debate, and afterwards in the executive cabinet, with as much persevering talent as any measure has ever experienced, and being supported by arguments which convinced minds as pure and as intelligent as this country can boast, it became a law. The original act was permitted to expire; but a short experience of the embarrassments to which the refusal to revive it exposed the government, convinced those who were most prejudiced against the measure of its necessity and induced the passage of the present law. It would require no ordinary share of intrepidity to assert that a measure adopted under these circumstances was a bold and plain usurpation, to which the constitution gave no countenance.

These observations belong to the cause; but

they are not made under the impression that, were the question entirely new, the law would be found irreconcilable with the constitution.

In discussing this question, the counsel for the state of Maryland have deemed it of some importance, in the construction of the constitution, to consider that instrument not as emanating from the people, but as the act of sovereign and independent states. The powers of the general government, it has been said, are delegated by the states, who alone are truly sovereign; and must be exercised in subordination to the states, who alone possess supreme dominion.

It would be difficult to sustain this proposition. The convention which framed the constitution was indeed elected by the state legislatures. But the instrument, when it came from their hands, was a mere proposal, without obligation, or pretensions to it. It was reported to the then existing Congress of the United States, with a request that it might "be submitted to a convention of delegates, chosen in each state by the people thereof, under the recommendation of its legislature, for their assent and ratification." This mode of proceeding was adopted; and by the convention, by Congress, and by the state legislatures, the instrument was submitted to the people. They acted upon it in the only manner in which they can act safely, effectively, and wisely on such a subject, by assembling in convention. It is true, they assembled in their several states—and where else should they have assembled? No political dreamer was ever wild enough to think of breaking down the lines which separate the states, and of compounding the American people into one common mass. Of consequence, when they act, they act in their states. But the measures they adopt do not, on that account, cease to be the measures of the people themselves, or become the measures of the state governments.

From these conventions the constitution derives its whole authority. The government proceeds directly from the people; is "ordained and established" in the name of the people; and is declared to be ordained, "in order to form a more perfect union, establish justice, insure domestic tranquility, and secure the blessings of liberty to themselves and to their posterity." The assent of the states, in their sovereign capacity, is implied in calling a convention, and thus submitting that instrument to the people. But the people were at perfect liberty to accept or reject it; and their act was final. It required not the affirmance, and could not be negatived, by the state governments. The constitution, when thus adopted, was of complete obligation, and bound the state sovereignties. . . .

The government of the Union, then (whatever may be the influence of this fact on the case), is, emphatically, and truly, a government of the people. In form and in substance it emanates from them. Its powers are granted by them, and are to be exercised directly on them, and for their benefit.

This government is acknowledged by all to be one of enumerated powers. The principle, that it can exercise only the powers granted to it, would seem too apparent to have required to be enforced by all those arguments which its enlightened friends, while it was depending before the people, found it necessary to urge. That principle is now universally admitted. But the question respecting the extent of the powers actually granted, is perpetually arising, and will probably continue to arise, as long as our system shall exist. . . .

If any one proposition could command the universal assent of mankind, we might expect it would be this—that the government of the Union, though limited in its powers, is supreme within its sphere of action. This would seem to result necessarily from its nature. It is the government of all; its powers are delegated by all; it represents all, and acts for all. Though any one state may be willing to control its operations, no state is willing to allow others to control them. The nation, on those subjects on which it can act, must necessarily bind its component parts. But this question is not left to mere reason; the people have, in express terms, decided it by saying, "this constitution, and the laws of the United States, which shall be made in pursuance thereof," "shall be the supreme law of the land," and by requiring that the members of the state legislatures, and the officers of the executive and judicial departments of the states shall take the oath of fidelity to it.

The government of the United States, then, though limited in its powers, is supreme; and its laws, when made in pursuance of the constitution, form the supreme law of the land, "anything in the constitution or laws of any state to the contrary notwithstanding."

Among the enumerated powers, we do not find that of establishing a bank or creating a corporation. But there is no phrase in the instrument which, like the articles of confederation, excludes incidental or implied powers; and which requires that everything granted shall be expressly and minutely described. Even the 10th amendment, which was framed for the purpose of quieting the excessive jealousies which had been excited, omits the word "expressly," and declares only that the powers "not delegated to the United States, nor prohibited to the states, are reserved to the states or to the people;" thus leaving the question, whether the particular power which may become the subject of contest, has been delegated to the one government, or prohibited to the other, to depend on a fair construction of the whole instrument. The men who drew and adopted this amendment had experienced the embarrassments resulting from the insertion of this word in the articles of confederation, and probably omitted it to avoid those embarrassments. A constitution, to contain an accurate detail of all the subdivisions of which its great powers will admit, and of all the means by which they may be carried into execution, would partake of the prolixity of a legal code, and could scarcely be embraced by the human mind. It would probably never be understood by the public. Its nature, therefore, requires, that only its great outlines should be marked, its important objects designated, and the minor ingredients which compose those objects be deduced from the nature of the objects themselves. That this idea was entertained by the framers of the American constitution, is not only to be inferred from the nature of the instrument, but from the language. Why else were some of the limitations, found in the ninth section of the 1st article, introduced? It is also, in some degree, warranted by their having omitted to use any restrictive term which might prevent its receiving a fair and just interpretation. In considering this question, then, we must never forget, that it is a constitution we are expounding.

Although, among the enumerated powers of government, we do not find the word "bank" or "incorporation," we find the great powers to lay and collect taxes; to borrow money; to regulate commerce; to declare and conduct a war; and to raise and support armies and navies. The sword and the purse, all the external relations, and no inconsiderable portion of the industry of the nation, are entrusted to its government. It can never be pretended that these vast powers draw after them others of inferior importance, merely because they are inferior. Such an idea can never be advanced. But it may with great reason be contended, that a government, entrusted with such ample powers, on the due execution of which the happiness and prosperity of the nation so vitally depends, must also be entrusted with ample means for their execution. The power being given, it is the interest of the nation to facilitate its execution. It can never be their interest, and cannot be presumed to have been their intention, to clog and embarrass its execution by withholding the most appropriate means. . . . If, indeed, such be the mandate of the constitution, we have only to obey; but that instrument does not profess to enumerate the means by which the powers it confers may be executed; nor does it prohibit the creation of a corporation, if the existence of such a being be essential to the beneficial exercise of those powers. It is, then, the subject of fair inquiry, how far such means may be employed. . . .

The government which has a right to do an act, and has imposed on it the duty of performing that act, must, according to the dictates of reason, be allowed to select the means; and those who contend that it may not select any appropriate means, that one particular mode of effecting the object is excepted, take upon themselves the burden of establishing that exception. . . .

But the constitution of the United States has not left the right of Congress to employ the necessary means, for the execution of the powers conferred on the government, to general reasoning. To its enumeration of powers is added that of making "all laws which shall be necessary and proper, for carrying into execution the foregoing powers, and all other powers vested by this constitution, in the government of the United States, or in any department [or officer] thereof."

The counsel for the state of Maryland have urged various arguments, to prove that this clause, though in terms a grant of power, is not so in effect; but is really restrictive of the general right, which might otherwise be implied, of selecting means for executing the enumerated powers. . . .

But the argument on which most reliance is placed, is drawn from the peculiar language of this clause. Congress is not empowered by it to make all laws, which may have relation to the powers conferred on the government, but such only as may be "necessary and proper" for carrying them into execution. The word "necessary" is considered as controlling the whole sentence, and as limiting the right to pass laws for the execution of the granted powers, to such as are indispensable, and without which the power would be nugatory. Thus it excludes the choice of means, and leaves to Congress, in each case, that only which is most direct and simple.

Is it true, that this is the sense in which the word "necessary" is always used? Does it always import an absolute physical necessity, so strong that one thing, to which another may be termed necessary, cannot exist without that other? We think it does not. If reference be had to its use, in the common affairs of the world, or

in approved authors, we find that it frequently imports no more than that one thing is convenient, or useful, or essential to another. To employ the means necessary to an end, is generally understood as employing any means calculated to produce the end, and not as being confined to those single means, without which the end would be entirely unattainable. . . .

Let this be done in the case under consideration. The subject is the execution of those great powers on which the welfare of a nation essentially depends. It must have been the intention of those who gave these powers, to insure, as far as human prudence could insure, their beneficial execution. This could not be done by confiding the choice of means to such narrow limits as not to leave it in the power of Congress to adopt any which might be appropriate, and which were conducive to the end. This provision is made in a constitution intended to endure for ages to come, and consequently, to be adapted to the various crises of human affairs. To have prescribed the means by which government should, in all future time, execute its powers, would have been to change, entirely, the character of the instrument, and give it the properties of a legal code. It would have been an unwise attempt to provide, by immutable rules, for exigencies which, if foreseen at all, must have been seen dimly, and which can be best provided for as they occur. To have declared that the best means shall not be used, but those alone without which the power given would be nugatory, would have been to deprive the legislature of the capacity to avil itself of experience, to exercise its reason, and to accommodate its legislation to circumstances. If we apply this principle of construction to any of the powers of the government, we shall find it so pernicious in its operation that we shall be compelled to discard it. . . .

In ascertaining the sense in which the word "necessary" is used in this clause of the constitution, we may derive some aid from that with which it is associated. Congress shall have power "to make all laws which shall be necessary and proper to carry into execution" the powers of the government. If the word "necessary" was used in that strict and rigorous sense for which the counsel for the state of Maryland contend, it would be an extraordinary departure from the usual course of the human mind, as exhibited in composition, to add a word, the only possible effect of which is to qualify that strict and rigorous meaning; to present to the mind the idea of some choice of means of legislation not straightened and compressed within the narrow limits for which gentlemen contend.

But the argument which most conclusively demonstrates the error of the construction contended for by the counsel for the state of Maryland, is found on the intention of the convention, as manifested in the whole clause. . . .

. . . 1st. The clause is placed among the powers of Congress, not among the limitations on those powers.

2d. Its terms purport to enlarge, not to diminish the powers vested in the government. It purports to be an additional power, not a restriction on those already granted. No reason has been, or can be assigned for thus concealing an intention to narrow the discretion of the national legislature under words which purport to enlarge it. . . .

The result of the most careful and attentive consideration bestowed upon this clause is, that if it does not enlarge, it cannot be construed to restrain the powers of Congress, or to impair the right of the legislature to exercise its best judgment in the selection of measures to carry into execution the constitutional powers of the government. If no other motive for its insertion can be suggested, a sufficient one is found in the desire to remove all doubts respecting the right to legislate on that vast mass of incidental powers which must be involved in the constitution, if that instrument be not a splendid bauble.

We admit, as all must admit, that the powers of the government are limited, and that its limits are not to be transcended. But we think the sound construction of the constitution must allow to the national legislature that discretion, with respect to the means by which the powers it confers are to be carried into execution, which will enable that body to perform the high duties assigned to it, in the manner most beneficial to the people. Let the end be legitimate, let it be within the scope of the constitution, and all means which are appropriate, which are plainly adapted to that end, which are not prohibited, but consist with the letter and spirit of the constitution, are constitutional. . . .

If a corporation may be employed indiscriminately with other means to carry into execution the powers of the government, no particular reason can be assigned for excluding the use of a bank, if required for its fiscal operations. To use one, must be within the discretion of Congress, if it be an appropriate mode of executing the powers of government. That it is a convenient, a useful, and essential instrument in the prosecution of its fiscal operations, is not now a subject of controversy. . . .

But, were its necessity less apparent, none can deny its being an appropriate measure; and if it is, the degree of its necessity, as has been very justly observed, is to be discussed in another place. Should Congress, in the execution of its powers, adopt measures which are prohibited by the constitution; or should Congress, under the pretext of executing its powers, pass laws for the accomplishment of objects not entrusted to the government; it would become the painful duty of this tribunal, should a case requiring such a decision come before it, to say that such an act was not the law of the land. But where the law is not prohibited, and is really calculated to effect any of the objects entrusted to the government, to undertake here to inquire into the degree of its necessity, would be to pass the line which circumscribes the judicial department, and to tread on legislative ground. This court disclaims all pretensions to such a power. . . .

It being the opinion of the court that the act incorporating the bank is constitutional, and that the power of establishing a branch in the state of Maryland might be properly exercised by the bank itself, we proceed to inquire:

Whether the state of Maryland may, without violating the constitution, tax that branch?

That the power of taxation is one of vital importance; that it is retained by the states; that it is not abridged by the grant of a similar power to the government of the Union; that it is to be concurrently exercised by the two governments; are truths which have never been denied. But, such is the paramount character of the constitution that its capacity to withdraw any subject from the action of even this power, is admitted. The states are expressly forbidden to lay any duties on imports or exports, except what may be absolutely necessary for executing their inspection laws. If the obligation of this prohibition must be conceded—if it may restrain a state from the exercise of its taxing power on imports and exports—the same paramount character would seem to restrain, as it certainly may restrain, a state from such other exercise of this power, as is in its nature incompatible with, and repugnant to, the constitutional laws of the Union. A law, absolutely repugnant to another, as entirely repeals that other as if express terms of repeal were used.

On this ground, the counsel for the bank place its claim to be exempted from the power of a state to tax its operations. There is no express provision for the case, but the claim has been sustained on a principle which so entirely pervades the constitution, is so intermixed with the materials which compose it, so interwoven with its web, so blended with its texture, as to be incapable of being separated from it, without rending it into shreds.

This great principle is, that the constitution and the laws made in pursuance thereof are supreme; that they control the constitution and laws of the respective states, and cannot be controlled by them. From this, which may be almost termed an axiom, other propositions are adduced as corollaries, on the truth or error of which, and on their application to this case, the cause has been supposed to depend. These are,

1st. that a power to create implies a power to preserve. 2d. That a power to destroy, if wielded by a different hand, is hostile to, and incompatible with, these powers to create and to preserve. 3d. That where this repugnance exists, that authority which is supreme must control, not yield to that over which it is supreme. . . .

The power of Congress to create, and of course to continue, the bank, was the subject of the preceding part of this opinion; and is no longer to be considered as questionable.

That the power of taxing [the bank] by the states may be exercised so as to destroy it, is too obvious to be denied. But taxation is said to be an absolute power, which acknowledges no other limits than those expressly prescribed in the constitution, and like sovereign powers of every other description, is trusted to the discretion of those who use it. But the very terms of this argument admit that the sovereignty of the state, in the article of taxation itself, is subordinate to, and may be controlled by the constitution of the United States. How far it has been controlled by that instrument must be a question of construction. In making this construction, no principle not declared can be admissible, which would defeat the legitimate operations of a supreme government. It is of the very essence of supremacy to remove all obstacles to its action within its own sphere, and so to modify every power vested in subordinate governments as to exempt its own operations from their own influence. This effect need not be stated in terms. It is so involved in the declaration of supremacy, so necessarily implied in it, that the expression of it could not make it more certain. We must, therefore, keep it in view while construing the constitution.

The argument on the part of the state of Maryland, is, not that the states may directly resist a law of Congress, but that they may exercise their acknowledged powers upon it, and that the constitution leaves them this right in the confidence that they will not abuse it.

But we proceed to examine this argument,

and to subject it to the test of the constitution, we must be permitted to bestow a few considerations on the nature and extent of this original right of taxation, which is acknowledged to remain with the states. It is admitted that the power of taxing the people and their property is essential to the very existence of government, and may be legitimately exercised on the objects to which it is applicable, to the utmost extent to which the government may choose to carry it. The only security against the abuse of this power is found in the structure of the government itself. In imposing a tax the legislature acts upon its constituents. This is in general a sufficient security against erroneous and oppressive taxation.

The people of a state, therefore, give to their government a right of taxing themselves and their property, and as the exigencies of government cannot be limited, they prescribe no limits to the exercise of this right, resting confidently on the interest of the legislator, and on the influence of the constituent over their representative, to guard them against its abuse. But the means employed by the government of the Union have no such security, nor is the right of a state to tax them sustained by the same theory. Those means are not given by the people of a particular state, not given by the constituents of the legislature, which claim the right to tax them, but by the people of all the states. They are given by all, for the benefit of all—and upon theory, should be subjected to that government only which belongs to all. . . .

. . . All subjects over which the sovereign power of a state extends, are objects of taxation; but those over which it does not extend, are, upon the soundest principles, exempt from taxation. This proposition may almost be pronounced self-evident.

The sovereignty of a state extends to everything which exists by its own authority, or is introduced by its permission; but does it extend to those means which are employed by Congress to carry into execution—powers conferred on that body by the people of the United States?

We think it demonstrable that it does not. Those powers are not given by the people of a single state. They are given by the people of the United States, to a government whose laws, made in pursuance of the constitution, are declared to be supreme. Consequently, the people of a single state cannot confer a sovereignty which will extend over them. . . .

That the power to tax involves the power to destroy; that the power to destroy may defeat and render useless the power to create; that there is a plain repugnance, in conferring on one government a power to control the constitutional measures of another, which other, with respect to those very measures, is declared to be supreme over that which exerts the control, are propositions not to be denied. But all inconsistencies are to be reconciled by the magic of the word CONFIDENCE. Taxation, it is said, does not necessarily and unavoidably destroy. To carry it to the excess of destruction would be an abuse, to presume which, would banish that confidence which is essential to all government.

But is this a case of confidence? Would the people of any one state trust those of another with a power to control the most insignificant operations of their state government? We know they would not. Why, then, should we suppose that the people of any one state should be willing to trust those of another with a power to control the operations of a government to which they have confided the most important and most valuable interests? In the legislature of the Union alone, are all represented. The legislature of the Union alone, therefore, can be trusted by the people with the power of controlling measures which concern all, in the confidence that it will not be abused. This, then, is not a case of confidence, and we must consider it as it really is.

If we apply the principle for which the state of Maryland contends, to the constitution generally, we shall find it capable of changing totally the character of that instrument. We shall find it capable of arresting all the measures of the government, and of prostrating it at the foot of the states. The American people have de-clared their constitution, and the laws made in pursuance thereof, to be supreme; but this prin-ciple would transfer the supremacy, in fact, to the states. . . .

. . . If the controlling power of the states be established; if their supremacy as to taxation be acknowledged; what is to restrain their exercis-ing this control in any shape they may please to give it? Their sovereignty is not confined to tax-ation. That is not the only mode in which it might be displayed. The question is, in truth, a question of supremacy; and if the right of the states to tax the means employed by the general government be conceded, the declaration that the constitution, and the laws made in pur-suance thereof, shall be the supreme law of the land, is empty and unmeaning declamation. . . .

It has also been insisted, that, as the power of taxation in the general and state governments is acknowledged to be concurrent, every argu-ment which would sustain the right of the gen-eral government to tax banks chartered by the states, will equally sustain the right of the states to tax banks chartered by the general govern-ment.

But the two cases are not on the same reason. The people of all the states have created the general government, and have conferred upon it the general power of taxation. The people of all the states, and the states themselves, are rep-resented in Congress, and, by their representa-tives, exercise this power. When they tax the chartered institutions of the states, they tax their constituents; and these taxes must be uniform. But, when a state taxes the operations of the government of the United States, it acts upon institutions created, not by their own constitu-ents, but by people over whom they claim no con-trol. It acts upon the measures of a government created by others as well as themselves, for the

benefit of others in common with themselves. The difference is that which always exists, and always must exist, between the action of the whole on a part, and the action of a part on the whole—between the laws of a government de-clared to be supreme, and those of a government which, when in opposition to those laws, is not supreme.

But if the full application of this argument could be admitted, it might bring into question the right of Congress to tax the state banks, and could not prove the right of the states to tax the Bank of the United States.

The court has bestowed on this subject its most deliberate consideration. The result is a conviction that the states have no power, by tax-ation or otherwise, to retard, impede, burden, or in any manner control the operations of the constitutional laws enacted by Congress to carry into execution the powers vested in the general government. This is, we think, the un-avoidable consequence of that supremacy which the Constitution has declared.

We are unanimously of opinion, that the law passed by the legislature of Maryland, imposing a tax on the Bank of the United States, is un-constitutional and void.

This opinion does not deprive the states of any resources which they originally possessed. It does not extend to a tax paid by the real prop-erty of the bank, in common with other real property within the state, nor to a tax imposed on the interest which the citizens of Maryland may hold in this institution, in common with other property of the same description through-out the state. But this is a tax on the operations of the bank, and is, consequently, a tax on the operation of an instrument employed by the government of the Union to carry its powers into execution. Such a tax must be unconstitu-tional.

Note: The "necessary and proper" power has been extensively used and upheld. See, for example, *United States* v. *Oregon,* 366 U.S. 643 (1961), which involved rival state and federal claims to the property of a deceased Oregon resident who died in a federal veterans' hospital, leaving no heirs and no will. By Oregon law his property would escheat to the state; by federal law it would go to the federal government for the benefit of military personnel. The Court upheld the federal law as "necessary and proper" with respect to the military power.

Lichter v. *United States,* above, upheld as "necessary and proper," vis-à-vis the military power, federal authority to renegotiate war supply contracts to prevent "excess profits."

Julliard v. *Greenman,* 110 U.S. 421 (1884), upheld congressional authorization of "paper money" as incidental to the express power to tax, borrow, and "coin money."

4

Federalism: The Nation and the States in the Making of Public Policy (State Authority)

STATE REGULATION OF INTERSTATE COMMERCE

H. P. Hood & Sons v. *Du Mond* (excerpt)
336 U.S. 525 (1949)

. . . [The] principle that our economic unit is the Nation, which alone has the gamut of powers necessary to control of the economy, including the vital power of erecting customs barriers against foreign competition, has as its corollary that the states are not separable economic units. As the Court said in *Baldwin* v. *G. A. F. Seelig, Inc.,* 294 U.S. 511, 527, "What is ultimate is the principle that one state in its dealings with another may not place itself in a position of economic isolation." In so speaking it but followed the principle that the state may not use its admitted powers to protect the health and safety of its people as a basis for suppressing competition. In *Buck* v. *Kuykendall,* 267 U.S. 307, the Court struck down a state act because, in the language of Mr. Justice Brandeis, "Its primary purpose is not regulation with a view to safety or to conservation of the highways, but the prohibition of competition." The same argument here advanced, that limitation of competition would itself contribute to safety and conserva-

tion, and therefore indirectly serve an end permissible to the state, was there declared "not sound." 267 U.S. 307, 315. It is no better here. . . .

The material success that has come to inhabitants of the states which make up this federal free trade unit has been the most impressive in the history of commerce, but the established interdependence of the states only emphasizes the necessity of protecting interstate movement of goods against local burdens and repressions. . . .

Our system, fostered by the Commerce Clause, is that every farmer and every craftsman shall be encouraged to produce by the certainty that he will have free access to every market in the Nation, that no home embargoes will withhold his export, and no [sister] state will by customs duties or regulations exclude them. Likewise, every consumer may look to the free competition from every producing area in the Nation to protect him from exploitation by any. Such was the vision of the Founders; such has been the doctrine of this Court which has given it reality. . . .

Hughes v. *Oklahoma* (excerpt)
99 S. Ct. 1727 (1979)

The few simple words of the Commerce Clause—"The Congress shall have Power . . . To regulate Commerce . . . among the several States . . ."—reflected a central concern of the Framers that was an immediate reason for calling the Constitutional Convention: the conviction that in order to succeed, the new union would have to avoid the tendencies toward economic Balkanization that had plagued relations among the Colonies and later among the States under the Articles of Confederation. See *H. P. Hood & Sons, Inc.* v. *Du Mond,* 336 U.S. 525, 533–534 (1949). The Commerce Clause has accordingly been interpreted by this Court not only as an authorization for congressional action, but, even in the absence of a conflicting federal statute, as a restriction on permissible state regulation. The cases defining the scope of permissible state regulation in areas of congressional silence reflect an often controversial evolution of rules to accommodate federal and state interests.

Gibbons v. *Ogden*
See p. 93, above.

Willson v. *Blackbird Creek Marsh Co.*
2 Peters 245 (1829)

Delaware authorized a dam across a small but navigable stream. Its purpose was to dry up a marsh or swampy area and thus eliminate the risk of malaria. No doubt this would also improve property values. In upholding the dam the Marshall Court seems to distinguish between state commercial regulations (*Gibbons*) and local health or safety (police power) regulations.

Mr. Chief Justice Marshall delivered the opinion of the Court. . . .

The act of assembly by which the plaintiffs were authorized to construct their dam, shows plainly that this is one of those many creeks, passing through a deep level marsh adjoining the Delaware, up which the tide flows for some distance. The value of the property on its banks must be enhanced by excluding the water from the marsh, and the health of the inhabitants probably improved. Measures calculated to produce these objects, provided they do not come into collision with the powers of the general government, are undoubtedly within those which are reserved to the states. But the measure authorised by this act stops a navigable creek, and must be supposed to abridge the rights of those who have been accustomed to use it. . . .

The counsel for the plaintiffs in error insist that it comes in conflict with the power of the United States "to regulate commerce with foreign nations and among the several states."

If Congress had passed any act which bore upon the case; any act in execution of the power to regulate commerce, the object of which was to control state legislation over those small navigable creeks into which the tide flows, and which abound throughout the lower country of the middle and southern states; we should feel not much difficulty in saying that a state law coming in conflict with such act would be void. But Congress has passed no such act. The repugnancy of the law of Delaware to the constitution is placed entirely on its repugnancy to the power to regulate commerce with foreign nations and among the several states; a power which has not been so exercised as to affect the question.

We do not think that the act empowering the Black Bird Creek Marsh Company to place a dam across the creeks, can, under all the circumstances of the case, be considered as repugnant to the power to regulate commerce in its dormant state, or as being in conflict with any law passed on the subject.

Note: In *Gibbons*, Daniel Webster had argued that as the Commerce Clause "implied in its nature, full power over the thing to be regulated, it excludes, necessarily, the action of all others that would perform the same operation on the same thing." Marshall responded crypitcally, "There is great force in this argument, and the Court is not satisfied that it has been refuted." But decision on the point was avoided. Later other Justices, particularly President Jackson's appointees, vigorously repudiated Marshall's suggestion of the exclusive nature of the national power. As Chief Justice Taney observed in *The License Cases*, 5 Howard 504, 579 (1847):

. . . it appears to me to be very clear, that the mere grant of power to the general government cannot, upon any just principles of construction, be construed to be an absolute prohibition to the exercise of any power over the same subject by the states. The controlling and supreme power over commerce with foreign nations and the several states is undoubtedly conferred upon Congress. Yet in my judgment, the State may nevertheless . . . make regulations for its own territory; and such regulations are valid unless they come in conflict with a law of Congress.

Whether the national power is exclusive, as Marshall apparently thought, or concurrent, as Taney clearly supposed, is one of the classic problems of constitutional law. The exclusive view in effect means that the affirmative grant of the commerce power to Congress implies a negative: a denial of such power to the states. The concurrent view admits no negative implications; that is, the Commerce Clause merely authorizes Congress to act. Such negatives as the Founding Fathers saw fit to impose on the states are to be found in Article I, Section 10 of the Constitution, and no general denial or commercial powers for the states is included there.

Which of the two conflicting views has prevailed? After years of conflict and uncertainty a compromise, silently acquiesced in by Taney, was reached in *Cooley* v. *Board of Wardens* (below): ". . . the power to regulate commerce, embraces a vast field, containing not only many, but exceedingly various subjects, quite unlike in nature; some imperatively demanding a single uniform rule . . . ; and some . . . as imperatively demanding that diversity, which alone can meet the local necessities. . . ."

It followed that in the one category the commerce power was exclusively national, in the other it was concurrent. In either situation, of course, Congress may legislate, if it so desires! The point of the *Cooley* rule is that *state* regulation of interstate commerce is never permissible in the one category but is permissible in the other, provided Congress has not exercised its power in a manner inconsistent with state regulation. *Cooley* involved a Pennsylvania regulation of pilotage in the Philadelphia harbor. Of course, the measure applied to interstate and foreign commerce. But in view of the great diversity of harbor conditions in the several ports throughout the country, and in the absence of any congressional effort to deal with the problem, state regulation was sustained. A modern application of the *Cooley* approach in a context amenable to local treatment is seen in *California* v. *Thompson,* and in a context susceptible only of uniform, national treatment in *Southern Pacific* v. *Arizona* (below).

Cooley v. *Board of Port Wardens*
12 Howard 299 (1851)

A Pennsylvania law provided that all ships entering or leaving the Philadelphia harbor must hire and use a local pilot. Failure to do so entailed a fine payable to a welfare fund for pilots and their dependents.

Mr. Justice Curtis delivered the opinion of the court: . . .

That the power to regulate commerce includes the regulation of navigation, we consider settled. And when we look to the nature of the service performed by pilots, to the relations which that service and its compensations bear to navigation between the several States, and between the ports of the United States and foreign countries, we are brought to the conclusion, that the regulation of the qualifications of pilots, of the modes and times of offering and rendering their services, of the responsibilities which shall rest upon them, of the powers they shall possess, of the compensation they may demand, and of the penalties by which their rights and duties may be enforced, do constitute regulations of navigation, and consequently of commerce, within the just meaning of this clause of the Constitution. . . .

If the law of Pennsylvania, now in question, had been in existence at the date of this Act of Congress (quoted below), we might hold it to have been adopted by Congress, and thus made a law of the United States, and so valid. Because this Act does, in effect, give the force of an Act of Congress, to the then existing State laws on this subject, so long as they should continue unrepealed by the State which enacted them.

But the law on which these actions were founded was not enacted till 1803. What effect, then, can be attributed to so much of the Act of 1789 as declares that pilots shall continue to be regulated in conformity "with such laws as the States may respectively hereafter enact for the purpose, until further legislative provision shall be made by Congress"?

If the States were divested of the power to legislate on this subject by the grant of the commercial power to Congress, it is plain this Act could not confer upon them power thus to legislate. If the Constitution excluded the States from making any law regulating commerce, certainly Congress cannot regrant, or in any manner reconvey to the States that power. And yet this Act of 1789 gives its sanction only to laws enacted by the States. This necessarily implies a constitutional power to legislate; for only a rule created by the sovereign power of a State acting in its legislative capacity, can be deemed a law, enacted by a State; and if the State has so limited its sovereign power that it no longer extends to a particular subject, manifestly it cannot, in any proper sense, be said to enact laws thereon. Entertaining these views we are brought directly and unavoidably to the consideration of the question, whether the grant of the commercial power to Congress, did *per se* deprive the States of all power to regulate pilots. This question has never been decided by this court, nor, in our judgment, has any case depending upon all the considerations which must govern this one, come before this court. The grant of commercial power to Congress does not contain any terms which expressly exclude the States from exercising an authority over its subject matter. If they are excluded it must be because the nature of the power, thus granted to Congress, requires that a similar authority should not exist in the States. . . .

The diversities of opinion, therefore, which have existed on this subject, have arisen from the different views taken of the nature of this power. But when the nature of a power like this is spoken of, when it is said that the nature of the power requires that it should be exercised exclusively by Congress, it must be intended to refer to the subjects of that power, and to say they are of such a nature as to require exclusive legislation by Congress. Now the power to regulate commerce, embraces a vast field, containing not only many, but exceedingly various subjects, quite unlike in their nature; some imperatively demanding a single uniform rule, operating equally on the commerce of the United States in every port; and some, like the subject now in question, as imperatively demanding that diversity, which alone can meet the local necessities of navigation.

Either absolutely to affirm, or deny, that the nature of this power requires exclusive legislation by Congress, is to lose sight of the nature of the subjects of this power, and to assert concerning all of them, what is really applicable but to a part. Whatever subjects of this power are in their nature national, or admit only of one uniform system, or plan of regulation, may justly be said to be of such a nature as to require exclusive legislation by Congress. That this cannot be affirmed of laws for the regulation of pilots and pilotage is plain. The Act of 1789 contains a clear and authoritative declaration by the first Congress, that the nature of this subject is such, that until Congress should find it necessary to exert its power, it should be left to the legislation of the States; that it is local and not national; that it is likely to be the best provided for, not by one system, or plan of regulations, but by as many as the legislative discretion of the several States should deem applicable to the local peculiarities of the ports within their limits.

Viewed in this light, so much of this Act of 1789 as declares that pilots shall continue to be regulated "by such laws as the States may respectively hereafter enact for that purpose," instead of being held to be inoperative, as an attempt to confer on the States a power to legislate, of which the Constitution had deprived them, is allowed an appropriate and important signification. It manifests the understanding of Congress, at the outset of the government, that the nature of this subject is not such as to require its exclusive legislation. The practice of the States, and of the national government, has been in conformity with this declaration, from the origin of the national government to this time; and the nature of the subject, when examined, is such as to leave no doubt of the superior fitness and propriety, not to say the absolute necessity, of different systems or regulation, drawn from local knowledge and experience, and conformed to local wants. How, then, can we say, that by the mere grant of power to regulate commerce, the States are deprived of all the power to legislate on this subject, because from the nature of the power the legislation of Congress must be exclusive. . . .

It is the opinion of a majority of the court that the mere grant to Congress of the power to regulate commerce, did not deprive the States of power to regulate pilots, and that although Congress has legislated on this subject, its legislation manifests an intntion, with a single exception, not to regulate this subject, but to leave its regulation to the several States. To these precise questions, which are all we are called on to decide, this opinion must be understood to be confined. It does not extend to the question what other subjects, under the commercial power, are within the exclusive control of Congress, or may be regulated by the States in the absence of all congressional legislation; nor to the general question how far any regulation of a subject by Congress may be deemed to operate as an exclusion of all legislation by the States upon the same subject. . . .

If the grant of commercial power in the Constitution has deprived the States of all power to legislate for the regulation of pilots, if their laws on this subject are mere usurpations upon the exclusive power of the general government, and utterly void it may be doubted whether Congress could, with propriety, recognize them as laws, and adopt them as its own acts; and how are the Legislatures of the States to proceed in the future, to watch over and amend these laws, as the progressive wants of a growing commerce will require, when the members of those legislatures are made aware that they cannot legislate on this subject without violating the oaths they have taken to support the Constitution of the United States?

We are of the opinion that this State law was enacted by virtue of a power, residing in the State to legislate; that it is not in conflict with any law of Congress; that it does not interefere with any system which Congress has established by making regulations, or by intentionally leaving individuals to their own unrestricted action; that this law is therefore valid and the judgment of the Supreme Court of Pennsylvania in each case must be affirmed.

Mr. Justice McLean and Mr. Justice Wayne dissented; and Mr. Justice Daniel, although he concurred in the judgment of the Court, yet dissented from its reasoning.

Mr. Justice McLean: . . .

That a state may regulate foreign commerce, or commerce among the states, is a doctrine which has been advanced by individual judges of this Court; but never before, I believe, has such a power been sanctioned by the decision of this Court. In this case, the power to regulate pilots is admitted to belong to the commecial power of Congress; and yet it is held, that a state, by virtue of its inherent power, may regulate the subject, until such regulation shall be annulled by Congress. This is the principle es-

tablished by this decision. Its language is guarded, in order to apply the decision only to the case before the Court. But such restrictions can never operate, so as to render the principle inapplicable to other cases. And it is in this light that the decision is chiefly to be regretted. . . .

From this race of legislation between Congress and the states, and between the states, if this principle be maintained, will arise a conflict similar to that which existed before the adoption of the Constitution. . . .

. . . Congress, to whom the subject peculiarly belongs, should have been applied to, and no doubt it would have adopted the act of the state.

Mr. Justice Daniel: . . .

The true question here is, whether the power to enact pilot laws is appropriate and necessary, or rather more appropriate and necessary to the state or the federal governments. It being conceded that this power has been exercised by the states from their very dawn of existence; that it can be practically and beneficially applied by the local authorities only; it being conceded, as it must be, that the power to pass pilot laws, as such, has not been in any express terms delegated to Congress, and does not necessarily conflict with the right to establish commercial regulations, I am forced to conclude that this is an original and inherent power in the states, and not one to be merely tolerated, or held subject to the sanction of the federal government.

Di Santo v. *Pennsylvania*
273 U.S. 34 (1927)

For years the Court often seemed to forget the *Cooley* test. Thus it frequently decided *Cooley*-type problems in terms of whether the challenged state regulation was a "burden," an "undue burden," or a "substantial burden" on interstate commerce; or whether its effect was "direct" or merely "indirect"; or whether indeed it fell "on" interstate commerce, or was merely an exercise of the state's "police power." Were these different ways of expressing the *Cooley* test, or did they constitute a new approach—a reflection, perhaps, of laissez-faire, as in *Lochner* v. *New York* (below, Chapter 6).

The problem is illustrated in the present case. It arose when Di Santo violated a state statute which—for reasons stated in the Brandeis dissent—sought by licensing to prevent fraud in the sale of steamship tickets. Di Santo was convicted for violating the statute.

Mr. Justice Butler delivered the opinion of the Court. . . .

The soliciting of passengers and the sale of steamship tickets and orders for passage between the United States and Europe constitute a well-recognized part of foreign commerce. . . . A state statute which by its necessary operation directly interferes with or burdens foreign commerce is a prohibited regulation and invalid, regardless of the purpose with which it was passed. . . . Such legislation cannot be sustained as an exertion of the police power of the state to prevent possible fraud. . . . The Congress has complete and paramount authority to regulate foreign commerce and, by appropriate measures, to protect the public against the frauds of those who sell these tickets and orders. The sales here in question are related to foreign commerce as directly as are sales made in ticket offices maintained by the carriers and operated by their servants and employees. The license fee and other things imposed by the act on plaintiff in error, who initiates for his principals a transaction in foreign commerce, constitute a direct burden on that commerce. This case is controlled by *Texas Transport Co.* v. *New Orleans*, 264 U.S. 150, and *McCall* v. *California*, 136 U.S. 104.

Judgment reversed.

Mr. Justice Brandeis, with whom Mr. Justice Holmes concurs, dissenting:

The statute is an exertion of the police power of the state. Its evident purpose is to prevent a particular species of fraud and imposition found to have been practiced in Pennsylvania upon persons of small means, unfamiliar with our language and institutions. Much of the immigration into the United States is effected by arrangements made here for remittance of the means of travel. The individual immigrant is often an advance guard. After gaining a foothold here, he has his wife and children, aged parents, brothers, sisters or other relatives follow. To this end he remits steamship tickets or orders for transportation. The purchase of the tickets involves trust in the dealer. This is so not only because of the nature of the transaction, but also because a purchaser when unable to pay the whole price at one time makes successive deposits on account, the ticket or order not being delivered until full payment is made. The facilities for remitting both cash and steamship tickets are commonly furnished by private bankers of the same nationality as the immigrant. It was natural that the supervision of persons engaged in the business of supplying steamship tickets should be committed by the statute to the commissioner of banking.

Although the purchase made is of an ocean steamship ticket, the transaction regulated is wholly intrastate—as much so as if the purchase were of local real estate or of local theater tickets. There is no purpose on the part of the state to regulate foreign commerce. The statute is not an obstruction to foreign commerce. It does not discriminate against foreign commerce. It places no direct burden upon such commerce. It does not affect the commerce except indirectly. Congress could, of course, deal with the subject, because it is connected with foreign commerce. But it has not done so. Nor has it legislated on any allied subject. Thus, there can be no contention that Congress has occupied the field. And obviously, also, this is not a case in which the silence of Congress can be interpreted as a prohibition of state action—as a declaration that in the sale of ocean steamship tickets fraud may be practiced without let or hindrance. If Pennsylvania must submit to seeing its citizens defrauded, it is not because Congress has so willed, but because the Constitution so commands. I cannot believe that it does. . . .

Mr. Justice Stone, dissenting: . . .

In this case the traditional test of the limit of state action by inquiring whether the interference with commerce is direct or indirect seems to me too mechanical, too uncertain in its application, and too remote from actualities, to be of value. In thus making use of the expressions, "direct" and "indirect interference" with commerce, we are doing little more than using labels to describe a result rather than any trustworthy formula by which it is reached. . . .

I am not persuaded that the regulation here is more than local in character or that it interposes any barrier to commerce. Until Congress undertakes the protection of local communities from the dishonesty of the sellers of steamship tickets, it would seem that there is no adequate ground for holding that the regulation here involved is a prohibited interference with commerce.

Mr. Justice Holmes and Mr. Justice Brandeis concur in this opinion.

California v. *Thompson*
313 U.S. 109 (1941)

Californa law requires the licensing and bonding of those who sell, or negotiate for, transportation over the public highways of the state. Thompson was convicted of violating this law with respect to interstate commerce.

Mr. Justice Stone delivered the opinion of the Court. . . .

As this Court has often had occasion to point out, the Commerce Clause, in conferring on Congress power to regulate commerce, did not wholly withdraw from the states the power to regulate matters of local concern with respect to which Congress has not exercised its power, even though the regulation affects interstate commerce. Ever since *Willson* v. *Blackbird Creek Marsh Co.*, 2 Pet. 245, and *Cooley* v. *Board of Port Wardens*, 12 How. 299, it has been recognized that there are matters of local concern, the regulation of which unavoidably involves some regulation of interstate commerce, but which because of their local character and their number and diversity may naver be adequately dealt with by Congress. Because of their local character, also, there is wide scope for local regulation without impairing the uniformity of control of the national commerce in matters of national concern and without materially obstructing the free flow of commerce which were the principal objects sought to be secured by the Commerce Clause. Notwithstanding the Commerce Clause, such regulation in the absence of Congressional action has, for the most part, been left to the states by the decisions of this Court, subject only to other applicable constitutional restraints. See cases collected in *Di Santo* v. *Pennsylvania, supra*, 273 U.S. 40.

A state may license trainmen engaged in interstate commerce in order to insure their skill and fitness. *Smith* v. *Alabama*, 124 U.S. 465; *Nashville, Chattanooga & St. Louis Railroad* v. *Alabama*, 128 U.S. 96. It may define the size of crews manning interstate trains. *Chicago, R. I. & P. R. Co.* v. *Arkansas*, 219 U.S. 453; *Missouri Pacific R. Co.* v. *Norwood*, 283 U.S. 249, and prescribe regulations for payment of their wages. *Erie R. Co.* v. *Williams,* 233 U.S. 685. It may require interstate passenger cars to be heated and guard posts to be placed on bridges of an interstate railroad. *New York, New Haven & Hartford R. Co.* v. *New York,* 165 U.S. 628. It may limit the speed of interstate trains within city limits. *Erb* v. *Morasch,* 177 U.S. 584. It may require an interstate railroad to eliminate grade crossings. *Erie R. Co.* v. *Board of Public Utility Commissioners,* 254 U.S. 394, 409, 412. It may pass local quarantine laws applicable to merchandise moving in interstate commerce as a means of protecting local health. *Morgan's etc., S. S. Co.* v. *Board of Health of State of Louisiana,* 118 U.S. 455; *Compagnie Française* v. *Board of Health,* 186 U.S. 380. It may regulate and protect the safe and convenient use of its harbors and navigable waterways unless there is conflict with some act of Congress. *Willson* v. *Blackbird Creek Marsh Co., supra,* see *Clyde Mallory Lines* v. *State of Alabama,* 296 U.S. 261. It may regulate pilots and pilotage in its harbors. *Cooley* v. *Board of Port Wardens, supra.* Where, as here, Congress has not entered the field, a state may pass inspection laws and regulations applicable to articles of interstate commerce designed to safeguard the inhabitants of the state from fraud, provided only that the regulation neither discriminates against nor substantially obstructs the commerce. *Turner* v. *Maryland,* 107 U.S. 38; *Plumley* v. *Massachusetts,* 155 U.S. 461; *Patapsco Guana Co.* v. *Board of Agriculture of North Carolina,* 171 U.S. 345, 357, 358; *Savage* v. *Jones,* 225 U.S. 501; see, also, *Minnesota Rate cases,* 230 U.S. 352 398–412, 33 S.Ct. 729, 739–745, and cases cited; *South Carolina State Highway Dept.* v. *Barnwell Bros.,* 303 U.S. 177, 185–191, and cases cited.

The present case is not one of prohibiting interstate commerce or licensing it on conditions which restrict or obstruct it. Cf. *Crutcher* v. *Kentucky,* 141 U.S. 47; *Dahnke-Walker Co.* v. *Bondurant,* 257 U.S. 282. For here the regulation is applied to one who is not himself engaged in the transportation but who acts only as broker or intermediary in negotiating a transportation contract between the passengers and the carrier. The license required of those engaged in such business is not conditioned upon any control or restriction of the movement of the traffic interstate but only on the good character and responsibility of those engaged locally as transportation brokers.

Fraudulent or unconscionable conduct of those so engaged which is injurious to their patrons, is peculiarly a subject of local concern and the appropriate subject of local regulation. In every practical sense regulation of such conduct is beyond the effective reach of Congressional action. Unless some measure of local control is permissible, it must go largely unregulated. In any case until Congress undertakes its regulation we can find no adequate basis for saying that the Constitution, interpreted as a working instrument of government, has foreclosed regulation, such as the present, by local authority.

In *Di Santo* v. *Pennsylvania,* this Court took a different view. Following what it conceived to be the reasoning of *McCall* v. *California,* 136 U.S. 104, it held that a Pennsylvania statute requiring others than railroad or steamship companies, who engage in the interstate sale of steamship tickets or of orders for transportation to and from foreign countries, to procure a license by giving proof of good moral character and filing a bond as security against fraud and misrepresentation to purchasers, was an infringement of the Commerce Clause. Since the decision in that case this Court has been repeatedly called upon to examine the constitutionality of numerous local regulations affecting interstate motor vehicle traffic. It has uniformly held that in the absence of pertinent Congressional legislation there is constitutional power in the states to regulate interstate commerce by motor vehicle wherever it affects the safety of the public or the safety and convenient use of its highways, provided only that the regulation does not in any other respect unnecessarily obstruct interstate commerce. *Continental Baking Co.* v. *Woodring,* 286 U.S. 352, 371;

Bradley v. *Public Utilities Commission*, 289 U.S. 92, 95; see *South Carolina State Highway Dept.* v. *Barnwell Bros., supra,* and cases cited; *H. P. Welch Co.* v. *New Hampshire*, 306 U.S. 79, 83; *Eichholz* v. *Public Service Commission*, 306 U.S. 268; *Maurer* v. *Hamilton*, 309 U.S. 598, 603; and see *Ziffrin, Inc.* v. *Reeves*, 308 U.S. 132.

If there is authority in the state, in the exercise of its police power, to adopt such regulations affecting interstate transportation, it must be deemed to possess the power to regulate the negotiations for such transportation where they affect matters of local concern which are in other respects within state regulatory power, and where the regulation does not infringe the national interest in maintaining the free flow of commerce and in preserving uniformity in the regulation of the commerce in matters of national concern. See *Hartford Accident & Indemnity Co.* v. *Illinois*, 298 U.S. 155.

The decision in the *Di Santo* case was a departure from this principle which has been recognized since *Cooley* v. *Board of Port Wardens, supra.* It cannot be reconciled with later decisions of this Court which have likewise recognized and applied the principle, and it can no longer be regarded as controlling authority.

Quaere: Does *Thompson*—in addition to overruling *Di Santo*—suggest via the numerous cases it cites that in practice the *Cooley* doctrine is quite lenient with respect to local "police power" regulations (i.e., those concerning health, safety, or fraud)—as distinct from commercial regulations calculated to achieve local economic advantages at the expense of outsiders? Does one find a similar dichotomy in Chief Justice Marshall's opinion in *Blackbird Creek Marsh* vis-à-vis his opinion in *Gibbons?*

Southern Pacific Co. v. *Arizona*
325 U.S. 761 (1945)

A n Arizona statute of 1912 prohibited trains in excess of 70 freight, or 14 passenger, cars within that state. The Southern Pacific was prosecuted for violating this limitation.

Mr. Chief Justice Stone delivered the opinion of the Court: . . .

Although the commerce clause conferred on the national government power to regulate commerce, its possession of the power does not exclude all state power of regulation. Ever since *Willson* v. *Blackbird Creek Marsh Co.*, 2 Pet. 245, and *Cooley* v. *Board of Port Wardens*, 12 How. 299, it has been recognized that, in the absence of conflicting legislation by Congress, there is a residuum of power in the state to make laws governing matters of local concern which nevertheless in some measure affect interstate commerce or even, to some extent, regulate it. . . .

But ever since *Gibbons* v. *Ogden*, 9 Wheat. 1, the states have not been deemed to have authority to impede substantially the free flow of commerce from state to state, or to regulate those phases of the national commerce which, because of the need of national uniformity, demand that their regulation, if any, be prescribed by a single authority.

For a hundred years it has been accepted constitutional doctrine that the commerce clause, without the aid of Congressional legislation, thus affords some protection from state legislation inimical to the national commerce, and that in such cases, where Congress has not acted, this Court, and not the state legislature, is under the commerce clause the final arbiter between the competing demands of state and national interests. . . .

Congress has undoubted power to redefine

the distribution of power over interstate commerce. It may either permit the states to regulate the commerce in a manner which would otherwise not be permissible. . . . or exclude state regulation even of matters of peculiarly local concern which nevertheless affect interstate commerce. . . .[1]

But in general Congress has left it to the courts to formulate the rules thus interpreting the commerce clause in its application, doubtless because it has appreciated the destructive consequences to the commerce of the nation if their protection were withdrawn, *Gwin, etc., Inc.* v. *Henneford* [305 U.S. 434], and has been aware that in their application state laws will not be invalidated without the support of relevant factual material which will "afford a sure basis" for an informed judgment. *Terminal R. Association* v. *Brotherhood of Railroad Trainmen* [318 U.S. 8]; *Southern R. Co.* v. *King*, 217 U.S. 524. Meanwhile, Congress has accommodated its legislation, as have the states, to these rules as an established feature of our constitutional system. There has thus been left to the states wide scope for the regulation of matters of local state concern, even though it in some measure affects the commerce, provided it does not materially restrict the free flow of commerce across state lines, or interfere with it in matters with respect to which uniformity of regulation is of predominant national concern.

Hence the matters for ultimate determination here are the nature and extent of the burden which the state regulation of interstate trains, adopted as a safety measure, imposes on interstate commerce, and whether the relative weights of the state and national interests involved are such as to make inapplicable the rule, generally observed, that the free flow of interstate commerce and its freedom from local restraints in matters requiring uniformity of regulation are interests safeguarded by the commerce clause from state inference.

While this Court is not bound by the findings

of the state court, and may determine for itself the facts of a case upon which an asserted federal right depends, *Hooven & Allison* v. *Evatt*, *supra*, p. 659, and cases cited, the facts found by the state trial court showing the nature of the interstate commerce involved, and the effect upon it of the train limit law, are not seriously questioned. Its findings with respect to the need for and effect of the statute as a safety measure, although challenged in some particulars which we do not regard as material to our decision, are likewise supported by evidence. Taken together the findings supply an adequate basis for decision of the constitutional issue.

The findings show that the operation of long trains, that is trains of more than fourteen passengers and more than seventy freight cars, is standard practice over the main lines of the railroads of the United States, and that, if the length of trains is to be regulated at all, national uniformity in the regulation adopted, such as only Congress can prescribe, is practically indispensable to the operation of an efficient and economical national railway system. On many railroads passenger trains of more than fourteen cars and freight trains of more than seventy cars are operated, and on some systems freight trains are run ranging from one hundred and twenty-five to one hundred and sixty cars in length. Outside of Arizona, where the length of trains is not restricted, appellant runs a substantial proportion of long trains. In 1939 on its comparable route for through traffic through Utah and Nevada from 66 to 85% of its freight trains were over 70 cars in length and over 43% of its passenger trains included more than fourteen passenger cars.

In Arizona, approximately 93% of the freight traffic and 95% of the passenger traffic is interstate. Because of the Train Limit Law appellant is required to haul over 30% more trains in Arizona than would otherwise have been necessary. The record shows a definite relationship between operating costs and the length of trains, the increase in length resulting in a reduction of operating costs per car. The addi-

---

[1] [See page 183 below—Editor's note].

tional cost of operation of trains complying with the Train Limit Law in Arizona amounts for the two railroads traversing that state to about $1,000,000 a year. The reduction in train lengths also impedes efficient operation. More locomotives and more manpower are required; the necessary conversion and reconversion of train lengths at terminals and the delay caused by breaking up and remaking long trains upon entering and leaving the state in order to comply with the law, delays the traffic and diminishes its volume moved in a given time, especially when traffic is heavy. . . .

The unchallenged findings leave no doubt that the Arizona Train Limit Law imposes a serious burden on the interstate commerce conducted by appellant. It materially impedes the movement of appellant's interstate trains through that state and interposes a substantial obstruction to the national policy proclaimed by Congress, to promote adequate, economical and efficient railway transportation service. Interstate Commerce Act, preceding § 1, 54 Stat. 899. Enforcement of the law in Arizona, while train lengths remain unregulated or are regulated by varying standards in other states, must inevitably result in an impairment of uniformity of efficient railroad operation because the railroads are subjected to regulation which is not uniform in its application. Compliance with a state statute limiting train lengths requires interstate trains of a length lawful in other states to be broken up and reconstituted as they enter each state according as it may impose varying limitations upon train lengths. The alternative is for the carrier to conform to the lowest train limit restriction of any of the states through which its trains pass, whose laws thus control the carriers' operations both within and without the regulating state. . . .

At present the seventy freight car laws are enforced only in Arizona and Oklahoma, with a fourteen car passenger car limit in Arizona. The record here shows that the enforcement of the Arizona statute results in freight trains being broken up and reformed at the California border

and in New Mexico, some distance from the Arizona line. Frequently it is not feasible to operate a newly assembled train from the New Mexico yard nearest to Arizona, with the result that the Arizona limitation governs the flow of traffic as far east as El Paso, Texas. For similar reasons the Arizona law often controls the length of passenger trains all the way from Los Angeles to El Paso.

If one state may regulate train lengths, so may all the others, and they need not prescribe the same maximum limitations. The practical effect of such regulations is to control train operations beyond the boundaries of the state exacting it because of the necessity of breaking up and reassembling long trains at the nearest terminal points before entering and after leaving the regulating state. The serious impediment to the free flow of commerce by the local regulation of train lengths and the practical necessity that such regulation, if any, must be prescribed by a single body having a nation-wide authority are apparent.

The trial court found that the Arizona law had no reasonable relation to safety, and made train operation more dangerous. Examination of the evidence and the detailed findings makes it clear that this conclusion was rested on facts found which indicate that such increased danger of accident and personal injury as may result from the greater length of trains is more than offset by the increase in the number of accidents resulting from the larger number of trains when train lengths are reduced. In considering the effect of the statute as a safety measure, therefore, the factor of controlling significance for present purposes is not whether there is basis for the conclusion of the Arizona Supreme Court that the increase in length of trains beyond the statutory maximum has an adverse effect upon safety of operation. The decisive question is whether in the circumstances the total effect of the law as a safety measure in reducing accidents and casualties is so slight or problematical as not to outweigh the national interest in keeping interstate commerce free from interferences which seriously impede it and subject it to local regulation which does not have a uniform effect on the interstate train journey which it interrupts.

The principal source of danger of accident from increased length of trains is the resulting increase of "slack action" of the train. Slack action is the amount of free movement of one car before it transmits its motion to an adjoining coupled car. This free movement results from the fact that in railroad practice cars are loosely coupled, and the coupling is often combined with a shock-absorbing device, a "draft gear," which, under stress, substantially increases the free movement as the train is started or stopped. . . .

On comparison of the number of slack action accidents in Arizona with those in Nevada, where the length of trains is now unregulated, the trial court found that with substantially the same amount of traffic in each state the number of accidents was relatively the same in long as in short train operations. While accidents from slack action do occur in the operation of passenger trains, it does not appear that they are more frequent or the resulting shocks more severe on long than on short passenger trains. Nor does it appear that slack action accidents occurring on passenger trains, whatever their length, are of sufficient severity to cause serious injury or damage.

As the trial court found, reduction of the length of trains also tends to increase the number of accidents because of the increase in the number of trains. The application of the Arizona law compelled appellant to operate 30.08%, or 4,304, more freight trains in 1938 than would otherwise have been necessary. And the record amply supports the trial court's conclusion that the frequency of accidents is closely related to the number of trains run. The number of accidents due to grade crossing collisions between trains and motor vehicles and pedestrians, and to collisions between trains, which are usually far more serious than those due to slack action, and accidents due to

locomotive failures, in general vary with the number of trains. Increase in the number of trains results in more starts and stops, more "meets" and "passes," and more switching movements, all tending to increase the number of accidents not only to train operatives and other railroad employees, but to passengers and members of the public exposed to danger by train operations.

Railroad statistics introduced into the record tend to show that this is the result of the application of the Arizona Train Limit Law to appellant, both with respect to all railroad casualties within the state and those affecting only trainmen whom the train limit law is supposed to protect. The accident rate in Arizona is much higher than on comparable lines elsewhere, where there is no regulation of length of trains. The record lends support to the trial court's conclusion that the train length limitation increased rather than diminished the number of accidents. This is shown by comparison of appellant's operations in Arizona with those in Nevada, and by comparison of operations of appellant and of the Sante Fe Railroad in Arizona with those of the same roads in New Mexico, and by like comparison between appellant's operations in Arizona and operations throughout the country.

Upon an examination of the whole case the trial court found that "if short-train operation may or should result in any decrease in the number of severity of the 'slack' or 'slack-surge' type of accidents or casualties, such decrease is substantially more than offset by the increased number of accidents and casualties from other causes that follow the arbitrary limitation of freight trains to 70 cars . . . and passenger trains to 14 cars."

We think, as the trial court found, that the Arizona Train Limit Law, viewed as a safety measure, affords at most slight and dubious advantage, if any, over unregulated train lengths, because it results in an increase in the number of trains and train operations and the consequent increase in train accidents of a character generally more severe than those due to slack action. Its undoubted effect on the commerce is the regulation, without securing uniformity, of the length of trains operated in interstate commerce, which lack is itself a primary cause of preventing the free flow of commerce by delaying it and by substantially increasing its cost and impairing its efficiency. In these respects the case differs from those where a state, by regulatory measures affecting the commerce, has removed or reduced safety hazards without substantial interference with the interstate movement of trains.

Here we conclude that the state does go too far. Its regulation of train lengths, admittedly obstructive to interstate train operation, and having a seriously adverse effect on transportation efficiency and economy, passes beyond what is plainly essential for safety since it does not appear that it will lessen rather than increase the danger of accident. Its attempted regulation of the operation of interstate trains cannot establish nation-wide control such as is essential to the maintenance of an efficient transportation system, which Congress alone can prescribe. The state interest cannot be preserved at the expense of the national interest by an enactment which regulates interstate train lengths without securing such control, which is a matter of national concern. To this the interest of the state here asserted is subordinate.

Reversed.

Mr. Justice Rutledge concurs in the result.

Mr. Justice Black, dissenting: . . .

For more than a quarter of a century, railroads and their employees have engaged in controversies over the relative virtues and dangers of long trains. . . . This controversy between the railroads and their employees, which was nationwide, was carried to Congress. Extensive hearings took place. . . . It is significant, however, that American railroads never once asked Congress to exercise its unquestioned

power to enact uniform legislation on that subject, and thereby invalidate the Arizona law. That which for some unexplained reason they did not ask Congress to do when it had the very subject of train length limitations under consideration, they shortly thereafter asked an Arizona state court to do.

In the state court a rather extraordinary "trial" took place. Charged with violating the law, the railroad admitted the charge. It alleged that the law was unconstitutional, however, and sought a trial of facts on that issue. The essence of its charge of unconstitutionality rested on one of these two grounds: (1) the legislature and people of Arizona erred in 1912 in determining that the running of long cars was dangerous; or (2) railroad conditions had so improved since 1912 that previous dangers did not exist to the same extent, and that the statute should be stricken down either because it cast an undue burden on interstate commerce by reason of the added cost, or because the changed conditions had rendered the Act "arbitrary and unreasonable." Thus, the issue which the court "tried" was not whether the railroad was guilty of violating the law, but whether the law was unconstitutional either because the legislature had been guilty of misjudging the facts concerning the degree of the danger of long trains, or because the 1912 conditions of danger no longer existed.

Before the state trial judge finally determined that the dangers found by the legislature in 1912 no longer existed, he heard evidence over a period of 5½ months which appears in about 3,000 pages of the printed record before us. It then adopted findings of fact submitted to it by the railroad, which cover 148 printed pages, and conclusions of law which cover 5 pages. We can best understand the nature of this "trial" by analogizing the same procedure to a defendant charged with violating a state or national safety appliance act, where the defendant comes into court and admits violation of the act. In such cases, the ordinary procedure would be for the court to pass upon the constitutionality of the act, and either discharge or convict the defendants. The procedure here, however, would justify quite a different trial method. Under it, a defendant is permitted to offer voluminous evidence to show that a legislative body has erroneously resolved disputed facts in finding a danger great enough to justify the passage of the law. This new pattern of trial procedure makes it necessary for a judge to hear all the evidence offered as to why a legislature passed a law and to make findings of fact as to the validity of those reasons. If under today's ruling a court does make findings, as to a danger contrary to the findings of the legislature, and the evidence heard "lends support" to those findings, a court can then invalidate the law. In this respect, the Arizona County Court acted, and this Court today is acting, as a "superlegislature."

Even if this method of invalidating legislative acts is a correct one, I still think that the "findings" of the state court do not authorize today's decision. That court did not find that there is no unusual danger from slack movements in long trains. It did decide on disputed evidence that the long train "slack movement" dangers were more than offset by prospective dangers as a result of running a larger number of short trains, since many people might be hurt at grade crossings. There was undoubtedly some evidence before the state court from which it could have reached such a conclusion. There was undoubtedly as much evidence before it which would have justified a different conclusion.

Under those circumstances, the determination of whether it is in the interest of society for the length of trains to be governmentally regulated is a matter of public policy. Someone must fix that policy—either the Congress, or the state, or the courts. A century and a half of constitutional history and government admonishes this Court to leave that choice to the elected legislative representatives of the people themselves, where it properly belongs both on democratic principles and the requirements of efficient government. . . .

The Supreme Court of Arizona did not discuss the County Court's so-called findings of fact. It properly designated the Arizona statute as a safety measure, and finding that it bore a reasonable relation to its purpose declined to review the judgment of the legislature as to the necessity for the passage of the act. In so doing it was well fortified by a long line of decisions of this Court. Today's decision marks an abrupt departure from that line of cases. . . .

The history of congressional consideration of this problem leaves little if any room to doubt that the choice of Congress to leave the state free in this field was a deliberate choice, which was taken with a full knowledge of the complexities of the problems and the probable need for diverse regulations in different localities. I am therefore compelled to reach the conclusion that today's decision is the result of the belief of a majority of this Court that both the legislature of Arizona and the Congress made wrong policy decisions in permitting a law to stand which limits the length of railroad trains. . . .

Mr. Justice Douglas, dissenting:

I have expressed my doubts whether the courts should intervene in situations like the present and strike down state legislation on the grounds that it burdens interstate commerce. *McCarroll* v. *Dixie Greyhound Lines*, 309 U.S. 176, 183–189. My view has been that the courts should intervene only where the state legislation discriminated against interstate commerce or was out of harmony with laws which Congress had enacted. . . . Whether the question arises under the commerce clause or the Fourteenth Amendment, I think the legislation is entitled to a presumption of validity. . . .

Note and Quaere: Do you think the Arizona Train Limit Law was in fact adopted as a safety measure, or was the safety language merely a "sugar coating" for a labor featherbedding measure? Note how the Court—surely with tongue in cheek—respects the state's characterization of the act as safety legislation.

Those who find that the language of *Southern Pacific* does not precisely conform with that of the *Cooley* case may find a reconciliation in *California v. Zook,* 336 U.S. 725 (1949), where the Court said, ". . . if a case falls within an area in commerce thought to demand a uniform national rule, state activity is struck down. If the activity is one of predominantly local interest, state action is sustained. More accurately, the question is whether the state interest is outweighed by a national interest in the unhampered operation of interstate commerce."

A generation after *Southern Pacific* in *Pike v. Bruce Church, Inc.,* 397 U.S. 137 (1970), the Court observed:

. . . Although the criteria for determining the validity of state statutes affecting in-

terstate commerce have been variously stated, the general rule that emerges can be phrased as follows: Where the statute regulates even-handedly to effectuate a legitimate local public interest, and its effects on interstate commerce are only incidental, it will be upheld unless the burden imposed on such commerce is clearly excessive in relation to the putative local benefits. *Huron Cement Co.* v. *Detroit,* 362 U.S. 440, 443. If a legitimate local purpose is found, then the question becomes one of degree. And the extent of the burden that will be tolerated will of course depend on the nature of the local interest involved, and on whether it could be promoted as well with a lesser impact on interstate activities. Occasionally the Court has candidly undertaken a balancing approach in resolving these issues, *Southern Pacific Co.* v. *Arizona,* 325 U.S. 761, but more frequently it has spoken in terms of "direct" and "indirect" effects and burdens. See *e.g., Shafer* v. *Farmers Grain Co.,* [268 U.S. 189 (1925)]. . . .

Philadelphia v. *New Jersey*
98 S. Ct. 2531 (1978)

A New Jersey law prohibited the importation of most "solid or liquid waste which originated or was collected outside . . . the State." Private operators of New Jersey landfills and several outside of New Jersey cities that had contracts with these operators challenged the law on Commerce Clause grounds.

Mr. Justice Stewart delivered the opinion of the Court . . . .

A
. . .

The opinions of the Court through the years have reflected an alertness to the evils of "economic isolation" and protectionism, while at the same time recognizing that incidental burdens on interstate commerce may be unavoidable when a State legislates to safeguard the

health and safety of its people. Thus, where simple economic protectionism is effected by state legislation, a virtually per se rule of invalidity has been erected. See, e.g., *Hood & Sons* v. *Du Mond* [336 U.S. 525]; *Toomer* v. *Witsell,* 334 U.S. 385, 403–406; *Baldwin* v. *G. A. F. Seelig, supra; Buck* v. *Kuykendall,* 267 U.S. 307, 315–316. The clearest example of such legislation is a law that overtly blocks the flow of interstate commerce at a State's borders. Cf. *Welton* v. *Missouri,* 91 U.S. 275. But where other legislative objectives are credibly advanced and there is no patent discrimination against interstate trade, the Court has adopted a much more flexible approach, the general contours of which were outlined in *Pike v. Bruce Church, Inc.*, 397 U.S. 137, 142. . . .

. . . The crucial inquiry, therefore, must be directed to determining whether ch. 363 is basically a protectionist measure, or whether it can fairly be viewed as a law directed to legitimate local concerns, with effects upon interstate commerce that are only incidental.

B

The purpose of ch. 363 is set in the statute itself as follows:

The Legislature finds and determines that . . . the volume of solid and liquid waste continues to rapidly increase, that the treatment and disposal of these wastes continues to pose an even greater threat to the quality of the environment of New Jersey, that the available and appropriate land fill sites within the State are being diminished, that the environment continues to be threatened by the treatment and disposal of waste which originated or was collected outside the State and that the public health, safety and welfare require that the treatment and disposal within this State of all wastes generated outside of the State be prohibited.

The New Jersey Supreme Court accepted this statement of the state legislature's purpose. The state court additionally found that New Jersey's existing landfill sites will be exhausted within a few years; that to go on using these sites or to develop new ones will take a heavy environmental toll, both from pollution and from loss of scarce open lands; that new techniques to divert waste from landfills to other methods of disposal and resource recovery processes are under development, but that these changes will require time; and finally, that "the extension of the lifespan of existing landfills, resulting from

the exclusion of out-of-state waste, may be of crucial importance in preventing further virgin wetlands or other undeveloped lands from being devoted to landfill purposes." 68 N.J., at 460–465, 348 A.2d, at 509–512. Based on these findings, the court concluded that ch. 363 was designed to protect not the State's economy, but its environment, and that its substantial benefits outweigh its "slight" burden on interstate commerce. Id., at 471–478, 348 A.2d, at 515–519.

The appellants strenuously contend that ch. 363, "while outwardly cloaked 'in the currently fashionable garb of environmental protection,' . . . is actually no more than a legislative effort to suppress competition and stabilize the cost of solid waste disposal for New Jersey residents. . . ." . . .

The appellees, on the other hand, deny that ch. 363 was motivated by financial concerns or economic protectionism. . . .

This dispute about ultimate legislative purpose need not be resolved, because its resolution would not be relevant to the constitutional issue to be decided in this case. Contrary to the evident assumption of the state court and the parties, the evil of protectionism can reside in legislative means as well as legislative ends. Thus, it does not matter whether the ultimate aim of ch. 363 is to reduce the waste disposal costs of New Jersey residents or to save remaining open lands from pollution, for we assume New Jersey has every right to protect its residents' pocketbooks as well as their environment. And it may be assumed as well that New Jersey may pursue those ends by slowing the flow of all waste into the State's remaining landfills, even though interstate commerce may incidentally be affected. But whatever New Jersey's ultimate purpose, it may not be accomplished by discriminating against articles of commerce coming from outside the State unless there is some reason, apart from their origin, to treat them differently. Both on its face and in its plain effect, ch. 363 violates this principle of nondiscrimination.

The Court has consistently found parochial legislation of this kind to be constitutionally invalid, whether the ultimate aim of the legislation was to assure a steady supply of milk by erecting barriers to allegedly ruinous outside competition, *Baldwin* v. *G. A. F. Seelig, supra,* at 522–524; or to create jobs by keeping industry within the State, *Foster Packing Co.* v. *Haydel,* 278 U.S. 1, 10; *Johnson* v. *Haydel,* 278 U.S. 16; *Toomer* v. *Witsell, supra,* at 403–404; or to preserve the State's financial resources from depletion by fencing out indigent immigrants, *Edwards* v. *California,* 314 U.S. 160, 173–174. In each of these cases, a presumably legitimate goal was sought to be achieved by the illegitimate means of isolating the State from the national economy.

Also relevant here are the Court's decisions holding that a State may not accord its own inhabitants a preferred right of access over consumers in other States to natural resources located within its borders. *Oklahoma* v. *Kansas Natural Gas Co.,* 221 U.S. 229; *Pennsylvania* v. *West Virginia,* 262 U.S. 553. These cases stand for the basic principle that a "State is without power to prevent privately owned articles of trade from being shipped and sold in interstate commerce on the ground that they are required to satisfy local demands or because they are needed by the people of the State." *Foster Packing Co.* v. *Haydel, supra,* at 10.

The New Jersey law at issue in this case falls squarely within the area that the Commerce Clause puts off-limits to state regulation. On its face, it imposes on out-of-state commercial interests the full burden of conserving the State's remaining landfill space. It is true that in our previous cases the scarce natural resource was itself the article of commerce, whereas here the scarce resource and the article of commerce are distinct. But that difference is without consequence. In both instances, the State has overtly moved to slow or freeze the flow of commerce for protectionist reasons. It does not matter that the State has shut the article of commerce inside the State in one case and out-

side the State in the other. What is crucial is the attempt by one State to isolate itself from a problem common to many by erecting a barrier against the movement of interstate trade.

The appellees argue that not all laws which facially discriminate against out-of-state commerce are forbidden protectionist regulations. In particular, they point to quarantine laws, which this Court has repeatedly upheld even though they appear to single out interstate commerce for special treatment. See *Baldwin* v. *G. A. F. Seelig, supra,* at 525; *Bowman* v. *Chicago & Northwestern R. Co., supra,* at 489. In the appellees' view, ch. 363 is analogous to such health-protective measures, since it reduces the exposure of New Jersey residents to the allegedly harmful effects of landfill sites.

It is true that certain quarantine laws have not been considered forbidden protectionist measures, even though they were directed against out-of-state commerce. . . . But those quarantine laws banned the importation of articles such as diseased livestock that required destruction as soon as possible because their very movement risked contagion and other evils. Those laws thus did not discriminate against interstate commerce as such, but simply prevented traffic in noxious articles, whatever their origin.

The New Jersey statute is not such a quarantine law. There has been no claim here that the very movement of waste into or through New Jersey endangers health, or that waste must be disposed of as soon as close to its point of generation as possible. The harms caused by waste are said to arise after its disposal in landfill sites, and at that point, as New Jersey concedes, there is no basis to distinguish out-of-state waste from domestic waste. If one is inherently harmful, so is the other. Yet New Jersey has banned the former while leaving its landfill sites open to the latter. The New Jersey law blocks the importation of waste in an obvious effort to saddle those outside the State with the entire burden of slowing the flow of refuse into New Jersey's remaining landfill sites. That legislative effort is clearly impermissible under the Commerce Clause of the Constitution.

Today, cities in Pennsylvania and New York find it expedient or necessary to send their waste into New Jersey for disposal, and New Jersey claims the right to close its borders to such traffic. Tomorrow, cities in New Jersey may find it expedient or necessary to send their waste into Pennsylvania or New York for disposal, and those States might then claim the right to close their borders. The Commerce Clause will protect New Jersey in the future, just as it protects her neighbors now, from efforts by one State to isolate itself in the stream of interstate commerce from a problem shared by all.

The judgment is reversed.

Mr. Justice Rehnquist, with whom The Chief Justice joins, dissenting. . . .

[T]he Court implies that the challenged laws must be invalidated because New Jersey has left its landfills open to domestic waste. But, as the Court notes . . . this Court has repeatedly upheld quarantine laws "even though they appear to single out interstate commerce for spe-

cial treatment." The fact that New Jersey has left its landfill sites open for domestic waste does not, of course, mean that solid waste is not innately harmful. Nor does it mean that New Jersey prohibits importation of solid waste for reasons other than the health and safety of its population. New Jersey must out of sheer necessity treat and dispose of its solid waste in some fashion, just as it must treat New Jersey cattle suffering from hoof-and-mouth disease. It does not follow that New Jersey must, under the Commerce Clause, accept solid waste or diseased cattle from outside its borders and thereby exacerbate its problems.

The Supreme Court of New Jersey expressly found that ch. 363 was passed "to preserve the health of New Jersey residents by keeping their exposure to solid waste and landfill areas to a minimum." . . . The Court points to absolutely no evidence that would contradict this finding by the New Jersey Supreme Court. Because I find no basis for distinguishing the laws under challenge here from our past cases upholding state laws that prohibit the importation of items that could endanger the population of the State, I dissent.

STATE TAXATION OF INTERSTATE COMMERCE

Introduction

American experience under the Articles of Confederation demonstrated for all time the danger of leaving with the separate states a power to tax interstate trade. The effort of each to gain advantages for itself by discriminatory tax burdens doomed the welfare of all. Moreover, interstate commerce has peculiarly seductive charms for state legislatures, always hard pressed by increasing needs for revenue. It is rich, and it has special political appeal. To tap it is in large measure to impose burdens on those outside the taxing state; that is, those who cannot vote the imposing legislators out of office. This is reminiscent of the old problem of taxation without representation. For all of these reasons state taxation—along with regulation—of interstate (i.e., national) commerce is a perennial problem. In the long view, perhaps it has raised more litigation than any other constitutional issue. It is, in sum, our "common market" problem.

Because there are so many different kinds of taxes with such different burdens—to say nothing of the elusive nature of tax incidence—the *Cooley* test has not been used extensively in state tax cases. It is too simple an approach for the subtleties involved. Or to put it more accurately, there was once a long-established doctrine that all interstate commerce demands uniformity of treatment for tax purposes, and so the states could not tax it at all: *The Passenger Cases,* 7 Howard 283 (1849); *State Freight Tax Case,* 15 Wallace 232 (1873). But if this cured one problem, it raised another. To give national trade full immunity means that competing, local businesses will have to pay an undue share of the cost of state government—whose benefits interstate trade also enjoys. The problem, then, is to protect the national market from strangulation by the states and yet make national commerce pay its fair share of the cost of state government. Surely there is no obvious solution.

The four cases presented here are offered simply to give a hint of some elements of a very complex problem.

Best v. *Maxwell*
311 U.S. 454 (1940)

Mr. Justice Reed delivered the opinion of the Court:

Appellant, a New York retail merchandise establishment, rented a display room in a North Carolina hotel for several days during February, 1938, and took orders for goods corresponding to samples; it filled the orders by shipping direct to the customers from New York City. Before using the room appellant paid under protest the tax required by chapter 127 § 121 (e), of the North Carolina Laws of 1937, which levies an annual privilege tax of $250 on every person or corporation, not a regular retail merchant in the state, who displays samples in any hotel room rented or occupied temporarily for the purpose of securing retail orders. Appellant not being a regular retail merchant of North Carolina admittedly comes within the statute. Asserting, however, that the tax was unconstitutional, especially in view of the commerce clause, it brought this suit for a refund and succeeded in the trial court. The Supreme Court of North Carolina reversed and then, being evenly divided on rehearing, allowed the reversal to stand. The prevailing opinion characterized the tax as one on the commercial use of temporary quarters, which in its operation did not discriminate against interstate

commerce and therefore did not come into conflict with the commerce clause.

The commerce clause forbids discrimination, whether forthright or ingenious. In each case it is our duty to determine whether the statute under attack, whatever its name may be, will in its practical operation work discrimination against interstate commerce. This standard we think condemns the tax at bar. Nominally the statute taxes all who are not regular retail merchants in North Carolina, regardless of whether they are residents or non-residents. We must assume, however, on this record that those North Carolina residents competing with appellant for the sale of similar merchandise will normally be regular retail merchants. The retail stores of the state are the natural outlets for merchandise, not those who sell only by sample. Some of these local shops may, like appellant, rent temporary display rooms in sections of North Carolina where they have no permanent store, but even these escape the tax at bar because the location of their central retail store somewhere within the state will qualify them as "regular retail merchants in the State of North Carolina." The only corresponding fixed-sum license tax to which appellant's real competitors are subject is a tax of $1 per annum for the privilege of doing business. Nonresidents wishing to display their wares must either establish themselves at regular North Carolina retail merchants at prohibitive expense, or else pay this

$250 tax that bears no relation to actual or probable sales but must be paid in advance no matter how small the sales turn out to be. Interstate commerce can hardly survive in so hostile an atmosphere. A $250 investment in advance, required of out-of-state retailers but not of their real local competitors, can operate only to discourage and hinder the appearance of interstate commerce in the North Carolina retail market. Extra-state merchants would be compelled to turn over their North Carolina trade to regular local merchants selling by sample. North Carolina regular retail merchants would benefit, but to the same extent the commerce of the Nation would suffer discrimination.

The freedom of commerce which allows the merchants of each state a regional or national market for their goods is not to be fettered by legislation, the actual effect of which is to discriminate in favor of intra-state businesses, whatever may be the ostensible reach of the language.

Judgment reversed.

Michigan-Wisconsin Pipe Line Co. v. *Calvert*
347 U.S. 157 (1954)

Mr. Justice Clark delivered the opinion of the Court. . . .

The question presented is whether the Commerce Clause is infringed by a Texas tax on the occupation of "gathering gas," measured by the entire volume of gas "taken," as applied to an interstate natural gas pipeline company, where the taxable incidence is the taking of gas from the outlet of an independent gasoline plant within the State for the purpose of immediate interstate transmission. . . . It is now well settled that a tax imposed on a local activity related to interstate commerce is valid if, and only if, the local activity is not such an integral part of the interstate process, the flow of commerce, that it cannot realistically be separated from it. *Mephis Natural Gas. Co.* v. *Stone*, 335 U.S. 80, 87 (1948). . . . This economic process is inherently unsusceptible of division into a distinct local activity capable of forming the basis for the tax here imposed, on the one hand, and a separate movement in commerce, on the other. It is difficult to conceive of a factual situation where the incidence of taking or loading for transmission is more closely related to the transmission itself. This Court has held that much less integrated activity is "so closely related to interstate transportation as to be practically a part of it." We are therefore of the opinion that the taking of the gas here is essentially a part of interstate commerce itself.

Here it is perhaps sufficient that the privilege taxed, namely the taking of the gas, is not so separate and distinct from interstate transportation as to support the tax. But additional objection is present if the tax be upheld. It would "permit a multiple burden upon that commerce," *Joseph* v. *Carter & Weekes Stevedoring Co.* (330 U.S. at 429), for if Texas may impose this "first taking" tax measured by the total volume of gas so taken, then Michigan and the other recipient states have at least equal right to tax the first taking or "unloading" from the pipeline of the same gas when it arrives for distribution. Oklahoma might then seek to tax the first taking of the gas as it crossed into that State. The net effect would be substantially to resurrect the customs barriers which the Commerce Clause was designed to eliminate. "The very purpose of the Commerce Clause was to create an area of free trade among the several States. That clause vested the power of taxing a transaction forming an unbroken process of interstate commerce in the Congress, not in the States." *McLeod* v. *J. E. Dilworth Co.*, 322 U.S. 327, 330, 331.

Evansville-Vanderburgh Airport Authority District v. *Delta Airlines*
405 U.S. 707 (1972)

Mr. Justice Brennan delivered the opinion of the Court.

The question is whether a charge by a State or municipality of $1 per commercial airline passenger to help defray the costs of airport construction and maintenance violates the Federal Constitution. Our answer is that, as imposed in these two cases, the charge does not violate the Federal Constitution. . . .

We being our analysis with consideration of the contention of the commercial airlines in both cases that the charge is constitutionally invalid under the Court's decision in *Crandall* v. *Nevada*, 73 U.S. 35, 6 Wall. 35 (1867). There the Court invalidated a Nevada statute that levied a "tax of one dollar upon every person leaving the State by any railroad, stagecoach, or other vehicle engaged or employed in the business of transporting passengers for hire." . . .

The Nevada charge, however, was not limited, as are the Indiana and New Hampshire charges before us, to travelers asked to bear a fair share of the costs of providing public facilities that further travel. The Nevada tax applied to passengers traveling interstate by privately owned transportation, such as railroads. Thus the tax was charged without regard to whether Nevada provided any facilities for the passengers required to pay the tax. Cases decided since *Crandall* have distinguished it on that ground and have sustained taxes "designed to make [interstate] commerce bear a fair share of the cost of the local government whose protection it enjoys." *Freeman* v. *Hewit*, 329 U.S. 249, 253 (1946). . . .

We therefore regard it as settled that a charge designed only to make the user of state-provided facilities pay a reasonable charge to help defray the costs of their construction and maintenance may constitutionally be imposed on interstate and domestic users alike. The principle that burdens on the right to travel are constitutional only if shown to be necessary to promote a compelling state interest has no application in this context. See *Shapiro* v. *Thompson*, 394 U.S. 618 (1969). The facility provided at public expense aids rather than hinders the right to travel. A permissible charge to help

defray the cost of the facility is therefore not a burden in the constitutional sense. . . .

Thus, while state or local tolls must reflect a "uniform, fair and practical standard" relating to public expenditures, it is the amount of the tax, not its formula, that is of central concern. At least so long as the toll is based on some fair approximation of use or privilege for use, as was that before us in *Capitol Greyhound* [339 U.S. 542 (1950)] and is neither discriminatory against interstate commerce nor excessive in comparison with the governmental benefit conferred, it will pass constitutional muster, even though some other formula might reflect more exactly the relative use of the state facilities by individual users.

The Indiana and New Hampshire charges meet those standards. *First*, neither fee discriminates against interstate commerce and travel. While the vast majority of passengers who board flights at the airports involved are traveling interstate, both interstate and domestic flights are subject to the same charges. Furthermore, there is no showing of any inherent difference between these two classes of flights, such that the application of the same fee to both would amount to discrimination against one or the other. See *Nippert* v. *City of Richmond*, 327 U.S. 416 (1946).

Second, these charges reflect a fair if imperfect approximation of the use of facilities for whose benefit they are imposed. We recognize that in imposing a fee on the boarding of commercial flights, both the Indiana and New Hampshire measures exempt in whole or part a majority of the actual number of persons who use facilities of the airports involved. Their number include certain classes of passengers, such as active members of the military and temporary layovers, deplaning commercial passengers, and passengers on noncommercial flights, nonscheduled commercial flights, and commercial flights on light aircraft. Also exempt are nonpassenger users, such as persons delivering or receiving air freight shipments, meeting or seeing off passengers, dining at airport restaurants, and working for employers located on airport grounds. Nevertheless, these exceptions are not wholly unreasonable. . . .

The measures before us also reflect rational distinctions among different classes of passengers and aircraft. . . .

Third, the airlines have not shown these fees to be excessive in relation to costs incurred by the taxing authorities. . . .

This omission . . . suffices to dispose of the final attack by appellants in that case on the New Hampshire statute. Appellants argue that the statute "on its face belies any legislative intent to impose an exaction based solely on use" because only 50% of its revenue is allocated to the state aeronautical fund while "the remaining fifty percent is allocated to the municipalities or airport authorities owning the landing areas at which the fees were imposed in the form of unrestricted general revenues." Brief, at 51–52. Yet so long as the funds received by local authorities under the statute are not shown to exceed their airport costs, it is immaterial whether those funds are expressly earmarked for airport use. The State's choice to reimburse local expenditures through unrestricted rather than restricted revenues is not a matter of concern to these appellants. . . .

We conclude, therefore, that the provisions before us impose valid charges on the use of airport facilities constructed and maintained with public funds. Furthermore, we do not think that they conflict with any federal policies furthering uniform national regulation of air transportation. No federal statute or specific congressional action or declaration evidences a Congressional purpose to deny or pre-empt state and local power to levy charges designed to help defray the costs of airport construction and maintenance. . . .

The commercial airlines argue in these cases that a proliferation of these charges in airports over the country will eventually follow in the wake of a decision sustaining the validity of the Indiana and New Hampshire fees, and that this is itself sufficient reason to adjudge the charges

repugnant to the Commerce Clause. "If such levies were imposed by each airport along a traveller's route, the total effect on the cost of air transportation could be prohibitive, the competitive structure of air carriers could be affected, and air transportation, compared to other forms of transportation, could be seriously impaired." Brief for appellants in No. 70-212, at 44. The argument relies on *Bibb* v. *Navajo Freight Lines, Inc.,* 359 U.S. 520 (1959). . . . But there is no suggestion that the Indiana and New Hampshire charges do not in fact advance the constitutionally permissible objective of having interstate commerce bear a fair share of the costs to the States of airports constructed and maintained for the purpose of aiding interstate air travel. In that circumstance, "[a]t least until Congress chooses to enact a nation-wide rule, the power will not be denied to the State[s]." *Freeman* v. *Hewit,* 329 U.S., at 253. . . .

Mr. Justice Powell took no part in the consideration or decision of these cases.

Mr. Justice Douglas, dissenting. . . .

Of course interstate commerce can be made to pay its fair share of the cost of the local government whose protection it enjoys. But though a local resident can be made to pay taxes to support his community, he cannot be required to pay a fee for making a speech or exercising any other First Amendment right. Like prohibitions obtain when licensing is exacted for exercising constitutional rights. *Lovell* v. *Griffin,* 303 U.S. 444, 451–452; *Thomas* v. *Collins,* 323 U.S. 516, 540–541; *Harman* v. *Forssenius,* 380 U.S. 528, 542. Heretofore we have treated the right to participate in interstate commerce in precisely the same way on the theory that the "power to tax the exercise of a privilege is the power to control or suppress its enjoyment." *Murdock* v. *Pennsylvania,* 319 U.S. 105, 112. I adhere to that view; federal constitutional rights should neither be "chilled" nor "suffocated." . . .

Note: After *Evansville* numerous state airline-passenger taxes were enacted. In 1973 Congress used its commerce power to outlaw them (49 U.S.C., Section 1513).

Norton Co. v. *Department of Revenue*
340 U.S. 534 (1951)

Mr. Justice Jackson delivered the opinion of the Court.

Petitioner, a Massachusetts corporation, manufactures and sells abrasive machines and supplies. . . . [I]t operates a branch office and warehouse in Chicago from which it makes local sales at retail. These sales admittedly subject it to an Illinois Occupation Tax "upon persons engaged in the business of selling tangible personal property at retail in this State." The base for computation of the tax is gross receipts. . . .

Not all of petitioner's sales to Illinois customers are over-the-counter, but the State has collected, under protest, the tax on the entire gross income of this company from sales to its inhabitants. . . . [T]he question is whether the State has exceeded the constitutional range of its taxing power by taxing all of petitioner's Illinois derived income.

In Worcester, Massachusetts, petitioner manufactures some 225,000 items, 18,000 of which it usually carries in stock. There are its general management, accounting, and credit offices, where it accepts or rejects all direct mail orders and orders forwarded by its Chicago office. If an order calls for specially built machines, it is there studied and accepted or rejected. Orders are filled by shipment f. o. b. Worcester either directly to the customer or via the Chicago office.

The Chicago place of business performs several functions. It carries an inventory of about 3,000 most frequently purchased items. From

these it serves cash customers and those whose credit the home office has approved, by consummating direct sales. Income from these sales petitioner admits to be constitutionally taxable. But this office also performs useful functions for other classes of customers. For those of no established credit, those who order items not in local stock, and those who want special equipment, it receives their order and forwards it to the home office for action there. For many of these Illinois customers it also acts as an intermediary to reduce freight charges. Worcester packages and marks each customer's goods but accumulates them until a carload lot can be consigned to the Chicago office. Chicago breaks the carload and reconsigns the separate orders in their original package to customers. The Chicago office thus intervenes between vendor and Illinois vendees and performs service helpful to petitioner's competition for that trade in all Illinois sales except when the buyer orders directly from Worcester, and the goods are shipped from there directly to the buyer.

The Illinois Supreme Court recognized that it was dealing with interstate commerce. It reiterated its former holdings "that there could be no tax on solicitation of orders only" in the State. But no solicitors work the territory out of either the home office or the Chicago branch . . . . The Illinois court held that the presence of petitioner's local retail outlet . . . was sufficient to attribute all income derived from Illinois sales to that outlet and render it all taxable.

Where a corporation chooses to stay at home in all respects except to send abroad advertising or drummers to solicit orders which are sent directly to the home office for acceptance, filling, and delivery back to the buyer, it is obvious that the State of the buyer has no local grip on the seller. Unless some local incident occurs sufficient to bring the transaction within its taxing power, the vendor is not taxable. *McLeod* v. *Dilworth Co.*, 322 U.S. 327. Of course, a state imposing a sales or use tax can more easily meet this burden, because the impact of those taxes is on the local buyer or user. Cases involving them are not controlling here, for this tax falls on the vendor.

But when, as here, the corporation has gone into the State to do local business by state permission and has submitted itself to the taxing power of the State, it can avoid taxation on some Illinois sales only by showing that particular transactions are dissociated from the local business and interstate in nature. The general rule, applicable here, is that a taxpayer claiming immunity from a tax has the burden of establishing his exemption.

This burden is never met merely by showing a fair difference of opinion which as an original matter might be decided differently. This corporation, by submitting itself to the taxing power of Illinois, likewise submitted itself to its judicial power to construe and apply its taxing statute insofar as it keeps within constitutional bounds. Of course, in constitutional cases, we have power to examine the whole record . . . but that does not mean that we will re-examine, as a court of first instance, findings of fact supported by substantial evidence.

This corporation has so mingled taxable business with that which it contends is not taxable that it requires administrative and judicial judgment to separate the two. We conclude that, in the light of all the evidence, the judgment attributing to the Chicago branch income from all sales that utilized it either in receiving the orders or distributing the goods was within the realm of permissible judgment. Petitioner has not established that such services as were rendered by the Chicago office were not decisive factors in establishing and holding this market.
. . .

This corporation could have approached the Illinois market through solicitors only and it would have been entitled to the immunity of interstate commerce as set out in the *Dilworth* case. But, from a competitive point of view, that system has disadvantages. The trade may view the seller as remote and inaccessible. He cannot be reached with process of local courts for breach of contract, or for service if the goods are defective or in need of replacement. Petitioner elected to localize itself in the Illinois market with the advantages of a retail outlet in the State . . . . Although the concern does not, by engaging in business within the State, lose its right to do interstate business with tax immunity, . . . it cannot channel business through a local outlet to gain the advantage of a local business and also hold the immunities of an interstate business.

The only items that are so clearly interstate in character that the State could not reasonably attribute their proceeds to the local business are orders sent directly to Worcester by the customer and shipped directly to the customer from Worcester. Income from those we think was not subject to this tax. . . .

Mr. Justice Reed concurs with the Court's opinion and judgment except as it permits Illinois to use as a base for the tax computation petitioner's sales, consummated in Massachusetts by the acceptance of orders forwarded to petitioner there by its Illinois branch office, filled in Massachusetts, and shipped from Massachusetts directly, and not by transhipment through the Illinois branch, to the buyer. In those sales title passes to buyer in Massachusetts. . . . The transactions described above are interstate business.

. . . [In the *Dilworth* case,] we made it clear that a tax cannot be collected by the buyer's state on orders solicited in one state, accepted in another, and shipped at the purchaser's risk. That later clarifying holding seems to me to state the true rule applicable here. I can see no difference, constitutionally, between solicitation by salesmen in a branch office or on the road. Such sales, consummated by direct shipment to Illinois buyers from out of the state are interstate business and free of the tax Illinois has levied. . . .

Mr. Justice Clark, dissenting in part.

I believe the respondent reasonably attributed all of the proceeds of petitioner's sales in

Illinois to the company's local activities. I therefore agree with the Illinois Supreme Court that under the circumstances shipments sent directly to Illinois customers on orders sent directly to Worcester were subject to the tax. . . . Surely the Court's conclusion, that "Petitioner has not established that such services as were rendered by the Chicago office were not decisive factors in establishing and holding this market," applies with equal validity to the direct sales.

In maintaining a local establishment of such magnitude, petitioner has adopted the label of a home-town merchant. After it has received the manifold advantages of that label, we should not give our sanction to its claim made at tax-paying time that with respect to direct sales it is only an itinerant drummer. . . .

Mr. Justice Black and Mr. Justice Douglas join in this opinion.

STATE INTRUSION ON FEDERAL FUNCTIONS

McCulloch v. *Maryland*
See p. 148, above.

Miller v. *Arkansas*
352 U.S. 187 (1956)

Per Curiam.

Appellant submitted a bid in May 1954 for construction of facilities at an Air Force Base in Arkansas over which the United States had not acquired jurisdiction pursuant to 54 Stat. 19, 40 U.S.C. § 255. The United States accepted appellant's bid, and in June appellant began work on the project. In September, the State of Arkansas filed an information accusing appellant of violation of Ark.Stat., 1947, §§ 71-701 through 71-721, for submitting a bid, executing a contract, and commencing work as a contractor in the State of Arkansas without having obtained a license under Arkansas law for such activity from its Contractors Licensing Board. The case was tried on stipulated facts. Appellant was found guilty and fined. The trial court's judgment was affirmed by the Arkansas Supreme Court, 225 Ark. 285, 281 S.W.2d 946, and the case came here on appeal. 351 U.S. 948. Appellant and the United States as *amicus curiae* contend that the application of the Arkansas statute to this contractor interferes with the Federal Government's power to select contractors and schedule construction and is in conflict with the federal law regulating procurement.

Congress provided in § 3 of the Armed Services Procurement Act of 1947, 62 Stat. 21, 23, 41 U.S.C. § 152, that awards on advertised bids "shall be made . . . to that responsible bidder whose bid, conforming to the invitation for bids, will be most advantageous to the Government, price and other factors considered . . . ." The report from the Committee on Armed Services of the House of Representatives indicated some of the factors to be considered: "The question whether a particular bidder is a 'responsible bidder' requires some business judgment, and involves an evaluation of the bidder's experience, facilities, technical organization, reputation, financial resources, and other factors." H.R.Rep.No.109, 80th Cong., 1st Sess. 18; see S.Rep.No.571, 80th Cong., 1st Sess. 16. The Armed Services Procurement Regulations, promulgated under the Act, set forth a list of guiding considerations, defining a responsible contractor as one who

"(a) Is a manufacturer, construction contractor, or regular dealer. . . .

"(b) Has adequate financial resources, or ability to secure such resources;

"(c) Has the necessary experience, organization, and technical qualifications, and has or can acquire the necessary facilities (including probable subcontractor arrangements) to perform the proposed contract;

"(d) Is able to comply with the required delivery or performance schedule (taking into consideration all existing business commitments);

"(e) Has a satisfactory record of performance, integrity, judgment, and skills; and

"(f) Is otherwise qualified and eligible to receive an award under applicable laws and regulations." 32 CRF § 1.307; see also 32 CFR § 2.406-3.

Under the Arkansas licensing law similar factors are set forth to guide the Contractors Licensing Board:

"The Board, in determining the qualifications of any applicant for original license . . . shall, among other things, consider the following: (a) experience, (b) ability, (c) character, (d) the manner of performance of previous contracts, (e) financial conditions, (f) equipment, (g) any other fact tending to show ability and willingness to conserve the public health and safety, and (h) default in complying with the provisions of this act . . . or any other law of the State. . . ." Ark.Stats., 1947 § 71-709.

Mere enumeration of the similar grounds for licensing under the state statute and for finding "responsibility" under the federal statute and regulations is sufficient to indicate conflict between this license requirement which Arkansas places on a federal contractor and the action which Congress and the Department of Defense have taken to insure the reliability of persons and companies contracting with the Federal Government. Subjecting a federal contractor to the Arkansas contractor license requirements would give the State's licensing board a virtual power of review over the federal determination of "responsibility" and would thus frustrate the expressed federal policy of selecting the lowest responsible bidder. In view of the federal statute and regulations, the rationale of *Johnson* v. *State of Maryland*, 254 U.S. 51, 57, is applicable:

"It seems to us that the immunity of the instruments of the United States from state control in the performance of their duties extends to a requirement that they desist from performance until they satisfy a state officer upon examination that they are competent for a necessary part of them and pay a fee for permission to go on. Such a requirement does not merely touch the Government servants remotely by a general rule of conduct; it lays hold of them in their specific attempt to obey orders and requires qualifications in addition to those that the Government has pronounced sufficient. It is the duty of the Department to employ persons competent for their work and that duty it must be presumed has been performed. . . ."

The judgment of the Supreme Court of Arkansas is reversed and the cause is remanded for further proceedings not inconsistent with this opinion.

THE EFFECT OF FEDERAL LEGISLATION ON STATE AUTHORITY

Introduction

In the absence of pertinent acts of Congress, the validity of state regulation or taxation of interstate commerce is determined by the *Cooley* and related tax doctrines, as we have seen. On the other hand, *when there is pertinent congressional legislation,* the validity of relevant state laws depends on which of these three circumstances prevails: (1) direct incompatibility of the state and federal laws (e.g., the *Pensacola Telegraph Case,* above, Chapter 3), (2) Congress has preempted or taken over the whole field (e.g., *Burbank* v. *Lockheed Air Terminal, Inc.,* below); and (3) Congress, exercising its commerce (or other) power, authorizes the state measure; an example is *Prudential Life Insurance Co.* v. *Benjamin,* 328 U.S. 408 (1946), which upheld the McCarran Act authorizing state regulation of interstate as well as local insurance business.

Burbank v. *Lockheed Air Terminal, Inc.*
411 U.S. 624 (1973)

Mr. Justice Douglas delivered the opinion of the Court. . . .

This suit brought by appellees asked for an injunction against the enforcement of an ordinance adopted by the City Council of Burbank, California, which made it unlawful for a so-called pure jet aircraft to take off from the Hollywood-Burbank Airport between 11 p.m. of one day and 7 a.m. the next day, and making it unlawful for the operator of that airport to allow any such aircraft to take off from that airport during such periods. The only regularly scheduled flight affected by the ordinance was an intrastate flight of Pacific Southwest Airlines originating in Oakland, California, and departing from Hollywood-Burbank Airport for San Diego every Sunday night at 11:30 p.m.

The District Court found the ordinance to be unconstitutional on both Supremacy Clause and Commerce Clause grounds. The Court of Appeals affirmed on the grounds of the Supremacy Clause both as respects pre-emption and as respects conflict. The case is here on appeal. . . . We affirm the Court of Appeals. . . .

[The Federal Aviation Act] provides in part, "The United States of America is declared to possess and exercise complete and exclusive national sovereignty in the airspace of the United States. . . ." [T]he Administrator of the Federal Aeronautics Act (FAA) has been given broad authority to regulate the use of the navigable airspace, "in order to insure the safety of aircraft and the efficient utilization of such airspace . . ." and "for the protection of persons and property on the ground . . . ."

The Solicitor General, though arguing against pre-emption, concedes that as respects "airspace management" there is pre-emption. That, however, is a fatal concession, for as the District Court found: "The imposition of curfew ordinances on a nationwide basis would result in a bunching of flights in those hours immediately preceding the curfew. This bunching of flights during these hours would have the two-fold effect of increasing an already serious congestion problem and actually increasing, rather than relieving, the noise problem by increasing flights in the period of greatest annoyance to surrounding communities. Such a result is totally inconsistent with the objectives of the federal statutory and regulatory scheme." It also found "[t]he imposition of curfew ordinances on a nationwide basis would cause a serious loss of efficiency in the use of the navigable airspace." . . .

Our prior cases on pre-emption are not precise guidelines in the present controversy, for each case turns on the peculiarities and special features of the federal regulatory scheme in question. Control of noise is of course deep-seated in the police power of the States. Yet the pervasive control vested in EPA and in FAA under the 1972 [Noise Control] Act seems to us to leave no room for local curfews or other local controls. What the ultimate remedy may be for aircraft noise which plagues many communities and tens of thousands of people is not known. The procedures under the 1972 Act are under way. In addition, the Administrator has imposed a variety of regulations relating to takeoff and landing procedures and runway preferences. The Federal Aviation Act requires a delicate balance between safety and efficiency, and the protection of persons on the ground. Any regulations adopted by the Administrator to control noise pollution must be consistent with the "highest degree of safety." The interdependence of these factors requires a uniform and exclusive system of federal regulation if the congressional objectives underlying the Federal Aviation Act are to be fulfilled.

If we were to uphold the Burbank ordinance and a significant number of municipalities followed suit, it is obvious that fractionalized control of the timing of takeoffs and landings would severely limit the flexibility of the FAA in controlling air traffic flow. The difficulties of scheduling flights to avoid congestion and the concomitant decrease in safety would be compounded. . . . We are not at liberty to diffuse the powers given by Congress to FAA and EPA by letting the States or municipalities in on the planning. If that change is to be made, Congress alone must do it.

Mr. Justice Rehnquist, with whom Mr. Justice Stewart, Mr. Justice White, and Mr. Justice Marshall join, dissenting. . . .

. . . Because noise regulation has traditionally been an area of local, not national, concern, in determining whether congressional legislation has, by implication, foreclosed remedial local enactments "we start with the assumption that the historic police powers of the States were not to be superseded by the Federal Act unless that was the clear and manifest purpose of Congress." This assumption derives from our basic constitutional division of legislative competence between the States and Congress; from "due regard for the presuppositions of our embracing federal system, *including the principle of diffusion of power not as a matter of doctrinaire localism but as a promoter of democracy . . . .*" (emphasis added).

Note: In *Askew* v. *American Waterways Operators, Inc.,* 411 U.S. 325 (1973), the Court held the Federal Water Quality Improvement Act (1970), providing no-fault liability for cleaning up oil spills and authorizing presidential regulations to prevent them, did not invalidate state laws concerning liability to the state and private parties for oil spill damage. In sum, the federal *clean-up law* and the state *liability for damage* law were found not mutually incompatible.

part

II

LIMITATIONS ON
GOVERNMENTAL
POWER AS A SHIELD
FOR FREEDOM

5

The Bill of Rights and the Fourteenth Amendment

THE ORIGINAL UNDERSTANDING

Barron v. *Baltimore*
7 Peters 243 (1833)

In paving and grading its streets, the city of Baltimore diverted certain streams from their natural courses, causing silt to pile up in front of Barron's wharf. This seriously diminished its commercial value, and Barron sued for compensation under the Fifth Amendment.

Mr. Chief Justice Marshall delivered the opinion of the Court. . . .

The question [is], we think, of great importance, but not of much difficulty. The constitution was ordained and established by the people of the United States for themselves, for their own government, and not for the government of the individual states. Each state established a constitution for itself, and, in that constitution, provided such limitations and restrictions on the powers of its particular government as its judgment dictated. The people of the United States framed such a government for the United States as they supposed best adapted to

their situation, and best calculated to promote their interests. The powers they conferred on this government were to be exercised by itself; and the limitations on power, if expressed in general terms, are naturally, and, we think, necessarily applicable to the government created by the instrument. They are limitations of power, granted in the instrument itself; not of distinct governments, framed by different persons and for different purposes. . . .

If these propositions be correct, the fifth amendment must be understood as restraining the power of the general government, not as applicable to the states. In their several constitutions they have imposed such restrictions on their respective governments as their own wisdom suggested; such as they deemed most proper for themselves. . . .

The ninth section [of Art. I] having enumerated, in the nature of a bill of rights, the limitations intended to be imposed on the powers of the general government, the tenth proceeds to enumerate those which were to operate on the state legislatures. These restrictions are brought together in the same section, and are by express words applied to the states. "No state shall enter into any treaty," &c. Perceiving that in a constitution framed by the people of the United States for the government of all, no limitation of the action of government on the people would apply to the state government, unless expressed in terms; the restrictions contained in the tenth section are in direct words so applied to the states. . . .

If the original constitution, in the ninth and tenth sections of the first article, draws this plain and marked line of discrimination between the limitations it imposes on the powers of the general government, and on those of the states; if in every inhibition intended to act on state power, words are employed which directly express that intent; some strong reason must be assigned for departing from this safe and judicious course in framing the amendments, before that departure can be assumed.

We search in vain for that reason.

Had the people of the several states, or any of them, required changes in their constitutions; had they required additional safeguards to liberty from the apprehended encroachments of their particular governments; the remedy was in their own hands, and would have been applied by themselves. A convention would have been assembled by the discontented state, and the required improvements would have been made by itself. The unwieldy and cumbrous machinery of procuring a recommendation from two-thirds of congress, and the assent of three-fourths of their sister states, could never have occurred to any human being as a mode of doing that which might be effected by the state

itself. Had the framers of these amendments intended them to be limitations on the powers of the state governments, they would have imitated the framers of the original constitution, and have expressed that intention. Had congress engaged in the extraordinary occupation of improving the constitutions of the several states by affording the people additional protection from the exercise of power by their own governments in matters which concerned themselves alone, they would have declared this purpose in plain and intelligible language.

But it is universally understood, it is a part of the history of the day, that the great revolution which established the constitution of the United States, was not effected without immense opposition. Serious fears were extensively entertained that those powers which the patriot statesmen, who then watched over the interests of our country, deemed essential to union, and to the attainment of those invaluable objects for which union was sought, might be exercised in a manner dangerous to liberty. In almost every convention by which the constitution was adopted, amendments to guard against the abuse of power were recommended. These amendments demanded security against the apprehended encroachments of the general government—not against those of the local governments.

In compliance with a sentiment thus generally expressed, to quiet fears thus extensively entertained, amendments were proposed by the required majority in congress, and adopted by the states. These amendments contain no expression indicating an intention to apply them to the state governments. This court cannot so apply them.

We are of opinion that the provision in the fifth amendment to the constitution, declaring that private property shall not be taken for public use without just compensation, is intended solely as a limitation on the exercise of power by the government of the United States, and is not applicable to the legislation of the states. We are therefore of opinion that there is no repugnancy between the several acts of the general assembly of Maryland, given in evidence by the defendants at the trial of this cause, in the court of that state, and the constitution of the United States. This court, therefore, has no jurisdiction of the cause; and it is dismissed.

The Slaughter House Cases
83 U.S. 36 (1873)

To "remove from the more densely populated part of the city, the noxious slaughterhouses, and large and offensive collections of animals," a Louisiana law prohibited all slaughtering in the New Orleans area except at a specified place south of the city. There, the law authorized a corporation to provide public slaughtering facilities open for use by anyone upon payment of a state approved fee—and subject to state health regulations. The corporation was given a 25-year exclusive franchise to provide and maintain these facilities and to collect the approved fees as compensation for its efforts. (The law had been enacted by a carpet-bag legislature apparently not immune to bribery—which of course has nothing to do with the purpose and meaning of the 14th Amendment.)

Mr. Justice Miller delivered the opinion of the Court: . . .

It is not, and cannot be successfully controverted, that it is both the right and the duty of the legislative body—the supreme power of the State or municipality—to prescribe and determine the localities where the business of slaughtering for a great city may be conducted. To do this effectively it is indispensable that all persons who slaughter animals for food shall do it in those places *and nowhere else.*

The statute under consideration defines these localities and forbids slaughtering in any other. It does not, as has been asserted, prevent the butcher from doing his own slaughtering. On the contrary, the Slaughter-House Company is required, under a heavy penalty, to permit any person who wishes to do so, to slaughter in their houses; and they are bound to make ample provision for the convenience of all slaughtering for the entire city. The butcher then is still permitted to slaughter, to prepare, and to sell his own meats; but he is required to slaughter at a specified place and to pay reasonable compensation for the use of the accommodations furnished him at that place.

The wisdom of the monopoly granted by the legislature may be open to question, but it is difficult to see a justification for the assertion that the butchers are deprived of the right to labor in their occupation, or the people of their daily service in preparing food, or how this statute, with the duties and guards imposed upon the company, can be said to destroy the business of the butcher, or seriously interfere with its pursuit.

The power here exercised by the legislature of Louisiana is, in its essential nature, one which has been, up to the present period in the constitutional history of this country, always conceded to belong to the States, however, it may *now* be questioned in some of its details. . . .

Unless, therefore, it can be maintained that the exclusive privilege granted by this charter to the corporation is beyond the power of the legislature of Louisiana, there can be no just exception to the validity of the statute. And in this respect we are not able to see that these privileges are especially odious or objectionable. The duty imposed as a consideration for the privilege is well defined, and its enforcement well guarded. The prices or charges to be made by the company are limited by the statute, and we are not advised that they are on the whole exorbitant or unjust.

The proposition is, therefore, reduced to these terms: Can any exclusive privileges be granted to any of its citizens, or to a corporation, by the legislature of a State? . . .

The plaintiffs in error accepting this issue, allege that the statute is a violation of the Constitution of the United States in these several particulars:

That it creates an involuntary servitude forbidden by the thirteenth article of amendment;

That it abridges the privileges and immunities of citizens of the United States;

That it denies to the plaintiffs the equal protection of the laws; and,

That it deprives them of their property without due process of law; contrary to the provisions of the first section of the fourteenth article of amendment.

This court is thus called upon for the first time to give construction to these articles.

We do not conceal from ourselves the great responsibility which this duty devolves upon us. No questions so far-reaching and pervading in their consequences, so profoundly interesting to the people of this country, and so important in their bearing upon the relations of the United States, and of the several States to each other and to the citizens of the States and of the United States, have been before this court during the official life of any of its present members. We have given every opportunity for a full hearing at the bar; we have discussed it freely and compared views among ourselves; we have taken ample time for careful deliberation, and we now propose to announce the judgments which we have formed in the construction of those articles, so far as we have found them necessary to the decision of the cases before us, and beyond that we have neither the inclination nor the right to go. . . .

On the most casual examination of the language of these [Civil War] amendments, no one can fail to be impressed with the one pervading

purpose found in them all, lying at the foundation of each, and without which none of them would have been even suggested; we mean the freedom of the slave race, the security and firm establishment of that freedom, and the protection of the newly-made freeman and citizen from the oppressions of those who had formerly exercised unlimited dominion over him. It is true that only the fifteenth amendment, in terms, mentions the Negro by speaking of his color and his slavery. But it is just as true that each of the other articles was addressed to the grievances of that race, and designed to remedy them as the fifteenth.

We do not say that no one else but the Negro can share in this protection. Both the language and spirit of these articles are to have their fair and just weight in any question of construction. Undoubtedly while Negro slavery alone was in the mind of the Congress which proposed the thirteenth article, it forbids any other kind of slavery, now or hereafter. If Mexican peonage or the Chinese cooly labor system shall develop slavery of the Mexican or Chinese race within our territory, this amendment may safely be trusted to make it void. And so if other rights are assailed by the States which properly and necessarily fall within the protection of these articles, that protection will apply, though the party interested may not be of African descent. But what we do say, and what we wish to be understood is, that in any fair and just construction of any section or phrase of these amendments, it is necessary to look to the purpose which we have said was the pervading spirit of them all, the evil which they were designed to remedy, and the process of continued addition to the Constitution, until that purpose was supposed to be accomplished, as far as constitutional law can accomplish it. . . . [The Court held that the Thirteenth Amendment had nothing whatsoever to do with the Louisiana butchering law.]

The next observation is more important in view of the arguments of counsel in the present case. It is, that the distinction between citizenship of the United States and citizenship of a State is clearly recognized and established. Not only may a man be a citizen of the United States without being a citizen of a State, but an important element is necessary to convert the former into the latter. He must reside within the State to make him a citizen of it, but it is only necessary that he should be born or naturalized in the United States to be a citizen of the Union.

It is quite clear, then, that there is a citizenship of the United States, and a citizenship of a State, which are distinct from each other, and which depend upon different characteristics or circumstances in the individual.

We think this distinction and its explicit recognition in this [the Fourteenth] amendment of great weight in this argument, because the next paragraph of this same section, which is the one mainly relied on by the plaintiffs in error, speaks only of privileges and immunities of citizens of the United States, and does not speak of those of citizens of the several States. The argument, however, in favor of the plaintiffs rests wholly on the assumption that the citizenship is the same, and the privileges and immunities guaranteed by the clause are the same.

The language is, "No State shall make or enforce any law which shall abridge the privileges or immunities of citizens of *the United States.*" It is a little remarkable, if this clause was intended as a protection to the citizens of a State against the legislative power of his own State, that the word citizen of the State should be left out when it is so carefully used, and used in contradistinction to citizens of the United States, in the very sentence which precedes it. It is too clear for argument that the change in phraseology was adopted understandingly and with a purpose.

Of the privileges and immunities of the citizen of the United States, and of the privileges and immunities of the citizen of the State, and what they respectively are, we will presently consider; but we wish to state here that it is only the former which are placed by this clause under the protection of the Federal Constitution, and that the latter, whatever they may be, are not

intended to have any additional protection by this paragraph of the amendment.

If, then, there is a difference between the privileges and immunities belonging to a citizen of the United States as such, and those belonging to the citizen of the State as such the latter must rest for their security and protection where they have heretofore rested; for they are not embraced by this paragraph of the amendment. . . .

Fortunately we are not without judicial construction of [the state citizenship clause in Article 4, Section 2] of the Constitution. The first and the leading case on the subject is that of *Corfield* v. *Coryell*, 6 Fed. Cas. 3230, decided by Mr. Justice Washington in the Circuit Court for the District of Pennsylvania in 1823.

"The inquiry," he says, "is, what are the privileges and immunities of citizens of the several States? We feel no hesitation in confining these expressions to those privileges and immunities which are fundamental; which belong of right to the citizens of all free governments, and which have at all times been enjoyed by citizens of the several States which compose this Union, from the time of their becoming free, independent, and sovereign. What these fundamental principles are, it would be more tedious than difficult to enumerate. They may all, however, be comprehended under the following general heads: protection by the government, with the right to acquire and possess property of every kind, and to pursue and obtain happiness and safety, subject, nevertheless, to such restraints as the government may prescribe for the general good of the whole." . . .

It would be the vainest show of learning to attempt to prove by citations of authority, that up to the adoption of the recent amendments, no claim or pretense was set up that those rights depended on the Federal government for their existence or protection, beyond the very few express limitations which the Federal Constitution imposed upon the States—such, for instance, as the prohibition against ex post facto laws, bills of attainder, and laws impairing the obligation of contracts. But with the exception of these and a few other restrictions, the entire domain of the privileges and immunities of citizens of the States, as above defined, lay within the constitutional and legislative power of the States, and without that of the Federal government. Was it the purpose of the four-teenth amendment, by the simple declaration that no State should make or enforce any law which shall abridge the privileges and im-munities of *citizens of the United States*, to trans-fer the security and protection of all the civil rights which we have mentioned, from the States to the Federal government? And where it is declared that Congress shall have the power to enforce that article, was it intended to bring within the power of Congress the entire domain of civil rights heretofore belonging exclusively to the States?

All this and more must follow, if the proposi-tion of the plaintiffs in error be sound. For not only are these rights subject to the control of Congress whenever in its discretion any of them are supposed to be abridged by State legisla-tion, but that body may also pass laws in ad-vance, limiting and restricting the exercise of legislative power by the States, in their most ordinary and usual functions, as in its judgment it may think proper on all such subjects. And still further, such a construction followed by the reversal of the judgments of the Supreme Court of Louisiana in these cases, would constitute this court a perpetual censor upon all legislation of the States, on the civil rights of their own citizens, with authority to nullify such as it did not approve as consistent with those rights, as they existed at the time of the adoption of this amendment. The argument we admit is not al-ways the most conclusive which is drawn from the consequences urged against the adoption of a particular construction of an instrument. But when, as in the case before us, these conse-quences are so serious, so far-reaching and per-vading, so great a departure from the structure and spirit of our institutions; when the effect is

to fetter and degrade the State governments by subjecting them to the control of Congress, in the exercise of powers heretofore universally conceded to them of the most ordinary and fun-damental character; when in fact it radically changes the whole theory of the relations of the State and Federal governments to each other and of both these governments to the people; the argument has a force that is irresistible, in the absence of language which expresses such a purpose too clearly to admit of doubt.

We are convinced that no such results were intended by the Congress which proposed these amendments, nor by the legislatures of the States which ratified them.

Having shown that the privileges and im-munities relied on in the argument are those which belong to citizens of the States as such, and that they are left to the State governments for security and protection, and not by this arti-cle placed under the special care of the Federal government, we may hold ourselves excused from defining the privileges and immunities of citizens of the United States which no State can abridge, until some case involving those privi-leges may make it necessary to do so.

But lest it be said that no such privileges and immunities are to be found if those we have been considering are excluded, we venture to suggest some which owe their existence to the Federal government, its National character, its Constitution, or its laws.

One of these is well described in the case of *Crandall* v. *Nevada*, 6 Wall. 35. It is said to be the right of the citizens of this great country, protected by implied guarantees of its Constitu-tion, "to come to the seat of government to as-sert any claim he may have upon that govern-ment, to transact any business he may have with it, to seek its protection, to share its offices, to engage in administering its functions. He has the right of free access to its seaports, through which all operations of foreign commerce are conducted, to the sub-treasuries, land offices, and courts of justice in the several States." And quoting from the language of Chief Justice

Taney in another case, it is said "that for all the great purposes for which the Federal government was established, we are one people, with one common country, we are all citizens of the United States;" and it is, as such citizens, that their rights are supported in this court in *Crandall* v. *Nevada*.

Another privilege of a citizen of the United States is to demand the care and protection of the Federal government over his life, liberty, and property when on the high seas or within the jurisdiction of a foreign government. Of this there can be no doubt, nor that the right depends upon his character as a citizen of the United States. The right to peaceably assemble and petition for redress of grievances, the privilege of the writ of habeas corpus, are rights of the citizen guaranteed by the Federal Constitution. The right to use the navigable waters of the United States, however they may penetrate the territory of the several States, all rights secured to our citizens by treaties with foreign nations, are dependent upon citizenship of the United States, and not citizenship of a State. One of these privileges is conferred by the very article under consideration. It is that a citizen of the United States can, of his own volition, become a citizen of any State of the Union by a bona fide residence therein, with the same rights as other citizens of that State. To these may be added the rights secured by the thirteenth and fifteenth articles of amendment, and by the other clause of the fourteenth, next to be considered.

But it is useless to pursue this branch of the inquiry, since we are of opinion that the rights claimed by these plaintiffs in error, if they have any existence, are not privileges and immunities of citizens of the United States within the meaning of the clause of the fourteenth amendment under consideration. . . .

The argument has not been much pressed in these cases that the defendant's charter deprives the plaintiffs of their property without due process of law, or that it denies to them the equal protection of the law. The first of these paragraphs has been in the Constitution since the

adoption of the fifth amendment, as a restraint upon the federal power. It is also to be found in some form of expression in the constitutions of nearly all the States, as a restraint upon the power of the States. This law, then, has practically been the same as it now is during the existence of the government, except so far as the present amendment may place the restraining power over the States in this matter in the hands of the Federal government.

We are not without judicial interpretation, therefore, both State and National, of the meaning of this clause. And it is sufficient to say that under no construction of that provision that we have ever seen, or any that we deem admissible, can the restraint imposed by the State of Louisiana upon the exercise of their trade by the butchers of New Orleans be held to be a deprivation of property within the meaning of that provision.

"Nor shall any State deny to any person within its jurisdiction the equal protection of the laws."

In the light of the history of these amendments, and the pervading purpose of them, which we have already discussed, it is not difficult to give a meaning to this clause. The existence of laws in the States where the newly emancipated Negroes resided, which discriminated with gross injustice and hardship against them as a class, was the evil to be remedied by this clause, and by it such laws are forbidden.

If, however, the States did not conform their laws to its requirements, then by the fifth section of the article of amendment Congress was authorized to enforce it by suitable legislation. We doubt very much whether any action of a State not directed by way of discrimination against the Negroes as a class, or on account of their race, will ever be held to come within the purview of this provision. It is so clearly a provision for that race and that emergency, that a strong case would be necessary for its application to any other. But as it is a State that is to be dealt with, and not alone the validity of its laws, we may safely leave that matter until Congress shall have exercised its power, or some case of State oppression, by denial of equal justice in its courts, shall have claimed a decision at our hands. We find no such case in the one before us, and do not deem it necessary to go over the argument again, as it may have relation to this particular clause of the amendment. . . .

The judgments of the Supreme Court of Louisiana in these cases are affirmed.

Mr. Justice Field, dissenting: . . .

The question presented is . . . one of the gravest importance, not merely to the parties here, but to the whole country. It is nothing less than the question whether the recent amendments to the Federal Constitution protect the citizens of the United States against the deprivation of their common rights by State legislation. In my judgment the fourteenth amendment does afford such protection, and was so intended by the Congress which framed and the States which adopted it.

The amendment does not attempt to confer any new privileges or immunities upon citizens, or to enumerate or define those already existing. It assumes that there are such privileges and immunities which belong of right to citizens as such, and ordains that they shall not be abridged by State legislation. If this inhibition has no reference to privileges and immunities of this character, but only refers, as held by the majority of the court in their opinion, to such privileges and immunities as were before its adoption specially designated in the Constitution or necessarily implied as belonging to citizens of the United States, it was a vain and idle enactment, which accomplished nothing, and most unnecessarily excited Congress and the people on its passage. With privileges and immunities thus designated or implied no State could ever have interfered by its laws, and no new constitutional provision was required to inhibit such interference. The supremacy of the Constitution and the laws of the United States always controlled any State legislation of that character. But if the amendment refers to the

natural and inalienable rights which belong to all citizens, the inhibition has a profound significance and consequence.

What, then, are the privileges and immunities which are secured against abridgment by State legislation? . . .

The terms, privileges and immunities, are not new in the Amendment; they were in the Constitution before the Amendment was adopted. They are found in the Second Section of the Fourth Article, which declares that "the citizens of each State shall be entitled to all privileges and immunities of citizens in the several States," and they have been the subject of frequent consideration in judicial decisions. In *Corfield* v. *Coryell,* Mr. Justice Washington said he had "no hesitation in confining these expressions to those privileges and immunities which were, in their nature, fundamental; which belong of right to citizens of all free governments, and which have at all times been enjoyed by the citizens of the several States which composed the Union, from the time of their becoming free, independent, and sovereign;" and, in considering what those fundamental privileges were, he said that perhaps it would be more tedious than difficult to enumerate them, but that they might be "all comprehended under the following general heads: protection by the government; the enjoyment of life and liberty, with the right to acquire and possess property of every kind, and to pursue and obtain happiness and safety, subject, nevertheless, to such restraints as the government may justly prescribe for the general good of the whole." This appears to me to be a sound construction of the clause in question. The privileges and immunities designated are those *which of right belong to the citizens of all free governments.* Clearly among these must be placed the right to pursue a lawful employment in a lawful manner, without other restraint than such as equally affects all persons. In the discussions in Congress upon the passage of the Civil Rights Act repeated reference was made to this language of Mr. Justice Washington. It was cited by Senator Trumbull with the observation that it enumerated the very rights belonging to a citizen of the United States set forth in the first section of the act, and with the statement that all persons born in the United States, being declared by the act citizens of the United States, would thenceforth be entitled to the rights of citizens, and that these were the great fundamental rights set forth in the act; and that they were set forth "as appertaining to every freeman." . . .

This equality of right, with exemption from all disparaging and partial enactments, in the lawful pursuits of life, throughout the whole country, is the distinguishing privilege of citizens of the United States. To them, everywhere, all pursuits, all professions, all avocations are open without other restrictions than such as are imposed equally upon all others of the same age, sex, and condition. The State may prescribe such regulations for every pursuit and calling of life as will promote the public health, secure the good order and advance the general prosperity of society, but when once prescribed, the pursuit or calling must be free to be followed by every citizen who is within the conditions designated, and will conform to the regulations. This is the fundamental idea upon which our institutions rest, and unless adhered to in the legislation of the country our government will be a republic only in name. The fourteenth amendment, in my judgment, makes it essential to the validity of the legislation of every State that this equality of right should be respected. How widely this equality has been departed from, how entirely rejected and trampled upon by the act of Louisiana, I have already shown. And it is to me a matter of profound regret that its validity is recognized by a majority of this court, for by it the right of free labor, one of the most sacred and imprescriptible rights of man, is violated. . . .

I am authorized by the Chief Justice [Chase], Mr. Justice Swayne, and Mr. Justice Bradley, to state that they concur with me in this dissenting opinion.

Justices Bradley and Swayne delivered separate dissenting opinions.

Note and quaere: The *Slaughter House* interpretation of the privileges and immunities of United States citizenship has remained essentially as outlined by Mr. Justice Miller. Like the Tenth Amendment it seems tautological; that is, apparently it protects only interests which would be protected in any event by other constitutional provisions. To put it differently, such meaning as the Court has found in the general provisions of the Fourteenth Amendment, it has found in the due Process and Equal Protection clauses. The net effect has been hardly restrictive, however, for as Holmes observed apropos the laissez-faire Court, only the sky was the limit to what could be found in due process. Putting the eggs in the equal protection–due process basket (which protects "persons") at least had the effect of encompassing aliens. Such protection would not have been possible if the Court had relied chiefly on the Privileges and Immunities Clause (which covers only citizens). But was this the crucial consideration? Or was it that the laissez-faire Justices settled upon equal protection–due process rather than privileges and immunities because business corporations could more plausibly be treated as "persons" under the former than as "citizens" under the latter?

Munn v. *Illinois*
94 U.S. 113 (1877)

This is one of the famous *Granger Cases* which together tested the validity of state regulation of rates (prices) charged by grain warehouses and railroads. Among other things, it was alleged that such regulations violated the Fourteenth Amendment by depriving the owners of their property without due process of law.

Mr. Chief Justice Waite delivered the opinion of the Court. . . .

. . . Every statute is presumed to be constitutional. The courts ought not to declare one to be unconstitutional, unless it is clearly so. If there is doubt, the expressed will of the legislature should be sustained. . . .

When one becomes a member of society, he necessarily parts with some rights or privileges which, as an individual not affected by his relations to others, he might retain. "A body politic," as aptly defined in the preamble of the constitution of Massachusetts, "is a social compact by which the whole people covenants with each citizen, and each citizen with the whole people, that all shall be governed by certain laws for the common good." This does not confer power upon the whole people to control rights which are purely and exclusively private, *Thorpe* v. *R. & B. Railroad Co.*, 27 Vt. 140; but it does authorize the establishment of laws requiring each citizen to so conduct himself, and so use his own property, as not unnecessarily to injure another. This is the very essence of government, and has found expression in the maxim, *sic utere tuo ut alienum non laedas.* From this source come the police powers, which . . . "are nothing more or less than the powers of government inherent in every sovereignty, . . . that is to say, . . . the power to govern men and things." Under these powers the government regulates the conduct of its citizens one towards another, and the manner in which each shall use his own property, when such regulation becomes necessary for the public good. In their exercise it has been customary in England from time immemorial, and in this country from its first colonization, to regulate ferries, common carriers, hackmen, bakers, millers, wharfingers, innkeepers, etc., and in so doing to fix a maximum of charge to be made for services rendered, accommodations furnished, and articles sold. To this day, statutes are to be found in many of the states upon some or all these subjects; and we think it has never yet been successfully contended that such legislation came

within any of the constitutional prohibitions against interference with private property. . . .

From this it is apparent that, down to the time of the adoption of the Fourteenth Amendment, it was not supposed that statutes regulating the use, or even the price of the use, of private property necessarily deprived an owner of his property without due process of law. Under some circumstances they may, but not under all. The amendment does not change the law in this particular: it simply prevents the states from doing that which will operate as such a deprivation.

This brings us to inquire as to the principles upon which this power of regulation rests, in order that we may determine what is within and what without its operative effect. Looking, then, to the common law, from whence came the right which the Constitution protects, we find that when private property is "affected with a public interest, it ceases to be *juris privati* only." This was said by Lord Chief Justice Hale more than two hundred years ago. . . . Property does become clothed with a public interest when used in a manner to make it of public consequence, and affect the community at large. When, therefore, one devotes his property to a use in which the public has an interest, he, in effect, grants to the public an interest in that use, and must submit to be controlled by the public for the common good, to the extent of the interest he has thus created. He may withdraw his grant by discontinuing the use; but, so long as he maintains the use, he must submit to the control. . . .

And the same has been held as to warehouses and warehousemen. . . .

From the same source comes the power to regulate the charges of common carriers, which was done in England as long ago as the third year of the reign of William and Mary, and continued until within a comparatively recent period. . . .

Common carriers exercise a sort of public office, and have duties to perform in which the public is interested. . . . Their business is, therefore, "affected with a public interest," within the meaning of the doctrine which Lord Hale has no forcibly stated.

But we need not go further. Enough has already been said to show that, when private property is devoted to a public use, it is subject to public regulation. It remains only to ascertain whether the warehouses of these plaintiffs in error, and the business which is carried on there, come within the operation of this principle.

For this purpose we accept as true the statements of fact contained in the elaborate brief of one of the counsel of the plaintiffs in error. From these it appears that ". . . The quantity [of grain] received in Chicago has made it the greatest grain market in the world. This business has created a demand for means by which the immense quantity of grain can be handled or stored, and these have been found in grain warehouses. . . . In this way the largest traffic between the citizens of the country north and west of Chicago and the citizens of the country lying on the Atlantic coast north of Washington is in grain which passes through the elevators of Chicago. In this way the trade in grain is carried on by the inhabitants of seven or eight of the great states of the west with four or five of the states lying on the seashore, and forms the largest part of interstate commerce in these states. The grain warehouses or elevators in Chicago are immense structures, holding from 300,000 to 1,000,000 bushels at one time, according to size. . . . It has been found impossible to preserve each owner's grain separate, and this has given rise to a system of inspection and grading, by which the grain of different owners is mixed, and receipts issued for the number of bushels, which are negotiable, and redeemable in like kind, upon demand. This mode of conducting the business was inaugurated more than twenty years ago, and has grown to immense proportions. The railways have found it impracticable to own such elevators, and public policy forbids the transaction of such business by the carrier; the ownership has, therefore, been by private individuals, who have embarked their capital and devoted their industry to such business as a private pursuit."

In this connection it must also be borne in mind that, although in 1874 there were in Chicago fourteen warehouses adapted to this particular business, and owned by about thirty persons, nine business firms controlled them, and that the price charged and received for storage were such "as have been from year to year agreed upon and established by the different elevators or warehouses in the city of Chicago, and which rates have been annually published in one or more newspapers printed in said city, in the month of January in each year, as the established rates for the year then next ensuing such publication." Thus it is apparent that all the elevating facilities through which these vast productions "of seven or eight great states of the west" must pass on the way "to four or five of the states on the seashore" may be a "virtual" monopoly.

Under such circumstances it is difficult to see why, if the common carrier, or the miller, or the ferryman, or the innkeeper, or the wharfinger, or the baker, or the cartman, or the hackney-coachman, pursues a public employment and exercises "a sort of public office," these plaintiffs in error do not. They stand, to use again the language of their counsel, in the very "gateway of commerce," and take toll from all who pass. Their business most certainly "tends to a common charge, and is become a thing of public interest and use." . . . Certainly, if any business can be clothed "with a public interest and cease to be *juris privati* only," this has been. It may not be made so by the operation of the constitution of Illinois or this statute, but it is by the facts.

We also are not permitted to overlook the fact that, for some reason, the people of Illinois, when they revised their constitution in 1870, saw fit to make it the duty of the general assembly to pass laws "for the protection of producers, shippers, and receivers of grain and product," article 13, section 7; and by section 5 of the same article, to require all railroad companies receiving and transporting grain in bulk or otherwise to deliver the same at any elevator to which it might be consigned, that could be reached by any track that was or could be used by such company, and that all railroad companies should permit connections to be made with their tracks, so that any public warehouse, etc., might be reached by the cars on their railroads. This indicates very clearly that during the twenty years in which this peculiar business had been assuming its present "immense proportions," something had occurred which led the whole body of the people to suppose that remedies such as are usually employed to prevent abuses by virtual monopolies might not be inappropriate here. For our purposes we must assume that, if a state of facts could exist that would justify such legislation, it actually did exist when the statute now under consideration was passed. For us the question is one of power, not of expediency. If no state of circumstances could exist to justify such a statute, then we may declare this one void, because in excess of the legislative power of the state. But if it could, we must presume it did. Of the propriety of legislative interference within the scope of legislative power, the legislature is the exclusive judge. . . .

We know that this is a power which may be abused; but that is no argument against its existence. For portection against abuses by legislatures the people must resort to the polls, not to the courts. . . .

We come now to consider the effect upon this statute of the power of Congress to regulate commerce.

It was very properly said in the case of the *State Tax on Railway Gross Receipts*, 15 Wallace 284, that "it is not everything that affects commerce that amounts to a regulation of it, within the meaning of the Constitution." The warehouses of these plaintiffs in error are situated and their business carried on exclusively within the limits of the State of Illinois. They are used as instruments by those engaged in state as well as those engaged in interstate commerce, but they are no more necessarily a part of commerce itself than the dray or the cart by which, but for them, grain would be trans-ferred from one railroad station to another. Incidentally they may become connected with interstate commerce, but not necessarily so. Their regulation is a thing of domestic concern, and, certainly, until Congress acts in reference to their interstate relations, the state may exercise all the powers of government over them, even though in so doing it may indirectly operate upon commerce outside its immediate jurisdiction. We do not say that a case may not arise in which it will be found that a state, under the form of regulating its own affairs, has encroached upon the exclusive domain of Congress in respect to interstate commerce, but we do say that, upon the facts as they are represented to us in this record, that has not been done. . . .

We conclude, therefore, that the statute in question is not repugnant to the Constitution of the United States, and that there is no error in the judgment. . . .

Judgment affirmed.

Mr. Justice Field and Mr. Justice Strong dissented.

Mr. Justice Field. . . . I am compelled to dissent from the decision of the court in this case, and from the reasons upon which that decision is founded. The principle upon which the opinion of the majority proceeds is, in my judgment, subversive of the rights of private property, heretofore believed to be protected by constitutional guaranties against legislative interference, and is in conflict with the authorities cited in its support. . . .

If this be sound law, if there be no protection, either in the principles upon which our republican government is founded, or in the prohibitions of the Constitution against such invasion of private rights, all property and all business in the State are held at the mercy of a majority of its legislature. The public has no greater interest in the use of buildings for the storage of grain than it has in the use of buildings for the residences of families, nor, indeed, any thing like so great an interest; and, according to the doctrine announced, the legislature may fix the rent of all tenements used for residences, without reference to the cost of their erection. If the owner does not like the rates prescribed, he may cease renting his houses. He has granted to the public, says the court, an interest in the use of the buildings, and "he may withdraw his grant by discontinuing the use; but, so long as he maintains the use, he must submit to the control." The public is interested in the manufacture of cotton, woollen, and silken fabrics, in the construction of machinery, in the printing and publication of books and periodicals, and in the making of utensils of every variety, useful and ornamental; indeed, there is hardly an enterprise or business engaging the attention and labor of any considerable portion of the community, in which the public has not an interest in the sense in which that term is used by the court in its opinion; and the doctrine which allows the legislature to interfere with and regulate the charges which the owners of property thus employed shall make for its use, that is, the rates at which all these different kinds of business shall be carried on, has never before been asserted, so far as I am aware, by any judicial tribunal in the United States. . . .

No State "shall deprive any person of life, liberty, or property without due process of law," says the Fourteenth Amendment to the Constitution. By the term "life," as here used, something more is meant than mere animal existence. The inhibition against its deprivation extends to all those limbs and faculties by which life is enjoyed. The provision equally prohibits the multilation of the body by the amputation of an arm or leg, or the putting out of an eye, or the destruction of any other organ of the body through which the soul communicates with the outer world. The deprivation not only of life, but of whatever God has given to every one with life, for its growth and enjoyment, is prohibited by the provision in question, if its efficacy be not frittered away by judicial decision.

By the term "liberty," as used in the provision, something more is meant than mere freedom from physical restraint or the bounds of a prison. It means freedom to go where one may choose, and to act in such manner, not inconsistent with the equal rights of others, as his judgment may dictate for the promotion of his happiness; that is, to pursue such callings and avocations as may be most suitable to develop his capacities, and give to them their highest enjoyment.

The same liberal construction which is required for the protection of life and liberty, in all particulars in which life and liberty are of any value, should be applied to the protection of private property. If the legislature of a State, under pretense of providing for the public good, or for any other reason, can determine, against the consent of the owner, the uses to which private property shall be devoted, or the prices which the owner shall receive for its uses, it can deprive him of the property as completely as by a special act for its confiscation or destruction. If, for instance, the owner is prohibited from using his building for the purposes for which it was designed, it is of little consequence that he is permitted to retain the title and possession; or, if he is compelled to take as compensation for its use less than the expenses to which he is subjected by its ownership, he is, for all practical purposes, deprived of the property, as effectually as if the legislature had ordered his forcible dispossession. If it be admitted that the legislature has any control over the compensation, the extent of that compensation becomes a mere matter of legislative discretion. The amount fixed will operate as a partial destruction of the value of the property, if it fall below the amount which the owner would obtain by contract, and, practically, as a complete destruction, if it be less than the cost of retaining its possession. There is, indeed, no protection of any value under the constitutional provision, which does not extend to the use and income of the property, as well as to its title and possession. . . .

Strauder v. *West Virginia* (excerpt)
100 U.S. 303 (1880)

A black man was convicted of murder by a state court jury from which blacks had been excluded by state law. Reversing the conviction, the Court observed:

This [Fourteenth Amendment] is one of a series of constitutional provisions having a common purpose; namely, securing to a race recently emancipated, a race that through many generations had been held in slavery, all the civil rights that the [white] race enjoy. It was designed to assure to the colored race the enjoyment of all the civil rights that under the law are enjoyed by white persons, and to give to that race the protection of the general government, in that enjoyment, whenever it should be denied by the States. It not only gave citizenship and the privileges of citizenship to persons of color, but it denied to any State the power to withhold from them the equal protection of the laws, and authorized Congress to enforce its provisions by appropriate legislation. . . . What is this but declaring that the law in the States shall be the same for the black as for the white; that all persons, whether colored or white, shall stand equal before the laws of the States, and, in regard to the colored race, for whose protection the amendment was primarily designed, that no discrimination shall be made against them by law because of their color? The words of the amendment, it is true, are prohibitory, but they contain a necessary implication of a positive immunity, or right, most valuable to the colored race,—the right to exemption from unfriendly legislation against them distinctively as colored,—exemption from legal discriminations, implying inferiority in civil society, lessening the security of their enjoyment of the rights which others enjoy, and discriminations which are steps towards reducing them to the condition of a subject race.

[Justices Field and Clifford dissented.]

Note: In *Twitchell* v. *Pennsylvania*, 7 Wallace 321 (1869), the petitioner had been sentenced to death for murder. His appeal to the Supreme Court alleged denial of Fifth and Sixth Amendment rights. On the basis of *Barron* v. *Baltimore*, above (which held that the Bill of Rights does not apply to the states), the Court unanimously dismissed the appeal—and *Twitchell* went to his death. If the Fourteenth Amendment "incorporated" the Bill of Rights (as *later* alleged), Twitchell's conviction would have had to be reversed. Counsel and all of the Justices had just lived through the era of the drafting, discussion, and public adoption of the Fourteenth Amendment. Yet none of them seemed aware of what later became the doctrine of incorporation (i.e., that somehow the Fourteenth Amendment "reverses" *Barron* and imposes the Bill of Rights on the states).

THE EVOLVING FOURTEENTH AMENDMENT

The Thirteenth Amendment abolished slavery in the United States. The South responded with discriminatory Black Codes calculated to maintain the essence of the old system (though not without some benefits for blacks). This was the basic problem that begot the Fourteenth Amendment.

As though recognizing the impossibility of defining precisely the forms of racism that they sought to outlaw, the authors of the Fourteenth Amendment resorted to generalities: the Privileges and Immunities, Due Process, and Equal Protection Clauses. Nowhere did they specify what they meant by "privileges or immunities" of

United States citizenship. Indeed the term is so lacking in standards for the guidance of judges that, with one exception (*Colgate* v. *Harvey*, 296 U.S. 404 [1935]) soon overruled (*Madden* v. *Kentucky*, 309 U.S. 83 [1940]), the Court has never upheld any claim based upon it. Literally, the Due Process Clause is also highly obscure. What "process" is "due" in what circumstances? Those who gave us the Fourteenth Amendment did not explain (though perhaps that was not necessary, for the phrase was laden with history which ran back to Magna Carta). The Equal Protection Clause has a fine ring—until one recognizes that virtually every law (good or bad) necessarily treats different people differently. Some must pay income taxes at a higher rate than others; some are entitled to welfare benefits, others are not; some may vote, some may practice medicine, some may drive automobiles—others may not. Such distinctions or classifications are inherent in all legal systems. The Equal Protection Clause does not tell us which classifications are permissible and which are forbidden.

The Court might have treated due process and equal protection as it has treated privileges or immunities, that is, as too ambiguous to be enforced judicially. Or it might have recognized that while the letter of the amendment is vague, its spirit or purpose (read in historical context) is quite clear—to eliminate racial discrimination, *period*. This, of course, was the Court's initial understanding, as *Slaughter House* indicates.

Neither of these two approaches has prevailed. What has happened rather has been a series of changing renditions (called "interpretations" by those who like them; "usurpations" by those who do not). Indeed, the Fourteenth Amendment has undergone more changes of meaning than any other provision of the Constitution. The "original understanding," as we have seen, was quite clear. It was adopted to outlaw racial discrimination (*Slaughter House*); it did just that (*Strauder*); it did not impede state regulation of business (*Munn*); and it had nothing to do with the Bill of Rights (*Twitchell*). By the mid–1890s, however, as we shall see, it began to embody laissez-faire restrictions on business regulation (*Lochner*) and to permit racial segregation (*Plessy*). Then in what can be called the era of reform beginning in 1937, the laissez-faire (*Skrupa*) and racial segregation (*Brown*) components were dropped. Professor E. S. Corwin called this a "return to the Constitution," that is, to the "original understanding." Then in the "flaming 1960s" the Fourteenth Amendment became a sword by which the Court imposed reapportionment (*Sims*), a new "code" of criminal procedure (e.g., *Miranda*), and busing, that is, integration (*Swann*) on the states. Finally, beginning about 1973, came a period of retrenchment best symbolized, perhaps, in the *Bakke* case and the refusal to require equal per-pupil expenditures for public schools (*Rodriguez*).

This brief outline touches only the high points. Other shifting crosscurrents of meaning will be found in the numerous additional Fourteenth Amendment cases that follow. Do these often clashing "interpretations" reflect what judges have perceived as "the goals of American society"? (See quotation from Miller and Howell in Chapter 1, above.) Does variation prove subjectivity? Do these significantly different meanings constitute in effect judicial amendments of the Fourteenth Amendment? Is this an encroachment on Article V of the Constitution?

6

The Right to Privacy (Autonomy): Old and New

PRIVATE PROPERTY AND PRIVATE ENTERPRISE

Introduction: The Contract Clause

Early in our history—prior to the Fourteenth Amendment—the Contract Clause (Constitution, Article I, Section 10) served as a shield for private property and entrepreneurial interests. *Fletcher* v. *Peck,* 6 Cranch 87 (1810)—the first case in which state legislation was found unconstitutional—held the clause applicable to state contracts with private entrepreneurs, despite the argument that it was meant to protect only contracts between private parties. The *Dartmouth Case,* (below) treated state-granted corporate charters as contracts protected from infringement by state legislation.

Later in *Providence Bank* v. *Billings,* 4 Peters 514 (1830), and *Charles River Bridge Co.* v. *Warren Bridge Co.,* 11 Peters 420 (1837), the Court, apparently in an effort to guard against excessively broad interpretations of public grants, developed a doctrine of strict construction: ". . . any ambiguity in the terms of [a public grant or] contract, must operate against the adventures [i.e., grantees] in favor of the public." Later still it held that a "legislature cannot bargain away the police power." Thus the grant of a charter to operate a lottery, or to sell beer, could subsequently be withdrawn by general prohibition of such activity: *Stone* v. *Mississippi,* 101 U.S. 814 (1880); *Beer Co.* v. *Massachusetts,* 97 U.S. 25 (1878). The now quiescent nature of the Contract Clause is seen in *Home Building & Loan Association* v. *Blaisdell,* below. Yet in extreme cases it may spring to life, as in *Allied Structural Steel Co.* v. *Spannaus,* 98 S. Ct. 2716 (1978), which struck down a state law that would have substantially increased—retroactively—pension fund obligations undertaken by a private employer.

It is noteworthy that beginning in the 1890s (after the decline of the Contract Clause), laissez-faire economic theory seemed to engulf the Court. It then began to use the Due Process Clause to protect privacy or autonomy interests similar to those earlier protected in *Fletcher* and *Dartmouth* by the Contract Clause. See the cases on substantive due process, below.

Dartmouth College v. *Woodward*
4 Wheaton 518 (1819)

A royal charter of 1769 established Dartmouth College and authorized a self-perpetuating board of trustees to manage it. After the American Revolution the state of New Hampshire enacted legislation to convert the college into a state university by placing it under a board of overseers appointed by the state governor. The trustees brought suit to test the validity of the new arrangement.

The opinion of the Court was delivered by Mr. Chief Justice Marshall: . . .

It can require no argument to prove, that the circumstances of this case constitute a contract. An application is made to the crown for a charter to incorporate a religious and literary institution. In the application, it is stated that large contributions have been made for the object, which will be conferred on the corporation, as soon as it shall be created. The charter is granted, and on its faith the property is conveyed. Surely in this transaction every ingredient of a complete and legitimate contract is to be found.

The points for consideration are,

1. Is this contract protected by the Constitution of the United States?

2. Is it impaired by the [legislative] acts under which the defendant holds?

1. On the first point it has been argued, that the word "contract," in its broadest sense, would comprehend the political relations between the government and its citizens, would extend to offices held within a State for State purposes, and to many of those laws concerning civil institutions, which must change with circumstances, and be modified by ordinary legislation; which deeply concern the public, and which, to preserve good government, the public judgment must control. That even marriage is a contract, and its obligations are affected by the laws respecting divorces. That the clause in the Constitution, if construed in its greatest latitude, would prohibit these laws. Taken in its broad unlimited sense, the clause would be an unprofitable and vexatious interference with the internal concerns of a State, would unnecessarily and unwisely embarrass its legislation, and render immutable those civil institutions, which are established for purposes of internal government, and which, to subserve those purposes, ought to vary with varying circumstances. That as the framers of the Constitution could never have intended to insert in that instrument a provision so unnecessary, so mischievous, and so repugnant to its general spirit, the term "contract" must be understood in a more limited sense. That it must be understood as intended to guard against a power of at least doubtful utility, the abuse of which had been extensively felt; and to restrain the legislature in future from violating the right to property. That anterior to the formation of the Constitution, a course of legislation had prevailed in many, if not in all, of the States, which weakened the confidence of man in man, and embarrassed all transactions between individuals, by dispensing with a faithful performance of engagements. To correct this mischief, by restraining the

power which produced it, the State legislatures were forbidden "to pass any law impairing the obligation of contracts," that is, of contracts respecting property, under which some individual could claim a right to something beneficial to himself; and that since the clause in the Constitution must in construction receive some limitation, it may be confined, and ought to be confined, to cases of this description; to cases within the mischief it was intended to remedy.

The general correctness of these observations cannot be controverted. That the framers of the Constitution did not intend to restrain the States in the regulation of their civil institutions, adopted for internal government, and that the instrument they have given us, is not to be so construed, may be admitted. The provision of the Constitution never has been understood to embrace other contracts, than those which respect property, or some object of value, and confer rights which may be asserted in a court of justice. It never has been understood to restrict the general right of the legislature to legislate on the subject of divorces. Those acts enable some tribunal, not to impair a marriage contract, but to liberate one of the parties because it has been broken by the other. When any State legislature shall pass an act annulling all marriage contracts, or allowing either party to annul it without the consent of the other, it will be time enough to inquire, whether such an act be constitutional. . . .

This is plainly a contract to which the donors, the trustees, and the crown (to whose rights and obligations New Hampshire succeeds) were the original parties. It is a contract made on a valuable consideration. It is a contract for the security and disposition of property. It is a contract on the faith of which real and personal estate has been conveyed to the corporation. It is then a contract within the letter of the Constitution, and within its spirit also, unless the fact that the property is invested by the donors in trustees, for the promotion of religion and education, for the benefit of persons who are perpetually changing, though the objects remain the same,

shall create a particular exception, taking this case out of the prohibition contained in the Constitution.

It is more than possible that the preservation of rights of this description was not particularly in the view of the framers of the Constitution, when the clause under consideration was introduced into that instrument. It is probable that interferences of more frequent recurrence, to which the temptation was stronger, and of which the mischief was more extensive, constituted the great motive for imposing this restriction on the State legislatures. But although a particular and a rare case may not, in itself, be of sufficient magnitude to induce a rule, yet it must be governed by the rule, when established, unless some plain and strong reason for excluding it can be given. It is not enough to say, that this particular case was not in the mind of the Convention when the article was framed, nor of the American people when it was adopted. It is necessary to go further, and to say that, had this particular case been suggested, the language would have been so varied as to exclude it, or it would have been made a special exception. The case being within the words of the rule, must be within its operation likewise, unless there be something in the literal construction so obviously absurd or mischievous, or repugnant to the general spirit of the instrument, as to justify those who expound the Constitution in making it an exception. . . .

The opinion of the Court, after mature deliberation, is, that this is a contract, the obligation of which cannot be impaired, without violating the Constitution of the United States. This opinion appears to us to be equally supported by reason, and by the former decisions of this Court.

2.   We next proceed to the inquiry, whether its obligation has been impaired by those acts of the legislature of New Hampshire, to which the special verdict refers.

From the review of this charter, which has been taken, it appears, that the whole power of governing the college, of appointing and removing tutors, of fixing their salaries, of directing the course of study to be pursued by the students, and of filling up vacancies created in their own body, was vested in the trustees. On the part of the crown it was expressly stipulated, that this corporation, thus constituted, should continue forever; and that the number of trustees should forever consist of twelve, and no more. By this contract the crown was bound, and could have made no violent alteration in its essential terms, without impairing its obligation.

By the revolution, the duties, as well as the powers, of government devolved on the people of New Hampshire. It is admitted, that among the latter was comprehended the transcendent power of parliament, as well as that of the executive department. It is too clear to require the support of argument, that all contracts, and rights, respecting property, remained unchanged by the revolution. The obligations then, which were created by the charter to Dartmouth College, were the same in the new, that they had been in the old government. The power of the government was also the same. A repeal of this charter at any time prior to the adoption of the present Constitution of the United States, would have been an extraordinary and unprecedented act of power, but one which could have been contested only by the restrictions upon the legislature, to be found in the constitution of the State. But the Constitution of the United States has imposed this additional limitation, that the legislature of a State shall pass no act "impairing the obligation of contracts." . . .

On the effect of this law [of 1816], two opinions cannot be entertained. Between acting directly, and acting through the agency of trustees and overseers, no essential difference is perceived. The whole power of governing the college is transferred from trustees appointed according to the will of the founder, expressed in the charter to the executive of New Hampshire. The management and application of the funds of this eleemosynary institution, which are placed by the donors in the hands of trustees named in the charter, and empowered to perpetuate themselves, are placed by this act under the control of the government of the State. The will of the State is substituted for the will of the donors, in every essential operation of the college. This is not an immaterial change.

It results from this opinion, that the acts of the legislature of New Hampshire, which are stated in the special verdict found in this cause, are repugnant to the Constitution of the United States; and that the judgment on this special verdict ought to have been for the plaintiffs. The judgment of the State Court must, therefore, be reversed.

[Justices Washington and Story concurred in separate opinions. Mr. Justice Duvall dissented without discussion.]

Home Building & Loan Association v. *Blaisdell*
290 U.S. 398 (1934)

In response to the Great Depression that began in 1929, the Minnesota Mortgage Moratorium Law of 1933 authorized state courts in effect to delay the foreclosure of mortgages by giving mortgage debtors an extended period of time to repay their debts (but not beyond May 1, 1935). The law required the debtor to pay to the creditor during the delay period the income of the property or its rental value. Blaisdell got a court-ordered delay conditioned on payment of $40 per month rental value. His creditor argued the moratorium law violated the Contract Clause and that accordingly immediate foreclosure was permissible.

Mr. Chief Justice Hughes delivered the opinion of the Court. . . .

In determining whether the provision for this temporary and conditional relief exceeds the power of the state by reason of the clause in the Federal Constitution prohibiting impairment of the obligations of contracts, we must consider the relation of emergency to constitutional power, the historical setting of the contract clause, the development of the jurisprudence of this Court in the construction of that clause, and the principles of construction which we may consider to be established.

Emergency does not create power. Emergency does not increase granted power or remove or diminish the restrictions imposed upon power granted or reserved. The Constitution was adopted in a period of grave emergency. Its grants of power to the federal government and its limitations of the power of the States were determined in the light of emergency, and they are not altered by emergency. What power was thus granted and what limitations were thus imposed are questions which have always been, and always will be, the subject of close examination under one constitutional system.

While emergency does not create power, emergency may furnish the occasion for the exercise of power. "Although an emergency may not call into life a power which has never lived, nevertheless emergency may afford a reason for the exertion of a living power already enjoyed." *Wilson* v. *New*, 243 U.S. 332, 348. The constitutional question presented in the light of an emergency is whether the power possessed embraces the particular exercise of it in response to particular conditions. Thus, the war power of the federal government is not created by the emergency of war, but it is a power given to meet that emergency. . . .

. . . To ascertain the scope of the constitutional prohibition, we examine the course of judicial decisions in its application. These put it beyond question that the prohibition is not an absolute one and is not to be read with literal exactness like a mathematical formula. . . .

The inescapable problems of construction have been: What is a contract? What are the obligations of contracts? What constitutes impairment of these obligations? What residuum of power is there still in the States, in relation to the operation of contracts, to protect the vital interests of the community? Questions of this character, "of no small nicety and intricacy, have vexed the legislative halls, as well as the judicial tribunals, with an uncounted variety and frequency of litigation and speculation." Story on the Constitution, § 1375.

The obligation of a contract is the law which binds the parties to perform their agreement. *Sturges* v. *Crowninshield*, 4 Wheat. 122, 197; Story, *op. cit.*, . . .

The obligations of a contract are impaired by a law which renders them invalid, or releases or extinguishes them (*Sturges* v. *Crowninshield, supra*, 4 Wheat. 197, 198), and impairment, as above noted, has been predicated of laws which without destroying contracts derogate from substantial contractual rights. In *Sturges* v. *Crowninshield, supra*, a state insolvent law, which discharged the debtor from liability, was held to be invalid as applied to contracts in existence when the law was passed. See *Ogden* v. *Saunders* [12 Wheat. 213]. In *Green* v. *Biddle*, 8 Wheat. 1, 5 L.Ed. 547, the Legislative acts, which were successfully assailed, exempted the occupant of land from the payment of rents and profits to the rightful owner, and were "parts of a system the object of which was to compel the rightful owner to relinquish his lands or pay for all lasting improvements made upon them, without his consent or default." In *Bronson* v. *Kinzie*, 1 How. 311, 11 L.Ed. 143, state legislation, which had been enacted for the relief of debtors in view of the seriously depressed condition of business, following the panic of 1837, and which provided that the equitable estate of the mortgagor should not be extinguished for twelve months after sale on foreclosure, and further prevented any sale unless two-thirds of the appraised value of the property should be bid therefor, was held to violate the constitutional provision. . . .

Not only is the constitutional provision qualified by the measure of control which the state retains over remedial processes, but the state also continues to possess authority to safeguard the vital interests of its people. It does not matter that legislation appropriate to that end "has the result of modifying or abrogating contracts already in effect." *Stephenson* v. *Binford,* 287 U.S. 251, 276. Not only are existing laws read into contracts in order to fix obligations as between the parties, but the reservation of essential attributes of sovereign power is also read into contracts as a postulate of the legal order. The policy of protecting contracts against impairment presupposes the maintenance of a government by virtue of which contractual relations are worth while,—a government which retains adequate authority to secure the peace and good order of society. This principle of harmonizing the constitutional prohibition with the necessary residuum of state power has had progressive recognition in the decisions of this Court.

While the charters of private corporations constitute contracts, a grant of exclusive privilege is not to be implied as against the state. *Charles River Bridge* v. *Warren Bridge,* 11 Pet. 420. And all contracts are subject to the right of eminent domain. *West River Bridge* v. *Dix,* 6 How. 507. The reservation of this necessary authority of the state is deemed to be a part of the contract. . . .

The Legislature cannot "bargain away the public health or the public morals." Thus the constitutional provision against the impairment of contracts was held not to be violated by an amendment of the state Constitution which put an end to a lottery theretofore authorized by the Legislature. *Stone* v. *Mississippi,* 101 U.S. 814, 819. . . .

The economic interests of the state may jus-

tify the exercise of its continuing and dominant protective power notwithstanding interference with contracts. In *Manigault* v. *Springs,* 199 U.S. 473, riparian owners in South Carolina had made a contract for a clear passage through a creek by the removal of existing obstructions. Later, the Legislature of the state, by virtue of its broad authority to make public improvements, and in order to increase the taxable value of the lowlands which would be drained, authorized the construction of a dam across the creek. The Court sustained the statute upon the ground that the private interests were subservient to the public right. . . .

Undoubtedly, whatever is reserved of state power must be consistent with the fair intent of the constitutional limitation of that power. The reserved power cannot be construed so as to destroy the limitation, nor is the limitation to be construed to destroy the reserved power in its essential aspects. They must be construed in harmoney with each other. This principle precludes a construction which would permit the state to adopt as its policy the repudiation of debts or the destruction of contracts or the denial of means to enforce them. But it does not follow that conditions may not arise in which a temporary restraint of enforcement may be consistent with the spirit and purpose of the constitutional provision and thus be found to be within the range of the reserved power of the state to protect the vital interests of the community. . . .

Whatever doubt there may have been that the protective power of the State, its police power, may be exercised—without violating the true intent of the provision of the Federal Constitution—in directly preventing the immediate and literal enforcement of contractual obligations by a temporary and conditional restraint, where vital public interests would otherwise suffer, was removed by our decisions relating to the enforcement of provisions of leases during a period of scarcity of housing. *Block* v. *Hirsh,* 256 U.S. 135; *Marcus Brown Hold-*

ing Co. v. *Feldman,* 256 U.S. 170; *Edgar A. Levy Leasing Co.* v. *Siegel,* 258 U.S. 242. The case of *Block* v. *Hirsh, supra,* arose in the District of Columbia and involved the due process clause of the Fifth Amendment. The cases of the Marcus Brown Company and the Levy Leasing Company arose under legislation of New York and the constitutional provision against the impairment of the obligation of contracts was invoked. The statutes of New York, declaring that a public emergency existed, directly interfered with the enforcement of covenants for the surrender of the possession of premises on the expiration of leases. Within the City of New York and contiguous counties, the owners of dwellings, including apartment and tenement houses (but excepting buildings under construction in September, 1920, lodging houses for transients and the larger hotels), were wholly deprived until November 1, 1922, of all possessory remedies for the purpose of removing from their premises the tenants or occupants in possession when the laws took effect (save in certain specified instances), providing the tenants or occupants were ready, able and willing to pay a reasonable rent or price for their use and occupation. . . .

It is manifest from this review of our decisions that there has been a growing appreciation of public needs and of the necessity of finding ground for a rational compromise between individual rights and public welfare. The settlement and consequent contraction of the public domain, the pressure of a constantly increasing density of population, the interrelation of the activities of our people and the complexity of our economic interests, have inevitably led to an increased use of the organization of society in order to protect the very bases of individual opportunity. Where, in earlier days, it was thought that only the concerns of individuals or of classes were involved, and that those of the state itself were touched only remotely, it has later been found that the fundamental interests of the state are directly affected; and that the question is no longer merely that of

one party to a contract as against another, but of the use of reasonable means to safeguard the economic structure upon which the good of all depends.

It is no answer to say that this public need was not apprehended a century ago, or to insist that what the provision of the Constitution meant to the vision of that day it must mean to the vision of our time. If by the statement that what the Constitution meant at the time of its adoption it means to-day, it is intended to say that the great clauses of the Constitution must be confined to the interpretation which the framers, with the conditions and outlook of their time, would have placed upon them, the statement carries its own refutation. It was to guard against such a narrow conception that Chief Justice Marshall uttered the memorable warning: "We must never forget, that it is *a constitution* we are expounding" (*McCulloch* v. *Maryland,* 4 Wheat. 316, 407); "a constitution intended to endure for ages to come, and, consequently, to be adapted to the various *crises* of human affairs." *Id.* page 415 of 4 Wheat. When we are dealing with the words of the Constitution, said this Court in *Missouri* v. *Holland,* 252 U.S. 416, 433, "we must realize that they have called into life a being the development of which could not have been foreseen completely by the most gifted of its begetters. . . . The case before us must be considered in the light of our whole experience and not merely in that of what was said a hundred years ago." . . .

Applying the criteria established by our decisions, we conclude:

1. An emergency existed in Minnesota which furnished a proper occasion for the exercise of the reserved power of the state to protect the vital interests of the community. The declarations of the existence of this emergency by the Legislature and by the Supreme Court of Minnesota cannot be regarded as a subterfuge or as lacking in adequate basis. . . .

2. The legislation was addressed to a legitimate end; that is, the legislation was not for the mere advantage of particular individuals

but for the protection of a basic interest of society.

3. In view of the nature of the contracts in question—mortgages of unquestionable validity—the relief afforded and justified by the emergency, in order not to contravene the constitutional provision, could only be of a character appropriate to that emergency, and could be granted only upon reasonable conditions.

4. The conditions upon which the period of redemption is extended do not appear to be unreasonable. . . .

5. The legislation is temporary in operation. . . .

We are of the opinion that the Minnesota statute as here applied does not violate the contract clause of the Federal Constitution. Whether the legislation is wise or unwise as a matter of policy is a question with which we are not concerned.

What has been said on that point is also applicable to the contention presented under the due process clause. . . .

Nor do we think that the statute denies to the appellant the equal protection of the laws. The classification which the statute makes cannot be said to be an arbitrary one. . . .

Mr. Justice Sutherland, dissenting.

. . . A candid consideration of the history and circumstances which led up to and accompanied the framing and adoption of this clause will demonstrate conclusively that it was framed and adopted with the specific and studied purpose of preventing legislation designed to relieve debtors *especially* in time of financial distress. Indeed, it is not probable that any other purpose was definitely in the minds of those who composed the framers' convention or the ratifying state conventions which followed, although the restriction has been given a wider application upon principles clearly stated by Chief Justice Marshall in the *Dartmouth College Case*, 4 Wheat. 518, 644–645. . . .

If it be possible by resort to the testimony of history to put any question of constitutional intent beyond the domain of uncertainty, the foregoing leaves no reasonable ground upon which to base a denial that the clause of the Constitution now under consideration was meant to foreclose state action impairing the obligation of contracts *primarily and especially* in respect of such action aimed at giving relief to debtors *in time of emergency*. And, if further proof be required to strengthen what already is inexpugnable, such proof will be found in the previous decisions of this court. [Discussion of the cases is omitted.]

The Minnesota statute either impairs the obligation of contracts or it does not. If it does not, the occasion to which it relates becomes immaterial, since then the passage of the statute is the exercise of a normal, unrestricted, state power and requires no special occasion to render it effective. If it does, the emergency no more furnishes a proper occasion for its exercise than if the emergency were non-existent. . . .

A statute which materially delays enforcement of the mortgagee's contractual right of ownership and possession does not modify the remedy merely; it destroys, for the period of delay, *all* remedy so far as the enforcement of that right is concerned. The phrase "obligation of a contract" in the constitutional sense imports a legal duty to perform the specified obligation of *that* contract, not to substitute and perform, against the will of one of the parties, a different, albeit equally valuable, obligation. And a state, under the contract impairment clause, has no more power to accomplish such a substitution than has one of the parties to the contract against the will of the other. It cannot do so either by acting directly upon the contract or by bringing about the result under the guise of a statute in form acting only upon the remedy. . . .

I am authorized to say that Mr. Justice Van Devanter, Mr. Justice McReynolds, and Mr. Justice Butler concur in this opinion.

The Old Substantive Due Process

Munn v. *Illinois*
See p. 197, above.

Lochner v. *New York*
198 U.S. 45 (1905)

Mr. Justice Peckham delivered the opinion of the Court. . . .

The indictment, it will be seen, charges that the plaintiff in error violated the 110th section of article 8, chapter 415, of the Laws of 1897, known as the labor law of the state of New York, in that he wrongfully and unlawfully required and permitted an employee working for him to work more than sixty hours in one week. . . .

It is not an act merely fixing the number of hours which shall constitute a legal day's work, but an absolute prohibition upon the employer permitting, under any circumstances, more than ten hours' work to be done in his establishment. The employee may desire to earn the extra money which would arise from his working more than the prescribed time, but this statute forbids the employer from permitting the employee to earn it.

The statute necessarily interferes with the right of contract between the employer and employees, concerning the number of hours in which the latter may labor in the bakery of the employer. The general right to make a contract in relation to his business is part of the liberty of the individual protected by the 14th Amendment of the Federal Constitution. *Allgeyer* v. *Louisiana,* 165 U.S. 578. Under that provision no state can deprive any person of life, liberty, or property without due process of law. The right to purchase or to sell labor is part of the liberty protected by this amendment, unless there are circumstances which exclude the right. There are, however, certain powers, existing in the sovereignty of each state in the Union,

somewhat vaguely termed police powers, the exact description and limitation of which have not been attempted by the courts. Those powers, broadly stated, and without, at present, any attempt at a more specific limitation, relate to the safety, health, morals, and general welfare of the public. Both property and liberty are held on such reasonable conditions as may be imposed by the governing power of the state in the exercise of those powers, and with such conditions the 14th Amendment was not designed to interfere. *Mugler* v. *Kansas,* 123 U.S. 623. . . .

Therefore, when the state, by its legislature, in the assumed exercise of its police powers, has passed an act which seriously limits the right to labor or the right of contract in regard to their means of livelihood between persons who are *sui juris* (both employer and employee), it becomes of great importance to determine which shall prevail,—the right of the individual to labor for such time as he may choose, or the right of the state to prevent the individual from laboring, or from entering into any contract to labor, beyond a certain time prescribed by the state.

This court has recognized the existence and upheld the exercise of the police powers of the states in many cases which might fairly be considered as border ones, and it has, in the course of its determination of questions regarding the asserted invalidity of such statutes, on the ground of their violation of the rights secured by the Federal Constitution, been guided by rules of a very liberal nature, the application of which has resulted, in numerous instances, in upholding the validity of state statutes thus assailed. Among the later cases where the state law has been upheld by this court is that of *Holden* v. *Hardy,* 169 U.S. 366. A provision in the act of the legislature of Utah was there under consideration, the act limiting the employment of workmen in all underground mines or workings, to eight hours per day, "except in cases of emergency, where life or property is in imminent danger." It also limited the hours of labor in smelting and other institutions for the reduction or refining of ores or metals to eight hours per day, except in like cases of emergency. The act was held to be a valid exercise of the police powers of the state. . . .

It must, of course, be conceded that there is a limit to the valid exercise of the police power by the state. . . . In every case that comes before this court, therefore, where legislation of this character is concerned, and where the protection of the Federal Constitution is sought, the question necessarily arises: Is this a fair, reasonable, and appropriate exercise of the police power of the state, or is it an unreasonable, unnecessary, and arbitrary interference with the right of the individual to his personal liberty, or to enter into those contracts in relation to labor which may seem to him appropriate or necessary for the support of himself and his family? Of course the liberty of contract relating to labor includes both parties to it. The one has as much right to purchase as the other to sell labor.

This is not a question of substituting the judgment of the court for that of the legislature. If the act be within the power of the state it is valid, although the judgment of the court might be totally opposed to the enactment of such a law. But the question would still remain: Is it within the police power of the state? and that question must be answered by the court.

The question whether this act is valid as a labor law, pure and simple, may be dismissed in a few words. There is no reasonable ground for interfering with the liberty of persons or the right of free contract, by determining the hours of labor, in the occupation of a baker. . . . Viewed in the light of a purely labor law with no reference whatever to the question of health, we think that a law like the one before us involves neither the safety, the morals, nor the welfare of the public, and that the interest of the public is not in the slightest degree affected by such an act. The law must be upheld, if at all, as a law pertaining to the health of the individual engaged in the occupation of a baker. . . .

We think the limit of the police power has been reached and passed in this case. There is,

in our judgment, no reasonable foundation for holding this to be necessary or appropriate as a health law to safeguard the public health, or the health of the individuals who are following the trade of a baker. . . .

It is also urged, pursuing the same line of argument, that it is to the interest of the state that its population should be strong and robust, and therefore any legislation which may be said to tend to make people healthy must be valid as health laws, enacted under the police power. If this be a valid argument and a justification for this kind of legislation, it follows that the protection of the Federal Constitution from undue interference with liberty of person and freedom of contract is visionary, wherever the law is sought to be justified as a valid exercise of the police power. Scarcely any law but might find shelter under such assumptions, and conduct, properly so called, as well as contract, would come under the restrictive sway of the legislature. Not only the hours of employees, but the hours of employers, could be regulated, and doctors, lawyers, scientists, all professional men, as well as athletes and artisans, could be forbidden to fatigue their brains and bodies by prolonged hours of exercise, lest the fighting strength of the state be impaired. We mention these extreme cases because the contention is extreme. We do not believe in the soundness of the views which uphold this law. . . . Statutes of the nature of that under review, limiting the hours in which grown and intelligent men may labor to earn their living, are mere meddlesome interferences with the rights of the individual, and they are not saved from condemnation by the claim that they are passed in the exercise of the police power and upon the subject of the health of the individual whose rights are interfered with, unless there be some fair ground, reasonable in and of itself, to say that there is material danger to the public health, or to the health of the employees, if the hours of labor are not curtailed. . . .

It is impossible, for us to shut our eyes to the fact that many of the laws of this character, while passed under what is claimed to be the police power for the purpose of protecting the public health or welfare, are, in reality, passed from other motives. We are justified in saying so when, from the character of the law and the subject upon which it legislates, it is apparent that the public health or welfare bears but the most remote relation to the law. The purpose of a statute must be determined from the natural and legal effect of the language employed; and whether it is or is not repugnant to the Constitution of the United States must be determined from the natural effect of such statutes when put into operation, and not from their proclaimed purpose. . . .

It is manifest to us that the limitation of the hours of labor as provided for in this section of the statute under which the indictment was found, and the plaintiff in error convicted, has no such direct relation to, and no such substantial effect upon, the health of the employee, as to justify us in regarding the section as really a health law. It seems to us that the real object and purpose were simply to regulate the hours of labor between the master and his employees (all being men, *sui juris*), in a private business, not dangerous in any degree to morals, or in any real and substantial degree to the health of the employees. Under such circumstances the freedom of master and employee to contract with each other in relation to their employment, and in defining the same, cannot be prohibited or interfered with, without violating the Federal Constitution. . . .

Reversed.

Mr. Justice Holmes dissenting:

I regret sincerely that I am unable to agree with the judgment in this case, and that I think it my duty to express my dissent.

This case is decided upon an economic theory which a large part of the country does not entertain. If it were a question whether I agreed with that theory, I should desire to study it further and long before making up my mind. But I do not conceive that to be my duty, because I strongly believe that my agreement or disagreement has nothing to do with the right of a majority to embody their opinions in law. It is settled by various decisions of this court that state constitutions and state laws may regulate life in many ways which we as legislators might think as injudicious, or if you like as tyrannical, as this, and which, equally with this, interfere with the liberty to contract. Sunday laws and usury laws are ancient examples. A more modern one is the prohibition of lotteries. The liberty of the citizen to do as he likes so long as he does not interfere with the liberty of others to do the same, which has been a shibboleth for some well-known writers, is interfered with by school laws, by the Postoffice, by every state or municipal institution which takes his money for purposes thought desirable, whether he likes it or not. The 14th Amendment does not enact Mr. Herbert Spencer's Social Statics. The other day we sustained the Massachusetts vaccination law. *Jacobson* v. *Massachusetts*, 197 U.S. 11. United States and state statutes and decisions cutting down the liberty to contract by way of combination are familiar to this court. *Northern Securities Co.* v. *United States*, 193 U.S. 197. Two years ago we upheld the prohibition of sales of stock on margins, or for future delivery, in the Constitution of California. *Otis* v. *Parker*, 187 U.S. 606. The decision sustaining an eight-hour law for miners is still recent. *Holden* v. *Hardy*, 169 U.S. 366. Some of these laws embody convictions or prejudices which judges are likely to share. Some may not. But a Constitution is not intended to embody a particular economic theory, whether of paternalism and the organic relation of the citizen to the state or of *laissez faire*. It is made for people of fundamentally differing views, and the accident of our finding certain opinions natural and familiar, or novel, and even shocking, ought not to conclude our judgment upon the question whether statutes embodying them conflict with the Constitution of the United States.

General propositions do not decide concrete cases. The decision will depend on a judgment or intuition more subtle than any articulate major premise. But I think that the proposition just stated, if it is accepted, will carry us far toward the end. Every opinion tends to become a law. I think that the word "liberty," in the 14th Amendment, is perverted when it is held to prevent the natural outcome of a dominant opinion, unless it can be said that a rational and fair man necessarily would admit that the statute proposed would infringe fundamental principles as they have been understood by the traditions of our people and our law. It does not need research to show that no such sweeping condemnation can be passed upon the statute before us. A reasonable man might think it a proper measure on the score of health. Men whom I certainly could not pronounce unreasonable would uphold it as a first instalment of a general regulation of the hours of work. Whether in the latter aspect it would be open to the charge of inequality I think it unnecessary to discuss.

Mr. Justice Harlan (with whom Mr. Justice White and Mr. Justice Day concurred) also dissented.

Note: In *Adair* v. *United States,* 208 U.S. 161 (1908), the Court struck down a federal statute making it an offense for an interstate carrier to discharge an employee because of union membership. The Court said this took the carrier's liberty without due process of law, and moreover was no proper regulation of interstate commerce. Justices McKenna and Holmes dissented. In *Coppage* v. *Kansas,* 236 U.S. 1 (1915), the Court pronounced a like judgment upon a state statute, making it an offense to require an agreement not to join a union as a condition of employment. The Court, speaking through Mr. Justice Pitney, held this a taking of the employer's "freedom of contract." Justices Holmes, Day, and Hughes dissented.

Muller v. *Oregon*
208 U.S. 412 (1908)

Muller was convicted in a state court for employing a woman for more than ten hours a day—in violation of an Oregon statute.

Mr. Justice Brewer delivered the opinion of the court.

. . . In patent cases counsel are apt to open the argument with a discussion of the state of the art. It may not be amiss, in the present case, before examining the constitutional question, to notice the course of legislation as well as expressions of opinion from other than judicial sources. In the brief filed by Mr. Louis D. Brandeis, for the defendant in error, is a very copious collection of all these matters, an epitome of which is found in the margin.[1]

---

[1] The following legislation of the States imposes restrictions in some form or another upon the hours of labor that may be required of women: [Mr. Brandeis here listed laws of 19 states.]

In foreign legislation Mr. Brandeis calls attention to these statutes: [English, French, Swiss, Austrian, Dutch, Italian, and German laws are listed.]

The legislation and opinions referred to in the margin may not be, technically speaking, authorities, and in them is little or no discussion

---

Then follow extracts from over ninety reports of committees, bureaus of statistics, commissioners of hygiene, inspectors of factories, both in this country and in Europe, to the effect that long hours of labor are dangerous for women, primarily because of their special physical organization. The matter is discussed in these reports in different aspects, but all agree as to the danger. It would of course take too much space to give these reports in detail. Following them are extracts from similar reports discussing the general benefits of short hours from an economic aspect of the question. In many of these reports individual instances are given tending to support the general conclusion. Perhaps the general scope and character of all these reports may be summed up in what an inspector for Hanover says: "The reasons for the reduction of the working day to ten hours— (a) the physical organization of women, (b) her maternal functions, (c) the rearing and education of the children, (d) the maintenance of the home—are all so important and so far reaching that the need for such reduction need hardly be discussed."

of the constitutional question presented to us for determination, yet they are significant of a widespread belief that woman's physical structure, and the functions she performs in consequence thereof, justify special legislation restricting or qualifying the conditions under which she should be permitted to toil. Constitutional questions, if it is true, are not settled by even a consensus of present public opinion, for it is the peculiar value of a written constitution that it places in unchanging form limitations upon legislative action, and thus gives a permanence and stability to popular government which otherwise would be lacking. At the same time, when a question of fact is debated and debatable, and the extent to which a special constitutional limitation goes is affected by the truth in respect to that fact, a widespread and long continued belief concerning it is worthy of consideration. We take judicial cognizance of all matters of general knowledge.

It is undoubtedly true, as more than once declared by this court, that the general right to contract in relation to one's business is part of the liberty of the individual, protected by the Fourteenth Amendment to the Federal Constitution; yet it is equally well settled that this liberty is not absolute and extending to all contracts, and that a State may, without conflicting with the provisions of the Fourteenth Amendment, restrict in many respects the individual's power of contract. Without stopping to discuss at length the extent to which a State may act in this respect, we refer to the following cases in which the question has been considered: *Allgeyer* v. *Louisiana*, 165 U.S. 578; *Holden* v. *Hardy*, 169 U.S. 366; *Lochner* v. *New York*, 198 U.S. 45.

That woman's physical structure and the performance of maternal functions place her at a disadvantage in the struggle for subsistence is obvious. This is especially true when the burdens of motherhood are upon her. Even when they are not, by abundant testimony of the medical fraternity continuance for a long time on her feet at work, repeating this from day to day, tends to injurious effects upon the body, and as healthy mothers are essential to vigorous offspring, the physical well-being of woman becomes an object of public interest and care in order to preserve the strength and vigor of the race.

Still again, history discloses the fact that woman has always been dependent upon man. He established his control at the outset by superior physical strength, and this control in various forms, with diminishing intensity, has continued to the present. As minors, though not to the same extent, she has been looked upon in the courts as needing especial care that her rights may be preserved. Education was long denied her, and while now the doors of the schoolroom are opened and her opportunities for acquiring knowledge are great, yet even with that and the consequent increase of capacity for business affairs it is still true that in the struggle for subsistence she is not an equal competitor with her brother. Though limitations upon personal and contractual rights may be removed by legislation, there is that in her disposition and habits of life which will operate against a full assertion of those rights. She will still be where some legislation to protect her seems necessary to secure a real equality of right. Doubtless there are individual exceptions, and there are many respects in which she has an advantage over him; but looking at it from the viewpoint of the effort to maintain an independent position in life, she is not upon an equality. Differentiated by these matters from the other sex, she is properly placed in a class by herself, and legislation designed for her protection may be sustained, even when like legislation is not necessary for men and could not be sustained. It is impossible to close one's eyes to the fact that she still looks to her brother and depends upon him. Even though all restrictions on political, personal and contractual rights were taken away, and she stood, so far as statutes are concerned, upon an absolutely equal plane with him, it would still be true that she is so constituted that she will rest upon and look to him for protection; that her physical structure and a proper discharge of her maternal functions—having in view not merely her own health, but the well-being of the race—justify legislation to protect her from the greed as well as the passion of man. The limitations which this statute places upon her contractual powers, upon her right to agree with her employer as to the time she shall labor, are not imposed solely for her benefit, but also largely for the benefit of all. Many words cannot make this plainer. The two sexes differ in structure of body, in the functions to be performed by each, in the amount of physical strength, in the capacity for long-continued labor, particularly when done standing, the influence of vigorous health upon the future well-being of the race, the self-reliance which enables one to assert full rights, and in the capacity to maintain the struggle for subsistence. This difference justifies a difference in legislation and upholds that which is designed to compensate for some of the burdens which rest upon her.

We have not referred in this discussion to the denial of the elective franchise in the State of Oregon, for while it may disclose a lack of political equality in all things with her brother, that is not of itself decisive. The reason runs deeper, and rests in the inherent difference between the two sexes, and in the different functions in life which they perform.

For these reasons, and without questioning in any respect the decision in *Lochner* v. *New York*, we are of the opinion that it cannot be adjudged that the act in question is in conflict with the Federal Constitution, so far as it respects the work of a female in a laundry, and the judgment of the Supreme Court of Oregon is affirmed.

Adkins v. *Children's Hospital*
261 U.S. 525 (1923)

Mr. Justice Sutherland delivered the opinion of the court:

The question presented for determination by these appeals is the constitutionality of the Act of September 19, 1918, providing for the fixing of minimum wages for women and children in the District of Columbia. . . .

The appellee in the first case is a corporation maintaining a hospital for children in the District. It employs a large number of women in various capacities, with whom it had agreed upon rates of wages and compensation satisfactory to such employees, but which, in some instances, were less than the minimum wage fixed by an order of the board, made in pursuance of the act. The women with whom appellee had so contracted were all of full age and under no legal disability. The instant suit was brought by the appellee in the supreme court of the District to restrain the board from enforcing or attempting to enforce its order, on the ground that the same was in contravention of the Constitution, and particularly the due process clause of the 5th Amendment.

In the second case the appellee, a woman twenty-one years of age, was employed by the Congress Hall Hotel Company as an elevator operator, at a salary of $35 per month and two meals a day. She alleges that the work was light and healthful, the hours short, with surroundings clean and moral, and that she was anxious to continue it for the compensation she was receiving, and that she did not earn more. Her services were satisfactory to the Hotel Company and it would have been glad to retain her, but was obliged to dispense with her services by reason of the order of the board and on account of the penalties prescribed by the act. The wages received by this appellee were the best she was able to obtain for any work she was capable of performing, and the enforcement of the order, she alleges, deprived her of such employment and wages. She further averred that she could not secure any other position at which she could make a living, with as good physical and moral surroundings, and earn as good wages, and that she was desirous of continuing and would continue the employment but for the order of the board. An injunction was prayed, as in the other case.

The supreme court of the District denied the injunction and dismissed the bill in each case. Upon appeal, the court of appeals, by a majority, first affirmed, and subsequently, on a rehearing, reversed, the trial court. . . .

In the *Muller* case the validity of an Oregon statute, forbidding the employment of any female in certain industries more than ten hours during any one day, was upheld. The decision proceeded upon the theory that the difference between the sexes may justify a different rule respecting hours of labor in the case of women than in the case of men. It is pointed out that these consist in differences of physical structure, especially in respect of the maternal functions, and also in the fact that historically woman has always been dependent upon man, who has established his control by superior physical strength. The cases of *Riley*, *Miller*, and *Bosley* follow in this respect the *Muller Case*. But the ancient inequality of the sexes, otherwise than physical, as suggested in the *Muller* case, has continued "with diminishing intensity." In view of the great—not to say revolutionary— changes which have taken place since that utterance, in the contractual, political, and civil status of women, culminating in the 19th Amendment, it is not unreasonable to say that these differences have now come almost, if not quite, to the vanishing point. In this aspect of the matter, while the physical differences must be recognized in appropriate cases, and legislation fixing hours or conditions of work may properly take them into account, we cannot accept the doctrine that women of mature age, sui juris, require or may be subjected to restrictions upon their liberty of contract which could not lawfully be imposed in the case of men under similar circumstances. To do so would be to ignore all the implications to be drawn from the present-day trend of legislation, as well as that of common thought and usage, by which woman is accorded emancipation from the old doctrine that she must be given special protection or be subjected to special restraint in her contractual and civil relationships. In passing, it

may be noted that the instant statute applies in the case of a woman employee as it does when the former is a man.

The essential characteristics of the statute now under consideration, which differentiate it from the laws fixing hours of labor, will be made as we proceed. It is sufficient now to point out that the latter, deal with incidents of the employment having no necessary effect upon the heart of the contract: that is, the amount of wages to be paid and received. A law forbidding work to continue beyond a given number of hours leaves the parties free to contract about wages and thereby equalize whatever additional burdens may be imposed upon the employer as a result of the restrictions as to hours, by an adjustment in respect of the amount of wages. Enough has been said to show that the authority to fix hours of labor cannot be exercised except in respect of those occupations where work of long-continued duration is detrimental to health. This court has been careful in every case where the question has been raised, to place its decision upon this limited authority of the legislature to regulate hours of labor, and to disclaim any purpose to uphold the legislation as fixing wages, thus recognizing an essential difference between the two. It seems plain that these decisions afford no real support for any form of law establishing minimum wages.

If now, in the light furnished by the foregoing exceptions to the general rule forbidding legislative interference with freedom of contract, we examine and analyze the statute in question, we shall see that it differs from them in every material respect. It is not a law dealing with any business charged with a public interest or with public work, or to meet and tide over a temporary emergency. It has nothing to do with the character, methods, or periods of wage payments. It does not prescribe hours of labor or conditions under which labor is to be done. It is not for the protection of persons under legal disability, or for the prevention of fraud. It is simply and exclusively a price-fixing law, confined to adult women (for we are not now considering the provisions relating to minors), who are legally as capable of contracting for themselves as men. It forbids two parties having lawful capacity—under penalties as to the employer—to freely contract with one another in respect of the price for which one shall render service to the other in a purely private employment where both are willing, perhaps anxious, to agree, even though the consequences may be to oblige one to surrender a desirable engagement, and the other to dispense with the services of a desirable employee. (This case is the exact situation in the *Lyons* case, as is shown by the statement in the first part of this opinion.) The price fixed by the board need have no relation to the capacity or earning power of the employee, the number of hours which may happen to constitute the day's work, the character of the place where the work is to be done, or the circumstances or surroundings of the employment; and, while it has no other basis to support its validity than the assumed necessities of the employee, it takes no account of any independent resources she may have. It is based wholly on the opinions of the members of the board and their advisers—perhaps an average of their opinions, if they do not precisely agree—as to what will be necessary to provide a living for a woman, keep her in health, and preserve her morals. It applies to any and every occupation in the District, without regard to its nature or the character of the work. . . .

It has been said that legislation of the kind now under review is required in the interest of social justice, for whose ends freedom of contract may lawfully be subjected to restraint. The liberty of the individual to do as he pleases, even in innocent matters, is not absolute. It must frequently yield to the common good, and the line beyond which the power of interference may not be pressed is neither definite nor unalterable, but may be made to move, within limits not well defined, with changing need and circumstances. Any attempt to fix a rigid boundary would be unwise as well as futile. But,

nevertheless, there are limits to the power, and when these have been passed, it becomes the plain duty of the courts, in the proper exercise of their authority, to so declare. To sustain the individual freedom of action contemplated by the Constitution is not to strike down the common good, but to exalt it; for surely the good of society as a whole cannot be better served than by the preservation against arbitrary restraint of the liberties of its constituent members.

It follows from what has been said that the act in question passes the limit prescribed by the Constitution, and, accordingly, the decrees of the court below are affirmed.

Mr. Justice Brandeis took no part in the consideration or decision of these cases.

Mr. Chief Justice Taft, and Mr. Justice Sanford, dissented with an opinion.

Mr. Justice Holmes, dissenting:

The question in this case is the broad one, whether Congress can establish minimum rates of wages for women in the District of Columbia, with due provision for special circumstances, or whether we must say that Congress has no power to meddle with the matter at all. To me, notwithstanding the deference due to the prevailing judgment of the court, the power of Congress seems absolutely free from doubt. The end—to remove conditions leading to ill health, immorality, and the deterioration of the race—no one would deny to be within the scope of constitutional legislation. The means are means that have the approval of Congress, of many states, and of those governments from which we have learned our greatest lessons. When so many intelligent persons, who have studied the matter more than any of us can, have thought that the means are effective and are worth the price, it seems to me impossible to deny that the belief reasonably may be held by reasonable men. If the law encountered no other objection than that the means bore no relation to the end, or that they cost too much, I do not suppose that anyone would venture to say that it was bad. I agree, of course, that a law answering the foregoing requirements might be invalidated by specific provisions of the Constitution. For instance, it might take private property without just compensation. But, in the present instance, the only objection that can be urged is found within the vague contours of the 5th Amendment, prohibiting the depriving any person of liberty or property without due process of law. To that I turn.

The earlier decisions upon the same words in the 14th Amendment began within our memory, and went no farther than an unpretentious assertion of the liberty to follow ordinary callings. Later that innocuous generality was expanded into the dogma, Liberty of Contract. Contract is not specially mentioned in the text that we have to construe. It is merely an example of doing what you want to do, embodied in the word "liberty." But pretty much all law consists in forbidding men to do some things that they want to do, and contract is no more exempt from law than other acts. Without enumerating all the restrictive laws that have been upheld, I will mention a few that seem to me to have interfered with liberty of contract quite as seriously and directly as the one before us. Usury laws prohibit contracts by which a man receives more than so much interest for the money that he lends. Statutes of frauds restrict many contracts to certain forms. Some Sunday laws prohibit practically all contracts during one seventh of our whole life. Insurance rates may be regulated. (I concurred in that decision without regard to the public interest with which insurance was said to be clothed. It seemed to me that the principle was general.) Contracts may be forced upon the companies. Employers of miners may be required to pay for coal by weight before screening. Employers generally may be required to redeem in cash store orders accepted by their employees in payment. Payment of sailors in advance may be forbidden. The size of a loaf of bread may be established. The responsibility of employers to their em-

ployees may be profoundly modified. Finally women's hours of labor may be fixed. And the principle was extended to men, with the allowance of a limited overtime, to be paid for "at the rate of time and one half of the regular wage," in *Bunting* v. *Oregon* [243 U.S. 426 (1917)].

I confess that I do not understand the principle on which the power to fix a minimum for the wages of women can be denied by those who admit the power to fix a maximum for their hours of work. I fully assent to the proposition that here, as elsewhere, the distinctions of the law are distinctions of degree; but I perceive no difference in the kind or degree of interference with liberty, the only matter with which we have any concern, between the one case and the other. The bargain is equally affected whichever half you regulate. *Muller* v. *Oregon*, I take it, is as good law today as it was in 1908. It will need more than the 19th Amendment to convince me that there are no differences between men and women, or that legislation cannot take those differences into account. I should not hesitate to take them into account if I thought it necessary to sustain this. But after *Bunting* v. *Oregon*, *supra*, I had supposed that it was not necessary, and that *Lochner* v. *New York* would be allowed a deserved repose. . . .

The criterion of constitutionality is not whether we believe the law to be for the public good. We certainly cannot be prepared to deny that a reasonable man reasonably might have that belief, in view of the legislation of Great Britain, Victoria, and a number of the states of this Union. The belief is fortified by a very remarkable collection of documents submitted on behalf of the appellants, material here, I conceive, only as showing that the belief reasonably may be held. In Australia the power to fix a minimum for wages in the case of industrial disputes extending beyond the limits of any one state was given to a court, and its President wrote a most interesting account of its operation. 29 *Harvard L. Rev.* 13. If a legislature should adopt what he thinks the doctrine of modern economists of all schools, that "freedom of contract is a misnomer as applied to a contract between an employer and an ordinary individual employee" (id. 25), I could not pronounce an opinion with which I agree impossible to be entertained by reasonable men. If the same legislature should accept his further opinion that industrial peace was best attained by the device of a court having the above powers, I should not feel myself able to contradict it, or to deny that the end justified restrictive legislation quite as adequately as beliefs concerning Sunday, or exploded theories about usury. I should have my doubts, as I have them about this statute; but they would be whether the bill that has to be paid for every gain, although hidden as interstitial detriments, was not greater than the gain was worth,—a matter that it is not for me to decide.

I am of opinion that the statute is valid and that the decree should be reversed.

Baldwin v. *Missouri* (excerpt)
281 U.S. 586 (1930)

I n this case the Court struck down a Missouri inheritance tax on securities located in that state, but owned by a person who died in Illinois.

Mr. Justice Holmes dissenting. . . .

I have not yet adequately expressed the more than anxiety that I feel at the ever increasing scope given to the Fourteenth Amendment in cutting down what I believe to be the constitutional rights of the States. As the decisions now stand, I see hardly any limit but the sky to the invalidating of those rights if they happen to strike a majority of this Court as for any reason undesirable. I cannot believe that the Amendment was intended to give us *carte blanche* to embody our economic or moral beliefs in its prohibitions. Yet I can think of no narrower reason that seems to me to justify the present and the earlier decisions to which I have referred. Of course, the words "due process of law," if taken in their literal meaning, have no application to this case: and while it is too late to deny that they have been given a much more extended and artificial signification, still we ought to remember the great caution shown by the Constitution in limiting the power of the States, and should be slow to construe the clause in the Fourteenth Amendment as committing to the Court, with no guide but the Court's own discretion, the validity of whatever laws the States may pass.

West Coast Hotel Co. v. *Parrish*
300 U.S. 379 (1937)

T his case began as a suit by Parrish to recover the differences between the lower wages paid her and the state-prescribed minimum wage of $14.50 for 48 hours of work. The employer, having lost below, sought review on the basis of *Adkins* v. *Children's Hospital*.

Mr. Chief Justice Hughes delivered the opinion of the Court. . . .

The principle which must control our decision is not in doubt. The constitutional provi-sion invoked is the due process clause of the Fourteenth Amendment governing the states, as the due process clause invoked in the *Adkins Case* governed Congress. In each case the violation alleged by those attacking minimum wage regulation for women is deprivation of freedom of contract. What is this freedom? The Constitution does not speak of freedom of contract. It speaks of liberty and prohibits the deprivation of liberty without due process of law. In prohibiting that deprivation, the Constitution does not recognize an absolute and uncontrollable liberty. Liberty in each of its phases has its history and connotation. But the liberty safeguarded is liberty in a social organization which requires the protection of law against the evils which menace the health, safety, morals, and welfare of the people. Liberty under the Constitution is thus necessarily subject to the restraints of due process, and regulation which is reasonable in relation to its subject and is adopted in the interests of the community is due process.

This essential limitation of liberty in general governs freedom of contract in particular. More than twenty-five years ago we set forth the applicable principle in these words, after referring to the cases where the liberty guaranteed by the Fourteenth Amendment had been broadly described.

"But it was recognized in the cases cited, as in many others, that freedom of contract is a qualified, and not an absolute right. There is no absolute freedom to do as one wills or to contract as one choose. . . . Liberty implies the absence of arbitrary restraint, not immunity from reasonable regulations and prohibitions imposed in the interests of the community." *Chicago, Burlington & Quincy R. Co.* v. *McGuire,* 219 U.S. 549, 565, 31 S.Ct. 259, 262, 55 L.Ed. 328.

This power under the Constitution to restrict freedom of contract has had many illustrations. That it may be exercised in the public interest with respect to contracts between employer and employee is undeniable. Thus statutes have been sustained limiting employment in underground mines and smelters to eight hours a day . . . ; in requiring redemption in cash of store orders or other evidences of indebtedness issued in the payment of wages . . . ; in forbid-

ding the payment of seamen's wages in advance . . . ; in making it unlawful to contract to pay miners employed at quantity rates upon the basis of screened coal instead of the weight of the coal as originally produced in the mine . . . ; in prohibiting contracts limiting liability for injuries to employees . . . ; in limiting hours of work of employees in manufacturing establishments . . . ; and in maintaining workmen's compensation laws. . . . In dealing with the relation of employer and employed, the Legislature has necessarily a wide field of discretion in order that there may be suitable protection of health and safety, and that peace and good order may be promoted through regulations designed to insure wholesome conditions of work and freedom from oppression. . . .

With full recognition of the earnestness and vigor which characterize the prevailing opinion in the *Adkins* case, we find it impossible to reconcile that ruling with these well-considered declarations. What can be closer to the public interest than the health of women and their protection from unscrupulous and overreaching employers? And if the protection of women is a legitimate end of the exercise of state power, how can it be said that the requirement of the payment of a minimum wage fairly fixed in order to meet the very necessities of existence is not an admissible means to that end? The Legislature of the state was clearly entitled to consider the situation of women in employment, the fact that they are in the class receiving the least pay, that their bargaining power is relatively weak, and that they are the ready victims of those who would take advantage of their necessitous circumstances. The Legislature was entitled to adopt measures to reduce the evils of the "sweating system," the exploiting of workers at wages so low as to be insufficient to meet the bare cost of living, thus making their very helplessness the occasion of a most injurious competition. The Legislature had the right to consider that its minimum wage requirements would be an important aid in carrying out its policy of protection. The adoption of similar requirements by many states evidences a deep-seated conviction both as to the presence of the evil and as to the means adapted to check it. Legislative response to that conviction cannot be regarded as arbitrary or capricious and that is all we have to decide. Even if the wisdom of the policy be regarded as debatable and its effects uncertain, still the Legislature is entitled to its judgment.

There is an additional and compelling consideration which recent economic experience has brought into a strong light. The exploitation of a class of workers who are in an unequal position with respect to bargaining power and are thus relatively defenseless against the denial of a living wage is not only detrimental to their health and well being, but casts a direct burden for their support upon the community. What these workers lose in wages the taxpayers are called upon to pay. The bare cost of living must be met. We may take judicial notice of the unparalleled demands for relief which arose during the recent period of depression and still continue to an alarming extent despite the degree of economic recovery which has been achieved. It is unnecessary to cite official statistics to establish what is of common knowledge through the length and breadth of the land. While in the instant case no factual brief has been presented, there is no reason to doubt that the state of Washington has encountered the same social problem that is present elsewhere. The community is not bound to provide what is in effect a subsidy for unconscionable employers. The community may direct its law-making power to correct the abuse which springs from their

selfish disregard of the public interest. The argument that the legislation in question constitutes an arbitrary discrimination, because it does not extend to men, is unavailing. This Court has frequently held that the legislative authority, acting within its proper field, is not bound to extend its regulation to call cases which it might possibly reach. The Legislature "is free to recognize degrees of harm and it may confine its restrictions to those classes of cases where the need is deemed to be clearest." If "the law presumably hits the evil where it is most felt, it is not to be overthrown because there are other instances to which it might have been applied." There is no "doctrinaire requirement" that the legislation should be couched in all embracing terms. . . . This familiar principle has repeatedly been applied to legislation which singles out women, and particular classes of women, in the exercise of the state's protective power. . . . Their relative need in the presence of the evil, no less than the existence of the evil itself, is a matter for the legislative judgment.

Our conclusion is that the case of *Adkins* v. *Children's Hospital, supra,* should be, and it is, overruled. The judgment of the Supreme Court of the state of Washington is affirmed.

Affirmed.

Mr. Justice Sutherland.

Mr. Justice Van Devanter, Mr. Justice McReynolds, Mr. Justice Butler, and I think the judgment of the court below should be reversed. . . .

Ferguson v. *Skrupa*
372 U.S. 726 (1963)

In *Adams* v. *Tanner,* 244 U.S. 590 (1917), the Court held unconstitutional a state statute outlawing employment agencies which collect fees from workers. Relying on *Adams,* a federal district court enjoined enforcement of a Kansas law prohibiting the business of debt adjustment (a debt adjuster, for a fee, collects agreed-upon sums periodically from debtors and distributes them to creditors).

Mr. Justice Black delivered the opinion of the Court. . . .

. . . Under the system of government created by our Constitution, it is up to legislatures, not courts, to decide on the wisdom and utility of legislation. There was a time when the Due Process Clause was used by this Court to strike down laws which were thought unreasonable, that is, unwise or incompatible with some particular economic or social philosophy. . . .

The doctrine that prevailed in *Lochner, Coppage, Adkins* . . . has long since been discarded. We have returned to the original constitutional proposition that courts do not substitute their social and economic beliefs for the judgment of legislative bodies, who are elected to pass laws. . . .

In face of our abandonment of the use of the "vague contours" of the Due Process Clause to nullify laws which a majority of the Court believed to be economically unwise, . . . [w]e conclude that the Kansas legislature was free to decide for itself that legislation was needed to deal with the business of debt adjusting. Unquestionably, there are arguments showing that the business of debt adjusting has social utility, but such arguments are properly addressed to the legislature, not to us. . . . Whether the legislature takes for its textbook Adam Smith, Herbert Spencer, Lord Keynes, or some other is no concern of ours. The Kansas debt adjusting statute may be wise or unwise. But relief, if any be needed, lies not with us but with the body constituted to pass laws for the State of Kansas. See *Day-Brite Lighting, Inc.* v. *Missouri*, 342 U.S. 421 (1952); *Williamson* v. *Lee Optical Co.*, 348 U.S. 483 (1955).

THE NEW RIGHT TO PRIVACY (AUTONOMY): NEOSUBSTANTIVE DUE PROCESS

Griswold v. *Connecticut*
381 U.S. 479 (1965)

Mr. Justice Douglas delivered the opinion of the Court.

Appellant Griswold is Executive Director of the Planned Parenthood League of Connecticut. Appellant Buxton is a licensed physician and a professor at the Yale Medical School who served as Medical Director for the League at its Center in New Haven—a center open and operating from November 1 to November 10, 1961, when appellants were arrested.

They gave information, instruction, and medical advice to *married persons* as to the means of preventing conception. They examined the wife and prescribed the best contraceptive device or material for her use. Fees were usually charged, although some couples were serviced free.

The statutes whose constitutionality is involved in this appeal are §§ 53-32 and 54-196 of the General Statutes of Connecticut (1938). The former provides:

"Any person who uses any drug, medicinal article or instrument for the purpose of preventing conception shall be fined not less than fifty dollars or imprisoned not less than sixty days nor more than one year or be both fined and imprisoned."

Section 54-196 provides:

"Any person who assists, abets, counsels, causes, hires or commands another to commit any offense may be prosecuted and punished as if he were the principal offender."

The appellants were found guilty as accessories and fined $100 each, against the claim that the accessory statute as so applied violated the Fourteenth Amendment. The Appellate Division of the Circuit Court affirmed. The Court of Errors affirmed that judgment. 151 Conn. 544, 200 A.2d 479. We noted probable jurisdiction. 379 U.S. 926. . . .

Coming to the merits, we are met with a wide range of questions that implicate the Due Process Clause of the Fourteenth Amendment. Overtones of some arguments suggest that *Lochner* v. *State of New York*, 198 U.S. 45, should be our guide. But we decline that invitation as we did in *West Coast Hotel Co.* v. *Parrish*, 300 U.S. 379; *Olsen* v. *State of Nebraska*, 313 U.S. 236; *Lincoln Federal Labor Union* v. *Northwestern Co.*, 335 U.S. 525; *Williamson* v. *Lee Optical Co.*, 348 U.S. 483; *Giboney* v. *Empire Storage Co.*, 336 U.S. 490. We do not sit as a super-legislature to determine the widsom, need, and propriety of laws that touch economic problems, business affairs, or social conditions. This law, however, operates directly on an intimate relation of husband and wife and their physician's role in one aspect of that relation.

The association of people is not mentioned in the Constitution nor in the Bill of Rights. The right to educate a child in a school of the parents' choice—whether public or private or parochial—is also not mentioned. Nor is the right to study any particular subject or any foreign language. Yet the First Amendment has been construed to include certain of those rights.

By *Pierce* v. *Society of Sisters, supra*, the right to educate one's children as one chooses is made applicable to the States by the force of the First and Fourteenth Amendments. By *Meyer* v. *State of Nebraska* [262 U.S. 390 (1923)], *supra*, the same dignity is given the right to study the German language in a private school. In other words, the State may not, consistently with the spirit of the First Amendment, contract the spectrum of available knowledge. The right of freedom of speech and press includes not only the right to utter or to print, but the right to distribute, the right to receive, the right to read

(*Martin* v. *City of Struthers*, 319 U.S. 141, 143) and freedom of inquiry, freedom of thought, and freedom to teach (see *Wieman* v. *Updegraff*, 344 U.S. 183, 195)—indeed the freedom of the entire university community. *Sweezy* v. *State of New Hampshire*, 354 U.S. 234, 249–250, 261–263; *Barenblatt* v. *United States*, 360 U.S. 109, 112; *Baggett* v. *Bullitt*, 377 U.S. 360, 369. Without those peripheral rights the specific rights would be less secure. And so we reaffirm the principle of the *Pierce* and the *Meyer* cases. . . .

The foregoing cases suggest that specific guarantees in the Bill of Rights have penumbras, formed by emanations from those guarantees that help give them life and substance. See *Poe* v. *Ullman*, 367 U.S. 497, 516–522 (dissenting opinion). Various guarantees create zones of privacy. The right of association contained in the penumbra of the First Amendment is one, as we have seen. The Third Amendment in its prohibition against the quartering of soldiers "in any house" in time of peace without the consent of the owner is another facet of that privacy. The Fourth Amendment explicitly affirms the "right of the people to be secure in their persons, houses, papers, and effects, against unreasonable searches and seizures." The Fifth Amendment in its Self-Incrimination Clause enables the citizen to create a zone of privacy which government may not force him to surrender to his detriment. The Ninth Amendment provies: "The enumeration in the Constitution, of certain rights, shall not be construed to deny or disparage others retained by the people."

The Fourth and Fifth Amendments were described in *Boyd* v. *United States*, 116 U.S. 616, 630, as protection against all governmental invasions "of the sanctity of a man's home and the privacies of life." We recently referred in *Mapp* v. *Ohio*, 367 U.S. 643, 656, to the Fourth Amendment as creating a "right to privacy, no less important than any other right carefully and particularly reserved to the people." See Beaney, The Constitutional Right to Privacy,

1962 *Sup.Ct.Rev.* 212; Griswold, The Right to be Let Alone, 55 *N.W.U.L.Rev.* 216 (1960).

We have had many controversies over these penumbral rights of "privacy and repose." . . . These cases bear witness that the right of privacy which presses for recognition here is a legitimate one.

The present case, then, concerns a relationship lying within the zone of privacy created by several fundamental constitutional guarantees. And it concerns a law which, in forbidding the *use* of contraceptives rather than regulating their manufacture or sale, seeks to achieve its goals by means having a maximum destructive impact upon that relationship. Such a law cannot stand in light of the familiar principle, so often applied by this Court, that a "governmental purpose to control or prevent activities constitutionally subject to state regulation may not be achieved by means which sweep unnecessarily broadly and thereby invade the area of protected freedoms." *NAACP* v. *Alabama*, 377 U.S. 288, 307. Would we allow the police to search the sacred precincts of marital bedrooms for telltale signs of the use of contraceptives? The very idea is repulsive to the notions of privacy surrounding the marriage relationship.

We deal with a right of privacy older than the Bill of Rights—older than our political parties, older than our school system. Marriage is a coming together for better or for worse, hopefully enduring, and intimate to the degree of being sacred. It is an association that promotes a way of life, not causes; a harmony in living, not political faiths; a bilateral loyalty, not commercial or social projects. Yet it is an association for as noble a purpose as any involved in our prior decisions.

Reversed.

Mr. Justice Goldberg, whom The Chief Justice and Mr. Justice Brennan join, concurring.

I agree with the Court that Connecticut's birth control law unconstitutionally intrudes upon the right of marital privacy, and I join in

its opinion and judgment. Although I have not accepted the view that " 'due process' as used in the Fourteenth Amendment includes all of the first eight Amendments," *id.*, 367 U.S. at 516 (see my concurring opinion in *Pointer* v. *Texas*, 380 U.S. 400, 410, and the dissenting opinion of Mr. Justice Brennan in *Cohen* v. *Hurley*, 366 U.S. 117), I do agree that the concept of liberty protects those personal rights that are fundamental, and is not confined to the specific terms of the Bill of Rights. My conclusion that the concept of liberty is not so restricted and that it embraces the right of marital privacy though that right is not mentioned explicitly in the Constitution is supported both by numerous decisions of this Court, referred to in the Court's opinion, and by the language and history of the Ninth Amendment. In reaching the conclusion that the right of marital privacy is protected, as being within the protected penumbra of specific guarantees of the Bill of Rights, the Court refers to the Ninth Amendment, *ante*, at 1681. I add these words to emphasize the relevance of that Amendment to the Court's holding. . . .

The Ninth Amendment reads, "The enumeration in the Constitution, of certain rights, shall not be construed to deny or disparage others retained by the people."

While this Court has had little occasion to interpret the Ninth Amendment, "[i]t cannot be presumed that any clause in the constitution is intended to be without effect." *Marbury* v. *Madison*, 1 Cranch 137, 174. In interpreting the Constitution, "real effect should be given to all the words it uses." *Myers* v. *United States*, 272 U.S. 52, 151. The Ninth Amendment to the Constitution may be regarded by some as a recent discovery but since 1791 it has been a basic part of the Constitution which we are sworn to uphold. To hold that a right so basic and fundamental and so deep-rooted in our society as the right of privacy in marriage may be infringed because that right is not guaranteed in so many words by the first eight amendments to the Constitution is to ignore the Ninth

Amendment and to give it no effect whatsoever. Moreover, a judicial construction that this fundamental right is not protected by the Constitution because it is not mentioned in explicit terms by one of the first eight amendments or elsewhere in the Constitution would violate the Ninth Amendment, which specifically states that "[t]he enumeration in the Constitution, of certain rights shall not be *construed* to deny or disparage others retained by the people." (Emphasis added.) . . .

The entire fabric of the Constitution and the purposes that clearly underlie its specific guarantees demonstrate that the rights to marital privacy and to marry and raise a family are of similar order and magnitude as the fundamental rights specifically protected.

Although the Constitution does not speak in so many words of the right of privacy in marriage, I cannot believe that it offers these fundamental rights no protection. The fact that no particular provision of the Constitution explicitly forbids the State from disrupting the traditional relation of the family—a relation as old and as fundamental as our entire civilization—surely does not show that the Government was meant to have the power to do so. Rather, as the Ninth Amendment expressly recognizes, there are fundamental personal rights such as this one, which are protected from abridgment by the Government though not specifically mentioned in the Constitution. . . .

The logic of the dissents would sanction federal or state legislation that seems to me even more plainly unconstitutional than the statute before us. . . . [I]f upon a showing of a slender basis of rationality, a law outlawing voluntary birth control by married persons is valid, then, by the same reasoning, a law requiring compulsory birth control also would seem to be valid. In my view, however, both types of law would unjustifiably intrude upon rights of marital privacy which are constitutionally protected. . . .

In sum, I believe that the right of privacy in the marital relation is fundamental and basic—a personal right "retained by the people" within the meaning of the Ninth Amendment. Connecticut cannot constitutionally abridge this fundamental right, which is protected by the Fourteenth Amendment from infringement by the States. I agree with the Court that petitioners' convictions must therefore be reversed.

Mr. Justice Harlan, concurring in the judgment.

I fully agree with the judgment of reversal, but find myself unable to join the Court's opinion. The reason is that it seems to me to evince an approach to this case very much like that taken by my Brothers Black and Stewart in dissent, namely: the Due Process Clause of the Fourteenth Amendment does not touch this Connecticut statute unless the enactment is found to violate some right assured by the letter or penumbra of the Bill of Rights.

In other words, what I find implicit in the Court's opinion is that the "incorporation" doctrine may be used to *restrict* the reach of Fourteenth Amendment Due Process. For me this is just as unacceptable constitutional doctrine as is the use of the "incorporation" approach to *impose* upon the States all the requirements of the Bill of Rights as found in the provisions of the first eight amendments and in the decisions of this Court interpreting them. . . .

Mr. Justice White, concurring in the judgment.

In my view this Connecticut law as applied to married couples deprives them of "liberty" without due process of law, as that concept is used in the Fourteenth Amendment. I therefore concur in the judgment of the Court reversing these convictions under Connecticut's aiding and abetting statute. . . .

Mr. Justice Black, with whom Mr. Justice Stewart joins, dissenting.

I agree with my Brother Sewart's dissenting opinion. And like him I do not to any extent whatever base my view that this Connecticut law is constitutional on a belief that the law is wise or that its policy is a good one. In order that there may be no room at all to doubt why I vote as I do, I feel constrained to add that the law is every bit as offensive to me as it is to my Brethren of the majority and my Brothers Harlan, White and Goldberg who, reciting reasons why it is offensive to them, hold it unconstitutional. There is no single one of the graphic and eloquent strictures and criticisms fired at the policy of this Connecticut law either by the Court's opinion or by those of my concurring Brethren to which I cannot subscribe—except their conclusion that the evil qualities they see in the law make it unconstitutional. . . .

The Court talks about a constitutional "right of privacy" as though there is some constitutional provision or provisions forbidding any law ever to be passed which might abridge the "privacy" of individuals. But there is not. . . .

I realize that many good and able men have eloquently spoken and written, sometimes in rhapsodical strains, about the duty of this Court to keep the Constitution in tune with the times. The idea is that the Constitution must be changed from time to time and that this Court is charged with a duty to make those changes. For myself, I must with all deference reject that philosophy. The Constitution makers knew the need for change and provided for it. Amendments suggested by the people's elected representatives can be submitted to the people or their selected agents for ratification. That method of change was good for our Fathers, and being somewhat old-fashioned I must add it is good enough for me. And so, I cannot rely on the Due Process Clause or the Ninth Amendment or any mysterious and uncertain natural law concept as a reason for striking down this state law. The Due Process Clause with an "arbitrary and capricious" or "shocking to the conscience" formula was liberally used by this Court to strike down economic legislation in the early decades of this century, threatening, many people thought, the tranquility and sta-

bility of the Nation. See, e.g., *Lochner* v. *State of New York*, 198 U.S. 45. That formula, based on subjective considerations of "natural justice," is no less dangerous when used to enforce this Court's views about personal rights than those about economic rights. I had thought that we had laid that formula, as a means for striking down state legislation, to rest once and for all in cases like *West Coast Hotel Co.* v. *Parrish*, 300 U.S. 379; *Olsen* v. *State of Nebraska ex rel. Western Reference & Bond Assn.*, 313 U.S. 236, and many other opinions. . . .

. . . The late Judge Learned Hand, after emphasizing his view that judges should not use the due process formula suggested in the concurring opinions today or any other formula like it to invalidate legislation offensive to their "personal preferences," made the statements, with which I fully agree, that: "For myself it would be most irksome to be ruled by a bevy of Platonic Guardians, even if I knew how to choose them, which I assuredly do not." So far as I am concerned, Connecticut's law as applied here is not forbidden by any provision of the Federal Constitution as that Constitution was written, and I would therefore affirm.

Mr. Justice Stewart, whom Mr. Justice Black joins, dissenting.

Since 1879 Connecticut has had on its books a law which forbids the use of contraceptives by anyone. I think this is an uncommonly silly law. As a practical matter, the law is obviously unenforceable, except in the oblique context of the present case. As a philosophical matter, I believe the use of contraceptives in the relationship of marriage should be left to personal and private choice, based upon each individual's moral, ethical, and religious beliefs. As a matter of social policy, I think professional counsel about methods of birth control should be available to all, so that each individual's choice can be meaningfully made. But we are not asked in this case to say whether we think this law is unwise, or even asinine. We are asked to hold that it violates the United States Constitution. And that I cannot do. . . .

What provision of the Constitution, then, does make this state law invalid? The Court says it is the right of privacy "created by several fundamental constitutional guarantees." With all deference, I can find no such general right of privacy in the Bill of Rights, in any other part of the Constitution, or in any case ever before decided by this Court. . . .

Roe v. *Wade*
410 U.S. 113 (1973)

Mr. Justice Blackmun delivered the opinion of the Court.

This Texas appeal and its Georgia companion, *Doe* v. *Bolton*, 410 U.S. 179, present constitutional challenges to state criminal abortion legislation. The Texas statutes under attack here are typical of those that have been in effect in many States for approximately a century. . . .

Our task, of course, is to resolve the issue by constitutional measurement, free of emotion and of predilection. We seek earnestly to do this, and, because we do, we have inquired into, and in this opinion place some emphasis upon, medical and medical-legal history and what that history reveals about man's attitudes toward the abortion procedure over the centuries. . . .

The Texas statutes . . . make it a crime to "procure an abortion," as therein defined, or to attempt one, except with respect to "an abortion procured or attempted by medical advice for the purpose of saving the life of the mother." . . .

Jane Roe, a single woman . . . sought a declaratory judgment that the Texas criminal abortion statutes were unconstitutional on their face, and an injunction restraining the defendant from enforcing the statutes.

Roe alleged that she was unmarried and pregnant; that she wished to terminate her pregnancy by an abortion "performed by a competent, licensed physician, under safe, clinical conditions"; that she was unable to get a "legal" abortion in Texas because her life did not appear to be threatened by the continuation of her pregnancy; and that she could not afford to travel to another jurisdiction in order to secure a legal abortion under safe conditions. . . .

It perhaps is not generally appreciated that the restrictive criminal abortion laws in effect in a majority of States today are of relatively recent vintage. Those laws, generally proscribing abortion or its attempt at any time during pregnancy except when necessary to preserve the pregnant woman's life, are not of ancient or even of common-law origin. Instead, they derive from statutory changes effected, for the most part, in the latter half of the 19th century. . . .

Three reasons have been advanced to explain historically the enactment of criminal abortion laws in the 19th century and to justify their continued existence.

It has been argued occasionally that these laws were the product of a Victorian social concern to discourage illicit sexual conduct. Texas, however, does not advance this justification in the present case, and it appears that no court or commentator has taken the argument seriously. . . .

A second reason is concerned with abortion as a medical procedure. When most criminal abortion laws were first enacted, the procedure was a hazardous one for the woman. . . .

Modern medical techniques have altered this situation. Appellants and various amici refer to medical data indicating that abortion in early pregnancy, that is, prior to the end of the first trimester, although not without its risk, is now relatively safe. Mortality rates for women undergoing early abortions, where the procedure is legal, appear to be as low as or lower than the rates for normal childbirth. Consequently, any interest of the State in protecting the woman from an inherently hazardous procedure, except when it would be equally dangerous for her to forgo it, has largely disappeared. Of course, important state interests in the area of health and medical standards do remain.

The State has a legitimate interest in seeing to it that abortion, like any other medical procedure, is performed under circumstances that insure maximum safety for the patient. This interest obviously extends at least to the performing physician and his staff, to the facilities involved, to the availability of after-care, and to adequate provision for any complication or emergency that might arise. The prevalence of high mortality rates at illegal "abortion mills" strengthens, rather than weakens, the State's interest in regulating the conditions under which abortions are performed. Moreover, the risk to the woman increases as her pregnancy continues. Thus, the State retains a definite interest in protecting the woman's own health and safety when an abortion is proposed at a late stage of pregnancy.

The third reason is the State's interest—some phrase it in terms of duty—in protecting prenatal life. Some of the argument for this justification rests on the theory that a new human life is present from the moment of conception. The State's interest and general obligation to protect life then extends, it is argued, to prenatal life. Only when the life of the pregnant mother herself is at stake, balanced against the life she carries within her, should the interest of the embryo or fetus not prevail. Logically, of course, a legitimate state interest in this area need not stand or fall on acceptance of the belief that life begins at conception or at some other point prior to live birth. In assessing the State's interest, recognition may be given to the less rigid claim that as long as at least *potential* life is involved, the State may assert interests beyond the protection of the pregnant woman alone.

Parties challenging state abortion laws have sharply disputed in some courts the contention that a purpose of these laws, when enacted, was to protect prenatal life. . . . [T]hey claim that most state laws were designed solely to protect the woman. Because medical advances have les-

sened this concern, at least with respect to abortion in the early pregnancy, they argue that with respect to such abortions the laws can no longer be justified by any state interest. . . .

It is with these interests, and the weight to be attached to them, that this case is concerned.

The Constitution does not explicitly mention any right of privacy. In a line of decisions, the Court has recognized that a right of personal privacy, or a guarantee of certain areas or zones of privacy, does exist under the Constitution. . . .

This right of privacy, whether it be founded in the Fourteenth Amendment's concept of personal liberty and restrictions upon state action, as we feel it is, or, as the District Court determined, in the Ninth Amendment's reservation of rights to the people, is broad enough to encompass a woman's decision whether or not to terminate her pregnancy. The detriment that the State would impose upon the pregnant woman by denying this choice altogether is apparent. Specific and direct harm medically diagnosable even in early pregnancy may be involved. Maternity, or additional offspring, may force upon the woman a distressful life and future. Psychological harm may be imminent. Mental and physical health may be taxed by child care. There is also the distress, for all concerned, associated with the unwanted child, and there is the problem of bringing a child into a family already unable, psychologically and otherwise, to care for it. In other cases, as in this one, the additional difficulties and continuing stigma of unwed motherhood may be involved. All these are factors the woman and her responsible physician necessarily will consider in consultation.

On the basis of elements such as these, appellant and some amici argue that the woman's right is absolute and that she is entitled to terminate her pregnancy at whatever time, in whatever way, and for whatever reason she alone chooses. With this we do not agree. . . . The Court's decisions recognizing a right of privacy also acknowledge that some state regulation in areas protected by that right is appropriate. As noted above, a State may properly assert important interests in safeguarding health, in maintaining medical standards, and in protecting potential life. At some point in pregnancy, these respective interests become sufficiently compelling to sustain regulation of the factors that govern the abortion decision. The privacy right involved, therefore, cannot be said to be absolute. In fact, it is not clear to us that the claim asserted by some amici that one has an unlimited right to do with one's body as one pleases bears a close relationship to the right of privacy previously articulated in the Court's decisions. The Court has refused to recognize an unlimited right of this kind in the past. *Jacobson* v. *Massachusetts*, 197 U.S. 11 (1905) (vaccination); *Buck* v. *Bell*, 274 U.S. 200 (1927) (sterilization).

We, therefore, conclude that the right of personal privacy includes the abortion decision, but that this right is not unqualified and must be considered against important state interests in regulation. . . .

Where certain fundamental "rights" are involved, the Court has held that regulation limiting these rights may be justified only by a "compelling state interest," [citing equal protection and first amendment cases], and that legislative enactments must be narrowly drawn to express only the legitimate state interests at stake. . . .

The appellee and certain amici argue that the fetus is a "person" within the language and meaning of the Fourteenth Amendment. In support of this, they outline at length and in detail the well-known facts of fetal development. If this suggestion of personhood is established, the appellant's case, of course, collapses, for the fetus' right to life is then guaranteed specifically by the Amendment. . . . On the other hand, the appellee conceded on the reargument that no case could be cited that holds that a fetus is a person within the meaning of the Fourteenth Amendment.

The Constitution does not define "person" in so many words. [The opinion here reviews all references to "person" in the Constitution.] But in nearly all these instances, the use of the word is such that it has application only postnatally. None indicates, with any assurance, that it has any possible prenatal application.

All this, together with our observation, that throughout the major portion of the 19th century prevailing legal abortion practices were far freer than they are today, persuades us that the word "person," as used in the Fourteenth Amendment, does not include the unborn. . . .

This conclusion, however, does not of itself fully answer the contentions raised by Texas, and we pass on to other considerations.

The pregnant woman cannot be isolated in her privacy. She carries an embryo and, later, a fetus, if one accepts the medical definitions of the developing young in the human uterus. The situation therefore is inherently different from marital intimacy, or bedroom possession of obscene material, or marriage, or procreation, or education, with which *Eisenstadt, Griswold, Stanley, Loving, Skinner, Pierce*, and *Meyer* were respectively concerned. . . .

Texas urges that, apart from the Fourteenth Amendment, life begins at conception and is present throughout pregnancy, and that, therefore, the State has a compelling interest in protecting that life from and after conception. We need not resolve the difficult question of when life begins. When those trained in the respective disciplines of medicine, philosophy, and theology are unable to arrive at any consensus, the judiciary, at this point in the development of man's knowledge, is not in a position to speculate as to the answer. . . .

In view of all this, we do not agree that, by adopting one theory of life, Texas may override the rights of the pregnant woman that are at stake. We repeat, however, that the State does have an important and legitimate interest in preserving and protecting the health of the pregnant woman, whether she be a resident of the State or a nonresident who seeks medical consultation and treatment there, and that it has still *another* important and legitimate interest in protecting the potentiality of human life. These interests are separate and distinct. Each grows in substantiality as the woman approaches term and, at a point during pregnancy, each becomes "compelling."

With respect to the State's important and legitimate interest in the health of the mother, the "compelling" point, in the light of present medical knowledge, is at approximately the end of the first trimester. This is so because of the now-established medical fact, that until the end of the first trimester mortality in abortion may be less than mortality in normal childbirth. It follows that, from and after this point, a State may regulate the abortion procedure to the extent that the regulation reasonably relates to the preservation and protection of maternal health. Examples of permissible state regulation in this area are requirements as to the qualifications of the person who is to perform the abortion; as to the licensure of that person; as to the facility in which the procedure is to be performed, that is, whether it must be a hospital or may be a clinic or some other place of less-than-hospital status; as to the licensing of the facility; and the like.

This means, on the other hand, that, for the period of pregnancy prior to this "compelling" point, the attending physician, in consultation with his patient, is free to determine, without regulation by the State, that, in his medical judgment, the patient's pregnancy should be terminated. If that decision is reached, the judgment may be effectuated by an abortion free of interference by the State.

With respect to the State's important and legitimate interest in potential life, the "compelling" point is at viability. This is so because the fetus then presumably has the capability of meaningful life outside the mother's womb. State regulation protective of fetal life after viability thus has both logical and biological justifications. If the State is interested in protecting fetal life after viability, it may go so far as to proscribe abortion during that period, except when it is necessary to preserve the life or health of the mother.

Measured against these standards . . . the Texas Penal Code, . . . sweeps too broadly. The statute makes no distinction between abortions performed early in pregnancy and those performed later, and it limits to a single reason, "saving" the mother's life, the legal justification for the procedure. The statute, therefore, cannot survive the constitutional attack made upon it here.

This holding, we feel, is consistent with the relative weights of the respective interests involved, with the lessons and examples of medical and legal history, with the lenity of the common law, and with the demands of the profound problems of the present day. The decision leaves the State free to place increasing restrictions on abortion as the period of pregnancy lengthens, so long as those restrictions are tailored to the recognized state interests. The decision vindicates the right of the physician to administer medical treatment according to his professional judgment up to the points where important state interests provide compelling justifications for intervention. Up to those points, the abortion decision in all its aspects is inherently, and primarily, a medical decision, and basic responsibility for it must rest with the physician. If an individual practitioner abuses the privilege of exercising proper medical judgment, the usual remedies, judicial and intra-professional, are available. . . .

Mr. Justice Douglas, concurring.

While I join the opinion of the Court [except on the abstention issue], I add a few words. . . .

The Ninth Amendment obviously does not create federally enforceable rights. It merely says, "The enumeration in the Constitution, of certain rights, shall not be construed to deny or disparage others retained by the people." But a catalogue of these rights includes customary, traditional, and time-honored rights, amenities, privileges, and immunities that come within the sweep of "the Blessings of Liberty" mentioned in the preamble to the Constitution. Many of them, in my view, come within the meaning of the term "liberty" as used in the Fourteenth Amendment.

First is the autonomous control over the development and expression of one's intellect, interests, tastes, and personality.

These are rights protected by the First Amendment and, in my view, they are absolute, permitting of no exceptions. The Free Exercise Clause of the First Amendment is one facet of this constitutional right. The right to remain silent as respects one's own beliefs, is protected by the First and the Fifth. The First Amendment grants the privacy of first-class mail. All of these aspects of the right of privacy are rights "retained by the people" in the meaning of the Ninth Amendment.

Second is freedom of choice in the basic decisions of one's life respecting marriage, divorce, procreation, contraception, and the education and upbringing of children.

These rights, unlike those protected by the First Amendment, are subject to some control by the police power. These rights are "fundamental," and we have held that in order to support legislative action the statute must be narrowly and precisely drawn and that a "compelling state interest" must be shown in support of the limitation. . . .

Third is the freedom to care for one's health and person, freedom from bodily restraint or compulsion, freedom to walk, stroll, or loaf.

These rights, though fundamental, are likewise subject to regulation on a showing of "compelling state interest." . . .

. . . [A] woman is free to make the basic decision whether to bear an unwanted child. Elaborate argument is hardly necessary to demonstrate that childbirth may deprive a woman of her preferred lifestyle and force upon her a radically different and undesired future. For example, rejected applicants under the Georgia statute are required to endure the discomforts of pregnancy; to incur the pain, higher mortality rate, and aftereffects of childbirth; to abandon educational plans; to sustain loss of income; to forgo the satisfactions of careers; to tax further mental and physical health in providing child care; and, in some cases, to bear the lifelong stigma of unwed motherhood, a badge which may haunt, if not deter, later legitimate family relationships. . . .

Justice Stewart, concurring.

In 1963, this Court, in *Ferguson* v. *Skrupa*, purported to sound the death knell for the doctrine of substantive due process. . . .

Barely two years later, in *Griswold* v. *Connecticut*, 381 U.S. 479, the Court held a Connecticut-birth control law unconstitutional. In view of what had been so recently said in *Skrupa*, the Court's opinion in *Griswold* understandably did its best to avoid reliance on the Due Process Clause of the Fourteenth Amendment as the ground for decision. Yet, the Connecticut law did not violate any provision of the Bill of Rights, nor any other specific provision of the Constitution. So it was clear to me then, and it is equally clear to me now, that the *Griswold* decision can be rationally understood only as a holding that the Connecticut statute substantively invaded the "liberty" that is protected by the Due Process Clause of the Fourteenth Amendment. As so understood, *Griswold* stands as one in a long line of pre-*Skrupa* cases decided under the doctrine of substantive due process, and I now accept it as such. . . .

Clearly, therefore, the Court today is correct in holding that the right asserted by Jane Roe is embraced within the personal liberty protected by the Due Process Clause of the Fourteenth Amendment.

It is evident that the Texas abortion statute infringes that right directly. Indeed, it is difficult to imagine a more complete abridgment of a constitutional freedom than that worked by the inflexible criminal statute now in force in Texas. The question then becomes whether the state interests advanced to justify this abridgment can survive the "particularly careful scrutiny" that the Fourteenth Amendment here requires.

. . . I think the Court today has thoroughly demonstrated that [the] state interests cannot constitutionally support the broad abridgment of personal liberty worked by the existing Texas law. . . .

Justice White, with whom Justice Rehnquist joins, dissenting. . . .

. . . I find nothing in the language or history of the Constitution to support the Court's judgment. The Court simply fashions and announces a new constitutional right for pregnant mothers and, with scarcely any reason or authority for its action, invests that right with sufficient substance to override most existing state abortion statutes. The upshot is that the people and the legislatures of the 50 States are constitutionally disentitled to weigh the relative importance of the continued existence and development of the fetus, on the one hand, against a spectrum of possible impacts on the mother, on the other hand. As an exercise of raw judicial power, the Court perhaps has authority to do what it does today; but in my view its judgment is an improvident and extravagant exercise of the power of judicial review that the Constitution extends to this Court. . . .

Justice Rehnquist, dissenting. . . .

. . . I have difficulty in concluding, as the Court does, that the right of "privacy" is involved in this case. Texas, by the statute here challenged, bars the performance of a medical abortion by a licensed physician on a plaintiff such as Roe. A transaction resulting in an operation such as this is not "private" in the ordinary usage of that word. Nor is the "privacy"

that the Court finds here even a distant relative of the freedom from searches and seizures protected by the Fourth Amendment to the Constitution, which the Court has referred to as embodying a right to privacy.

If the Court means by the term "privacy" no more than that the claim of a person to be free from unwanted state regulation of consensual transactions may be a form of "liberty" protected by the Fourteenth Amendment, there is no doubt that similar claims have been upheld in our earlier decisions on the basis of that liberty. I agree with the statement of Mr. Justice Stewart in his concurring opinion that the "liberty," against deprivation of which without due process the Fourteenth Amendment protects, embraces more than the rights found in the Bill of Rights. But that liberty is not guaranteed absolutely against deprivation, only against deprivation without due process of law. The test traditionally applied in the area of social and economic legislation is whether or not a law such as that challenged has a rational relation to a valid state objective. The Due Process Clause of the Fourteenth Amendment undoubtedly does place a limit, albeit a broad one, on legislative power to enact laws such as this. If the Texas statute were to prohibit an abortion even where the mother's life is in jeopardy, I have little doubt that such a statute would lack a rational relation to a valid state objective. . . . But the Court's sweeping invalidation of any restrictions on abortion during the first trimester is impossible to justify under that standard, and the conscious weighing of competing factors that the Court's opinion apparently substitutes for the established test is far more appropriate to a legislative judgment than to a judicial one.

The Court eschews the history of the Fourteenth Amendment in its reliance on the "compelling state interest" test. But the Court adds a new wrinkle to this test by transposing it from the legal considerations associated with the Equal Protection Clause of the Fourteenth

Amendment to this case arising under the Due Process Clause of the Fourteenth Amendment. Unless I misapprehended the consequences of this transplanting of the "compelling state interest test," the Court's opinion will accomplish the seemingly impossible feat of leaving this area of the law more confused than it found it.

While the Court's opinion quotes from the dissent of Mr. Justice Holmes in *Lochner* v. *New York*, 198 U.S. 45 (1905), the result it reaches is more closely attuned to the majority opinion of Mr. Justice Peckham in that case. As in *Lochner* and similar cases applying substantive due process standards to economic and social welfare legislation, the adoption of the compelling state interest standard will inevitably require this Court to examine the legislative policies and pass on the wisdom of these policies in the very process of deciding whether a particular state interest put forward may or may not be "compelling." The decision here to break pregnancy into three distinct terms and to outline the permissible restrictions the State may impose in each one, for example, partakes more of judicial legislation than it does of a determination of the intent of the drafters of the Fourteenth Amendment.

The fact that a majority of the States reflecting, after all, the majority sentiment in those States, have had restrictions on abortions for at least a century is a strong indication, it seems to me, that the asserted right to an abortion is not "so rooted in the traditions and conscience of our people as to be ranked as fundamental," *Snyder* v. *Massachusetts*, 291 U.S. 97 (1934). Even today, when society's views on abortion are changing, the very existence of the debate is evidence that the "right" to an abortion is not so universally accepted as the appellants would have us believe. . . .

Note: Doe v. *Bolton,* 410 U.S. 179 (1973), held invalid a Georgia law requiring that abortions be accomplished only in accredited hospitals; that they be approved by a hospital staff abortion committee; that the operating physician's judgment be confirmed by independent examinations of the patient by two other licensed physicians; and that abortions be given only to Georgia residents.

Planned Parenthood of Central Missouri v. *Danforth*
428 U.S. 52 (1976)

In response to *Roe* v. *Wade,* Missouri required (among other things) that any unmarried female under 18 obtain written consent of a parent or person *in loco parentis* as a prerequisite to an abortion, and in the case of a married female, her husband's written consent.

Mr. Justice Blackmun delivered the opinion of the Court . . . .

Clearly, since the State cannot regulate or proscribe abortion during the first stage, when the physician and his patient make that decision, the State cannot delegate authority to any particular person, even the spouse, to prevent abortion during that same period.

We are not unaware of the deep and proper concern and interest that a devoted and protective husband has in his wife's pregnancy and in the growth and development of the fetus she is carrying. Neither has this Court failed to appreciate the importance of the marital relationship in our society. See, e.g., *Griswold* v. *Connecticut*, 381 U.S. 479, 486 (1965); *Maynard* v. *Hill*, 125 U.S. 190, 211 (1888). Moreover, we recognize that the decision whether to undergo or to forgo an abortion may have profound effects on the future of any marriage, effects that are both physical and mental, and possibly deleterious. Notwithstanding these factors, we cannot hold that the State has the constitutional authority to give the spouse unilaterally the ability to prohibit the wife from terminating her pregnancy, when the State itself lacks that right. See *Eisenstadt* v. *Baird*, 405 U.S. 438, 453 (1972).

It seems manifest that, ideally, the decision to terminate a pregnancy should be one concurred in by both the wife and her husband. No marriage may be viewed as harmonious or successful if the marriage partners are fundamentally divided on so important and vital an issue. But it is difficult to believe that the goal of fostering mutuality and trust in a marriage, and of strengthening the marital relationship and the marriage institution, will be achieved by giving the husband a veto power exercisable for any reason whatsoever or for no reason at all. Even if the State had the ability to delegate to the husband a power it itself could not exercise, it is not at all likely that such action would further, as the District Court majority phrase it, the interest of the state in protecting the mutuality of decisions vital to the marriage relationship. 392 F.Supp., at 1370.

We recognize, of course, that when a woman, with the approval of her physician but without the approval of her husband, decides to terminate her pregnancy, it could be said that she is acting unilaterally. The obvious fact is that when the wife and the husband disagree on this decision, the view of only one of the two marriage partners can prevail. Since it is the woman who physically bears the child and who is the more directly and immediately affected by the pregnancy, as between the two, the balance weighs in her favor. Cf. *Roe* v. *Wade*, 410 U.S., at 153. . . .

Just as with the requirement of consent from the spouse, so here, the State does not have the constitutional authority to give a third party [parent or guardian] an absolute, and possibly arbitrary, veto over the decision of the physician and his patient to terminate the patient's pregnancy, regardless of the reason for withholding the consent.

Constitutional rights do not mature and come into being magically only when one attains the state-defined age of majority. Minors, as well as adults, are protected by the Constitution and possess constitutional rights. See, e.g., *Breed* v. *Jones*, 421 U.S. 519 (1975); *Goss* v. *Lopez*, 419 U.S. 565 (1975); *Tinker* v. *Des Moines School District*, 393 U.S. 503 (1969); *In re Gault*, 387 U.S. 1 (1967). The Court indeed, however, long has recognized that the State has somewhat broader authority to regulate the activities of children than of adults. *Prince* v. *Massachusetts*, 321 U.S., at 170; *Ginsberg* v. *New York*, 390 U.S. 629 (1968). It remains, then, to examine whether there is any significant state interest in conditioning an abortion on the consent of a parent or person *in loco parentis* that is not present in the case of an adult.

One suggested interest is the safeguarding of the family unit and of parental authority. 392 F.Supp., at 1370. It is difficult, however, to conclude that providing a parent with absolute power to overrule a determination, made by the physician and his minor patient, to terminate the patient's pregnancy will serve to strengthen the family unit. Neither is it likely that such veto power will enhance parental authority or control where the minor and the nonconsenting parent are so fundamentally in conflict and the very existence of the pregnancy already has fractured the family structure. Any independent interest the parent may have in the termination of the minor daughter's pregnancy is no more weighty than the right of privacy of the competent minor mature enough to have become pregnant.

We emphasize that our holding that § 3(4) is invalid does not suggest that every minor, regardless of age or maturity, may give effective consent for termination of her pregnancy. See *Bellotti* v. *Baird, post*. The fault with § 3(4) is that it imposes a special consent provision, exercisable by a person other than the women and her physician, as a prerequisite to a minor's termination of her pregnancy and does so without a sufficient justification for restriction. It violates the strictures of *Roe* and *Doe*.

[Justices White, Burger, and Rehnquist, dissenting.]

Section 3(3) of the Act provides that a married woman may not obtain an abortion without her husband's consent. The Court strikes down this statute in one sentence. It says that "since the State cannot . . . proscribe abortion . . . the State cannot delegate authority to any particular person, even the spouse, to prevent abortion . . . ." . . . But the State is not—under § 3(3)—delegating to the husband the power to vindicate the *State's* interest in the future life of the fetus. It is instead recognizing that the husband has an interest of his own in the life of the fetus which should not be extinguished by the unilateral decision of the wife. It by no means follows, from the fact that the mother's interest in deciding "whether or not to terminate her pregnancy" outweighs the *State's* interest in the potential life of the fetus, that the husband's interest is also outweighed and may not be protected by the State. A father's interest in having a child—perhaps his only child—may be unmatched by any other interest in his life. See *Stanley* v. *Illinois*, 405 U.S. 645, 651, and cases there cited. It is truly surprising that the majority finds in the United States Constitution, as it must in order to justify the result it reaches, a rule that the State must assign a greater value to a mother's decision to cut off a potential human life by abortion than to a father's decision to let it mature into a live child. Such a rule cannot be found there, nor can it be found in *Roe* v. *Wade, supra*. These are matters which a State should be able to decide free from the suffocating power of the federal judge, purporting to act in the name of the Constitution.

In describing the nature of a mother's interest in terminating a pregnancy, the Court in *Roe* v. *Wade* mentioned only the post-birth burdens of rearing a child, id., at p. 153, and rejected a rule based on her interest in controlling her own body during pregnancy. *Id.*, at 154. Missouri has a law which prevents a woman from putting a child up for adoption over her husband's objection, § 453.030 R.S.Mo.1969. This law represents a judgment by the State that the mother's interest in avoiding the burdens of child rearing do not outweigh or snuff out the father's interest in participating in bringing up his own child. That law is plainly valid, but no more so than § 3(3) of the Act now before us, resting as it does on precisely the same judgment.

. . . [T]he purpose of the parental consent requirement is not merely to vindicate any interest of the parent or of the State. The purpose of the requirement is to vindicate the very right created in *Roe* v. *Wade, supra*—the right of the pregnant woman to decide "whether *or not* to terminate her pregnancy". *Id.*, at 153 (emphasis added). The abortion decision is unquestionably important and has irrevocable consequences whichever way it is made. Missouri is entitled to protect the minor unmarried woman from making the decision in a way which is not in her own best interests, and it seeks to achieve this goal by requiring parental consultation and consent. This is the traditional way by which States have sought to protect children from their own immature and improvident decisions; and there is absolutely no reason expressed by the majority why the State may not utilize that method here.

[Mr. Justice Stevens dissenting.]

In my opinion, however, the parental consent requirement is consistent with the holding in *Roe*. The State's interest in the welfare of its young citizens justifies a variety of protective measures. Because he may not foresee the consequences of his decision, a minor may not make an enforceable bargain. He may not lawfully work or travel where he pleases, or even attend exhibitions of constitutionally protected adult motion pictures. Persons below a certain age may not marry without parental consent. Indeed, such consent is essential even when the young woman is already pregnant. The State's interest in protecting a young person from harm justifies the imposition of restraints on his or her freedom even though comparable restraints on adults would be constitutionally impermissible. Therefore, the holding in *Roe* v. *Wade* that the abortion decision is entitled to constitutional protection merely emphasizes the importance of the decision; it does not lead to the conclusion that the state legislature has no power to enact legislation for the purpose of protecting a young pregnant woman from the consequences of an incorrect decision.

The abortion decision is, of course, more important than the decision to attend or to avoid an adult motion picture, or the decision to work long hours in a factory. It is not necessarily any more important than the decision to run away from home or the decision to marry. But even if it is the most important kind of a decision a young person may ever make, that assumption merely enhances the quality of the State's interest in maximizing the probability that the decision be made correctly and with full understanding of the consequences of either alternative.

The Court recognizes that the State may insist that the decision not be made without the benefit of medical advice. But since the most significant consequences of the decision are not medical in character, it would seem to me that the State may, with equal legitimacy, insist that the decision be made only after other appropriate counsel has been had as well. Whatever choice a pregnant young woman makes—to marry, to abort, to bear her child out of wedlock—the consequences of her decision may have a profound impact on her entire future

life. A legislative determination that such a choice will be made more wisely in most cases if the advice and moral support of a parent play a part in the decisionmaking process is surely not irrational. Moreover, it is perfectly clear the parental consent requirement will necessarily involve a parent in the decisional process.

If there is no parental consent requirement, many minors will submit to the abortion procedure without ever informing their parents. An assumption that the parental reaction will be hostile, disparaging or violent no doubt persuades many children simply to bypass parental counsel which would in fact be loving, supportive and, indeed, for some indispensable. It is unrealistic, in my judgment, to assume that every parent-child relationship is either (a) so perfect that communication and accord will take place routinely or (b) so imperfect that the absence of communication reflects the child's correct prediction that the parent will exercise his or her veto arbitrarily to further a selfish interest rather than the child's interest. A state legislature may conclude that most parents will be primarily interested in the welfare of their children, and further, that the imposition of a parental consent requirement is an appropriate method of giving the parents an opportunity to foster that welfare by helping a pregnant distressed child to make and to implement a correct decision.

The State's interest is not dependent on an estimate of the impact the parental consent requirement may have on the total number of abortions that may take place. I assume that parents will sometimes prevent abortions which might better be performed; other parents may advise abortions that should not be performed. Similarly, even doctors are not omniscient; specialists in performing abortions may incorrectly conclude that the immediate advantages of the procedure outweigh the disadvantages which a parent could evaluate in better perspective. In each individual case factors much more profound than a mere medical judgment may weigh heavily in the scales. The overriding consideration is that the right to make the choice be exercised as wisely as possible.

The Court assumes that parental consent is an appropriate requirement if the minor is not "capable of understanding the procedure and of appreciating its consequences and those of available alternatives." . . . This assumption is, of course, correct and consistent with the predicate which underlies all State legislation seeking to protect minors from the consequences of decisions they are not yet prepared to make. In all such situations chronological age has been the basis for imposition of a restraint on the minor's freedom of choice even though it is perfectly obvious that such a yardstick is imprecise and perhaps even unjust in particular cases. The Court seems to assume that the capacity to conceive a child and the judgment of the physician are the only constitutionally permissible yardsticks for determining whether a young woman can independently make the abortion decision. I doubt the accuracy of the Court's empirical judgment. Even if it were correct, however, as a matter of constitutional law I think a State has power to conclude otherwise and to select a chronological age as its standard.

In short, the State's interest in the welfare of its young citizens is sufficient, in my judgment, to support the parental consent requirement.

Note: In *Bellotti* v. *Baird*, 99 S. Ct. (1979), four Justices held that, if a state decides to require a pregnant minor to obtain one or both parents' consent to an abortion, it must also provide an alternative procedure whereby authorization for the abortion can be obtained. A pregnant minor is entitled in such a proceeding to show either that she is mature enough and well enough informed to make her abortion decision, in consultation with her physician, independently of her parents' wishes, or that even if she is not able to make this decision independently, the desired abortion would be in her best interests. The alternative procedure was found inadequate in the present case because it permitted a court to withhold authorization for an abortion even though the minor is found mature and competent to decide for herself, and also because it did not permit a minor to go directly to court without first consulting or notifying her parents.

Four other Justices found both the requirement and the modifying alternative invalid because no matter how mature and capable of informed decision-making a minor might be, her decision would be subject to an absolute, third-party veto. One judge dissented.

Maher v. *Roe* (excerpt)
432 U.S. 464 (1977)

Connecticut law provided medical aid for the indigent, including aid with respect to childbirth, but not with respect to nontherapeutic abortions.

[*Roe* v. *Wade*] did not declare an unqualified "constitutional right to an abortion," as the District Court seemed to think. Rather the right protects the woman from unduly burdensome interference with her freedom to decide whether to terminate her pregnancy. It implies no limitation on the authority of a State to make a value judgment favoring childbirth over abortion, and to implement that judgment by the allocation of public funds.

The Connecticut regulation before us is different in kind from the laws invalidated in our previous abortion decisions. The Connecticut regulation places no obstacles—absolute or otherwise—in the pregnant woman's path to an abortion. An indigent woman who desires an abortion suffers no disadvantage as a consequence of Connecticut's decision to fund childbirth; she continues as before to be dependent on private sources for the service she desires. The State may have made childbirth a more attractive alternative, thereby influencing the woman's decision, but it has imposed no restriction on access to abortions that was not already there. The indigency that may make it difficult—and in some cases, perhaps, impossible—for some women to have abortions is neither created nor in any way affected by the Connecticut regulation. We conclude that the Connecticut regulation does not impinge upon the fundamental right recognized in *Roe*.

[Justices Brennan, Marshall, and Blackman dissenting:]

Roe v. *Wade* and cases following it hold that an area of privacy invulnerable to the State's intrusion surrounds the decision of a pregnant woman whether or not to carry her pregnancy to term. The Connecticut scheme clearly infringes upon that area of privacy by bringing financial pressures on indigent women that force them to bear children they would not otherwise have. That is an obvious impairment of the fundamental right established by *Roe*. Yet the Court concludes that "the Connecticut regulation does not impinge upon [that] fundamental right." This conclusion is based on a perceived distinction, on the one hand, between the imposition of criminal penalties for the procurement of an abortion present in *Roe* v. *Wade* and *Doe* v. *Bolton* and the absolute prohibition present in *Planned Parenthood of Missouri* v. *Danforth*, 428 U.S. 52 (1976), and, on the other, the assertedly lesser inhibition imposed by the Connecticut scheme.

Paris Adult Theatre I v. Slaton (excerpt)
413 U.S. 49 (1973)

This case began as a state proceeding to enjoin the showing of obscene films. In the course of its opinion (presented more fully in Chapter 8, below), the Court made these observations with respect to privacy:

It is asserted, however, that standards for evaluating state commercial regulations are inapposite in the present context, as state regulation of access by consenting adults to obscene material violates the constitutionally protected right to privacy enjoyed by petitioners' customers. Even assuming that petitioners have vicarious standing to assert potential customers' rights, it is unavailing to compare a theater, open to the public for a fee, with the private home of *Stanley* v. *Georgia*, 394 U.S. at 568, and the marital bedroom of *Griswold* v. *Connecticut, supra*, at 485–486. This Court, has, on numerous occasions, refused to hold that commerical ventures such as a motion-picture house are "private" for the purpose of civil rights litigation and civil rights statutes. See *Sullivan* v. *Little Hunting Park, Inc.*, 396 U.S. 229, 236 (1969). . . .

Our prior decisions recognizing a right to privacy guaranteed by the Fourteenth Amendment included "only personal rights that can be deemed 'fundamental' or 'implicit in the concept of ordered liberty.' *Palko* v. *Connecticut*, 302 U.S. 319, 325 (1937)." *Roe* v. *Wade*, 410 U.S. 113, 152 (1973). This privacy right encompasses and protects the personal intimacies of the home, the family, marriage, motherhood, procreation, and child rearing. Cf. *Eisenstadt* v. *Baird*, 405 U.S. 438, 453–454 (1972); *id.*, at 460, 463–465 (White, J., concurring); *Stanley* v. *Georgia, supra*, at 568; *Loving* v. *Virginia*, 388 U.S. 1, 12 (1967); *Griswold* v. *Connecticut, supra*, at 486;

Prince v. *Massachusetts*, 321 U.S. 158, 166 (1944); *Skinner* v. *Oklahoma*, 316 U.S. 535, 541 (1942); *Pierce* v. *Society of Sisters*, 268 U.S. 510, 535 (1925); *Meyer* v. *Nebraska*, 262 U.S. 390, 399 (1923). Nothing however, in this Court's decisions intimates that there is any "fundamental" privacy right "implicit in the concept of ordered liberty" to watch obscene movies in places of public accommodation.

If obscene material unprotected by the First Amendment in itself carried with it a "penumbra" of constitutionally protected privacy, this Court would not have found it necessary to decide *Stanley* on the narrow basis of the "privacy of the home," which was hardly more than a reaffirmation that "a man's home is his castle." Cf. *Stanley* v. *Georgia, supra*, at 564. Moreover, we have declined to equate the privacy of

the home relied on in *Stanley* with a "zone" of "privacy" that follows a distributor or a consumer of obscene materials wherever he goes. See *United States* v. *Orito*, 413 U.S. at 141–143. . . . (opinion of White, J.); *United States* v. *Reidel* [402 U.S. 351 (1971)] at 355. The idea of a "privacy" right and a place of public accommodation are, in this context, mutually exclusive. Conduct or depictions of conduct that the state police power can prohibit on a public street do not become automatically protected by the Constitution merely because the conduct is moved to a bar or a "live" theater stage, any more than a "live" performance of a man locked in a sexual embrace at high noon in Times Square is protected by the Constitution because they simultaneously engage in a valid political dialogue.

Note and quaere: Paul v. Davis, 424 U.S. 693 (1976), was a suit for damages said to have resulted from a memo to merchants in which the police listed the plaintiff as a shoplifter. The Court held the listing was not a violation of *constitutionally protected privacy* (regardless of plaintiff's guilt or innocence), since such privacy included only "matters relating to marriage, procreation, contraception, family relationships, and child rearing and education." The Court reached a similar conclusion in *Kelley* v. *Johnson,* 425 U.S. 328 (1976), with respect to a hair-length regulation for *policement*—even assuming "the citizenry at large has some sort of 'liberty' interest within the Fourteenth Amendment in matters of appearance." *Doe* v. *Commonwealth's Attorney,* 425 U.S. 901 (1976), found privacy no defense against a charge of sodomy between consenting adults in private. *Whalen* v. *Roe,* 429 U.S. 589 (1977), found no violation of constitutionally protected privacy in a New York Drug-control statute which required that the names of persons obtaining certain dangerous drugs by medical prescription be recorded in a computer file. *Runyon* v. *McCrary,* 427 U.S. 160 (1976), held that a federal law which

prohibits private schools from excluding qualified children because of race does not violate the "right of privacy." (This and related "race privacy" cases are considered in Chapters 9 and 10, below.)

Do these cases suggest the Court's terminology in *Griswold* and *Roe* is misleadingly broad? Surely the sale and purchase of contraceptives, like abortion, do not fit easily into the traditional concept of privacy. Would it not be more accurate (and less deluding) to call the *Griswold-Roe* right a qualified right of autonomy with respect to pregnancy (and perhaps other highly personal matters)? Doesn't virtually every governmental act—good or bad—disturb the privacy of some or all of us? Consider, for example, the federal income tax, which requires listing of all sources and amounts of one's income—and, if one claims itemized deductions, the amounts and beneficiaries even of religious and charitable donations.

On essentially First Amendment grounds, *Stanley* v. *Georgia,* 394 U.S. 557 (1969), upholds the freedom to use pornographic materials in the privacy of one's home. The case is discussed in *United States* v. *Orito,* Chapter 8, below.

7

Rights of the Accused:
The Fair Hearing

INTRODUCTION: THE INCORPORATION DOCTRINE

Barron v. *Baltimore*
See p. 189, above.

The Slaughter House Cases
See p. 191, above.

Twitchell v. *Pennsylvania*
See p. 202, above.

Twining v. *New Jersey*
211 U.S. 78 (1908)

Twining and his associate were indicted for fraud. At their trial they refused to take the witness stand in their own defense. The trial judge, in his instructions to the jury, mentioned this fact. Twining claimed that doing so made his silence "speak" against (incriminate) him. On the basis of *Slaughter House* (above, Chapter 5), the Supreme Court held exemption from self-incrimination is not a privilege or immunity of United States citizenship. It then turned to a related claim.

Mr. Justice Moody delivered the opinion of the court. . . .

The defendants, however, do not stop here. They appeal to another clause of the 14th Amendment, and insist that the self-incrimination which they allege the instruction to the jury compelled was a denial of due process of law. This contention requires separate consideration, for it is possible that some of the personal rights safeguarded by the first eight Amendments against national action may also be safeguarded against state action, because a denial of them would be a denial of due process of law. *Chicago, B. & Q. R. Co.* v. *Chicago,* 166 U.S. 226. If this is so, it is not because those rights are enumerated in the first eight Amendments, but because they are of such a nature that they are included in the conception of due process of law. Few phrases of the law are so elusive of exact apprehension as this. Doubtless the difficulties of ascertaining its connotation have been increased in American jurisprudence, where it has been embodied in constitutions and put to new uses as a limit on legislative power. This court has always declined to give a comprehensive definition of it, and has preferred that its full meaning should be gradually ascertained by the process of inclusion and exclusion in the course of the decisions of cases as they arise. There are certain general principles, well settled, however, which narrow the field of discussion, and may serve as helps to correct conclusions. These principles grow out of the proposition universally accepted by American courts on the authority of Coke, that the words "due process of law" are equivalent in meaning to the words "law of the land," contained in that chapter of Magna Charta which provides that "no freeman shall be taken, or imprisoned, or disseised, or outlawed, or exiled, or any wise destroyed; nor shall we go upon him, nor send upon him, but by the lawful judgment of his peers or by the law of the land." *Den ex dem. Murray* v. *Hoboken Land & Improv. Co.,* 18 How. 272; *Davidson* v. *New Orleans,* 96 U.S. 97; *Jones* v. *Robbins,* 8 Gray, 329; Cooley, *Const.Lim.* 7th ed. 500; McGehee, *Due Process of Law,* 16. From the consideration of the meaning of the words in the light of their historical origin this court has drawn the following conclusions:

First. What is due process of law may be ascertained by an examination of those settled usages and modes of proceedings existing in the common and statute law of England before the emigration of our ancestors, and shown not to have been unsuited to their civil and political condition by having been acted on by them after the settlement of this country. This test was adopted by the court, speaking through Mr. Justice Curtis, in *Den ex dem. Murray* v. *Hoboken Land & Improv. Co.,* 18 How. 272, 280 (approved in *Hallinger* v. *Davis,* 146 U.S. 314, 320; *Holden* v. *Hardy,* 169 U.S. 366, 390; but see *Lowe* v. *Kansas,* 163 U.S. 81, 85. Of course, the part of the Constitution then before the court was the 5th Amendment. If any different meaning of the same words, as they are used in the 14th Amendment, can be conceived, none has yet appeared in judicial decision. "A process of law," said Mr. Justice Matthews, commenting on this statement of Mr. Justice Curtis, "which is not otherwise forbidden, must be taken to be due process of law, if it can show the sanction of settled usage both in England and in this country." *Hurtado* v. *California,* 110 U.S. 516, 528.

Second. It does not follow, however, that a procedure settled in English law at the time of the emigration, and brought to this country and practised by our ancestors, is an essential element of due process of law. If that were so, the procedure of the first half of the seventeenth century would be fastened upon the American jurisprudence like a straightjacket, only to be unloosed by constitutional amendment. That, said Mr. Justice Matthews, in the same case, p. 529, "would be to deny every quality of the law but its age, and to render it incapable of progress or improvement." *Holden* v. *Hardy,* 169 U.S. 366, 388. *Brown* v. *New Jersey,* 175 U.S. 172, 175.

Third. But, consistently with the requirements of due process, no change in ancient procedure can be made which disregards those fundamental principles, to be ascertained from time to time by judicial action, which have relation to process of law, and protect the citizen in his private law, and guard him against the arbitrary action of government. This idea has been many times expressed in differing words by this court, and it seems well to cite some expressions of it. The words "due process of law" "were intended to secure the individual from the arbitrary exercise of the powers of government, unrestrained by the established principles of private rights and distributive justice." *Bank of Columbia* v. *Okely*, 4 Wheat. 235, 244 (approved in *Hurtado* v. *California*, 110, U.S. 516, 527; *Leeper* v. *Texas*, 139 U.S. 462, 468; *Scott* v. *McNeal*, 154 U.S. 34, 45; "This court has never attempted to define with precision the words 'due process of law.' . . . It is sufficient to say that there are certain immutable principles of justice which inhere in the very idea of free government which no member of the Union may disregard." *Holden* v. *Hardy*, 169 U.S. 366, 389. "The same words refer to that law of the land in each state, which derives its authority from the inherent and reserved powers of the state, exerted within the limits of those fundamental principles of liberty and justice which lie at the base of all our civil and political institutions." *Re Kemmler*, 136 U.S. 436, 448. "The limit of the full control which the state has in the proceedings of its courts, both in civil and criminal cases is subject only to the qualification that such procedure must not work a denial of fundamental rights or conflict with specific and applicable provisions of the Federal Constitution." *West* v. *Louisiana*, 194 U.S. 258, 263.

The question under consideration may first be tested by the application of these settled doctrines of this court. If the statement of Mr. Justice Curtis, as elucidated in *Hurtado* v. *California*, is to be taken literally, that alone might almost be decisive. For nothing is more certain, in point of historical fact, than that the practice of compulsory self-incrimination in the courts and elsewhere existed for four hundred years after the granting of Magna Charta, continued throughout the reign of Charles I. (though then beginning to be seriously questioned), gained at least some foothold among the early colonists of this country, and was not entirely omitted at trials in England until the eighteenth century. Wigmore, Ev. § 2250 (see the Colonies, note 108). . . .

But, without repudiating or questioning the test proposed by Mr. Justice Curtis for the court, or rejecting the inference drawn from English law, we prefer to rest our decision on broader grounds, and inquire whether the exemption from self-incrimination is of such a nature that it must be included in the conception of due process. Is it a fundamental principle of liberty and justice which inheres in the very idea of free government and is the inalienable right of a citizen of such a government? In approaching such a question it must not be forgotten that in a free representative government nothing is more fundamental than the right of the people, through their appointed servants, to govern themselves in accordance with their own will, except so far as they have restrained themselves by constitutional limits specifically established, and that, in our peculiar dual form of government, nothing is more fundamental than the full power of the state to order its own affairs and govern its own people, except so far as the Federal Constitution, expressly or by fair implication, has withdrawn that power. . . . One aid to the solution of the question is to inquire how the right was rated during the time when the meaning of due process was in a formative state, and before it was incorporated in American constitutional law. Did those who then were formulating and insisting upon the rights of the people entertain the view that the right was so fundamental that there could be no due process without it? . . .

Thus it appears that four only of the thirteen original states insisted upon incorporating the privilege in the Constitution, and they separately and simultaneously with the requirement of due process of law, and that three states proposing amendments were silent upon this subject. It is worthy of note that two of these four states did not incorporate the privilege in their own Constitutions, where it would have had a much wider field of usefulness, until many years after. New York in 1821 and Rhode Island in 1842 (its first Constitution). This survey does not tend to show that it was then in this country the universal or even general belief that the privilege ranked among the fundamental and inalienable rights of mankind; and what is more important here, it affirmatively shows that the privilege was not conceived to be inherent in due process of law, but, on the other hand, a right separate, independent, and outside of due process. Congress, in submitting the Amendments to the several states, treated the two rights as exclusive of each other. Such also has been the view of the states in framing their own Constitutions, for in every case, except in New Jersey and Iowa, where the due process clause or its equivalent is included, it has been thought necessary to include separately the privilege clause. Nor have we been referred to any decision of a state court save one (*State* v. *Height*, 117 Iowa 650, 91 N.W. 935), where the exemption has been held to be required by due process of law. The inference is irresistible that it has been the opinion of constitution makers that the privilege, if fundamental in any sense, is not fundamental in due process of law, nor an essential part of it. We believe that this opinion is proved to have been correct by every historical test by which the meaning of the phrase can be tried.

The decisions of this court, though they are silent on the precise question before us, ought to be searched to discover if they present any analogies which are helpful in its decision. The essential elements of due process of law, already established by them, are singularly few, though of wide application and deep significance. We are not here concerned with the effect of due process in restraining substantive laws, as, for example, that which forbids the taking of private property for public use without compensation. We need notice now only those cases which deal with the principles which must be observed in the trial of criminal and civil causes. Due process requires that the court which assumes to determine the rights of parties shall have jurisdiction (*Pennoyer* v. *Neff*, 95 U.S. 714, 733), . . . and that there shall be notice and opportunity for hearing given the parties (*Hovey* v. *Elliott*, 167 U.S. 409, 17 S.Ct. 841). . . . Subject to these two fundamental conditions, which seem to be universally prescribed in all systems of law established by civilized countries, this court has, up to this time, sustained all state laws, statutory or judicially declared, regulating procedure, evidence, and methods of trial, and held them to be consistent with due process of law.

. . . In *Missouri* v. *Lewis* (*Bowman* v. *Lewis*) 101 U.S. 22, Mr. Justice Bradley, speaking for the whole court, said, in effect, that the 14th Amendment would not prevent a state from adopting or continuing the Civil Law instead of the common law. This dictum has been approved and made an essential part of the reasoning of the decision in *Holden* v. *Hardy*, 169 U.S. 387, 389, and *Maxwell* v. *Dow*, [176 U.S. 581] *supra*, 598. The statement excludes the possibility that the privilege is essential to due process, for it hardly need be said that the interrogation of the accused at his trial is the practice in the Civil Law.

Even if the historical meaning of due process of law and the decisions of this court did not exclude the privilege from it, it would be going far to rate it as an immutable principle of justice which is the inalienable possession of every citizen of a free government. Salutary as the principle may seem to the great majority, it cannot be ranked with the right to hearing before condemnation, the immunity from arbitrary power not acting by general laws, and the inviolability of private property. . . . It has no place in the jurisprudence of civilized and free countries outside the domain of the common law, and it is nowhere observed among our own people in the search for truth outside the administration of the law. . . .

We have assumed only for the purpose of discussion that what was done in the case at bar was an infringement of the privilege against self-incrimination. . . .

Judgment affirmed.

Mr. Justice Harlan, dissenting:

. . . In my judgment, immunity from self-incrimination is protected against hostile state action, not only by that clause in the 14th Amendment declaring that "no state shall make or enforce any law which shall abridge the privileges or immunities of citizens of the United States," but by the clause, in the same Amendment, "nor shall any state deprive any person of life, liberty, or property, without due process of law." . . .

I am of opinion that as immunity from self-incrimination was recognized in the Fifth Amendment of the Constitution and placed beyond violation by any Federal agency, it should be deemed one of the immunities of citizens of the United States which the Fourteenth Amendment in express terms forbids any State from abridging—as much so, for instance, as the right of free speech (1st Amend.), or the exemption from cruel or unusual punishments (8th Amend.), or the exemption from being put twice in jeopardy of life or limb for the same offense (5th Amend.), or the exemption from unreasonable searches and seizures of one's person, house, papers or effects (4th Amend.). Even if I were anxious or willing to cripple the operation of the Fourteenth Amendment by strained or narrow interpretations, I should feel obliged to hold that when that Amendment was adopted all these last-mentioned exemptions were among the immunities belonging to citizens of the United States, which, after the adoption of the Fourteenth Amendment, no State could impair or destroy. But, as I read the opinion of the court, it will follow from the general principles underlying it, or from the reasoning pursued therein, that the Fourteenth Amendment would be no obstacle whatever in the way of a state law or practice under which, for instance, cruel or unusual punishments (such as the thumb screw, or the rack or burning at the stake) might be inflicted. So of a state law which infringed the right of free speech, or authorized unreasonable searches or seizures of persons, their houses, papers or effects, or a state law under which one accused of crime could be put in jeopardy twice or oftener, at the pleasure of the prosecution, for the same offense.

Palko v. *Connecticut*
302 U.S. 319 (1937)

Mr. Justice Cardozo delivered the opinion of the Court.

A statute of Connecticut permitting appeals in criminal cases to be taken by the state is challenged by appellant as an infringement of the Fourteenth Amendment of the Constitution of the United States. Whether the challenge should be upheld is now to be determined.

Appellant was indicted in Fairfield County, Conn., for the crime of murder in the first degree. A jury found him guilty of murder in the second degree, and he was sentenced to confinement in the state prison for life. Thereafter the State of Connecticut, with the permission of the judge presiding at the trial, gave notice of appeal to the Supreme Court of Errors. This it did pursuant to an act adopted in 1886. . . . Upon such appeal, the Supreme Court of Errors reversed the judgment and ordered a new trial. *State* v. *Palko*, 121 Conn. 669, 186 A. 657. It found that there had been error of law to the prejudice of the state (1) in excluding testimony as to a confession by defendant; (2) in excluding testimony upon cross-examination of defendant to impeach his credibility; and (3) in the instructions to the jury as to the difference between first and second degree murder.

Pursuant to the mandate of the Supreme Court of Errors, defendant was brought to trial again. Before a jury was impaneled, and also at later stages of the case, he made the objection that the effect of the new trial was to place him twice in jeopardy for the same offense, and in so doing to violate the Fourteenth Amendment of the Constitution of the United States. Upon the overruling of the objection the trial proceeded. The jury returned a verdict of murder in the first degree, and the court sentenced the defendant to the punishment of death. The Supreme Court of Errors affirmed the judgment of conviction (122 Conn. 529, 191 A. 320). . . .

1.   The execution of the sentence will not

deprive appellant of his life without the process of law assured to him by the Fourteenth Amendment of the Federal Constitution.

The argument for appellant is that whatever is forbidden by the Fifth Amendment is forbidden by the Fourteenth also. The Fifth Amendment, which is not directed to the States, but solely to the federal government, creates immunity from double jeopardy. No person shall be "subject for the same offense to be twice put in jeopardy of life or limb." The Fourteenth Amendment ordains, "nor shall any State deprive any person of life, liberty, or property, without due process of law." To retry a defendant, though under one indictment and only one, subjects him, it is said, to double jeopardy in violation of the Fifth Amendment, if the prosecution is one on behalf of the United States. From this the consequence is said to follow that there is a denial of life or liberty without due process of law, if the prosecution is one on behalf of the people of a state. Thirty-five years ago a like argument was made to this court in *Dreyer* v. *Illinois*, 187 U.S. 71, 85, and was passed without consideration of its merits as unnecessary to a decision. The question is now here.

We do not find it profitable to mark the precise limits of the prohibition of double jeopardy in federal prosecutions. The subject was much considered in *Kepner* v. *United States*, 195 U.S. 100, decided in 1904 by a closely divided court. The view was there expressed for a majority of the court that the prohibition was not confined to jeopardy in a new and independent case. It forbade jeopardy in the same case if the new trial was at the instance of the government and not upon defendant's motion. . . . All this may be assumed for the purpose of the case at hand, though the dissenting opinions . . . show how much was to be said in favor of a different ruling. Right-minded men, as we learn from those opinions, could reasonably, even if mistakenly, believe that a second trial was lawful in prosecutions subject to the Fifth Amendment, if it was all in the same case. Even more plainly, right-minded men could reasonably believe that in espousing that conclusion they were not favoring a practice repugnant to the conscience of mankind. Is double jeopardy in such circumstances, if double jeopardy it must be called, a denial of due process forbidden to the States? The tyranny of labels . . . must not lead us to leap to a conclusion that a word which in one set of facts may stand for oppression or enormity is of like effect in every other.

We have said that in appellant's view the Fourteenth Amendment is to be taken as embodying the prohibitions of the Fifth. His thesis is even broader. Whatever would be a violation of the original bill of rights (Amendments 1 to 8) if done by the federal government is now equally unlawful by force of the Fourteenth Amendment if done by a state. There is no such general rule.

The Fifth Amendment provides, among other things, that no person shall be held to answer for a capital or otherwise infamous crime unless on presentment or indictment of a grand jury. This court has held that, in prosecutions by a state, presentment or indictment by a grand jury may give way to informations at the instance of a public officer. *Hurtado* v. *California*, 110 U.S. 516. . . . The Fifth Amendment provides also that no person shall be compelled in any criminal case to be a witness against himself. This court has said that, in prosecutions by a state, the exemption will fail if the state elects to end it. *Twining* v. *New Jersey*, 211 U.S. 78, 106, 111, 112. . . . The Sixth Amendment calls for a jury trial in criminal cases and the Seventh for a jury trial in civil cases at common law where the value in controversy shall exceed $20. This court has ruled that consistently with those amendments trial by jury may be modified by a state or abolished altogether. *Walker* v. *Sauvinet*, 92 U.S. 90; *Maxwell* v. *Dow*, 176 U.S. 581. . . .

On the other hand, the due process clause of the Fourteenth Amendment may make it unlawful for a state to abridge by its statutes the freedom of speech which the First Amendment safeguards against encroachment by the Congress . . . of the like freedom of the press, . . . or the free exercise of religion, . . . or the right of peaceable assembly, without which speech would be unduly trammeled, . . . or the right of one accused of crime to the benefit of counsel (*Powell* v. *Alabama,* 287 U.S. 45). In these and other situations immunities that are valid as against the federal government by force of the specific pledges of particular amendments have been found to be implicit in the concept of ordered liberty, and thus, through the Fourteenth Amendment, become valid as against the states.

The line of division may seem to be wavering and broken if there is a hasty catalogue of the cases on the one side and the other. Reflection and analysis will induce a different view. There emerges the perception of a rationalizing principle which gives to discrete instances a proper order and coherence. The right to trial by jury and the immunity from prosecution except as the result of an indictment may have value and importance. Even so, they are not of the very essence of a scheme of ordered liberty. To abolish them is not to violate a "principle of justice so rooted in the traditions and conscience of our people as to be ranked as fundamental." *Snyder* v. *Massachusetts,* 291 U.S. 97, at page 105; *Brown* v. *Mississippi,* 297 U.S. 278, at page 285; *Hebert* v. *Louisiana,* 272 U.S. 312, 316. Few would be so narrow or provincial as to maintain that a fair and enlightened system of justice would be impossible without them. What is true of jury trials and indictments is true also, as the cases show, of the immunity from compulsory self-incrimination. *Twining* v. *New Jersey, supra.* This too might be lost, and justice still be done. Indeed, today as in the past there are students of our penal system who look upon the immunity as a mischief rather than a benefit, and who would limit its scope, or destroy it altogether.[1]

No doubt there would remain the need to give protection against torture, physical or mental. *Brown* v. *Mississippi, supra.* Justice, however, would not perish if the accused were subject to a duty to respond to orderly inquiry. The exclusion of these immunities and privileges from the privileges and immunities protected against the action of the States has not been arbitrary or casual. It has been dictated by a study and appreciation of the meaning, the essential implications, of liberty itself.

We reach a different plane of social and moral values when we pass to the privileges and immunities that have been taken over from the earlier articles of the Federal Bill of Rights and brought within the Fourteenth Amendment by a process of absorption. These in their origin were effective against the federal government alone. If the Fourteenth Amendment has absorbed them, the process of absorption has had its source in the belief that neither liberty nor justice would exist if they were sacrificed. . . . This is true, for illustration, of freedom of thought and speech. Of that freedom one may say that it is the matrix, the indispensable condition, of nearly every other form of freedom. With rare aberrations a pervasive recognition of that truth can be traced in our history, political and legal. So it has come about that the domain of liberty, withdrawn by the Fourteenth Amendment from encroachment by the states, has been enlarged by latter-day judgments to include liberty of the mind as well as liberty of action. The extension became, indeed, a logical imperative when once it was recognized, as long ago it was, that liberty is something more than exemption from physical restraint, and that even in the field of substantive rights and duties the legislative judgment, if oppressive and arbitrary, may be overridden by the courts.

---

[1] See, e.g., Bentham, *Rationale of Judicial Evidence,* Book IX, Pt. 4, c. III; Glueck, *Crime and Justice,* p. 94. Cf. Wigmore, *Evidence,* vol. 4, § 2251.

Compulsory self-incrimination is part of the established procedure in the law of Continental Europe. Wigmore, *supra,* p. 824; Garner, Criminal Procedure in France, 25 *Yale L.J.* 255, 260; Sherman, *Roman Law in the Modern World,* vol. 2, pp. 493, 494; Stumberg, *Guide to the Law and Legal Literature of France,* p. 184. Double jeopardy too is not everywhere forbidden. Radin, *Anglo American Legal History,* p. 228.

. . . Fundamental too in the concept of due process, and so in that of liberty, is the thought that condemnation shall be rendered only after trial. . . . The hearing, moreover, must be a real one, not a sham or a pretense. *Moore* v. *Dempsey,* 261 U.S. 86; *Mooney v. Holohan,* 294 U.S. 103. For that reason, ignorant defendants in a capital case were held to have been condemned unlawfully when in truth, though not in form, they were refused the aid of counsel. *Powell* v. *Alabama, supra,* 287 U.S. 45, at pages 67, 68. The decision did not turn upon the fact that the benefit of counsel would have been guaranteed to the defendants by the provisions of the Sixth Amendment if they had been prosecuted in a federal court. The decision turned upon the fact that in the particular situation laid before us in the evidence the benefit of counsel was essential to the substance of a hearing.

Our survey of the cases serves, we think, to justify the statement that the dividing line between them, if not unfaltering throughout its course, has been true for the most part to a unifying principle. On which side of the line the case made out by the appellant has appropriate location must be the next inquiry and the final one. Is that kind of double jeopardy to which the statute has subjected him a hardship so acute and shocking that our polity will not endure it? Does it violate those "fundamental principles of liberty and justice which lie at the base of all our civil and political institutions"? *Hebert* v. *Louisiana, supra.* The answer surely must be "no." What the answer would have to be if the state were permitted after a trial free from error to try the accused over again or to bring another case against him, we have no occasion to consider. We deal with the statute before us and no other. The state is not attempting to wear the accused out by a multitude of cases with accumulated trials. It asks no more than this, that the case against him shall go on until there shall be a trial free from the corrosion of substantial legal error. . . . This is not cruelty at all, nor even vexation in any immoderate degree. If the trial had been infected with error adverse to the accused, there might have been review at his instance, and as often as necessary to purge the vicious taint. A reciprocal privilege, subject at all times to the discretion of the presiding judge . . . has now been granted to the state. There is here no seismic innovation. The edifice of justice stands, its symmetry, to many, greater than before.

2. The conviction of appellant is not in derogation of any privileges or immunities that belong to him as a citizen of the United States.

There is argument in his behalf that the privileges and immunities clause of the Fourteenth Amendment as well as the due process clause has been flouted by the judgment. *Maxwell* v. *Dow, supra,* 176 U.S. 581, at page 584, gives all the answer that is necessary.

The judgment is affirmed.

Mr. Justice Butler dissents.

Note: See Benton v. Maryland, below.

Adamson v. *California*
332 U.S. 46 (1947)

Here, the Court upheld a state statute permitting comment on a defendant's failure to testify in his own defense. In doing so the Court reaffirmed *Twining,* as well as the approach set forth in *Palko.* The case is crucial because of the concurring and dissenting opinions which are presented here.

Mr. Justice Frankfurter, concurring. . . .

For historical reasons a limited immunity from the common duty to testify was written into the Federal Bill of Rights, and I am prepared to agree that, as part of that immunity, comment on the failure of an accused to take the witness stand is forbidden in federal prosecutions. It is so, of course, by explicit act of Congress. . . . But to suggest that such a limitation can be drawn out of "due process" in its protection of ultimate decency in a civilized society is to suggest that the Due Process Clause fastened fetters of unreason upon the States. . . .

Between the incorporation of the Fourteenth Amendment into the Constitution and the beginning of the present membership of the Court—a period of seventy years—the scope of that Amendment was passed upon by forty-three judges. Of all these judges, only one, who may respectfully be called an eccentric exception, ever indicated the belief that the Fourteenth Amendment was a shorthand summary of the first eight Amendments. . . .

The short answer to the suggestion that the [due process clause] was a way of saying that every State must thereafter initiate prosecutions through indictment by a grand jury, must have a trial by a jury of twelve in criminal cases, and must have trial by such a jury in common law suits where the amount in controversy exceeds twenty dollars, is that it is a strange way of saying it. It would be extraordinarily strange for a Constitution to convey such specific commands in such a roundabout and inexplicit way. . . . The notion that the Fourteenth Amendment was a covert way of imposing upon the States all the rules which it seemed important to Eighteenth Century statesmen to write into the Federal Amendments, was rejected by judges who were themselves witnesses of the process by which the Fourteenth Amendment became part of the Constitution. . . . [A]t the time of the ratification of the Fourteenth Amendment the constitutions of nearly half of the ratifying States did not have the rigorous requirements of the Fifth Amendment for instituting criminal proceedings through a grand jury. It could hardly have occurred to these States that by ratifying the Amendment they uprooted their established methods for prosecuting crime and fastened upon themselves a new prosecutorial system.

Indeed, the suggestion that the Fourteenth Amendment incorporates the first eight Amendments as such is not unambiguously urged. . . . There is suggested merely a selective incorporation of the first eight Amendments into the Fourteenth Amendment. Some are in and some are out, but we are left in the dark as to which are in and which are out. Nor are we given the calculus for determining which go in and which stay out. If the basis of selection is merely that those provisions of the first eight Amendments are incorporated which commend themselves to individual justices as indispensable to the dignity and happiness of a free man, we are thrown back to a merely subjective test. . . . If all that is meant is that due process contains within itself certain minimal standards which are "of the very essence of a scheme of ordered liberty," *Palko* v. *Connecticut* . . ., putting upon this Court the duty of applying these standards from time to time, then we have merely arrived at the insight which our predecessors long ago expressed.

. . . The Amendment neither comprehends the specific provisions by which the founders deemed it appropriate to restrict the federal government nor is it confined to them. The Due Process Clause of the Fourteenth Amendment has an independent potency, precisely as does the Due Process Clause of the Fifth Amendment in relation to the Federal Government. It ought not to require argument to reject the notion that due process of law meant one thing in the Fifth Amendment and another in the Fourteenth. . . . Are Madison and his contemporaries in the framing of the Bill of Rights to be charged with writing into it a meaningless clause? . . .

A construction which gives to due process no independent function but turns it into a summary of the specific provisions of the Bill of

Rights would . . . assume that no other abuses would reveal themselves in the course of time than those which had become manifest in 1791. Such a view not only disregards the historic meaning of "due process." It leads inevitably to a warped construction of specific provisions of the Bill of Rights to bring within their scope conduct clearly condemned by due process but not easily fitting into the pigeon-holes of the specific provisions. It seems pretty late in the day to suggest that a phrase so laden with historic meaning should be given an improvised content consisting of some but not all of the provisions of the first eight Amendments, selected on an undefined basis, with improvisation of content for the provisions so selected.

And so, when, as in a case like the present, a conviction in a State court is here for review under a claim that a right protected by the Due Process Clause of the Fourteenth Amendment has been denied, the issue is not whether an infraction of one of the specific provisions of the first eight Amendments is disclosed by the record. The relevant question is whether the criminal proceedings which resulted in conviction deprived the accused of the due process of law to which the United States Constitution entitled him. Judicial review of that guaranty of the Fourteenth Amendment inescapably imposes upon this Court an exercise of judgment upon the whole course of the proceedings in order to ascertain whether they offend those canons of decency and fairness which express the notions of justice of English-speaking peoples even toward those charged with the most heinous offenses. These standards of justice are not authoritatively formulated anywhere as though they were prescriptions in a pharmacopoeia. But neither does the application of the Due Process Clause imply that judges are wholly at large. The judicial judgment in applying the Due Process Clause must move within the limits of accepted notions of justice and is not to be based upon the idiosyncrasies of a merely personal judgment. The fact that judges among themselves may differ whether in a particular case a trial offends accepted notions of justice is not disproof that general rather than idiosyncratic standards are applied. An important safeguard against such merely individual judgment is an alert deference to the judgment of the State court under review.

Mr. Justice Black, dissenting. . . .

This decision reasserts a constitutional theory spelled out in *Twining* v. *New Jersey*, 211 U.S. 78, that this Court is endowed by the Constitution with boundless power under "natural law" periodically to expand and contract constitutional standards to conform to the Court's conception of what at a particular time constitutes "civilized decency" and "fundamental liberty and justice." Invoking this *Twining* rule, the Court concludes that although comment upon testimony in a federal court would violate the Fifth Amendment, identical comment in a state court does not violate today's fashion in civilized decency and fundamentals and is therefore not prohibited by the Federal Constitution as amended.

. . . I would not reaffirm the *Twining* decision. I think that decision and the "natural law" theory of the Constitution upon which it relies degrade the constitutional safeguards of the Bill of Rights and simultaneously appropriate for this Court a broad power which we are not authorized by the Constitution to exercise. My reasons for believing that the *Twining* decision should not be revitalized can best be understood by reference to the constitutional, judicial, and general history that preceded and followed the case. . . .

. . . I am attaching to this dissent an appendix which contains a résumé, by no means complete, of the Amendment's history. In my judgment that history conclusively demonstrates that the language of the first section of the Fourteenth Amendment, taken as a whole, was thought by those responsible for its submission to the people, and by those who opposed its submission, sufficiently explicit to guarantee that thereafter no state could deprive its citizens of the privileges and protections of the Bill of Rights. Whether this Court ever will, or whether it now should, in the light of past decisions, give full effect to what the Amendment was intended to accomplish is not necessarily essential to a decision here. However that may be, our prior decisions, including *Twining*, do not prevent our carrying out that purpose, at least to the extent of making applicable to the states, not a mere part, as the Court has, but the full protection of the Fifth Amendment's provision against compelling evidence from an accused to convict him of crime. And I further contend that the "natural law" formula which the Court uses to reach its conclusion in this case should be abandoned as an incongruous excrescence on our Constitution. . . .

. . . I fear to see the consequences of the Court's practice of substituting its own concepts of decency and fundamental justice for the language of the Bill of Rights as its point of departure in interpreting and enforcing that Bill of Rights. If the choice must be between the selective process of the *Palko* decision applying some of the Bill of Rights to the States, or the *Twining* rule applying none of them, I would choose the *Palko* selective process. But rather than accept either of these choices, I would follow what I believe was the original purpose of the Fourteenth Amendment—to extend to all the people of the nation the complete protection of the Bill of Rights. To hold that this Court can determine what, if any, provisions of the Bill of Rights will be enforced, and if so to what degree, is to frustrate the great design of a written Constitution.

It is an illusory apprehension that literal application of some or all of the provisions of the Bill of Rights to the States would unwisely increase the sum total of the powers of this Court to invalidate state legislation. . . . It must be conceded, of course, that the natural-law–due-process formula, which the Court today reaffirms, has been interpreted to limit substan-

tially this Court's power to prevent state violations of the individual civil liberties guaranteed by the Bill of Rights. But this formula also has been used in the past, and can be used in the future, to license this Court, in considering regulatory legislation, to roam at large in the broad expanses of policy and morals and to trespass, all too freely, on the legislative domain of the States as well as the Federal Government.

. . . [S]ince words can have many meanings, interpretation obviously may result in contraction or extension of the original purpose of a constitutional provision, thereby affecting policy. But to pass upon the constitutionality of statutes by looking to the particular standards enumerated in the Bill of Rights and other parts of the Constitution is one thing; to invalidate statutes because of application of "natural law" deemed to be above and undefined by the Constitution is another. . . .

Mr. Justice Douglas joins in this opinion.

Mr. Justice Murphy, with whom Mr. Justice Rutledge concurs, dissenting.

While in substantial agreement with the views of Mr. Justice Black, I have one reservation and one addition to make.

I agree that the specific guarantees of the Bill of Rights should be carried over intact into the first section of the Fourteenth Amendment. But I am not prepared to say that the latter is entirely and necessarily limited by the Bill of Rights. Occasions may arise where a proceeding falls so far short of conforming to fundamental standards of procedure as to warrant constitutional condemnation in terms of a lack of due process despite the absence of a specific provision in the Bill of Rights.

That point, however, need not be pursued here inasmuch as the Fifth Amendment . . . guarantee against self-incrimination has been violated in this case. . . .

Duncan v. *Louisiana*
391 U.S. 145 (1968)

Mr. Justice White delivered the opinion of the Court.

Appellant, Gary Duncan, was convicted of simple battery in the Twenty-fifth Judicial District Court of Louisiana. Under Louisiana law simple battery is a misdemeanor, punishable by two years' imprisonment and a $300 fine. Appellant sought trial by jury, but because the Louisiana Constitution grants jury trials only in cases in which capital punishment or imprisonment at hard labor may be imposed, the trial judge denied the request. Appellant was convicted and sentenced to serve 60 days in the parish prison and pay a fine of $150. . . .

I.

The Fourteenth Amendment denies the States the power to "deprive any person of life, liberty, or property, without due process of law." In resolving conflicting claims concerning the meaning of this spacious language, the Court has looked increasingly to the Bill of Rights for guidance; many of the rights guaranteed by the first eight Amendments to the Constitution have been held to be protected against state action by the Due Process Clause of the Fourteenth Amendment. That clause now protects the right to compensation for property taken by the State;[1] the rights of speech, press, and religion covered by the First Amendment,[2] the Fourth Amendment rights to be free from unreasonable searches and seizures and to have excluded from criminal trials any evidence illegally seized;[3] the right guaranteed by the Fifth Amendment to be free of compelled self-incrimination;[4] and the Sixth Amendment

rights to counsel,[5] to a speedy[6] and public[7] trial, to confrontation of opposing witnesses[8] and to compulsory process for obtaining witnesses.[9]

The test for determining whether a right extended by the Fifth and Sixth Amendments with respect to federal criminal proceedings is also protected against state action by the Fourteenth Amendment has been phrased in a variety of ways in the opinions of this Court. The question has been asked whether a right is among those " 'fundamental principles of liberty and justice which lie at the base of all our civil and political institutions,' " *Powell* v. *Alabama*, 287 U.S. 45, 67 (1932); whether it is "basic in our system of jurisprudence," *In re Oliver*, 333 U.S. 257, 273 (1948); and whether it is "a fundamental right, essential to a fair trial," *Gideon* v. *Wainwright*, 372 U.S. 335, 343–344 (1963); *Malloy* v. *Hogan*, 378 U.S. 1, 6 (1964); *Pointer* v. *Texas*, 380 U.S. 400, 403 (1965). The claim before us is that the right to trial by jury guaranteed by the Sixth Amendment meets these tests. The position of Louisiana, on the other hand, is that the Constitution imposes upon the States no duty to give a jury trial in any criminal case, regardless of the seriousness of the crime or the size of the punishment which may be imposed. Because we believe that trial by jury in criminal cases is fundamental to the American scheme of justice, we hold that the Fourteenth Amendment guarantees a right of jury trial in all criminal cases which—were they to be tried in a federal court—would come within the Sixth Amendment's guarantee.[10] Since we consider

---

[1] Chicago, B. & Q. R. Co. v. Chicago, 166 U.S. 226 (1897).

[2] See, e.g., Fiske v. Kansas, 274 U.S. 380 (1927).

[3] See Mapp v. Ohio, 367 U.S. 643 (1961).

[4] Malloy v. Hogan, 378 U.S. 1 (1964).

[5] Gideon v. Wainwright, 372 U.S. 335 (1963).

[6] Klopfer v. North Carolina, 386 U.S. 213 (1967).

[7] In re Oliver, 333 U.S. 257 (1948).

[8] Pointer v. Texas, 380 U.S. 400 (1965).

[9] Washington v. Texas, 388 U.S. 14 (1967).

[10] In one sense recent cases applying provisions of the first eight amendments to the States represent a new approach to the "incorporation" debate. Earlier the Court can be seen as having asked, when inquiring into whether some particular procedural safeguard was required of a State, if a civilized system could be imagined that would not accord the particular protection. For example, Palko v. Connecticut,

the appeal before us to be such a case, we hold that the Constitution was violated when appellant's demand for jury trial was refused.

The history of trial by jury in criminal cases has been frequently told. . . .

---

302 U.S. 319, 325 (1937), stated: "The right to trial by jury and the immunity from prosecution except as the result of an indictment may have value and importance. Even so, they are not of the very essence of a scheme of ordered liberty . . . . Few would be so narrow or provincial as to maintain that a fair and enlightened system of justice would be impossible without them." The recent cases, on the other hand, have proceeded upon the valid assumption that state criminal processes are not imaginary and theoretical schemes but actual systems bearing virtually every characteristic of the common-law system that has been developing contemporaneously in England and in this country. The question thus is whether given this kind of system a particular procedure is fundamental—whether, that is, a procedure is necessary to an Anglo-American regime of ordered liberty. It is this sort of inquiry that can justify the conclusions that state courts must exclude evidence seized in violation of the Fourth Amendment, Mapp v. Ohio, 367 U.S. 643 (1961); that state prosecutors may not comment on a defendant's failure to testify, Griffin v. California, 380 U.S. 609 (1965); and that criminal punishment may not be imposed for the status of narcotics addiction, Robinson v. California, 370 U.S. 660 (1962). Of immediate relevance for this case are the Court's holdings that the States must comply with certain provisions of the Sixth Amendment, specifically that the States may not refuse a speedy trial, confrontation of witnesses, and the assistance, at state expense if necessary, of counsel. See cases cited in nn. [5–9], supra. Of each of these determinations that a constitutional provision originally written to bind the Federal Government should bind the States as well it might be said that the limitation in question is not necessarily fundamental to fairness in every criminal system that might be imagined but is fundamental in the context of the criminal processes maintained by the American States.

When the inquiry is approached in this way the question whether the States can impose criminal punishment without granting a jury trial appears quite different from the way it appeared in the older cases opining that States might abolish jury trial. See, e.g., Maxwell v. Dow, 176 U.S. 581 (1900). A criminal process which was fair and equitable but used no juries is easy to imagine. It would make use of alternative guarantees and protections which would serve the purposes that the jury serves in the English and American systems. Yet no American State has undertaken to construct such a system. Instead, every American State, including Louisiana, uses the jury extensively, and imposes very serious punishments only after a trial at which the defendant has a right to a jury's verdict. In every State, including Louisiana, the structure and style of the criminal process—the supporting framework and the subsidiary procedures—are of the sort that naturally complement jury trial, and have developed in connection with and in reliance upon jury trial.

Even such skeletal history is impressive support for considering the right to jury trial in criminal cases to be fundamental to our system of justice, an importance frequently recognized in the opinions of this Court. . . .

Jury trial continues to receive strong support. The laws of every State guarantee a right to jury trial in serious criminal cases; no State has dispensed with it; nor are there significant movements underway to do so. . . .

We are aware of prior cases in this Court in which the prevailing opinion contains statements contrary to our holding today that the right to jury trial in serious criminal cases is a fundamental right and hence must be recognized by the States as part of their obligation to extend due process of law to all persons within their jurisdiction. . . . None of these cases, however, dealt with a State which had purported to dispense entirely with a jury trial in serious criminal cases. . . . Respectfully, we reject the prior dicta regarding jury trial in criminal cases.

The guarantees of jury trial in the Federal and State Constitutions reflect a profound judgment about the way in which law should be enforced and justice administered. A right to jury trial is granted to criminal defendants in order to prevent oppression by the Government. . . . The deep commitment of the Nation to the right of jury trial in serious criminal cases as a defense against arbitrary law enforcement qualifies for protection under the Due Process Clause of the Fourteenth Amendment, and must therefore be respected by the States.

Of course jury trial has "its weaknesses and the potential for misuse," Singer v. United States, 380 U.S. 24, 35 (1965). We are aware of the long debate, especially in this century, among those who write about the administration of justice, as to the wisdom of permitting untrained laymen to determine the facts in civil and criminal proceedings. Although the debate has been intense, with powerful voices on either side, most of the controversy has centered on the jury in civil cases. Indeed, some of the severest critics of civil juries acknowledge that the arguments for criminal juries are much stronger. . . .

The State of Louisiana urges that holding that the Fourteenth Amendment assures a right to jury trial will cast doubt on the integrity of every trial conducted without a jury. Plainly, this is not the import of our holding. Our conclusion is that in the American States, as in the federal judicial system, a general grant of jury trial for serious offenses is a fundamental right, essential for preventing miscarriages of justice and for assuring that fair trials are provided for all defendants. We would not assert, however, that every criminal trial—or any particular trial—held before a judge alone is unfair or that a defendant may never be as fairly treated by a judge as he would be by a jury. Thus we hold no constitutional doubts about the practices, common in both federal and state courts, of accepting waivers of jury trial and prosecuting petty crimes without extending a right to jury trial. However, the fact is that in most places more trials for serious crimes are to juries than to a court alone; a great many defendants prefer the judgment of a jury to that of a court. Even where defendants are satisfied with bench trials, the right to a jury trial very likely serves its intended purpose of making judicial or prosecutorial unfairness less likely.

II.

Louisiana's final contention is that even if it must grant jury trials in serious criminal cases, the conviction before us is valid and constitutional because here the petitioner was tried for simple battery and was sentenced to only 60 days in the parish prison. We are not persuaded. It is doubtless true that there is a category of petty crimes or offenses which is not subject to the Sixth Amendment jury trial provision and should not be subject to the Fourteenth Amendment jury trial requirement here applied to the States. Crimes carrying possible penalties up to six months do not require a jury trial if they otherwise qualify as petty offenses, *Cheff* v. *Schnackenberg*, 384 U.S. 373 (1966). But the penalty authorized for a particular crime is of major relevance in determining whether it is serious or not and may in itself, if severe enough, subject the trial to the mandates of the Sixth Amendment. *District of Columbia* v. *Clawans*, 300 U.S. 617 (1937). The penalty authorized by the law of the locality may be taken "as a gauge of its social and ethical judgments," 300 U.S., at 628 of the crime in question. In *Clawans* the defendant was jailed for 60 days, but it was the 90-day authorized punishment on which the Court focused in determining that the offense was not one for which the Constitution assured trial by jury. In the case before us the Legislature of Louisiana has made simple battery a criminal offense punishable by imprisonment for two years and a fine. The question, then is whether a crime carrying such a penalty is an offense which Louisiana may insist on trying without a jury.

We think not. . . .

The judgment below is reversed and the case is remanded for proceedings not inconsistent with this opinion.

Mr. Justice Black, with whom Mr. Justice Douglas joins, concurring.

The Court today holds that the right to trial by jury guaranteed defendants in criminal cases in federal courts by Art. III of the United States Constitution and by the Sixth Amendment is also guaranteed by the Fourteenth Amendment to defendants tried in state courts. With this holding I agree for reasons given by the Court. I also agree because of reasons given in my dissent in *Adamson* v. *California*, 332 U.S. 46, 68. . . .

While I do not wish at this time to discuss at length my disagreement with Brother Harlan's forthright and frank restatement of the now discredited *Twining* doctrine, I do want to point out what appears to me to be the basic difference between us. His view, as was indeed the view of *Twining*, is that "due process is an evolving concept" and therefore that it entails a "gradual process of judicial inclusion and exclusion" to ascertain those "immutable principles of free government which no member of the Union may disregard." Thus the Due Process Clause is treated as prescribing no specific and clearly ascertainable constitutional command that judges must obey in interpreting the Constitution, but rather as leaving judges free to decide at any particular time whether a particular rule or judicial formulation embodies an "immutable principle[s] of free government" or "is implicit in the concept of ordered liberty," or whether certain conduct "shocks the judge's conscience" or runs counter to some other similar, undefined and undefinable standard. Thus due process, according to my Brother Harlan, is to be a word with no permanent meaning, but one which is found to shift from time to time in accordance with judges' predilections and understandings of what is best for the country. If due process means this, the Fourteenth Amendment, in my opinion, might as well have been written that "no person shall be deprived of life, liberty or property except by laws that the judges of the United States Supreme Court shall find to be consistent with the immutable principles of free government." It is impossible for me to believe that such unconfined power is given to judges in our Constitution that it is a written one in order to limit governmental power.

Another tenet of the *Twining* doctrine as restated by my Brother Harlan is that "due process of law requires only fundamental fairness." But the "fundamental fairness" test is one on a par with that of shocking the conscience of the Court. Each of such tests depends entirely on the particular judge's idea of ethics and morals instead of requiring him to depend on the boundaries fixed by the written words of the Constitution. Nothing in the history of the phrase "due process of law" suggests that constitutional controls are to depend on any particular judge's sense of values. . . .

Finally I want to add that I am not bothered by the argument that applying the Bill of Rights to the States, "according to the same standards that protect those rights against federal encroachment," interferes with our concept of federalism in that it may prevent States from trying novel social and economic experiments. I have never believed that under the guise of federalism the States should be able to experiment with the protections afforded our citizens through the Bill of Rights. . . . It seems to me totally inconsistent to advocate on the one hand, the power of this Court to strike down any state law or practice which it finds "unreasonable" or "unfair," and on the other hand urge that the States be given maximum power to develop their own laws and procedures. Yet the due process approach of my Brothers Harlan and Fortas (see other concurring opinion) does just that since in effect it restricts the States to practices which a majority of this Court is willing to approve on a case-by-case basis. No one is more concerned than I that the States be allowed to use the full scope of their powers as their citizens see fit. And that is why I have continually fought against the expansion of this Court's authority over the States through the use of a broad, general interpretation of due process that permits judges to strike down state laws they do not like.

In closing I want to emphasize that I believe as strongly as ever that the Fourteenth Amendment was intended to make the Bill of Rights applicable to the States. I have been willing to support the selective incorporation doctrine, however, as an alternative, although perhaps less historically supportable than complete incorporation. The selective incorporation process, if used properly, does limit the Supreme Court in the Fourteenth Amendment field to specific Bill of Rights' protections only and keeps judges from roaming at will in their own notions of what policies outside the Bill of Rights are desirable and what are not. And, most importantly for me, the selective incorporation process has the virtue of having already worked to make most of the Bill of Rights' protections applicable to the States.

Mr. Justice Fortas, concurring.

I join the judgments and opinions of the Court in these cases because I agree that the Due Process Clause of the Fourteenth Amendment requires that the States accord the right to jury trial in prosecutions for offenses that are not petty. . . .

Mr. Justice Harlan, whom Mr. Justice Stewart joins, dissenting.

Every American jurisdiction provides for trial by jury in criminal cases. The question before us is not whether jury trial is an ancient institution, which it is; nor whether it plays a significant role in the administration of criminal justice, which it does; nor whether it will endure, which it shall. The question in this case is whether the State of Louisiana, which provides trial by jury for all felonies, is prohibited by the Constitution from trying charges of simple battery to the court alone. In my view, the answer to that question, mandated alike by our constitutional history and by the longer history of trial by jury, is clearly "no." . . .

I.

I believe I am correct in saying that every member of the Court for at least the last 135 years has agreed that our Founders did not consider the requirements of the Bill of Rights so fundamental that they should operate directly against the States. They were wont to believe rather that the security of liberty in America rested primarily upon the dispersion of governmental power across a federal system. The Bill of Rights was considered unnecessary by some but insisted upon by others in order to curb the possibility of abuse of power by the strong central government they were creating.

The Civil War Amendments dramatically altered the relation of the Federal Government to the States. The first section of the Fourteenth Amendment imposes highly significant restrictions on state action. But the restrictions are couched in very broad and general terms: citizenship, privileges and immunities; due process of law; equal protection of the laws. Consequently, for 100 years this Court has been engaged in the difficult process Professor Jaffe has well called "the search for intermediate premises." The question has been, "Where does the Court properly look to find the specific rules that define and give content to such terms as 'life, liberty, or property' and 'due process of law'?"

A few members of the Court have taken the position that the intention of those who drafted the first section of the Fourteenth Amendment was simply, and exclusively, to make the provisions of the first eight amendments applicable to state action. This view has never been accepted by this Court. In my view, often expressed elsewhere, the first section of the Fourteenth Amendment was meant neither to incorporate, nor to be limited to, the specific guarantees of the first eight amendments. The overwhelming historical evidence marshalled by Professor Fairman demonstrates, to me conclusively, that the Congressmen and state legislators who wrote, debated, and ratified the Fourteenth Amendment did not think they were "incorporating" the Bill of Rights[11] and the very

---

[11] Fairman, Does the Fourteenth Amendment Incorporate the Bill of Rights? The Original Understanding, 2 *Stan.L.Rev.* 5 (1949). Professor Fairman was not content to rest upon the overwhelming fact that the great words of the four clauses of the first section of the Fourteenth Amendment would have been an exceedingly peculiar way to say that "The rights heretofore guaranteed against federal intrusion by the first eight Amendments are henceforth guaranteed against state intrusion as well." He therefore sifted the mountain of material comprising the debates and committee reports relating to the Amendment in both Houses of Congress and in the state legislatures that passed upon it. He found that in the immense corpus of comments on the purpose and effects of the proposed amendment, and on its virtues and defects, there is almost no evidence whatever for "incorporation." The first eight amendments are so much as mentioned by only two members of Congress, one of whom effectively demonstrated (a) that he did not understand Barron v. Baltimore, 7 Pet. 243, and therefore did not under-

breadth and generality of the Amendment's provisions suggests that its authors did not suppose that the Nation would always be limited to mid-19th century conceptions of "liberty" and "due process of law" but that the increasing experience and evolving conscience of the American people would add new "intermediate premises." In short, neither history, nor sense, supports using the Fourteenth Amendment to put the States in a constitutional straitjacket with respect to their own development in the administration of criminal or civil law.

Although I therefore fundamentally disagree with the total incorporation view of the Fourteenth Amendment, it seems to me that such a position does at least have the virtue, lacking in the Court's selective incorporation approach, of internal consistency: we look to the Bill of Rights, word for word, clause for clause, precedent for precedent because, it is said, the men who wrote the Amendment wanted it that way. For those who do not accept this "history," a different source of "intermediate premises" must be found. The Bill of Rights is not necessarily irrelevant to the search for guidance in interpreting the Fourteenth Amendment, but the reason for and the nature of its relevance must be articulated.

Apart from the approach taken by the absolute incorporationists, I can see only one

method of analysis that has any internal logic. That is to start with the words "liberty" and "due process of law" and attempt to define them in a way that accords with American traditions and our system of government. This approach, involving a much more discriminating process of adjudication than does "incorporation," is, albeit difficult, the one that was followed throughout the Nineteenth and most of the present century. It entails a "gradual process of judicial inclusion and exclusion," seeking, with due recognition of constitutional tolerance for state experimentation and disparity, to ascertain those "immutable principles of free government which no member of the Union may disregard." . . .

Today's Court still remains unwilling to accept the total incorporationists' view of the history of the Fourteenth Amendment. This, if accepted, would afford a cogent reason for applying the Sixth Amendment to the States. The Court is also, apparently, unwilling to face the task of determining whether denial of trial by jury in the situation before us, or in other situations, is fundamentally unfair. Consequently, the Court has compromised on the ease of the incorporationist position, without its internal logic. It has simply assumed that the question before us is whether the Jury Trial Clause of the Sixth Amendment should be incorporated into the Fourteenth, jot-for-jot and case-for-case, or ignored. Then the Court merely declares that the clause in question is "in" rather than "out." . . .

The Court has justified neither its starting place nor its conclusion. . . .

II.

Since, as I see it, the Court has not even come to grips with the issues in this case, it is necessary to start from the beginning. When a criminal defendant contends that his state conviction lacked "due process of law," the question before this Court, in my view, is whether he was denied any element of fundamental procedural

---

stand the question of incorporation, and (b) that he was not himself understood by his colleagues. One state legislative committee report, rejected by the legislature as a whole, found § I of the Fourteenth Amendment superfluous because it duplicated the Bill of Rights: the committee obviously did not understand Barron v. Baltimore either. That is all Professor Fairman could find, in hundreds of pages of legislative discussion prior to passage of the Amendment, that even suggests incorporation.

To this negative evidence the judicial history of the Amendment could be added. For example, it proved possible for a court whose members had lived through Reconstruction to reiterate the doctrine of Barron v. Baltimore, that the Bill of Rights did not apply to the States, without so much as questioning whether the Fourteenth Amendment had any effect on the continued validity of that principle. *E.g.*, Walker v. Sauvinet, 92 U.S. 90; see generally Morrison, Does the Fourteenth Amendment Incorporate the Bill of Rights? The Judicial Interpretation, 2 *Stan.L.Rev.* 140 (1949).

fairness. Believing, as I do, that due process is an evolving concept and that old principles are subject to re-evaluation in light of later experience, I think it appropriate to deal on its merits with the question whether Louisiana denied appellant due process of law when it tried him for simple assault without a jury. . . .

In sum, there is a wide range of views on the desirability of trial by jury, and on the ways to make it most effective when it is used; there is also considerable variation from State to State in local conditions such as the size of the criminal caseload, the ease or difficulty of summoning jurors, and other trial conditions bearing on fairness. We have before us, therefore, an almost perfect example of a situation in which the celebrated dictum of Mr. Justice Brandeis should be invoked. It is, he said, "one of the happy incidents of the federal system that a single courageous State may, if its citizens choose, serve as a laboratory . . . ." *New State Ice Co.* v. *Liebmann*, 285 U.S. 262, 280, 311 (dissenting opinion). This Court, other courts, and the political process are available to correct any experiments in criminal procedure that prove fundamentally unfair to defendants. That is not what is being done today: instead, and quite without reason, the Court has chosen to impose upon every State one means of trying criminal cases; it is a good means, but it is not the only fair means, and it is not demonstrably better than the alternatives States might devise.

I would affirm the judgment of the Supreme Court of Louisiana.

ARREST—STOP AND FRISK

Henry v. *United States*
361 U.S. 98 (1959)

Mr. Justice Douglas delivered the opinion of the Court.

Petitioner stands convicted of unlawfully possessing three cartons of radios valued at more than $100 which had been stolen from an interstate shipment. See 18 U.S.C. § 659. The issue in the case is whether there was probable cause for the arrest leading to the search that produced the evidence on which the conviction rests. A timely motion to suppress the evidence was made by petitioner and overruled by the District Court; and the judgment of conviction was affirmed by the Court of Appeals on a divided vote. 259 F.2d 725. The case is here on a petition for a writ of certiorari, 359 U.S. 904.

There was a theft from an interstate shipment of whisky at a terminal in Chicago. The next day two FBI agents were in the neighborhood investigating it. They saw petitioner and one Pierotti walk across a street from a tavern and get into an automobile. The agents had been given, by the employer of Pierotti, information of an undisclosed nature "concerning the implication of the defendant Pierotti with interstate shipments." But, so far as the record shows, he never went so far as to tell the agents he suspected Pierotti of any such thefts. The agents followed the car and saw it enter an alley and stop. Petitioner got out of the car, entered a gangway leading to residential premises and returned in a few minutes with some cartons. He placed them in the car and he and Pierotti drove off. The agents were unable to follow the car. But later they found it parked at the same place near the tavern. Shortly they saw petitioner and Pierotti leave the tavern, get into the car, and drive off. The car stopped in the same alley as before; petitioner entered the same gangway and returned with more cartons. The agents observed this transaction from a distance of some 300 feet and could not determine the size, number or contents of the cartons. As the car drove off the agents followed it and finally, when they met it, waved it to a stop. As he got out of the car, petitioner was heard to say, "Hold it; it is the G's." This was followed by, "Tell him he [you] just picked me up." The agents searched the car, placed the cartons (which bore the name "Admiral" and were addressed to an out-of-state company) in their car, took the merchandise and petitioner and Pierotti to their office and held them for about two hours when the agents learned that the cartons contained stolen radios. They then placed the men under formal arrest.

The statutory authority of FBI officers and agents to make felony arrests without a warrant is restricted to offenses committed "in their presence" or to instances where they have "reasonable grounds to believe that the person to be arrested has committed or is committing" a felony. 18 U.S.C. § 3052. The statute states the constitutional standard, for it is the command of the Fourth Amendment that no warrants for either searches or arrests shall issue except "upon probable cause, supported by oath or affirmation, and particularly describing the place to be searched, and the persons or things to be seized."

The requirement of probable cause has roots that are deep in our history. The general warrant, in which the name of the person to be arrested was left blank, and the writs of assitance, against which James Otis inveighed, both perpetuated the oppressive practice of allowing the police to arrest and search on suspicion. Police control took the place of judicial control, since no showing of "probable cause" before a magistrate was required. The Virginia Declaration of Rights, adopted June 12, 1776, rebelled against that practice:

> "That general warrants, whereby any officer or messenger may be commanded to search suspected places without evidence of a fact committed, or to seize any person or persons not named, or whose offence is not particularly described and supported by evidence, are grievous and oppressive, and ought not to be granted."

The Maryland Declaration of Rights (1776), Art. XXIII, was equally emphatic:

> "That all warrants, without oath or affirmation, to search suspected places, or to seize any person or property, are griev-

ous and oppressive; and all general warrants—to search suspected places, or to apprehend suspected persons, without naming or describing the place, or the person in special—are illegal, and ought not to be granted."

And see North Carolina Declaration of Rights (1776), Art. XI; Pennsylvania Constitution (1776), Art. X; Massachusetts Constitution (1780), Pt. I, Art. XIV.

That philosophy later was reflected in the Fourth Amendment. And as the early American decisions both before and immediately after its adoption show, common rumor or report, suspicion, or even "strong reason to suspect" was not adequate to support a warrant for arrest. And that principle has survived to this day. See *United States* v. *Di Re*, 332 U.S. 581, 593–595; *Johnson* v. *United States*, 333 U.S. 10, 13–15; *Giordenello* v. *United States*, 357 U.S. 480, 486. Its high water was *Johnson* v. *United States, supra*, where the smell of opium coming from a closed room was not enough to support an arrest and search without a warrant. It was against this background that two scholars recently wrote, "Arrest on mere suspicion collides violently with the basic human right of liberty."

Evidence required to establish guilt is not necessary. *Brinegar* v. *United States*, 338 U.S. 160; *Draper* v. *United States*, 358 U.S. 307. On the other hand, good faith on the part of the arresting officers is not enough. Probable cause exists if the facts and circumstances known to the officer warrant a prudent man in believing that the offense has been committed. *Stacey* v. *Emery*, 97 U.S. 642, 645. And see *Director General* v. *Kastenbaum*, 263 U.S. 25, 28; *United States* v. *Di Re, supra*, at 592; *Giordenello* v. *United States, supra*, at 486. It is important, we think, that this requirement be strictly enforced, for the standard set by the Constitution protects both the officer and the citizen. If the officer acts with probable cause, he is protected even though it turns out that the citizen is innocent. *Carroll* v. *United States*, 267 U.S. 132, 156. And while a search without a warrant is, within limits, permissible if incident to a lawful arrest, if an arrest without a warrant is to support an incidental search, it must be made with probable cause. *Carroll* v. *United States, supra*, at 155–156. This immunity of officers cannot fairly be enlarged without jeopardizing the privacy or security of the citizen. We turn then to the question whether prudent men in the shoes of these officers (*Brinegar* v. *United States, supra*, at 175) would have seen enough to permit them to believe that petitioner was violating or had violated the law. We think not.

The prosecution conceded below, and adheres to the concession here, that the arrest took place when the federal agent stopped the car. That is our view on the facts of this particular case. When the officers interrupted the two men and restricted their liberty of movement, the arrest, for purposes of this case, was complete. It is, therefore, necessary to determine whether at or before that time they had reasonable cause to believe that a crime had been committed. The fact that afterwards contraband was discovered is not enough. An arrest is not justified by what the subsequent search discloses, as *Johnson* v. *United States, supra*, holds.

It is true that a federal crime had been committed at a terminal in the neighborhood, whisky having been stolen from an interstate shipment. Petitioner's friend, Pierotti, had been suspected of some implication in some interstate shipments, as we have said. But as this record stands, what those shipments were and the manner in which he was implicated remain unexplained and undefined. The rumor about him is therefore practically meaningless. On the record there was far from enough evidence against him to justify a magistrate in issuing a warrant. So far as the record shows, petitioner had not even been suspected of criminal activity prior to this time. Riding in the car, stopping in an alley, picking up packages, driving away—these were all acts that were outwardly innocent. Their movements in the car

had no mark of fleeing men or men acting furtively. The case might be different if the packages had been taken from a terminal or from an interstate trucking platform. But they were not. As we have said, the alley where the packages were picked up was in a residential section. The fact that packages have been stolen does not make every man who carries a package subject to arrest nor the package subject to seizure. The police must have reasonable grounds to believe that the particular package carried by the citizen is contraband. Its shape and design might at times be adequate. The weight of it and the manner in which it is carried might at times be enough. But there was nothing to indicate that the cartons here in issue probably contained liquor. The fact that they contained other contraband appeared only some hours after the arrest. What transpired at or after the time the car was stopped by the officers is, as we have said, irrelevant to the narrow issue before us. To repeat, an arrest is not justified by what the subsequent search discloses. Under our system suspicion is not enough for an officer to lay hands on a citizen. It is better, so the Fourth Amendment teaches, that the guilty sometimes go free than that citizens be subject to easy arrest.

The fact that the suspects were in an automobile is not enough. *Carroll* v. *United States, supra*, liberalized the rule governing searches when a moving vehicle is involved. But that decision merely relaxed the requirements for a warrant on grounds of practicality. It did not dispense with the need for probable cause.

Reversed.

Mr. Justice Black concurs in the result.

Mr. Justice Clark, whom The Chief Justice [Warren] joins, dissenting.

The Court decides this case on the narrow ground that the arrest took place at the moment the Federal Bureau of Investigation agents stopped the car in which petitioner was riding.

and at that time probable cause for it did not exist. While the Government, unnecessarily it seems to me, conceded that the arrest was made at the time the car was stopped, this Court is not bound by the Government's mistakes.

The record shows beyond dispute that the agents had received information from co-defendant Pierotti's employer implicating Pierotti with interstate shipments. The agents began a surveillance of petitioner and Pierotti after recognizing them as they came out of a bar. Later the agents observed them loading cartons into an automobile from a gangway up an alley in Chicago. The agents had been trailing them, and after it appeared that they had delivered the first load of cartons, the suspects returned to the same platform by a circuitous route through streets and alleys. The agents then saw petitioner load another set of cartons into the car and drive off with the same. A few minutes later the agents stopped the car, alighted from their own car, and approached the petitioner. As they did so, petitioner was overheard to say: "Hold it; it is the G's," and "Tell him he [you] just picked me up." Since the agents had actually seen the two suspects together for several hours, it was apparent to them that the statement was untrue. Upon being questioned, the defendants stated that they had borrowed the car from a friend. During the questioning and after petitioner had stepped out of the car one of the agents happened to look through the door of the car which petitioner had left open and saw three cartons stacked up inside which resembled those petitioner had just loaded into the car from the gangway. The agent saw that the cartons bore Admiral shipping labels and were addressed to a company in Cincinnati, Ohio. Upon further questioning, the agent was told that the cartons were in the car when the defendants borrowed it. Knowing this to be untrue, the agents then searched the car, arrested petitioner and his companion, and seized the cartons.

The Court seems to say that the mere stopping of the car amounted to an arrest of the petitioner. I cannot agree. The suspicious activities of the petitioner during the somewhat prolonged surveillance by the agents warranted the stopping of the car. The sighting of the cartons with their interstate labels in the car gave the agents reasonable ground to believe that a crime was in the course of its commission in their very presence. The search of the car and the subsequent arrest were therefore lawful and the motion to suppress was properly overruled.

In my view, the time at which the agents were required to have reasonable grounds to believe that petitioner was committing a felony was when they began the search of the automobile, which was after they had seen the cartons with interstate labels in the car. The earlier events certainly disclosed ample grounds to justify the following of the car, the subsequent stopping thereof, and the questioning of petitioner by the agents. This interrogation, together with the sighting of the cartons and the labels, gave the agents indisputable probable cause for the search and arrest.

When an investigation proceeds to the point where an agent has reasonable grounds to believe that an offense is being committed in his presence, he is obligated to proceed to make such searches, seizures, and arrests as the circumstances require. It is only by such alertness that crime is discovered, interrupted, prevented, and punished. We should not place additional burdens on law enforcement agencies.

I would affirm the judgments on the rationale of *Brinegar* v. *United States*, 338 U.S. 160 (1949), and *Carroll* v. *United States*, 267 U.S. 132 (1925).

Terry v. *Ohio*
392 U.S. 1 (1968)

Mr. Chief Justice Warren delivered the opinion of the Court . . . .

This case presents serious questions concerning the role of the Fourth Amendment in the confrontation on the street between the citizen and the policeman investigating suspicious circumstances.

Petitioner Terry was convicted of carrying a concealed weapon and sentenced to the statutorily prescribed term of one to three years in the penitentiary. Following the denial of a pretrial motion to suppress, the prosecution introduced in evidence two revolvers and a number of bullets seized from Terry and a codefendant, Richard Chilton, by Cleveland Police Detective Martin McFadden. At the hearing on the motion to suppress this evidence, Officer McFadden testified that while he was patrolling in plain clothes in downtown Cleveland at approximately 2:30 in the afternoon of October 31, 1963, his attention was attracted by two men, Chilton and Terry, standing on the corner of Huron Road and Euclid Avenue. He had never seen the two men before, and he was unable to say precisely what first drew his eye to them. However, he testified that he had been a policemen for 39 years and a detective for 35 and that he had been assigned to patrol this vicinity of downtown Cleveland for shoplifters and pickpockets for 30 years. He explained that he had developed routine habits of observation over the years and that he would "stand and watch people or walk and watch people at many intervals of the day." He added: "Now, in this case when I looked over they didn't look right to me at the time."

His interest aroused, Officer McFadden took up a post of observation in the entrance to a store 300 to 400 feet away from the two men. "I got more purpose to watch them when I seen their movements," he testified. He saw one of the men leave the other one and walk southwest on Huron Road, past some stores. The man paused for a moment and looked in a store window, then walked on a short distance, turned around and walked back toward the corner, pausing once again to look in the same store window. He rejoined his companion at the corner, and the two conferred briefly. Then the second man went through the same series of motions, strolling down Huron Road, looking in the same window, walking on a short distance, turning back, peering in the store window again, and returning to confer with the first man at the corner. The two men repeated this ritual alternately between five and six times apiece—in all, roughly a dozen trips. At one point, while the two were standing together on the corner, a third man approached them and engaged them briefly in conversation. This man then left the two others and walked west on Euclid Avenue. Chilton and Terry resumed their measured pacing, peering, and conferring. After this had gone on for 10 to 12 minutes, the two men walked off together, heading west on Euclid Avenue, following the path taken earlier by the third man.

By this time Officer McFadden had become thoroughly suspicious. He testified that after observing their elaborately casual and oft-repeated reconnaissance of the store window on Huron Road, he suspected the two men of "casing a job, a stick-up," and that he considered it his duty as a police officer to investigate further. He added that he feared "they may have a gun." Thus, Officer McFadden followed Chilton and Terry and saw them stop in front of Zucker's store to talk to the same man who had conferred with them earlier on the street corner. Deciding that the situation was ripe for direct action, Officer McFadden approached the three men, identified himself as a police officer and asked for their names. At this point his knowledge was confined to what he had observed. He was not acquainted with any of the three men by name or by sight, and he had received no information concerning them from any other source. When the man "mumbled something" in response to his inquiries, Officer McFadden grabbed petitioner Terry, spun him around so that they were facing the other two, with Terry between McFadden and the others, and patted down the outside of his clothing. In the left breast pocket of Terry's overcoat Officer McFadden felt a pistol. He reached inside the overcoat pocket, but was unable to remove the gun. At this point, keeping Terry between himself and the others, the officer ordered all three men to enter Zucker's store. As they went in, he removed Terry's overcoat completely, retrieved a .38 caliber revolver from the pocket and ordered all three men to face the wall with their hands raised. Officer McFadden proceeded to pat down the outer clothing of Chilton and the third man, Katz. He discovered another revolver in the outer pocket of Chilton's overcoat, but no weapons were found on Katz. The officer testified that he only patted the men down to see whether they had weapons, and that he did not put his hands beneath the outer garments of either Terry or Chilton until he felt their guns. So far as appears from the record, he never placed his hands beneath Katz's outer garments. Officer McFadden seized Chilton's gun, asked the proprietor of the store to call a police wagon, and took all three men to the station, where Chilton and Terry were formally charged with carrying concealed weapons.

On the motion to suppress the guns the prosecution took the position that they had been seized following a search incident to a lawful arrest. The trial court rejected this theory, stating that it "would be stretching the facts beyond reasonable comprehension" to find that Officer McFadden had had probable cause to arrest the men before he patted them down for weapons. However, the court denied the defendant's motion on the ground that Officer McFadden, on the basis of his experience, "had reasonable cause to believe . . . that the defendants were conducting themselves suspiciously, and some interrogation should be made of their action." Purely for his own protection, the court held, the officer had the right to pat down the outer clothing of these men, whom he had reasonable cause to believe might be armed. The court distinguished between an investigatory "stop" and an arrest, and between a "frisk" of the outer clothing for weapons and a full-blown search for evidence of crime. The frisk, it held, was essential to the proper per-

formance of the officer's investigatory duties, for without it "the answer to the police officer may be a bullet, and a loaded pistol discovered during the frisk is admissible."

After the court denied their motion to suppress, Chilton and Terry waived jury trial and pleaded not guilty. The court adjudged them guilty. . . . We granted certiorari to determine whether the admission of the revolvers in evidence violated petitioner's rights under the Fourth Amendment, made applicable to the States by the Fourteenth. *Mapp* v. *Ohio*, 367 U.S. 643 (1961). We affirm the conviction. . . .

II.

Our first task is to establish at what point in this encounter the Fourth Amendment becomes relevant. That is, we must decide whether and when Officer McFadden "seized" Terry and whether and when he conducted a "search." There is some suggestion in the use of such terms as "stop" and "frisk" that such police conduct is outside the purview of the Fourth Amendment because neither action rises to the level of a "search" or "seizure" within the meaning of the Constitution. We emphatically reject this notion. It is quite plain that the Fourth Amendment governs "seizures" of the person which do not eventuate in a trip to the station house and prosecution for crime— "arrests" in traditional terminology. It must be recognized that whenever a police officer accosts an individual and restrains his freedom to walk away, he has "seized" that person. And it is nothing less than sheer torture of the English language to suggest that a careful exploration of the outer surfaces of a person's clothing all over his or her body in an attempt to find weapons is not a "search." Moreover, it is simply fantastic to urge that such a procedure performed in public by a policeman while the citizen stands helpless, perhaps facing a wall with his hands raised, is a "petty indignity." It is a serious intrusion upon the sanctity of the person, which may inflict great indignity and arouse strong resentment, and it is not to be undertaken lightly.

The danger in the logic which proceeds upon distinctions between a "stop" and an "arrest," or "seizure" of the person and between a "frisk" and a "search" is twofold. It seeks to isolate from constitutional scrutiny the initial stages of the contact between the policeman and the citizen. And by suggesting a rigid all-or-nothing model of justification and regulation under the Amendment, it obscures the utility of limitations upon the scope, as well as the initiation, of police action as a means of constitutional regulation. This Court has held in the past that a search which is reasonable at its inception may violate the Fourth Amendment by virtue of its intolerable intensity and scope. . . . The scope of the search must be "strictly tied to and justified by" the circumstances which rendered its initiation permissible. *Warden* v. *Hayden*, 387 U.S. 294 (1967) (Mr. Justice Fortas, concurring). . . .

The distinctions of classical "stop-and-frisk" theory thus serve to divert attention from the central inquiry under the Fourth Amendment—the reasonableness in all the circumstances of the particular governmental invasion of a citizen's personal security. "Search" and "seizure" are not talismans. We therefore reject the notions that the Fourth Amendment does not come into play at all as a limitation upon police conduct if the officers stop short of something called "technical arrest" or a "full-blown search."

In this case there can be no question, then, that Officer McFadden "seized" petitioner and subjected him to a "search" when he took hold of him and patted down the outer surfaces of his clothing. We must decide whether at that point it was reasonable for Officer McFadden to have interfered with petitioner's personal security as he did. And in determining whether the seizure and search were "unreasonable" our inquiry is a dual one—whether the officer's action was justified at its inception, and whether it was reasonably related in scope to the circumstances which justified the interference in the first place.

III.

If this case involved police conduct subject to the Warrant Clause of the Fourth Amendment, we would have to ascertain whether "probable cause" existed to justify the search and seizure which took place. However, that is not the case. We do not retreat from our holdings that the police must, whenever practicable, obtain advance judicial approval of searches and seizures through the warrant procedure, see, e.g., *Katz* v. *United States*, 389 U.S. 347 (1967) . . . , or that in most instances failure to comply with the warrant requirement can only be excused by exigent circumstances, see, e.g., *Warden* v. *Hayden* (hot pursuit); cf. *Preston* v. *United States*, 376 U.S. 364 (1964). But we deal here with an entire rubric of police conduct—necessarily swift action predicated upon the on-the-spot observations of the officer on the beat—which historically has not been, and as a practical matter could not be, subjected to the warrant procedure. Instead, the conduct involved in this case must be tested by the Fourth Amendment's general proscription against unreasonable searches and seizures.

Nonetheless, the notions which underlie both the warrant procedure and the requirement of probable cause remain fully relevant in this context. In order to assess the reasonableness of Officer McFadden's conduct as a general proposition, it is necessary "first to focus upon the governmental interest which allegedly justifies official intrusion upon the constitutionally protected interests of the private citizen," for there is "no ready test for determining reasonableness other than by balancing the need to search [or seize] against the invasion which the search [or seizure] entails." *Camara* v. *Municipal Court*, 387 U.S. 523 (1967). And in justifying the particular intrusion the police officer must be able to point to specific and articulable facts which, taken together with rational inferences from those facts reasonably warrant that intrusion. . . .

Applying these principles to this case, we consider first the nature and extent of the governmental interests involved. One general interest is of course that of effective crime prevention and detection; it is this interest which underlies the recognition that a police officer may in appropriate circumstances and in an appropriate manner approach a person for purposes of investigating possibly criminal behavior even though there is no probable cause to make an arrest. It was this legitimate investigative function Officer McFadden was discharging when he decided to approach petitioner and his companions. He had observed Terry, Chilton, and Katz go through a series of acts, each of them perhaps innocent in itself, but which taken together warranted further investigation. . . .

The crux of this case, however, is not the propriety of Officer McFadden's taking steps to investigate petitioner's suspicious behavior, but rather, whether there was justification for McFadden's invasion of Terry's personal security by searching him for weapons in the course of that investigation. . . .

Petitioner does not argue that a police officer should refrain from making any investigation of suspicious circumstances until such time as he has probable cause to make an arrest; nor does he deny that police officers in properly discharging their investigative function may find themselves confronting persons who might well be armed and dangerous. Moreover, he does not say that an officer is always unjustified in searching a suspect to discover weapons. Rather, he says it is unreasonable for the policeman to take that step until such time as the situation evolves to a point where there is probable cause to make an arrest. When that point has been reached, petitioner would concede the officer's right to conduct a search of the sus-

pect for weapons, fruits or instrumentalities of the crime,' or "mere" evidence, incident to the arrest.

There are two weaknesses in this line of reasoning, however. First, it fails to take account of traditional limitations upon the scope of searches, and thus recognizes no distinction in purpose, character, and extent between a search incident to an arrest and a limited search for weapons. The former, although justified in part by the acknowledged necessity to protect the arresting officer from assault with a concealed weapon . . . , is also justified on other grounds and can therefore involve a relatively extensive exploration of the person. A search for weapons in the absence of probable cause to arrest, however, must, like any other search, be strictly circumscribed by the exigencies which justify its initiation. . . . Thus it must be limited to that which is necessary for the discovery of weapons which might be used to harm the officer or others nearby, and may realistically be characterized as something less than a "full" search, even though it remains a serious intrusion.

A second, and related, objection to petitioner's argument is that it assumes that the law of arrest has already worked out the balance between the particular interests involved here—the neutralization of danger to the policeman in the investigative circumstance and the sanctity of the individual. But this is not so. An arrest is a wholly different kind of intrusion upon individual freedom from a limited search for weapons, and the interests each is designed to serve are likewise quite different. An arrest is the initial stage of a criminal prosecution. It is intended to vindicate society's interest in having its laws obeyed, and it is inevitably accompanied by future interference with the individual's freedom of movement, whether or not trial or conviction ultimately follows. The protective search for weapons, on the other hand, constitutes a brief, though far from inconsiderable, intrusion upon the sanctity of the person. It does not follow that because an officer may lawfully arrest a person only when he is apprised of facts sufficient to warrant a belief that the person has committed or is committing a crime, the officer is equally unjustified, absent that kind of evidence, in making any intrusions short of an arrest. Moreover, a perfectly reasonable apprehension of danger may arise long before the officer is possessed of adequate information to justify taking a person into custody for the purpose of prosecuting him for a crime. Petitioner's reliance on cases which have worked out standards of reasonableness with regard to "seizures" constituting arrests and searches incident thereto is thus misplaced. It assumes that the interests sought to be vindicated and the invasions of personal security may be equated in the two cases, and thereby ignores a vital aspect of the analysis of the reasonableness of particular types of conduct under the Fourth Amendment. . . .

Our evaluation of the proper balance that has to be struck in this type of case leads us to conclude that there must be a narrowly drawn authority to permit a reasonable search for weapons for the protection of the police officer, where he has reason to believe that he is dealing with an armed and dangerous individual, regardless of whether he has probable cause to arrest the individual for a crime. The officer need not be absolutely certain that the individual is armed; the issue is whether he has probable cause to arrest the individual for a crime. The officer need not be absolutely certain that the individual is armed; the issue is whether a reasonably prudent man in the circumstances would be warranted in the belief that his safety or that of others was in danger. . . . And in determining whether the officer acted reasonably in such circumstances, due weight must be given, not to his inchoate and unparticularized suspicion or "hunch," but to the specific reasonable inferences which he is entitled to draw from the facts in light of his experience. . . .

IV.

We must now examine the conduct of Officer McFadden in this case to determine whether his search and seizure of petitioner were reasonable, both at their inception and as conducted. He had observed Terry, together with Chilton and another man, acting in a manner he took to be preface to a "stick-up." We think on the facts and circumstances Officer McFadden detailed before the trial judge a reasonably prudent man would have been warranted in believing petitioner was armed and thus presented a threat to the officer's safety while he was investigating his suspicious behavior. . . .

The scope of the search in this case presents no serious problem in light of these standards. Officer McFadden patted down the outer clothing of petitioner and his two companions. He did not place his hands in their pockets or under the outer surface of their garments until he had felt weapons, and then he merely reached for and removed the guns. He never did invade Katz's person beyond the outer surfaces of his clothes, since he discovered nothing in his pat down which might have been a weapon. Officer McFadden confined his search strictly to what was minimally necessary to learn whether the men were armed and to disarm them once he discovered the weapons. He did not conduct a general exploratory search for whatever evidence of criminal activity he might find.

V.

We conclude that the revolver seized from Terry was properly admitted in evidence against him. At the time he seized petitioner and searched him for weapons, Officer McFadden had reasonable grounds to believe that petitioner was armed and dangerous, and it was necessary for the protection of himself and others to take swift measures to discover the true facts and neutralize the threat of harm if it materialized. The policeman carefully restricted his search to what was appropriate to the discovery of the particular items which he sought. Each case of this sort will, of course, have to be decided on its own facts. We merely hold today that where a police officer observes unusual conduct which leads him reasonably to conclude in light of his experience that criminal activity may be afoot and that the persons with whom he is dealing may be armed and presently dangerous: where in the course of investigating this behavior he identifies himself as a policeman and makes reasonable inquiries; and where nothing in the initial stages of the encounter serves to dispel his reasonable fear for his own or others' safety, he is entitled for the protection of himself and others in the area to conduct a carefully limited search of the outer clothing of such persons in an attempt to discover weapons which might be used to assault him. Such a search is reasonable search under the Fourth Amendment, and any weapons seized may properly be introduced in evidence against the person from whom they were taken.

Mr. Justice Black concurs in the judgment and the opinions except where the opinion quotes from and relies upon this Court's opinion in *Katz* v. *United States* and the concurring opinion in *Warden* v. *Hayden.*

[Justices Harlan and White wrote concurring opinions.]

Mr. Justice Douglas, dissenting. . . .

I agree that petitioner was "seized" within the meaning of the Fourth Amendment. I also agree that frisking petitioner and his companions for guns was a "search." But it is a mystery how that "search" and that "seizure" can be constitutional by Fourth Amendment standards, unless there was "probable cause" to believe that (1) a crime had been committed or (2) a crime was in the process of being committed or (3) a crime was about to be committed.

The opinion of the Court disclaims the existence of "probable cause." If loitering were an issue and that was the offense charged, there would be "probable cause" shown. But the crime here is carrying concealed weapons; and there is no basis for concluding that the officer had "probable cause" for believing that crime was being committed. Had a warrant been sought, a magistrate would, therefore, have been unauthorized to issue one, for he can act only if there is a showing of "probable cause." We hold today that the police have greater authority to make a "seizure" and conduct a "search" than a judge has to authorize such action. We have said precisely the opposite over and over again. . . .

Note: Terry does not give the police a free "stopping" hand. *Brown* v. *Texas,* 99 S. Ct. 2637 (1979), permits them to "stop and frisk" only when circumstances justify a reasonable suspicion that the detainee is involved in criminal conduct. Stopping a man who was walking in an alley near another man in a neighborhood with a high incidence of drug traffice—without any "objective facts" to justify suspicion—was found unconstitutional.

Adams v. *Williams*
407 U.S. 143 (1972)

Williams was convicted in a Connecticut court of illegal possession of a handgun found during a "stop and frisk," and also of possession of heroin found during a full search incident to the handgun arrest. The conviction was reversed by a United States court of appeals via writ of habeas corpus.

Mr. Justice Rehnquist delivered the opinion of the Court.

Police Sgt. John Connolly was alone early in the morning on car patrol duty in a high-crime area of Bridgeport, Connecticut. At approximately 2:15 a. m. a person known to Sgt. Connolly approached his cruiser and informed him that an individual seated in a nearby vehicle was carrying narcotics and had a gun at his waist.

After calling for assistance on his car radio, Sgt. Connolly approached the vehicle to investigate the informant's report. Connolly tapped on the car window and asked the occupant, Robert Williams, to open the door. When Williams rolled down the window instead, the sergeant reached into the car and removed a fully loaded revolver from Williams' waistband. The gun had not been visible to Connolly from outside the car, but it was in precisely the place indicated by the informant. Williams was then arrested by Connolly for unlawful possession of the pistol. A search incident to that arrest was conducted after other officers arrived. They found substantial quantities of heroin on Williams' person and in the car, and they found a machete and a second revolver hidden in the automobile.

Respondent contends that the initial seizure of his pistol, upon which rested the later search and seizure of other weapons and narcotics, was not justified by the informant's tip to Sgt. Connolly. He claims that absent a more reliable informant, or some corroboration of the tip, the policeman's actions were unreasonable under the standards set forth in *Terry* v. *Ohio, supra.*

In *Terry* this Court recognized that "a police officer may in appropriate circumstances and in an appropriate manner approach a person for purposes of investigating possible criminal behavior even though there is no probable cause to make an arrest." *Id.,* at 22. The Fourth Amendment does not require a policeman who lacks the precise level of information necessary for probable cause to arrest to simply shrug his shoulders and allow a crime to occur or a criminal to escape. On the contrary, *Terry* recognizes that it may be the essence of good police work to adopt an intermediate response. See *id.,* at 23. A brief stop of a suspicious individual, in order to determine his identity or to maintain the status quo momentarily while obtaining more information, may be most reasonable in light of the facts known to the officer at the time. *Id.,* at 21–22; see *Gaines* v. *Craven,* 448 F.2d 1236 (CA9 1971); *United States* v. *Unverzagt,* 424 F.2d 396 (CA8 1970).

The Court recognized in *Terry* that the policeman making a reasonable investigatory stop should not be denied the opportunity to protect himself from attack by a hostile suspect. "When an officer is justified in believing that the individual whose suspicious behavior he is investigating at close range is armed and presently dangerous to the officer or to others," he may conduct a limited protective search for concealed weapons. 392 U.S., at 24. The purpose of this limited search is not to discover evidence of crime, but to allow the officer to pursue his investigation without fear of violence, and thus the frisk for weapons might be equally necessary and reasonable, whether or not carrying a concealed weapon violated any applicable state law. So long as the officer is entitled to make a forcible stop, and has reason to believe that the suspect is armed and dangerous, he may conduct a weapons search limited in scope to this protective purpose. *Id.,* at 30.

Applying these principles to the present case, we believe that Sgt. Connolly acted justifiably in responding to his informant's tip. The informant was known to him personally and had provided him with information in the past. This is a stronger case than obtains in the case of an anonymous telephone tip. The informant was known to him personally and had provided him with information in the past. This is a stronger case than obtains in the case of an anonymous telephone tip. The informant here came forward personally to give information that was immediately verifiable at the scene. Indeed, under

Connecticut law, the informant might have been subject to immediate arrest for making a false complaint had Sgt. Connolly's investigation proved the tip incorrect. Thus, while the Court's decisions indicate that this informant's unverified tip may have been insufficient for a narcotics arrest or search warrant, . . . the information carried enough indicia of reliability to justify the officer's forcible stop of Williams.

In reaching this conclusion, we reject respondent's argument that reasonable cause for a stop and frisk can only be based on the officer's personal observation, rather than on information supplied by another person. Informants' tips, like all other clues and evidence coming to a policeman on the scene, may vary greatly in their value and reliability. One simple rule will not cover every situation. Some tips, completely lacking in indicia of reliability, would either warrant no police response or require further investigation before a forcible stop of a suspect would be authorized. But in some situations— for example, when the victim of a street crime seeks immediate police aid and gives a description of his assailant, or when a credible informant warns of a specific impending crime—the subtleties of the hearsay rule should not thwart an appropriate police response.

While properly investigating the activity of a person who was reported to be carrying narcotics and a concealed weapon and who was sitting alone in a car in a high-crime area at 2:15 in the morning, Sgt. Connolly had ample reason to fear for his safety. When Williams rolled down his window, rather than complying with the policeman's request to step out of the car so that his movements could more easily be seen, the revolver allegedly at Williams' waist became an even greater threat. Under these circumstances the policeman's action in reaching to the spot where the gun was thought to be hidden constituted a limited intrusion designed to insure his safety, and we conclude that it was reasonable. The loaded gun seized as a result of this intrusion was therefore admissible at Williams' trial. . . .

Once Sgt. Connolly had found the gun precisely where the informant had predicted, probable cause existed to arrest Williams for unlawful possession of the weapon. Probable cause to arrest depends "upon whether, at the moment the arrest was made . . . the facts and circumstances within [the arresting officers'] knowledge and of which they had reasonably trustworthy information were sufficient to warrant a prudent man in believing that the [suspect] had committed or was committing an offense." *Beck* v. *Ohio*, 379 U.S. 89, 91 (1964). In the present case the policeman found Williams in possession of a gun in precisely the place predicted by the informant. This tended to corroborate the reliability of the informant's further report of narcotics and, together with the surrounding circumstances, certainly suggested no lawful explanation for possession of the gun. Probable cause does not require the same type of specific evidence of each element of the offense as would be needed to support a conviction. . . . Rather, the court will evaluate generally the circumstances at the time of the arrest to decide if the officer had probable cause for his action:

> "In dealing with probable cause, however, as the very name implies, we deal with probabilities. These are not technical; they are the factual and practical considerations of everyday life on which reasonable and prudent men, not legal technicians, act." *Brinegar* v. *United States*, 338 U.S. 160, 175 (1949).

See also *id.*, at 177. Under the circumstances surrounding Williams' possession of the gun seized by Sgt. Connolly, the arrest on the weapons charge was supported by probable cause, and the search of his person and of the car incident to that arrest was lawful. . . . The fruits of the search were therefore properly admitted at Williams' trial, and the Court of Appeals erred in reaching a contrary conclusion.

Mr. Justice Douglas, with whom Mr. Justice Marshall concurs, dissenting. . . .

The police problem is an acute one not because of the Fourth Amendment, but because of the ease with which anyone can acquire a pistol. A powerful lobby dins into the ears of our citizenry that these gun purchases are constitutional rights protected by the Second Amendment which reads, ''A well regulated Militia, being necessary to the security of a free State, the right of the people to keep and bear Arms, shall not be infringed.''

There is under our decisions no reason why stiff state laws governing the purchase and possession of pistols may not be enacted. There is no reason why pistols may not be barred from anyone with a police record. There is no reason why a State may not require a purchaser of a pistol to pass a psychiatric test. There is no reason why all pistols should not be barred to everyone except the police.

The leading case is *United States* v. *Miller*, 307 U.S. 174, upholding a federal law making criminal the shipment in interstate commerce of a sawed-off shotgun. The law was upheld, there being no evidence that a sawed-off shotgun had ''some reasonable relationship to the preservation or efficiency of a well regulated militia.'' *Id.*, at 178. The Second Amendment, it was held, ''must be interpreted and applied'' with the view of maintaining a ''militia.''

> ''The Militia which the States were expected to maintain and train is set in contrast with Troops which they were forbidden to keep without the consent of Congress. The sentiment of the time strongly disfavored standing armies; the common view was that adequate defense of country and laws could be secured through the Militia—civilians primarily, soldiers on occasion.'' *Id.*, at 178–179.

Critics say that proposals like this water down the Second Amendment. Our decisions belie that argument, for the Second Amendment, as noted, was designed to keep alive the militia. But if watering-down is the mood of the day, I would prefer to water down the Second rather than the Fourth Amendment. I share with Judge Friendly a concern that the easy extension of *Terry* v. *Ohio*, 392 U.S. 1, to ''possessory offenses'' is a serious intrusion on Fourth Amendment safeguards. . . .

Mr. Justice Brennan, dissenting.

The crucial question on which this case turns, as the Court concedes, is whether, there being no contention that Williams acted voluntarily in rolling down the window of his car, the State had shown sufficient cause to justify Sgt. Connolly's ''forcible'' stop. I would affirm, believing, for the following reasons stated by Judge, now Chief Judge, Friendly, dissenting, 436 F.2d, at 38–39, that the State did not make that showing:

> ''To begin, I have the gravest hesitancy in extending [*Terry* v. *Ohio*, 392 U.S. 1 (1968)] to crimes like the possession of narcotics. . . . There is too much danger that, instead of the stop being the object and the protective frisk and incident thereto, the reverse will be true. Against that we have here the added fact of the report that Williams had a gun on his person. . . . [But] Connecticut allows its citizens to carry weapons, concealed or otherwise, at will, provided only they have a permit, Conn.Gen.Stat. §§ 29–35 and 29–38, and gives its police officers no special authority to stop for the purpose of determining whether the citizen has one. . . .
>
> ''If I am wrong in thinking that *Terry* should not be applied at all to mere possessory offenses, . . . I would not find the combination of Officer Connolly's almost meaningless observation and the tip in this case to be sufficient justification for the intrusion. The tip suffered from a threefold defect, with each fold compounding the

others. The informer was unnamed, he was not shown to have been reliable with respect to guns or narcotics, and he gave no information which demonstrated personal knowledge or—what is worse—could not readily have been manufactured by the officer after the event. To my mind, it has not been sufficiently recognized that the difference between this sort of tip and the accurate prediction of an unusual event is as important on the latter score as on the former. [In *Draper* v. *United States*, 358 U.S. 307 (1959),] Narcotics Agent Marsh would hardly have been at the Denver Station at the exact moment of the arrival of the train Draper had taken from Chicago unless *someone* had told him *something* important, although the agent might later have embroidered the details to fit the observed facts. . . . There is no such guarantee of a patrolling officer's veracity when he testifies to a "tip" from an unnamed informer saying no more than that the officer will find a gun and narcotics on a man across the street, as he later does. If the state wishes to rely on a tip of that nature to validate a stop and frisk, revelation of the name of the informer or demonstration that his name is unknown and could not reasonably have been ascertained should be the price.

"*Terry* v. *Ohio* was intended to free a police officer from the rigidity of a rule that would prevent his doing anything to a man reasonably suspected of being about to commit or having just committed a crime of violence, no matter how grave the problem or impelling the need for swift action, unless the officer had what a court would later determine to be probable cause for arrest. It was meant for the serious cases of imminent danger or of harm recently perpetrated to persons or property, not the conventional ones of possessory offenses. If it is to be extended to the latter at all, this should be only where observation by the officer himself or well authenticated information shows "that criminal activity may be afoot." 392 U.S., at 30. . . . I greatly fear that if the [contrary view] should be followed, *Terry* will have opened the sluicegates for serious and unintended erosion of the protection of the Fourth Amendment."

[The separate dissent of Mr. Justice Marshall is omitted.]

Note: Pennsylvania v. *Mimms,* 98 S. Ct. 330 (1977), held that a "stop and frisk" search of the driver of a car that had been stopped for a routine traffic offense was not unconstitutional. But *Delaware* v. *Prouse,* 99 S. Ct. 1391 (1979), held that stopping a car and detaining the driver merely to check the driver's license and registration, when there is no basis for believing that there has been a law violation, is forbidden by the Fourth and Fourteenth Amendments as an unreasonable seizure.

RIGHT TO COUNSEL

Powell v. *Alabama* (excerpt)
287 U.S. 45 (1932)

Under English law at the time of the Declaration of Independence persons charged with felony were not permitted to be represented by counsel except in treason cases. Apparently to correct this, that is, to permit the hiring of counsel by defendants, the Founding Fathers gave us the Sixth Amendment. See W. M. Beaney, *The Right to Counsel in American Courts*, 24–33 (1955); D. Fellman, *The Defendant's Rights Today*, 208–210 (1976). In this, the famous *Scottsboro* case, the Court found for the first time that in some circumstances *appointment* of counsel is required by the Due Process Clause of the Fourteenth Amendment.

Mr. Justice Sutherland delivered the opinion of the Court. . . .

In the light of the facts outlined in the forepart of this opinion—the ignorance and illiteracy of the defendants, their youth, the circumstances of public hostility, the imprisonment and the close surveillance of the defendants by the military forces, the fact that their friends and families were all in other states and communication with them necessarily difficult, and above all that they stood in deadly peril of their lives—we think the failure of the trial court to give them reasonable time and opportunity to secure counsel was a clear denial of due process.

But passing that, and assuming their inability, even if opportunity had been given, to employ counsel, as the trial court evidently did assume, we are of opinion that, under the circumstances just stated, the necessity of counsel was so vital and imperative that the failure of the trial court to make an effective appointment of counsel was likewise a denial of due process within the meaning of the Fourteenth Amendment. Whether this would be so in other criminal prosecutions, or under other circumstances, we need not determine. All that it is necessary now to decide, as we do decide, is that in a capital case, where the defendant is unable to employ counsel, and is incapable adequately of making his own defense because of ignorance, feeblemindedness, illiteracy, or the like, it is the duty of the court, whether requested or not, to assign counsel for him as a necessary requisite of due process of law; and that duty is not discharged by an assignment at such a time or under such circumstances as to preclude the giving of effective aid in the preparation and trial of the case. . . .

Gideon v. *Wainwright*
372 U.S. 335 (1963)

Mr. Justice Black delivered the opinion of the Court.

Petitioner was charged in a Florida state court with having broken and entered a poolroom with intent to commit a misdemeanor. This offense is a felony under Florida law. Appearing in court without funds and without a lawyer, petitioner asked the court to appoint counsel for him, whereupon the following colloquy took place:

The Court: Mr. Gideon, I am sorry, but I cannot appoint Counsel to represent you in this case. Under the laws of the State of Florida, the only time the Court can appoint Counsel to represent a Defendant is when that person is charged with a capital offense. I am sorry, but I will have to deny your request to appoint Counsel to defend you in this case.

The Defendant: The United States Supreme Court says I am entitled to be represented by Counsel.

Put to trial before a jury, Gideon conducted his defense about as well as could be expected from a layman. He made an opening statement to the jury, cross-examined the State's witnesses, presented witnesses in his own defense, declined to testify himself, and made a short argument "emphasizing his innocence to the charge contained in the Information filed in this case." The jury returned a verdict of guilty, and petitioner was sentenced to serve five years in the state prison. Later, petitioner filed in the Florida Supreme Court this habeas corpus petition attacking his conviction and sentence on the ground that the trial court's refusal to appoint counsel for him denied him rights "guaranteed by the Constitution and the Bill of Rights by the United States Government." Treating the petition for habeas corpus as properly before it, the State Supreme Court, "upon consideration thereof" but without an opinion, denied all relief. Since 1942, when *Betts* v. *Brady*, 316 U.S. 455, was decided by a divided Court, the problem of a defendant's federal constitutional right to counsel in a state court has been a continuing source of controversy and litigation in both state and federal courts. To give this problem another review here, we granted certiorari. 370 U.S. 908. Since Gideon was proceeding *in forma pauperis*, we appointed counsel to represent him and requested both sides to discuss in their briefs and oral arguments the following: "Should this Court's holding in *Betts* v. *Brady*, 316 U.S. 455, be reconsidered?"

I.

The facts upon which Betts claimed that he had been unconstitutionally denied the right to have counsel appointed to assist him are strikingly like the facts upon which Gideon here bases his federal constitutional claim. Betts was indicted for robbery in a Maryland state court. On arraignment, he told the trial judge of his lack of funds to hire a lawyer and asked the court to appoint one for him. Betts was advised that it was not the practice in that county to appoint counsel for indigent defendants except in murder and rape cases. He then pleaded not guilty, had witnesses summoned, cross-examined the State's witnesses, examined his own, and chose not to testify himself. He was found guilty by the judge, sitting without a jury, and sentenced to eight years in prison. Like Gideon, Betts sought release by habeas corpus, alleging that he had been denied the right to assistance of counsel in violation of the Fourteenth Amendment. Betts was denied any relief, and on review this Court affirmed. It was

held that a refusal to appoint counsel for an indigent defendant charged with a felony did not necessarily violate the Due Process Clause of the Fourteenth Amendment, which for reasons given the Court deemed to be the only applicable federal constitutional provision. The Court said:

"Asserted denial [of due process] is to be tested by an appraisal of the totality of facts in a given case. That which may, in one setting, constitute a denial of fundamental fairness, shocking to the universal sense of justice, may, in other circumstances, and in the light of other considerations, fall short of such denial." 316 U.S., at 462.

Treating due process as "a concept less rigid and more fluid than those envisaged in other specific and particular provisions of the Bill of Rights," the Court held that refusal to appoint counsel under the particular facts and circumstances in the *Betts* case was not so "offensive to the common and fundamental ideas of fairness" as to amount to a denial of due process. Since the facts and circumstances of the two cases are so nearly indistinguishable, we think the *Betts* v. *Brady* holding if left standing would require us to reject Gideon's claim that the Constitution guarantees him the assistance of counsel. Upon full reconsideration we conclude that *Betts* v. *Brady* should be overruled.

II.

The Sixth Amendment provides, "In all criminal prosecutions, the accused shall enjoy the right . . . . to have the Assistance of Counsel for his defence." We have construed this to mean that in federal courts counsel must be provided for defendants unable to employ counsel unless the right is competently and intelligently waived. *Betts* argued that this right is extended to indigent defendants in state courts by the Fourteenth Amendment. In response the Court stated that, while the Sixth Amendment laid down "no rule for the conduct of the states, the question recurs whether the constraint laid by the amendment upon the national courts expresses a rule so fundamental and essential to a fair trial, and so, to due process of law, that it is made obligatory upon the states by the Fourteenth Amendment." 316 U.S., at 465. In order to decide whether the Sixth Amendment's guarantee of counsel is of this fundamental nature, the Court in *Betts* set out and considered "[r]elevant data on the subject . . . afforded by constitutional and statutory provisions subsisting in the colonies and the states prior to the inclusion of the Bill of Rights in the national Constitution, and in the constitutional, legislative, and judicial history of the states to the present date." 316 U.S., at 465. On the basis of this historical data the Court concluded that "appointment of counsel is not a fundamental right, essential to a fair trial." . . .

We accept *Betts* v. *Brady's* assumption, based as it was on our prior cases, that a provision of the Bill of Rights which is "fundamental and essential to a fair trial" is made obligatory upon the States by the Fourteenth Amendment. We think the Court in *Betts* was wrong, however, in concluding that the Sixth Amendment's guarantee of counsel is not one of these fundamental rights. Ten years before *Betts* v. *Brady*, this Court, after full consideration of all the historical data examined in *Betts*, had unequivocally declared that "the right to the aid of counsel is of this fundamental character." *Powell* v. *Alabama*, 287 U.S. 45, 68 (1932). While the Court at the close of its *Powell* opinion did by its language, as this Court frequently does, limit its holding to the particular facts and circumstances of that case, its conclusions about the fundamental nature of the right to counsel are unmistakable. . . . The fact is that in deciding as it did—that "appointment of counsel is not a fundamental right, essential to a fair trial"—the Court in *Betts* v. *Brady* made an abrupt break with its own well-considered precedents. In returning to these old precedents, sounder we

believe than the new, we but restore constitutional principles established to achieve a fair system of justice. Not only these precedents but also reason and reflection require us to recognize that in our adversary system of criminal justice, any person haled into court, who is too poor to hire a lawyer, cannot be assured a fair trial unless counsel is provided for him. This seems to us to be an obvious truth. Governments, both state and federal, quite properly spend vast sums of money to establish machinery to try defendants accused of crime. Lawyers to prosecute are everywhere deemed essential to protect the public's interest in an orderly society. Similarly, there are few defendants charged with crime, few indeed, who fail to hire the best lawyers they can get to prepare and present their defenses. That government hires lawyers to prosecute and defendants who have the money hire lawyers to defend are the strongest indications of the wide-spread belief that lawyers in criminal courts are necessities, not luxuries. The right of one charged with crime to counsel may not be deemed fundamental and essential to fair trials in some countries, but it is in ours. From the very beginning, our state and national constitutions and laws have laid great emphasis on procedural and substantive safeguards designed to assure fair trials before impartial tribunals in which every defendant stands equal before the law. This noble ideal cannot be realized if the poor man charged with crime has to face his accusers without a lawyer to assist him. . . . The Court in *Betts* v. *Brady* departed from the sound wisdom upon which the Court's holding in *Powell* v. *Alabama* rested. Florida, supported by two other States, has asked that *Betts* v. *Brady* be left intact. Twenty-two States, as friends of the Court, argue that *Betts* was "an anachronism when handed down" and that it should now be overruled. We agree.

The judgment is reversed and the cause is remanded to the Supreme Court of Florida for further action not inconsistent with this opinion.

[Justices Douglas and Clark wrote concurring opinions.]

Mr. Justice Harlan, concurring.

I agree that *Betts* v. *Brady* should be overruled, but consider it entitled to a more respectful burial than has been accorded, at least on the part of those of us who were not on the Court when that case was decided.

I cannot subscribe to the view that *Betts* v. *Brady* represented "an abrupt break with its own well-considered precedents." . . . In 1932, in *Powell* v. *Alabama*, 287 U.S. 45, a capital case, this Court declared that under the particular facts there presented—"the ignorance and illiteracy of the defendants, their youth, the circumstances of public hostility . . . and above all that they stood in deadly peril of their lives" (287 U.S., at 71)—the state court had a duty to assign counsel for the trial as a necessary requisite of due process of law. It is evident that these limiting facts were not added to the opinion as an afterthought; they were repeatedly emphasized, see 287 U.S., at 52, 57–58, 71, and were clearly regarded as important to the result.

Thus when this Court, a decade later, decided *Betts* v. *Brady*, it did no more than to admit of the possible existence of special circumstances in noncapital as well as capital trials, while at the same time insisting that such circumstances be shown in order to establish a denial of due process. The right to appointed counsel had been recognized as being considerably broader in federal prosecutions, see *Johnson* v. *Zerbst*, 304 U.S. 458, but to have imposed these requirements on the States would indeed have been "an abrupt break" with the almost immediate past. The declaration that the right to appointed counsel in state prosecutions, as established in *Powell* v. *Alabama*, was not limited to capital cases was in truth not a departure from, but an extension of, existing precedent.

The principles declared in *Powell* and in *Betts*, however, have had a troubled journey throughout the years that have followed first the one case and then the other. Even by the time of the *Betts* decision, dictum in at least one of the Court's opinions had indicated that there was an absolute right to the services of counsel in the trial of state capital cases. Such dicta continued to appear in subsequent decisions, and any lingering doubts were finally eliminated by the holding of *Hamilton* v. *Alabama*, 368 U.S. 52.

In noncapital cases, the "special circumstances" rule has continued to exist in form while its substance has been substantially and steadily eroded. In the first decade after *Betts*, there were cases in which the Court found special circumstances to be lacking, but usually by a sharply divided vote. However, no such decision has been cited to us, and I have found none, after *Quicksall* v. *Michigan*, 339 U.S. 660, decided in 1950. At the same time, there have been not a few cases in which special circumstances were found in little or nothing more than the "complexity" of the legal questions presented, although those questions were often of only routine difficulty. The Court has come to recognize, in other words, that the mere existence of a serious criminal charge constituted in itself special circumstances requiring the services of counsel at trial. In truth the *Betts* v. *Brady* rule is no longer a reality.

This evolution, however, appears not to have been fully recognized by many state courts, in this instance charged with the frontline responsibility for the enforcement of constitutional rights. To continue a rule which is honored by this Court only with lip service is not a healthy thing and in the long run will do disservice to the federal system.

The special circumstances rule has been formally abandoned in capital cases, and the time has now come when it should be similarly abandoned in noncapital cases, at least as to offenses which, as the one involved here, carry the possibility of a substantial prison sentence. (Whether the rule should extend to *all* criminal cases need not now be decided.) This indeed does no more than to make explicit something that has long since been foreshadowed in our decisions.

Note: The *Gideon* doctrine was extended in *Argersinger* v. *Hamlin*, 407 U.S. 25 (1972), to non-felony cases involving imprisonment. But *Scott* v. *Illinois*, 99 S. Ct. 1158 (1979), held that, if in fact only a fine has been imposed (though imprisonment was a possibility), a conviction will not be reversed for want of counsel.

A *pretrial* right to assistance of counsel has been recognized with respect to police in-custody interrogation (see *Miranda* v. *Arizona*, below), and police lineups (*United States* v. *Wade*, 388 U.S. 218 [1967], and *Gilbert* v. *California*, 388 U.S. 263 [1967]); but the *Wade-Gilbert* right was confined in *Kirby* v. *Illinois*, 406 U.S. 682 (1972), to postindictment and preliminary hearing lineups—unless "unnecessarily suggestive and conducive to irreparable mistaken identification."

Ross v. *Moffit*
417 U.S. 600 (1974)

Douglas v. *California*, 372 U.S. 353 (1963), recognized an indigent's right to appointed counsel for review of a felony conviction on a first appeal available as a matter of right. *Griffin* v. *Illinois*, 351 U.S. 12 (1956), ruled a state must provide indigents with copies of trial transcripts necessary for a first appeal as a matter of right. In the present case, the Court refused to extend these decisions.

Mr. Justice Rehnquist delivered the opinion of the Court. . . .

. . . [T]here are significant differences between the trial and appellate stages of a criminal proceeding. [A] defendant needs an attorney on appeal not as a shield to protect him against being 'haled into court' by the State and stripped of his presumption of innocence, but rather as a sword to upset the prior determination of guilt. This difference is significant for, while no one would agree that the State may simply dispense with the trial stage of proceedings without a criminal defendant's consent, it is clear that the State need not provide any appeal at all. The fact that an appeal *has* been provided does not automatically mean that a State then acts unfairly by refusing to provide counsel to indigent defendants at every stage of the way. Unfairness results only if indigents are singled out by the State and denied meaningful access to that system because of their poverty. That question is more profitably considered under an equal protection analysis.

[Fourteenth Amendment "equality"] "does not require absolute equality or precisely equal advantages," *San Antonio Independent School District* v. *Rodriquez* [411 U.S. 1 (1973)] nor does it require the State to "equalize economic conditions." *Griffin* (Frankfurter, J., concurring). It does require that the state appellate system be "free of unreasoned distinctions" and that indigents have an adequate opportunity to present their claims fairly within the adversarial system. The State cannot adopt procedures which leave an indigent defendant "entirely cut off from any appeal at all," by virtue of his indigency or extend to such indigent defendants merely a "meaningless ritual" while others in better economic circumstances have a "meaningful appeal." *Douglas*.

. . . [P]rior to his seeking discretionary review in the State Supreme Court, [respondent's] claims "had once been presented by a lawyer and passed upon by an [intermediate] appellate court." *Douglas*. We do not believe that it can be said, therefore, that [such a defendant] is denied meaningful access to the North Carolina Supreme Court simply because the State does not appoint counsel to aid him in seeking review in that court. At that stage he will have, at the very least, [a record] of trial proceedings, a brief on his behalf in the Court of Appeals setting forth his claims of error, and in many cases an opinion by the Court of Appeals disposing of his case. These materials, supplemented by whatever submission respondent may make pro se, would appear to provide the Supreme Court of North Carolina with an adequate basis on which to base its decision to grant or deny review.

We are fortified in this conclusion by our understanding of the function served by discretionary review in the North Carolina Supreme Court. The critical issue in that court [is] whether "the subject matter of the appeal has significant public interest," whether "the cause involves legal principles of major significance to the jurisprudence of the state," or whether the decision below is in probable conflict with a decision of the Supreme Court. The Supreme Court may deny certiorari even though it believes that the decision [below] was incorrect, since a decision which appears incorrect may nevertheless fail to satisfy any of the criteria discussed above. Once a defendant's claims of error are organized and presented in a lawyer-like fashion to the Court of Appeals, the [North Carolina Supreme Court] should be able to ascertain whether his case satisfies the standards established by the legislature for [discretionary] review.

This is not to say, of course, that a skilled lawyer, particularly one trained in the somewhat arcane art of preparing petitions for discretionary review, would not prove helpful to any litigant able to employ him. An indigent defendant seeking review in the Supreme Court of North Carolina is therefore somewhat handicapped in comparison with a wealthy defendant who has counsel assiting him in every conceivable manner at every stage in the proceeding. But both the opportunity to have counsel prepare an initial brief in the Court of Appeals and the nature of discretionary review in the Supreme Court of North Carolina make this rel-

ative handicap far less than the handicap borne by the indigent defendant denied counsel on his initial appeal as of right in *Douglas*. And the fact that a particular service might be of benefit to an indigent defendant does not mean that the service is constitutionally required. The duty of the State under our cases is not to duplicate the legal arsenal that may be privately retained by a criminal defendant in a continuing effort to reverse his conviction, but only to assure the indigent defendant an adequate opportunity to present his claims fairly in the context of the State's appellate process. We think respondent was given that opportunity under the existing North Carolina system.

Much of the discussion in the preceding section is equally relevant to the question of whether a State must provide counsel for a defendant seeking review of his conviction in this Court. . . . There is also a significant difference between the source of the right to seek discretionary review in the Supreme Court of North Carolina and the source of the right to seek discretionary review in this Court. The former is conferred by the statutes of the State of North Carolina, but the latter is granted by statutes enacted by Congress. Thus the argument relied upon in the *Griffin* and *Douglas* cases, that the State having once created a right of appeal must give all persons an equal opportunity to enjoy the right, is by its terms inapplicable. The right to seek certiorari in this Court is not granted by any State, and exists by virtue of federal statute with or without the consent of the State whose judgment is sought to be reviewed.

The suggestion that a State is responsible for providing counsel to one petitioning this Court simply because it initiated the prosecution which led to the judgment sought to be reviewed is unsupported by either reason or authority. It would be quite as logical under the rationale of *Douglas* and *Griffin*, and indeed perhaps more so, to require that the Federal Government or this Court furnish and compensate counsel for petitioners who seek certiorari here to review state judgments of conviction. Yet this Court has followed a consistent policy of denying applications for appointment of counsel by persons seeking to file jurisdictional statements or petitions for certiorari in this Court. In the light of these authorities, it would be odd, indeed, to read the Fourteenth Amendment to impose such a requirement on the States, and we decline to do so.

Mr. Justice Douglas, with whom Mr. Justice Brennan and Mr. Justice Marshall concur, dissenting. . . .

. . . [Douglas] did not deal with the appointment of counsel [beyond the first appeal as of right], but we noted [there] that "there can be no equal justice where the kind of appeal a man enjoys "depends on the amount of money he has.'" . . . More familiar with the functioning of the North Carolina criminal justice system than are we, [Chief Judge Haynsworth concluded for a unanimous panel in the U.S. Court of Appeals] that "in the context of constitutional questions arising in criminal prosecutions, permissive review in the state's highest court may be predictably the most meaningful review the conviction will receive." The North Carolina Court of Appeals, for example, will be constrained in diverging from an earlier opinion of the State Supreme Court, even if subsequent developments have rendered the earlier Supreme Court decision suspect. "[T]he state's highest court remains the ultimate arbiter of the rights of its citizens." Judge Haynsworth also correctly observed that the indigent defendant, proceeding without counsel, is at a substantial disadvantage relative to wealthy defendants represented by counsel when he is forced to fend for himself in seeking discretionary review . . . . It may well not be enough to allege error in the courts below in layman's terms; a more sophisticated approach may be demanded. . . .

Douglas was grounded on concepts of fairness and equality. The right to discretionary review is a substantial one, and one where a lawyer can be of significant assistance to an indigent defendant. It was correctly perceived below that the "same concepts of fairness and equality, which require counsel in a first appeal of right, require counsel in other and subsequent discretionary appeals."

> *Note:* The Supreme Court has never reversed a conviction on the basis of counsel's incompetence. In *McMann* v. *Richardson*, 397 U.S. 759 (1970), it said (with respect to a lawyer's advice on pleading guilty) that "defendants cannot be left to the mercies of incompetent counsel [but] the matter, for the most part, should be left to the good sense and discretion of the trial courts." It concluded that a guilty plea will not be set aside unless defendant can "demonstrate gross error on the part of counsel."

TRIAL BY JURY (DISINCORPORATION?)

Duncan v. *Louisiana*
See p. 253, above.

> *Note:* What is a jury as that term is used in the Bill of Rights? As recently as 1952 the Court—recognizing a centuries-old tradition—observed in *Rochin* v. *California*, 342 U.S. 165:
>
> > Words being symbols do not speak without a gloss. [T]he gloss may be the deposit of history, whereby a term gains technical content. Thus the requirements of the Sixth and Seventh Amendments for trial by jury in the federal courts have a rigid meaning. No changes or chances can alter the content of the verbal symbol of "jury"—a body of twelve men who must reach a unanimous conclusion if the verdict is to go against the defendant.

Williams v. *Florida*
399 U.S. 78 (1970)

A six-person jury (as authorized by Florida law in noncapital cases) found Williams guilty of robbery. He claimed that a less than twelve-person jury violated the Sixth Amendment applicable to the states via the Fourteenth Amendment.

Mr. Justice White delivered the opinion of the Court. . . .

. . . The question in this case then is whether the constitutional guarantee of a trial by "jury" necessarily requires trial by exactly 12 persons, rather than some lesser number—in this case six. We hold that the 12-man panel is not a necessary ingredient of "trial by jury," and that respondent's refusal to impanel more than the six members provided for by Florida law did not violate petitioner's Sixth Amendment rights as applied to the States through the Fourteenth.

We had occasion in *Duncan* v. *Louisiana*, *supra*, to review briefly the oft-told history of the development of trial by jury in criminal cases. That history revealed a long tradition attaching great importance to the concept of relying on a body of one's peers to determine guilt or innocence as a safeguard against arbitrary law enforcement. That same history, however, affords little insight into the considerations that gradually led the size of that body to be generally fixed at 12. Some have suggested that the number 12 was fixed upon simply because that was the number of the presentment jury from the hundred, from which the petit jury developed. Other, less circular but more fanciful reasons for the number 12 have been given, "but they were all brought forward after the number was fixed," and rest on little more than mystical or superstitious insights into the significance of "12." Lord Coke's explanation that the *"number of twelve* is much respected *in holy writ,* as 12 *apostles,* 12 *stones,* 12 *tribes, etc."* is typical. In short, while sometime in the 14th century the size of the jury at common law came to be fixed generally at 12, that particular feature of the jury system appears to have been a historical acci-

dent, unrelated to the great purposes which gave rise to the jury in the first place. The question before us is whether this accidental feature of the jury has been immutably codified into our Constitution. . . .

While "the intent of the Framers" is often an elusive quarry, the relevant constitutional history casts considerable doubt on the easy assumption in our past decisions that if a given feature existed in a jury at common law in 1789, then it was necessarily preserved in the Constitution. Provisions for jury trial were first placed in the Constitution in Article III's provision that "[t]he Trial of all Crimes . . . shall be by Jury; and such Trial shall be held in the State where the said Crimes shall have been committed." The "very scanty history [of this provision] in the records of the Constitutional Convention" sheds little light either way on the intended correlation between Article III's "jury" and the features of the jury at common law. . . .

We do not pretend to be able to divine precisely what the word "jury" imported to the Framers, the First Congress, or the States in 1789. It may well be that the usual expectation was that the jury would consist of 12, and that hence, the most likely conclusion to be drawn is simply that little thought was actually given to the specific questions we face today. But there is absolutely no indication in "the intent of the Framers" of an explicit decision to equate the constitutional and common-law characteristics of the jury. Nothing in this history suggests, then, that we do violence to the letter of the Constitution by turning to other than purely historical considerations to determine which features of the justice system, as it existed at common law, were preserved in the Constitution. The relevant inquiry, as we see it, must be the function that the particular feature performs and its relation to the purposes of the jury trial. Measured by this standard, the 12-man requirement cannot be regarded as an indispensable component of the Sixth Amendment.

The purpose of the jury trial, as we noted in *Duncan*, is to prevent oppression by the Government. "Providing an accused with the right to be tried by a jury of his peers gave him an inestimable safeguard against the corrupt or overzealous prosecutor and against the compliant, biased, or eccentric judge." . . . Given this purpose, the essential feature of a jury obviously lies in the interposition between the accused and his accuser of the commonsense judgment of a group of laymen, and in the community participation and shared responsibility that results from that group's determination of guilt or innocence. The performance of this role is not a function of the particular number of the body that makes up the jury. To be sure, the number should probably be large enough to promote group deliberation, free from outside attempts at intimidation, and to provide a fair possibility for obtaining a representative cross-section of the community. But we find little reason to think that these goals are in any meaningful sense less likely to be achieved when the jury numbers six, than when it numbers 12—particularly if the requirement of unanimity is retained. And certainly the reliability of the jury as a factfinder hardly seems likely to be a function of its size.

It might be suggested that the 12-man jury gives a defendant a greater advantage since he has more "chances" of finding a juror who will insist on acquittal and thus prevent conviction. But the advantage might just as easily belong to the State, which also needs only one juror out of twelve insisting on guilt to prevent acquittal. What few experiments have occurred—usually in the civil area—indicate that there is no discernible difference between the results reached by the two different-sized juries. In short, neither currently available evidence nor theory suggests that the 12-man jury is necessarily more advantageous to the defendant than a jury composed of fewer members.

Similarly, while in theory the number of viewpoints represented on a randomly selected jury ought to increase as the size of the jury increases, in practice the difference between the 12-man and the six-man jury in terms of the cross-section of the community represented seems likely to be neglible. Even the 12-man jury cannot insure representation of every distinct voice in the community, particularly given the use of the peremptory challenge. As long as arbitrary exclusions of a particular class from the jury rolls are forbidden . . . the concern that the cross-section will be significantly diminished if the jury is decreased in size from 12 to six seems an unrealistic one.

We conclude, in short, as we began: the fact that the jury at common law was composed of precisely 12 is a historical accident, unnecessary to effect the purposes of the jury system and wholly without significance "except to mystics." . . . To read the Sixth Amendment as forever codifying a feature so incidental to the real purpose of the Amendment is to ascribe a blind formalism to the Framers which would require considerably more evidence than we have been able to discover in the history and language of the Constitution or in the reasoning of our past decisions. We do not mean to intimate that legislatures can never have good reasons for concluding that the 12-man jury is preferable to the smaller jury, or that such conclusions—reflected in the provisions of most States and in our federal system—are in any sense unwise. Legislatures may well have their own views about the relative value of the larger and smaller juries, and may conclude that, wholly apart from the jury's primary function, it is desirable to spread the collective responsibility for the determination of guilt among the larger group. In capital cases, for example, it appears that no State provides for less than 12 jurors—a fact that suggests implicit recognition of the value of the larger body as a means of legitimating society's decision to impose the death penalty. Our holding does no more than leave these considerations to Congress and the States, unrestrained by an interpretation of the Sixth Amendment that would forever dictate the precise number that can constitute a jury. Consistent with this holding, we conclude that petitioner's Sixth Amendment rights, as applied to the States through the Fourteenth Amendment, were not violated by Florida's decision to provide a six-man rather than a 12-man jury.

Mr. Justice Black, with whom Mr. Justice Douglas joins, concurring. . . .

Mr. Justice Harlan, . . . concurring in the result. . . .

The historical argument by which the Court undertakes to justify its view that the Sixth Amendment does not require 12-member juries is, in my opinion, much too thin to mask the true thrust of this decision. The decision evinces, I think, a recognition that the "incorporationist" view of the Due Process Clause of the Fourteenth Amendment, which underlay *Duncan* and is now carried forward . . . must be tempered to allow the States more elbow room in ordering their own criminal systems. With that much I agree. But to accomplish this by diluting constitutional protections within the federal system itself is something to which I cannot possibly subscribe. Tempering the rigor of *Duncan* should be done forthrightly, by facing up to the fact that at least in this area the "incorporation" doctrine does not fit well with our federal structure, and by the same token that *Duncan* was wrongly decided. . . .

. . . With all respect, I consider that before today it would have been unthinkable to suggest that the Sixth Amendment's right to a trial by jury is satisfied by a jury of six or less, as is left open by the Court's opinion in *Williams,* or by less than a unanimous verdict, a question also reserved in today's decision.

The Court, in stripping off the livery of his-

tory from the jury trial, relies on a two-step analysis. With arduous effort the Court first liberates itself from the "intent of the Framers" and "the easy assumption in our past decisions that if a given feature existed in a jury at common law in 1789, then it was necessarily preserved in the Constitution." . . . Unburdened by the yoke of history the Court then concludes that the policy protected by the jury guarantee does not require its perpetuation in common-law form.

Neither argument is, in my view, an acceptable reason for disregarding history and numerous pronouncements of this Court that have made "the easy assumption" that the Sixth Amendment's jury was one composed of 12 individuals. . . .

The principle of *stare decisis* is multifaceted. It is a solid foundation for our legal system; yet care must be taken not to use it to create an unmovable structure. It provides the stability and predictability required for the ordering of human affairs over the course of time and a basis of "public faith in the judiciary as a source of impersonal and reasoned judgments." . . . Surely, if the principle of *stare decisis* means anything in the law, it means that precedent should not be jettisoned when the rule of yesterday remains viable, creates no injustice, and can reasonably be said to be no less sound than the rule sponsored by those who seek change, let alone incapable of being demonstrated wrong. The decision in *Williams,* however, casts aside workability and relevance and substitutes uncertainty. The only reason I can discern for today's decision that discards numerous judicial pronouncements and historical precedent that sound constitutional interpretation would look to as controlling, is the Court's disquietude with the tension between the jurisprudential consequences wrought by "incorporation" in *Duncan* . . . and the counterpulls of the situation in *Williams* which presents the prospect of invalidating the common practice in the States of providing less than a 12-member jury for the trial of misdemeanor cases.

These decisions demonstrate that the difference between a "due process" approach, that considers each particular case on its own bottom to see whether the right alleged is one "implicit in the concept of ordered liberty" . . . and "selective incorporation" is not an abstract one whereby different verbal formulae achieve the same results. The internal logic of the selective incorporation doctrine cannot be respected if the Court is both committed to interpreting faithfully the meaning of the Federal Bill of Rights and recognizing the governmental diversity that exists in this country. The "backlash" in *Williams* exposes the malaise, for there the Court dilutes a federal guarantee in order to reconcile the logic of "incorporation," the "jot-for-jot and case-for-case" application of the federal right to the States, with the reality of federalism. Can one doubt that had Congress tried to undermine the common-law right to trial by jury before *Duncan* came on the books the history today recited would have barred such action? Can we expect repeat performances when this Court is called upon to give definition and meaning to other federal guarantees that have been "incorporated"? . . .

But the best evidence of the vitality of federalism is today's decision in *Williams*. The merits or demerits of the jury system can, of course, be debated and those States that have diluted the common-law requirements evince a conclusion that the protection as known at common law is not necessary for a fair trial, or is only such marginal assurance of a fair trial that the inconvenience of assembling 12 individuals outweighs other gains in the administration of justice achieved by using only six individuals. . . .

It is time, I submit, for this Court to face up to the reality implicit in today's holdings and reconsider the "incorporation" doctrine before its leveling tendencies further retard development in the field of criminal procedure by stifling flexibility in the States and by discarding the possibility of federal leadership by example.

[Mr. Justice Stewart wrote a concurring opinion.]
[Mr. Justice Marshall dissented.]
[Mr. Justice Blackmun took no part in the consideration or decision of this case.]

Note: Ballew v. *Georgia,* 98 S. Ct. 1029 (1978), held that a five-person jury in a misdemeanor case deprives a defendant of his trial-by-jury rights: "recent empirical data suggest that progressively smaller juries are less likely to foster effective deliberation" and "at some point this decline leads to inaccurate fact-finding"—moreover, reduction below six would prevent juries from adequately representing a cross section of the community.

Apodaca v. *Oregon* (summary)
406 U.S. 404 (1972)

In this case four Justices (White, Burger, Blackmun and Rehnquist)—finding nothing conclusive in the history of the Sixth Amendment—upheld state convictions by a nonunanimous jury in votes of 10 to 2 and 11 to 1. In their view the essential function of a jury lay in the interposition, between the accused and the accuser, of the commonsense judgment of a body of laymen. This function, they held, was adequately served by the juries in question.

Four other Justices (Douglas, Stewart, Brennan, and Marshall), dissenting, insisted that "until to-day" it had been universally understood that a unanimous verdict was an essential element of Sixth Amendment trial by jury.

In this impasse Mr. Justice Powell provided the controlling opinion:

I concur in the plurality opinion . . . insofar as it concludes that a defendant in a state court may constitutionally be convicted by less than a unanimous verdict, but I am not in accord with a major premise upon which that judgment is based. Its premise is that the concept of jury trial, as applicable to the States under the Fourteenth Amendment, must be identical in every detail to the concept required in federal courts by the Sixth Amendment. I do not think that all of the elements of jury trial within the meaning of the Sixth Amendment are necessarily embodied in or incorporated into the Due Process Clause of the Fourteenth Amendment.

Note: It follows as a result of *Apodaca* that unanimous jury verdicts are required in federal, but not in state, criminal trials. This, Mr. Justice Douglas claimed, constituted a "watered down" application of the Bill of Rights to state trials. *Burch* v. *Louisiana*, 99 S. Ct. 1623 (1979), held invalid a state law permitting conviction by five members of a six-person jury in a case involving a nonpetty offense: " . . . having already departed from the strictly historical requirements of jury trial [*Williams, Apodaca*], it is inevitable that lines must be drawn somewhere if the substance of the jury trial right is to be preserved."

FAIR TRIBUNAL AND PROSECUTOR

Nebraska Press Association v. *Stuart* (excerpt)
427 U.S. 539 (1976)

This case is considered below in Chapter 8. Here is the Court's summary of several leading cases involving media interference with the right to a fair trial.

Mr. Chief Justice Burger delivered the opinion of the Court. . . .

The Sixth Amendment in terms guarantees "trial by an impartial jury . . ." in federal criminal prosecutions. Because "trial by jury in criminal cases is fundamental to the American scheme of justice," the Due Process Clause of the Fourteenth Amendment guarantees the same right in state criminal prosecutions. . . .

In the overwhelming majority of criminal trials, pretrial publicity presents few unmanageable threats to this important right. But when the case is a "sensational" one, tensions develop between the right of the accused to trial by an impartial jury and the rights guaranteed others by the First Amendment. The relevant decisions of this Court, even if not dispositive, are instructive by way of background.

In *Irvin* v. *Dowd*, 366 U.S. 726 (1961), for example, the defendant was convicted of murder following intensive and hostile news coverage. The trial judge had granted a defense motion for a change of venue, but only to an adjacent county, which had been exposed to essentially the same news coverage. At trial, 430 persons were called for jury service; 268 were excused because they had fixed opinions as to guilt. Eight of the 12 who served as jurors thought the defendant guilty, but said they could nevertheless render an impartial verdict. On review the Court vacated the conviction and death sentence and remanded to allow a new trial for, "[w]ith his life at stake, it is not requiring too much that petitioner be tried in an atmosphere undisturbed by so huge a wave of public passion. . . ." *Id.,* at 728.

Similarly, in *Rideau* v. *Louisiana,* 373 U.S. 723 (1963), the Court reversed the conviction of a defendant whose staged, highly emotional confession had been filmed with the cooperation of local police and later broadcast on television for three days while he was awaiting trial, saying "[a]ny subsequent court proceedings in a community so pervasively exposed to such a spectacle could be but a hollow formality." *Id.,* at 726. And in *Estes* v. *Texas,* 381 U.S. 532 (1965), the Court held that the defendant had not been afforded due process where the volume of trial publicity, the judge's failure to control the proceedings, and the telecast of a hearing and of the trial itself "inherently prevented a sober search for the truth." *Id.,* at 551. See also *Marshall* v. *United States,* 360 U.S. 310 (1959).

In *Sheppard* v. *Maxwell,* 384 U.S. 333 (1966), the Court focused sharply on the impact of pretrial publicity and a trial court's duty to protect the defendant's constitutional right to a fair trial. With only Justice Black dissenting, and he without opinion, the Court ordered a new trial for the petitioner, even though the first trial had occurred 12 years before. Beyond doubt the press had shown no responsible concern for the constitutional guarantee of a fair trial; the community from which the jury was drawn had been inundated by publicity hostile to the defendant. But the trial judge "did not fulfill his duty to protect [the defendant] from the inherently prejudicial publicity which saturated the community and to control disruptive influences in the courtroom." *Id.,* at 363. The Court noted that "unfair and prejudicial news comment on pending trials has become increasing prevalent," *id.,* at 362, and issued a strong warning:

> "Due process requires that the accused receive a trial by an impartial jury free from outside influences. Given the pervasiveness of modern communications and the difficulty of effacing prejudicial public-

ity from the minds of the jurors, *the trial courts must take strong measures to ensure that the balance is never weighed against the accused. . . .* Of course, there is nothing that proscribes the press from reporting events that transpire in the courtroom. But where there is a reasonable likelihood that prejudicial news prior to trial will prevent a fair trial, the judge should *continue the case* until the threat abates, *or transfer it* to another county not so permeated with publicity. In addition, *sequestration of the jury* was something the judge should have raised sua sponte with counsel. If publicity during the proceedings threatens the fairness of the trial, a new trial should be ordered. But we must remember that reversals are but palliatives; the cure lies in those remedial measures that will prevent the prejudice at its inception. The courts must take such steps by rule and regulation that will protect their processes from prejudicial outside interferences. *Neither prosecutors, counsel for defense, the accused, witnesses, court staff nor enforcement officers coming under the jurisdiction of the court should be permitted to frustrate its function.* Collaboration between counsel and the press as to information affecting the fairness of a criminal trial is not only subject to regulation, but is highly censurable and worthy of disciplinary measures." *Id.,* at 362–363 (emphasis added).

Because the trial court had failed to use even minimal efforts to insulate the trial and the jurors from the "deluge of publicity," *id.,* at 357, the Court vacated the judgment of conviction and a new trial followed, in which the accused was acquitted.

Cases such as these are relatively rare, and we have held in other cases that trials have been fair in spite of widespread publicity. In *Stroble* v. *California,* 343 U.S. 181 (1951), for example, the Court affirmed a conviction and death sentence challenged on the ground that pretrial news accounts, including the prosecutor's release of the defendant's recorded confession, were allegedly so inflammatory as to amount to a denial of due process. The Court disapproved of the prosecutor's conduct, but noted that the publicity had receded some six weeks before trial, that the defendant had not moved for a change of venue, and that the confession had been found voluntary and admitted in evidence at trial. The Court also noted the thorough examination of jurors on *voir dire* and the careful review of the facts by the state courts, and held that petitioner had failed to demonstrate a denial of due process. See also *Murphy* v. *Florida*, 421 U.S. 794 (1975); *Beck* v. *Washington*, 369 U.S. 541 (1962).

Taken together, these cases demonstrate that pretrial publicity—even pervasive, adverse publicity—does not inevitably lead to an unfair trial. The capacity of the jury eventually impaneled to decide the case fairly is influenced by the tone and extent of the publicity, which is in part, and often in large part, shaped by what attorneys, police, and other officials do to precipitate news coverage. The trial judge has a major responsibility. What the judge says about a case, in or out of the courtroom, is likely to appear in newspapers and broadcasts. More important, the measures a judge takes or fails to take to mitigate the effects of pretrial publicity—the measures described in *Sheppard*—may well determine whether the defendant receives a trial consistent with the requirements of due process. That this responsibility has not always been properly discharged is apparent from the decisions just reviewed.

The costs of failure to afford a fair trial are high. In the most extreme cases, like *Sheppard* and *Estes*, the risk of injustice was avoided when the convictions were reversed. But a reversal means that justice has been delayed for both the defendant and the State; in some cases, because of lapse of time retrial is impossible or further prosecution is gravely handicapped. Moreover, in borderline cases in which the con-

viction is not reversed, there is some possibility of an injustice unredressed. The "strong measures" outlined in *Sheppard* v. *Maxwell* are means by which a trial judge can try to avoid exacting these costs from society or from the accused.

Note: Gannett Co. v. *De Pasquale*, 99 S. Ct. 2898 (1979), held that to protect the accused from prejudicial, pretrial publicity a trial judge may deny the press and the public access to a pretrial hearing when all parties to the litigation agree. In the Court's view the Sixth Amendment guarantee of a public trial is for the benefit of the accused alone (not for the benefit of the press or the public). Here obviously the accused waived the benefit because he felt it would do him more harm than good.

Justices Blackmun, Brennan, White, and Marshall dissented in part (they recognized that in some circumstances some closure is permissible). All of the Justices treated that case as it was presented to them on Sixth, not First, Amendment grounds.

Hernandez v. *Texas*
347 U.S. 475 (1954)

Mr. Chief Justice Warren delivered the opinion of the Court.

The petitioner, Pete Hernandez, was indicted for the murder of one Joe Espinosa by a grand jury in Jackson County, Texas. He was convicted and sentenced to life imprisonment. The Texas Court of Criminal Appeals affirmed the judgment of the trial court. 251 S.W.2d 531. Prior to the trial, the petitioner, by his counsel, offered timely motions to quash the indictment and the jury panel. He alleged that persons of Mexican descent were systematically excluded from service as jury commissioners, grand jurors, and petit jurors, although there were such persons fully qualified to serve residing in

Jackson County. The petitioner asserted that exclusion of this class deprived him, as a member of the class, of the equal protection of the laws guaranteed by the Fourteenth Amendment of the Constitution. After a hearing, the trial court denied the motions. At the trial, the motions were renewed, further evidence taken, and the motions again denied. An allegation that the trial court erred in denying the motions was the sole basis of petitioner's appeal. . . .

In numerous decisions, this Court has held that it is a denial of the equal protection of the laws to try a defendant of a particular race or color under an indictment issued by a grand jury, or before a petit jury, from which all persons of his race or color have, solely because of that race or color, been excluded by the State, whether acting through its legislature, its courts, or its executive or administrative officers. Although the Court has had little occasion to rule on the question directly, it has been recognized since *Strauder* v. *State of West Virginia*, 100 U.S. 303, that the exclusion of a class of persons from jury service on grounds other than race or color may also deprive a defendant who is a member of that class of the constitutional guarantee of equal protection of the laws. The State of Texas would have us hold that there are only two classes—white and Negro—within the contemplation of the Fourteenth Amendment. The decisions of this Court do not support that view. And, except where the question presented involves the exclusion of persons of Mexican descent from juries, Texas courts have taken a broader view of the scope of the equal protection clause.

Throughout our history differences in race and color have defined easily identifiable groups which have at times required the aid of the courts in securing equal treatment under the laws. But community prejudices are not static, and from time to time other differences from the community norm may define other groups which need the same protection. Whether such a group exists within a community is a question of fact. When the existence of a distinct class is demonstrated, and it is further shown that the laws, as written or as supplied, single out that class for different treatment not based on some reasonable classification, the guarantees of the Constitution have been violated. The Fourteenth Amendment is not directed solely against discrimination due to a "two-class theory"— that is, based upon differences between "white" and Negro.

As the petitioner acknowledges, the Texas system of selecting grand and petit jurors by the use of jury commissions is fair on its face and capable of being utilized without discrimination. But as this Court has held, the system is susceptible to abuse and can be employed in a discriminatory manner. The exclusion of otherwise eligible persons from jury service solely because of their ancestry or national origin is discrimination prohibited by the Fourteenth Amendment. The Texas statute makes no such discrimination, but the petitioner alleges that those administering the law do.

The petitioner's initial burden in substantiating his charge of group discrimination was to prove that persons of Mexican descent constitute a separate class in Jackson County, distinct from "whites." One method by which this may be demonstrated is by showing the attitude of the community. Here the testimony of responsible officials and citizens contained the admission that residents of the community distinguished between "white" and "Mexican." The participation of persons of Mexican descent in business and community groups was shown to be slight. Until very recent times, children of Mexican descent were required to attend a segregated school for the first four grades. At least one restaurant in town prominently displayed a sign announcing "No Mexicans Served." On the courthouse grounds at the time of the hearing, there were two men's toilets, one unmarked, and the other marked "Colored Men" and "Hombres Aqui" ("Men Here"). No substantial evidence was offered to rebut the logical inference to be drawn from these facts, and it must be concluded that petitioner succeeded in his proof.

Having established the existence of a class, petitioner was then charged with the burden of proving discrimination. To do so, he relied on the pattern of proof established by *Norris* v. *State of Alabama*, 294 U.S. 587. In that case, proof that Negroes constituted a substantial segment of the population of the jurisdiction, that some Negroes were qualified to serve as jurors, and that none had been called for jury service over an extended period of time, was held to constitute prima facie proof of the systematic exclusion of Negroes from jury service. This holding, sometimes called the "rule of exclusion," has been applied in other cases, and it is available in supplying proof of discrimination against any delineated class.

The petitioner established that 14% of the population of Jackson County were persons with Mexican or Latin American surnames, and that 11% of the males over 21 bore such names. The County Tax Assessor testified that 6 or 7 percent of the freeholders on the tax rolls of the County were persons of Mexican descent. The State of Texas stipulated that "for the last twenty-five years there is no record of any person with a Mexican or Latin American name having served on a jury commission, grand jury or petit jury in Jackson County." The parties also stipulated that "there are some male persons of Mexican or Latin American descent in Jackson County who, by virtue of being citizens, freeholders, and having all other legal prerequisites to jury service, are eligible to serve as members of a jury commission, grand jury and/or petit jury."

The petitioner met the burden of proof imposed in *Norris* v. *Alabama, supra*. To rebut the strong prima facie case of the denial of the equal protection of the laws guaranteed by the Constitution thus established, the State offered the testimony of five jury commissioners that they had not discriminated against persons of Mexican or Latin American descent in selecting jurors. They stated that their only objective had been to select those whom they thought were best qualified. This testimony is not enough to overcome the petitioner's case. As the Court said in *Norris* v. *Alabama*:

"That showing as to the long-continued exclusion of Negroes from jury service, and as to the many Negroes qualified for that service, could not be met by mere generalities. If, in the presence of such testimony as defendant adduced, the mere general assertions by officials of their performance of duty were to be accepted as an adequate justification for the complete exclusion of Negroes from jury service, the constitutional provision . . . would be but a vain and illusory requirement."

The same reasoning is applicable to these facts.

Circumstances or chance may well dictate that no persons in a certain class will serve on a particular jury or during some particular period. But it taxes our credulity to say that mere chance resulted in there being no members of this class among the over six thousand jurors called in the past 25 years. The result bespeaks discrimination, whether or not it was a conscious decision on the part of any individual jury commissioner. The judgment of conviction must be reversed.

To say that this decision revives the rejected contention that the Fourteenth Amendment requires proportional representation of all the component ethnic groups of the community on every jury ignores the facts. The petitioner did not seek proportional representation, nor did he claim a right to have persons of Mexican descent sit on the particular juries which he faced. His only claim is the right to be indicted and tried by juries from which all members of his class are not systematically excluded—juries selected from among all qualified persons regardless of national origin or descent. To this much, he is entitled by the Constitution.

Note: Louisiana gave women a blanket exemption from jury duty, subject to a right to serve for any woman who had filed a declaration of her desire to do so. This was held an invalid interference with a male defendant's right to an impartial jury drawn from a fair cross section of the community, as guaranteed by the Sixth and Fourteenth Amendments (Taylor v. Louisiana, 419 U.S. 522 [1975]). In the Court's view the state law in question operated largely to exclude females from jury service.

Alcorta v. Texas
355 U.S. 28 (1957)

Per Curiam.

Petitioner, Alvaro Alcorta, was indicted for murder in a Texas state court for stabbing his wife to death. Vernon's Tex. Pen. Code, 1948, Art. 1256. He admitted the killing but claimed it occurred in a fit of passion when he discovered his wife, whom he had already suspected of marital infidelity, kissing one Castilleja late at night in a parked car. Petitioner relied on Texas statutes which treat killing under the influence of a "sudden passion arising from an adequate cause . . . as would commonly produce a degree of anger, rage, resentment, or terror in a person of ordinary temper sufficient to render the mind incapable of cool reflection" as murder without malice punishable by a maximum sentence of five years imprisonment. Vernon's Tex. Pen. Code, 1948, Arts. 1257a, 1257b, 1257c. The jury, however, found him guilty of murder with malice and, acting under broad statutory authority to determine the extent of punishment, sentenced him to death. The judgment and sentence were affirmed by the Texas Court of Criminal Appeals. 294 S.W.2d 112.

Castilleja, the only eye witness to the killing, testified for the state at petitioner's trial. In response to inquiries by the prosecutor about his relationship with the petitioner's wife, Castilleja said that he had simply driven her home from work a couple of times, and in substance testified that his relationship with her had been nothing more than a casual friendship. He stated that he had given her a ride on the night she was killed and was parked in front of her home with his car lights out at two o'clock in the morning because of engine trouble. The prosecutor then asked what had transpired between Castilleja and petitioner's wife in the parked car:

"Q. Did you have a conversation with Herlinda? A. Yes; she opened the door. She was going to get off [sic] and, then, she told me to tell my sister to come and pick her up in the morning so she could go to church.
"Q. To tell your sister, Delfina Cabrera, to come pick her up in the morning so she could go to church? A. Yes."

At the conclusion of Castilleja's testimony the following colloquy took place between him and the prosecutor:

"Q. Natividad [Castilleja], were you in love with Herlinda? A. No.
"Q. Was she in love with you? A. No.
"Q. Had you ever talked about love? A. No.
"Q. Had you ever had any dates with her other than to take her home? A. No. Well, just when I brought her from there.
"Q. Just when you brought her from work? A. Yes."

All this testimony was quite plainly inconsistent with petitioner's claim that he had come upon his wife kissing Castilleja in the parked car.

Some time after petitioner's conviction had been affirmed Castilleja issued a sworn statement in which he declared that he had given false testimony at the trial. Relying on this statement petitioner asked the trial court to issue a writ of habeas corpus. He contended that he had been denied a fair trial in violation of State and Federal Constitutions because Castilleja had testified falsely, with the knowledge of the prosecutor, that his relationship with petitioner's wife had been only "that of a friend and neighbor, and that he had had no 'dates,' nor other relations with her, when in truth and in fact the witness had been her lover and paramour, and had had sexual intercourse with her on many occasions. . . ." Petitioner further alleged that he had no knowledge of this illicit intercourse at the time of his trial.

A hearing was held on the petition for habeas corpus. Castilleja was called as a witness. He confessed having sexual intercourse with petitioner's wife on five or six occasions within a relatively brief period before her death. He testified that he had informed the prosecutor of this before trial and the prosecutor had told him he should not volunteer any information about such intercourse but if specifically asked about it to answer truthfully. The prosecutor took the stand and admitted that these statements were true. He conceded that he had not told petitioner about Castilleja's illicit intercourse with his wife. He also admitted that he had not included this information in a written statement taken from Castilleja prior to the trial but instead had noted it in a separate record. At the conclusion of the hearing the trial judge denied the petition for habeas corpus. Petitioner then applied to the Texas Court of Criminal Appeals for a writ of habeas corpus but that court, acting

on the record made at the hearing before the trial court, also refused to issue the writ. We granted certiorari, 353 U.S. 972. Texas concedes that petitioner has exhausted all remedies available to him under state law.

Under the general principles laid down by this Court in *Mooney* v. *Holohan*, 294 U.S. 103, and *Pyle* v. *State of Kansas*, 317 U.S. 213, petitioner was not accorded due process of law. It cannot seriously be disputed that Castilleja's testimony, taken as a whole, gave the jury the false impression that his relationship with petitioner's wife was nothing more than that of casual friendship. This testimony was elicited by the prosecutor who knew of the illicit intercourse between Castilleja and petitioner's wife. Undoubtedly Castilleja's testimony was seriously prejudicial to petitioner. It tended squarely to refute his claim that he had adequate cause for a surge of "sudden passion" in which he killed his wife. If Castilleja's relationship with petitioner's wife had been truthfully portrayed to the jury, it would have, apart from impeaching his credibility, tended to corroborate petitioner's contention that he had found his wife embracing Castilleja. If petitioner's defense had been accepted by the jury, as it might well have been if Castilleja had not been allowed to testify falsely, to the knowledge of the prosecutor, his offense would have been reduced to "murder without malice" precluding the death penalty now imposed upon him.

SEARCH AND SEIZURE

Introduction

Search warrants are issued on the same basis as are warrants for arrest. The process is described in *Henry* v. *United States,* above. As the Court has said, "Over and again . . . the [Fourth] Amendment requires adherence to judicial processes [which means that] searches conducted outside the judicial process, without prior approval by judge or magistrate, are *per se* unreasonable under the Fourth Amendment—subject only to a few specifically established and well-delineated exceptions [based on necessity]." Two of the more common of these exceptions (searches in conjunction with valid arrests, and consent searches) are considered in the next four cases.

Another exception (searches to prevent loss or destruction of evidence) is considered in *Carroll* v. *United States,* 267 U.S. 132 (1925) and in *Schmerber,* below.

Chimel v. *California*
395 U.S. 752 (1969)

Mr. Justice Stewart delivered the opinion of the Court.

This case raises basic questions concerning the permissible scope under the Fourth Amendment of a search incident to a lawful arrest.

The relevant facts are essentially undisputed. Late in the afternoon of September 13, 1965, three police officers arrived at the Santa Ana, California, home of the petitioner with a warrant authorizing his arrest for the burglary of a coin shop. The officers knocked on the door, identified themselves to the petitioner's wife, and asked if they might come inside. She ushered them into the house, where they waited 10 or 15 minutes until the petitioner returned home from work. When the petitioner entered the house, one of the officers handed him the arrest warrant and asked for permission to "look around." The petitioner objected, but was advised that "on the basis of the lawful arrest," the officers would nonetheless conduct a search. No search warrant had been issued.

Accompanied by the petitioner's wife, the officers then looked through the entire three-bedroom house, including the attic, the garage, and a small workshop. In some rooms the search was relatively cursory. In the master bedroom and sewing room, however, the officers directed the petitioner's wife to open drawers and "to physically move contents of the drawers from side to side so that [they] might view any items that would have come from [the] burglary." After completing the search, they seized numerous items—primarily coins, but also several medals, tokens, and a few other objects. The entire search took between 45 minutes and an hour.

At the petitioner's subsequent state trial on two charges of burglary, the items taken from his house were admitted into evidence against him, over his objection that they had been unconstitutionally seized. . . .

. . . [W]e proceed on the hypothesis . . . that the arrest of the petitioner was valid under the Constitution. This brings us directly to the question whether the warrantless search of the petitioner's entire house can be constitutionally justified as incident to that arrest. The decisions of this Court bearing upon that question have been far from consistent, as even the most cursory review makes evident.

. . . [In] *Harris* v. *United States,* 331 U.S. 145, decided in 1947, . . . officers had obtained a warrant for Harris' arrest on the basis of his alleged involvement with the cashing and interstate transportation of a forged check. He was arrested in the living room of his four-room apartment, and in an attempt to recover two canceled checks thought to have been used in effecting the forgery, the officers undertook a thorough search of the entire apartment. Inside a desk drawer they found a sealed envelope marked "George Harris, personal papers." The envelope, which was then torn open, was found to contain altered Selective Service documents, and those documents were used to secure Harris' conviction for violating the Selective Training and Service Act of 1940. The Court rejected Harris' Fourth Amendment claim, sustaining the search as "incident to arrest." *Id.,* at 151.

Only a year after *Harris,* however, the pendulum swung again. In *Trupiano* v. *United States,* 334 U.S. 699, agents raided the site of an illicit distillery, saw one of several conspirators operating the still, and arrested him, contemporaneously "seiz[ing] the illicit distillery." *Id.,* at 702. The Court held that the arrest and others made subsequently had been valid, but that the unexplained failure of the agents to procure a search warrant—in spite of the fact that they had had more than enough time before the raid to do so—rendered the search unlawful. The opinion stated:

> "It is a cardinal rule that, in seizing goods and articles, law enforcement agents must secure and use search warrants wherever reasonably practicable. . . .
>
> A search or seizure without a warrant as an incident to a lawful arrest has always been considered to be a strictly limited right. It grows out of the inherent necessities of the situation at the time of the arrest. But there must be something more in the way of necessity than merely a lawful arrest." *Id.*, at 705, 708.

In 1950, two years after *Trupiano*, came *United States* v. *Rabinowitz*, 339 U.S. 56, the decision upon which California primarily relies in the case now before us. . . .

Rabinowitz has come to stand for the proposition, *inter alia*, that a warrantless search "incident to a lawful arrest" may generally extend to the area that is considered to be in the "possession" or under the "control" of the person arrested. And it was on the basis of that proposition that the California courts upheld the search of the petitioner's entire house in this case. That doctrine, however, at least in the broad sense in which it was applied by the California courts in this case, can withstand neither historical nor rational analysis. . . .

Only last Term in *Terry* v. *Ohio*, 392 U.S. 1, we emphasized that "the police must, whenever practicable, obtain advance judicial approval of searches and seizures through the warrant procedure," *id.*, at 20 and that "[t]he scope of [a] search must be 'strictly tied to and justified by' the circumstances which rendered its initiation permissible." *Id.*, at 19. . . .

A similar analysis underlies the "search incident to arrest" principle, and marks its proper extent. When an arrest is made, it is reasonable for the arresting officer to search the person arrested in order to remove any weapons that the latter might seek to use in order to resist arrest or effect his escape. Otherwise, the officer's safety might well be endangered, and the arrest itself frustrated. In addition, it is entirely reasonable for the arresting officer to search for and seize any evidence on the arrestee's person in order to prevent its concealment or destruction. And the area into which an arrestee might reach in order to grab a weapon or evidentiary items must, of course, be governed by a like rule. A gun on a table or in a drawer in front of one who is arrested can be as dangerous to the arresting officer as one concealed in the clothing of the person arrested. There is ample justification, therefore, for a search of the arrestee's person and the area "within his immediate control"—construing that phrase to mean the area from within which he might gain possession of a weapon or destructible evidence.

There is no comparable justification, however, for routinely searching any room other than that in which an arrest occurs—or, for that matter, for searching through all the desk drawers or other closed or concealed areas in that room itself. Such searches, in the absence of well-recognized exceptions, may be made only under the authority of a search warrant. The "adherence to judicial processes" mandated by the Fourth Amendment requires no less. . . .

It is argued in the present case that it is "reasonable" to search a man's house when he is arrested in it. But that argument is founded on little more than a subjective view regarding the acceptability of certain sorts of police conduct, and not on considerations relevant to Fourth Amendment interests. Under such an unconfined analysis, Fourth Amendment protection in this area would approach the evaporation point. It is not easy to explain why, for instance, it is less subjectively "reasonable" to search a man's house when he is arrested on his front lawn—or just down the street—than it is when he happens to be in the house at the time of arrest. . . .

It would be possible, of course, to draw a line between *Rabinowitz* and *Harris* on the one hand, and this case on the other. For *Rabinowitz* involved a single room, and *Harris* a four-room apartment, while in the case before us an entire house was searched. But such a distinction would be highly artificial. The rationale that allowed the searches and seizures in *Rabinowitz* and *Harris* would allow the searches and seizures in this case. No consideration relevant to the Fourth Amendment suggests any point of rational limitation, once the search is allowed to go beyond the area from which the person arrested might obtain weapons or evidentiary items. The only reasoned distinction is one between a search of the person arrested and the area within his reach on the one hand, and more extensive searches on the other.

The petitioner correctly points out that one result of decisions such as *Rabinowitz* and *Harris* is to give law enforcement officials the opportunity to engage in searches not justified by probable cause, by the simple expedient of arranging to arrest suspects at home rather than elsewhere. We do not suggest that the petitioner is necessarily correct in his assertion that such a strategy was utilized here, but the fact remains that had he been arrested earlier in the day, at his place of employment rather than at home, no search of his house could have been made without a search warrant. . . .

Application of sound Fourth Amendment principles to the facts of this case produces a clear result. The search here went far beyond the petitioner's person and the area from within which he might have obtained either a weapon or something that could have been used as evidence against him. There was no constitutional justification, in the absence of a search warrant, for extending the search beyond that area. The scope of the search was, therefore, "unreasonable" under the Fourth and Fourteenth Amendments, and the petitioner's conviction cannot stand.

Mr. Justice Harlan concurring. . . .

Mr. Justice White, with whom Mr. Justice Black joins, dissenting.

. . . [T]he Court must decide whether a given search is reasonable. The Amendment does not proscribe "warrantless searches" but instead it proscribes "unreasonable searches" and this Court has never held nor does the majority today assert that warrantless searches are necessarily unreasonable.

Applying this reasonableness test to the area of searches incident to arrests, one thing is clear at the outset. Search of an arrested man and of the items within his immediate reach must in almost every case be reasonable. There is always a danger that the suspect will try to escape, seizing concealed weapons with which to overpower and injure the arresting officers, and there is a danger that he may destroy evidence vital to the prosecution. Circumstances in which these justifications would not apply are sufficiently rare that inquiry is not made into searches of this scope, which have been considered reasonable throughout.

The justifications which make such a search reasonable obviously do not apply to the search of areas to which the accused does not have ready physical access. This is not enough, however, to prove such searches unconstitutional. The Court has always held, and does not today deny, that when there is probable cause to search and it is "impracticable" for one reason or another to get a search warrant, then a warrantless search may be reasonable. E.g., even *Trupiano* v. *United States*, 334 U.S. 699 (1948). This is the case whether an arrest was made at the time of the search or not.

This is not to say that a search can be reasonable without regard to the probable cause to believe that seizable items are on the premises. But when there are exigent circumstances, and probable cause, then the search may be made without a warrant, reasonably. An arrest itself may often create an emergency situation making it impracticable to obtain a warrant before embarking on a related search. Again assuming that there is probable cause to search premises at the spot where a suspect is arrested, it seems to me unreasonable to require the police to leave the scene in order to obtain a search warrant when they are already legally there to make a valid arrest, and when there must almost always be a strong possibility that confederates of the arrested man will in the meanwhile remove the items for which the police have probable cause to search. This must so often be the case that it seems to me as unreasonable to require a warrant for a search of the premises as to require a warrant for search of the person and his very immediate surroundings.

This case provides a good illustration of my point that it is unreasonable to require police to leave the scene of an arrest in order to obtain a search warrant when they already have probable cause to search and there is a clear danger that the items for which they may reasonably search will be removed before they return with a warrant. Petitioner was arrested in his home after an arrest whose validity will be explored below, but which I will now assume was valid. There was doubtless probable cause not only to arrest petitioner, but also to search his house. He had obliquely admitted, both to a neighbor and to the owner of the burglarized store, that he had committed the burglary. In light of this, and the fact that the neighbor had seen other admittedly stolen property in petitioner's house, there was surely probable cause on which a warrant could have issued to search the house for the stolen coins. Moreover, had the police simply arrested petitioner, taken him off to the station house, and later returned with a warrant, it seems very likely that petitioner's wife, who in view of petitioner's generally garrulous nature must have known of the robbery, would have removed the coins. For the police to search the house while the evidence they had probable cause to search out and seize was still there cannot be considered unreasonable.

This line of analysis, supported by the precedents of this Court, hinges on two assumptions. One is that the arrest of petitioner without a

valid warrant was constitutional as the majority assumes; the other is that the police were not required to obtain a search warrant in advance, even though they knew that the effect of the arrest might well be to alert petitioner's wife that the coins had better be removed soon. . . .

If circumstances so often require the warrantless arrest that the law generally permits it, the typical situation will find the arresting officers lawfully on the premises without arrest or search warrant. Like the majority, I would permit the police to search the person of a suspect and the area under his immediate control either to assure the safety of the officers or to prevent the destruction of evidence. And like the majority, I see nothing in the arrest alone furnishing probable cause for a search of any broader scope. However, where as here the existence of probable cause is independently established and would justify a warrant for a broader search for evidence, I would follow past cases and permit such a search to be carried out without a warrant, since the fact of arrest supplies an exigent circumstance justifying police action before the evidence can be removed, and also alerts the suspect to the fact of the search so that he can immediately seek judicial determination of probable cause in an adversary proceeding, and appropriate redress.

This view, consistent with past cases, would not authorize the general search against which the Fourth Amendment was meant to guard, nor would it broaden or render uncertain in any way whatsoever the scope of searches permitted under the Fourth Amendment. The issue in this case is not the breadth of the search, since there was clearly probable cause for the search which was carried out. No broader search than if the officers had a warrant would be permitted. The only issue is whether a search warrant was required as a precondition to that search. It is agreed that such a warrant would be required absent exigent circumstances. I would hold that the fact of arrest supplies such an exigent circumstance, since the police had lawfully gained entry to the premises to effect the arrest and since delaying the search to secure a warrant would have involved the risk of not recovering the fruits of the crime. . . .

In considering searches incident to arrest, it must be remembered that there will be immedi- ate opportunity to challenge the probable cause for the search in an adversary proceeding. The suspect has been apprised of the search by his very presence at the scene, and having been ar- rested, he will soon be brought into contact with people who can explain his rights. . . .

United States v. *Chadwick* (excerpt)
433 U.S. 1 (1977)

In *Carroll* v. *United States*, 267 U.S. 132 (1925), it was first recognized that when a vehicle has been stopped *legally* a probable-cause search without a warrant is permissible, lest the vehicle and the evidence disappear before a warrant can be obtained. *Cardwell* v. *Lewis*, 417 U.S. 583 (1974), indicated the Court is supplement- ing the disappearance rationale with a broader one which recognizes that one's automobile is less private in nature than one's home, office—and in the present case—one's luggage.

. . . [T]he Government views . . . luggage as analogous to motor vehicles for Fourth Amendment purposes. It is true that, like the footlocker in issue here, automobiles are "ef- fects" under the Fourth Amendment, and searches and seizures of automobiles are there- fore subject to the constitutional standard of reasonableness. But this Court has recognized significant differences between motor vehicles and other property which permit warrantless searches of automobiles in circumstances in which warrantless searches would not be rea- sonable in other contexts. *Carroll* v. *United States*, 267 U.S. 132 (1925); *Preston* v. *United States*, 376 U.S., at 366–367 (1964); *Chambers* v. *Maroney*, 399 U.S. 42 (1970). See also *South Dakota* v. *Opperman*, 428 U.S., at 367.

Our treatment of automobiles has been based in part on their inherent mobility, which often makes obtaining a judicial warrant impractica- ble. Nevertheless, we have also sustained "war- rantless searches of vehicles . . . in cases in which the possibilities of the vehicle's being removed or evidence in it destroyed were re- mote, if not non-existent." *Cady* v. *Dombrowski*, 413 U.S. 433, 441–442 (1973); accord, *South Dakota* v. *Opperman*, *supra*, at 367; see *Texas* v.

White, 423 U.S. 67 (1975); *Chambers* v. *Maroney*, *supra*; *Cooper* v. *California*, 386 U.S. 58 (1967).

The answer lies in the diminished expecta- tion of privacy which surrounds the automo- bile:

"One has a lesser expectation of privacy in a motor vehicle because its function is transportation and it seldom serves as one's residence or as the repository of per- sonal effects. . . . It travels public thoroughfares where both its occupants and its contents are in plain view." *Cardwell* v. *Lewis*, 417 U.S. 583, 590 (1974) (plurality opinion).

Other factors reduce automobile privacy. "All States require vehicles to be registered and operators to be licensed. States and localities have enacted extensive and detailed codes regulating the condition and manner in which motor vehicles may be operated on public streets and highways." *Cady* v. *Dombrowski*, 413 U.S., at 441. Automobiles periodically undergo official inspection, and they are often taken into police custody in the interests of public safety. *South Dakota* v. *Opperman*, 428 U.S., at 368.

The factors which diminish the privacy aspects of an automobile do not apply to respondents' footlocker. Luggage contents are not open to public view, except as a condition to a border entry or common carrier travel; nor is luggage subject to regular inspections and official scrutiny on a continuing basis. Unlike an automobile whose primary function is transportation, luggage is intended as a repository of personal effects. In sum, a person's expectations of privacy in personal luggage are substantially greater than in an automobile.

Nor does the footlocker's mobility justify dispensing with the added protections of the Warrant Clause. Once the federal agents had seized it at the railroad station and had safely transferred it to the Boston federal building under their exclusive control, there was not the slightest danger that the footlocker or its contents could have been removed before a valid search warrant could be obtained. The initial seizure and detention of the footlocker, the validity of which respondents do not contest, were sufficient to guard against any risk that evidence might be lost. With the footlocker safely immobilized, it was unreasonable to undertake the additional and greater intrusion of a search without a warrant.

United States v. *Robinson*
414 U.S. 218 (1973)

Robinson was lawfully stopped and arrested for driving after revocation of his driver's license. During a full search incident to this arrest, heroin was found in a cigarette package taken from Robinson's coat pocket. The Court rejected the argument that a search in such circumstances must be *limited* as prescribed in *Terry* v. *Ohio,* above.

Mr. Justice Rehnquist delivered the opinion of the Court. . . .

A police officer's determination as to how and where to search the person of a suspect whom he has arrested is necessarily a quick ad hoc judgment which the Fourth Amendment does not require to be broken down in each instance into an analysis of each step in the search. The authority to search the person incident to a lawful custodial arrest, while based upon the need to disarm and to discover evidence, does not depend on what a court may later decide was the probability in a particular arrest situation that weapons or evidence would in fact be found upon the person of the suspect. A custodial arrest of a suspect based on probable cause is a reasonable intrusion under the Fourth Amendment; that intrusion being lawful, a search incident to the arrest requires no additional justification. [I]n the case of a lawful custodial arrest a full search of the person is not only an exception to the warrant requirement of the Fourth Amendment, but is also a "reasonable" search under that Amendment. . . . Since it is the fact of custodial arrest [as opposed to "a routine traffic stop," whose ramifications the Court did not reach] which gives rise to the authority to search, it is of no moment that [the arresting officer] did not indicate any subjective fear of the respondent or that he did not himself suspect that respondent was armed.

[Justices Marshall, Douglas, and Brennan dissenting.]

. . . [T]he only rationale for a search in this case removal of weapons—"is identical to the rationale of the search permitted in *Terry.* [E]ven were we to assume, arguendo, that it was reasonable for [the officer] to remove the object he felt in respondent's pocket, clearly there was no justification consistent with the Fourth Amendment which would authorize his opening the package and looking inside. [E]ven if the crumpled up cigarette package had in fact contained some sort of small weapon [and there is no indication the officer so believed or had reason to], it would have been impossible for respondent to have used it once [it] was in the officer's hands. Opening the package therefore did not further the protective purpose of the search. [The suggestion] that since the custodial arrest itself represents a significant intrusion into the privacy of the person, any additional intrusion by way of opening or examining effects found on the person is not worthy of constitutional protection . . . was expressly rejected in *Chimel*.

Schneckloth v. *Bustamonte*
412 U.S. 218 (1973)

A policeman stopped a car which was being driven at night with defective lights. When the driver failed to produce a driver's license, the officer asked for, and got, permission to search the car. The search produced some stolen checks. On the basis of this, and other, evidence, Bustamonte was convicted of improper possession of a check.

Mr. Justice Stewart delivered the opinion of the Court.

It is well settled under the Fourth and Fourteenth Amendments that a search conducted without a warrant issued upon probable cause is "per se unreasonable . . . subject only to a few specifically established and well-delineated exceptions." . . . . It is equally well settled that one of the specifically established exceptions to the requirements of both a warrant and probable cause is a search that is conducted pursuant to consent. . . . The constitutional question in the present case concerns the definition of "consent" in this Fourth and Fourteenth Amendment context. . . .

Our decision today is a narrow one. We hold only that when the subject of a search is not in custody and the State attempts to justify a search on the basis of his consent, the Fourth and Fourteenth Amendments require that it demonstrate that the consent was in fact voluntarily given, and not the result of duress or coercion, express or implied. Voluntariness is a question of fact to be determined from all the circumstances, and while the subject's knowledge of a right to refuse is a factor to be taken into account, the prosecution is not required to demonstrate such knowledge as a prerequisite to establishing a voluntary consent.

Judgment of Court of Appeals reversed.

Mr. Justice Douglas, dissenting.

I agree with the Court of Appeals that "verbal assent" to a search is not enough; that the fact that consent was given to the search does not imply that the suspect knew that the alternative of a refusal existed. 448 F.2d, at 700. As that court stated "under many circumstances a reasonable person might read an officer's 'May I' as the courteous expression of a demand backed by force of law." *Id.*, at 701.

A considerable constitutional guarantee rides on this narrow issue. At the time of the search there was no probable cause to believe that the car contained contraband or other unlawful articles. The car was stopped only because a headlight and the license plate light were burned out. The car belonged to Alcala's brother from whom it was borrowed and Alcala had a driver's license. Traffic citations were appropriately issued. The car was searched, the present record showing that Alcala consented. But whether Alcala knew he had the right to refuse, we do not know. All the Court of Appeals did was to remand the case to the District Court for a finding—and if necessary, a hearing on that issue.

I would let the case go forward on that basis. The long, time-consuming contest in this Court might well wash out. At least we could be assured that, if it came back, we would not be rendering an advisory opinion. Had I voted to grant this petition, I would suggest we dismiss it as improvidently granted. But being in the minority, I am bound by the rule of four.

[Justices Brennan and Marshall also dissented.]

Wolf v. *Colorado*
338 U.S. 25 (1949)

Mr. Justice Frankfurter delivered the opinion of the Court.

The precise question for consideration is this: Does a conviction by a State court for a State offense deny the "due process of law" required by the Fourteenth Amendment, solely because evidence that was admitted at the trial was obtained under circumstances which would have rendered it inadmissible in a prosecution for violation of a federal law in a court of the United States because there deemed to be an infraction of the Fourth Amendment as applied in *Weeks* v. *United States*, 232 U.S. 383? The Supreme Court of Colorado has sustained convictions in which such evidence was admitted, and we brought the cases here.

Unlike the specific requirements and restrictions placed by the Bill of Rights (Amendments I to VIII) upon the administration of criminal justice by federal authority, the Fourteenth Amendment did not subject criminal justice in the States to specific limitations. The notion that

the "due process of law" guaranteed by the Fourteenth Amendment is shorthand for the first eight amendments of the Constitution and thereby incorporates them has been rejected by this Court again and again, after impressive consideration. . . . The issue is closed.

For purposes of ascertaining the restrictions which the Due Process Clause imposed upon the States in the enforcement of their criminal law, we adhere to the views expressed in *Palko* v. *Connecticut*, 302 U.S. 319. That decision speaks to us with the great weight of the authority, particularly in matters of civil liberty, of a court that included Mr. Chief Justice Hughes, Mr. Justice Brandeis, Mr. Justice Stone and Mr. Justice Cardozo, to name only the dead. In rejecting the suggestion that the Due Process Clause incorporated the original Bill of Rights, Mr. Justice Cardozo reaffirmed on behalf of that Court a different but deeper and more pervasive conception of the Due Process Clause. This Clause exacts from the States for the lowliest and the most outcast all that is "implicit in the concept of ordered liberty." 302 U.S. at 325.

Due process of law thus conveys neither formal nor fixed nor narrow requirements. It is the compendious expression for all those rights which the courts must enforce because they are basic to our free society. But basic rights do not become petrified as of any one time, even though, as a matter of human experience, some may not too rhetorically be called eternal verities. It is of the very nature of a free society to advance in its standards of what is deemed reasonable and right. Representing as it does a living principle, due process is not confined within a permanent catalogue of what may at a given time be deemed the limits or the essentials of fundamental rights.

To rely on a tidy formula for the easy determination of what is a fundamental right for purposes of legal enforcement may satisfy a longing for certainty but ignores the movements of a free society. It belittles the scale of the conception of due process. The real clue to the problem confronting the judiciary in the application of the Due Process Clause is not to ask where the line is once and for all to be drawn but to recognize that it is for the Court to draw it by the gradual and empiric process of "inclusion and exclusion." *Davidson* v. *New Orleans*, 96 U.S. 97, 104. . . .

The security of one's privacy against arbitrary intrusion by the police—which is at the core of the Fourth Amendment—is basic to a free society. It is therefore implicit in "the concept of ordered liberty" and as such enforceable against the States through the Due Process Clause. The knock at the door, whether by day or by night, as a prelude to a search, without authority of law but solely on the authority of the police, did not need the commentary of recent history to be condemned as inconsistent with the conception of human rights enshrined in the history and the basic constitutional documents of English-speaking peoples.

Accordingly, we have no hesitation in saying that were a State affirmatively to sanction such police incursion into privacy it would run counter to the guaranty of the Fourteenth Amendment. But the ways of enforcing such a basic right raise questions of a different order. How such arbitrary conduct should be checked, what remedies against it should be afforded, the means by which the right should be made effective, are all questions that are not to be so dogmatically answered as to preclude the varying solutions which spring from an allowable range of judgment on issues not susceptible of quantitative solution.

In *Weeks* v. *United States*, *supra*, this Court held that in a federal prosecution the Fourth Amendment barred the use of evidence secured through an illegal search and seizure. This ruling was made for the first time in 1914. It was not derived from the explicit requirements of the Fourth Amendment; it was not based on legislation expressing Congressional policy in the enforcement of the Constitution. The decision was a matter of judicial implication. Since then it has been frequently applied and we stoutly adhere to it. But the immediate question

is whether the basic right to protection against arbitrary intrusion by the police demands the exclusion of logically relevant evidence obtained by an unreasonable search and seizure because, in a federal prosecution for a federal crime, it would be excluded. As a matter of inherent reason, one would suppose this to be an issue as to which men with complete devotion to the protection of the right of privacy might give different answers. When we find that in fact most of the English-speaking world does not regard as vital to such protection the exclusion of evidence thus obtained, we must hesitate to treat this remedy as an essential ingredient of the right. The contrariety of views of the States is particularly impressive in view of the careful reconsideration which they have given the problem in the light of the *Weeks* decision. . . .

The jurisdictions which have rejected the *Weeks* doctrine have not left the right to privacy without other means of protection. Indeed, the exclusion of evidence is a remedy which directly serves only to protect those upon whose person or premises something incriminating has been found. We cannot, therefore, regard it as a departure from basic standards to remand such persons, together with those who emerge scatheless from a search, to the remedies of private action and such protection as the internal discipline of the police, under the eyes of an alert public opinion, may afford. Granting that in practice the exclusion of evidence may be an effective way of deterring unreasonable searches, it is not for this Court to condemn as falling below the minimal standards assured by the Due Process Clause a State's reliance upon other methods which, if consistently enforced, would be equally effective. . . . We cannot brush aside the experience of States which deem the incidence of such conduct by the police too slight to call for a deterrent remedy not by way of disciplinary measures but by overriding the relevant rules of evidence. There are, moreover, reasons for excluding evidence unreasonably obtained by the federal police which are less compelling in the case of police under State or local authority. The public opinion of a community can far more effectively be exerted against oppressive conduct on the part of police directly responsible to the community itself than can local opinion, sporadically aroused, be brought to bear upon remote authority pervasively exerted throughout the country.

We hold, therefore, that in a prosecution in a State court for a State crime the Fourteenth Amendment does not forbid the admission of evidence obtained by an unreasonable search and seizure. And though we have interpreted the Fourth Amendment to forbid the admission of such evidence, a different question would be presented if Congress under its legislative powers were to pass a statute purporting to negate the *Weeks* doctrine. We would then be faced with the problem of the respect to be accorded the legislative judgment on an issue as to which, in default of that judgment, we have been forced to depend upon our own. Problems of a converse character, also not before us, would be presented should Congress under § 5 of the Fourteenth Amendment undertake to enforce the rights there guaranteed by attempting to make the *Weeks* doctrine binding upon the States.

Affirmed.

[Mr. Justice Black concurred; Justice Douglas dissented.]

Mr. Justice Murphy, with whom Mr. Justice Rutledge joins, dissenting.

It is disheartening to find so much that is right in an opinion which seems to me so fundamentally wrong. Of course I agree with the Court that the Fourteenth Amendment prohibits activities which are proscribed by the search and seizure clause of the Fourth Amendment. . . . It is difficult for me to understand how the Court can go this far and yet be unwilling to make the step which can give some meaning to the pronouncements it utters.

Imagination and zeal may invent a dozen methods to give content to the commands of the Fourth Amendment. But this Court is limited to the remedies currently available. It cannot legislate the ideal system. If we would attempt the enforcement of the search and seizure clause in the ordinary case today, we are limited to three devices: judicial exclusion of the illegally obtained evidence; criminal prosecution of violators; and civil action against violators in the action of trespass.

Alternatives are deceptive. Their very statement conveys the impression that one possibility is as effective as the next. In this case their statement is blinding. For there is but one alternative to the rule of exclusion. That is no sanction at all. . . .

. . . Little need be said concerning the possibilities of criminal prosecution. Self-scrutiny is a lofty ideal, but its exaltation reaches new heights if we expect a District Attorney to prosecute himself or his associates for well-meaning violations of the search and seizure clause during a raid the District Attorney or his associates have ordered. But there is an appealing ring in another alternative. A trespass action for damages is a venerable means of securing reparation for unauthorized invasion of the home. Why not put the old writ to a new use? When the Court cites cases permitting the action, the remedy seems complete.

But what an illusory remedy this is, if by "remedy" we mean a positive deterrent to police and prosecutors tempted to violate the Fourth Amendment. The appealing ring softens when we recall that in a trespass action the measure of damages is simply the extent of the injury to physical property. If the officer searches with care, he can avoid all but nominal damages—a penny, or a dollar. Are punitive damages possible? Perhaps. But a few states permit none, whatever the circumstances. In those that do, the plaintiff must show the real ill will or malice of the defendant, and surely it is not unreasonable to assume that one in honest pursuit of crime bears no malice toward the search victim. If that burden is carried, recovery may yet be defeated by the rule that there must be physical damages before punitive damages may be awarded. In addition, some states limit punitive damages to the actual expenses of litigation. See 61 *Harv.L.Rev.* 113, 119–120. Others demand some arbitrary ratio between actual and punitive damages before a verdict may stand. Even assuming the ill will of the officer, his reasonable grounds for belief that the home he searched harbored evidence of crime is admissible in mitigation of punitive damages. The bad reputation of the plaintiff is likewise admissible. If the evidence seized was actually used at a trial, that fact has been held a complete justification of the search, and a defense against the trespass action. And even if the plaintiff hurdles all these obstacles, and gains a substantial verdict, the individual officer's finances may well make the judgment useless—for the municipality, of course, is not liable without its consent. Is it surprising that there is so little in the books concerning trespass actions for violation of the search and seizure clause?

The conclusion is inescapable that but one remedy exists to deter violations of the search and seizure clause. That is the rule which excludes illegally obtained evidence. Only by exclusion can we impress upon the zealous prosecutor that violation of the Constitution will do him no good. And only when that point is driven home can the prosecutor be expected to emphasize the importance of observing constitutional demands in his instructions to the police.

If proof of the efficacy of the federal rule were needed, there is testimony in abundance in the recruit training programs and in-service courses provided the police in states which follow the federal rule. St. Louis, for example, demands extensive training in the rules of search and seizure, with emphasis upon the ease with which a case may collapse if it depends upon evidence obtained unlawfully. Current court decisions are digested and read at roll calls. The same general pattern prevails in Washington, D.C. In Dallas, officers are thoroughly briefed and instructed that "the courts will follow the rules very closely and will detect any frauds." In Milwaukee, a stout volume on the law of arrest and search and seizure is made the basis of extended instruction. Officer preparation in the applicable rules in Jackson, Mississippi, has included the lectures of an Associate Justice of the Mississippi Supreme Court. The instructions on evidence and search and seizure given to trainees in San Antonio carefully note the rule of exclusion in Texas, and close with this statement: "Every police officer should know the laws and the rules of evidence. Upon knowledge of these facts determines whether the . . . defendant will be convicted or acquitted. . . . When you investigate a case . . . remember throughout your investigation that only admissible evidence can be used."

But in New York City, we are informed simply that "copies of the State Penal Law and Code of Criminal Procedure" are given to officers, and that they are "kept advised" that illegally obtained evidence may be admitted in New York courts. In Baltimore, a "Digest of Laws" is distributed, and it is made clear that the statutory section excluding evidence "is limited in its application to the trial of misdemeanors. . . . It would appear . . . that . . . evidence illegally obtained may still be admissible in the trial of felonies." In Cleveland, recruits and other officers are told of the rules of search and seizure, but "instructed that it is admissible in the courts of Ohio. The Ohio Supreme Court has indicated very definitely and clearly that Ohio belongs to the 'admissionist' group of states when evidence obtained by an illegal search is presented to the court." A similar pattern emerges in Birmingham, Alabama.

The contrast between states with the federal rule and those without it is thus a positive demonstration of its efficacy. . . . [T]he examples cited above serve to ground an assumption that has motivated this Court since the *Weeks* case: that this is an area in which judicial action has positive effect upon the breach of law; and that, without judicial action, there are simply no effective sanctions presently available. . . .

Mapp v. *Ohio*
367 U.S. 643 (1961)

Mr. Justice Clark delivered the opinion of the Court.

. . . The Court's reasons [in *Wolf*] for not considering essential to the right to privacy, as a curb imposed upon the States by Due Process Clause, that which decades before had been posited as part and parcel of the Fourth Amendment's limitation upon federal encroachment of individual privacy, were bottomed on factual considerations.

While they are not basically relevant to a decision that the exclusionary rule is an essential ingredient of the Fourth Amendment as the right it embodies is vouchsafed against the States by Due Process Clause, we will consider the current validity of the factual ground upon which *Wolf* was based.

. . . While in 1949, prior to the *Wolf* case, almost two-thirds of the States were opposed to the use of the exclusionary rule, now, despite the *Wolf* case, more than half of those since passing upon it, by their own legislative or judicial decision, have wholly or partly adopted or adhered to the *Weeks* rule. Significantly, among those now following the rule is California, which, according to its highest court, was "compelled to reach that conclusion because other remedies have completely failed to secure compliance with the constitutional provisions. . . ." In connection with this California case, we note that the second basis elaborated in *Wolf* in support of its failure to enforce the exclusionary doctrine against the States was that "other means of protection" have been afforded "the right to privacy." 338 U.S., at 30. The experience of California that such other remedies have been worthless and futile is buttressed by the experience of other States. . . .

It, therefore, plainly appears that the factual considerations supporting the failure of the *Wolf* Court to include the *Weeks* exclusionary rule when it recognized the enforceability of the right to privacy against the States in 1949, while not basically relevant to the constitutional consideration, could not, in any analysis, now be deemed controlling. . . .

. . . Today we once again examine *Wolf's* constitutional documentation of the right to privacy free from unreasonable state intrusion, and, after its dozen years on our books, are led by it to close the only courtroom door remaining open to evidence secured by official lawlessness in flagrant abuse of that basic right, reserved to all persons as a specific guarantee against that very same unlawful conduct. We hold that all evidence obtained by searches and seizures in violation of the Constitution is, by that same authority, inadmissible in a state court.

Since the Fourth Amendment's right of privacy has been declared enforceable against the States through the Due Process Clause of the Fourteenth, it is enforceable against them by the same sanction of exclusion as is used against the Federal Government. Were it otherwise, then just as without the *Weeks* rule the assurance against unreasonable federal searches and seizures would be "a form of words," valueless and undeserving of mention in a perpetual charter of inestimable human liberties, so too, without that rule the freedom from state invasions of privacy would be so ephemeral and so neatly severed from its conceptual nexus with the freedom from all brutish means of coercing evidence as not to merit this Court's high regard as a freedom "implicit in the concept of ordered liberty." . . . To hold otherwise is to grant the right but in reality to withhold its privilege and enjoyment. Only last year the Court itself recognized that the purpose of the exclusionary rule "is to deter—to compel respect for the constitutional guaranty in the only effectively available way—by removing the incentive to disregard it." *Elkins* v. *United States* [364 U.S. 206, 217 (1960)].

Indeed, we are aware of no restraint, similar to that rejected today, conditioning the enforcement of any other basic constitutional right. The right to privacy, no less important than any other right carefully and particularly reserved to the people, would stand in marked contrast to all other rights declared as "basic to a free society." *Wolf* v. *Colorado, supra,* at 27. This Court has not hesitated to enforce as strictly against the States as it does against the Federal Government the rights of free speech and of a free press, the rights to notice and to a fair, public trial, including, as it does, the right not to be convicted by use of a coerced confession, however logically relevant it be, and without regard to its reliability. *Rogers* v. *Richmond,* 365 U.S. 534 (1961). And nothing could be more certain than that when a coerced confession is involved, "the relevant rules of evidence" are overridden without regard to "the incidence of such conduct by the police," slight or frequent. Why should not the same rule apply to what is tantamount to coerced testimony by way of unconstitutional seizure of goods, papers, effects, documents, etc.? . . .

Moreover, our holding that the exclusionary rule is an essential part of both the Fourth and Fourteenth Amendments is not only the logical dictate of prior cases, but it also makes very good sense. There is no war between the Constitution and common sense. Presently, a federal prosecutor may make no use of evidence illegally seized, but a State's attorney across the street may, although he supposedly is operating under the enforceable prohibitions of the same Amendment. Thus the State, by admitting evidence unlawfully seized, serves to encourage disobedience to the Federal Constitution which it is bound to uphold. Moreover, as was said in *Elkins,* "[t]he very essence of a healthy federalism depends upon the avoidance of needless conflict between state and federal courts." 364 U.S., at 221. Such a conflict, hereafter needless, arose this very Term, in *Wilson* v. *Schnettler,* 365 U.S. 381 (1961), in which, and in spite of the promise made by *Rea,* we gave full recognition to our practice in this regard by refusing to restrain a federal officer from testifying in a state court as to evidence unconstitutionally seized by him in the performance of his duties. Yet the double standard recognized until today hardly put such a thesis into practice. In nonexclusionary States, federal officers, being human, were by it invited to and did, as our cases indicate, step across the street to the State's attorney with their unconstitutionally seized evidence. Prosecution on the basis of that evidence was then had in a state court in utter disregard of the enforceable Fourth Amendment. If the fruits of an unconstitutional search had been inadmissible in both state and federal courts, this inducement to evasion would have been sooner eliminated. . . .

Federal-state cooperation in the solution of crime under constitutional standards will be promoted, if only by recognition of their now mutual obligation to respect the same fundamental criteria in their approaches. . . .

There are those who say, as did Justice (then Judge) Cardozo, that under our constitutional exclusionary doctrine "[t]he criminal is to go free because the constable has blundered." *People* v. *Defore,* 242 N.Y., at 21, 150 N.E., at 587. In some cases this will undoubtedly be the result. But, as was said in *Elkins,* "there is another consideration—the imperative of judicial integrity." 364 U.S., at 222. The criminal goes free, if he must, but it is the law that sets him free. Nothing can destroy a government more quickly than its failure to observe its own laws, or worse, its disregard of the charter of its own existence. As Mr. Justice Brandeis, dissenting, said in *Olmstead* v. *United States,* 277 U.S. 438, 485 (1928): "Our Government is the potent, the omnipresent teacher. For good or for ill, it teaches the whole people by its example. . . . If the Government becomes a lawbreaker, it breeds contempt for law; it invites every man to become a law unto himself; it invites anarchy." Nor can it lightly be assumed that, as a practical matter, adoption of the exclusionary rule fetters law enforcement. Only last year this Court expressly considered that contention and found that "pragmatic evidence of a sort" to the contrary was not wanting. *Elkins* v. *United States, supra,* at 218. The Court noted that

> "The federal courts themselves have operated under the exclusionary rule of *Weeks* for almost half a century; yet it has not been suggested either that the Federal Bureau of Investigation has thereby been rendered ineffective, or that the administration of criminal justice in the federal courts has thereby been disrupted. Moreover, the experience of the states is impressive. . . . The movement towards the rule of exclusion has been halting but seemingly inexorable." *Id.,* at 218–219.

[Justices Black, Douglas, and Stewart concurred; Justices Frankfurter, Whittaker, and Harlan dissented.]

Note: Evidence outlawed by the exclusionary rule may lead the police to *other* evidence. Use of the latter is outlawed as "fruit of the poisonous tree." See *Wong Sun* v. *United States,* 371 U.S. 338 (1974).

Linkletter v. *Walker*
381 U.S. 618 (1965)

Mr. Justice Clark delivered the opinion of the Court.

. . . heretofore, without discussion, we have applied new constitutional rules to cases finalized before promulgation of the rule [but] the Constitution neither prohibits nor requires retrospective effect.

[In deciding whether to apply a new rule retroactively, we must look to the] prior history of the rule in question, its purpose and effect, and whether retrospective operation will further or retard its operation. [*Mapp's*] prime purpose [was] enforcement of the Fourth Amendment through the [exclusionary rule]. This, it was found, was the only effective deterrence against lawless police action. [T]his purpose [would not] be advanced by making the rule retrospective. The misconduct of the police prior to *Mapp* has already occurred and will not be corrected by releasing the prisoners involved. Nor would it add harmony to the delicate state-federal relationship of which we have spoken as part and parcel of the purpose of *Mapp.* Finally, the ruptured privacy of the victim's homes and effects cannot be restored. Reparation comes too late.

[Moreover, the deterrence purpose of *Mapp*] will not at this late date be served by the wholesale release of the guilty victims [of improper searches].

[To] make [*Mapp*] retrospective would tax the administration of justice to the utmost. Hearings would have to be held on the excludability of evidence long since destroyed, misplaced or deteriorated. If it is excluded, [witnesses may no longer be available] or if located their memory will be dimmed. To thus legitimate such an extraordinary procedural weapon that has no bearing on guilt would seriously disrupt the administration of justice.

[Although we have applied *Gideon, Griffin* v. *Illinois* and "coerced confession" cases retrospectively, those principles] went to the fairness of the trial—the very integrity of the fact-finding process. [Here,] the fairness of the trial is not under attack.

Mr. Justice Black, with whom Mr. Justice Douglas joins, dissenting. . . .

. . . Despite the Court's resounding promises throughout the *Mapp* opinion that convictions based on such "unconstitutional evidence" would " 'find no sanction in the judgments of the courts,' " Linkletter, convicted in the state court by use of "unconstitutional evidence," is today denied relief by the judgment of this Court because his conviction became "final" before *Mapp* was decided. Linkletter must stay in jail; Miss Mapp, whose offense was committed before Linkletter's, is free. This different treatment of Miss Mapp and Linkletter points up at once the arbitrary and discriminatory nature of the judicial contrivance utilized here to break the promise of *Mapp* by keeping all people in jail who are unfortunate enough to

have had their unconstitutional convictions affirmed before June 19, 1961.

> *Quaere: Linkletter* gives some people a "right", yet denies it to others similarly situated. Would the Court permit a legislature to classify or "discriminate" in a similar fashion? See Chapter 9, "Equal Protection of the Law," below.

What the Court Gives It May Take Away: The Decline of the Exclusionary Rule

The Warren Court's decision in *Linkletter* surely suggests something less than full sympathy for the exclusionary rule. In *Bivens* v. *Six Unknown Named Agents*, 403 U.S. 388 (1971), Chief Justice Burger in dissent launched the following attack upon it:

> Some clear demonstration of the benefits and effectiveness of the Exclusionary Rule is required to justify it in view of the high price it extracts from society—the release of countless guilty criminals. But there is no empirical evidence to support the claim that the rule actually deters illegal conduct of law enforcement officials. Oaks, Studying the Exclusionary Rule in Search and Seizure, 37 *U.Chi. L.Rev.* 665, 667 (1970).
>
> There are several reasons for this failure. The rule does not apply any direct sanction to the individual official whose illegal conduct results in the exclusion of evidence in a criminal trial. With rare exceptions law enforcement agencies do not impose direct sanctions on the individual officer responsible for a particular judicial application of the Suppression Doctrine. Oaks at 710. Thus there is virtually nothing done to bring about a change in his practices. The immediate sanction triggered by the application of the rule is visited upon the prosecutor whose case against a criminal is either weakened or destroyed. The doctrine deprives the police in no real sense; except that apprehending wrongdoers is their business, police have no more stake in successful prosecutions than prosecutors or the public.
>
> The Suppression Doctrine vaguely assumes that law enforcement is a monolithic governmental enterprise. . . . But the prosecutor who loses his case because of police misconduct is not an official in the police department; he can rarely set in motion any corrective action or administrative penalties. Moreover, he does not have control or direction over police procedures or police action that lead to the exclusion of evidence. It is the rare exception when a prosecutor takes part in arrests, searches, or seizures so that he can guide police action.
>
> Whatever educational effect the rule conceivably might have in theory is greatly diminished in fact by the realities of law enforcement work. Policemen do not have the time, inclination, or training to read and grasp the nuances of the appellate opinions that ultimately define the standards of conduct they are to follow. . . . The presumed educational effect of judicial opinions is also reduced by the long time lapse—often several years—between the original police action and its final judicial evaluation. Given a policeman's pressing responsibilities, it would be surprising if he ever becomes aware of the final result after such a delay. Finally the Exclusionary Rule's deterrent impact is diluted by the fact that there are large areas of police activity which do not result in

criminal prosecutions—hence the rule has virtually no applicability and no effect in such situations. . . .

Although unfortunately ineffective, the Exclusionary Rule has increasingly been characterized by a single, monolithic, and drastic judicial response to all official violations of legal norms. Inadvertent errors of judgment that do not work any grave injustice will inevitably occur under the pressure of police work. These honest mistakes have been treated in the same way as deliberate and flagrant *Irvine*-type violations of the Fourth Amendment. . . .

I submit that society has at least as much right to expect rationally graded responses from judges in place of the universal "capital punishment" we inflict on all evidence when police error is shown in its acquisition. See ALI, *A Model Code of Pre-Arraignment Procedure* § 8.02(2), at 23 (Tent. Draft No. 4, 1971) [providing that evidence obtained in violation of the proposed code shall be excluded "only if the court finds that such violation was substantial," taking into account such factors as "the extent to which the violation was willful," "the extent to which privacy was invaded," and "the extent to which exclusion will tend to prevent violations of this Code."] Yet for over 55 years . . . our legal system has treated vastly dissimilar cases as if they were the same. . . .

Instead of continuing to enforce the Suppression Doctrine, inflexibly, rigidly, and mechanically, we should view it as one of the experimental steps in the great tradition of the Common Law and acknowledge its shortcomings. But in the same spirit we should be prepared to discontinue what the experience of over half a century has shown neither deters errant officers nor affords a remedy to the totally innocent victims of official misconduct.

I do not propose, however, that we abandon the Suppression Doctrine until some meaningful alternative can be developed. In a sense our legal system has become the captive of its own creation. To overrule *Weeks* and *Mapp,* even assuming the Court was now prepared to take that step, could raise yet new problems. Obviously the public interest would be poorly served if law enforcement officials were suddenly to gain the impression, however erroneous, that all constitutional restraints on police had somehow been removed—that an open season on "criminals" had been declared. I am concerned lest some such mistaken impression might be fostered by a flat overruling of the Suppression Doctrine cases. For years we have relied upon it as the exclusive remedy for unlawful official conduct; in a sense we are in a situation akin to the narcotics addict whose dependence on drugs precludes any drastic or immediate withdrawal of the supposed prop, regardless of how futile its continued use may be.

Reasonable and effective substitutes can be formulated if Congress would take the lead, as it did for example in 1946 in the Federal Tort Claims Act. I see no insuperable obstacle to the elimination of the Suppression Doctrine if Congress would provide some meaningful and effective remedy against unlawful conduct by government officials. . . .

I conclude, therefore, that an entirely different remedy is necessary but it is [beyond our judicial power]. Congress should develop an administrative or quasi-judicial remedy against the government itself to afford compensation and restitution for persons whose Fourth Amendment rights have been violated. . . .

Once the constitutional validity of [the appropriate] statute is established, it can reasonably be assumed that the States would develop their own remedial systems on the federal model. Indeed there is nothing to prevent a State from enacting a comparable statutory scheme without waiting on the Congress. . . . Independent of the alternative embraced in this dissenting opinion, I believe the time has come to re-examine the scope of the Exclusionary Rule and consider at least some narrowing of its thrust so as to eliminate the anomalies it has produced.

In *United States* v. *Calandra*, 414 U.S. 338 (1971), six of the Justices refused extension of the exclusionary rule to grand jury proceedings:

> Any incremental deterrent effect which might be achieved by extending the rule to grand jury proceedings is uncertain at best. Whatever deterrence of police misconduct may result from the exclusion of illegally seized evidence from criminal trials, it is unrealistic to assume that the application of the rule to grand jury proceedings would significantly further that goal. Such an extension would deter only police investigation consciously directed toward the discovery of evidence solely for use in a grand jury investigation. . . .
>
> We therefore decline to embrace a view that would achieve a speculative and undoubtedly minimal advance in the deterrence of police misconduct at the expense of substantially impeding the role of the grand jury.

For similar reasons (after a lengthy examination of the whole matter), the Court held in *Stone* v. *Powell,* 428 U.S. 465 (1976), that

> . . . where the State has provided an opportunity for full and fair litigation of a Fourth Amendment claim, a state prisoner may not be granted federal habeas corpus relief on the ground that evidence obtained in an unconstitutional search or seizure was introduced at his trial. In this context the contribution of the exclusionary rule, if any, to the effectuation of the Fourth Amendment is minimal and the substantial societal costs of application of the rule persist with special force.

Only Justices Brennan and Marshall rejected their colleagues' obvious disenchantment with the exclusionary rule. In their view *Mapp* still stands undiminished, but "to-day's holding portends evisceration of federal habeas corpus . . . ."

CONFESSIONS AND SELF–INCRIMINATION

Watts v. *Indiana*
388 U.S. 49 (1949)

The prevailing opinion here relates only to *Watts*. Mr. Justice Jackson's concurring opinion covers *Watts* and two other cases.

Mr. Justice Frankfurter announced the judgment of the Court and an opinion in which Mr. Justice Murphy and Mr. Justice Rutledge join. . . .

. . . There is torture of mind as well as body; the will is as much affected by fear as by force. And there comes a point where this Court should not be ignorant as judges of what we know as men. See Taft, C. J., in the *Child Labor Tax Case,* 259 U.S. 20, 37.

This brings us to the undisputed circumstances which must determine the issue of due process in this case. Thanks to the forthrightness of counsel for Indiana, these circumstances may be briefly stated.

On November 12, 1947, a Wednesday, petitioner was arrested and held as the suspected perpetrator of an alleged criminal assault earlier in the day. Later the same day, in the vicinity of this occurrence, a woman was found dead under conditions suggesting murder in the course of an attempted criminal assault. Suspicion of murder quickly turned towards petitioner and the police began to question him. They took him from the county jail to State Police Headquarters, where he was questioned by officers in relays from about 11:30 that night until sometime between 2:30 and 3 o'clock the following morning. The same procedure of persistent interrogation from about 5:30 in the afternoon until about 3 o'clock the following morning, by a relay of six to eight officers, was pursued on Thursday the 13th, Friday the 14th, Saturday the 15th, Monday the 17th. Sunday was a day of rest from interrogation. About 3 o'clock on Tuesday morning, November 18, the petitioner made an incriminating statement after continuous questioning since 6 o'clock of the preceding evening. The statement did not satisfy the prosecutor who had been called in and he then took petitioner in hand. Petitioner, questioned by an interrogator of twenty years' experience as lawyer, judge and prosecutor, yielded a more incriminating document.

Until his inculpatory statements were secured, the petitioner was a prisoner in the exclusive control of the prosecuting authorities. He was kept for the first two days in solitary confinement in a cell aptly enough called "the hole" in view of its physical conditions as described by the State's witnesses. Apart from the five night sessions, the police intermittently interrogated Watts during the day and on three days drove him around town, hours at a time, with a view to eliciting identifications and other disclosures. Although the law of Indiana required that petitioner be given a prompt preliminary hearing before a magistrate, with all the protection a hearing was intended to give him, the petitioner was not only given no hearing during the entire period of interrogation but was without friendly or professional aid and without advice as to his constitutional rights. Disregard of rudimentary needs of life—opportunities for sleep and a decent allowance of food—are also relevant, not as aggravating

elements of petitioner's treatment, but as part of the total situation out of which his confessions came and which stamped their character.

A confession by which life becomes forfeit must be the expression of free choice. A statement to be voluntary of course need not be volunteered. But if it is the product of sustained pressure by the police it does not issue from a free choice. When a suspect speaks because he is overborne, it is immaterial whether he has been subjected to a physical or a mental ordeal. Eventual yielding to questioning under such circumstances is plainly the product of the suction process of interrogation and therefore the reverse of voluntary. We would have to shut our minds to the plain significance of what here transpired to deny that this was a calculated endeavor to secure a confession through the pressure of unrelenting interrogation. The very relentlessness of such interrogation implies that it is better for the prisoner to answer than to persist in the refusal of disclosure which is his constitutional right. To turn the detention of an accused into a process of wrenching from him evidence which could not be extorted in open court with all its safeguards, is so grave an abuse of the power of arrest as to offend the procedural standards of due process.

This is so because it violates the underlying principle in our enforcement of the criminal law. Ours is the accusatorial as opposed to the inquisitorial system. Such has been the characteristic of Anglo-American criminal justice since it freed itself from practices borrowed by the Star Chamber from the Continent whereby an accused was interrogated in secret for hours on end. See Ploscowe, The Development of Present-Day Criminal Procedures in Europe and America, 48 *Harv.L.Rev.* 433, 457–58, 467–473 (1935). Under our system society carries the burden of proving its charge against the accused not out of his own mouth. It must establish its case, not by interrogation of the accused even under judicial safeguards, but by evidence independently secured through skillful investigation. "The law will not suffer a prisoner to be made the deluded instrument of his own conviction." 2 Hawkins, *Pleas of the Crown*, c. 46, § 34 (8th ed., 1824). The requirement of specific charges, their proof beyond a reasonable doubt, the protection of the accused from confessions extorted through whatever form of police pressures, the right to a prompt hearing before a magistrate, the right to assistance of counsel, to be supplied by government when circumstances make it necessary, the duty to advise an accused of his constitutional rights—these are all characteristics of the accusatorial system and manifestations of its demands. Protracted, systematic and uncontrolled subjection of an accused to interrogation by the police for the purpose of eliciting disclosures or confessions is subversive of the accusatorial system. It is the inquisitorial system without its safeguards. For while under that system the accused is subjected to judicial interrogation, he is protected by the disinterestedness of the judge in the presence of counsel. See Keedy, The Preliminary Investigation of Crime in France, 88 *U. of Pa.L.Rev.* 692, 708–712 (1940).

In holding that the Due Process Clause bars police procedure which violates the basic notions of our accusatorial mode of prosecuting crime and vitiates a conviction based on the fruits of such procedure, we apply the Due Process Clause to its historic function of assuring appropriate procedure before liberty is curtailed or life is taken. We are deeply mindful of the anguishing problems which the incidence of crime presents to the States. But the history of the criminal law proves overwhelmingly that brutal methods of law enforcement are essentially self-defeating, whatever may be their effect in a particular case. See, e.g., Radzinowicz, *A History of English Criminal Law and its Administration from 1750, passim* (1948). Law triumphs when the natural impulses aroused by a shocking crime yield to the safeguards which our civilization has evolved for an administration of criminal justice at once rational and effective.

We have examined petitioner's other contentions and do not sustain them.

[The concurring opinions of Justices Black and Douglas are omitted.]

Mr. Justice Jackson concurring in the result in No. 610 and dissenting in Nos. 76 and 107.

These three cases, from widely separated states, present essentially the same problem. Its recurrence suggests that it has roots in some condition fundamental and general to our criminal system.

In each case police were confronted with one or more brutal murders which the authorities were under the highest duty to solve. Each of these murders was unwitnessed, and the only positive knowledge on which a solution could be based was possessed by the killer. In each there was reasonable ground to *suspect* an individual but not enough legal evidence to *charge* him with guilt. In each the police attempted to meet the situation by taking the suspect into custody and interrogating him. This extended over varying periods. In each, confessions were made and received in evidence at the trial. Checked with external evidence, they are inherently believable, and were not shaken as to truth by anything that occurred at the trial. Each confessor was convicted by a jury and state courts affirmed. This Court sets all three convictions aside.

The seriousness of the Court's judgment is that no one suggests that any course held promise of solution of these murders other than to take the suspect into custody for questioning. The alternative was to close the books on the crime and forget it, with the suspect at large. This is a grave choice for a society in which two-thirds of the murders already are closed out as insoluble.

A concurring opinion, however, goes to the very limit and seems to declare for outlawing any confession, however freely given, if obtained during a period of custody between arrest and arraignment—which, in practice, means all of them.

Others would strike down these confessions because of conditions which they say make them "involuntary." In this, on only a printed record, they pit their judgment against that of the trial judge and the jury. Both, with the great advantage of hearing and seeing the confessor and also the officers whose conduct and bearing toward him is in question, have found that the confessions were voluntary. In addition, the majority overrule in each case one or more state appellate courts, which have the same limited opportunity to know the truth that we do.

Amid much that is irrelevant or trivial, one serious situation seems to me to stand out in these cases. The suspect neither had nor was advised of his right to get counsel. This presents a real dilemma in a free society. To subject one without counsel to questioning which may and is intended to convict him, is a real peril to individual freedom. To bring in a lawyer means a real peril to solution of the crime, because, under our adversary system, he deems that his sole duty is to protect his client—guilty or innocent—and that in such a capacity he owes no duty whatever to help society solve its crime problem. Under this conception of criminal procedure, any lawyer worth his salt will tell the suspect in no uncertain terms to make no statement to police under any circumstances.

If the State may arrest on suspicion and interrogate without counsel, there is no denying the fact that it largely negates the benefits of the constitutional guaranty of the right to assistance of counsel. Any lawyer who has ever been called into a case after his client has "told all" and turned any evidence he has over to the Government, knows how helpless he is to protect his client against the facts thus disclosed.

I suppose the view one takes will turn on what one thinks should be the right of an accused person against the State. Is it his right to have the judgment on the facts? Or is it his right to have a judgment based on only such evidence as he cannot conceal from the authorities, who cannot compel him to testify in court and also cannot question him before? Our system comes close to the latter by any interpretation, for the defendant is shielded by such safeguards as no system of law except the Anglo-American concedes to him.

Of course, no confession that has been obtained by any form of physical violence to the person is reliable and hence no conviction should rest upon one obtained in that manner. Such treatment not only breaks the will to conceal or lie, but may even break the will to stand by the truth. Nor is it questioned that the same result can sometimes be achieved by threats, promises, or inducements, which torture the mind but put no scar on the body. . . . But if [the] ultimate quest in a criminal trial is the truth and if the circumstances indicate no violence or threats of it, should society be deprived of the suspect's help in solving a crime merely because he was confined and questioned when uncounseled?

We must not overlook that, in these as in some previous cases, once a confession is obtained it supplies ways of verifying its trustworthiness. In these cases before us the verification is sufficient to leave me in no doubt that the admissions of guilt were genuine and truthful. Such corroboration consists in one case of finding a weapon where the accused has said he hid it, and in others that conditions which could only have been known to one who was implicated correspond with his story. It is possible, but it is rare, that a confession, if repudiated on the trial, standing alone will convict unless there is external proof of its verity.

In all such cases, along with other conditions criticized, the continuity and duration of the questioning is invoked and it is called an "inquiry," "inquest" or "inquisition," depending mainly on the emotional state of the writer. But as in some of the cases here, if interrogation is permissible at all, there are sound reasons for prolonging it—which the opinions here ignore. The suspect at first perhaps makes an effort to exculpate himself by alibis or other statements. These are verified, found false, and he is then confronted with his falsehood. Sometimes (though such cases do not reach us) verification proves them true or credible and the suspect is released. Sometimes, as here, more than one crime is involved. The duration of an interrogation may well depend on the temperament, shrewdness and cunning of the accused and the competence of the examiner. But, assuming a right to examine at all, the right must include what is made reasonably necessary by the facts of the particular case.

If the right of interrogation be admitted, then it seems to me that we must leave it to trial judges and juries and state appellate courts to decide individual cases, unless they show some want of proper standards of decision. I find nothing to indicate that any of the courts below in these cases did not have a correct understanding of the Fourteenth Amendment, unless this Court thinks it means absolute prohibition of interrogation while in custody before arraignment.

I suppose no one would doubt that our Constitution and Bill of Rights, grounded in revolt against the arbitrary measures of George III and in the philosophy of the French Revolution, represent the maximum restrictions upon the power of organized society over the individual that are compatible with the maintenance of organized society itself. They were so intended and should be so interpreted. It cannot be denied that, even if construed as these provisions traditionally have been, they contain an aggregate of restrictions which seriously limit the power of society to solve such crimes as confront us in these cases. Those restrictions we should not for that reason cast aside, but that is good reason for indulging in no unnecessary expansion of them.

I doubt very much if they require us to hold that the State may not take into custody and question one suspected reasonably of an unwitnessed murder. If it does, the people of this country must discipline themselves to seeing their police stand by helplessly while those suspected of murder prowl about unmolested. Is it a necessary price to pay for the fairness which we know as "due process of law"? And if not a necessary one, should it be demanded by this Court? I do not know the ultimate answer to these questions; but, for the present, I should not increase the handicap on society.

Mallory v. *United States*
354 U.S. 449 (1957)

Both *Watts* (above) and *Schmerber* (below) involve state proceedings and constitutional requirements. The present case involves a federal trial and the Federal Rules of Criminal Procedure. Reversing a conviction for rape, the Court, per Mr. Justice Frankfurter, said in part:

In *McNabb* v. *United States*, 318 U.S. 332, 343–344, . . . the Court held that police detention of defendants beyond the time when a committing magistrate was readily accessible constituted "wilful disobedience of law." In order adequately to enforce the congressional requirement of prompt arraignment, it was deemed necessary to render inadmissible incriminating statements elicited from defendants during a period of unlawful detention.

In *Upshaw* v. *United States*, 335 U.S. 410, which came here after the Federal Rules of Criminal Procedure had been in operation, the Court made it clear that Rule 5(a)'s standard of "without unnecessary delay" implied no relaxation of the McNabb doctrine.

The requirement of Rule 5(a) is part of the procedure devised by Congress for safeguarding individual rights without hampering effective and intelligent law enforcement. Provisions related to Rule 5(a) contemplate a procedure that allows arresting officers little more leeway than the interval between arrest and the ordinary administrative steps required to bring a suspect before the nearest available magistrate. . . .

The scheme for initiating a federal prosecution is plainly defined. The police may not arrest upon mere suspicion but only on "probable cause." The next step in the proceeding is to arraign the arrested person before a judicial officer as quickly as possible so that he may be advised of his rights and so that the issue of probable cause may be promptly determined. The arrested person may, of course, be "booked" by the police. But he is not to be taken to police headquarters in order to carry out a process of inquiry that lends itself, even if not so designed, to eliciting damaging statements to support the arrest and ultimately his guilt.

The duty enjoined upon arresting officers to arraign "without unnecessary delay" indicates that the command does not call for mechanical or automatic obedience. Circumstances may justify a brief delay between arrest and arraignment, as for instance, where the story volunteered by the accused is susceptible of quick verification through third parties. But the delay must not be of a nature to give opportunity for the extraction of a confession.

The circumstances of this case preclude a holding that arraignment was "without unnecessary delay." Petitioner was arrested in the early afternoon and was detained at headquarters within the vicinity of numerous committing magistrates. Even though the police had ample evidence from other sources than the petitioner for regarding the petitioner as the chief suspect, they first questioned him for ap-

proximately a half hour. When this inquiry of a nineteen-year-old lad of limited intelligence produced no confession, the police asked him to submit to a "lie-detector" test. He was not told of his rights to counsel or to a preliminary examination before a magistrate, nor was he warned that he might keep silent and "that any statement made by him may be used against him." After four hours of further detention at headquarters, during which arraignment could easily have been made in the same building in which the police headquarters were housed, petitioner was examined by the lie-detector operator for another hour and a half before his story began to waver. Not until he had confessed, when any judicial caution had lost its purpose, did the police arraign him.

We cannot sanction this extended delay, resulting in confession, without subordinating the general rule of prompt arraignment to the discretion of arresting officers in finding exceptional circumstances for its disregard. In every case where the police resort to interrogation of an arrested person and secure a confession, they may well claim, and quite sincerely, that they were merely trying to check on the information given by him. Against such a claim and the evil potentialities of the practice for which it is urged stands Rule 5(a) as a barrier. Nor is there an escape from the constraint laid upon the police by that Rule in that two other suspects were involved for the same crime. Presumably, whomever the police arrest they must arrest on "probable cause." It is not the function of the police to arrest, as it were, at large and to use an interrogating process at police headquarters in order to determine whom they should charge before a committing magistrate on "probable cause."

Miranda v. *Arizona* (and two related cases)
384 U.S. 436 (1966)

Here, as in so many rape cases, there were no outside witnesses. In a police lineup the complaining witness identified Miranda as her assailant. There could be no prosecution on that basis alone, for it would be merely her word against his. *Convic-*

tion requires proof of guilt beyond reasonable doubt! Thus, as usual when no other probative evidence is available (two) policemen (in an "interrogation room") questioned Miranda. Within two hours they emerged with a written, signed confession. This, plus the identification by the complainant, produced a conviction. Miranda, age 23, had left school midway through the ninth grade. A medical report indicated he had an "emotional illness" of a schizophrenic nature.

Mr. Chief Justice Warren delivered the opinion of the Court.

The cases before us raise questions which go to the roots of our concepts of American criminal jurisprudence: the restraints society must observe consistent with the Federal Constitution in prosecuting individuals of crime. More specifically, we deal with the admissibility of statements obtained from an individual who is subjected to custodial police interrogation and the necessity for procedures which assure that the individual is accorded his privilege under the Fifth Amendment to the Constitution not to be compelled to incriminate himself.

We dealt with certain phases of this problem recently in *Escobedo* v. *Illinois*, 378 U.S. 478 (1964). There, as in the four cases before us, law enforcement officials took the defendant into custody and interrogated him in a police station for the purpose of obtaining a confession. The police did not effectively advise him of his right to remain silent or of his right to consult with his attorney. Rather, they confronted him with an alleged accomplice who accused him of having perpetrated a murder. When the defendant denied the accusation and said "I didn't shoot Manuel, you did it," they handcuffed him and took him to an interrogation room. There, while handcuffed and standing, he was questioned for four hours until he confessed. During this interrogation, the police denied his request to speak to his attorney, and they prevented his retained attorney, who had come to the police station, from consulting with him. At his trial, the State, over his objection, introduced the confession against him. We held that the statements thus made were constitutionally inadmissible.

This case has been the subject of judicial in-terpretation and spirited legal debate since it was decided two years ago. Both state and federal courts, in assessing its implications, have arrived at varying conclusions. A wealth of scholarly material has been written tracing its ramifications and underpinnings. Police and prosecutor have speculated on its range and desirability. We granted certiorari in these cases . . . in order further to explore some facets of the problems, thus exposed, of applying the privilege against self-incrimination to incustody interrogation, and to give concrete constitutional guidelines for law enforcement agencies and courts to follow.

We start here, as we did in *Escobedo*, with the premise that our holding is not an innovation in our jurisprudence, but is an application of principles long recognized and applied in other settings. We have undertaken a thorough reexamination of the *Escobedo* decision and the principles it announced, and we reaffirm it. That case was but an explication of basic rights that are enshrined in our Constitution—that "No person . . . shall be compelled in any criminal case to be a witness against himself," and that "the accused shall . . . have the Assistance of Counsel"—rights which were put in jeopardy in that case through official overbearing. These precious rights were fixed in our Constitution only after centuries of persecution and struggle. And in the words of Chief Justice Marshall, they were secured "for ages to come, and . . . designed to approach immortality as nearly as human institutions can approach it". . . . Our holding will be spelled out with some specificity in the pages which follow but briefly stated it is this: the prosecution may not use statements, whether exculpatory or inculpatory, stemming from custodial interrogation of the defendant unless it demonstrates the use of procedural safeguards effective to secure the privilege against self-incrimination. By custodial interrogation, we mean questioning initiated by law enforcement officers after a person has been taken into custody or otherwise deprived of his freedom of action in any significant way. As for the procedural safeguards to be employed, unless other fully effective means are devised to inform accused persons of their right of silence and to assure a continuous opportunity to exercise it, the following measures are required. Prior to any questioning, the person must be warned that he has a right to remain silent, that any statement he does make may be used as evidence against him, and that he has a right to the presence of an attorney, either retained or appointed. The defendant may waive effectuation of these rights, provided the waiver is made voluntarily, knowingly and intelligently. If, however, he indicates in any manner and at any stage of the process that he wishes to consult with an attorney before speaking there can be no questioning. Likewise, if the individual is alone and indicates in any manner that he does not wish to be interrogated, the police may not question him. The mere fact that he may have answered some questions or volunteered some statements on his own does not deprive him of the right to refrain from answering any further inquiries until he has consulted with an attorney and thereafter consents to be questioned.

I.

The constitutional issue we decide in each of these cases is the admissibility of statements obtained from a defendant questioned while in custody or otherwise deprived of his freedom of action in any significant way. In each, the defendant was questioned by police officers, detectives, or a prosecuting attorney in a room in which he was cut off from the outside world. In none of these cases was the defendant given a full and effective warning of his rights at the outset of the interrogation process. In all the

cases, the questioning elicited oral admissions, and in three of them, signed statements as well which were admitted at their trials. They all thus share salient features—incommunicado interrogation of individuals in a police-dominated atmosphere, resulting in self-incriminating statements without full warnings of constitutional rights.

An understanding of the nature and setting of this in-custody interrogation is essential to our decisions today. The difficulty in depicting what transpires at such interrogations stems from the fact that in this country they have largely taken place incommunicado. From extensive factual studies undertaken in the early 1930's, including the famous Wickersham Report to Congress by a Presidential Commission, it is clear that police violence and the "third degree" flourished at that time. In a series of cases decided by this Court long after these studies, the police resorted to physical brutality—beating, hanging, whipping—and to sustained and protracted questioning incommunicado in order to extort confessions. The Commission on Civil Rights in 1961 found much evidence to indicate that "some policemen still resort to physical force to obtain confessions," 1961 Comm'n. on Civil Rights Rep., *Justice*, pt. 5, 17. The use of physical brutality and violence is not, unfortunately, relegated to the past or to any part of the country. Only recently in Kings County, New York, the police brutally beat, kicked and placed lighted cigarette butts on the back of a potential witness under interrogation for the purpose of securing a statement incriminating a third party. . . .

The examples given above are undoubtedly the exception now, but they are sufficiently widespread to be the object of concern. Unless a proper limitation upon custodial interrogation is achieved—such as these decisions will advance—there can be no assurance that practices of this nature will be eradicated in the foreseeable future. . . .

. . . [W]e stress that the modern practice of

in-custody interrogation is psychologically rather than physically oriented. As we have stated before . . . this Court has recognized that "coercion can be mental as well as physical, and that the blood of the accused is not the only hallmark of an unconstitutional inquisition." . . . Interrogation still takes place in privacy. Privacy results in secrecy and this in turn results in a gap in our knowledge as to what in fact goes on in the interrogation rooms. A valuable source of information about present police practices, however, may be found in various police manuals and texts which document procedures employed with success in the past, and which recommend various other effective tactics. These texts are used by law enforcement agencies themselves as guides. It should be noted that these texts professedly present the most enlightened and effective means presently used to obtain statements through custodial interrogation. . . .

From . . . representative samples of interrogation techniques, the setting prescribed by the manuals and observed in practice becomes clear. In essence, it is this: To be alone with the subject is essential to prevent distraction and to deprive him of any outside support. The aura of confidence in his guilt undermines his will to resist. He merely confirms the preconceived story the police seek to have him describe. Patience and persistence, at times relentless questioning, are employed. To obtain a confession the interrogator must "patiently maneuver himself or his quarry into a position from which the desired objective may be attained." When normal procedures fail to produce the needed result, the police may resort to deceptive stratagems such as giving false legal advice. It is important to keep the subject off balance, for example, by trading on his insecurity about himself or his surroundings. The police then persuade, trick, or cajole him out of exercising his constitutional rights.

Even without employing brutality, the "third degree" or the specific stratagems described above, the very fact of custodial interrogation exacts a heavy toll on individual liberty and trades on the weakness of individuals. . . .

. . . [T]he constitutional foundation underlying the privilege is the respect a government—state or federal—must accord to the dignity and integrity of its citizens. To maintain a "fair state-individual balance," to require the government "to shoulder the entire load" . . . to respect the inviolability of the human personality, our accusatory system of criminal justice demands that the government seeking to punish an individual produce the evidence against him by its own independent labors, rather than by the cruel, simple expedient of compelling it from his own mouth. . . .

. . . We are satisfied that all the principles embodied in the privilege apply to informal compulsion exerted by law-enforcement officers during in-custody questioning. An individual swept from familiar surroundings into police custody, surrounded by antagonistic forces, and subjected to the techniques of persuasion described above cannot be otherwise than under compulsion to speak. As a practical matter, the compulsion to speak in the isolated setting of the police station may well be greater than in courts or other official investigations, where there are often impartial observers to guard against intimidation or trickery. . . .

III.

Today, then, there can be no doubt that the Fifth Amendment privilege is available outside of criminal court proceedings and serves to protect persons in all settings in which their freedom of action is curtailed in any significant way from being compelled to incriminate themselves. We have concluded that without proper safeguards the process of in-custody interrogation of persons suspected or accused of crime contains inherently compelling pressures which work to undermine the individual's will to resist and to compel him to speak where he would not otherwise do so freely. In order to combat these pressures and to permit a full opportunity to exercise the privilege against self-incrimination, the accused must be adequately and effectively apprised of his rights and the exercise of those rights must be fully honored.

It is impossible for us to foresee the potential alternatives for protecting the privilege which might be devised by Congress or the States in the exercise of their creative rule-making capacities. Therefore we cannot say that the Constitution necessarily requires adherence to any particular solution for the inherent compulsions of the interrogation process as it is presently conducted. Our decision in no way creates a constitutional straitjacket which will handicap sound efforts at reform, nor is it intended to have this effect. We encourage Congress and the States to continue their laudable search for increasingly effective ways of protecting the rights of the individual while promoting efficient enforcement of our criminal laws. However, unless we are shown other procedures which are at least as effective in apprising accused persons of their right of silence and in assuring a continuous opportunity to exercise it, the following safeguards must be observed.

At the outset, if a person in custody is to be subjected to interrogation, he must first be informed in clear and unequivocal terms that he has the right to remain silent. For those unaware of the privilege, the warning is needed simply to make them aware of it—the threshold requirement for an intelligent decision as to its exercise. More important, such a warning is an absolute prerequisite in overcoming the inherent pressures of the interrogation atmosphere. It is not just the subnormal or woefully ignorant who succumb to an interrogator's imprecations, whether implied or expressly stated, that the interrogation will continue until a confession is obtained or that silence in the face of accusation is itself damning and will bode ill when presented to a jury. Further, the warning will show the individual that his interrogators are prepared to recognize his privilege should he choose to exercise it. . . .

The principles announced today deal with the protection which must be given to the privilege against self-incrimination when the individual is first subjected to police interrogation while in custody at the station or otherwise deprived of his freedom of action in any significant way. . . .

Our decision is not intended to hamper the traditional function of police officers in investigating crime. . . . When an individual is in custody on probable cause, the police may, of course, seek out evidence in the field to be used at trial against him. Such investigation may include inquiry of persons not under restraint. General on-the-scene questioning as to facts surrounding a crime or other general questioning of citizens in the fact-finding process is not affected by our holding. It is an act of responsible citizenship for individuals to give whatever information they may have to aid in law enforcement. In such situations the compelling atmosphere inherent in the process of in-custody interrogation is not necessarily present.

In dealing with statements obtained through interrogation, we do not purport to find all confessions inadmissible. Confessions remain a proper element in law enforcement. Any statement given freely and voluntarily without any compelling influences is, of course, admissible in evidence. The fundamental import of the privilege while an individual is in custody is not whether he is allowed to talk to the police without the benefit of warnings and counsel, but whether he can be interrogated. There is no requirement that police stop a person who enters a police station and states that he wishes to confess a crime, or a person who calls the police to offer a confession or any other statement he desires to make. Volunteered statements of any kind are not barred by the Fifth Amendment and their admissibility is not affected by our holding today.

To summarize, we hold that when an individual is taken into custody or otherwise deprived of his freedom by the authorities in any significant way and is subjected to questioning, the privilege against self-incrimination is jeopardized. Procedural safeguards must be employed to protect the privilege, and unless other fully effective means are adopted to notify the person of his right of silence and to assure that the exercise of the right will be scrupulously honored, the following measures are required. He must be warned prior to any questioning that he has the right to remain silent, that anything he says can be used against him in a court of law, that he has the right to the presence of an attorney, and that if he cannot afford an attorney one will be appointed for him prior to any questioning if he so desires. Opportunity to exercise these rights must be afforded to him throughout the interrogation. After such warnings have been given, and such opportunity afforded him, the individual may knowingly and intelligently waive these rights and agree to answer questions or make a statement. But unless and until such warnings and waiver are demonstrated by the prosecution at trial, no evidence obtained as a result of interrogation can be used against him.

IV.

. . . If the individual desires to exercise his privilege, he has the right to do so. This is not for the authorities to decide. An attorney may advise his client not to talk to police until he has had an opportunity to investigate the case, or he may wish to be present with his client during any police questioning. In doing so an attorney is merely exercising the good professional judgment he has been taught. This is not cause for considering the attorney a menace to law enforcement. He is merely carrying out what he is sworn to do under his oath—to protect to the extent of his ability the rights of his client. In fulfilling this responsibility the attorney plays a vital role in the administration of criminal justice under our Constitution.

In announcing these principles, we are not unmindful of the burdens which law enforcement officials must bear, often under trying circumstances. We also fully recognize the obliga-

tion of all citizens to aid in enforcing the criminal laws. . . .

Mr. Justice Harlan, whom Mr. Justice Stewart and Mr. Justice White join, dissenting.

I believe the decision of the Court represents poor constitutional law and entails harmful consequences for the country at large. How serious these consequences may prove to be only time can tell. But the basic flaws in the Court's justification seem to me readily apparent now once all sides of the problem are considered. . . .

While the fine points of this scheme are far less clear than the Court admits, the tenor is quite apparent. The new rules are not designed to guard against police brutality or other unmistakably banned forms of coercion. Those who use third-degree tactics and deny them in court are equally able and destined to lie as skillfully about warnings and waivers. Rather, the thrust of the new rules is to negate all pressures, to reinforce the nervous or ignorant suspect, and ultimately to discourage any confession at all. The aim in short is toward "voluntariness" in a utopian sense, or to view it from a different angle voluntariness with a vengeance.

To incorporate this notion into the Constitution requires a strained reading of history and precedent and a disregard of the very pragmatic concerns that alone may on occasion justify such strains. I believe that reasoned examination will show that the Due Process Clauses provide an adequate tool for coping with confessions and that, even if the Fifth Amendment privilege against self-incrimination be invoked, its precedents taken as a whole do not sustain the present rules. Viewed as a choice based on pure policy, these new rules prove to be a highly debatable, if not one-sided, appraisal of the competing interests, imposed over widespread objection, at the very time when judicial restraint is most called for by the circumstances.

Without at all subscribing to the generally black picture of police conduct painted by the Court, I think it must be frankly recognized at the outset that police questioning allowable under due process precedents may inherently entail some pressure on the suspect and may seek advantage in his ignorance or weaknesses. The atmosphere and questioning techniques, proper and fair though they be, can in themselves exert a tug on the suspect to confess, and in this light "(t)o speak of any confessions of crime made after arrest at being 'voluntary' or 'uncoerced' is somewhat inaccurate, although traditional. A confession is wholly and incontestably voluntary only if a guilty person gives himself up to the law and becomes his own accuser." *Ashcraft* v. *Tennessee*, 322 U.S. 143, (Jackson, J., dissenting). Until today, the role of the Constitution has been only to sift out *undue* pressure, not to assure spontaneous confessions. . . .

What the Court largely ignores is that its rules impair, if they will not eventually serve wholly to frustrate, an instrument of law enforcement that has long and quite reasonably been thought worth the price paid for it. There can be little doubt that the Court's new code would markedly decrease the number of confessions. To warn the suspect that he may remain silent and remind him that his confession may be used in court are minor obstructions. To require also an express waiver by the suspect and an end to questioning whenever he demurs must heavily handicap questioning. And to suggest or provide counsel for the suspect simply invites the end of the interrogation.

How much harm this decision will inflict on law enforcement cannot fairly be predicted with accuracy. Evidence on the role of confessions is notoriously incomplete. . . . We do know that some crimes cannot be solved without confessions, that ample expert testimony attests to their importance in crime control, and that the Court is taking a real risk with society's welfare in imposing its new regime on the country. The social costs of crime are too great to call the new rules anything but a hazardous experimentation.

While passing over the costs and risks of its experiment, the Court portrays the evils of normal police questioning in terms which I think are exaggerated. Albeit stringently confined by the due process standards interrogation is no doubt often inconvenient and unpleasant for the suspect. However, it is no less so for a man to be arrested and jailed, to have his house searched, or to stand trial in court, yet all this may properly happen to the most innocent given probable cause, a warrant, or an indictment. Society has always paid a stiff price for law and order, and peaceful interrogation is not one of the dark moments of the law.

This brief statement of the competing considerations seems to me ample proof that the Court's preference is highly debatable at best and therefore not to be read into the Constitution. . . .

. . . Nothing in the letter or the spirit of the Constitution or in the precedents squares with the heavy-handed and one-sided action that is so precipitously taken by the Court in the name of fulfilling its constitutional responsibilities. . . .

[Mr. Justice Clark gave a separate dissenting opinion.]

Note: Dunaway v. *New York,* 99 S. Ct. 2248 (1979), confirms *Brown* v. *Illinois,* 422 U.S. 590 (1975). In these cases the defendants were illegally arrested. Then after full *Miranda* warnings they made inculpatory statements which led to convictions. In both cases the convictions were overruled. Citing *Wong Sun* v. *United States,* 371 U.S. 471 (1963), the Court said in *Brown:*

> If *Miranda* warnings, by themselves, were held to attenuate the taint of an unconstitutional arrest, [the] effect of the exclusionary rule would be substantially diluted. Arrests made without warrant or without probable cause, for questioning or "investigation," would be encouraged by the knowledge that evidence derived therefrom hopefully could be made admissible at trial by the simple expedient of giving *Miranda* warnings.

> It is entirely possible [that] persons arrested illegally frequently may desire to confess, as an act of free will unaffected by the initial illegality. But the *Miranda* warnings, *alone* and *per se,* cannot always make the

act sufficiently a product of free will to break, for Fourth Amendment purposes, the causal connection between the illegality and the confession. They cannot assure in every case that the Fourth Amendment violation has not been unduly exploited.

> While we therefore reject the *per se* rule [accepted below] we also decline to adopt any alternative *per se* or 'but for' rule. [W]hether a confession is the product of a free will under *Wong Sun* must be answered on the facts of each case. [The] *Miranda* warnings are an important factor [but other factors to be considered are] the temporal proximity of the arrest and the confession, the presence of intervening circumstances, and, particularly, the purpose and flagrancy of the official misconduct. [T]he burden of showing admissibility rests, of course, on the prosecution.

Note: Johnson v. *New Jersey,* 384 U.S. 719 (1966)—following the rationale of *Linkletter*— declined to give retroactive effect to *Miranda.*

Harris v. New York
401 U.S. 222 (1971)

Harris was taken into custody for twice selling heroin to an undercover police officer. He was not given the *Miranda* warnings. At his trial he testified that he had not made the first sale at all, and that the second sale involved only baking powder. When asked whether he had made statements at the time of arrest which contradicted his testimony, Harris claimed he could not remember. Police testimony was then introduced, alleging prior statements by Harris *inconsistent* with his trial testimony. The purpose of the police testimony was not to prove the criminal acts, but to impeach the credibility of the Harris testimony.

Mr. Chief Justice Burger delivered the opinion of the Court.

We granted the writ in this case to consider petitioner's claim that a statement made by him to police under circumstances rendering it

inadmissible to establish the prosecution's case in chief under *Miranda* v. *Arizona,* 384 U.S. 436 (1966), may not be used to impeach his credibility. . . .

Some comments in the *Miranda* opinion can indeed be read as indicating a bar to use of an uncounseled statement for any purpose, but discussion of that issue was not at all necessary to the Court's holding and cannot be regarded as controlling. *Miranda* barred the prosecution from making its case with statements of an accused made while in custody prior to having or effectively waiving counsel. It does not follow from *Miranda* that evidence inadmissible against an accused in the prosecution's case in chief is barred for all purposes, provided of course that the trustworthiness of the evidence satisfies legal standards.

In *Walder* v. *United States*, 347 U.S. 62 (1954), the Court permitted physical evidence, inadmissible in the case in chief, to be used for impeachment purposes:

> "It is one thing to say that the Government cannot make an affirmative use of evidence unlawfully obtained. It is quite another to say that the defendant can turn the illegal method by which evidence in the Government's possession was obtained to his own advantage, and provide himself with a shield against contradiction of his untruths. Such an extension of the *Weeks* doctrine would be a perversion of the Fourth Amendment.
>
> "[T]here is hardly justification for letting the defendant affirmatively resort to perjurious testimony in reliance on the Government's disability to challenge his credibility." 347 U.S., at 65.

It is true that Walder was impeached as to collateral matters included in his direct examination, whereas petitioner here was impeached as to testimony bearing more directly on the crimes charged. We are not persuaded that there is a difference in principle that warrants a result different from that reached by the Court in *Walder*. Petitioner's testimony in his own behalf concerning the events of January 7 contrasted sharply with what he told the police shortly after his arrest. The impeachment process here

undoubtedly provided valuable aid to the jury in assessing petitioner's credibility, and the benefits of this process should not be lost, in our view, because of the speculative possibility that impermissible police conduct will be encouraged thereby. Assuming that the exclusionary rule has a deterrent effect on proscribed police conduct, sufficient deterrence flows when the evidence in question is made unavailable to the prosecution in its case in chief.

Every criminal defendant is privileged to testify in his own defense, or to refuse to do so. But that privilege cannot be construed to include the right to commit perjury. . . . Having voluntarily taken the stand, petitioner was under an obligation to speak truthfully and accurately, and the prosecution here did no more than utilize the traditional truth-testing devices of the adversary process. Had inconsistent statements been made by the accused to some third person, it could hardly be contended that the conflict could not be laid before the jury by way of cross-examination and impeachment.

The shield provided by *Miranda* cannot be perverted into a license to use perjury by way of a defense, free from the risk of confrontation with prior inconsistent utterances. We hold, therefore, that petitioner's credibility was appropriately impeached by use of his earlier conflicting statements.

Affirmed.

Mr. Justice Brennan, with whom Mr. Justice Douglas and Mr. Justice Marshall join, dissenting.

It is conceded that the question-and-answer statement used to impeach petitioner's direct testimony was, under *Miranda* v. *Arizona* . . . constitutionally inadmissible as part of the State's direct case against petitioner. I think that the Constitution also denied the State the use of the statement on cross-examination to impeach the credibility of petitioner's testimony given in his own defense. The decision in *Walder* v.

United States . . . is not, as the Court today holds, dispositive to the contrary. Rather, that case supports my conclusion. . . .

The objective of deterring improper police conduct is only part of the larger objective of safeguarding the integrity of our adversary system. The "essential mainstay" of that system . . . is the privilege against self-incrimination, which for that reason has occupied a central place in our jurisprudence since before the Nation's birth. Moreover, "we may view the historical development of the privilege as one which groped for the proper scope of governmental power over the citizen. . . . All these policies point to one overriding thought: the constitutional foundation underlying the privilege is the respect a government . . . must accord to the dignity and integrity of its citizens." These values are plainly jeopardized if an exception against admission of tainted statements is made for those used for impeachment purposes. Moreover, it is monstrous that

courts should aid or abet the lawbreaking police officer. It is abiding truth that "[n]othing can destroy a government more quickly than its failure to observe its own laws, or worse, its disregard of the charter of its own existence." . . . Thus, even to the extent that *Miranda* was aimed at deterring police practices in disregard of the Constitution, I fear that today's holding will seriously undermine the achievement of that objective. The Court today tells the police that they may freely interrogate an accused incommunicado and without counsel and know that although any statement they obtain in violation of *Miranda* cannot be used on the State's direct case, it may be introduced if the defendant has the temerity to testify in his own defense. This goes far toward undoing much of the progress made in conforming police methods to the Constitution. I dissent.

[Mr. Justice Black gave a separate dissenting opinion.]

Note: As of mid–1977, the Burger Court had not found any evidence inadmissible on *Miranda* grounds. The problem had come up in eleven cases. See G. R. Stone, "The Miranda Doctrine and the Burger Court," *The Supreme Court Review* (1977).

Title II of the Crime Control Act of 1968 undertakes to "repeal" the *Miranda* rule in federal cases by making any voluntary confession admissible, essentially as it would have been prior to *Miranda*. Thus only coerced confessions (as in *Watts*) would be excluded in federal courts. With reference to *Mallory*, the act provides that in District of Columbia cases an in-custody confession within six hours of arrest shall not be inadmissible "solely because of delay" in presenting the suspect for arraignment.

Note: Ullman v. *United States,* 350 U.S. 422 (1956), held that when the federal government gives a witness full immunity from prosecution (state and federal) for certain conduct, he cannot be prosecuted for such conduct—and to that extent can claim no privilege against self-incrimination under the Fifth Amendment. Justices Black and Douglas dissented on the ground that a witness in such circumstances might have to subject himself to various noncriminal "penalties," as well as social and economic reprisals.

Kastigar v. *United States,* 406 U.S. 441 (1972), held that when a witness is given *Ullman* immunity his *testimony* may never be used against him, but he may be prosecuted for offenses about which he was compelled to testify, provided such prosecution rests on other, independent evidence.

OTHER QUESTIONABLY OBTAINED EVIDENCE

Schmerber v. *California*
384 U.S. 757 (1966)

Mr. Justice Brennan delivered the opinion of the Court.

Petitioner was convicted in Los Angeles Municipal Court of the criminal offense of driving an automobile while under the influence of intoxicating liquor. He had been arrested at a hospital while receiving treatment for injuries suffered in an accident involving the automobile that he had apparently been driving. At the direction of a police officer, a blood sample was then withdrawn from petitioner's body by a physician at the hospital. The chemical analysis of this sample revealed a percent by weight of alcohol in his blood at the time of the offense which indicated intoxication, and the report of this analysis was admitted in evidence at the trial. Petitioner objected to receipt of this evidence of the analysis on the ground that the blood had been withdrawn despite his refusal, on the advice of his counsel, to consent to the test. He contended that in that circumstance the withdrawal of the blood and the admission of the analysis in evidence denied him due process of law under the Fourteenth Amendment, as well as specific guarantees of the Bill of Rights secured against the States by that Amendment: his privilege against self-incrimination under the Fifth Amendment; his right to counsel under the Sixth Amendment; and his right not to be subjected to unreasonable searches and seizures in violation of the Fourth Amendment.

. . .

I.

THE DUE PROCESS CLAUSE CLAIM

Breithaupt [v. *Abram*, 352 U.S. 432] was also a case in which police officers caused blood to be withdrawn from the driver of an automobile involved in an accident, and in which there was ample justification for the officer's conclusion that the driver was under the influence of alcohol. There, as here, the extraction was made by a physician in a simple, medically acceptable manner in a hospital environment. There, however, the driver was unconscious at the time the blood was withdrawn and hence had no opportunity to object to the procedure. We affirmed the conviction there resulting from the use of the test in evidence, holding that under such circumstances the withdrawal did not offend "that 'sense of justice' of which we spoke in *Rochin* v. *California*, 342 U.S. 165." 352 U.S., at 435. *Breithaupt* thus requires the rejection of petitioner's due process argument, and nothing in the circumstances of this case or in supervening events persuades us that this aspect of *Breithaupt* should be overruled.

II.

THE PRIVILEGE AGAINST SELF-INCRIMINATION CLAIM

Breithaupt summarily rejected an argument that the withdrawal of blood and the admission of the analysis report involved in that state case violated the Fifth Amendment privilege of any person not to "be compelled in any criminal case to be a witness against himself," citing *Twining* v. *New Jersey*, 211 U.S. 78. But that case, holding that the protections of the Fourteenth Amendment do not embrace this Fifth Amendment privilege, has been succeeded by *Malloy* v. *Hogan*, 378 U.S. 1, 8. We there held that "[t]he Fourteenth Amendment secures against state invasion the same privilege that the Fifth Amendment guarantees against federal infringement—the right of a person to remain silent unless he chooses to speak in the unfettered exercise of his own will, and to suffer no penalty . . . for such silence." We therefore must now decide whether the withdrawal of the blood and admission in evidence of the analysis involved in this case violated petitioner's privilege. We hold that the privilege protects an accused only from being compelled to testify against himself, or otherwise provide the State with evidence of a testimonial or communicative nature, and that the withdrawal of blood and use of the analysis in question in this case did not involve compulsion to these ends. . . .

It is clear that the protection of the privilege reaches an accused's communications, whatever form they might take, and the compulsion of responses which are also communications, for example, compliance with a subpoena to produce one's papers. *Boyd* v. *United States,* 116 U.S. 616. On the other hand, both federal and state courts have usually held that it offers no protection against compulsion to submit to fingerprinting, photographing, or measurements, to write or speak for identification, to appear in court, to stand, to assume a stance, to walk, or to make a particular gesture. The distinction which has emerged, often expressed in different ways, is that the privilege is a bar against compelling "communications" or "testimony," but that compulsion which makes a suspect or accused the source of "real or physical evidence" does not violate it.

Although we agree that this distinction is a helpful framework for analysis, we are not to be understood to agree with past applications in all instances. There will be many cases in which such a distinction is not readily drawn. Some tests seemingly directed to obtain "physical evidence," for example, lie detector test measuring changes in body function during interrogation, may actually be directed to eliciting responses which are essentially testimonial. To compel a person to submit to testing in which an effort will be made to determine his guilt or innocence on the basis of physiological responses, whether willed or not, is to evoke the spirit and history of the Fifth Amendment. Such situations call to mind the principle that the protection of the privilege "is as broad as the mischief against which it seeks to guard," *Counselman* v. *Hitchcock,* 142 U.S. 547, 562.

In the present case, however, no such problem of application is presented. Not even a shadow of testimonial compulsion upon or enforced communication by the accused was involved either in the extraction or in the chemical analysis. Petitioner's testimonial capacities were in no way implicated; indeed, his participation, except as a donor, was irrelevant to the results of the test, which depend on chemical analysis and on that alone. Since the blood test evidence, although an incriminating product of compulsion, was neither petitioner's testimony nor evidence relating to some communicative act or writing by the petitioner, it was not inadmissible on privilege grounds . . . .

IV.

THE SEARCH AND SEIZURE CLAIM

In *Breithaupt,* as here, it was also contended that the chemical analysis should be excluded from evidence as the product of an unlawful search and seizure in violation of the Fourth and Fourteenth Amendments. The Court did not decide whether the extraction of blood in that case was unlawful, but rejected the claim on the basis of *Wolf* v. *Colorado,* 338 U.S. 25. . . . [Since *Wolf* has been overruled] [t]he question is squarely presented . . . whether the chemical analysis introduced in evidence in this case should have been excluded as the product of an unconstitutional search and seizure.

Because we are dealing with intrusions into the human body rather than with state interferences with property relationships or private papers—"houses, papers, and effects"—we write on a clean slate. Limitations on the kinds of property which may be seized under warrant, as distinct from the procedures for search and the permissible scope of search, are not instructive in this context. We begin with the assumption that once the privilege against self-incrimination has been found not to bar compelled intrusions into the body for blood to be analyzed for alcohol content, the Fourth

Amendment's proper function is to constrain, not against all intrusions as such, but against intrusions which are not justified in the circumstances, or which are made in an improper manner. In other words, the questions we must decide in this case are whether the police were justified in requiring petitioner to submit to the blood test, and whether the means and procedures employed in taking his blood respected relevant Fourth Amendment standards of reasonableness.

In this case, as will often be true when charges of driving under the influence of alcohol are pressed, these questions arise in the context of an arrest made by an officer without a warrant. Here, there was plainly probable cause for the officer to arrest petitioner and charge him with driving an automobile while under the influence of intoxicating liquor. The police officer who arrived at the scene shortly after the accident smelled liquor on petitioner's breath, and testified that petitioner's eyes were "bloodshot, watery, sort of a glassy appearance." The officer saw petitioner again at the hospital, within two hours of the accident. There he noticed similar symptoms of drunkenness. He thereupon informed petitioner "that he was under arrest and that he was entitled to the services of an attorney, and that he could remain silent, and that anything that he told me would be used against him in evidence."

While early cases suggest that there is an unrestricted "right on the part of the Government, always recognized under English and American law, to search the person of the accused when legally arrested to discover and seize the fruits or evidences of crime," *Weeks* v. *United States,* 232 U.S. 383, 392; *People* v. *Chiagles,* 237 N.Y. 193, 142 N.E. 583 (1923) (Cardozo, J.), the mere fact of a lawful arrest does not end our inquiry. The suggestion of these cases apparently rests on two factors—first, there may be more immediate danger of concealed weapons or of destruction of evidence under the direct control of the accused, . . . ; second, once a search of the arrested person for weapons is permitted, it

would be both impractical and unnecessary to enforcement of the Fourth Amendment's purpose to attempt to confine the search to those objects alone. . . . Whatever the validity of these considerations in general, they have little applicability with respect to searches involving intrusions beyond the body's surface. The interests in human dignity and privacy which the Fourth Amendment protects forbid any such intrusions on the mere chance that desired evidence might be obtained. In the absence of a clear indication that in fact such evidence will be found, these fundamental human interests require law officers to suffer the risk that such evidence may disappear unless there is an immediate search.

Although the facts which established probable cause to arrest in this case also suggested the required relevance and likely success of a test of petitioner's blood for alcohol, the question remains whether the arresting officer was permitted to draw these inferences himself, or was required instead to procure a warrant before proceeding with the test. Search warrants are ordinarily required for searches of dwellings, and, absent an emergency, no less could be required where intrusions into the human body are concerned. . . .

The officer in the present case, however, might reasonably have believed that he was confronted with an emergency, in which the delay necessary to obtain a warrant, under the circumstances, threatened "the destruction of evidence," *Preston* v. *United States,* 376 U.S. 364, 367. We are told that the percentage of alcohol in the blood begins to diminish shortly after drinking stops, as the body functions to eliminate it from the system. Particularly in a case such as this, where time had to be taken to bring the accused to a hospital and to investigate the scene of the accident, there was no time to seek out a magistrate and secure a warrant. Given these special facts, we conclude that the attempt to secure evidence of blood-alcohol content in this case was an appropriate incident to petitioner's arrest.

Similarly, we are satisfied that the test chosen to measure petitioner's blood-alcohol level was a reasonable one. Extraction of blood samples for testing is a highly effective means of determining the degree to which a person is under the influence of alcohol. . . . Such tests are a commonplace in these days of periodic physical examinations and experience with them teaches that the quantity of blood extracted is minimal, and that for most people the procedure involves virtually no risk, trauma, or pain. Petitioner is not one of the few who on grounds of fear, concern for health, or religious scruple might prefer some other means of testing, such as the "breathalyzer" test petitioner refused . . . . We need not decide whether such wishes would have to be respected.

Finally, the record shows that the test was performed in a reasonable manner. Petitioner's blood was taken by a physician in a hospital environment according to accepted medical practices. We are thus not presented with the serious questions which would arise if a search involving use of a medical technique, even of the most rudimentary sort, were made by other than medical personnel or in other than a medical environment—for example, if it were administered by police in the privacy of the stationhouse. To tolerate searches under these conditions might be to invite an unjustified element of personal risk of infection and pain.

We thus conclude that the present record shows no violation of petitioner's right under the Fourth and Fourteenth Amendments to be free of unreasonable searches and seizures. It bears repeating, however, that we reach this judgment only on the facts of the present record. The integrity of an individual's person is a cherished value of our society. That we today hold that the Constitution does not forbid the States minor intrusions into an individual's body under stringently limited conditions in no way indicates that it permits more substantial intrusions, or intrusions under other conditions.

Mr. Justice Black with whom Mr. Justice Douglas joins, dissenting.

I would reverse petitioner's conviction. I agree with the Court that the Fourteenth Amendment made applicable to the States the Fifth Amendment's provision that "no person . . . shall be compelled in any criminal case to be a witness against himself . . . ." But I disagree with the Court's holding that California did not violate petitioner's constitutional right against self-incrimination when it compelled him, against his will, to allow a doctor to puncture his blood vessels in order to extract a sample of blood and analyze it for alcoholic content, and then used that analysis as evidence to convict petitioner of a crime.

The Court admits that "the State compelled [petitioner] to submit to an attempt to discover evidence [in his blood] that might be [and was] used to prosecute him for a criminal offense." To reach the conclusion that compelling a person to give his blood to help the State convict him is not equivalent to compelling him to be a witness against himself strikes me as quite an extraordinary feat. . . .

In the first place it seems to me that the compulsory extraction of petitioner's blood for analysis so that the person who analyzed it could give evidence to convict him had both a "testimonial" and a "communicative nature." The sole purpose of this project which proved to be successful was to obtain "testimony" from some person to prove that petitioner had alcohol in his blood at the time he was arrested. And the purpose of the project was certainly "communicative" in that the analysis of the blood was to supply information to enable a witness to communicate to the court and jury that petitioner was more or less drunk.

I think it unfortunate that the Court rests so heavily for its very restrictive reading of the Fifth Amendment's privilege against self-incrimination on the words "testimonial" and "communicative." These words are not models of clarity and precision as the Court's rather labored explication shows. Nor can the Court, so far as I know, find precedent in the former opinions of this Court for using these particular words to limit the scope of the Fifth Amendment's protection. There is a scholarly precedent, however, in the late Professor Wigmore's learned treatise on evidence. He used "testimonial" which, according to the latest edition of his treatise revised by McNaughton, means "communicative" (8 Wigmore, *Evidence* § 2263 [McNaughton rev. 1961], p. 378), as a key word in his vigorous and extensive campaign designed to keep the privilege against self-incrimination "within limits the strictest possible." 8 Wigmore, *Evidence* § 2251 [3d ed. 1940], p. 318. Though my admiration for Professor Wigmore's scholarship is great, I regret to see the word he used to narrow the Fifth Amendment's protection play such a major part in any of this Court's opinions.

I am happy that the Court itself refuses to follow Professor Wigmore's implication that the Fifth Amendment goes no further than to bar the use of forced self-incriminating statements coming from a "person's own lips." It concedes, as it must so long as *Boyd* v. *United States,* 116 U.S. 616, stands, that the Fifth Amendment bars a State from compelling a person to produce papers he has that might tend to incriminate him. It is a strange hierarchy of values that allows the State to extract a human being's blood to convict him of a crime because of the blood's content but proscribes compelled production of his lifeless papers. Certainly there could be few papers that would have any more "testimonial" value to convict a man of drunken driving than would an analysis of the alcoholic content of a human being's blood introduced in evidence at a trial for driving while under the influence of alcohol. In such a situation blood, of course, is not oral testimony given by an accused but it can certainly "communicate" to a court and jury the fact of guilt. . . .

[A brief concurring statement by Justices Harlan and Stewart is omitted—as are brief dissents by the Chief Justice and Mr. Justice Fortas.]

Note: Schmerber was decided one week after *Miranda.* It is noteworthy that only Mr. Justice Brennan was with the majority in both cases. In short, eight of the Justices found the two decisions incompatible.

Note: In accordance with a long tradition, an accused may be compelled to furnish a voice exemplar, *United States* v. *Dionisio,* 410 U.S. 1 (1973); a handwriting exemplar, *United States* v. *Mara,* 410 U.S. 19 (1973); fingerprints, *Davis* v. *Mississippi,* 394 U.S. 721 (1969); and perhaps other evidence of "physical characteristics . . . constantly exposed to the public."

Katz v. *United States*
389 U.S. 347 (1967)

In *Olmstead* v. *United States,* 277 U.S. 478 (1928), listening in on a telephone conversation via wiretapping was held not to be a search and seizure within the meaning of the Fourth Amendment. The dissenting views of Justices Holmes and Brandeis were adopted by an act of Congress which in effect forbade the use in federal courts of wire-tap evidence: *Nardone* v. *United States,* 302 U.S. 379 (1937); *Benanti* v. *United States,* 355 U.S. 96 (1957). In *On Lee* v. *United States,* 343 U.S. 747 (1952), the *Olmstead* principle sustained use of damaging evidence obtained by an undercover agent in a conversation with a suspect. The agent was equipped with a concealed radio transmitter which broadcast the conversation to a government recording device. The Court held that neither the Constitution nor the act of Congress was applicable. Justices Black, Frankfurter, Douglas, and Burton dissented. See also *Lopez* v. *United States,* 373 U.S. 427 (1963).

Mr. Justice Stewart delivered the opinion of the Court.

The petitioner was convicted in the District Court for the Southern District of California under an eight-count indictment charging him with transmitting wagering information by telephone from Los Angeles to Miami and Boston, in violation of a federal statute. At trial the Government was permitted, over the petitioner's objection, to introduce evidence of the petitioner's end of telephone conversations, overheard by FBI agents who had attached an electronic listening and recording device to the outside of the public telephone booth from which he had placed his calls. In affirming his conviction, the Court of Appeals rejected the contention that the recordings had been obtained in violation of the Fourth Amendment, because "[t]here was no physical entrance into the area occupied by [the petitioner]." We granted certiorari in order to consider the constitutional questions thus presented.

The petitioner has phrased those questions as follows:

> "A. Whether a public telephone booth is a constitutionally protected area so that evidence obtained by attaching an electronic listening recording device to the top of such a booth is obtained in violation of the right of privacy of the user of the booth.
>
> "B. Whether physical penetration of a constitutionally protected area is necessary before a search and seizure can be said to be violative of the Fourth Amendment to the United States Constitution."

We decline to adopt this formulation of the issues. In the first place, the correct solution of Fourth Amendment problems is not necessarily promoted by incantation of the phrase "con-stitutionally protected area." Secondly, the Fourth Amendment cannot be translated into a general constitutional "right to privacy." That Amendment protects individual privacy against certain kinds of governmental intrusion but its protections go further, and often have nothing to do with privacy at all. Other provisions of the Constitution protect personal privacy from other forms of governmental invasion. But the protection of a person's *general* right to privacy—his right to be let alone by other people—is, like the protection of his property and of his very life, left largely to the law of the individual States.

Because of the misleading way the issues have been formulated, the parties have attached great significance to the characterization of the telephone booth from which the petitioner placed his calls. The petitioner has strenuously argued that the booth was a "constitutionally protected area." The Government has maintained with equal vigor that it was not. But this effort to decide whether or not a given "area," viewed in the abstract, is "constitutionally protected" deflects attention from the problem presented by his case. For the Fourth Amendment protects people, not places. What a person knowingly exposes to the public, even in his own home or office, is not a subject of Fourth Amendment protection. See *Lewis* v. *United States,* 385 U.S. 206, 210; *United States* v. *Lee,* 274 U.S. 559, 563. But what he seeks to preserve as private, even in an area accessible to the public, may be constitutionally protected. See *Rios* v. *United States,* 364 U.S. 253; *Ex parte Jackson,* 96 U.S. 727, 733.

The Government stresses the fact that the telephone booth from which the petitioner made his calls was constructed partly of glass, so that he was as visible after he entered it as he would have been if he had remained outside. But what he sought to exclude when he entered the booth was not the intruding eye—it was the uninvited ear. He did not shed his right to do so simply because he made his calls from a place where he might be seen. No less than an individual in a business office, in a friend's apartment, or in a taxicab, a person in a telephone booth may rely upon the protection of the Fourth Amendment. One who occupies it, shuts the door behind him, and pays the toll that permits him to place a call is surely entitled to assume that the words he utters into the mouthpiece will not be broadcast to the world. To read the Constitution more narrowly is to ignore the vital role that the public telephone has come to play in private communication.

The Government contends, however, that the activities of its agents in this case should not be tested by Fourth Amendment requirements, for the surveillance technique they employed involved no physical penetration of the telephone booth from which the petitioner placed his calls. It is true that the absence of such penetration was at one time thought to foreclose further Fourth Amendment inquiry, *Olmstead* v. *United States*, 277 U.S. 438, 457, 464, 466; *Goldman* v. *United States*, 316 U.S. 129, 134–136, for that Amendment was thought to limit only searches and seizures of tangible property. But "[t]he premise that property interests control the right of the Government to search and seize has been discredited." *Warden* v. *Hayden*, 387 U.S. 294, 304. Thus, although a closely divided Court supposed in Olmstead that surveillance without any trespass and without the seizure of any material object fell outside the ambit of the Constitution, we have since departed from the narrow view on which that decision rested. Indeed, we have expressly held that the Fourth Amendment governs not only the seizure of tangible items, but extends as well to the recording of oral statements, overheard without any "technical trespass under . . . local property law." *Silverman* v. *United States*, 365 U.S. 505, 511. Once this much is acknowledged, and once it is recognized that the Fourth Amendment protects people—and not simply "areas"—against unreasonable searches and seizures, it

becomes clear that the reach of that Amendment cannot turn upon the presence or absence of a physical intrusion into any given enclosure.

We conclude that the underpinnings of *Olmstead* and *Goldman* have been so eroded by our subsequent decisions that the "trespass" doctrine there enunciated can no longer be regarded as controlling. The Government's activities in electronically listening to and recording the petitioner's words violated the privacy upon which he justifiably relied while using the telephone booth and thus constituted a "search and seizure" within the meaning of the Fourth Amendment. The fact that the electronic device employed to achieve that end did not happen to penetrate the wall of the booth can have no constitutional significance.

The question remaining for decision, then, is whether the search and seizure conducted in this case complied with constitutional standards. In that regard, the Government's position is that its agents acted in an entirely defensible manner: They did not begin their electronic surveillance until investigation of the petitioner's activities had established a strong probability that he was using the telephone in question to transmit gambling information to persons in other States, in violation of federal law. Moreover, the surveillance was limited, both in scope and in duration, to the specific purpose of establishing the contents of the petitioner's unlawful telephonic communications. The agents confined their surveillance to the brief periods during which he used the telephone booth, and they took great care to overhear only the conversations of the petitioner himself.

Accepting this account of the Government's actions as accurate, it is clear that this surveillance was so narrowly circumscribed that a duly authorized magistrate, properly notified of the need for such investigation, specifically informed of the basis on which it was to proceed, and clearly apprised of the precise intrusion it would entail, could constitutionally have authorized, with appropriate safeguards, the very limited search and seizure that the Government asserts in fact took place. . . .

The Government urges that, because its agents relied upon the decisions in *Olmstead* and *Goldman*, and because they did no more here than they might properly have done with prior judicial sanction, we should retroactively validate their conduct. That we cannot do. It is apparent that the agents in this case acted with restraint. Yet the inescapable fact is that this restraint was imposed by the agents themselves, not by a judicial officer. They were not required, before commencing the search, to present their estimate of probable cause for detached scrutiny by a neutral magistrate. They were not compelled, during the conduct of the search itself, to observe precise limits established in advance by a specific court order. Nor were they directed, after the search had been completed, to notify the authorizing magistrate in detail of all that had been seized. In the absence of such safeguards, this Court has never sustained a search upon the sole ground that officers reasonably expected to find evidence of a particular crime and voluntarily confined their activities to the least intrusive means consistent with that end. . . . "Over and again this Court has emphasized that the mandate of the [Fourth] Amendment requires adherence to judicial processes," *United States* v. *Jeffers*, 342 U.S. 48, 51, and that searches conducted outside the judicial process, without prior approval by judge or magistrate, are per se unreasonable under the Fourth Amendment—subject only to a few specifically established and well-delineated exceptions. . . .

The Government does not question these basic principles. Rather, it urges the creation of a new exception to cover this case. It argues that surveillance of a telephone booth should be exempted from the usual requirement of advance authorization by a magistrate upon a showing of probable cause. We cannot agree. Omission of such authorization "bypasses the safeguards provided by an objective predetermination of probable cause, and substitutes intsead the far less reliable procedure of an after-the-event justification for the . . . search, too likely to be subtly influenced by the familiar shortcomings of hindsight judgment." *Beck* v. *Ohio*, 379 U.S. 89, 96. And bypassing a neutral predetermination of the *scope* of a search leaves individuals secure from the Fourth Amendment violations "only in the discretion of the police." *Id.*, at 97.

These considerations do not vanish when the search in question is transferred from the setting of a home, an office, or a hotel room to that of a telephone booth. Wherever a man may be, he is entitled to know that he will remain free from unreasonable searches and seizures. The government agents here ignored "the procedure of antecedent justification . . . that is central to the Fourth Amendment," a procedure that we hold to be a constitutional precondition of the kind of electronic surveillance involved in this case. Because the surveillance here failed to meet that condition, and because it led to the petitioner's conviction, the judgment must be reversed.

Mr. Justice Marshall took no part in the consideration or decision of this case.

Mr. Justice Douglas, with whom Mr. Justice Brennan joins, concurring.

While I join the opinion of the Court, I feel compelled to reply to the separate concurring opinion of my Brother White, which I view as a wholly unwarranted green light for the Executive Branch to resort to electronic eavesdropping without a warrant in cases which the Executive Branch itself labels as "national security" matters.

Neither the President nor the Attorney General is a magistrate. In matters where they believe national security may be involved they are not detached, disinterested, and neutral as a court or magistrate must be. Under the separation of powers created by the Constitution, the Executive Branch is not supposed to be neutral and disinterested. Rather it should vigorously investigate and prevent breaches of national security and prosecute those who violate the pertinent federal laws. The President and Attorney

General are properly interested parties, cast in the role of adversary, in national security cases. They may even be the intended victims of subversive action. Since spies and saboteurs are as entitled to the protection of the Fourth Amendment as suspected gamblers like petitioner, I cannot agree that where spies and saboteurs are involved adequate protection of Fourth Amendment rights is assured when the President and Attorney General assume both the position of adversary and prosecutor and disinterested neutral magistrate.

There is, so far as I understand constitutional history, no distinction under the Fourth Amendment between types of crimes. Article III, § 3, gives "treason" a very narrow definition and puts restrictions on its proof. But the Fourth Amendment draws no lines between various substantive offenses. The arrests in cases of "hot pursuit" and the arrests on visible or other evidence of probable cause cut across the board and are not peculiar to any kind of crime.

I would respect the present lines of distinction and not improvise because a particular crime seems particularly heinous. When the Framers took that step, as they did with treason, the worst crime of all, they made their purpose manifest.

Mr. Justice Harlan, concurring.

I join the opinion of the Court, which I read to hold only (a) that an enclosed telephone booth is an area where, like a home, *Weeks* v. *United States*, 232 U.S. 383, and unlike a field, *Hester* v. *United States*, 265 U.S. 57, a person has a constitutionally protected reasonable expectation of privacy; (b) that electronic as well as physical intrusion into a place that is in this sense private may constitute a violation of the Fourth Amendment; and (c) that the invasion of a constitutionally protected area by federal authorities is, as the Court has long held, presumptively unreasonable in the absence of a search warrant. . . .

The critical fact in this case is that "[o]ne who

occupies it, [a telephone booth] shuts the door behind him, and pays the toll that permits him to place a call is surely entitled to assume" that his conversation is not being intercepted. *Ante*, p. 352. The point is not that the booth is "accessible to the public" at other times, *ante*, p. 351, but that it is a temporarily private place whose momentary occupants' expectations of freedom from intrusion are recognized as reasonable. Cf. *Rios* v. *United States*, 364 U.S. 253. . . .

Mr. Justice White, concurring.

I agree that the official surveillance of petitioner's telephone conversations in a public booth must be subjected to the test of reasonableness under the Fourth Amendment and that on the record now before us the particular surveillance undertaken was unreasonable absent a warrant properly authorizing it. This application of the Fourth Amendment need not interfere with legitimate needs of law enforcement.

In joining the Court's opinion, I note the Court's acknowledgement that there are circumstances in which it is reasonable to search without a warrant. In this connection, . . . the Court points out that today's decision does not reach national security cases. Wiretapping to protect the security of the Nation has been authorized by successive Presidents. The present Administration would apparently save national security cases from restrictions against wiretapping. See *Berger* v. *New York*, 388 U.S. 41, 112–118 (1967) (White, J., dissenting). We should not require the warrant procedure and the magistrate's judgment if the President of the United States or his chief legal officer, the Attorney General, has considered the requirements of national security and authorized electronic surveillance as reasonable.

[Mr. Justice Black, in an extended dissent based on *Olmstead* and the language of the Fourth Amendment, insisted that eavesdropping did not constitute a search and seizure.]

Note: United States v. *White,* 401 U.S. 745 (1971), involved electronic eavesdropping similar to that in *On Lee* (see above). Four Justices (Burger, White, Stewart, and Blackmun) thought *Katz* did not overrule *On Lee.* Four judges (Douglas, Brennan, Harlan, and Marshall) thought it did. Mr. Justice Black's vote was thus controlling. It was based on his *Katz* dissent to the effect that the Fourth Amendment does not preclude eavesdropping evidence.

Note: A pen register is a monitoring device which records the numbers dialed on a telephone. It does not "hear" or record phone conversations. At police request such a device was installed at the phone company's central office to monitor a suspect's phone calls. This led to evidence that produced a conviction.

Smith v. *Maryland,* 99 S. Ct. 2577 (1979), held this did not constitute a Fourth Amendment "search." The rationale was that Smith (using his home phone) lacked what *Katz* held is indispensable in such cases; namely, a "reasonable" or "legitimate expectation of privacy." There could be no such expectation with respect to dialed phone numbers, since they are voluntarily "conveyed" to the phone company and "All subscribers realize . . . that the phone company has facilities for making permanent records of the numbers they dial, for they see a list of their long distance (toll) calls on their monthly bills." Moreover, pen registers are routinely used by phone companies for numerous lawful purposes with respect, for example, to billing, fraud detection, and obscene phone calls. Three Justices dissented. As Mr. Justice Marshall put it:

Applying the standards set forth in *Katz* v. *United States,* 389 U.S. 347, 361 (1967) (Harlan, J., concurring), the Court first determines that telephone subscribers have no subjective expectations of privacy concerning the numbers they dial. To reach this conclusion, the Court posits that individuals somehow infer from the long distance listings on their phone bills, and from the cryptic assurances of "help" in tracing obscene calls included in "most" phone books, that pen registers are regularly used for recording local calls. See *ante,* at 7. But even assuming, as I do not, that individuals "typically know" that a phone company monitors calls for internal reasons, *ibid.,* it does not follow that they expect this information to be made available to the public in general or the government in particular. Privacy is not a discrete commodity, possessed absolutely or not at all. Those who disclose certain facts to a bank or phone company for a limited business purpose need not assume that this information will be released to other persons for other purposes.

Hoffa v. *United States*
385 U.S. 293 (1966)

Hoffa was convicted of attempting to bribe a juror. A major part of the evidence against him was the testimony of a Mr. Partin. The latter (whom Hoffa considered an old friend) overheard with Hoffa's permission several conversations between Hoffa and his lawyers. This "eavesdropping" was the basis of Partin's testimony. Partin had been released from jail (where he was being held on pending criminal charges) apparently in exchange for his "informer" services. The Supreme Court upheld the convication with these remarks concerning search and seizure.

Mr. Justice Stewart delivered the opinion of the Court. . . .

It is contended that only by violating the petitioner's rights under the Fourth Amendment was Partin able to hear the petitioner's incriminating statements in the hotel suite, and that Partin's testimony was therefore inadmissible under the exclusionary rule of *Weeks* v. *United States*, 232 U.S. 383. The argument is that Partin's failure to disclose his role as a government informer vitiated the consent that the petitioner gave to Partin's repeated entries into the suite, and that by listening to the petitioner's statements Partin conducted an illegal "search" for verbal evidence.

The preliminary steps of this argument are on solid ground. A hotel room can clearly be the object of Fourth Amendment protection as much as a home or an office. *United States* v. *Jeffers*, 342 U.S. 48. The Fourth Amendment can certainly be violated by guileful as well as by forcible intrusions into a constitutionally protected area. *Gouled* v. *United States*, 255 U.S. 298. And the protections of the Fourth Amendment are surely not limited to tangibles, but can extend as well to oral statements. *Silverman* v. *United States*, 365 U.S. 505.

Where the argument falls is in its misapprehension of the fundamental nature and scope of Fourth Amendment protection. What the Fourth Amendment protects is the security a man relies upon when he places himself or his property within a constitutionally protected area, be it his home or his office, his hotel room or his automobile. There he is protected from unwarranted governmental intrusion. And when he puts something in his filing cabinet, in his desk drawer, or in his pocket, he has the right to know it will be secure from an unreasonable search or an unreasonable seizure. So it was that the Fourth Amendment could not tolerate the warrantless search of the hotel room in *Jeffers*, the purloining of the petitioner's private papers in *Gouled*, or the surreptitious electronic surveillance in *Silverman*. Countless other cases which have come to this Court over the years have involved a myriad of differing factual contexts in which the protections of the Fourth Amendment have been appropriately invoked. No doubt the future will bring countless others. By nothing we say here do we either foresee or foreclose factual situations to which the Fourth Amendment may be applicable.

In the present case, however, it is evident that no interest legitimately protected by the Fourth Amendment is involved. It is obvious that the petitioner was not relying on the security of his hotel suite when he made the incriminating statements to Partin or in Partin's presence. Partin did not enter the suite by force or by stealth. He was not a surreptitious eavesdropper. Partin was in the suite by invitation, and every conversation which he heard was either directed to him or knowingly carried on in his presence. The petitioner, in a word, was not relying on the security of the hotel room; he was relying upon his misplaced confidence that Partin would not reveal his wrongdoing. As counsel for the petitioner himself points out, some of the communications with Partin did not take place in the suite at all, but in the "hall of the hotel" in the "Andrew Jackson Hotel lobby," and "at the courthouse."

Neither this Court nor any member of it has ever expressed the view that the Fourth Amendment protects a wrongdoer's misplaced belief that a person to whom he voluntarily confides his wrongdoing will not reveal it. Indeed, the Court unanimously rejected that very contention less than four years ago in *Lopez* v. *United States*, 373 U.S. 427. In that case the petitioner had been convicted of attempted bribery of an internal revenue agent named Davis. The Court was divided with regard to the admissibility in evidence of a surreptitious electronic recording of an incriminating conversation Lopez had had in his private office with Davis. But there was no dissent to the view that testimony about the conversation by Davis himself was clearly admissible.

As the Court put it, "Davis was not guilty of

an unlawful invasion of petitioner's office simply because his apparent willingness to accept a bribe was not real. Compare *Wong Sun* v. *United States*, 371 U.S. 471. He was in the office with petitioner's consent, and while there he did not violate the privacy of the office by seizing something surreptitiously without petitioner's knowledge. Compare *Gouled* v. *United States*, *supra*. The only evidence obtained consisted of statements made by Lopez to Davis, statements which Lopez knew full well could be used against him by Davis if he wished. . . . " 373 U.S. at 438. In the words of the dissenting opinion in *Lopez*, "The risk of being overheard by an eavesdropper or betrayed by an informer or deceived as to the identity of one with whom one deals is probably inherent in the conditions of human society. It is the kind of risk we necessarily assume whenever we speak." *Id.*, 373 U.S. at 465. See also *Lewis* v. *United States*, 385 U.S. 206.

Adhering to these views, we hold that no right protected by the Fourth Amendment was violated in the present case.

Mr. Justice White and Mr. Justice Fortas took no part in the consideration or decision of these cases.

Mr. Chief Justice Warren, dissenting.

. . . [A]lthough petitioners make their main argument on constitutional grounds . . . it should not be necessary for the Court to reach those questions. For the affront to the quality and fairness of federal law enforcement is sufficient to require an exercise of our supervisory powers [to preclude such evidence in federal courts].

[Justices Clark and Douglas thought the writs of certiorari should have been dismissed as improvidently granted.]

Note: Title III of the Omnibus Crime Control Act of 1968 authorizes "interception of wire or oral communications" to obtain evidence relating to a large number of federal offenses. The procedures for interception (in effect for obtaining and using search warrants) are prescribed in detail.

Dalia v. *United States*, 99 S. Ct. 1682 (1979), held that by this legislation Congress gave the courts authority to approve covert entries for the purpose of installing electronic surveillance equipment; and that if such entries are reasonable under the circumstances, they do not violate the Fourth Amendment.

DOUBLE JEOPARDY

Benton v. *Maryland*
395 U.S. 784 (1969)

Benton was charged in a single indictment for burglary and larceny. He was acquitted of larceny, but convicted of burglary. On his appeal the indictment was invalidated because of a defect in selection of the grand jury. He was reindicted for both offenses and convicted for both.

Mr. Justice Marshall delivered the opinion of the Court. . . .

In 1937, this Court decided the landmark case of *Palko* v. *Connecticut*, 302 U.S. 319 (1937).

Palko, although indicted for first-degree murder, had been convicted of murder in the second degree after a jury trial in a Connecticut state court. The State appealed and won a new trial. Palko argued that the Fourteenth Amendment incorporated, as against the States, the Fifth Amendment requirement that no person "be twice put in jeopardy of life or limb." The Court disagreed. Federal double jeopardy standards were not applicable against the States. Only when a kind of jeopardy subjected a defendant to "a hardship so acute and shocking that our polity will not endure it," . . . did the Fourteenth Amendment apply. The order for a new trial was affirmed. In subsequent appeals from state courts, the Court continued to apply this lesser Palko standard. . . .

. . . [W]e today find that the double jeopardy prohibition of the Fifth Amendment represents a fundamental ideal in our constitutional heritage, and that it should apply to the States through the Fourteenth Amendment. Insofar as it is inconsistent with this holding, *Palko* v. *Connecticut* is overruled. . . . The validity of petitioner's larceny conviction must be judged, not by the watered-down standard enunciated in *Palko*, but under this Court's interpretations of the Fifth Amendment double jeopardy provision.

It is clear that petitioner's larceny conviction cannot stand once federal double jeopardy standards are applied. Petitioner was acquitted of larceny in his first trial. Because he decided to appeal his burglary conviction, he is forced to suffer retrial on the larceny count as well. As this Court held in *Green* v. *United States,* 335 U.S. 184, "[c]onditioning an appeal of one offense on a coerced surrender of a valid plea of former jeopardy on another offense exacts a forfeiture in plain conflict with the constitutional bar against double jeopardy." . . .

Mr. Justice White, concurring. . . .

Mr. Justice Harlan, whom Mr. Justice Stewart joins, dissenting. . .

. . . I conclude that the concurrent sentence doctrine is applicable here. . . . [Benton's sentence on the still valid burglary conviction was much longer than his sentence on the *concurrent* larceny conviction. Eliminating the shorter larceny sentence would not relieve the convict of his longer sentence for burglary.] I . . . conclude that the real reason for reaching the "double jeopardy" issue . . . is the Court's eagerness to see that provision "incorporated" into the Fourteenth Amendment. . . .

[Mr. Justice White explained the "concurrent sentence doctrine" as follows:]

In a time of increasingly congested judicial dockets, often requiring long delays before trial and upon appeal, judicial resources have become scarce. Where a man has been convicted on several counts and sentenced concurrently upon each, and where judicial review of one count sustains its validity, the need for review of the other counts is not a pressing one since, regardless of the outcome, the prisoner will remain in jail for the same length of time under the count upheld. Rather than permit other cases to languish while careful review of these redundant counts is carried to its futile conclusion, judicial resources might be better employed by moving on to more pressing business. This is not a rule of convenience to the judge, but rather of fairness to other litigants.

Ashe v. *Swenson*
397 U.S. 436 (1970)

Ashe was acquitted of robbing one of six poker players. He was later indicted and convicted of robbing another one of them.

Mr. Justice Stewart delivered the opinion of the Court. . . .

As the District Court and the Court of Appeals correctly noted, the operative facts here are virtually identical to those of *Hoag* v. *New Jersey*, 356 U.S. 464. Viewing the question presented solely in terms of Fourteenth Amendment due process—whether the course that New Jersey had pursued had "led to fundamental unfairness," . . .—this Court declined to reverse the judgment of conviction, because "in the circumstances shown by this record, we cannot say that petitioner's later prosecution and conviction violated due process." . . . The Court found it unnecessary to decide whether "collateral estoppel"—the principle that bars relitigation between the same parties of issues actually determined at a previous trial—is a due process requirement in a state criminal trial. . . . And in the view the Court took of the issues presented, it did not, of course, even approach consideration of whether collateral estoppel is an ingredient of the Fifth Amendment guarantee against double jeopardy.

The doctrine of *Benton* v. *Maryland*, 395 U.S. 784 (1969), puts the issues in the present case in a perspective quite different from that in which the issues were perceived in *Hoag* v. *New Jersey*. The question is no longer whether collateral estoppel is a requirement of due process, but whether it is a part of the Fifth Amendment's guarantee against double jeopardy. . . .

"Collateral estoppel" is an awkward phrase, but it stands for an extremely important principle in our adversary system of justice. It means simply that when an issue of ultimate fact has once been determined by a valid and final judgment, that issue cannot again be litigated between the same parties in any future lawsuit. . . . The federal decisions have made clear that the rule of collateral estoppel in criminal cases is not to be applied with the hypertechnical and archaic approach of a 19th century pleading book, but with realism and rationality. Where a previous judgment of acquittal was based upon a general verdict, as is usually the case, this approach requires a court to "examine the record of a prior proceeding, taking into account the pleadings, evidence, charge, and other relevant matter, and conclude whether a rational jury could have grounded its verdict upon an issue other than that which the defendant seeks to foreclose from consideration." . . .

Straightforward application of the federal rule to the present case can lead to but one conclusion. . . . The single rationally conceivable issue in dispute before the jury was whether the petitioner had been one of the robbers. And the jury by its verdict found that he had not. . . .

The ultimate question to be determined, then, in the light of *Benton* v. *Maryland, supra,* is whether this established rule of federal law is embodied in the Fifth Amendment guarantee against double jeopardy. We do not hesitate to hold that it is. For whatever else that constitutional guarantee may embrace, . . . it surely protects a man who has been acquitted from having to "run the gantlet" a second time. . . .

The question is not whether Missouri could validly charge the petitioner with six separate offenses for the robbery of the six poker players. It is not whether he could have received a total of six punishments if he had been convicted in a single trial of robbing the six victims. It is simply whether, after a jury determined by its verdict that the petitioner was not one of the robbers, the State could constitutionally hale him before a new jury to litigate that issue again. . . .

The judgment is reversed. . . .

Mr. Justice Black, concurring. . . .

Mr. Justice Harlan, concurring.

If I were to judge this case under the traditional standards of Fourteenth Amendment due process, I would adhere to the decision in *Hoag* v. *New Jersey* . . . believing that regardless of the reach of the federal rule of collateral estoppel, it would have been open to a state court to treat the issue differently. However, having acceded . . . to the decision in *Benton* v. *Maryland* . . . which, over my dissent, held that the Fourteenth Amendment imposes on the States the standards of the Double Jeopardy Clause of the Fifth Amendment, I am satisfied that on this present record Ashe's acquittal in the first trial brought double jeopardy standards into play. Hence, I join the Court's opinion. In doing so I wish to make explicit my understanding that the Court's opinion in no way intimates that the Double Jeopardy Clause embraces to any degree the "same transaction" concept reflected in the concurring opinion of my Brother Brennan.

Mr. Justice Brennan, whom Mr. Justice Douglas and Mr. Justice Marshall join, concurring.

I agree that the Double Jeopardy Clause incorporates collateral estoppel as a constitutional requirement and therefore join the Court's opinion. However, even if the rule of collateral estoppel had been inapplicable to the facts of this case, it is my view that the Double Jeopardy Clause nevertheless bars the prosecution of petitioner a second time for armed robbery. The two prosecutions, the first for the robbery of Knight and the second for the robbery of Roberts, grew out of one criminal episode, and therefore I think it clear on the facts of this case that the Double Jeopardy Clause prohibited Missouri from prosecuting petitioner for each robbery at a different trial. . . .

The Double Jeopardy Clause . . . guarantee is expressed as a prohibition against multiple prosecutions for the "same offence. Although the phrase "same offence" appeared in most of the early common-law articulations of the double-jeopardy principle, questions of its precise meaning rarely arose prior to the 18th century, and by the time the Bill of Rights was adopted it had not been authoritatively defined.

When the common law did finally attempt a definition, in *The King* v. *Vandercomb*, 2 Leach 708, 720, 168 Eng. Rep. 455, 461 (Crown 1796), it adopted the "same evidence" test, which provided little protection from multiple prosecution:

"[U]nless the first indictment were such as the prisoner might have been convicted upon by proof of the facts contained in the second indictment, an acquittal on the first indictment can be no bar to the second."

The "same evidence" test of "same offence" was soon followed by a majority of American jurisdictions, but its deficiencies are obvious. It does not enforce but virtually annuls the constitutional guarantee. For example, where a single criminal episode involves several victims, under the "same evidence" test a separate prosecution may be brought as to each. . . .

The "same evidence" test permits multiple prosecutions where a single transaction is divisible into chronologically discrete crimes . . . (e.g., each of 75 poker hands a separate "offense"). Even a single criminal act may lead to multiple prosecutions if it is viewed from the perspectives of different statues. . . . Given the tendency of modern criminal legislation to divide the phases of a criminal transaction into numerous separate crimes, the opportunities for multiple prosecutions for an essentially unitary criminal episode are frightening. And given our tradition of virtually unreviewable prosecutorial discretion concerning the initiation and scope of a criminal prosecution, the potentialities for abuse inherent in the "same evidence" test are simply intolerable.

The "same evidence" test is not constitutionally required. It was first expounded *after* the adoption of the Fifth Amendment, and . . . had never been squarely held by this Court to be the required construction of the constitutional phrase "same offence" in a case involving multiple trials; indeed, in that context it has been rejected. . . .

The "same evidence" test may once have been defensible at English common law, which, for reasons peculiar to English criminal procedure, severely restricted the power of prosecutors to combine several charges in a single trial. In vivid contrast, American criminal procedure generally allows a prosecutor freedom, subject to judicial control, to prosecute a person at one trial for all the crimes arising out of a single criminal transaction.

In my view, the Double Jeopardy Clause requires the prosecution, except in most limited circumstances, to join at one trial all the charges against a defendant that grow out of a single criminal act, occurrence, episode, or transaction. This "same transaction" test of "same offence" not only enforces the ancient prohibition against vexatious multiple prosecutions embodied in the Double Jeopardy Clause, but responds as well to the increasingly widespread recognition that the consolidation in one lawsuit of all issues arising out of a single transaction or occurrence best promotes justice, economy, and convenience. Modern rules of criminal and civil procedure reflect this recognition.

. . . Although in 1935 the American Law Institute adopted the "same evidence" test, it has since replaced it with the "same transaction" test. England, too, has abandoned its surviving rules against joinder of charges and has adopted the "same transaction" test. The Federal Rules of Criminal Procedure liberally encourage the joining of parties and charges in a single trial. Rule 8(a) provides for joinder of charges that are similar in character, or arise from the same transaction or from connected transactions or form part of a common scheme or plan. Rule 8(b) provides for joinder of defendants. Rule 13 provides for joinder of separate indictments or informations in a single trial where the offenses alleged could have been included in one indictment or information. These rules represent considered modern thought concerning the proper structuring of criminal litigation. . . .

. . . Some flexibility in the structuring of criminal litigation is also desirable and consistent with our traditions. But the Double Jeopardy Clause stands as a constitutional barrier against possible tyranny by the overzealous prosecutor. The considerations of justice, economy, and convenience that have propelled the movement for consolidation of civil cases apply with even greater force in the criminal context because of the constitutional principle that no man shall be vexed more than once by trial for the same offense. Yet, if the Double Jeopardy Clause were interpreted by this Court

to incorporate the "same evidence" test, criminal defendants would have less protection from multiple trials than civil defendants. This anomaly would be intolerable. . . .

. . . Correction of the abuse of criminal process should not in any event be made to depend on the availability of collateral estoppel. Abuse of the criminal process is foremost among the feared evils that led to the inclusion of the Double Jeopardy Clause in the Bill of Rights. That evil will be most effectively avoided, and the Clause can thus best serve its worthy ends, if "same offence" is construed to embody the "same transaction" standard. Then both federal and state prosecutors will be prohibited from mounting successive prosecutions for offenses growing out of the same criminal episode, at least in the absence of a showing of unavoidable necessity for successive prosecutions in the particular case.

Mr. Chief Justice Burger, dissenting.

The Fifth Amendment to the Constitution of the United States provides in part: "nor shall any person be subject for the same offence to be twice put in jeopardy of life or limb. . . ." Nothing in the language or gloss previously placed on this provision of the Fifth Amendment remotely justifies the treatment that the Court today accords to the collateral-estoppel doctrine. Nothing in the purpose of the authors of the Constitution commands or even justifies what the Court decides today; this is truly a case of expanding a sound basic principle beyond the bounds—or needs—of its rational and legitimate objectives to preclude harassment of an accused. . . .

The concept of double jeopardy and our firm constitutional commitment is against repeated trials "for the *same offence.*" This Court, like most American jurisdictions, has expanded that part of the Constitution into a "same evidence" test. For example, in *Blockburger* v. *United States,* 284 U.S. 299, 304 (1932), it was stated, so far as here relevant, that "the test to be applied to determine whether there are two offenses or only one, is whether each provision (i.e., each charge) requires *proof of a fact which the other does not.*"

Clearly and beyond dispute the charge against Ashe in the second trial required proof of a fact—robbery of Roberts—which the charge involving Knight did not. The Court, therefore, has had to reach out far beyond the accepted offense-defining rule to reach its decision in this case. What it has done is to superimpose on the same-evidence test a new and novel collateral-estoppel gloss.

The majority rests its holding in part on a series of cases . . . which did not involve constitutional double jeopardy but applied collateral estoppel as developed in civil litigation to federal criminal prosecutions as a matter of this Court's supervisory power over the federal court system. The Court now finds the federal collateral estoppel rule to be an "ingredient" of the Fifth Amendment guarantee against double jeopardy and applies it to the States through the Fourteenth Amendment. This is an ingredient that eluded judges and justices for nearly two centuries.

The collateral-estoppel concept—originally a product only of civil litigation—is a strange mutant as it is transformed to control this criminal case. In civil cases the doctrine was justified as conserving judicial resources as well as those of the parties to the actions and additionally as providing the finality needed to plan for the future. It ordinarily applies to parties on each side of the litigation who have the same interest as or who are identical with the parties in the initial litigation. Here the complainant in the second trial is not the same as in the first even though the State is a party in both cases. Very properly, in criminal cases, finality and conservation of private, public, and judicial resources are lesser values than in civil litigation. Also, courts that have applied the collateral-estoppel concept to criminal actions would certainly not apply it to *both* parties, as is true in civil cases, i.e., here, if Ashe had been convicted at the first trial, presumably no court would then hold that he

was thereby foreclosed from litigating the identification issue at the second trial.

Perhaps, then, it comes as no surprise to find that the only expressed rationale for the majority's decision is that Ashe has "run the gantlet" once before. This is not a doctrine of the law or legal reasoning but a colorful and graphic phrase, which, as used originally in an opinion of the Court written by Mr. Justice Black, was intended to mean something entirely different. The full phrase is "run the gantlet once *on that charge* . . ." . . . found in *Green* v. *United States*, 355 U.S. 184, 190 (1957), where no question of multiple crimes against multiple victims was involved. Green, having been found guilty of second degree murder on a charge of first degree, secured a new trial. This Court held nothing more than that Green, once put in jeopardy—once having "run the gantlet . . . on *that charge*"—of first degree murder, could not be compelled to defend against that charge again on retrial.

Today's step in this area of constitutional law ought not be taken on no more basis that casual reliance on the "gantlet" phrase lifted out of the context in which it was originally used. This is decision by slogan.

Some commentators have concluded that the harassment inherent in standing trial a second time is a sufficient reason for use of collateral estoppel in criminal trials. If the Court is today relying on a harassment concept to superimpose a new brand of collateral-estoppel gloss on the "same evidence" test, there is a short answer; this case does not remotely suggest harassment of an accused who robbed six victims and the harassment aspect does not rise to constitutional levels.

Finally, the majority's opinion tells us "that the rule of collateral estoppel in criminal cases is not to be applied with the hypertechnical and archaic approach of a 19th century pleading book, but with realism and rationality." . . . With deference I am bound to pose the question: what is reasonable and rational about holding that an acquittal of Ashe for robbing

Knight bars a trial for robbing Roberts? To borrow a phrase from the Court's opinion, what could conceivably be more "hypertechnical and archaic" and more like the stilted formalisms of 17th and 18th century common-law England, than to stretch jeopardy for robbing Knight into jeopardy for robbing Roberts?

After examining the facts of this case the Court concludes that the first jury must have concluded that Ashe was not one of the robbers—that he was not present at the time. Also, since the second jury necessarily reached its decision by finding he was present, the collateral-estoppel doctrine applies. . . .

. . . Even the facts in this case, which the Court's opinion considers to "lead to but one conclusion," are susceptible of an interpretation that the first jury did not base its acquittal on the identity ground which the Court finds so compelling. The Court bases its holding on sheer "guesswork," which should have no place particularly in our review of state convictions by way of habeas corpus. . . .

The essence of Mr. Justice Brennan's concurrence is that this was all one transaction, one episode, or, if I may so characterize it, one frolic, and, hence, only one crime. His approach, like that taken by the Court, totally overlooks the significance of there being *six entirely separate charges of robbery* against six individuals.

This "single frolic" concept is not a novel notion; it has been urged in various courts including this Court. One of the theses underlying the "single frolic" notion is that the criminal episode is "indivisible." The short answer to that is that to the victims, the criminal conduct is readily divisible and intensely personal; each offense is an offense against *a person*. For me it demeans the dignity of the human personality and individuality to talk of "a single transaction" in the context of six separate assaults on six individuals.

No court that elevates the individual rights and human dignity of the accused to a high place—as we should—ought to be so casual as to treat the victims as a single homogenized lump of human clay. I would grant the dignity of individual status to the victims as much as to those accused, not more but surely no less.

If it be suggested that multiple crimes can be separately punished but must be collectively tried, one can point to the firm trend in the law to allow severance of defendants and offenses into separate trials so as to avoid possible prejudice of one criminal act or of the conduct of one defendant to "spill over" on another.

What the Court holds today must be related to its impact on crimes more serious than ordinary house-breaking, followed by physical assault on six men and robbery of all of them. To understand its full impact we must view the holding in the context of four men who break and enter, rob, and then kill six victims. The concurrence tells us that unless all the crimes are joined in one trial the alleged killers cannot be tried for more than one of the killings even if the evidence is that they personally killed two, three, or more of the victims. Or alter the crime to four men breaking into a college dormitory and assaulting six girls. What the Court is holding is, in effect, that the second and third and fourth criminal acts are "free," unless the accused is tried for the multiple crimes in a single trial—something defendants frantically use every legal device to avoid, and often succeed in avoiding. This is the reality of what the Court holds today; it does not make good sense and it cannot make good law.

I therefore join with the four courts that have found no double jeopardy in this case. . . .

Waller v. *Florida*
397 U.S. 387 (1970)

Mr. Chief Justice Burger delivered the opinion of the Court. . . .

Petitioner was one of a number of persons who removed a canvas mural which was affixed to a wall inside the City Hall of St. Petersburg,

Florida. After the mural was removed, the petitioner and others carried it through the streets of St. Petersburg until they were confronted by police officers. After a scuffle, the officers recovered the mural, but in a damaged condition.

The petitioner was charged by the City of St. Petersburg with the violation of two ordinances: first, destruction of city property; and second, disorderly breach of the peace. He was found guilty in the municipal court on both counts, and a sentence of 180 days in the county jail was imposed.

Thereafter an information was filed against the petitioner by the State of Florida charging him with grand larceny. It is conceded that this information was based on the same acts of the petitioner as were involved in the violation of the two city ordinances. . . . Thereafter petitioner was tried in the Circuit Court of Florida by a jury and was found guilty of the felony of grand larceny. . . .

On appeal, the District Court of Appeal of Florida considered and rejected petitioner's claim that he had twice been put in jeopardy because prior to his conviction of grand larceny, he had been convicted by the municipal court of an included offense of the crime of grand larceny. . . . [The District Court quoted the Florida Supreme Court saying:]

" 'This double jeopardy argument has long been settled contrary to the claims of the petitioner. We see no reason to recede from our established precedent on the subject. Long ago it was decided that an act committed within municipal limits may be punished by city ordinance even though the same act is also proscribed as a crime by a state statute. An offender may be tried for the municipal offense in the city court and for the crime in the proper state court. Conviction or acquittal in either does not bar prosecution in the other.' " . . .

. . . Whether in fact and law petitioner committed separate offenses which could support separate charges was not decided by the Florida courts, nor do we reach that question. What is before us is the asserted power of the two courts within one State to place petitioner on trial for the same alleged crime.

In *Benton* v. *Maryland*, 395 U.S. 784, this Court declared the double jeopardy provisions of the Fifth Amendment applicable to the States. . . . Here, as in *North Carolina* v. *Pearce*, 395 U.S. 711, *Benton* should be applied to test petitioner's conviction. . . .

Florida does not stand alone in treating municipalities and the State as separate sovereign entities, each capable of imposing punishment for the same alleged crime. Here, respondent State of Florida seeks to justify this separate sovereignty theory by asserting that the relationship between a municipality and the state is analogous to the relationship between a State and the Federal Government. Florida's chief reliance is placed upon this Court's holdings in *Bartkus* v. *Illinois*, 359 U.S. 121, and *Abbate* v. *United States*, 359 U.S. 187, which permitted successive prosecutions by the Federal and State Governments as separate sovereigns. . . .

. . . [The] provisions of the Florida Constitution demonstrate that the judicial power to try petitioner on the first charges in municipal court springs from the same organic law that created the state court of general jurisdiction in which petitioner was tried and convicted for a felony. Accordingly, the apt analogy to the relationship between municipal and state governments is to be found in the relationship between the government of a Territory and the Government of the United States. The legal consequence of that relationship was settled in *Grafton* v. *United States*, 206 U.S. 333 (1907), where this Court held that a prosecution in a court of the United States is a bar to a subsequent prosecution in a territorial court, since both are arms of the same sovereign. . . .

Thus *Grafton*, not . . . *Bartkus* v. *Illinois* . . .

or *Abbate* v. *United States* . . . controls, and we hold that on the basis of facts upon which the Florida District Court of Appeal relied petitioner could not lawfully be tried both by the municipal government and by the State of Florida. In this context a "dual sovereignty" theory is an anachronism, and the second trial constituted double jeopardy violative of the Fifth and Fourteenth Amendments to the United States Constitution. . . .

[Justices Black and Brennan wrote concurring opinions.]

> *Note:* Following *Bartkus* and *Abbate* (mentioned in *Waller*), the Department of Justice announced that "After a state prosecution there should be no federal trial for the same act unless the reasons [for it are unusually] compelling."

> *Note: United States* v. *Scott,* 98 S. Ct. 2187 (1978), held that the prohibition of double jeopardy does not outlaw a second trial when the original trial ended *upon the defendant's own motion* (based on preindictment delay) before introduction of any evidence of guilt or innocence. The Court stressed that element of the double jeopardy provision which protects against retrial *after acquittal.* Justices Brennan, White, Marshall, and Stevens, in dissent, thought the majority's acquittal rule was merely an aspect of a larger principle, namely "the gross unfairness of requiring the accused to undergo the strain and agony of more than one trial for any single offense."
>
> When a trial ends before conviction or acquittal *upon motion of the prosecutor,* the general rule is that reprosecution is permissible only if the "mistrial was dictated by 'manifest necessity' or the "ends of public justice' [and does not involve] prosecutorial manipulation. . . ." See *Illinois* v. *Somerville,* 410 U.S. 458 (1973).

CRUEL AND UNUSUAL PUNISHMENT

Gregg v. *Georgia*
428 U.S. 153 (1976)

In *Furman* v. *Georgia,* 408 U.S. 238 (1972), the Court—split 5 to 4—apparently invalidated capital punishment as we had known it. Only Justice Brennan and Marshall thought the death penalty as such was unconstitutional. The other three members of the majority (Justices Douglas, White, and Stewart) found fault only in our manner of imposing it. All three were concerned about the wide, *unguided* discretion given to judges and juries. Mr. Justice Douglas stressed its potential for discrimination against minorities. Justices Stewart and White stressed the sporadic and capricious way death sentences had been imposed.

The four dissenters (Burger, Blackmun, Powell, and Rehnquist) found nothing in the Constitution prohibiting capital punishment as traditionally imposed. Any state wanting to retain the death penalty thus had four supporting votes and needed only (as it developed) to rewrite its laws to meet the unguided-discretion problem stressed by Justices Douglas, Stewart, and White.

Mr. Justice Stewart, Mr. Justice Powell, and Mr. Justice Stevens, announced the judgment of the Court and filed an opinion delivered by Mr. Justice Stewart.

The issue in this case is whether the imposition of the sentence of death for the crime of murder under the law of Georgia violates the Eighth and Fourteenth Amendments. . . .

II.

. . . The Georgia statute, as amended after our decision in *Furman* v. *Georgia*, 408 U.S. 238 (1972), retains the death penalty for six categories of crime: murder and kidnapping for ransom or where the victim is harmed, armed robbery and rape, treason and aircraft hijacking. . . .

The capital defendants' guilt or innocence is determined in the traditional manner, either by a trial judge or a jury, in the first stage of a bifurcated trial.

If trial is by jury, the trial judge is required to charge lesser included offenses when they are supported by any view of the evidence. . . . After a verdict, finding, or plea of guilty to a capital crime, a presentence hearing is conducted before whomever made the determination of guilt. The sentencing procedures are essentially the same in both bench and jury trials. . . .

The defendant is accorded substantial latitude as to the types of evidence that he may introduce. . . . Evidence considered during the guilt stage may be considered during the sentencing stage without being resubmitted. . . .

In the assessment of the appropriate sentence to be imposed the judge is also required to consider or to include in his instructions to the jury "any mitigating circumstances or aggravating circumstances otherwise authorized by law and any of [10] statutory aggravating circumstances which may be supported by the evidence. . . ." . . . The scope of the nonstatutory aggravating or mitigating circumstances is not

delineated in the statute. Before a convicted defendant may be sentenced to death, however, except in cases of treason or aircraft hijacking, the jury, or the trial judge in cases tried without a jury, must find beyond a reasonable doubt one of the 10 aggravating circumstances specified in the statute.[1] The sentence of death

---

[1] The statute provides in part:

"(a) The death penalty may be imposed for the offenses of aircraft hijacking or treason, in any case.

"(b) In all cases of other offenses for which the death penalty may be authorized, the judge shall consider, or he shall include in his instructions to the jury for it to consider, any mitigating circumstances or aggravating circumstances otherwise authorized by law and any of the following statutory aggravating circumstances which may be supported by the evidence:

"(1) The offense of murder, rape, armed robbery, or kidnapping was committed by a person with a prior record of conviction for a capital felony, or the offense of murder was committed by a person who has a substantial history of serious assaultive criminal convictions.

"(2) The offense of murder, rape, armed robbery, or kidnapping was committed while the offender was engaged in the commission of another capital felony, or aggravated battery, or the offense of murder was committed while the offender was engaged in the commission of burglary or arson in the first degree.

"(3) The offender by his act of murder, armed robbery, or kidnapping knowingly created a great risk of death to more than one person in a public place by means of a weapon or device which would normally be hazardous to the lives of more than one person.

"(4) The offender committed the offense of murder for himself or another, for the purpose of receiving money or any other thing of monetary value.

"(5) The murder of a judicial officer, former judicial officer, district attorney or solicitor or former district attorney or solicitor during or because of the exercise of his official duty.

"(6) The offender caused or directed another to commit murder or committed murder as an agent or employee of another person.

"(7) The offense of murder, rape, armed robbery, or kidnapping was outrageously or wantonly vile, horrible or inhuman in that it involved torture, depravity of mind, or an aggravated battery to the victim.

"(8) The offense of murder was committed against any peace officer, corrections employee or fireman while engaged in the performance of his official duties.

"(9) The offense of murder was committed by a

may be imposed only if the jury (or judge) finds one of the statutory aggravating circumstances and then elects to impose that sentence. . . . If the verdict is death the jury or judge must specify the aggravating circumstances(s) found. . . . In jury cases, the trial judge is bound by the jury's recommended sentence. . . .

In addition to the conventional appellate process available in all criminal cases, provision is made for special expedited direct review by the Supreme Court of Georgia of the appropriateness of imposing the sentence of death in the particular case. The court is directed to consider "the punishment as well as any errors enumerated by way of appeal." . . . If the court affirms a death sentence, it is required to include in its decision reference to similar cases that it has taken into consideration. . . .

A transcript and complete record of the trial, as well as a separate report by the trial judge, are transmitted to the court for its use in reviewing the sentence. . . . Under its special review authority, the court may either affirm the death sentence or remand the case for resentencing. In cases in which the death sentence is affirmed there remains the possibility of executive clemency.

III.

We address initially the basic contention that the punishment of death for the crime of murder is, under all circumstances, "cruel and unusual" in violation of the Eighth and Fourteenth Amendments of the Constitution. . . .

. . . [U]ntil *Furman* v. *Georgia*, 408 U.S. 238 (1972), the Court never confronted squarely the fundamental claim that the punishment of death always, regardless of the enormity of the offense or the procedure followed in imposing the sentence, is cruel and unusual punishment

in violation of the Constitution. Although this issue was presented and addressed in Furman, it was not resolved by the Court. Four Justices would have held that capital punishment is not unconstitutional per se; two Justices would have reached the opposite conclusion; and three Justices, while agreeing that the statutes then before the Court were invalid as applied, left open the question whether such punishment may ever be imposed. We now hold that the punishment of death does not invariably violate the Constitution.

A

. . . The American draftsmen . . . in drafting the Eighth Amendment were primarily concerned, however, with proscribing "tortures" and other "barbarous" methods of punishment. . . .

In the earliest cases raising Eighth Amendment claims, the Court focused on particular methods of execution to determine whether they were too cruel to pass constitutional muster. The constitutionality of the sentence of death itself was not at issue, and the criterion used to evaluate the mode of execution was its similarity to "torture" and other "barbarous" methods. . . .

But the Court has not confined the prohibition embodied in the Eighth Amendment to "barbarous" methods that were generally outlawed in the 18th century. Instead, the Amendment has been interpreted in a flexible and dynamic manner. . . . Thus the clause forbidding "cruel and unusual" punishments "is not fastened to the obsolete but may acquire meaning as public opinion becomes enlightened by a humane justice." . . .

. . . [T]he Eighth Amendment has not been regarded as a static concept. As Chief Justice Warren said, in an oft-quoted phrase. "[T]he Amendment must draw its meaning from the evolving standards of decency that mark the progress of a maturing society." *Trop* v. *Dulles*, 356 U.S. 86, 101 (1958). . . . Thus, an assess-

---

person in, or who has escaped from, the lawful custody of a peace officer or place of lawful confinement.

"(10) The murder was committed for the purpose of avoiding, interfering with, or preventing a lawful arrest or custody in a place of lawful confinement, of himself or another. . . ."

ment of contemporary values concerning the infliction of a challenged sanction is relevant to the application of the Eighth Amendment. . . . [A]ssessment does not call for a subjective judgment. It requires, rather, that we look to objective indicia that reflect the public attitude toward a given sanction.

But our cases also make clear that public perceptions of standards of decency with respect to criminal sanctions are not conclusive. A penalty also must accord with "the dignity of man," which is the "basic concept underlying the Eighth Amendment." *Trop* v. *Dulles, supra* at 100 (plurality opinion). This means, at least, that the punishment in the abstract (in this case, whether capital punishment may ever be imposed as a sanction for murder) rather than in the particular (the propriety of death as a penalty to be applied to a specific defendant for a specific crime) is under consideration, the inquiry into "excessiveness" has two aspects. First, the punishment must not involve the unnecessary and wanton infliction of pain. . . . Second, the punishment must not be grossly out of proportion to the severity of the crime. . . .

B

Of course, the requirements of the Eighth Amendment must be applied with an awareness of the limited role to be played by the courts. This does not mean that judges have no role to play, for the Eighth Amendment is a restraint upon the exercise of legislative power. . . .

But, while we have an obligation to insure that constitutional bounds are not overreached we may not act as judges as we might as legislators. . . .

Therefore, in assessing a punishment selected by a democratically elected legislature against the constitutional measure, we presume its validity. We may not require the legislature to select the least severe penalty possible so long as the penalty selected is not cruelly inhumane or

disproportionate to the crime involved. And a heavy burden rests on those who would attack the judgment of the representatives of the people. . . .

C

. . . We now consider specifically whether the sentence of death for the crime of murder is a per se violation of the Eighth and Fourteenth Amendments to the Constitution. We note first that history and precedent strongly support a negative answer to this question.

The imposition of the death penalty for the crime of murder has a long history of acceptance both in the United States and in England. The common-law rule imposed a mandatory death sentence on all convicted murderers. . . . And the penalty continued to be used into the 20th century by most American States, although the breadth of the common-law rule was diminished, initially by narrowing the class of murders to be punished by death and subsequently by widespread adoption of laws expressly granting juries the discretion to recommend mercy. . . .

It is apparent from the text of the Constitution itself that the existence of capital punishment was accepted by the Framers. At the time the Eighth Amendment was ratified, capital punishment was a common sanction in every State. Indeed, the First Congress of the United States enacted legislation providing death as the penalty for specified crimes. 1 Stat. 112 (1790). The Fifth Amendment, adopted at the same time as the Eighth, contemplated the continued existence of the capital sanction by imposing certain limits on the prosecution of capital cases:

"No person shall be held to answer for a capital, or otherwise infamous crime, unless on a presentment or indictment of a Grand Jury . . . ; nor shall any person be subject for the same offence to be twice put in jeopardy of life or limb; . . . nor be deprived of life, liberty, or property, without due process of law. . . ."

And the Fourteenth Amendment, adopted over three-quarters of a century later, similarly contemplates the existence of the capital sanction in providing that no State shall deprive any person of "life, liberty, or property" without due process of law.

For nearly two centuries, this Court, repeatedly and often expressly, has recognized that capital punishment is not invalid per se. . . .

Four years ago, the petitioners in *Furman* and its companion cases predicated their argument primarily upon the asserted proposition that standards of decency had evolved to the point where capital punishment no longer could be tolerated. . . . This view was accepted by two Justices. Three other Justices were unwilling to go so far; focusing on the procedures by which convicted defendants were selected for the death penalty rather than on the actual punishment inflicted, they joined in the conclusion that the statutes before the Court were constitutionally invalid.

The petitioners in the capital cases before the Court today renew the "standards of decency" argument, but developments during the four years since *Furman* have undercut substantially the assumptions upon which their argument rested. Despite the continuing debate, dating back to the 19th century, over the morality and utility of capital punishment, it is now evident that a large proportion of American society continues to regard it as an appropriate and necessary criminal sanction.

The most marked indication of society's endorsement of the death penalty for murder is the legislative response to *Furman*. The legislatures of at least 35 States have enacted new statutes that provide for the death penalty for at least some crimes that result in the death of another person. And the Congress of the United States, in 1974, enacted a statute providing the death penalty for aircraft piracy that results in death. . . . [A]ll of the post-*Furman* statutes make clear that capital punishment itself has not been rejected by the elected representatives of the people.

In the only statewide referendum occurring since *Furman* and brought to our attention the people of California adopted a constitutional amendment that authorized capital punishment, in effect negating a prior ruling by the Supreme Court of California in *People* v. *Anderson*, 6 Cal. 3d 628, 493 P.2d 880, cert. denied, 406 U.S. 958 (1972), that the death penalty violated the California Constitution.[2]

. . . [The] relative infrequency of jury verdicts imposing the death sentence does not indicate rejection of capital punishment per se. Rather, the reluctance of juries in many cases to impose the sentence may well reflect the humane feeling that this most irrevocable of sanctions should be reserved for a small number of extreme cases. . . . Indeed, the actions of juries in many States since *Furman* is fully compatible with the legislative judgments, reflected in the new statutes, as to the continued utility and necessity of capital punishment in appropriate cases. At the close of 1974 at least 254 persons had been sentenced to death since *Furman*, and by the end of March 1976, more than 460 persons were subject to death sentences.

As we have seen, however, the Eighth Amendment demands more than that a chal-

---

[2] In 1968, the people of Massachusetts were asked "Shall the commonwealth . . . retain the death penalty for crime?" A substantial majority of the ballots cast answered "Yes." Of 2,348,005 ballots cast, 1,159,348 voted "Yes," 730,649 voted "No," and 458,008 were blank. See Commonwealth v. O'Neal, 339 N.E.2d 676, 708 and n.1 (Mass. 1975) (Reardon, J., dissenting). A December 1972 Gallup poll indicated that 57% of the people favored the death penalty, while a June 1973 Harris survey showed support of 59%. Vidmar and Ellsworth, Public Opinion and the Death Penalty, 26 Stan. L. Rev. 1245, 1249 n.22 (1974). In a December 1970 referendum, the voters of Illinois also rejected the abolition of capital punishment by 1,218,791 votes to 676,320 votes. Report of the Governor's Study Commission on Capital Punishment, p. 43 (Pa. 1973).

lenged punishment be acceptable to contemporary society. The Court also must ask whether it comports with the basic concept of human dignity at the core of the Amendment. *Trop* v. *Dulles*, 356 U.S. at 100 (plurality opinion). . . . [The] sanction imposed cannot be so totally without penological justification that it results in the gratuitous infliction of suffering. . . .

The death penalty is said to serve two principal social purposes: retribution and deterrence of capital crimes by prospective offenders.[3]

In part, capital punishment is an expression of society's moral outrage at particularly offensive conduct. This function may be unappealing to many, but it is essential in an ordered society that asks its citizens to rely on legal processes rather than self-help to vindicate their wrongs. . . .

"Retribution is no longer the dominant objective of the criminal law." . . . but neither is it a forbidden objective nor one inconsistent with our respect for the dignity of men. . . . Indeed, the decision that capital punishment may be the appropriate sanction in extreme cases is an expression of the community's belief that certain crimes are themselves so grievous an affront to humanity that the only adequate response may be the penalty of death.

Statistical attempts to evaluate the worth of the death penalty as a deterrent to crimes by potential offenders have occasioned a great deal of debate. The results simply have been inconclusive. . . .

Although some of the studies suggest that the death penalty may not function as a significantly greater deterrent than lesser penalties, there is no convincing empirical evidence either supporting or refuting this view. We may nevertheless assume safely that there are murders, such as those who act in passion, for whom the threat of death has little or no deterrent effect. But for many others, the death penalty undoubtedly is a significant deterrent. There are carefully contemplated murders, such as murder for hire, where the possible penalty of death may well enter into the cold calculus that precedes the decision to act. And there are some categories of murder, such as murder by a life prisoner, where other sanctions may not be adequate.[4]

The value of capital punishment as a deterrent of crime is a complex factual issue the resolution of which properly rests with the legislatures, which can evaluate the results of statistical studies in terms of their own local conditions and with a flexibility of approach that is not available to the courts. . . . Indeed, many of the post-*Furman* statutes reflect just such a responsible effort to define those crimes and those criminals for which capital punishment is most probably an effective deterrent.

In sum, we cannot say that the judgment of the Georgia legislature that capital punishment may be necessary in some cases is clearly wrong. Considerations of federalism, as well as respect for the ability of a legislature to evaluate, in terms of its particular state, the moral consensus concerning the death penalty and its social utility as a sanction, require us to conclude, in the absence of more convincing evidence, that the infliction of death as a punishment for murder is not without justification and thus is not unconstitutionally severe.

Finally, we must consider whether the punishment of death is disproportionate in relation to the crime for which it is imposed. There is no question that death as a punishment is unique in its severity and irrevocability.

---

[3] Another purpose that has been discussed is the incapacitation of dangerous criminals and the consequent prevention of crimes that they may otherwise commit in the future. . . .

[4] . . . In 1964, reported murders totaled an estimated 9,250. During the ensuing decade, the number reported increased 123% until it totaled approximately 20,600 in 1974. In 1972, the year Furman was announced, the total estimated was 18,550. Despite a fractional decrease in 1975 as compared with 1974, the number of murders increased in the three years immediately following Furman to approximately 20,400, an increase of almost 10%. See Federal Bureau of Investigation, *Crime in the United States*, Uniform Crime Reports, for 1964, 1972, and 1974; 1975 Preliminary Annual Release, Uniform Crime Reports.

. . . When a defendant's life is at stake, the Court has been particularly sensitive to insure that every safeguard is observed. . . . But we are concerned here only with the imposition of capital punishment for the crime of murder, and when a life has been taken deliberately by the offender we cannot say that the punishment is invariably disproportionate to the crime. It is an extreme sanction, suitable to the most extreme of crimes.

We hold that the death penalty is not a form of punishment that may never be imposed, regardless of the circumstances of the offense, regardless of the character of the offender, and regardless of the procedure followed in reaching the decision to impose it.

IV.

We now consider whether Georgia may impose the death penalty on the petitioner in this case.

A

While *Furman* did not hold that the infliction of the death penalty per se violates the Constitution's ban on cruel and unusual punishments, it did recognize that the penalty of death is different in kind from any other punishment imposed under our system of criminal justice. Because of the uniqueness of the death penalty, *Furman* held that it could not be imposed under sentencing procedures that created a substantial risk that it would be inflicted in an arbitrary and capricious manner. . . .

Furman mandates that where discretion is afforded a sentencing body on a matter so grave as the determination of whether a human life should be taken or spared, that discretion must be suitably directed and limited so as to minimize the risk of wholly arbitrary and capricious action.

It is certainly not a novel proposition that discretion in the area of sentencing be exercised in an informed manner. We have long recog-

nized that "[f]or the determination of sentences, justice generally requires . . . that there be taken into account the circumstances of the offense together with the character and propensities of the offender." . . .

. . . When a human life is at stake and when the jury must have information prejudicial to the question of guilt but relevant to the question of penalty in order to impose a rational sentence, a bifurcated system is more likely to ensure elimination of the constitutional deficiencies identified in *Furman*.

But the provision of relevant information under fair procedural rules is not alone sufficient to guarantee that the information will be properly used in the imposition of punishment, especially if sentencing is performed by a jury. Since the members of a jury will have had little, if any, previous experience in sentencing, they are unlikely to be skilled in dealing with the information they are given. . . . To the extent that this problem is inherent in jury sentencing, it may not be totally correctible. It seems clear, however, that the problem will be alleviated if the jury is given guidance regarding the factors about the crime and the defendant that the State, representing organized society, deems particularly relevant to the sentencing decision.

The idea that a jury should be given guidance in its decision making is also hardly a novel proposition. Juries are invariably given careful instructions on the law and how to apply it before they are authorized to decide the merits of a lawsuit. . . .

. . . While such standards are by necessity somewhat general, they do provide guidance to the sentencing authority and thereby reduce the likelihood that it will impose a sentence that fairly can be called capricious or arbitrary. Where the sentencing authority is required to specify the factors it relied upon in reaching its decision, the further safeguard of meaningful appellate review is available to ensure that death sentences are not imposed capriciously or in a freakish manner.

In summary, the concerns expressed in *Fur-*

man that the penalty of death not be imposed in an arbitrary or capricious manner can be met by a carefully drafted statute that ensures that the sentencing authority is given adequate information and guidance. As a general proposition these concerns are best met by a system that provides for a bifurcated proceeding at which the sentencing authority is apprised of the information relevant to the imposition of sentence and provided with standards to guide its use of the information.

We do not intend to suggest that only the above described procedures would be permissible under *Furman* or that any sentencing system constructed along these general lines would inevitably satisfy the concerns of *Furman*, for each distinct system must be examined on an individual basis. . . .

B

We now turn to consideration of the constitutionality of Georgia's capital-sentencing procedures. In the wake of *Furman*, Georgia amended its capital punishment statute, but chose not to narrow the scope of its murder privisions. . . .

Georgia did act, however, to narrow the class of murders subject to capital punishment by specifying 10 statutory aggravating circumstances, one of which must be found by the jury to exist beyond a reasonable doubt before a death sentence can ever be imposed. In addition, the jury is authorized to consider any other appropriate aggravating or mitigating circumstances. . . . The jury is not required to find any mitigating circumstance in order to make a recommendation of mercy that is binding on the trial court . . . but it must find a *statutory* aggravating circumstance before recommending a sentence of death.

These procedures require the jury to consider the circumstances of the crime and the criminal before it recommends sentence. No longer can a Georgia jury do as *Furman's* jury did: reach a finding of the defendant's guilt and then, without guidance or direction, decide whether he

should live or die. Instead, the jury's attention is directed to the specific circumstances of the crime: Was it committed in the course of another capital felony? Was it committed for money? Was it committed upon a peace officer or judicial officer? Was it committed in a particularly heinous way or in a manner that endangered the lives of many persons? In addition, the jury's attention is focused on the characteristics of the person who committed the crime: Does he have a record of prior convictions for capital offenses? Are there any special facts about this defendant that mitigate against imposing capital punishment (e.g., his youth, the extent of his cooperation with the police, his emotional state at the time of the crime)? As a result, while some jury discretion still exists, "the discretion to be exercised is controlled by clear and objective standards so as to produce nondiscriminatory application." *Coley* v. *State*, 231 Ga. 829, 834, 204 S.E.2d 612, 615.

As an important additional safeguard against arbitrariness and caprice, the Georgia statutory scheme provides for automatic appeal of all death sentences to the State's Supreme Court. That court is required by statute to review each sentence of death and determine whether it was imposed under the influence of passion or prejudice, whether the evidence supports the jury's finding of a statutory, aggravating circumstance, and whether the sentence is disproportionate compared to those sentences imposed in similar cases. . . .

In short, Georgia's new sentencing procedures require as a prerequisite to the imposition of the death penalty, specific jury findings as to the circumstances of the crime or the character of the defendant. Moreover, to guard further against a situation comparable to that presented in *Furman*, the Supreme Court of Georgia compares each death sentence with the sentences imposed on similarly situated defendants to ensure that the sentence of death in a particular case is not disproportionate. On their face these procedures seem to satisfy the concerns of *Furman*. . . .

The petitioner contends, however, that the changes in the Georgia sentencing procedures are only cosmetic, that the arbitrariness and capriciousness condemned by *Furman* continue to exist in Georgia—both in traditional practices that still remain and in the new sentencing procedures adopted in response to Furman.

1.

First, the petitioner focuses on the opportunities for discretionary action that are inherent in the processing of any murder case under Georgia law. He notes that the state prosecutor has unfettered authority to select those persons whom he wishes to prosecute for a capital offense and to plea bargain with them. Further, at the trial the jury may choose to convict a defendant of a lesser included offense rather than find him guilty of a crime punishable by death, even if the evidence would support a capital verdict. And finally, a defendant who is convicted and sentenced to die may have his sentence commuted by the Governor of the State and the Georgia Board of Pardons and Paroles.

The existence of these discretionary stages is not determinative of the issues before us. At each of these stages an actor in the criminal justice system makes a decision which may remove a defendant from consideration as a candidate for the death penalty. *Furman*, in contrast, dealt with the decision to impose the death sentence on a specific individual who had been convicted of a capital offense. Nothing in any of our cases suggests that the decision to afford an individual defendant mercy violates the Constitution. *Furman* held only that, in order to minimize the risk that the death penalty would be imposed on a capriciously selected group of offenders, the decision to impose it had to be guided by standards so that the sentencing authority would focus on the particularized circumstances of the crime and the defendant.

The petitioner further contends that the capital-sentencing procedures adopted by Georgia in response to *Furman* do not eliminate

the dangers of arbitrariness and caprice in jury sentencing that were held in *Furman* to be violative of the Eighth and Fourteenth Amendments. He claims that the statute is so broad and vague as to leave juries free to act as arbitrarily and capriciously as they wish in deciding whether to impose the death penalty. . . . Specifically, Gregg urges that the statutory aggravating circumstances are too broad and too vague, that the sentencing procedure allows for arbitrary grants of mercy, and that the scope of the evidence and argument that can be considered at the presentence hearing is too wide.

The petitioner attacks the seventh statutory aggravating circumstance, which authorizes imposition of the death penalty if the murder was "outrageously or wantonly vile, horrible or inhuman in that it involved torture, depravity of mind, or an aggravated battery to the victim," contending that it is so broad that capital punishment could be imposed in any murder case. It is, of course, arguable that any murder involves depravity of mind or an aggravated battery. But this language need not be construed in this way and there is no reason to assume that the Supreme Court of Georgia will adopt such an open-ended construction. . . .

The petitioner also argues that two of the statutory aggravating circumstances are vague and therefore susceptible to widely differing interpretations, thus creating a substantial risk that the death penalty will be arbitrarily inflicted by Georgia juries. In light of the decisions of the Supreme Court of Georgia we must disagree. . . .

The petitioner next argues that the requirements of *Furman* are not met here because the jury has the power to decline to impose the death penalty even if it finds that one or more statutory aggravating circumstances is present in the case. This contention misinterprets *Furman*. . . . Moreover, it ignores the role of the Supreme Court of Georgia which reviews each death sentence to determine whether it is proportional to other sentences imposed for similar crimes. . . .

The petitioner objects, finally to the wide scope of evidence and argument allowed at the presentence hearings. We think that the Georgia court wisely has chosen not to impose unnecessary restrictions on the evidence that can be offered at such a hearing and to approve open and far-ranging argument. . . . So long as the evidence introduced and the arguments made at the presentence hearing do not prejudice a defendant, it is preferable not to impose restrictions. We think it desirable for the jury to have as much information before it as possible when it makes the sentencing decision. . . .

3.

Finally, the Georgia statute has an additional provision designed to assure that the death penalty will not be imposed on a capriciously selected group of convicted defendants. The new sentencing procedures require that the State Supreme Court review every death sentence to determine whether it was imposed under the influence of passion, prejudice, or any other arbitrary factor, whether the evidence supports the findings of a statutory aggravating circumstance, and "[w]hether the sentence of death is excessive or disproportionate to the penalty imposed in similar cases, considering both the crime and the defendant." . . . In performing its sentence review function the Georgia court has held that "if the death penalty is only rarely imposed for an act or it is substantially out of line with sentences imposed for other acts it will be set aside as excessive." *Coley* v. *State*, 231 Ga. 829, 834, 204 S.E.2d 612, 616 (1974). . . .

It is apparent that the Supreme Court of Georgia has taken its review responsibilities seriously. . . .

The provision for appellate review in the Georgia capital-sentencing system serves as a check against the random or arbitrary imposition of the death penalty. In particular, the proportionality review substantially eliminates the possibility that a person will be sentenced to die by the action of an aberrant jury. If a time comes when juries generally do not impose the death sentence in a certain kind of murder case, the appellate review procedures assure that no defendant convicted under such circumstances will suffer a sentence of death.

V.

The basic concern of *Furman* centered on those defendants who were being condemned to death capriciously and arbitrarily. . . . The new Georgia sentencing procedures, by contrast, focus the jury's attention on the particularized nature of the crime and the particularized characteristics of the individual defendant. While the jury is permitted to consider any aggravating or mitigating circumstances, it must find and identify at least one statutory aggravating factor before it may impose a penalty of death. In this way the jury's discretion is channeled. No longer can a jury wantonly and freakishly impose the death sentence; it is always circumscribed by the legislative guidelines. In addition, the review function of the Supreme Court of Georgia affords additional assurance that the concerns that prompted our decision in *Furman* are not present to any significant degree in the Georgia procedure applied here.

For the reasons expressed in this opinion, we hold that the statutory system under which Gregg was sentenced to death does not violate the Constitution. Accordingly, the judgment of the Georgia Supreme Court is affirmed.

Mr. Justice White, with whom the Chief Justice [Burger] and Mr. Justice Rehnquist join, concurring in the judgment. . . .

. . . The Georgia Legislature has made an effort to identify those aggravating factors which it considers necessary and relevant to the question whether a defendant convicted of capital murder should be sentenced to death. The jury which imposes sentence is instructed on all statutory aggravating factors which are supported by the evidence, and is told that it may not impose the death penalty unless it unanimously finds at least one of those factors to have been established beyond a reasonable doubt. The Georgia Legislature has plainly made an effort to guide the jury in the exercise of its discretion, while at the same time permitting the jury to dispense mercy on the basis of factors too intengible to write into a statute and I cannot accept a naked assertion that the effort is bound to fail. As the types of murders for which the death penalty may be imposed become more narrowly defined and are limited to those which are particularly serious or for which the death penalty is peculiarly appropriate as they are in Georgia by reason of the aggravating circumstance requirement, it becomes reasonable to expect that juries—even given discretion *not* to impose the death penalty—will impose the death penalty in a substantial portion of the cases so defined. If they do, it can no longer be said that the penalty is being imposed wantonly and freakishly or so infrequently that it loses its usefulness as a sentencing device. There is, therefore, reason to expect that Georgia's current system would escape the infirmities which invalidated its previous system under *Furman*. . . .

Petitioner's argument that prosecutors behave in a standardless fashion in deciding which cases to try as capital felonies is unsupported by any facts. Petitioner simply asserts that since prosecutors have the power not to charge capital felonies they will exercise that power in a standardless fashion. This is untenable. Absent facts to the contrary, it cannot be assumed that prosecutors will be motivated in their charging decision by factors other than the strength of their case and the likelihood that a jury would impose the death penalty if it convicts. Unless prosecutors are incompetent in their judgments, the standards by which they decide whether to charge a capital felony will be the same as those by which the jury will decide the questions of guilt and sentence.

Thus defendants will escape the death penalty through prosecutorial charging decisions only because the offense is not sufficiently serious; or because the proof is insufficiently strong. This does not cause the system to be standardless any more than the jury's decision to impose life imprisonment on a defendant whose crime is deemed insufficiently serious or its decision to acquit someone who is probably guilty but whose guilt is not established beyond a reasonable doubt. Thus the prosecutor's charging decisions are unlikely to have removed from the sample of cases considered by the Georgia Supreme Court any which are truly "similar." If the cases really were "similar" in relevant respects, it is unlikely that prosecutors would fail to prosecute them as capital cases; and I am unwilling to assume the contrary.

Petitioner's argument that there is an unconstitutional amount of discretion in the system which separates those suspects who receive the death penalty from those who receive life imprisonment, a lesser penalty, or are acquitted or never charged, seems to be in final analysis of indictment of our entire system of justice. Petitioner has argued, in effect, that no matter how effective the death penalty may be as a punishment, government, created and run as it must be by humans, is inevitably incompetent to administer it. This cannot be accepted as a proposition of constitutional law. Imposition of the death penalty is surely an awesome responsibility for any system of justice and those who participate in it. Mistakes will be made and discriminations will occur which will be difficult to explain. However, one of society's most basic tasks is that of protecting the lives of its citizens and one of the most basic ways in which it achieves the task is through criminal laws against murder. I decline to interfere with the manner in which Georgia has chosen to enforce such laws on what is simply an assertion of lack of faith in the ability of the system of justice to operate in a fundamentally fair manner.

. . . [N]either can I agree with the petitioner's other basic argument that the death penalty, however imposed and for whatever crime, is cruel and unusual punishment.

I therefore concur in the judgment of affirmance.

Statement of the Chief Justice [Burger] and Mr. Justice Rehnquist.

We join the opinion of Mr. Justice White, agreeing with its analysis that Georgia's system of capital punishment comports with the Court's holding in *Furman* v. *Georgia*, 408 U.S. 238 (1972).

[Mr. Justice Blackmun concurred without opinion.]

Mr. Justice Brennan, dissenting.

The Cruel and Unusual Punishments Clause "must draw its meaning from the evolving standards of decency that mark the progress of a maturing society." The opinions of Mr. Justice Stewart, Mr. Justice Powell, and Mr. Justice Stevens today hold that "evolving standards of decency" require focus not on the essence of the death penalty itself but primarily upon the procedures employed by the state to single out persons to suffer the penalty of death. Those opinions hold further that, so viewed, the Clause invalidates the mandatory infliction of the death penalty but not its infliction under sentencing procedures that Mr. Justice Stewart, Mr. Justice Powell, and Mr. Justice Stevens conclude adequately safeguard against the risk that the death penalty was imposed in an arbitrary and capricious manner. . . .

This Court inescapably has the duty, as the ultimate arbiter of the meaning of our Constitution, to say whether, when individuals condemned to death stand before our Bar, "moral concepts" require us to hold that the law has progressed to the point where we should declare that the punishment of death, like punishments on the rack, the screw and the wheel, is no longer morally tolerable in our civilized society. My opinion in *Furman* v. *Georgia*

concluded that our civilization and the law had progressed to this point and that therefore the punishment of death, for whatever crime and under all circumstances, is "cruel and unusual" in violation of the Eighth and Fourteenth Amendments of the Constitution. I shall not again canvass the reasons that led to that conclusion. I emphasize only that foremost among the "moral concepts" recognized in our cases and inherent in the Clause is the primary moral principle that the State, even as it punishes, must treat its citizens in a manner consistent with their intrinsic worth as human beings—a punishment must not be so severe as to be degrading to human dignity. A judicial determination whether the punishment of death comports with human dignity is therefore not only permitted but compelled by the Clause. . . .

The fatal constitutional infirmity in the punishment of death is that it treats "members of the human race as nonhumans, as objects to be toyed with and discarded. [It is] thus inconsistent with the fundamental premise of the Clause that even the vilest criminal remains a human being possessed of common human dignity." . . . As such it is a penalty that "subjects the individual to a fate forbidden by the principle of civilized treatment guaranteed by the [Clause]." I therefore would hold, on that ground alone, that death is today a cruel and unusual punishment prohibited by the Clause. "Justice of this kind is obviously no less shocking than that crime itself, and the new 'official' murder, far from offering redress for the offense committed against society, adds instead a second defilement to the first."

Mr. Justice Marshall, dissenting. . . .

In *Furman*, I concluded that the death penalty is constitutionally invalid for two reasons. First, the death penalty is excessive. . . . And second, the American people, fully informed as to the purposes of the death penalty and its liabilities, would in my view reject it as morally unacceptable. . . .

Since the decision in *Furman*, the legislatures of 35 states have enacted new statutes authorizing the imposition of the death sentence for certain crimes, and Congress has enacted a law providing the death penalty for air piracy resulting in death. . . . I would be less than candid if I did not acknowledge that these developments have a significant bearing on a realistic assessment of the moral acceptability of the death penalty to the American people. But if the constitutionality of the death penalty turns, as I have urged, on the opinion of an *informed* citizenry, then even the enactment of new death statutes cannot be viewed as conclusive. In *Furman*, I observed that the American people are largely unaware of the information critical to a judgment on the morality of the death penalty, and concluded that if they were better informed they would consider it shocking, unjust, and unacceptable. . . . A recent study, conducted after the enactment of the post-*Furman* statutes, has confirmed that the American people know little about the death penalty, and that the opinions of an informed public would differ significantly from those of a public unaware of the consequences and effects of the death penalty.[5]

Even assuming, however, that the post-*Furman* enactment of statutes authorizing the death penalty renders the prediction of the views of an informed citizenry an uncertain basis for a constitutional decision, the enactment of those statutes has no bearing whatsoever on the conclusion that the death penalty is unconstitutional because it is excessive. An excessive penalty is invalid under the Cruel and Unusual Punishments Clause "even though popular sentiment may favor" it. . . .

The two purposes that sustain the death penalty as nonexcessive in the Court's view are general deterrence and retribution. In *Furman* I canvassed the relevant data on the deterrent effect of capital punishment. . . . The available evidence, I concluded in *Furman*, was convinc-

ing that "capital punishment is not necessary as a deterrent to crime to our society. . . .

The Solicitor General in his amicus brief in these cases relies heavily on a study by Isaac Ehrlich,[6] reported a year after *Furman*, to support the contention that the death penalty does deter murder. Since the Ehrlich study was not available at the time of *Furman* and since it is the first scientific study to suggest that the death penalty may have a deterrent effect, I will briefly consider its import.

The Ehrlich study focused on the relationship in the Nation as a whole between the homicide rate and "execution risk"—the fraction of persons convicted of murder who were actually executed. Comparing the differences in homicide rate and execution risk for the years 1933 and 1969, Ehrlich found that increases in the execution risk were associated with increases in the homicide rate. But when he employed the statistical technique of multiple regression analysis to control for the influence of other variables posited to have an impact on the homicide rate, Ehrlich found a negative correlation between changes in the homicide rate and changes in execution risk. His tentative conclusion was that for the period from 1933 to 1967 each additional execution in the United States might have saved eight lives.

The methods and conclusions of the Ehrlich study have been severely criticized on a number of grounds. It has been suggested, for example, that the study is defective because it compares execution and homicide rates on a nationwide, rather than a State by State basis. . . .

The most compelling criticism of the Ehrlich study is that its conclusions are extremely sensitive to the choice of the time period included in the regression analysis. Analysis of Ehrlich's data reveals that all empirical support for the deterrent effect of capital punishment disap-

---

[5] Sarat and Vidmar, Public Opinion, The Death Penalty, and the Eighth Amendment: Testing the Marshall Hypothesis, 1976 *Wisc. L. Rev.* 171.

[6] I. Ehrlich, The Deterrent Effect of Capital Punishment: A Question of Life and Death (Working Paper No. 18, National Bureau of Economic Research, November 1973); Ehrlich, The Deterrent Effect of Capital Punishment: A Question of Life and Death, 65 *Am. Econ. Rev.* 397 (1975).

pears when the five most recent years are removed from his time series—that is to say, whether a decrease in the execution risk corresponds to an increase or a decrease in the murder rate depends on the ending point of the sample period. . . .

The Ehrlich study, in short, is of little, if any, assistance in assessing the deterrent impact of the death penalty. . . . The evidence I reviewed in *Furman* remains convincing, in my view, that "capital punishment is not necessary as a deterrent to crime in our society." . . . The justification for the death penalty must be found elsewhere.

The other principal purpose said to be served by the death penalty is retribution. The notion that retribution can serve as a moral justification for the sanction of death finds credence in the opinion of my Brothers Stewart, Powell, and Stevens, and that of my Brother White in [Stanislaus] *Roberts* v. *Louisiana,* 428 U.S. 325 (1976). It is this notion that I find to be the most disturbing aspect of today's unfortunate decision.

. . . [O]ur recognition that retribution plays a crucial role in determining who may be punished by no means requires approval of retribution as a general justification for punishment. It is the question whether retribution can provide a moral justification for punishment—in particular, capital punishment—that we must consider. . . .

It simply defies belief to suggest that the death penalty is necessary to prevent the American people from taking the law into their own hands.

In a related vein, it may be suggested that the expression of moral outrage through the imposition of the death penalty serves to reinforce basic moral values—that it marks some crimes as particularly offensive and therefore to be avoided. . . . This contention, like the previous one, provides no support for the death penalty. It is inconceivable that any individual concerned about conforming his conduct to what society says is "right" would fail to realize that

murder is "wrong" if the penalty were simply life imprisonment.

The foregoing contentions—that society's expression of moral outrage through the imposition of the death penalty pre-empts the citizenry from taking the law into its own hands and reinforces moral values—are not retributive in the purest sense. They are essentially utilitarian in that they portray the death penalty as valuable because of its beneficial results. These justifications for the death penalty are inadequate because the penalty is, quite clearly I think, not necessary to the accomplishment of those results.

There remains for consideration, however, what might be termed the purely retributive justification for the death penalty—that the death penalty is appropriate, not because of its beneficial effect on society, but because the taking of the murderer's life is itself morally good. . . .

. . . The mere fact that the community demands the murderer's life in return for the evil he has done cannot sustain the death penalty, for as the plurality reminds us, "the Eighth Amendment demands more than that a challenged punishment be acceptable to contemporary society." . . . To be sustained under the Eighth Amendment, the death penalty must "[comport] with the basic concept of human dignity at the core of the Amendment", . . . the objective in imposing it must be "[consistent] with our respect for the dignity of other men." . . . Under these standards, the taking of life "because the wrong-doer deserves it" surely must fall, for such a punishment has as its very basis the total denial of the wrong-doer's dignity and worth.

The death penalty, unnecessary to promote the goal of deterrence or to further any legitimate notion of retribution, is an excessive penalty forbidden by the Eighth and Fourteenth Amendments. I respectfully dissent from the Court's judgment upholding the sentences of death imposed upon the petitioners in these cases.

Woodson v. *North Carolina*
428 U.S. 280 (1976)

Unlike Georgia, North Carolina responded to the *Furman* unguided-discretion problem by making death a *mandatory* sentence for all persons convicted of first-degree murder.

[Mr. Justice Stewart announced the judgment of the court.]

II.

The petitioners argue that the imposition of the death penalty under any circumstances is cruel and unusual punishment in violation of the Eighth and Fourteenth Amendments. We reject this argument for the reasons stated in *Gregg* v. *Georgia*, 428 U.S. 153 (1976).

III.

. . . North Carolina, unlike Florida, Georgia, and Texas, has thus responded to the *Furman* decision by making death the mandatory sentence for all persons convicted of first-degree murder. In ruling on the constitutionality of the sentences imposed on the petitioners under this North Carolina statute, the Court now addresses for the first time the question whether a death sentence returned pursuant to a law imposing a mandatory death penalty for a broad category of homicidal offenses constitutes cruel and unusual punishment within the meaning of the Eighth and Fourteenth Amendments. The issue, like that explored in *Furman*, involves the procedure employed by the State to select persons for the unique and irreversible penalty of death.

A

The Eighth Amendment stands to assure that the State's power to punish is "exercised within the limits of civilized standards." *Trop* v. *Dulles*, 356 U.S. 86, 100 (1958) (plurality opinion). . . .

Central to the application of the Amendment is a determination of contemporary standards regarding the infliction of punishment. As discussed in *Gregg* v. *Georgia*, indicia of societal values identified in prior opinions include history and traditional usage, legislative enactments, and jury determinations.

In order to provide a frame for assessing the relevancy of these factors in this case we begin by sketching the history of mandatory death penalty statutes in the United States. At the time the Eighth Amendment was adopted in 1791, the States uniformly followed the common-law practice of making death the exclusive and mandatory sentence for certain specified offenses. Although the range of capital offenses in the American colonies was quite limited in comparison to the more than 200 offenses then punishable by death in England, the colonies at the time of the Revolution imposed death sentences on all persons convicted of any of a considerable number of crimes, typically including at a minimum, murder, treason, piracy, arson, rape, robbery, burglary, and sodomy. As at common law, all homicides that were not involuntary, provoked, justified, or excused constituted murder and were automatically punished by death. Almost from the outset jurors reacted unfavorably to the harshness of mandatory death sentences. The States initially responded to this expression of public dissatisfaction with mandatory statutes by limiting the classes of capital offenses. . . .

Despite the broad acceptance of the division of murder into degrees . . . juries continued to find the death penalty inappropriate in a significant number of first-degree murder cases and refused to return guilty verdicts for that crime.

The inadequacy of distinguishing between murderers solely on the basis of legislative criteria narrowing the definition of the capital offense led the States to grant juries sentencing discretion in capital cases. Tennessee in 1838, followed by Alabama in 1841, and Louisiana in 1846, were the first States to abandon mandatory death sentences in favor of discretionary death penalty statutes. This flexibility remedied the harshness of mandatory statutes by permitting the jury to respond to mitigating factors by withholding the death penalty. By the turn of the century, 23 States and the Federal Government had made death sentences discretionary for first-degree murder and other capital offenses. During the next two decades 14 additional States replaced their mandatory death statutes. Thus, by the end of World War I, all but eight States, Hawaii, and the District of Columbia either had adopted discretionary death penalty schemes or abolished the death penalty altogether. By 1963, all of these remaining jurisdictions had replaced their automatic death penalty statutes with discretionary jury sentencing.

The history of mandatory death penalty statutes in the United States thus reveals that the practice of sentencing to death all persons convicted of a particular offense has been rejected as unduly harsh and unworkably rigid. The two crucial indicators of evolving standards of decency respecting the imposition of punishment in our society—jury determinations and legislative enactments—both point conclusively to the repudiation of automatic death sentences. . . .

. . . [L]egislative measures adopted by the people's chosen representatives weigh heavily in ascertaining contemporary standards of decency. The consistent course charted by the state legislatures and by Congress since the middle of the past century demonstrates that the aversion of jurors to mandatory death penalty statutes is shared by society at large.

Still further evidence of the incompatibility of mandatory death penalties with contemporary values is provided by the results of jury sentencing under discretionary statutes. . . . Various studies indicate that even in first-degree mur-

der cases juries with sentencing discretion do not impose the death penalty "with any great frequency," H. Kalven and H. Zeisel, *The American Jury* 436 (1966).[1] The actions of sentencing juries suggest that under contemporary standards of decency death is viewed as an inappropriate punishment for a substantial portion of convicted first-degree murderers.

Although the Court has never ruled on the constitutionality of mandatory death penalty statutes, on several occasions dating back to 1899 it has commented upon our society's aversion to automatic death sentences. . . .

Although it seems beyond dispute that, at the time of the *Furman* decision in 1972 mandatory death penalty statutes had been renounced by American juries and legislatures, there remains the question whether the mandatory statutes adopted by North Carolina and a number of other States following *Furman* evince a sudden reversal of societal values regarding the imposition of capital punishment. In view of the persistent and unswerving legislative rejection of mandatory death penalty statutes beginning in 1838 and continuing for more than 130 years until *Furman*, it seems evident that the post-*Furman* enactments reflect attempts by the States to retain the death penalty in a form consistent with the Constitution, rather than a renewed societal acceptance of mandatory death sentencing. The fact that some States have adopted mandatory measures following *Furman* while others have legislated standards to guide jury discretion appears attributable to diverse readings of this Court's multi-opinioned decision in that case. . . .

It is now well established that the Eighth Amendment draws much of its meaning from "the evolving standards of decency that mark the progress of a maturing society." *Trop* v. *Dulles,* 356 U.S., at 101 (plurality opinion). As the

---

[1] Data compiled on discretionary jury sentencing of persons convicted of capital murder indicate that the penalty of death is generally imposed in less than 20% of the cases. . . .

above discussion makes clear, one of the most significant developments in our society's treatment of capital punishment has been the rejection of the common-law practice of inexorably imposing a death sentence upon every person convicted of a specified offense. North Carolina's mandatory death penalty statute for first-degree murder departs markedly from contemporary standards respecting the imposition of the punishment of death and thus cannot be applied consistently with the Eighth and Fourteenth Amendments' requirement that the State's power to punish "be exercised within the limits of civilized standards." . . .

B

A separate deficiency of North Carolina's mandatory death sentence statute is its failure to provide a constitutionally tolerable response to *Furman's* rejection of unbridled jury discretion in the imposition of capital sentences. Central to the limited holding in *Furman* was the conviction that the vesting of standardless sentencing power in the jury violated the Eighth and Fourteenth Amendments. . . . When one considers the long and consistent American experience with the death penalty in first-degree murder cases, it becomes evident that mandatory statutes enacted in response to *Furman* have simply papered over the problem of unguided and unchecked jury discretion. . . .

North Carolina's mandatory death penalty statute provides no standards to guide the jury in its inevitable exercise of the power to determine which first-degree murderers shall live and which shall die. And there is no way under the North Carolina law for the judiciary to check arbitrary and capricious exercise of that power through a review of death sentences. . . . Instead of rationalizing the sentencing process, a mandatory scheme may well exacerbate the problem identified in *Furman* by resting the penalty determination on the particular jury's willingness to act lawlessly. While a mandatory death penalty statute may reasonably be ex-

pected to increase the number of persons sentenced to death, it does not fulfill *Furman's* basic requirement by replacing arbitrary and wanton jury discretion with objective standards to guide, regularize and make rationally reviewable the process for imposing a sentence of death.

C

A third constitutional shortcoming of the North Carolina statute is its failure to allow the particularized consideration of relevant aspects of the character and record of each convicted defendant before the imposition upon him of a sentence of death. . . . A process that accords no significance to relevant facets of the character and record of the individual offender or the circumstances of the particular offenses excludes from consideration in fixing the ultimate punishment of death the possibility of compassionate or mitigating factors stemming from the diverse frailties of humankind. It treats all persons convicted of a designated offense not as uniquely individual human beings, but as members of a faceless, undifferentiated mass to be subjected to the blind infliction of the penalty of death. . . .

While the prevailing practice of individualizing sentencing determinations generally reflects simply enlightened policy rather than a constitutional imperative, we believe that in capital cases the fundamental respect for humanity underlying the Eighth Amendment . . . requires consideration of the character and record of the individual offender and the circumstances of the particular offense as a constitutionally indispensable part of the process of inflicting the penalty of death.

This conclusion rests squarely on the predicate that the penalty of death is qualitatively different from a sentence of imprisonment, however long. Death, in its finality, differs more from life imprisonment than a 100 year prison term differs from one of only a year or two. Because of that qualitative difference there is a corresponding difference in the need for reliability in the determination that death is the appropriate punishment in a specific case.

For the reasons stated, we conclude that the death sentences imposed upon the petitioners under North Carolina's mandatory death sentence statute violated the Eighth and Fourteenth Amendments and therefore must be set aside. The judgment of the Supreme Court of North Carolina is reversed insofar as it upheld the death sentences imposed upon the petitioners, and the case is remanded for further proceedings not inconsistent with this opinion.

Mr. Justice Brennan, concurring in the judgment.

For the reasons stated in my dissenting opinion in *Gregg* v. *Georgia*, 428 U.S. 153, 227 (1976), I concur in the judgment that sets aside the death sentences imposed under the North Carolina death sentence statute as violative of the Eighth and Fourteenth Amendments.

Mr. Justice Marshall, concurring in the judgment.

For the reasons stated in my dissenting opinion in *Gregg* v. *Georgia*, 428 U.S. 153, 231 (1976), I am of the view that the death penalty is a cruel and unusual punishment forbidden by the Eighth and Fourteenth Amendments. I therefore concur in the Court's judgment.

Mr. Justice White, with whom The Chief Justice [Burger] and Mr. Justice Rehnquist join, dissenting. . . .

. . . I reject petitioners' arguments that the death penalty in any circumstances is a violation of the Eighth Amendment and that the North Carolina statute, although making the imposition of the death penalty mandatory upon proof of guilt and a verdict of first-degree murder, will nevertheless result in the death penalty being imposed so seldom and arbitrarily that it is void under *Furman* v. *Georgia*. . . . I also disagree with the two additional grounds

which the plurality sua sponte offers for invalidating the North Carolina statute. I would affirm the judgment of the North Carolina Supreme Court.

Mr. Justice Blackmun, dissenting.

I dissent for the reasons set forth in my dissent in *Furman* v. *Georgia*, 408 U.S. 238, 405–414 (1972), and in the other dissenting opinions I joined in that case. *Id.*, at 375, 414, and 465.

Mr. Justice Rehnquist, dissenting. . . .

. . . It is by no means clear that the prohibition against cruel and unusual punishments embodied in the Eighth Amendment, and made applicable to the States by the Fourteenth Amendment, *Robinson* v. *California*, 370 U.S. 660 (1962), was not limited to those punishments deemed cruel and unusual at the time of the adoption of the Bill of Rights. *McGautha* v. *California*, 402 U.S. 183, 225 (1971) (Black, J., concurring). . . . Thus for the plurality to begin its analysis with the assumption that it need only demonstrate that "evolving standards of decency" show that contemporary "society" has rejected such provisions is itself a somewhat shaky point of departure. But even if the assumption be conceded, the plurality opinion's analysis nonetheless founders.

The plurality relies first upon its conclusion that society has turned away from the mandatory imposition of death sentences, and second upon its conclusion that the North Carolina system has "simply papered over" the problem of unbridled jury discretion which two of the separate opinions in *Furman* v. *Georgia*, 408 U.S. 238 (1972), identified as the basis for the judgment rendering the death sentences there reviewed unconstitutional. The third "constitutional shortcoming" of the North Carolina statute is said to be "its failure to allow the particularized consideration of relevant aspects of the character and record of each convicted defendant before the imposition upon him of a sentence of death." . . .

I do not believe that any one of these reasons singly, nor all of them together, can withstand careful analysis. Contrary to the plurality's assertions, they would import into the Cruel and Unusual Punishments Clause procedural requirements which find no support in our cases. Their application will result in the invalidation of a death sentence imposed upon a defendant convicted of first-degree murder under the North Carolina system and the upholding of the same sentence imposed on an identical defendant convicted on identical evidence of first-degree murder under the Florida, Georgia, or Texas systems—a result surely as "freakish" as that condemned in the separate opinions in *Furman*. . . .

. . . What the plurality opinion has actually done is to import into the Due Process Clause of the Fourteenth Amendment what it conceives to be desirable procedural guarantees where the punishment of death, concededly not cruel and unusual for the crime of which the defendant was convicted, is to be imposed. . . .

I agree with the conclusion of the plurality, and with that of Mr. Justice White, that death is not a cruel and unusual punishment for the offense of which these petitioners were convicted. Since no member of the Court suggests that the trial which led to those convictions in any way fell short of the standards mandated by the Constitution, the judgments of conviction should be affirmed. The Fourteenth Amendment, giving the fullest scope to its "majestic generalities," *Fay* v. *New York*, 322 U.S. 261, 282 (1947), is conscripted rather than interpreted when used to permit one but not another system for imposition of the death penalty.

Lockett v. *Ohio*
98 S. Ct. 2954 (1978)

Mr. Chief Justice Burger delivered the opinion of the Court with respect to the constitutionality of petitioner's conviction (Parts I and II), together with an opinion (Part III), in which Mr. Justice Stewart, Mr. Justice Powell, and Mr. Justice Stevens, joined, on the constitutionality of the statute under which petitioner was sentenced to death and announced the judgment of the Court. . . .

Lockett challenges the constitutionality of Ohio's death penalty statute on a number of grounds. We find it necessary to consider only her contention that her death sentence is invalid because the statute under which it was imposed did not permit the sentencing judge to consider, as mitigating factors, her character, prior record, age, lack of specific intent to cause death, and her relatively minor part in the crime. To address her contention from the proper perspective, it is helpful to review the developments in our recent cases where we have applied the Eighth and Fourteenth Amendments to death penalty statutes. We do not write on a "clean slate."

Prior to *Furman* v. *Georgia*, 408 U.S. 238, (1972), every State that authorized capital punishment had abandoned mandatory death penalties, and instead permitted the jury unguided and unrestrained discretion regarding the imposition of the death penalty in a particular capital case. Mandatory death penalties had proven unsatisfactory, as the plurality noted in *Woodson* v. *North Carolina*, 428 U.S. 280, 293, in part because juries "with some regularity disregarded their oaths and refused to convict defendants where a death sentence was the automatic consequence of a guilty verdict."

This Court had never intimated prior to *Furman* that discretion in sentencing offended the Constitution. . . . As recently as *McGautha* v. *California*, 402 U.S. 183 (1971), the Court had specifically rejected the contention that discretion in imposing the death penalty violated the fundamental standards of fairness embodied in Fourteenth Amendment due process. . . .

Predictably, the variety of opinions supporting the judgment in *Furman* engendered confusion as to what was required in order to impose the death penalty in accord with the Eighth

Amendment. Some States responded to what was thought to be the command of *Furman* by adopting mandatory death penalties for a limited category of specific crimes thus eliminating all discretion from the sentencing process in capital cases. Other States attempted to continue the practice of individually assessing the culpability of each individual defendant convicted of a capital offense and, at the same time, to comply with *Furman,* by providing standards to guide the sentencing decision.

Four years after *Furman,* we considered Eighth Amendment issues posed by five of the post-*Furman* death penalty statutes. Four Justices took the position that all five statutes complied with the Constitution; two Justices took the position that none of them complied. Hence, the disposition of each case varied according to the votes of a plurality of three Justices who delivered a joint opinion in each of the five cases upholding the constitutionality of the statutes of Georgia, Florida, and Texas, and holding those of North Carolina and Louisiana unconstitutional. . . .

In the last decade, many of the States have been obliged to revise their death penalty statutes in response to the various opinions supporting the judgments in *Furman, supra,* and *Gregg* [*Gregg* v. *Georgia,* 428 U.S. 153 (1976)], and it companion cases. The signals from this Court have not, however, always been easy to decipher. The States now deserve the clearest guidance that the Court can provide; we have an obligation to reconcile previously differing views in order to provide that guidance. . . .

We begin by recognizing that the concept of individualized sentencing in criminal cases generally, although not constitutionally required, has long been accepted in this country. . . . And where sentencing discretion is granted, it generally has been agreed that the sentencing judge's "possession of the fullest information possible concerning the defendant's life and characteristics" is "[h]ighly relevant— *if not essential*—[to the] selection of an appropriate sentence. . . ." (Emphasis added). . . .

We . . . conclude that the Eighth and Fourteenth Amendments require that the sentencer, in all but the rarest kind of capital case,[1] not be precluded from considering *as a mitigating factor,* any aspect of a defendant's character of record and any of the circumstances of the offense that the defendant proffers as a basis for a sentence less than death. . . . The need for treating each defendant in a capital case with that degree of respect due the uniqueness of the individual is far more important than in noncapital cases. A variety of flexible techniques— probation, parole, work furloughs, to name a few—and various post conviction remedies, may be available to modify an initial sentence of confinement in noncapital cases. The nonavailability of corrective or modifying mechanisms with respect to an executed capital sentence underscores the need for individualized consideration as a constitutional requirement in imposing the death sentence. . . .

The limited range of mitigating circumstances which may be considered by the sentencer under the Ohio statute is incompatible with the Eighth and Fourteenth Amendments. To meet constitutional requirements, a death penalty statute must not preclude consideration of relevant mitigating factors.

Accordingly, the judgment under review is reversed to the extent that it sustains the imposition of the death penalty; the case is remanded for further proceedings.

Mr. Justice Brennan took no part in the consideration or decision of this case.

Mr. Justice Marshall, concurring in the judgment.

I continue to adhere to my view that the death penalty is, under all circumstances, a

---

[1] We express no opinion as to whether the need to deter certain kinds of homicide would justify a mandatory death sentence as, for example, when a prisoner—or escapee— under a life sentence is found guilty of murder. See Roberts (Harry) v. Louisiana, 431 U.S. 633, 637 (1977).

cruel and unusual punishment prohibited by the Eighth Amendment. . . .

Mr. Justice Blackmun, concurring in part and concurring in the judgment. . . .

Mr. Justice White, dissenting in part and concurring in the judgments of the Court. . . .

The Court has now completed its about-face since *Furman.* . . .

With all due respect, I dissent. I continue to be of the view, for the reasons set forth in my dissenting opinion in *Roberts* v. *Louisiana,* 428 U.S., at 337, that it does not violate the Eighth Amendment for a State to impose the death penalty on a mandatory basis when the defendant has been found guilty beyond a reasonable doubt of committing a deliberate, unjustified killing. . . .

Mr. Justice Rehnquist, concurring in part and dissenting.

. . . [T]he Court has gone from pillar to post, with the result that the sort of reasonable predictability upon which legislatures, trial courts, and appellate courts must of necessity rely has been all but completely sacrificed. . . .

It seems to me indisputably clear from today's opinion that, while we may not be writing on a clean slate, the Court is scarcely faithful to what has been written before. . . . By encouraging defendants in capital cases, and presumably sentencing judges and juries, to take into consideration anything under the sun as a "mitigating circumstance," it will not guide sentencing discretion but will totally unleash it. . . .

> *Quaere:* It has been suggested that "In *Lockett,* the Court has downgraded *Furman* and its premise that broad jury discretion in capital sentencing is constitutionally suspect. The decision reflects a disenchantment with legislative efforts to control arbitrariness and represents a reaffirmation of faith in the informed discretion of the sentencer to reach the fairest, if not the most consistent outcome." Do you agree?

Coker v. *Georgia*
433 U.S. 584 (1977)

While serving life sentences for murder, rape, and kidnapping, Coker escaped from prison. Within a few hours he raped and abducted a 16-year-old female in the presence of her husband (whom he had robbed and tied up). After his conviction, a sentencing hearing was held as recommended by the Court in *Gregg* (above). The jury found that Coker's earlier conviction for a capital felony, plus the rape in conjunction with the felonious robbery of the victim's husband, constituted aggravating circumstance, and thus warranted a death sentence under the Georgia statute (outlined in *Gregg*).

Mr. Justice White announced the judgment of the Court and filed an opinion in which Mr. Justice Stewart, Mr. Justice Blackmun, and Mr. Justice Stevens joined. . . .

II.

. . .

In sustaining the imposition of the death penalty in *Gregg* [v. *Georgia,* 428 U.S. 153 (1976)]

. . . the Court firmly embraced the holdings and dicta from prior cases, *Furman* v. *Georgia* [408 U.S. 238 (1972)]; *Robinson* v. *California,* 370 U.S. 660 (1963); *Trop* v. *Dulles,* 356 U.S. 86 (1958); and *Weems* v. *United States,* 217 U.S. 349 (1910), to the effect that the Eighth Amendment bars not only those punishments that are "barbaric" but also those that are "excessive" in relation to the crime committed. Under *Gregg,* a punishment is "excessive" and unconstitutional if it (1) makes no measureable contribution to acceptable goals of punishment and hence is nothing more than the purposeless and needless imposition of pain and suffering; or (2) is grossly out of proportion to the severity of the crime. A punishment might fail the test on either ground. Furthermore, these Eighth Amendment judgments should not be, or appear to be, merely the subjective views of individual Justices; judgment should be informed by objective factors to the maximum possible extent. To this end, attention must be given to the public attitudes concerning a particular sentence—history and precedent, legislative attitudes, and the response of juries reflected in their sentencing decisions are to be consulted. In *Gregg*, after giving due regard to such sources, the Court's judgment was that the death penalty for deliberate murder was neither the purposeless imposition of severe punishment nor a punishment grossly disproportionate to the crime. But the Court reserved the question of the constitutionality of the death penalty when imposed for other crimes. . . .

III.

That question with respect to rape of an adult woman, is now before us. We have concluded that a sentence of death is grossly disproportionate and excessive punishment for the crime of rape and is therefore forbidden by the Eighth Amendment as cruel and unusual punishment.

A

. . . At no time in the last 50 years has a majority of the States authorized death as a punishment for rape. In 1925, 18 States, the District of Columbia, and the Federal Government authorized capital punishment for the rape of an adult female. By 1971 just prior to the decision in *Furman* v. *Georgia*, that number had declined, but not substantially, to 16 States plus the Federal Government. *Furman* then invalidated most of the capital punishment statutes in this country, including the rape statutes, because,

among other reasons, of the manner in which the death penalty was imposed and utilized under those laws.

With their death penalty statutes for the most part invalidated, the States were faced with the choice of enacting modified capital punishment laws in an attempt to satisfy the requirements of *Furman* or of being satisfied with life imprisonment as the ultimate punishment of *any* offense. Thirty-five States immediately reinstituted the death penalty for at least limited kinds of crime. . . .

This public judgment as to the acceptability of capital punishment, evidenced by the immediate, post-*Furman* legislative reaction in a large majority of the States, heavily influenced the Court to sustain the death penalty for murder in *Gregg* v. *Georgia*. . . .

But if the "most marked indication of a society's endorsement of the death penalty for murder is the legislative response to *Furman*," *Gregg* v. *Georgia*, *supra*, at 179–180, it should also be a telling datum that the public judgment with respect to rape, as reflected in the statutes providing the punishment for that crime, has been dramatically different. In reviving death penalty laws to satisfy *Furman's* mandate, none of the States that had not previously authorized death for rape chose to include rape among capital felonies. Of the 16 States in which rape had been a capital offense, only three provided the death penalty for rape of an adult woman in their revised statutes—Georgia, North Carolina, and Louisiana. In the latter two States, the death penalty was mandatory for those found guilty, and those laws were invalidated by *Woodson* and *Roberts*. When Louisiana and North Carolina, responding to those decisions, again revised their capital punishment laws, they reenacted the death penalty for murder but not for rape; none of the seven other legislatures that to our knowledge have amended or replaced their death penalty statutes since July 2, 1976, including four States (in addition to Louisiana and North Carolina) that had authorized the death sentence for rape prior to 1972 and had reacted to *Furman* with mandatory statutes, included rape among the crimes for which death was an authorized punishment.

Georgia argues that 11 of the 16 states that authorized death for rape in 1972 attempted to comply with *Furman* by enacting arguably mandatory death penalty legislation and that it is very likely that aside from Louisiana and North Carolina, these States simply chose to eliminate rape as a capital offense rather than to *require* death for *each* and *every* instance of rape. The argument is not without force; but four of the 16 States did not take the mandatory course and also did *not* continue rape of an adult woman as a capital offense. Further, as we have indicated, the legislatures of six of the 11 arguably mandatory States have revised their death penalty laws since *Woodson* and *Roberts* without enacting a new death penalty for rape. And this is to say nothing of 19 other States that enacted nonmandatory, post-*Furman* statutes and chose not to sentence rapists to death.

It should be noted that Florida, Mississippi, and Tennessee also authorized the death penalty in some rape cases, but only where the victim was a child and the rapist an adult. The Tennessee statute has since been invalidated because the death sentence was mandatory. *Collins* v. *State*, 550 S.W. 2d 643 (1977). The upshot is that Georgia is the sole jurisdiction in the United States at the present time that authorizes a sentence of death when the rape victim is an adult woman, and only two other jurisdictions provide capital punishment when the victim is a child.

The current judgment with respect to the death penalty for rape is not wholly unanimous among state legislatures, but it obviously weighs very heavily on the side of rejecting capital punishment as a suitable penalty for raping an adult woman.

B

It was also observed in Gregg that "[t]he jury . . . is a significant and reliable index of con-

temporary values because it is so directly involved," 428 U.S., at 181, and that it is thus important to look to the sentencing decisions that juries have made in the course of assessing whether capital punishment is an appropriate penalty for the crime being tried. Of course, the jury's judgment is meaningful only where the jury has an appropriate measure of choice as to whether the death penalty is to be imposed. As far as execution for rape is concerned, this is now true only in Georgia and in Florida; and in the latter State, capital punishment is authorized only for the rape of children.

According to the factual submissions in this Court, out of all rape convictions in Georgia since 1973—and that total number has not been tendered—63 cases had been reviewed by the Georgia Supreme Court as of the time of oral argument; and of these, six involved a death sentence, one of which was set aside, leaving five convicted rapists now under sentence of death in the State of Georgia. Georgia juries have thus sentenced rapists to death six times since 1973. This obviously is not a negligible number; and the State argues that as a practical matter juries simply reserve the extreme sanction for extreme cases of rape and that recent experience surely does not prove that jurors consider the death penalty to be a disproportionate punishment for every conceivable instance of rape, no matter how aggravated. Nevertheless, it is true that in the vast majority of cases, at least nine out of 10, juries have not imposed the death sentence.

IV.

These recent events evidencing the attitude of state legislatures and sentencing juries do not wholly determine this controversy, for the Constitution contemplates that in the end our own judgment will be brought to bear on the question of the acceptability of the death penalty under the Eighth Amendment. Nevertheless, the legislative rejection of capital punishment for rape strongly confirms our own judgment, which is that death is indeed a disproportionate penalty for the crime of raping an adult woman.

We do not discount the seriousness of rape as a crime. It is highly reprehensible, both in a moral sense and in its almost total contempt for the personal integrity and autonomy of the female victim and for the latter's privilege of choosing those with whom intimate relationships are to be established. Short of homicide, it is the "ultimate violation of self." It is also a violent crime because it normally involves force, or the threat of force or intimidation, to overcome the will and the capacity of the victim to resist. Rape is very often accompanied by physical injury to the female and can also inflict mental and psychological damage. Because it undermines the community's sense of security, there is public injury as well.

Rape is without doubt deserving of serious punishment; but in terms of moral depravity and of the injury to the person and to the public, it does not compare with murder, which does involve the unjustified taking of human life. Although it may be accompanied by another crime, rape by definition does not include the death or even the serious injury of another person. The murderer kills; the rapist, if no more than that, does not. Life is over for the victim of murderers; for the rape victim, life may not be nearly so happy as it was, but it is not over and normally is not beyond repair. We have the abiding conviction that the death penalty, which "is unique in its severity and revocability," 428 U.S. 187, is an excessive penalty for the rapist who, as such, does not take human life.

This does not end the matter, for under Georgia law, death may not be imposed for any capital offense, including rape, unless the jury or judge finds one of the statutory aggravating circumstances and then elects to impose that sentence. . . . For the rapist to be executed in Georgia, it must therefore be found not only that he committed rape but also that one or more of the following aggravating circumstances were present: (1) that the rape was committed by a person with a prior record of conviction for a capital felony; (2) that the rape was committed while the offender was engaged in the commission of another capital felony, or aggravated battery; or (3) the rape "was outrageously or wantonly vile, horrible or inhuman in that it involved torture, depravity of mind, or aggravated battery to the victim." Here, the first two of these aggravating circumstances were alleged and found by the jury.

Neither of these circumstances, nor both of them together, change our conclusion that the death sentence imposed on Coker is a disproportionate punishment for rape. Coker had prior convictions for capital felonies—rape, murder and kidnapping—but these prior convictions do not change the fact that the instant crime being punished is a rape not involving the taking of life.

It is also true that the present rape occurred while Coker was committing armed robbery, a felony for which the Georgia statutes authorize the death penalty. But Coker was tried for the robbery offense as well as for rape and received a separate life sentence for this crime; the jury did not deem the robbery itself deserving of the death penalty, even though accompanied by the aggravating circumstance, which was stipulated, that Coker had been convicted of a prior capital crime.

We note finally that in Georgia a person commits murder when he unlawfully and with malice aforethought, either express or implied, causes the death of another human being. He also commits that crime when in the commission of a felony he causes the death of another human being, irrespective of malice. But even where the killing is deliberate, it is not punishable by death absent proof of aggravating circumstances. It is difficult to accept the notion, and we do not, that the rape, with or without aggravating circumstances, should be punished more heavily than the deliberate killing as long as the rapist does not himself take the life of his victim. The judgment of the Georgia Supreme Court upholding the death sentence is reversed and the case is remanded to that court for further proceedings not inconsistent with this opinion.

Mr. Justice Brennan, concurring in the judgment.

Adhering to my view that the death penalty is in all circumstances cruel and unusual punishment prohibited by the Eighth and Fourteenth Amendments, *Gregg* v. *Georgia*, 428 U.S. 153, 227 (1976), I concur in the judgment of the Court setting aside the death sentence imposed under the Georgia rape statute.

Mr. Justice Marshall concurring in the judgment of the Court.

In *Gregg* v. *Georgia*, 428 U.S. 153, 231 (1976), I stated, "In *Furman* v. *Georgia*, 408 U.S. 238, 314 (1972) (concurring), I set forth at some length my views on the basic issue presented to the Court in these cases. The death penalty, I concluded, is a cruel and unusual punishment prohibited by the Eighth and Fourteenth Amendments. That continues to be my view."

I then explained in some detail my reasons for reaffirming my position. I continue to adhere to those views in concurring in the judgment of the Court in this case.

Mr. Justice Powell, concurring in part and dissenting in part.

I concur in the judgment of the Court on the facts of this case, and also in its reasoning supporting the view that ordinarily death is disproportionate punishment for the crime of raping an adult woman. Although rape invariably is a reprehensible crime, there is no indication that petitioner's offense was committed with excessive brutality or that the victim sustained serious or lasting injury. The plurality, however, does not limit its holding to the case before us or to similar cases. Rather, in an opinion that ranges well beyond what is necessary, it holds that capital punishment *always*—regardless of the circumstances—is a disproportionate penalty for the crime of rape.

The Georgia statute, sustained in *Gregg* v. *Georgia*, 428 U.S. 153 (1976), specifies aggravating circumstances that may be considered by the jury when appropriate. With respect to the crime of rape, only three such circumstances are specified: (i) the offense was committed by a person with a prior record of conviction of a capital felony; (ii) the offense was committed while the offender was engaged in another capital felony or in aggravated battery; and (iii) the offense was "outrageously or wantonly vile, horrible or inhuman in that it involved torture, depravity of mind, or an aggravated battery to the victim." . . . Only the third circumstance describes in general the offense of aggravated rape, often identified as a separate and more heinous offense than rape. . . . That third circumstance was not submitted to the jury in this case, as the evidence would not have supported such a finding. It is therefore quite unnecessary for the plurality to write in terms so sweeping as to foreclose each of the 50 state legislatures from creating a narrowly defined substantive crime of aggravated rape punishable by death. . . .

Today, in a case that does not require such an expansive pronouncement, the plurality draws a bright line between murder and all rapes—regardless of the degree of brutality of the rape or the effect upon the victim. I dissent because I am not persuaded that such a bright line is appropriate. . . .

. . . [I]t may be that the death penalty is not disproportionate punishment for the crime of aggravated rape. Final resolution of the question must await careful inquiry into objective indicators of society's "evolving standards of decency," particularly legislative enactments and the responses of juries in capital cases. . . . In a proper case a more discriminating inquiry than the plurality undertakes well might discover that both juries and legislatures have reserved the ultimate penalty for the case of an outrageous rape resulting in serious, lasting harm to the victim. I would not prejudge the issue. To this extent, I respectfully dissent.

Mr. Chief Justice Burger, with whom Mr. Justice Rehnquist joins, dissenting. . . .

My first disagreement with the Court's holding is its unnecessary breadth. The narrow issue here presented is whether the State of Georgia may constitutionally execute this petitioner for the particular rape which he has committed, in light of all the facts and circumstances shown by this record. The plurality opinion goes to great lengths to consider societal mores and attitudes toward the generic crime of rape and the punishment for it; however, the opinion gives little attention on the special circumstances which bear directly on whether imposition of the death penalty is an appropriate societal response to Coker's criminal acts: (a) On account of his prior offenses, Coker is already serving such lengthy prison sentences that imposition of additional periods of imprisonment would have no incremental punitive effect; (b) by his life pattern Coker has shown that he presents a particular danger to the safety, welfare, and chastity of women, and on his record the likelihood is therefore great that he will repeat his crime at first opportunity; (c) petitioner escaped from prison, only a year and a half after he commenced serving his latest sentences; he has nothing to lose by further escape attempts; and (d) should he again succeed in escaping from prison, it is reasonably predictable that he will repeat his pattern of attacks on women—and with impunity since the threat of added prison sentences will be no deterrent.

Unlike the Court, I would narrow the inquiry in this case to the question actually presented: Does the Eighth Amendment's ban against cruel and unusual punishment prohibit the State of Georgia from executing a person who has, within the space of three years, raped three separate women, killing one and attempting to kill another, who is serving prison terms exceeding his probable lifetime and who has not hesitated to escape confinement at the first available

opportunity? Whatever one's view may be as to the State's constitutional power to impose the death penalty upon a rapist who stands before a court convicted for the first time, this case reveals a chronic rapist whose continuing danger to the community is abundantly clear. . . .

In my view, the Eighth Amendment does not prevent the State from taking an individual's "well demonstrated propensity for life-endangering behavior" into account in devising punitive measures which will prevent inflicting further harm upon innocent victims. See *Gregg* v. *Georgia*, 428 U.S. 153, 183 n.28 (1976). Only one year ago Mr. Justice White succinctly noted: "Death finally forecloses the possibility that a prisoner will commit further crimes, whereas life imprisonment does not." *Roberts* v. *Louisiana*, 428 U.S. 325, 354 (1976) (White, J., dissenting). . . .

In sum, once the Court has held that "the punishment of death does not invariably violate the Constitution," *Gregg* v. *Georgia*, 428 U.S., at 169, it seriously impinges upon the State's legislative judgment to hold that it may not impose such sentence upon an individual who has shown total and repeated disregard for the welfare, safety, personal integrity and human worth of others, and who seemingly cannot be deterred from continuing such conduct. I therefore would hold that the death sentence here imposed is within the power reserved to the State and leave for another day the question of whether such sanction would be proper under other circumstances. . . . Since the Court now invalidates the death penalty as a sanction for all rapes of adults at all times under all circumstances, I reluctantly turn to what I see as the broader issues raised by this holding. . . .

Despite its strong condemnation of rape, the Court reaches the inexplicable conclusion that "the death penalty . . . is an excessive penalty" for the perpetrator of this heinous offense.[1] This,

---

[1] While only three Justices have joined Mr. Justice White in this portion of his opinion, see separate opinion of Mr. Justice Powell, *ante.* I take this to be the view of the Court in light of Mr. Justice Brennan's and Mr. Justice Marshall's statements joining the judgment.

the Court holds, is true even though in Georgia the death penalty may be imposed only where the rape is coupled with one or more aggravating circumstances. The process by which this conclusion is reached is as startling as it is disquieting. It represents a clear departure from precedent by making this Court "under the aegis of the Cruel and Unusual Punishments Clause, the ultimate arbiter of the standards of criminal responsibility in diverse areas of the criminal law, throughout the country." *Powell* v. *Texas*, 392 U.S. 514, 533 (1968) (opinion of Marshall, J.). This seriously strains and distorts our federal system, removing much of the flexibility from which it has drawn strength for two centuries. . . .

The plurality opinion bases its analysis, in part, on the fact that "Georgia is the sole jurisdiction in the United States at the present time that authorizes the sentence of death when the rape victim is an adult woman." . . .

Surely, however, this statistic cannot be deemed determinative, or even particularly relevant. As the opinion concedes . . . two other States—Louisiana and North Carolina—have enacted death penalty statutes for adult rape since this Court's 1972 decision in *Furman* v. *Georgia*, 408 U.S. 238 (1972). If the Court is to rely on some "public opinion" process does this not suggest the beginning of a "trend"? . . .

In any case, when considered in light of the experience since the turn of the century, where more than one-third of American jurisdictions have consistently provided the death penalty for rape, the plurality's focus on the experience of the immediate past must be viewed as truly disingenuous. Having in mind the swift changes in positions of some Members of this Court in the short span of five years, can it rationally be considered a relevant indicator of what our society deems "cruel and unusual" to look solely to what legislatures have *refrained* from doing under conditions of great uncertainty arising from our less than lucid holdings on the Eighth Amendment? Far more representative of societal mores of the 20th Century is the accepted practice in a substantial number of

jurisdictions preceding the *Furman* decision. "The problem . . . is the suddenness of the Court's perception of progress in the human attitude since decisions of only a short while ago." *Furman* v. *Georgia*, 408 U.S., at 410 (Blackmun, J., dissenting). Cf. *Rudolph* v. *Alabama*, 375 U.S. 889 (1963).

However, even were one to give the most charitable acceptance to the plurality's statistical analysis, it still does not, to my mind, support its conclusion. The most that can be claimed is that for the past year Georgia has been the only State whose adult rape death penalty statute has not otherwise been invalidated; two other state legislatures had enacted rape death penalty statutes in the last five years, but these were invalidated for reasons unrelated to rape under the Court's decisions last Term. *Woodson* v. *North Carolina*, 428 U.S. 280 (1976); [Stanislaus] *Roberts* v. *Louisiana*, 428 U.S. 325 (1976). Even if these figures could be read as indicating that no other States view the death penalty as an appropriate punishment for the rape of an adult woman, it would not necessarily follow that Georgia's imposition of such sanction violates the Eighth Amendment. . . .

Statutory provisions in criminal justice applied in one part of the country can be carefully watched by other state legislatures, so that the experience of one State becomes available to all. Although human lives are in the balance, it must be remembered that failure to allow flexibility may also jeopardize human lives—those of the victims of undeterred criminal conduct. . . . Our concern for the accused ought not foreclose legislative judgments showing a modicum of consideration for the potential victims.

Three state legislatures have, in the past five years, determined that the taking of human life and the devastating consequences of rape will be minimized if rapists may, in a limited class of cases, be executed for their offenses. That these States are presently a minority does not, in my view, make their judgment less worthy of deference. Our concern for human life must not be confined to the guilty; a state legislature is not to be thought insensitive to human values because it acts firmly to protect the lives and related values of the innocent. In this area, the choices for legislatures are at best painful and difficult and deserve a high degree of deference. . . .

In order for Georgia's legislative program to develop it must be given time to take effect so that data may be evaluated for comparison with the experience of States which have not enacted death penalty statutes. Today, the Court repudiates the State's solemn judgment on how best to deal with the crime of rape before anyone can know whether the death penalty is an effective deterrent for one of the most horrible of all crimes. And this is done a few short years after Justice Powell's excellent statement:

> "In a period in our country's history when the frequency of [rape] is increasing alarmingly, it is indeed a grave event for the Court to take from the States whatever deterrent and retributive weight the death penalty retains." *Furman* v. *Georgia,* 408 U.S., at 459 (Powell, J., dissenting) (footnote omitted).

To deprive States of this authority as the Court does, on the basis that "the current judgment with respect to the death penalty for rape . . . weighs very heavily on the side of an adult woman," . . . is impermissibly rash. The current judgment of some Members of this Court has undergone significant change in the short time since *Furman.* Social change on great issues generally reveals itself in small increments, and the "current judgment" of many States could well be altered on the basis of Georgia's experience, were we to allow its statute to stand.

The subjective judgment that the death penalty is simply disproportionate for the crime of rape is even more disturbing than the "objective" analysis discussed *supra.* The plurality's conclusion on this point is based upon the bare fact that murder necessarily results in the physical death of the victim, while rape does not. . . . However, no Member of the Court explains why this distinction has rele-

vance, much less constitutional significance. It is, after all, not irrational—nor constitutionally impermissible—for a legislature to make the penalty more severe than the criminal act it punishes in the hope it would deter wrongdoing. . . . Until now, the issue under the Eighth Amendment has not been the state of any particular victim after the crime, but rather whether the punishment imposed is grossly disproportionate to the evil committed by the perpetrator. . . . As a matter of constitutional principle, that test cannot have the primitive simplicity of "life for life, eye for eye, tooth for tooth." Rather States must be permitted to engage in a more sophisiticated weighing of values in dealing with criminal activity which consistently poses serious danger of death or grave bodily harm. If innocent life and limb is to be preserved I see no constitutional barrier in punishing by death all who engage in such activity, regardless of whether the risk comes to fruition in any particular instance. . . .

Only one year ago the Court held it constitutionally permissible to impose the death penalty for the crime of murder provided that certain procedural safeguards are followed. . . . Today, the Court readily admits that "[s]hort of homicide, [rape] is the 'ultimate violation of self.'" . . . Rape thus is not a crime "light-years" removed from murder in the degree of its heinousness; it certainly poses a serious potential danger to the life and safety of innocent victims—apart from the devastating psychic consequences. It would seem to follow therefore that, affording the States proper leeway under the broad standard of the Eighth Amendment, if murder is properly punishable by death, rape should be also, if that is the considered judgment of the legislators.

The Court's conclusion to the contrary is very disturbing indeed. The clear implication of today's holding appears to be that the death penalty may be properly imposed only as to crimes resulting in death of the victim. This casts serious doubt upon the constitutional validity of statutes imposing the death penalty for a variety of conduct which, though dangerous, may not necessarily result in any immediate death, e.g., treason, airplane hijacking, and kidnapping. In that respect, today's holding does even more harm than is initially apparent. We cannot avoid judicial notice that crimes such as airplane hijacking, kidnapping, and mass terrorist activity constitute a serious and increasing danger to the safety of the public. It would be unfortunate indeed if the effect of today's holding were to inhibit States and the Federal Government from experimenting with various remedies—including possibly imposition of the penalty of death—to prevent and deter such crimes. . . .

Whatever our individual views as to the wisdom of capital punishment, I cannot agree that it is constitutionally impermissible for a state legislature to make the "solemn judgment" to impose such penalty for the crime of rape. Accordingly, I would leave to the States the task of legislating in this area of the law.

Department of Justice (LEAA) News
Release, July 2, 1979

There were 445 persons under death sentence in the United States at the end of 1978, an increase of 35 over the previous year, the Law Enforcement Assistance Administration (LEAA) announced today.

During the year, death sentences were given to 183 and lifted from 148 others. Ohio removed 99 from death row after the U.S. Supreme Court ruled its capital punishment statute was unconstitutional. A Colorado law also was struck down.

No one was executed in 1978. One person was executed in 1977, and another this year.

During 1978, Oregon, Maryland, and Pennsylvania enacted death penalty laws, but 10 of the 34 states with such statutes had no death-row prisoners on December 31.

Southern states held 87 percent of the death-row prisoners—including 121 in Florida and 100 in Texas.

Western states held nine percent and the north-central states three percent. The Northeast's only death-row prisoners were two in Rhode Island, the report said.

Other states with 10 or more were Georgia, 57; Alabama, 41; Oklahoma, 16; Arkansas, 11; and Mississippi, 10.

> Note: Witherspoon v. Illinois, 391 U.S. 510 (1968), held "a sentence of death cannot be carried out if the jury that imposed or recommended it was chosen by excluding veniremen for cause simply because they voiced general objections to the death penalty or expressed conscientious or religious scruples against its infliction." Thus unless a venireman is "irrevocably committed, before trial has begun, to vote against the penalty of death regardless of the . . . circumstances," he cannot be excluded.

> Note: Trop v. Dulles, 356 U.S. 86 (1958), found "cruel and unusual punishment" in a loss-of-citizenship penalty prescribed by Congress for wartime desertion from the armed forces. Robinson v. California, 370 U.S. 660 (1962), similarly held invalid a state effort to punish narcotics addiction as a crime. A related problem arose in Powell v. Texas, 392 U.S. 514 (1968), with respect to the difference, if any, between drunkenness and alcoholism.

PLEA BARGAINING

Introduction

The negotiated—or bargained—guilty plea is today one of our chief methods of enforcing criminal law. As one observer put it, "Conviction by guilty plea is normal and a trial the exception." Overall, around 90 percent of all convictions are obtained by pleas of guilt. As the Supreme Court recently observed in *Blackledge* v. *Allison*, 431 U.S. 63, 71 (1977):

> Whatever might be the situation in an ideal world, the fact is that the guilty plea and the often concomitant plea bargain are important components of this country's criminal justice system. Properly administered, they can benefit all concerned. The defendant avoids extended pretrial incarceration and the anxieties and uncertainties of a trial; he gains a speedy disposition of his case, the chance to acknowledge his guilt, and a prompt start in realizing whatever potential there may be for rehabilitation. Judges and prosecutors conserve vital and scarce resources. The public is protected from the risks posed by those charged with criminal offenses who are at large on bail while awaiting completion of criminal proceedings.

There are, of course, difficulties. See L. Weinreb, *Denial of Justice* (1977); A. Rosett and D. Cressey, *Justice by Consent* (1976).

One specialist in these matters concludes that the incorporation "revolution" has greatly augmented

> the pressures for plea negotiation. . . . [P]rosecutors were able to keep conviction rates fairly constant in the face of both burgeoning caseloads and procedural developments apparently favoring the defense. . . . [P]rocedural reforms did not benefit defendants primarily through increased judicial control of the criminal process. Rather, these reforms became levers in the bargaining process and had their principal impact in reducing the punishment that guilty plea defendants received. (A. W. Alschuler, "Plea Bargaining and Its History," 79 *Columbia Law Review* 1, 38–40 [1979])

Boykin v. *Alabama*
395 U.S. 238 (1969)

Mr. Justice Douglas delivered the opinion of the Court.

In the spring of 1966, within the period of a fortnight, a series of armed robberies occurred in Mobile, Alabama. The victims, in each case, were local shopkeepers open at night who were forced by a gunman to hand over money. While robbing one grocery store, the assailant fired his gun once, sending a bullet through a door into the ceiling. A few days earlier in a drugstore, the robber had allowed his gun to discharge in such a way that the bullet, on ricochet from the floor, struck a customer in the leg. Shortly thereafter, a local grand jury returned five indictments against petitioner, a 27-year-old Negro, for common-law robbery—an offense punishable in Alabama by death.

Before the matter came to trial, the court determined that petitioner was indigent and appointed counsel to represent him. Three days later, at his arraignment, petitioner pleaded guilty to all five indictments. So far as the record shows, the judge asked no questions of petitioner concerning his plea, and petitioner did not address the court.

Trial strategy may of course make a plea of guilty seem the desirable course. But the record is wholly silent on that point and throws no light on it.

Alabama provides that when a defendant pleads guilty, "the court must cause the punishment to be determined by a jury" (except where it is required to be fixed by the court) and may "cause witnesses to be examined to ascertain the character of the offense." . . .

In the present case a trial of that dimension was held, the prosecution presenting its case largely through eyewitness testimony. Although counsel for petitioner engaged in cursory cross-examination, petitioner neither testified himself nor presented testimony concerning his character and background. There was nothing to indicate that he had a prior criminal record.

In instructing the jury, the judge stressed that petitioner had pleaded guilty in five cases of robbery, defined as "the felonious taking of money . . . from another against his will . . . by violence or by putting him in fear . . . (carrying) from ten years minimum in the penitentiary to the supreme penalty of death by electrocution." The jury, upon deliberation, found petitioner guilty and sentenced him severally to die on each of the five indictments.

Taking an automatic appeal to the Alabama Supreme Court, petitioner argued that a sentence of death for common-law robbery was cruel and unusual punishment within the meaning of the Federal Constitution, a suggestion which that court unanimously rejected. . . . On their own motion, however, four of the seven justices discussed the constitutionality of the process by which the trial judge had accepted petitioner's guilty plea. From the order affirming the trial court, three justices dissented on the ground that the record was inadequate to show that petitioner had intelligently and knowingly pleaded guilty. The fourth member concurred separately, conceding that "a trial judge should not accept a guilty plea unless he has determined that such a plea was voluntarily and knowingly entered by the defendant," but refusing "[f]or aught appearing" "to presume that the trial judge failed to do his duty." . . . We granted certiorari. . . .

It was error, plain on the face of the record, for the trial judge to accept petitioner's guilty plea without an affirmative showing that it was intelligent and voluntary. That error, under Alabama procedure, was properly before the court below and considered explicitly by a majority of the justices and is properly before us on review.

A plea of guilty is more than a confession which admits that the accused did various acts; it is itself a conviction; nothing remains but to give judgement and determine punishment. Admissibility of a confession must be based on a "reliable determination on the voluntariness issue which satisfies the constitutional rights of the defendant." The requirement that the prosecution spread on the record the prerequisites of a valid waiver is no constitutional innovation. In *Carnley* v. *Cochran*, 369 U.S. 506, 516 (1962), we dealt with a problem of waiver of the right to counsel, a Sixth Amendment right. We held: "Presuming waiver from a silent record is impermissible. The record must show, or there must be an allegation and evidence which show, that an accused was offered counsel but intelligently and understandingly rejected the offer. Anything less is not waiver."

We think that the same standard must be applied to determining whether a guilty plea is voluntarily made. For, as we have said, a plea of guilty is more than an admission of conduct; it is a conviction. Ignorance, incomprehension, coercion, terror, inducements, subtle or blatant threats might be a perfect cover-up of unconstitutionality. The question of an effective waiver of a federal constitutional right in a proceeding is of course governed by federal standards. . . .

Several federal constitutional rights are involved in a waiver that takes place when a plea of guilty is entered in a state criminal trial. First, is the privilege against compulsory self-incrimination guaranteed by the Fifth Amendment and applicable to the States by reason of the Fourteenth. . . . Second, is the right to trial by jury. . . . Third, is the right to confront one's accusers. . . . We cannot presume a waiver of these three important federal rights from a silent record.

What is at stake for an accused facing death or imprisonment demands the utmost solicitude of which courts are capable in canvassing the matter with the accused to make sure he has a full understanding of what the plea connotes and of its consequence. When the judge discharges that function, he leaves a record adequate for any review that may be later sought

. . . and forestalls the spin-off of collateral proceedings that seek to probe murky memories.

The three dissenting justices in the Alabama Supreme Court stated the law accurately when they concluded that there was reversible error "because the record does not disclose that the defendant voluntarily and understandingly entered his pleas of guilty." . . .

Mr. Justice Harlan, whom Mr. Justice Black joins, dissenting.

The Court today holds that petitioner Boykin was denied due process of law, and that his robbery convictions must be reversed outright, solely because "the record [is] inadequate to show that petitioner . . . intelligently and knowingly pleaded guilty." . . . The Court thus in effect fastens upon the States, as a matter of federal constitutional law, the rigid prophylactic requirements of Rule 11 of the Federal Rules of Criminal Procedure. It does so in circumstances where the Court itself has only very recently held application of Rule 11 to be unnecessary in the federal courts. See *Halliday* v. *United States*, 394 U.S. 831 (1969). Moreover, the Court does all this at the behest of a petitioner who has never at any time alleged that his guilty plea was involuntary or made without knowledge of the consequences. I cannot possibly subscribe to so bizarre a result.

I.

. . .

The record does not show what inquiries were made by the arraigning judge to confirm that the plea was made voluntarily and knowingly.

Petitioner was not sentenced immediately after the acceptance of his plea. Instead, pursuant to an Alabama statute, the court ordered that "witnesses . . . be examined, to ascertain the character of the offense," in the presence of a jury which would then fix petitioner's sentence.

. . . That proceeding occurred some two months after petitioner pleaded guilty. During that period, petitioner made no attempt to withdraw his plea. Petitioner was present in court with his attorney when the witnesses were examined. Petitioner heard the judge state the elements of common-law robbery and heard him announce that petitioner had pleaded guilty to that offense and might be sentenced to death. Again, petitioner made no effort to withdraw his plea.

On his appeal to the Alabama Supreme Court, petitioner did not claim that his guilty plea was made involuntarily or without full knowledge of the consequences. In fact, petitioner raised no questions at all concerning the plea. In his petition and brief in this Court, and in oral argument by counsel, petitioner has never asserted that the plea was coerced or made in ignorance of the consequences.

II.

Against this background, the Court holds that the Due Process Clause of the Fourteenth Amendment requires the outright reversal of petitioner's conviction. This result is wholly unprecedented. There are past holdings of this Court to the effect that a federal habeas corpus petitioner who makes sufficiently credible allegations that his state guilty plea involuntary is entitled to a hearing as to the truth of those allegations. . . . These holdings suggest that if equally convincing allegations were made in a petition for certiorari on direct review, the petitioner might in some circumstances be entitled to have a judgment of affirmance vacated and the case remanded for a state hearing on voluntariness. . . . However, as has been noted, this petitioner makes no allegations of actual involuntariness.

The Court's reversal is therefore predicated entirely upon the failure of the arraigning state judge to make an "adequate" record. In holding that this is a ground for reversal, the Court quotes copiously from *McCarthy* v. *United*

States, 394 U.S. 459 (1969), in which we held earlier this Term that when a *federal* district judge fails to comply in every respect with the procedure for accepting a guilty plea which is prescribed in Rule 11 of the Federal Rules of Criminal Procedure, the plea must be set aside and the defendant permitted to replead, regardless of lower-court findings that the plea was in fact voluntary. What the Court omits to mention is that in *McCarthy* we stated that our decision was based "solely upon our construction of Rule 11," and explicitly disavowed any reliance upon the Constitution. . . . Thus *McCarthy* can provide no support whatever for today's constitutional edict.

III.

So far as one can make out from the Court's opinion, what is now in effect being held is that the prophylactic procedures of Criminal Rule 11 are substantially applicable to the States as a matter of federal constitutional due process. If this is the basis upon which Boykin's conviction is being reversed, then the Court's disposition is plainly out of keeping with a sequel case to *McCarthy,* decided only last month. For the Court held, *Halliday* v. *United States,* 394 U.S. 831 (1969), that "in view of the large number of constitutionally valid convictions that may have been obtained without full compliance with Rule 11, we decline to apply McCarthy retroactively." . . . The Court quite evidently found Halliday's conviction to be "constitutionally valid," for it affirmed the conviction even though Halliday's guilty plea was accepted in

1954 without any explicit inquiry into whether it was knowingly and understandingly made, as now required by present Rule 11. In justification, the Court noted that two lower courts had found in collateral proceedings that the plea was voluntary. The Court declared that:

> "[A] defendant whose plea has been accepted without full compliance with Rule 11 may still resort to appropriate post-conviction remedies to attack his plea's voluntariness. Thus, if his plea was accepted prior to our decision in McCarthy, he is not without a remedy to correct constitutional defects in his conviction." . . .

It seems elementary that the Fifth Amendment due process to which petitioner Halliday was entitled must be at least as demanding as the Fourteenth Amendment process due petitioner Boykin. Yet petitioner Halliday's federal conviction has been affirmed as "constitutionally valid," despite the omission of any judicial inquiry of record at the time of his plea, because he initiated collateral proceedings which revealed that the plea was actually voluntary. Petitioner Boykin, on the other hand, today has his Alabama conviction reversed because of exactly the same omission, even though he too "may . . . resort to appropriate post-conviction remedies to attack his plea's voluntariness" and thus "is not without a remedy to correct constitutional defects in his conviction." In short, I find it utterly impossible to square today's holding with what the Court has so recently done. . . .

Bordenkircher v. *Hayes*
98 S. Ct. 663 (1978)

The prosecutor threatened that unless defendant pleaded guilty to forgery as charged, he would be prosecuted under a habitual-criminal recidivist statute which carried a greater penalty. The Court rejected the argument that this violated due process.

Mr. Justice Stewart delivered the opinion of the Court . . . .

II.

It may be helpful to clarify at the outset the nature of the issue in this case. While the prosecutor did not actually obtain the recidivist indictment until after the plea conferences had ended, his intention to do so was clearly put forth at the outset of the plea negotiations. Hayes was thus fully informed of the true terms of the offer when he made his decision to plead not guilty. This is not a situation, therefore, where the prosecutor without notice brought an additional and more serious charge after plea negotiations relating only to the original indictment had ended with the defendant's insistence on pleading not guilty. As a practical matter, in short, this case would be no different if the grand jury had indicted Hayes as a recidivist from the outset, and the prosecutor had offered to drop that charge as part of the plea bargain.

The Court of Appeals nonetheless drew a distinction between "concessions relating to prosecution under an existing indictment," and threats to bring more severe charges not contained in the original indictment—a line it thought necessary in order to establish a prophylactic rule to guard against the evil of prosecutorial vindictiveness. Quite apart from this chronological distinction, however, the Court of Appeals found that the prosecutor had acted vindictively in the present case since he had conceded that the indictment was influenced by his desire to induce a guilty plea. The ultimate conclusion of the Court of Appeals thus seems to have been that a prosecutor acts vindictively and in violation of due process of law whenever his charging decision is influenced by what he hopes to gain in the course of plea bargaining negotiations.

III.

We have recently had occasion to observe that "[w]hatever might be the situation in an ideal world, the fact is that the guilty plea and the often concomitant plea bargain are important components of this country's criminal justice system. Properly administered, they can benefit all concerned." *Blackledge* v. *Allison*, 431 U.S. 63, 71. The open acknowledgment of this previously clandestine practice has led this Court to recognize the importance of counsel during plea negotiations, *Brady* v. *United States*, 397 U.S. 742, 758, the need for a public record indicating that a plea was knowingly and voluntarily made, *Boykin* v. *Alabama*, 395 U.S. 238, 242, and the requirement that a prosecutor's plea bargaining promise must be kept, *Santobello* v. *New York*, 404 U.S. 257, 262. The decision of the Court of Appeals in the present case, however, did not deal with considerations such as these, but held that the substance of the plea offer itself violated the limitations imposed by the Due Process Clause of the Fourteenth Amendment. Cf. *Brady* v. *United States*, *supra*, 397 U.S., at 751 n. 8. For the reasons that follow, we have concluded that the Court of Appeals was mistaken in so ruling.

IV.

This Court held in *North Carolina* v. *Pearce*, 395 U.S. 711, 725, that the Due Process Clause of the Fourteenth Amendment "requires that vindictiveness against a defendant for having successfully attacked his first conviction must play no part in the sentence he receives after a new trial." The same principle was later applied to prohibit a prosecutor from reindicting a convicted misdemeanant on a felony charge after the defendant had invoked an appellate remedy, since in this situation there was also a "realistic likelihood of 'vindictiveness.' " *Blackledge* v. *Perry*, 417 U.S., at 27.

In those cases the Court was dealing with the State's unilateral imposition of a penalty upon a defendant who had chosen to exercise a legal right to attack his original conviction—a situation "very different from the give-and-take negotiation common in plea bargaining between the prosecution and the defense, which arguably possess relatively equal bargaining power." *Parker* v. *North Carolina,* 397 U.S. 790, 809 (opinion of Brennan, J.). The Court has emphasized that the due process violation in cases such as *Pearce* and *Perry* lay not in the possibility that a defendant might be deterred from the exercise of a legal right, see *Colten* v. *Kentucky,* 407 U.S. 104; *Chaffin* v. *Stynchcombe,* 412 U.S. 17, but rather in the danger that the State might be retaliating against the accused for lawfully attacking his conviction. See *Blackledge* v. *Perry, supra,* 417 U.S., at 26–28.

To punish a person because he has done what the law plainly allows him to do is a due process violation of the most basic sort, see *North Carolina* v. *Pearce, supra,* 395 U.S., at 738 (opinion of Black, J.), and for an agent of the State to pursue a course of action whose objective is to penalize a person's reliance on his legal rights is "patently unconstitutional." *Chaffin* v. *Stynchcombe, supra,* 412 U.S., at 32–33, n. 20. See *United States* v. *Jackson,* 390 U.S. 570. But in the "give-and-take" of plea bargaining, there is no such element of punishment or retaliation so long as the accused is free to accept or reject the prosecution's offer.

Plea bargaining flows from "the mutuality of advantage" to defendants and prosecutors, each with his own reasons for wanting to avoid trial. *Brady* v. *United States, supra,* 397 U.S., at 752. Defendants advised by competent counsel and protected by other procedural safeguards are presumptively capable of intelligent choice in response to prosecutorial persuasion, and unlikely to be driven to false self-condemnation. *Id.,* at 758. Indeed, acceptance of the basic legitimacy of plea bargaining necessarily implies rejection of any notion that a guilty plea is involuntary in a constitutional sense simply because it is the end result of the bargaining process. By hypothesis, the plea may have been induced by promises of a recommendation of a lenient sentence or a reduction of charges, and thus by fear of the possibility of a greater penalty upon conviction after a trial. See ABA Standards Relating to Pleas of Guilty § 3.1 (1968);

Note, Plea Bargaining and the Transformation of the Criminal Process, 90 *Harv.L.Rev.* 564 (1977). Cf. *Brady* v. *United States, supra,* 397 U.S., at 751, *North Carolina* v. *Alford,* 400 U.S. 25.

While confronting a defendant with the risk of more severe punishment clearly may have a "discouraging effect on the defendant's assertion of his trial rights, the imposition of these difficult choices [is] an inevitable"—and permissible—"attribute of any legitimate system which tolerates and encourages the negotiation of pleas." *Chaffin* v. *Stynchcombe, supra,* 412 U.S., at 31. It follows that, by tolerating and encouraging the negotiation of pleas, this Court has necessarily accepted as constitutionally legitimate the simple reality that the prosecutor's interest at the bargaining table is to persuade the defendant to forego his right to plead not guilty.

It is not disputed here that Hayes was properly chargeable under the recidivist statute, since he had in fact been convicted of two previous felonies. In our system, so long as the prosecutor has probable cause to believe that the accused committed an offense defined by statute, the decision whether or not to prosecute, and what charge to file or bring before a grand jury, generally rests entirely in his discretion. Within the limits set by the legislature's constitutionally valid definition of chargeable offenses, "the conscious exercise of some selectivity in enforcement is not in itself a federal constitutional violation" so long as "the selection was [not] deliberately based upon an unjustifiable standard such as race, religion, or other arbitrary classification." *Oyler* v. *Boles,* 368 U.S. 448, 456. To hold that the prosecutor's desire to induce a guilty plea is an "unjustifiable standard," which, like race or religion, may play no part in his charging decision, would contradict the very premises that underlie the concept of plea bargaining itself. Moreover, a rigid constitutional rule that would prohibit a prosecutor from acting forthrightly in his dealings with the defense could only invite unhealthy subterfuge that would drive the practice of plea bargaining back into the shadows from which it has so recently emerged. See *Blackledge* v. *Allison, supra,* 431 U.S., at 76.

There is no doubt that the breadth of discretion that our country's legal system vests in prosecuting attorneys carries with it the potential for both individual and institutional abuse. And broad though that discretion may be, there are undoubtedly constitutional limits upon its exercise. We hold only that the course of conduct engaged in by the prosecutor in this case, which no more than openly presented the defendant with the unpleasant alternatives of foregoing trial or facing charges on which he was plainly subject to prosecution, did not violate the Due Process Clause of the Fourteenth Amendment.

Mr. Justice Blackmun, with whom Mr. Justice Brennan and Mr. Justice Marshall join, dissenting. . . .

Mr. Justice Powell, dissenting.

Although I agree with much of the Court's opinion, I am not satisfied that the result in this case is just or that the conduct of the plea bargaining met the requirements of due process.

Respondent was charged with the uttering of a single forged check in the amount of $88.30. Under Kentucky law, this offense was punishable by a prison term of from two to 10 years, apparently without regard to the amount of the forgery. During the course of plea bargaining, the prosecutor offered respondent a sentence of five years in consideration of a guilty plea. I observe, at this point, that five years in prison for the offense charged hardly could be characterized as a generous offer. Apparently respondent viewed the offer in this light and declined to accept it; he protested that he was innocent and insisted on going to trial. Respondent adhered to this position even when the prosecutor advised that he would seek a new indictment under the State's Habitual Criminal Act which would subject respondent, if convicted,

to a mandatory life sentence because of two prior felony convictions.

The prosecutor's initial assessment of respondent's case led him to forego an indictment under the habitual criminal statute. The circumstances of respondent's prior convictions are relevant to this assessment and to my view of the case. Respondent was 17 years old when he committed his first offense. He was charged with rape but pled guilty to the lesser included offense of "detaining a female." One of the other participants in the incident was sentenced to life imprisonment. Respondent was sent not to prison but to a reformatory where he served five years. Respondent's second offense was robbery. This time he was found guilty by a jury and was sentenced to five years in prison, but he was placed on probation and served no time. Although respondent's prior convictions brought him within the terms of the Habitual Criminal Act, the offenses themselves did not result in imprisonment; yet the addition of a conviction on a charge involving $88.30 subjected respondent to a mandatory sentence of imprisonment for life. Persons convicted of rape and murder often are not punished so severely.

No explanation appears in the record for the prosecutor's decision to escalate the charge against respondent other than respondent's refusal to plead guilty. The prosecutor has conceded that his purpose was to discourage respondent's assertion of constitutional rights, and the majority accepts this characterization of events. See *ante* . . . .

It seems to me that the question to be asked under the circumstances is whether the prosecutor reasonably might have charged respondent under the Habitual Criminal Act in the first place. The deferrence that courts properly accord the exercise of a prosecutor's discretion perhaps would foreclose judicial criticism if the prosecutor originally had sought an indictment under that act, as unreasonable as it would have seemed. But here the prosecutor evidently made a reasonable, responsible judgment not to subject an individual to a mandatory life sentence when his only new offense had societal implications as limited as those accompanying the uttering of a single $88 forged check and when the circumstances of his prior convictions confirmed the inappropriateness of applying the habitual criminal statute. I think it may be inferred that the prosecutor himself deemed it unreasonable and not in the public interest to put this defendant in jeopardy of a sentence of life imprisonment.

There may be situations in which a prosecutor would be fully justified in seeking a fresh indictment for a more serious offense. The most plausible justification might be that it would have been reasonable and in the public interest initially to have charged the defendant with the greater offense. In most cases a court could not know why the harsher indictment was sought, and an inquiry into the prosecutor's motive would neither be indicated nor likely to be fruitful. In those cases, I would agree with the majority that the situation would not differ materially from one in which the higher charge was brought at the outset. See *ante* . . . .

But this is not such a case. Here, any inquiry into the prosecutor's purpose is made unnecessary by his candid acknowledgement that he threatened to procure and in fact procured the habitual criminal indictment because of respondent's insistence on exercising his constitutional rights. We have stated in unequivocal terms, in discussing *United States* v. *Jackson*, 390 U.S. 570 (1968), and *North Carolina* v. *Pearce*, 395 U.S. 711 (1969), that "*Jackson* and *Pearce* are clear and subsequent cases have not diluted their force: if the only objective of a state practice is to discourage the assertion of constitutional rights it is 'patently unconstitutional.'" *Chaffin* v. *Stynchcombe*, 412 U.S. 17, 32 n. 20 (1973). And in *Brady* v. *United States*, 397 U.S. 742 (1970), we drew a distinction between the situation there approved and the "situation where the prosecutor or judge, or both, deliberately employ their charging and sentencing powers to induce a particular defendant to tender a plea of guilty." *Id.*, at 751 n. 8.

The plea-bargaining process, as recognized by this Court, is essential to the functioning of the criminal-justice system. It normally affords genuine benefits to defendants as well as to society. And if the system is to work effectively, prosecutors must be accorded the widest discretion, within constitutional limits, in conducting bargaining. . . . This is especially true when a defendant is represented by counsel and presumably is fully advised of his rights. Only in the most exceptional case should a court conclude that the scales of the bargaining are so unevenly balanced as to arouse suspicion. In this case, the prosecutor's actions denied respondent due process because their admitted purpose was to discourage and then to penalize with unique severity his exercise of constitutional rights. Implementation of a strategy calculated solely to deter the exercise of constitutional rights is not a constitutionally permissible exercise of discretion. I would affirm the opinion of the Court of Appeals on the facts of this case.

North Carolina v. *Alford*
400 U.S. 25 (1970)

Mr. Justice White delivered the opinion of the Court.

On December 2, 1963, Alford was indicted for first-degree murder, a capital offense under North Carolina law. The court appointed an attorney to represent him, and this attorney questioned all but one of the various witnesses who appellee said would substantiate his claim of innocence. The witnesses, however, did not support Alford's story but gave statements that strongly indicated his guilt. Faced with strong evidence of guilt and no substantial evidentiary support for the claim of innocence, Alford's attorney recommended that he plead guilty, but left the ultimate decision to Alford himself. The prosecutor agreed to accept a plea of guilty to a charge of second-degree murder, and on

December 10, 1963, Alford pleaded guilty to the reduced charge.

Before the plea was finally accepted by the trial court, the court heard the sworn testimony of a police officer who summarized the State's case. Two other witnesses besides Alford were also heard. Although there was no eyewitness to the crime, the testimony indicated that shortly before the killing Alford took his gun from his house, stated his intention to kill the victim, and returned home with the declaration that he had carried out the killing. After the summary presentation of the State's case, Alford took the stand and testified that he had not committed the murder but that he was pleading guilty because he faced the threat of the death penalty if he did not do so. In response to the question of his counsel, he acknowledged that his counsel had informed him of the difference between second- and first-degree murder and of his rights in case he chose to go to trial. The trial court then asked appellee if, in light of his denial of guilt, he still desired to plead guilty to second-degree murder and appellee answered, "Yes, sir, I plead guilty on—from the circumstances that he [Alford's attorney] told me." After eliciting information about Alford's prior criminal record, which was a long one, the trial court sentenced him to 30 years' imprisonment, the maximum penalty for second-degree murder.

Alford sought post-conviction relief in the state court. Among the claims raised was the claim that his plea of guilty was invalid because it was the product of fear and coercion. After a hearing, the state court in 1965 found that the plea was "willingly, knowingly, and understandingly" made on the advice of competent counsel and in the face of a strong prosecution case. Subsequently, Alford petitioned for a writ of habeas corpus, first in the United States District Court for the Middle District of North Carolina, and then in the Court of Appeals for the Fourth District. Both courts denied the writ on the basis of the state court's findings that Alford voluntarily and knowingly agreed to

plead guilty. In 1967, Alford again petitioned for a writ of habeas corpus in the District Court for the Middle District of North Carolina. That court, without an evidentiary hearing, again denied relief on the grounds that the guilty plea was voluntary and waived all defenses and nonjurisdictional defects in any prior stage of the proceedings, and that the findings of the state court in 1965 clearly required rejection of Alford's claim that he was denied effective assistance of counsel prior to pleading guilty. On appeal, a divided panel of the Court of Appeals for the Fourth Circuit reversed on the ground that Alford's guilty plea was made involuntarily. . . . In reaching its conclusion, the Court of Appeals relied heavily on *United States* v. *Jackson*, 390 U.S. 570 (1968), which the Court read to require invalidation of the North Carolina statutory framework for the imposition of the death penalty because North Carolina statutes encouraged defendants to waive constitutional rights by the promise of no more than life imprisonment if a guilty plea was offered and accepted. Conceding that Jackson did not require the automatic invalidation of pleas of guilty entered under the North Carolina statutes, the Court of Appeals ruled that Alford's guilty plea was involuntary because its principal motivation was fear of the death penalty. By this standard, even if both the judge and the jury had possessed the power to impose the death penalty for first-degree murder or if guilty pleas to capital charges had not been permitted, Alford's plea of guilty to second-degree murder should still have been rejected because impermissibly induced by his desire to eliminate the possibility of a death sentence. We noted probable jurisdiction. . . . We vacate the judgment of the Court of Appeals and remand the case for further proceedings.

We held in *Brady* v. *United States*, 397 U.S. 742 (1970), that a plea of guilty which would not have been entered except for the defendant's desire to avoid a possible death penalty and to limit the maximum penalty to life imprisonment or a term of years was not for that reason compelled within the meaning of the Fifth Amendment. Jackson established no new test for determining the validity of guilty pleas. The standard was and remains whether the plea represents a voluntary and intelligent choice among the alternative courses of action open to the defendant. . . . That he would not have pleaded except for the opportunity to limit the possible penalty does not necessarily demonstrate that the plea of guilty was not the product of a free and rational choice, especially where the defendant was represented by competent counsel whose advice was that the plea would be to the defendant's advantage. The standard fashioned and applied by the Court of Appeals was therefore erroneous and we would, without more, vacate and remand the case for further proceedings with respect to any other claims of Alford which are properly before that court, if it were not for other circumstances appearing in the record which might seem to warrant an affirmance of the Court of Appeals.

As previously recounted, after Alford's plea of guilty was offered and the State's case was placed before the judge, Alford denied that he had committed the murder but reaffirmed his desire to plead guilty to avoid a possible death sentence and to limit the penalty to the 30-year maximum provided for second-degree murder. Ordinarily, a judgment of conviction resting on a plea of guilty is justified by the defendant's admission that he committed the crime charged against him and his consent that judgment be entered without a trial of any kind. The plea usually subsumes both elements, and justifiably so, even though there is no separate, express admission by the defendant that he committed the particular acts claimed to constitute the crime charged in the indictment. . . . Here Alford entered his plea but accompanied it with the statement that he had not shot the victim.

If Alford's statements were to be credited as sincere assertions of his innocence, there obviously existed a factual and legal dispute between him and the State. Without more, it might be argued that the conviction entered on

his guilty plea was invalid, since his assertion of innocence negatived any admission of guilt, which, as we observed last Term in *Brady*, is normally "[c]entral to the plea and the foundation for entering judgment against the defendant . . . ."

In addition to Alford's statement, however, the court had heard an account of the events on the night of the murder, including information from Alford's acquaintances that he had departed from his home with his gun stating his intention to kill and that he had later declared that he had carried out his intention. Nor had Alford wavered in his desire to have the trial court determine his guilt without a jury trial. Although denying the charge against him, he nevertheless preferred the dispute between him and the State to be settled by the judge in the context of a guilty plea proceeding rather than by a formal trial. Thereupon, with the State's telling evidence and Alford's denial before it, the trial court proceeded to convict and sentence Alford for second-degree murder.

State and lower federal courts are divided upon whether a guilty plea can be accepted when it is accompanied by protestations of innocence and hence contains only a waiver of trial but no admission of guilt. Some courts, giving expression to the principle that "[o]ur law only authorizes a conviction where guilt is shown," *Harris* v. *State*, 172 S.W. 975, 977 (1915), require that trial judges reject such pleas. . . . But others have concluded that they should not "force any defense on a defendant in a criminal case," particularly when advancement of the defense might "end in disaster . . . ." *Tremblay* v. *Overholser*, 199 F. Supp. 569, 570 (D.C. 1961). They have argued that, since "guilt, or the degree of guilt, is at times uncertain and elusive," "[a]n accused, though believing in or entertaining doubts respecting his innocence, might reasonably conclude a jury would be convinced of his guilt and that he would fare better in the sentence by pleading guilty . . . ." *McCoy* v. *United States*, 363 F.2d 306, 308 (1966). As one state court observed nearly a century ago, "[r]easons other than the fact that he is guilty may induce a defendant to so plead, . . . [and] [h]e must be permitted to judge for himself in this respect." *State* v. *Kaufman*, 51 Iowa 578, 580, 2 N.W. 275, 276 (1879) (dictum) . . . .

This Court has not confronted this precise issue, but prior decisions do yield relevant principles. In *Lynch* v. *Overholser*, 369 U.S. 705 (1962), Lynch, who had been charged in the Municipal Court of the District of Columbia with drawing and negotiating bad checks, a misdemeanor punishable by a maximum of one year in jail, sought to enter a plea of guilty, but the trial judge refused to accept the plea since a psychiatric report in the judge's possession indicated that Lynch had been suffering from "a manic depressive psychosis, at the time of the crime charged," and hence might have been not guilty by reason of insanity. Although at the subsequent trial Lynch did not rely on the insanity defense, he was found not guilty by reason of insanity and committed for an indeterminate period to a mental institution. On habeas corpus, the Court ordered his release, construing the congressional legislation seemingly authorizing the commitment as not reaching a case where the accused preferred a guilty plea to a plea of insanity. The Court expressly refused to rule that Lynch had an absolute right to have his guilty plea accepted, . . . but implied that there would have been no constitutional error had his plea been accepted even though evidence before the judge indicated that there was a valid defense.

The issue in *Hudson* v. *United States*, 272 U.S. 451 (1926), was whether a federal court has power to impose a prison sentence after accepting a plea of nolo contendere, a plea by which a defendant does not expressly admit his guilt, but nonetheless waives his right to a trial and authorizes the court for purposes of the case to treat him as if he were guilty. The Court held that a trial court does have such power, and, except for the cases which were rejected in *Hudson*, the federal courts have uniformly followed

this rule, even in cases involving moral turpitude. . . . Implicit in the nolo contendere cases is a recognition that the Constitution does not bar imposition of a prison sentence upon an accused who is unwilling expressly to admit his guilt but who, faced with grim alternatives, is willing to waive his trial and accept the sentence.

These cases would be directly in point if Alford had simply insisted on his plea but refused to admit the crime. The fact that his plea was denominated a plea of guilty rather than a plea of nolo contendere is of no constitutional significance with respect to the issue now before us, for the Constitution is concerned with the practical consequences, not the formal categorizations, of state law. . . . Thus, while most pleas of guilty consist of both a waiver of trial and an express admission of guilt, the latter element is not a constitutional requisite to the imposition of criminal penalty. An individual accused of crime may voluntarily, knowingly, and understandingly consent to the imposition of a prison sentence even if he is unwilling or unable to admit his participation in the acts constituting the crime.

Nor can we perceive any material difference between a plea that refuses to admit commission of the criminal act and a plea containing a protestation of innocence when, as in the instant case, a defendant intelligently concludes that his interests require entry of a guilty plea and the record before the judge contains strong evidence of actual guilt. Here the State had a strong case of first-degree murder against Alford. Whether he realized or disbelieved his guilt, he insisted on his plea because in his view he had absolutely nothing to gain by a trial and much to gain by pleading. Because of the overwhelming evidence against him, a trial was precisely what neither Alford nor his attorney desired. Confronted with the choice between a trial for first-degree murder, on the one hand, and a plea of guilty to second-degree murder, on the other, Alford quite reasonably chose the latter and thereby limited the maximum penalty to a 30-year term. When his plea is viewed in light of the evidence against him, which substantially negated his claim of innocence and which further provided a means by which the judge could test whether the plea was being intelligently entered . . . its validity cannot be seriously questioned. In view of the strong factual basis for the plea demonstrated by the State and Alford's clearly expressed desire to enter it despite his professed belief in his innocence, we hold that the trial judge did not commit constitutional error in accepting it.

Relying on *United States* v. *Jackson, supra*, Alford now argues in effect that the State should not have allowed him this choice but should have insisted on proving him guilty of murder in the first degree. The States in their wisdom may take this course by statute or otherwise and may prohibit the practice of accepting pleas to lesser included offenses under any circumstances. But this is not the mandate of the Fourteenth Amendment and the Bill of Rights. The prohibitions against involuntary or unintelligent pleas should not be relaxed, but neither should an exercise in arid logic render those constitutional guarantees counterproductive and put in jeopardy the very human values they were meant to preserve.

The Court of Appeals for the Fourth Circuit was in error to find Alford's plea of guilty invalid because it was made to avoid the possibility of the death penalty. That court's judgment directing the issuance of the writ of habeas corpus is vacated and the case is remanded to the Court of Appeals for further proceedings consistent with this opinion. . . .

Mr. Justice Black . . . concurs in the judgment and substantially all of the opinion in this case.

Mr. Justice Brennan, with whom Mr. Justice Douglas and Mr. Justice Marshall join, dissenting.

Last Term, this Court held, over my dissent, that a plea of guilty may validly be induced by an unconstitutional threat to subject the defendant to the risk of death, so long as the plea is entered in open court and the defendant is represented by competent counsel who is aware of the threat, albeit not of its unconstitutionality. *Brady* v. *United States*, 397 U.S. 742, 745–758 (1970). . . . Today the Court makes clear that its previous holding was intended to apply even when the record demonstrates that the actual effect of the unconstitutional threat was to induce a guilty plea from a defendant who was unwilling to admit his guilt.

I adhere to the view that, in any given case, the influence of such an unconstitutional threat "must necessarily be given weight in determining the voluntariness of a plea." *Parker* v. *North Carolina*, 397 U.S., at 805 (dissent). And, without reaching the question whether due process permits the entry of judgment upon a plea of guilty accompanied by a contemporaneous denial of acts constituting the crime, I believe that at the very least such a denial of guilt is also a relevant factor in determining whether the plea was voluntarily and intelligently made. With these factors in mind, it is sufficient in my view to state that the facts set out in the majority opinion demonstrate that Alford was "so gripped by fear of the death penalty" that his decision to plead guilty was not voluntary but was "the product of duress as much so as choice reflecting physical constraint." . . . Accordingly, I would affirm the judgment of the Court of Appeals.

Note: Tollett v. *Henderson*, 411 U.S. 258 (1973), held that a defendant who, on advice of reasonably competent counsel, pleads guilty in open court may not later raise independent claims of deprivation of constitutional rights (here improper grand jury selection) that preceded the guilty plea.

8

Free Speech, Press, and Association

INTRODUCTION

John Milton, *Areopagitica* (excerpt)

. . . And though all the winds of doctrine were let loose to play upon the earth, so truth be in the field, we do injuriously by licensing and prohibiting to misdoubt her strength. Let her and Falsehood grapple; who ever knew truth put to the worse in a free and open encounter?

John Stuart Mill, *Utilitarianism, Liberty, and Representative Government* (excerpt)

. . . But the peculiar evil of silencing the expression of an opinion is, that it is robbing the human race; posterity as well as the existing generation; those who dissent from the opinion, still more than those who hold it. If the opinion is right, they are deprived of the opportunity of exchanging error for truth; if wrong, they lose, what is almost as great a benefit, the clearer per-

ception and livelier impression of truth, produced by its collision with error.

Alexander Meiklejohn, *Free Speech and Its Relation to Self-Government* (excerpt)*

. . . [T]he vital point, as stated negatively, is that no suggestion of policy shall be denied a hearing because it is on one side of the issue rather than another. And this means that though citizens may, on other grounds, be barred from speaking, they may not be barred because their views are thought to be false or dangerous. No plan of action shall be outlawed because someone in control thinks it unwise, unfair, un-American. No speaker may be declared "out of order" because we disagree with what he intends to say. And the reason for this equality of status in the fields of ideas lies deep in the very foundations of the self-governing process. When men govern themselves, it is they—and no one else—who must pass judgment upon unwisdom and unfairness and

* New York: Harper & Brothers (1948), pp. 26–27.

382

danger. And that means that unwise ideas must have a hearing as well as wise ones, unfair as well as fair, dangerous as well as safe, un-American as well as American. Just so far as, at any point, the citizens who are to decide an issue are denied acquaintance with information or opinion or doubt or disbelief or criticism which is relevant to that issue, just so far the result must be ill-considered, ill-balanced planning for the general good. *It is that mutilation of the thinking process of the community against which the First Amendment to the Constitution is directed.* The principle of the freedom of speech springs from the necessities of the program of self-government. It is not a Law of Nature or of Reason in the abstract. It is a deduction from the basic American agreement that public issues shall be decided by universal suffrage.

If, then, on any occasion in the United States it is allowable to say that the Constitution is a good document it is equally allowable, in that situation, to say that the Constitution is a bad document. If a public building may be used in which to say, in time of war, that the war is justified, then the same building may be used in which to say that it is not justified. If it be publicly argued that conscription for armed service is moral and necessary, it may likewise be publicly argued that it is immoral and unnecessary. If it may be said that American political institutions are superior to those of England or Russia or Germany, it may, with equal freedom, be said that those of England or Russia or Germany are superior to ours. These conflicting views may be expressed, must be expressed, not because they are valid, but because they are relevant. If they are responsibly entertained by anyone, we, the voters, need to hear them. When a question of policy is "before the house," free men choose to meet it not with their eyes shut, but with their eyes open. To be afraid of ideas, any idea, is to be unfit for self-government. Any such suppression of ideas about the common good, the First Amendment condemns with its absolute disapproval. The freedom of ideas shall not be abridged.

PRIOR RESTRAINT—CENSORSHIP

William Blackstone, *Commentaries on the Laws of England* (1769) (excerpt)

The liberty of the press is indeed essential to the nature of a free state; but this consists in laying no *previous* restraints upon publications, and not in freedom from censure for criminal matter when published. Every freeman has an undoubted right to lay what sentiments he pleases before the public: to forbid this is to destroy the freedom of the press, but if he publishes what is improper, mischievous, or illegal, he must take the consequences of his own temerity. To subject the press to the restrictive power of a licenser, as was formerly done, both before and since the Revolution, is to subject all freedom of sentiment to the prejudices of one man, and make him the arbitrary and infallible judge of all controverted points in learning, religion, and government. But to punish (as the law does at present) any dangerous or offensive writings which, when published, shall on a fair and impartial trial be ajudged of a pernicious tendency, is necessary for the preservation of peace and good order, of government and religion,—the only solid foundations of civil liberty. Thus the will of individuals is still left free; the abuse only of that free will is the object of legal punishment. . . . (Book IV, p. 151)

New York Times Co. v. United States (The Pentagon Papers Cases)
403 U.S. 713 (1971)

Per Curiam.

We granted certiorari, in these cases in which the United States seeks to enjoin the *New York Times* and the *Washington Post* from publishing the contents of a classified study entitled "History of U.S. Decision-Making Process on Viet Nam Policy."

"Any system of prior restraints of expression comes to this Court bearing a heavy presumption against its constitutional validity." *Bantam Books, Inc.* v. *Sullivan,* 372 U.S. 58, 70 (1963). The Government "thus carries a heavy burden of showing justification for the imposition of such a restraint." *Organization for a Better Austin* v. *Keefe,* 401 U.S. [415] (1971). The District Court for the Southern District of New York in the *New York Times* case, and the District Court for the District of Columbia and the Court of Appeals for the District of Columbia Circuit in the *Washington Post* case held that the Government had not met that burden. We agree. . . .

Mr. Justice Black, with whom Mr. Justice Douglas joins, concurring. . . .

. . . [F]or the first time in the 182 years since the founding of the Republic, the federal courts are asked to hold that the First Amendment does not mean what it says, but rather means that the Government can halt the publication of current news of vital importance to the people of this country.

. . . Both the history and language of the First Amendment support the view that the press must be left free to publish news, whatever the source, without censorship, injunctions, or prior restraints.

In the First Amendment the Founding Fathers gave the free press the protection it must have to fulfill its essential role in our democracy. The press was to serve the governed, not the governors. The Government's power to censor the press was abolished so that the press would remain forever free to censure the Government. The press was protected so that it could bare the secrets of government and inform the people. Only a free and unrestrained press can effectively expose deception in government. . . .

The Government does not even attempt to rely on any act of Congress. Instead it makes the bold and dangerously far-reaching contention that the courts should take it upon themselves to "make" a law abridging freedom of the press in the name of equity, presidential power and national security, even when the representatives of the people in Congress have adhered to the command of the First Amendment and refused to make such a law. To find that the President has "inherent power" to halt the publication of news by resort to the courts would wipe out the First Amendment and destroy the fundamental liberty and security of the very people the Government hopes to make "secure." . . .

The word "security" is a broad, vague generality whose contours should not be invoked to abrogate the fundamental law embodied in the First Amendment. The guarding of military and diplomatic secrets at the expense of informed representative government provides no real security for our Republic. . . .

Mr. Justice Douglas, with whom Mr. Justice Black joins, concurring.

While I join the opinion of the Court I believe it necessary to express my views more fully.

[T]he First Amendment . . . leaves, in my view, no room for governmental restraint on the press.

There is, moreover, no statute barring the publication by the press of the material which the Times and Post seek to use. . . .

These disclosures may have a serious impact. But that is no basis for sanctioning a previous restraint on the press. . . .

The dominant purpose of the First Amendment was to prohibit the widespread practice of governmental suppression of embarrassing information. It is common knowledge that the First Amendment was adopted against the widespread use of the common law of seditious libel to punish the dissemination of material that is embarassing to the powers-that-be. The present cases will, I think, go down in history as the most dramatic illustration of that principle.

A debate of large proportions goes on in the Nation over our posture in Vietnam. That debate antedated the disclosure of the contents of the present documents. The latter are highly relevant to the debate in progress.

Secrecy in government is fundamentally anti-democratic, perpetuating bureaucratic errors. Open debate and discussion of public issues are vital to our national health. On public questions there should be "open and robust debate." *New York Times, Inc.* v. *Sullivan*. . . .

The stays in these cases that have been in effect for more than a week constitute a flouting of the principles of the First Amendment as interpreted in [*Near* v. *Minnesota*, 283 U.S. 697].

Mr. Justice Brennan, concurring.

I write separately in these cases only to emphasize what should be apparent: that our judgment in the present cases may not be taken to indicate the propriety, in the future, or issuing temporary stays and restraining orders to block the publication of material sought to be suppressed by the Government. So far as I can determine, never before has the United States sought to enjoin a newspaper from publishing information in its possession. . . .

The entire thrust of the Government's claim throughout these cases has been that publication of the material sought to be enjoined "could," or "might," or "may" prejudice the national interest in various ways. But the First Amendment tolerates absolutely no prior judicial restraints of the press predicated upon surmise or conjecture that untoward consequences may result. Our cases, it is true, have indicated that there is a single, extremely narrow class of cases in which the First Amendment's ban on prior judicial restraint may be overriden. Our cases have thus far indicated that such cases may arise only when the Nation "is at war," *Schenck* v. *United States*, 249 U.S. 470. Even if the present world situation were assumed to be tantamount to a time of war, or if the power of presently available armaments would justify even in peacetime the suppression of information that would set in motion a nuclear holocaust, in neither of these actions has the Government presented or even alleged that publication of items from or based upon the material at issue would cause the happening of an event of that nature. . . . Thus, only governmental allegation and proof that publication must inevitably, directly and immediately cause the occurrence of an event kindred to imperiling the safety of a transport already at sea can support even the issuance of an interim restraining order. In no event may mere conclusions be sufficient: for if the Executive Branch seeks judicial aid in preventing publication, it must inevitably submit the basis upon which that aid is sought to scrutiny by the judiciary. And therefore, every restraint issued in this case, whatever its form, has violated the First Amendment—and nonetheless so because that restraint was justified as necessary to afford the court an opportunity to examine the claim more thoroughly. Unless and until the Government has clearly made out its case, the First Amendment commands that no injunction may issue.

Mr. Justice Stewart, with whom Mr. Justice White joins, concurring.

. . . [I]n the cases before us we are asked neither to construe specific regulations nor to apply specific laws. We are asked, instead, to perform a function that the Constitution gave to the Executive, not the judiciary. We are asked, quite simply, to prevent the publication by two newspapers of material that the Executive Branch insists should not, in the national interest, be published. I am convinced that the Executive is correct with respect to some of the documents involved. But I cannot say that disclosure of any of them will surely result in direct, immediate, and irreparable damage to our Nation or its people. That being so, there can under the First Amendment be but one judicial resolution of the issues before us. I join the judgments of the Court.

Mr. Justice White, with whom Mr. Justice Stewart joins, concurring.

I concur in today's judgments, but only because of the concededly extraordinary protection against prior restraints enjoyed by the press under our constitutional system. I do not say that in no circumstances would the First Amendment permit an injunction against publishing information about government plans or operations. Nor, after examining the materials the Government characterizes as the most sensitive and destructive, can I deny that revelation of these documents will do substantial damage to public interests. Indeed, I am confident that their disclosure will have that result. But I nevertheless agree that the United States has not satisfied the very heavy burden which it must meet to warrant an injunction against publication in these cases, at least in the absence of express and appropriately limited congressional authorization for prior restraints in circumstances such as these.

The Government's position is simply stated: The responsibility of the Executive for the conduct of the foreign affairs and for the security of the Nation is so basic that the President is entitled to an injunction against publication of a newspaper story whenever he can convince a court that the information to be revealed threatens "grave and irreparable" injury to the public interest; and the injunction should issue whether or not the material to be published is classified, whether or not publication would be lawful under relevant criminal statutes enacted by Congress and regardless of the circumstances by which the newspaper came into possession of the information.

At least in the absence of legislation by Congress, based on its own investigations and findings, I am quite unable to agree that the inherent powers of the Executive and the courts reach so far as to authorize remedies having such sweeping potential for inhibiting publications by the press. [To] sustain the Government in these cases would start the courts down a long and hazardous road that I am not willing to travel at least without congressional guidance and direction.

. . . Prior restraints require an unusually heavy justification under the First Amendment; but failure by the Government to justify prior restraints does not measure its constitutional entitlement to a conviction for criminal publication. That the Government mistakenly chose to proceed by injunction does not mean that it could not successfully proceed in another way.

. . . Congress has addressed itself to the problems of protecting the security of the country and the national defense from unauthorized disclosure of potentially damaging information. Cf. [*Steel Seizure* case]. It has not, however, authorized the injunctive remedy against threatened publication. It has apparently been satisfied to rely on criminal sanctions and their deterrent effect on the responsible as well as the irresponsible press. . . .

[Mr. Justice Marshall, concurring, did not deal with First Amendment problems. In his view the case presented a basic separation-of-powers issue—an executive effort to secure by judicial order relief which Congress had refused to authorize.]

Mr. Chief Justice Burger, dissenting.

So clear are the constitutional limitations on prior restraint against expression, that . . . we have had little occasion to be concerned with cases involving prior restraints against news reporting on matters of public interest. There is, therefore, little variation among the members of the Court in terms of resistance to prior restraints against publication. Adherence to this basic constitutional principle, however, does not make this case a simple one. In this case, the imperative of a free and unfettered press comes into collision with another imperative, the effective functioning of a complex modern government and specifically the effective exercise of certain constitutional powers of the Executive.

Only those who view the First Amendment as an absolute in all circumstances—a view I respect, but reject—can find such a case as this to be simple or easy.

This case is not simple for another and more immediate reason. We do not know the facts of the case. . . . Why are we in this posture, in which only those judges to whom the First Amendment is absolute and permits of no restraint in any circumstances or for any reason, are really in a position to act? I suggest we are in this posture because these cases have been conducted in unseemly haste. . . . Here, moreover, the frenetic haste is due in large part to the manner in which the *Times* proceeded from the date it obtained the purloined documents. It seems reasonably clear now that the haste precluded reasonable and deliberate judicial treatment of these cases and was not warranted. . . .

The newspapers make a derivative claim under the First Amendment; they denominate this right as the public right-to-know; by implication, the *Times* asserts a sole trusteeship of that right by virtue of its journalist "scoop." The right is asserted as an absolute. Of course, the First Amendment right itself is not an absolute, as Justice Holmes so long as pointed out in his aphorism concerning the right to shout of fire in a crowded theater. There are other exceptions, some of which Chief Justice Hughes mentioned by way of example in *Near* v. *Minnesota*. There are no doubt other exceptions no one has had occasion to describe or discuss. Conceivably such exceptions may be lurking in these cases and would have been flushed had they been properly considered in the trial courts, free from unwarranted deadlines and frenetic pressures. A great issue of this kind should be tried in a judicial atmosphere conducive to thoughtful, reflective deliberation, especially when haste, in terms of hours, is unwarranted in light of the long period the *Times,* by its own choice, deferred publication.

It is not disputed that the *Times* has had unauthorized possession of the documents for three to four months, during which it has had its expert analysts studying them, presumably digesting them and preparing the material for publication. During all of this time, the *Times,* presumably in its capacity as trustee of the public's "right to know," has held up publication for purposes it considered proper and thus public knowledge was delayed. No doubt this was for a good reason; the analysis of 7,000 pages of complex material drawn from a vastly greater volume of material would inevitably take time and the writing of good news stories takes time. But why should the United States Government, from whom this information was illegally acquired by someone, along with all the counsel, trial judges, and appellate judges be placed under needless pressure? After these months of deferral, the alleged right-to-know has somehow and suddenly become a right that must be vindicated instanter.

Would it have been unreasonable, since the newspaper could anticipate the government's objections to release of secret material, to give the government an opportunity to review the entire collection and determine whether agreement could be reached on publication? Stolen or not, if security was not in fact jeopardized, much of the material could no doubt have been declassified, since it spans a period ending in 1968. With such an approach—one that great newspapers having in the past practiced and stated editorially to be the duty of an honorable press—the newspapers and government might well have narrowed the area of disagreement as to what was and was not publishable, leaving the remainder to be resolved in orderly litigation if necessary. To me it is hardly believeable that a newspaper long regarded as a great institution in American life would fail to perform one of the basic and simple duties of every citizen with respect to the discovery or possession of stolen property or secret government documents. That duty, I had thought—perhaps naively—was to report forthwith, to responsible public officers. This duty rests on taxi drivers, Justices and the *New York Times.* The course followed by the *Times,* whether so calculated or

not, removed any possibility of orderly litigation of the issues. If the action of the judges up
to now has been correct, that result is sheer
happenstance.[1] . . .

The consequence of all this melancholy series
of events is that we literally do not know what
we are acting on. . . . I agree with Mr. Justice
Harlan and Mr. Justice Blackmun but I am not
prepared to reach the merits. . . .

I should add that I am in general agreement
with much of what Mr. Justice White has expressed with respect to penal sanctions concerning communication or retention of documents
or information relating to the national defense.

We all crave speedier judicial processes but
when judges are pressured as in these cases the
result is a parody of the judicial process.

Mr. Justice Harlan, with whom The Chief
Justice [Burger] and Mr. Justice Blackmun join,
dissenting.

. . . With all respect, I consider that the
Court has been almost irresponsibly feverish in
dealing with these cases. . . . This frenzied
train of events took place in the name of the
presumption against prior restraints created by
the First Amendment. Due regard for the extraordinarily important and difficult questions
involved in these litigations should have led the
Court to shun such a precipitate timetable. In
order to decide the merits of these cases properly, some or all of the following questions
should have been faced:

1.   Whether the Attorney General is authorized to bring these suits in the name of the
United States. . . . This question involves as
well the construction and validity of a singularly
opaque statue—the Espionage Act, 18 U.S.C.
§ 793(e).

2.   Whether the First Amendment permits
the federal courts to enjoin publication of
stories which would present a serious threat to
national security. See *Near* v. *Minnesota*, 283
U.S. 697, 716 (1931) (dictum).

3.   Whether the threat to publish highly secret documents is of itself a sufficient implication
of national security to justify an injunction on
the theory that regardless of the contents of the
documents harm enough results simply from
the demonstration of such a breach of secrecy.

4.   Whether the unauthorized disclosure of
any of these particular documents would seriously impair the national security.

5.   What weight should be given to the
opinion of high officers in the Executive Branch
of the Government with respect to questions 3
and 4.

6.   Whether the newspapers are entitled to
retain and use the documents notwithstanding
the seemingly uncontested facts that the documents, or the originals of which they are dupli-
cates, were purloined from the Government's
possession and that the newspapers received
them with knowledge that they had been
feloniously acquired. Cf. *Liberty Lobby, Inc.* v.
Pearson, 390 F.2d 489 (CADC 1968).

7.   Whether the threatened harm to the national security or the Government's possessory
interest in the documents justifies the issuance
of an injunction against publication in light of—

a.   The strong First Amendment policy
against prior restraints on publication;

b.   The doctrine against enjoining conduct
in violation of criminal statutes; and

c.   The extent to which the materials at issue
have apparently already been otherwise dis-
seminated.

These are difficult questions of fact, of law,
and of judgment; the potential consequences of
erroneous decision are enormous. The time
which has been available to us, to the lower
courts, and to the parties has been wholly inadequate for giving these cases the kind of consideration they deserve. It is a reflection on the
stability of the judicial process that these great

---

[1] Interestingly the *Times* explained its refusal to allow the
government to examine its own purloined documents by
saying in substance this might compromise *their* sources
and informants! The *Times* thus asserts a right to guard the
secrecy of its sources while denying that the Government of
the United States has that power.

issues—as important as any that have arisen during my time on the Court—should have been decided under the pressures engendered by the torrent of publicity that has attended these litigations from their inception.

Forced as I am to reach the merits of these cases, I dissent from the opinion and judgments of the Court. Within the severe limitations imposed by the time constraints under which I have been required to operate, I can only state my reasons in telescoped form, even though in different circumstances I would have felt constrained to deal with the cases in the fuller sweep indicated above.

It is a sufficient basis for affirming the Court of Appeals for the Second Circuit in the Times litigation to observe that its order must rest on the conclusion that because of the time elements the Government had not been given an adequate opportunity to present its case to the District Court. At the least this conclusion was not an abuse of discretion.

In the Post litigation the Government had more time to prepare; this was apparently the basis for the refusal of the Court of Appeals for the District of Columbia Circuit on rehearing to conform its judgment to that of the Second Circuit. But I think there is another and more fundamental reason why this judgment cannot stand—a reason which also furnishes an additional ground for not reinstating the judgment of the District Court in the Times litigation, set aside by the Court of Appeals. It is plain to me that the scope of the judicial function in passing upon the activities of the executive Branch of the Government in the field of foreign affairs is very narrowly restricted. This view is, I think, dictated by the concept of separation of powers upon which our constitutional system rests.

[The Executive possesses] constitutional primacy in the field of foreign affairs. . . . The power to evaluate the "pernicious influence" of premature disclosure is not, however, lodged in the Executive alone. I agree that, in performance of its duty to protect the values of the First Amendment against political pressures, the judiciary must review the initial Executive determination to the point of satisfying itself that the subject matter of the dispute does lie within the proper compass of the President's foreign relations power. Constitutional considerations forbid "a complete abandonment of judicial control." Moreover, the judiciary may properly insist that the determination that disclosure of the subject matter would irreparably impair the national security be made by the head of the Executive Department concerned—here the Secretary of State or the Secretary of Defense—after actual personal consideration by that officer. . . . But in my judgment the judiciary may not properly go beyond these two inquiries and redetermine for itself the probable impact of disclosure on the national security. "[T]he very nature of executive decisions as to foreign policy is political, not judicial. . . . They are delicate, complex, and involve large elements of prophecy. They are and should be undertaken only by those directly responsible to the people whose welfare they advance or imperil. They are decisions of a kind for which the Judiciary has neither aptitude, facilities nor responsibility. . . ." *Chicago & Southern Air Lines* v. *Waterman Steamship Corp.*, 333 U.S. 103, 111 (1948) (Jackson, J.).

Even if there is some room for the judiciary to override the executive determination, it is plain that the scope of review must be exceedingly narrow. I can see no indication in the opinions of [the lower courts] in the *Post* litigation that the conclusions of the Executive were given even the deference owing to an administrative agency, much less that owing to a co-equal branch of the Government operating within the field of its constitutional prerogative. . . .

Pending further hearings in each case conducted under the appropriate ground rules, I would continue the restraints on publication. I cannot believe that the doctrine prohibiting prior restraints reaches to the point of preventing courts from maintaining the *status quo* long enough to act responsibly in matters of such national importance as those involved here.

Mr. Justice Blackmun.

I join Mr. Justice Harlan in his dissent. I also am in substantial accord with much that Mr. Justice White says, by way of admonition, in the latter part of his opinion. . . .

Two federal district courts, two United States courts of appeals, and this Court—within a period of less than three weeks from inception until today—have been pressed into hurried decision of profound constitutional issues on inadequately developed and largely assumed facts without the careful deliberation that, hopefully, should characterize the American judicial process. There has been much writing about the law and little knowledge and less digestion of the facts. . . . The country would be none the worse off were the cases tried quickly, to be sure, but in the customary and properly deliberative manner. . . .

The First Amendment, after all, is only one part of an entire Constitution. . . . First Amendment absolutism has never commanded a majority of this Court. What is needed here is a weighing, upon properly developed standards, of the broad right of the press to print and of the very narrow right of the Government to prevent. Such standards are not yet developed. The parties here are in disagreement as to what those standards should be. But even the newspapers concede that there are situations where restraint is in order and is constitutional. . . . I therefore would remand these cases to be developed expeditiously, of course, but on a schedule permitting [orderly presentation of evidence].

The Court, however, decides the cases today the other way. I therefore add one final comment.

I strongly urge, and sincerely hope, that these two newspapers will be fully aware of their ultimate responsibilities to the United States of America. Judge Wilkey, dissenting in the District of Columbia case, after a review of only the affidavits before this court (the basic papers had not then been made available by either party), concluded that there were a number of examples of documents that, if in the possession of the *Post,* and if published, "could clearly result in great harm to the nation," and he defined "harm" to mean "the death of soldiers, the destruction of alliances, the greatly increased difficulty of negotiation with our enemies, the inability of our diplomats to negotiate. . . ." I, for one, have now been able to give at least some cursory study not only to the affidavits, but to the material itself. I regret to say that from this examination I fear that Judge Wilkey's statements have possible foundation. I therefore share his concern. I hope that damage already has not been done. If, however, damage has been done, and if, with the Court's action today, these newspapers proceed to publish the critical documents and there results therefrom "the death of soldiers, the destruction of alliances, the greatly increased difficulty of negotiation with our enemies, the inability of our diplomats to negotiate," to which list I might add the factors of prolongation of the war and of further delay in the freeing of United States prisoners, then the Nation's people will know where the responsibility for these sad consequences rests.

Nebraska Press Association v. *Stuart*
427 U.S. 539 (1976)

In the section titled "Fair Tribunal and Prosecutor" in Chapter 7, an excerpt from the present case provides a resumé of decisions involving clashes between freedom of the press and the right to a fair trial. Nebraska courts had tried to avoid such a clash in a widely publicized mass murder trial by prohibiting news-media reports on "the existence and nature of any confessions or admissions made by the defendant [Simants] to law enforcement officers [or] third parties, except members of the press, and . . . other facts 'strongly implicative' of the accused.''

Mr. Chief Justice Burger delivered the opinion of the Court . . . .

The thread running through all these cases [see excerpt from this case, Chapter 7 above, and *New York Times Co.,* above] is that prior restraints on speech and publication are the most serious and the least tolerable infringement on First Amendment rights. . . .

A prior restraint, . . . has an immediate and irreversible sanction. It if can be said that a threat of criminal or civil sanctions after publication "chills" speech, prior restraint "freezes" it at least for the time.

The damage can be particularly great when the prior restraint falls upon the communication of news and commentary on current events. Truthful reports of public judicial proceedings have been afforded special protection against subsequent punishment. See *Cox Broadcasting Corp.* v. *Cohn,* 420 U.S. 469, 492–493 (1975); see also, *Craig* v. *Harney,* 331 U.S. 367, 374 (1947). For the same reasons the protection against prior restraint should have particular force as applied to reporting of criminal proceedings, whether the crime in question is a single isolated act or a pattern of criminal conduct. . . . The extraordinary protections afforded by the First Amendment carry with them something in the nature of a fiduciary duty to exercise the protected rights responsibly—a duty widely acknowledged but not always observed by editors and publishers. It is not asking too much to suggest that those whose exercise First Amendment rights in newspapers or broadcasting enterprises direct some effort to protect the rights of an accused to a fair trial by unbiased jurors.

Of course, the order at issue—like the order requested in *New York Times*—does not prohibit but only postpones publication. Some news can be delayed and most commentary can even more readily be delayed without serious injury, and there often is a self-imposed delay when responsible editors call for verification of information. But such delays are normally slight and they are self-imposed. Delays imposed by governmental authority are a different matter. . . . As a practical matter, moreover, the element of time is not unimportant if press coverage is to fulfill its traditional function of bringing news to the public promptly.

The authors of the Bill of Rights did not undertake to assign priorities as between First Amendment and Sixth Amendment rights, ranking one as superior to the other. In this case, the petitioners would have us declare the right of an accused subordinate to their right to publish in all circumstances. But if the authors of these guarantees, fully aware of the potential conflicts between them, were unwilling or unable to resolve the issue by assigning to one priority over the other, it is not for us to rewrite the Constitution by undertaking what they declined. It is unnecessary, after nearly two centuries, to establish a priority applicable in all circumstances. Yet it is nonetheless clear that the barriers to prior restraint remain high unless we are to abandon what the Court has said for nearly a quarter of our national existence and implied throughout all of it. The history of even wartime suspension of categorical guarantees, such as habeas corpus or the right to trial by civilian courts, see *Ex parte Milligan,* 4 Wall. 2 (1867), cautions against suspending explicit guarantees.

VI.

We turn now to the record in this case to determine whether, as Learned Hand put it, "the gravity of the 'evil,' discounted by its improbability, justifies such invasion of free speech as is necessary to avoid the danger." *Dennis* v. *United States,* 183 F.2d 201, 212 (1950), aff'd, 341 U.S. 494 (1951); see also L. Hand, *The Bill of Rights* 58–61 (1958). To do so, we must examine the evidence before the trial judge when the order was entered to determine (*a*) the nature and extent of pretrial news coverage; (*b*) whether other measures would be likely to mitigate the effects of unrestrained pretrial publicity; (*c*) how effectively a restraining order would operate to prevent the threatened danger. The precise terms of the restraining order are also important. We must then consider whether the record supports the entry of a prior restraint on publication, one of the most extraordinary remedies known to our jurisprudence. . . .

A

Our review of the pretrial record persuades us that the trial judge was justified in concluding that there would be intense and pervasive pretrial publicity concerning this case. He could also reasonably conclude, based on common human experience, that publicity might impair the defendant's right to a fair trial. He did not purport to say more, for he found only "a clear and present danger that pretrial publicity *could* impinge upon the defendant's right to a fair trial." (Emphasis added.) His conclusion as to the impact of such publicity on prospective jurors was of necessity speculative, dealing as he was with factors unknown and unknowable.

B

We find little in the record that goes to another aspect of our task, determining whether measures short of an order restraining all publication would have insured the defendant a fair trial. Although the entry of the order might be read as a judicial determination that other measures would not suffice, the trial court made no express findings to that effect; the Nebraska Supreme Court referred to the issue only by implication. See 194 Neb., at 797–798.

Most of the alternatives to prior restraint of publication in these circumstances were discussed with obvious approval in *Sheppard* v. *Maxwell*, 384 U.S., at 357–362: (*a*) change of trial venue to a place less exposed to the intense publicity that seemed imminent in Lincoln County; (*b*) postponement of the trial to allow public attention to subside; (*c*) use of searching questioning of prospective jurors, as Chief Justice Marshall did in the *Burr* case, to screen out those with fixed opinions as to guilt or innocence; (*d*) the use of emphatic and clear instructions on the sworn duty of each juror to decide the issues only on evidence presented in open court. Sequestration of jurors is, of course, always available. Although that measure insulates jurors only after they are sworn, it also enhances the likelihood of dissipating the impact of pretrial publicity and emphasizes the elements of the jurors' oaths.

This Court has outlined other measures short of prior restraints on publication tending to blunt the impact of pretrial publicity. See *Sheppard* v. *Maxwell*, 384 U.S., at 361–362. Professional studies have filled out these suggestions, recommending that trial courts in appropriate cases limit what the contending lawyers, the police, and witnesses may say to anyone. See American Bar Association, Standards for Criminal Justice, Fair Trial and Free Press 2–15 (Approved Draft, 1968).

We have noted earlier that pretrial publicity, even if pervasive and concentrated, cannot be regarded as leading automatically and in every kind of criminal case to an unfair trial. The decided cases "cannot be made to stand for the proposition that juror exposure to information about a state defendant's prior convictions or to news accounts of the crime with which he is charged alone presumptively deprives the defendant of due process." *Murphy* v. *Florida*, 421 U.S. 794, 799 (1975). Appellate evaluations as to the impact of publicity take into account what other measures were used to mitigate the adverse effects of publicity. The more difficult prospective or predictive assessment that a trial judge must make also calls for a judgment as to whether other precautionary steps will suffice.

We have therefore examined this record to determine the probable efficacy of the measures short of prior restraint on the press and speech. There is no finding that alternative measures would not have protected Simants' rights, and the Nebraska Supreme Court did no more than imply that such measures might not be adequate. Moreover, the record is lacking in evidence to support such a finding.

C

We must also assess the probable efficacy of prior restraint on publication as a workable method of protecting Simants' right to a fair trial, and we cannot ignore the reality of the problems of managing and enforcing pretrial restraining orders. The territorial jurisdiction of the issuing court is limited by concepts of sovereignty, see, *e.g., Hanson* v. *Denckla*, 357 U.S. 235 (1958); *Pennoyer* v. *Neff*, 95 U.S. 714 (1878). The need for *in personam* jurisdiction also presents an obstacle to a restraining order that applies to publication at-large as distinguished from restraining publication within a given jurisdiction. See generally American Bar Association, Legal Advisory Committee on Fair Trial and Free Press, Recommended Court Procedures to Accommodate Rights of Fair Trial and Free Press (Revised Draft, November 1975); Rendleman, Free Press-Fair Trial: Review of Silence Orders, 52 *N.C.L.Rev.* 127, 149–155 (1973).[1]

The Nebraska Supreme Court narrowed the

---

[1] Assuming, *arguendo*, that these problems are within reach of legislative enactment, or that some application of evolving concepts of long-arm jurisdiction would solve the problems of personal jurisdiction, even a cursory examination suggests how awkwardly broad prior restraints on publication, directed not at named parties but at-large, would fit into our jurisprudence. The British experience is in sharp contrast for a variety of reasons; Great Britain has a smaller and unitary court system permitting the development of a manageable system of prior restraints by the application of the constructive contempt doctrine. . . . [S]ee generally Maryland v. Baltimore Radio Show, 338 U.S. 912, 921–936 (1950) (App. to Opinion of Frankfurter, J., respecting denial of certiorari); Gillmor, Free Press and Fair Trial in English Law, 22 *Wash. & Lee L.Rev.* 17 (1965). Moreover, any comparison between the two systems must take into account that although England gives a very high place to freedom of the press and speech, its courts are not subject to the explicit strictures of a written Constitution.

scope of the restrictive order, and its opinion reflects awareness of the tensions between the need to protect the accused as fully as possible and the need to restrict publication as little as possible. The dilemma posed underscores how difficult it is for trial judges to predict what information will in fact undermine the impartiality of jurors, and the difficulty of drafting an order that will effectively keep prejudicial information from prospective jurors. When a restrictive order is sought, a court can anticipate only part of what will develop that may injure the accused. But information not so obviously prejudicial may emerge, and what may properly be published in these "gray zone" circumstances may not violate the restrictive order and yet be prejudicial.

Finally, we note that the events disclosed by the record took place in a community of 850 people. It is reasonable to assume that, without any news accounts being printed or broadcast, rumors would travel swiftly by word of mouth. One can only speculate on the accuracy of such reports, given the generative propensities of rumors; they could well be more damaging than reasonably accurate news accounts. But plainly a whole community cannot be restrained from discussing a subject intimately affecting life within it.

Given these practical problems, it is far from clear that prior restraint on publication would have protected Simants' rights.

D

Finally, another feature of this case leads us to conclude that the restrictive order entered here is not supportable. At the outset the County Court entered a very broad restrictive order, the terms of which are not before us; it then held a preliminary hearing open to the public and the press. There was testimony concerning at least two incriminating statements made by Simants to private persons; the statement—evidently a confession—that he gave to law enforcement officials was also introduced. The State District Court's later order was entered after this public hearing and, as modified by the Nebraska Supreme Court, enjoined reporting of (1) "[c]onfessions or admissions against interests made by the accused to law enforcement officials"; (2) "[c]onfessions or admissions against interest, oral or written, if any, made by the accused to third parties, excepting any statements, if any, made by the accused to representatives of the news media"; and (3) all "[o]ther information strongly implicative of the accused as the perpetrator of the slayings."

To the extent that this order prohibited the reporting of evidence adduced at the open preliminary hearing, it plainly violated settled principles: "there is nothing that proscribes the press from reporting events that transpire in the courtroom." *Sheppard* v. *Maxwell, supra,* at 362–363. See also *Cox Broadcasting Corp.* v. *Cohn, supra; Craig* v. *Harney, supra.* The County Court could not know that closure of the preliminary hearing was an alternative open to it until the Nebraska Supreme Court so construed state law; but once a public hearing had been held, what transpired there could not be subject to prior restraint.

The third prohibition of the order was defective in another respect as well. As part of a final order, entered after plenary review, this prohibition regarding "implicative" information is too vague and too broad to survive the scrutiny we have given to restraints on First Amendment rights. See, *e.g., Hynes* v. *Oradell Mayor & Council,* 425 U.S. 610 (1976); *Buckley* v. *Valeo,* 424 U.S. 1, 76–82 (1976); *NAACP* v. *Button,* 371 U.S. 415 (1963). The third phase of the order entered falls outside permissible limits.

E

The record demonstrates, as the Nebraska courts held, that there was indeed a risk that pretrial news accounts, true or false, would have some adverse impact on the attitudes of those who might be called as jurors. But on the record now before us it is not clear that further

publicity, unchecked, would so distort the views of potential jurors that 12 could not be found who would, under proper instructions, fulfill their sworn duty to render a just verdict exclusively on the evidence presented in open court. We cannot say on this record that alternatives to a prior restraint on petitioners would not have sufficiently mitigated the adverse effects of pretrial publicity so as to make prior restraint unnecessary. Nor can we conclude that the restraining order actually entered would serve its intended purpose. Reasonable minds can have few doubts about the gravity of the evil pretrial publicity can work, but the probability that it would do so here was not demonstrated with the degree of certainty our cases on prior restraint require.

Of necessity our holding is confined to the record before us. But our conclusion is not simply a result of assessing the adequacy of the showing made in this case; it results in part from the problems inherent in meeting the heavy burden of demonstrating, in advance of trial, that without prior restraint a fair trial will be denied. The practical problems of managing and enforcing restrictive orders will always be present. In this sense, the record now before us is illustrative rather than exceptional. It is significant that when this Court has reversed a state conviction because of prejudicial publicity, it has carefully noted that some course of action short of prior restraint would have made a critical difference. See *Sheppard* v. *Maxwell, supra,* at 363; *Estes* v. *Texas, supra,* 550–551; *Rideau* v. *Louisiana, supra,* at 726; *Irvin* v. *Dowd, supra,* at 728. However difficult it may be, we need not rule out the possibility of showing the kind of threat to fair trial rights that would possess the requisite degree of certainty to justify restraint. This Court has frequently denied that First Amendment rights are absolute and has consistently rejected the proposition that a prior restraint can never be employed. See *New York Times* v. *United States, supra; Organization for a Better Austin* v. *Keefe, supra; Near* v. *Minnesota, supra.*

Our analysis ends as it began, with a confrontation between prior restraint imposed to protect one vital constitutional guarantee and the explicit comman of another that the freedom to speak and publish shall not be abridged. We reaffirm that the guarantees of freedom of expression are not an absolute prohibition under all circumstances, but the barriers to prior restrain remain high and the presumption against its use continues intact. We hold that, with respect to the order entered in this case prohibiting reporting or commentary on judicial proceedings held in public, the barriers have not been overcome; to the extent that this order restrained publication of such material, it is clearly invalid. To the extent that is prohibited publication based on information gained from other sources, we conclude that the heavy burden imposed as a condition to securing a prior restraint was not met and the judgment of the Nebraska Supreme Court is therefore reversed.

Mr. Justice Brennan, with whom Mr. Justice Stewart and Mr. Justice Marshall concur, concurring in the judgment.

The question presented in this case is whether, consistently with the First Amendment, a court may enjoin the press, in advance of publication, from reporting or commenting on information acquired from public court proceedings, public court records, or other sources about pending judicial proceedings. . . . The right to a fair trial by a jury of one's peers is unquestionably one of the most precious and sacred safeguards enshrined in the Bill of Rights. I would hold, however, that resort to prior restraints on the freedom of the press is a constitutionally impermissible method for enforcing that right; judges have at their disposal a broad spectrum of devices for ensuring that fundamental fairness is accorded the accused without necessitating so drastic an incursion on the equally fundamental and salutary constitutional mandate that discussion of public affairs in a free society cannot depend on the preliminary grace of judicial censors. . . .

. . . However, the press may be arrogant, tyrannical, abusive, and sensationalist, just as it may be incisive, probing, and informative. But at least in the context of prior restraints on publication, the decision of what, when, and how to publish is for editors, not judges. . . . Every restrictive order imposed on the press in this case was accordingly an unconstitutional prior restraint on the freedom of the press, and I would therefore reverse the judgment of the Nebraska Supreme Court and remand for further proceedings not inconsistent with this opinion.

Mr. Justice White, concurring.

Technically there is no need to go farther than the Court does to dispose of this case, and I join the Court's opinion. I should add, however, that for the reasons which the Court itself canvasses there is grave doubt in my mind whether orders with respect to the press such as were entered in this case would ever be justifiable. It may be the better part of discretion, however, not to announce such a rule in the first case in which the issue has been squarely presented here. Perhaps we should go no farther than absolutely necessary until the federal courts, and ourselves, have been exposed to a broader spectrum of cases presenting similar issues. If the recurring result, however, in case after case is to be similar to our judgment today, we should at some point announce a more general rule and avoid the interminable litigation that our failure to do so would necessarily entail.

Mr. Justice Powell, concurring.

Although I join the opinion of the Court, in view of the importance of the case I write to emphasize the unique burden that rests upon the party, whether it be the state or a defendant, who undertakes to show the necessity for prior restraint on pretrial publicity.

In my judgment a prior restraint properly may issue only when it is shown to be necessary to prevent the dissemination of prejudicial publicity that otherwise poses a high likelihood of preventing, directly and irreparably, the impaneling of a jury meeting the Sixth Amendment requirement of impartiality. This requires a showing that (i) there is a clear threat to the fairness of trial, (ii) such a threat is posed by the actual publicity to be restrained, and (iii) no less restrictive alternatives are available. Notwithstanding such a showing, a restraint may not issue unless it also is shown that previous publicity or publicity from unrestrained sources will not render the restraint inefficacious. The threat to the fairness of the trial is to be evaluated in the context of Sixth Amendment law on impartiality, and any restraint must comply with the standards of specificity always required in the First Amendment context.

I believe these factors are sufficiently addressed in the Court's opinion to demonstrate beyond question that the prior restraint here was impermissible.

Mr. Justice Stevens, concurring in the judgment.

For the reasons eloquently stated by Mr. Justice Brennan, I agree that the judiciary is capable of protecting the defendant's right to a fair trial without enjoining the press from publishing information in the public domain, and that it may not do so. Whether the same absolute protection would apply no matter how shabby or illegal the means by which the information is obtained, no matter how serious an intrusion on privacy might be involved, no matter how demonstrably false the information might be, no matter how prejudicial it might be to the interests of innocent persons, and no matter how perverse the motivation for publishing it, is a question I would not answer without further argument. See *Ashwander* v. *Valley Authority*, 297 U.S. 288, 346–347 Brandeis, J., concurring). I do, however, subscribe to most of what Mr. Justice Brennan says and, if ever required to face the issue squarely, may well accept his ultimate conclusion.

INCITEMENT OR DISCUSSION?

Masses Publishing Co. v. *Patten* (excerpt)
244 Fed. 535 (S.D.N.Y. 1917)

The court here enjoined the New York Postmaster from excluding an issue of a left-wing publication from the mails. (The decision was reversed on appeal—246 Fed. 24.) Holding that the Espionage Act could not be construed to outlaw the statements involved, Judge Learned Hand distinguished between protected and unprotected speech as follows:

One may not counsel or advise others to violate the law as it stands. Words are not only the keys of persuasion, but the triggers of action, and those which have no purport but to counsel the violation of law cannot by any latitude of interpretation be a part of that public opinion which is the final source of government in a democratic state. . . . Political agitation, by the passions it arouses or the convictions it engenders, may in fact stimulate men to the violation of law. Detestation of existing policies is easily transformed into forcible resistance of the authority which puts them in execution, and it would be folly to disregard the causal relation between the two. Yet to assimilate agitation, legitimate as such, with direct incitement to violent resistance, is to disregard the tolerance of all methods of political agitation which in normal times is a safeguard of free government. The distinction is not a scholastic subterfuge, but a hard-bought acquisition in the fight for freedom, and the purpose to disregard it must be evident when the power exists. If one stops short of urging upon others that it is their duty or their interest to resist the law, it seems to me one should not be held to have attempted to cause its violation. If that be not the test, I can see no escape from the conclusion that under this section every political agitation which can be shown to be apt to create a seditious temper is illegal. I am confident that by such language Congress had no such revolutionary purpose in view.

Schenck v. *United States*
249 U.W. 47 (1919)

Schenck and others were convicted under the Espionage Act of 1917 of conspiracy to obstruct the draft by sending to drafted (but not yet inducted) men circulars asserting that conscription violated the Thirteenth Amendment and served only Wall Street despotism. While the message "in form at least confined itself to peaceful measures," it did urge draftees not to "submit to intimidation."

Mr. Justice Holmes delivered the opinion of the Court. . . .

. . . Of course the document would not have been sent unless it had been intended to have some effect, and we do not see what effect it could be expected to have upon persons subject to the draft except to influence them to obstruct the carrying of it out. The defendants do not deny that the jury might find against them on this point.

But it is said, suppose that that was the tendency of this circular, it is protected by the First Amendment to the Constitution. Two of the strongest expressions are said to be quoted respectively from well-known public men. It well may be that the prohibition of laws abridging the freedom of speech is not confined to previous restraints, although to prevent them may have been the main purpose, as intimated in *Patterson* v. *Colorado*, 205 U.S. 454, 462. We admit that in many places and in ordinary times the defendants in saying all that was said in the circular would have been within their constitutional rights. But the character of every act depends upon the circumstances in which it is done. *Aikens* v. *Wisconsin*, 195 U.S. 194, 205, 206. The most stringent protection of free speech would not protect a man in falsely shouting fire in a theatre and causing a panic. It does not even protect a man from an injunction against uttering words that may have all the effect of force. *Gompers* v. *Buck's Stove & Range Co.*, 221 U.S. 418, 439. The question in every case is whether the words used are in such circumstances and are of such a nature as to create a clear and present danger that they will bring about the substantive evils that Congress has a right to prevent. It is a question of proximity and degree. When a nation is at war many things that might be said in time of peace are such a hindrance to its effort that their utterance will not be endured so long as men fight and that no Court could regard them as protected by any constitutional right. It seems to be admitted that if an actual obstruction of the recruiting service were proved, liability for words that produced that effect might be enforced. The statute of 1917 in section 4 (Comp. St. 1918, § 10212d) punishes conspiracies to obstruct as well as actual obstruction. If the act (speaking, or circulating a paper), its tendency and the intent with which it is ·done are the same, we perceive no ground for saying that success alone warrants making the act a crime. *Goldman* v. *United States*, 245 U.S. 474, 477. . . .

Abrams v. *United States* (excerpt)
250 U.S. 616 (1919)

Abrams and others were convicted under the Espionage Act of 1917, as amended in 1918, for publishing leaflets "intended to incite, provoke and encourage resistance to the United States" during World War I, and of conspiring "to urge, incite and advocate curtailment of production of . . . ammunition . . . ." The Court upheld the convictions.

[Mr. Justice Holmes, joined by Mr. Justice Brandeis, dissenting:]

. . . This indictment is founded wholly upon the publication of two leaflets. . . . The first . . . says that the President's cowardly silence about the intervention in Russia reveals the hypocrisy of the plutocratic gang in Washington. . . . It says that there is only one enemy of the workers of the world and that is capitalism; that it is a crime for workers of America, &c., to fight the workers' republic of Russia, and ends "Awake! Awake, you Workers of the World! Revolutionists." . . .

The other leaflet [is] headed "Workers—Wake Up," . . . . It tells the Russian emigrants that they now must spit in the face of the false military propaganda by which their sympathy and help to the prosecution of the war have been called forth and says that with the money they have lent or are going to lend "they will make bullets not only for the Germans but also for the Workers Soviets of Russia" . . . . The leaflet winds up by saying "Workers, our reply to this barbaric intervention has to be a general strike!," and after a few words on the spirit of revolution, exhortations not to be afraid, and some usual tall talk ends "Woe unto those who will be in the way of progress. Let solidarity live! The Rebels."

. . . [I]t seems too plain to be denied that the suggestion to workers in the ammunition factories that they are producing bullets to murder their dearest, and the further advocacy of a general strike, both in the second leaflet, do urge curtailment of production of things necessary to the prosecution of the war within the meaning of the Act . . . . But to make the conduct criminal that statute requires that it should be "with intent by such curtailment to cripple or hinder the United States in the prosecution of the war." It seems to me that no such intent is proved.

I am aware of course that the word intent as vaguely used in ordinary legal discussion means no more than knowledge at the time of the act that the consequences said to be intended will ensue. Even less than that will satisfy the general principle of civil and criminal liability. A man may have to pay damages, may be sent to prison, at common law might be hanged, if at the time of his act he knew facts from which common experience showed that the consequences would follow, whether he individually could foresee them or not. But, when words are used exactly, a deed is not done with intent to produce a consequence unless that consequence is the aim of the deed. It may be obvious, and obvious to the actor, that the consequence will follow, and he may be liable for it even if he regrets it, but he does not do the act with intent to produce it unless the aim to produce it is the proximate motive of the specific act, although there may be some deeper motive behind.

It seems to me that this statute must be taken to use its words in a strict and accurate sense. They would be absurd in any other. A patriot might think that we were wasting money on aeroplanes, or making more cannon of a certain kind than we needed, and might advocate curtailment with success, yet even if it turned out that the curtailment hindered and was thought by other minds to have been obviously likely to hinder the United States in the prosecution of the war, no one would hold such conduct a crime. I admit that my illustration does not answer all that might be said but it is enough to show what I think and to let me pass to a more important aspect of the case. I refer to the First Amendment to the Constitution that Congress shall make no law abridging the freedom of speech.

I never have seen any reason to doubt that the questions of law that alone were before this Court in the cases of *Schenck, Frohwerk* and *Debs,* 249 U.S. 47, 204, 211, were rightly decided. I do not doubt for a moment that by the same reasoning that would justify punishing persuasion to murder, the United States constitutionally may punish speech that produces or is intended to produce a clear and imminent danger that it will bring about forthwith certain substantive evils that the United States constitutionally may seek to prevent. The power undoubtedly is greater in time of war than in time of peace because war opens dangers that do not exist at other times.

But as against dangers peculiar to war, as against others, the principle of the right to free speech is always the same. It is only the present danger of immediate evil or an intent to bring it about that warrants Congress in setting a limit to the expression of opinion where private rights are not concerned. Congress certainly cannot forbid all effort to change the mind of the country. Now nobody can suppose that the surreptitious publishing of a silly leaflet by an unknown man, without more, would present any immediate danger that its opinions would hinder the success of the government arms or have

any appreciable tendency to do so. Publishing those opinions for the very purpose of obstructing however, might indicate a greater danger and at any rate would have the quality of an attempt. . . .

I do not see how anyone can find the intent required by the statute in any of the defendants' words. . . .

In this case sentences of twenty years imprisonment have been imposed for the publishing of two leaflets that I believe the defendants had as much right to publish as the Government has to publish the Constitution of the United States now vainly invoked by them. Even if I am technically wrong and enough can be squeezed from these poor and puny anonymities to turn the color of legal litmus paper; I will add, even if what I think the necessary intent were shown; the most nominal punishment seems to me all that possibly could be inflicted, unless the defendants are to be made to suffer not for what the indictment alleges but for the creed that they avow—a creed that I believe to be the creed of ignorance and immaturity when honestly held, as I see no reason to doubt that it was held here, but which, although made the subject of examination at the trial, no one has a right even to consider in dealing with the charges before the Court.

Persecution for the expression of opinions seems to me perfectly logical. If you have no doubt of your premises or your power and want a certain result with all your heart you naturally express your wishes in law and sweep away all opposition. To allow opposition by speech seems to indicate that you think the speech impotent, as when a man says that he has squared the circle, or that you do not care wholeheartedly for the result, or that you doubt either your power or your premises. But when men have realized that time has upset many fighting faiths, they may come to believe even more than they believe the very foundations of their own conduct that the ultimate good desired is better reached by free trade in ideas—that the best test of truth is the power of the thought to get itself accepted in the competition of the market, and that truth is the only ground upon which their wishes safely can be carried out. That at any rate is the theory of our Constitution. It is an experiment, as all life is an experiment. Every year if not every day we have to wager our salvation upon some prophecy based upon imperfect knowledge. While that experiment is part of our system I think that we should be eternally vigilant against attempts to check the expression of opinions that we loathe and believe to be fraught with death, unless they so imminently threaten immediate interference with the lawful and pressing purposes of the law that an immediate check is required to save the country. I wholly disagree with the argument of the Government that the First Amendment left the common law as to seditious libel in force. History seems to me against the notion. I had conceived that the United States through many years had shown its repentance for the Sedition Act of 1798, by repaying fines that it imposed. Only the emergency that makes it immediately dangerous to leave the correction of evil counsels to time warrants making any exception to the sweeping command, "Congress shall make no law . . . abridging the freedom of speech." Of course I am speaking only of expressions of opinion and exhortations, which were all that were uttered here, but I regret that I cannot put into more impressive words my belief that in their conviction upon this indictment the defendants were deprived of their rights under the Constitution of the United States.

Gitlow v. *New York*
268 U.S. 652 (1925)

Gitlow was found guilty of "criminal anarchy" in that he had "advocated, advised and taught the duty, necessity, and propriety of overthrowing . . . government by force [in] certain writings" [namely, "The Left Wing Manifesto" and "The Revolutionary Age"]. His defense was that there was no evidence of any concrete result flowing from such publications, or of the likelihood of such result, and that therefore the statute under which he was charged was unconstitutional as applied to mere utterance of doctrine in such circumstances.

Mr. Justice Sanford delivered the opinion of the Court: . . .

The statute does not penalize the utterance or publication of abstract "doctrine" or academic discussion having no quality of incitement to any concrete action. It is not aimed against mere historical or philosophical essays. It does not restrain the advocacy of changes in the form of government by constitutional and lawful means. What it prohibits is language advocating, advising, or teaching the overthrow of organized government by unlawful means. These words imply urging to action. . . .

The Manifesto, plainly, is neither the statement of abstract doctrine nor, as suggested by counsel, mere prediction that industrial disturbances and revolutionary mass strikes will result spontaneously in an inevitable process of evolution in the economic system. It advocates and urges in fervent language mass action which shall progressively foment industrial disturbances and through political mass strikes and revolutionary mass action overthrow and destroy organized parliamentary government. It concludes with a call to action in these words: "The proletariat revolution and the Communist reconstruction of society—*the struggle for these*—is now indispensable. . . . The Communist International calls the proletariat of the world to the final struggle!" This is not the expression of philosophical abstractions, the mere prediction of future events; it is the language of direct incitement. . . .

. . . That the jury were warranted in finding that the Manifesto advocated not merely the abstract doctrine of overthrowing organized government by force, violence and unlawful means, but action to that end is clear.

For present purposes we may and do assume that freedom of speech and of the press—which are protected by the First Amendment from abridgment by Congress—are among the fundamental personal rights and "liberties" protected by the due process clause of the Fourteenth Amendment from impairment by the states. . . .

It is a fundamental principle, long established, that the freedom of speech and of the press which is secured by the Constitution, does not confer an absolute right to speak or publish, without responsibility, whatever one may choose, or an unrestricted and unbridled license that gives immunity for every possible use of language and prevents the punishment of those who abuse this freedom. . . .

That a State in the exercise of its police power may punish those who abuse this freedom by utterances inimical to the public welfare, tending to corrupt public morals, incite to crime, or disturb the public peace, is not open to question. . . .

And, for yet more imperative reasons, a State may punish utterances endangering the foundations of organized government and threatening its overthrow by unlawful means. These imperil its own existence as a constitutional State. Freedom of speech and press, said Story, does not protect disturbances to the public peace or attempts to subvert the government. . . .

By enacting the present statute the State has determined, through its legislative body, that utterances advocating the overthrow of organized government by force, violence and unlawful means, are so inimical to the general welfare and involve such danger of substantive evil that they may be penalized in the exercise of its police power. That determination must be

given great weight. Every presumption is to be indulged in favor of the validity of the statute. . . . That utterances inciting to the overthrow of organized government by unlawful means, present a sufficient danger of substantive evil to bring their punishment within the range of legislative discretion, is clear. Such utterances, by their very nature, involve danger to the public peace and to the security of the State. They threaten breaches of the peace and ultimate revolution. And the immediate danger is none the less real and substantial, because the effect of a given utterance cannot be accurately foreseen. The State cannot reasonably be required to measure the danger from every such utterance in the nice balance of a jeweler's scale. A single revolutionary spark may kindle a fire that, smouldering for a time, may burst into a sweeping and destructive conflagration. It cannot be said that the State is acting arbitrarily or unreasonably when in the exercise of its judgment as to the measures necessary to protect the public peace and safety, it seeks to extinguish the spark without waiting until it has enkindled the flame or blazed into the conflagration. It cannot reasonably be required to defer the adoption of measures for its own peace and safety until the revolutionary utterances lead to actual disturbances of the public peace or imminent and immediate danger of its own destruction; but it may, in the exercise of its judgment, suppress the threatened danger in its incipiency. . . .

We cannot hold that the present statute is an arbitrary or unreasonable exercise of the police power of the State unwarrantably infringing the freedom of speech or press; and we must and do sustain its constitutionality.

This being so it may be applied to every utterance—not too trivial to be beneath the notice of the law—which is of such a character and used with such intent and purpose as to bring it within the prohibition of the statute. . . .

It is clear that the question in such cases is entirely different from that involved in those cases where the statute merely prohibits certain acts involving the danger of substantive evil, without any reference to language itself, and it is sought to apply its provisions to language used by the defendant for the purpose of bringing about the prohibited results. There, if it be contended that the statute cannot be applied to the language used by the defendant because of its protection by the freedom of speech or press, it must necessarily be found, as an original question, without any previous determination by the legislative body, whether the specific language used involved such likelihood of bringing about the substantive evil as to deprive it of the constitutional protection. In such cases it has been held that the general provisions of the statute may be constitutionally applied to the specific utterance of the defendant if its natural tendency and probable effect was to bring about the substantive evil which the legislative body might prevent. *Schenck* v. *United States,* 249 U.S. 47; *Debs* v. *United States,* 249 U.S. 211. And the general statement in the *Schenck* case that the "question in every case is whether the words used are used in such circumstances and are of such a nature as to create a clear and present danger that they will bring about the substantive evils,"—upon which great reliance is placed in the defendant's argument—was manifestly intended, as shown by the context, to apply only in cases of this class, and has no application to those like the present, where the legislative body itself has previously determined the danger of substantive evil arising from utterances of a specified character. . . .

Affirmed.

Mr. Justice Holmes, dissenting.

Mr. Justice Brandeis and I are of opinion that this judgment should be reversed. The general principle of free speech, it seems to me, must be taken to be included in the Fourteenth Amendment, in view of the scope that has been given to the word "liberty" as there used, although perhaps it may be accepted with a somewhat larger latitude of interpretation than is allowed to Congress by the sweeping language that governs or ought to govern the laws of the United States. If I am right, then I think that the criterion sanctioned by the full court in *Schenck* v. *United States, supra,* applies. "The question in every case is whether the words used are used in such circumstances and are of such a nature as to create a clear and present danger that they will bring about the substantive evils that [the state] has a right to prevent." It is true that in my opinion this criterion was departed from in *Abrams* v. *United States,* 250 U.S. 616, but the convictions that I expressed in that case are too deep for it to be possible for me as yet to believe that it and *Schaefer* v. *United States,* 251 U.S. 466, have settled the law. If what I think the correct test is applied, it is manifest that there was no present danger of an attempt to overthrow the government by force on the part of the admittedly small minority who shared the defendant's views. It is said that this manifesto was more than a theory, that it was an incitement. Every idea is an incitement. It offers itself for belief and if believed it is acted on unless some other belief outweighs it or some failure of energy stifles the movement at its birth. The only difference between the expression of an opinion and an incitement in the narrower sense is the speaker's enthusiasm for the result. Eloquence may set fire to reason. But whatever may be thought of the redundant discourse before us it had no chance of starting a present conflagration. If in the long run the beliefs expressed in proletarian dictatorship are destined to be accepted by the dominant forces of the community, the only meaning of free speech is that they should be given their chance and have their way. . . .

Whitney v. *California* (excerpt)
274 U.S. 357 (1927)

Miss Whitney, heiress of a famous fortune, was convicted of violating a state criminal syndicalism law by organizing, and being a member of, a group advocating unlawful force as a political weapon. The conviction was sustained on appeal on grounds similar to those laid out in *Gitlow*.

Following is the concurring opinion of Mr. Justice Brandeis in which Mr. Justice Holmes joined: . . .

The felony which the statute created is a crime very unlike the old felony of conspiracy or the old misdemeanor of unlawful assembly. The mere act of assisting in forming a society for teaching syndicalism, of becoming a member of it, or assembling with others for that purpose is given the dynamic quality of crime. There is guilt although the society may not contemplate immediate promulgation of the doctrine. Thus the accused is to be punished, not for attempt, incitement, or conspiracy, but for a step in preparation, which, if it threatens the public order at all, does so only remotely. The novelty in the prohibition introduced is that the statute aims, not at the practice of criminal syndicalism, nor even directly at the preaching of it, but at association with those who propose to preach it.

Despite arguments to the contrary which had seemed to me persuasive, it is settled that the due process clause of the Fourteenth Amendment applies to matters of substantive law as well as to matters of procedure. Thus all fundamental rights comprised within the term liberty are protected by the federal Constitution from invasion by the states. The right of free speech, the right to teach and the right of assembly are, of course, fundamental rights. . . . These may not be denied or abridged. But, although the rights of free speech and assembly are fundamental, they are not in their nature absolute. Their exercise is subject to restriction, if the particular restriction proposed is required in order to protect the state from destruction or from serious injury, political, economic or moral. That the necessity which is essential to a valid restriction does not exist unless speech would produce, or is intended to produce, a clear and imminent danger of some substantive evil which the state constitutionally may seek to prevent has been settled. See *Schenck* v. *United States*, 249 U.S. 47, 52.

It is said to be the function of the Legislature to determine whether at a particular time and under the particular circumstances the formation of, or assembly with, a society organized to advocate criminal syndicalism constitutes a clear and present danger of substantive evil; and that by enacting the law here in question the Legislature of California determined that question in the affirmative. Compare *Gitlow* v. *New York*. . . . The Legislature must obviously decide, in the first instance, whether a danger exists which calls for a particular protective measure. But where a statute is valid only in case certain conditions exist, the enactment of the statute cannot alone establish the facts which are essential to its validity. Prohibitory legislation has repeatedly been held invalid, because unnecessary, where the denial of liberty involved was that of engaging in a particular business. The powers of the courts to strike down an offending law are no less when the interests involved are not property rights, but the fundamental personal rights of free speech and assembly.

This court has not yet fixed the standard by which to determine when a danger shall be deemed clear; how remote the danger may be and yet be deemed present; and what degree of evil shall be deemed sufficiently substantial to justify resort to abridgment of free speech and assembly as the means of protection. To reach sound conclusions on these matters, we must bear in mind why a state is, ordinarily, denied the power to prohibit dissemination of social, economic and political doctrine which a vast majority of its citizens believes to be false and fraught with evil consequence.

Those who won our independence believed that the final end of the state was to make men free to develop their faculties, and that in its government the deliberative forces should prevail over the arbitrary. They valued liberty both as an end and as a means. They believed liberty to be the secret of happiness and courage to be the secret of liberty. They believed that freedom to think as you will and to speak as you think are means indispensable to the discovery and spread of political truth; that without free speech and assembly discussion would be futile; that with them, discussion affords ordinarily adequate protection against the dissemination of noxious doctrine; that the greatest menace to freedom is an inert people; that public discussion is a political duty; and that this should be a fundamental principle of the American government. They recognized the risks to which all human institutions are subject. But they knew that order cannot be secured merely through fear of punishment for its infraction; that it is hazardous to discourage thought, hope and imagination; that fear breeds repression; that repression breeds hate; that hate menaces stable government; that the path of safety lies in the opportunity to discuss freely supposed grievances and proposed remedies; and that the fitting remedy for evil counsels is good ones. Believing in the power of reason as applied through public discussion, they eschewed silence coerced by law—the argument of force in its worst form. Recognizing the occasional tyrannies of governing majorities, they amended the Constitution so that free speech and assembly should be guaranteed.

Fear of serious injury cannot alone justify

suppression of free speech and assembly. Men feared witches and burnt women. It is the function of speech to free men from the bondage of irrational fears. To justify suppression of free speech there must be reasonable ground to fear that serious evil will result if free speech is practiced. There must be reasonable ground to believe that the danger apprehended is imminent. There must be reasonable ground to believe that the evil to be prevented is a serious one. . . . The wide difference between advocacy and incitement, between preparation and attempt, between assembling and conspiracy, must be borne in mind. In order to support a finding of clear and present danger it must be shown either that immediate serious violence was to be expected or was advocated, or that the past conduct furnished reason to believe that such advocacy was then contemplated.

Those who won our independence by revolution were not cowards. They did not fear political change. They did not exalt order at the cost of liberty. To courageous, self-reliant men, with confidence in the power of free and fearless reasoning applied through the processes of popular government, no danger flowing from speech can be deemed clear and present, unless the incidence of the evil apprehended is so imminent that it may befall before there is opportunity for full discussion. If there be time to expose through discussion the falsehood and fallacies, to avert the evil by the process of education, the remedy to be applied is more speech, not enforced silence. Only an emergency can justify repression. Such must be the rule if authority is to be reconciled with freedom. Such, in my opinion, is the command of the Constitution. It is therefore always open to Americans to challenge a law abridging free speech and assembly by showing that there was no emergency justifying it.

Moreover, even imminent danger cannot justify resort to prohibition of these functions essential to effective democracy, unless the evil apprehended is relatively serious. Prohibition of free speech and assembly is a measure so stringent that it would be inappropriate as the means for averting a relatively trivial harm to society. A police measure may be unconstitutional merely because the remedy, although effective as means of protection, is unduly harsh or oppressive. . . . The fact that speech is likely to result in some violence or in destruction of property is not enough to justify its suppression. There must be the probability of serious injury to the State. Among free men, the deterrents ordinarily to be applied to prevent crime are education and punishment for violations of the law, not abridgment of the rights of free speech and assembly. . . .

Whether in 1919, when Miss Whitney did the things complained of, there was in California such clear and present danger of serious evil, might have been made the important issue in this case. She might have required that the issue be determined either by the court or by the jury. She claimed below that the statute as applied to her violated the federal Constitution; but she did not claim that it was void because there was no clear and present danger of serious evil, nor did she request that the existence of these conditions of a valid measure thus restricting the rights of free speech and assembly be passed upon by the court of a jury. On the other hand, there was evidence on which the court or jury might have found that such danger existed. [We are] unable to assent to the suggestion in the opinion of the court that assembling with a political party, formed to advocate the desirability of a proletarian revolution by mass action at some date necessarily far in the future, is not a right within the protection of the Fourteenth Amendment. In the present case, however, there was other testimony which tended to establish the existence of a conspiracy, on the part of members of the International Workers of the World, to commit present serious crimes, and likewise to show that such a conspiracy would be furthered by the activity of the society of which Miss Whitney was a member. Under these circumstances the judgment of the State court cannot be disturbed. . . .

Dennis v. *United States*
341 U.S. 494 (1951)

Mr. Chief Justice Vinson announced the judgment of the Court and an opinion in which Mr. Justice Reed, Mr. Justice Burton and Mr. Justice Minton join.

Petitioners were indicted in July, 1948, for violation of the conspiracy provisions of the Smith Act during the period of April, 1945, to July, 1948. . . . A verdict of guilty as to all the petitioners was returned by the jury on October 14, 1949. The Court of Appeals affirmed the convictions. 183 F.2d 201. We granted certiorari, limited to the following two questions: (1) Whether either § 2 or § 3 of the Smith Act, inherently or as construed and applied in the instant case, violates the First Amendment and other provisions of the Bill of Rights; (2) whether either § 2 or § 3 of the Act, inherently or as construed and applied in the instant case, violates the First and Fifth Amendments because of indefiniteness.

Sections 2 and 3 of the Smith Act provide as follows:

"Sec. 2.
"(a) It shall be unlawful for any person—
"(1) to knowingly or willfully advocate, abet, advise, or teach the duty, necessity, desirability, or propriety of overthrowing or destroying any government in the United States by force or violence, or by the assassination of any officer of any such government; . . .
"(3) to organize or help to organize any society, group, or assembly of persons who teach, advocate, or encourage the overthrow or destruction of any government in the United States by force or violence; or to be or become a member of, or affiliate with, any such society, group, or assembly of persons, knowing the purposes thereof. . . .
"Sec. 3. It shall be unlawful for any person to attempt to commit, or to con-

spire to commit, any of the acts prohibited by the provisions of this title."

The indictment charged the petitioners with wilfully and knowingly conspiring (1) to organize as the Communist Party of the United States of America a society, group and assembly of persons who teach and advocate the overthrow and destruction of the Government of the United States by force and violence, and (2) knowingly and wilfully to advocate and teach the duty and necessity of overthrowing and destroying the Government of the United States by force and violence. The indictment further alleged that § 2 of the Smith Act proscribes these acts and that any conspiracy to take such action is a violation of § 3 of the Act.

. . . Our limited grant of the writ of certiorari has removed from our consideration any question as to the sufficiency of the evidence to support the jury's determination that petitioners are guilty of the offense charged. Whether on this record petitioners did in fact advocate the overthrow of the Government by force and violence is not before us, and we must base any discussion of this point upon the conclusions state in the opinion of the Court of Appeals, which treated the issue in great detail. That court held that the record amply supports the necessary finding of the jury that petitioners, the leaders of the Communist Party in this country, . . . intended to initiate a violent revolution whenever the propitious occasion appeared. . . .

The obvious purpose of the statute is to protect existing Government, not from change by peaceable, lawful and constitutional means, but from change by violence, revolution and terrorism. That it is within the *power* of the Congress to protect the Government of the United States from armed rebellion is a proposition which requires little discussion. Whatever theoretical merit there may be to the argument that there is a "right" to rebellion against dictatorial governments is without force where the existing structure of the government provides for peaceful and orderly change. We reject any principle of governmental helplessness in the face of preparation for revolution, which principle, carried to its logical conclusion, must lead to anarchy. No one could conceive that it is not within the power of Congress to prohibit acts intended to overthrow the Government by force and violence. The question with which we are concerned here is not whether Congress has such *power*, but whether the *means* which it has employed conflict with the First and Fifth Amendments to the Constitution.

One of the bases for the contention that the means which Congress has employed are invalid takes the form of an attack on the face of the statute on the grounds that by its terms it prohibits academic discussion of the merits of Marxism-Leninism, that it stifles ideas and is contrary to all concepts of a free speech and a free press. . . .

The very language of the Smith Act negates the interpretation which petitioners would have us impose on that Act. It is directed at advocacy, not discussion. Thus, the trial judge properly charged the jury that they could not convict if they found that petitioners did "no more than pursue peaceful studies and discussions or teaching and advocacy in the realm of ideas." He further charged that it was not unlawful "to conduct in an American college and university a course explaining the philosophical theories set forth in the books which have been placed in evidence." Such a charge is in strict accord with the statutory language, and illustrates the meaning to be placed on those words. Congress did not intend to eradicate the free discussion of political theories, to destroy the traditional rights of Americans to discuss and evaluate ideas without fear of governmental sanction. Rather Congress was concerned with the very kind of activity in which the evidence showed these petitioners engaged.

But although the statute is not directed at the hypothetical cases which petitioners have conjured, its application in this case has resulted in convictions for the teaching and advocacy of the overthrow of the Government by force and violence, which, even though coupled with the intent to accomplish that overthrow, contains an element of speech. For this reason, we must pay special heed to the demands of the First Amendment marking out the boundaries of speech. . . .

The rule we deduce from [prior] cases is that where an offense is specified by a statute in nonspeech or nonpress terms, a conviction relying upon speech or press as evidence of violation may be sustained only when the speech or publication created a "clear and present danger" of attempting or accomplishing the prohibited crime, *e.g.*, interference with enlistment. The dissents, we repeat, in emphasizing the value of speech, were addressed to the argument of the sufficiency of the evidence. . . .

Although no case subsequent to *Whitney* and *Gitlow* has expressly overruled the majority opinions in those cases, there is little doubt that subsequent opinions have inclined toward the Holmes-Brandeis rationale. . . .

[N]either Justice Holmes nor Justice Brandeis ever envisioned that a shorthand phrase should be crystallized into a rigid rule to be applied inflexibly without regard to the circumstances of each case. Speech is not an absolute, above and beyond control by the legislature when its judgment, above and beyond control by the legislature when its judgment, subject to review here, is that certain kinds of speech are so undesirable as to warrant criminal sanction. Nothing is more certain in modern society than the principle that there are no absolutes, that a name, a phrase, a standard has meaning only when associated with the considerations which gave birth to the nomenclature. To those who would paralyze our Government in the face of impending threat by encasing it in a semantic straitjacket we must reply that all concepts are relative.

In this case we are squarely presented with the application of the "clear and present danger" test, and must decide what that phrase imports. . . . Overthrow of the Government by

force and violence is certainly a substantial enough interest for the Government to limit speech. Indeed, this is the ultimate value of any society, for if a society cannot protect its very structure from armed internal attack, it must follow that no subordinate value can be protected. If, then, this interest may be protected, the literal problem which is presented is what has been meant by the use of the phrase "clear and present danger" of the utterances bringing about the evil within the power of Congress to punish.

Obviously, the words cannot mean that before the Government may act, it must wait until the *putsch* is about to be executed, the plans have been laid and the signal awaited. If Government is aware that a group aiming at its overthrow is attempting to indoctrinate its members and to commit them to a course whereby they will strike when the leaders feel the circumstances permit, action by the Government is required. . . . a sufficient evil for Congress to prevent. The damage which such attempts create both physically and politically to a nation makes it impossible to measure the validity in terms of the probability of success, or the immediacy of a successful attempt. In the instant case the trial judge charged the jury that they could not convict unless they found that petitioners intended to overthrow the Government "as speedily as circumstances would permit." This does not mean, and could not properly mean, that they would not strike until there was certainty of success. What was meant was that the revolutionists would strike when they thought the time was ripe. We must therefore reject the contention that success or probability of success is the criterion.

The situation with which Justices Holmes and Brandeis were concerned in *Gitlow* was a comparatively isolated event, bearing little relation in their minds to any substantial threat to the safety of the community. . . . They were not confronted with any situation comparable to the instant one—the development of an apparatus designed and dedicated to the overthrow of the Government, in the context of world crisis after crisis.

Chief Judge Learned Hand, writing for the majority below, interpreted the phrase as follows: "In each case [courts] must ask whether the gravity of the 'evil,' discounted by its improbability, justifies such invasion of free speech as is necessary to avoid the danger." 183 F.2d at 212. We adopt this statement of the rule. As articulated by Chief Judge Hand, it is as succinct and inclusive as any other we might devise at this time. It takes into consideration those factors which we deem relevant, and relates their significances. More we cannot expect from words.

Likewise, we are in accord with the court below, which affirmed the trial court's finding that the requisite danger existed. The mere fact that from the period 1945 to 1948 petitioners' activities did not result in an attempt to overthrow the Government by force and violence is of course no answer to the fact that there was a group that was ready to make the attempt. The formation by petitioners of such a highly organized conspiracy, with rigidly disciplined members subject to call when the leaders, these petitioners, felt that the time had come for action, coupled with the inflammable nature of world conditions, similar uprisings in other countries, and the touch-and-go nature of our relations with countries with whom petitioners were in the very least ideologically attuned, convince us that their convictions were justified on this score. And this analysis disposes of the contention that a conspiracy to advocate, as distinguished from the advocacy itself, cannot be constitutionally restrained, because it comprises only the preparation. It is the existence of the conspiracy which creates the danger. If the ingredients of the reaction are present, we cannot bind the Government to wait until the catalyst is added. . . .

We hold that §§ 2(a) (1), 2(a) (3) and 3 of the Smith Act, do not inherently, or as construed or applied in the instant case, violate the First Amendment and other provisions of the Bill of Rights, or the First and Fifth Amendments because of indefiniteness. Petitioners intended to overthrow the Government of the United States as speedily as the circumstances would permit. Their conspiracy to organize the Communist Party and to teach and advocate the overthrow of the Government of the United States by force and violence created a "clear and present danger" of an attempt to overthrow the Government by force and violence. They were properly and constitutionally convicted for violation of the Smith Act. The judgments of conviction are affirmed.

Mr. Justice Clark took no part in the consideration or decision of this case.

Mr. Justice Frankfurter, concurring in affirmance of the judgment. . . .

. . . Absolute rules would inevitably lead to absolute exceptions, and such exceptions would eventually corrode the rules. The demands of free speech in a democratic society as well as the interest in national security are better served by candid and informed weighing of the competing interests, within the confines of the judicial process, than by announcing dogmas too inflexible for the non-Euclidian problems to be solved.

But how are competing interests to be assessed? Since they are not subject to quantitative ascertainment, the issue necessarily resolves itself into asking, who is to make the adjustment?—who is to balance the relevant factors and ascertain which interest is in the circumstances to prevail? Full responsibility for the choice cannot be given to the courts. Courts are not representative bodies. They are not designed to be a good reflex of a democratic society. Their judgment is best informed, and therefore most dependable, within narrow limits. Their essential quality is detachment, founded on independence. History teaches that the independence of the judiciary is jeopardized when courts become embroiled in the passions of the day and assume primary responsibility in choosing between competing political, economic and social pressures.

Primary responsibility for adjusting the interests which compete in the situation before us of necessity belongs to the Congress. The nature of the power to be exercised by this Court has been delineated in decisions not charged with the emotional appeal of situations such as that now before us. We are to set aside the judgment of those whose duty it is to legislate only if there is no reasonable basis for it. We are to determine whether a statute is sufficiently definite to meet the constitutional requirements of due process, and whether it respects the safeguards against undue concentration of authority secured by separation of power. . . .

Mr. Justice Jackson, concurring.

This prosecution is the latest of never-ending, because never successful, quests for some legal formula that will secure an existing order against revolutionary radicalism. It requires us to reappraise, in the light of our own times and conditions, constitutional doctrines devised under other circumstances to strike a balance between authority and liberty. . . .

The Communist Party . . . does not seek its strength primarily in numbers. Its aim is a relatively small party whose strength is in selected, dedicated, indoctrinated, and rigidly disciplined members. From established policy it tolerates no deviation and no debate. It seeks members that are, or may be, secreted in strategic posts in transportation, communications, industry, government, and especially in labor unions where it can compel employers to accept and retain its members. It also seeks to infiltrate and control organizations of professional and other groups. Through these placements in positions of power it seeks a leverage over society that will make up in power of coercion what it lacks in power of persuasion.

. . . [V]iolence is not with them, as with the anarchists, an end in itself. The Communist Party advocates force only when prudent and profitable. . . . They resort to violence as to truth, not as a principle but as an expedient. Force or violence, as they would resort to it, may never be necessary, because infiltration and deception may be enough. . . .

The United States, fortunately, has experienced Communism only in its preparatory stages and for its pattern of final action must look abroad. . . . But Communist technique in the overturn of a free government was disclosed by the *coup d'etat* in which they seized power in Czechoslovakia. . . .

The foregoing is enough to indicate that, either by accident or design, the Communist stratagem outwits the anti-anarchist pattern of a statute aimed against "overthrow by force and violence" if qualified by the doctrine that only "clear and present danger" of accomplishing that result will sustain the prosecution. . . .

If we must decide that this Act and its application are constitutional only if we are convinced that petitioner's conduct creates a "clear and present danger" of violent overthrow, we must appraise imponderables, including international and national phenomena which baffle the best informed foreign offices and our most experienced politicians. . . . No doctrine can be sound whose application requires us to make a prophecy of that sort in the guise of a legal decision. The judicial process simply is not adequate to a trial of such far-flung issues. The answers given would reflect our own political predilections and nothing more.

The authors of the clear and present danger test never applied it to a case like this, nor would I. If applied as it is proposed here, it means that the Communist plotting is protected during its period of incubation; its preliminary stages of organization and preparation are immune from the law; the Government can move only after imminent action is manifest, when it would, of course, be too late. . . .

What really is under review here is a conviction of conspiracy, after a trial for conspiracy, on an indictment charging conspiracy, brought under a statute outlawing conspiracy. With due respect to my colleagues, they seem to me to discuss anything under the sun except the law of conspiracy. . . .

The Constitution does not make conspiracy a civil right. . . . While I consider criminal conspiracy a dragnet device capable of perversion into an instrument of injustice in the hands of a partisan or complacent judiciary, it has an established place in our system of law, and no reason appears for applying it only to concerted action claimed to disturb interstate commerce and withholding it from those claimed to undermine our whole Government. . . .

. . . The Communist Party realistically is a state within a state, an authoritarian dictatorship within a republic. . . . The law of conspiracy has been the chief means at the Government's disposal to deal with the growing problems created by such organizations. I happen to think it is an awkward and inept remedy, but I find no constitutional authority for taking this weapon from the Government. There is no constitutional right to "gang up" on the Government.

While I think there was power in Congress to enact this statute and that as applied in this case, it cannot be held unconstitutional, I add that I have little faith in the long-range effectiveness of this conviction to stop the rise of the Communist movement. . . . No decision by this Court can forestall revolution whenever the existing government fails to command the respect and loyalty of the people and sufficient distress and discontent is allowed to grow up among the masses. . . . Corruption, ineptitude, inflation, oppressive taxation, militarization, injustice, and loss of leadership capable of intellectual initiative in domestic or foreign affairs are allies on which the Communists count to bring opportunity knocking to their

door. Sometimes I think they may be mistaken. But the Communists are not building just for today—the rest of us might profit by their example.

Mr. Justice Black, dissenting. . . .

Mr. Justice Douglas, dissenting. . . .

The vice of treating speech as the equivalent of overt acts of a treasonable or seditious character is emphasized by a concurring opinion, which by invoking the law of conspiracy makes speech do service for deeds which are dangerous to society. The doctrine of conspiracy has served divers and oppressive purposes and in its broad reach can be made to do great evil. But never until today has anyone seriously thought that the ancient law of conspiracy could constitutionally be used to turn speech into seditious conduct. Yet that is precisely what is suggested. I repeat that we deal here with speech alone, not with speech *plus* acts of sabotage or unlawful conduct. Not a single seditious act is charged in the indictment. To make a lawful speech unlawful because two men conceive it is to raise the law of conspiracy to appalling proportions. That course is to make a radical break with the past and to violate one of the cardinal principles of our constitutional scheme. . . .

There comes a time when even speech loses its constitutional immunity. Speech innocuous one year may at another time fan such destructive flames that it must be halted in the interests of the safety of the Republic. That is the meaning of the clear and present danger test. When conditions are so critical that there will be no time to avoid the evil that the speech threatens, it is time to call a halt. Otherwise, free speech which is the strength of the Nation will be the cause of its destruction.

Note and Quaere: If in *Dennis* the Court was not very respectful of the discourse there at issue, was that because the defendants had spoken in secret and underground, that is, conspiratorially? Their views had not been offered for what Holmes and Brandeis called "public discussion" as part of the "free trade in ideas" in the "competition of the market," where the public is offered exposure to conflicting views so that it can choose intelligently among them: *Abrams* v. *United States,* 250 U.S. 616, 630 (1919), Justice Holmes, dissenting. Recall John Milton's famous line in *Areopagitica:* "[W]ho ever knew truth put to the worse, in a *free and open encounter?*" (J. Milton, *Areopagitica,* in 2 *The Prose Works of John Milton* 96 [J. St. John ed., 1900; emphasis supplied]) John Stuart Mill's *On Liberty* rests on what he called "the morality of public discussion" (J. Mill, *On Liberty* 99 [1887]). Thomas Jefferson put it briefly: truth is "the proper and sufficient antagonist to error, and has nothing to fear from the conflict unless by human interposition [*e.g.,* secrecy] disarmed of her natural weapons, *free argument and debate . . . .*" (2 The *Papers of Thomas Jefferson* 546 [J. Boyd ed., 1950; emphasis supplied]). Benjamin Franklin has it thus: "[W]hen Men differ in Opinion, both Sides ought equally to have the Advantage of being heard by the Publick . . . ." (B. Franklin, "An Apology for Printers" [1731], in 1 *The Papers of Benjamin Franklin* 194–95 [L. Labaree ed., 1959]). In Z. Chafee's view, "the fundamental pol-icy of the First Amendment [is] the *open discussion* of public affairs." Z. Chafee, *Freedom of Speech* 30 [1920; emphasis supplied]). As Alexander Meiklejohn put it:

What, then, does the First Amendment forbid? Here again the town meeting suggests an answer. That meeting is called to discuss and, on the basis of such discussion, to decide matters of public policy. . . . *The voters, therefore, must be made as wise as possible.* . . . And this, in turn, requires that . . . all facts and interests relevant to the problem shall be fully and fairly presented to the meeting. . . .

. . . [The fifth amendment's] limited guarantee of the freedom . . . to speak is radically different in intent from the unlimited guarantee of the freedom of *public discussion,* which is given by the First Amendment. A. Meiklejohn, *Free Speech and Its Relation to Self-Government* 24-25, 39 [1948; emphasis supplied]).

Thus all of these great founts of our free-speech ideal seem to have anticipated the Court's apparent stand in *Dennis;* namely, that freedom of speech means open, public discussion, not underground activity designed to achieve its goals by circumventing, rather than winning, community consent.

Yates v. *United States* (summary)
354 U.S. 298 (1957)

Yates and 13 other secondary leaders of the Communist Party of the United States were convicted on charges essentially identical to those in *Dennis* (above). Their convictions were reversed on the ground that the trial judge—unlike the trial judge in *Dennis*—had failed in his charge to the jury to distinguish between "advocacy of abstract doctrine [which the Constitution protects] and advocacy directed at promoting unlawful action [a distinction] that has been consistently recognized in the decisions of this Court. . . ." In the course of its opinion the Court restated its understanding of the earlier decision:

The essence of the *Dennis* holding was that indoctrination of a group in preparation for future violent action, as well as exhortation to immediate action, by advocacy found to be directed to "action for the accomplishment" of forcible overthrow, to violence "as a rule or principle of action," and employing "language of incitement," . . . is not constitutionally protected when the group is of sufficient size and cohesiveness, is sufficiently oriented towards action, and other circumstances are such as reasonably to justify apprehension that action will occur.

Mr. Justice Clark, dissenting, found *Dennis* and *Yates* inconsistent. In his view, (1) the restatement of *Dennis* was incompatible with what the Court had in fact decided; and (2) the *Yates* "trial judge charged in essence all that was required under the *Dennis* opinions."

The contribution of *Yates,* as some liberals saw it, was that the First Amendment protects advocacy of abstract doctrine—that only advocacy (incitement) of illegal action is punishable.

Scales v. *United States*
367 U.S. 203 (1961)

Mr. Justice Harlan delivered the opinion of the Court.

Our writ issued in this case (358 U.S. 917) to review a judgment of the Court of Appeals (260 F.2d 21) affirming petitioner's conviction under the so-called membership clause of the Smith Act. 18 U.S.C. § 2385. The Act, among other things, makes a felony the acquisition or holding of knowing membership in any organization which advocates the overthrow of the Government of the United States by force or violence. The indictment charged that from January 1946 to the date of its filing (November 18, 1954) the Communist Party of the United States was such an organization, and that petitioner throughout that period was a member thereof, with knowledge of the Party's illegal purpose and a specific intent to accomplish overthrow "as speedily as circumstances would permit." . . .

It will bring the constitutional issues into clearer focus to notice first the premises on which the case was submitted to the jury. The jury was instructed that in order to convict it must find that within the three-year limitations period (1) the Communist Party advocated the violent overthrow of the Government, in the sense of present "advocacy of action" to accom-

plish that end as soon as circumstances were propitious; and (2) petitioner was an "active" member of the Party, and not merely "a nominal, passive, inactive or purely technical" member, with knowledge of the Party's illegal advocacy and a specific intent to bring about violent overthrow "as speedily as circumstances would permit."

The constitutional attack upon the membership clause, as thus construed, is that the statute offends (1) the Fifth Amendment, in that it impermissibly imputes guilt to an individual merely on the basis of his associations and sympathies, rather than because of some concrete personal involvement in criminal conduct; and (2) the First Amendment, in that it infringes free political expression and association. . . .

FIFTH AMENDMENT

In our jurisprudence guilt is personal, and when the imposition of punishment on a status or on conduct can only be justified by reference to the relationship of that status or conduct to other concededly criminal activity (here advocacy of violent overthrow), that relationship must be sufficiently substantial to satisfy the concept of personal guilt in order to withstand attack under the Due Process Clause of the Fifth Amendment. Membership, without more, in an organization engaged in illegal advocacy, it is now said, has not heretofore been recognized by this Court to be such a relationship. This claim stands and we shall examine it, independently of that made under the First Amendment.

Any thought that due process puts beyond the reach of the criminal law all individual associational relationships, unless accompanied by the commission of specific acts of criminality, is dispelled by familiar concepts of the law of conspiracy and complicity. While both are commonplace in the landscape of the criminal law, they are not natural features. Rather they are particular legal concepts manifesting the more general principle that society, having the power to punish dangerous behavior, cannot be powerless against those who work to bring about that behavior. The fact that Congress has not resorted to either of these familiar concepts means only that the enquiry here must direct itself to an analysis of the relationship between the fact of membership and the underlying substantive illegal conduct, in order to determine whether that relationship is indeed too tenuous to permit its use as the basis of criminal liability. In this instance it is an organization which engages in criminal activity, and we can perceive no reason why one who actively and knowingly works in the ranks of that organization, intending to contribute to the success of those specifically illegal activities, should be any more immune from prosecution than he to whom the organization has assigned the task of carrying out the substantive criminal act. . . .

What must be met, then, is the argument that membership, even when accompanied by the elements of knowledge and specific intent, affords an insufficient quantum of participation in the organization's alleged criminal activity, that is, an insufficiently significant form of aid and encouragement to permit the imposition of criminal sanctions on that basis. It must indeed be recognized that a person who merely becomes a member of an illegal organization, by that "act" alone need be doing nothing more than signifying his assent to its purposes and activities on one hand, and providing, on the other, only the sort of moral encouragement which comes from the knowledge that others believe in what the organization is doing. It may indeed be argued that such assent and encouragement do fall short of the concrete, practical impetus given to a criminal enterprise which is lent for instance by a commitment on the part of a conspirator to act in furtherance of that enterprise. A member, as distinguished from a conspirator, may indicate his approval of a criminal enterprise by the very fact of his membership without thereby necessarily committing himself to further it by any act or course of conduct whatever.

In an area of the criminal law which this Court has indicated more than once demands its watchful scrutiny . . . these factors have weight and must be found to be overborne in a total constitutional assessment of the statute. We think, however, they are duly met when the statute is found to reach only "active" members having also a guilty knowledge and intent, and which therefore prevents a conviction on what otherwise might be regarded as merely an expression of sympathy with the alleged criminal enterprise, unaccompanied by any significant action in its support or any commitment to undertake such action.

Thus, given the construction of the membership clause already discussed, we think the factors called for in rendering members criminally responsible for the illegal advocacy of the organization fall within established, and therefore presumably constitutional standards of criminal imputability.

FIRST AMENDMENT

Little remains to be said concerning the claim that the statute infringes First Amendment freedoms. It was settled in *Dennis* that the advocacy with which we are here concerned is not constitutionally protected speech, and it was further established that a combination to promote such advocacy, albeit under the aegis of what purports to be a political party, is not such association as is protected by the First Amendment. We can discern no reason why membership, when it constitutes a purposeful form of complicity in a group engaging in this same forbidden advocacy, should receive any greater degree of protection from the guarantees of that Amendment.

If it is said that the mere existence of such an enactment tends to inhibit the exercise of constitutionally protected rights, in that it engenders an unhealthy fear that one may find himself unwittingly embroiled in criminal liability, the answer surely is that the statute provides that a defendant must be proven to have knowledge of the proscribed advocacy before he may be convicted. It is, of course, true that quasi-political parties or other groups that may embrace both legal and illegal aims differ from a technical conspiracy, which is defined by its criminal purpose, so that *all* knowing association with the conspiracy is a proper subject for criminal proscription as far as First Amendment liberties are concerned. If there were a similar blanket prohibition of association with a group having both legal and illegal aims, there would indeed be a real danger that legitimate political expression or association would be impaired, but the membership clause, as here construed, does not cut deeper into the freedom of association than is necessary to deal with "the substantive evils that Congress has a right to prevent." *Schenck* v. *United States,* 249 U.S. 47, 52. The clause does not make criminal all association with an organization, which has been shown to engage in illegal advocacy. There must be clear proof that a defendant "specifically intend[s] to accomplish [the aims of the organization] by resort to violence." *Notto* v. *United States, post,* . . . Thus the member for whom the organization is a vehicle for the advancement of legitimate aims and policies does not fall within the ban of the statute: he lacks the requisite specific intent "to bring about the overthrow of the government as speedily as circumstances would permit." Such a person may be foolish, de-

luded, or perhaps merely optimistic, but he is not by this statute made a criminal.

We conclude that petitioner's constitutional challenge must be overruled.

Mr. Justice Black, dissenting. . . .

I think it is important to point out the manner in which this case re-emphasizes the freedom-destroying nature of the "balancing test" presently in use by the Court to justify its refusal to apply specific constitutional protections of the Bill of Rights. In some of the recent cases in which it has "balanced" away the protections of the First Amendment, the Court has suggested that it was justified in the application of this "test" because no direct abridgment of First Amendment freedoms was involved, the abridgment in each of these cases being, in the Court's opinion, nothing more than "an incident of the informed exercise of a valid governmental function." A possible implication of that suggestion was that if the Court were confronted with what it would call a direct abridgment of speech, it would not apply the "balancing test" but would enforce the protections of the First Amendment according to its own terms. This case causes me to doubt that such an implication is justified. Petitioner is being sent to jail for the express reason that he has associated with people who have entertained unlawful ideas and said unlawful things, and that of course is a *direct* abridgment of his freedoms of speech and assembly—under any definition that has ever been used for that term. Nevertheless, even as to this admittedly direct abridgment, the Court relies upon its prior decisions to the effect that the Government has power to abridge speech and assembly if its interest in doing so is sufficient to outweigh the interest in protecting these First Amendment freedoms. . . .

Mr. Justice Douglas, dissenting. . . .

Even the Alien and Sedition Laws—shameful reminders of an early chapter in intolerance—never went to far as we go today. . . . There is here no charge of conspiracy, no charge of any overt act to overthrow the Government by force and violence, no charge of any other criminal act. . . .

We legalize today guilt by association, sending a man to prison when he committed no unlawful act. Today's break with tradition is a serious one. It borrows from the totalitarian philosophy. . . .

[Justices Brennan, Warren, and Douglas in dissent thought Sections 4 (f) of the Internal Security Act gave immunity from prosecution under the membership clause of the Smith Act.]

Brandenburg v. *Ohio*
395 U.S. 444 (1969)

Per Curiam.

The appellant, a leader of a Ku Klux Klan group, was convicted under the Ohio Criminal Syndicalism statute for "advocat[ing] . . . the duty, necessity, or propriety of crime, sabotage, violence, or unlawful methods of terrorism as a means of accomplishing industrial or political reform" and for "voluntarily assembl[ing] with any society, group, or assemblage of persons formed to teach or advocate the doctrines of criminal syndicalism." Ohio Rev.Code Ann. § 2923.13. He was fined $1,000 and sentenced to one to 10 years' imprisonment. The appellant challenged the constitutionality of the criminal syndicalism statute under the First and Fourteenth Amendments to the United States Constitution, but the intermediate appellate court of Ohio affirmed his conviction without opinion. The Supreme Court of Ohio dismissed his appeal, *sua sponte*, "for the reason that no substantial constitutional question exists herein." . . . Appeal was taken to this Court, . . . We reverse.

The record shows that a man, identified at trial as the appellant, telephoned an announcer-reporter on the staff of a Cincinnati television station and invited him to come to a Ku Klux Klan "rally" to be held at a farm in Hamilton County. With the cooperation of the organizers, the reporter and a cameraman attended the meting and filmed the events. Portions of the films were later broadcast on the local station and on a national network.

The prosecution's case rested on the films and on testimony identifying the appellant as the person who communicated with the reporter and who spoke at the rally. The State also introduced into evidence several articles appearing in the film, including a pistol, a rifle, a shotgun, ammunition, a Bible, and a red hood worn by the speaker in the films.

One film showed 12 hooded figures, some of whom carried firearms. They were gathered around a large wooden cross, which they burned. No one was present other than the participants and the newsmen who made the film. Most of the words uttered during the scene were incomprehensible when the film was projected, but scattered phrases could be understood that were derogatory of Negroes and, in one instance, of Jews. Another scene of the same film showed the appellant, in Klan regalia, making a speech. The speech, in full, was as follows:

"This is an organizers' meeting. We have had quite a few members here today which are—we have hundreds, hundreds of members throughout the State of Ohio. I can quote from a newspaper clipping from the Columbus, Ohio *Dispatch*, five weeks ago Sunday morning. The Klan has more members in the State of Ohio than does any other organization. We're not a revengent organization, but if our President, our Congress, our Supreme Court, continues to suppress the white, Caucasian race, it's possible that there might have to be some revengeance taken.

"We are marching on Congress July the Fourth, four hundred thousand strong. From there we are dividing into two groups, one group to march on St. Augustine, Florida, the other group to march into Mississippi. Thank you."

The second film showed six hooded figures one of whom, later identified as the appellant, repeated a speech very similar to that recorded on the first film. The reference to the possibility of "revengeance" was omitted, and one sentence was added: "Personally, I believe the nigger should be returned to Africa, the Jew returned to Israel." Though some of the figures in the films carried weapons, the speaker did not.

The Ohio Criminal Syndicalism Statute was enacted in 1919. From 1917 to 1920, identical or quite similar laws were adopted by 20 States and two territories. E. Dowell, *A History of Criminal Syndicalism Legislation in the United States* 21 (1939). In 1927, this Court sustained the constitutionality of California's Criminal Syndicalism Act, the text of which is quite similar to that of the laws of Ohio. *Whitney* v. *California,* 274 U.S. 357 (1927). The Court upheld the statute on the ground that, without more, "advocating" violent means to effect political and economic change involves such danger to the security of the State that the State may outlaw it. Cf. *Fiske* v. *Kansas,* 274 U.S. 380 (1927). But *Whitney* has been thoroughly discredited by later decisions. See *Dennis* v. *United States,* 341 U.S. 494, at 507 (1951). These later decisions have fashioned the principle that the constitutional guarantees of free speech and free press do not permit a State to forbid or proscribe advocacy of the use of force or of law violation except where such advocacy is directed to inciting or producing imminent lawless action and is likely to incite or produce such action.[1] As we said in *Noto* v. *United States,* 367 U.S. 290, 297–298 (1961), "the mere abstract teaching . . . of the moral propriety or even moral necessity for a resort to force

---

[1] It was on the theory that the Smith Act, 54 Stat. 670, 18 U.S.C. § 2385, embodied such a principle and that it had been applied only in conformity with it that this Court sustained the Act's constitutionality. Dennis v. United States, 341 U.S. 494 (1951). That this was the basis for *Dennis* was emphasized in Yates v. United States, 354 U.S. 298, 320–324 (1957), in which the Court overturned convictions for advocacy of the forcible overthrow of the Government under the Smith Act, because the trial judge's instructions had allowed conviction for mere advocacy, unrelated to its tendency to produce forcible action.

and violence, is not the same as preparing a group for violent action and steeling it to such action." See also *Herndon* v. *Lowry,* 301 U.S. 242, 259–261 (1937); *Bond* v. *Floyd,* 385 U.S. 116, 134 (1966). A statute which fails to draw this distinction impermissibly intrudes upon the freedoms guaranteed by the First and Fourteenth Amendments. It sweeps within its condemnation speech which our Constitution has immunized from governmental control. Cf. *Yates* v. *United States,* 354 U.S. 298 (1957); *De Jonge* v. *Oregon,* 299 U.S. 353 (1937); *Stromberg* v. *California,* 283 U.S. 359 (1931). . . .

Measured by this test, Ohio's Criminal Syndicalism Act cannot be sustained. The Act punishes persons who "advocate or teach the duty, necessity, or propriety" of violence "as a means of accomplishing industrial or political reform"; or who publish or circulate or display any book or paper containing such advocacy; or who "justify" the commission of violent acts "with intent to exemplify, spread or advocate the propriety of the doctrines of criminal syndicalism"; or who "voluntarily assemble" with a group formed "to teach or advocate the doctrines of criminal syndicalism." Neither the indictment nor the trial judge's instructions to the jury in any way refined the statute's bald definition of the crime in terms of mere advocacy not distinguished from incitement to imminent lawless action.

Accordingly, we are here confronted with a statute which, by its own words and as applied, purports to punish mere advocacy and to forbid, on pain of criminal punishment, assembly with others merely to advocate the described type of action. Such a statute falls within the condemnation of the First and Fourteenth Amendments. The contrary teaching of *Whitney* v. *California, supra,* cannot be supported, and that decision is therefore overruled.

Mr. Justice Black, concurring.

I agree with the views expressed by Mr. Justice Douglas in his concurring opinion in this case that the "clear and present danger" doctrine should have no place in the interpretation of the First Amendment.

Mr. Justice Douglas, concurring.

While I join the opinion of the Court, I desire to enter a *caveat*. . . .

. . . I see no place in the regime of the First Amendment for any "clear and present danger" test, whether strict and tight as some would make it, or free-wheeling as the Court in *Dennis* rephrased it.

When one reads the opinions closely and sees when and how the "clear and present danger" test has been applied, great misgivings are aroused. First, the threats were often loud but always puny and made serious only by judges so wedded to the *status quo* that critical analysis made them nervous. Second, the test was so twisted and perverted in *Dennis* as to make the trial of those teachers of Marxism an all-out political trial which was part and parcel of the cold war that has eroded substantial parts of the First Amendment. . . .

The line between what is permissible and not subject to control and what may be made impermissible and subject to regulation is the line between ideas and overt acts.

The example usually given by those who would punish speech is the case of one who falsely shouts fire in a crowded theatre.

This is, however, a classic case where speech is brigaded with action. They are indeed inseparable and a prosecution can be launched for the overt acts actually caused. Apart from rare instances of that kind, speech is, I think, immune from prosecution. Certainly there is no constitutional line between advocacy of abstract ideas as in *Yates* and advocacy of political action as in *Scales*. The quality of advocacy turns on the depth of the conviction; and government has no power to invade that sanctuary of belief and conscience.

Note and quaere: In *Masses*, above, and in his private correspondence Judge Learned Hand seemed to focus on the *form* of the speaker's language: Did the challenged words *explicitly* urge a criminal act? This, he thought, was a more objective test, and it would give speech and press more protection than the Holmesian "clear and present danger" test, which focuses on the *possible effects* of the speaker's words. Hand thought the latter would give judges too much leeway. According to Professor Gerald Gunther, *Brandenburg* gives us the best of Hand and Holmes: "Under *Brandenburg*, probability of harm is no longer the central criterion for speech limitations. The inciting language of the speaker—the Hand focus on 'objective' words—is the major consideration. And punishment of the harmless inciter is prevented by the *Schenck*-derived requirement of a likelihood of dangerous consequences." (See Gunther, "Learned Hand and the Origins of Modern First Amendment Doctrine . . . ," *27 Stanford Law Review* 719 [1975]).

Would Justices Black and Douglas, who dissented in *Brandenburg,* agree with Gunther's interpretation of that case? If the Court had intended to float a new doctrine, is it apt to have done so in a brief, per curiam opinion—and without explicit acknowledgment of what it was doing?

THE DOCTRINES OF VAGUENESS, OVERBREADTH, AND LESS DRASTIC MEANS

Coates v. *Cincinnati*
402 U.S. 611 (1971)

Mr. Justice Stewart delivered the opinion of the Court.

A Cincinnati, Ohio, ordinance makes it a criminal offense for "three or more persons to assemble . . . on any of the sidewalks . . . and there conduct themselves in a manner annoying to persons passing by. . . ." The issue before us is whether this ordinance is unconstitutional on its face.

The appellants were convicted of violating the ordinance, and the convictions were ultimately affirmed by a closely divided vote in the Supreme Court of Ohio, upholding the constitutional validity of the ordinance. 21 Ohio St.2d 66. An appeal from that judgment was brought here. . . . The record brought before the reviewing courts tells us no more than that the appellant Coates was a student involved in a demonstration and the other appellants were pickets involved in a labor dispute. For throughout this litigation it has been the appellants' position that the ordinance on its face violates the First and Fourteenth Amendments of the Constitution. Cf. *Times Film Corp.* v. *Chicago,* 365 U.S. 43.

In rejecting this claim and affirming the convictions the Ohio Supreme Court did not give the ordinance any construction at variance with the apparent plain import of its language. . . .

We are thus relegated, at best, to the words of the ordinance itself. If three or more people meet together on a sidewalk or street corner, they must conduct themselves so as not to annoy any police officer or other person who should happen to pass by. In our opinion this ordinance is unconstitutionally vague because it subjects the exercise of the right of assembly to an unascertainable standard, and unconstitutionally broad because it authorizes the punishment of constitutionally protected conduct.

Conduct that annoys some people does not annoy others. Thus, the ordinance is vague not in the sense that it requires a person to conform his conduct to an imprecise but comprehensible normative standard, but rather in the sense that no standard of conduct is specified at all. As a result, "men of common intelligence must necessarily guess at its meaning." *Connally* v. *General Construction Co.,* 269 U.S. 385, 391.

It is said that the ordinance is broad enough to encompass many types of conduct clearly within the city's constitutional power to pro-

hibit. And so, indeed, it is. The city is free to prevent people from blocking sidewalks, obstructing traffic, littering streets, committing assaults, or engaging in countless other forms of anti-social conduct. It can do so through the enactment and enforcement of ordinances directed with reasonable specificity toward the conduct to be prohibited. *Gregory* v. *Chicago,* 394 U.S. 111, 118, 124–125 (concurring opinion of Mr. Justice Black). It cannot constitutionally do so through the enactment and enforcement of an ordinance whose violation may entirely depend upon whether or not a policeman is annoyed.

But the vice of the ordinance lies not alone in its violation of the due process standard of vagueness. The ordinance also violates the constitutional right of free assembly and association. Our decisions establish that mere public intolerance or animosity cannot be the basis for abridgment of these constitutional freedoms. . . . The First and Fourteenth Amendments do not permit a State to make criminal the exercise of the right of assembly simply because its exercise may be "annoying" to some people. If this were not the rule, the right of the people to gather in public places for social or political purposes would be continually subject to summary suspension through the good-faith enforcement of a prohibition against annoying conduct. And such a prohibition, in addition, contains an obvious invitation to discriminatory enforcement against those whose association together is "annoying" because their ideas, their lifestyle or their physical appearance is resented by the majority of their fellow citizens.

The ordinance before us makes a crime out of what under the Constitution cannot be a crime. It is aimed directly at activity protected by the Constitution. We need not lament that we do not have before us the details of the conduct found to be annoying. It is the ordinance on its face that sets the standard of conduct and warns against transgression. The details of the offense could no more serve to validate this ordinance than could the details of an offense charged under an ordinance suspending unconditionally the right of assembly and free speech.

Mr. Justice White, with whom The Chief Justice and Mr. Justice Blackmun join, dissenting.

The claim in this case, in part, is that the Cincinnati ordinance is so vague that it may not constitutionally be applied to any conduct. But the ordinance prohibits persons from assembling with others and "conduct[ing] themselves in a manner annoying to persons passing by. . . ." Cincinnati Code of Ordinances § 901–L6. Any man of average comprehension should know that some kinds of conduct, such as assault or blocking passage on the street, will annoy others and are clearly covered by the "annoying conduct" standard of the ordinance. It would be frivolous to say that these and many other kinds of conduct are not within the foreseeable reach of the law.

It is possible that a whole range of other acts, defined with unconstitutional imprecision, is forbidden by the ordinance. But as a general rule, when a criminal charge is based on conduct constitutionally subject to proscription and clearly forbidden by a statute, it is no defense that the law would be unconstitutionally vague if applied to other behavior. Such a statute is not vague on its face. It may be vague as applied in some circumstances, but ruling on such a challenge obviously requires knowledge of the conduct with which a defendant is charged. . . .

So in *United States* v. *National Dairy Prod. Corp.*, 372 U.S. 29 (1963), where we considered a statute forbidding sales of goods at "unreasonably" low prices to injure or eliminate a competitor, 15 U.S.C § 13a, we thought the statute gave a seller adequate notice that sales below cost were illegal. The statute was therefore not facially vague, although it might be difficult to tell whether certain other kinds of conduct fell within this language. We said: "In determining the sufficiency of the notice a statute must of necessity be examined in the light of the conduct with which a defendant is charged." *Id.*, at 33. See also *United States* v. *Harriss*, 347 U.S. 612 (1954). This approach is consistent with the host of cases holding that "one to whom application of a statute is constitutional will not be heard to attack the statute on the ground that impliedly it might also be taken as applying to other persons or other situations in which its application might be unconstitutional." *United States* v. *Raines*, 362 U.S. 17, 21 (1960), and cases there cited.

Our cases, however, including *National Dairy*, recognize a different approach where the statute at issue purports to regulate or proscribe rights of speech or press protected by the First Amendment. See *United States* v. *Robel*, 389 U.S. 258 (1967); *Keyishian* v. *Board of Regents*, 385 U.S. 589 (1967); *Kunz* v. *New York*, 340 U.S. 290 (1951). Although a statute may be neither vague, overbroad, nor otherwise invalid as applied to the conduct charged against a particular defendant, he is permitted to raise its vagueness or unconstitutional overbreadth as applied to others. And if the law is found deficient in one of these respects, it may not be applied to him either, until and unless a satisfactory limiting construction is placed on the statute. *Dombrowski* v. *Pfister*, 380 U.S. 479, 491–492 (1965). The statute, in effect, is stricken down on its face. This result is deemed justified since the otherwise continued existence of the statute in unnarrowed form would tend to suppress constitutionally protected rights. See *United States* v. *National Dairy Prod. Corp.*, *supra*, at 36.

Even accepting the overbreadth doctrine with respect to statutes clearly reaching speech, the Cincinnati ordinance does not purport to bar or regulate speech as such. It prohibits persons from assembling and "conduct[ing]" themselves in a manner annoying to other persons. Even if the assembled defendants in this case were demonstrating and picketing, we have long recognized that picketing is not solely a communicative endeavor and has aspects which the State is entitled to regulate even though there is incidental impact on speech. In *Cox* v. *Louisiana*, 379 U.S. 559 (1965), the Court held valid on its face a statute forbidding picketing and parading near a courthouse. This was deemed a valid regulation of conduct rather than pure speech. The conduct reached by the statute was "subject to regulation even though [it was] intertwined with expression and association." *Id.*, at 563. The Court then went on to consider the statute as applied to the facts of record.

In the case before us, I would deal with the Cincinnati ordinance as we would with the ordinary criminal statute. The ordinance clearly reaches certain conduct but may be illegally vague with respect to other conduct. The statute is not infirm on its face and since we have no information from this record as to what conduct was charged against these defendants, we are in no position to judge the statute as applied. That the ordinance may confer wide discretion in a wide range of circumstances is irrelevant when we may be dealing with conduct at its core.

I would therefore affirm the judgment of the Ohio court.

Mr. Justice Black. . . .

[T]he First Amendment which forbids the State to abridge freedom of speech, would invalidate this city ordinance if it were used to punish the making of a political speech, even if that speech were to annoy other persons. In contrast, however, the ordinance could properly be applied to prohibit the gathering of persons in the mouths of alleys to annoy passersby by throwing rocks or by some other conduct not at all connected with speech. It is a matter of no little difficulty to determine when a law can be held void on its face and when such summary action is inappropriate. This difficulty has been aggravated in this case, because the record fails to show in what conduct these defendants had engaged to annoy other people. In my view, a record showing the facts surrounding the conviction is essential to adjudicate the important constitutional issues in this case. I would therefore, vacate the judgment and remand the case to the court below to give both parties an opportunity to supplement the record so that we may determine whether the conduct actually punished is the kind of conduct which it is within the power of the State to punish.

Gooding v. *Wilson* (summary)
405 U.S. 518 (1972)

This case involved the conviction of a person who in the course of antiwar picketing of an Army building refused a police request to stop blocking access to inductees. In the ensuing struggle he said to a policeman, ". . . white son of a bitch, I'll kill you . . . I'll choke you to death," and "You son of a bitch, if you put your hands on me again, I'll cut you all to pieces." He was convicted under a statute making it a misdemeanor to "use to or of another, and in his presence . . . opprobrious words or abusive language, tending to cause a breach of the peace." In the Court's view the statutory terms "opprobrious" and "abusive" make it a " 'breach of the peace' merely to speak words offensive to some who hear them, and so sweep . . . too broadly." In sum, while the defendant's words were indeed punishable as "fighting words" (see *Chaplinsky*, below) the statutory language was broad enough to include nonfighting, that is, less provocative, terms, and so the conviction was reversed.

Schneider v. *Irvington* (summary)
308 U.S. 147 (1939)

In *Feiner* v. *New York,* 340 U.S. 315 (1951), Mr. Justice Black summarized *Schneider* as follows:

> In *Schneider* v. *State,* 308 U.S. 147, we held that a purpose to prevent littering of the streets was insufficient to justify an ordinance which prohibited a person lawfully on the street from handing literature to one willing to receive it. We said at page 162, "There are obvious methods of preventing littering. Amongst these is the punishment of those who actually throw papers on the streets." In the present case as well, the threat of one person to assault a speaker does not justify suppression of the speech. There are obvious available alternative methods of preserving public order. One of these is to arrest the person who threatens an assault. Cf. *Dean Milk Co.* v. *Madison,* 340 U.S. 349, decided today, in which the Court invalidates a municipal health ordinance under the Commerce Clause because of a belief that the city could have accomplished its purposes by reasonably adequate alternatives. The Court certainly should not be less alert to protect freedom of speech than it is to protect freedom of trade.

Note: The vagueness and overbreadth doctrines are concerned with form, not substance. Thus, unlike the clear and present danger and other tests, they permit legislatures to reenact the invalidated laws, if they so desire, in more precise terms. The less drastic means test requires only a change in the law's sanction, not in its substance.

DEFAMATION AND INVASION OF PRIVACY

New York Times Co. v. *Sullivan*
376 U.S. 254 (1964)

Mr. Justice Brennan delivered the opinion of the Court.

We are required for the first time in this case to determine the extent to which the constitutional protections for speech and press limit a State's power to award damages in a libel action brought by a public official against critics of his official conduct.

Respondent L. B. Sullivan is one of the three elected Commissioners of the City of Montgomery, Alabama. He testified that he was "Commissioner of Public Affairs and the duties are supervision of the Police Department, Fire Department, Department of Cemetery and Department of Scales." . . . A jury in the Circuit Court of Montgomery County awarded him damages of $500,000, the full amount claimed, against all the petitioners, and the Supreme Court of Alabama affirmed.

Respondent's complaint alleged that he had been libeled by statements in a full-page advertisement that was carried in the *New York Times* on March 29, 1960. Entitled "Heed Their Rising Voices," . . . .

Of the 10 paragraphs of text in the advertisement, the third and a portion of the sixth were the basis of respondent's claim of libel. They read as follows:

Third paragraph:

> "In Montgomery, Alabama, after students sang 'My Country, 'Tis of Thee' on the State Capitol steps, their leaders were expelled from school, and truckloads of police armed with shotguns and tear-gas ringed the Alabama State College Campus. When the entire student body protested to state authorities by refusing to re-register, their dining hall was padlocked in an attempt to starve them into submission."

Sixth paragraph:

"Again and again the Southern violators have answered Dr. King's peaceful protests with intimidation and violence. They have bombed his home almost killing his wife and child. They have assaulted his person. They have arrested him seven times—for 'speeding,' 'loitering' and similar 'offenses.' And now they have charged him with 'perjury'—a *felony* under which they would imprison him for *ten years. . . ."*

Although neither of these statements mentions respondent by name, . . . [r]espondent and six other Montgomery residents testified that they read some or all of the statements as referring to him in his capacity as Commissioner.

It is uncontroverted that some of the statements contained in the two paragraphs were not accurate descriptions of events which occurred in Montgomery. . . .

Under Alabama law as applied in this case, a publication is "libelous per se" if the words "tend to injure a person . . . in his reputation" or to "bring [him] into public contempt"; the trial court stated that the standard was met if the words are such as to "injure him in his public office, or impute misconduct to him in his office, or want of official integrity, or want of fidelity to a public trust. . . ." The jury must find that the words were published "of and concerning" the plaintiff, but where the plaintiff is a public official his place in the governmental hierarchy is sufficient evidence to support a finding that his reputation has been affected by statements that reflect upon the agency of which he is in charge. Once "libel per se" has been established, the defendant has no defense as to stated facts unless he can persuade the jury that they were true in all their particulars. . . . Unless he can discharge the burden of proving truth, general damages are presumed, and may be awarded without proof of pecuniary injury. . . .

The question before us is whether this rule of liability, as applied to an action brought by a public official against critics of his official conduct, abridges the freedom of speech and of the press that is guaranteed by the First and Fourteenth Amendments.

Respondent relies heavily, as did the Alabama courts, on statements of this Court to the effect that the Constitution does not protect libelous publications. Those statements do not foreclose our inquiry here. None of the cases sustained the use of libel laws to impose sanctions upon expression critical of the official conduct of public officials. . . . Like insurrection, contempt, advocacy of unlawful acts, breach of the peace, obscenity, solicitation of legal business, and the various other formulae for the repression of expression that have been challenged in this Court, libel can claim no talismanic immunity from constitutional limitations. It must be measured by standards that satisfy the First Amendment.

The general proposition that freedom of expression upon public questions is secured by the First Amendment has long been settled by our decisions. The constitutional safeguard, we have said, "was fashioned to assure unfettered interchange of ideas for the bringing about of political and social changes desired by the people." *Roth* v. *United States*, 354 U.S. 476, 484. . . .

Thus we consider this case against the background of a profound national commitment to the principle that debate on public issues should be uninhibited, robust, and wide-open, and that it may well include vehement, caustic, and sometimes unpleasantly sharp attacks on government and public officials. See *Terminiello* v. *Chicago*, 337 U.S. 1; *De Jonge* v. *Oregon*, 299 U.S. 353, 365. The present advertisement, as an expression of grievance and protest on one of the major public issues of our time, would seem clearly to qualify for the constitutional protection. The question is whether it forfeits that protection by the falsity of some of its factual statements and by its alleged defamation of respondent.

Authoritative interpretations of the First

Amendment guarantees have consistently refused to recognize an exception for any test of truth, whether administered by judges, juries, or administrative officials—and especially not one that puts the burden or proving truth on the speaker. Cf. *Speiser* v. *Randall*, 357 U.S. 513, 525–526. The constitutional protection does not turn upon "the truth, popularity, or social utility of the ideas and beliefs which are offered." N. A. A. C. P. v. *Button*, 371 U.S. 415, 445. As Madison said, "Some degree of abuse is inseparable from the proper use of every thing; and in no instance is this more true than in that of the press." 4 *Elliot's Debates on the Federal Constitution* (1876), p. 571. . . .

Just as factual error affords no warrant for repressing speech that would otherwise be free, the same is true of injury to official reputation. Where judicial officers are involved, this Court has held that concern for the dignity and reputation of the courts does not justify the punishment as criminal contempt of criticism of the judge or his decision. *Bridges* v. *California*, 314 U.S. 252. . . .

If neither factual error nor defamatory content suffices to remove the constitutional shield from criticism of official conduct, the combination of the two elements is no less inadequate. This is the lesson to be drawn from the great controversy over the Sedition Act of 1798, 1 Stat. 596, which first crystallized a national awareness of the central meaning of the First Amendment. See Levy, *Legacy of Suppression* (1960), at 258 *et seq.*; Smith, *Freedom's Fetters* (1956), at 426, 431 and *passim.* . . .

Although the Sedition Act was never tested in this Court, the attack upon its validity has carried the day in the court of history. . . .

. . . These views reflect a broad consensus that the Act, because of the restraint it imposed upon criticism of government and public officials, was inconsistent with the First Amendment.

There is no force in respondent's argument that the constitutional limitations implicit in the history of the Sedition Act apply only to Congress and not to the States. It is true that the First Amendment was originally addressed only to action by the Federal Government, and that Jefferson, for one, while denying the power of Congress "to controul the freedom of the press," recognized such a power in the States. See the 1804 Letter to Abigail Adams quoted in *Dennis* v. *United States*, 341 U.S. 494, 522, n. 4. (concurring opinion). But this distinction was eliminated with the adoption of the Fourteenth Amendment and the application to the States of the First Amendment's restrictions. See, *e.g.*, *Gitlow* v. *New York*, 268 U.S. 652, 666. . . .

What a State may not constitutionally bring about by means of a criminal statute is likewise beyond the reach of its civil law of libel. The fear of damage awards under a rule such as that invoked by the Alabama courts here may be markedly more inhibiting than the fear of prosecution under a criminal statute. . . . The judgment awarded in this case—without the need for any proof of actual pecuniary loss—was one thousand times greater than the maximum fine provided by the Alabama criminal statute, and one hundred times greater than that provided by the Sedition Act. And since there is no double-jeopardy limitation applicable to civil lawsuits, this is not the only judgment that may be awarded against petitioners for the same publication. Whether or not a newspaper can survive a succession of such judgments, the pall of fear and timidity imposed upon those who would give voice to public criticism is an atmosphere in which the First Amendment freedoms cannot survive. Plainly the Alabama law of civil libel is "a form of regulation that creates hazards to protected freedoms markedly greater than those that attend reliance upon the criminal law." *Bantam Books, Inc.* v. *Sullivan*, 372 U.S. 58, 70.

The state rule of law is not saved by its allowance of the defense of truth. . . . Allowance of the defense of truth, with the burden of proving it on the defendant, does not mean that only false speech will be deterred. . . . Under such a rule, would-be critics of official conduct may be deterred from voicing their criticism, even though it is believed to be true and even though it is in fact true, because of doubt whether it can be proved in court or fear of the expense of having to do so. They tend to make only statements which "steer far wider of the unlawful zone." *Speiser* v. *Randall, supra,* 357 U.S., at 526. The rule thus dampens the vigor and limits the variety of public debate. It is inconsistent with the First and Fourteenth Amendments.

The constitutional guarantees require, we think, a federal rule that prohibits a public official from recovering damages for a defamatory falsehood relating to his official conduct unless he proves that the statement was made with "actual malice"—that is, with knowledge that it was false or with reckless disregard of whether it was false or not. . . .

We think the evidence against the *Times* supports at most a finding of negligence in failing to discover the misstatements, and is constitutionally insufficient to show the recklessness that is required for a finding of actual malice. . . .

We also think the evidence was constitutionally defective in another respect: it was incapable of supporting the jury's finding that the allegedly libelous statements were made "of and concerning" respondent. Respondent relies on the words of the advertisement and the testimony of six witnesses to establish a connection between it and himself. . . .

Mr. Justice Black, with whom Mr. Justice Douglas joins (concurring).

I concur in reversing this half-million-dollar judgment against the *New York Times* and the four individual defendants. In reversing the Court holds that "the First and Fourteenth Amendments delimit a State's power to award damages for libel in an action brought by a public official against critics of his official conduct." I base my vote to reverse on the belief that the First and Fourteenth Amendments not merely "delimit" a State's power to award damages to "a public official against critics of his official conduct" but completely prohibit a State from

exercising such a power. The Court goes on to hold that a State can subject such critics to damages if "actual malice" can be proved against them. "Malice," even as defined by the Court, is an elusive, abstract concept, hard to prove and hard to disprove. The requirement that malice be proved provides at best an evanescent protection for the right critically to discuss public affairs and certainly does not measure up to the sturdy safeguard embodied in the First Amendment. Unlike the Court, therefore, I vote to reverse exclusively on the ground that the Times and the individual defendants had an absolute, unconditional constitutional right to publish in the Times advertisement their criticisms of the Montgomery agencies and officials. . . .

Mr. Justice Goldberg, with whom Mr. Justice Douglas joins (concurring in the result). . . .

In my view, the First and Fourteenth Amendments to the Constitution afford to the citizen and to the press an absolute, unconditional privilege to criticize official conduct despite the harm which may flow from excesses and abuses. . . .

Note: A "public figure" for purposes of the law of defamation is one who "thrusts" himself into a public controversy in order to affect its outcome. An otherwise little-known person unwillingly caught up in a matter of public interest is not a public figure and thus need prove only negligence (not "actual malice") to prevail against a defamer. Thus, a former State Department translator (whose refusal to testify in an investigation of Soviet intelligence operations brought a flurry of newspaper publicity) was held not to be a public figure when he sued the author and publisher of a book which listed him as an "identified" Soviet agent. *Wolston* v. *Reader's Digest Association,* 99 S. Ct. 2701 (1979). A similar result was reached in *Hutchinson* v. *Proxmire,* 99 S. Ct. 2675 (1979), where the plaintiff was a scientist whose publicly funded research was ridiculed by a United States Senator.

Gertz v. *Robert Welch, Inc.*
418 U.S. 323 (1974)

The *New York Times Co.* v. *Sullivan* rule was extended to cover not merely public officials but public figures and also private persons caught up in matters of public interest. This development is summarized in the present Burger Court case—and modified in favor of the privacy of private persons.

Gertz, a lawyer, represented (for civil damage purposes) the family of a young person slain by a policeman. He sued defendant for accusing him in print of being a "Communist-Fronter" and the architect of a "frame-up" of the policeman.

Mr. Justice Powell delivered the opinion of the Court. . . .

Three years after *New York Times*, a majority of the Court agreed to extend the constitutional privilege to defamatory criticism of "public figures." This extension was announced in *Curtis Publishing Co.* v. *Butts* and its companion *Associated Press* v. *Walker*, 388 U.S. 130, 162 (1967). The first case involved the *Saturday Evening Post's* charge that Coach Wally Butts of the University of Georgia had conspired with Coach Bear Bryant of the Univeristy of Alabama to fix a football game between their respective schools *Walker* involved an erroneous Associated Press account of Brigadier General Edwin Walker's participation in a University of Mississippi campus riot. Because Butts was paid by a private alumni association and Walker had retired from the Army, neither could be classified as a "public official" under *New York Times*. Although Mr. Justice Harlan announced the result in both cases, a majority of the Court agreed with Mr. Chief Justice Warren's conclusion that the *New York Times* test should apply to criticism of "public figures" as well as "public officials." The Court extended the constitutional privilege announced, in that case to protect defamatory criticism of nonpublic officials who "are nevertheless intimately involved in the resolution of important public questions, or, by reason of their fame, shape events in areas of concern to society at large." *Id.*, at 164.

In his opinion for the plurality in *Rosenbloom* v. *Metromedia, Inc.*, 403 U.S. 29 (1971), Mr. Jus-

tice Brennan took the *New York Times* privilege one step further. He concluded that its protection should extend to defamatory falsehoods relating to private persons if the statements concerned matters of general or public interest. He abjured the suggested distinction between public officials and public figures on the one hand and private individuals on the other. He focused instead on society's interest in learning about certain issues: "If a matter is a subject of public or general interest, it cannot suddenly become less so merely because a private individual is involved or because in some sense the individual did not choose to become involved." 403 U.S., at 43. Thus, under the plurality opinion, a private citizen involuntarily associated with a matter of general interest has no recourse for injury to his reputation unless he can satisfy the demanding requirements of the *New York Times* test.

Two members of the Court concurred in the result in *Rosenbloom* but departed from the reasoning of the plurality. Mr. Justice Black restated his view, long shared by Mr. Justice Douglas, that the First Amendment cloaks the news media with an absolute and indefeasible immunity from liability for defamation. *Id.*, at 57. Mr. Justice White concurred on a narrower ground. *Ibid.* He concluded that "the First Amendment gives the press and the broadcast media a privilege to report and comment upon the official actions of public servants in full detail, with no requirement that the reputation or privacy of an individual involved in or affected by the official action be spared from public view." *Id.*, at 62. He therefore declined to reach the broader questions addressed by the other Justices. . . .

Mr. Justice Marshall dissented in *Rosenbloom* in an opinion joined by Mr. Justice Stewart. The principal point of disagreement among the three dissenters concerned punitive charges. Whereas Mr. Justice Harlan thought that the States could allow punitive damages in amounts bearing "a reasonable and purposeful relationship to the actual harm done . . . ," *id.*, at 75, Mr. Justice Marshall concluded that the size and unpredictability of jury awards of exemplary damages unnecessarily exacerbated the problems of media self-censorship and that such damages should therefore be forbidden.

III.

We begin with the common ground. Under the First Amendment there is no such thing as a false idea. However pernicious an opinion may seem, we depend for its correction not on the conscience of judges and juries but on the competition of other ideas. But there is no constitutional value in false statements of fact. Neither the intentional lie nor the careless error materially advances society's interest in "uninhibited, robust, and wide-open" debate on public issues. *New York Times Co.* v. *Sullivan*, 376 U.S., at 270. . . .

Although the erroneous statement of fact is not worthy of constitutional protection, it is nevertheless inevitable in free debate. . . . And punishment of error runs the risk of inducing a cautious and restrictive exercise of the constitutionally guaranteed freedoms of speech and press. Our decisions recognize that a rule of strict liability that compels a publisher or broadcaster to guarantee the accuracy of his factual assertions may lead to intolerable self-censorship. Allowing the media to avoid liability only by proving the truth of all injurious statements does not accord adequate protection to First Amendment liberties. As the Court stated in *New York Times Co.* v. *Sullivan, supra,*

376 U.S., at 279, "Allowance of the defense of truth, with the burden of proving it on the defendant, does not mean that only false speech will be deterred." The First Amendment requires that we protect some falsehood in order to protect speech that matters.

The need to avoid self-censorship by the news media is, however, not the only societal value at issue. If it were, this Court would have embraced long ago the view that publishers and broadcasters enjoy an unconditional and indefeasible immunity from liability for defamation. . . . Such a rule would indeed obviate the fear that the prospect of civil liability for injurious falsehood might dissuade a timorous press from the effective exercise of First Amendment freedoms. Yet absolute protection for the communications media requires a total sacrifice of the competing value served by the law of defamation.

The legitimate state interest underlying the law of libel is the compensation of individuals for the harm inflicted on them by defamatory falsehoods. We would not lightly require the State to abandon this purpose, for, as Mr. Justice Stewart has reminded us, the individual's right to the protection of his own good name "reflects no more than our basic concept of the essential dignity and worth of every human being—a concept at the root of any decent system of ordered liberty. The protection of private personality, like the protection of life itself, is left primarily to the individual states under the Ninth and Tenth Amendments. But this does not mean that the right is entitled to any less recognition by this Court as a basic of our constitutional system." *Rosenblatt* v. *Baer*, 383 U.S. 75, 92–93 (1963) (opinion of Stewart, J.).

Some tension necessarily exists between the need for a vigorous and uninhibited press and the legitimate interest in redressing wrongful injury. . . . In our continuing effort to define the proper accommodation between these competing concerns, we have been especially anxious to assure to the freedoms of speech and press that "breathing space" essential to their fruitful exercise. *NAACP* v. *Button*, 371 U.S. 415, 433 (1963). To that end this Court has extended a measure of strategic protection to defamatory falsehood.

The *New York Times* standard defines the level of constitutional protection appropriate to the context of defamation of a public person. Those who, by reason of the notoriety of their achievements or the vigor and success with which they seek the public's attention, are properly classed as public figures and those who hold governmental office may recover for injury to reputation only on clear and convincing proof that the defamatory falsehood was made with knowledge of its falsity or with reckless disregard for the truth. This standard administers an extremely powerful antidote to the inducement to media self-censorship of the common law rule of strict liability for libel and slander. And it exacts a correspondingly high price from the victims of defamatory falsehood. Plainly many deserving plaintiffs, including some intentionally subjected to injury, will be unable to surmount the barrier of the *New York Times* test. Despite this substantial abridgement of the state law right to compensation for wrongful hurt to one's reputation, the Court has concluded that the protection of the *New York Times* privilege should be available to publishers and broadcasters of defamatory falsehoods concerning public officials and public figures. . . . We think that these decisions are correct, but we do not find their holdings justified solely by reference to the interest of the press and broadcast media in immunity from liability. Rather, we believe that the *New York Times* rule states an accommodation between this concern and the limited state interest present in the context of libel actions brought by public persons. For the reasons stated below, we conclude that the state interest in compensating injury to the reputation of private individuals requires that a different rule should obtain with respect to them. . . .

. . . [W]e have no difficulty in distinguishing among defamation plaintiffs. The first remedy of any victim of defamation is self-help—using available opportunities to contradict the lie or correct the error and thereby to minimize its adverse impact on reputation. Public officials and public figures usually enjoy significantly greater access to the channels of effective communication and hence have a more realistic opportunity to counteract false statements than private individuals normally enjoy. Private individuals are therefore more vulnerable to injury, and the state interest in protecting them is correspondingly greater.

More important than the likelihood that private individuals will lack effective opportunities for rebuttal, there is a compelling normative consideration underlying the distinction between public and private defamation plaintiffs. An individual who decides to seek governmental office must accept certain necessary consequences of that involvement in public affairs. He runs the risk of closer public scrutiny than might otherwise be the case. And society's interest in the officers of government is not strictly limited to the formal discharge of official duties. . . .

Those classed as public figures stand in a similar position. Hypothetically, it may be possible for someone to become a public figure through no purposeful action of his own, but the instances of truly involuntary public figures must be exceedingly rare. For the most part those who attain this status have assumed roles of especial prominence in the affairs of society. Some occupy positions of such persuasive power and influence that they are deemed public figures for all purposes. More commonly, those classed as public figures have thrust themselves to the forefront of particular public controversies in order to influence the resolution of the issues involved. In either event, they invite attention and comment.

Even if the foregoing generalities do not obtain in every instance, the communications media are entitled to act on the assumption that public officials and public figures have voluntarily exposed themselves to increased risk of injury from defamatory falsehoods concerning them. No such assumption is justified with respect to a private individual. He has not accepted public office nor assumed an "influential role in ordering society." *Curtis Publishing Co.* v. *Butts, supra,* 388 U.S., at 164 (opinion of Warren, C. J.). He has relinquished no part of his interest in the protection of his own good name, and consequently he has a more compelling call on the courts for redress of injury inflicted by defamatory falsehood. Thus, private individuals are not only more vulnerable to injury than public officials and public figures; they are also more deserving of recovery.

For these reasons we conclude that the States should retain substantial latitude in their efforts to enforce a legal remedy for defamatory falsehood injurious to the reputation of a private individual. The extension of the *New York Times* test proposed by the *Rosenbloom* plurality would abridge this legitimate state interest to a degree that we find unacceptable. . . .

We hold that, so long as they do not impose liability without fault, the States may define for themselves the appropriate standard of liability for a publisher or broadcaster of defamatory falsehood injurious to a private individual. This approach provides a more equitable boundary between the competing concerns involved here. It recognizes the strength of the legitimate state interest in compensating private individuals for wrongful injury to reputation, yet shields the press and broadcast media from the rigors of strict liability for defamation. At least this conclusion obtains where, as here, the substance of the defamatory statement "makes substantial danger to reputation apparent." This phrase places in perspective the conclusion we announce today. Our inquiry would involve considerations somewhat different from those discussed above if a State purported to condition civil liability on a factual misstatement whose content did not warn a reasonably prudent editor or broadcaster of its defamatory potential. Cf. *Time, Inc.* v. *Hill,* 385 U.S. 374 (1967). Such a case is not now before us, and we intimate no view as to its proper resolution.

IV.

Our accommodation of the competing values at stake in defamation suits by private individuals allows the States to impose liability on the publisher or broadcaster of defamatory falsehoods on a less demanding showing than that required by *New York Times.* This conclusion is not based on a belief that the considerations which prompted the adoption of the *New York Times* privilege for defamation of public officials and its extension to public figures are wholly inapplicable to the context of private individuals. Rather, we endorse this approach in recognition of the strong and legitimate state interest in compensating private individuals for injury to reputation. But this countervailing state interest extends no further than compensation for actual injury. For the reasons stated below, we hold that the States may not permit recovery of presumed or punitive damages, at least when liability is not based on a showing of knowledge of falsity or reckless disregard for the truth.

The common law of defamation is an oddity of tort law, for it allows recovery of purportedly compensatory damages without evidence of actual loss. Under the traditional rules pertaining to actions for libel, the existence of injury is presumed from the fact of publication. Juries may award substantial sums of compensation for supposed damage to reputation without any proof that such harm actually occurred. The largely uncontrolled discretion of juries to award damages where there is no loss unnecessarily compounds the potential of any system of liability for defamatory falsehood to inhibit the vigorous exercise of First Amendment freedoms. Additionally, the doctrine of presumed damages invites injuries to punish unpopular opinion rather than to compensate individuals for injury sustained by the publication of a false fact. More to the point, the States have no substantial interest in securing for plaintiffs such as this petitioner gratuitous awards of money damages far in excess of any actual injury.

We would not, of course, invalidate state law

simply because we doubt its wisdom, but here we are attempting to reconcile state law with a competing interest grounded in the constitutional command of the First Amendment. It is therefore appropriate to require that state remedies for defamatory falsehood reach no farther than is necessary to protect the legitimate interest involved. It is necessary to restrict defamation plaintiffs who do not prove knowledge of falsity or reckless disregard for the truth to compensation for actual injury. We need not define "actual injury," as trial courts have wide experience in framing appropriate jury instructions in tort action. Suffice it to say that actual injury is not limited to out-of-pocket loss. Indeed, the more customary types of actual harm inflicted by defamatory falsehood include impairment of reputation and standing in the community, personal humiliation, and mental anguish and suffering. Of course, juries must be limited by appropriate instructions, and all awards must be supported by competent evidence concerning the injury, although there need be no evidence which assigns an actual dollar value to the injury.

We also find no justification for allowing awards of punitive damages against publishers and broadcasters held liable under state-defined standards of liability for defamation. In most jurisdictions jury discretion over the amounts awarded is limited only by the gentle rule that they not be excessive. Consequently, juries assess punitive damages in wholly unpredictable amounts bearing no necessary relation to the actual harm caused. And they remain free to use their discretion selectively to punish expressions of unpopular views. Like the doctrine of presumed damages, jury discretion to award punitive damages unnecessarily exacerbates the danger of media self-censorship, but, unlike the former rule, punitive damages are wholly irrelevant to the state interest that justifies a negligence standard for private defamation actions. They are not compensation for injury. Instead, they are private fines levied by civil juries to punish reprehensible conduct and to deter its future occurrence. In short, the private defama-

tion plaintiff who establishes liability under a less demanding standard than that stated by New York Times may recover only such damages as are sufficient to compensate him for actual injury.

V.

Notwithstanding our refusal to extend the New York Times privilege to defamation of private individuals, respondent contends that we should affirm the judgment below on the ground that petitioner is either a public official or a public figure. There is little basis for the former assertion. Several years prior to the present incident, petitioner had served briefly on housing committees appointed by the mayor of Chicago, but at the time of publication he had never held any remunerative governmental position. Respondent admits this but argues that petitioner's appearance at the coroner's inquest rendered him a "de facto public official." Our cases recognize no such concept. Respondent's suggestion would sweep all lawyers under the New York Times rule as officers of the court and distort the plain meaning of the "public official" category beyond all recognition. We decline to follow it.

Respondent's characterization of petitioner as a public figure raises a different question. That designation may rest on either of two alternative bases. In some instances an individual may achieve such pervasive fame or notoriety that he becomes a public figure for all purposes and in all contexts. More commonly, an individual voluntarily injects himself or is drawn into a particular public controversy and thereby becomes a public figure for a limited range of issues. In either case such persons assume special prominence in the resolution of public questions.

Petitioner has long been active in community and professional affairs. He has served as an officer of local civil groups and of various professional organizations, and he has published several books and articles on legal subjects. Although petitioner was consequently well-known in some circles, he had achieved no general fame or notoriety in the community. None of the prospective jurors called at the trial had ever heard of petitioner prior to this litigation, and respondent offered no proof that this response was atypical of the local population. We would not lightly assume that a citizen's participation in community and professional affairs rendered him a public figure for all purposes. Absent clear evidence of general fame or notoriety in the community, and pervasive involvement in the affairs of society, an individual should not be deemed a public personality for all aspects of his life. It is preferable to reduce the public figure question to a more meaningful context by looking to the nature and extent of an individual's participation in the particular controversy giving rise to the defamation.

In this context it is plain that petitioner was not a public figure. He played a minimal role at the coroner's inquest, and his participation related solely to his representation of a private client. He took no part in the criminal prosecution of officer Nuccio. Moreover, he never discussed either the criminal or civil litigation with the press and was never quoted as having done so. He plainly did not thrust himself into the vortex of this public issue, nor did he engage the public's attention in an attempt to influence its outcome. We are persuaded that the trial court did not err in refusing to characterize petitioner as a public figure for the purpose of this litigation.

We therefore conclude that the *New York Times* standard is inapplicable to this case and that the trial court erred in entering judgment for respondent. Because the jury was allowed to impose liability without fault and was permitted to presume damages without proof of injury, a new trial is necessary.

Mr. Justice Blackmun, concurring.

I joined Mr. Justice Brennan's opinion for the plurality in *Rosenbloom* v. *Metromedia, Inc.*, 403 U.S. 29 (1971). . . . Although the Court's opin-

ion in the present case departs from the rationale of the *Rosenbloom* plurality, in that the Court now conditions a libel action by a private person upon a showing of negligence, as contrasted with a showing of willful or reckless disregard, I am willing to join, and do join, the Court's opinion and its judgment for two reasons:

1. By removing the spectres of presumed and punitive damages in the absence of *New York Times* malice, the Court eliminates significant and powerful motives for self-censorship that otherwise are present in the traditional libel action. By so doing, the Court leaves what should prove to be sufficient and adequate breathing space for a vigorous press. What the Court has done, I believe, will have little, if any, practical effect on the functioning of responsible journalism.

2. The Court was sadly fractionated in *Rosenbloom*. A result of that kind inevitably leads to uncertainty. I feel that it is of profound importance for the Court to come to rest in the defamation area and to have a clearly defined majority position that eliminates the unsureness engendered by *Rosenbloom's* diversity. If my vote were not needed to create a majority, I would adhere to my prior view. A definitive ruling, however, is paramount. . . .

For these reasons, I join the opinion and the judgment of the Court.

Mr. Chief Justice Burger, dissenting.

The doctrines of the law of defamation have had a gradual evolution primarily in the state courts. In *New York Times Co.* v. *Sullivan*, 376 U.S. 254 (1964), and its progeny this Court entered this field.

Agreement or disagreement with the law as it has evolved to this time does not alter the fact that it has been orderly development with a consistent basic rationale. In today's opinion the Court abandons the traditional thread so far as the ordinary private citizen is concerned and introduces the concept that the media will be liable for negligence in publishing defamatory statements with respect to such persons. Although I agree with much of what Mr. Justice White states, I do not read the Court's new doctrinal approach in quite the way he does. I am frank to say I do not know the parameters of a "negligence" doctrine as applied to the news media. Conceivably this new doctrine could inhibit some editors, as the dissents of Mr. Justice Douglas and Mr. Justice Brennan suggest. But I would prefer to allow this area of law to continue to evolve as it has up to now with respect to private citizens rather than embark on a new doctrinal theory which has no jurisprudential ancestry.

The petitioner here was performing a professional representative role as an advocate in the highest tradition of the law, and under that tradition the advocate is not to be invidiously identified with his client. The important public policy which underlies this tradition—the right to counsel—would be gravely jeopardized if every lawyer who takes an "unpopular" case, civil or criminal, would automatically become fair game for irresponsible reporters and editors who might, for example, describe the lawyer as a "mob mouthpiece" for representing a client with a serious prior criminal record, or as an "ambulance chaser" for representing a claimant in a personal injury action.

I would reverse the judgment of the Court of Appeals and remand for reinstatement of the verdict of the jury and the entry of an appropriate judgment on that verdict.

Mr. Justice Douglas, dissenting.

The Court describes this case as a return to the struggle of "defin[ing] the proper accommodation between the law of defamation and the freedoms of speech and press protected by the First Amendment." It is indeed a struggle, once described by Mr. Justice Black as "the same quagmire" in which the Court "is helplessly struggling in the field of obscenity." *Curtis Publishing Co.* v. *Butts*, 388 U.S. 130, 171

(concurring). I would suggest that the struggle is a quite hopeless one, for, in light of the command of the First Amendment, no "accommodation" of its freedoms can be "proper" except those made by the Framers themselves. . . .

Mr. Justice Brennan, dissenting.

I agree with the conclusion, expressed in Part V of the Court's opinion, that, at the time of publication of respondent's article, petitioner could not properly have been viewed as either a "public official" or "public figure"; instead, respondent's article, dealing with an alleged conspiracy to discredit local police forces, concerned petitioner's purported involvement in "an event of public or general interest." *Rosenbloom* v. *Metromedia, Inc.*, 403 U.S. 29, 31–32 (1971); see, . . . , *ante.* I cannot agree, however, that free and robust debate—so essential to the proper functioning of our system of government—is permitted adequate "breathing space," *N. A. A. C. P.* v. *Button*, 371 U.S. 415, 433 (1963), when, as the Court holds, the States may impose all but strict liability for defamation if the defamed party is a private person and "the substance of the defamatory statement 'makes substantial danger to reputation apparent.'" *Ante*, . . . I adhere to my view expressed in *Rosenbloom* v. *Metromedia, Inc.*, *supra*, that we strike the proper accommodation between avoidance of media self-censorship and protection of individual reputations only when we require States to apply the *New York Times Co.* v. *Sullivan*, 376 U.S. 254 (1964), knowing-or-reckless-falsity standard in civil libel actions concerning media reports of the involvement of private individuals in events of public or general interest. . . .

Mr. Justice White, dissenting.

For some 200 years—from the very founding of the Nation—the law of defamation and right of the ordinary citizen to recover for false publication injurious to his reputation have been almost exclusively the business of state courts and legislatures. Under typical state defamation law, the defamed private citizen had to prove only a false publication that would subject him to hatred, contempt or ridicule. Given such publication, general damages to reputation were presumed, while punitive damages required proof of additional facts. The law governing the defamation of private citizens remained untouched by the First Amendment because until relatively recently, the consistent view of the Court was that libelous words constitute a class of speech wholly unprotected by the First Amendment, subject only to limited exceptions carved out since 1964.

But now, using that amendment as the chosen instrument, the Court, in a few printed pages, has federalized major aspects of libel law by declaring unconstitutional in important respects the prevailing defamation law in all or most of the 50 States. That result is accomplished by requiring the plaintiff in each and every defamation action to prove not only the defendant's culpability beyond his act of publishing defamatory material but also actual damage to reputation resulting from the publication. Moreover, punitive damages may not be recovered by showing malice in the traditional sense of ill will; knowing falsehood or reckless disregard of the truth will now be required.

I assume these sweeping changes will be popular with the press, but this is not the road to salvation for a court of law. As I see it, there are wholly insufficient grounds for scuttling the libel laws of the States in such wholesale fashion, to say nothing of deprecating the reputation interest of ordinary citizens and rendering them powerless to protect themselves. I do not suggest that the decision is illegitimate or beyond the bounds of judicial review, but it is an ill-considered exercise of the power entrusted to this Court, particularly when the Court has not had the benefit of briefs and argument addressed to most of the major issues which the Court now decides. I respectfully dissent. . . .

Note and quaere: Herbert v. Lando, 99 S. Ct. 1635 (1979), held that in a defamation suit against press persons, a public-figure plaintiff whose case rests on the *Sullivan* "acutal malice" rule may question the defendants as to their editoral processes and state of mind with respect to the alleged damaging, false publications.

Refining its rule of "actual malice," the Warren Court, in *Saint Amant* v. *Thompson,* 390 U.S. 727 (1968), had said a plaintiff must prove "that the defendant in fact entertained serious doubts as to the truth of his publication." Thus, as the Court observed in *Lando,*

> . . . *New York Times* [v. *Sullivan*] and its progeny made it essential to proving liability that plaintiffs focus on the conduct and state of mind of the defendant. To be liable, the alleged defamer of public officials or of public figures must know or have reason to suspect that his publication is false . . . .

Inevitably, unless liability [for damaging falsehoods] is to be completely foreclosed, the thoughts and editorial processes of the alleged defamer would be open to examination.

Mr. Justice Brennan dissented in part. Justices Stewart and Marshall filed separate dissenting opinions. None of the dissenters accepted the lower court's view according an absolute privilege to the editorial process of a media defendant in defamation cases. Mr. Justice Brennan argued for a limited privilege "to shield the editorial process from general claims of damaged reputation. If, however, a public figure plaintiff is able to establish, to the prima facie satisfaction of a trial judge, that the publication . . . constitutes defamatory falsehood . . . the editorial privilege must yield." Mr. Justice Marshall "would foreclose [inquiry] in defamation cases as to the substance of editorial conversations" but not as to "state of mind." Mr.

Justice Stewart would confine inquiry to "the publisher's state of knowledge of the falsity of what he published . . ." and exclude inquiry as to "motivation . . . in other words [as to] actual malice as those words are ordinarily understood."

It is noteworthy that in the face of need for relevant evidence by trial courts, all of the Justices rejected claims of absolute editorial, as well as executive, privilege. See *United States* v. *Nixon* (above, Chapter 2).

Does *Lando* suggest that the malice rule is not a good device for striking a balance between freedom of the press and the individual's interest in protecting his or her good name and reputation?

Note: In a landmark article, "The Right to Privacy," 4 *Harvard Law Review* 193 (1890), Warren and Brandeis argued that growing excesses of the press called for a legal remedy to protect private persons against unjustifiable journalistic intrusion into their personal affairs. *Time, Inc.,* v. *Hill,* 385 U.S. 374 (1967), held the *New York Times Co.* rule applicable under a state privacy law in a case for damages for an inaccurate (but no unflattering) press story—three years after the fact—of a family's misfortune in being held hostage by escaped convicts.

Cox Broadcasting Corp. v. *Cohn,* 420 U.S. 469 (1975)—recognizing the "impressive credentials for a right of privacy"—denied damages where a father had sued because of a broadcast of the fact that his daughter was a rape victim. The decision rested on the narrow ground that the defendant had truthfully published only what was already available to the public in official court records. The Court found it unnecessary to decide whether "truthful publications [however unwelcome] may ever be subjected to civil or criminal liability."

FREEDOM OF ASSOCIATION

NAACP v. *Alabama*
357 U.S. 449 (1958)

An Alabama statute similar to those in many other states required certain out-of-state corporations, before doing business in the state, to file the corporate charter and designate a place of business and an agent to receive service of process. NAACP, a New York, nonprofit corporation, thought itself exempt from the statute and operated in Alabama without complying therewith. In 1956 the attorney general of Alabama brought an equity suit to enjoy any further NAACP activities within, and to oust the Association from, the state. Before trial, upon a motion by the attorney general, the trial court ordered NAACP to submit certain papers, including a list of all its Alabama members and agents. NAACP, still disclaiming the applicability of the statute, offered to comply with its requirements, but refused to produce the membership lists. For this refusal it was fined $100,000 for contempt of court.

Mr. Justice Harlan delivered the opinion of the court. . . .

We thus reach petitioner's claim that the production order in the state litigation trespasses upon fundamental freedoms protected by the due process clause of the Fourteenth Amendment. Petitioner argues that in view of the facts and circumstances shown in the record, the effect of compelled disclosure of the membership lists will be to abridge the rights of its rank-and-file members to engage in lawful association in support of their common beliefs. It contends that governmental action which, although not directly suppressing association, nevertheless carries this consequence, can be justified only upon some overriding valid interest of the State.

Effective advocacy of both public and private points of view, particularly controversial ones, is undeniably enhanced by group association, as this Court has more than once recognized by remarking upon the close nexus between the freedoms of speech and assembly. *De Jonge* v. *Oregon*, 299 U.S. 353, 364; *Thomas* v. *Collins*, 323 U.S. 516, 530. It is beyond debate that freedom to engage in association for the advancement of beliefs and ideas is an inseparable aspect of the "liberty" assured by the due process clause of the Fourteenth Amendment, which embraces freedom of speech. See *Gitlow* v. *New York*, 268 U.S. 652, 666; *Palko* v. *Connecticut*, 302 U.S. 319, 324; *Cantwell* v. *Connecticut*, 310 U.S. 296, 303; *Staub* v. *City of Baxley*, 355 U.S. 313, 321. Of course, it is immaterial whether the beliefs sought to be advanced by association pertain to political, economic, religious, or cultural matters, and state action which may have the effect of curtailing the freedom to associate is subject to the closest scrutiny.

The fact that Alabama, so far as is relevant to the validity of the contempt judgment presently under review, has taken no direct action, cf. *De Jonge* v. *Oregon, supra; Near* v. *Minnesota*, 283 U.S. 697, to restrict the right of petitioner's members to associate freely, does not end inquiry into the effect of the production order. See *American Communications Assn.* v. *Douds*, 339 U.S. 382, 402. In the domain of these indispensable liberties, whether of speech, press, or association, the decisions of this Court recognize that abridgment of such rights, even though unintended, may inevitably follow from varied forms of governmental action. Thus in *Douds*, the Court stressed that the legislation there challenged, which on its face sought to regulate labor unions and to secure stability in interstate commerce, would have the practical effect "of discouraging" the exercise of constitutionally protected political rights, 339 U.S., at 393, and it upheld the statute only after concluding that the reasons advanced for its enactment were constitutionally sufficient to justify its possible deterrent effect upon such freedoms. Similar recognition of possible unconstitutional intimidation of the free exercise of the right to advocate underlay this Court's narrow construction of the authority of a congressional committee investigating lobbying and of an Act regulating lobbying, although in neither case was there an effort to suppress speech. *United States* v. *Rumely*, 345 U.S. 41, 46–47; *United States* v. *Harriss*, 347 U.S. 612, 625–626. The governmental action challenged may appear to be totally unrelated to protected liberties. Statutes imposing taxes upon rather than prohibiting particular activity have been struck down when perceived to have the consequence of unduly curtailing the liberty of freedom of press assured under the Fourteenth Amendment. *Grosjean* v. *American Press Co.*, 297 U.S. 233; *Murdock* v. *Pennsylvania*, 319 U.S. 105.

It is hardly a novel perception that compelled disclosure of affiliation with groups engaged in advocacy may constitute as effective a restraint on freedom of association as the forms of governmental action in the cases above were thought likely to produce upon the particular constitutional rights there involved. This court has recognized the vital relationship between freedom to associate and privacy in one's associations. When referring to the varied forms of governmental action which might interfere with freedom of assembly, it said in *American Communications Assn.* v. *Douds, supra.* at 402: "A requirement that adherents of particular religious faiths or political parties wear identifying armbands, for example, is obviously of this nature." Compelled disclosure of membership in an organization engaged in advocacy of particular beliefs is of the same order. Inviolability of privacy in group association may in many circumstances be indispensable to preservation of freedom of association, particularly where a group espouses dissident beliefs. Cf. *United States* v. *Rumely, supra*, at 56–58 (concurring opinion).

We think that the production order, in the respects here drawn in question, must be regarded as entailing the likelihood of a substantial restraint upon the exercise by petitioner's members of their right to freedom of association. Petitioner has made an uncontroverted showing that on past occasions revelation of the identity of its rank-and-file members has exposed these members to economic reprisal, loss of employment, threat of physical coercion, and other manifestations of public hostility. . . .

We turn to the final question whether Alabama has demonstrated an interest in obtaining the disclosures it seeks from petitioner which is sufficient to justify the deterrent effect which we have concluded these disclosures may well have on the free exercise by petitioner's members of their constitutionally protected right of association. See *American Communications Assn.* v. *Douds, supra*, at 400; *Schneider* v. *State*, 308 U.S. 147, 161. Such a ". . . subordinating interest of the state must be compelling," *Sweezy* v. *New Hampshire*, 354 U.S. 234, 265 (concurring opinion). It is not of moment that the state has here acted solely through its judicial branch, for whether legislative or judicial, it is still the application of state power which we are asked to scrutinize.

It is important to bear in mind that petitioner asserts no right to absolute immunity from state investigation, and no right to disregard Alabama's laws. As shown by its substantial compliance with the production order, petitioner does not deny Alabama's right to obtain from it such information as the state desires concerning the purposes of the Association and its activities within the state. Petitioner has not objected to divulging the identity of its members who are employed by or hold official positions with it. It has urged the rights solely of its ordinary rank-and-file members. This is therefore not analogous to a case involving the interest of a state in protecting its citizens in their dealings with paid solicitors or agents of foreign corporations by requiring identification. See *Cantwell* v. *Connecticut, supra*, at 306; *Thomas* v. *Collins, supra*, at 538.

Whether there was "justification" in this instance turns solely on the substantiality of Alabama's interest in obtaining the membership lists. During the course of a hearing before the Alabama Circuit Court on a motion of petitioner to set aside the production order, the State Attorney General presented at length, under examination by petitioner, the state's reason for requesting the membership lists. The exclusive purpose was to determine whether petitioner was conducting intrastate business in violation of the Alabama foreign corporation registration statute, and the membership lists were expected to help resolve this question. The issues in the litigation commenced by Alabama by its bill in equity were whether the character of petitioner and its activities in Alabama had been such as to make petitioner subject to the registration statute, and whether the extent of petitioner's activities without qualifying suggested its permanent ouster from the state. Without intimating the slightest view upon the merits of these issues, we are unable to perceive that the disclosure of the names of petitioner's rank-and-file members has a substantial bearing on either of them. . . .

From what has already been said, we think it apparent that *Bryant* v. *Zimmerman,* 278 U.S. 63, cannot be relied on in support of the state's position, for that case involved markedly different considerations in terms of the interest of the state in obtaining disclosure. There, this Court upheld, as applied to a member of a local chapter of the Ku Klux Klan, a New York statute requiring any unincorporated association which demanded an oath as a condition to membership to file with state officials copies of its " . . . constitution, bylaws, rules, regulations and oath of membership, together with a roster of its membership and a list of its officers for the current year." N.Y. Laws 1923, c. 664, §§ 53, 56. In its opinion, the Court took care to emphasize the nature of the organization which New York sought to regulate. The decision was based on the particular character of the Klan's activities, involving acts of unlawful intimidation and violence, which the Court assumed was before the state legislature when it enacted the statute, and of which the Court itself took judicial notice. Furthermore, the situation before us is significantly different from that in *Bryant,* because the organization there had made no effort to comply with any of the requirements of New York's statute but rather had refused to furnish the state with *any* information as to its local activities. . . .

Note: In the face of a Virginia barratry statute, *NAACP* v. *Button,* 371 U.S. 415 (1963), upheld the NAACP's right to sponsor and promote litigation: " . . . abstract discussion is not the only form of communication which the Constitution protects . . . . Groups which find themselves unable to achieve their objectives through the ballot frequently turn to the courts . . . . For such a group, association for litigation may be the most effective form of political association." In sum, litigation "is thus a form of political expression."

Scales v. *United States*
See p. 412, above.

Note: Bryant v. *Zimmerman* (discussed in *NAACP* v. *Alabama,* above) upheld a law requiring the Ku Klux Klan to reveal a roster of its members. *Communist Party* v. *SACB,* 367 U.S. 1 (1961), upheld a similar requirement for similar reasons with respect to the Communist Party. But later *Albertson* v. *SACB,* 382 U.S. 70 (1965), in effect held the required "registration" by the Communist Party was unconstitutional on self-incrimination grounds. (In the earlier *SACB* case the claim of self-incrimination had been held premature in the posture of the proceeding at that time.)

Jones v. *North Carolina Prisoners' Union,* 433 U.S. 119 (1977) upheld regulations calculated to inhibit organizing efforts of a prisoners' union: "The fact of confinement and the needs of the penal institution impose limits on constitutional rights, including those derived from the First Amendment, which are implicit in incarceration."

ACCESS TO THE NEWS MEDIA

Red Lion Broadcasting Co. v. *FCC*
395 U.S. 367 :1969)

Mr. Justice White delivered the opinion of the Court.

The Federal Communications Commission has for many years imposed on radio and television broadcasters the requirement that discussion of public issues be presented on broadcast stations, and that each side of those issues must be given fair coverage. This is known as the fairness doctrine, which originated very early in the history of broadcasting and has maintained its present outlines for some time. It is an obligation whose content has been defined in a long series of FCC rulings in particular cases, and which is distinct from the statutory requirement of § 315 of the Communications Act that equal time be allotted all qualified candidates for public office. . . .

The broadcasters challenge the fairness doctrine and its specific manifestations in the personal attack and political editorial rules on conventional First Amendment grounds, alleging that the rules abridge their freedom of speech and press. Their contention is that the First Amendment protects their desire to use their allotted frequencies continuously to broadcast whatever they choose, and to exclude whomever they choose from ever using that frequency. No man may be prevented from saying or publishing what he thinks, or from refusing in his speech or other utterances to give equal weight to the views of his opponents. This right, they say, applies equally to broadcasters. . . .

. . . It would be strange if the First Amendment, aimed at protecting and furthering communications, prevented the Government from making radio communication possibly by requiring licenses to broadcast and by limiting the number of licenses so as not to overcrowd the spectrum.

. . . No one has a First Amendment right to a license or to monopolize a radio frequency; to deny a station license because "the public interest" requires it "is not a denial of free speech." *National Broadcasting Co.* v. *United States*, 319 U.S. 190, 227 (1943).

. . . There is nothing in the First Amendment which prevents the Government from requiring a licensee to share his frequency with others and to conduct himself as a proxy or fiduciary with obligations to present those views and voices which are representative of his community and which would otherwise, by necessity, be barred from the airwaves.

This is not to say that the First Amendment is irrelevant to public broadcasting. On the contrary, it has a major role to play as the Congress itself recognized in § 326, which forbids FCC interference with "the right of free speech by means of radio communication." Because of the scarcity of radio frequencies, the Government is permitted to put restraints on licensees in favor of others whose views should be expressed on this unique medium. But the people as a whole retain their interest in free speech by radio and their collective right to have the medium function consistently with the ends and purposes of the First Amendment. It is the right of the viewers and listeners, not the right of the broadcasters, which is paramount. It is the purpose of the First Amendment to preserve an uninhibited marketplace of ideas in which truth will ultimately prevail, rather than to countenance monopolization of that market, whether it be by the Government itself or a private licensee. . . . It is the right of the public to receive suitable access to social, political, esthetic, moral, and other ideas and experiences which is crucial here. That right may not constitutionally be abridged either by Congress or by the FCC. . . .

Nor can we say that it is inconsistent with the First Amendment goal of producing an informed public capable of conducting its own affairs to require a broadcaster to permit answers to personal attacks occurring in the course of discussing controversial issues, or to require that the political opponents of those endorsed by the station be given a chance to communicate with the public. Otherwise, station owners and a few networks would have unfettered power to make time available only to the highest bidders, to communicate only their own views on public issues, people and candidates, and to permit on the air only those with whom they agreed. There is no sanctuary in the First Amendment for unlimited private censorship operating in a medium not open to all. "Freedom of the press from governmental interference under the First Amendment does not sanction repression of that freedom by private interests." . . .

. . . [I]f present licensees should suddenly prove timorous, the Commission is not powerless to insist that they give adequate and fair attention to public issues. It does not violate the First Amendment to treat licensees given the privilege of using scarce radio frequencies as proxies for the entire community, obligated to give suitable time and attention to matters of great public concern. To condition the granting or renewal of licenses on a willingness to present representative community views on controversial issues is consistent with the ends and purposes of those constitutional provisions forbidding the abridgment of freedom of speech and freedom of the press. Congress need not stand idly by and permit those with licenses to ignore the problems which beset the people or to exclude from the airways anything but their own views of fundamental questions. . . .

> *Note: Columbia Broadcasting System* v. *Democratic National Committee,* 412 U.S. 94 (1973), qualifies *Red Lion* by upholding the right of broadcasters to refuse to accept paid-for, editorial "advertisements" of a political nature—emphasizing broadcasters' freedom to control the content of their programs. Justices Brennan and Marshall in dissent stressed the public's right of access to the airwaves. For a parallel decision with respect to the press, see *Miami Herald,* below.
>
> Are *Red Lion* and *Columbia Broadcasting* reconcilable on the ground that a right of access to the air waves is not necessary, because the fairness doctrine adequately protects the public interest in being fully and fairly informed?
>
> Are *Red Lion* and *Miami Herald,* below, reconcilable on the ground that broadcasters enjoy a legal monopoly, while newspapers do not?

Miami Herald Publishing Co. v. *Tornillo*
418 U.S. 241 (1974)

Mr. Chief Justice Burger delivered the opinion of the Court.

The issue in this case is whether a state statute granting a political candidate a right to equal space to reply to criticism and attacks on his record by a newspaper, violates the guarantees of a free press.

In the fall of 1972, appellee, Executive Director of the Classroom Teachers Association, apparently a teachers' collective-bargaining agent, was a candidate for the Florida House of Representatives. On September 20, 1972, and again on September 29, 1972, appellant printed editorials critical of appellee's candidacy. In response to these editorials appellee demanded that appellant print verbatim his replies, defending the role of the Classroom Teachers Association and the organization's accomplishments for the citizens of Dade County. Appellant declined to print the appellee's replies, and appellee brought suit in Circuit Court, Dade County, seeking declaratory and injunctive relief and actual and punitive damages in excess of $5,000. The action was premised on Florida Statute § 104.38, a "right of reply" statute which provides that if a candidate for nomination or election is assailed regarding his personal character or official record by any newspaper, the candidate has the right to demand that the newspaper print, free of cost to the candidate, any reply the candidate may make to the newspaper's charges. The reply must appear in as conspicuous a place and in the same kind of type as the charges which prompted the reply, provided it does not take up more space than the charges. Failure to comply with the statute constitutes a first-degree misdemeanor. . . .

Appellant contends the statute is void on its face because it purports to regulate the content of a newspaper in violation of the First Amendment. Alternatively it is urged that the statute is void for vagueness since no editor could know exactly what words would call the statute into operation. It is also contended that the statute fails to distinguish between critical comment which is and is not defamatory.

The appellee and supporting advocates of an enforceable right of access to the press vigorously argue that Government has an obligation to ensure that a wide variety of views reach the public. The contentions of access proponents will be set out in some detail. It is urged that at the time the First Amendment to the Constitution was enacted in 1791 as part of our Bill of Rights the press was broadly representative of the people it was serving. While many of the newspapers were intensely partisan and narrow in their views, the press collectively presented a broad range of opinions to readers. Entry into publishing was inexpensive; pamphlets and books provided meaningful alternatives to the organized press for the expression of unpopular ideas and often treated events and expressed views not covered by conventional newspapers. A true marketplace of ideas existed in which there was relatively easy access to the channels of communication.

Access advocates submit that although newspapers of the present are superficially similar to those of 1791 the press of today is in reality very different from that known in the early years of our national existence. In the past half century a communications revolution has seen the introduction of radio and television into our lives, the promise of a global community through the use of communications satellites, and the spectre of a "wired" nation by means of an expanding cable television network with two-way capabilities. The printed press, it is said, has not escaped the effects of this revolution. Newspapers have become big business and there are far fewer of them to serve a larger literate population. Chains of newspapers, national newspapers, national wire and news services, and one-newspaper towns, are the dominant features of a press that has become noncompetitive and enormously powerful and influential in its capacity to manipulate popular opinion and change the course of events. Major metropolitan newspapers have collaborated to establish news services national in scope. Such national news organizations provide syndicated "interpretative reporting" as well as syndicated features and commentary, all of which can serve as part of the new school of "advocacy journalism."

The elimination of competing newspapers in most of our large cities, and the concentration of control of media that results from the only newspaper being owned by the same interests which own a television station and a radio station, are important components of this trend toward concentration of control of outlets to inform the public.

The result of these vast changes has been to place in a few hands the power to inform the American people and shape public opinion. Much of the editorial opinion and commentary that is printed is that of syndicated columnists distributed nationwide and, as a result, we are told, on national and world issues there tends to be a homogeneity of editorial opinion, commentary, and interpretative analysis. The abuses of bias and manipulative reportage are, likewise, said to be the result of the vast accumulations of unreviewable power in the modern media empires. In effect, it is claimed, the public has lost any ability to respond or to contribute in a meaningful way to the debate on issues. The monopoly of the means of communication allows for little or no critical analysis of the media except in professional journals of very limited readership. . . .

. . . [I]t is reasoned that the only effective way to insure fairness and accuracy and to provide for some accountability is for government to take affirmative action. The First Amendment interest of the public in being informed is said to be in peril because the "marketplace of ideas" is today a monopoly controlled by the owners of the market.

Proponents of enforced access to the press take comfort from language in several of this Court's decisions which suggests that the First Amendment acts as a sword as well as a shield, that it imposes obligations on the owners of the press in addition to protecting the press from government regulation. . . .

In *New York Times Co.* v. *Sullivan,* the Court spoke of "a profound national commitment to the principle that debate on public issues should be uninhibited, robust, and wide-open." It is argued that the "uninhibited, robust" debate is not "wide-open" but open only to a monopoly in control of the press. Appellee cites the plurality opinion in *Rosenbloom* v. *Metromedia, Inc.*, which he suggests seemed to invite experimentation by the States in right to access regulation of the press.

. . . They also claim the qualified support of Professor Thomas I. Emerson, who has written that "[a] limited right of access to the press can be safely enforced," although he believes that "[g]overnment measures to encourage a multiplicity of outlets, rather than compelling a few outlets to represent everybody, seems a preferable course of action." T. Emerson, *The System of Freedom of Expression* 671 (1970).

However much validity may be found in these arguments, at each point the implementation of a remedy such as an enforceable right of access necessarily calls for some mechanism, either governmental or consensual. If it is governmental coercion, this at once brings about a confrontation with the express provisions of the First Amendment and the judicial gloss on that amendment developed over the years. . . .

. . . [T]he Court has expressed sensitivity as to whether a restriction or requirement constituted the compulsion exerted by government on a newspaper to print that which it would not otherwise print. The clear implication has been that any such a compulsion to publish that which "'reason' tells them should not be published" is unconstitutional. A responsible press is an undoubtedly desirable goal, but press responsibility is not mandated by the Constitution and like many other virtues it cannot be legislated.

Appellee's argument that the Florida statute does not amount to a restriction of appellant's right to speak because "the statute in question here has not prevented the *Miami Herald* from saying anything it wished" begs the core question. Compelling editors or publishers to publish that which "'reason' tells them should not be published" is what is at issue in this case. The Florida statute operates as a command in the same sense as a statute or regulation forbid-

ding appellant from publishing specified matter. Governmental restraint on publishing need not fall into familiar or traditional patterns to be subject to constitutional limitations on governmental powers. The Florida statute exacts a penalty on the basis of the content of a newspaper. The first phase of the penalty resulting from the compelled printing of a reply is exacted in terms of the cost in printing and composing time and materials and in taking up space that could be devoted to other material the newspapers may have preferred to print. It is correct, as appellee contends, that a newspaper is not subject to the finite technological limitations of time that confront a broadcaster but it is not correct to say that, as an economic reality, a newspaper can proceed to infinite expansion of its column space to accommodate the replies that a government agency determines or a statute commands the readers should have available.

Faced with the penalties that would accrue to any newspaper that published news or commentary arguably within the reach of the right of access statute, editors might well conclude that the safe course is to avoid controversy and that, under the operation of the Florida statute, political and electoral coverage would be blunted or reduced. Government enforced right of access inescapably "dampens the vigor and limits the variety of public debate," *New York Times Co.* v. *Sullivan*. . . .

Even if a newspaper would face no additional costs to comply with a compulsory access law and would not be forced to forego publication of news or opinion by the inclusion of a reply, the Florida statute fails to clear the barriers of the First Amendment because of its intrusion into the function of editors. A newspaper is more than a passive receptacle or conduit for news, comment, and advertising. The choice of material to go into a newspaper, and the decisions made as to limitations on the size of the paper, and content, and treatment of public issues and public officials—whether fair or unfair—constitutes the exercise of editorial control and judgment. It has yet to be demonstrated how governmental regulation of this crucial process can be exercised consistent with First Amendment guarantees of a free press as they have evolved to this time. Accordingly, the judgment of the Supreme Court of Florida is reversed.

Mr. Justice Brennan, with whom Mr. Justice Rehnquist joins, concurring.

I join the Court's opinion which, as I understand it, addresses only "right of reply" statutes and implies no view upon the constitutionality of "retraction" statutes affording plaintiffs able to prove defamatory falsehoods a statutory action to require publication of a retraction. See generally Note, Vindication of the Reputation of a Public Official, 80 *Harv. L. Rev.* 1730, 1739–1747 (1967).

Note: *Valentine* v. *Chrestensen*, 316 U.S. 52 (1942), held that commercial speech (e.g., advertising) is not protected by the First Amendment. That view has now "all but passed from the scene." *Bigelow* v. *Virginia*, 421 U.S. 809 (1975), invalidated a law prohibiting advertisements to promote abortions. For similar decisions with respect to laws prohibiting ads by pharmacists and lawyers, see *Virginia Board of Pharmacy* v. *Virginia Citizens Consumer Council*, 425 U.S. 748 (1976) and *Bates* v. *State Bar of Arizona*, 433 U.S. 350 (1977).

THE PUBLIC FORUM

Hague v. *CIO* (excerpt)
307 U.S. 496 (1939):

Wherever the title of streets and parks may rest they have immemorially been held in trust for the use of the public and, time out of mind, have been used for purposes of assembly, communicating thoughts between citizens, and discussing public questions. Such use of the streets and public places has, from ancient times, been a part of the privileges, immunities, rights and liberties of citizens. The privilege [to] use the streets and parks for communication of views on national questions may be regulated in the interest of all; . . . but it must not, in the guise of regulation, be abridged or denied.

Feiner v. *New York*
340 U.S. 315 (1951)

Mr. Chief Justice Vinson delivered the opinion of the Court.

Petitioner was convicted of the offense of disorderly conduct, a misdemeanor under the New York penal laws, in the Court of Special Sessions of the City of Syracuse and was sentenced to thirty days in the county penitentiary. . . .

In the review of state decisions where First Amendment rights are drawn in question, we of course make an examination of the evidence to ascertain independently whether the right has been violated. Here, the trial judge, who heard the case without jury, rendered an oral decision at the end of the trial, setting forth his determination of the facts upon which he found the petitioner guilty. His decision indicated generally that he believed the state's witnesses, and his summation of the testimony was used by the two New York Courts on review in stating the facts. Our appraisal of the facts is, therefore, based upon the uncontroverted facts and, where controversy exists, upon that testimony which the trial judge did reasonably conclude to be true.

On the evening of March 8, 1949, petitioner Irving Feiner was addressing an open-air meeting at the corner of South McBride and Harrison Streets in the City of Syracuse. At approximately 6,30 p.m., the police received a telephone complaint concerning the meeting, and two officers were detailed to investigate. One of these officers went to the scene immediately, the other arriving some twelve minutes later. They found a crowd of about seventy-five or eighty people, both Negro and white, filling the sidewalk and spreading out into the street. Petitioner, standing on a large wooden box on the sidewalk, was addressing the crowd through a loud-speaker system attached to an automobile. Although the purpose of his speech was to urge his listeners to attend a meeting to be held that night in the Syracuse Hotel, in its course he was making derogatory remarks concerning President Truman, the American Legion, the Mayor of Syracuse, and other local political officials.

The police officers made no effort to interfere with petitioner's speech, but were first concerned with the effect of the crowd on both pedestrian and vehicular traffic. They observed the situation from the opposite side of the street, noting that some pedestrians were forced to walk in the street to avoid the crowd. Since traffic was passing at the time, the officers attempted to get the people listening to petitioner back on the sidewalk. The crowd was restless and there was some pushing, shoving and milling around. One of the officers telephoned the police station from a nearby store, and then both policemen crossed the street and mingled with the crowd without any intention of arresting the speaker.

At this time, petitioner was speaking in a "loud, high-pitched voice." He gave the impression that he was endeavoring to arouse the Negro people against the whites, urging that they rise up in arms and fight for equal rights. The statements before such a mixed audience "stirred up a little excitement." Some of the onlookers made remarks to the police about their inability to handle the crowd and at least one threatened violence if the police did not act. There were others who appeared to be favoring petitioner's arguments. Because of the feeling that existed in the crowd both for and against the speaker, the officers finally "stepped in to prevent it from resulting in a fight." One of the officers approached the petitioner, not for the purpose of arresting him, but to get him to

break up the crowd. He asked petitioner to get down off the box, but the latter refused to accede to his request and continued talking. The officer waited for a minute and then demanded that he cease talking. Although the officer had thus twice requested petitioner to stop over the course of several minutes, petitioner not only ignored him but continued talking. During all this time, the crowd was pressing closer around petitioner and the officer. Finally, the officer told petitioner he was under arrest and ordered him to get down from the box, reaching up to grab him. Petitioner stepped down, announcing over the microphone that "the law has arrived, and I suppose they will take over now." In all, the officer had asked petitioner to get down off the box three times over a space of four or five minutes. Petitioner had been speaking for over a half hour.

On these facts, petitioner was specifically charged with violation of § 722 of the Penal Law of New York. . . . The bill of particulars, demanded by petitioner and furnished by the State, gave in detail the facts upon which the prosecution relied to support the charge of disorderly conduct. Paragraph C is particularly pertinent here:

"By ignoring and refusing to heed and obey reasonable police orders issued at the time and place mentioned in the Information to regulate and control said crowd and to prevent a breach or breaches of the peace and to prevent injury to pedestrians attempting to use said walk, and being forced into the highway adjacent to the place in question, and prevent injury to the public generally."

We are not faced here with blind condonation by a state court of arbitrary police action. Petitioner was accorded a full, fair trial. The trial judge heard testimony supporting and contradicting the judgment of the police officers that a clear danger of disorder was threatened. After weighing this contradictory evidence, the trial judge reached the conclusion that the police officers were justified in taking action to prevent a breach of the peace. The exercise of the police officers' proper discretionary power to prevent a breach of the peace was thus approved by the trial court and later by two courts on review. The courts below recognized petitioner's right to hold a street meeting at this locality, to make use of loud-speaking equipment in giving his speech, and to make derogatory remarks concerning public officials and the American Legion. They found that the officers in making the arrest were motivated solely by a proper concern for the preservation of order and protection of the general welfare, and that there was no evidence which could lend color to a claim that the acts of the police were a cover for suppression of petitioner's views and opinions. Petitioner was thus neither arrested nor convicted for the making or the content of his speech. Rather, it was the reaction which it actually engendered.

The language of *Cantwell* v. *Connecticut*, 310 U.S. 296 (1940), is appropriate here.

"The offense known as breach of the peace embraces a great variety of conduct destroying or menacing public order and tranquility. It includes not only violent acts but acts and words likely to produce violence in others. No one would have the hardihood to suggest that the principle of freedom of speech sanctions incitement to riot or that religious liberty connotes the privilege to exhort others to physical attack upon those belonging to another sect. When clear and present danger of riot, disorder, interference with traffic upon the public streets, or other immediate threat to public safety, peace, or order appears, the power of the State to prevent or punish is obvious. (310 U.S. at 308.)"

The findings of New York courts as to the condition of the crowd and the refusal of petitioner to obey the police requests, supported as they are by the record of this case, are

persuasive that the conviction of petitioner for violation of public peace, order and authority does not exceed the bounds of proper state police action. This Court respects, as it must, the interest of the community in maintaining peace and order on its streets. *Schneider* v. *State*, 308 U.S. 147, 160 (1939); *Kovacs* v. *Cooper*, 336 U.S. 77, 82 (1949). We cannot say that the preservation of that interest here encroaches on the constitutional rights of this petitioner.

We are well aware that the ordinary murmurings and objections of a hostile audience cannot be allowed to silence a speaker, and are also mindful of the possible danger of giving overzealous police officials complete discretion to break up otherwise lawful public meetings. "A State may not unduly suppress free communication of views, religious or other, under the guise of conserving desirable conditions." *Cantwell* v. *Connecticut, supra*, at 308. But we are not faced here with such a situation. It is one thing to say that the police cannot be used as an instrument for the suppression of unpopular views, and another to say that, when as here, the speaker passes the bounds of argument or persuasion and undertakes incitement to riot, they are powerless to prevent a breach of the peace. Nor in this case can we condemn the considered judgment of three New York courts approving the means which the police, faced with a crisis, used in the exercise of their power and duty to preserve peace and order. The findings of the state courts as to the existing situation and the imminence of greater disorder coupled with petitioner's deliberate defiance of the police officers convince us that we should not reverse this conviction in the name of free speech.

Affirmed.

[Mr. Justice Frankfurter concurred in a separate opinion emphasizing the unanimity of the highest court of New York in accepting the trial court's finding that Feiner was stopped because the police honestly believed that a breach of the peace was imminent. "It is not," said the Justice, "a constitutional principle that, in acting to preserve order, the police must proceed against the crowd, whatever its size and temper, and not against the speaker."

Justices Black, Douglas, and Minton dissented on the ground that the evidence showed no serious threat of immediate disorder and that the police, if they were to intervene at all, should have thrown their weight on the side of the speaker, not of the unsympathetic crowd.]

Cox v. *Louisiana* (*Cox* I, No. 24)
379 U.S. 536 (1965)

Mr. Justice Goldberg delivered the opinion of the Court. . . .

THE BREACH OF THE PEACE CONVICTION

Appellant was convicted of violating a Louisiana "disturbing the peace" statute. . . .

Appellant led a group of young college students who wished "to protest segregation" and discrimination against Negroes and the arrest of 23 fellow students. They assembled peaceably at the State Capitol building and marched to the courthouse where they sang, prayed and listened to a speech. A reading of the record reveals agreement on the part of the State's witnesses that Cox had the demonstration "very well controlled," and until the end of Cox's speech, the group was perfectly "orderly." Sheriff Clemmons testified that the crowd's activities were not "objectionable" before that time. They became objectionable, according to the Sheriff himself, when Cox, concluding his speech, urged the students to go uptown and sit in at lunch counters. The Sheriff testified that the sole aspect of the program to which he objected was "[t]he inflammatory manner in which he [Cox] addressed that crowd and told them to go up town, go to four places on the protest list, sit down and if they don't feed you, sit there for one hour." Yet this part of Cox's

speech obviously did not deprive the demonstration of its protected character under the Constitution as free speech and assembly. . . .

The State argues, however, that while the demonstrators started out to be orderly, the loud cheering and clapping by the students in response to the singing from the jail converted the peaceful assembly into a riotous one. The record, however, does not support this assertion. It is true that the students, in response to the singing of their fellows who were in custody, cheered and applauded. However, the meeting was an outdoor meeting and a key state witness testified that while the singing was loud, it was not disorderly. There is, moreover, no indication that the mood of the students was ever hostile, aggressive, or unfriendly. Our conclusion that the entire meeting from the beginning until its dispersal by tear gas was orderly and not riotous is confirmed by a film of the events taken by a television news photographer, which was offered in evidence as a state exhibit. We have viewed the film, and it reveals that the students, though they undoubtedly cheered and clapped, were well-behaved throughout. My Brother Black, concurring in this opinion . . . agrees "that the record does not show boisterous or violent conduct or indecent language on the part of the . . ." students. *Post*, at p. 583. The singing and cheering do not seem to us to differ significantly from the constitutionally protected activity of the demonstrators in Edwards, who loudly sang "while stamping their feet and clapping their hands." *Edwards* v. *South Carolina, supra,* 372 U.S., at 233.

Finally, the State contends that the conviction should be sustained because of fear expressed by some of the state witnesses that "violence was about to erupt" because of the demonstration. It is virtually undisputed, however, that the students themselves were not violent and threatened no violence. The fear of violence seems to have been based upon the reaction of the group of white citizens looking on from across the street. . . . There is no indication, however, that any member of the white group threatened violence. And this small crowd estimated at between 100 and 300 was separated from the students by "seventy-five to eighty" armed policemen, including "every available shift of the City Police," the "Sheriff's Office in full complement," and "additional help from the State Police," along with a "fire truck and the Fire Department." As Inspector Trigg testified, they could have handled the crowd.

This situation, like that in Edwards, is "a far cry from the situation in *Feiner* v. *New York*, 340 U.S. 315." . . .

There is an additional reason why this conviction cannot be sustained. The statute at issue in this case, as authoritatively interpreted by the Louisiana Supreme Court, is unconstitutionally vague in its overly broad scope.

THE OBSTRUCTING PUBLIC PASSAGES CONVICTION

We now turn to the issue of the validity of appellant's conviction for violating the Louisiana statute [which] provides:

"No person shall wilfully obstruct the free, convenient and normal use of any public sidewalk, street, . . . or other passageway, or the entrance , corridor or passage of any public building, . . . by impeding, hindering, stifling, retarding or restraining traffic or passage thereon or therein.

"Providing however nothing herein contained shall apply to a bona fide legitimate labor organization or to any of its legal activities such as picketing . . . ."

Appellant was convicted under this statute [for] leading the meeting on the sidewalk across the street from the courthouse. . . .

[Appellant's free speech contention] raises an issue with which this Court has dealt in many decisions. . . . From these decisions certain clear principles emerge. The rights of free speech and assembly, while fundamental in our

democratic society, still do not mean that everyone with opinions or beliefs to express may address a group at any public place and at any time. The constitutional guarantee of liberty implies the existence of an organized society maintaining public order, without which liberty itself would be lost in the excesses of anarchy. The control of travel on the streets is a clear example of governmental responsibility to insure this necessary order. A restriction in that relation, designed to promote the public convenience in the interest of all, and not susceptible to abuses of discriminatory application, cannot be disregarded by the attempted exercise of some civil right which, in other circumstances, would be entitled to protection. One would not be justified in ignoring the familiar red light because this was thought to be a means of social protest. Nor could one, contrary to traffic regulations, insist upon a street meeting in the middle of Times Square at the rush hour as a form of freedom of speech or assembly. Governmental authorities have the duty and responsibility to keep their streets open and available for movement. A group of demonstrators could not insist upon the right to cordon off a street, or entrance to a public or private building, and allow no one to pass who did not agree to listen to their exhortations. . . .

We emphatically reject the notion urged by appellant that the First and Fourteenth Amendments afford the same kind of freedom to those who would communicate ideas by conduct such as patrolling, marching, and picketing on streets and highways, as these amendments afford to those who communicate ideas by pure speech. . . . We reaffirm the statement of the Court in *Giboney* v. *Empire Storage & Ice Co.*, that "it has never been deemed an abridgment of freedom of speech or press to make a course of conduct illegal merely because the conduct was in part initiated, evidence, or carried out by means of language, either spoken, written, or printed."

We have no occasion in this case to consider the constitutionality of the uniform, consistent, and nondiscriminatory application of a statute forbidding all access to streets and other public facilities for parades and meetings. Although the statute here involved on its face precludes all street assemblies and parades, it has not been so applied and enforced by the Baton Rouge authorities. City officials who testified for the State clearly indicated that certain meetings and parades are permitted in Baton Rouge, even though they have the effect of obstructing traffic, provided prior approval is obtained. . . . The statute itself provides no standards for the determination of local officials as to which assemblies to permit or which to prohibit. . . . From all the evidence before us it appears that the authorities in Baton Rouge permit or prohibit parades or street meetings in their completely uncontrolled discretion.

The situation is thus the same as if the statute itself expressly provided that there could only be peaceful parades or demonstrations in the unbridled discretion of the local officials. The pervasive restraint on freedom of discussion by the practice of the authorities under the statute is not any less effective than a statute expressly permitting such selective enforcement. . . .

This Court has recognized that the lodging of such broad discretion in a public official allows him to determine which expressions of view will be permitted and which will not. This thus sanctions a device for the suppression of the communication of ideas and permits the official to act as a censor. . . . Also inherent in such a system allowing parades or meetings only with the prior permission of an official is the obvious danger to the right of a person or group not to be denied equal protection of the laws. . . . It is clearly unconstitutional to enable a public official to determine which expressions of view will be permitted and which will not or to engage in invidious discrimination among persons or groups either by use of a statute providing a system of broad discretionary licensing power or, as in this case, the equivalent of such a system by selective enforcement of an extremely broad prohibitory statute. . . . It is, of course,

undisputed that appropriate, limited discretion, under properly drawn statutes or ordinances, concerning the time, place, duration, or manner of use of the streets for public assemblies may be vested in administrative officials. . . .

[Justices Black and Clark concurred on vagueness-of-the-statute grounds. Justices White and Harlan, concurring, stressed that one may not be convicted for expressing unpopular views. See their opinions in *Cox* II, below.]

Cox v. *Louisiana* (*Cox* II, No. 49)
379 U.S. 559 (1965)

Mr. Justice Goldberg delivered the opinion of the Court.

Appellant was convicted of violating a Louisiana statute which provides:

"Whoever, with the intent of interfering with, obstructing, or impeding the administration of justice, or with the intent of influencing any judge, juror, witness, or court officer, in the discharge of his duty pickets or parades in or near a building housing a court of the State of Louisiana . . . shall be fined not more than five thousand dollars or imprisoned not more than one year, or both."

This charge was based upon the same set of facts as [the] charges involved and set forth in No. 24 [above]. . . .

We shall first consider appellant's contention that this statute must be declared invalid on its face as an unjustified restriction upon freedoms guaranteed by the First and Fourteenth Amendments to the United States Constitution.

This statute was passed by Louisiana in 1950 and was modeled after a [federal law of 1950 which] resulted from the picketing of federal courthouses by partisans of the defendants during trials involving leaders of the Communist Party.

This statute, unlike the two previously considered, is a precise, narrowly drawn regulatory statute which proscribes certain specific behavior. . . . It prohibits a particular type of conduct, namely, picketing and parading, in a few specified locations, in or near courthouses.

There can be no question that a State has a legitimate interest in protecting its judicial system from the pressures which picketing near a courthouse might create. Since we are committed to a government of laws and not of men, it is of the utmost importance that the administration of justice be absolutely fair and orderly. This Court has recognized that the unhindered and untrammeled functioning of our courts is part of the very foundation of our constitutional democracy. See *Wood* v. *Georgia*, 370 U.S. 375, 383. The constitutional safeguards relating to the integrity of the criminal process attend every stage of a criminal proceeding [and] they exclude influence or domination by either a hostile or friendly mob. There is no room at any stage of judicial proceedings for such intervention; mob law is the very antithesis of due process. . . . A State may adopt safeguards necessary and appropriate to assure that the administration of justice at all stages is free from outside control and influence. A narrowly drawn statute such as the one under review is obviously a safeguard both necessary and appropriate to vindicate the State's interest in assuring justice under law.

Nor does such a statute infringe upon the constitutionally protected rights of free speech and free assembly. The conduct which is the subject of this statute—picketing and parading—is subject to regulation even though intertwined with expression and association. The examples are many of the application by this Court of the principle that certain forms of conduct mixed with speech may be regulated or prohibited.

Bridges v. *California*, 314 U.S. 252, and *Pennekamp* v. *Florida*, 328 U.S. 331 [cases applying the clear and present danger test in reversing contempt of court convictions] do not hold to the contrary. . . . Here we deal not with the contempt power [but with] a statute narrowly drawn. . . . We are not concerned here with such a pure form of expression as newspaper comment or a telegram by a citizen to a public official. We deal in this case not with free speech alone, but with expression mixed with particular conduct. . . .

We hold that this statute on its face is a valid law dealing with conduct subject to regulation so as to vindicate important interests of society and that the fact that free speech is intermingled with such conduct does not bring with it constitutional protection.

We now deal with the Louisiana statute as applied to the conduct in this case. The group of 2,000, led by appellant, paraded and demonstrated before the courthouse. Judges and court officers were in attendance to discharge their respective functions. It is undisputed that a major purpose of the demonstration was to protest what the demonstrators considered an "illegal" arrest of 23 students the previous day. . . .

It is, of course, true that most judges will be influenced only by what they see and hear in court. However, judges are human; and the legislature has the right to recognize the danger that some judges, jurors, and other court officials, will be consciously or unconsciously influenced by demonstrations in or near their courtrooms both prior to and at the time of the trial. A State may also properly protect the judicial process from being misjudged in the minds of the public. Suppose demonstrators paraded and picketed for weeks with signs asking that indictments be dismissed, and that a judge completely uninfluenced by these demonstrations, dismissed the indictments. A State may protect against the possibility of a conclusion by the public under these circumstances that the judge's action was in part a product of intimidation and did not flow only from the fair and orderly working of the judicial process. . . .

Appellant invokes the clear and present danger doctrine in support of his argument that the statute cannot constitutionally be applied to the conduct involved here [relying upon *Pennekamp* and *Bridges*]. He defines the standard to be applied [to] be whether the expression of opinion presents a clear and present danger to the administration of justice.

We have already pointed out the important differences between the contempt cases and the present one. . . . Here we deal not with the contempt power but with a narrowly drafted statute and not with speech in its pristine form but with conduct of a totally different character. Even assuming the applicability of a general clear and present danger test, it is one thing to conclude that the mere publication of a newspaper editorial or a telegram to a Secretary of Labor, however critical of a court, presents no clear and present danger to the administration of justice and quite another thing to conclude that crowds, such as this, demonstrating before a courthouse may not be prohibited by a legislative determination based on experience that such conduct inherently threatens the judicial process. We therefore reject the clear and present danger argument of appellant. . . .

There are, however, more substantial constitutional objections arising from appellant's conviction on the particular facts of this case. Appellant was convicted for demonstrating not "in," but "near" the courthouse. [T]here is some lack of specificity in a word such as "near." While this lack of specificity may not render the statute unconstitutionally vague, at least as applied to a demonstration within the sight and hearing of those in the courthouse, it is clear that the statute, with respect to the determination of how near the courthouse a particular demonstration can be, foresees a degree of on-the-spot administrative interpretation by officials charged with responsibility for administering and enforcing it. [The] administrative discretion to construe the term "near" [is] the type of narrow discretion which this Court has recognized as the proper role of responsible offi-

cials in making determinations concerning the time, place, duration, and manner of demonstrations. . . .

The record here clearly shows that the officials present gave permission for the demonstration to take place across the street from the courthouse. In effect, appellant was advised that a demonstration at the place it was held would not be one "near" the courthouse within the terms of the statute. [U]nder all the circumstances of this case, after the public officials acted as they did, to sustain appellant's later conviction for demonstrating where they told him he could "would be to sanction an indefensible sort of entrapment by the State—convicting a citizen for exercising a privilege which the State had clearly told him was available to him." [*Raley* v. *Ohio*, 360 U.S. 423.] The Due Process Clause does not permit convictions to be obtained under such circumstances. . . . There remains just one final point: the effect of the Sheriff's order to disperse. The State in effect argues that this order somehow removed the prior grant of permission and reliance on the officials' construction that the demonstration on the far side of the street was not illegal as being "near" the courthouse. This, however, we cannot accept. [I]t is our conclusion from the record that the dispersal order had nothing to do with any time or place limitation, and thus, on this ground alone, it is clear that the dispersal order did not remove the protection accorded appellant by the original grant of permission. . . .

Nothing we have said here or in No. 24, *ante*, is to be interpreted as sanctioning riotous conduct in any form or demonstrations, however peaceful their conduct or commendable their motives, which conflict with properly drawn statutes and ordinances designed to promote law and order, protect the community against disorder, regulate traffic, safeguard legitimate interests in private and public property, or protect the administration of justice and other essential governmental functions.

. . . We reaffirm the repeated holdings of this

Court that our constitutional command of free speech and assembly is basic and fundamental and encompasses peaceful social protest, so important to the preservation of the freedoms treasured in a democratic society. We also reaffirm the repeated decisions of this Court that there is no place for violence in a democratic society dedicated to liberty under law, and that the right of peaceful protest does not mean that everyone with opinions or beliefs to express may do so at any time and at any place. There is a proper time and place for even the most peaceful protest and a plain duty and responsibility on the part of all citizens to obey all valid laws and regulations.

Reversed.

Mr. Justice Black, concurring in No. 24 and dissenting in No. 49. . . .

The First and Fourteenth Amendments, I think, take away from government, state and federal, all power to restrict freedom of speech, press, and assembly *where people have a right to be for such purposes.* This does not mean, however, that these amendments also grant a constitutional right to engage in the conduct of picketing or patrolling, whether on publicly owned streets or on privately owned property. . . . Were the law otherwise, people on the streets, in their homes and anywhere else could be compelled to listen against their will to speakers they did not want to hear. Picketing, though it may be utilized to communicate ideas, is not speech, and therefore is not of itself protected by the First Amendment. . . . However, because Louisiana's breach-of-peace statute is not narrowly drawn to assure nondiscriminatory application, I think it is constitutionally invalid under our holding in [*Edwards* v. *South Carolina*, 372 U.S. 229].

[As to the obstructing-public-passages conviction], I believe that the First and Fourteenth Amendments require that if the streets of a town are open to some views, they must be open to all. [B]y specifically permitting picketing for the publication of labor union views, Louisiana is attempting to pick and choose among the views it is willing to have discussed on its streets [in violation of equal protection as well as the First Amendment].

I would sustain the conviction [for picketing near a courthouse]. Certainly the most obvious reason for their protest at the courthouse was to influence the judge and other court officials. . . . The Court attempts to support its holding by its inference that the Chief of Police gave his consent to picketing the courthouse. But quite apart from the fact that a police chief cannot authorize violations of his State's criminal laws, there was strong, emphatic testimony that if any consent was given it was limited to telling Cox and his group to come no closer to the courthouse than they had already come without the consent of any official, city, state, or federal. And there was also testimony that when told to leave appellant Cox defied the order by telling the crowd not to move. I fail to understand how the Court can justify the reversal of this conviction because of a permission which testimony in the record denies was given, which could not have been authoritatively given anyway, and which even if given was soon afterwards revoked. . . .

. . . Those who encourage minority groups to believe that the United States Constitution and federal laws give them a right to patrol and picket in the streets whenever they choose, in order to advance what they think to be a just and noble end, do no service to those minority groups, their cause, or their country. I am confident from this record that this appellant violated the Louisiana statute because of a mistaken belief that he and his followers had a constitutional right to do so, because of what they believed were just grievances. But the history of the past 25 years if it shows nothing else shows that his group's constitutional and statutory rights have to be protected by the courts, which must be kept free from intimidation and coercive pressures of any kind. . . . [Justice Clark concurred in Cox I and dissented in Cox II.]

Mr. Justice White, with whom Mr. Justice Harlan joins, concurring in part and dissenting in part.

In No. 49, I agree with the dissent filed by my Brother Black in [the last part] of his opinion. In No. 24, although I do not agree with everything the Court says concerning the breach of peace conviction, particularly its statement concerning the unqualified protection to be extended to Cox's exhortations to engage in sit-ins in restaurants, I agree that the conviction for breach of peace is governed by [*Edwards*] and must be reversed.

Regretfully, I also dissent from the reversal of the conviction for obstruction of public passages. The Louisiana statute is not invalidated on its face but only in its application. But this remarkable emasculation of a prohibitory statute is based on only very vague evidence that other meetings and parades have been allowed by the authorities. . . . There is no evidence in the record that other meetings of this magnitude had been allowed on the city streets, had been allowed in the vicinity of the courthouse or had been permitted completely to obstruct the sidewalk and to block access to abutting buildings. . . .

Furthermore, even if the obstruction statute, because of prior permission granted to others, could not be applied in this case so as to prevent the demonstration, it does not necessarily follow that the federal license to use the streets is unlimited as to time and circumstance. [A]t some point the authorities were entitled to apply the statute and to clear the streets. That point was reached here. To reverse the conviction under these circumstances makes it only rhetoric to talk of local power to control the streets under a properly drawn ordinance.

Adderley v. *Florida*
385 U.S. 39 (1966)

Mr. Justice Black delivered the opinion of the Court.

Petitioners, Harriett Louise Adderley and 31 other persons, were convicted by a jury in a joint trial in the County Judge's Court of Leon County, Florida, on a charge of "trespass with a malicious and mischievous intent" upon the premises of the county jail contrary to § 821.18 of the Florida statutes. . . . Petitioners, apparently all students of the Florida A. & M. University in Tallahassee, had gone from the school to the jail about a mile away, along with many other students, to "demonstrate" at the jail their protests because of arrests of other protesting students the day before, and perhaps to protest more generally against state and local policies and practices of racial segregation, including segregation of the jail. The county sheriff, legal custodian of the jail and jail grounds, tried to persuade the students to leave the jail grounds. When this did not work, he notified them that they must leave, notified them that they must leave or he would arrest them for trespassing, and notified them further that if they resisted arrest he would arrest them for resisting arrest as well. Some of the students left but others, including petitioners, remained and they were arrested. . . .

Petitioners have insisted from the beginning of these cases that they are controlled and must be reversed because of our prior cases of *Edwards* v. *South Carolina*, 372 U.S. 229, and *Cox* v. *Louisiana*, 379 U.S. 536, 559. We cannot agree. . . .

In Edwards, the demonstrators went to the South Carolina State Capitol grounds to protest. In this case they went to jail. Traditionally, state capitol grounds are open to the public. Jails, built for security purposes, are not. The demonstrators at the South Carolina Capitol went in through a public driveway and as they entered they were told by state officials there that they had a right as citizens to go through the State House grounds as long as they were peaceful. Here the demonstrators entered the jail grounds through a driveway used only for jail purposes and without warning to or permission from the sheriff. More importantly, South Carolina sought to prosecute its State Capitol demonstrators by charging them with the common-law crime of breach of the peace. The South Carolina breach-of-the-peace statute was . . . struck down as being so broad and all-embracing as to jeopardize speech, press, assembly and petition, under the constitutional doctrine enunciated in *Cantwell* v. *State of Connecticut*, 310 U.S. 296, 307–308 and followed in many subsequent cases. And it was on this same ground of vagueness that in *Cox* v. *Louisiana, supra,* 379 U.S. at 551–552, the Louisiana breach-of-the-peace law used to prosecute Cox was invalidated.

The Florida trespass statute under which these petitioners were charged cannot be challenged on this ground. It is aimed at conduct of one limited kind, that is for one person or persons to trespass upon the property of another with a malicious and mischievous intent. There is no lack of notice in this law, nothing to entrap or fool the unwary.

Petitioners seem to argue that the Florida trespass law is void for vagueness because it requires a trespass to be "with a malicious and mischievous intent . . . ." But these words do not broaden the scope of trespass so as to make it cover a multitude of types of conduct as does the common-law breach-of-the-peace charge. On the contrary, these words narrow the scope of the offense. . . .

Under the foregoing testimony the jury was authorized to find that the State had proven every essential element of the crime, as it was defined by the state court. That interpretation is, of course, binding on us, leaving only the question of whether conviction of the state offense, thus defined, unconstitutionally deprives petitioners of their rights to freedom of speech, press, assembly or petition. We hold it does not. The sheriff, as jail custodian, had power, as the state courts have here held, to direct that this large crowd of people get off the grounds. There is not a shred of evidence in this record that this power was exercised, or that its exercise was sanctioned by the lower courts, because the sheriff objected to what was being sung or said by the demonstrators or because he disagreed with the objectives of their protest. The record reveals that he objected only to their presence on that part of the jail grounds reserved for jail uses. There is no evidence at all that on any other occasion had similarly large groups of the public been permitted to gather on this portion of the jail grounds for any purpose. Nothing in the Constitution of the United States prevents Florida from even-handed enforcement of its general trespass statute against those refusing to obey the sheriff's order to remove themselves from what amounted to the curtilage of the jailhouse. The State, no less than a private owner of property, has power to preserve the property under its control for the use to which it is lawfully dedicated. For this reason there is no merit to the petitioners' argument that they had a constitutional right to stay on the property, over the jail custodian's objections, because this "area chosen for the peaceful civil rights demonstration was not only 'reasonable' but also particularly appropriate . . . ." Such an argument has as its major unarticulated premise the assumption that people who want to propagandize protests or views have a constitutional right to do so whenever and however and wherever they please. That concept of constitutional law was vigorously and forthrightfully rejected in two of the cases petitioners rely on, *Cox* v. *State of Louisiana, supra,* at 554–555 and 563–564. We reject it again. The United States Constitution does not forbid a State to control the use of its own property for its own lawful nondiscriminatory purpose.

Mr. Justice Douglas, with whom The Chief Justice, Mr. Justice Brennan, and Mr. Justice Fortas concur, dissenting. . . .

The jailhouse, like an executive mansion, a legislative chamber, a courthouse, or the statehouse itself (*Edwards* v. *South Carolina, supra*) is one of the seats of government whether it be the Tower of London, the Bastille, or a small county jail. And when it houses political prisoners or those whom many think are unjustly held, it is an obvious center for protest. . . .

There is no question that petitioners had as their purpose a protest against the arrest of Florida A. & M. students for trying to integrate public theatres. The sheriff's testimony indicates that he well understood the purpose of the rally. . . . *Cox* v. *State of Louisiana,* 379 U.S. 536, 546–548. There was no violence; no threats of violence; no attempted jail break; no storming of a prison; no plan or plot to do anything but protest. . . .

We do violence to the First Amendment when we permit this "petition for redress of grievances" to be turned into a trespass action. . . .

There may be some public places which are so clearly committed to other purposes that their use for the airing of grievances is anomalous. There may be some instances in which assemblies and petitions for redress of grievances are not consistent with other necessary purposes of public property. A noisy meeting may be out of keeping with the serenity of the statehouse or the quiet of the courthouse. . . . But this is quite different than saying that all public places are off-limits to people with grievances. . . . And it is farther yet from saying that the "custodian" of the public property in his discretion can decide when public places shall be used for the communication of ideas, especially the constitutional right to assemble and petition for redress of grievances. . . .

Tinker v. *Des Moines School District*
393 U.S. 503 (1969)

School authorities outlawed the wearing of black armbands in school to publicize opposition to the Vietnam War. Tinker and others defied this ruling and were suspended. This case was initiated to overturn the suspension.

Mr. Justice Fortas delivered the opinion of the Court. . . .

The District Court recognized that the wearing of an armband for the purpose of expressing certain views is the type of symbolic act that is within the Free Speech Clause of the First Amendment. See *West Virginia State Board of Education* v. *Barnette,* 319 U.S. 624 (1943); *Stromberg* v. *California,* 283 U.S. 359 (1931) . . . . As we shall discuss, the wearing of armbands in the circumstances of this case was entirely divorced from actually or potentially disruptive conduct by those particiating in it. It was closely akin to "pure speech" which, we have repeatedly held, is entitled to comprehensive protection under the First Amendment. Compare *Cox* v. *Louisiana,* 379 U.S. 536, 555 (1965); *Adderley* v. *Florida,* 385 U.S. 39 (1966).

First Amendment rights, applied in light of the special characteristics of the school environment, are available to teachers and students. It can hardly be argued that either students or teachers shed their constitutional rights to freedom of speech or expression at the schoolhouse gate. This has been the unmistakable holding of this Court for almost 50 years. In *Meyer* v. *Nebraska,* 262 U.S. 390 (1923), and *Bartels* v. *Iowa,* 262 U.S. 404 (1923), this Court, in opinions by Mr. Justice McReynolds, held that the Due Process Clause of the Fourteenth Amendment prevents States from forbidding the teaching of a foreign language to young students. Statutes to this effect, the Court held, unconstitutionally interfere with the liberty of teacher, student, and parent. . . .

On the other hand, the Court has repeatedly emphasized the need for affirming the comprehensive authority of the States and of school authorities, consistent with fundamental constitutional safeguards, to prescribe and control conduct in the schools. See *Epperson* v. *Arkansas, supra,* 393 U.S. at 104; *Meyer* v. *Nebraska, supra,* 262 U.S. at 402. Our problem lies in the area where students in the exercise of First Amendment rights collide with the rules of the school authorities.

The problem presented by the present case does not relate to regulation of the length of skirts or the type of clothing, to hair style or deportment. . . . It does not concern aggressive, disruptive action or even group demonstrations. Our problem involves direct, primary First Amendment rights akin to "pure speech."

The school officials banned and sought to punish petitioners for a silent, passive, expression of opinion, unaccompanied by any disorder or disturbance on the part of petitioners. There is here no evidence whatever of petitioners' interference, actual or nascent, with the school's work or of collision with the rights of other students to be secure and to be let alone. . . .

The District Court concluded that the action of the school authorities was reasonable because it was based upon their fear of a disturbance from the wearing of the armbands. But, in our system, undifferentiated fear or apprehension of disturbance is not enough to overcome the right to freedom of expression. Any departure from absolute regimentation may cause trouble. . . .

In order for the State in the person of school officials to justify prohibition of a particular expression of opinion, it must be able to show that its action was caused by something more than a mere desire to avoid the discomfort and unpleasantness that always accompany an unpopular viewpoint. Certainly where there is no finding and no showing that the exercise of the forbidden right would "materially and substantially interfere with the requirements of appropriate discipline in the operation of the school," the prohibition cannot be sustained. *Burnside* v. *Byars,* 363 F.2d at 749.

In the present case, the District Court made no such finding, and our independent examination of the record fails to yield evidence that the school authorities had reason to anticipate that the wearing of the armbands would substantially interfere with the work of the school or impinge upon the rights of other students. Even an official memorandum prepared after the suspension that listed the reasons for the ban on wearing the armbands made no reference to the anticipation of such disruption.

On the contrary, the action of the school authorities appears to have been based upon an urgent wish to avoid the controversy which might result from the expression, even by the silent symbol of armbands, of opposition to this Nation's part in the conflagration in Vietnam. . . .

It is also relevant that the school authorities did not purport to prohibit the wearing of all symbols of political or controversial significance. The record shows that students in some of the schools wore buttons relating to national political campaigns, and some even wore the Iron Cross, traditionally a symbol of Nazism. The order prohibiting the wearing of armbands did not extend to these. Instead, a particular symbol—black armbands worn to exhibit opposition to this Nation's involvement in Vietnam—was singled out for prohibition. Clearly, the prohibition of expression of one particular opinion, at least without evidence that it is necessary to avoid material and substantial interference with school work or discipline, is not constitutionally permissible. . . .

The principal use to which the schools are dedicated is to accommodate students during prescribed hours for the purpose of certain types of activities. Among those activities is personal intercommunication among the students. This is not only an inevitable part of the process of attending school, it is also an important part of the educational process. A student's rights therefore, do not embrace merely the classroom hours. When he is in the cafeteria, or on the playing field, or on the campus during the authorized hours, he may express his opinions, even on controversial subjects like the conflict in Vietnam, if he does so "[without] materially and substantially interfering with . . . appropriate discipline in the operation of the school" and without colliding with the rights of others. *Burnside* v. *Byars*, 363 F.2d at 749. But conduct by the student, in class or out of it, which for any reason—whether it stems from time, place, or type of behavior—materially disrupts classwork or involves substantial disorder or invasion of the rights of others is, of course, not immunized by the constitutional guaranty of freedom of speech. . . .

As we have discussed, the record does not demonstrate any facts which might reasonably have led school authorities to forecast substantial disruption of or material interference with school activities, and no disturbances or disorders on the school premises in fact occurred. These petitioners merely went about their ordained rounds in school. Their deviation consisted only in wearing on their sleeve a band of black cloth, not more than two inches wide. They wore it to exhibit their disapproval of the Vietnam hostilities and their advocacy of a truce, to make their views known, and by their example, to influence others to adopt them. They neither interrupted school activities nor sought to intrude in the school affairs or the lives of others. They caused discussion outside of the classrooms, but no interference with work and no disorder. In the circumstances, our Constitution does not permit officials of the State to deny their form of expression.

We express no opinion as to the form of relief which should be granted, this being a matter for the lower courts to determine. We reverse and remand for further proceedings consistent with this opinion.

Mr. Justice Stewart, concurring.

Although I agree with much of what is said in the Court's opinion, and with its judgment in this case, I cannot share the Court's uncritical assumption that, school discipline aside, the

First Amendment rights of children are co-extensive with those of adults. . . .

Mr. Justice White, concurring.

While I join the Court's opinion, I deem it appropriate to note, first, that the Court continues to recognize a distinction between communicating by words and communicating by acts or conduct which sufficiently impinge on some valid state interest. . . .

Mr. Justice Black, dissenting. . . .

While the record does not show that any of these armband students shouted, used profane language or were violent in any manner, a detailed report by some of them shows their armbands caused comments, warnings by other students, the poking of fun at them, and a warning by an older football player that other, non-protesting students had better let them alone. There is also evidence that the professor of mathematics had his lesson period practically "wrecked" chiefly by disputes with Beth Tinker, who wore her armband for her "demonstration." Even a casual reading of the record shows that this armband did divert students' minds from their regular lessons, and that talk, comments, etc., made John Tinker "self-conscious" in attending school with his armband. While the absence of obscene or boisterous and loud disorder perhaps justifies the Court's statement that the few armband students did not actually "disrupt" the classwork, I think the record overwhelmingly shows that the armbands did exactly what the elected school officials and principals foresaw it would, that is, took the students' minds off their classwork and diverted them to thoughts about the highly emotional subject of the Vietnam war. . . .

I deny . . . that it has been the "unmistakable holding of this Court for almost 50 years" that "students" and "teachers" take with them into the "schoolhouse gate" constitutional rights to "freedom of speech or expression." . . . The truth is that a teacher of kindergarten, grammar school, or high school pupils no more carries into a school with him a complete right to freedom of speech and expression than an anti-Catholic or anti-Semitic carries with him a complete freedom of speech and religion into a Catholic church or Jewish synagogue. Nor does a person carry with him into the United States Senate or House, or to the Supreme Court, or any other court, a complete constitutional right to go into those places contrary to their rules and speak his mind on any subject he pleases. It is a myth to say that any person has a constitutional right to say what he pleases, where he pleases, and when he pleases. Our Court has decided precisely the opposite. See, *e.g.*, *Cox* v. *Louisiana*, 379 U.S. 536, 555. . . .

Mr. Justice Harlan, dissenting. . . .

Note: Grayned v. *Rockford,* 408 U.S. 104 (1972), upheld a conviction for a demonstration in violation of a statute penalizing "the making of any noise or diversion which disturbs or tends to disturb the peace or good order of [a school]"— despite charges of vagueness and overbreadth.

THE PRIVATE FORUM

Hynes v. *Mayor and Council of Oradell*
425 U.S. 610 (1976)

A city ordinance required advance notice to the police department by anyone intending to "call from house to house for a recognized charitable . . . or political campaign or cause . . . in writing for identification only . . . ." The Court found this measure invalid on vagueness grounds, but indicated that otherwise such laws are acceptable.

Mr. Chief Justice Burger delivered the opinion of the Court . . . .

. . . [T]his Court has in several cases reviewed attempts by municipalities to regulate activities like canvassing and soliciting. Regulation in this area "must be done, and the restriction applied, in such a manner as not to intrude upon the rights of free speech and free assembly," *Thomas* v. *Collins,* 323 U.S. 516, 540–541 (1945). But in these very cases the Court has consistently recognized a municipality's power to protect its citizens from crime and undue annoyance by regulating soliciting and canvassing. A narrowly drawn ordinance, that does not vest in municipal officials the undefined power to determine what messages residents will hear may serve these important interests without running afoul of the First Amendment.

In reaching these results, the Court acknowledged the valid and important interests these ordinances sought to serve. In *Martin* [v. Struthers], 319 U.S. at 144, Mr. Justice Black writing for the Court stated:

"Ordinances of the sort now before us may be aimed at the protection of the householders from annoyance, including intrusion upon the hours of rest, and at the prevention of crime. Constant callers, whether selling pots or distributing leaflets, may lessen the peaceful enjoyment of a home as much as a neighborhood glue factory or railroad yard which zoning ordinances may prohibit. . . .

"In addition, burglars frequently pose as canvassers, either in order that they may have a pretense to discover whether a house is empty and hence ripe for burglary, or for the purpose of spying out the premises in order that they may return later. Crime prevention may thus be the purpose of regulatory ordinances."

As Mr. Justice Black suggested, the lone housewife has no way of knowing whether the purposes of the putative solicitor are benign or malignant, and even an innocuous caller "may lessen the peaceful enjoyment of a home." *Ibid.* In his view a municipality "can by identification devices" regulate canvassers in order to deter criminal conduct by persons "posing as canvassers," . . . Professor Zechariah Chafee articulated something of the householder's right-to-be-let-alone, saying:

> "Of all the methods of spreading unpopular ideas, [house to house canvassing] seems the least entitled to extensive protection. The possibilities of persuasion are slight compared with the certainties of annoyance. Great as is the value of exposing citizens to novel views, home is one place where a man ought to be able to shut himself up in his own ideas if he desires." *Free Speech in the United States* (2d ed., 1941) 406–407.

Professor Chafee went on to note that these cases "do not invalidate all ordinances that include within their scope . . . doorway dissemination of thought. Several sentences in the opinions state that ordinances suitably designed to take care of legitimate social interests are not void." *Id.*, at 407.

There is, of course, no absolute right under the Federal Constitution to enter on the private premises of another and knock on a door for any purpose, and the police power permits reasonable regulation for public safety. We cannot say, and indeed appellants do not argue, that door-to-door canvassing and solicitation are immune from regulation under the State's police power, whether the purpose of the regulation is to protect from danger or to protect the peaceful enjoyment of the home. See *Rowan* v. *Post Office Dept.*, 397 U.S. 728, 735–738 (1970). . . .

[Justices Brennan and Marshall agreed with the Court on the vagueness issue, but disagreed otherwise, as follows:]

. . . Contrary to the thrust . . . of the Court's opinion, it seems inescapable that ordinances of the Oradell type, however precisely drafted to avoid the pitfalls of vagueness, must present substantial First Amendment questions. The imperiling of precious constitutional values, for reasons however justifiable, cannot be taken lightly. The prevention of crime is of course one of the most serious of modern-day problems. But our perception as individuals of the need to solve that particular problem should not color our judgment as to the constitutionality of measures aimed at that end.

[Mr. Justice Rehnquist dissented on the vagueness issue. Mr. Justice Stevens did not participate in the decision.]

Hudgens v. *NLRB*
424 U.S. 507 (1976)

This case involved picketing at a retail store in a *privately owned shopping center* by a union involved in a dispute with the store owner with respect to his operation of a distant warehouse.

Marsh v. *Alabama*, 326 U.S. 501 (1946), involved freedom of speech on the sidewalk of a privately owned "company town." The Court held that such a town came within the protection of the First and Fourteenth Amendments because it was the functional equivalent of "any other [i.e., public] town." (See the "state-action" problem in Chapter 10, below.)

Mr. Justice Stewart delivered the opinion of the Court . . . .

It was the *Marsh* case that in 1968 provided the foundation for the Court's decision in *Amalgamated Food Employees Union Local 590* v. *Logan Valley Plaza, Inc.*, 391 U.S. 308. That case involved peaceful picketing within a large shopping center near Altoona, Pa. One of the tenants of the shopping center was a retail store that employed a wholly nonunion staff. Members of a local union picketed the store, carrying signs proclaiming that it was nonunion and that its employees were not receiving union wages or other union benefits. The picketing took place on the shopping center's property in the immediate vicinity of the store. A Pennsylvania court issued an injunction that required all picketing to be confined to public areas outside the shopping center, and the Supreme Court of Pennsylvania affirmed the issuance of this injunction. This Court held that the doctrine of the *Marsh* case required reversal of that judgment. . . .

Four years later the Court had occasion to reconsider the *Logan Valley* doctrine in *Lloyd Corp.* v. *Tanner*, 407 U.S. 551. That case involved a shopping center covering some 50 acres in downtown Portland, Ore. On a November day in 1968 five young people entered the mall of the shopping center and distributed handbills protesting the then ongoing American military operations in Vietnam. Security guards told them to leave, and they did so, "to avoid arrest." 407 U.S., at 556. They subsequently brought suit in a federal district court, seeking declaratory and injunctive relief. The trial court ruled in their favor, holding that the distribution of handbills on the shopping center's property was protected by the First and Fourteenth Amendments. The Court of Appeals for the Ninth Circuit affirmed the judgment, 446 F.2d 545, expressly relying on this Court's *Marsh* and *Logan*

Valley decisions. This Court reversed the judgment of the Court of Appeals.

The Court in its *Lloyd* opinion did not say that it was overruling the *Logan Valley* decision. Indeed a substantial portion of the Court's opinion in *Lloyd* was devoted to pointing out the differences between the two cases, noting particularly that, in contrast to the handbilling in *Lloyd,* the picketing in *Logan Valley* had been specifically directed to a store in the shopping center and the picketers had had no other reasonable opportunity to reach their intended audience. 407 U.S., at 561–567. But the fact is that the reasoning of the Court's opinion in *Lloyd* cannot be squared with the reasoning of the Court's opinion in *Logan Valley.*

It matters not that some members of the Court may continue to believe that the *Logan Valley* case was rightly decided. Our institutional duty is to follow until changed the law as it now is, not as some members of the Court might wish it to be. And in the performance of that duty we make clear now, if it was not clear before, that the rationale of *Logan Valley* did not survive the Court's decision in the *Lloyd* case. . . .

If a large self-contained shopping center *is* the functional equivalent of a municipality, as *Logan Valley* held, then the First and Fourteenth Amendments would not permit control of speech within such a center to depend upon the speech's content. For while a municipality may constitutionally impose reasonable time, place, and manner regulations on the use of its streets and sidewalks for First Amendment purposes, see *Cox* v. *New Hampshire,* 312 U.S. 569, *Poulos* v. *New Hampshire,* 345 U.S. 395, and may even forbid altogether such use of some of its facilities, see *Adderley* v. *Florida,* 385 U.S. 39, what a municipality may *not* do under the First and Fourteenth Amendments is to discriminate in the regulation of expression on the basis of the content of that expression. *Erznoznik* v. *City of Jacksonville*, 422 U.S. 205. "[A]bove all else, the First Amendment means that government has no power to restrict expression because of its message, its ideas, its subject matter, or its content." *Police Department of Chicago* v. *Mosley*, 408 U.S. 92, 95. It conversely follows, therefore, that if the respondents in the *Lloyd* case did not have a First Amendment right to enter that shopping center to distribute handbills concerning Vietnam, then the respondents in the present case did not have a First Amendment right to enter this shopping center for the purpose of advertising their strike against the Butler Shoe Company.

We conclude, in short, that under the present state of the law the constitutional guarantee of free expression has no part to play in a case such as this.

From what has been said it follows that the rights and liabilities of the parties in this case are dependent exclusively upon the National Labor Relations Act. . . .

For the reasons stated in this opinion, the judgment is vacated and the case is remanded to the Court of Appeals with directions to remand to the National Labor Relations Board, so that the case may be there considered under the statutory criteria on the National Labor Relations Act alone.

Mr. Justice Stevens took no part in the consideration or decision of this case.

Mr. Justice Powell, with whom the Chief Justice joins, concurring.

Although I agree with Mr. Justice White's concurring view that *Lloyd Corp.* v. *Tanner*, 407 U.S. 551 (1972), did not overrule *Amalgamated Food Employees Union* v. *Logan Valley Plaza*, 391 U.S. 308 (1968), and that the present case can be distinguished narrowly from *Logan Valley*, I nevertheless have joined the opinion of the Court today. . . .

Mr. Justice White, concurring in the judgment.

While I concur in the result reached by the Court, I find it unnecessary to inter *Amalgamated Food Employees Union Local 590* v. *Logan Valley Plaza, Inc.*, 391 U.S. 308 (1968), and therefore do not join the Court's opinion. I agree that "the constitutional guarantee of free expression has no part to play in a case such as this," *ante*, p. 1037; but *Lloyd Corp.* v. *Tanner*, 407 U.S. 551 (1972), did not overrule *Logan Valley*, either expressly or implicitly, and I would not, somewhat after the fact, say that it did. . . .

Mr. Justice Marshall, with whom Mr. Justice Brennan joins, dissenting. . . .

In the final analysis, the Court's rejection of any role for the First Amendment in the privately owned shopping center complex stems, I believe, from an overly formalistic view of the relationship between the institution of private ownership of property and the First Amendment's guarantee of freedom of speech. No one would seriously question the legitimacy of the values of privacy and individual autonomy traditionally associated with privately owned property. But property that is privately owned is not always held for private use, and when a property owner opens his property to public use the force of those values diminishes. A degree of privacy is necessarily surrendered; thus, the privacy interest that petitioner retains when he leases space to 60 retail businesses and invites the public onto his land for the transaction of business with other members of the public is small indeed. Cf. *Paris Adult Theatre I* v. *Slaton*, 413 U.S. 49, 65–67 (1973). And while the owner of property open to public use may not automatically surrender any of his autonomy interest in managing the property as he sees fit, there is nothing new about the notion that that autonomy interest must be accommodated with the interests of the public. . . .

The interest of members of the public in communicating with one another on subjects relating to the businesses that occupy a modern shopping center is substantial. Not only employees with a labor dispute, but also consumers with complaints against business establishments, may look to the location of a retail store as the only reasonable avenue for effective communication with the public. As far as these groups are concerned, the shopping center owner has assumed the traditional role of the state in its control of historical First Amendment forums. *Lloyd* and *Logan Valley* recognized the vital role the First Amendment has to play in such cases, and I believe that this Court errs when it holds otherwise.

OFFENSIVE WORDS AND THE HOSTILE AUDIENCE

Chaplinsky v. *New Hampshire* (summary)
315 U.S. 568 (1942)

New Hampshire law prohibited words in a public place "likely to cause an average addressee to fight—face-to-face words plainly likely to cause a breach of the peace by the addressee." The Court deemed it "unnecessary to demonstrate" that the words appellant had applied to a city official—"damned racketeer" and "damned Fascist"—"are likely to provoke the average person to retaliation." This was in 1942! Upholding appellant's conviction, the Court unanimously made this famous observation:

> There are certain well-defined and narrowly limited classes of speech, the prevention and punishment of which have never been thought to raise any Constitutional problem. These include the lewd and obscene, the profane, the libelous, and the insulting or "fighting" words—those which by their very utterance inflict injury or tend to incite an immediate breach of the peace. It has been well observed that such utterances are no essential part of any exposition of ideas, and are of such slight social value as a step to truth that any benefit that may be derived from them is clearly outweighed by the social interest in order and morality. "Resort to epithets or personal abuse is not in any proper sense communication of information or opinion safeguarded by the Constitution, and its punishment as a criminal act would raise no question under that instrument." *Cantwell* v. *Connecticut,* 310 U.S. 296, 309–310.

Gooding v. *Wilson*
See p. 420, above. In the course of its opinion in this case, the Court reaffirmed the *Chaplinsky* fighting-words doctrine.

Feiner v. *New York*
See p. 441, above.

Cohen v. *California*
403 U.S. 15 (1971)

Mr. Justice Harlan delivered the opinion of the Court.

This case may seem at first blush too inconsequential to find its way into our books, but the issue it presents is of no small constitutional significance.

Appellant Paul Robert Cohen was convicted in the Los Angeles Municipal Court of violating that part of California Penal Code § 415 which prohibits "maliciously and willfully disturb[ing] the peace or quiet of any neighborhood or person [by] offensive conduct." He was given 30 days' imprisonment. The facts upon which his conviction rests are detailed in the opinion of the Court of Appeal of California:

> "On April 26, 1968, the defendant was observed in the Los Angeles County Courthouse in the corridor outside of Division 20 of the Municipal Court wearing a jacket bearing the words 'Fuck the Draft' which were plainly visible. There were women and children present in the corridor. The defendant was arrested. The defendant testified that he wore the jacket as a means of informing the public of the depth of his feelings against the Vietnam War and the draft.
>
> "The defendant did not engage in, nor threaten to engage in, nor did anyone as the result of his conduct in fact commit or threaten to commit any act of violence. The defendant did not make any loud or unusual noise, nor was there any evidence that he uttered any sound prior to his arrest."

In affirming the conviction the Court of Appeal held that "offensive conduct" means "behavior which has a tendency to provoke *others* to acts of violence or to in turn disturb the peace," and that the State had proved this element because, on the facts of this, "[i]t was certainly reasonably foreseeable that such conduct might cause others to rise up to commit a violent act against the person of the defendant or attempt to forceably remove his jacket."

. . . [A]s it comes to us, this case cannot be said to fall within those relatively few categories of instances where prior decisions have established the power of government to deal more comprehensively with certain forms of individual expression simply upon a showing that such a form was employed. This is not, for example, an obscenity case. Whatever else may be necessary to give rise to the States' broader power to prohibit obscene expression, such expression must be, in some significant way, erotic. *Roth* v. *United States,* 354 U.S. 476 (1957). It cannot plausibly be maintained that this vulgar allusion to the Selective Service System would conjure up such psychic stimulation in anyone likely to be confronted with Cohen's crudely defaced jacket.

This Court has also held that the States are free to ban the simple use, without a demonstration of additional justifying circumstances, of so-called "fighting words," those personally abusive epithets which, when addressed to the ordinary citizen, are, as a matter of common knowledge, inherently likely to provoke violent reaction. *Chaplinsky* v. *New Hampshire,* 315 U.S. 568 (1942). While the four-letter word displayed by Cohen in relation to the draft is not uncommonly employed in a personally provocative fashion, in this instance it was clearly not "directed to the person of the hearer." *Cantwell* v. *Connecticut,* 310 U.S. 296, 309 (1940). No individual actually or likely to be present could reasonably have regarded the words on appellant's jacket as a direct personal insult. Nor do we have here an instance of the exercise of the State's police power to prevent a speaker from intentionally provoking a given group to hostile reaction. Cf. *Feiner* v. *New York,* 340 U.S. 315 (1951); *Terminiello* v. *Chicago,* 337 U.S. 1 (1949). There is, as noted above, no showing that anyone who saw Cohen was in fact violently aroused or that appellant intended such a result.

Finally, in arguments before this Court much has been made of the claim that Cohen's distasteful mode of expression was thrust upon unwilling or unsuspecting viewers, and that the State might therefore legitimately act as it did in order to protect the sensitive from otherwise unavoidable exposure to appellant's crude form of protest. Of course, the mere presumed presence of unwitting listeners or viewers does not serve automatically to justify curtailing all speech capable of giving offense. See *e.g., Organization For a Better Austin* v. *Keefe*, 402 U.S. 415 (1971). While this Court has recognized that government may properly act in many situations to prohibit intrusion into the privacy of the home of unwelcome views and ideas which cannot be totally banned from the public dialogue, *e.g., Rowan* v. *Postmaster General*, 397 U.S. 728 (1970), we have at the same time consistently stressed that "we are often 'captives' outside the sanctuary of the home and subject to objectionable speech." *Id.*, at 738. The ability of government, consonant with the Constitution, to shut off discourse solely to protect others from hearing it is, in other words, dependent upon a showing that substantial privacy interests are being invaded in an essentially intolerable manner. Any broader view of this authority would effectively empower a majority to silence dissidents simply as a matter of personal predilections.

In this regard, persons confronted with Cohen's jacket were in a quite different posture than, say, those subjected to the raucous emissions of sound trucks blaring outside their residences. Those in the Los Angeles courthouse could effectively avoid further bombardment of their sensibilities simply by averting their eyes. And while it may be that one has a more substantial claim to a recognizable privacy interest when walking through a courthouse corridor than, for example, strolling through Central Park, surely it is nothing like the interest in being free from unwanted expression in the confines of one's own home. Cf. *Keefe, supra.* Given the subtlety and complexity of the factors involved, if Cohen's "speech" was otherwise entitled to constitutional protection, we do not think the fact that some unwilling "listeners" in a public building may have been briefly exposed to it can serve to justify this breach of the peace conviction where, as here, there was no evidence that persons powerless to avoid appel-

lant's conduct did in fact object to it, and where that portion of the statute upon which Cohen's conviction rests evinces no concern, either on its face or as construed by the California courts, with the special plight of the captive auditor, but, instead, indiscriminately sweeps within its prohibitions all "offensive conduct" that disturbs "any neighborhood or person."

Against this background, the issue flushed by this case stands out in bold relief. It is whether California can excise, as "offensive conduct," one particular scurrilous epithet from the public discourse, either upon the theory of the court below that its use is inherently likely to cause violent reaction or upon a more general assertion that the States, acting as guardians of public morality, may properly remove this offensive word from the public vocabulary.

The rationale of the California court is plainly untenable. . . . We have been shown no evidence that substantial numbers of citizens are standing ready to strike out physically at whoever may assault their sensibilities with execrations like that uttered by Cohen. . . .

Admittedly, it is not so obvious that the First and Fourteenth Amendments must be taken to disable the States from punishing public utterance of this unseemly expletive in order to maintain what they regard as a suitable level of discourse within the body politic. We think, however, that examination and reflection will reveal the shortcomings of a contrary viewpoint. . . .

Against this perception of the constitutional policies involved, we discern certain more particularized considerations that peculiarly call for reversal of this conviction. First, the principle contended for by the State seems inherently boundless. How is one to distinguish this from any other offensive word? . . . For, while the particular four-letter word being litigated here is perhaps more distasteful than most others of its genre, it is nevertheless often true that one man's vulgarity is another's lyric. Indeed, we think it is largely because governmental officials cannot make principled distinctions in this area that the Constitution leaves matters of taste and style so largely to the individual.

Additionally, we cannot overlook the fact, because it is well illustrated by the episode involved here, that much linguistic expression serves a dual communicative function: it conveys not only ideas capable of relatively precise, detached explication, but otherwise inexpressible emotions as well. In fact, words are often chosen as much for their emotive as their cognitive force. . . .

Finally, and in the same vein, we cannot indulge the facile assumption that one can forbid particular words without also running a substantial risk of suppressing ideas in the process. Indeed, governments might soon seize upon the censorship of particular words as a convenient guise for banning the expression of unpopular views. . . .

It is, in sum, our judgment that, absent a more particularized and compelling reason for its actions, the State may not, consistently with the First and Fourteenth Amendments, make the simple public display here involved of this single four-letter expletive a criminal offense. . . .

Mr. Justice Blackmun, with whom The Chief Justice and Mr. Justice Black join.

I dissent. . . .

Cohen's absurd and immature antic, in my view, was mainly conduct and little speech.

FCC v. *Pacifica Foundation* (excerpt)
98 S. Ct. 3026 (1978)

The FCC penalized a radio station for broadcasting a 12-minute selection called "Filthy Words" from a satirical comedy album by a Mr. Carlin. His effort was part of a program devoted to contemporary attitudes toward language. Seven very crude words were repeated over and over in a variety of usages. The Court upheld the penalty with these observations:

We have long recognized that each medium of expression presents special First Amendment problems. *Joseph Burstyn, Inc.* v. *Wilson*, 343 U.S. 495, 502–503. And of all forms of communication, it is broadcasting that has received the most limited First Amendment protection. Thus, although other speakers cannot be licensed except under laws that carefully define and narrow official discretion, a broadcaster may be deprived of his license and his forum if the Commission decides that such an action would serve "the public interest, convenience, and necessity." Similarly, although the First Amendment protects newspaper publishers from being required to print the replies of those whom they criticize, *Miami Herald Publishing Co.* v. *Tornillo*, 418 U.S. 241, it affords no such protection to broadcasters; on the contrary, they must give free time to the victims of their criticism. *Red Lion Broadcasting Co., Inc.* v. *FCC*, 395 U.S. 367.

The reasons for these distinctions are complex, but two have relevance to the present case. First, the broadcast media have established a uniquely pervasive presence in the lives of all Americans. Patently offensive, indecent material presented over the airwaves confronts the citizen, not only in public, but also in the privacy of the home, where the individual's right to be let alone plainly outweighs the First Amendment rights of an intruder. *Rowan* v. *Post Office Department*, 397 U.S. 728. Because the broadcast audience is constantly tuning in and out, prior warnings cannot completely protect the listener or viewer from unexpected program content. To say that one may avoid further offense by turning off the radio when he hears indecent language is like saying that the remedy for an assault is to run away after the first blow. One may hang up on an indecent phone call, but that option does not give the caller a constitutional immunity or avoid a harm that has already taken place.

Second, broadcasting is uniquely accessible to children, even those too young to read. Although Cohen's written message might have been incomprehensible to a first grader, Pacifica's broadcast could have enlarged a child's vocabulary in an instant. Other forms of offensive expression may be withheld from the young without restricting the expression at its source. Bookstores and motion picture theaters, for example, may be prohibited from making indecent material available to children. We held in *Ginsberg* v. *New York*, 390 U.S. 629, that the government's interest in the "well being of its youth" and in supporting "parents' claim to authority in their own household" justified the regulation of otherwise protected expression. . . . The ease with which children may obtain access to broadcast material, coupled with the concerns recognized in *Ginsberg*, amply justify special treatment of indecent broadcasting.

It is appropriate, in conclusion, to emphasize the narrowness of our holding. This case does not involve a two-way radio conversation between a cab driver and a dispatcher, or a telecast of an Elizabethan comedy. We have not decided that an occasional expletive in either setting would justify any sanction or, indeed, that this broadcast would justify a criminal prosecution. The Commission's decision rested entirely on a nuisance rationale under which context is all-important. The concept requires consideration of a host of variables. The time of day was emphasized by the Commission. The content of the program in which the language is used will also affect the composition of the audience, and differences between radio, television, and perhaps closed-circuit transmissions, may also be relevant. As Mr. Justice Sutherland wrote, a "nuisance may be merely a right thing in the wrong place—like a pig in the parlor instead of the barnyard." *Euclid* v. *Amber Realty Co.*, 272 U.S. 365, 388. We simply hold that when the Commission finds that a pig has entered the parlor, the exercise of its regulatory power does not depend on proof that the pig is obscene.

Mr. Justice Powell, with whom Mr. Justice Blackmun joins, concurring. . . .

Mr. Justice Brennan, with whom Mr. Justice Marshall joins, dissenting.

I.

For the second time in two years, see *Young* v. *American Mini Theatres*, 427 U.S. 50 (1976), the Court refuses to embrace the notion, completely antithetical to basic First Amendment values, that the degree of protection the First Amendment affords protected speech varies with the social value ascribed to that speech by five Members of this Court. . . . Moreover, as do all parties, all Members of the Court agree that the Carlin monologue aired by Station WBAI does not fall within one of the categories of speech, such as "fighting words," . . . or obscenity, . . . that is totally without First Amendment protection. This conclusion, of course, is compelled by our cases expressly holding that communications containing some of the words found condemnable here are fully protected by the First Amendment in other contexts. . . . Yet despite the Court's refusal to create a sliding scale of First Amendment protection calibrated to this Court's perception of the worth of a communication's content, and despite our unanimous agreement that the Carlin monologue is protected speech, a majority of the Court nevertheless finds that, on the facts of this case, the FCC is not constitutionally barred from imposing sanctions on Pacifica for its airing of the Carlin monologue. This majority apparently believes that the FCC's disapproval of Pacifica's afternoon broadcast of Carlin's "Dirty Words" recording is a permissible time, place, and manner regulation. *Kovacs* v. *Cooper*, 336 U.S. 77 (1949). Both the opinion of my Brother Stevens and the opinion of my Brother Powell rely principally on two factors in reaching this conclusion: (1) the capacity of a radio broadcast to intrude into the unwilling listener's home, and (2) the presence of children in the listening audience. Dispassionate analysis, removed from individual notions as to what is proper and what is not, starkly reveals that these justifications, whether individually or together, simply do not support even the professedly moderate degree of governmental homogenization of radio communications—if, indeed, such homogenization can ever be moderate given the pre-eminent status of the right of free speech in our constitutional scheme—that the Court today permits.

A

Without question, the privacy interests of an individual in his home are substantial and deserving of significant protection. In finding these interests sufficient to justify the content regulation of protected speech, however, the Court commits two errors. First, it misconceives the nature of the privacy interests involved where an individual voluntarily chooses to admit radio communications into his home. Second, it ignores the constitutionally protected interests of both those who wish to transmit and those who desire to receive broadcasts that many—including the FCC and this Court— might find offensive.

. . . I believe that an individual's actions in switching on and listening to communications transmitted over the public airways and directed to the public at-large do not implicate fundamental privacy interests, even when engaged in within the home. Instead, because the radio is undeniably a public medium, these actions are more properly viewed as a decision to take part, if only as a listener, in an ongoing public discourse. . . . Although an individual's decision to allow public radio communications into his home undoubtedly does not abrogate all of his privacy interests, the residual privacy interests he retains vis-à-vis the communication he voluntarily admits into his home are surely no greater than those of the people present in the corridor of the Los Angeles courthouse in *Cohen* who bore witness to the words "Fuck the Draft" emblazoned across Cohen's jacket. Their privacy interests were held insufficient to justify punishing Cohen for his offensive communication.

Even if an individual who voluntarily opens his home to radio communications retains privacy interests of sufficient moment to justify a ban on protected speech if those interests are "invaded in an essentially intolerable manner," *Cohen* v. *California, supra,* at 21, the very fact that those interests are threatened only by a radio broadcast precludes any intolerable invasion of privacy; for unlike other intrusive modes of communication, such as sound trucks, "[t]he radio can be turned off," . . . Where the individuals comprising the offended majority may freely choose to reject the material being offered, we have never found their privacy interests of such moment to warrant the suppression of speech on privacy grounds. . . .

B

Most parents will undoubtedly find understandable as well as commendable the Court's sympathy with the FCC's desire to prevent offensive broadcasts from reaching the ears of unsupervised children. Unfortunately, the facial appeal of this justification for radio censorship masks its constitutional insufficiency. . . . The opinion of my Brother Powell acknowledges that there lurks in today's decision a potential for "'reduc[ing] the adult population . . . to [hearing] only what is fit for children,'" . . . but expresses faith that the FCC will vigilantly prevent this potential from ever becoming a reality. I am far less certain than my Brother Powell that such faith in the Commission is warranted, . . . and even if I shared it, I could not so easily shirk the responsibility assumed by each Member of this Court jealously to guard against encorachments on First Amendment freedoms.

In concluding that the presence of children in the listening audience provides an adequate basis for the FCC to impose sanctions for Pacifica's broadcast of the Carlin monologue, the opinions of my Brother Powell, . . . and my Brother Stevens, *ante*, at 21, both stress the time-honored right of a parent to raise his child as he sees fit—a right this Court has consistently been vigilant to protect. See *Wisconsin* v. *Yoder*, 406 U.S. 205 (1972); *Pierce* v. *Society of Sisters*, 268 U.S. 510 (1925). Yet this principle supports a result directly contrary to that reached by the Court. *Yoder* and *Pierce* hold that parents, *not* the government, have the right to make certain decisions regarding the upbringing of their children. As surprising as it may be to individual Members of this Court, some parents may actually find Mr. Carlin's unabashed attitude towards the seven "dirty words" healthy, and deem it desirable to expose their children to the manner in which Mr. Carlin defuses the taboo surrounding the words. Such parents may constitute a minority of the American public, but the absence of great numbers willing to exercise the right to raise their children in this fashion does not alter the right's nature or its existence. Only the Court's regrettable decision does that. . . .

III.

It is quite evident that I find the Court's attempt to unstitch the warp and woof of First Amendment law in an effort to reshape its fabric to cover the patently wrong result the Court reaches in this case dangerous as well as lamentable. Yet there runs throughout the opinions of my Brothers Powell and Stevens another vein I find equally disturbing: a depressing inability to appreciate that in our land of cultural pluralism, there are many who think, act, and talk differently from the Members of this Court, and who do not share their fragile sensibilities. It is only an acute ethnocentric myopia that enables the Court to approve the censorship of communications solely because of the words they contain. . . .

Today's decision will thus have its greatest impact on broadcasters desiring to reach, and listening audiences comprised of, persons who do not share the Court's view as to which words or expressions are acceptable and who, for a variety of reasons, including a conscious desire to flout majoritarian conventions, express themselves using words that may be regarded as offensive by those from different socio-economic backgrounds. In this context, the Court's decision may be seen for what, in the broader perspective, it really is: another of the dominant culture's inevitable efforts to force those groups who do not share its mores to conform to its way of thinking, acting, and speaking. . . .

Mr. Justice Stewart, with whom Mr. Justice Brennan, Mr. Justice White, and Mr. Justice Marshall join, dissenting. . . .

. . . I think that "indecent" should properly be read as meaning no more than "obscene." Since the Carlin monologue concededly was not "obscene," I believe that the Commission lacked statutory authority to ban it. Under this construction of the statute, it is unnecessary to address the difficult and important issue of the Commission's constitutional power to prohibit speech that would be constitutionally protected outside the context of electronic broadcasting.

SYMBOLISM: ACTION THAT SPEAKS

Tinker v. *Des Moines School District*
See p. 452, above.

United States v. *O'Brien*
391 U.S. 367 (1968)

A s part of an antiwar demonstration, O'Brien burned his draft registration card before a large crowd. He was convicted for violating a federal law prohibiting destruction or mutilation of such cards.

Chief Justice Warren delivered the opinion of the Court . . . .

O'Brien first argues that the [statute] is unconstitutional as applied to him because his act of burning his registration certificate was protected "symbolic speech" within the First Amendment. His argument is that the freedom of expression which the First Amendment guarantees includes all modes of "communication of ideas by conduct," and that his conduct is within this definition because he did it in "demonstration against the war and against the draft."

We cannot accept the view that an apparently limitless variety of conduct can be labelled "speech" whenever the person engaging in the conduct intends thereby to express an idea. However, even on the assumption that the alleged communicative element in O'Brien's conduct is sufficient to bring into play the First Amendment, it does not necessarily follow that the destruction of a registration certificate is constitutionally protected activity. This Court has held that when "speech" and "nonspeech" elements are combined in the same course of conduct, a sufficiently important governmental interest in regulating the nonspeech element can justify incidental limitations on First Amendment freedoms. To characterize the quality of the governmental interest which must appear, the Court has employed a variety of descriptive terms: compelling; substantial; subor-

dinating; paramount; cogent; strong. Whatever imprecision inheres in these terms, we think it clear that a government regulation is sufficiently justified if it is within the constitutional power of the government; if it furthers an important or substantial governmental interest; if the governmental interest is unrelated to the suppression of free expression; and if the incidental restriction on alleged First Amendment freedom is no greater than is essential to the furtherance of that interest. We find that the [statute] meets all of these requrements, and consequently that O'Brien can be constitutionally convicted for violating it. . . .

The many functions performed by Selective Service certificates establish beyond doubt that Congress has a legitimate and substantial interest in preventing their wanton and unrestrained destruction and assuring their continuing availability by punishing people who knowingly and wilfully destroy or mutilate them. . . .

. . . The governmental interest and the scope of the [statute] are limited to preventing a harm to the smooth and efficient functioning of the Selective Service System. When O'Brien deliberately rendered unavailable his registration certificate, he wilfully frustrated this governmental interest. For this noncommunicative impact of his conduct, and nothing else, he was convicted.

The case at bar is therefore unlike one where the alleged governmental interest in regulating conduct arises in some measure because the communication allegedly integral to the conduct is itself thought to be harmful. In *Stromberg v. California,* 283 U.S. 359 (1931), for example, this Court struck down a statutory phrase which punished people who expressed their "opposition to organized government" by displaying "any flag, badge, banner, or device." Since the statute there was aimed at suppressing communication it could not be sustained as a regulation of noncommunicative conduct. . . .

In conclusion, we find that because of the Government's substantial interest in assuring the continuing availability of issued Selective Service certificates, because amended § 462(b) is an appropriately narrow means of protecting this interest and condemns only the independent noncommunicative impact of conduct within its reach, and because the noncommunicative impact of O'Brien's act of burning his registration certificate frustrated the Government's interest, a sufficient governmental interest has been shown to justify O'Brien's conviction. . . .

. . . O'Brien finally argues that the 1965 Amendment is unconstitutional as enacted because what he calls the "purpose" of Congress was "to suppress freedom of speech." We reject this argument because under settled principles the purpose of Congress, as O'Brien uses that term, is not a basis for declaring this legislation unconstitutional. . . .

Inquiries into congressional motives or purposes are a hazardous matter. When the issue is simply the interpretation of legislation, the Court will look to statements by legislators for guidance as to the purpose of the legislature, because the benefit to sound decision-making in this circumstance is thought sufficient to risk the possibility of misreading Congress' purpose. It is entirely a different matter when we are asked to void a statute that is, under well-settled criteria, constitutional on its face, on the basis of what fewer than a handful of Congressmen said about it. What motivates one legislator to make a speech about a statute is not necessarily what motivates scores of others to enact it, and the stakes are sufficiently high for us to eschew guesswork. We decline to void essentially on the ground that it is unwise [to void] legislation which Congress had the undoubted power to enact and which could be reenacted in its exact form if the same or another legislator made a "wiser" speech about it.

[Mr. Justice Douglas, dissenting, thought the case should be reargued on the issue of the constitutionality of peace-time conscription.]

> *Note:* At least as early as *Fletcher* v. *Peck,* 6 Cranch 87 (1810), and in a long string of cases thereafter (e.g., *Darby Lumber,* above, Chapter 3), the Court has held that judicial review is concerned with the *power* of a legislative, not its motives. In sum, good motives will not validate an unconstitutional act, nor will improper motives invalidate an otherwise constitutional act. But see the section entitled "Separation of Church and State" in Chapter 11, below, and *Washington* v. *Davis,* Chapter 9, below.

Spence v. *Washington*
418 U.S. 405 (1974)

Spence was convicted not of desecration, but of improper use, of his United States flag.

Per Curiam. . . .

The State based its case on the flag itself and the testimony of the three arresting officers, who testified that they had observed the flag displayed from appellant's window and that on the flag was superimposed what they identified as a peace symbol. Appellant took the stand in his own defense. He testified that he put a peace symbol on the flag and displayed it to public view as a protest to the invasion of Cambodia and the killings at Kent State University, events which occurred a few days prior to his arrest. He said that his purpose was to associate the American flag with peace instead of war and violence:

> "I felt there had been so much killing and that this was not what America stood for. I felt that the flag stood for America and I wanted people to know that I thought America stood for peace."

Appellant further testified that he chose to fashion the peace symbol from tape so that it could be removed without damaging the flag. The State made no effort to controvert any of appellant's testimony.

The trial court instructed the jury in essence that the mere act of displaying the flag with the peace symbol attached, if proven beyond a reasonable doubt, was sufficient to convict. There was no requirement of specific intent to do anything more than display the flag in that manner. The jury returned a verdict of guilty. The court sentenced appellant to 10 days in jail, suspended, and to a $75 fine. The Washington Court of Appeals reversed the conviction. 5 Wash.App. 752, 490 P.2d 1321 (1971). It held the improper use statute overbroad and invalid on its face under the First and Fourteenth Amendments. With one justice dissenting and two concurring in the result, the Washington Supreme Court reversed and reinstated the conviction. 81 Wash.2d 788, 506 P.2d 293 (1973).

A number of factors are important in the instant case. First, this was a privately-owned flag. In a technical property sense it was not the property of any government. We have no doubt that the state or national governments constitutionally may forbid anyone from mishandling in any manner a flag that is public property. But this is a different case. Second, appellant displayed his flag on private property. He engaged in no trespass or disorderly conduct. Nor is this

a case that might be analyzed in terms of reasonable time, place or manner restraints on access to a public area. Third, the record is devoid of proof of any risk of breach of the peace. It was not appellant's purpose to incite violence or even stimulate a public demonstration. There is no evidence that any crowd gathered or that appellant made any effort to attract attention beyond hanging the flag out of his own window. Indeed, on the facts stipulated by the parties there is no evidence that anyone other than the three police officers observed the flag.

Fourth, the State concedes, as did the Washington Supreme Court, that appellant engaged in a form of communication. Although the stipulated facts fail to show that any member of the general public viewed the flag, the State's concession is inevitable on this record. The undisputed facts are that appellant "wanted people to know that I thought America stood for peace." To be sure, appellant did not choose to articulate his views through printed or spoken words. It is therefore necessary to determine whether his activity was sufficiently imbued with elements of communication to fall within the scope of the First and Fourteenth Amendments, for as the Court noted in *United States* v. *O'Brient*, 391 U.S. 367, 376 (1968), "[w]e cannot accept the view that an apparently limitless variety of conduct can be labeled 'speech' whenever the person engaging in the conduct intends thereby to express an idea." But the nature of appellant's activity, combined with the factual context and environment in which it was undertaken, lead to the conclusion that he engaged in a form of protected expression.

The Court for decades has recognized the communicative connotations of the use of flags. E.g., *Stromberg* v. *California*, 283 U.S. 359 (1931). In many of their uses flags are a form of symbolism comprising a "primitive but effective way of communicating ideas . . . ," and "a short cut from mind to mind." *Board of Education* v. *Barnette*, 319 U.S. 624, 632 (1943). On this record there can be little doubt that appellant communicated through the use of symbols. The symbolism included not only the flag but also the superimposed peace symbol.

Moreover, the context in which a symbol is used for purposes of expression is important, for the context may give meaning to the symbol. See *Tinker* v. *Des Moines School District*, 393 U.S. 503 (1969). In *Tinker*, the wearing of black armbands in a school environment conveyed an unmistakable message about a contemporaneous issue of intense public concern—the Vietnam hostilities. *Id.*, at 505–514. In this case, appellant's activity was roughly simultaneous with and concededly triggered by the Cambodian incursion and the Kent State tragedy, also issues of great public moment. Cf. *Scheuer* v. *Rhodes*, 416 U.S. 232 (1974). A flag bearing a peace symbol and displayed upside down by a student today might be interpreted as nothing more than bizarre behavior, but it would have been difficult for the great majority of citizens to miss the drift of appellant's point at the time that he made it.

It may be noted, further, that this was not an act of mindless nihilism. Rather, it was a pointed expression of anguish by appellant about the then current domestic and foreign affairs of his government. An intent to convey a particularized message was present, and in the surrounding circumstances the likelihood was great that the message would be understood by those who viewed it.

We are confronted then with a case of prosecution for the expression of an idea through activity. Moreover, the activity occurred on private property, rather than in an environment over which the state by necessity must have certain supervisory powers unrelated to expression. . . . Accordingly, we must examine with particular care the interests advanced by appellee to support its prosecution. . . . The first interest at issue is prevention of breach of the peace. In our view, the Washington Supreme Court correctly rejected this notion. It is totally without support in the record.

We are also unable to affirm the judgment below on the ground that the State may have desired to protect the sensibilities of passersby. "It is firmly settled that under our Constitution the public expression of ideas may not be prohibited merely because the ideas are themselves offensive to some of their hearers." *Street* v. *New York*, *supra* [314 U.S. 576], at 592. Moreover, appellant did not impose his ideas upon a captive audience. Anyone who might have been offended could easily have avoided the display. See *Cohen* v. *California*, 403 U.S. 15 (1971). Nor may appellant be punished for failing to show proper respect for our national emblem. *Street* v. *New York*, *supra*, at 593; *Board of Education* v. *Barnette*, *supra*.

We are brought, then, to the state court's thesis that Washington has an interest in preserving the national flag as an unalloyed symbol of our country. The court did not define this interest; it simply asserted it. See 81 Wash.2d, at 799, 506 P.2d, at 300. The dissenting opinion today . . . adopts essentially the same approach. Presumably, this interest might be seen as an effort to prevent the appropriation of a revered national symbol by an individual, interest group, or enterprise where there was a risk that association of the symbol with a particular product or viewpoint might be taken erroneously as evidence of governmental endorsement. Alternatively, it might be argued that the interest asserted by the state court is based on the uniquely universal character of the national flag as a symbol. For the great majority of us, the flag is a symbol of patriotism, of pride in the history of our country, and of the service, sacrifice and valor of the millions of Americans who in peace and war have joined together to build and to defend a Nation in which self-government and personal liberty endure. It evidences both the unity and diversity which are America. For others the flag carries in varying degrees a different message. "A person gets from a symbol the meaning he puts into it, and what is one man's comfort and inspiration is another's jest and scorn." *Board of Education* v. *Barnette*, *supra*, at 632–633. It might be said that we all draw something from our national symbol, for it is capable of conveying simultaneously a spectrum of meanings. If it may be destroyed or permanently disfigured, it could be argued that it will lose its capability of mirroring the sentiments of all who view it.

But we need not decide in this case whether the interest advanced by the court below is valid. We assume *arguendo* that it is. The statute is nonetheless unconstitutional as applied to appellant's activity. There was no risk that appellant's acts would mislead viewers into assuming that the Government endorsed his viewpoint. To the contrary, he was plainly and peacefully protesting the fact that it did not. Appellant was not charged under the desecration statute, . . . nor did he permanently disfigure the flag or destroy it. He displayed it as a flag of his country in a way closely analogous to the manner in which flags have always been used to convey ideas. Moreover, his message was direct, likely to be understood, and within the contours of the First Amendment. Given the protected character of his expression and in light of the fact that no interest the State may have in preserving the physical integrity of a privately-owned flat was significantly impaired on these facts, the conviction must be invalidated.

Mr. Justice Blackmun concurs in the result.

Mr. Justice Douglas, concurring. . . .

Mr. Chief Justice Burger, dissenting.

If the constitutional role of this Court were to strike down unwise laws or restrict unwise application of some laws, I could agree with the result reached by the Court. That is not our function, however, and it should be left to each state and ultimately the common sense of its people to decide how the flag, as a symbol of national unity, should be protected.

Mr. Justice Rehnquist, with whom The Chief Justice and Mr. Justice White join, dissenting.

The Court holds that a Washington statute prohibiting persons from attaching material to the American flag was unconstitutionally applied to petitioner. Although I agree with the Court that petitioner's activity was a form of communication, I do not agree that the First Amendment prohibits the State from restricting this activity in furtherance of other important interests. And I believe the rationale by which the Court reaches its conclusion is unsound. . . .

The true nature of the State's interest in this case is not only one of preserving "the physical integrity of the flag," but also one of preserving the flag as "an important symbol of nationhood and unity." . . .

The value of this interest has been emphasized in recent as well as distant times. Mr. Justice Fortas, for example, noted in *Street* v. *New York*, 394 U.S. 576, 616 (1969), that "the flag is a special kind of personalty," a form of property "burdened with peculiar obligations and restrictions." *Id.*, at 617. Mr. Justice White has observed that "the flag is a national property, and the Nation may regulate those who would make, imitate, sell, possess, or use it." *Smith* v. *Goguen*, 415 U.S. 566 (1974) (concurring opinion). I agree. What petitioner here seeks is simply license to use the flag however he pleases, so long as the activity can be tied to a concept of speech, regardless of any state interest in having the flag used only for more limited purposes. I find no reasoning in the Court's opinion which convinces me that the Constitution requires such license to be given.

The fact that the State has a valid interest in preserving the character of the flag does not mean, of course, that it can employ all conceivable means to enforce it. It certainly could not require all citizens to own the flag or compel citizens to salute one. *West Virginia State Board of Education* v. *Barnette*, 319 U.S. 624 (1943). It presumably cannot punish criticism of the flag, or the principles for which it stands, anymore than it could punish criticism of this country's policies or ideas. But the statute in this case demands no such allegiance. Its operation does not depend upon whether the flag is used for communicative or noncommunicative purposes; upon whether a particular message is deemed commercial or political; upon whether the use of the flag is respectful or contemptuous; or upon whether any particular segment of the State's citizenry might applaud or oppose the intended message. It simply withdraws a unique national symbol from the roster of materials that may be used as a background for communications. Since I do not believe the Constitution prohibits Washington from making that decision, I dissent.

THE ELECTION PROCESS

United States CSC v. National Association of Letter Carriers
413 U.S. 548 (1973)

Mr. Justice White delivered the opinion of the Court.

On December 11, 1972, we noted probable jurisdiction of this appeal based on a jurisdictional statement presenting the single question whether the prohibition in § 9(a) of the Hatch Act, now codified in 5 U.S.C. § 7324 (a)(2), against federal employees taking "an active part in political management or in political campaigns," is unconstitutional on its face. . . .

II.

As the District Court recognized, the constitutionality of the Hatch Act's ban on taking an active part in political management or politi-

cal campaigns has been here before. This very prohibition was attacked in [*United Public Workers v. Mitchell,* 330 U.S. 73 (1947)] . . .

We unhesitatingly reaffirm the *Mitchell* holding that Congress had, and has, the power to prevent Mr. Poole and others like him from holding a party office, working at the polls, and acting as party paymaster for other party workers. An Act of Congress going no farther would in our view unquestionably be valid. So would it be if, in plain and understandable language, the statute forbade activities such as organizing a political party or club; actively participating in fund-raising activities for a partisan candidate or political party; becoming a partisan candidate for, or campaigning for, an elective public office; actively managing the campaign of a partisan candidate for public office; initiating or circulating a partisan nominating petition or soliciting votes for a partisan candidate for public office; or serving as a delegate, alternate or proxy to a political party convention. Our judgment is that neither the First Amendment nor any other provision of the Constitution invalidates a law barring this kind of partisan political conduct by federal employees. . . .

Until now, the judgment of Congress, the Executive and the country appears to have been that partisan political activities by federal employees must be limited if the Government is to operate effectively and fairly, elections are to play their proper part in representative government and employees themselves are to be sufficiently free from improper influences. E.g., 84 *Cong.Rec.* 9598, 9603; 86 *Cong.Rec.* 2360, 2621, 2864, 9376. The restrictions so far imposed on federal employees are not aimed at particular parties, groups or points of view, but apply equally to all partisan activities of the type described. They discriminate against no racial, ethnic or religious minorities. Nor do they seek to control political opinions or beliefs, or to interfere with or influence anyone's vote at the polls.

But as the Court held in *Pickering* v. *Board of*

Education, 391 U.S. 563, 568 (1968), the government has an interest in regulating the conduct and "the speech of its employees that differ[s] significantly from those it possesses in connection with regulation of the speech of the citizenry in general. The problem in any case is to arrive at a balance between the interest of the [employee], as a citizen, in commenting upon matters of public concern and the interest of the [government], as an employer, in promoting the efficiency of the public services it performs through its employees." Although Congress is free to strike a different balance than it has, if it so chooses, we think the balance it has so far struck is sustainable by the obviously important interests sought to be served by the limitations on partisan political activities now contained in the Hatch Act. . . .

Neither the right to associate nor the right to participate in political activities is absolute in any event. See, e.g., *Rosario* v. *Rockefeller*, 410 U.S. 752 (1973); *Dunn* v. *Blumstein*, 405 U.S. 330, 336 (1972) . . . *Williams* v. *Rhodes*, 393 U.S. 23, 30–31 (1968). Nor are the management, financing and conduct of political campaigns wholly free from governmental regulation. We agree with the basic holding of *Mitchell* that plainly identifiable acts of political management and political campaigning may constitutionally be prohibited on the part of federal employees. Until now this has been the judgment of the lower federal courts, and we do not understand the District Court in this case to have questioned the constitutionality of a law that was specifically limited to prohibiting the conduct in which Mr. Poole in the *Mitchell* case admittedly engaged.

III.

But however constitutional the proscription of identifiable partisan conduct in understandable language may be, the District Court's judgment was that § 7324(a)(2) was both unconstitutionally vague and fatally overbroad. Appellees make the same contentions here, but we cannot agree that the section is unconstitutional on its face for either reason. . . .

[Justice Douglas's dissent, joined by Justices Brennan and Marshall, insisted that *Mitchell* should not be followed: it "is of a different vintage than the present cases"; it applied a "rational basis" standard no longer permissible in the First Amendment area; it came before the "host of decisions" requiring "narrowly drawn statutes" in the free speech context. He thought the "chilling effect of these vague and generalized prohibitions" was "so obvious as not to need elaboration." And he commented that "it is of no concern to Government what an employee does in his or her spare time, whether religion, recreation, social work, or politics is his hobby—unless what he or she does impairs efficiency or other facets of the merits of his job. Some things, some activities, do affect or may be thought to affect the employee's job performance. But his political creed, like his religion, is irrelevant."]

Buckley v. *Valeo*
424 U.S. 1 (1976)

The Federal Elections Campaign Act of 1971 as amended in 1974 contains numerous provisions for reform of presidential elections. One of these provisions, which authorizes a Federal Election Commission, is considered above, p. 81. Another, dealing with public financing, is considered above, p. 146.

Per Curiam.

CONTRIBUTION AND EXPENDITURE LIMITATIONS

The intricate statutory scheme adopted by Congress to regulate federal election campaigns includes restrictions on political contributions and expenditures that apply broadly to all phases of and all participants in the election process. The major contribution and expenditure limitations in the Act prohibit individuals from contributing more than $25,000 in a single year or more than $1,000 to any single candidate for an election campaign and from spending more than $1,000 a year "relative to a clearly identified candidate." Other provisions restrict a candidate's use of personal and family resources in his campaign and limit the overall amount that can be spent by a candidate in campaigning for federal office.

In upholding the constitutional validity of the Act's contribution and expenditure provisions on the ground that those provisions should be viewed as regulating conduct, not speech, the Court of Appeals relied upon *United States* v. *O'Brien*, . . .

We cannot share the view that the present Act's contribution and expenditure limitations are comparable to the restrictions on conduct upheld in *O'Brien*. The expenditure of money simply cannot be equated with such conduct as destruction of a draft card. . . . [T]his Court has never suggested that the dependence of a communication on the expenditure of money operates itself to introduce a nonspeech element or to reduce the exacting scrutiny required by the First Amendment. . . .

A restriction on the amount of money a person or group can spend on political communication during a campaign necessarily reduces the quantity of expression by restricting the number of issues discussed, the depth of their exploration, and the size of the audience reached. This is because virtually every means of com-

municating ideas in today's mass society requires the expenditure of money.

The electorate's increasing dependence on television, radio, and other mass media for news and information has made these expensive modes of communication indispensable instruments of effective political speech.

The expenditure limitations contained in the Act represent substantial rather than merely theoretical restraints on the quantity and diversity of political speech. . . .

By contrast [a] limitation on the amount of money a person may give to a candidate or campaign organization . . . involves little direct restraint on his political communication, for it permits the symbolic expression of support evidenced by a contribution but does not in any way infringe the contributor's freedom to discuss candidates and issues. While contributions may result in political expression if spent by a candidate or an association to present views to the voters, the transformation of contributions into political debate involves speech by someone other than the contributor. . . .

There is no indication that the contribution limitations imposed by the Act would have any dramatic adverse effect on the funding of campaigns and political associations. The overall effect by the Act's contribution ceilings is merely to require candidates and political committees to raise funds from a greater number of persons and to compel people who would otherwise contribute amounts greater than the statutory limits to expend such funds on direct political expression, rather than to reduce the total amount of money potentially available to promote political expression.

The Act's contribution and expenditure limitations also impinge on protected associational freedoms. Making a contribution, like joining a political party, serves to affiliate a person with a candidate. In addition, it enables like-minded persons to pool their resources in furtherance of common political goals. The Act's contribution ceilings thus limit one important means of associating with a candidate or committee, but leave the contributor free to become a member of any political association and to assist personally in the association's efforts on behalf of candidates. And the Act's contribution limitations permit associations and candidates to aggregate large sums of money to promote effective advocacy. By contrast, the Act's $1,000 limitation on independent expenditures "relative to a clearly identified candidate" precludes most associations from effectively amplifying the voice of their adherents, the original basis for the recognition of First Amendment protection of the freedom of association. . . .

In sum, although the Act's contribution and expenditure limitations both implicate fundamental First Amendment interests, its expenditure ceilings impose significantly more severe restrictions on protected freedoms of political expression and association than do its limitations on financial contributions.

Contribution Limitations

. . . In view of the fundamental nature of the right to associate, governmental "action which may have the effect of curtailing the freedom to associate is subject to the closest scrutiny." *NAACP* v. *Alabama*. Yet, it is clear that "[n]either the right to associate nor the right to participate in political activities is absolute." *United States Civil Service Comm'n* v. *National Association of Letter Carriers*. Even a " 'significant interference' with protected rights of political association" may be sustained if the State demonstrates a sufficiently important interest and employs means closely drawn to avoid unnecessary abridgment of associational freedoms. . . .

It is unnecessary to look beyond the Act's primary purpose—to limit the actuality and appearance of corruption resulting from large individual financial contributions—in order to find a constitutionally sufficient justification for the $1,000 contribution limitation. . . . To the extent that large contributions are given to se-

cure political *quid pro quos* from current and potential office holders, the integrity of our system of representative democracy is undermined. Although the scope of such pernicious practices can never be reliably ascertained, the deeply disturbing examples surfacing after the 1972 election demonstrate that the problem is not an illusory one.

Of almost equal concern as the danger of actual *quid pro quo* arrangements is the impact of the appearance of corruption stemming from public awareness of the opportunities for abuse inherent in a regime of large individual financial contributions. . . .

Appellants contend that the contribution limitations must be invalidated because bribery laws and narrowly-drawn disclosure requirements constitute a less restrictive means of dealing with "proven and suspected *quid pro quo* arrangements." But laws making criminal the giving and taking of bribes deal with only the most blatant and specific attempts of those with money to influence governmental action. And while disclosure reqirements serve the many salutary purposes discussed elsewhere in this opinion, Congress was surely entitled to conclude that disclosure was only a partial measure, and that contribution ceilings were a necessary legislative concomitant to deal with the reality or appearance of corruption inherent in a system permitting unlimited financial contributions, even when the identities of the contributors and the amounts of their contributions are fully disclosed.

The Act's $1,000 contribution limitation focuses precisely on the problem of large campaign contributions—the narrow aspect of political association where the actuality and potential for corruption have been identified. . . . Significantly, the Act's contribution limitations in themselves do not undermine to any material degree the potential for robust and effective discussion of candidates and campaign issues by individual citizens, associations, the institutional press, candidates, and political parties.

We find that, under the rigorous standard of

review established by our prior decisions, the weighty interests served by restricting the size of financial contributions to political candidates are sufficient to justify the limited effect upon First Amendment freedoms caused by the $1,000 contribution ceiling. . . .

Expenditure Limitations

The $1,000 Limitation on Expenditures "Relative to a Clearly Identified Candidate."

Section 608(e)(1) provides that "[n]o person may make any expenditure . . . relative to a clearly identified candidate during a calendar year which, when added to all other expenditures made by such person during the year advocating the election or defeat of such candidate, exceeds $1,000." The plain effect of section 608(e)(1) is to prohibit all individuals, who are neither candidates nor owners of instututional press facilities, and all groups, except political parties and campaign organizations, from voicing their views "relative to a clearly identified candidate" through means that entail aggregate expenditures of more than $1,000 during a calendar year. The provision, for example, would make it a federal criminal offense for a person or association to place a single one-quarter page advertisement "relative to a clearly identified candidate" in a major metropolitan newspaper. . . .

We find that the governmental interest in preventing corruption and the appearance of corruption is inadequate to justify section 608(e)(1)'s ceiling on independent expenditures. First, assuming *arguendo* that large independent expenditures pose the same dangers of actual or apparent *quid pro quo* arrangements as do large contributions, section 608(e)(1) does not provide an answer that sufficiently relates to the elimination of those dangers. Unlike the contribution limitations' total ban on the giving of large amounts of money to candidates, section 608(e)(1) prevents only some large expenditures. So long as persons and groups eschew

expenditures that in express terms advocate the election or defeat of a clearly identified candidate, they are free to spend as much as they want to promote the candidate and his views. . . . It would naively underestimate the ingenuity and resourcefulness of persons and groups desiring to buy influence to believe that they would have much difficulty devising expenditures that skirted the restriction on express advocacy of election or defeat but nevertheless benefited the candidate's campaign. Yet no substantial societal interest would be served by a loophole-closing provision designed to check corruption that permitted unscrupulous persons and organizations to expend unlimited sums of money in order to obtain improper influence over candidates for elective office. . . .

. . . While the independent expenditure ceiling thus fails to serve any substantial governmental interest in stemming the reality or appearance of corruption in the electoral process, it heavily burdens core First Amendment expression. For the First Amendment right to "'speak one's mind . . . on all public institutions'" includes the right to engage in "'vigorous advocacy' no less than 'abstract discussion.'" Advocacy of the election or defeat of candidates for federal office is no less entitled to protection under the First Amendment than the discussion of political policy generally or advocacy of the passage or defeat of legislation.

It is argued, however, that the ancillary governmental interest in equalizing the relative ability of individuals and groups to influence the outcome of elections serves to justify the limitation on express advocacy of the election or defeat of candidates imposed by section 608(e)(1)'s expenditure ceiling. But the concept that government may restrict the speech of some elements of our society in order to enhance the relative voice of others is wholly foreign to the First Amendment, which was designed "to secure 'the widest possible dissemination of information from diverse and antagonistic sources,'" and "'to assure unfettered interchange of ideas for the bringing about of political and social changes desired by the people.'"'. . .

The ceiling on personal expenditures by candidates on their own behalf, like the limitations on independent expenditures contained in section 608(e)(1), imposes a substantial restraint on the ability of persons to engage in protected First Amendment expression. The candidate, no less than any other person, has a First Amendment right to engage in the discussion of public issues and vigorously and tirelessly to advocate his own election and the election of other candidates. . . .

The primary governmental interest served by the Act—the prevention of actual and apparent corruption of the political process—does not support the limitation on the candidate's expenditure of his own personal funds. . . . Indeed, the use of personal funds reduces the candidate's dependence on outside contributions and thereby counteracts the coercive pressures and attendant risks of abuse to which the Act's contribution limitations are directed.

The ancillary interest in equalizing the relative financial resources of candidates competing for elective office, therefore, provides the sole relevant rationale for [an] . . . expenditure ceiling. That interest is clearly not sufficient to justify the provision's infringement of fundamental First Amendment rights. . . . The First Amendment simply cannot tolerate . . . [a] restriction upon the freedom of a candidate to speak without legislative limit on behalf of his own candidacy. We therefore hold that . . . restrictions on a candidate's personal expenditures is unconstitutional.

. . . In sum, the provisions of the Act that impose a $1,000 limitation on contributions to a single candidate, section 608(b)(1), a $5,000 limitation on contributions by a political committee to a single candidate, section 608(b)(2), and a $25,000 limitation on total contributions by an individual during any calendar year, section 608(b)(3), are constitutionally valid. . . . The contribution ceilings . . . serve the basic governmental interest in safeguarding the integrity

of the electoral process without directly impinging upon the rights of individual citizens and candidates to engage in political debate and discussion. By contrast, the First Amendment requires the invalidation of the Act's independent expenditure ceiling, section 608(e)(1), its limitation on a candidate's expenditures from his own personal funds, section 608(a), and its ceilings on overall campaign expenditures, section 608(c). These provisions place substantial and direct restrictions on the ability of candidates, citizens, and associations to engage in protected political expression, restrictions that the First Amendment cannot tolerate.

REPORTING AND DISCLOSURE REQUIREMENTS

General Principles

. . . Unlike the overall limitations on contributions and expenditures, the disclosure requirements impose no ceiling on campaign-related activities. But we have repeatedly found that compelled disclosure, in itself, can seriously infringe on privacy of association and belief guaranteed by the First Amendment, *NAACP* v. *Alabama*. . . .

We long have recognized that significant encroachments on First Amendment rights of the sort that compelled disclosure imposes cannot be justified by a mere showing of some legitimate governmental interest. Since *Alabama* we have required that the subordinating interests of the State must survive exacting scrutiny. . . .

The governmental interests sought to be vindicated by the disclosure requirements . . . fall into three categories. First, disclosure provides the electorate with information "as to where political campaign money comes from and how it is spent by the candidate" in order to aid the voters in evaluating those who seek Federal office. . . .

Second, disclosure requirements deter actual corruption and avoid the appearance of corruption by exposing large contributions and expenditures to the light of publicity. . . .

Third, and not least significant, recordkeeping, reporting and disclosure requirements are an essential means of gathering the data necessary to detect violations of the contribution limitations described above. . . .

It is undoubtedly true that public disclosure of contributions to candidates and political parties will deter some individuals who otherwise might contribute. In some instances, disclosure may even expose contributors to harassment or retaliation. These are not insignificant burdens on individual rights, and they must be weighed carefully against the interests which Congress has sought to promote by this legislation. In this process, we note and agree with appellants' concession that disclosure requirements—certainly in most applications—appear to be the least restrictive means of curbing the evils of campaign ignorance and corruption that Congress found to exist. Appellants argue, however, that the balance tips against disclosure when it is required of contributors to certain [minor] parties and candidates. We turn now to this contention.

Application to Minor Parties and Independents

. . . Appellants agree that "the record here does not reflect the kind of focused and insistent harassment of contributors and members that existed in the NAACP cases." They argue, however, that a blanket exemption for minor parties is necessary lest irreparable injury be done before the required evidence can be gathered.

. . . We recognize that unduly strict requirements of proof could impose a heavy burden, but it does not follow that a blanket exemption for minor parties is necessary. Minor parties must be allowed sufficient flexibility in the proof of injury to assure a fair consideration of their claim. . . .

Where it exists the type of chill and harassment identified in Alabama can be shown. We

cannot assume that courts will be insensitive to similar showings when made in future cases. We therefore conclude that a blanket exemption is not required. . . .

[W]e sustain . . . the disclosure and reporting provisions, . . .

Mr. Justice Stevens took no part in the consideration or decision of these cases.

Mr. Chief Justice Burger, concurring in part and dissenting in part.

. . . I dissent from those parts of the Court's holding sustaining the Act's provisions (a) for disclosure of small contributions, (b) for limitations on contributions, and (c) for public financing of Presidential campaigns. . . . The Act's system for public financing of Presidential campaigns is, in my judgment, an impermissible intrusion by the Government into the traditionally private political process.

More broadly, the Court's result does violence to the intent of Congress in this comprehensive scheme of campaign finance. By dissecting the Act bit by bit, and casting off vital parts, the Court fails to recognize that the whole of this Act is greater than the sum of its parts. Congress intended to regulate all aspects of federal campaign finances, but what remains after today's holding leaves no more than a shadow of what Congress contemplated. I question whether the residue leaves a workable program.

DISCLOSURE PROVISIONS

. . . [G]iven the objectives to which disclosure is directed, I agree that the need for disclosure outweighs individual constitutional claims.

Disclosure is, however, subject to First Amendment limitations which are to be defined by looking to the relevant public interests. The legitimate public interest is the elimination of the appearance and reality of corrupting influences. Serious dangers to the very processes of government justify disclosure of contributions of such dimensions reasonably thought likely to purchase special favors. . . .

The Court's theory, however, goes beyond permissible limits. Under the Court's view, disclosure serves broad informational purposes, enabling the public to be fully informed on matters of acute public interest. Forced disclosure of one aspect of a citizen's political activity, under this analysis, serves the public right-to-know. This open-ended approach is the only plausible justification for the otherwise irrationally low ceilings of $10 and $100 for anonymous contributions. The burdens of these low ceilings seem to me obvious, and the Court does not try to question this. . . . Examples come readily to mind. Rank-and-file union members or rising junior executives may now think twice before making even modest contributions to a candidate who is disfavored by the union or management hierarchy. Similarly, potential contributors may well decline to take the obvious risks entailed in making a reportable contribution to the opponent of a well-entrenched incumbent. . . .

The public right-to-know ought not be absolute when its exercise reveals private political convictions. . . . In other contexts, this Court has seen to it that governmental power cannot be used to force a citizen to disclose his private affiliations. . . . For me it is far too late in the day to recognize an ill-defined "public interest" to breach the historic safeguards guaranteed by the First Amendment.

. . . The balancing test used by the Court requires that fair recognition be given to competing interests. With respect, I suggest the Court has failed to give the traditional standing to some of the First Amendment values at stake here. "In the area of First Amendment freedoms government has the duty to confine itself to the *least* intrusive regulations which are adequate for the purpose. . . .

In light of these views, it seems to me that the threshold limits fixed at $10 and $100 for anonymous contributions are constitutionally impermissible on their face. . . . To argue that a

1976 contribution of $10 or $100 entails a risk of corruption or its appearance is simply too extravagant to be maintained. No public right-to-know justifies the compelled disclosure of such contributions, at the risk of discouraging them. There is, in short, no relation whatever between the means used and the legitimate goal of ventilating possible undue influence. Congress has used a shotgun to kill wrens as well as hawks.

In saying that the lines drawn by Congress are "not wholly without rationality," the Court plainly fails to apply the traditional test:

> "Precision of regulation must be the touchstone in an area so closely touching on our most precious freedoms. . . ."

CONTRIBUTION AND EXPENDITURE LIMITS

I agree fully with that part of the Court's opinion that holds unconstitutional the limitations the Act puts on campaign expenditures which "place substantial and direct restrictions on the ability of candidates, citizens, and associations to engage in protected political expression, restrictions that the First Amendment cannot tolerate. . . ." Yet when it approves similarly stringent limitations on contributions, the Court ignores the reasons it finds so persuasive in the context of expenditures. For me contributions and expenditures are two sides of the same First Amendment coin.

By limiting campaign contributions, the Act restricts the amount of money that will be spent on political activity—and does so directly. . . . In treating campaign expenditure limitations, the Court says that the "First Amendment denies government the power to determine that spending to promote one's political views is wasteful, excessive, or unwise. . . ." Limiting contributions, as a practical matter, will limit expenditures and will put an effective ceiling on the amount of political activity and debate that the Government will permit to take place. . . .

At any rate, the contribution limits are a far

more severe restriction on First Amendment activity than the sort of "chilling" legislation for which the Court has shown such extraordinary concern in the past. . . . There are many prices we pay for the freedoms secured by the First Amendment; the risk of undue influence is one of them, confirming what we have long known: freedom is hazardous, but some restraints are worse.

Mr. Justice White, concurring in part and dissenting in part. . . .

. . . In the interest of preventing undue influence that large contributors would have or that the public might think they would have, the Court upholds the provision that an individual may not give to a candidate, or spend on his behalf if requested or authorized by the candidate to do so, more than $1,000 in any one election. . . .

It would make little sense to me, and apparently made none to Congress, to limit the amounts an individual may give to a candidate or spend with his approval but fail to limit the amounts that could be spent on his behalf. Yet the Court permits the former while striking down the latter limitation. No more than $1,000 may be given to a candidate or spent at his request or with his approval or cooperation; but otherwise, apparently, a contributor is to be constitutionally protected in spending unlimited amounts of money in support of his chosen candidates.

Let us suppose that each of two brothers spends one million dollars on TV spot announcements that he has individually prepared and in which he appears, urging the election of the same named candidate in identical words. One brother has sought and obtained the approval of the candidate; the other has not. The former may validly be prosecuted under section 608(e); under the Court's view, the latter may not, even though the candidate could scarcely help knowing about and appreciating the expensive favor. For constitutional purposes it is difficult to see the difference between the two situations. I would take the word of those who know—that limiting independent expenditures is essential to prevent transparent and widespread evasion of the contribution limits. . . .

Proceeding from the maxim that "money talks," the Court finds that the expenditure limitations will seriously curtail political expression by candidates and interfere substantially with their chances for election. . . . The record before us no more supports the conclusion that the communicative efforts of congressional and Presidential candidates will be crippled by the expenditure limitations that it supports the contrary. The judgment of Congress was that reasonably effective campaigns could be conducted within the limits established by the Act and that the communicative efforts of these campaigns would not seriously suffer. In this posture of the case, there is no sound basis for invalidating the expenditure limitations, so long as the purposes they serve are legitimate and sufficiently substantial, which in my view they are. . . .

By limiting the importance of personal wealth, section 608(a) helps to assure that only individuals with a modicum of support from others will be viable candidates. This in turn would tend to discourage any notion that the outcome of elections is primarily a function of money. Similarly, section 608(a) tends to equalize access to the political arena, encouraging the less wealthy, unable to bankroll their own campaigns, to run for political office.

As with the campaign expenditure limits, Congress was entitled to determine that personal wealth ought to play a less important role in political campaigns than it has in the past. Nothing in the First Amendment stands in the way of that determination.

Mr. Justice Rehnquist, concurring in part and dissenting in part. . . .

. . . I join in all of the Court's opinion except [the part] which sustains, against appellants' First and Fifth Amendment challenges, the disparities found in the congressional plan for financing general Presidential elections between the two major parties, on the one hand and minor parties and candidates on the other. . . .

Congress, of course, does have an interest in not "funding hopeless candidacies with large sums of public money," . . . and may for that purpose legitimately require "'some preliminary showing of a significant modicum of support,' *Jenness* v. *Fortson* as an eligibility requirement for public funds." . . . But Congress

in this legislation has done a good deal more than that. It has enshrined the Republican and Democratic Parties in a permanently preferred position, and has established requirements for funding minor party and independent candidates to which the two major parties are not subject. . . . I find it impossible to subscribe to the Court's reasoning that because no third party has posed a credible threat to the two major parties in Presidential elections since 1860, Congress may by law attempt to assure that this pattern will endure forever.

Note: First National Bank v. Bellotti, 98 S. Ct. 1407 (1978), recognizes that free speech is "indispensable to decision-making in a democracy, and this is no less true because the speech comes from a corporation rather than an individual."

Abood v. *Detroit Board of Education*, 431 U.S. 209 (1977), involved a state law authorizing "agency shop" arrangements whereby all local government workers represented by a union (even though not themselves members) must pay "service charges" to the union equal to union dues. The school board made such an arrangement with a union. Some teachers objected. They did not want to pay the charges; they opposed unions in the public sector; and they did not approve of the union's political views and activities. The Court

held that "insofar as the service charge is used to finance expenditures by the union for purposes of collective bargaining, contract administration, and grievance adjustment," the agency-shop measure was valid—but that union spending of service-charge money "to contribute to political candidates and to express political views unrelated to [union] duties as exclusive bargaining representative" violates the free-speech rights of objecting teachers.

Elrod v. *Burns*, 427 U.S. 347 (1976), held that the First Amendment prohibits the patronage system whereby government employees lose their jobs when their party loses an election: "The cost of the practice of patronage is the restraint it places on freedoms of belief and association."

PRESS PROBLEMS: FREEDOM OR PRIVILEGE?

Nebraska Press Association v. *Stuart*
See p. 390, above.

Craig v. *Harney*
331 U.S. 367 (1947)

Opinion of the Court by Mr. Justice Douglas, announced by Mr. Justice Reed.

Petitioners were adjudged guilty of constructive criminal contempt by the County Court of Nueces County, Texas, and sentenced to jail for three days. They sought to challenge the legality of their confinement by applying to the Court of Criminal Appeals for a writ of habeas corpus. That court by a divided vote denied the writ and remanded petitioners to the custody of the county sheriff. 149 Tex. Cr.—, 193 S.W.2d. 178. The case is here on a petition for a writ of certiorari which we granted because of the importance of the problem and because the ruling of the Texas court raised doubts whether it conformed to the principles, announced in *Bridges v. California*, 314 U.S. 252, and *Pennekamp v. Florida*, 328 U.S. 331.

Petitioners are a publisher, an editorial writer, and a news reporter of newspapers published in Corpus Christi, Texas. The County Court had before it a forcible detainer case, *Jackson v. Mayes*, whereby Jackson sought to regain possession from Mayes of a business building in Corpus Christi which Mayes (who was at the time in the armed services and whose affairs were being handled by an agent, one Burchard) claimed under a lease. That case turned on whether Mayes' lease was forfeited because of non-payment of rent. At the close of the testimony each side moved for an instructed verdict. The judge instructed the jury to return a verdict for Jackson. That was on May 26, 1945. The jury returned with a verdict for Mayes. The judge refused to accept it and again instructed the jury to return a verdict for Jackson. The jury returned a second time with a verdict for Mayes. Once more the judge refused to accept it and repeated his prior instruction. It being the evening of May 26th and the jury not having complied, the judge recessed the court until the morning of May 27. Again the jury balked at returning the instructed verdict. But finally it complied, stating that it acted under coercion of the court and against its conscience.

On May 29th Mayes moved for a new trial. That motion was denied on June 6th. On June 4th an officer of the County Court filed with that court a complaint charging petitioners with contempt by publication. The publications referred to were an editorial and news stories published on May 26, 27, 28, 30, and 31 in the newspapers with which petitioners are connected. We have set forth the relevant parts of the publications in the appendix to this opinion. Browning, the judge, who is a layman and who holds an elective office, was criticised for taking the case from the jury. That ruling was called "arbitrary action" and a "travesty on justice." It was deplored that a layman, rather than a lawyer, sat as judge. Groups of local citizens

were reported as petitioning the judge to grant Mayes a new trial and it was said that one group had labeled the judge's ruling as a "gross miscarriage of justice." It was also said that the judge's behavior had properly brought down "the wrath of public opinion upon his head," that the people were aroused because a serviceman "seems to be getting a raw deal," and that there was "no way of knowing whether justice was done, because the first rule of justice, giving both sides an opportunity to be heard, was repudiated." And the fact that there could be no appeal from the judge's ruling to a court "familiar with proper procedure and able to interpret and weigh motions and arguments by opposing counsel" was deplored.

The trial judge concluded that the reports and editorial were designed falsely to represent to the public the nature of the proceedings and to prejudice and influence the court in its ruling on the motion for a new trial then pending. Petitioners contended at the hearing that all that was reported did no more than to create the same impression that would have been created upon the mind of an average intelligent layman who sat through the trial. They disclaimed any purpose to impute unworthy motives to the judge or to advise him how the case should be decided or to bring the court into disrepute. The purpose was to "quicken the conscience of the judge" and to "make him more careful in discharging his duty."

The Court of Criminal Appeals, in denying the writ of habeas corpus, stated that the "issue before us" is "whether the publications . . . were reasonably calculated to interfere with the due administration of justice" in the pending case. 193 S.W.2d p. 186. It held that "there is no escape from the conclusion that it was the purpose and intent of the publishers . . . to force, compel, and coerce Judge Browning to grant Mayes a new trial. The only reason or motive for so doing was because the publishers did not agree with Judge Browning's decision or conduct of the case. According to their viewpoint, Judge Browning was wrong and they took it upon themselves to make him change his decision." *Id.*, pp. 188–189. The court went on to say that "It is hard to conceive how the public press could have been more forcibly or substantially used or applied to make, force, and compel a judge to change a ruling or decision in a case pending before him that was here done." *Id.*, p. 189. The court distinguished the *Bridges* case, noting that there the published statements carried threats of future adverse criticism and action on the part of the publisher if the pending matter was not disposed of in accordance with the views of the publisher, that the views of the publisher in the matter were already well known, and that the *Bridges* case was not private litigation but a suit in the outcome of which the public had an interest. *Id.*, p. 188. It concluded that the facts of this case satisfied the "clear and present danger" rule of the *Bridges* case. The test was, in the view of the court, satisfied "because the publications and their purpose were to impress upon Judge Browning (*a*) that unless he granted the motion for a new trial he would be subjected to suspicion as to his integrity and fairness and to odium and hatred in the public mind; (*b*) that the safe and secure course to avoid the criticism of the press and public opinion would be to grant the motion and disqualify himself from again presiding at the trial of the case; and (*c*) that if he overruled the motion for a new trial, there would be produced in the public mind such a disregard for the court over which he presided as to give rise to a purpose in practice to refuse to respect and obey any order, judgment, or decree which he might render in conflict with the views of the public press. (*Id.*, p. 189.)"

The court's statement of the issue before it and the reasons it gave for holding that the "clear and present danger" test was satisfied have a striking resemblance to the findings which the Court in *Toledo Newspaper Co.* v. *United States*, 247 U.S. 402, held adequate to sustain an adjudication of contempt by publication. That case held that comment on a pending case in a federal court was punishable by con-

tempt if it had a "reasonable tendency" to obstruct the administration of justice. We revisited that case in *Nye* v. *United States*, 313 U.S. 33, 52, and disapproved it. And in *Bridges* v. *California*, *supra*, we held that the compulsion of the First Amendment, made applicable to the States by the Fourteenth (*Schneider* v. *Irvington*, 308 U.S. 147; *Murdock* v. *Pennsylvania*, 319 U.S. 105, 108) forbade the punishment by contempt for comment on pending cases in absence of a showing that the utterances created a "clear and present danger" to the administration of justice. 314 U.S. pp. 260–264. We reaffirmed and reapplied that standard in *Pennekamp* v. *Florida*, *supra*, which also involved comment on matters pending before the court. We stated, p. 347:

> "Courts must have power to protect the interests of prisoners and litigants before them from unseemly efforts to pervert judicial action. In the borderline instances where it is difficult to say upon which side the alleged offense falls, we think the specific freedom of public comment should weigh heavily against a possible tendency to influence pending cases. Freedom of discussion should be given the widest range compatible with the essential requirement of the fair and orderly administration of justice."

Neither those cases nor the present one raises questions concerning the full reach of the power of the state to protect the administration of justice by its courts. The problem presented is only a narrow, albeit important, phase of that problem—the power of a court promptly and without a jury trial to punish for comment on cases pending before it and awaiting disposition. The history of the power to punish for contempt (see *Nye* v. *United States*, *supra*; *Bridges* v. *California*, *supra*) and the unequivocal command of the First Amendment serve as constant reminders that freedom of speech and of the press should not be impaired through the exercise of that power, unless there is no doubt that the utterances in question are a serious and imminent threat to the administration of justice.

In a case where it is asserted that a person has been deprived by a state court of a fundamental right secured by the Constitution, an independent examination of the facts by this Court is often required to be made. . . .

We start with the news articles. A trial is a public event. What transpires in the court room is public property. If a transcript of the court proceedings had been published, we suppose none would claim that the judge could punish the publisher for contempt. And we can see no difference though the conduct of the attorneys, of the jury, or even of the judge himself, may have reflected on the court. Those who see and hear what transpired can report it with impunity. There is no special prerequisite of the judiciary which enables it, as distinguished from other institutions of democratic government, to suppress, edit, or censor events which transpire in proceedings before it.

The articles of May 26, 27, and 28 were partial reports of what transpired at the trial. They did not reflect good reporting, for they failed to reveal the precise issue before the judge. They said that Mayes, the tenant, had tendered a rental check. They did not disclose that the rental check was post-dated and hence, in the opinion of the judge, not a valid tender. In that sense the news articles were by any standard an unfair report of what transpired. But inaccuracies in reporting are commonplace. Certainly a reporter could not be laid by the heels for contempt because he missed the essential point in a trial or failed to summarize the issues to accord with the views of the judge who sat on the case. Conceivably, a plan of reporting on a case could be so designed and executed as to poison the public mind, to cause a march on the court house, or otherwise so disturb the delicate balance in a highly wrought situation as to imperil the fair and orderly functioning of the judicial process. But it takes more imagination than we possess to find in this rather sketchy and one-sided report of a case any imminent or serious threat to

a judge of reasonable fortitude. See *Pennekamp* v. *Florida, supra.*

The accounts of May 30 and 31 dealt with the news of what certain groups of citizens proposed to do about the judge's ruling in the case. So far as we are advised, it was a fact that they planned to take the proposed action. The episodes were community events of legitimate interest. Whatever might be the responsibility of the group which took the action, those who reported it stand in a different position. Even if the former were guilty of contempt, freedom of the press may not be denied a newspaper which brings their conduct to the public eye.

The only substantial question raised pertains to the editorial. It called the judge's refusal to hear both sides "high-handed," a "travesty on justice," and the reason that public opinion was "outraged." It said that his ruling properly "brought down the wrath of public opinion upon his head" since a serviceman "seems to be getting a raw deal." The fact that there was no appeal from his decision to a "judge who is familiar with proper procedure and able to interpret and weigh motions and arguments by opposing counsel and to make his decisions accordingly" was a "tragedy." It deplored the fact that the judge was a "layman" and not a "competent attorney." It concluded that the "first rule of justice" was to give both sides an opportunity to be heard and when that rule was "repudiated," there was "no way of knowing whether justice was done."

This was strong language, intemperate language, and, we assume, an unfair criticism. But a judge may not hold in contempt one "who ventures to publish anything that tends to make him unpopular or to belittle him. . . ." See *Craig* v. *Hecht*, 263 U.S. 255, 281. Mr. Justice Holmes dissenting. The vehemence of the language used is not alone the measure of the power to punish for contempt. The fires which it kindles must constitute an imminent, not merely a likely, threat to the administration of justice. The danger must not be remote or even probable; it must immediately imperil.

We agree with the court below that the editorial must be appraised in the setting of the news articles which both preceded and followed it. It must also be appraised in light of the community environment which prevailed at that time. The fact that the jury was recalcitrant and balked, the fact that it acted under coercion and contrary to its conscience and said so were some index of popular opinion. A judge who is part of such a dramatic episode can hardly help but know that his decision is apt to be unpopular. But the law of contempt is not made for the protection of judges who may be sensitive to the winds of public opinion. Judges are supposed to be men of fortitude, able to thrive in a hardy climate. Conceivably a campaign could be so managed and so aimed at the sensibilities of a particular judge and the matter pending before him as to cross the forbidden line. But the episodes we have here do not fall in that category. Nor can we assume that the trial judge was not a man of fortitude.

The editorial's complaint was two-fold. One objection or criticism was that a layman rather than a lawyer sat on the bench. That is legitimate comment; and its relevancy could hardly be denied at least where judges are elected. In the circumstances of the present case, it amounts at the very most to an intimation that come the next election the newspaper in question will not support the incumbent. But it contained no threat to oppose him in the campaign if the decision on the merits was not overruled, nor any implied reward if it was changed. Judges who stand for reelection run on their records. That may be a rugged environment. Criticism is expected. Discussion of their conduct is appropriate, if not necessary. The fact that the discussion at this particular point of time was not in good taste falls far short of meeting the clear and present danger test.

The other complaint of the editorial was directed at the court's procedure—its failure to hear both sides before the case was decided. There was no attempt to pass on the merits of the case. The editorial, indeed, stated that there was no way of knowing whether justice was done. That criticism of the court's procedure—that it decided the case without giving both sides a chance to be heard—reduces the salient point of the case to a narrow issue. If the point had been made in a petition for rehearing, and reduced to lawyer's language, it would be of trifling consequence. The fact that it was put in layman's language, colorfully phrased for popular consumption, and printed in a newspaper does not seem to us to elevate it to the criminal level. It might well have a tendency to lower the standing of the judge in the public eye. But it is hard to see on these facts how it could obstruct the course of justice in the case before the court. The only demand was for a hearing. There was no demand that the judge reverse his position—or else.

"Legal trials are not like elections, to be won through the use of the meeting-hall, the radio, and the newspaper." *Bridges* v. *California, supra,* p. 271. But there was here no threat or menace to the integrity of the trial. The editorial challenged the propriety of the court's procedure, not the merits of its ruling. Any such challenge, whether made prior or subsequent to the final disposition of a case, would likely reflect on the competence of the judge in handling cases. But as we have said, the power to punish for contempt depends on a more substantial showing. Giving the editorial all of the vehemence which the court below found in it we fail to see how it could in any realistic sense create an imminent and serious threst to the ability of the court to give fair consideration to the motion for rehearing.

There is a suggestion that the case is different from *Bridges* v. *California, supra,* in that we have here only private litigation, while in the *Bridges* case labor controversies were involved, some of them being criminal cases. The thought apparently is that the range of permissible comment is greater where the pending case generates a public concern. The nature of the case may, of course, be relevant in determining whether the clear and present danger test is satisfied. But, the rule of the *Bridges* and *Pennekamp* cases is fashioned to serve the needs of all litigation, not merely select types of pending cases.

Reversed.

Mr. Justice Murphy concurred in a separate opinion.

Mr. Justice Frankfurter, joined by Chief Justice Vinson, dissented.

[He emphasized that the effect of the Court's position was to destroy a theretofore unquestioned state power. And he observed that the *Toledo*, *Nye*, and *Hecht* cases on which the Court relied were not relevant because they dealt not with the constitutional authority of the states, but merely with the interpretation of federal legislation narrowly restricting the contempt power of federal courts. He then continued as follows:]

We are not dealing here with criticisms, whether temperate or unbridled, of action in a case after a judge is through with it, or of his judicial qualifications, or of his conduct in general. Comment on what a judge has done—criticism of the judicial process in a particular case after it has exhausted itself—no matter how ill-informed or irresponsible or misrepresentative, is part of the precious right of the free play of opinion. Whatever violence there may be to truth in such utterances must be left to the correction of truth.

The publications now in question did not constitute merely a narrative of a judge's conduct in a particular case nor a general commentary upon his competence or his philosophy. Nor were they a plea for reform of the Texas legal system to the end that county court judges should be learned in the law and that a judgment in a suit of forcible detainer may be appealable. The thrust of the articles was directed to what the judge should do on a matter immediately before him, namely to grant a motion for a new trial. So the Texas Court found. And it found this not in the abstract but on the particu-

lar stage of the happenings and in the circumstances disclosed by the record. The Texas Court made its findings with reference to the locality where the events took place and in circumstances which may easily impart significance to the Texas Court but may elude full appreciation here.

Corpus Christi, the locale of the drama, had a population of less than 60,000 at the last census, and Nueces County about 92,000. The three papers which published the articles complained of are under common control and are the only papers of general circulation in the area. It can hardly be a compelling presumption that such papers so controlled had no influence, at a time when patriotic fervor was running high, in stirring up sentiment of powerful groups in a small community in favor of a veteran to whom, it was charged, a great wrong had been done. It would seem a natural inference, as the court below in effect found, that these newspapers whipped up public opinion against the judge to secure reversal of his action and then professed merely to report public opinion. We cannot say that the Texas Court could not properly find that these newspapers asked of the judge, and instigated powerful sections of the community to ask of the judge, that which no one has any business to ask of a judge, except the parties and their counsel in open court, namely, that he should decide one way rather than another. Only if we can say that the Texas Court had no basis in reason to find what it did find, can we deny that the purpose of the articles in their setting was to induce the judge to grant a new trial. Surely a jury could reach such a conclusion on these facts. We ought not to allow less leeway to the Texas Court in drawing inferences than we would to a jury. Because it is a question of degree, the field in which a court, like a jury, may "exercise its judgment is, necessarily, a wide one." Mr. Justice Brandeis in *Schafer* v. *United States*, 251 U.S. 466, 483. Of course, the findings by a State court of what are usually deemed facts cannot foreclose our scrutiny of them if a constitutional right depends on a fair appraisal of those facts. But it would be novel doctrine indeed to say that we may consider the record as it comes before us from a State court as though it were our duty or right to ascertain the facts in the first instance. A State cannot by torturing facts preclude us from considering whether it has thereby denied a constitutional right. Neither can this Court find a violation of a constitutional right by denying to a State its right to a fair appraisal of facts and circumstances peculiarly its concern. Otherwise, in every case coming here from a State court this Court might make independent examination of the facts, because every right claimed under the Constitution is a fundamental right. The "most respectful attention" which we have been told is due to a State would then be merely an empty profession. See *Pennekamp* v. *Florida*, 328 U.S. 331, 335.

If under all the circumstances the Texas Court here was not justified in finding that these publications created "a clear and present danger" of the substantive evil that Texas had a right to prevent, namely the purposeful exertion of extraneous influence in having the motion for a new trial granted, "clear and present danger" becomes merely a phrase for covering up a novel, iron constitutional doctrine. Hereafter the States cannot deal with direct attempts to influence the disposition of a pending controversy by a summary proceeding, except when the misbehavior physically prevents proceedings from going on in court, or occurs in its immediate proximity. Only the pungent pen of Mr. Justice Holmes could adequately comment on such a perversion of his phrase. . . .

Mr. Justice Jackson, dissenting.

This is one of those cases in which the reasons we give for our decision are more important to the development of the law than the decision itself.

It seems to me that the Court is assigning two untenable, if not harmful, reasons for its action. The first is that this newspaper publisher has done no wrong. I take it that we could not deny the right of the state to punish him if he had done wrong and I do not suppose we could say that the traditional remedy was an unconstitutional one.

The right of the people to have a free press is a vital one, but so is the right to have a calm and fair trial free from outside pressures and influences. Every other right, including the right of a free press itself, may depend on the ability to get a judicial hearing as dispassionate and impartial as the weakness inherent in men will permit. I think this publisher passed beyond the legitimate use of press freedom and infringed the citizen's right to a calm and impartial trial. I do not think we can say that it is beyond the power of the state to exert safeguards against such interference with the course of trial as we have here.

This was a private lawsuit between individuals. It involved an issue of no greater public importance than which of two claimants should be the tenant of the "Playboy Cafe." The public interest in the litigation was that dispassionate justice be done by the court and that it appear to be done. . . .

For this Court to imply that this kind of attack during a pending case is all right seems to me to compound the wrong. The press of the country may rightfully take the decision of this Court to mean indifference toward, if not approval of, such attacks upon courts during pending cases. I think this opinion conveys a wrong impression of the responsibilities of a free press for the calm and dispassionate administration of justice and that we should not hesitate to condemn what has been done here.

But even worse is that this Court appears to sponsor the myth that judges are not as other men are, and that therefore newspaper attacks on them are negligible because they do not penetrate the judicial armor. Says the opinion: "But the law of contempt is not made for the protection of judges who may be sensitive to the winds of public opinion. Judges are supposed to be men of fortitude, able to thrive in a hardy climate." With due respect to those who think otherwise, to me this is an ill-founded opinion, and to inform the press that it may be irresponsible in attacking judges because they have so much fortitude is ill-advised, or worse. I do not know whether it is the view of the Court that a judge must be thick-skinned or just thick-headed, but nothing in my experience or observation confirms the idea that he is insensitive to publicity. Who does not prefer good to ill report of his work? And if fame—a good public name—is, as Milton said, the "last infirmity of noble mind," it is frequently the first infirmity of a mediocre one.

From our sheltered position, fortified by life tenure and other defenses to judicial independence, it is easy to say that this local judge ought to have shown more fortitude in the face of criticism. But he had no such protection. He was an elective judge, who held for a short term. I do not take it that an ambition of a judge to remain a judge is either unusual or dishonorable. Moreover, he was not a lawyer, and I regard

this as a matter of some consequence. A lawyer may gain courage to render a decision that temporarily is unpopular because he has confidence that his profession over the years will approve it, despite its unpopular reception, as has been the case with many great decisions. But this judge had no anchor in professional opinion. Of course, the blasts of these little papers in this small community do not jolt us, but I am not so confident that we would be indifferent if a news monopoly in our entire jurisdiction should perpetrate this kind of an attack on us. . . .

> *Quaere:* Were those who interfered with the judicial process in the cases summarized in *Nebraska Press Association* (p. 284) guilty of contempt of court? Would *Craig* (and cases cited therein) shield them? Is invalidation of a judgment tainted by improper outside interference—and immunity for the taintor—required by the Constitution? For a more recent contempt case, see *Wood* v. *Georgia*, 370 U.S. 375 (1962).

Smith v. *Daily Mail Publishing Co.*
99 Sm Ct. 2667 (1979)

The defendant newspaper published articles containing the name of a juvenile who had been arrested for alleged homicide. The newspaper got the information from a police-band radio broadcast and from eyewitnesses. It was indicted for violating a state law making it a crime for a newspaper to publish, without approval of the juvenile court, the name of anyone charged as a juvenile offender.

Mr. Chief Justice Burter delivered the opinion of the Court . . . .

The sole interest advanced by the State to justify its criminal statute is to protect the anonymity of the juvenile offender. It is asserted that confidentiality will further his rehabilitation because publication of the name may encourage further antisocial conduct and also may cause the juvenile to lose future employment or suffer other consequences for this single offense. . . .

The magnitude of the State's interest in this statute is not sufficient to justify application of a criminal penalty to respondents. Moreover, the statute's approach does not satisfy constitutional requirements. The statute does not restrict the electronic media or any form of publication, except "newspaper," from printing the names of youths charged in a juvenile proceeding. In this very case, three radio stations announced the alleged assailant's name before the *Daily Mail* decided to publish it. Thus, even assuming the statute served a state interest of the highest order, it does not accomplish its stated purpose.

Mr. Justice Powell took no part in the consideration or decision of this case.

Mr. Justice Rehnquist, concurring. [Justice Rehnquist agreed with the Court that the state law "does not accomplish its stated purpose", but in his view:]

. . . So valued is the liberty of speech and of the press that there is a tendency in cases such as this to accept virtually any contention supported by a claim of interference with speech or the press. See *Jones* v. *Opelika*, 316 U.S. 584, 595 (1942). I would resist that temptation. In my view, a State's interest in preserving the anonymity of its juvenile offenders—an interest that I consider to be, in the words of the Court, of the "highest order"—far outweighs any minimal interference with freedom of the press that a ban on publication of the youth's names entails.

Cox Broadcasting Corp. v. *Cohn*
See p. 433, above.

Miami Herald Publishing Co. v. *Tornillo*
See p. 438, above.

New York Times Co. v. *Sullivan*
See p. 421, above.

Gertz v. *Robert Welch, Inc.*
See p. 425, above.

Pittsburgh Press Co. v. *Pittsburgh Commission on Human Relations*
413 U.S. 376 (1973)

Mr. Justice Powell delivered the opinion of the Court.

The Human Relations Ordinance of the City of Pittsburgh (the "Ordinance") has been construed below by the courts of Pennsylvania as forbidding newspapers to carry "help-wanted" advertisements in sex-designated columns except where the employer or advertiser is free to make hiring or employment referral decisions on the basis of sex. We are called upon to decide whether the Ordinance as so construed violates the freedoms of speech, and of the press guaranteed by the First and Fourteenth Amendments. . . .

There is little need to reiterate that the freedoms of speech and of the press are among our most cherished liberties. . . . The durability of our system of self-government hinges upon the preservation of these freedoms. . . .

The repeated emphasis accorded this theme in the decisions of this Court serves to underline the narrowness of the recognized exceptions to the principle that the press may not be regulated by the Government. Our inquiry must therefore be whether the challenged order falls within any of these exceptions.

At the outset, however, it is important to identify with some care the nature of the alleged abridgment. This is not a case in which the challenged law arguably disables the press by undermining its institutional viability. As the press has evolved from an assortment of small printers into a diverse aggregation including large publishing empires as well, the parallel growth and complexity of the economy have led to extensive regulatory legislation from which "[t]he publisher of a newspaper has no special immunity." *Associated Press* v. *NLRB*, 301 U.S. 103, 132 (1937). Accordingly, this Court has upheld application to the press of the National Labor Relations Act, . . . and the Sherman Antitrust Act, ... Yet the Court has recognized on several occasions the special institutional needs of a vigorous press by striking down laws taxing the advertising revenue of newspapers with circulations in excess of 20,000, *Grosjean* v. *American Press Co., supra* [297 U.S. 233], requiring a license for the distribution of printed matter, *Lovell* v. *Griffin*, 303 U.S. 444 (1938), and prohibiting the door-to-door distribution of leaflets, *Martin* v. *Struthers*, 319 U.S. 141 (1943).

But no suggestion is made in this case that the Pittsburgh Ordinance was passed with any purpose of muzzling or curbing the press. Nor does [the] *Pittsburgh Press* argue that the Ordinance threatens its financial viability or impairs in any significant way its ability to publish and distribute its newspaper. In any event, such a contention would not be supported by the record. . . .

Respondents rely principally on the argument that this regulation is permissible because the speech is commercial speech unprotected by the First Amendment. The commercial speech doctrine is traceable to the brief opinion in *Valentine* v. *Chrestensen*, 316 U.S. 52 (1942). . . .

But *Pittsburgh Press* contends that *Chrestensen* is not applicable, as the focus in this case must be upon the exercise of editorial judgment by the newspaper as to where to place the advertisement rather than upon its commercial content. . . .

As for the present case, we are not persuaded that either the decision to accept a commercial advertisement which the advertiser directs to be placed in a sex-designated column or the actual placement there lifts the newspaper's actions from the category of commercial speech. By implication at least, an advertiser whose want-ad appears in the "Jobs—Male Interest" column is likely to discriminate against women in his hiring decisions. Nothing in a sex-designated column heading sufficiently dissociates the designation from the want-ads placed beneath it to make the placement severable for First Amendment purposes from the want-ads themselves. The combination, which conveys essentially the same message as an overtly discriminatory want-ad, is in practical effect an integrated commercial statement.

Pittsburgh Press goes on to argue that if this package of advertisement and placement is commercial speech, then commercial speech should be accorded a higher level of protection than *Chrestensen* and its progeny would suggest. Insisting that the exchange of information is as important in the commercial realm as in any other, the newspaper here would have us abrogate the distinction between commercial and other speech.

Whatever the merits of this contention may be in other contexts, it is unpersuasive in this case. Discrimination in employment is not only commercial activity, it is *illegal* commercial activity under the Ordinance. We have no doubt that a newspaper constitutionally could be forbidden to publish a want-ad proposing a sale of narcotics or soliciting prostitutes. Nor would the result be different if the nature of the transaction were indicated by placement under columns captioned "Narcotics for Sale" and "Prostitutes Wanted" rather than stated within the four corners of the advertisement. . . .

We emphasize that nothing in our holding allows government at any level to forbid *Pittsburgh Press* to publish and distribute advertisements commenting on the Ordinance, the enforcement practices of the Commission, or the propriety of sex preferences in employment. Nor, *a fortiorari*, does our decision authorize any restriction whatever, whether of content or layout, on stories or commentary originated by *Pittsburgh Press*, its columnists, or its contributors. On the contrary, we reaffirm unequivocally the protection afforded to editorial judgment and to the free expression of views on these and other issues, however controversial. We hold only that the Commission's modified order, narrowly drawn to prohibit placement in sex-designated columns of advertisements for nonexempt job opportunities, does not infringe the First Amendment rights of *Pittsburgh Press*.

Mr. Chief Justice Burger, dissenting.

Despite the Court's efforts to decide only the most narrow question presented in this case, the holding represents, for me, a disturbing en-largement of the "commercial speech" doctrine, *Valentine* v. *Chrestensen*, 316 U.S. 52 (1942), and a serious encroachment on the freedom of press guaranteed by the First Amendment. It also launches the courts on what I perceive to be a treacherous path of defining what layout and organizational decisions of newspapers are "suf-ficiently associated" with the "commercial" parts of the papers as to be constitutionally un-protected and therefore subject to governmental regulation. Assuming, *arguendo,* that the First Amendment permits the States to place restric-tions on the content of commercial advertise-ments, I would not enlarge that power to reach the layout and organizational decisions of a newspaper. . . .

Mr. Justice Douglas, dissenting. . . .

Mr. Justice Stewart, with whom Mr. Justice Douglas joins, dissenting. . . .

. . . [W]hat the Court approves today is wholly different. It approves a government order dictating to a publisher in advance how he must arrange the layout of pages in his news-paper.

Nothing in *Valentine* v. *Chrestensen*, 316 U.S. 52, remotely supports the Court's decision. . . .

So far as I know, this is the first case in this or any other American court that permits a gov-ernment agency to enter a composing room of a newspaper and dictate to the publisher the

layout and makeup of the newspaper's pages. This is the first such case, but I fear it may not be the last. The camel's nose is in the tent. . . .

So long as Members of this Court view the First Amendment as no more than a set of "val-ues" to be balanced against other "values," that Amendment will remain in grave jeopardy. . . .

Those who think the First Amendment can and should be subordinated to other socially desirable interests will hail today's decision. But I find it frightening. For I believe the constitu-tional guarantee of a free press is more than prec-atory. I believe it is a clear command that Gov-ernment must never be allowed to lay its heavy editorial hand on any newspaper in this coun-try.

Mr. Justice Blackmun, dissenting.

I dissent substantially for the reasons stated by Mr. Justice Stewart in his opinion. . . .

Note: FCC regulations prohibited (prospec-tively) joint ownership of broadcasting stations and newspapers located in any single community. The Court unanimously rejected a claim that this violated the First Amendment rights of newspaper owners; ". . . the regulations are not content-related; moreover their purpose and effect are to promote free speech [by promoting the public interest in a diversity of media voices], not to re-strict it" *F.C.C.* v. *National Citizens Committee for Broadcasting,* 98 S. Ct. 2906 [1978].

Branzburg v. *Hayes*
408 U.S. 665 (1972)

This and two related cases (*Pappas* and *Caldwell*) present the issue of whether the free speech and press provisions of the First Amendment give journalists special immunity from testifying before grand juries—an immunity not available to people in general.

Opinion of the Court by Mr. Justice White, announced by the Chief Justice. . . .

Petitioners Branzburg and Pappas and re-spondent Caldwell press First Amendment claims that may be simply put: that to gather news it is often necessary to agree either not to identify the source of information published or to publish only part of the facts revealed, or both; that if the reporter is nevertheless forced to reveal these confidences to a grand jury, the source so identified and other confidential sources of other reporters will be measurably deterred from furnishing publishable information, all to the detriment of the free flow of information protected by the First Amendment. Although petitioners do not claim an absolute privilege against official interrogation in all circumstances, they assert that the reporter should not be forced either to appear or to testify before a grand jury or at trial until and unless sufficient grounds are shown for believing that the reporter possesses information relevant to a crime the grand jury is investigating, that the information the reporter has is unavailable from other sources, and that the need for the information is sufficiently compelling to override the claimed invasion of First Amendment interests occasioned by the disclosure. . . .

We do not question the significance of free speech, press or assembly to the country's welfare. Nor is it suggested that news gathering does not qualify for First Amendment protection; without some protection for seeking out the news, freedom of the press could be eviscerated. But this case involves no intrusions upon speech or assembly, no prior restraint or restriction on what the press may publish, and no express or implied command that the press publish what it prefers to withhold. . . .

The sole issue before us is the obligation of reporters to respond to grand jury subpoenas as other citizens do and to answer questions relevant to an investigation into the commission of crime. . . .

Despite the fact that news gathering may be hampered, the press is regularly excluded from grand jury proceedings, our own conferences, the meetings of other official bodies gathered in executive session, and the meetings of private organizations. Newsmen have no constitutional

right of access to the scenes of crime or disaster when the general public is excluded, and they may be prohibited from attending or publishing information about trials if such restrictions are necessary to assure a defendant a fair trial before an impartial tribunal. *Sheppard* v. *Maxwell*, 384 U.S. 333 (1966) . . .

It is thus not surprising that the great weight of authority is that newsmen are not exempt from the normal duty of appearing before a grand jury and answering questions relevant to a criminal investigation. At common law, courts consistently refused to recognize the existence of any privilege authorizing a newsman to refuse to reveal confidential information to a grand jury. . . . See generally Annot., 7 A.L.R.3d 591 (1966).

The prevailing constitutional view of the newsman's privilege is very much rooted in the ancient role of the grand jury which has the dual function of determining if there is probable cause to believe that a crime has been committed and of protecting citizens against unfounded criminal prosecutions. . . . Because its task is to inquire into the existence of possible criminal conduct and to return only well-founded indictments, its investigative powers are necessarily broad. . . .

A number of States have provided newsmen a statutory privilege of varying breadth, but the majority have not done so, and none has been provided by federal statute. Until now the only testimonial privilege for unofficial witnesses that is rooted in the Federal Constitution is the Fifth Amendment privilege against compelled self-incrimination. We are asked to create another by interpreting the First Amendment to grant newsmen a testimonial privilege that other citizens do not enjoy. This we decline to do. . . .

This conclusion itself involves no restraint on what newspapers may publish or on the type or quality of information reporters may seek to acquire, nor does it threaten the vast bulk of confidential relationships between reporters and their sources. Grand juries address themselves to the issues of whether crimes have been committed and who committed them. Only where news sources themselves are implicated in crime or possess information relevant to the grand jury's task need they or the reporter be concerned about grand jury subpoenas. Nothing before us indicates that a large number or percentage of *all* confidential news sources fall into either category and would in any way be deterred by our holding that the Constitution does not, as it never has, exempt the newsman from performing the citizen's normal duty of appearing and furnishing information relevant to the grand jury's task. . . .

The argument that the flow of news will be diminished by compelling reporters to aid the grand jury in a criminal investigation is not irrational, nor are the records before us silent on the matter. But we remain unclear how often and to what extent informers are actually deterred from furnishing information when newsmen are forced to testify before a grand jury. The available data indicates that some newsmen rely a great deal on confidential sources and that some informants are particularly sensitive to the threat of exposure and may be silenced if it is held by this Court that, ordinarily, newsmen must testify pursuant to subpoenas, but the evidence fails to demonstrate that there would be a significant constriction of the flow of news to the public if this Court reaffirms the prior common law and constitutional rule regarding the testimonial obligations of newsmen. Estimates of the inhibiting effect of such subpoenas on the willingness of informants to make disclosures to newsmen are widely divergent and to a great extent speculative. . . .

Accepting the fact, however, that an undetermined number of informatants not themselves implicated in crime will nevertheless, for whatever reason, refuse to talk to newsmen if they fear identification by a reporter in an official investigation, we cannot accept the argument that the public interest in possible future news about crime from undisclosed, unverified

sources must take precedence over the public interest in pursuing and prosecuting those crimes reported to the press by informants and in thus deterring the commission of such crimes in the future. . . .

It is said that currently press subpoenas have multiplied, that mutual distrust and tension between press and officialdom have increased, that reporting styles have changed, and that there is now more need for confidential sources, particularly where the press seeks news about minority cultural and political groups or dissident organizations suspicious of the law and public officials. These developments, even if true, are treacherous grounds for a far-reaching interpretation of the First Amendment fastening a nationwide rule on courts, grand juries, and prosecuting officials everywhere. . . .

The privilege claimed here is conditional, not absolute; given the suggested preliminary showings and compelling need, the reporter would be required to testify. Presumably, such a rule would reduce the instances in which reporters could be required to appear, but predicting in advance when and in what circumstances they could be compelled to do so would be difficult. . . .

We are unwilling to embark the judiciary on a long and difficult journey to such an uncertain destination. The administration of a constitutional newsman's privilege would present practical and conceptual difficulties of a high order. Sooner or later, it would be necessary to define those categories of newsmen who qualified for the privilege, a questionable procedure in light of the traditional doctrine that liberty of the press is the right of the lonely pamphleteer who uses carbon paper or a mimeograph just as much as of the large metropolitan publisher who utilizes the latest photocomposition methods. . . .

In each instance where a reporter is subpoenaed to testify, the courts would also be embroiled in preliminary factual and legal determinations with respect to whether the proper predicate had been laid for the reporters' appearance: Is there probable cause to believe a crime has been committed? Is it likely that the reporter has useful information gained in confidence? Could the grand jury obtain the information elsewhere? Is the official interest sufficient to outweigh the claimed privilege?

Thus, in the end, by considering whether enforcement of a particular law served a "compelling" government interest, the courts would be inextricably involved in distinguishing between the value of enforcing different criminal laws. By requiring testimony from a reporter in investigations involving some crimes but not in others, they would be making a value judgment which a legislature had declined to make, since in each case the criminal law involved would represent a considered legislative judgment, not constitutionally suspect, of what conduct is liable to criminal prosecution. The task of judges, like other officials outside the legislative branch is not to make the law but to uphold it in accordance with their oaths.

At the federal level, Congress has freedom to determine whether a statutory newsman's privilege is necessary and desirable and to fashion standards and rules as narrow or broad as deemed necessary to address the evil discerned and, equally important, to re-fashion those rules as experience from time to time may dictate. There is also merit in leaving state legislatures free, within First Amendment limits, to fashion their own standards in light of the conditions and problems with respect to the relations between law enforcement officials and press in their own areas. It goes without saying, of course, that we are powerless to erect any bar to state courts responding in their own way and construing their own constitutions so as to recognize a newsman's privilege, either qualified or absolute. . . .

Finally, as we have earlier indicated, news gathering is not without its First Amendment protections, and grand jury investigations if instituted or conducted other than in good faith, would pose wholly different issues for resolution under the First Amendment. Official harassment of the press undertaken not for purposes of law enforcement but to disrupt a reporter's relationship with his news sources would have no justification. Grand juries are subject to judicial control and subpoenas to motions to quash. We do not expect courts will forget that grand juries must operate within the limits of the First Amendment as well as the Fifth. . . .

Mr. Justice Powell, concurring in the opinion of the Court.

I add this brief statement to emphasize what seems to me to be the limited nature of the Court's holding. The Court does not hold that newsmen, subpoenaed to testify before a grand jury, are without constitutional rights with respect to the gathering of news or in safeguarding their sources. Certainly, we do not hold, as suggested in the dissenting opinion, that state and federal authorities are free to "annex" the news media as "an investigative arm of government." The solicitude repeatedly shown by this Court for First Amendment freedoms should be sufficient assurance against any such effort, even if one seriously believed that the media—properly free and untrammeled in the fullest sense of these terms—were not able to protect themselves.

As indicated in the concluding portion of the opinion, the Court states that no harassment of newsmen will be tolerated. If a newsman believes that the grand jury investigation is not being conducted in good faith he is not without remedy. Indeed, if the newsman is called upon to give information bearing only a remote and tenuous relationship to the subject of the investigation, or if he has some other reason to believe that his testimony implicates confidential source relationships without a legitimate need of law enforcement, he will have access to the Court on a motion to quash and an appropriate protective order may be entered. The asserted claim to privilege should be judged on its facts by the striking of a proper balance between freedom of the press and the obligation of all citizens to give relevant testimony with respect to criminal conduct. The balance of these vital constitutional and societal interests on a case-by-case basis accords with the tried and traditional way of adjudicating such questions.

In short, the courts will be available to newsmen under circumstances where legitimate First Amendment interests require protection.

Mr. Justice Douglas, dissenting. . . .

It is my view that there is no "compelling need" that can be shown which qualifies the reporter's immunity from appearing or testifying before a grand jury, unless the reporter himself is implicated in a crime. His immunity in my view is therefore quite complete, for absent his involvement in a crime, the First Amendment protects him against an appearance before a grand jury and if he is involved in a crime, the Fifth Amendment stands as a barrier. Since in my view there is no area of inquiry not protected by a privilege, the reporter need not appear for the futile purpose of invoking one to each question. And, since in my view a newsman has an absolute right not to appear before a grand jury it follows for me that a journalist who voluntarily appears before that body may invoke his First Amendment privilege to specific questions. The basic issue is the extent to which the First Amendment . . . must yield to the Government's asserted need to know a reporter's unprinted information. . . .

A reporter is no better than his source of information. Unless he has a privilege to withhold the identity of his source, he will be the victim of governmental intrigue or aggression. If he can be summoned to testify in secret before a grand jury, his sources will dry up and the attempted exposure, the effort to enlighten the public, will be ended. If what the Court sanctions today becomes settled law, then the repor-

ter's main function in America society will be to pass on to the public the press releases which the various departments of government issue. . . .

Mr. Justice Stewart, with whom Mr. Justice Brennan and Mr. Justice Marshall join, dissenting.

The Court's crabbed view of the First Amendment reflects a disturbing insensitivity to the critical role of an independent press in our society. The question whether a reporter has a constitutional right to a confidential relationship with his source is of first impression here, but the principles which should guide our decision are as basic as any to be found in the Constitution. While Mr. Justice Powell's enigmatic concurring opinion gives some hope of a more flexible view in the future, the Court in these cases holds that a newsman has no First Amendment right to protect his sources when called before a grand jury. The Court thus invites state and federal authorities to undermine the historic independence of the press by attempting to annex the journalistic profession as an investigative arm of government. Not only will this decision impair performance of the press constitutionally protected functions, but it will, I am convinced, in the long run, harm rather than help the administration of justice. . . .

The reporter's constitutional right to a confidential relationship with his source stems from the broad societal interest in a full and free flow of information to the public. . . .

It is obvious that informants are necessary to the news-gathering process as we know it today. . . .

It is equally obvious that the promise of confidentiality may be a necessary prerequisite to a productive relationship between a newsman and his informants. . . .

Finally, and most important, when governmental officials possess an unchecked power to compel newsmen to disclose information received in confidence, sources will clearly be deterred from giving information, and reporters will clearly be deterred from publishing it, because uncertainty about exercise of the power will lead to "self-censorship." . . .

The impairment of the flow of news cannot, of course, be proven with scientific precision, as the Court seems to demand. . . .

Posed against the First Amendment's protection of the newsman's confidential relationship in these cases is society's interest in the use of the grand jury to administer justice fairly and effectively. . . .

Yet the longstanding rule making every person's evidence available to the grand jury is not absolute. The rule has been limited by the Fifth Amendment, the Fourth Amendment, and the evidentiary privileges of the common law. . . .

Such an interest must surely be the First Amendment protection of a confidential relationship that I have discussed above. . . .

Accordingly, when a reporter is asked to appear before a grand jury and reveal confidences, I would hold that the government must (1) show that there is probable cause to believe that the newsman has information which is clearly relevant to a specific probable violation of law; (2) demonstrate that the information sought cannot be obtained by alternative means less destructive of First Amendment rights; and (3) demonstrate a compelling and overriding interest in the information.

This is not to say that a grand jury could not issue a subpoena until such a showing were made, and it is not to say that a newsman would be in any way privileged to ignore any subpoena that was issued. Obviously, before the government's burden to make such a showing were triggered, the reporter would have to move to quash the subpoena, asserting the basis on which he considered the particular relationship a confidential one. . . .

Note: Compare *United States* v. *Nixon* (above, Chapter 2) with Branzburg. *Pell* v. *Procunier,* 417 U.S. 817 (1974), and *Houchins* v. *KQED,* 98 S. Ct. 2588 (1978), held that journalists have no constitutional privilege (or right) of access to prisons or their inmates beyond that afforded to the general public. *Nixon* v. *Warner Communications, Inc.,* 98 S. Ct. 1306 (1978)—involving the Nixon tapes then in custody of a federal district court—held that "The First Amendment generally grants the press no right to information about a trial superior to that of the general public." *Zurcher* v. *Stanford Daily,* 98 S. Ct. 1970 (1978), held that a newspaper office is no less subject to *search warrants* for law enforcement purposes than are other offices—or indeed homes.

For a history of the consistent development of the doctrine that the press enjoys under the First Amendment only the same rights and is bound by the same obligations as the individual, see Blanchard, "The Institutional Press and Its First Amendment Privileges," *The Supreme Court Review* (The University of Chicago Press, 1978, p. 225).

A RIGHT TO SILENCE? (PRIVACY?)

McGrain v. *Daugherty* (excerpt)
273 U.S. 135 (1927)

The power of inquiry—with process to enforce it—is an essential and appropriate auxiliary to the legislative function. A legislative body cannot legislate wisely or effectively in the absence of information respecting the conditions which the legislation is intended to affect or change; and where the legislative body does not itself possess the requisite information—which is not infrequently true—recourse must be had to others who do possess it.

Watkins v. *United States* (excerpt)
354 U.S. 178 (1957)

The power of the Congress to conduct investigations is inherent in the legislative process. . . . But, broad as is this power of inquiry, it is not unlimited. There is no general authority to expose the private affairs of individuals without justification in terms of the functions of the Congress. . . . Nor is the Congress a law enforcement or trial agency. These are functions of the executive and judicial departments of government. No inquiry is an end in itself; it must be related to, and in furtherance of, a legitimate task of the Congress. Investigations conducted solely for the personal aggrandizement of the investigators or to "punish" those investigated are indefensible.

It is unquestionably the duty of all citizens to cooperate with the Congress in its efforts to obtain the facts needed for intelligent legislative action. . . . This, of course, assumes that the constitutional rights of witnesses will be respected by the Congress as they are in a court of justice. The Bill of Rights is applicable to investigations as to all forms of governmental action. Witnesses cannot be compelled to give evidence against themselves. They cannot be subjected to unreasonable search and seizure. Nor can the First Amendment freedoms of speech, press, religion, or political belief and association be abridged. . . .

We have no doubt that there is no congressional power to expose for the sake of exposure. The public is, of course, entitled to be informed concerning the workings of its government. That cannot be inflated into a general power to expose where the predominant result can only be an invasion of the private rights of individuals. But a solution to our problem is not to be found in testing the motives of committee members for this purpose. Such is not our function. Their motives alone would not vitiate an investigation which had been instituted by a House of Congress if that assembly's legislative purpose is being served. . . .

It is the responsibility of the Congress, in the first instance, to insure that compulsory process is used only in furtherance of a legislative purpose. That requires that the instructions to an investigating committee spell out that group's jurisdiction and purpose with sufficient particularity. Those instructions are embodied in the authorizing resolution. That document is the committee's charter. Broadly drafted and loosely worded, however, such resolutions can leave tremendous latitutde to the discretion of the investigators. The more vague the committee's charter is, the greater becomes the possibility that the committee's specific actions are not in conformity with the will of the parent House of Congress. . . .

An excessively broad charter, like that of the House Un-American Activities Committee, places the courts in an untenable position if they are to strike a balance between the public need for a particular interrogation and the right of citizens to carry on their affairs free from unnecessary governmental interference. It is impossible in such a situation to ascertain whether any legislative purpose justifies the disclosures sought and, if so, the importance of that information to the Congress in furtherance of its legislative function. . . .

There are several sources that can outline the question under inquiry in such a way that the rules against vagueness are satisfied. The authorizing resolution, the remarks of the chairman or members of the committee, or even the nature of the proceedings themselves, might sometimes make the topic clear.

Barrenblatt v. *United States*
360 U.S. 109 (1959)

Mr. Justice Harlan delivered the opinion of the Court. . . .

We here review petitioner's conviction under 2 U.S.C. § 192 for contempt of Congress, arising from his refusal to answer certain questions put to him by a Subcommittee of the House Committee on Un-American Activities during the course of an inquiry concerning alleged Communist infiltration into the field of education. . . .

Petitioner's various contentions resolve themselves into three propositions: First, the compelling of testimony by the Subcommittee was neither legislatively authorized nor constitutionally permissible because of the vagueness of Rule XI of the House of Representatives, Eighty-third Congress, the charter of authority of the parent Committee. Second, petitioner was not adequately apprised of the pertinency of the Subcommittee's questions to the subject matter of the inquiry. Third, the questions petitioner refused to answer infringed rights protected by the First Amendment.

SUBCOMMITTEE'S AUTHORITY TO COMPEL TESTIMONY

At the outset it should be noted that Rule XI authorized this Subcommittee to compel testimony within the framework of the investigative authority conferred on the Un-American Activities Committee. Petitioner contends that *Watkins* v. *United States*, 354 U.S. 178, nevertheless held the grant of this power in all circumstances ineffective because of the vagueness of Rule XI in delineating the Committee jursidiction to which its exercise was to be appurtenant. This view of *Watkins* was accepted by two of the dissenting judges below. 252 F.2d at page 136.

The *Watkins* case cannot properly be read as standing for such a proposition. A principal contention in *Watkins* was that the refusals to answer were justified because the requirement of 2 U.S.C. § 192 that the questions asked be "pertinent to the question under inquiry" had not been satisfied. . . . This Court reversed the conviction solely on that ground, holding that Watkins had not been adequately apprised of the subject matter of the Subcommittee's inves-

tigation or the pertinency thereto of the questions he refused to answer, *id.*, 354 U.S. at pages 206–209, 214–215; and see the concurring opinion in that case, *id.*, 354 U.S. at page 216. In so deciding the Court drew upon Rule XI only as one of the facets in the total *mise en scène* in its search for the "question under inquiry" in that particular investigation. *Id.*, 354 U.S. at pages 209–215. The Court, in other words, was not dealing with Rule XI at large, and indeed in effect stated that no such issue was before it, *id.*, 354 U.S. at page 209. That the vagueness of Rule XI was not alone determinative is also shown by the Court's further statement that aside from the Rule "the remarks of the chairman or members of the committee, or even the nature of the proceedings themselves, might sometimes make the topic [under inquiry] clear." *Ibid.* In short, while *Watkins* was critical of Rule XI, it did not involve the broad and inflexible holding petitioner now attributes to it. . . .

We are urged, however, to construe Rule XI so as at least to exclude the field of education from the Committee's compulsory authority. Two of the four dissenting judges below relied entirely, the other two alternatively, on this ground. 252 F.2d at pages 136, 138. The contention is premised on the course we took in *United States* v. *Rumely*, 345 U.S. 41, where in order to avoid constitutional issues we construed narrowly the authority of the congressional committee there involved. We cannot follow that route here for this is not a case where Rule XI has to "speak for itself, since Congress put no gloss upon it at the time of its passage," nor one where the subsequent history of the Rule has the "infirmity of *post litem motam*, self-serving declarations." See *United States* v. *Rumely, supra*, 345 U.S. at pages 44–45, 48.

To the contrary, the legislative gloss on Rule XI is again compelling. Not only is there no indication that the House ever viewed the field of education as being outside the Committee's authority under Rule XI, but the legislative history affirmatively evinces House approval of this phase of the Committee's work. . . .

PERTINENCY CLAIM

Undeniably a conviction for contempt under 2 U.S.C § 192, 2 U.S.C.A. § 192 cannot stand unless the questions asked are pertinent to the subject matter of the investigation. *Watkins* v. *United States, supra,* 354 U.S. at pages 214–215. But the factors which led us to rest decision on this ground in *Watkins* were very different from those involved here.

In *Watkins* the petitioner had made specific objection to the Subcommittee's questions on the ground of pertinency; the question under inquiry had not been disclosed in any illuminating manner; and the questions asked the petitioner were not only amorphous on their face, but·in some instances clearly foreign to the alleged subject matter of the investigation— "Communism in labor." *Id.,* 354 U.S. at pages 185, 209–215.

In contrast, petitioner in the case before us raised no objections on the ground of pertinency at the time any of the questions were put to him. . . . We need not, however, rest decision on petitioner's failure to object on this score, for here "pertinency" was made to appear "with undisputable clarity" [the Subcommittee having clearly indicated that the subject under inquiry was Communist infiltration into the field of education].

CONSTITUTIONAL CONTENTIONS

Our function, at this point, is purely one of constitutional adjudication in the particular case and upon the particular record before us, not to pass judgment upon the general wisdom or efficacy of the activities of this Committee in a vexing and complicated field.

The precise constitutional issue confronting us is whether the Subcommittee's inquiry into petitioner's past or present membership in the Communist Party transgressed the provisions of the First Amendment, which of course reach and limit congressional investigations. *Watkins, supra,* 354 U.S. at page 197.

The Court's past cases establish sure guides to decision. Undeniably, the First Amendment in some circumstances protects an individual from being compelled to disclose his associational relationships. However, the protections of the First Amendment, unlike a proper claim of the privilege against self-incrimination under the Fifth Amendment, do not afford a witness the right to resist inquiry in all circumstances. Where the First Amendment rights are asserted to bar governmental interrogation resolution of the issue always involves a balancing by the courts of the competing private and public interests at stake in the particular circumstances shown. . . .

The first question is whether this investigation was related to a valid legislative purpose, for Congress may not constitutionally require an individual to disclose his political relationships or other private affairs except in relation to such a purpose. See *Watkins* v. *United States, supra,* 354 U.S. at page 198.

That Congress has wide power to legislate in the field of Communist activity in this Country, and to conduct appropriate investigations in aid thereof, is hardly debatable. The existence of such power has never been questioned by this Court, and it is sufficient to say, without particularization, that Congress has enacted or considered in this field a wide range of legislative measures, not a few of which have stemmed from recommendations of the very Committee whose actions have been drawn in question here. In the last analysis this power rests on the right of self-preservation, "the ultimate value of any society," *Dennis* v. *United States,* 341 U.S. 494, 509. Justification for its exercise in turn rests on the long and widely accepted view that the tenets of the Communist Party include the ultimate overthrow of the Government of the United States by force and violence, a view which has been given formal expression by the Congress.

On these premises, this Court in its constitutional adjudications has consistently refused to view the Communist Party as an ordinary political party, and has upheld federal legislation aimed at the Communist problem which in a different context would certainly have raised constitutional issues of the gravest character. . . .

. . . [W]e do not understand petitioner here to suggest that Congress in no circumstances may inquire into Communist activity in the field of education. Rather, his position is in effect that this particular investigation was aimed not at the revolutionary aspects but at the theoretical classroom discussion of communism.

In our opinion this position rests on a too constricted view of the nature of the investigatory process, and is not supported by a fair assessment of the record before us. An investigation of advocacy of or preparation for overthrow certainly embraces the right to identify a witness as a member of the Communist Party, see *Barsky* v. *United States,* 167 F.2d 241, and to inquire into the various manifestations of the Party's tenets. The strict requirements of a prosecution under the Smith Act, see *Dennis* v. *United States, supra,* and *Yates* v. *United States,* 354 U.S. 298, are not the measure of the permissible scope of a congressional investigation into "overthrow," for of necessity the investigatory process must proceed step by step. Nor can it fairly be concluded that this investigation was directed at controlling what is being taught at our universities rather than at overthrow. The statement of the Subcommittee Chairman at the opening of the investigation evinces no such intention, and so far as this record reveals nothing thereafter transpired which would justify our holding that the thrust of the investigation later changed. The record discloses considerable testimony concerning the foreign domination and revolutionary purposes and efforts of the Communist Party. That there was also testimony on the abstract philosophical level does not detract from the dominant theme of this investigation—Communist infiltration furthering the alleged ultimate purpose of overthrow. And certainly the conclusion would not be justified that the questioning of petitioner would

have exceeded permissible bounds had he not shut off the Subcommittee at the threshold.

Nor can we accept the further contention that this investigation should not be deemed to have been in furtherance of a legislative purpose because the true objective of the Committee and of the Congress was purely "exposure." So long as Congress acts in pursuance of its constitutional power, the judiciary lacks authority to intervene on the basis of the motives which spurred the exercise of that power. *State of Arizona* v. *State of California,* 283 U.S. 423, 455, and cases there cited. "It is, of course, true," as was said in *McCray* v. *United States,* 195 U.S. 27, 55, "that if there be no authority in the judiciary to restrain a lawful exercise of power by another department of the government, where a wrong motive or purpose has impelled to the exertion of the power, that abuses of a power conferred may be temporarily effectual. The remedy for this, however, lies, not in abuse by the judicial authority of its functions, but in the people, upon whom, after all, under our institutions, reliance must be placed for the correction of abuses committed in the exercise of a lawful power." These principles of course apply as well to committee investigations into the need for legislation as to the enactments which such investigations may produce. Cf. *Tennèy* v. *Brandhove,* 341 U.S. 367, 377–378. Thus, in stating in the *Watkins* case, 354 U.S. at page 200, that "there is no congressional power to expose for the sake of exposure," we at the same time declined to inquire into the "motives of committee members," and recognized that their "motives alone would not vitiate an investigation which had been instituted by a House of Congress if that assembly's legislative purpose is being served." Having scrutinized this record we cannot say that the unanimous panel of the Court of Appeals which first considered this case was wrong in concluding that "the primary purposes of the inquiry were in aid of legislative processes." 240 F.2d at page 881. Certainly this is not a case like *Kilbourn* v. *Thomspon,* 103 U.S. 168, 192, where "the House of Representatives not only exceeded the limit of its own authority, but assumed a power which could only be properly exercised by another branch of the government, because it was in its nature clearly judicial." See *McGrain* v. *Daugherty*, 273 U.S. 135, 171. The constitutional legislative power of Congress in this instance is beyond question. . . .

We conclude that the balance between the individual and the governmental interests here at stake must be struck in favor of the latter, and that therefore the provisions of the First Amendment have not been offended.

We hold that petitioner's conviction for contempt of Congress discloses no infirmity, and that the judgment of the Court of Appeals must be affirmed.

Mr. Justice Black, with whom The Chief Justice, and Mr. Justice Douglas concur, dissenting. . . .

I do not agree that laws directly abridging First Amendment freedoms can be justified by a congressional or judicial balancing process. There are, of course, cases suggesting that a law which primarily regulates conduct but which might also indirectly affect speech can be upheld if the effect on speech is minor in relation to the need for control of the conduct. With these cases I agree. Typical of them are *Cantwell* v. *State of Connecticut*, 310 U.S. 296, and *Schneider* v. *State of New Jersey, Town of Irvington*, 308 U.S. 147. Both of these involved the right of a city to control its streets. . . . But we did not in Schneider, any more than in Cantwell, even remotely suggest that a law directly aimed at curtailing speech and political persuasion could be saved through a balancing process. Neither these cases, nor any others, can be read as allowing legislative bodies to pass laws abridging freedom of speech, press and association merely because of hostility to views peacefully expressed in a place where the speaker had a right to be. Rule XI, on its face and as here applied, since it attempts inquiry into beliefs, not action—ideas and associations, not conduct, does just that.

To apply the Court's balancing test under such circumstances is to read the First Amendment to say "Congress shall pass no law abridging freedom of speech, press, assembly and petition, unless Congress and the Supreme Court reach the joint conclusion that on balance the interests of the Government in stifling these freedoms is greater than the interest of the people in having them exercised." This is closely akin to the notion that neither the First Amendment nor any other provision of the Bill of Rights should be enforced unless the Court believes it is *reasonable* to do so. Not only does this violate the genius of our *written* Constitution, but it runs expressly counter to the injunction to Court and Congress made by Madison when he introduced the Bill of Rights. "If they [the first ten amendments] are incorporated into the Constitution, independent tribunals of justice will consider themselves in a peculiar manner the guardians of those rights; they will be an impenetrable bulwark against *every* assumption of power in the Legislative or Executive; they will be naturally led to resist *every* encroachment upon rights expressly stipulated for in the Constitution by the declaration of rights." Unless we return to this view of our judicial function, unless we once again accept the notion that the Bill of Rights means what it says and that this Court must enforce that meaning, I am of the opinion that our great charter of liberty will be more honored in the breach than in the observance.

But even assuming what I cannot assume, that some balancing is proper in this case, I feel that the Court after stating the test ignores it completely. At most it balances the right of the Government to preserve itself, against Barenblatt's right to refrain from revealing Communist affiliations. Such a balance, however, mistakes the factors to be weighed. In the first place, it completely leaves out the real interest in Barenblatt's silence, the interest of the people as a whole in being able to join organizations, advocate causes and make political "mistakes" without later being subjected to governmental penalties for having dared to think for themselves. It is this right, the right to err politically, which keeps us strong as a Nation. For no number of laws against communism can have as much effect as the personal conviction which comes from having heard its arguments and rejected them, or from having once accepted its tenets and later recognized their worthlessness. Instead, the obloquy which results from investigations such as this not only stifles "mistakes" but prevents all but the most courageous from hazarding any views which might at some later time become disfavored. This result, whose importance cannot be overestimated, is doubly crucial when it affects the universities, on which we must largely rely for the experimentation and development of new ideas essential to our country's welfare. It is these interests of society, rather than Barenblatt's own right to silence, which I think the Court should put on the balance against the demands of the Government, if any balancing process is to be tolerated. Instead they are not mentioned, while on the other side the demands of the Government are vastly overstated and called "self preservation." It is admitted that this Committee can only seek information for the purpose of suggesting laws, and that Congress' power to make laws in the realm of speech and association is quite limited, even on the Court's test. Its interest in making such laws in the field of education, primarily a state function, is clearly narrow still. Yet the Court styles this attenuated interest self-preservation and allows it to overcome the need our country has to let us all think, speak, and associate politically as we like and without fear of reprisal. . . .

Finally, I think Barenblatt's conviction violates the Constitution because the chief aim, purpose and practice of the House Un-American Activities Committee, as disclosed by its many reports, is to try witnesses and punish them because they are or have been Communists or because they refuse to admit or deny Communist affiliations. The punishment imposed is generally punishment by humiliation and public shame. There is nothing strange or novel about this kind of punishment. It is in fact one of the oldest forms of governmental punishment known to mankind; branding, the pillory, ostracism and subjection to public hatred being but a few examples of it. . . .

Mr. Justice Brennan, dissenting.

I would reverse this conviction. It is sufficient that I state my complete agreement with my Brother Black that no purpose for the investigation of Barenblatt is revealed by the record except exposure purely for the sake of exposure. This is not a purpose to which Barenblatt's rights under the First Amendment can validly be subordinated. . . .

Cole v. *Richardson*
405 U.S. 676 (1972)

Chief Justice Burger delivered the opinion of the Court.

In this appeal we review the decision of the three-judge District Court holding a Massachusetts loyalty oath unconstitutional, 300 F. Supp. 1321.

The appellee, Richardson, was hired as a research sociologist by the Boston State Hospital. The appellant is superintendent of the hospital. Soon after she entered on duty Mrs. Richardson was asked to subscribe to the oath required of all public employees in Massachusetts. The oath is as follows:

"I do solemnly swear (or affirm) that I will uphold and defend the Constitution of the United States of America and the Constitution of the Commonwealth of Massachusetts and that I will oppose the overthrow of the government of the United States of America or of this Commonwealth by force, violence or by any illegal or unconstitutional method."

Mrs. Richardson informed that hospital's personnel department that she could not take the oath as ordered because of her belief that it was in violation of the United States Constitution. Approximately 10 days later appellant Cole personally informed Mrs. Richardson that under state law she could not continue as an employee of the Boston State Hospital unless she subscribed to the oath. Again she refused. On November 25, 1968, Mrs. Richardson's employment was terminated and she was paid through that date. . . .

We conclude that the Massachusetts oath is constitutionally permissible. . . .

A review of the oath cases in this Court will put the instant oath into context. We have made clear that neither federal nor state governments may condition employment on taking oaths which impinge rights guaranteed by the First and Fourteenth Amendments respectively, as for example those relating to political beliefs. *Law Students . . . v. Woodmond*, 401 U.S. 154. . . . Nor may employment be conditioned on an oath that one has not engaged, or will not engage, in protected speech activities such as the following: criticizing institutions of government; discussing political doctrine that approves the overthrow of certain forms of government; and supporting candidates for political office. *Keyishian* v. *Board of Regents*, 385 U.S. 589 (1967); *Baggett* v. *Bullitt*, 377 U.S. 360 (1964). Employment may not be conditioned on an oath denying past, or abjuring future, associational activities within constitutional protection; such protected activities include membership in organizations having illegal purposes unless one knows of the purpose and shares a specific intent to promote the illegal purpose. *Whitehill* v. *Elkins*, 389 U.S. 54 (1967); *Keyishian* v. *Board of Regents, supra; Elfbrandt* v. *Russell*, 384 U.S. 11 (1966). . . . Concern for vagueness in the oath cases has been especially great because uncertainty as to an oath's meaning may deter individuals from engaging in constitutionally protected activity conceivably within the scope of the oath. . . . *Bond* v. *Floyd*, 385 U.S. 116.

Several cases recently decided by the Court stand out among our oath cases because they have upheld the constitutionality of oaths, ad-

dressed to the future, promising constitutional support in broad terms. . . .

The District Court in the instant case properly recognized that the first clause of the Massachusetts oath, in which the individual swears to "uphold and defend" the constitutions of the United States and the Commonwealth, is indistinguishable from the oaths this Court has recently approved. Yet the District Court applied a highly literalistic approach to the second clause to strike it down. We view the second clause of the oath as essentially the same as the first.

The second clause of the oath contains a promise to "oppose the overthrow of the government of the United States of America or of this Commonwealth by force, violence or by any illegal or unconstitutional method." The District Court sought to give a dictionary meaning to this language and found "oppose" to raise the specter of vague, undefinable responsibilities actively to combat a potential overthrow of the government. That reading of the oath understandably troubled the court because of what it saw as vagueness in terms of what threats would constitute sufficient danger of overthrow to require the oathgiver to actively oppose overthrow, and exactly what actions he would have to take in that respect.

But such a literal approach to the second clause is inconsistent with the Court's approach to the "support" oaths. One could make a literal argument that "support" involves nebulous, undefined responsibilities for action in some hypothetical situations. . . . We have rejected such rigidly literal notions and recognized that the purpose leading legislatures to enact such oaths, jut as the purpose leading the Framers of our Constitution to include to two explicit constitutional oaths, was not to create specific responsibilities but to assure that those in positions of public trust were willing to commit themselves to live by the constitutional processes of our system. . . . Here the second clause does not require specific action in some hypothetical or actual situation. Plainly "force, violence or . . . any illegal or unconstitutional method" modifies "overthrow" and does not commit the oath taker to meet force with force. Just as the connotatively active word "support" has been interpreted to mean simply a commitment to abide by our constitutional system, the second clause of this oath is merely oriented to the negative implication of this notion; it is a commitment not to use illegal and constitutionally unprotected force to change the constitutional system. The second clause does not expand the obligation of the first; it simply makes clear the application of the first clause to a particular issue. Such repetition, whether for emphasis or cadence, seems to be wont with authors of oaths. That the second clause may be redundant is no ground to strike it down; we are not charged with correcting grammar but with enforcing a constitution.

The purpose of the oath is clear on its face. We cannot presume that the Massachusetts legislature intended by its use of such general terms as "uphold," "defend," and "oppose" to impose obligations of specific, positive action on oath takers. Any such construction would raise serious questions whether the oath was so vague as to amount to denial of due process.

Nor is the oath as interpreted void for vagueness. As Mr. Justice Harlan pointed out in his opinion on our earlier consideration of this case, the oath is "no more than an amenity." It is punishable only by a prosecution for perjury and, since perjury is a knowing and willful falsehood, the constitutional vice of punishment without fair warning cannot occur here. Nor here is there any problem of the punishment inflicted by mere prosecution. There has been no prosecution under this statute since its 1948 enactment, and there is no indication that prosecutions have been planned or begun. The oath "triggered no serious possibility of prosecution" by the Commonwealth. Were we confronted with a record of actual prosecutions or harassment through threatened prosecutions, we might be faced with a different question. Those who view the Massachusetts oath in terms of an endless "parade of horribles" would do well to bear in mind that many of the hazards of human existence that can be imagined are circumscribed by the classic observation of Mr. Justice Holmes, when confronted with the prophecy of dire consequences of certain judicial action, that it would not occur "while this Court sits."

Appellee mounts an additional attack on the Massachusetts oath program in that it does not provide for a hearing prior to the determination not to hire the individual based on the refusal to subscribe to the oath. All of the cases in this Court which require a hearing before discharge for failure to take an oath involved impermissible oaths. . . . In the circumstances of those cases only by holding a hearing, showing evidence of disloyalty, and allowing the employee an opportunity to respond might the State develop a permissible basis for concluding that the employee was to be discharged.

Since there is no constitutionally protected right to overthrow a government by force, violence, or illegal or unconstitutional means, no constitutional right is infringed by an oath to abide by the constitutional system in the future. Therefore there is no requirement that one who refuses to take the Massachusetts oath be granted a hearing for the determination of some other fact before being discharged.

The judgment of the District Court is reversed and the case is remanded for further proceedings consistent with this opinion.

Justice Powell and Justice Rehnquist took no part in the consideration or decision in this case.

Justice Douglas, dissenting. . . .

Justice Marshall with whom Justice Brennan joins, dissenting. . . .

It is the second half of the oath to which I object. I find the language . . . to be impermissibly vague and overbroad. . . .

I would also strike down the second half of

this oath as an overbroad infringement of protected expression and conduct.

The Court's prior decisions represent a judgment that simple affirmative oaths of support are less suspect and less evil than negative oaths requiring a disaffirmance of political ties, group affiliations, or beliefs.

Yet, I think that it is plain that affirmative oaths of loyalty, no less than negative ones, have odious connotations and that they present dangers. We have tolerated support oaths as applied to all government employees only because we view these affirmations as an expression of "minimal loyalty to the Government." Such oaths are merely indications by the employee "in entirely familiar and traditional language that he will endeavor to perform his public duties lawfully."

It is precisely because these oaths are minimal, requiring only that nominal expression of allegiance "which, by the common law, every citizen was understood to owe his sovereign that they have been sustained." That they are minimal intrusions into the freedom of government officials and employees to think, speak, and act makes them constitutional; it does not mean that greater intrusions will be tolerated. On the contrary, each time this Court has been faced with an attempt by government to make the traditional support oath more comprehensive or demanding, it has struck the oath down.

When faced with an "imminent clear and present danger," governments may be able to compel citizens to do things which would ordinarily be beyond their authority to mandate. But, such emergency governmental power is a far cry from compelling every state employee in advance of any such danger to promise in any and all circumstances to conform speech and conduct to opposing an "overthrow" of the government. The Constitution severely circumscribes the power of government to force its citizens to perform symbolic gestures of loyalty. Since the overbreadth of the oath tends to infringe areas of speech and conduct which may be protected by the Constitution, I believe that it cannot stand. . . .

NAACP v. *Alabama*

See p. 433, above.

Buckley v. *Valeo*

See p. 472, above, for that part of this case which deals with reporting and disclosure requirements.

Note: Wooley v. *Maynard,* 430 U.S. 705 (1978), held a state may not impose criminal penalties upon a person for covering the state motto, "Live Free or Die," on automobile license plates because that motto violates that person's moral and religious beliefs: "The freedom of thought protected by the First Amendment . . . includes . . . the right to refrain from speaking at all." Two Justices, dissenting, thought "The State has not forced appellees to 'say' anything. . . . Appellees have not been forced to affirm or reject that motto. . . ."

There is, of course, a qualified privilege of silence in the context of self-incrimination (see Chapter 7, above).

OBSCENITY

Warren Court Difficulties

The supreme Court has long recognized that obscenity is not protected by the First Amendment. (See, for example, *Gooding* and *Chaplinsky,* above.) Not until the Warren era, however, did the Supreme Court get involved in obscenity problems. In

Roth v. *United States,* 354 U.S. 476 (1957), it undertook to define obscenity and squarely determine its status under the Constitution. The venture was less than successful; never after Roth was a majority of the Warren Court able to agree on what constituted obscenity. In a dissenting opinion in *Paris Adult Theatre I* v. *Slaton,* 413 U.S. 39 (1973), Justice Brennan traced the evolution of the Warren Court's difficulties:

> In [*Roth*], the Court held that obscenity, although expression, falls outside the area of speech or press constitutionally protected under the First and Fourteenth Amendments against state or federal infringement. But at the same time we emphasized in *Roth* that "sex and obscenity are not synonymous," and that matter which is sexually oriented but not obscene is fully protected by the Constitution. [*Roth*] rested, in other words, on what has been termed a two-level approach to the question of obscenity. While much criticized, that approach has been endorsed by all but two members of this Court who have addressed the question since *Roth.* Yet our efforts to implement that approach demonstrate that agreement on the existence of something called "obscenity" is still a long and painful step from agreement on a workable definition of the term.
>
> [W]e have demanded that "sensitive tools" be used to carry out the "separation of legitimate from illegitimate speech." The essence of our problem in the obscenity area is that we have been unable to provide "sensitive tools" to separate obscenity from other sexually oriented but constitutionally protected speech, so that efforts to suppress the former do not spill over into the suppression of the latter. . . .
>
> To be sure, five members of the Court did agree in *Roth* that obscenity could be determined by asking "whether to the average person, applying contemporary community standards, the dominant theme of the material taken as a whole appeals to prurient interest." But agreement on that test—achieved in the abstract and without reference to the particular material before the Court—was, to say the least, short lived. By 1967 the following views had emerged: Mr. Justice Black and Mr. Justice Douglas consistently maintained that government is wholly powerless to regulate any sexually oriented matter on the ground of its obscenity. Mr. Justice Harlan, on the other hand, believed that the Federal Government in the exercise of its enumerated powers could control the distribution of "hard core" pornography, while the States were afforded more latitude to "[ban] any material which, taken as a whole, has been reasonably found in state judicial proceedings to treat with sex in a fundamentally offensive manner, under rationally established criteria for judging such material." *Jacobellis* v. *Ohio,* [378 U.S. 184 (1964)]. Mr. Justice Stewart regarded "hard core" pornography as the limit of both federal and state power. See, e.g., *Ginzburg* v. *United States,* 383 U.S. 463 (1966) (dissenting opinion); [*Jacobellis*] (concurring opinion).
>
> The view that, until today, enjoyed the most, but not majority, support was an interpretation of *Roth* (and not, as the Court suggests [in *Miller,* below], a veering "sharply away from the *Roth* concept" and the articulation of "a new test of obscenity") adopted by Mr. Chief Justice Warren, Mr. Justice Fortas, and the author of this opinion in *Memoirs* v. *Massachusetts,* 383 U.S. 413 (1966). We expressed the view that Federal or State Governments could control the distribution of material where "three elements . . . coalesce: it must be established that (a) the dominent theme of the material taken as a whole appeals to a prurient interest in sex; (b) the material is patently offensive because it affronts contemporary community standards relating to the description or representation of sexual matters; and (c) the material is utterly without redeeming social value." Even this formulation, however, concealed differences of opinion. Compare *Jacobellis* v. *Ohio, supra,* at 192–195 (Brennan, J., joined by Goldberg, J.) (community standards national), with *id.,* at 200–201 (Warren, C. J., joined by Clark, J., dissenting) (community

standards local). Moreover, it did not provide a definition covering all situations. See *Mishkin* v. *New York*, 383 U.S. 502 (1966) (prurient appeal defined in terms of a deviant sexual group); *Ginzburg* v. *United States, supra* ("pandering" probative evidence of obscenity in close cases). See also *Ginsberg* v. *New York,* 390 U.S. 629 (1968) (obscenity for juveniles). Nor, finally, did it ever command a majority of the Court. Aside from the other views described above, Mr. Justice Clark believed that "social importance" could only "be considered together with evidence that the material in question appeals to prurient interest and is patently offensive." *Memoirs* v. *Massachusetts, supra,* at 445 (dissenting opinion). Similarly, Mr. Justice White regarded "a publication to be obscene if its predominant theme appeals to the prurient interest in a manner exceeding customary limits of candor," *id.,* at 460–461 (dissenting opinion), and regarded " 'social importance' . . . not [as] an independent test of obscenity but [as] relevant only to determining the predominant prurient interest of the material . . . ." *Id.,* at 462.

In the face of this divergence of opinion the Court began the practice in *Redrup* v. *New York,* 386 U.S. 767 (1967), of *per curiam* reversals of convictions for the dissemination of materials that at least five members of the Court, applying their separate tests, deemed not to be obscene. This approach capped the attempt in Roth to separate all forms of sexually oriented expression into two categories—the one subject to full governmental suppression and the other beyond the reach of governmental regulation to the same extent as any other protected form of speech or press.

Miller v. *California*
413 U.S. 1 (1973)

Building on the difficulties of its predecessor, the Burger Court, in the present case, was able for the first time since *Roth* (16 years earlier) to muster a majority in favor of a definition of obscenity.

Chief Jusice Burger delivered the opinion of the Court . . . .

II.

This much has been categorically settled by the Court, that obscene material is unprotected by the First Amendment. *Roth* v. *United States,* 354 U.S. 476, 485 (1957) . . . We acknowledge, however, the inherent dangers of undertaking to regulate any form of expression. State statutes designed to regulate obscene materials must be carefully limited. See *Interstate Circuit, Inc.* v. *Dallas, supra,* 390 U.S., at 682–685 (1968). As a result, we now confine the permissible scope of such regulation to works which depict or describe sexual conduct. That conduct must be specifically defined by the applicable state law, as written or authoritatively construed. A

state offense must also be limited to works which, taken as a whole, appeal to the prurient interest in sex, which portray sexual conduct in a patently offensive way, and which, taken as a whole, do not have serious literary, artistic, political, or scientific value.

The basic guidelines for the trier of fact must be: (*a*) whether "the average person, applying contemporary community standards" would find that the work, taken as a whole, appeals to the prurient interest, (*b*) whether the work depicts or describes, in a patently offensive way, sexual conduct specifically defined by the applicable state law, and (*c*) whether the work, taken as a whole, lacks serious literary, artistic, political, or scientific value. We do not adopt as a constitutional standard the "*utterly* without redeeming social value" test of *Memoirs* v. *Massachusetts, supra,* 383 U.S., at 419 (1966) that concept has never commanded the adherence of more than three Justices at one time. If a state law that regulates obscene material is thus limited, as written or construed, the First Amendment values applicable to the States through the Fourteenth Amendment are adequately protected by the ultimate power of appellate courts to conduct an independent review of constitutional claims when necessary . . . .

We emphasize that it is not our function to propose regulatory schemes for the States. That must await their concrete legislative efforts. It is possible, however, to give a few plain examples of what a state statute could define for regulation under the second part (*b*) of the standard announced in this opinion, *supra:*

(*a*) Patently offensive representations or descriptions of ultimate sexual acts, normal or perverted, actual or simulated.

(*b*) Patently offensive representation or descriptions of masturbation, excretory functions, and lewd exhibition of the genitals.

Sex and nudity may not be exploited without limit by films or pictures exhibited or sold in places of public accommodation any more than live sex and nudity can be exhibited or sold without limit in such public places. At a minimum, prurient, patently offensive depiction or description of sexual conduct must have serious literary, artistic, political, or scientific value to merit First Amendment protection. . . . For example, medical books for the education of physicians and related personnel necessarily use graphic illustrations and descriptions of human anatomy. In resolving the inevitably sensitive questions of fact and law, we must continue to rely on the jury system, accompanied by the safeguards that judges, rules of evidence, presumption of innocence and other protective features provide, as we do with rape, murder and a host of other offenses against society and its individual members.[1]

---

[1] The mere fact that juries may reach different conclusions as to the same material does not mean that constitutional rights are abridged. . . .

Mr. Justice Brennan, author of the opinions of the Court, or the plurality opinions, in *Roth* v. *United States, supra, Jacobellis* v. *Ohio, supra, Ginzburg* v. *United States*, 383 U.S. 463 (1966), *Mishkin* v. *New York*, 383 U.S. 502 (1966), and *Memoirs* v. *Massachusetts, supra*, has abandoned his former positions and now maintains that no formulation of this Court, the Congress, or the States can adequately distinguish obscene material unprotected by the First Amendment from protected expression, *Paris Adult Theatre I* v. *Slaton*, 413 U.S. 49, 73 (1973) (Brennan, J., dissenting). Paradoxically, Mr. Justice Brennan indicates that suppression of unprotected obscene material is permissible to avoid exposure to unconsenting adults, as in this case, and to juveniles, although he gives no indication of how the division between protected and nonprotected materials may be drawn with greater precision for these purposes than for regulation of commercial exposure to consenting adults only. Nor does he indicate where in the Constitution he finds the authority to distinguish between a willing "adult" one month past the state law age of majority and a willing "juvenile" one month younger.

Under the holdings announced today, no one will be subject to prosecution for the sale or exposure of obscene materials unless these materials depict or describe patently offensive "hard core" sexual conduct specifically defined by the regulating state law, as written or construed. We are satisfied that these specific prerequisites will provide fair notice to a dealer in such materials that his public and commercial activities may bring prosecution. . . .

It is certainly true that the absence, since *Roth*, of a single majority view of this Court as to proper standards for testing obscenity has placed a strain on both state and federal courts. But today, for the first time since *Roth* was decided in 1957, a majority of this Court has agreed on concrete guidelines to isolate "hard core" pornography from expression protected by the First Amendment. Now we may abandon the casual practice of *Redrup* v. *New York, supra*, and attempt to provide positive guidance to the federal and state courts alike. . . .

III.

Under a national Constitution, fundamental First Amendment limitations on the powers of the States do not vary from community to community, but this does not mean that there are, or should or can be, fixed, uniform national standards of precisely what appeals to the "prurient interest" or is "patently offensive." These are essentially questions of fact, and our nation is simply too big and too diverse for this Court to reasonably expect that such standards could be articulated for all 50 States in a single formulation, even assuming the prerequisite consensus exists. When triers of fact are asked to decide whether "the average person, applying contemporary community standards" would consider certain materials "prurient," it would be unrealistic to require that the answer be based on some abstract formulation. The adversary system, with lay jurors as the usual ultimate fact-finders in criminal prosecutions, has historically permitted triers-of-fact to draw on the standards of their community, guided always by limiting instructions on the law. To require a State to structure obscenity proceedings around evidence of a *national* "community standard" would be an exercise in futility. . . .

It is neither realistic nor constitutionally sound to read the First Amendment as requiring that the people of Maine or Mississippi accept public depiction of conduct found tolerable in Las Vegas, or New York City. . . . People in different States vary in their tastes and attitudes, and this diversity is not to be strangled by the absolutism of imposed uniformity. As the Court made clear in *Mishkin* v. *New York*, 383 U.S. 502, 508–509 (1966), the primary concern with requiring a jury to apply the standard of "the average person, applying contemporary community standards" is to be certain that, so far as material is not aimed at a deviant group, it will be judged by its impact on an average person, rather than a particularly susceptible or sensitive person—or indeed a totally insensitive one. We hold the requirement that the jury evaluate the materials with reference to "contemporary standards of the State of California" serves this protective purpose and is constitutionally adequate.

IV.

The dissenting Justices sound the alarm of repression. But, in our view, to equate the free and robust exchange of ideas and political debate with commercial exploitation of obscene material demeans the grand conception of the First Amendment and its high purposes in the historic struggle for freedom. . . .

The First Amendment protects works which, taken as a whole, have serious literary, artistic, political or scientific value, regardless of whether the government or a majority of the people approve of the ideas these works represent. "The protection given speech and press was fashioned to assure unfettered interchange of *ideas* for the bringing about of political and social changes desired by the people," *Roth* v. *United States, supra*, 354 U.S., at 484 (1957) (emphasis added). But the public portrayal of hard core sexual conduct for its own sake, and for the ensuing commercial gain, is a different matter. . . .

Mr. Justice Brennan finds "it is hard to see how state-ordered regimentation of our minds can ever be forestalled." *Paris Adult Theatre I* v. *Slaton, supra*, 413 U.S., at 110 (1973) (Brennan, J., dissenting). These doleful anticipations assume that courts cannot distinguish commerce in ideas, protected by the First Amendment, from commercial exploitation of obscene material. Moreover, state regulation of hard core pornography so as to make it unavailable to nonadults, a regulation which Mr. Justice Brennan finds constitutionally permissible, has all the elements of "censorship" for adults; indeed even more rigid enforcement techniques may be called for with such dichotomy of regulation.

See *Interstate Circuit* v. *Dallas, supra,* 390 U.S., at 690 (1968). . . .

In sum we (*a*) reaffirm the *Roth* holding that obscene material is not protected by the First Amendment, (*b*) hold that such material can be regulated by the States, subject to the specific safeguards enunciated above, without a showing that the material is *"utterly* without redeeming social value," and (*c*) hold that obscenity is to be determined by applying "contemporary community standards," see *Kois* v. *Wisconsin, supra,* 408 U.S., at 230 (1972), and *Roth* v. *United States, supra,* 354 U.S., at 489 (1957), not "national standards." The judgment of the Appellate Department of the Superior Court, Orange County, California, is vacated and the case remanded to that court for further proceedings not inconsistent with the First Amendment standards established by this opinion. See *United States* v. *12 200-Ft. Reels,* 413 U.S. 123, 130, n. 7 (1973).

[Justices Douglas, Brennan, Stewart, and Marshall dissented. See their opinions in *Paris,* below.]

Paris Adult Theatre I v. *Slaton*
413 U.S. 39 (1973)

The Burger Court not only redefined obscenity (see *Miller,* above), it offered a more extensive discussion of the interests perceived as justifying obscenity control than the Court had ever before presented.

Mr. Chief Justice Burger delivered the opinion of the Court. . . .

We categorically disapprove the theory, apparently adopted by the trial judge, that obscene, pornographic films acquire constitutional immunity from state regulation simply because they are exhibited for consenting adults only. . . .

In particular, we hold that there are legitimate state interests at stake in stemming the tide of commercialized obscenity, even assuming it is feasible to enforce effective safeguards against exposure to juveniles and to the passerby. Rights and interests "other than those of the advocates are involved." Cf. *Breard* v. *Alexandria,* 341 U.S. 622, 642 (1951). These include the interest of the public in the quality of life and the total community environment, the tone of commerce in the great city centers, and, possibly, the public safety itself. The Hill-Link Minority Report of the Commission on Obscenity and Pornography indicates that there is at least an arguable correlation between obscene material and crime. Quite apart from sex crimes, however, there remains one problem of large proportions apty described by Professor Bickel:

> "It concerns the tone of the society, the mode, or to use terms that have perhaps greater currency, the style and quality of life, now and in the future. A man may be entitled to read an obscene book in his room, or expose himself indecently there. . . . We should protect his privacy. But if he demands a right to obtain the books and pictures he wants in the market, and to foregather in public places—discreet, if you will, but accessible to all—with others who share his tastes, *then to grant him his right is to affect the world about the rest of us, and to impinge on other privacies.* Even supposing that each of us can, if he wishes, effectively avert the eye and stop the ear (which, in truth, we cannot), what is commonly read and seen and heard and done intrudes upon us all, want it or not." 22 *The Public Interest* 25, 25–26 (Winter, 1971). (Emphasis supplied.)

As Chief Justice Warren stated there is a "right of the Nation and of the States to maintain a decent society. . . ." *Jacobellis* v. *Ohio*, 378 U.S. 184, 199 (1964) (Warren, C. J., dissenting). . . .

But, if is argued, there is no scientific data which conclusively demonstrates that exposure to obscene materials adversely affects men and women or their society. It is urged on behalf of the petitioner that, absent such a demonstration, any kind of state regulation is "impermissible." We reject this argument. It is not for us to resolve empirical uncertainties underlying state legislation, save in the exceptional case where that legislation plainly impinges upon rights protected by the Constitution itself. . . . Although there is no conclusive proof of a connection between antisocial behavior and obscene material, the legislature of Georiga could quite reasonably determine that such a connection does or might exist. In deciding *Roth*, this Court implicitly accepted that a legislature could legitimately act on such a conclusion to protect *"the social interest in order and morality."* *Roth* v. *United States, supra,* 354 U.S., at 485 (1957), quoting *Chaplinsky* v. *New Hampshire,* 315 U.S. 568, 572 (1942) (emphasis added in *Roth*).

From the beginning of civilized societies, legislators and judges have acted on various unprovable assumptions. Such assumptions underlie much lawful state regulation of commercial and business affairs. See *Ferguson* v. *Skrupa,* 372 U.S. 726, 730 (1963); *Breard* v. *Alexandria,* 341 U.S. 622, 632–633, 641–645 (1951); *Lincoln Federal Labor Union* v. *Northwestern Iron & Metal Co.,* 335 U.S. 525, 536–537 (1949). . . . On the basis of these assumptions both Congress and state legislatures have, for example, drastically restricted associational rights by adopting antitrust laws, and have strictly regulated public expression by issuers of and dealers in securities, profit sharing "coupons," and "trading stamps," commanding what they must and may not publish and announce. . . . Understandably those who entertain an absolutist view of the First Amendment find it uncomfortable to explain why

rights of association, speech, and press should be severaly restrained in the marketplace of goods and money, but not in the marketplace of pronography. . . .

If we accept the unprovable assumption that a complete education requires certain books . . . and the well nigh universal belief that good books, plays and art lift the spirit, improve the mind, enrich the human personality and develop character, can we then say that a state legislature may not act on the corollary assumption that commerce in obscene books, or public exhibitions focused on obscene conduct, have a tendency to exert a corrupting and debasing impact leading to antisocial behavior? . . . The sum of experience, including that of the past two decades, affords an ample basis for legislatures to conclude that a sensitive, key relationship of human existence, central to family life, community welfare, and the development of human personality, can be debased and distorted by crass commercial exploitation of sex. Nothing in the Constitution prohibits a State from reaching such a conclusion and acting on it legislatively simply because there is no conclusive evidence or empirical data.

It is argued that individual "free will" must govern, even in activities beyond the protection of the First Amendment and other constitutional guarantees of privacy, and that Government cannot legitimately impede an individual's desire to see or acquire obscene plays, movies, and books. We do indeed base our society on certain assumptions that people have the capacity for free choice. Most exercises of individual free choice—those in politics, religion and expression of ideas—are explicitly protected by the Constitution. Totally unlimited play for free will, however, is not allowed in ours or any other society. We have just noted, for example, that neither the First Amendment, nor "free will" precludes States from having "blue sky" laws to regulate what sellers of securities may write or publish about their wares. See . . . *supra.* Such laws are to protect the weak, the uninformed, the unsuspecting, and the gullible from the exercise of their own volition. Nor do modern societies leave disposal of garbage and sewage up to the individual "free will," but impose regulation to protect both public health and the appearance of public places. States are told by some that they must await a "laissez faire" market solution to the obscenity-pornography problem, paradoxically "by people who have never otherwise had a kind work to say for laissez-faire," particularly in solving urban, commercial, and environmental pollution problems. See Kristol, *On the Democratic Idea in America* (1972 ed.) . . .

It is asserted, however, that standards for evaluating state commercial regulations are inapposite in the present context, as state regulation of access by consenting adults to obscene material violates the constitutionally protected right to privacy enjoyed by petitioners' customers. Even assuming that petitioners have vicarious standing to assert potential customers' rights, it is unavailing to compare a theatre, open to the public for a fee, with the private home of *Stanley* v. *Georgia,* 394 U.S. 557, 568 (1969), and the marital bedroom of *Griswold* v. *Connecticut,* 381 U.S. 479, 485–486 (1965). This Court, has, on numerous occasions, refused to hold that commercial ventures such as a motion-picture house are "private" for the purpose of civil rights litigation and civil rights statutes. See *Sullivan* v. *Little Hunting Park, Inc.,* 396 U.S. 229, 236 (1969). . . .

It is also argued that the State has no legitimate interest in "control [of] the moral content of a person's thoughts," *Stanley* v. *Georgia, supra,* 394 U.S., at 565 (1969), and we need not quarrel with this. But we reject the claim that the State of Georgia is here attempting to control the minds or thoughts of those who patronize theatres. . . . Where communication of ideas, protected by the First Amendment, is not involved, nor the particular privacy of the home protected by *Stanley,* nor any of the other "areas or zones" of constitutionally protected privacy, the mere fact that, as a consequence, some human "utterances" or "thoughts" may be in-

cidentally affected does not bar the State from acting to protect legitimate state interests. . .

Finally, petitioners argue that conduct which directly involves "consenting adults" only has, for that sole reason, a special claim to constitutional protection. Our Constitution establishes a broad range of conditions on the exercise of power by the States, but for us to say that our Constitution incorporates the proposition that conduct involving consenting adults only is always beyond state regulation, that is a step we are unable to take. Commercial exploitation of depictions, descriptions, or exhibitions of obscene conduct on commercial premises open to the adult public falls within a State's broad power to regulate commerce and protect the public environment. The issue in this context goes beyond whether someone, or even the majority, considers the conduct depicted as "wrong" or "sinful." The States have the power to make a morally neutral judgment that public exhibition of obscene material, or commerce in such material, has a tendency to injure the community as a whole, to endanger the public safety, or to jeopardize in Chief Justice Warren's words, the States' "right . . . to maintain a decent society." *Jacobellis* v. *Ohio, supra,* 378 U.S., at 199 (1964) (dissenting opinion).

To summarize, we have today reaffirmed the basic holding of *United States* v. *Roth, supra,* that obscene material has no protection under the First Amendment. See *Miller* v. *California, supra,* and *Kaplan* v. *California,* 413 U.S. 115 (1973). We have directed our holdings, not at thoughts or speech, but at depiction and description of specifically defined sexual conduct that States may regulate within limits designed to prevent infringement of First Amendment rights. We have also reaffirmed the holdings of *United States* v. *Reidel, supra,* and *United States* v. *Thirty-Seven Photographs, supra,* that commerce in obscene material is unprotected by any constitutional doctrine of privacy. *United States* v. *Orito,* 413 U.S. 139, at pp. 141–143 (1973); *United States* v. *Twelve 200-Ft. Reels,* 413 U.S. 123, at pp. 126–129 (1973). In this case we hold that the States have a legitimate interest in regulating commerce in obscene material and in regulating exhibition of obscene material in places of public accommodation, including so-called "adult" theatres from which minors are excluded. In light of these holdings, nothing precludes the State of Georgia from the regulation of the allegedly obscene materials exhibited in Paris Adult Theatre I or II, provided that the applicable Georgia law, as written or authoritatively interpreted by the Georgia courts, meets the First Amendment standards set forth in *Miller* v. *California, supra,* 413 U.S., at pp. 23–25. The judgment is vacated and the case remanded to the Georgia Supreme Court for further proceedings not inconsistent with this opinion and Miller v. California, supra. See *United States* v. *12 220-Ft. Reels,* 413 U.S. 123, p. 130, n. 7 (1973). . . .

Mr. Justice Brennan, with whom Mr. Justice Stewart and Mr. Justice Marshall join, dissenting. . . .

I am convinced that the approach initiated 15 years ago in *Roth* v. *United States,* and culminating in the Court's decision today, cannot bring stability to this area of the law without jeopardizing fundamental First Amendment values, and I have concluded that the time has come to make a significant departure from that approach. . . .

. . . The essence of our problem in the obscenity area is that we have been unable to provide "sensitive tools" to separate obscenity from other sexually oriented but constitutionally protected speech, so that efforts to suppress the former do not spill over into the suppression of the latter. . . .

Our experience with the *Roth* approach has certainly taught us that the outright suppression of obscenity cannot be reconciled with the fundamental principles of the First and Fourteenth Amendments. For we have failed to formulate a standard that sharply distinguishes protected from unprotected speech, and out of

necessity, we have resorted to the *Redrup* approach, which resolves cases as between the parties, but offers only the most obscure guidance to legislation, adjudication by other courts, and primary conduct. By disposing of cases through summary reversal or denial of certiorari we have deliberately and effectively obscured the rationale underlying the decision. It comes as no surprise that judicial attempts to follow our lead conscientiously have often ended in hopeless confusion.

Of course, the vagueness problem would be largely of our own creation if it stemmed primarily from our failure to reach a consensus on any one standard. But after 16 years of experimentation and debate I am reluctantly forced to the conclusion that none of the available formulas, including the one announced today, can reduce the vagueness to a tolerable level while at the same time striking an acceptable balance between the protections of the First and Fourteenth Amendments, on the one hand, and on the other the asserted state interest in regulating the dissemination of certain sexually oriented materials. Any effort to draw a constitutionally acceptable boundary on state power must resort to such indefinite concepts as "prurient interest," "patent offensiveness," "serious literary value," and the like. The meaning of these concepts necessarily varies with the experience, outlook, and even idiosyncracies of the person defining them. . . .

. . . [T]he uncertainty of the standards creates a continuing source of tension between state and federal courts, since the need for an independent determination by this Court seems to render superfluous even the most conscientious analysis by state tribunals. And our inability to justify our decisions with a persuasive rationale—or indeed, any rationale at all—necessarily creates the impression that we are merely second-guessing state court judges.

The severe problems arising from the lack of fair notice, from the chill on protected expression, and from the stress imposed on the state and federal judicial machinery persuade me that a significant change in direction is urgently required. I turn, therefore, to the alternatives that are now open.

1. The approach requiring the smallest deviation from our present course would be to draw a new line between protected and unprotected speech, still permitting the States to suppress all material on the unprotected side of the line. In my view, clarity cannot be obtained pursuant to this approach except by drawing a line that resolves all doubts in favor of state power and against the guarantees of the First Amendment. We could hold, for example, that any depiction or description of human sexual organs, irrespective of the manner or purpose of the portrayal, is outside the protection of the First Amendment and therefore open to suppression by the States. That formula would, no doubt, offer much fairer notice of the reach of any state statute drawn at the boundary of the State's constitutional power. And it would also, in all likelihood, give rise to a substantial probability of regularity in most judicial determinations under the standard. But such a standard would be appallingly overboard, permitting the suppression of a vast range of literary, scientific, and artistic masterprices. Neither the First Amendment nor any free community could possibly tolerate such a standard. Yet short of that extreme it is hard to see how any choice of words could reduce the vagueness problem to tolerable proportions, so long as we remain committed to the view that some class of materials is subject to outright suppression by the State.

2. The alternative adopted by the Court today recognizes that a prohibition against any depiction or description of human sexual organs could not be reconciled with the guarantees of the First Amendment. But the Court does retain the view that certain sexually oriented material can be considered obscene and therefore unprotected by the First and Fourteenth Amendments. To describe that unprotected class of expression, the Court adopts a restatement of the *Roth-Memoirs* definition of obscenity. . . .

The differences between this formulation and the three-pronged *Memoirs* test are, for the most part, academic. . . .

The Court evidently recognizes that difficulties with the *Roth* approach necessitate a significant change of direction. But the Court does not describe its understanding of those difficulties, nor does it indicate how the restatement of the *Memoirs* test is in any way responsive to the problems that have arisen. In my view, the restatement leaves unresolved the very difficulties that compel our rejection of the underlying *Roth* approach, while at the same time contributing substantial difficulties of its own. The modification of the *Memoirs* test may prove sufficient to jeopardize the analytic underpinnings of the entire scheme. And today's restatement will likely have the effect, whether or not intended, of permitting far more sweeping suppression of sexually oriented expression, including expression that would almost surely be held protected under our current formulation.

Although the Court's restatement substantially tracks the three-part test announced in *Memoirs* v. *Massachusetts*, it does purport to modify the "social value" component of the test. Instead of requiring, as did *Roth* and *Memoirs*, that state suppression be limited to materials utterly lacking in social value, the Court today permits suppression if the government can prove that the materials lack "serious literary, artistic, political or scientific value." But the definition of "obscenity" as expression utterly lacking in social importance is the key to the conceptual basis of *Roth* and our subsequent opinions. In *Roth* we held that certain expression is obscene, and thus outside the protection of the First Amendment, precisely *because* it lacks even the slightest redeeming social value. The Court's approach necessarily assumes that some works will be deemed obscene—even though they clearly have *some* social value—because the State was able to prove that the value, measured by some unspecified standard, was not sufficiently "serious" to warrant constitutional protection. That result is not merely inconsistent with our holding in *Roth;* it is nothing less than a rejection of the fundamental First Amendment premises and rationale of the *Roth* opinion and an invitation to widespread suppression of sexually oriented speech. Before today, the protections of the First Amendment have never been thought limited to expressions of *serious* literary or political value.

Although the Court concedes that "*Roth* presumed 'obscenity' to be 'utterly without redeeming social value,'" it argues that *Memoirs* produced "a drastically altered test that called on the prosecution to prove a negative, *i.e.,* that the material was 'utterly without redeeming social value'—a burden virtually impossible to discharge under our criminal standards of proof." One should hardly need to point out that under the third component of the Court's test the prosecution is still required to "prove a negative"—i.e., that the material lacks serious literary, artistic, political, or scientific value. Whether it will be easier to prove that material lacks "serious" value than to prove that it lacks any value at all remains, of course, to be seen.

In any case, even if the Court's approach left undamaged the conceptual framework of *Roth,* and even if it clearly barred the suppression of works with at least some social value, I would nevertheless be compelled to reject it. For it is beyond dispute that the approach can have no ameliorative impact on the cluster of problems that grow out of the vagueness of our current standards. Indeed, even the Court makes no argument that the reformulation will provide fairer notice to booksellers, theatre owners, and the reading and viewing public. Nor does the Court contend that the approach will provide clearer guidance to law enforcement officials or reduce the chill on protected expression. Nor, finally, does the Court suggest that the approach will mitigate to the slightest degree the institutional problems that have plagued this Court and the State and Federal Judiciary as a direct result of the uncertainty inherent in any definition of obscenity.

. . . The Court surely demonstrates little sensitivity to our own institutional problems, much less the other vagueness-related difficulties, in establishing a system that requires us to consider whether a description of human genitals is sufficiently "lewd" to deprive it of constitutional protection; whether a sexual act is "ultimate"; whether the conduct depicted in materials before us fits within one of the categories of conduct whose depiction the state or federal governments have attempted to suppress; and a host of equally pointless inquiries. In addition, adoption of such a test does not, presumably, obviate the need for consideration of the nuances of presentation of sexually oriented material, yet it hardly clarifies the application of those opaque but important factors.

If the application of the "physical conduct" test to pictorial material is fraught with difficulty, its application to textual material carries the potential for extraordinary abuse. Surely we have passed the point where the mere written description of sexual conduct is deprived of First Amendment protection. Yet the test offers no guidance to us, or anyone else, in determining which written descriptions of sexual conduct are protected, and which are not.

Ultimately, the reformulation must fail because it still leaves in this Court the responsibility of determining in each case whether the materials are protected by the First Amendment.
. . .

3. I have also considered the possibility of reducing our own role, and the role of appellate courts generally, in determining whether particular matter is obscene. Thus, we might conclude that juries are best suited to determine obscenity *vel non* and that jury verdicts in this area should not be set aside except in cases of extreme departure from prevailing standards. Or, more generally, we might adopt the position that where a lower federal or state court has conscientiously applied the constitutional standard, its finding of obscenity will be no more vulnerable to reversal by this Court than any finding of fact. While the point was not clearly resolved prior to our decision in *Redrup* v. *New*

York [386 U.S. 767], it is implicit in that decision that the First Amendment requires an independent review by appellate courts of the constitutional fact of obscenity. That result is required by principles applicable to the obscenity issue no less than to any other area involving free expression, or other constitutional right. In any event, even if the Constitution would permit us to refrain from judging for ourselves the alleged obscenity of particular materials, that approach would solve at best only a small part of our problem. For while it would mitigate the institutional stress produced by the *Roth* approach, it would neither offer nor produce any cure for the other vices of vagueness. Far from providing a clearer guide to permissible primary conduct, a approach would inevitably lead to even greater uncertainty and the consequent due process problems of fair notice. And the approach would expose much protected sexually oriented expression to the vagaries of jury determinations. Plainly, the institutional gain would be more than offset by the unprecedented infringement of First Amendment rights.

4. Finally, I have considered the view, urged so forcefully since 1957 by our Brothers Black and Douglas, that the First Amendment bars the suppression of any sexually oriented expression. That position would effect a sharp reduction, although perhaps not a total elimination, of the uncertainty that surrounds our current approach. Nevertheless, I am convinced that it would achieve that desirable goal only by stripping the States of power to an extent that cannot be justified by the commands of the Constitution, at least so long as there is available an alternative approach that strikes a better balance between the guarantee of free expression and the States' legitimate interests.

Our experience since *Roth* requires us not only to abandon the effort to pick out obscene materials on a case-by-case basis, but also to reconsider a fundamental postulate of *Roth:* that there exists a definable class of sexually oriented expression that may be totally suppressed by

the Federal and State Governments. Assuming that such a class of expression does in fact exist, I am forced to conclude that the concept of "obscenity" cannot be defined with sufficient specificity and clarity to provide fair notice to persons who create and distribute sexually oriented materials, to prevent substantial erosion of protected speech as a by-product of the attempt to suppress unprotected speech, and to avoid very costly institutional harms. Given these inevitable side-effects of state efforts to suppress what is assumed to be *unprotected* speech, we must scrutinize with care the state interest that is asserted to justify the suppression. For in the absence of some very substantial interest in suppressing such speech, we can hardly condone the ill-effects that seem to flow inevitably from the effort. . . .

In short, while I cannot say that the interests of the State—apart from the question of juveniles and unconsenting adults—are trivial or nonexistent, I am compelled to conclude that these interests cannot justify the substantial damage to constitutional rights and to this Nation's judicial machinery that inevitably results from state efforts to bar the distribution even of unprotected material to consenting adults. I would hold, therefore, that at least in the absence of distribution to juveniles or obtrusive exposure to unconsenting adults, the First and Fourteenth Amendments prohibit the state and federal governments from attempting wholly to suppress sexually oriented materials on the basis of their allegedly "obscene" contents. Nothing in this approach precludes those governments from taking action to serve what may be strong and legitimate interests through regulation of the manner of distribution of sexually oriented material.

Mr. Justice Douglas, dissenting. . . .

I applaud the effort of my Brother Brennan to forsake the low road which the Court has followed in this field. The new regime he would inaugurate is much closer than the old to the policy of abstention which the First Amendment proclaims. But since we do not have here the unique series of problems raised by government imposed or government approved captive audiences (cf. *Public Utilities Comm'n* v. *Pollak*, 343 U.S. 451), I see no constitutional basis for fashioning a rule that makes a publisher, producer, bookseller, librarian, or movie house criminally responsible, when he or she fails to take affirmative steps to protect the consumer against literature or books offensive[1] to those who temporarily occupy the seats of the mighty.

When man was first in the jungle he took care of himself. When he entered a societal group, controls were necessarily imposed. But our society—unlike most in the world—presupposes that freedom and liberty are in a frame of reference that make the individual, not government, the keeper of his tastes, beliefs, and ideas. That is the philosophy of the First Amendment. . . .

Quaere: Is the Court's discussion of "empirical uncertainties" and scientifically "unprovable assumptions" with respect to obscenity relevant with respect to capital punishment?

United States v. *Orito*
413 U.S. 139 (1973)

Mr. Chief Justice Burger delivered the opinion of the Court.

Appellee Orito was charged in the United States District Court for the Eastern District of Wisconsin with a violation of 18 U.S.C. § 1462 in that he did "knowingly transport and carry in

---

[1] What we do today is rather ominous as respects librarians. The net now designed by the Court is so finely meshed that taken literally it could result in raids on libraries. Libraries, I had always assumed, were sacrosanct, representing every part of the spectrum. If what is offensive to the most influential person or group in a community can be purged from a library, the library system would be destroyed. . . .

interstate commerce from San Francisco . . . to Milwaukee . . . by means of a common carrier, that is, Trans World Airlines and North Central Airlines, copies of lewd, lascivious, and filthy materials. . . ." The materials specified included some 83 reels of film, with as many as eight to 10 copies of some of the films. Appellee moved to dismiss the indictment on the ground that the statute violated his First and Ninth Amendment rights. The District Court granted his motion, holding that the statute was unconstitutionally overbroad since it failed to distinguish between "public" and "non-public" transportation of obscene materials. The District Court interpreted this Court's decisions in *Griswold* v. *Connecticut*, 381 U.S. 479 (1965), *Redrup* v. *New York*, 386 U.S. 767 (1967), and *Stanley* v. *Georgia*, 394 U.S. 557 (1969), to establish the proposition that "non-public transportation" of obscene materials was constitutionally protected. . . .

The District Court erred in striking down 18 U.S.C. § 1462 and dismissing respondent's indictment on these "privacy" grounds. The essence of respondent's contentions is that *Stanley* has firmly established the right to possess obscene material in the privacy of the home and that this creates a correlative right to receive it, transport it or distribute it. We have rejected that reasoning. This case was decided by the District Court before our decisions in *United States* v. *Thirty-Seven Photographs*, 402 U.S. 363 (1971); and *United States* v. *Reidel*, 402 U.S. 351 (1971). Those holdings negate the idea that some zone of constitutionally protected privacy follows such materials when they are moved outside the home area protected by *Stanley*. . . .

The Constitution extends special safeguards to the privacy of the home, just as it protects other special privacy rights such as those of marriage, procreation, motherhood, child rearing, and education. . . . But viewing obscene films in a commercial theater open to the adult public . . . or transporting such films in common carriers in interstate commerce, has no such claim to such special consideration. It is hardly necessary to catalog the myriad activities that may lawfully be engaged in within the privacy and confines of the home, but may be prohibited in public. . . .

Given (a) that obscene material is not protected under the First Amendment, *Miller* v. *California, supra, Roth* v. *United States, supra* (b) that the government has a legitimate interest in protecting the public commercial environment by preventing such materials from entering the stream of commerce, see *Paris Adult Theatre, supra,* 413 U.S., at pp. 57–64 (1973), and (c) that no constitutionally protected privacy is involved, *United States* v. *Thirty-Seven Photographs, supra,* 402 U.S., at 376 (1971) (opinion of White, J.), we cannot say that the Constitution forbids comprehensive federal regulation of interstate transportation of obscene material merely because such transport may be by private carriage, or because material is intended for the private use of the transporter. That the transporter has an abstract proprietary power to shield the obscene material from all others and to guard the material with the same privacy as in the home is not controlling. Congress may regulate on the basis of the natural tendency of material in the home being kept private and the contrary tendency once material leaves that area, regardless of a transporter's professed intent. Congress could reasonably determine such regulation to be necessary to effect permissible federal control of interstate commerce in obscene materials, based as that regulation is on a legislatively determined risk of ultimate exposure to juveniles or to the public and the harm that exposure could cause. . . . The decision of the District Court is vacated and the case is remanded for reconsideration of the sufficiency of the indictment in light of *Miller* v. *California, supra; United States* v. *Twelve 200-Ft. Reels* [413 U.S. 123], and this opinion.

Mr. Justice Douglas, dissenting.

We held in *Stanley* v. *Georgia,* 394 U.S. 557, that an individual reading or examining "ob-

scene" materials in the privacy of his home is protected against state prosecution by reason of the First Amendment made applicable to the States by reason of the Fourteenth.

By that reasoning a person who reads an "obscene" book on an airline or bus or train is protected. So is he who carries an "obscene" book in his pocket during a journey for his intended personal enjoyment. So is he who carries the book in his baggage or has a trucking company move his household effects to a new residence. Yet 18 U.S.C. § 1462 makes such interstate carriage unlawful.

The conclusion is too obvious for argument, unless we are to overrule *Stanley.* I would abide by *Stanley* and affirm this judgment, dismissing the indictment.

Mr. Justice Brennan, with whom Mr. Justice Stewart and Mr. Justice Marshall join, dissenting. . . .

Under the view expressed in my dissent today in *Paris Adult Theatre* v. *Slaton, supra,* it is clear that the statute before us cannot stand. . . .

Hamling v. *United States* (excerpt)
418 U.S. 87 (1974)

Mr. Justice Rehnquist delivered the opinion of the Court . . . .

Miller rejected the view that the First and Fourteenth Amendments require that the proscription of obscenity be based on uniform nationwide standards of what is obscene, describing such standards as "hypothetical and unascertainable," 413 U.S., at 31. But in so doing the Court did not require as a constitutional matter the substitution of some smaller geographical area into the same sort of formula; the test was stated in terms of the understanding of "the average person, applying contemporary community standards." 413 U.S., at 24. . . . A juror is entitled to draw on his own knowledge of the views of the average person in the community or vicinage from which he comes for making the required determination, just as he is entitled to draw on his knowledge of the propensities of a "reasonable" person in other areas of the law. . . . Our holding in *Miller* that California could constitutionally proscribe obscenity in terms of a "statewide" standard did not mean that any such precise geographic area is required as a matter of constitutional law. . . .

The result of the *Miller* cases, therefore, as a matter of constitutional law and federal statutory construction, is to permit a juror sitting in obscenity cases to draw on knowledge of the community or vicinage from which he comes in deciding what conclusion "the average person, applying contemporary community standards" would reach in a given case. Since this case was tried in the Southern District of California, and presumably jurors from throughout that judicial district were available to serve on the panel which tried petitioners, it would be the standards of that "community" upon which the jurors would draw. But this is not to say that a District Court would not be at liberty to admit evidence of standards existing in some place outside of this particular district, if it felt such evidence would assist the jury in the resolution of the issues which they were to decide.

Our Brother Brennan suggests in dissent that in holding that a federal obscenity case may be tried on local community standards, we do violence both to congressional prerogative and to the Constitution. Both of these arguments are foreclosed by our decision last Term in *United States* v. *12 200-ft. Reels of Film, supra*, that the *Miller* standards, including the "contemporary community standards" formulation, applied to federal legislation. The fact that distributors of allegedly obscene materials may be subjected to varying community standards in the various federal judicial districts into which they transmit the materials does not render a federal statute unconstitutional because of the failure of application of uniform national standards of obscenity. Those same distributors may be subjected to such varying degrees of criminal liability in prosecutions by the States for violations of state obscenity statutes; we see no constitutional impediment to a similar rule for federal prosecutions.

[Justices Douglas, Brennan, Stewart, and Marshall dissented.]

Jenkins v. *Georgia* (excerpt)
418 U.S. 153 (1974)

Mr. Justice Rehnquist delivered the opinion of the Court.

Appellee contends essentially that under *Miller* the obscenity *vel non* of the film "Carnal Knowledge" was a question for the jury, and that the jury having resolved the question against appellant, and there being some evidence to support its findings, the judgment of conviction should be affirmed. We turn to the language of *Miller* to evaluate appellee's contention. . . .

But all of this does not lead us to agree with the Supreme Court of Georgia's apparent conclusion that the jury's verdict against appellant virtually precluded all further appellate review of appellant's assertion that his exhibition of the film was protected by the First and Fourteenth Amendments. Even though questions of appeal to the "prurient interest" or of patent offensiveness are "essentially questions of fact," it would be a serious misreading of *Miller* to conclude that juries have unbridled discretion in determining what is "patently offensive." Not only did we there say that "the First Amendment values applicable to the States through the Fourteenth Amendment are adequately protected by the ultimate power of appellate courts to conduct an independent review of constitutional claims when necessary," 413 U.S., at 25, but we made it plain that under that holding "no one will be subject to prosecution for the sale or exposure of obscene materials unless these materials depict or describe patently offensive 'hard core' sexual conduct . . . ." 413 U.S., at 27.

We also took pains in *Miller* to "give a few plain examples of what a state statute could define for regulation under part (b) of the standard announced," that is, the requirement of patent offensiveness. 413 U.S., at 25. These examples included "representations or descriptions of ultimate sexual acts, normal or perverted, actual or simulated," and "representations or descriptions of masturbation, excretory functions, and lewd exhibition of the genitals." *Ibid.* While this did not purport to be an exhaustive catalog of what juries might find patently offensive, it was certainly intended to fix substantive constitutional limitations, deriving from the First Amendment, on the type of material subject to such a determination. It would be wholly at odds with this aspect of *Miller* to uphold an obscenity conviction based upon a defendant's depiction of a woman with a bare midriff, even though a properly charged jury unanimously agreed on a verdict of guilty.

Our own view of the film satisfies us that "Carnal Knowledge" could not be found under the *Miller* standards to depict sexual conduct in a patently offensive way. Nothing in the movie falls within either of the two examples given in *Miller* of material which may constitutionally be found to meet the "patently offensive" element of those standards, nor is there anything sufficiently similar to such material to justify similar treatment. While the subject matter of the picture is, in a broader sense, sex, and there are scenes in which sexual conduct including "ultimate sexual acts" is to be understood to be taking place, the camera does not focus on the bodies of the actors at such times. There is no exhibition whatever of the actors' genitals, lewd or otherwise, during these scenes. There are occasional scenes of nudity, but nudity alone is not enough to make material legally obscene under the *Miller* standards.

Appellant's showing of the film "Carnal Knowledge" is simply not the "public portrayal of hard core sexual conduct for its own sake, and for ensuing commercial gain" which we said was punishable in *Miller*. We hold that the film could not, as a matter of constitutional law, be found to depict sexual conduct in a patently offensive way, and that it is therefore not outside the protection of the First and Fourteenth Amendments because it is obscene. No other basis appearing in the record upon which the judgment of conviction can be sustained, we reverse the judgment of the Supreme Court of Georgia.

Mr. Justice Brennan, with whom Mr. Justice Stewart and Mr. Justice Marshall join, concurring in result.

. . . Today's decision confirms my observation in *Paris Adult Theatre I* v. *Slaton*, 413 U.S. 49 (1973), that the Court's new formulation does not extricate us from the mire of case-by-case determinations of obscenity. . . .

[Mr. Justice Douglas concurred.]

9

Equal Protection of the Law

WHAT CONSTITUTES DISCRIMINATION? EVOLVING JUDICIAL STANDARDS

Stage One: The Traditional Test

Lindsley v. *Natural Carbonic Gas Co.* (excerpt)
220 U.S. 61 (1911)

. . . The rules by which [the contention that a statutory classification violates the equal-protection clause] must be tested, as is shown by repeated decisions of this court, are these: 1. The equal-protection clause of the Fourteenth Amendment does not take from the state the power to classify in the adoption of police laws, but admits of the exercise of a wide scope of discretion in that regard, and avoids what is done only when it is without any reasonable basis, and therefore is purely arbitrary. 2. A classification having some reasonable basis does not offend against that clause merely because it is not made with mathematical nicety, or because in practice it results in some inequality. 3. When the classification in such a law is called in question, if any state of facts reasonably can be conceived that would sustain it, the existence of that state of facts at the time the law was enacted must be assumed. 4. One who assails the classification in such a law must carry the burden of showing that it does not rest upon any reasonable basis, but is essentially arbitrary.

Railway Express Agency v. *New York*
336 U.S. 106 (1949)

Mr. Justice Douglas delivered the opinion of the Court.

Section 124 of the Traffic Regulations of the City of New York promulgated by the Police Commissioner provides:

> "No person shall operate, or cause to be operated, in or upon any street an advertising vehicle; provided that nothing herein contained shall prevent the putting of business notices upon business delivery vehicles, so long as such vehicles are engaged in the usual business or regular work of the owner and not used merely or mainly for advertising."

Appellant is engaged in a nation-wide express business. It operates about 1,900 trucks in New York City and sells the space on the exterior sides of these trucks for advertising. That advertising is for the most part unconnected with its own business. It was convicted in the magistrates court and fined. The judgment of conviction was sustained in the Court of Special Sessions. . . . The Court of Appeals affirmed without opinion by a divided vote. . . . The case is here on appeal . . .

The Court of Special Sessions concluded that advertising on vehicles using the streets of New York City constitutes a distraction to vehicle drivers and to pedestrians alike and therefore affects the safety of the public in the use of the streets. We do not sit to weigh evidence on the due process issue in order to determine whether the regulation is sound or appropriate; nor is it our function to pass judgment on its wisdom. See *Olsen* v. *State of Nebraska*, 313 U.S. 236. We would be trespassing on one of the most intensely local and specialized of all municipal problems if we held that this regulation had no relation to the traffic problem of New York City. It is the judgment of the local authorities that it does have such a relation. And nothing has been advanced which shows that to be palpably false.

The question of equal protection of the laws is pressed more strenuously on us. It is pointed out that the regulation draws the line between advertisements of products sold by the owner of the truck and general advertisements. It is argued that unequal treatment on the basis of such a distinction is not justified by the aim and purpose of the regulation. It is said, for example, that one of appellant's trucks carrying the advertisement of a commercial house would not cause any greater distraction of pedestrians and vehicle drivers than if the commercial house carried the same advertisement on its own truck. Yet the regulation allows the latter to do what the former is forbidden from doing. It is therefore contended that the classification which the regulation makes has no relation to the traffic problem since a violation turns not on what kind of advertisements are carried on trucks but on whose trucks they are carried.

That, however, is a superficial way of analyzing the problem, even if we assume that it is premised on the correct construction of the regulation. The local authorities may well have concluded that those who advertised their own wares on their trucks do not present the same traffic problem in view of the nature or extent of the advertising which they use. It would take a degree of ominiscience which we lack to say that such is not the case. If that judgment is correct, the advertising displays that are exempt have less incidence on traffic than those of appellants.

We cannot say that that judgment is not an allowable one. Yet if it is, the classification has relation to the purpose for which it is made and does not contain the kind of discrimination against which the Equal Protection Clause affords protection. It is by such practical considerations based on experience rather than by theoretical inconsistencies that the question of equal protection is to be answered. *Patsone* v. *Commonwealth of Pennsylvania*, 232 U.S. 138, 144. . . . And the fact that New York City sees fit to eliminate from traffic this kind of distraction but does not touch what may be even greater ones in a different category, such as the vivid displays on Times Square, is immaterial. It is no requirement of equal protection that all evils of the same genus be eradicated or none at all. . . .

Mr. Justice Rutledge acquiesces in the Court's opinion and judgment, *dubitante* on the question of equal protection of the laws.

Mr. Justice Jackson, concurring. . . .

Note: An example of laissez-faire perversion of the traditional equal-protection test will be found in *Connolly* v. *Union Sewer Pipe Co.*, 184 U.S. 540 (1902). It was overruled in *Tigner* v. *Texas*, 310 U.S. 141 (1940).

Stage Two: A Warren Court Innovation

Shapiro v. *Thompson* (excerpt)
394 U.S. 618 (1969)

Mr. Justice Harlan, dissenting. . . .

In upholding the equal protection argument, the Court has applied an equal protection doctrine of relatively recent vintage: the rule that statutory classifications which either are based upon certain "suspect" criteria or affect "fundamental rights" will be held to deny equal protection unless justified by a "compelling" governmental interest. . . .

The "compelling interest" doctrine, which today is articulated more explicitly than ever before, constitutes an increasingly significant exception to the long-established rule that a statute does not deny equal protection if it is rationally related to a legitimate governmental objective. The "compelling interest" doctrine has two branches. The branch which requires that classifications based upon "suspect" criteria be supported by a compelling interest apparently had its genesis in cases involving racial classifications, which have at least since *Korematsu* v. *United States,* 323 U.S. 214, 216 (1944), been regarded as inherently "suspect." The criterion of "wealth" apparently was added to the list of "suspects" as an alternative justification for the rationale in *Harper* v. *Virginia Bd. of Elections,* 383 U.S. 663, 668 (1966), in which Virginia's poll tax was struck down. The criterion of political allegiance may have been added in *Williams* v. *Rhodes,* 393 U.S. 23 (1968). Today the list apparently has been further enlarged to include classifications based upon recent interstate movement, and perhaps those based upon the exercise of *any* constitutional right, . . .

I think that this branch of the "compelling interest" doctrine is sound when applied to racial classifications, for historically the Equal Protection Clause was largely a product of the desire to eradicate legal distinctions founded upon race. However, I believe that the more recent extensions have been unwise. . . .

The second branch of the "compelling interest" principle is even more troublesome. For it has been held that a statutory classification is subject to the "compelling interest" test if the result of the classification may be to affect a "fundamental right," regardless of the basis of the classification. . . .

I think this branch of the "compelling interest" doctrine particularly unfortunate and unnecessary. It is unfortunate because it creates an exception which threatens to swallow the standard equal protection rule. Virtually every state statute affects important rights. This Court has repeatedly held, for example, that the traditional equal protection standard is applicable to statutory classifications affecting such fundamental matters as the right to pursue a particular occupation, the right to receive greater or smaller wages or to work more or less hours, and the right to inherit property. Rights such as these are in principle indistinguishable from those involved here, and to extend the "compelling interest" rule to all cases in which such rights are affected would go far toward making this Court a "super-legislature." The branch of the doctrine is also unnecessary. When the right affected is one assured by the federal Constitution, any infringement can be dealt with under the Due Process Clause. But when a statute affects only matters not mentioned in the federal Constitution and is not arbitrary or irrational, I must reiterate that I know of nothing which entitles this Court to pick out particular human activities, characterize them as "fundamental," and give them added protection under an unusually stringent equal protection test. . . .

Stage Three: Post-Warren Revisions

Dandridge v. *Williams* (excerpt)
397 U.S. 471 (1970)

Under the federal Aid to Families with Dependent Children (AFDC) program, Maryland gave standard aid per child but imposed a monthly limit of $250 per family. Large-family recipients challenged the limitation as discriminatory against them merely because of family size. The Court was careful not to repudiate, but to confine, the new Warren era "strict scrutiny" test (see *Shapiro,* above) to classifications intruding on "constitutionally protected freedom", that is, to interests recognized by the Constitution. Other interests—including those involved in the present case—were subject to regulation in accordance with the traditional equal-protection test of reasonableness.

Mr. Justice Stewart delivered the opinion of the Court. . . .

. . . Maryland says that its maximum grant regulation is wholly free of any invidiously discriminatory purpose or effect, and that the regulation is rationally supportable on at least four entirely valid grounds. The regulation can be clearly justified, Maryland argues, in terms of legitimate state interests in encouraging gainful employment, in maintaining an equitable balance in economic status as between welfare families and those supported by a wage-earner, in providing incentives for family planning, and in allocating available public funds in such a way as fully to meet the needs of the largest possible number of families. The District Court, while apparently recognizing the validity of at least some of these state concerns, nonetheless held that the regulation "is invalid on its face for overreaching,"—that it violates the Equal Protection Clause "[b]ecause it cuts too broad a swath on an indiscriminate basis as applied to the entire group of AFDC eligibles to which it purports to apply . . . ."

If this were a case involving government action claimed to violate the First Amendment guarantee of free speech, a finding of "overreaching" would be significant and might be crucial. For when otherwise valid governmental regulation sweeps so broadly as to impinge upon activity protected by the First Amendment, its very overbreadth may make it unconstitutional. See, e.g., *Shelton* v. *Tucker,* 364 U.S. 479. But the concept of "overreaching" has no place in this case. For here we deal with state regulation in the social and economic field, not affecting freedoms guaranteed by the Bill of Rights, and claimed to violate the Fourteenth Amendment only because the regulation results in some disparity in grants of welfare payments to the largest AFDC families. For this Court to approve the invalidation of state economic or social regulation as "overreaching" would be far too reminiscent of an era when the Court thought the Fourteenth Amendment gave it power to strike down state laws "because they may be unwise, improvident, or out of harmony with a particular school of thought." *Williamson* v. *Lee Optical Co.,* 348 U.S. 483, 488. That era long ago passed into history. *Ferguson* v. *Skrupa,* 372 U.S. 726.

In the area of economics and social welfare, a State does not violate the Equal Protection Clause merely because the classifications made by its laws are imperfect. If the classification has some "reasonable basis," it does not offend the Constitution simply because the classification "is not made with mathematical nicety or because in practice it results in some inequality."

Lindsley v. *Natural Carbonic Gas Co.*, 220 U.S. 61, 78. . . . "A statutory discrimination will not be set aside if any state of facts reasonably may be conceived to justify it." *McGowan* v. *Maryland*, 366 U.S. 420, 426.

To be sure, the cases cited, and many others enunciating this fundamental standard under the Equal Protection Clause, have in the main involved state regulation of business or industry. The administration of public welfare assistance, by contrast, involves the most basic economic needs of impoverished human beings. We recognize the dramatically real factual difference between the cited cases and this one, but we can find no basis for applying a different constitutional standard. It is a standard that has consistently been applied to state legislation restricting the availability of employment opportunities. *Goesaert* v. *Cleary*, 335 U.S. 464; *Kotch* v. *Board of River Port Pilot Comm'rs*, 330 U.S. 552. And it is a standard that is true to the principle that the Fourteenth Amendment gives the federal courts no power to impose upon the States their views of what constitutes wise economic or social policy.

Under this long-established meaning of the Equal Protection Clause, it is clear that the Maryland maximum grant regulation is constitutionally valid. We need not explore all the reasons that the State advances in justification of the regulation. It is enough that a solid foundation for the regulation can be found in the State's legitimate interest in encouraging employment and in avoiding discrimination between welfare families and the families of the working poor. By combining a limit on the recipient's grant with permission to retain money earned, without reduction in the amount of the grant, Maryland provides an incentive to seek gainful employment. And by keying the maximum family AFDC grants to the minimum wage a steadily employed head of a household receives, the State maintains some semblance of an equitable balance between families on welfare and those supported by an employed breadwinner.

[Justices Douglas, Brennan, and Marshall dissented.]

Massachusetts Board of Retirement v. *Murgia* (excerpt)
427 U.S. 307 (1976)

State law required the retirement of police officers at age 50. The Court—following the traditional "rational basis" test—upheld the measure in the face of an equal-protection attack.

Mr. Justice Marshall, dissenting. . . .

Although there are signs that its grasp on the law is weakening, the rigid two-tier model still holds sway as the Court's articulated description of the equal protection test. Again, I must object to its perpetuation. The model's two fixed modes of analysis, strict scrutiny and mere rationality, simply do not describe the inquiry the Court has undertaken—or should undertake—in equal protection cases. Rather, the inquiry has been much more sophisticated

and the Court should admit as much. It has focused upon the character of the classification in question, the relative importance to individuals in the class discriminated against of the governmental benefits that they do not receive, and the state interests asserted in support of the classification. . . .

Although the Court outwardly adheres to the two-tier model, it has apparently lost interest in recognizing further "fundamental" rights and "suspect" classes. See *San Antonio School District* v. *Rodriguez, supra* (rejecting education as a fundamental right); *Frontiero* v. *Richardson*, 411 U.S. 677 (1973) (declining to treat women as a suspect class). In my view, this result is the natural consequence of the limitations of the Court's traditional equal protection analysis. If a statute invades a "fundamental" right or discriminates against a "suspect" class, it is subject to strict scrutiny. If a statute is subject to strict scrutiny, the statute always, or nearly always, see *Korematsu* v. *United States*, 323 U.S. 214 (1944), is struck down. Quite obviously, the only critical decision is whether strict scrutiny should be invoked at all. It should be no surpirse, then, that the Court is hesitant to expand the number of categories of rights and classes subject to strict scrutiny, when each expansion involves the invalidation of virtually every classification bearing upon a newly covered category.[1]

But however understandable the Court's hesitancy to invoke strict scrutiny, all remaining legislation should not drop into the bottom tier, and be measured by the mere rationality test. For that test, too, when applied as articulated, leaves little doubt about the outcome; the challenged legislation is always upheld. See *New Orleans* v. *Dukes*, 427 U.S. 297 (1976) (overruling *Morey* v. *Doud*; 354 U.S. 457 [1957], the only modern case in which this Court has struck down an economic classification as irrational). It cannot be gainsaid that there remain rights, not now classified as "fundamental," that remain vital to the flourishing of a free society, and classes, not now classified as "suspect," that are unfairly burdened by invidious discrimination unrelated to the individual worth of their members. Whatever we call these rights and classes, we simply cannot forgo all judicial protection against discriminatory legislation bearing upon them, but for the rare instances when the legislative choice can be termed "wholly irrelevant" to the legislative goal. *McGowan* v. *Maryland*, 366 U.S. 420, 425 (1961).

While the Court's traditional articulation of the rational basis test does suggest just such an abdication, happily the Court's deeds have not matched its words. Time and again, met with cases touching upon the prized rights and burdened classes of our society, the Court has acted only after a reasonably probing look at the legislative goals and means, and at the significance of the personal rights and interests invaded. *Stanton* v. *Stanton*, 421 U.S. 7 (1975); *Weinberger* v. *Weisenfeld*, 420 U.S. 636 (1975); *United States Dept. of Agriculture* v. *Moreno*, 413 U.S. 528 (1973); *Frontiero* v. *Richardson*, 411 U.S., at 691 (Powell, J., concurring in the judgment); *James* v. *Strange*, 407 U.S. 128 (1972); *Weber* v. *Aetna Casualty & Surety Co.*, 406 U.S. 164 (1972); *Eisenstadt* v. *Baird*, 405 U.S. 438 (1972); *Reed* v. *Reed*, 404 U.S. 71 (1971). See *San Antonio School District* v. *Rodriguez*, 411 U.S., at 98–110 (Marshall, J., dissenting). These cases make clear that the court has rejected, albeit *sub silentio*, its most deferential statements of the rationality standard in assessing the validity under the Equal Protection Clause of much noneconomic legislation.

But there are problems with deciding cases based on factors not encompassed by the applicable standards. First, the approach is rudderless, affording no notice to interested parties of the standards governing particular cases and giving no firm guidance to judges who, as a consequence, must assess the constitutionality of legislation before them on an *ad hoc* basis. Second, and not unrelatedly, the approach is unpredictable and requires holding this Court to standards it has never publicly adopted. Thus,

---

[1] Some classifications are so invidious that they should be struck down automatically absent the most compelling state interest, and by suggesting the limitations of strict scrutiny analysis I do not mean to imply otherwise. The analysis should be accomplished, however, not by stratified notions of "suspect" classes and "fundamental" rights, but by individualized assessments of the particular classes and rights involved in each case. Of course, the traditional suspect classes and fundamental rights would still rank at the top of the list of protected categories, so that in cases involving those categories analysis would be functionally equivalent to strict scrutiny. Thus, the advantages of the approach I favor do not appear in such cases, but rather emerge in those dealing with traditionally less protected classes and rights.

the approach presents the danger that, as I suggest has happened here, relevant factors will be misapplied or ignored. All interests not "fundamental" and all cases not "suspect" are not the same; and it is time for the Court to drop the pretense that, for purposes of the Equal Protection Clause, they are. . . .

Note: In a famous article, "Foreword: In Search of Evolving Doctrine on a Changing Court: A Model for a Newer Equal Protection," 86 *Harvard Law Review* 1 (1972), G. Gunther traced the evolution of the Court's various equal-protection tests or standards and suggested that the Burger Court may be developing a "newer equal protection" which in effect embodies the traditional (rational basis) test, but "with bite." This may be explained as follows: In the Warren era application of the *new* strict-scrutiny test was *automatically* a death sentence for state laws; under the traditional rational-basis test it was almost equally automatic that state legislation (except in race cases after 1937) would be upheld. The "newer" traditional test "with bite" seemingly falls between these two extremes. Under it, for example, the Court would be less cavalier than it was in its treatment of the claimant's interests in *Railway Express,* above—and less cavalier with state interests than it was in *Shapiro,* below. Careful readers may detect such developments in the cases that follow. For extended, recent judicial discussion of the whole problem, see *Craig* v. *Boren,* below.

RACIAL CLASSIFICATIONS

Introduction

A state which *on its face* obviously mandated discrimination was invalidated in *Strauder* v. *West Virginia* (above, Chapter 5). Not all cases are that simple. *Yick Wo* v. *Hopkins,* 118 U.S. 356 (1886), is important for its recognition that a statute fair on its face may be administered in a discriminatory manner, that is, in violation of the Equal Protection Clause. *Washington* v. *Davis,* below, presents a third possibility: disproportionate *impact* of an otherwise neutral law.

Dred Scott v. *Sandford*
See p. 6, above.

Loving v. *Virginia*
388 U.S. 1 (1967)

Chief Justice Warren delivered the opinion of the Court.

This case presents a constitutional question never addressed by this Court: whether a statutory scheme adopted by the State of Virginia to prevent marriages between persons solely on the basis of racial classifications violates the Equal Protection and Due Process Clauses of the Fourteenth Amendment. For reasons which seem to us to reflect the central meaning of those constitutional commands, we conclude that these statutes cannot stand consistently with the Fourteenth Amendment.

In June 1958, two residents of Virginia, Mildred Jeter, a Negro woman, and Richard Loving, a white man, were married in the District of Columbia pursuant to its laws. Shortly after their marriage, the Lovings returned to Virginia and established their marital abode in Caroline County. . . .

[They were then convicted of violating Virginia's ban on interracial marriages. The state supreme court of appeals affirmed the convictions.]

In upholding the constitutionality of these provisions in the decision below, the Supreme Court of Appeals of Virginia referred to its 1955 decision in *Naim* v. *Naim*, 197 Va. 80, 87 S.E.2d 749 . . . that the State's legitimate purposes were "to preserve the racial integrity of its citizens," and to prevent "the corruption of blood," "a mongrel breed of citizens," and "the obliteration of racial pride,' obviously an endorsement of the doctrine of White Supremacy. The court also reasoned that marriage has traditionally been subject to state regulation without federal intervention, and, consequently, the regulation of marriage should be left to exclusive state control by the Tenth Amendment.

While the state court is no doubt correct in asserting that marriage is a social relation subject to the State's police power, the State does not contend in its argument before this Court that its powers to regulate marriage are unlimited notwithstanding the commands of the Fourteenth Amendment. . . .

Because we reject the notion that the mere "equal application" of a statute containing racial classifications is enough to remove the classifications from the Fourteenth Amendment's proscription of all invidious racial discriminations, we do not accept the State's contention that these statutes should be upheld if there is any possible basis for concluding that they serve a rational purpose. The mere fact of equal application does not mean that our analysis of these statutes should follow the approach we have taken in cases involving no racial discrimination. . . . In these cases, involving distinctions not drawn according to race, the Court has merely asked whether there is any rational foundation for the discriminations, and has deferred to the wisdom of the state legislatures. In the case at bar, however, we deal with statutes containing racial classifications, and the fact of equal application does not immunize the statute

from the very heavy burden of justification which the Fourteenth Amendment has traditionally required of state statutes drawn according to race. . . .

. . . We have rejected the proposition that the debates in the Thirty-ninth Congress or in the state legislatures which ratified the Fourteenth Amendment supported the theory advanced by the State, that the requirement of equal protection of the laws is satisfied by penal laws defining offenses based on racial classifications so long as white and Negro participants in the offense were similarly punished. *McLaughlin* v. *State of Florida*, 379 U.S. 184 (1964). . . .

There can be no question but that Virginia's miscegenation statutes rest solely upon distinctions drawn according to race. The statutes proscribe generally accepted conduct if engaged in by members of different races. Over the years, this Court has consistently repudiated "[d]istinctions between citizens solely because of their ancestry" as being "odious to a free people whose institutions are found upon the doctrine of equality." *Hirabayashi* v. *United States*, 320 U.S. 81, 100 (1943). At the very least, the Equal Protection Clause demands that racial classifications, especially suspect in criminal statutes, be subjected to the "most rigid scrutiny," *Korematsu* v. *United States*, 323 U.S. 214, 216 (1944), and, if they are ever to be upheld, they must be shown to be necessary to the accomplishment of some permissible state objective, independent of the racial discrimination which it was the object of the Fourteenth Amendment to eliminate. Indeed, two members of this Court have already stated that they "cannot conceive of a valid legislative purpose . . . which makes the color of a person's skin the test of whether his conduct is a criminal offense." *McLaughlin* v. *Florida* (Stewart, J., joined by Douglas, J., concurring).

There is patently no legitimate overriding purpose independent of invidious racial discrimination which justifies this classification. The fact that Virginia prohibits only interracial marriages involving white persons demonstrates that the racial classifications must stand on their own justification, as measures designed to maintain White Supremacy. We have consistently denied the constitutionality of measures which restrict the rights of citizens on account of race. There can be no doubt that restricting the freedom to marry solely because of racial classifications violates the central meaning of the Equal Protection Clause.

These statutes also deprive the Lovings of liberty without due process of law in violation of the Due Process Clause of the Fourteenth Amendment. The freedom to marry has long been recognized as one of the vital personal rights essential to the orderly pursuit of happiness by free men.

Marriage is one of the "basic civil rights of man," fundamental to our very existence and survival. *Skinner* v. *State of Oklahoma*, 316 U.S. 535 (1942). To deny this fundamental freedom on so unsupportable a basis as the racial classifications embodied in these statutes, classifications so directly subversive of the principle of equality at the heart of the Fourteenth Amendment, is surely to deprive all the State's citizens of liberty without due process of law. The Fourteenth Amendment requires that the freedom of choice to marry not be restricted by invidious racial discriminations. Under our Constitution, the freedom to marry or not marry, a person of another race resides with the individual and cannot be infringed by the State. . . .

Washington v. *Davis*
426 U.S. 229 (1976)

This case, in contrast to the *Strauder* racial-mandate problem and the *Yick Wo* administration problem, is concerned with the disproportionate *impact* or results of legislation.

Mr. Justice White delivered the opinion of the Court.

This case involves the validity of a qualifying test administered to applicants for positions as police officers in the District of Columbia Metropolitan Police Department. The test was sustained by the District Court but invalidated by the Court of Appeals. We are in agreement with the District Court and hence reverse the judgment of the Court of Appeals. . . .

I.

According to the findings and conclusions of the District Court, to be accepted by the Department and to enter an intensive 17-week training program, the police recruit was required to satisfy certain physical and character standards, to be a high school graduate or its

equivalent and to receive a grade of at least 40 on "Test 21," which is "an examination that is used generally throughout the federal service," which "was developed by the Civil Service Commission not the Police Department" and which was "designed to test verbal ability, vocabulary, reading and comprehension." 348 F.Supp., at 16.

The validity of Test 21 was the sole issue before the court on the motions for summary judgment. The District Court noted that there was no claim of "an intentional discrimination or purposeful discriminatory actions" but only a claim that Test 21 bore no relationship to job performance and "has a highly discriminatory impact in screening out black candiates." 348 F.Supp., at 16. Petitioners' evidence, the District Court said, warranted three conclusions: "(a) The number of black police officers, while substantial, is not proportionate to the population mix of the city. (*b*) A higher percentage of blacks fail the Test than whites. (*c*) The Test has not been validated to establish its reliability for measuring subsequent job performance." *Ibid.* This showing was deemed sufficient to shift the burden of proof to the defendants in the action, petitioners here; but the court nevertheless concluded that on the undisputed facts respondents were not entitled to relief. The District Court relied on several factors. Since August 1969, 44% of new police force recruits had been black; that figure also represented the proportion of blacks on the total force and was roughly equivalent to 20–29-year-old blacks in the 50-mile radius in which the recruiting efforts of the Police Department had been concentrated. It was undisputed that the Department had systematically and affirmatively sought to enroll black officers many of whom passed the test but failed to report for duty. The District Court rejected the assertion that Test 21 was culturally slanted to favor whites and was "satisfied that the undisputable facts prove the test to be reasonably and directly related to the requirements of the police recruit training program and that it is neither so designed nor operated to discriminate against otherwise qualified blacks." 348 F.Supp., at 17. It was thus not necessary to show that Test 21 was not only a useful indicator of training school performance but had also been validated in terms of job performance—"the lack of job performance validation does not defeat the test, given its direct relationship to recruiting and the valid part it plays in this process." The District Court ultimately concluded that "the proof is wholly lacking that a police officer qualifies on the color of his skin rather than ability" and that the Department "should not be required on this showing to lower standards or to abandon efforts to achieve excellence." 348 F.Supp., at 18.

Having lost on both constitutional and statutory issues in the District Court, respondents brought the case to the Court of Appeals claiming that their summary judgment motion, which rested on purely constitutional grounds,

should have been granted. The tendered constitutional issue was whether the use of Test 21 invidiously discriminated against Negroes and hence denied them due process of law contrary to the commands of the Fifth Amendment. The Court of Appeals, addressing that issue, announced that it would be guided by *Griggs* v. *Duke Power Co.*, 401 U.S. 424 (1971), a case involving the interpretation and application of Title VII of the Civil Rights Act of 1964, and held that the statutory standards elucidated in that case were to govern the due process question tendered in this one. 168 U.S.App.D.C. 42, 512 F.2d 956 (1975). The court went on to declare that lack of discriminatory intent in designing and administering Test 21 was irrelevant; the critical fact was rather that a far greater proportion of blacks—four times as many—failed the test than did whites. This disproportionate impact, standing alone and without regard to whether it indicated a discriminatory purpose, was held sufficient to establish a constitutional violation, absent proof by petitioners that the test was an adequate measure of job performance in addition to being an indicator of probable success in the training program, a burden which the court ruled petitioners had failed to discharge. . . .

II.

The central purpose of the Equal Protection Clause of the Fourteenth Amendment is the prevention of official conduct discriminating on the basis of race. It is also true that the Due Process Clause of the Fifth Amendment contains an equal protection component prohibiting the United States from invidiously discriminating between individuals or groups. *Bolling* v. *Sharpe*, 347 U.S. 497 (1954). But our cases have not embraced the proposition that a law or other official act, without regard to whether it reflects a racially discriminatory purpose, is unconstitutional *solely* because it has a racially disproportionate impact.

Almost 100 years ago, *Strauder* v. *West Vir-*

ginia, 100 U.S. 303 (1879), established that the exclusion of Negroes from grand and petit juries in criminal proceedings violated the Equal Protection Clause, but the fact that a particular jury or a series of juries does not statistically reflect the racial composition of the community does not in itself make out an invidious discrimination forbidden by the Clause. "A purpose to discriminate must be present which may be proven by systematic exclusion of eligible jurymen of the prescribed race or by an unequal application of the law to such an extent as to show intentional discrimination." *Akins* v. *Texas,* 325 U.S. 398, 403–404 (1945). A defendant in a criminal case is entitled "to require that the State not deliberately and systematically deny to the members of his race the right to participate as jurors in the administration of justice." See also *Carter* v. *Jury Commission,* 396 U.S. 320, 335–337, 339 (1970); *Cassell* v. *Texas,* 339 U.S. 282, 287–290 (1950); *Patton* v. *Mississippi,* 332 U.S. 463, 468–469 (1947).

The rule is the same in other contexts. *Wright* v. *Rockefeller,* 376 U.S. 52 (1964), upheld a New York congressional apportionment statute against claims that district lines had been racially gerrymandered. The challenged districts were made up predominantly of whites or of minority races, and their boundaries were irregularly drawn. The challengers did not prevail because they failed to prove that the New York legislature "was either motivated by racial considerations or in fact drew the districts on racial lines"; the plaintiffs had not shown that the statute "was the product of a state contrivance to segregate on the basis of race or place of origin." 376 U.S., at 56, 58. The dissenters were in agreement that the issue was whether the "boundaries . . . were purposefully drawn on racial lines." 376 U.S., at 67.

The school desegregation cases have also adhered to the basic equal protection principle that the invidious quality of a law claimed to be racially discriminatory must ultimately be traced to a racially discriminatory purpose. That there are both predominantly black and pre-

dominantly white schools in a community is not alone violative of the Equal Protection Clause. The essential element of *de jure* segregation is "a current condition of segregation resulting from intentional state action . . . the differentiating factor between *de jure* segregation and so-called *de facto* segregation . . . is *purpose* or *intent* to segregate." *Keyes* v. *School District No. 1,* 413 U.S. 189, 205, 208 (1973). See also *id.,* at 199, 211, 213. The Court has also recently rejected allegations of racial discrimination based solely on the statistically disproportionate racial impact of various provisions of the Social Security Act because "the acceptance of appellant's constitutional theory would render suspect each difference in treatment among the grant classes, however lacking the racial motivation and however rational the treatment might be." *Jefferson* v. *Hackney,* 406 U.S. 535, 548 (1972). And compare *Hunter* v. *Erickson,* 393 U.S. 385 (1969), with *James* v. *Valtierra,* 402 U.S. 137 (1971).

This is not to say that the necessary discriminatory racial purpose must be express or appear on the face of the statute, or that a law's disproportionate impact is irrelevant in cases involving Constitution-based claims of racial discrimination. A statute, otherwise neutral on its face, must not be applied so as invidiously to discriminate on the basis of race. *Yick Wo* v. *Hopkins,* 118 U.S. 356 (1886). It is also clear from the cases dealing with racial discrimination in the selection of juries that the systematic exclusion of Negroes is itself such an "unequal application of the law . . . as to show intentional discrimination." *Akins* v. *Texas, supra,* at 404. *Smith* v. *Texas,* 311 U.S. 128 (1940); *Pierre* v. *Louisiana,* 306 U.S. 354 (1939); *Neal* v. *Delaware,* 103 U.S. 370 (1881). A prima facie case of discriminatory purpose may be proved as well by the absence of Negroes on a particular jury combined with the failure of the jury commissioners to be informed of eligible Negro jurors in a community, *Hill* v. *Texas,* 316 U.S. 400, 404 (1942), or with racially nonneutral selection procedures, *Alexander* v. *Louisiana,* 405 U.S. 625 (1972); *Avery* v. *Georgia,* 345 U.S. 559 (1953);

Whitus v. *Georgia*, 385 U.S. 545 (1967). With a *prima facie* case made out, "the burden of proof shifts to the State to rebut the presumption of unconstitutional action by showing that permissible racially neutral selection criteria and procedures have produced the monochromatic result." *Alexander, supra*, at 632. See also *Turner* v. *Fouche*, 396 U.S. 346, 361 (1970); *Eubanks* v. *Louisiana*, 356 U.S. 584, 587 (1958).

Necessarily, an invidious discriminatory purpose may often be inferred from the totality of the relevant facts, including the fact, if it is true, that the law bears more heavily on one race than another. It is also not infrequently true that the discriminatory impact—in the jury cases for example, the total or seriously disproportionate exclusion of Negroes from jury venires—may for all practical purposes demonstrate unconstitutionality because in various circumstances the discrimination is very difficult to explain on nonracial grounds. Nevertheless, we have not held that a law, neutral on its face and serving ends otherwise within the power of government to pursue, is invalid under the Equal Protection Clause simply because it may affect a greater proportion of one race than of another. Disproportionate impact is not irrelevant, but it is not the sole touchstone of an invidious racial discrimination forbidden by the Constitution. Standing alone, it does not trigger the rule, *McLaughlin* v. *Florida*, 379 U.S. 184 (1964), that racial classifications are to be subjected to the strictest scrutiny and are justifiable only by the weightiest of considerations.

There are some indications to the contrary in our cases. In *Palmer* v. *Thompson*, 403 U.S. 217 (1971), the city of Jackson, Miss., following a court decree to this effect, desegregated all of its public facilities save five swimming pools which had been operated by the city and which, following the decree, were closed by ordinance pursuant to a determination by the city council that closure was necessary to preserve peace and order and that integrated pools could not be economically operated. Accepting the finding that the pools were closed to avoid violence and economic loss, this Court rejected the argument that the abandonment of this service was inconsistent with the outstanding desegregation decree and that the otherwise seemingly permissible ends served by the ordinance could be impeached by demonstrating that racially invidious motivations had prompted the city council's action. The holding was that the city was not overtly or covertly operating segregated pools and was extending identical treatment to both whites and Negroes. The opinion warned against grounding decision on legislative purpose or motivation, thereby lending support for the proposition that the operative effect of the law rather than its purpose is the paramount factor. But the holding of the case was that the legitimate purposes of the ordinance—to preserve peace and avoid deficits—were not open to impeachment by evidence that the councilmen were actually motivated by racial considerations. Whatever dicta the opinion may contain, the decision did not involve, much less invalidate, a statute or ordinance having neutral purposes but disproportionate racial consequences.

Wright v. *Council of the City of Emporia*, 407 U.S. 451 (1972), also indicates that in proper circumstances, the racial impact of a law, rather than its discriminatory purpose, is the critical factor. That case involved the division of a school district. The issue was whether the division was consistent with an outstanding order of a federal court to desegregate the dual school system found to have existed in the area. The constitutional predicate for the District Court's invalidation of the divided district was "the enforcement until 1969 of racial segregation in the public school system of which Emporia had always been a part." *Id.*, at 459. There was thus no need to find "an independent constitutional violation." *Ibid.* Citing *Palmer* v. *Thompson*, we agreed with the District Court that the division of the district had the effect of interfering with the federal decree and should be set aside.

That neither *Palmer* nor *Wright* was understood to have changed the prevailing rule is apparent from *Keyes* v. *School District No. 1, supra,* where the principal issue in litigation was whether and to what extent there had been purposeful discrimination resulting in a partially or wholly segregated school system. Nor did other later cases, *Alexander* v. *Louisiana, supra,* and *Jefferson* v. *Hackney, supra,* indicate that either Palmer or Wright had worked a fundamental change in equal protection law.

Both before and after *Palmer* v. *Thompson,* however, various Courts of Appeals have held in several contexts, including public employment, that the substantially disproportionate racial impact of a statute or official practice standing alone and without regard to discriminatory purpose, suffices to prove racial discrimination violating the Equal Protection Clause absent some justification going substantially beyond what would be necessary to validate most other legislative classifications. The cases impressively demonstrate that there is another side to the issue; but, with all due respect, to the extent that those cases rested on or expressed the view that proof of discriminatory racial purpose is unnecessary in making out an equal protection violation, we are in disagreement.

As an initial matter, we have difficulty understanding how a law establishing a racially neutral qualification for employment is nevertheless racially discriminatory and denies "any person equal protection of the laws" simply because a greater proportion of Negroes fail to qualify than members of other racial or ethnic groups. Had respondents, along with all others who had failed Test 21, whether white or black, brought an action claiming that the test denied each of them equal protection of the laws as compared with those who had passed with high enough scores to qualify them as police recruits, it is most unlikely that their challenge would have been sustained. Test 21, which is administered generally to prospective government employees, concededly seeks to ascertain whether those who take it have acquired a particular level of verbal skill; and it is untenable that the

Constitution prevents the government from seeking modestly to upgrade the communicative abilities of its employees rather than to be satisfied with some lower level of competence, particularly where the job requires special ability to communicate orally and in writing. Respondents, as Negroes, could no more successfully claim that the test denied them equal protection than could white applicants who also failed. The conclusion would not be different in the face of proof that more Negroes than whites had been disqualified by Test 21. That other Negroes also failed to score well would, alone, not demonstrate that respondents individually were being denied equal protection of the laws by the application of an otherwise valid qualifying test being administered to prospective police recruits.

Nor on the facts of the case before us would the disproportionate impact of Test 21 warrant the conclusion that it is a purposeful device to discriminate against Negroes and hence an infringement of the constitutional rights of respondents as well as other black applicants. As we have said, the test is neutral on its face and rationally may be said to serve a purpose the government is constitutionally empowered to pursue. Even agreeing with the District Court that the differential racial effect of Test 21 called for further inquiry, we think the District Court correctly held that the affirmative efforts of the Metropolitan Police Department to recruit black officers, the changing racial composition of the recruit classes and of the force in general, and the relationship of the test to the training program negated any inference that the Department discriminated on the basis of race or that "a police officer qualifies on the color of his skin rather than ability." 348 F.Supp., at 18.

Under Title VII, Congress provided that when hiring and promotion practices disqualifying substantially disproportionate numbers of blacks are challenged, discriminatory purpose need not be proved, and that it is an insufficient response to demonstrate some rational basis for the challenged practices. It is necessary, in addition, that they be "validated" in terms of job performance in any one of several ways, perhaps by ascertaining the minimum skill, ability or potential necessary for the position at issue and determining whether the qualifying tests are appropriate for the selection of qualified applicants for the job in question. However this process proceeds, it involves a more probing judicial review of, and less deference to, the seemingly reasonable acts of administrators and executives than is appropriate under the Constitution where special racial impact, without discriminatory purpose, is claimed. We are not disposed to adopt this more rigorous standard for the purposes of applying the Fifth and the Fourteenth Amendments in cases such as this.

A rule that a statute designed to serve neutral ends is nevertheless invalid, absent compelling justification, if in practice it benefits or burdens one race more than another would be far reaching and would raise serious questions about, and perhaps invalidate, a whole range of tax, welfare, public service, regulatory, and licensing statutes that may be more burdensome to the poor and to the average black than to the more affluent white.

Given that rule, such consequences would perhaps be likely to follow. However, in our view, extension of the rule beyond those areas where it is already applicable by reason of statute, such as in the field of public employment, should await legislative prescription.

As we have indicated, it was error to direct summary judgment for respondents based on the Fifth Amendment.

III.

We also hold that the Court of Appeals should have affirmed the judgment of the District Court granting the motions for summary judgment filed by petitioners and the federal parties. Respondents were entitled to relief on neither constitutional nor statutory grounds.

The submission of the defendants in the Dis-

trict Court was that Test 21 complied with all applicable statutory as well as constitutional requirements; and they appear not to have disputed that under the statutes and regulations governing their conduct standards similar to those obtaining under Title VII had to be satisfied. The District Court also assumed that Title VII standards were to control the case, identified the determinative issue as whether Test 21 was sufficiently job related and proceeded to uphold use of the test because it was "directly related to a determination of whether the applicant possesses sufficient skills requisite to the demands of the curriculum a recruit must master at the police academy." 348 F.Supp., at 17. The Court of Appeals reversed because the relationship between Test 21 and training school success, if demonstrated at all, did not satisfy what it deemed to be the crucial requirement of a direct relationship between performance on Test 21 and performance on the policeman's job.

We agree with petitioners and the federal respondents that this was error. The advisability of the police recruit training course informing the recruit about his upcoming job, acquainting him with its demands and attempting to impart a modicum of required skills seems conceded. It is also apparent to us, as it was to the District Judge, that some minimum verbal and communicative skill would be very useful, if not essential, to satisfactory progress in the training regimen. Based on the evidence before him, the District Judge concluded that Test 21 was directly related to the requirements of the police training program and that a positive relationship between the test and training course performance was sufficient to validate the former, wholly aside from its possible relationship to actual performance as a police officer. This conclusion of the District Judge that training-program validation may itself be sufficient is supported by regulations of the Civil Service Commission, by the opinion evidence placed before the District Judge and by the current views of the Civil Service Commissioners who were parties to the case. Nor is the conclusion foreclosed by either *Griggs* or *Albemarle Paper Co.* v. *Moody*, 422 U.S. 405 (1975); and it seems to us the much more sensible construction of the job relatedness requirement.

The District Court's accompanying conclusion that Test 21 was in fact directly related to the requirements of the police training program was supported by a validation study, as well as by other evidence of record; and we are not convinced that this conclusion was erroneous. . . .

The judgment of the Court of Appeals accordingly is reversed.

Mr. Justice Stevens, concurring.

While I agree with the Court's disposition of this case, I add these comments on the constitutional issue discussed in Part II. . . .

Frequently the most probative evidence of intent will be objective evidence of what actually happened rather than evidence describing the subjective state of mind of the actor. . . .

My point in making this observation is to suggest that the line between discriminatory purpose and discriminatory impact is not nearly as bright, and perhaps not quite as critical, as the reader of the Court's opinion might assume. I agree, of course, that a constitutional issue does not arise every time some disproportionate impact is shown. On the other hand, when the disproportion is as dramatic as in *Gomillion* or *Yick Wo*, it really does not matter whether the standard is phrased in terms of purpose or effect. Therefore, although I accept the statement of the general rule in the Court's opinion, I am not yet prepared to indicate how that standard should be applied in the many cases which have formulated the governing standard in different language.

[Mr. Justice Stewart joined in the Court's constitutional views as set out above. Justices Brennan and Marshall did not reach the constitutional issues but dissented on statutory grounds.]

Village of Arlington Heights v. *Metropolitan Housing Development Corp.* (excerpt)
429 U.S. 252 (1977)

Mr. Justice Powell delivered the opinion of the Court . . . .

Our decision last Term in *Washington* v. *Davis*, 426 U.S. 229 (1976), made it clear that official action will not be held unconstitutional solely because it results in a racially disproportionate impact. "Disproportionate impact is not irrelevant, but it is not the sole touchstone of an invidious racial discrimination." *Id.*, at 242. Proof of racially discriminatory intent or purpose is required to show a violation of the Equal Protection Clause. Although some contrary indications may be drawn from some of our cases the holding in *Davis* reaffirmed a principle well established in a variety of contexts. E.g., *Keyes* v. *School District No. 1*, 413 U.S. 189, 208 (1973) (schools); *Wright* v. *Rockefeller*, 376 U.S. 52, 56–57 (1974) (election districting); *Akins* v. *Texas*, 325 U.S. 398, 403–404 (1945) (jury selection).

Davis does not require a plaintiff to prove that the challenged action rested solely on racially discriminatory purposes. Rarely can it be said that a legislature or administrative body operating under a broad mandate made a decision motivated solely by a single concern, or even that a particular purpose was the "dominant" or "primary" one. In fact, it is because legislators and administrators are properly concerned with balancing numerous competing considerations that courts refrain from reviewing the merits of their decisions, absent a showing or arbitrariness or irrationality. But racial discrimination is not just another competing consideration. When there is a proof that a discriminatory purpose has been a motivating factor in the decision, this judicial deference is no longer justified.

Determining whether invidious discriminatory purpose was a motivating factor demands a sensitive inquiry into such circumstantial and direct evidence of intent as may be available. The impact of the official action—whether it "bears more heavily on one race than another," *Washington* v. *Davis,* 426 U.S., at 242—may provide an important starting point. Sometimes a clear pattern, unexplainable on grounds other than race, emerges from the effect of the state action even when the governing legislation appears neutral on its face. *Yick Wo* v. *Hopkins,* 118 U.S. 356 (1886); *Guinn* v. *United States,* 238 U.S. 347 (1915); *Lane* v. *Wilson,* 307 U.S. 268 (1939); *Gomillion* v. *Lightfoot,* 364 U.S. 339 (1960). The evidentiary inquiry is then relatively easy. But such cases are rare. Absent a pattern as stark as that in *Gomillion* or *Yick Wo,* impact alone is not determinative, and the Court must look to other evidence.

The historical background of the decision is one evidentiary source, particularly if it reveals a series of official actions taken for invidious purposes. See *Lane* v. *Wilson, supra; Griffin* v. *County School Board,* 377 U.S. 218 (1964); *Davis* v. *Schnell,* 81 F.Supp. 872 (S.D.Ala.) aff'd per curiam, 336 U.S. 933 (1949); cf. *Keyes* v. *School District No. 1,* 413 U.S., at 207. The specific sequence of events leading up to the challenged decision also may shed some light on the decisionmaker's purposes. *Reitman* v. *Mulkey,* 387 U.S. 369, 373–376 (1967); *Grosjean* v. *American Press,* 297 U.S. 233, 250 (1936). For example, if the property involved here always had been zoned R–5 but suddenly was changed to R–3 when the town learned of MHDC's plans to erect integrated housing, we would have a far different case. Departues from the normal procedural sequence also might afford evidence that improper purposes are playing a role. Substantive departures too may be relevant, particularly if the factors usually considered important by the decisionmaker strongly favor a decision contrary to the one reached.

The legislative or administrative history may be highly relevant, especially where there are contemporary statements by members of the decisionmaking body, minutes of its meetings, or reports. In some extraordinary instances the members might be called to the stand at trial to testify concerning the purpose of the official action, although even then such testimony frequently will be barred by privilege. See *Tenney* v. *Brandhove,* 341 U.S. 367 (1951); *United States* v. *Nixon,* 418 U.S. 683, 705 (1974); 8 Wigmore, *Evidence* § 2371 (McNaughton rev.ed. 1961).

The foregoing summary identifes, without purporting to be exhaustive, subjects of proper inquiry in determining whether racially discriminatory intent existed.

Racial Segregation

Strauder v. *West Virginia*
See p. 202, above.

Plessy v. *Ferguson*
163 U.S. 537 (1896)

Mr. Justice Brown . . . delivered the opinion of the court.

This case turns upon the constitutionality of [a Louisiana statute providing that] "all railway companies carrying passengers . . . in this State, shall provide equal but separate accommodations for white, and colored, races . . ."

The constitutionality of this act is attacked upon the ground that it conflicts both with the Thirteenth Amendment of the Constitution, abolishing slavery, and the Fourteenth Amendment, which prohibits certain restrictive legislation on the part of the states.

That it does not conflict with the Thirteenth Amendment, which abolished slavery and involuntary servitude, except as a punishment for crime, is too clear for argument. . . .

The object of the [Fourteenth] amendment was undoubtedly to enforce the absolute equality of the two races before the law, but in the nature of things it could not have been intended to abolish distinctions based upon color, or to enforce social, as distinguished from political, equality, or a commingling of the two races upon terms unsatisfactory to either. Laws permitting, and even requiring, their separation in places where they are liable to be brought into contact do not necessarily imply the inferiority of either race to the other, and have been generally, if not universally, recognized as within the competency of the state legislatures in the exercise of their police power. The most common instance of this is connected with the establishment of separate schools for white and colored children, which has been held to be a valid exercise of the legislative power even by courts of states where the political rights of the colored race have been longest and most earnestly enforced.

One of the earliest of these cases is that of *Roberts* v. *City of Boston*, 5 Cush. 198 (1849), in which the Supreme Judicial Court of Massachusetts held that the general school committee of Boston had power to make provision for the instruction of colored children in separate schools established exclusively for them, and to prohibit their attendance upon the other schools. "The great principle," said Chief Justice Shaw, p. 206, "advanced by the learned and eloquent advocate for the plaintiff" (Mr. Charles Sumner), "is, that by the constitution and laws of Massachusetts, all persons without distinction of age or sex, birth or color, origin or condition, are equal before the law. . . . But, when this great principle comes to be applied to the actual and various conditions of persons in society, it will not warrant the assertion, that men and women are legally clothed with the same civil and political powers, and that children and adults are legally to have the same functions and be subject to the same treatment; but only that the rights of all, as they are settled and regulated by law, are equally entitled to the paternal consideration and protection of the law for their maintenance and security." It was held that the powers of the committee extended to the establishment of separate schools for children of different ages, sexes and colors, and that they

might also establish special schools for poor and neglected children, who have become too old or attend the primary school, and yet have not acquired the rudiments of learning, to enable them to enter the ordinary schools. Similar laws have been enacted by Congress under its general power of legislation over the District of Columbia . . . as well as by the legislatures of many of the states, and have been generally, if not uniformly, sustained by the courts. . . .

The distinction between laws interfering with the political equality of the Negro and those requiring the separation of the two races in schools, theatres, and railway carriages has been frequently drawn by this court. Thus in *Strauder* v. *West Virginia*, 100 U.S. 303, it was held that a law of West Virginia limiting to white male persons, 21 years of age and citizens of the state, the right to sit upon juries, was a discrimination which implied a legal inferiority in civil society, which lessened the security of the right of the colored race, and was a step toward reducing them to a condition of servility. Indeed, the right of a colored man that, in the selection of jurors to pass upon his life, liberty and property, there shall be no exclusion of his race, and no discrimination against them because of color, has been asserted in a number of cases. . . .

So far, then, as a conflict with the Fourteenth Amendment is concerned, the case reduces itself to the question whether the statute of Louisiana is a reasonable regulation, and with respect to this there must necessarily be a large discretion on the part of the legislature. In determining the question of reasonableness it is at liberty to act with reference to the established usages, customs and traditions of the people, and with a view to the promotion of their comfort, and the preservation of the public peace and good order. Gauged by this standard, we cannot say that a law which authorizes or even requires the separation of the two races in public conveyances is unreasonable or more obnoxious to the Fourteenth Amendment than the acts of Congress requiring separate schools for colored children in the District of Columbia, the constitutionality of which does not seem to have been questioned, or the corresponding acts of state legislatures.

We consider the underlying fallacy of the plaintiff's argument to consist in the assumption that the enforced separation of the two races stamps the colored race with a badge of inferiority. If this be so, it is not by reason of anything found in the act, but solely because the colored race chooses to put that construction upon it. The argument necessarily assumes that if, as has been more than once the case, and is not unlikely to be so again, the colored race should become the dominant power in the state legislature, and should enact a law in precisely similar terms, it would thereby relegate the white race to an inferior position. We imagine that the white race, at least, would not acquiesce in this assumption. The argument also assumes that social prejudices may be overcome by legislation and that equal rights cannot be secured to the Negro except by an enforced commingling of the two races. We cannot accept this proposition. If the two races are to meet upon terms of social equality, it must be the result of natural affinities, a mutual appreciation of each other's merits, and a voluntary consent of individuals. As was said by the Court of Appeals of New York in *People* v. *Gallagher*, 93 N.Y. 438, 448,

> "this end can neither be accomplished nor prompted by laws which conflict with the general sentiment of the community upon whom they are designed to operate.
>
> "When the government, therefore, has secured to each of its citizens equal rights before the law and equal opportunities for improvement and progress, it has accomplished the end for which it was organized and performed all of the functions respecting social advantages with which it is endowed."

Legislation is powerless to eradicate racial instincts or to abolish distinctions based upon physical differences, and the attempt to do so can only result in accentuating the difficulties of the present situation. If the civil and political rights of both races be equal, one cannot be inferior to the other civilly or politically. If one race be inferior to the other socially, the Constitution of the United States cannot put them upon the same plane. . . .

The judgment of the court below is, therefore, affirmed.

Mr. Justice Harlan, dissenting:

In respect of civil rights, common to all citizens, the Constitution of the United States does not, I think, permit any public authority to know the race of those entitled to be protected in the enjoyment of such rights. Every true man has pride of race, and under appropriate circumstances when the rights of others, his equals before the law, are not to be affected, it is his privilege to express such pride and to take such action based upon it as to him seems proper. But I deny that any legislative body or judicial tribunal may have regard to the race of citizens when the civil rights of those citizens are involved. Indeed, such legislation as that here in question is inconsistent not only with that equality of rights which pertains to citizenship, national and state, but with the personal liberty enjoyed by everyone within the United States. . . .

It was said in argument that the statute of Louisiana does not discriminate against either race but prescribes a rule applicable alike to white and colored citizens. But this argument does not meet the difficulty. Everyone knows that the statute in question had its origin in the purpose, not so much to exclude white persons from railroad cars occupied by blacks, as to exclude colored people from coaches occupied by or assigned to white persons. Railroad corporations of Louisiana did not make discrimination among white in the matter of accommodation for travellers. The thing to accomplish was, under the guise of giving equal accommodations for whites and blacks, to compel the latter to keep to themselves while travelling in railroad passenger coaches. No one would be so wanting in candor as to assert the contrary. The fundamental objection, therefore, to the statute is that it interferes with the personal freedom of citizens. . . . If a white man and a black man choose to occupy the same public conveyance on a public highway, it is their right to do so, and no government, proceeding alone on grounds of race, can prevent it without infringing the personal liberty of each. . . .

The white race deems itself to be the dominant race in this country. And so it is, in prestige, in achievements, in education, in wealth, and in power. So, I doubt not, it will continue to be for all time, if it remains true to its great heritage and holds fast to the principles of constitutional liberty. But in the view of the Constitution, in the eye of the law, there is in this country no superior, dominant, ruling class of citizens. There is no caste here. Our Constitution is color-blind and neither knows nor tolerates classes among citizens. In respect of civil rights, all citizens are equal before the law. The humblest is the peer of the most powerful. The law regards man as man and takes no account of his surroundings or of his color when his civil rights as guaranteed by the supreme law of the land are involved. . . .

The arbitrary separation of citizens, on the basis of race, while they are on a public highway, is a badge of servitude wholly inconsistent with the civil freedom and the equality before the law established by the Constitution. It cannot be justified upon any legal grounds. . . .

Mr. Justice Brewer did not hear the argument or participate in the decision of this case.

The Roosevelt Court

The phenomenon called the Roosevelt Court began when the old laissez-faire Justices "surrendered" in the face of President Franklin D. Roosevelt's court reorganization bill in the spring of 1937. The turning points were the *Jones & Laughlin* and *Steward Machine Co.* (Chapter 3, above), and *West Coast Hotel* (Chapter 6, above) cases. These in a matter of weeks restored the national commerce power, the state police power, and the national spending power to what they had been prior to the era of laissez-faire activism which began in the 1890s. See particularly *E. C. Knight* and *Pollock* (Chapter 3, above) and *Lochner* (Chapter 6, above).

After the "surrender," the "nine old men" left the bench one by one, giving President Roosevelt an opportunity to appoint eight new Justices and to elevate Mr. Justice Stone (a dissenter on the "old Court") to the Chief Justiceship. These—the Roosevelt—judges constituted a majority on the Supreme Court from 1940 until the death of Mr. Justice Jackson in 1954—*several months after the landmark desegregation case of* Brown v. Board of Education of Topeka (below).

The Roosevelt, or New Deal, Court was plainly a reform institution in the sense that it overruled or abandoned all of the activist constitutional innovations of laissez-faire jurisprudence. E. S. Corwin called this process "a return to the Constitution." Not the least of the reforms was a return to *Strauder* v. *West Virginia* (1880), above—the first desegregation decision! The initial blow fell in 1938 in *Missouri ex rel. Gaines* v. *Canada,* 305 U.S. 337. That case sprang from a Missouri law barring blacks from the state university. Gaines, a black resident of Missouri, was denied admission to the university's law school, though he was entitled by state law (as a black) to have Missouri pay his tuition "at the university of any adjacent state." The Roosevelt Court held this arrangement unconstitutional:

> Here, petitioner's right was a personal one. It was as an individual that he was entitled to the equal protection of the laws, and the state was bound to furnish him within its borders facilities for legal education substantially equal to those which the state there afforded for persons of the white race, whether or not other Negroes sought the same opportunity.

The *Gaines* case is an important landmark because in it, *for the first time,* the Court enforced the "equal" aspect of the "separate but equal" rule. Oklahoma, responding to the *Gaines* decision, admitted blacks to its state university but separated them from whites in classes, the library, and the cafeteria. This was held to be a denial of equal protection because it impaired the black plaintiff's "ability to study, [and] to engage in discussions and exchange views with other students . . . ": *McLaurin* v. *Oklahoma State Regents,* 339 U.S. 637 (1950). In *Sweatt* v. *Painter,* 339 U.S. 629 (1950), the requirement of real equality was so far stressed as to suggest that nothing short of identical treatment would satisfy the Constitution. As a practical matter separate-but-equal was doomed:

> Whether the University of Texas Law School is compared with the original or the new law school for Negroes, we cannot find substantial equality in the educational opportunities offered white and Negro law students by the State. In terms of number of the faculty, variety of courses and opportunity for specialization, size of the student body, scope of the library, availability of law review and similar activities, the University of Texas Law School is superior. What is more important, the University of Texas Law School possesses to a far greater degree those qualities which are incapable of objective measurement but which make for greatness in a law school. Such qualities, to name but a few, include reputation of the faculty, experience of the administration, position and influence of the alumni, standing in the community, traditions and prestige. It is difficult to believe that one who had a free choice between these law schools would consider the question close.
>
> Moreover, although the law is a highly learned profession, we are well aware that it is an intensely practical one. The law school, the proving ground for legal learning and practice, cannot be effective in isolation from the individuals and institutions with which the law interacts. Few students and no one who has practiced law would choose to study in an academic vacuum, removed from the interplay of ideas and the exchange of views with which the law is concerned. The law school to which Texas is willing to admit petitioner excludes from its student body members of the racial groups which number 85 percent of the population of the State and include most of the lawyers, witnesses, jurors, judges, and other officials with whom petitioner will inevitably be dealing when he becomes a member of the Texas Bar. With such a substantial and significant segment of society excluded, we cannot conclude that the education offered petitioner is substantially equal to that which he would receive if admitted to the University of Texas Law School.

It is crucial that in each of these cases since *Gaines* the decision was unanimous. It is crucial, too, that the Court did not have to face the separate-but-equal rule in any of them, for each entailed such grossly unequal treatment for blacks that decision could, and did, turn on that point alone. What was wanting was a case in which blacks and others were in fact treated with substantial equality—in short, a case that would squarely raise the issue of *equal but separate* treatment of the races. The NAACP obliged by bringing *Brown* to the Supreme Court, *still dominated by Roosevelt appointees,* each of whom had always, consistently, voted against racism.

Brown v. *Board of Education of Topeka* (No. I)
347 U.S. 483 (1954)

Mr. Chief Justice Warren delivered the opinion of the Court.

These cases come to us from the States of Kansas, South Carolina, Virginia, and Delaware. They are premised on different facts and different local conditions, but a common legal question justifies their consideration together in this consolidated opinion.

In each of the cases, minors of the Negro race, through their legal representatives, seek the aid of the courts in obtaining admission to the public schools of their community on a nonsegregated basis. In each instance, they have been denied admission to schools attended by white children under laws requiring or permitting segregation according to race. This segregation was alleged to deprive the plaintiffs of the equal protection of the laws under the Fourteenth Amendment. In each of the cases other than the Delaware case, a three-judge federal district court denied relief to the plaintiffs on the so-called "separate but equal" doctrine announced by this Court in *Plessy* v. *Ferguson,* 163 U.S. 537. Under that doctrine, equality of treatment is accorded when the races are provided substantially equal facilities, even though these facilities be separate. In the Delaware case, the Supreme Court of Delaware adhered to that doctrine, but ordered that the plaintiffs be admitted to the white schools because of their superiority to the Negro schools.

The plaintiffs contend that segregated public schools are not "equal" and cannot be made "equal," and that hence they are deprived of the equal protection of the laws. Because of the obvious importance of the question presented, the Court took jurisdiction. Argument was heard in the 1952 Term, and reargument was heard this Term on certain questions propounded by the Court.

Reargument was largely devoted to the circumstances surrounding the adoption of the Fourteenth Amendment in 1868. It covered exhaustively consideration of the Amendment in Congress, ratification by the states, then existing practices in racial segregation, and the views of proponents and opponents of the Amendment. This discussion and our own investigation convince us that, although these sources cast some light, it is not enough to resolve the problem with which we are faced. At best, they are inconclusive. The most avid proponents of the post-War Amendments undoubtedly intended them to remove all legal distinctions among "all persons born or naturalized in the United States." Their opponents, just as certainly, were antagonistic to both the letter and the spirit of the Amendments and wished them to have the most limited effect. What others in Congress and the state legislatures had in mind cannot be determined with any degree of certainty.

An additional reason for the inconclusive nature of the Amendment's history, with respect to segregated schools, is the status of public education at that time. In the South, the movement toward free common schools, supported by general taxation, had not yet taken hold. Education of white children was largely in the hands of private groups. Education of Negroes was almost nonexistent, and practically all of the race were illiterate. In fact, any education of

Negroes was forbidden by law in some states. Today, in contrast, many Negroes have achieved outstanding success in the arts and sciences as well as in the business and professional world. It is true that public school education at the time of the Amendment had advanced further in the North, but the effect of the Amendment on Northern States was generally ignored in the congressional debates. Even in the North, the conditions of public education did not approximate those existing today. The curriculum was usually rudimentary; ungraded schools were common in rural areas; the school term was but three months a year in many states; and compulsory school attendance was virtually unknown. As a consequence, it is not surprising that there should be so little in the history of the Fourteenth Amendment relating to its intended effect on public education.

In the first cases in this Court construing the Fourteenth Amendment, decided shortly after its adoption, the Court interpreted it as proscribing all state-imposed discriminations against the Negro race.[1] The doctrine of "separate but equal" did not make its appearance in this Court until 1896 in the case of *Plessy* v. *Ferguson, supra,* involving not education but transportation. American courts have since labored with the doctrine for over half a century. In this Court, there have been six cases involving the "separate but equal" doctrine in the field of public education. In *Cumming* v. *Board of Education of Richmond County,* 175 U.S. 528, and *Gong Lum* v. *Rice,* 275 U.S. 78, the validity of the doctrine itself was not challenged. In more recent cases, all on the graduate school level, inequality was found in that specific benefits enjoyed by white students were denied to Negro students of the same educational qualifications. *State of Missouri ex rel. Gaines* v. *Canada,* 305 U.S. 337; *Sipuel* v. *Board of Regents of University of Oklahoma,* 332 U.S. 631; *Sweatt* v. *Painter,* 339

U.S. 629; *McLaurin* v. *Oklahoma State Regents,* 339 U.S. 637. In none of these cases was it necessary to reexamine the doctrine to grant relief to the Negro plaintiff. And in *Sweatt* v. *Painter, supra,* the Court expressly reserved decision on the question whether *Plessy* v. *Ferguson* should be held inapplicable to public education.

In the instant cases, that question is directly presented. Here, unlike *Sweatt* v. *Painter,* there are findings below that the Negro and white schools involved have been equalized, or are being equalized, with respect to buildings, curricula, qualifications and salaries of teachers, and other "tangible" factors. Our decision, therefore, cannot turn on merely a comparison of these tangible factors in the Negro and white schools involved in each of the cases. We must look instead to the effect of segregation itself on public education.

In approaching this problem, we cannot turn the clock back to 1868 when the Amendment was adopted, or even to 1896 when *Plessy* v. *Ferguson* was written. We must consider public education in the light of its full development and its present place in American life throughout the Nation. Only in this way can it be determined if segregation in public schools deprives these plaintiffs of the equal protection of the laws.

Today, education is perhaps the most important function of state and local governments. Compulsory school attendance laws and the great expenditures for education both demonstrate our recognition of the importance of education to our democratic society. It is required in the performance of our most basic public responsibilities, even service in the armed forces. It is the very foundation of good citizenship. Today it is a principal instrument in awakening the child to cultural values, in preparing him for later professional training, and in helping him to adjust normally to his environment. In these days, it is doubtful that any child may reasonably be expected to succeed in life if he is denied the opportunity of an education. Such

---

[1] In re Slaughter House Cases, 1873, 16 Wall. 36, 67–72; Strauder v. West Virginia, 1880, 100 U.S. 303, 307–308: . . .

an opportunity, where the state has undertaken to provide it, is a right which must be made available to all on equal terms.

We come then to the question presented: Does segregation of children in public schools solely on the basis of race, even though the physical facilities and other "tangible" factors may be equal, deprive the children of the minority group of equal educational opportunities? We believe that it does.

In *Sweatt* v. *Painter, supra,* in finding that a segregated law school for Negroes could not provide them equal educational opportunities, this Court relied in large part on "those qualities which are incapable of objective measurement but which make for greatness in a law school." In *McLaurin* v. *Oklahoma State Regents, supra,* the Court, in requiring that a Negro admitted to a white graduate school be treated like all other students, again resorted to intangible considerations: ". . . his ability to study, to engage in discussions and exchange views with other students, and, in general, to learn his profession." Such considerations apply with added force to children in grade and high schools. To separate them from others of similar age and qualifications solely because of their race generates a feeling of inferiority as to their status in the community that may affect their hearts and minds in a way unlikely ever to be undone. The effect of this separation on their educational opportunities was well stated by a finding in the Kansas case by a court which nevertheless felt compelled to rule against the Negro plaintiffs:

> "Segregation of white and colored children in public schools has a detrimental effect upon the colored children. The impact is greater when it has the sanction of the law; for the policy of separating the races is usually interpreted as denoting the inferiority of the negro group. A sense of inferiority affects the motivation of a child to learn. Segregation with the sanction of law, therefore, has a tendency to [retard] the educational and mental development of negro children and to deprive them of some of the benefits they would receive in a racial[ly] integrated school system."

Whatever may have been the extent of psychological knowledge at the time of *Plessy* v. *Ferguson,* this finding is amply supported by modern authority. Any language in *Plessy* v. *Ferguson* contrary to this finding is rejected.

We conclude that in the field of public education the doctrine of "separate but equal" has no place. Separate educational facilities are inherently unequal. Therefore, we hold that the plaintiffs and others similarly situated for whom the actions have been brought are, by reason of the segregation complained of, deprived of the equal protection of the laws guaranteed by the Fourteenth Amendment. This disposition makes unnecessary any discussion whether such segregation also violates the Due Process Clause of the Fourteenth Amendment.

Because these are class actions, because of the wide applicability of this decision, and because of the great variety of local conditions, the formulation of decrees in these cases presents problems of considerable complexity. On reargument, the consideration of appropriate relief was necessarily subordinated to the primary question—the constitutionality of segregation in public education. We have now announced that such segregation is a denial of the equal protection of the laws. In order that we may have the full assistance of the parties in formulating decrees, the cases will be restored to the docket, and the parties are requested to present further argument on Questions 4 and 5 previously propounded by the Court for the reargument this Term. The Attorney General of the United States is again invited to participate. The Attorneys General of the states requiring or permitting segregation in public education will also be permitted to appear as *amici curiae* upon request to do so by September 15, 1954, and submission of briefs by October 1, 1954.

Note: *Bolling* v. *Sharp*, 347 U.S. 497 (1954)—a companion case to *Brown*—struck down segregation in the District of Columbia public schools with this equation:

The Fifth Amendment, which is applicable to the District of Columbia, does not contain an equal protection clause as does the Fourteenth Amendment which applies only to the states. But the concepts of equal protection and due process, both stemming from the American ideal of fairness, are not mutually exclusive. The "equal protection of the laws" is a more explicit safeguard of prohibited unfairness than "due process of law," and, therefore, we do not imply that the two are always interchangeable phrases. But, as this Court has recognized, discrimination may be so unjustifiable as to be violative of due process.

Brown v. *Board of Education of Topeka* (No. II)
349 U.S. 294 (1955)

Mr. Chief Justice Warren delivered the opinion of the Court:

These cases were decided on May 17, 1954. The opinions of that date, declaring the fundamental principle that racial discrimination in public education is unconstitutional, are incorporated herein by reference. All provisions of federal, state, or local law requiring or permitting such discrimination must yield to this principle. There remains for consideration the manner in which relief is to be accorded.

Because these cases arose under different local conditions and their disposition will involve a variety of local problems, we requested further argument on the question of relief. In view of the nation-wide importance of the decision, we invited the Attorney General of the United States and the Attorneys General of all states requiring or permitting racial discrimination in public education to present their views on that question. The parties, the United States, and the States of Florida, North Carolina, Arkansas, Oklahoma, Maryland, and Texas filed briefs and participated in the oral argument.

These presentations were informative and helpful to the Court in its consideration of the complexities arising from the transition to a system of public education freed of racial discrimination. The presentations also demonstrated that substantial steps to eliminate racial discrimination in public schools have already been taken, not only in some of the communities in which these cases arose, but in some of the states appearing as *amici curiae*, and in other states as well. Substantial progress has been made in the District of Columbia and in the communities in Kansas and Delaware involved in this litigation. The defendants in the cases coming to us from South Carolina and Virginia are awaiting the decision of this Court concerning relief.

Full implementation of these constitutional principles may require solution of varied local school problems. School authorities have the primary responsibility for elucidating, assessing, and solving these problems; courts will have to consider whether the action of school authorities constitutes good faith implementation of the governing constitutional principles. Because of their proximity to local conditions and the possible need for further hearings, the courts which originally heard these cases can best perform this judicial appraisal. Accordingly, we believe it appropriate to remand the cases to those courts.

In fashioning and effectuating the decrees, the courts will be guided by equitable principles. Traditionally, equity has been characterized by a practical flexibility in shaping its remedies and by a facility for adjusting the reconciling public and private needs. These cases call for the exercise of these traditional attributes of equity power. At stake is the personal interest of the plaintiffs in admission to public schools as soon as practicable on a nondiscriminatory basis. To effectuate this interest may call for elimination of a variety of obstacles in making the transition to school systems operated in accordance with the constitutional principles set forth in our May 17, 1954, decision. Courts of equity may properly take into account the public interest in the elimination of such obstacles in a systematic and effective manner. But it should go without saying that the vitality of these constitutional principles cannot be allowed to yield simply because of disagreement with them.

While giving weight to these public and private considerations, the courts will require that the defendants make a prompt and reasonable start toward full compliance with our May 17, 1954, ruling. Once such a start has been made, the courts may find that additional time is necessary to carry out the ruling in an effective manner. The burden rests upon the defendants to establish that such time is necessary in the public interest and is consistent with good faith compliance at the earliest practicable date. To that end, the courts may consider problems related to administration, arising from the physical condition of the school plant, the school transportation system, personnel, revision of school districts and attendance areas into compact units to achieve a system of determining admission to the public schools on a nonracial basis, and revision of local laws and regulations which may be necessary in solving the foregoing problems. They will also consider the adequacy of any plans the defendants may propose to meet these problems and to effectuate a transition to a racially nondiscriminatory school system. During this period of transition, the courts will retain jurisdiction of these cases.

From *Brown* to *Swann*

Some school boards responded to *Brown* by voluntary compliance. Others—sometimes with state encouragement—reacted with "massive resistance." This took many forms. The most unfortunate perhaps was the use by Governor Faubus of the National Guard to block court-ordered desegregation of a Little Rock high school. President Eisenhower responded with federal troops, the Supreme Court with a ringing reaffirmation of *Brown* in *Cooper* v. *Aaron*, 358 U.S. 1 (1958). An effort to evade *Brown* by closing all public schools and giving county money to white children to attend private schools was held unconstitutional in *Griffin* v. *Prince Edward County School Board*, 377 U.S. 218 (1964). The often-used device of voluntary student transfer plans (to soften the impact of rezoning) was held invalid in *Goss* v. *Board of Education*, 373 U.S. 683 (1963), since it was based "solely on racial factors." *Green* v. *County School Board*, 391 U.S. 430 (1968), held invalid "freedom of choice" attendance plans which produced little desegregation. By the end of the 1960s the Court announced that "continued operation of segregated schools under a standard of allowing 'all deliberate speed' for desegregation is no longer constitutionally permissible. Under explicit holdings of this Court the obligation of every school district is to terminate dual schools at once and to operate now and hereafter only unitary schools" (*Alexander* v. *Holmes County Board of Education*, 396 U.S. 19 [1969]).

Each of the pre–1970 desegregation cases until *Green* was decided on the ground that the challenged desegregation program was invalid because on its face it was racially oriented. *Green* marks a crucial turning point because it shifted the emphasis from the *form* of a desegregation plan to its effect: "The burden on a school board today is to come forward with a plan that promises realistically to work, and promises realistically to work *now*." But this leaves open a crucial question: "work" to what end? This problem came before the Court in *Swann*.

Swann v. *Charlotte-Mecklenburg Board of Education*
402 U.S. 1 (1971)

Government action to compel separation of the races is one thing; government action to compel mingling of the races is another. Did *Brown* require that school districts merely stop separating—or that they begin mingling—the races? Some lower court judges and others have read it the one way; some the other way. *Swann* is crucial because of its response to that issue—and also because, building on *Green*, it focuses on *remedies* and realism (rather than *forms* of school board action).

This case arose in a large metropolitan school district. About 30 percent of its students were black. By 1969, after several years under a court-approved desegregation plan, about half of the blacks were still attending virtually all-black schools. Following *Green* a federal district court ordered what it considered a more effective desegregation plan.

Chief Justice Burger delivered the opinion of the Court. . . .

This case and those argued with it arose in states having a long history of maintaining two sets of schools in a single school system deliberately operated to carry out a governmental policy to separate pupils in schools solely on the basis of race. That was what *Brown* v. *Board of Education* was all about. These cases present us with the problem of defining in more precise terms than heretofore the scope of the duty of school authorities and district courts in implementing *Brown I* and the mandate to eliminate dual systems and establish unitary systems at once. . . .

The objective today remains to eliminate from the public schools all vestiges of state-imposed [ie. *de jure*] segregation. . . .

We turn . . . to the problem of defining with more particularity the responsibilities of school authorities in desegregating a state-enforced dual school system in light of the Equal Protection Clause. Although the several related cases before us are primarily concerned with problems of student assignment, it may be helpful to begin with a brief discussion of other aspects of the process.

In *Green*, we pointed out that existing policy and practice with regard to faculty, staff, transportation, extracurricular activities, and facilities were among the most important indicia of a segregated system. Independent of student assignment, where it is possible to identify a "white school" or a "Negro school" simply by reference to the racial composition of teachers and staff, the quality of school buildings and equipment, or the organization of sports activities, a *prima facie* case of violation of substantive constitutional rights under the Equal Protection Clause is shown.

When a system has been dual is these respects, the first remedial responsibility of school authorities is to eliminate invidious racial distinctions. With respect to such matters as transportation, supporting personnel, and extracurricular activities, no more than this may be necessary. Similar corrective action must be taken with regard to the maintenance of buildings and the distribution of equipment. In these areas, normal administrative practice should produce schools of like quality, facilities, and staffs. Something more must be said, however, as to faculty assignment and new school construction.

In the companion *Davis* case [402 U.S. 33], the Mobile school board has argued that the Constitution requires that teachers be assigned on a "color blind" basis. It also argues that the Constitution prohibits district courts from using their equity power to order assignment of teachers to achieve a particular degree of faculty desegregation. We reject that contention. . . .

The construction of new schools and the closing of old ones is one of the most important functions of local school authorities and also one of the most complex. They must decide questions of location and capacity in light of population growth, finances, land values, site availability, through an almost endless list of factors to be considered. The result of this will be a decision which, when combined with one technique or another of student assignment, will determine the racial composition of the student body in each school in the system. Over the long run, the consequences of the choices will be far reaching. People gravitate toward school facilities, just as schools are located in response to the needs of people. The location of schools may thus influence the patterns of residential development of a metropolitan area and have important impact on composition of inner city neighborhoods.

In the past, choices in this respect have been used as a potent weapon for creating or maintaining a state-segregated school system. . . . Upon a proper showing a district court may consider this in fashioning a remedy.

In ascertaining the existence of legally imposed school segregation, the existence of a pattern of school construction and abandonment is thus a factor of great weight. In devising remedies where legally imposed segregation has been established, it is the responsibility of local authorities and district courts to see to it that future school construction and abandonment is not used and does not serve to perpetuate or re-establish the dual system. When necessary, district courts should retain jurisdiction to assure that these responsibilities are carried out.

The central issue in this case is that of student assignment, and there are essentially four problem areas: . . .

1. Racial Balances or Racial Quotas

. . . We do not reach in this case the question whether a showing that school segregation is a consequence of other types of state action, without any discriminatory action by the school authorities, is a constitutional violation requiring remedial action by the school desegregation decree. This case does not present that question and we therefore do not decide it.

Our objective in dealing with the issues presented by these cases is to see that school authorities exclude no pupil of a racial minority from any school, directly or indirectly, on account of race; it does not and cannot embrace all the problems of racial prejudice, even when those problems contribute to disproportionate racial concentrations in some schools.

In this case it is urged that the District Court has imposed a racial balance requirement of 71%–29% on individual schools. . . .

[The District Court opinion] contains intimations that the "norm" is a fixed mathematical racial balance reflecting the pupil constituency of the system. If we were to read the holding of the District Court to require, as a matter of substantive constitutional right, any particular degree of racial balance or mixing, that approach would be disapproved and we would be obliged to reverse. The constitutional command to desegregate schools does not mean that every school in every community must always reflect the racial composition of the school system as a whole. . . .

[But, in this case] the use made of mathematical ratios was no more than a starting point in the process of shaping a remedy, rather than an inflexible requirement. . . . As we said in *Green*, a school authority's remedial plan or a district court's remedial decree is to be judged by its effectiveness. Awareness of the racial composition of the whole school system is likely to be a useful starting point in shaping a remedy to correct past constitutional violations. In sum, the very limited use made of mathematical ratios was within the equitable remedial discretion of the District Court.

2. One-Race Schools

The record in this case reveals the familiar phenomenon that in metropolitan areas minority groups are often found concentrated in one part of the city. In some circumstances certain schools may remain all or largely of one race until new schools can be provided or neighborhood patterns change. Schools all or predominately of one race in a district of mixed population will require close scrutiny to determine that school assignments are not part of state-enforced segregation.

In light of the above, it should be clear that the existence of some small number of one-race, or virtually one-race, schools within a district is not in and of itself the mark of a system which still practices segregation by law. . . . The court should scrutinize such schools, and the burden upon the school authorities will be to satisfy the court that their racial composition is not the result of present or past discriminatory action on their part.

An optional majority-to-minority transfer provision has long been recognized as a useful part of every desegregation plan. Provision for optional transfer of those in the majority racial group of a particular school to other schools where they will be in the minority is an indispensable remedy for those students willing to transfer to other schools in order to lessen the impact on them of the state-imposed stigma of segregation. In order to be effective, such a transfer arrangement must grant the transferring student free transportation and space must be made available in the school to which he desires to move. . . .

3. Remedial Altering of Attendance Zones

. . .

Absent a constitutional violation there would be no basis for judicially ordering assignment of students on a racial basis. All things being equal, with no history of discrimination, it might well be desirable to assign pupils to schools nearest their homes. But all things are not equal in a system that has been deliberately constructed and maintained to enforce racial segregation. The remedy for such segregation may be administratively awkward, inconvenient and even bizarre in some situations and may impose burdens on some; but all awkwardness and inconvenience cannot be avoided in the interim period when remedial adjustments are being made to eliminate the dual school systems. . . .

In this area, we must of necessity rely to a large extent, as this Court has for more than 16 years, on the informed judgment of the district courts in the first instance and on courts of appeals.

We hold that the pairing and grouping of non-contiguous school zones is a permissible tool and such action is to be considered in light of the objectives sought. . . .

4. Transportation of Students

. . . No rigid guidelines as to student transportation can be given for application to the infinite variety of problems presented in thousands of situations. Bus transportation has been an integral part of the public education system for years, and was perhaps the single most important factor in the transition from the one-room schoolhouse to the consolidated school. Eighteen milion of the nation's public school children, approximately 39%, were transported to their schools by bus in 1969–1970 in all parts of the country.

The importance of bus transportation as a normal and accepted tool of educational policy is readily discernible in this and the companion case. . . .

An objection to transportation of students may have validity when the time or distance of travel is so great as to risk either the health of the children or significantly impinge on the educational process. . . .

. . . On the facts of this case, we are unable to conclude that the order of the District Court is not reasonable, feasible and workable. However, in seeking to define the scope of remedial power or the limits on remedial power of courts in an area as sensitive as we deal with here, words are poor instruments to convey the sense of basic fairness inherent in equity. Substance, not semantics, must govern, and we have sought to suggest the nature of limitations without frustrating the appropriate scope of equity.

At some point, these school authorities and others like them should have achieved full compliance with this Court's decision in *Brown I*. The systems will then be "unitary" in the sense required by our decisions in *Green* and *Alexander*.

It does not follow that the communities served by such systems will remain demographically stable, for in a growing, mobile society, few will do so. Neither school authorities nor district courts are constitutionally required to make year-by-year adjustments of the racial composition of student bodies once the affirmative duty to desegregate has been accomplished and racial discrimination through official action is eliminated from the system. This does not mean that federal courts are without power to deal with future problems; but in the absence of a showing that either the school authorities or some other agency of the State has deliberately attempted to fix or alter demographic patterns to affect the racial composition of the schools [i.e. where racial imbalance is merely *de facto*], further intervention by a district court should not be necessary.

Note: The dicta in the last paragraph of *Swann* became a decision in *Pasadena City Board of Education* v. *Spangler*, 427 U.S. 424 (1976). Thus, once a school district has attained "racial neutrality" in school attendance, *resegregation* resulting from private, voluntary "white flight"—rather than from governmental action—does not violate the Constitution. See the state-action cases in Chapter 10, below.

Keyes v. *School District No. 1, Denver*
413 U.S. 189 (1973)

Here for the first time the Court faced a race imbalance problem in the North. It did not question the *de jure–de facto* distinction which is so crucial in the South. Yet one may wonder whether, as a practical matter, it did not largely undermine that distinction by making it quite easy to find *systemwide, de jure* (i.e., governmentally imposed) segregation, even in a community and state with an extraordinary record of racial fairness.

Justice Brennan delivered the opinion of the Court.

. . . [T]he gravamen of this action, brought in June 1969 in the District Court for the District of Colorado by parents of Denver school children, is that respondent School Board alone, by use of various techniques such as the manipulation of student attendance zones, school site selection and a neighborhood school policy, created or maintained racially or ethnically (or both racially and ethnically) segregated schools throughout the school district, entitling petitioners to a decree directing desegregation of the entire school district. . . .

. . . [W]here plaintiffs prove that the school authorities have carried out a systematic program of segregation affecting a substantial portion of the students, schools, teachers and facilities within the school system, it is only common sense to conclude that there exists a predicate for a finding of the existence of a dual school system. Several considerations support this conclusion. First, it is obvious that a practice of concentrating Negroes in certain schools by structuring attendance zones or designating "feeder" schools on the basis of race has the reciprocal effect of keeping other nearby schools predominantly white. Similarly, the practice of building a school . . . to a certain size and in a certain location, "with conscious knowledge that it would be a segregated school," has a substantial reciprocal effect on the racial composition of other nearby schools. So also, the use of mobile classrooms, the drafting of student transfer policies, the transportation of students, and the assignment of faculty and staff, on racially identifiable bases, have the clear effect of earmarking schools according to their racial composition, and this, in turn, together with the elements of student assignment and school construction, may have a profound reciprocal effect on the racial composition of residential neighborhoods within a metropolitan area, thereby causing further racial concentration within the schools. . . .

. . . [W]e hold that a finding of intentionally segregative school board actions in a meaningful portion of a school system, as in this case, creates a presumption that other segregated schooling within the system is not adventitious. It establishes, in other words, a prima facie case of unlawful segregative design on the part of school authorities, and shifts to those authorities the burden of proving that other segregated schools within the system are not also the result of intentionally segregative actions. This is true even if it is determined that different areas of the school district should be viewed independently of each other because, even in that situation, there is a high probability that where school authorities have effectuated an intentionally segregative policy in a meaningful portion of the school system, similar impermissible considerations have motivated their actions in other areas of the system. We emphasize that the differentiating factor between *de jure* segregation and so-called *de facto* segregation to which we referred in *Swann* is *purpose* or *intent* to segregate. Where school authorities have been found to have practiced purposeful segregation in part of a school system, they may be expected to oppose system-wide desegregation, as did the respondents in this case, on the ground that their purposefully segregative actions were isolated and individual events, thus leaving plaintiffs with the burden of proving otherwise. But at that point where an intentionally segregative policy is practiced in a meaningful or significant segment of a school system, as in this case, the school authorities can not be heard to argue that plaintiffs have proved only "isolated and individual" unlawfully segregative actions. In that circumstance, it is both fair and reasonable to require that the school authorities bear the burden of showing that their actions as to other segregated schools within the system were not also motivated by segregative intent. . . .

In discharging that burden, it is not enough, of course, that the school authorities rely upon some allegedly logical, racially neutral explanation for their actions. Their burden is to adduce proof sufficient to support a finding that segregative intent was not among the factors that motivated their actions. . . . We reject any suggestion that remoteness in time has any relevance to the issue of intent. If the actions of school authorities were to any degree motivated by segregative intent and the segregation resulting from those actions continues to exist, the fact of remoteness in time certainly does not make those actions any less "intentional."

This is not to say, however, that the prima

facie case may not be met by evidence supporting a finding that a lesser degree of segregated schooling in the core city area would not have resulted even if the Board had not acted as it did. . . . [I]f respondent School Board cannot disprove segregative intent, it can rebut the prima facie case only by showing that its past segregative acts did not create or contribute to the current segregated condition of the core city schools.

The respondent School Board invoked at trial its "neighborhood school policy" as explaining racial and ethnic concentrations within the core city schools, arguing that since the core city area population had long been Negro and Hispano, the concentrations were necessarily the result of residential patterns and not of purposefully segregative policies. We have no occasion to consider in this case whether a "neighborhood school policy" of itself will justify racial or ethnic concentrations in the absence of a finding that school authorities have committed acts constituting *de jure* segregation. It is enough that we hold that the mere assertion of such a policy is not dispositive where, as in this case, the school authorities have been found to have practiced *de jure* segregation in a meaningful portion of the school system by techniques that indicate that the "neighborhood school" concept has not been maintained free of manipulation. . . .

Justice White took no part in the decision of this case.

Justice Powell concurring in part and dissenting in part.

. . . I concur in the Court's position that the public school authorities are the responsible agency of the State, and that if the affirmative duty doctrine is sound constitutional law for Charlotte, it is equally so for Denver. I would not, however, perpetuate the *de jure/de facto* distinction nor would I leave to petitioners the initial tortuous effort of identifying "segregative acts" and deducing "segregatory intent." I would hold, quite simply, that where segregated public schools exist within a school district to a substantial degree, there is a prima facie case that the duly constituted public authorities (I will usually refer to them collectively as the "school board") are sufficiently responsible to impose upon them a nationally applicable burden to demonstrate they nevertheless are operating a genuinely integrated school system.

The principal reason for abandonment of the *de jure/de facto* distinction is that, in view of the evolution of the holding in *Brown I* into the affirmative duty doctrine, the distinction no longer can be justified on a principled basis. In decreeing remedial requirements for the Charlotte/Mecklenburg school district, *Swann* dealt with a metropolitan, urbanized area in which the basic causes of segregation were generally similar to those in all sections of the country, and also largely irrelevant to the existence of historic, state-imposed segregation at the time of the *Brown* decision. Further, the extension of the affirmative duty concept to include compulsory student transportation went well beyond the mere remedying of that portion of school segregation for which former state segregation laws were ever responsible. Moreover, as the Court's opinion today abundantly demonstrates, the facts deemed necessary to establish *de jure* discrimination present problems of subjective intent which the courts cannot fairly resolve. . . .

Justice Rehnquist, dissenting.

. . . [I]n a school district the size of Denver's, it is quite conceivable that the school board might have engaged in the racial gerrymandering of the attendance boundary between two particular schools in order to keep one largely Negro and Hispano, and the other largely Anglo, as the District Court found to have been the fact in this case. Such action would have deprived affected minority students who were the victims of such gerrymandering of their constitutional right to equal protection of the law. But if the school board had been evenhanded in its drawing of the attendance lines for other schools in the district, minority students required to attend other schools within the district would have suffered no such deprivation. It certainly would not reflect normal English usage to describe the entire district as "segregated" on such a state of facts, and it would be a quite unprecedented application of principles of equitable relief to determine that if the gerrymandering of one attendance zone were proven, particular racial mixtures could be required by a federal district court for every school in the district.

. . . [U]nless the Equal Protection Clause of the Fourteenth Amendment now be held to embody a principle of "taint," found in some primitive legal systems but discarded centuries ago in ours, such a result can only be described as the product of judicial fiat. . . .

Note: By 1976 the Supreme Court seemed to be backing away from the integration implications of *Keyes.* In three cases, *School District of Omaha* v. *United States,* 431 U.S. 667 (1977); *Dayton Board of Education* v. *Brinkman,* 433 U.S. 406 (1977); *Austin Independent School District* v. *United States,* 429 U.S. 990 (1976), it remanded systemwide integration (busing) orders for reconsideration in light of the *Washington* v. *Davis* and *Arlington Heights* (above) "purpose and intent" standard. In sum, the Court seemed to be stressing the *de jure* and the *desegregation* (rather than the *de facto* and *integration*) elements of the problem.

In *Dayton,* for example, it found the evidence of state-imposed (i.e., *de jure*) segregation too thin to justify an overall integration order. Moreover, only if a school board's misconduct has had "a systemwide impact may there be a system-wide remedy. *Keyes.*" Some two years later, in *Columbus Board of Education* v. *Penick* (below), a majority seemed to have moved in the other direction.

Columbus Board of Education v. Penick (excerpt)
99 S. Ct. 2941 (1979)

Traditionally a plaintiff (alleging unlawful conduct) has the burden of proof. In this case the Court held that when a plaintiff proves purposeful segregation at the time of *Brown I* in 1954 (i.e., a generation earlier), the burden of proving present innocence shifts to the defendant (school board). As Mr. Justice Stewart, joined by Chief Justice Burger, explained in dissent on this point in *Penick* and *Dayton II:*

As I understand the Court's opinions in these cases, if such an officially authorized segregated school system can be found to have existed in 1954, then any current racial separation in the schools will be presumed to have been caused by acts in violation of the Constitution. Even if, as the Court says, this presumption is rebuttable, the burden is on the school board to rebut it. And, when the factual issues are as elusive as these, who bears the burden of proof can easily determine who prevails in the litigation. *Speiser* v. *Randall,* 357 U.S. 513, 525–526.

I agree that a school district in violation of the Constitution in 1954 was under a duty to remedy that violation. So was a school district violating the Constitution in 1964, and so is one violating the Constitution today. But this duty does not justify a complete shift of the normal burden of proof.[1]

---

[1] In Keyes the Court did discuss the affirmative duty of a school board to desegregate the school district, but limited its discussion to cases "where a dual system was compelled or authorized by statute at the time of our decision in Brown v. Board of Education . . . ." 413 U.S., at 200. It is undisputed that Ohio has forbidden its school boards racially to segregate the public schools since at least 1888.

[Justices Powell and Rehnquist, dissenting, put it this way:]

The Court suggests a radical new approach to desegregation cases in systems without a history of statutorily mandated separation of the races: if a district court concludes—employing what in honesty must be characterized as an irrebuttable presumption—that there was a "dual" school system at the time of *Brown I*, 347 U.S. 483 (1954), it must find post–1954 constitutional violations in a school board's failure to take every affirmative step to integrate the system. Put differently, *racial imbalance* at the time the complaint is filed is sufficient to support a systemwide, racial balance school busing remedy if the district court can find *some* evidence of discriminatory purpose prior to 1954, without any inquiry into the causal relationship between those pre–1954 violations and current segregation in the school system.

[In a separate opinion Mr. Justice Powell, who had had substantial experience fighting school segregation before he became a judge, offered an "overall" view of the problem, as follows:]

I . . . .

There are unintegrated schools in every major urban area in the country that contains a substantial minority population. This condition results primarily from familiar segregated housing patterns, which—in turn—are caused by social, economic, and demographic forces for which no school board is responsible. These causes of the greater part of the school segregation problem are not newly discovered. Nearly a decade ago, Professor Bickel wrote:

> In most of the larger urban areas, demographic conditions are such that no policy that a court can order, and a school board, a city or even a state has the capability to put into effect, will in fact result in the foreseeable future in racially balanced public schools. Only a reordering of the

environment involving economic and social policy on the broadest conceivable front might have an appreciable impact." A. Bickel, *The Supreme Court and the Idea of Progress* 132, n. 7 (1979).[2]

Federal courts, including this Court today, continue to ignore these indisputable facts. Relying upon fictions and presumptions in school cases that are irreconcilable with principles of equal protection law applied in all other cases, see, *e.g., Personnel Administrator* v. *Feeney*, __ U.S. __ (1979); *Arlington Heights* v. *Metropolitan Housing Development Corp.*, 429 U.S. 252 (1977); *Washington* v. *Davis*, 426 U.S. 229 (1976), federal courts prescribe systemwide remedies without relation to the causes of the segregation found to exist, and implement their decrees by requiring extensive transportation of children of all school ages.

The type of state-enforced segregation that *Brown* properly condemned no longer exists in this country. This is not to say that school boards—particularly in the great cities of the North, Midwest, and West—are taking all reasonable measures to provide integrated educational opportunities. As I indicated in my separate opinion in *Keyes* v. *School District No. 1*, 413 U.S. 189, 223–236 (1973), *de facto* segregation has existed on a large scale in many of these cities, and often it is indistinguishable in effect from the type of *de jure* segregation outlawed by *Brown*. Where there is proof of intentional segregative action or inaction, the federal courts must act, but their remedies should not exceed the scope of the constitutional violation. *Dayton* v. *Brinkman*, 433 U.S. 406 (1977); *Austin Independent School District* v. *United States*, 429 U.S. 900, 991 (1976) (Powell, J., concurring); *Pasadena City Board of Education* v. *Spangler*, 427 U.S. 424 (1976); *Milliken* v. *Bradley*, 418 U.S. 717 (1974); *Swann* v. *Charlotte-Mecklenburg Board of Educa-*

---

[2] See also Farley, Residential Segregation and Its Implications for School Integration, 39 *L. & Contemp. Probs.* 164 (1975); K. Taeuber & A. Taeuber, *Negroes in Cities* (1965). The Court of Appeals below treated the residential segregation in Dayton and Columbus as irrelevant.

tion, 402 U.S. 1, 16 (1971). Systemwide remedies such as were ordered by the courts below, and today are approved by this Court, lack any principled basis when the absence of integration in all schools cannot reasonably be attributed to discriminatory conduct.[3]

Mr. Justice Rehnquist has dealt devastatingly with the way in which the Court of Appeals endowed prior precedents with new and wonderous meanings. I can add little to what he has said. I therefore move to more general but, in my view, important considerations that the Court simply ignores.

II.

Holding the school boards of these two cities responsible for *all* of the segregation in the Dayton and Columbus systems and prescribing fixed racial ratios in every school as the constitutionally required remedy necessarily implies a belief that the same school boards—under court supervision—will be capable of bringing about and maintaining the desired racial balance in each of these schools. The experience in city after city demonstrates that this is an illusion. The process of resegregation, stimulated by resentment against judicial coercion and concern as to the effect of court supervision of education, will follow today's decisions as surely as it has in other cities subjected to similar sweeping decrees.

The orders affirmed today typify intrusions on local and professional authorities that affect adversely the quality of education. They require an extensive reorganization of both school systems, including the reassignment of almost half of the 96,000 students in the Columbus system and the busing of some 15,000 students in Dayton. They also require reassignments of teachers and other staff personnel, reorganization of

grade structures, and the closing of certain schools. The orders substantially dismantle and displace neighborhood schools in the face of compelling economic and educational reasons for preserving them. This wholesale substitution of judicial legislation for the judgments of elected officials and professional educators derogates the entire process of public education. Moreover, it constitutes a serious interference with the private decisions of parents as to how their children will be educated. These harmful consequences are the inevitable byproducts of a judicial approach that ignores other relevant factors in favor of an exclusive focus on racial balance in every school.

These harmful consequences, moreover, in all likelihood will provoke responses that will defeat the integrative purpose of the court's order. Parents, unlike school officials, are not bound by these decrees and may frustrate them through the simple expedient of withdrawing their children from a public school system in which they have lost confidence. In spite of the substantial costs often involved in relocation of the family or in resort to private education, experience demonstrates that many parents view these alternatives as preferable to submitting their children to court-run school systems. In the words of a leading authority:

> "An implication that should have been seen all along but can no longer be ignored is that a child's enrollment in a given public school is not determined by a governmental decision alone. It is a joint result of a governmental decision (the making of school assignments) and parental decisions, whether to remain in the same residential location, whether to send their child to a private school, or which school district to move into when moving into a metropolitan area. The fact that the child's enrollment is a result of two decisions operating jointly means that government policies must, to be effective, anticipate parental decisions and obtain the parents' active cooperation in implementing school

---

[3] As I suggested in my separate opinion in Keyes, it is essential to identify the constitutional right that is asserted in school desegregation cases. The Court's decisions hardly have been lucid on this point. In Brown II, 348 U.S. 294 (1955), the Court identified the "fundamental principle" enunciated in Brown I, as being the unconstitutionality "of racial discrimination in public education." *Id.*, at 298. . . .

policies." Coleman, New Incentives for Desegregation, 7 *Human Rights* 10, 13 (1978).

At least where inner-city populations comprise a large proportion of racial minorities and surrounding suburbs remain white, conditions that exist in most large American cities, the demonstrated effect of compulsory integration is a substantial exodus of whites from the system. See J. Coleman, S. Kelly, and J. Moore, *Trends in School Segregation, 1968–1973*, at 66, 76–77 (1975). It would be unfair and misleading to attribute this phenomenon to a racist response to integration *per se*. It is at least as likely that the exodus is in substantial part a natural reaction to the displacement of professional and local control that occurs when courts go into the business of restructuring and operating school systems.

Nor will this resegregation be the only negative effect of court-coerced integration on minority children. Public schools depend on community support for their effectiveness. When substantial elements of the community are driven to abandon these schools, their quality tends to decline, sometimes markedly. Members of minority groups, who have relied especially on education as a means of advancing themselves, also are likely to react to this decline in quality by removing their children from public schools.[4] As a result, public school enroll-

ment increasingly will become limited to children from families that either lack the resources to choose alternatives or are indifferent to the quality of education. The net effect is an overall deterioration in public education, the one national resource that traditionally has made this country a land of opportunity for diverse ethnic and racial groups. See *Keyes, supra,* at 250 (opinion of Powell, J.).

III.

If public education is not to suffer further, we must "return to a more balanced evaluation of the recognized interests of our society in achieving desegregation with other educational and societal interests a community may legitimately assert." *Id.*, at 253. The ultimate goal is to have quality school systems in which racial discrimination is neither practiced nor tolerated. It has been thought that ethnic and racial diversity in the classroom is a desirable component of sound education in our country to diverse populations, a view to which I subscribe. The question that courts in their single-minded pursuit of racial balance seem to ignore is how best to move toward this goal.

For a decade or more after *Brown*, the courts properly focused on dismantling segregated school systems as a means of eliminating state-imposed discrimination and furthering wholesome diversity in the schools.[5] Experience in re-

---

[4] Academic debate has intensified as to the degree of educational benefit realized by children due to integration. See R. Crain & R. Mahard, *The Influence of High School Racial Composition on Black College Attendance and Test Performance* (1978); Coleman, New Incentives for Desegregation, 7 *Human Rights* 10 (1978); Weinberg, The Relationship Between School Desegregation and Academic Achievement: A Review of the Research, 39 *L. & Contemp. Probs.* 240 (1975). Much of the dispute seems beside the point. It is essential that the diverse peoples of our country learn to live in harmony and mutual respect. This end is furthered when young people attend schools with diverse student bodies. But the benefits that may be achieved through this experience often will be compromised where the methods employed to promote integration include coercive measures such as forced transportation to achieve some theoretically desirable racial balance. Cf. N. St. John, *School Desegregation Outcomes for Children* (1975).

[5] During this period the issues confronted by the courts by and large involved combatting the devices by which States deliberately perpetuated dual school systems and dismantling segregated systems in small, rural areas. *E.g.,* Green v. County School Board, 391 U.S. 430 (1968); Griffin v. School Board, 377 U.S. 218 (1964); Goss v. Board of Education, 373 U.S. 683 (1963); Cooper v. Aaron, 358 U.S. 1 (1958). See Wilkinson, The Supreme Court and Southern School Desegregation, 1955–1970: A History and Analysis, 64 *Va. L. Rev.* 485 (1978). This Court did not begin to face the difficult administrative and social problems associated with *de facto* segregation in large urban school systems until Swann v. Charlotte-Mecklenburg Board of Education, 402 U.S. 1 (1971). It is especially unfortunate that the Court today refuses to acknowledge these problems and chooses instead to sanction methods that, although often appropriate and salutary in the earlier context, are disruptive and counterproductive in school systems like those in Columbus and Dayton.

cent years, however, has cast serious doubt upon the efficacy of far-reaching judicial remedies directed not against specific constitutional violations, but rather imposed on an entire school system on the fictional assumption that the existence of identifiable black or white schools is caused entirely by intentional segregative conduct, and is evidence of systemwide discrimination. In my view, some federal courts—now led by this Court—are pursuing a path away from rather than toward this desired goal. While these courts conscientiously view their judgments as mandated by the Constitution (a view that would have astonished constitutional scholars throughout most of our history), the fact is that restructuring and overseeing the operation of major public school systems—as ordered in these cases—fairly can be viewed as social engineering that hardly is appropriate for the federal judiciary. . . .

After all, and in spite of what many view as excessive government regulation, we are a free society—perhaps the most free of any in the world. Our people instinctively resent coercion, and perhaps most of all when it affects their children and the opportunities that only education affords them. It is now reasonably clear that the goal of diversity that we call integration, if it is to be lasting and conducive to quality education, must have the support of parents who so frequently have the option to choose where their children will attend school. Courts, of course, should confront discrimination wherever it is found to exist. But they should recognize limitations on judicial action inherent in our system and also the limits of effective judicial power. The primary and continuing responsibility for public education, including the bringing about and maintaining of desired diversity, must be left with school officials and public authorities.

Quaere: Does *Penick* suggest a judicial return—after the Omaha, Dayton, Austin and Pasadena interval—to the pro-integration spirit of *Keyes*? The *Penick* burden-of-proof rule rests on a judicially created presumption of guilt that is said to spring from pre-*Brown* (1954) segregation. Is this calculated to undercut the distinction between *de facto* and *de jure* separation—in the interest of promoting systemwide, compulsory integration? If so, why does the Court not say openly and directly that the Constitution requires integration? What is gained by the *Swann-Pasadena* rule that integration is not a constitutional *right*, but merely a *remedy* to be used in *de jure* segregation cases—when the Court then "adjusts" (manipulates?) the burden of proof in a manner that makes virtually all racial separation in effect *de jure*?

Milliken v. *Bradley* (I)
418 U.S. 717 (1974)

The Detroit Public School System was found to be *de jure* segregated, but desegregation could not be accomplished within the system because virtually all of its pupils were black. The trial court ordered busing between the Detroit system and 53 outside, separate, suburban school districts, none of which had been found to have indulged in relevant racial segregation.

Chief Justice Burger delivered the opinion of the Court.

We granted certiorari in these consolidated cases to determine whether a federal court may impose a multidistrict, areawide remedy to a single district *de jure* segregation problem absent any finding that the other included school districts have failed to operate unitary school systems within their districts, absent any claim or finding that the boundary lines of any affected school district were established with the purpose of fostering racial segregation in public schools, absent any finding that the included districts committed acts which effected segregation within the other districts, and absent a meaningful opportunity for the included neighboring school districts to present evidence or be heard on the propriety of a multidistrict remedy or on the question of constitutional violations by those neighboring districts. . . .

Viewing the record as a whole, it seems clear that the District Court and the Court of Appeals shifted the primary focus from a Detroit remedy to the metropolitan area only because of their conclusion that total desegregation of Detroit would not produce the racial balance which they perceived as desirable. Both courts proceeded on an assumption that the Detroit schools could not be truly desegregated—in their view of what constituted desegregation—unless the racial composition of the student body of each school substantially reflected the racial composition of the population of the metropolitan area as a whole. The metropolitan area as a whole. The metropolitan area was then defined as Detroit plus 53 of the outlying school districts. . . .

. . . The clear import of . . . *Swann* is that desegregation, in the sense of dismantling a dual school system, does not require any particular racial balance in each "school, grade or classroom."

Here the District Court's approach to what constituted "actual desegregation" raises the fundamental question, not presented in *Swann*, as to the circumstances in which a federal court may order desegregation relief that embraces more than a single school district. The court's analytical starting point was its conclusion that school district lines are no more than arbitrary lines on a map "drawn for political convenience." Boundary lines may be bridged where there has been a constitutional violation calling for inter-district relief but, the notion that

school district lines may be casually ignored or treated as a mere administrative convenience is contrary to the history of public education in our country. No single tradition in public education is more deeply rooted than local control over the operation of schools; local autonomy has long been thought essential. . . .

Of course, no state law is above the Constitution. School district lines and the present laws with respect to local control, are not sacrosanct and if they conflict with the Fourteenth Amendment federal courts have a duty to prescribe appropriate remedies. . . . But our prior holdings have been confined to violations and remedies within a single school district. We therefore turn to address, for the first time, the validity of a remedy mandating cross-district or inter-district consolidation to remedy a condition of segregation found to exist in only one district.

The controlling principle consistently expounded in our holdings is that the scope of the remedy is determined by the nature and extent of the constitutional violation. Before the boundaries of separate and autonomous school districts may be set aside by consolidating the separate units for remedial purposes or by imposing a cross-district remedy, it must first be shown that there has been a constitutional violation within one district that produces a significant segregative effect in another district. Specifically it must be shown that racially discriminatory acts of the state or local school districts, or of a single school district have been a substantial cause of inter-district segregation. Thus an inter-district remedy might be in order where the racially discriminatory acts of one or more school districts caused racial segregation in an adjacent district, or where district lines have been deliberately drawn on the basis of race. In such circumstances an inter-district remedy would be appropriate to eliminate the inter-district segregation directly caused by the constitutional violation. Conversely, without an inter-district violation and inter-district effect, there is no constitutional wrong calling for an inter-district remedy.

The record before us, voluminous as it is, contains evidence of *de jure* segregated conditions only in the Detroit schools; indeed, that was the theory on which the litigation was initially based and on which the Detroit Court took evidence. With no showing of significant violation by the 53 outlying school districts and no evidence of any inter-district violation or effect, the court went beyond the original theory of the case as framed by the pleadings and mandated a metropolitan area remedy. To approve the remedy ordered by the court would impose on the outlying districts, not shown to have committed any constitutional violation, a wholly impermissible remedy based on a standard not hinted at in *Brown I* and *II* or any holding of this Court. . . .

The constitutional right of the Negro respondents residing in Detroit is to attend a unitary school system in that district. Unless petitioners drew the district lines in a discriminatory fashion, or arranged for White students residing in the Detroit district to attend schools in Oakland and Macomb Counties, they were under no constitutional duty to make provisions for Negro students to do so. The view of the dissenters . . . can be supported only by drastic expansion of the constitutional right itself, an expansion without any support in either constitutional principle or precedent. . . .

We conclude that the relief ordered by the District Court and affirmed by the Court of Appeals was based upon an erroneous standard and was unsupported by record evidence that acts of the outlying districts affected the discrimination found to exist in the schools of Detroit. Accordingly, the judgment of the Court of Appeals is reversed and the case is remanded for further proceedings consistent with this opinion leading to prompt formulation of a decree directed to eliminating the segregation found to exist in Detroit city schools, a remedy which has been delayed since 1970.

Justice Marshall, with whom Justice Douglas, Justice Brennan, and Justice White join, dissenting. . . .

. . . [S]everal factors in this case coalesce to support the District Court's ruling that it was the State of Michigan itself, not simply the Detroit Board of Education, which bore the obligation of curing the condition of segregation within the Detroit city schools. The actions of the State itself directly contributed to Detroit's segregation. Under the Fourteenth Amendment, the State is ultimately responsible for the actions of its local agencies. And finally, given the structure of Michigan's educational system, Detroit's segregation cannot be viewed as the problem of an independent and separate entity. Michigan operates a single statewide system of education, a substantial part of which was shown to be segregated in this case. . . .

After examining three plans limited to the city of Detroit, the District Court correctly concluded that none would eliminate root and branch the vestiges of unconstitutional segregation. . . .

The rippling effects on residential patterns caused by purposeful acts of segregation do not automatically subside at the school district border. With rare exceptions, these effects naturally spread through all the residential neighborhoods within a metropolitan area. See *Keyes*. . . .

The majority asserts, however, that involvement of outlying districts would do violence to the accepted principle that "the nature of the violation determines the scope of the remedy." . . . To read this principle as barring a District Court from imposing the only effective remedy for past segregation and remitting the court to a patently ineffective alternative is, in my view, to turn a simple commonsense rule into a cruel and meaningless paradox. Ironically, by ruling out an inter-district remedy, the only relief which promises to cure segregation in the Detroit public schools, the majority flouts the very principle on which it purports to rely.

Nor should it be of any significance that the suburban school districts were not shown to have themselves taken any direct action to promote segregation of the races. Given the State's broad powers over local school districts, it was well within the State's powers to require those districts surrounding the Detroit school district to participate in a metropolitan remedy. The State's duty should be no different here than in cases where it is shown that certain of a State's voting districts are malapportioned in violation of the Fourteenth Amendment. . . .

> *Note:* In *Milliken* v. *Bradley* (II), 433 U.S. 267 (1977), the Court for the first time held "remedial education programs" are permissible as part of a school desegregation decree. This approach—like busing, a costly one—was used in this case to make up for the failure of desegregation by busing in the special circumstances of *Milliken I* (above).
>
> *Hills* v. *Gautreaux,* 425 U.S. 284 (1976), involving public housing, held that intergovernmental remedies are permissible, if (unlike the *Milliken* situation) the "outside" governmental entity involved is guilty of race relevant discrimination.

Affirmative Action—Reverse Discrimination

Regents of the University of California v. *Bakke* (summary)
98 S. Ct. 2733 (1978)

In disposing of this case the Justices wrote six opinions comprising about 150 pages. While the Court was severely fragmented, the immediate effect of its decision was clear: Affirmative action in university admissions is not unconstitutional in principle, though the quota system at issue in this case is. The Medical School of the University of California at Davis (hereinafter Davis) had reserved 16 out of 100 places in its freshman class for disadvantaged minority students. Bakke, a white man, contended that this had caused his exclusion, in violation of the Equal Protection Clause of the Fourteenth Amendment and Title VI of the Civil Rights Act of 1964 (as well as the California Constitution).

Title VI provides "No person . . . shall on the ground of race . . . be subjected to discrimination under any program . . . receiving Federal financial assistance." Justice Stevens (joined by Justices Burger, Stewart, and Rhnquist; hereinafter the Stevens group) argued that the Davis program clearly violated Title VI—and in their view the latter had independent meaning; it was not merely a "constitutional appendage." Thus these four judges did not address the constitutional issue at all.

All of the other Justices thought Title VI embraces, and is equivalent to, the constitutional standard of the Equal Protection Clause. Accordingly they decided the case on constitutional grounds. Justices Brennan, White, Marshall, and Blackmun (hereinafter the Brennan group) concluded that "racial classifications designed to further remedial purposes 'must serve important governmental objectives and must be substantially related to achievement of those objectives.'" They insisted that even benign racial classifications must be given careful judicial review lest they be misused. A classification would be invalid, they said, if it (1) stigmatized any group, (2) hurt those least well represented in the political process, or (3) was not justified by "an important and articulated purpose." The Brennan group concluded that counteracting past social discrimination is important enough to justify race-conscious admissions when there is reason to believe minority underrepresentation is substantial and chronic and that past societal discrimination impedes minority access to the school. The Davis program was said to meet these tests—and was accordingly deemed permissible.

The Court being divided 4 to 4, Justice Powell wrote the "controlling" opinion. He insisted that racial distinctions "of any sort are inherently suspect and thus call for the most exacting judicial examination." He then considered four possible goals of the Davis admissions program and found that none of them satisfied the orthodox strict-scrutiny test; namely, that the state demonstrate a compelling governmental objective, and that the challenged classification be essential to achieve that objective. As to the four possible Davis objectives, Justice Powell found: (1) assuring within the student body a quota based merely on race or ethnic origin is an unconstitutional purpose; (2) improving health care to underserved communities might be compelling enough to justify a racial classification, but no evidence presented in this case established that the Davis program was necessary to promote this goal; (3) achieving a diverse student body is a compelling interest protected by the First Amendment's guarantee of academic freedom, but Davis had not demonstrated that its racial classification was necessary to achieve that end; (4) compensating for the effects of past social discrimination is legitimate, but Davis had no compelling basis for hurting one group for the benefit of another, in the absence of a judicial, legislative, or administrative finding of past unlawful conduct by Davis. It followed that the challenged quota admission system violated the Fourteenth Amendment's Equal Protection Clause.

The result was that Justice Powell, plus the Stevens group of four, formed a majority in favor of Bakke. But another majority (Justice Powell plus the Brennan group) held that race-conscious admissions for the purpose of increasing minority representation in a student body is not necessarily unconstitutional.

The chief difference between Justice Powell and the Brennan group concerned whether past discrimination as a justification for affirmative action can ever be permitted without a specific judicial, legislative, or administrative finding of past discrimination by the agency in question. Each side read the earlier decisions as supporting its position. How members of the Stevens group may read them in the future could be crucial.

Another difference between Justice Powell and the Brennan group was that only the latter accepted the quota system. Mr. Justice Powell supported a more flexible approach which "treats each applicant as an individual," whose race may be considered, along with other relevant considerations, but race itself (e.g., by quota), may not qualify or disqualify anyone.

Note: See *United Jewish Organization* v. *Carey*, below, decided shortly before *Bakke*.

United Steel Workers v. *Weber*
99 S. Ct. 2721 (1979)

In *Bakke,* racial quotas and preferences, that is, "reverse discrimination," was rejected. This case upholds it in a different setting. Since in the Court's view the challenged conduct "does not involve state action" (see Chapter 10, below), this case "does not present an alleged violation of the Equal Protection Clause." Apparently ignoring the problem of "federal action" (see Quaere, below), the Court reaches its conclusion by interpreting—or, as the dissent insists, by rewriting—an act of Congress. The majority and the main dissenting opinions are presented at length as classic examples of the use of "legislative history" as an aid to statutory interpretation.

The Court's *unanimous* remarks a few days earlier in *United States* v. *Rutherford,* 99 S. Ct. 2470 (1979), stated the orthodox approach to judicial explication of statutes. Congress had prohibited interstate shipment and sale of Laetril (a cancer-treatment drug not approved in accordance with the Food, Drug, and Cosmetic Act). Refusing to read an exception into the act at the request of terminally ill cancer victims, the Court observed,

> Under our constitutional framework federal courts do not sit as councils of revision, empowered to rewrite legislation in accord with their own conceptions of prudent public policy . . . . Only when a literal construction of a statute yields results so manifestly unreasonable that they could not fairly be attributed to congressional design will an exception to statutory language be judicially implied.

Mr. Justice Brennan delivered the opinion of the Court.

Challenged here is the legality of an affirmative action plan—collectively bargained by an employer and a union—that reserves for black employees 50% of the openings in an in-plant craft training program until the percentage of black craft workers in the plant is commensurate with the percentage of blacks in the local labor force. The question for decision is whether Congress, in Title VII of the Civil Rights Act of 1964 as amended, 42 U.S.C. § 2000e, left employers and unions in the private sector free to take such race-conscious steps to eliminate manifest racial imbalances in traditionally segregated job categories. We hold that Title VII does not prohibit such race-conscious affirmative action plans.

I.

In 1974 petitioner United Steelworkers of America (USWA) and petitioner Kaiser Alumi-

num & Chemical Corporation (Kaiser) entered into a master collective-bargaining agreement covering terms and conditions of employment at 15 Kaiser plants. The agreement contained, *inter alia,* and affirmative action plan designed to eliminate conspicuous racial imbalances in Kaiser's then almost exclusively white craft work forces. Black craft hiring goals were set for each Kaiser plant equal to the percentage of blacks in the respective local labor forces. To enable plants to meet these goals, on-the-job training programs were established to teach unskilled production workers—black and white— the skills necessary to become craft workers. The plan reserved for black employees 50% of the openings in these newly created in-plant training programs.

This case arose from the operation of the plan at Kaiser's plant in Gramercy, La. Until 1974 Kaiser hired as craft workers for that plant only persons who had had prior craft experience. Because blacks had long been excluded from craft unions, few were able to present such credentials. As a consequence, prior to 1974 only 1.83% (five out of 273) of the skilled craft workers at the Gramercy plant were black, even though the work force in the Gramercy area was approximately 39% black.

Pursuant to the national agreement Kaiser altered its craft hiring practice in the Gramercy plant. Rather than hiring already trained outsiders, Kaiser established a training program to train its production workers to fill craft openings. Selection of craft trainees was made on the basis of seniority, with the proviso that at least 50% of the new trainees were to be black until the percentage of black skilled craft workers in the Gramercy plant approximated the percentage of blacks in the local labor force. See 415 F. Supp. 761, 764.

During 1974, the first year of the operation of the Kaiser–USWA affirmative action plan, 13 craft trainees were selected from Gramercy's production work force. Of these, 7 were black and 6 white. The most junior black selected into the program had less seniority than several white production workers whose bids for admission were rejected. Thereafter one of those white production workers, respondent Brian Weber, instituted this class action in the United States District Court for the Eastern District of Louisiana.

The complaint alleged that the filling of craft trainee positions at the Gramercy plant pursuant to the affirmative action program had resulted in junior black employees receiving training in preference to more senior white employees, thus discriminating against respondent and other similarly situated white employees in violation of §§ 703(a)[1] and (d)[2] of Title VII. The District Court held that the plan violated

Title VII, entered a judgment in favor of the plaintiff class, and granted a permanent injunction prohibiting Kaiser and the USWA "from denying plaintiffs, Brian F. Weber and all other members of the class, access to on-the-job training programs on the basis of race." 415 F. Supp. 761 (1976). A divided panel of the Court of Appeals for the Fifth Circuit affirmed, holding that all employment preferences based upon race, including those preferences incidental to bona fide affirmative action plans, violated Title VII's prohibition against racial discrimination in employment. 563 F. 2d 216 (1978). . . . We reverse.

II.

We emphasize at the outset the narrowness of our inquiry. Since the Kaiser–USWA plan does not involve state action, this case does not present an alleged violation of the Equal Protection Clause of the Constitution. Further, since the Kaiser–USWA plan was adopted voluntarily, we are not concerned with what Title VII requires or with what a court might order to remedy a past proven violation of the Act. The only question before us is the narrow statutory issue of whether Title VII *forbids* private employers and unions from voluntarily agreeing upon bona fide affirmative action plans that accord racial preferences in the manner and for the

---

[1] Section 703(a), 42 U.S.C. § 2000e–2(a), provides:

"(a) It shall be unlawful employment practice for an employer—

"(1) to fail or refuse to hire or to discharge any individual, or otherwise to discriminate against any individual with respect to his compensation, terms, conditions, or privileges of employment, because of such

individual's race, color, religion, sex, or national origin; or

"(2) to limit or classify his employees or applicants for employment in any way which would deprive or tend to deprive any individual of employment opportunities or otherwise adversely affect his status as an employee, because of such individual's race, color, religion, sex, or national origin."

[2] Section 703(d), 42 U.S.C. § 2000e–2(d), provides:

"It shall be an unlawful employment practice for any employer, labor organization, or joint labor-management committee controlling apprenticeship or other training or retraining, including on-the-job training programs to discriminate against any individual because of his race, color, religion, sex, or national origin in admission to, or employment in, any program established to provide apprenticeship or other training."

purpose provided in the Kaiser–USWA plan. That question was expressly left open in *McDonald* v. *Sante Fe Trail Trans. Co.*, 427 U.S. 273, 281, n. 8 (1976),' which held, in a case not involving affirmative action, that Title VII protects whites as well as blacks from certain forms of racial discrimination.

Respondent argues that Congress intended in Title VII to prohibit all race-conscious affirmative action plans. Respondent's argument rests upon a literal interpretation of §§ 703(a) and (d) of the Act. Those sections make it unlawful to "discriminate . . . because of . . . race" in hiring and in the selection of apprentices for training programs. Since, the argument runs, *McDonald* v. *Santa Fe Trans. Co.*, *supra*, settled that Title VII forbids discrimination against whites as well as blacks, and since the Kaiser–USWA affirmative action plan operates to discriminate against white employees solely because they are white, it follows that the Kaiser–USWA plan violates Title VII.

Respondent's argument is not without force. But it overlooks the significance of the fact that the Kaiser–USWA plan is an affirmative action plan voluntarily adopted by private parties to eliminate traditional patterns of racial segregation. In this context respondent's reliance upon a literal construction of § 703(a) and (d) and upon *McDonald* is misplaced. See *McDonald* v. *Santa Fe Trail Trans. Co.*, *supra*, at 281, n. 8. It is a "familiar rule, that a thing may be within the letter of the statute and yet not within the statute, because not within its spirit, nor within the intention of its makers." *Holy Trinity Church* v. *United States*, 143 U.S. 457, 459 (1892). The prohibition against racial discrimination in §§ 703(a) and (d) of Title VII must therefore be read against the background of the legislative history of Title VII and the historical context from which the Act arose. See *Train* v. *Colorado Public Interest Research Group*, 426 U.S. 1, 10 (1976); *Woodworkers* v. *NLRB*, 386 U.S. 612, 620 (1967); *United States* v. *American Trucking Assns.*, 310 U.S. 534, 543–544 (1940). Examination of those sources makes clear that an interpretation

of the sections that forbade all race-conscious affirmative action would "bring about an end completely at variance with the purpose of the statute" and must be rejected. *United States* v. *Public Utilities Comm'n*, 345 U.S. 295, 315 (1953). See *Johansen* v. *United States*, 343 U.S. 427, 431 (1952); *International Union* v. *Juneau Spruce Corp.*, 342 U.S. 237, 243 (1952); *Texas & Pacific R. Co.* v. *Abilene Oil Co.*, 204 U.S. 426 (1907).

Congress' primary concern in enacting the prohibition against racial discrimination in Title VII of the Civil Rights Act of 1964 was with "the plight of the Negro in our economy." 110 *Cong. Rec.* 6548 (remarks of Sen. Humphrey). Before 1964, blacks were largely relegated to "unskilled and semi-skilled jobs." *Id.*, at 6548 (remarks of Sen. Humphrey); *id.*, at 7204 (remarks of Sen. Clark); *id.*, at 7279–7280 (remarks of Sen. Kennedy). Because of automation the number of such jobs was rapidly decreasing. See 110 *Cong. Rec.*, at 6548 (remarks of Sen. Humphrey); *id.*, at 7204 (remarks of Sen. Clark). As a consequence "the relative position of the Negro worker [was] steadily worsening. In 1947 the non-white unemployment rate was only 64 percent higher than the white rate; in 1962 it was 124 percent higher." *Id.*, at 6547 (remarks of Sen. Humphrey). See also *id.*, at 7204 (remarks of Sen. Clark). Congress considered this a serious social problem. As Senator Clark told the Senate:

> "The rate of Negro unemployment has gone up consistently as compared with white unemployment for the past 15 years. This is a social malaise and a social situation which we should not tolerate. That is one of the principal reasons why this bill should pass." *Id.*, at 7220.

Congress feared that the goals of the Civil Rights Act—the integration of blacks into the mainstream of American society—could not be achieved unless this trend were reversed. And Congress recognized that that would not be possible unless blacks were able to secure jobs "which have a future." *Id.*, at 7204 (remarks of

Sen. Clark). See also *id.*, at 7279–7280 (remarks of Sen. Kennedy). As Senator Humphrey explained to the Senate:

> "What good does it do a Negro to be able to eat in a fine restaurant if he cannot afford to pay the bill? What good does it do him to be accepted in a hotel that is too expensive for his modest income? How can a Negro child be motivated to take full advantage of integrated educational facilities if he has no hope of getting a job where he can use that education?" *Id.*, at 6547.

. . .

> "Without a job, one cannot afford public convenience and accommodations. Income from employment may be necessary to further a man's education, or that of his children. If his children have no hope of getting a good job, what will motivate them to take advantage of educational opportunities." *Id.*, at 6552.

These remarks echoed President Kennedy's original message to Congress upon the introduction of the Civil Rights Act in 1963: "There is little value in a Negro's obtaining the right to be admitted to hotels and restaurants if he has no cash in his pocket and no job." *Id.*, at 11159. Accordingly, it was clear to Congress that "the crux of the problem [was] to open employment opportunities for Negroes in occupations which have been traditionally closed to them," *id.*, at 6548 (remarks of Sen. Humphrey), and it was to this problem that Title VII's prohibition against racial discrimination in employment was primarily addressed.

It plainly appears from the House Report accompanying the Civil Rights Act that Congress did not intend wholly to prohibit private and voluntary affirmative action efforts as one method of solving this problem. The Report provides:

> "No bill can or should lay claim to eliminating all of the causes and consequences of racial and other types of discrimination against minorities. There is reason to believe, however, that national leadership provided by the enactment of Federal legislation dealing with the most troublesome problems *will create an atmosphere conducive to voluntary or local resolution of other forms of discrimination.*" H.R. Rep. No. 914. 88th Cong., 1st Sess. (1963), at 18. (Emphasis supplied.)

Given this legislative history, we cannot agree with respondent that Congress intended to prohibit the private sector from taking effective steps to accomplish the goal that Congress designed Title VII to achieve. The very statutory words intended as a spur or catalyst to cause "employers and unions to self-examine and to self-evaluate their employment practices and to endeavor to eliminate, so far as possible, the last vestiges of an unfortunate and ignominious page in this country's history," *Albemarle* v. *Moody*, 422 U.S. 405, 418 (1975), cannot be interpreted as an absolute prohibition against all private, voluntary, race-conscious affirmative action efforts to hasten the elimination of such vestiges. It would be ironic indeed if a law triggered by a Nation's concern over centuries of racial injustice and intended to improve the lot of those who had "been excluded from the American dream for so long," 110 Cong. Rec., at 6552 (remarks of Sen. Humphrey), constituted the first legislative prohibition of all voluntary, private, race-conscious efforts to abolish traditional patterns of racial segregation and hierarchy.

Our conclusion is further reinforced by examination of the language and legislative history of § 703(j) of Title VII.[3] Opponents of Title VII

---

[3] Section 703(j) of Title VII, 42 U.S.C. § 2000e–2(j), provides:

> "Nothing contained in this subchapter shall be interpreted to require any employer, employment agency, labor organization, or joint labor-management committee subject to this subchapter to grant preferential treatment to any individual or to any group because of the race, color, religion, sex,

raised two related arguments against the bill. First, they argued that the Act would be interpreted to *require* employers with racially imbalanced work forces to grant preferential treatment to racial minorities in order to integrate. Second, they argued that employers with racially imbalanced work forces would grant preferential treatment to racial minorities, even if not required to do so by the Act. See 110 Cong. Rec. 8618–8619 (remarks of Sen. Sparkman). Had Congress meant to prohibit all race-conscious affirmative action, as respondent urges, it easily could have answered both objections by providing that Title VII would not require or *permit* racially preferential integration efforts. But Congress did not choose such a course. Rather Congress added § 703(j) which addresses only the first objection. The section provides that nothing contained in Title VII "shall be interpreted to *require* any employer . . . to grant preferential treatment . . . to any group because of the race . . . of such . . . group on account of" a defacto racial imbalance in the employer's work force. The section does *not* state that "nothing in Title VII shall be interpreted to *permit*" voluntary affirmative efforts to correct racial imbalances. The natural inference is that Congress chose not to forbid all voluntary race-conscious affirmative action.

The reasons for this choice are evident from

the legislative record. Title VII could not have been enacted into law without substantial support from legislators in both Houses who traditionally resisted federal regulation of private business. Those legislators demanded as a price for their support that "management prerogatives and union freedoms . . . be left undisturbed to the greatest extent possible." H.R. Rep. No. 914, 88th Cong., 1st Sess., Pt. 2 (1963), at 29. Section 703(j) was proposed by Senator Dirksen to allay any fears that the Act might be interpreted in such a way as to upset this compromise. The section was designed to prevent § 703 of Title VII from being interpreted in such a way as to lead to undue "Federal Government interference with private businesses because of some Federal employee's ideas about racial balance or imbalance." 110 *Cong. Rec.*, at 14314 (remarks of Sen. Miller).[4] See also *Id.*, at 9881 (remarks of Sen. Allott); *id.*, at 10520 (remarks of Sen. Carlson); *id.*, at 11471 (remarks of Sen. Javits); *id.*, at 12817 (remarks of Sen. Dirksen). Clearly, a prohibition against all voluntary, race-conscious, affirmative action efforts would disserve these ends. Such a prohibition would augment the powers of the Federal Government and diminish traditional management prerogatives while at the same time impeding attainment of the ultimate statutory goals. In view of this legislative history and in view of Congress' desire to avoid undue federal regulation of private businesses, use of the word "require"

national origin of such individual or group on account of an imbalance which may exist with respect to the total number or percentage of persons of any race, color, religion, sex, or national origin employed by any employer, referred or classified for employment by any employment agency or labor organization, or admitted to, or employed in, any apprenticeship or other training program, in comparison with the total number or percentage or persons of such race, color, religion, sex, or national origin in any community, State, section, or other area, or in the available work force in any community, State, section, or other area."

Section 703(j) speaks to substantive liability under Title VII, but it does not preclude courts from considering racial imbalance as evidence of a Title VII violation. See *Teamsters* v. *United States*, 431 U.S. 324, 339–340, n. 20 (1977). Remedies for substantive violations are governed by § 706(g), 42 U.S.C. § 2000e–5(g).

[4] Title VI of the Civil Rights Act of 1964, considered in *University of California Regents* v. *Bakke*, 438 U.S. 265 (1978), contains no provision comparable to § 703(j). This is because Title VI was an exercise of federal power over a matter in which the Federal Government was already directly involved: the prohibitions against race-based conduct contained in Title VI governed "program[s] or activit[ies] receiving Federal financial assistance." 42 U.S.C. § 2000d. Congress was legislating to assure federal funds would not be used in an improper manner. Title VII, by contrast, was enacted pursuant to the Commerce power to regulate purely private decisionmaking and was not intended to incorporate and particularize the commands of the Fifth and Fourteenth Amendments. Title VII and Title VI, therefore, cannot be read *in pari materia*. See 110 *Cong. Rec.* 8315 (1964) (remarks of Sen. Cooper). See also *id.*, at 11615 (remarks of Sen. Cooper).

rather than the phrase "require or permit" in § 703(j) fortifies the conclusion that Congress did not intend to limit traditional business freedom to such a degree as to prohibit all voluntary, race-conscious affirmative action.[5]

We therefore hold that Title VII's prohibition in §§ 703(a) and (d) against racial discrimination does not condemn all private, voluntary, race-conscious affirmative action plans.

III.

We need not today define in detail the line of demarcation between permissible and impermissible affirmative action plans. It suffices to hold that the challenged Kaiser–USWA affirma-

[5] Respondent argues that our construction of § 703 conflicts with various remarks in the legislative record. See, e.g., 110 Cong. Rec. 7213 (Sens. Clark and Case); id., at 7218 (Sens. Clark and Case); id., at 6549 (Sen. Humphrey); id., at 8921 (Sen. Williams). We do not agree. In Senator Humphrey's words, these comments were intended as assurances that Title VII would not allow establishment of systems "to *maintain* racial balance in employment." id., at 11848. They were not addressed to temporary, voluntary, affirmative action measures undertaken to eliminate manifest racial imbalance in traditionally segregated job categories. Moreover, the comments referred to by respondent all preceded the adoption of § 703(j), 42 U.S.C. § 2000e–2(j). After § 703(j) was adopted congressional comments were all to the effect that employers would not be *required* to institute preferential quotas to avoid Title VII liability, see, e.g., id., at 12819 (remarks of Sen. Dirksen): id., at 13079–13080 (remarks of Sen. Clark): id., at 15876 (remarks of Rep. Lindsay). There was no suggestion after the adoption of § 703(j) that wholly voluntary, race-conscious, affirmative action efforts would in themselves constitute a violation of Title VII. On the contrary, as Representative MacGregor told the House shortly before the final vote on Title VII:

"Important as the scope and extent of this bill is, it is also vitally important that all Americans understand what this bill does not cover.

"Your mail and mine, your contacts and mine with our constituents, indicates a great degree of misunderstanding about this bill. People complain about . . . preferential treatment or quotas in employment. There is a mistaken belief that Congress is legislating in these areas in this bill. When we drafted this bill we excluded these issues largely because the problems raised by these controversial questions are more properly handled at a governmental level closer to the American people and by communities and individuals themselves." 110 Cong. Rec. 15893 (remarks of Rep. MacGregor).

tive action plan falls on the permissible side of the line. The purposes of the plan mirror those of the statute. Both were designed to break down old patterns of racial segregation and hierarchy. Both were structured to "open employment opportunities for Negroes in occupations which have been traditionally closed to them." 100 Cong. Rec. 6548 (remarks of Sen. Humphrey).

At the same time the plan does not unnecessarily trammel the interests of the white employees. The plan does not require the discharge of white workers and their replacement with new black hires. Cf. McDonald v. Santa Fe Trail Trans. Co., supra. Nor does the plan create an absolute bar to the advancement of white employees; half of those trained in the program will be white. Moreover, the plan is a temporary measure; it is not intended to maintain racial balance, but simply to eliminate a manifest racial imbalance. Preferential selection of craft trainees at the Gramercy plant will end as soon as the percentage of black skilled craft workers in the Gramercy plant approximates the percentage of blacks in the local labor force. See 415 F. Supp. 761, 783.

We conclude, therefore, that the adoption of the Kaiser–USWA plan for the Gramercy plant falls within the area of discretion left by Title VII to the private sector voluntarily to adopt affirmative action plans designed to eliminate conspicuous racial imbalance in traditionally segregated job categories. Accordingly, the judgment of the Court of Appeals for the Fifth Circuit is reversed.

Mr. Justice Powell and Mr. Justice Stevens took no part in the consideration or decision of this case.

Mr. Justice Blackmun, concurring. . . .

Mr. Chief Justice Burger dissenting. . . .

Mr. Justice Rehnquist, with whom The Chief Justice joins, dissenting. . . .

The operative sections of Title VII prohibit racial discrimination in employment *simpliciter*. Taken in its normal meaning, and as understood by all Members of Congress who spoke to the issue during the legislative debates, see *infra*, at __, this language prohibits a covered employer from considering race when making an employment decision, whether the race be black or white. Several years ago, however, a United States District Court held that "the dismissal of white employees charged with misappropriating company property while not dismissing a similarly charged Negro employee does not raise a claim upon which Title VII relief may be granted." *McDonald* v. *Santa Fe Trail Tranps. Co.*, 427 U.S. 273, 278 (1976). This Court unanimously reversed, concluding from the "uncontradicted legislative history" that "Title VII prohibits racial discrimination against the white petitioners in this case upon the same standards as would be applicable were they Negroes . . . ." 427 U.S., at 180.

We have never waivered in our understanding that Title VII "prohibits *all* racial discrimination in employment, without exception for any particular employees." *Id.*, at 283 (emphasis in original). In *Griggs* v. *Duke Power Co.*, 401 U.S. 424, 429 (1971), our first occasion to interpret Title VII, a unanimous court observed that "[d]iscriminatory preference, for any group, minority or majority, is precisely and only what Congress has proscribed." And in our most recent discussion of the issue, we uttered words seemingly dispositive of this case: "It is clear beyond cavil that the obligation imposed by Title VII is to provide an equal opportunity for *each* applicant regardless of race, without regard to whether members of the applicant's race are already proportionately represented in the work force." *Furnco Construction Corp.* v. *Waters*, 438 U.S. 567. __ (1978) (emphasis in original).[6]

---

[6] Our statements in *Griggs* and *Furnco Construction*, patently inconsistent with today's holding, are not even mentioned, much less distinguished, by the Court.

Today, however, the Court behaves much like the Orwellian speaker earlier described, as if it had been handed a note indicating that Title VII would lead to a result unacceptable to the Court if interpreted here as it was in our prior decisions. Accordingly, without even a break in syntax, the Court rejects "a literal construction of § 703(a)" in favor of newly discovered "legislative history," which leads it to a conclusion directly contrary to that compelled by the "uncontradicted legislative history" unearthed in *McDonald* and our other prior decisions. Now we are told that the legislative history of Title VII shows that employers are free to discriminate on the basis of race; an employer may, in the Court's words, "trammel the interests of white employees" in favor of black employees in order to eliminate "racial imbalance." *Ante*, at 12. Our earlier interpretations of Title VII, like the banners and posters decorating the square in Oceania, were all wrong.

As if this were not enough to make a reasonable observer question this Court's adherence to the oft-stated principle that our duty is to construe rather than rewrite legislation, *United States* v. *Rutherford* . . . the Court also seizes upon § 703(j) of Title VII as an independent, or at least partially independent, basis for its holding. Totally ignoring the wording of that section, which is obviously addressed to those charged with the responsibility of interpreting the law rather than those who are subject to its proscriptions, and totally ignoring the months of legislative debates preceding the section's introduction and passage, which demonstrate clearly that it was enacted to prevent precisely what occurred in this case, the Court infers from § 703(j) that "Congress chose not to forbid all voluntary race-conscious affirmative action." *Ante*, . . .

Thus, by a *tour de force* reminiscent not of jurists such as Hale, Holmes, and Hughes, but of escape artists such as Houdini, the Court eludes clear statutory language, "uncontradicted" legislative history, and uniform precedent in concluding that employers are, after all, permitted to consider race in making employment decisions. It may be that one or more of the principal sponsors of Title VII would have preferred to see a provision allowing preferential treatment of minorities written into the bill. Such a provision, however, would have to have been expressly or impliedly excepted from Title VII's explicit prohibition on all racial discrimination in employment. There is no such exception in the Act. And a reading of the legislative debates concerning Title VII, in which proponents and opponents alike uniformly denounced discrimination in favor of, as well as discrimination against, Negroes, demonstrates clearly that any legislator harboring an unspoken desire for such a provision could not possibly have succeeded in enacting it into law. . . .

II.

Were Congress to act today specifically to prohibit the type of racial discrimination suffered by Weber, it would be hard pressed to draft language better tailored to the task than that found in § 703(d) of Title VII:

"It shall be an unlawful employment practice for any employer, labor organization, or joint labor-management committee controlling apprenticeship or other training or retraining, including on-the-job training programs to discriminate against any individual because of his race, color, religion, sex, or national origin in admission to, or employment in, any program established to provide apprenticeship or other training." 43 U.S.C. § 2000e-2(d).

Equally suited to the task would be § 703(a)(2), which makes it unlawful for an employer to classify his employees "in any way which would deprive or tend to deprive any individual of employment opportunities or otherwise adversely affect his status as an employee, because of such individual's race, color, religion,

sex, or national origin." 42 U.S.C. § 2000e-2(a)(2).[7]

Entirely consistent with these two express prohibitions is the language of § 703(j) of Title VII, which provides that the Act is not to be interpreted "to require any employer . . . to grant preferential treatment to any individual or to any group because of the race . . . of such individual or group" to correct a racial imbalance in the employer's work force. 42 U.S.C. § 2000e-2(j).[8] Seizing on the word "require," the Court infers that Congress must have intended to "permit" this type of racial discrimination. Not only is this reading of § 703(j) outlandish in the light of the flat prohibitions of §§ 703(a) and (d), but, as explained in Part III, it is totally belied by the Act's legislative history.

Quite simply, Kaiser's racially discriminatory admission quota is flatly prohibited by the plain

---

[7] Section 703(a)(1) provides the third express prohibition in Title VII of Kaiser's discriminatory admission quota:

"It shall be an unlawful employment practice for an employer—

"(1) to fail or refuse to hire or to discharge an individual, or otherwise to discriminate against any individual with respect to his compensation, terms, conditions, or privileges of employment, because of such individual's race, color, religion, sex, or national origin . . . ." 42 U.S.C. § 2000e-2(a)(1).

[8] The full text of § 703(j), 42 U.S.C. § 2000e-2(j), provides as follows:

"(j) Nothing contained in this subchapter shall be interpreted to require any employer, employment agency, labor organization, or joint labor-management committee subject to this subchapter to grant preferential treatment to any individual or to any group because of the race, color, religion, sex, or national origin of such individual or group on account of an imbalance which may exist with respect to the total number or percentage of persons of any race, color, religion, sex, or national origin employed by any employer, referred or classified for employment by any employment agency or labor organization, admitted to membership or classified by any labor organization, or admitted to, or employed in, any apprenticeship or other training program, in comparison with the total number or percentage of persons of such race, color, religion, sex, or national origin in any community, State, section, or other area, or in the available work force in any community, State, section, or other area."

language of Title VII. This normally dispositive fact, however, gives the Court only momentary pause. An "interpretation" of the statute upholding Weber's claim would, according to the Court, " 'bring about an end completely at variance with the purpose of the statute.' " *Ante,* . . . , quoting *United States* v. *Public Utilities Comm'n,* 345 U.S. 295, 315 (1953). To support this conclusion, the Court calls upon the "spirit" of the Act, which it divines from passages in Title VII's legislative history indicating that enactment of the statute was prompted by Congress' desire "to open employment opportunities for Negroes in occupations which [had] been traditionally closed to them." *Ante,* . . . , quoting 110 *Cong. Rec.* 6548 (1964) (remarks of Sen. Humphrey).[9] But the legislative history invoked by the Court to avoid the plain language of §§ 703(a) and (d) simply misses the point. To be sure, the reality of employment discrimination against Negroes provided the primary impetus for passage of Title VII. But this fact by no means supports the proposition that Congress intended to leave employers free to discriminate against white persons.[10] In most

cases, "[l]egislative history . . . is more vague than the statute we are called upon to interpret." *United States* v. *Public Utilities Comm'n,*

reason to believe, however, that national leadership provided by the enactment of Federal legislation dealing with the most troublesome problems *will create an atmosphere conducive to voluntary or local resolution of other forms of discrimination.*" H.R. Rep. No. 914, 88th Cong., 1st Sess., 18 (1963) (thereinafter H.R. Rep.), . . .

The Court seizes on the italicized language to support its conclusion that Congress did not intend to prohibit voluntary imposition of racially discriminatory employment quotas. The Court, however, stops too short in its reading of the House Report. The words immediately following the material excerpted by the Court are as follows:

"It is, however, possible and necessary for the Congress to enact legislation which prohibits and provides the means of terminating *the most serious types of discrimination.* This H.R. 7152, as amended, would achieve in a number of related areas. It would reduce discriminatory obstacles to the exercise of the right to vote and provide means of expediting the vindication of that right. It would make it possible to remove the daily affront and humiliation involved in discriminatory denials of access to facilities ostensibly open to the general public. It would guarantee that there will be no discrimination upon recipients of Federal financial assistance. It would prohibit discrimination in employment and provide means to expedite termination of discrimination in public education. It would open additional avenues to deal with redress of denials of equal protection of the laws on account of race, color, religion, or national origin by State or local authorities." H.R. Rep., at 18 (emphasis added).

When thus read in context, the meaning of the italicized language in the Court's excerpt of the House Report becomes clear. By dealing with "the most serious types of discrimination," such as discrimination in voting, public accommodations, employment, etc., H.R. 7152 would hopefully inspire "voluntary or local resolution of other forms of discrimination," that is, forms other than discrimination in voting, public accommodations, employment, etc.

One can also infer from the House Report that the Judiciary Committee hoped that federal legislation would inspire voluntary elimination of discrimination against minority groups other than those protected under the bill, perhaps the aged and handicapped to name just two. In any event, the House Report does not support the Court's proposition that Congress, by banning racial discrimination in employment, intended to permit racial discrimination in employment.

Thus, examination of the House Judiciary Committee's report reveals that the Court's interpretation of Title VII, far from being compelled by the Act's legislative history, is utterly without support in that legislative history. Indeed, as demonstrated in Part III, *infra,* the Court's interpretation of Title VII is totally refuted by the Act's legislative history.

---

[9] In holding that Title VII cannot be interpreted to prohibit use of Kaiser's racially discriminatory admission quota, the Court reasons that it would be "ironic" if a law inspired by the history of racial discrimination in employment against blacks forbade employers from voluntarily discriminating against whites in favor of blacks. I see no irony in a law that prohibits *all* voluntary racial discrimination, even discrimination directed at whites in favor of blacks. The evil inherent in discrimination against Negroes is that it is based on an immutable characteristic, utterly irrelevant to employment decisions. The characteristic becomes no less immutable and irrelevant, and discrimination based thereon becomes no less evil, simply because the person excluded is a member of one race rather than another. Far from ironic, I find a prohibition on all preferential treatment based on race as elementary and fundamental as the principle that "two wrongs do not make a right."

[10] The only shred of legislative history cited by the Court in support of the proposition that "Congress did not intend wholly to prohibit private and voluntary affirmative action efforts," *ante,* . . . , is the following excerpt from the Judiciary Committee Report accompanying the civil rights bill reported to the House:

"No bill can or should lay claim to eliminating all of the causes and consequences of racial and other types of discrimination against minorities. There is

345 U.S. 295, 321 (1954) (Jackson, J., concurring). Here, however, the legislative history of Title VII is as clear as the language of §§ 703(a) and (d), and it irrefutably demonstrates that Congress meant precisely what it said in §§ 703(a) and (d)—that *no* racial discrimination in employment is permissible under Title VII, not even preferential treatment of minorities to correct racial imbalance.

III.

In undertaking to review the legislative history of Title VII, I am mindful that the topic hardly makes for light reading, but I am also fearful that nothing short of a thorough examination of the congressional debates will fully expose the magnitude of the Court's misinterpretation of Congress' intent.

A

Introduced on the floor of the House of Representatives on June 20, 1963, the bill—H.R. 7152—that ultimately became the Civil Rights Act of 1964 contained no compulsory provisions directed at private discrimination in employment. The bill was promptly referred to the Committee on the Judiciary, where it was amended to include Title VII. With two exceptions, the bill reported by the House Judiciary Committee contained §§ 703(a) and (d) as they were ultimately enacted. Amendments subsequently adopted on the House floor added § 703's prohibition against sex discrimination and § 703(d)'s coverage of "on the job training."

After noting that "[t]he purpose of [Title VII] is to eliminate . . . discrimination in employment based on race, color, religion, or national origin," the Judiciary Committee's report simply paraphrased the provisions of Title VII without elaboration. H.R. Rep. No. 914, 88th Cong., 1st Sess., 26 (1963) (thereinafter H.R. Rep.). In a separate Minority Report, however, opponents of the measure on the Committee advanced a line of attack which was reiterated throughout the debates in both the House and

Senate and which ultimately led to passage of § 703(j). Noting that the word "discrimination" was nowhere defined in H.R. 7152, the Minority Report charged that the absence from Title VII of any reference to "racial imbalance" was a "public relations" ruse and that "the administration intends to rely upon its own construction of "discrimination' as including the lack of racial balance . . . ." H.R. Rep., at 67–68. To demonstrate how the bill would operate in practice, the Minority Report posited a number of hypothetical employment situations, concluding in each example that the employer "*may be forced to hire according to race*, to 'racially balance' those who work for him *in every job classification* or be in violation of Federal law." *Id.*, at 69 (emphasis in original).

When H.R. 7152 reached the House floor, the opening speech in support of its passage was delivered by Representative Celler, Chairman of the House Judiciary Committee and the Congressman responsible for introducing the legislation. A portion of that speech responded to criticism "seriously misrepresent[ing] what the bill would do and grossly distort[ing] its effects":

> "[T]he charge has been made that the Equal Employment Opportunity Commission to be established by title VII of the bill would have the power to prevent a business from employing and promoting the people it wished, and that a 'Federal inspector' could then order the hiring and promotion only of employees of certain races or religious groups. This description of the bill is entirely wrong . . . .
>
> "Even [a] court could not order that any preference be given to any particular race, religion or other group, but would be limited to ordering an end of discrimination. The statement that a Federal inspector could order the employment and promotion only of members of a specific racial or religious group is therefore patently erroneous. . . .

". . . The Bill would do no more than prevent . . . employers from discriminating against *or in favor* of workers because of their race, religion, or national origin.

"It is likewise not true that the Equal Employment Opportunity Commission would have power to rectify existing 'racial or religious imbalance' in employment by requiring the hiring of certain people without regard to their qualifications simply because they are of a given race or religion. Only actual discrimination could be stopped." 110 *Cong. Rec.* 1518 (1964) (emphasis added).

Representative Celler's construction of Title VII was repeated by several other supporters during the House debate.[11]

---

[11] Representative Lindsay had this to say:

"This legislation . . . does not, as has been suggested heretofore both on and off the floor, force acceptance of people in . . . jobs . . . because they are Negro. It does not impose quotas or any special privileges of seniority or acceptance. There is nothing whatever in this bill about racial balance as appears so frequently in the minority report of the Committee.

"What the bill does do is prohibit discrimination because of race . . . ." 110 *Cong. Rec.* 1540 (1964).

Representative Minish added: "Under title VII, employment will be on the basis of merit, not of race. This means that no quota system will be set up, no one will be forced to hire incompetent help because of race or religion, and no one will be given a vested right to demand employment for certain jobs." *Id.*, at 1600. Representative Goodell, answering the charge that Title VII would be interpreted "to requir[e] a racial balance," *id.*, at 2557, responded: "There is nothing here as a matter of legislative history that would require racial balancing. . . . We are not talking about a union having to balance its membership or an employer having to balance a number of employees. There is no quota involved. It is a matter of an individual's rights having been violated, charges having been brought, investigation carried out, and conciliation having been attempted and then proof in court that there was discrimination and a denial of rights on the basis of race or color." *Id.*, at 2558. After H.R. 7152 had been passed and sent to the Senate, Republican supporters of the bill in the House prepared an interpretative memorandum making clear that "title VII *does not permit* the ordering of racial quotas in business or unions and does not permit interferences with seniority rights of employees or union members." *Id.*, at 6566 (emphasis added).

Thus, the battle lines were drawn early in the legislative struggle over Title VII, with opponents of the measure charging that agencies of the federal government such as the Equal Employment Opportunity Commission (EEOC), by interpreting the word "discrimination" to mean the existence of "racial imbalance," would "require" employers to grant preferential treatment to minorities, and supporters responding that the EEOC would be granted no such power and that, indeed, Title VII prohibits discrimination "in favor of workers because of their race." Supporters of H.R. 7152 in the House ultimately prevailed by a vote of 290 to 130, and the measure was sent to the Senate to begin what became the longest debate in that body's history.

B

The Senate debate was broken into three phases: the debate on sending the bill to Committee, the general debate on the bill prior to invocation of cloture, and the debate following cloture.

1

When debate on the motion to refer the bill to Committee opened, opponents of Title VII in the Senate immediately echoed the fears expressed by their counterparts in the House, as is demonstrated by the following colloquy between Senators Hill and Ervin:

"Mr. Ervin. I invite attention to . . . Section [703(a)] . . . .

"I ask the Senator from Alabama if the Commission could not tell an employer that he had too few employees, that he had limited his employment, and enter an order, under [Section 703(a)], requiring him to hire more persons, not because the employer thought he needed more persons, but because the Commission wanted to compel him to employ persons of a particular race.

"Mr. Hill. The Senator is correct. That power is written into the bill. The employer could be forced to hire additional persons . . . ." 110 *Cong. Rec.* 4764 (1964).

Senator Humphrey, perhaps the primary moving force behind H.R. 7152 in the Senate, was the first to state the proponents' understanding of Title VII. Responding to a political advertisement charging that federal agencies were at liberty to interpret the word "discrimination" in Title VII to require racial balance, Senator Humphrey stated: "[T]he meaning of racial or religious discrimination is perfectly clear. . . . [I]t means a distinction and treatment given to different individuals because of their different race, religion, or national origin." *Id.*, at 5423. Stressing that Title VII "does not limit the employer's freedom to hire, fire, promote, or demote for any reasons—or no reasons—so long as his action is not based on race," Senator Humphrey further stated that "nothing in the bill would permit any official or court to require any employer or labor union to give preferential treatment to any minority group." *Ibid.* [12]

After 17 days of debate the Senate voted to take up the bill directly, without referring it to a committee. *Id.*, at 6455. Consequently, there is no Committee Report in the Senate.

---

[12] Earlier in the debate, Senator Humphrey had introduced a newspaper article quoting the answers of a Justice Department "expert" to the "ten most common objections to Title VII." Insofar as is pertinent here, the article stated:

"Objection: The law would empower Federal 'inspectors' to require employers to hire by race. White people would be fired to make room for Negroes. Seniority rights would be destroyed . . . .

"Reply: The bill requires no such thing. The five-member Equal Employment Opportunity Commission that would be created would have no powers to order anything . . . .

". . . The bill would not authorize anyone to order hiring or firing to achieve racial or religious balance. An employer will remain wholly free to hire on the basis of his needs and of the job candidate's qualifications. What is prohibited is the refusal to hire someone because of his race or religion. Similarly, the law will have no effect on union seniority rights." 110 *Cong. Rec.* 5094 (1964).

2

Formal debate on the merits of H.R. 7152 began on March 30, 1964. Supporters of the bill in the Senate had made elaborate preparations for this second round. Senator Humphrey, the Majority Whip, and Senator Kuchel, the Minority Whip, were selected as the bipartisan floor managers on the entire civil rights bill. Responsibility for explaining and defending each important title of the bill was placed on bipartisan "captains." Senators Clark and Case were selected as the bipartisan captains responsible for Title VII. Vass, Title VII: Legislative History, 7 *B. C. Indus. & Com. L. Rev.* 431, 444–445 (1966) (hereinafter Title VII: Legislative History).

In the opening speech of the formal Senate debate on the bill, Senator Humphrey addressed the main concern of Title VII's opponents, advising that not only does Title VII not require use of racial quotas, *it does not permit* their use. "The truth," stated the floor leader of the bill, "is that this title forbids discriminating against anyone on account of race. This is the simple and complete truth about title VII." 110 *Cong. Rec.* 6549 (1964). Senator Humphrey continued:

"Contrary to the allegations of some opponents of this title, there is nothing in it that will give any power to the Commission or to any courts to require hiring, firing, or promotion of employees in order to meet a racial 'quota' or to achieve a certain racial balance.

"That bugaboo has been brought up a dozen times; but it is nonexistent. In fact, *the very opposite is true. Title VII prohibits discrimination.* In effect, it says that race, religion, and national origin are not to be used as the basis for hiring and firing. Title VII is designed to encourage hiring on the basis of ability and qualifications, not race or religion." *Ibid.* (emphasis added).

At the close of his speech, Senator Humphrey returned briefly to the subject of employment quotas: "It is claimed that the bill would require racial quotas for all hiring, when in fact it provides that race shall not be a basis for making personnel decisions." *Id.*, at 6553.

Senator Kuchel delivered the second major speech in support of H.R. 7152. In addressing the concerns of the opposition, he observed that "[n]othing could be further from the truth" than the charge that "Federal inspectors" would be empowered under Title VII to dictate racial balance and preferential advancement of minorities. *Id.*, at 6563. Senator Kuchel emphasized that seniority rights would in no way be affected by Title VII: "Employers and labor organizations could not discriminate *in favor of or against* a person because of his race, his religion, or his national origin. In such matters . . . the bill now before us . . . is color-blind." *Id.*, at 6564 (emphasis added).

A few days later the Senate's attention focused exclusively on Title VII, as Senators Clark and Case rose to discuss the title of H.R. 7152 on which they shared floor "captain" responsibilities. In an interpretative memorandum submitted jointly to the Senate, Senators Clark and Case took pains to refute the opposition's charge that Title VII would result in preferential treatment of minorities. Their words were clear and unequivocal:

> "There is no requirement in title VII that an employer maintain a racial balance in his work force. On the contrary, any deliberate attempt to maintain a racial balance, whatever such a balance may be, would involve a violation of title VII because maintaining such a balance would require an employer to hire or to refuse to hire on the basis of race. It must be emphasized that discrimination is prohibited as to any individual." *Id.*, at 7213.[13]

Of particular relevance to the instant case were their observations regarding seniority rights. As if directing their comments at Brian Weber, the Senators said:

> "Title VII would have no effect on established seniority rights. Its effect is prospective and not retrospective. Thus, for example, if a business has been discriminating in the past and as a result has an all-white working force, when the title comes into effect the employer's obligation would be simply to fill future vacancies on a nondiscriminatory basis. He would not be obliged—*or indeed permitted*—to fire whites in order to hire Negroes, *or to prefer Negroes for future vacancies, or, once Negroes are hired, to give them special seniority rights at the expense of the white workers hired earlier.*" *Ibid.* (emphasis added).[14]

[13] In obvious reference to the charge that the word "discrimination" in Title VII would be interpreted by federal agencies to mean the absence of racial balance, the interpretative memorandum stated:

"[Section 703] prohibits discrimination in employment because of race, color, religion, sex, or national origin. It has been suggested that the concept of discrimination is vague. In fact it is clear and simple and has no hidden meanings. To discriminate is to make a distinction, to make a difference in treatment *or favor,* and those distinctions or differences in treatment *or favor* which are prohibited by [Section 703] are those which are based on any five of the forbidden criteria: race, color, religion, sex, or national origin." 110 *Cong. Rec.* 7213 (1964) (emphasis added).

Earlier in his speech, Senator Clark introduced a memorandum prepared at his request by the Justice Department with the purpose of responding to criticisms of Title VII leveled by opponents of the measure, particularly Senator Hill. With regard to racial balance, the Justice Department stated:

"Finally, it has been asserted that title VII would impose a requirement for 'racial balance.' This is incorrect. There is no provision . . . in title VII . . . that requires or authorizes any Federal agency or Federal court to require preferential treatment for any individual or any group for the purpose of achieving racial balance. . . . No employer is required to maintain any ratio of Negroes to whites. . . . On the contrary, any deliberate attempt to maintain a given balance would almost certainly run afoul of title VII because it would involve a failure or refusal to hire some individual because of his race, color, religion, sex, or national origin. What title VII seeks to accomplish, what the civil rights bill seeks to accomplish is equal treatment for all." *Id.*, at 7207.

[14] A Justice Department memorandum earlier introduced by Senator Clark, see n. 13, *supra,* expressed the same view regarding Title VII's impact on seniority rights of employees:

"Title VII would have no effect on seniority rights existing at the time it takes effect. . . . This would be

Thus with virtual clairvoyance the Senate's leading supporters of Title VII anticipated precisely the circumstances of this case and advised their colleagues that the type of minority preference employed by Kaiser would violate Title VII's ban on racial discrimination. To further accentuate the point, Senator Clark introduced

> true even in the case where owing to discrimination prior to the effective date of the title, white workers had more seniority than Negroes. . . . [A]ssuming that seniority rights were built up over a period of time during which Negroes were not hired, these rights would not be set aside by the taking effect of title VII. Employers and labor organizations would simply be under a duty not to discriminate against Negroes because of their race." 110 *Cong. Rec.* 7207 (1964).

The interpretation of Title VII contained in the memoranda introduced by Senator Clark totally refutes the Court's implied suggestion that Title VII would prohibit an employer from discriminating on the basis of race in order to *maintain* a racial balance in his work force, but would permit him to do so in order to *achieve* racial balance. See *ante*, . . .

The maintain-achieve distinction is analytically indefensible in any event. Apparently, the Court is saying that an employer is free to *achieve* a racially balanced work force by discriminating against whites, but that once he has reached his goal, he is no longer free to discriminate in order to maintain that racial balance. In other words, once Kaiser reaches its goal of 39% minority representation in craft positions at the Gramercy plant, it can no longer consider race in admitting employees into its on-the-job training programs, even if the programs become as "all-white" as they were in April 1974.

Obviously, the Court is driven to this illogical position by the glaring statement, quoted in text, of Senators Clark and Case that "any deliberate attempt to *maintain* a racial balance . . . would involve a violation of Title VII because *maintaining* such a balance would require an employer to hire or to refuse to hire on the basis of race." 110 *Cong. Rec.* 7123 (1964) (emphasis added). Achieving a certain racial balance, however, no less than maintaining such a balance, would require an employer to hire or to refuse to hire on the basis of race. Further, the Court's own conclusion that Title VII's legislative history, coupled with the wording of § 703(j), evinces a congressional intent to leave employers free to employ "private, voluntary, race-conscious affirmative action plans," *ante*, . . . , is inconsistent with its maintain-achieve distinction. If Congress' primary purpose in enacting Title VII was to open employment opportunities previously closed to Negroes, it would seem to make little difference whether the employer opening those opportunities was achieving or maintaining a certain racial balance in his work force. Likewise, if § 703(j) evinces Congress' intent to permit imposition of race-conscious affirmative action plans, it would seem to make little difference whether the plan was adopted to achieve or maintain the desired racial balance.

another memorandum dealing with common criticisms of the bill, including the charge that racial quotas would be imposed under Title VII. The answer was simple and to the point: "Quotas are themselves discriminatory." *Id.*, at 7218.

Despite these clear statements from the bill's leading and most knowledgeable proponents, the fears of the opponents were not put to rest. Senator Robertson reiterated the view that "discrimination" could be interpreted by a federal "bureaucrat" to require hiring quotas. *Id.*, at 7418–7420. Senators Smathers and Sparkman, while conceding that Title VII does not in so many words require the use of hiring quotas, repeated the opposition's view that employers would be coerced to grant preferential hiring treatment to minorities by agencies of the Federal Government. Senator Williams was quick to respond:

> "Those opposed to H.R. 7152 should realize that to hire a Negro solely because he is a Negro is racial discrimination, just as much as a 'white only' employment policy. Both forms of discrimination are prohibited by title VII of this bill. The language of that title simply states that race is not a qualification for employment. . . . Some people charge that H.R. 7152 favors the Negro, at the expense of the white majority. But how can the language of equality favor one race or one religion over another? Equality can have only one meaning, and that meaning is self-evident to reasonable men. Those who say that equality means favoritism do violence to common sense." *Id.*, at 8921.

Senator Williams concluded his remarks by noting that Title VII's only purpose is "the elimination of racial and religious discrimination in employment." *Ibid.*[15] On May 25, Senator

---

[15] Several other proponents of H.R. 7152 commented briefly on Title VII, observing that it did not authorize the imposition of quotas to correct racial imbalance. See 110 *Cong. Rec.* 9113 (1964) (remarks of Sen. Keating), *id.*, at 9881–9882 (remarks of Sen. Allott), *id.*, at 10520 (remarks of Sen. Carlson), *id.*, at 11768 (remarks of Sen. McGovern).

Humphrey again took the floor to defend the bill against "the well-financed drive by certain opponents to confuse and mislead the American people." *Id.*, at 11846. Turning once again to the issue of preferential treatment. Senator Humphrey remained faithful to the view that he had repeatedly expressed:

> "The title does not provide that any preferential treatment in employment shall be given to Negroes or to any other persons or groups. It does not provide that any quota systems may be established to maintain racial balance in employment. In fact, *the title would prohibit preferential treatment for any particular group*, and any person, whether or not a member of any minority group, would be permitted to file a complaint of discriminatory employment practices." *Id.*, at 11848 (emphasis added).

While the debate in the Senate raged, a bipartisan coalition under the leadership of Senators Dirksen, Mansfield, Humphrey, and Kuchel was working with House leaders and representatives of the Johnson Administration on a number of amendments to H.R. 7152 designed to enhance its prospects of passage. The so-called "Dirksen-Mansfield" amendment was introduced on May 26 by Senator Dirksen as a substitute for the entire House-passed bill. The substitute bill, which ultimately became law, left unchanged the basis prohibitory language of §§ 703(a) and (d), as well as the remedial provisions in § 706(g). It added, however, several provisions defining and clarifying the scope of Title VII's substantive prohibitions. One of those clarifying amendments, § 703(j), was specifically directed at the opposition's concerns regarding racial balancing and preferential treatment of minorities, providing in pertinent part: "Nothing contained in [Title VII] shall be interpreted to require any employer . . . to grant preferential treatment to any individual or to any group because of the race . . . of such individual or group on account of" a racial imbalance in the employer's work force. 42 U.S.C. § 2000e–2(j); quoted in full, at n. 8, *supra*.

The Court draws from the language of § 703(j) primary support for its conclusion that Title VII's blanket prohibition on racial discrimination in employment does not prohibit preferential treatment of blacks to correct racial imbalance. Alleging that opponents of Title VII had argued (1) that the act would be interpreted to require employers with racially imbalanced work forces to grant preferential treatment to minorities and (2) that "employers with racially imbalanced work forces would grant preferential treatment to racial minorities, even if not required to do so by the Act," *ante*, . . . , the Court concludes that § 703(j) is responsive only to the opponents' first objection and that Congress therefore must have intended to permit voluntary, private discrimination against whites in order to correct racial imbalance.

Contrary to the Court's analysis, the language of § 703(j) is precisely tailored to the objection voiced time and again by Title VII's opponents. Not once during the 83 days of debate in the Senate did a speaker, proponent or opponent, suggest that the bill would allow employers *voluntarily* to prefer racial minorities over white persons.[16] In light of Title VII's flat prohibition on discrimination "against any individual . . .

[16] The Court cites the remarks of Senator Sparkman in support of its suggestion that opponents had argued that employers would take it upon themselves to balance their work forces by granting preferential treatment to racial minorities. In fact, Senator Sparkman's comments accurately reflected the opposition's "party line." He argued that while the language of Title VII does not expressly require imposition of racial quotas (no one, of course, had ever argued to the contrary), the law would be applied by federal agencies in such a way that "some kind of quota system will be used." 110 *Cong. Rec.* 8619 (1964). Senator Sparkman's view is reflected in the following exchange with Senator Stennis:

> "Mr. Sparkman. At any rate, when the Government agent came to interview an employer who had 100 persons in his employ, the first question would be, 'How many Negroes are you employing?' Suppose the population of that area was 20 percent Negro. Immediately the agent would say, 'You should have at least 20 Negroes in your employ, and they should be distributed among your supervisory personnel and in all the other categories': and the agent would *insist* that that be done immediately. . . .
> "Mr. Stennis. . . .
> "The Senator from Alabama has made very clear

because of such individual's race," § 703(a), 42 U.S.C. § 2000e–2(a), such a contention would have been, in any event, too preposterous to warrant response. Indeed, speakers on both sides of the issue, as the legislative history makes clear, recognized that Title VII would tolerate no *voluntary* racial preference, whether in favor of blacks or whites. The complaint consistently voiced by the opponents was that Title VII, particularly the word "discrimination," would be *interpreted* by federal agencies such as the Equal Employment Opportunity Commission to *require* the correction of racial imbalance through the granting of preferential treatment to minorities. Verbal assurances that Title VII would not require—indeed, would not permit—preferential treatment of blacks having failed, supporters of H.R. 7152 responded by proposing an amendment carefully worded to meet, and put to rest, the opposition's charge. Indeed, unlike §§ 703(a) and (d), which are by their terms directed at entities—*e.g.*, employers, labor unions—whose actions are restricted by Title VII's prohibitions, the language of § 703(j) is specifically directed at entities—federal agencies and courts—charged with the responsibility of interpreting Title VII's provisions.[17]

In light of the background and purpose of

§ 703(j), the irony of invoking the section to justify the result in this case is obvious. The Court's frequent references to the "voluntary" nature of Kaiser's racially discriminatory admission quota bear no relationship to the facts of this case. Kaiser and the Steelworkers acted under pressure from an agency of the Federal Government, the Office of Federal Contract Compliance, which found that minorities were being "underutilized" at Kaiser's plants. . . . That is, Kaiser's work force was racially imbalanced. Bowing to that pressure, Kaiser instituted an admissions quota preferring blacks over whites, thus confirming that the fears of Title VII's opponents were well founded. Today § 703(j), adopted to allay those fears, is invoked by the Court to uphold imposition of a racial quota under the very circumstances that the section was intended to prevent.[18]

Section 703(j) apparently calmed the fears of most of the opponents; after its introduction complaints concerning racial balance and preferential treatment died down considerably.

---

his point about employment on the quota basis. Would not the same basis be applied to promotions?

"Mr. Sparkman. Certainly it would. As I have said, when the Federal agents came to check on the situation in a small business which had 100 employees, and when the agents said to the employer, 'You must hire 20 Negroes, and some of them must be employed in supervisory capacities,' and so forth, and so on, the agent would also say, 'And you must promote the Negroes, too, in order to distribute them evenly among the various ranks of your employees.' " *Id.*, at 8618 (emphasis added).

Later in his remarks, Senator Sparkman stated: "Certainly the suggestion will be made to a small business that may have a small government contract . . . that if it does not carry out the suggestion that has been made to the company by an inspector, its Government contract will not be renewed." *Ibid.* Except for the size of the business, Senator Sparkman has seen his prophecy fulfilled in this case.

[17] Compare § 703(a), 42 U.S.C. § 2000e–2(a) ("It shall be an unlawful employment practice for an employer . . . .") with § 703(j), 42 U.S.C. § 2000e–2(j) ("Nothing contained in this subchapter shall be interpreted . . . .").

[18] In support of its reading of § 703(j), the Court argues that "a prohibition against all voluntary, race-conscious, affirmative action efforts would disserve" the important policy, expressed in the House Report on H.R. 7152, that Title VII leave "management prerogatives and union freedoms . . . undisturbed to the greatest extent possible." H. R. Rep., Part II, at 29 . . . . The Court thus concludes that "Congress did not intend to limit traditional business freedom to such a degree as to prohibit all voluntary, race-conscious affirmative action." *Ante*, . . .

The sentences in the House Report immediately following the statement quoted by the Court, however, belie the Court's conclusion:

"Internal affairs of employers and labor organizations must not be interfered with *except to the limited extent that correction is required in discrimination practices.* Its primary task is to make certain that the channels of employment are open to persons *regardless of their race* and that jobs in companies or membership in unions are strictly filled on the basis of qualification." H.R. Rep., Part II, at 29 (emphasis added).

Thus, the House Report invoked by the Court is perfectly consistent with the countless observations elsewhere in Title VII's voluminous legislative history that employers are free to make employment decisions without governmental interference, so long as those decisions are made *without regard to race.* The whole purpose of Title VII was to deprive employers of their "traditional business freedom" to discriminate on the basis of race. In this case, the "channels of employment" at Kaiser were hardly "open" to Brian Weber.

Proponents of the bill, however, continued to reassure the opposition that its concerns were unfounded. In a lengthy defense of the entire civil rights bill, Senator Muskie emphasized that the opposition's "torrent of words . . . cannot obscure this basic, simple truth: Every American citizen has the right to equal treatment—not favored treatment, not complete individual equality—just equal treatment." 110 *Cong. Rec.* 12614 (1964). With particular reference to Title VII, Senator Muskie noted that the measure "seeks to afford to all Americans equal opportunity in employment without discrimination. Not equal pay, not 'racial balance.' Only equal opportunity." *Id.*, at 12617.

Senator Saltonstall, Chairman of the Republican Conference of Senators participating in the drafting of the Dirksen-Mansfield amendment, spoke at length on the substitute bill. He advised the Senate that the Dirksen-Mansfield substitute, which included § 703(j), "provides no preferential treatment for any group of citizens. In fact, *it specifically prohibits such treatment.*" *Id.*, at 12691 (emphasis added).[19]

On June 9, Senator Ervin offered an amendment that would entirely delete Title VII from the bill. In answer to Senator Ervin's contention that Title VII "would make the members of a particular race special favorites of the laws," *id.*, at 13079, Senator Clark retorted:

> "The bill does not make anyone higher than anyone else. It establishes no quotas.

It leaves an employer free to select whomever he wishes to employ. . . .

"All this is subject to one qualification, and that qualification, is to state: 'In your activity as an employer . . . you must not discriminate because of the color of a man's skin. . . .

"That is all this provision does. . . . It merely says, "When you deal in interstate commerce, you must not discriminate on the basis of race . . . .'" *Id.*, at 13080.

The Ervin amendment was defeated, and the Senate turned its attention to an amendment proposed by Senator Cotton to limit application of Title VII to employers of at least 100 employees. During the course of the Senate's deliberations on the amendment, Senator Cotton had a revealing discussion with Senator Curtis, also an opponent of Title VII. Both men expressed dismay that Title VII would prohibit preferential hiring of "members of a minority race in order to enhance their opportunity":

> "Mr. Curtis. Is it not the opinion of the Senator that any individuals who provide jobs for a class of people who have perhaps not had sufficient opportunity for jobs should be commended rather than outlawed?
>
> "Mr. Cotton. Indeed it is." *Id.*, at 13086.

Thus in the only exchange on the Senate floor raising the possibility that an employer might wish to reserve jobs for minorities in order to assist them in overcoming their employment disadvantage, both speakers concluded that Title VII prohibits such, in the words of the Court, "voluntary, private, race-conscious efforts to abolish traditional patterns of racial segregation and hierarchy." *Ante,* . . . Immediately after this discussion, both Senator Dirksen and Senator Humphrey took the floor in defense of the 25-employee limit contained in the Dirksen-Mansfield substitute bill, and neither Senator disputed the conclusions of Senators Cotton and Curtis. The Cotton amendment was defeated.

---

[19] The Court states that congressional comments regarding § 703(j) "were all to the effect that employers would not be *required* to institute preferential quotas to avoid Title VII liability." *Ante* . . . (emphasis in original). Senator Saltenstall's statement that Title VII of the Dirksen-Mansfield substitute, which contained § 703(j), "specifically prohibits" preferential treatment for any racial group disproves the Court's observation. Further, in a major statement explaining the purpose of the Dirksen-Mansfield substitute amendments, Senator Humphrey said of § 703(j): "This subsection does not represent any change in the substance of the title. It does state clearly and accurately what we have mentioned all along about the bill's intent and meaning." 110 *Cong. Rec.* 12723 (1964). What Senator Humphrey had "mentioned all along about the bill's intent and meaning," was that it neither required *nor permitted* imposition of preferential quotas to eliminate racial imbalances.

3

On June 10 the Senate, for the second time in its history, imposed cloture on its members. The limited debate that followed centered on proposed amendments to the Dirksen-Mansfield substitute. Of some 24 proposed amendments, only 5 were adopted.

As the civil rights bill approached its final vote, several supporters rose to urge its passage. Senator Muskie adverted briefly to the issue of preferential treatment: "It has been said that the bill discriminates in favor of the Negro at the expense of the rest of us. It seeks to do nothing more than to lift the Negro from the status of inequality to one of *equality* of treatment." 110 *Cong. Rec.* 14328 (1964) (emphasis added). Senator Moss, in a speech delivered on the day that the civil rights bill was finally passed, had this to say about quotas:

> "The bill does not accord to any citizen advantage or preference—it does not fix quotas of employment or school population—it does not force personal association. What it does is to prohibit public officials and those who invite the public generally to patronize their businesses or to apply for employment, to utilize the offensive, humiliating, and cruel practice of discrimination on the basis of race. In short, the bill does not accord special consideration; it establishes *equality*." *Id.*, at 14484 (emphasis added).

Later that day, June 19, the issue was put to a vote, and the Dirksen-Mansfield substitute bill was passed.

C

The Act's return engagement in the House was brief. The House Committee on Rules reported the Senate version without amendments on June 30, 1964. By a vote of 289 to 126, the House adopted House Resolution 789, thus agreeing to the Senate's amendments of H.R. 7152.[20] Later that same day, July 2, the President signed the bill and the Civil Rights Act of 1964 became law.

IV.

Reading the language of Title VII, as the Court purports to do, "against the background of [its] legislative history . . . and the historical context from which the Act arose," *ante*, . . . , one is led inescapably to the conclusion that Congress fully understood what it was saying and meant precisely what it said. Opponents of the civil rights bill did not argue that employers would be permitted under Title VII voluntarily to grant preferential treatment to minorities to correct racial imbalance. The plain language of the statute too clearly prohibited such racial discrimination to admit of any doubt. They argued, tirelessly, that Title VII would be interpreted by federal agencies and their agents to require unwilling employers to racially balance their work forces by granting preferential treatment to minorities. Supporters of H.R. 7152 responded, equally tirelessly, that the Act would not be so interpreted because not only does it not require preferential treatment of minorities, it does not *permit* preferential treatment of minorities, it does not *permit* preferential treatment of any race for any reason. It cannot be doubted that the proponents of Title VII understood the meaning of their words, for "[s]eldom has similar legislation been debated

---

[20] Only three Congressmen spoke to the issue of racial quotas during the House's debate on the Senate amendments. Representative Lindsay stated: "[W]e wish to emphasize that this bill does not require quotas, racial balance, or any of the other things that the opponents have been saying about it." 110 *Cong. Rec.* 15876 (1964). Representative McCollugh echoed this understanding, remarking that "[t]he bill does not permit the Federal Government to require an employer or union to hire or accept for membership a quota for persons from a particular minority group." *Id.*, at 15893. The remarks of Representative MacGregor, quoted by the Court, *ante*, . . . , are singularly unhelpful. He merely noted that by adding § 703(j) to Title VII of the House bill, "[t]he Senate . . . spelled out [the House's] intentions more specifically." *Id.*, at 15893.

with greater consciousness for the need for 'legislative history' or with greater care in the making thereof, to guide the courts in interpreting and applying the law." Title VII: Legislative History, at 444.

To put an end to the dispute, supporters of the civil rights bill drafted and introduced § 703(j). Specifically addressed to the opposition's charge, § 703(j) simply enjoins federal agencies and courts from interpreting Title VII to require an employer to prefer certain racial groups to correct imbalances in his work force. The section says nothing about voluntary preferential treatment of minorities because such racial discrimination is plainly proscribed by §§ 703(a) and (d). Indeed, had Congress intended to except voluntary, race-conscious preferential treatment from the blanket prohibition on racial discrimination in §§ 703(a) and (d), it surely could have drafted language better suited to the task than § 703(j). It knew how. Section 703(i) provides:

"Nothing contained in [title VII] shall apply to any business or enterprise on or near an Indian reservation with respect to any publicly announced employment practice of such business or enterprise under which a preferential treatment is given to any individual because he is an Indian living on or near a reservation." § 703(i), 42 U.S.C. § 2000e–2(i).

V.

Our task in this case, like any other case involving the construction of a statute, is to give effect to the intent of Congress. To divine that intent, we traditionally look first to the words of the statute and, if they are unclear, then to the statute's legislative history. Finding the desired result hopelessly foreclosed by these conventional sources, the Court turns to a third source—the "spirit" of the Act. But close examination of what the Court proffers as the spirit of

the Act reveals it as the spirit animating the present majority, not the Eighty-eight Congress. For if the spirit of the Act eludes the cold words of the statute itself, it rings out with unmistakable clarity in the words of the elected representatives who made the Act law. It is *equality*. Senator Dirksen, I think, captured that spirit in a speech delivered on the floor of the Senate just moments before the bill was passed:

"[T]oday we come to grips finally with a bill that advances the enjoyment of living; but, more than that, it advances the equality of opportunity.

"I do not emphasize the word 'equality' standing by itself. It means equality of opportunity in the field of education. It means equality of opportunity in the field of employment. It means equality of opportunity in the field of participation in the affairs of government . . . .

"That is it.

"Equality of opportunity, if we are going to talk about conscience, is the mass conscience of mankind that speaks in every generation, and it will continue to speak long after we are dead and gone." 110 *Cong. Rec.* 14510 (1964).

There is perhaps no device more destructive to the notion of equality than the *numerus clausus*—the quota. Whether described as "benign discrimination" or "affirmative action," the racial quota is nonetheless a creator of castes, a two-edged sword that must demean one in order to prefer another. In passing Title VII Congress outlawed *all* racial discrimination, recognizing that no discrimination based on race is benign, that no action disadvantaging a person because of his color is affirmative. With today's holding, the Court introduces into Title VII a tolerance for the very evil that the law was intended to eradicate, without offering even a clue as to what the limits on that tolerance may be. We are told simply that Kaiser's racially discriminatory admission quota "falls on the permissible side of the line." *Ante*, . . . By going not merely *beyond*, but directly *against* Title VII's language and legislative history, the Court has sown the wind. Later courts will face the impossible task of reaping the whirlwind.

Quaere: Would it have been politically possible in 1964—or even in 1979—for Congress to enact the *Weber* version of Title VII? Is *Weber* another classic example of the Miller-Howell conception of the judicial function? (See Chapter 1, above.)

Does Title VII *as interpreted* in *Weber* raise a "federal action" problem? That is, does it "invalidly involve the [federal government] in racial discrimination in the [private employment] market" by "encouraging" private racism? (See *Reitman* v. *Mulkey*, below, Chapter 10). A response to this question must recognize, among other things, that Title VII as interpreted in *Weber* shields antiwhite job discrimination from state and local antidiscrimination laws.

Does *Weber* silently overrule *Reitman*? If so, why silently?

Note: The Brennan group of four in *Bakke* had the upper hand in *Weber*, since two of their *Bakke* opponents (Justices Powell and Stevens) did not participate in the *Weber* decision (the one apparently because of illness, the other because his former law firm had served one of the parties). Thus, going into *Weber,* the Brennan minority that supported racial quotas and racial preferences in *Bakke* had a four to three hold on a Court that had rejected these views in *Bakke*. The Brennan group became a majority of five because of a silent "shift" by Mr. Justice Stewart. In *Bakke* he found that the antidiscrimination language of Title VI outlawed racial quotas and preferences—in *Weber* he found that similar language in Title VII did not. Thus, as Mr. Justice Stewart saw it, Congress, in the great Civil Rights Act of 1964, rejected racial quotas and racial preferences in Title VI and embraced them in Title VII, though there is no significant difference in the antidiscrimination language of the two provisions. Assuming that Justices Powell and Stevens still mean what they seemed to say in *Bakke, eight* of the justices reject this bifurcated interpretation of the 1964 act. For these eight it is all fish or all fowl—though they are divided four to four on which it should be.

GENDER CLASSIFICATIONS

Muller v. *Oregon*
See p. 215, above.

Adkins v. *Children's Hospital*
See p. 217, above.

Goesaert v. *Cleary*
335 U.S. 464 (1948)

A Michigan law provided that no woman could obtain a bartender's license unless she was "the wife or daughter of the male owner" of a licensed liquor establishment. (This case should be read in conjunction with *Railway Express Agency*, above.)

Mr. Justice Frankfurter delivered the opinion of the Court. . . .

We are, to be sure, dealing with a historic calling. We meet the alewife, sprightly and ribald, in Shakespeare, but centuries before him she played a role in the social life of England. See, e.g., Jusserand, *English Wayfaring Life*, 133, 134, 136–37 (1889). The Fourteenth Amendment did not tear history up by the roots, and the regulation of the liquor traffic is one of the oldest and most untrammeled of legislative powers. Michigan could, beyond question, forbid all women from working behind a bar. This is so despite the vast changes in the social and legal position of women. The fact that women may now have achieved the virtues that men have long claimed as their prerogatives and now indulge in vices that men have long practiced, does not preclude the States from drawing a sharp line between the sexes, certainly, in such matters as the regulation of the liquor traffic. See the Twenty-First Amendment and *Carter* v. *Virginia*, 321 U.S. 131. The Constitution does not require legislatures to reflect sociological insight, or shifting social standards, any more than it requires them to keep abreast of the latest scientific standards.

While Michigan may deny to all women opportunities for bartending, Michigan cannot play favorites among women without rhyme or reason. The Constitution in enjoining the equal protection of the laws upon States precludes irrational discrimination as between persons or groups of persons in the incidence of a law. But the Constitution does not require situations "which are different in fact or opinion to be treated in law as though they were the same." *Tigner* v. *State of Texas*, 310 U.S. 141, 147. Since bartending by women may, in the allowable legislative judgment, give rise to moral and social problems against which it may devise preventive measures, the legislature need not go to the full length of prohibition if it believes that as to a defined group of females other factors are operating which either eliminate or reduce the moral and social problems otherwise calling for prohibition. Michigan evidently believes that the oversight assured through ownership of a bar by a barmaid's husband or father minimizes hazards that may confront a barmaid without such protecting oversight. This Court is certainly not in a position to gainsay such belief by the Michigan legislature. If it is entertainable, as we think it is, Michigan has not violated its duty to afford equal protection of its laws. We cannot cross-examine either actually or argumentatively the mind of Michigan legislatures nor question their motives. Since the line they have drawn is not without a basis in reason, we cannot give ear to the suggestion that the real impulse behind this legislature was an unchivalrous desire of male bartenders to try to monopolize the calling. . . .

Judgment affirmed.

Mr. Justice Rutledge, with whom Mr. Justice Douglas and Mr. Justice Murphy join, dissenting.

While the equal protection clause does not require a legislature to achieve "abstract symmetry" or to classify with "mathematical nicety," that clause does require lawmakers to refrain from invidious distinctions of the sort drawn by the statute challenged in this case.

The statute arbitrarily discriminates between male and female owners of liquor establishments. A male owner, although he himself is always absent from his bar, may employ his wife and daughter as barmaids. A female owner may neither work as a barmaid herself nor employ her daughter in that position, even if a man is always present in the establishment to keep order. This inevitable result of the classification belies the assumption that the statute was motivated by a legislative solicitude for the moral and physical well-being of women who, but for the law, would be employed as barmaids. Since there could be no other conceivable justification for such discrimination against women owners of liquor establishments, the statute should be held invalid as a denial of equal protection.

Frontiero v. *Richardson*
411 U.S. 677 (1973)

Mr. Justice Brennan announced the judgment of the Court in an opinion in which Mr. Justice Douglas, Mr. Justice White, and Mr. Justice Marshall join.

The question before us concerns the right of a female member of the uniformed services to claim her spouse as a "dependent" for the purposes of obtaining increased quarters allowances and medical and dental benefits under 37 U.S.C. §§ 401, 403, and 10 U.S.C. §§ 1072, 1076, on an equal footing with male members. Under these statutes, a serviceman may claim his wife as a "dependent" without regard to whether she is in fact dependent upon him for any part of her support. 37 U.S.C. § 401(1); 10 U.S.C. § 1072(2)(A). A servicewoman, on the other hand, may not claim her husband as a "dependent" under these programs unless he is in fact dependent upon her for over one-half of his support. 37 U.S.C. § 401; 10 U.S.C. § 1072(2)(C). Thus, the question for decision is whether this difference in treatment constitutes an unconstitutional discrimination against servicewomen in violation of the Due Process Clause of the Fifth Amendment. A three-judge District Court for the Middle District of Alabama, one judge dissenting, rejected this contention and sustained the constitutionality of the provisions of the statutes making this distinction. 341 F.Supp. 201 (1972). We noted probable jurisdiction. 409 U.S. 840 (1972). We reverse.

I.

In an effort to attract career personnel through reenlistment, Congress established, in 37 U.S.C. § 401 et seq., and 10 U.S.C. § 1071 et seq., a scheme for the provision of fringe benefits to members of the uniformed services on a competitive basis with business and industry. Thus, under 37 U.S.C. § 403, a member of the uniformed services with dependents is entitled to an increased "basic allowance for quarters" and, under 10 U.S.C. § 1076, a member's dependents are provided comprehensive medical and dental care.

Appellant Sharron Frontiero, a lieutenant in the United States Air Force, sought increased quarters allowances, and housing and medical benefits for her husband, appellant Joseph Frontiero, on the ground that he was her "dependent." Although such benefits would automatically have been granted with respect to the wife of a male member of the uniformed services, appellant's application was denied because she failed to demonstrate that her husband was dependent on her for more than one-half of his support. Appellants then commenced this suit, contending that, by making this distinction, the statutes unreasonably discriminate on the basis of sex in violation of the Due Process Clause of the Fifth Amendment. In essence, appellants asserted that the discriminatory impact of the statutes is two-fold: first, as a procedural matter, a female member is required to demonstrate her spouse's dependency, while no such burden is imposed upon male members; and second, as a substantive matter, a male member who does not provide more than one-half of his wife's support receives benefits, while a similarly situated female member is denied such benefits. Appellants therefore sought a permanent injunction against the continued enforcement of these statutes and an order directing the appellees to provide Lieutenant Frontiero with the same housing and medical benefits that a similarly situated male member would receive.

Although the legislative history of these statutes sheds virtually no light on the purposes underlying the differential treatment accorded male and female members, a majority of the three judge District Court surmised that Congress might reasonably have concluded that, since the husband in our society is generally the "breadwinner" in the family—and the wife typically the "dependent" partner—"it would be more economical to require married female members claiming husbands to prove actual dependency than to extend the presumption of dependency to such members." 341 F.Supp., at 207. Indeed, given the fact that approximately 99% of all members of the uniformed services are male, the District Court speculated that such differential treatment might conceivably lead to a "considerable saving of administrative expense and manpower." *Ibid.*

II.

At the outset, appellants contend that classifications based upon sex, like classifications based upon race, alienage, and national origin, are inherently suspect and must therefore be subjected to close judicial scrutiny. We agree and, indeed, find at least implicit support for such an approach in our unanimous decision only last Term in *Reed* v. *Reed*, 404 U.S. 71 (1971).

In *Reed*, the Court considered the constitutionality of an Idaho statute providing that, when two individuals are otherwise equally entitled to appointment as administrator of an estate, the male applicant must be preferred to the female. Appellant, the mother of the deceased, and appellee, the father, filed competing petitions for appointment as administrator of their son's estate. Since the parties, as parents of the deceased, were members of the same entitlement class, the statutory preference was invoked and the father's petition was therefore granted. Appellant claimed that this statute, by giving a mandatory preference to males over females without regard to their individual qualifications, violated the Equal Protection Clause of the Fourteenth Amendment.

The Court noted that the Idaho statute "provides that different treatment be accorded to the

applicants on the basis of their sex; it thus establishes a classification subject to scrutiny under the Equal Protection Clause." Under "traditional" equal protection analysis, a legislative classification must be sustained unless it is "patently arbitrary" and bears no rational relationship to a legitimate governmental interest.

In an effort to meet this standard, appellee contended that the statutory scheme was a reasonable measure designed to reduce the workload on probate courts by eliminating one class of contests. Moreover, appellee argued that the mandatory preference for male applicants was in itself reasonable since "men [are] as a rule more conversant with business affairs than . . . women." Indeed, appellee maintained that "it is a matter of common knowledge, that women still are not engaged in politics, the professions, business or industry to the extent that men are." And the Idaho Supreme Court, in upholding the constitutionality of this statute, suggested that the Idaho Legislature might reasonably have "concluded that in general men are better qualified to act as an administrator than are women."

Despite these contentions, however, the Court held the statutory preference for male applicants unconstitutional. In reaching this result, the Court implicitly rejected appellee's apparently rational explanation of the statutory scheme, and concluded that, by ignoring the individual qualifications of particular applicants, the challenged statute provided "dissimilar treatment for men and women who are . . . similarly situated." The Court therefore held that, even though the State's interest in achieving administrative efficiency "is not without some legitimacy," "[t]o give a mandatory preference to members of either sex over members of the other, merely to accomplish the elimination of hearings on the merits, is to make the very kind of arbitrary legislative choice forbidden by the [Constitution] . . . ." This departure from "traditional" rational-basis analysis with respect to sex-based classifications is clearly justified.

There can be no doubt that our Nation has had a long and unfortunate history of sex discrimination. Traditionally, such discrimination was rationalized by an attitude of "romantic paternalism" which, in practical effect, put women not on a pedestal, but in a cage. Indeed, this paternalistic attitude became so firmly rooted in our national consciousness that, exactly 100 years ago, a distinguished member of this Court was able to proclaim:

> "Man is, or should be, woman's protector and defender. The natural and proper timidity and delicacy which belongs to the female sex evidently unfits it for many of the occupations of civil life. The constitution of the family organization, which is founded in the divine ordinance, as well as in the nature of things, indicates the domestic sphere as that which properly belongs to the domain and functions of womanhood. The harmony, not to say identity, of interests and views which belong, or should belong, to the family institution is repugnant to the ideas of a woman adopting a distinct and independent career from that of her husband. . . .
>
> ". . . The paramount destiny and mission of woman are to fulfil the noble and benign offices of wife and mother. This is the law of the Creator." *Bradwell* v. *Illinois*, 83 U.S. [16 Wall.] 130, 141 (1873) (Bradley, J., concurring).

As a result of notions such as these, our statute books gradually became laden with gross, stereotypical distinctions between the sexes and, indeed, throughout much of the 19th century the position of women in our society was, in many respects, comparable to that of blacks under the pre–Civil War slave codes. Neither slaves nor women could hold office, serve on juries, or bring suit in their own names, and married women traditionally were denied the legal capacity to hold or convey property or to serve as legal guardians of their own children. See generally, L. Kantowitz, *Women and the Law: The Unfinished Revolution* 5–6 (1969); G. Mydral, *An American Dilemma* 1073 (2d ed., 1962). And although blacks were guaranteed the right to vote in 1870, women were denied even that right—which is itself "preservative of other basic civil and political rights"—until adoption on the Nineteenth Amendment half a century later.

It is true, of course, that the position of women in America has improved markedly in recent decades. Nevertheless, it can hardly be doubted that, in part because of the high visibility of the sex characteristic, women still face pervasive, although at times more subtle, discrimination in our educational institutions, on the job market and, perhaps most conspicuously, in the political arena. See generally, K. Amundsen, *The Silenced Majority: Women and American Democracy* (1971); The President's Task Force on Women's Rights and Responsibilities, *A Matter of Simple Justice* (1970).

Moreover, since sex, like race and national origin, is an immutable characteristic determined solely by the accident of birth, the imposition of special disabilities upon the members of a particular sex because of their sex would seem to violate "the basic concept of our system that legal burdens should bear some relationship to individual responsibility . . . ." *Weber* v. *Aetna Casualty & Surety Co.*, 406 U.S. 164, 175 (1972). And what differentiates sex from such nonsuspect statuses as intelligence or physical disability, and aligns it with the recognized suspect criteria, is that the sex characteristic frequently bears no relation to ability to perform or contribute to society. As a result, statutory distinctions between the sexes often have the effect of invidiously relegating the entire class of females to inferior legal status without regard to the actual capabilities of its individual members.

We might also note that, over the past decade, Congress has itself manifested an increasing sensitivity to sex-based classifications. In Tit. VII of the Civil Rights Act of 1964, for example, Congress expressly declared that no employer, labor union, or other organization subject to the provisions of the Act shall discriminate against any individual on the basis of "race, color, religion, *sex*, or national origin." Similarly, the Equal Pay Act of 1963 provides that no employer covered by the Act "shall discriminate . . . between employees on the basis of sex." And § 1 of the Equal Rights Amendment, passed by Congress on March 22, 1972, and submitted to the legislatures of the States for ratification, declares that "[e]quality of rights under the law shall not be denied or abridged by the United States or by any State on account of sex." Thus, Congress has itself concluded that classifications based upon sex are inherently invidious, and this conclusion of a coequal branch of Government is not without significance to the question presently under consideration. . . .

With these considerations in mind, we can only conclude that classifications based upon sex, like classifications based upon race, alienage, or national origin, are inherently suspect, and must therefore be subjected to strict judicial scrutiny. Applying the analysis mandated by that stricter standard of review, it is clear that the statutory scheme now before us is constitutionally invalid.

III.

The sole basis of the classification established in the challenged statutes is the sex of the individuals involved. . . .

Moreover, the Government concedes that the differential treatment accorded men and women under these statutes serves no purpose other than mere "administrative convenience." In essence, the Government maintains that, as an empirical matter, wives in our society frequently are dependent upon their husbands, while husbands rarely are dependent upon their wives. Thus, the Government argues that Congress might reasonably have concluded that it would be both cheaper and easier simply conclusively to presume that wives of male members are financially dependent upon their husbands, while burdening female members with the task of establishing dependency in fact.

The Government offers no concrete evidence, however, tending to support its view that such differential treatment in fact saves the Government any money. In order to satisfy the demands of strict judicial scrutiny, the Government must demonstrate, for example, that it is actually cheaper to grant increased benefits with respect to *all* male members, than it is to determine which male members are in fact entitled to such benefits and to grant increased benefits only to those members whose wives actually meet the dependency requirement. Here, however, there is substantial evidence that, if put to the test, many of the wives of male members would fail to qualify for benefits. And in light of the fact that the dependency determination with respect to the husbands of female members is presently made solely on the basis of affidavits rather than through the more costly hearing process, the Government's explanation of the statutory scheme is, to say the least, questionable.

In any case, our prior decisions make clear that, although efficacious administration of governmental programs is not without some importance, "the Constitution recognizes higher values than speed and efficiency." *Stanley* v. *Illinois*, 405 U.S. 645, 656 (1972). And when we enter the realm of "strict judicial scrutiny," there can be no doubt that "administrative convenience" is not a shibboleth, the mere recitation of which dictates constitutionality. See *Shapiro* v. *Thompson*, 394 U.S. 618 (1969); *Carrington* v. *Rash*, 380 U.S. 89 (1965). On the contrary, any statutory scheme which draws a sharp line between the sexes, *solely* for the purpose of achieving administrative convenience, necessarily commands "dissimilar treatment for men and women who are . . . similarly situated," and therefore involves the "very kind of arbitrary legislative choice forbidden by the [Constitution] . . . ." *Reed* v. *Reed*, 404 U.S., *supra*, at 77, 76. We therefore conclude that, by according differential treatment to male and female members of the uniformed services for the sole purpose of achieving administrative convenience, the challenged statutes violate the Due Process Clause of the Fifth Amendment insofar as they require a female member to prove the dependency of her husband. . . .

Mr. Justice Stewart concurs in the judgment, agreeing that the statutes before us work an invidious discrimination in violation of the Constitution. *Reed* v. *Reed*, 404 U.S. 71.

Mr. Justice Rehnquist dissents for the reasons stated by Judge Rives in his opinion for the District Court, *Frontiero* v. *Laird*, 341 F.Supp. 201 (1972).

Mr. Justice Powell, with whom The Chief Justice and Mr. Justice Blackmun join, concurring in the judgment.

I agree that the challenged statutes constitute an unconstitutional discrimination against service women in violation of the Due Process Clause of the Fifth Amendment, but I cannot join the opinion of Mr. Justice Brennan, which would hold that all classifications based upon sex, "like classifications based upon race, alienage, and national origin," are "inherently suspect and must therefore be subjected to close judicial scrutiny." *Supra*, at 1768. It is unnecessary for the Court in this case to characterize sex as a suspect classification, with all of the far-reaching implications of such a holding. *Reed* v. *Reed*, 404 U.S. 71 (1971), which abundantly supports our decision today,

did not add sex to the narrowly limited group of classifications which are inherently suspect. In my view, we can and should decide this case on the authority of *Reed* and reserve for the future any expansion of its rationale.

There is another, and I find compelling, reason for deferring a general categorizing of sex classifications as invoking the strictest test of judicial scrutiny. The Equal Rights Amendment, which if adopted will resolve the substance of this precise question, has been approved by the Congress and submitted for ratification by the States. If this Amendment is duly adopted, it will represent the will of the people accomplished in the manner prescribed by the Constitution. By acting prematurely and unnecessarily, as I view it, the Court has assumed a decisional responsibility at the very time when state legislatures, functioning within the traditional democratic process, are debating the proposed Amendment. It seems to me that this reaching out to pre-empt by judicial action a major political decision which is currently in process of resolution does not reflect appropriate respect for duly prescribed legislative processes.

There are times when this Court, under our system, cannot avoid a constitutional decision on issues which normally should be resolved by the elected representatives of the people. But democratic institutions are weakened, and confidence in the restraint of the Court is impaired, when we appear unnecessarily to decide sensitive issues of broad social and political importance at the very time they are under consideration within the prescribed constitutional processes.

Note: Orr v. *Orr,* 99 S. Ct. 1102 (1979), invalidated because of gender discrimination a state law providing that men, but not women, may be required to pay alimony. Similarly, *Caban* v. *Mohammed,* 99 S. Ct. 1760 (1979), held invalid a state law which permitted an unwed mother, but not an unwed father, to block adoption of their child simply by withholding consent.

Personnel Administrator v. *Feeney,* 99 S. Ct. 2282 (1979)—based on *Washington* v. *Davis* and *Arlington Heights,* both above—found no gender discrimination in a statutory preference for veterans in state employment, though there are far more male than female veterans. Justices Brennan and Marshall, dissenting, argued that "Where the foreseeable impact of a racially neutral policy is so disproportionate, the burden should rest on the State to establish that sex-based considerations played no part in the choice of the . . . legislative scheme."

Califino v. *Westcott,* 99 S. Ct. 2655 (1979), held invalid Section 407 of the Social Security Act, which provides benefits to families whose dependent children have been deprived of parental support because of the father's unemployment, but denies such benefits when the mother becomes unemployed. In the Court's view,

. . . [The] gender classification of § 407 is not substantially related to the attainment of any important and valid statutory goals; it is, rather, part of the "baggage of sexual stereotypes," *Orr* v. *Orr,* 440 U.S. __, that presumes the father has the "primary responsibility to provide a home and its essentials," *Stanton* v. *Stanton,* 421 U.S. 7, 10, while the mother is the "center of home and family life." *Taylor* v. *Louisiana,* 419 U.S. 522, 534, n. 15. Legislation that rests on such presumptions, without more, cannot survive scrutiny under the Due Process Clause of the Fifth Amendment.

Taylor v. *Louisiana*
See p. 289, above.

Craig v. *Boren*
429 U.S. 190 (1976)

Mr. Justice Brennan delivered the opinion of the Court.

The interaction of two sections of an Oklahoma statute, 37 Okla.Stat. §§ 241 and 245, prohibits the sale of "nonintoxicating" 3.2% beer to males under the age of 21 and to females under the age of 18. The question to be decided is whether such a gender-based differential constitutes a denial to males 18–20 years of age of the Equal Protection of the Laws in violation of the Fourteenth Amendment. . . .

A

. . .

Analysis may appropriately begin with the reminder that *Reed* v. *Reed,* [404 U.S. 71 (1971)] emphasized that statutory classifications that distinguish between males and females are "subject to scrutiny under the Equal Protection Clause." 404 U.S., at 75. To withstand constitutional challenge, previous cases establish that classifications by gender must serve important governmental objectives and must be substantially related to achievement of those objectives. Thus, in *Reed,* the objectives of "reducing the workload on probate courts," *id.,* at 76, and "avoiding intra-family controversy," *id.,* at 77, were deemed of insufficient importance to sustain use of an overt gender criterion in the appointment of interstate administrators. Decisions following *Reed* similarly have rejected administrative ease and convenience as sufficiently important objectives to justify gender-based classifications. See, *e.g., Stanley* v. *Illinois,* 405 U.S. 645, 656 (1972); *Frontiero* v. *Richardson,* 411 U.S. 677, 690 (1973); cf. *Schlesinger* v. *Ballard,* 419 U.S. 498, 506–507 (1975). And only two Terms ago *Stanton* v. *Stanton,* 421 U.S. 7 (1975), expressly stating that *Reed* v. *Reed* was "controlling," *id.,* at 13, held that *Reed* required invalidation of a Utah differential age-of-majority statute, notwithstanding the statute's coincidence with and furtherance of the State's purpose of fostering "old notions" of role-typing and preparing boys for their expected performance in the economic and political worlds. *Id.,* at 14–15.[1]

Reed v. *Reed* has also provided the underpinning for decisions that have invalidated statutes employing gender as an inaccurate proxy for other, more germane bases of classification. Hence, "archaic and overbroad" generalizations, *Schlesinger* v. *Ballard, supra,* 419 U.S., at 508, concerning the financial position of servicewomen, *Frontiero* v. *Richardson, supra,* 411 U.S., at 689, n. 3, and working women, *Weinberger* v. *Wiesenfeld,* 420 U.S. 636, 643 (1975), could not justify use of a gender line in determining eligibility for certain governmental entitlements. Similarly increasingly outdated misconceptions concerning the role of females in the home rather than in the "marketplace and world of ideas" were rejected as loose-fitting characterizations incapable of supporting state statutory schemes that were premised upon their accuracy. *Stanton* v. *Stanton, supra; Taylor* v. *Louisiana,* 419 U.S. 522, 535 n. 17 (1975). In light of the weak congruence between gender and the characteristic or trait that gender purported to represent, it was necessary that the legislatures choose either to realign their substantive laws in a gender-neutral fashion, or to adopt procedures for identifying those instances where the sex-centered generalization actually comported to fact. See, *e.g., Stanley* v. *Illinois, supra,* 405 U.S., at 658; cf. *Cleveland Board of Educ.* v. *LaFleur,* 414 U.S. 632, 650 (1974).

In this case, too, "*Reed* we feel, is controlling . . . ," *Stanton* v. *Stanton, supra,* 421 U.S., at 13.

---

[1] *Kahn* v. *Shevin,* 416 U.S. 351 (1974) and *Schlesinger* v. *Ballard,* 419 U.S. 498 (1975), upholding the use of gender-based classifications, rested upon the Court's perception of the laudatory purposes of those laws as remedying disadvantageous conditions suffered by women in economic and military life. . . .

We turn then to the question whether, under *Reed,* the difference between males and females with respect to the purchase of 3.2% beer warrants the differential in age drawn by the Oklahoma statute. We conclude that it does not.

B

The District Court recognized that *Reed* v. *Reed* was controlling. In applying the teachings of that case, the Court found the requisite important governmental objective in the traffic-safety goal proferred by the Oklahoma Attorney General. It then concluded that the statistics introduced by the appellees established that the gender-based distinction was substantially related to achievement of that goal.

C

We accept for purposes of discussion the District Court's identification of the objective underlying §§ 241 and 245 as the enhancement of traffic safety. Clearly, the protection of public health and safety represents an important function of state and local governments. However, appellees' statistics in our view cannot support the conclusion that the gender-based distinction closely serves to achieve that objective and therefore the distinction cannot under *Reed* withstand equal protection challenge.

The appellees introduced a variety of statistical surveys. First, an analysis of arrest statistics for 1973 demonstrated that 18–20-year-old male arrests for "driving under the influence" and "drunkenness" substantially exceeded female arrests for that same age period. Similarly, youths aged 17–21 were found to be overrepresented among those killed or injured in traffic accidents, with males again numerically exceeding females in this regard. Third, a random roadside survey in Oklahoma City revealed that young males were more inclined to drive and drink beer than were their female counterparts. Fourth, Federal Bureau of Investigation nationwide statistics exhibited a notable increase in arrests for "driving under the influence." Finally, statistical evidence gathered in other jurisdictions, particularly Minnesota and Michigan, was offered to corroborate Oklahoma's experience by indicating the pervasiveness of youthful participation in motor vehicle accidents following the imbibing of alcohol. Conceding that "the case is not free from doubt," 399 F.Supp., at 1314, the District Court nonetheless concluded that this statistical showing substantiated "a rational basis for the legislative judgment underlying the challenged classification." Id., at 1307.

Even were this statistical evidence accepted as accurate, it nevertheless offers only a weak answer to the equal protection question presented here. The most focused and relevant of the statistical surveys, arrests of 18–20-year-olds for alcohol-related driving offenses, exemplifies the ultimate unpersuasiveness of this evidentiary record. Viewed in terms of the correlation between sex and the actual activity that Oklahoma seeks to regulate—driving while under the influence of alcohol—the statistics broadly establish that .18% of females and 2% of males in that age group were arrested for that offense. While such a disparity is not trivial in a statistical sense, it hardly can form the basis for employment of a gender line as a classifying device. Certainly if maleness is to serve as a proxy for drinking and driving a correlation of 2% must be considered an unduly tenuous "fit." Indeed, prior cases have consistently rejected the use of sex as a decisionmaking factor even though the statutes in question certainly rested on far more predictive empirical relationships than this.

Moreover, the statistics exhibit a variety of other shortcomings that seriously impugn their value to equal protection analysis. Setting aside the obvious methodological problems, the surveys do not adequately justify the salient features of Oklahoma's gender-based traffic-safety law. None purports to measure the use and dangerousness of 3.2% beer as opposed to alcohol generally, a detail that is of particular impor-

tance since, in light of its low alcohol level, Oklahoma apparently considers the 3.2% beverage to be "non-intoxicating." 37 Okla.Stat. § 163.1 (1971); see State ex rel. Springer v. Bliss, 199 Okla. 198, 185 P.2d 220 (1947). Moreover, many of the studies, while graphically documenting the unfortunate increase in driving while under the influence of alcohol, make no effort to relate their findings to age-sex differentials as involved here. Indeed, the only survey that explicitly centered its attention upon young drivers and their use of beer—albeit apparently not of the diluted 3.2% variety—reached results that hardly can be viewed as impressive in justifying either a gender or age classification.

There is no reason to belabor this line of analysis. It is unrealistic to expect either members of the judiciary or state officials to be well versed in the rigors of experimental or statistical technique. But this merely illustrates that proving broad sociological propositions by statistics is a dubious business, and one that inevitably is in tension with the normative philosophy that underlies the Equal Protection Clause. Suffice to say that the showing offered by the appellees does not satisfy us that sex represents a legitimate, accurate proxy for the regulation of drinking and driving. In fact, when it is further recognized that Oklahoma's statute prohibits only the selling of 3.2% beer to young males and not their drinking the beverage once acquired (even after purchase by their 18–20-year-old female companions), the relationship between gender and traffic safety becomes far too tenuous to satisfy Reed's requirement that the gender-based difference be substantially related to achievement of the statutory objective.

We hold, therefore, that under Reed, Oklahoma's 3.2% beer statute invidiously discriminates against males 18–20 years of age.

Mr. Justice Stewart, concurring. . . .

Every State has broad power under the Twenty-first Amendment to control the dispensation of alcoholic beverages within its borders.

. . . But "[t]his is not to say that the Twenty-first Amendment empowers a State to act with total irrationality or invidious discrimination in controlling the dispensation of liquor . . . ." *California* v. *LaRue, supra,* 409 U.S. at 120 (concurring opinion).

The disparity created by these Oklahoma statutes amounts to total irrationality. For the statistics upon which the State now relies, whatever their other shortcomings, wholly fail to prove or even suggest that 3.2 beer is somehow more deleterious when it comes into the hands of a male aged 18–20 than of a female of like age. The disparate statutory treatment of the sexes here, without even a colorably valid justification or explanation, thus amounts to invidious discrimination. See *Reed* v. *Reed,* 404 U.S. 71.

Mr. Justice Blackmun, concurring.

Mr. Justice Powell, concurring. . . .

I join the opinion of the Court as I am in general agreement with it. I do have reservations as to some of the discussion concerning the appropriate standard for equal protection analysis and the relevance of the statistical evidence. Accordingly, I add this concurring statement.

With respect to the equal protection standard, I agree that *Reed* v. *Reed,* 404 U.S. 71 (1971), is the most relevant precedent. But I find it unnecessary, in deciding this case, to read that decision as broadly as some of the Court's language may imply. *Reed* and subsequent cases involving gender-based classifications make clear that the Court subjects such classifications to a more critical examination than is normally applied when "fundamental" constitutional rights and "suspect classes" are not present.

[T]he Court held, too, that the Twenty-first Amendment does not save an otherwise invalid gender-based discrimination.]

Califino v. *Goldfarb*
430 U.S. 199 (1977)

Mr. Justice Brennan announced the judgment of the Court and delivered an opinion in which Mr. Justice White, Mr. Justice Marshall, and Mr. Justice Powell joined.

Under the Federal Old-Age, Survivors, and Disability Insurance Benefits program (OASDI) 42 U.S.C. §§ 401–431, survivors' benefits based on the earnings of a deceased husband covered by the Act are payable to his widow. Such benefits on the basis of the earnings of a deceased wife covered by the Act are payable to the widower, however, only if he "was receiving at least one-half of his "support" from his deceased wife. The question in this case is whether this gender-based distinction violates the Due Process Clause of the Fifth Amendment.

The gender-based distinction drawn by § 402(f)(1)(D)—burdening a widower but not a widow with the task of proving dependency upon the deceased spouse—presents an equal protection question indistinguishable from that decided in *Weinberger* v. *Wiesenfeld,* 420 U.S. 636. That decision and the decision in *Frontiero* v. *Richardson,* 411 U.S. 677 (1973) plainly require affirmance of the judgment of the District Court.

Weinberger v. *Wiesenfeld,* like the instant case, presented the question in the context of the OASDI program. There the Court held unconstitutional a provision that denied father's insurance benefits to surviving widowers with children in their care, while authorizing similar mother's benefits to similarly situated widows. . . . [T]he gender-based distinction made by § 402(g) was "indistinguishable from that invalidated in *Frontiero,*" and therefore, while

". . . the notion that men are more likely than women to be the primary supporters of their spouses and children is not entirely without empirical support, . . . such a gender-based generalization cannot suffice to justify the denigration of the efforts of women who do work and whose earnings contribute significantly to their families' support.

"Section 402(g) clearly operates, as did the statutes invalidated by our judgment in *Frontiero*, to deprive women of protection for their families which men receive as a result of their employment."

Precisely the same reasoning condemns the gender-based distinction made by § 402(f)(1)(D) in this case. For that distinction too operates "to deprive women of protection for their families which men receive as a result of their employment." . . .

Appellant, however, would focus equal protection analysis not upon the discrimination against the covered wage earning female, but rather upon whether her surviving widower was unconstitutionally discriminated against by burdening him but not a surviving widow with proof of dependency. The gist of the argument is that, analyzed from the perspective of the widower, ". . . the denial of benefits reflected the congressional judgment that aged widowers as a class were sufficiently likely not to be dependent upon their wives, that it was appropriate to deny them benefits unless they were in fact dependent."

But *Weinberger* v. *Wiesenfeld* rejected the virtually identical argument when appellant's predecessor argued that the statutory classification there attacked should be regarded from the perspective of the prospective beneficiary and not from that of the covered wage earner. The Court, . . . , analyzed the classification from the perspective of the wage earner and concluded that the classification was unconstitutional because "benefits must be distributed according to classifications which do not without sufficient justification differentiate among covered employees solely on the basis of sex." Thus, contrary to appellant's insistence, *Wiesenfeld* is "dispositive here."

. . . Plainly then § 402(f)(1)(D) disadvan-

tages women contributors to the social security system as compared to similarly situated men. The section then "impermissibly discriminates against a female wage earner because it provides her family less protection than it provides that of a male wage earner, even though the family needs may be identical." . . .

. . . The Social Security Act is permeated with provisions that draw lines in classifying those who are to receive benefits. Congressional decisions in this regard are entitled to deference as those of the institution charged under our scheme of government with the primary responsibility for making such judgments in light of competing policies and interests. But "[t]o withstand constitutional challenge, . . . classifications by gender must serve important governmental objectives and must be substantially related to the achievement of those objectives." *Craig* v. *Boren*, 429 U.S. 190 (1976). Such classifications, however, have frequently been revealed on analysis to rest only upon "old notions" and "archaic and overbroad" generalizations, and so have been found to offend the prohibitions against denial of equal protection of the law. . . .

Appellant next argues that *Frontiero* and *Wiesenfeld* should be distinguished as involving statutes with different objectives than § 402(f)(1)(D). Rather than merely enacting presumptions designed to save the expense and trouble of determining which spouses are really dependent, providing benefits to all widows, but to such widowers as prove dependency, § 402(f)(1)(D), it is argued, rationally defines different standards of eligibility because of the differing social welfare needs of widowers and widows. That is, the argument runs, Congress may reasonably have presumed that nondependent widows, who receive benefits, are needier than nondependent widowers, who do not, because of job discrimination against women (particularly older women), see *Kahn* v. *Shevin*, and because they are more likely to have been more dependent on their spouses. . . .

We conclude, . . . that the differential treatment of nondependent widows and widowers results not, as appellant asserts, from a deliberate congressional intention to remedy the arguably greater needs of the former, but rather from an intention to aid the dependent spouses of decreased wage earners, coupled with a presumption that wives are usually dependent. This presents precisely the situation faced in *Frontiero* and *Wiesenfeld.* The only conceivable justification for writing the presumption of wives' dependency into the statute is the assumption, not verified by the Government in *Frontiero,* or here, but based simply on "archaic and overbroad" generalizations, that it would save the Government time, money, and effort simply to pay benefits to all widows, rather than to require proof of dependency of both sexes. We held in *Frontiero,* and again in *Wiesenfeld,* and therefore hold again here, that such assumptions do not suffice to justify a gender-based discrimination in the distribution of employment-related benefits.

Mr. Justice Stevens, concurring in the judgment.

I am . . . persuaded that this discrimination against a group of males is merely the accidental byproduct of a traditional way of thinking about females. I am also persuaded that a rule which effects an unequal distribution of economic benefits solely on the basis of sex is sufficiently questionable that "due process requires that there be a legitimate basis for presuming that the rule was actually intended to serve [the] interest" put forward by the government as its justification. In my judgment, something more than accident is necessary to justify the disparate treatment of persons who have as strong a claim to equal treatment as do similarly situated surviving spouses.

But if my judgment is correct, what is to be said about *Kahn* v. *Shevin?* . . . It seems clear, . . . that the Court upheld the Florida statute on the basis of a hypothetical justification for the discrimination which had nothing to do with the legislature's actual motivation. On this premise, I would be required to regard *Kahn* as controlling in this case, were it not for the fact that I believe precisely the same analysis applies to *Weinberger* v. *Wiesenfeld.*

. . . If there is inconsistency between *Kahn* and *Wiesenfeld,* as I believe there is, it is appropriate to follow the later unanimous holding rather than the earlier, sharply divided decision. And if the cases are distinguishable, *Wiesenfeld* is closer on its facts to this case than is *Kahn.* . . .

Mr. Justice Rehnquist, with whom The Chief Justice, Mr. Justice Stewart, and Mr. Justice Blackmun join, dissenting.

. . . [I]t seems to me that there are two largely separate principles which may be deduced from these cases which indicate that the Court has reached the wrong result.

The first of these principles is that cases requiring heightened levels of scrutiny for particular classifications under the Equal Protection Clause, which have originated in areas of the law outside of the field of social insurance legislation, will not be uncritically carried over into that field.

The second principle upon which I believe this legislative classification should be sustained is that set forth in our opinion in *Kahn* v. *Shevin.* The effect of the statutory scheme is to make it easier for widows to obtain benefits than it is for widowers, since the former qualify automatically while the latter must show proof of need. Such a requirement in no way perpetuates or exacerbates the economic disadvantage which has led the Court to conclude that gender-based discrimination must meet a different test than other types of classifications. It is, like the property tax exemption to widows in *Kahn,* a differing treatment which " 'rest[s] upon some ground of difference having a fair and substantial relation to the object of the legislation.'"

Califino v. Webster
430 U.S. 313 (1977)

Per Curiam.

Under § 215 of the Social Security Act, old-age insurance benefits are computed on the basis of the wage earner's "average monthly wage" earned during his "benefit computation years" which are the "elapsed years" (reduced by five) during which the wage earner's covered wages were highest. Until a 1972 amendment, "elapsed years" depended upon the sex of the wage earner. Section 215(b)(3) prescribed that the number of "elapsed years" for a male wage earner would be three higher than for an otherwise similarly situated female wage earner; for a male, the number of "elapsed years" equalled the number of years that elapsed after 1950 and before the year in which he attained age 65; for a male, the number of "elapsed years" equalled the number of years that elapsed after 1950 and before the year in which he attained age 65; for a female the number of "elapsed years" "elapsed years" on retirement at age 65 but a female born in the same year would have only 11. Accordingly, a female wage earner could exclude from the computation of her "average monthly wage" three more lower earning years than a similarly situated male wage earner could exclude. This would result in a slightly higher "average monthly wage" and a correspondingly higher level of monthly old-age benefits for the retired female wage earner. . . .

To withstand scrutiny under the equal protection component of the Fifth Amendment's Due Process Clause, "classifications by gender must serve important governmental objectives and must be substantially related to achievement of those objectives." *Craig* v. *Boren*. Reduction of the disparity in economic condition

between men and women caused by the long history of discrimination against women has been recognized as such an important governmental objective. *Schlesinger* v. *Ballard; Kahn* v. *Shevin*. But "the mere recitation of a benign, compensatory purpose is not an automatic shield that protects against any inquiry into the actual purposes underlying a legislative scheme." *Weinberger* v. *Wiesenfeld*. Accordingly, we have rejected attempts to justify gender classifications as compensation for past discrimination against women when the classifications in fact penalized women wage earners, *Califano* v. *Goldfarb; Weinberger* v. *Wiesenfeld*, or when its legislative history revealed that the classification was not enacted as compensation for past discrimination. [*Goldfarb; Wiesenfeld.*]

The statutory scheme involved here is more analogous to those upheld in *Kahn* and *Ballard* than to those struck down in *Wiesenfeld* and *Goldfarb*. The more favorable treatment of the female wage earner enacted here was not a result of "archaic and overbroad generalizations" about women, *Schlesinger* v. *Ballard*, or of "the role-typing society has long imposed" upon women, *Stanton* v. *Stanton*, such as casual assumptions that women are "the weaker sex" or are more likely to be child-rearers or dependents. Rather, "the only discernible purpose of [§ 215's more favorable treatment is] the permissible one of redressing our society's longstanding disparate treatment of women."

The challenged statute operated directly to compensate women for past economic discrimination. Retirement benefits under the Act are based on past earnings. But as we have recognized, "[w]hether from overt discrimination or from the socialization process of a male-dominated culture, the job market is inhospitable to the woman seeking any but the lowest paid jobs." *Kahn* v. *Shevin*. Thus, allowing women, who as such have been unfairly hindered from earning as much as men, to eliminate additional low-earning years from the calculation of their retirement benefits works directly to remedy some part of the effect of past discrimination.

The legislative history of § 215(b)(3) also reveals that Congress directly addressed the justification for differing treatment of men and women in the former version of that section and purposely enacted the more favorable treatment for female wage earners to compensate for past employment discrimination against women. [T]he legislative history is clear that the differing treatment of men and women in former § 215(b)(3) was not "the accidental byproduct of a traditional way of thinking about females," *Califano* v. *Goldfarb* (Stevens, J., concurring in the result), but rather was deliberately enacted to compensate for particular economic disabilities suffered by women.

That Congress changed its mind in 1972 and equalized the treatment of men and women does not, as the District Court concluded, constitute an admission by Congress that its previous policy was invidiously discriminatory. Congress has in recent years legislated directly upon the subject of unequal treatment of women in the job market. Congress may well have decided that "[t]hese congressional reforms [have] lessened the economic justification for the more favorable benefit computation formula in § 215(b)(3)." Moreover, elimination of the more favorable benefit computation for women wage earners, even in the remedial context, is wholly consistent with those reforms, which require equal treatment of men and women in preference to the attitudes of "romantic paternalism" that have contributed to the "long and unfortunate history of sex discrimination." *Frontiero*. . . .

Mr. Chief Justice Burger, with whom Mr. Justice Stewart, Mr. Justice Blackmun, and Mr. Justice Rehnquist join, concurring in the judgment.

While I am happy to concur in the Court's judgment, I find it somewhat difficult to distinguish the Social Security provision upheld here from that struck down so recently in *Califano* v. *Goldfarb*. Although the distinction drawn by the Court between this case and *Goldfarb* is not totally lacking in substance, I question whether certainty in the law is promoted by hinging the validity of important statutory schemes on whether five Justices view them to be more akin to the "offensive" provisions struck down in *Weinberger* v. *Wiesenfeld*, and *Frontiero* v. *Richardson*, or more like the "benign" provisions upheld in *Schlesinger* v. *Ballard* and *Kahn* v. *Shevin*. I therefore concur in the judgment of the Court for reasons stated by Mr. Justice Rehnquist in his dissenting opinion in Goldfarb. . . .

Geduldig v. *Aiello*
417 U.S. 484 (1974)

California's workers' disability insurance program, covering a vast range of disabilities, excluded from its coverage normal (but not abnormal) pregnancy.

Mr. Justice Stewart delivered the opinion of the Court. . . .

We cannot agree that the exclusion of this disability from coverage amounts to invidious discrimination under the Equal Protection Clause. California does not discriminate with respect to the persons or groups who are eligible for disability insurance protection under the program. The classification challenged in this case relates to the asserted under-inclusiveness of the set of risks that the State has selected to insure. Although California has created a program to insure most risks of employment disability, it has not chosen to insure all such risks, and this decision is reflected in the level of annual contribution exacted from participating employees. This Court has held that, consistently with the Equal Protection Clause, a State "may take one step at a time, addressing itself to the phase of the problem which seems most acute to the legislative mind. The legislature may select one phase of one field and apply a remedy there, neglecting the others. . . ." *Williams* v. *Lee Optical Co.*, 348 U.S. 483, 489; *Jefferson* v. *Hackney*, 406 U.S. 535 (1972). Particularly with respect to social welfare programs, so long as the line drawn by the State is rationally supportable, the courts will not interpose their judgment as to the appropriate stopping point. "[T]he Equal Protection Clause does not require that a State must choose between attacking every aspect of a problem or not attacking the problem at all." *Dandridge* v. *Williams*, 397 U.S. 471, 486–487 (1970).

The District Court suggested that moderate alterations in what it regarded as "variables" of the disability insurance program could be made to accommodate the substantial expense required to include normal pregnancy within the program's protection. The same can be said, however, with respect to the other expensive class of disabilities that are excluded from coverage—short-term disabilities. If the Equal Protection Clause were thought to compel disability payments for normal pregnancy, it is hard to perceive why it would not also compel payments for short-term disabilities suffered by participating employees.

It is evident that a totally comprehensive program would be substantially more costly than the present program and would inevitably require state subsidy, a higher rate of employee contribution, a lower scale of benefits for those suffering insured disabilities, or some combination of these measures. There is nothing in the Constitution, however, that requires the State to subordinate or compromise its legitimate interests solely to create a more comprehensive social insurance program than it already has.

The State has a legitimate interest in maintaining the self-supporting nature of its insurance program. Similarly, it has an interest in distributing the available resources in such a way as to keep benefit payments at an adequate level for disabilities that are covered, rather than to cover all disabilities inadequately. Finally, California has a legitimate concern in maintaining the contribution rate at a level that will not unduly burden participating employees, particularly low-income employees who may be most in need of the disability insurance.

These policies provide an objective and wholly non-invidious basis for the State's decision not to create a more comprehensive insurance program than it has. There is no evidence in the record that the selection of the risks insured by the program worked to discriminate against any definable group or class in terms of the aggregate risk protection derived by that group or class from the program.[1] There is no risk from which men are protected and women

---

[1] The dissenting opinion to the contrary, this case is thus a far cry from cases like Reed v. Reed, 404 U.S. 71, and Frontiero v. Richardson, 411 U.S. 677, involving discrimination based upon gender as such. The California insurance program does not exclude anyone from benefit eligibility because of gender but merely removes one physical condition—pregnancy—from the list of compensable disabilities. While it is true that only women can become pregnant, it does not follow that every legislative classification concerning pregnancy is a sex-based classification like those considered in Reed, *supra,* and Frontiero, *supra.* Normal pregnancy is an objectively identifiable physical condition with unique characteristics. Absent a showing that distinctions involving pregnancy are mere pretexts designed to effect an invidious discrimination against the members of one sex or the other, lawmakers are constitutionally free to include or exclude pregnancy from the coverage of legislation such as this on any reasonable basis, just as with respect to any other physical condition.

The lack of identity between the excluded disability and gender as such under this insurance program becomes clear upon the most cursory analysis. The program divides potential recipients into two groups—pregnant women and nonpregnant persons. While the first group is exclusively female, the second includes members of both sexes. The fiscal and actuarial benefits of the program thus accrue to members of both sexes.

are not. Likewise, there is no risk from which women are protected and men are not.[2]

The appellee simply contends that, although she has received insurance protection equiva-

_____

[2] Indeed, the appellant submitted to the District Court data that indicated that both the annual claim rate and the annual claim cost are greater for women than for men. As the District Court acknowledged, "women contribute 28 per cent of the total disability insurance fund and receive back about 38 per cent of the fund in benefits." 359 F.Supp., at 800. Several *amici curiae* have represented to the Court that they have had a similar experience under private disability insurance programs.

lent to that provided all other participating employees, she has suffered discrimination because she encountered a risk that was outside the program's protection. For the reasons we have stated, we hold that this contention is not a valid one under the Equal Protection Clause of the Fourteenth Amendment.

[Justices Brennan, Douglas, and Marshall dissented on the ground that *Frontiero* and *Reed* "mandate a stricter standard of scrutiny which the State's classification fails to satisfy."]

Los Angeles Department of Water and Power v. *Manhart*
98 S. Ct. 1370 (1978)

Many laws which treat women "differently" are based on old-fashioned, stereotypical conceptions, with little or no foundation in fact. The classification in the present case is based on an accurate, fact-based generalization; namely, that on the average women live longer than men. (Annual life insurance premiums favoring females have long been based on this proposition.) Here Manhart challenged a retirement system that provided equal benefits for men and women but required women to contribute 14.84 percent more per month, since actuarially they would receive that much more in benefits. The case arose, and was decided, under Title VII of the Civil Rights Act of 1964. The Court was silent with respect to the Constitution, but surely there are constitutional overtones in its discussion of *General Electric Co.* v. *Gilbert*, 429 U.S. 125 (1976).

Mr. Justice Stevens delivered the opinion of the Court . . . .

There are both real and fictional differences between women and men. It is true that the average man is taller than the average woman; it is not true that the average woman driver is more accident-prone than the average man. Before the Civil Rights Act of 1964 was enacted, an employer could fashion his personnel policies on the basis of assumptions about the differences between men and women, whether or not the assumptions were valid.

It is now well recognized that employment decisions cannot be predicated on mere "stereotyped" impressions about the characteristics of males or females. [This] case does not,

however, involve a fictional difference between men and women. It involves a generalization that the parties accept as unquestionably true: women, as a class, do live longer than men. The Department treated its women employees differently from its men employees because the two classes are in fact different. It is equally true, however, that all individuals in the respective classes do not share the characteristic which differentiates the average class representatives. Many women do not live as long as the average man and many men outlive the average woman. The question, therefore, is whether the existence or nonexistence of "discrimination" is to be determined by comparison of class characteristics or individual characteristics. A "stereotyped" answer to that question may not be the same as the answer which the language and purpose of the statute command.

The statute makes it unlawful "to discriminate against any *individual* with respect to his compensation, terms, conditions or privileges of employment, because of such *individual's* race, color, religion, sex, or national origin." 42 U.S.C. § 2000e–2(a)(1) (emphasis added). The statute's focus on the individual is unambiguous. It precludes treatment of individuals as simply components of a racial, religious, sexual, or national class. If height is required for a job, a tall woman may not be refused employment merely because, on the average, women are too short. Even a true generalization about the class is an insufficient reason for disqualifying an individual to whom the generalization does not apply.

That proposition is of critical importance in this case because there is no assurance that any individual woman working for the Department will actually fit the generalization on which the Department's policy is based. Many of those individuals will not live as long as the average man. While they were working, those individuals received smaller paychecks because of their sex, but they will receive no compensating advantage when they retire.

It is true, of course, that while contributions are being collected from the employees, the Department cannot know which individuals will predecease the average woman. Therefore, unless women as a class are assessed an extra charge, they will be subsidized, to some extent, by the class of male employees. It follows, according to the Department, that fairness to its class of male employees justifies the extra assessment against all of its female employees.

But the question of fairness to various classes affected by the statute is essentially a matter of policy for the legislature to address. Congress has decided that classifications based on sex, like those based on national origin or race, are unlawful. Actuarial studies could unquestionably identify differences in life expectancy based on race or national origin, as well as sex. But a statute which was designed to make race irrelevant in the employment market, see *Griggs* v. *Duke Power Co.*, 401 U.S. 424, 436, could not reasonably be construed to permit a take-home pay differential based on a racial classification.

Even if the statutory language were less clear, the basic policy of the statute requires that we focus on fairness to individuals rather than fairness to classes. Practices which classify employees in terms of religion, race, or sex tend to preserve traditional assumptions about groups rather than thoughtful scrutiny of individuals. The generalization involved in this case illustrates the point. Separate mortality tables are easily interpreted as reflecting innate differences between the sexes; but a significant part of the longevity differential may be explained by the social fact that men are heavier smokers than women. . . .

In *Gilbert* the Court held that the exclusion of pregnancy from an employer's disability benefit plan did not constitute sex discrimination within the meaning of Title VII. Relying on the reasoning in *Geduldig* v. *Aiello*, 417 U.S. 484, the Court first held that the General Electric plan did not involve "discrimination based upon gender as such." The two groups of potential recipients which that case concerned were pregnant women and nonpregnant persons. "While the first group is exclusively female, the second includes members of both sexes." 429 U.S., at 135. In contrast each of the two groups of employees involved in this case is composed entirely and exclusively of members of the same sex. On its face, this plan discriminates on the basis of sex whereas the General Electric plan discriminated on the basis of a special physical disability.

In *Gilbert* the Court did note that the plan as actually administered had provided more favorable benefits to women as a class than to men as a class. This evidence supported the conclusion that not only had plaintiffs failed to establish a prima facie case by proving that the plan was discriminatory on its face, but they had also failed to prove any discriminatory effect.

In this case, however, the Department argues that the absence of a discriminatory effect on women as a class justifies an employment practice which, on its face, discriminated against individual employees because of their sex. But even if the Department's actuarial evidence is sufficient to prevent plaintiffs from establishing a prima facie case on the theory that the effect of the practice on women as a class was discriminatory, that evidence does not defeat the claim that the practice, on its face, discriminated against every individual woman employed by the Department.

[Mr. Justice Brennan did not participate in the decision.]

[Mr. Justice Blackmun concurred, saying in part:]

Given the decisions in *Geduldig* and *General Electric*—the one constitutional, the other statutory—the present case just cannot be an easy one for the Court. I might have thought that those decisions would have required the Court to conclude that the critical difference in the Department's pension payments was based on life expectancy, a nonstigmatizing factor that demonstrably differentiates females from males and that is not measurable on an individual basis. I might have thought, too, that there is nothing arbitrary, irrational, or "discriminatory" about recognizing the objective and accepted . . . disparity in female-male life expectancies in computing rates for retirement plans. Moreover, it is unrealistic to attempt to force, as the Court does, an individualized analysis upon what is basically an insurance context. Unlike the possibility, for example, of properly testing job applicants for qualifications before employment, there is simply no way to determine in advance when a particular employee will die. . . .

The Court's distinction between the present case and *General Electric*—that the permitted classes there were "pregnant women and nonpregnant persons," both female and male, . . . seems to me to be just too easy. It is probably the only distinction that can be drawn. For me, it does not serve to distinguish the case on any

principled basis. I therefore must conclude that today's decision cuts back on *General Electric*, and inferentially on *Geduldig*, the reasoning of which was adopted there, . . . and, indeed, makes the recognition of those cases as continuing precedent somewhat questionable. I do not say that this is necessarily bad. If that is what Congress has chosen to do by Title VII—as the Court today with such assurance asserts—so be it. I feel, however, that we should meet the posture of the earlier cases head-on and not by thin rationalization that seeks to distinguish but fails in its quest.

[Chief Justice Burger, joined by Mr. Justice Rehnquist, dissenting, considered it "rational" to base pension systems "on statistically sound and proven disparities in longevity between men and women (and) irrational to assume Congress intended to outlaw use of the fact that, for whatever reasons . . . , women as a class outlive men." In the dissenter's view Title VII is not clear enough to justify such a revolutionary and profemale discriminatory undermining of pension systems.]

Note: In proposing the Equal Rights Amendment (ERA), Congress seemed to have approved *Geduldig* in advance:

The legal principle underlying the equal rights amendment (H.J. Res. 208) is that the law must deal with the individual attributes of the particular person and not with stereotypes of over-classification based on sex. However, the original resolution does not require that women must be treated in all respects the same as men. "Equality" does not mean "sameness." As a result, the original resolution would not prohibit reasonable classifications based on characteristics that are unique to one sex. ("Equal Rights for Men and Women," *Senate Report* No. 92-689, 92d Cong., 2d Sess. [1972]).

In *Manhart* the Court's interpretation of Title VII obviously ignores the distinction between "sameness" and "equality."

Pittsburgh Press Co. v. *Pittsburgh Commission on Human Relations*
See p. 488, above.

Note and quaere: On March 22, 1972, Congress submitted ERA to the state legislatures for ratification as the Twenty-seventh Amendment to the Constitution. By its terms:

Section 1. Equality of rights under the law shall not be denied or abridged by the United States or by any State on account of sex.

Section 2. The Congress shall have the power to enforce, by appropriate legislation, the provisions of this article.

Section 3. This amendment shall take effect two years after the date of ratification.

Would ERA have any effect on discrimination by private persons or businesses? (See the state-action problem in Chapter 10, below.) Would it outlaw "benign discrimination" in favor of women, as in *Webster,* above, on the ground that this constitutes discrimination against men? Would ERA add anything to the protections already afforded by decision under the Fifth and Fourteenth Amendments?

SUFFRAGE CLASSIFICATIONS

Colegrove v. *Green*
See p. 39, above.

Baker v. *Carr*
See p. 41, above.

Reynolds v. *Sims*
377 U.S. 533 (1964)

The Alabama Constitution provided that "each county shall be entitled to at least one representative," and that no county should have more than one senator. It required reapportionment decennially according to population, but this had not been done since 1901. As a result of the constitutional provisions plus failure to reapportion there were population variations from district to district of up to about 41 to 1 in the state Senate, and up to about 16 to 1 in the House. Voters challenged this inequality in a federal district court.

Mr. Chief Justice Warren delivered the opinion of the Court. . . .

In *Gary* v. *Sanders,* 372 U.S. 368, we held that the Georgia county unit system, applicable in statewide primary elections, was unconstitutional since it resulted in a dilution of the weight of the votes of certain Georgia voters merely because of where they resided. . . .

In *Wesberry* v. *Sanders,* 376 U.S. 1, decided

earlier this Term, we held that attacks on the constitutionality of congressional districting plans enacted by state legislatures do not present nonjusticiable questions and should not be dismissed generally for "want of equity." We determined that the constitutional test for the validity of congressional districting schemes was one of substantial equality of population among the various districts established by a state legislature for the election of members of the Federal House of Representatives. . . .

Gray and *Wesberry* are of course not dispositive of or directly controlling on our decision in these cases involving state legislative apportionment controversies. Admittedly, those decisions, in which we held that, in statewide and in congressional elections, one person's vote must be counted equally with those of all other voters in a State, were based on different constitutional considerations and were addressed to rather distinct problems. But neither are they wholly inapposite. *Gray*, though not determinative here since involving the weighting of votes in statewide elections, established the basic principle of equality among voters within a State, and held that voters cannot be classified, constitutionally, on the basis of where they live, at least with respect to voting in statewide elections. And our decision in *Wesberry* was of course grounded on that language of the Constitution which prescribes that members of the Federal House of Representatives are to be chosen "by the People," while attacks on state legislative apportionment schemes, such as that involved in the instant cases, are principally based on the Equal Protection Clause of the Fourteenth Amendment. Nevertheless, *Wesberry* clearly established that the fundamental principle of representative government in this country is one of equal representation for equal numbers of people, without regard to race, sex, economic status, or place of residence within a State. Our problem, then, is to ascertain, in the instant cases, whether there are any constitutionally cognizable principles which would justify departures from the basic standard of equality among voters in the apportionment of seats in state legislatures.

III.

A predominant consideration in determining whether a State's legislative apportionment scheme constitutes an invidious discrimination violative of rights asserted under the Equal Protection Clause is that the rights allegedly impaired are individual and personal in nature. . . .

Legislators represent people, not trees or acres. Legislators are elected by voters, not farms or cities or economic interests. As long as ours is a representative form of government, and our legislatures are those instruments of government elected directly by and directly representative of the people, the right to elect legislators in a free and unimpaired fashion is a bedrock of our political system. It could hardly be gainsaid that a constitutional claim had been asserted by an allegation that certain otherwise qualified voters had been entirely prohibited from voting for members of their state legislature. And, if a State should provide that the votes of citizens in one part of the State should be given two times, or five times, or 10 times the weight of votes of citizens in another part of the State, it could hardly be contended that the right to vote of those residing in the disfavored areas had not been effectively diluted. It would appear extraordinary to suggest that a state could be constitutionally permitted to enact a law providing that certain of the state's voters could vote two, five, or 10 times for their legislative representatives, while voters living elsewhere could vote only once. And it is inconceivable that a state law to the effect that, in counting votes for legislators, the votes of citizens in one part of the State would be multiplied by two, five, or 10, while the votes of persons in another area would be counted only at face value, could be constitutionally sustainable. Of course, the effect of state legislative districting schemes which give the same number of representatives to unequal numbers of constituents is identical. Overweighting and overvaluation of the votes of those living here has the certain effect of dilution and undervaluation of the votes of those living there. The resulting discrimination against those individual voters living in disfavored areas is easily demonstrable mathematically. Their right to vote is simply not the same right to vote as that of those living in a favored part of the State. Two, five, or 10 of them must vote before the effect of their voting is equivalent to that of their favored neighbor. Weighting the votes of citizens differently, by any method or means, merely because of where they happen to reside, hardly seems justifiable. . . .

. . . Since the achieving of fair and effective representation for all citizens is concededly the basic aim of legislative apportionment, we conclude that the Equal Protection Clause guarantees the opportunity for equal participation by all voters in the election of state legislators. Diluting the weight of votes because of place of residence impairs basic constitutional rights under the Fourteenth Amendment just as much as invidious discriminations based upon factors such as race, *Brown* v. *Board of Education*, 347 U.S. 483, or economic status, *Griffin* v. *People of State of Illinois*, 351 U.S. 12, *Douglas* v. *People of State of California*, 372 U.S. 353. Our constitutional system amply provides for the protection of minorities by means other than giving them majority control of state legislatures. And the democratic ideals of equality and majority rule, which have served this Nation so well in the past, are hardly of any less significance for the present and the future.

We are told that the matter of apportioning representation in a state legislature is a complex and many-faceted one. We are advised that States can rationally consider factors other than population in apportioning legislative representation. We are admonished not to restrict the power of the States to impose differing views as to political philosophy on their citizens. We are cautioned about the dangers of entering into

political thickets and mathematical quagmires. Our answer is this: a denial of constitutionally protected rights demands judicial protection; our oath and our office require no less of us.

. . . Population is, of necessity, the starting point for consideration and the controlling criterion for judgment in legislative apportionment controversies. A citizen, a qualified voter, is no more nor no less so because he lives in the city or on the farm. This is the clear and strong command of our Constitution's Equal Protection Clause. This is an essential part of the concept of a government of laws and not men. This is at the heart of Lincoln's vision of "government of the people, by the people, [and] for the people." The Equal Protection Clause demands no less than substantially equal state legislative representation for all citizens, of all places as well as of all races.

IV.

We hold that, as a basic constitutional standard, the Equal Protection Clause requires that the seats in both houses of a bicameral state legislature must be apportioned on a population basis. Simply stated, an individual's right to vote for state legislators is unconstitutionally impaired when its weight is in a substantial fashion diluted when compared with votes of citizens living in other parts of the State. Since, under neither the existing apportionment provisions nor under either of the proposed plans was either of the houses of the Alabama Legislature apportioned on a population basis, the District Court correctly held that all three of these schemes were constitutionally invalid. . . .

V.

. . .

The system of representation in the two Houses of the Federal Congress is one ingrained in our Constitution, as part of the law of the land. It is one conceived out of compromise and concession indispensable to the establishment of our federal republic. Arising from unique historical circumstances, it is based on the consideration that in establishing our type of federalism a group of formerly independent States bound themselves together under one national government. . . .

Political subdivisions of States—counties, cities, or whatever—never were and never have been considered as sovereign entities. Rather, they have been traditionally regarded as subordinate governmental instrumentalities created by the State to assist in the carrying out of state governmental functions. . . The relationship of the States to the Federal Government could hardly be less analogous. . . .

Since we find the so-called federal analogy inapposite to a consideration of the constitutional validity of state legislative apportionment schemes, we necessarily hold that the Equal Protection Clause requires both houses of a state legislature to be apportioned on a population basis. . . .

VI.

By holding that as a federal constitutional requisite both houses of a state legislature must be apportioned on a population basis, we mean that the Equal Protection Clause requires that a State make an honest and good faith effort to construct districts, in both houses of its legislature, as nearly of equal population as is practicable. We realize that it is a practical impossibility to arrange legislative districts so that each one has an identical number of residents, or citizens, or voters. Mathematical exactness or precision is hardly a workable constitutional requirement. . . .

A State may legitimately desire to maintain the integrity of various political subdivisions, insofar as possible, and provide for compact districts of contiguous territory in designing a legislative apportionment scheme. Valid considerations may underlie such aims. Indiscriminate districting, without any regard for political subdivision or natural or historical boundary lines, may be little more than an open invitation to partisan gerrymandering. Single-member districts may be the rule in one State, while another State might desire to achieve some flexibility by creating multimember or floterial districts. Whatever the means of accomplishment, the overriding objective must be substantial equality of population among the various districts, so that the vote of any citizen is approximately equal in weight to that of any other citizen in the State. . . .

But neither history alone, nor economic or other sorts of group interests, are permissible factors in attempting to justify disparities from population-based representation. Citizens, not history or economic interests, cast votes. Considerations of area alone provide an insufficient justification for deviations from the equal-population principle. Again, people, not land or trees or pastures, vote. Modern developments and improvements in transportation and communications make rather hollow, in the mid-1960's, most claims that deviations from population-based representation can validly be based solely on geographical considerations. Arguments for allowing such deviations in order to insure effective representation for sparsely settled areas and to prevent legislative districts from becoming so large that the availability of access of citizens to their representatives is impaired are today, for the most part, unconvincing.

A consideration that appears to be of more substance in justifying some deviations from population-based representation in state legislatures is that of insuring some voice to political subdivisions, as political subdivisions. Several factors make more than insubstantial claims that a State can rationally consider according political subdivisions some independent representation in at least one body of the state legislature, as long as the basic standard of equality of population among districts is maintained. . . .

VII.

That the Equal Protection Clause requires that both houses of a state legislature be apportioned on a population basis does not mean that States cannot adopt some reasonable plan for periodic revision of their apportionment schemes. Decennial reapportionment appears to be a rational approach to readjustment of legislative representation in order to take into account population shifts and growth. . . . In substance, we do not regard the Equal Protection Clause as requiring daily, monthly, annual or biennial reapportionment, so long as a State has reasonably conceived plan for periodic readjustment of legislative representation. . . .

[Justices Clark and Stewart concurred in separate opinions on the ground the Alabama apportionment was reminiscent of a crazy quilt, "completely lacking in rationality."]

Mr. Justice Harlan dissenting [in this and five related cases, including *Lucas,* below].

The Court's constitutional discussion [is] remarkable (as, indeed, is that found in the separate opinions of my Brothers Stewart and Clark) for its failure to address itself at all to the Fourteenth Amendment as a whole or to the legislative history of the Amendment pertinent to the matter at hand. . . .

The failure of the Court to consider any of these matters cannot be excused or explained by any concept of "developing" constitutionalism. It is meaningless to speak of constitutional "development" when both the language and history of the controlling provisions of the Constitution are wholly ignored. . . . Whatever one might take to be the application to these cases of the Equal Protection Clause if it stood alone, I am unable to understand the Court's utter disregard of [§ 2 of the fourteenth amendment], which expressly recognizes the States' power to deny "or in any way" abridge the right of their inhabitants to vote for "the members of the

[State] Legislature," and its express provision of a remedy for such denial or abridgment. The comprehensive scope of the second section and its particular reference to the state legislatures precludes the suggestion that the first section was intended to have the result reached by the Court. . . .

The history of the adoption of the Fourteenth Amendment provides conclusive evidence that neither those who proposed nor those who ratified the Amendment believed that the Equal Protection Clause limited the power of the States to apportion their legislatures as they saw fit. Moreover, the history demonstrates that the intention to leave this power undisturbed was deliberate and was widely believed to be essential to the adoption of the Amendment. . . .

In the three days of debate [in the House on the resolution proposing the fourteenth amendment] every speaker on the resolution, with a single doubtful exception, assumed without question that, as Mr. Bingham said, "the second section excludes the conclusion that by the first section suffrage is subjected to congressional law." The assumption was neither inadvertent nor silent. Much of the debate concerned the change in the basis of representation effected by the second section, and the speaker stated repeatedly, in express terms or by unmistakable implication, that the States retained the power to regulate suffrage within their borders. [In] the Senate, it was fully understood by everyone that neither the first nor the second section interfered with the right of the States to regulate the elective franchise. [Of] the 23 loyal States which ratified the Amendment before 1870, five had constitutional provisions for apportionment of at least one house of their respective legislatures which wholly disregarded the spread of population. Ten more had constitutional provisions which gave primary emphasis to population, but which applied also other principles, such as partial ratios and recognition of political subdivisions, which were intended to favor sparsely settled areas. Can it be seriously contended that the legislatures of these States, almost two-thirds of those concerned, would have ratified an amendment which might render their own States' constitutions unconstitutional?

[Each] of the 10 "reconstructed" States was required to ratify the Fourteenth Amendment before it was readmitted to the Union. The Constitution of each was scrutinized in Congress [and] six of the 10 States contained provisions departing substantially from the method of apportionment now held to be required by the Amendment. . . . It is incredible that Congress would have exacted ratification of the Fourteenth Amendment as the price of readmission, would have studied the State Constitutions for compliance with the Amendment, and would then have disregarded violations of it.

. . . There is here none of the difficulty which may attend the application of basic principles to situations not contemplated or understood when the principles were framed. The problems which concern the Court now were [b]y the deliberate choice of those responsible for the Amendment [left] untouched.

. . . As of 1961, the Constitutions of all but 11 States, roughly 20% of the total, recognized bases of apportionment other than geographic spread of population. . . . Since Tennessee, which was the subject of *Baker* v. *Carr*, and Virginia, scrutinized and disapproved today, are among the 11 states whose own Constitutions are sound from the standpoint of the Federal Constitution as construed today, it is evident that the actual practice of the States is even more uniformly than their theory opposed to the Court's view of what is constitutionally permissible.

In this summary of what the majority ignores, note should be taken of the Fifteenth and Nineteenth Amendments. [If] constitutional amendment was the only means by which all men and, later, women, could be guaranteed the right to vote at all, even for *federal* officers, how can it be that the far less obvious right to a particular kind of apportionment of *state* legislatures—a right to which is opposed a far more plausible conflicting interest of the State than the interest which opposes the general right to vote—can be conferred by judicial construction of the Fourteenth Amendment? . . .

Mention should be made finally of the decisions of this Court which are disregarded or, more accurately, silently overruled today. *Minor* v. *Happersett* [21 Wall. 162] held that the Fourteenth Amendment did *not* confer the right to vote on anyone . . . . Other cases are more directly in point [*Colegrove* v. *Barrett*, 330 U.S. 804; *Remmey* v. *Smith*, 342 U.S. 916; *Kidd* v. *McCanless*, 352 U.S. 920; *Radford* v. *Gary*, 352 U.S. 991.]

Each of these recent cases is distinguished on some ground or other in *Baker*. Their summary disposition prevent consideration whether these after-the-fact distinctions are real or imaginary. The fact remains, however, that between 1947 and 1957, four cases raising issues precisely the same as those decided today were presented to the Court. Three were dismissed because the issues presented were thought insubstantial and in the fourth the lower court's dismissal was affirmed.

. . . . The consequence of today's decision is that in all but the handful of States which may already staisfy the new requirements the local District Court or, it may be, the state courts, are given blanket authority and the constitutional duty to supervise apportionment of the State Legislatures. It is difficult to imagine a more intolerable and inappropriate interference by the judiciary with the independent legislatures of the States. . . .

Generalities cannot obscure the cold truth that cases of this type are not amenable to the development of judicial standards. No set of standards can guide a court which has to decide how many legislative districts a State shall have, or what the shape of the districts shall be, or . . . whether a State should have single-member districts or multi-member districts or some other combination of both. No such standard can control the balance between keeping up with population shifts and having stable districts. In all these respects, the courts will be called upon to make particular decisions with respect to which a principle of equally populated districts will be of no assistance whatsoever. Quite obviously, there are limitless possibilities for districting consistent with such a principle. Nor can these problems be avoided by judicial reliance on legislative judgments so far as possible. Reshaping or combining one or two districts, or modifying just a few district lines, is no less a matter of choosing among many possible solutions, with varying political consequences, than reapportionment broadside. . . .

Although the Court—necessarily, as I believe—provides only generalities in elaboration of its main thesis, its opinion nevertheless fully demonstrates how far removed these problems are from fields of judicial competence. Recognizing that "indiscriminate districting" is an invitation to "partisan gerrymandering," the Court nevertheless excludes virtually every basis for the formation of electoral districts other than "indiscriminate districting." In one or another of today's opinions, the Court declares it unconstitutional for a State to give effective consideration to any of the following in establishing legislative districts: (1) history; (2) "economic or other sorts of group interests"; (3) area; (4) geographical considerations; (5) a desire "to insure effective representation for sparsely settled areas"; (6) "availability of access of citizens to their representatives"; (7) theories of bicameralism (except those approved by the Court); (8) occupation; (9) "an attempt to balance urban and rural power"; (10) the preference of a majority of voters in the State. So far as presently appears, the *only* factor which a State

may consider, apart from numbers, is political subdivisions. But even "a clearly rational state policy" recognizing this factor is unconstitutional if "population is submerged as the controlling consideration . . . ."

I know of no principle of logic or practical or theoretical politics, still less any constitutional principle, which establishes all or any of these exclusions. [L]egislators can represent their electors only by speaking for their interests—economic, social, political—many of which do reflect the place where the electors live. The Court does not establish, or indeed even attempt to make a case for the proposition that conflicting interests within a State can only be adjusted by disregarding them when voters are grouped for purposes of representation. . . .

Finally, these decisions give support to a current mistaken view . . . that every major social ill in this country can find its cure in some constitutional "principle," and that this Court should "take the lead" in promoting reform when other branches of government fail to act. The Constitution is not a panacea for every blot upon the public welfare, nor should this Court, ordained as a judicial body, be thought of as a general haven for reform movements. The Constitution is an instrument of government, fundamental to which is the premise that in a diffusion of governmental authority lies the greatest promise that this Nation will realize liberty for all its citizens. This Court, limited in function in accordance with that premise, does not serve its high purpose when it exceeds its authority, even to satisfy justified impatience with the slow workings of the political process. For when, in the name of constitutional interpretation, the Court *adds* something to the Constitution that was deliberately excluded from it, the Court in reality substitutes its view of what should be so for the amending process. . . .

Lucas v. *Forty-Fourth General Assembly* (excerpt)
377 U.S. 713 (1964)

This, a companion case to *Reynolds,* merits special attention because here the people of Colorado, *in a statewide referendum,* had elected to copy Congress by providing geographic representation for their Senate and population representation for their House. Neither the federal analogy nor approval of the people themselves (by a majority in every county of the state) saved the measure from the *Reynolds* rule of apportionment.

Mr. Justice Stewart, whom Mr. Justice Clark joins, dissenting. . . .

The Colorado plan creates a General Assembly composed of a Senate of 39 members and a House of 65 members. The State is divided into 65 equal population representative districts, with one representative to be elected from each district, and 39 senatorial districts, 14 of which include more than one county. In the Colorado House, the majority unquestionably rules supreme, with the population factor untempered by other considerations. In the Senate rural minorities do not have effective control, and therefore do not have even a veto power over the will of the urban majorities. It is true that, as a matter of theoretical arithmetic, a minority of 36% of the voters could elect a majority of the Senate, but this percentage has no real meaning in terms of the legislative process.[1] Under the Colorado plan, no possible combination of Colorado senators from rural districts, even assuming arguendo that they would vote as a bloc, could control the Senate. To arrive at the 36%

figure, one must include with the rural districts a substantial number of urban districts, districts with substantially dissimilar interests. There is absolutely no reason to assume that this theoretical majority would ever vote together on any issue so as to thwart the wishes of the majority of the voters of Colorado. Indeed, when we eschew the world of numbers, and look to the real world of effective representation, the simple fact of the matter is that Colorado's three metropolitan areas, Denver, Pueblo, and Colorado Springs, elect a majority of the Senate. . . .

It is clear from the record that if per capita representation were the rule in both houses of the Colorado Legislature, counties having small populations would have to be merged with larger counties having totally dissimilar interests. Their representatives would not only be unfamiliar with the problems of the smaller county, but the interests of the smaller counties might well be totally submerged by the interests of the larger counties with which they are joined. Since representatives representing conflicting interests might well pay greater attention to the views of the majority, the minority interest could be denied any effective representation at all. Its votes would not be merely "diluted," an injury which the Court considers of constitutional dimensions, but rendered totally nugatory. . . .

The present apportionment, adopted overwhelmingly by the people in a 1962 popular referendum as a state constitutional amendment, is entirely rational, and the amendment by its terms provides for keeping the apportionment current. Thus the majority has consciously cho-

---

[1] The theoretical figure is arrived at by placing the legislative districts for each house in rank order of population, and by counting down the smallest population end of the list a sufficient distance to accumulate the minimum population which could elect a majority of the house in question. It is a meaningless abstraction as applied to a multimembered body because the factors of political party alignment and interest representation make such theoretical bloc voting a practical impossibility. For example, 31,000,000 people in the 26 least populous States representing only 17% of United States population have 52% of the Senators in the United States Senate. But no one contends that this bloc controls the Senate's legislative process. [Footnote by Justice Stewart.]

sen to protect the minority's interests, and under the liberal initiative provisions of the Colorado Constitution, it retains the power to reverse its decision to do so. Therefore, there can be no question of frustration of the basic principle of majority rule.

Note and quaere: In *Baker* v. *Carr* (above, Chapter 1), the Court said, "Judicial standards under the Equal Protection Clause are well developed and familiar [this was in 1961], and it has been open to courts since the enactment of the Fourteenth Amendment to determine, if on the particular facts they must, that a discrimination reflects *no* policy, but simply arbitrary and capricious action." The three concurring opinions also stress that it was the *traditional* view of Equal Protection that was to control apportionment. Does the Court in fact adhere to that view in *Sims* and *Lucas?* Did the Court take jurisdiction (*Baker*) on one basis, and then exercise that jurisdiction (*Sims* and *Lucas*) on another basis?

In the course of its opinion in *Baker* the Court said, "No effective political remedy to obtain relief against the alleged malapportionment appears to have been available." This thought is endlessly urged by commentators as justification for judicial intervention in the apportionment problem and elsewhere. Is this an acceptable view of the separation (and division) of powers; namely, that if one branch does not perform satisfactorily (from whose point of view?), another branch may intervene and indeed itself perform the other branch's function? Was there in *Lucas* no "political remedy" to cure the challenged apportionment?

The major premise of *Baker* seems to be that a representative body should be subject to control by a majority of the voters. Thus the *Baker* Court observed, "To conclude differently, and to sanction minority control of state bodies would appear to deny majority rights . . . ." Does the Court itself deny majority rights in *Lucas?* See the Bork quotation in Chapter 1, above.

Governor Earl Warren on Redistricting

Some 16 years before the *Reynolds* decision, California was considering a proposal to apportion the state senate in accordance with population. In a speech at Merced, California, on October 29, 1948, Governor Earl Warren (then the Republican candidate for the vice presidency of the United States) made the following remarks:

Many California counties are far more important in the life of the State than their population bears to the entire population of the State. It is for this reason that I have never been in favor of restricting the representation in the senate to a strictly population basis.

It is the same reason that the Founding Fathers of our country gave balanced representation to the States of the Union—equal representation in one house and proportionate representation based on population in the other.

Moves have been made to upset the balanced representation in our State, even though it has served us well and is strictly in accord with American tradition and the pattern of our National Government.

There was a time when California was completely dominated by boss rule. The liberal election laws and legislative reapportionment of the system have liberated us from such domination. Any weakening of the laws would invite a return to boss rule which we are now happily rid of.

Our State has made almost unbelievable progress under our present system of legislative representation. I believe we should keep it.

Note: With respect to congressional districts, the Court has adhered to a strict rule that the states must "make a good-faith effort to achieve precise mathematical equality," *White* v. *Weiser,* 412 U.S. 783 (1973). But with respect to state legislature districting it has been much less strict. *Mahan* v. *Howell,* 410 U.S. 315 (1973), permitted a deviation of 16.4 percent from district population equality in one house of the Virginia legislature. The greater flexibility with respect to state legislatures was said to be justified by "the state's policy of maintaining the integrity of political subdivision lines." See *Connor* v. *Rich,* 431 U.S. 407 (1977).

Avery v. *Midland County,* 390 U.S. 474 (1968), and *Hadley* v. *Junior College District,* 397 U.S. 50 (1970), held the *Reynolds* rule of equality applies to local governments.

Note and quaere: United Jewish Organizations v. *Carey,* 430 U.S. 114 (1977), upheld racial gerrymandering of state legislative districts in the following circumstances. Pursuant to Section 5 of the Voting Rights Act of 1965, the United States Attorney General "induced" the New York legislature to redraw district boundaries so as to ensure nonwhites in each of four state electoral districts a 65 percent majority. One result was that the voting strength of some 30,000 Hasidic Jews was significantly "diluted" (by being spread over two districts instead of one, as before). The Jewish plaintiffs argued that this reapportionment was invalid because it was deliberately based on racial considerations. The Court found no fault in that, for the reapportionment did not "stigmatize" any race; it did not "fence out" the white population (see *Gomillion* v. *Lightfoot,* 364 U.S. 339 [1960]); it was not unfair to whites as a whole. Chief Justice Burger dissented:

> Manipulating the racial composition of electoral districts to assure one minority or another its "deserved" representation will not promote the goal of a racially neutral legislature. On the contrary, such racial gerrymandering puts the imprimatur of the state on the concept that race is a proper consideration in the electoral process. . . .
>
> The result reached by the Court today in the name of the Voting Rights Act is ironic. The use of a mathematical formula tends to sustain the existence of ghettos by promoting the notion that political clout is to be gained or maintained by marshalling particular racial, ethnic or religious groups in enclaves. It suggests to the voter that only a candidate of the same race, religion or ethnic origins can properly represent that voter's interests, and that such candidate can be elected only from a district with a sufficient minority concentration. The de-vice employed by the State of New York and endorsed by the Court today, moves us one step farther away from a truly homogeneous society. . . .

Gaffney v. *Cummings,* 412 U.S. 735 (1973), found no constitutional infirmity in equal-size districts deliberately gerrymandered to give the two major political parties proportionate representation. The Court has consistently avoided getting itself involved in the gerrymander problem. Is that because all districting entails gerrymandering in the sense that no matter how it is done it will inevitably favor some interests at the expense of others? In *Whitcomb* v. *Chavis,* 403 U.S. 124 (1971), Justices Douglas, Brennan, and Marshall (dissenting) observed that ". . . gerrymandering is the other half of *Reynolds* v. *Sims*." (That is, it too "dilutes" votes.) Yet—except vis-à-vis race—they, like the Court, seem to have found it judicially unmanageable.

Does the crux of the problem lie in the fact that interests are not homogenized—that some interest groups are large, some small; some geographically compact, some widespread, some spotty; some strong and some weak for fiscal, organizational, and prestige reasons? Don't equal-sized voting districts imposed on such an uneven, crazy-quilt interest base inevitably produce uneven results, that is, diluted votes? Consider, for example, a state divided into equal-sized districts first by north-south boundary lines—and then alternatively by east-west lines. Both satisfy the *Reynolds* test. Yet, given the reality of nonhomogenized interests, is it not likely that the north-south lines would favor one set of interests, while the east-west lines would favor another? Surely, as Mr. Justice Douglas put it, gerrymandering—whether deliberate or the inadvertent result of nonfungible interests—"is the other half of Reynolds." Is there any way the Court can solve this problem?

Harper v. *Virginia State Board of Elections*
383 U.S. 663 (1966)

Mr. Justice Douglas delivered the opinion of the Court.

These are suits by Virginia residents to have declared unconstitutional Virginia's poll tax. The three-judge District Court, feeling bound by our decision in *Breedlove* v. *Suttles*, 302 U.S. 277, dismissed the complaint. See 240 F.Supp. 270. The cases came here on appeal and we noted probable jurisdiction. . . .

While the right to vote in federal elections is conferred by Art. I, § 2, of the Constitution . . . the right to vote in state elections is nowhere expressly mentioned. It is argued that the right to vote in state elections is implicit, particularly by reason of the First Amendment and that it may not constitutionally be conditioned upon the payment of a tax or fee. . . . We do not stop to canvass the relation between voting and political expression. For it is enough to say that once the franchise is granted to the electorate, lines may not be drawn which are inconsistent with the Equal Protection Clause of the Fourteenth Amendment. That is to say, the right of suffrage "is subject to the imposition of state standards which are not discriminatory and which do not contravene any restriction that Congress, acting pursuant to its constitutional powers, has imposed." *Lassiter* v. *Northampton County Board of Elections*, 360 U.S. 45, 51. We were speaking there of a state literacy test which we sustained, warning that the result would be different if a literacy test, fair on its face, were used to discriminate against a class. *Id.*, at 53. But the Lassiter case does not govern the result here, because, unlike a poll tax, the "ability to read and write . . . has some relation to standards designed to promote intelligent use of the ballot." *Id.*, at 51.

We conclude that a State violates the Equal Protection Clause of the Fourteenth Amendment whenever it makes the affluence of the voter or payment of any fee an electoral standard. Voter qualifications have no relation to wealth nor to paying or not paying this or any other tax. Our cases demonstrate that the Equal Protection Clause of the Fourteenth Amendment restrains the States from fixing voter qualifications which invidiously discriminate. Thus without questioning the power of a State to impose reasonable residence restrictions on the availability of the ballot (see *Pope* v. *Williams*, 193 U.S. 621), we held in *Carrington* v. *Rash*, 380 U.S. 89, that a State may not deny the opportunity to vote to a bona fide resident merely because he is a member of the armed services. "By forbidding a soldier ever to controvert the presumption of non-residence, the Texas Constitution imposes an invidious discrimination in violation of the Fourteenth Amendment." *Id.*, at 96. And see *Louisiana* v. *United States*, 380 U.S. 145. Previously we had said that neither homesite nor occupation "affords a permissible basis for distinguishing between qualified voters within the State." *Gray* v. *Sanders*, 372 U.S. 368, 380. We think the same must be true of requirements of wealth or affluence or payment of a fee.

Long ago in *Yick Wo* v. *Hopkins*, 118 U.S. 356, 370, the Court referred to "the political franchise of voting" as a "fundamental political right, because preservative of all rights." Recently in *Reynolds* v. *Sims*, 377 U.S. 533, 561–562, we said: "Undoubtedly, the right of suffrage is a fundamental matter in a free and democratic society. Especially since the right to exercise the franchise in a free and unimpaired manner is preservative of other basic civil and political rights, any alleged infringement of the right of citizens to vote must be carefully and meticulously scrutinized." . . .

It is argued that a State may exact fees from citizens for many different kinds of licenses; that if it can demand from all an equal fee for a driver's license, it can demand from all an equal poll tax for voting. But we must remember that the interest of the State, when it comes to voting, is limited to the power to fix qualifications. Wealth, like race, creed, or color, is not germane to one's ability to participate intelligently in the electoral process. Lines drawn on the basis of wealth or property, like those of race (*Korematsu v. United States,* 323 U.S. 214, 216), are traditionally disfavored. See *Edwards* v. *People of State of California,* 314 U.S. 160, 184–185 (Jackson, J., concurring); *Griffin* v. *People of State of Illinois,* 351 U.S. 12; *Douglas* v. *People of State of California,* 372 U.S. 353. To introduce wealth or payment of a fee as a measure of a voter's qualifications is to introduce a capricious or irrelevant factor. The degree of the discrimination is irrelevant. In this context—that is, as a condition of obtaining a ballot—the requirement of fee paying causes an "invidious" discrimination (*Skinner* v. *State of Oklahoma,* 316 U.S. 535, 541) that runs afoul of the Equal Protection Clause. Levy "by the poll," as stated in *Breedlove* v. *Suttles, supra,* 302 U.S. at 281, is an old familiar form of taxation; and we say nothing to impair its validity so long as it is not made a condition to the exercise of the franchise. *Breedlove* v. *Suttles* sanctioned its use as "a prerequisite of voting." *Id.,* at 283. To that extent the *Breedlove* case is overruled.

We agree, of course, with Mr. Justice Holmes that the Due Process Clause of the Fourteenth Amendment "does not enact Mr. Herbert Spencer's Social Statics" (*Lochner* v. *People of State of New York,* 198 U.S. 45, 75). Likewise, the Equal Protection Clause is not shackled to the political theory of a particular era. In determining what lines are unconstitutionally discriminatory, we have never been confined to historic notions of equality, any more than we have restricted due process to a fixed catalogue of what was at a given time deemed to be the limits of fundamental rights. See *Malloy* v. *Hogan,* 378 U.S. 1, 5–6. Notions of what constitutes equal treatment for purposes of the Equal Protection Clause *do* change. This Court in 1896 held that laws providing for separate public facilities for white and Negro citizens did not deprive the latter of the equal protection and treatment that the Fourteenth Amendment commands. *Plessy* v. *Ferguson,* 163 U.S. 537. Seven of the eight

Justices then sitting subscribed to the Court's opinion, thus joining in expressions of what constituted unequal and discriminatory treatment that sound strange to a contemporary ear. When, in 1954—more than a half-century later—we repudiated the "separate-but-equal" doctrine of Plessy as respects public education we stated: "In approaching this problem, we cannot turn the clock back to 1868 when the Amendment was adopted, or even to 1896 when *Plessy* v. *Ferguson* was written." *Brown* v. *Board of Education,* 347 U.S. 483, 492.

In a recent searching re-examination of the Equal Protection Clause, we held, as already noted, that "the opportunity for equal participation by all voters in the election of state legislators" is required. *Reynolds* v. *Sims, supra,* 377 U.S. at 566. We decline to qualify that principle by sustaining this poll tax. Our conclusion, like that in *Reynolds* v. *Sims,* is founded not on what we think governmental policy should be, but on what the Equal Protection Clause requires.

We have long been mindful that where fundamental rights and liberties are asserted under the Equal Protection Clause, classifications which might invade or restrain them must be closely scrutinized and carefully confined. See, *e.g., Skinner* v. *State of Oklahoma,* 316 U.S. 535, 541; *Reynolds* v. *Sims,* 377 U.S. 533, 561–562; *Carrington* v. *Rash, supra; Baxstrom* v. *Herold,* 383 U.S. 107; *Cox* v. *State of Louisiana,* 379 U.S. 536, 580–581 (Black, J., concurring).

Those principles apply here. For to repeat, wealth or free paying has, in our view, no relation to voting qualifications; the right to vote is too precious, too fundamental to be so burdened or conditioned. . . .

Mr. Justice Black, dissenting.

. . . The Court . . . overrules Breedlove in part, but its opinion reveals that it does so not by using its limited power to interpret the original meaning of the Equal Protection Clause, but by giving that clause a new meaning which it believes represents a better governmental policy. From this action I dissent. . . .

The Court's justification for consulting its own notions rather than following the original meaning of the Constitution, as I would, apparently is based on the belief of the majority of the Court that for this Court to be bound by the original meaning of the Constitution is an intolerable and debilitating evil; that our Constitution should not be "shackled to the political theory of a particular era," and that to save the country from the original Constitution the Court must have constant power to renew it and keep it abreast with this Court's more enlightening theories of what is best for our society. It seems to me that this is not only an attack on the great value of our Constitution itself but also on the concept of a written constitution which is to survive through the years as originally written unless changed through the amendment process which the Framers wisely provided. Moreover, when a "political theory" embodied in our Constitution becomes outdated, it seems to me that a majority of the nine members of this Court are not only without constitutional power but are far less qualified to choose a new constitutional political theory than the people of this country proceeding in the manner provided by Article V.

The people have not found it impossible to amend their Constitution to meet new conditions. The Equal Protection Clause itself is the product of the people's desire to use their constitutional power to amend the Constitution to meet new problems. . . .

Mr. Justice Harlan, whom Mr. Justice Stewart joins, dissenting.

The final demise of state poll taxes, already totally proscribed by the Twenty-Fourth Amendment with respect to federal elections and abolished by the States themselves in all but four States with respect to state elections, is perhaps in itself not of great moment. But the fact that the *coup de grace* has been administered

by this Court instead of being left to the affected States or to the federal political process should be a matter of continuing concern to all interested in maintaining the proper role of this tribunal under our scheme of government. . . .

Quaere: Should *Harper* be considered a wealth or a voting case? Only 14 months before the *Harper* decision we adopted the Twenty-fourth Amendment, abolishing poll taxes in *federal elections* only. May this be considered a judgment by the American people that the poll tax in state elections was a matter to be left to state discretion? It should be noted that in amending the Constitution the American people act in their ultimate sovereign capacity as a self-governing body. Does *Harper* in effect override a constitutional amendment?

WEALTH CLASSIFICATIONS

Shapiro v. *Thompson*
394 U.S. 618 (1969)

Justice Brennan delivered the opinion of the Court.

These three appeals were restored to the calendar for reargument. Each is an appeal from a decision of a three-judge District Court holding unconstitutional a State or District of Columbia statutory provision which denies welfare assistance to residents of the State or District who have ˜not resided within their jurisdictions for at least one year immediately preceding their applications for such assistance. We affirm the judgments of the District Courts in the three cases. . . .

There is no dispute that the effect of the waiting-period requirement in each case is to create two classes of needy resident families indistinguishable from each other except that one is composed of residents who have resided a year or more, and the second of residents who have resided less than a year, in the jurisdiction. On the basis of this sole difference the first class is granted and the second class is denied welfare aid upon which may depend the ability of the families to obtain the very means to subsist—food, shelter, and other necessities of life. In each case, the District Court found that appellees met the test for residence in their jurisdictions, as well as all other eligibility requirements except the requirement of residence for a full year prior to their applications. On reargument, appellees' central contention is that the statutory prohibition of benefits to residents of less than a year creates a classification which constitutes an invidious discrimination denying them equal protection of the laws. We agree. The interests which appellants assert are promoted by the classification either may not constitutionally be promoted by government or are not compelling governmental interests.

Primarily, appellants justify the waiting-period requirement as a protective device to preserve the fiscal integrity of state public assistance programs. It is asserted that people who require welfare assistance during their first year of residence in a State are likely to become continuing burdens on state welfare programs. Therefore, the argument runs, if such people can be deterred from entering the jursidiction by denying them welfare benefits during the first year, state programs to assist long-term residents will not be impaired by a substantial influx of indigent newcomers. . . .

We do not doubt that the one-year waiting period device is well suited to discourage the influx of poor families in need of assistance. An indigent who desires to migrate, resettle, find a new job, start a new life will doubtless hesitate if he knows that he must risk making the move without the possibility of falling back on state welfare assistance during his first year of residence, when his need may be most acute. But the purpose of inhibiting migration by needy persons into the State is constitutionally impermissible.

This Court long ago recognized that the nature of our Federal Union and our constitutional concepts of personal liberty unite to require that all citizens be free to travel throughout the length and breadth of our land uninhibited by statutes, rules, or regulations which unreasonably burden or restrict this movement. . . .

We have no occasion to ascribe the source of this right to travel interstate to a particular constitutional provision. It suffices that, as Mr. Justice Stewart said for the Court in *United States* v. *Guest*, 383 U.S. 745 (1966): "The constitutional right to travel from one State to another . . . occupies a position fundamental to the concept of our Federal Union. It is a right that has been firmly established and repeatedly recognized . . . [T]he right finds no explicit mention in the Constitution. The reason, it has been suggested, is that a right so elementary was conceived from the beginning to be a necessary concomitant of the stronger Union the Constitution created. . . ."

Thus, the purpose of deterring the inmigration of indigents cannot serve as justification for the classification created by the one-year waiting period, since that purpose is constitutionally impermissible. . . .

Alternatively, appellants argue that even if it is impermissible for a State to attempt to deter the entry of all indigents, the challenged classification may be justified as a permissible state attempt to discourage those indigents who would enter the State solely to obtain larger benefits. We observe first that none of the statutes before us is tailored to serve that objective. Rather, the class of barred newcomers is all-inclusive, lumping the great majority who come to the State for other purposes with those who come for the sole purpose of collecting higher benefits. . . .

More fundamentally, a State may no more try to fence out those indigents who seek higher welfare benefits than it may try to fence out indigents generally. Implicit in any such distinction is the notion that indigents who enter a State with the hope of securing higher welfare benefits are somehow less deserving than indigents who do not take this consideration into account. But we do not perceive why a mother who is seeking to make a new life for herself and her children should be regarded as less deserving because she considers, among other factors, the level of a State's public assistance. Surely such a mother is no less deserving than a mother who moves into a particular State in order to take advantage of its better educational facilities.

Appellants argue further that the challenged classification may be sustained as an attempt to distinguish between new and old residents on the basis of the contribution they have made to the community through the payment of taxes. We have difficulty seeing how long-term residents who qualify for welfare are making a greater present contribution to the State in taxes than indigent residents who have recently arrived. . . . Appellants' reasoning would logically permit the State to bar new residents from schools, parks, and libraries or deprive them of police and fire protection. Indeed it would permit the State to apportion all benefits and services according to the past tax contributions of its citizens. The Equal Protection Clause prohibits such an apportionment of state services. . . .

In sum, neither deterrence of indigents from migrating to the State nor limitation of welfare benefits to those regarded as contributing to the State is a constitutionally permissible state objective.

Appellants next advance as justification certain administrative and related governmental objectives allegedly served by the waiting-period requirement. They argue that the requirement (1) facilitates the planning of the welfare budget; (2) provides an objective test of residency; (3) minimizes the opportunity for recipients fraudulently to receive payments from more than one jurisdiction; and (4) encourages early entry of new residents into the labor force. . . .

We conclude . . . that appellants in these cases do not use and have no need to use the one-year requirement for the governmental purposes suggested. Thus, even under traditional equal protection tests a classification of welfare applicants according to whether they have lived in the State for one year would seem irrational and unconstitutional. But, of course, the traditional criteria do not apply in these cases. Since the classification here touches on the fundamental right of interstate movement, its constitutionality must be judged by the stricter standard of whether it promotes a *compelling* state interest. Under this standard, the waiting period requirement clearly violates the Equal Protection Clause.

The waiting-period requirement in the District of Columbia Code . . . violates the Due Process Clause of the Fifth Amendment. . . .

Mr. Justice Stewart, concurring.

In joining the opinion of the Court, I add a word in response to the dissent of my Brother Harlan, who, I think, has quite misapprehended what the Court's opinion says.

The Court today does *not* "pick out particular human activities, characterize them as 'fundamental,' and give them added protection . . . ." To the contrary, the Court simply recognizes, as it must, an established constitutional right, and gives to that right no less protection than the Constitution itself demands. . . .

Mr. Chief Justice Warren, with whom Mr. Justice Black joins, dissenting.

In my opinion the issue before us can be simply stated: may Congress, acting under one of its enumerated powers, impose minimal nationwide residence requirements or authorize the States to do so? Since I believe that Congress does have this power and has constitutionally exercised it in these cases, I must dissent. . . .

[The crux of Mr. Justice Harlan's dissent will be found in an excerpt from *Shapiro*, page 000, above.]

Dandridge v. *Williams*
See p. 523, above.

> *Note:* Under *Dandridge,* as we have seen, only constitutionally recognized interests are entitled to special strict-scrutiny protection. Thus *James* v. *Voltierra,* 402 U.S. 137 (1971), upheld on rational-basis grounds a referendum requirement for *low-rent* housing, whereas *Hunter* v. *Erickson,* 339 U.S. 385 (1969), had invalidated on strict-scrutiny grounds a similar requirement with respect to *open* housing. In each case "special burdens" fell on a "minority" group. The differentiating factor in the Court's decisions apparently was that the Constitution does not deal with poverty; it does deal with and outlaw racism.

San Antonio Independent School District v.
Rodriguez
411 U.S. 1 (1973)

Mr. Justice Powell delivered the opinion of the Court.

This suit attacking the Texas system of financing public education was initiated by Mexican-American parents . . . [as] a class action on behalf of school children throughout the State who are members of minority groups or who are poor and reside in school districts having a low property tax base. . . .

. . . The District Court held that the Texas system discriminates on the basis of wealth in the manner in which education is provided for its people. [337 F. Supp. 280]. Finding that wealth is a "suspect" classification and that education is a "fundamental" interest, the District Court held that the Texas system could be sustained only if the State could show that it was premised upon some compelling state interest. On this issue the court concluded that "[n]ot only are defendants unable to demonstrate compelling state interests . . . they fail even to establish a reasonable basis for these classifications."

I.

[Half of the educational expenditures in Texas come from the Texas Minimum Foundation School Program. Eighty percent of this program is financed by state revenues; the balance—called the Local Fund Assignment—comes from the individual school districts via a formula reflecting each district's relative property tax potential.]

The school district in which appellees reside, the Edgewood Independent School District, has been compared throughout this litigation with the Alamo Heights Independent School District. This comparison between the least and most affluent districts in the San Antonio area serves to illustrate the manner in which the dual system of finance operates and to indicate the extent to which substantial disparities exist despite the State's impressive progress in recent years. Edgewood is one of seven public school districts in the metropolitan area. Approximately 22,000 students are enrolled in its 25 elementary and secondary schools. The district is situated in the core-city sector of San Antonio in a residential neighborhood that has little commercial or industrial property. The residents are predominantly of Mexican-American descent: approximately 90% of the student population is Mexican-American and over 6% is Negro. The average assessed property value per pupil is $5,960—the lowest in the metropolitan area—and the median family income ($4,686) is also the lowest. At an equalized tax rate of $1.05 per $100 of assessed property—the highest in the metropolitan area—the district contributed $26 to the education of each child for the 1967–1968 school year above its Local Fund Assignment for the Minimum Foundation Program. The Foundation Program contributed $222 per pupil for a state-local total of $248. Federal funds added another $108 for a total of $356 per pupil.

Alamo Heights is the most affluent school district in San Antonio. Its six schools, housing approximately 5,000 students, are situated in a residential community quite unlike the Edgewood District. The school population is predominantly Anglo, having only 18% Mexican-Americans and less than 1% of Negroes. The assessed property value per pupil exceeds $49,000 and the median family income is $8,001. In 1967–1968 the local tax rate of $.85 per $100 of valuation yielded $333 per pupil over and above its contribution to the Foundation Program. Coupled with the $225 provided from that Program, the district was able to supply $558 per student. Supplemented by a $36 per pupil grant from federal sources, Alamo Heights spent $594 per pupil.

. . . [1970–1971] figures also reveal the extent to which these two districts' allotments were funded from their own required contributions to the Local Fund Assignment. Alamo Heights, because of its relative wealth, was required to contribute out of its local property tax collections approximately $100 per pupil, or about 20% of its Foundation grant. Edgewood, on the other hand, paid only $8.46 per pupil, which is about 2.4% of its grant. It does appear then that, at least as to these two districts, the Local Fund Assignment does reflect a rough approximation of the relative taxpaying potential of each.

Despite . . . recent increases, substantial interdistrict disparities in school expenditures found by the District Court to prevail in San Antonio and in varying degrees throughout the State still exist. And it was these disparities, largely attributable to differences in the amounts of money collected through local property taxation, that led the District Court to conclude that Texas' dual system of public school finance violated the Equal Protection Clause.
. . .

Texas virtually concedes that its historically rooted dual system of financing education could not withstand the strict judicial scrutiny that this Court has found appropriate in reviewing legislative judgments that interfere with fundamental constitutional rights or that involve suspect classifications. If, as previous decisions have indicated, strict scrutiny means that the State's system is not entitled to the usual pre-

sumption of validity, that the State rather than the complainants must carry a "heavy burden of justification," that the State must demonstrate that its educational system has been structured with "precision" and is "tailored" narrowly to serve legitimate objectives and that it has selected the "least drastic means" for effectuating its objectives, the Texas financing system and its counterpart in virtually every other State will not pass muster. The State candidly admits that "[n]o one familiar with the Texas system would contend that it has yet achieved perfection." Apart from its concession that educational finance in Texas has "defects" and "imperfections," the State defends the system's rationality with vigor and disputes the District Court's finding that it lacks a "reasonable basis."

This, then, establishes the framework for our analysis. We must decide, first, whether the Texas system of financing public education operates to the disadvantage of some suspect class or impinges upon a fundamental right explicitly or implicitly protected by the Constitution, thereby requiring strict judicial scrutiny. If so, the judgment of the District Court should be affirmed. If not, the Texas scheme must still be examined to determine whether it rationally furthers some legitimate, articulated state purpose and therefore does not constitute an invidious discrimination in violation of the Equal Protection Clause of the Fourteenth Amendment.

I.

. . .

A

The wealth discrimination discovered by the District Court in this case, and by several other courts that have recently struck down school financing laws in other States,[1] is quite unlike

---

[1] [E.g., *Serrano* v. *Priest*, 487 P.2d 1241 (1971)—Editor's note.]

any of the forms of wealth discrimination heretofore reviewed by this Court. Rather than focusing on the unique features of the alleged discrimination, the courts in these cases have virtually assumed their findings of a suspect classification through a simplistic process of analysis: since, under the traditional systems of financing public schools, some poorer people receive less expensive educations than other more affluent people, these systems discriminate on the basis of wealth. This approach largely ignores the hard threshold questions, including whether it makes a difference for purposes of consideration under the Constitution that the class of disadvantaged "poor" cannot be identified or defined in customary equal protection terms, and whether the relative—rather than absolute—nature of the asserted deprivation is of significant consequence. Before a State's laws and the justifications for the classifications they create are subjected to strict judicial scrutiny, we think these threshold considerations must be analyzed more closely than they were in the court below.

The case comes to us with no definitive description of the classifying facts or delineation of the disfavored class. Examination of the District Court's opinion and of appellees' complaint, briefs, and contentions at oral argument suggests, however, at least three ways in which the discrimination claimed here might be described. The Texas system of school finance might be regarded as discriminating (1) against "poor" persons whose incomes fall below some identifiable level of poverty or who might be characterized as functionally "indigent," or (2) against those who are relatively poorer than others, or (3) against all those who, irrespective of their personal incomes, happen to reside in relatively poorer school districts. Our task must be to ascertain whether, in fact, the Texas system has been shown to discriminate on any of these possible bases and, if so, whether the resulting classification may be regarded as suspect.

The precedents of this Court provide the proper starting point. The individuals or groups of individuals who constituted the class discriminated against in our prior cases shared two distinguishing characteristics: because of their impecunity they were completely unable to pay for some desired benefit, and as a consequence, they sustained an absolute deprivation of a meaningful opportunity to enjoy that benefit. In *Griffin* v. *Illinois*, 351 U.S. 12 (1956), and its progeny, the Court invalidated state laws that prevented an indigent criminal defendant from acquiring a transcript, or an adequate substitute for a transcript, for use at several stages of the trial and appeal process. The payment requirements in each case were found to occasion *de facto* discrimination against those who, because of their indigency, were totally unable to pay for transcripts. And, the Court in each case emphasized that no constitutional violation would have been shown if the State had provided some "adequate substitute" for a full stenographic transcript. . . .

Only appellees' first possible basis for describing the class disadvantaged by the Texas school finance system—discrimination against a class of definably "poor" persons—might arguably meet the criteria established in these prior cases. Even a cursory examination, however, demonstrates that neither of the two distinguishing characteristics of wealth classifications can be found here. First, in support of their charge that the system discriminates against the "poor," appellees have made no effort to demonstrate that it operates to the peculiar disadvantage of any class fairly definable as indigent, or as composed of persons whose incomes are beneath any designated poverty level. Indeed, there is reason to believe that the poorest families are not necessarily clustered in the poorest property districts. A recent and exhaustive study of school districts in Connecticut concluded that "[i]t is clearly incorrect . . . to contend that the 'poor' live in 'poor' districts . . . . Thus, the major factual assumption of *Serrano*—that the educational finance system discriminates against the 'poor'—is simply false in Connecticut."[2] Defining "poor" families as those below the Bureau of the Census "poverty level," the Connecticut study found, not surprisingly, that the poor were clustered around commercial and industrial areas—those same areas that provide the most attractive sources of property tax income for school districts. Whether a similar pattern would be discovered in Texas is not known, but there is no basis on the record in this case for assuming that the poorest people—defined by reference to any level of absolute impecunity—are concentrated in the poorest districts.

Second, neither appellees nor the District Court addressed the fact that, unlike each of the foregoing cases, lack of personal resources has not occasioned an absolute deprivation of the desired benefit. The argument here is not that the children in districts having relatively low assessable property values are receiving no public education; rather, it is that they are receiving a poorer quality education than that available to children in districts having more assessable wealth. . . .

For these two reasons—the absence of any evidence that the financing system discriminates against any definable category of "poor" people or that it results in the absolute deprivation of education—the disadvantaged class is not susceptible to identification in traditional terms.

As suggested above, appellees and the District Court may have embraced a second or third approach, the second of which might be characterized as a theory of relative or comparative discrimination based on family income. Appellees sought to prove that a direct correlation exists between the wealth of families within each district and the expenditures therein for education. That is, along a continuum, the poorer the family the lower the dollar amount of education received by the family's children.
. . .

If, in fact, these correlations could be sustained, then it might be argued that expenditures on education—equated by appellees to the quality of education—are dependent on personal wealth. . . . These questions need not be addressed in this case, however, since appellees' proof fails to support their allegations or the District Court's conclusions.

Professor Berke's affidavit is based on a survey of approximately 10% of the school districts in Texas. His findings, set out in the margin,[3] show only that the wealthiest few districts in the sample have the highest median family incomes and spend the most on education, and that the several poorest districts have the lowest family incomes and devote the least amount of money to education. For the remainder of the districts—96 districts comprising almost 90% of the sample—the correlation is inverted, i.e., the districts that spend next to the most money on education are populated by families having next to the lowest median family incomes while the districts spending the least have the highest median family incomes. It is evident that, even if the conceptual questions were answered favorably to appellees, no factual basis exists upon which to found a claim of comparative wealth discrimination.

This brings us, then, to the third way in which the classification scheme might be defined—district wealth discrimination. Since the only correlation indicated by the evidence is between district property wealth and expenditures, it may be argued that discrimination might be found without regard to the individual income characteristics of district residents. Assuming a perfect correlation between district

---

[2] Note, A Statistical Analysis of the School Finance Decisions: On Winning Battles and Losing Wars, 81 Yale L.J. 1303, 1328–1329 (1972).

[3]

Market Value of Taxable Property per Pupil	Median Family Income in 1960	State & Local Expenditures per Pupil
Above $100,000 (10 districts)	$5,900	$815
$100,000–$50,000 (26 districts)	$4,425	$544
$50,000–$30,000 (30 districts)	$4,900	$483
$30,000–$10,000 (40 districts)	$5,050	$462
Below $10,000 (4 districts)	$3,325	$305

property wealth and expenditures from top to bottom, the disadvantaged class might be viewed as encompassing every child in every district except the district that has the most assessable wealth and spends the most on education.[4] Alternatively, as suggested in Mr. Justice Marshall's dissenting opinion, *post*, . . . the class might be defined more restrictively to include children in districts with assessable property which falls below the statewide average, or median, or below some other artificially defined level.

However described, it is clear that appellees' suit asks this Court to extend its most exacting scrutiny to review a system that allegedly discriminates against a large, diverse, and amorphous class, unified only by the common factor of residence in districts that happen to have less taxable wealth than other districts. The system of alleged discrimination and the class it defines have none of the traditional indicia of suspectness: the class is not saddled with such disabilities, or subjected to such a history of purposeful unequal treatment, or relegated to such a position of political powerlessness as to command extraordinary protection from the majoritarian political process.

We thus conclude that the Texas system does not operate to the peculiar disadvantage of any suspect class. But in recognition of the fact that this Court has never heretofore held that wealth discrimination alone provides an adequate basis for invoking strict scrutiny, appellees have not relied solely on this contention. They also assert that the State's system impermissibly interferes with the exercise of a "fundamental" right and that accordingly the prior decisions of this Court require the application of the strict standard of judicial review. . . . It is this

question—whether education is a fundamental right, in the sense that it is among the rights and liberties protected by the Constitution—which has so consumed the attention of courts and commentators in recent years.

B

In *Brown* v. *Board of Education*, 347 U.S. 483 (1954), a unanimous Court recognized that "education is perhaps the most important function of state and local governments." *Id.*, at 493. What was said there in the context of racial discrimination has lost none of its vitality with the passage of time: . . .

Nothing this Court holds today in any way detracts from our historic dedication to public education. We are in complete agreement with the conclusion of the three-judge panel below that "the grave significance of education both to the individual and to our society" cannot be doubted. But the importance of a service performed by the State does not determine whether it must be regarded as fundamental for purposes of examination under the Equal Protection Clause. Mr. Justice Harlan, dissenting from the Court's application of strict scrutiny to a law impinging upon the right of interstate travel, admonished that "[v]irtually every state statute affects important rights." *Shapiro* v. *Thompson*, 394 U.S. 618, 655, 661 (1969). In his view, if the degree of judicial scrutiny of state legislation fluctuated depending on a majority's view of the importance of the interest affected, we would have gone "far toward making this Court a 'super-legislature.'" *Ibid.* We would indeed then be assuming a legislative role and one for which the Court lacks both authority and competence. But Mr. Justice Stewart's response in *Shapiro* to Mr. Justice Harlan's concern correctly articulates the limits of the fundamental rights rationale employed in the Court's equal protection decisions:

"The Court today does *not* 'pick out particular human activities, characterize them

---

[4] Indeed, this is precisely how the plaintiffs in Serrano v. Priest defined the class they purported to represent: "Plaintiff children claim to represent a class consisting of all public school pupils in California, 'except children in that school district . . . which . . . affords the greatest educational opportunity of all school districts within California.'" 96 *Cal.Rptr.*, at 604, 487 P.2d, at 1244, 5 Cal.3d, at 589. See also Van Dusartz v. Hatfield, 334 F.Supp., at 873.

as "fundamental," and give them added protection. . . .' To the contrary, the Court simply recognizes, as it must, an established constitutional right, and gives to that right no less protection that the Constitution itself demands." 394 U.S., at 642. (Emphasis from original.)

. . . The right to interstate travel had long been recognized as a right of constitutional significance, and the Court's decision therefore did not require an *ad hoc* determination as to the social or economic importance of that right. . . .

The lesson of these cases in addressing the question now before the Court is plain. It is not the province of this Court to create substantive constitutional rights in the name of guaranteeing equal protection of the laws. Thus the key to discovering whether education is "fundamental" is not to be found in comparisons of the relative societal significance of education as opposed to subsistence or housing. Nor is it to be found by weighing whether education is as important as the right to travel. Rather, the answer lies in assessing whether there is a right to education explicitly or implicitly guaranteed by the Constitution. *Eisenstadt* v. *Baird*, 405 U.S. 438 (1972); *Dunn* v. *Blumstein*, 405 U.S. 330 (1972);[5] *Police Department of the City of Chicago* v. *Mosley*, 408 U.S. 92 (1972);[6] *Skinner* v. *Oklahoma*, 316 U.S. 535 (1942).[7]

Education, of course, is not among the rights afforded explicit protection under our Federal Constitution. Nor do we find any basis for saying it is implicitly so protected. . . .

We have carefully considered each of the arguments supportive of the District Court's finding that education is a fundamental right or liberty and have found those arguments unpersuasive. In one further respect we find this a particularly inappropriate case in which to subject state action to strict judicial scrutiny. The present case, in another basic sense, is significantly different from any of the cases in which the Court has applied strict scrutiny to state or federal legislation touching upon constitutionally protected rights. Each of our prior cases involved legislation which "deprived," "infringed," or "interfered" with the free exercise of some such fundamental personal right or liberty. See *Skinner* v. *Oklahoma, supra,* at 536; *Shapiro* v. *Thompson, supra,* at 634; *Dunn* v. *Blumstein, supra,* at 338–343. A critical distinction between those cases and the one now before us lies in what Texas is endeavoring to do with respect to education. . . . The Texas system of school finance . . . was implemented in an effort to *extend* public education and to improve its quality. Of course, every reform that benefits some more than others may be criticized for what it fails to accomplish. But we think it plain that, in substance, the thrust of the Texas system is affirmative and reformatory and, therefore, should be scrutinized under judicial principles sensitive to the nature of the State's efforts and to the rights reserved to the States under the Constitution.

---

[5] Dunn fully canvasses this Court's voting rights cases and explains that "this Court has made clear that a citizen has a *constitutionally protected right* to participate in elections on an equal basis with other citizens in the jurisdiction." *Id.,* at 336 (emphasis supplied). The constitutional underpinnings of the right to equal treatment in the voting process can no longer be doubted even though, as the Court noted in Harper v. Virginia Bd. of Elections, 383 U.S. 663, 665 (1966), "the right to vote in state elections is nowhere expressly mentioned." See Oregon v. Mitchell, 400 U.S. 112, 135, 138–144 (Mr. Justice Douglas), 229, 241–242 (Opinion of Justices Brennan, White, and Marshall) (1970); Bullock v. Carter, 405 U.S. 134, 140–144 (1972); Kramer v. Union Free School District, 395 U.S. 621, 625–630 (1969); Williams v. Rhodes, 393 U.S. 23, 29, 30–31 (1968); Reynolds v. Sims, 377 U.S. 533, 554–562 (1964); Gray v. Sanders, 372 U.S. 368, 379–381 (1963).

[6] In Mosley, the Court struck down a Chicago antipicketing ordinance that exempted labor picketing from its pro-

hibitions. The ordinance was held invalid under the Equal Protection Clause after subjecting it to careful scrutiny and finding that the ordinance was not narrowly drawn. The stricter standard of review was appropriately applied since the ordinance was one "affecting First Amendment interests." *Id.,* at 101.

[7] Skinner applied the standard of close scrutiny to a state law permitting forced sterilization of "habitual criminals." Implicit in the Court's opinion is the recognition that the right of procreation is among the rights of personal privacy protected under the Constitution. See Roe v. Wade, 410 U.S. 113 (1973).

C

It should be clear, for the reasons stated above and in accord with the prior decisions of this Court, that this is not a case in which the challenged state action must be subjected to the searching judicial scrutiny reserved for laws that create suspect classifications or impinge upon constitutionally protected rights.

We need not rest our decision, however, solely on the inappropriateness of the strict scrutiny test. A century of Supreme Court adjudication under the Equal Protection Clause affirmatively supports the application of the traditional standard of review, which requires only that the State's system be shown to bear some rational relationship to legitimate state purposes. This case represents far more than a challenge to the manner in which Texas provides for the education of its children. We have here nothing less than a direct attack on the way in which Texas has chosen to raise and disburse state and local tax revenues. We are asked to condemn the State's judgment in conferring on political subdivisions the power to tax local property to supply revenues for local interests. In so doing, appellees would have the Court intrude in an area in which it has traditionally deferred to state legislatures. This Court has often admonished against such interferences with the State's fiscal policies under the Equal Protection Clause . . .

Thus we stand on familiar ground when we continue to acknowledge that the Justices of this Court lack both the expertise and the familiarity with local problems so necessary to the making of wise decisions with respect to the raising and disposition of public revenues. . . .

In addition to matters of fiscal policy, this case also involves the most persistent and difficult questions of educational policy, another area in which this Court's lack of specialized knowledge and experience counsels against premature interference with the informed judgments made at the state and local levels.
. . .

The foregoing considerations buttress our conclusion that Texas' system of public school finance is an inappropriate candidate for strict judicial scrutiny. These same considerations are relevant to the determination whether that system, with its conceded imperfections, nevertheless bears some rational relationship to a legitimate state purpose. It is to this question that we next turn our attention.

III.

. . .

In sum, to the extent that the Texas system of school finance results in unequal expenditures between children who happen to reside in different districts, we cannot say that such disparities are the product of a system that is so irrational as to be invidiously discriminatory. Texas has acknowledged its shortcomings and has persistently endeavored—not without some success—to ameliorate the differences in levels of expenditures without sacrificing the benefits of local participation. The Texas plan is not the result of hurried, ill-conceived legislation. It certainly is not the product of purposeful discrimination against any group or class. On the contrary, it is rooted in decades of experience in Texas and elsewhere, and in major part is the product of responsible studies by qualified people. In giving substance to the presumption of validity to which the Texas system is entitled, *Lindsey* v. *National Carbonic Gas Co.*, 220 U.S. 61, 78 (1911), it is important to remember that at every stage of its development it has constituted a "rough accommodation" of interests in an effort to arrive at practical and workable solutions. *Metropolis Theater Co.* v. *City of Chicago*, 228 U.S. 69–70 (1913). One also must remember that the system here challenged is not peculiar to Texas or to any other State. In its essential characteristics the Texas plan for financing public education reflects what many educators for a half century have thought was an enlightened approach to a problem for which there is no perfect solution. We are unwilling to assume for ourselves a level of wisdom superior to that of legislators, scholars, and educational authorities in 49 States, especially where the alternatives proposed are only recently conceived and nowhere yet tested. The constitutional standard under the Equal Protection Clause is whether the challenged state action rationally furthers a legitimate state purpose or interest. *McGinnis* v. *Royster*, 410 U.S. 263, 270 (1973). We hold that the Texas plan abundantly satisfies this standard. . . .

Mr. Justice Stewart, concurring. . . .

Unlike other provisions of the Constitution, the Equal Protection Clause confers no substantive rights and creates no substantive liberties.[8] The function of the Equal Protection Clause, rather, is simply to measure the validity of *classifications* created by state laws.

There is hardly a law on the books that does not affect some people differently from others. But the basic concern of the Equal Protection Clause is with state legislation whose purpose or effect is to create discrete and objectively identifiable classes. And with respect to such legislation, it has long been settled that the Equal Protection Clause is offended only by laws that are invidiously discriminatory—only by classifications that are wholly arbitrary or capricious. . . .

Mr. Justice Brennan, dissenting.

Although I agree with my Brother White that the Texas statutory scheme is devoid of any rational basis, and for that reason is violative of

the Equal Protection Clause, I also record my disagreement with the Court's rather distressing assertion that a right may be deemed "fundamental" for the purposes of equal protection analysis only if it is "explicitly or implicitly guaranteed by the Constitution." . . . As my Brother Marshall convincingly demonstrates, our prior cases stand for the proposition that "fundamentality" is, in large measure, a function of the right's importance in terms of the effectuation of those rights which are in fact constitutionally guaranteed. Thus, "[a]s the nexus between the specific constitutional guarantee and the unconstitutional interest draws closer, the nonconstitutional interest becomes more fundamental and the degree of judicial scrutiny applied when the interest is infringed on a discriminatory basis must be adjusted accordingly." . . .

Here, there can be no doubt that education is inextricably linked to the right to participate in the electoral process and to the rights of free speech and association guaranteed by the First Amendment. . . . This being so, any classification affecting education must be subjected to strict judicial scrutiny, and since even the State concedes that the statutory scheme now before us cannot pass constitutional muster under this stricter standard of review, I can only conclude that the Texas school financing scheme is constitutionally invalid.

Mr. Justice White, with whom Mr. Justice Douglas and Mr. Justice Brennan join, dissenting. . . .

The Equal Protection Clause permits discriminations between classes but requires that the classification bear some rational relationship to a permissible object sought to be attained by the statute. It is not enough that the Texas system before us seeks to achieve the valid, rational purpose of maximizing local initiative; the means chosen by the State must also be rationally related to the end sought to be achieved. . . .

---

[8] There is one notable exception to the above statement: It has been established in recent years that the Equal Protection Clause confers the substantive right to participate on an equal basis with other qualified voters whenever the State has adopted an electoral process for determining who will represent any segment of the State's population. See, *e.g.*, Reynolds v. Sims, 377 U.S. 533; Kramer v. Union School District, 395 U.S. 621; Dunn v. Blumstein, 405 U.S. 330, 336. But there is no constitutional right to vote, as such. Minor v. Happersett, 88 U.S. 162. If there were such a right, both the Fifteenth Amendment and the Nineteenth Amendment would have been wholly unnecessary.

Neither Texas nor the majority heeds this rule. If the State aims at maximizing local initiative and local choice, by permitting school districts to resort to the real property tax if they choose to do so, it utterly fails in achieving its purpose in districts with property tax bases so low that there is little if any opportunity for interested parents, rich or poor, to augment school district revenues. Requiring the State to establish only that unequal treatment is in furtherance of a permissible goal, without also requiring the State to show that the means chosen to effectuate that goal are rationally related to its achievement, makes equal protection analysis no more than an empty gesture. In my view, the parents and children in Edgewood, and in like districts, suffer from an invidious discrimination violative of the Equal Protection Clause. . . .

Mr. Justice Marshall, with whom Mr. Justice Douglas concurs, dissenting.

. . . [In the majority's view, the Texas scheme must be tested by nothing more than that lenient standard of rationality which we have traditionally applied to discriminatory state action in the context of economic and commercial matters. . . . By so doing the Court avoids the telling task of searching for a substantial state interest which the Texas financing scheme, with its variations in taxable district property wealth, is necessary to further. I cannot accept such an emasculation of the Equal Protection Clause in the context of this case.

A

To begin, I must once more voice my disagreement with the Court's rigidified approach to equal protection analysis. See *Dandridge* v. *Williams*, 397 U.S. 471, 519–521 (1970) (dissenting opinion); *Richardson* v. *Belcher*, 404 U.S. 78, 90 (1971) (dissenting opinion). The Court apparently seeks to establish today that equal protection cases fall into one of two neat categories which dictate the appropriate standard of

review—strict scrutiny or mere rationality. But this Court's decisions in the field of equal protection defy such easy categorization. A principled reading of what this Court has done reveals that it has applied a spectrum of standards in reviewing discrimination allegedly violative of the Equal Protection Clause. This spectrum clearly comprehends variations in the degree of care with which the Court will scrutinize particular classifications, depending, I believe, on the constitutional and societal importance of the interest adversely affected and the recognized invidiousness of the basis upon which the particular classsification is drawn. I find in fact that many of the Court's recent decisions embody the very sort of reasoned approach to equal protection analysis for which I previously argued—that is, an approach in which "concentration [is] placed upon the character of the classification in question, the relative importance to the individuals in the class discriminated against of the governmental benefits they do not receive, and the asserted state interests in support of the classification." *Dandridge* v. *Williams*, 397 U.S., at 520–521 (dissenting opinion).

I therefore cannot accept the majority's labored efforts to demonstrate that fundamental interests, which call for strict scrutiny of the challenged classification, encompass only established rights which we are somehow bound to recognize from the text of the Constitution itself. To be sure, some interests which the Court has deemed to be fundamental for purposes of equal protection analysis are themselves constitituionally protected rights. . . . But it will not do to suggest that the "answer" to whether an interest is fundamental for purposes of equal protection analysis is *always* determined by whether that interest "is a right . . . explicitly or implicitly guaranteed by the Constitution." . . .

The majority is, of course, correct when it suggests that the process of determining which interests are fundamental is a difficult one. But I do not think the problem is insurmountable.

And I certainly do not accept the view that the process need necessarily degenerate into an unprincipled, subjective "picking-and-choosing" between various interests or that it must involve this Court in creating "substantive constitutional rights in the name of guaranteeing equal protection of the laws." . . . Although not all fundamental interests are constitutionally guaranteed, the determination of which interests are fundamental should be firmly rooted in the text of the Constitution. The task in every case should be to determine the extent to which constitutionally guaranteed rights are dependent on interests not mentioned in the Constitution. As the nexus between the specific constitutional guarantee and the nonconstitutional interest draws closer, the nonconstitutional interest becomes more fundamental and the degree of judicial scrutiny applied when the interest is infringed on a discriminatory basis must be adjusted accordingly. Thus, it cannot be denied that interests such as procreation, the exercise of the state franchise, and access to criminal appellate processes are not fully guaranteed to the citizen by our Constitution. But these interests have nonetheless been afforded special judicial consideration in the face of discrimination because they are, to some extent, interrelated with constitutional guarantees. Procreation is now understood to be important because of its interaction with the established constitutional right of privacy. The exercise of the state franchise is closely tied to basic civil and political rights inherent in the First Amendment. And access to criminal appellate processes enhances the integrity of the range of rights implicit in the Fourteenth Amendment guarantee of due process of law. Only if we closely protect the related interests from state discrimination do we ultimately ensure the integrity of the constitutional guarantee itself. This is the real lesson that must be taken from our previous decisions involving interests deemed to be fundamental. . . .

In summary, it seems to me inescapably clear that this Court has consistently adjusted the care with which it will review state discrimination in light of the constitutional significance of the interests affected and the invidiousness of the particular classification. . . . The majority suggests, however, that a variable standard of review would give this Court the appearance of a "super-legislature." . . . I cannot agree. Such an approach seems to me a part of the guarantees of our Constitution and of the historic experiences with oppression of and discrimination against discrete, powerless minorities which underlie that Document. In truth, the Court itself will be open to the criticism raised by the majority so long as it continues on its present course of effectively selecting in private which cases will be afforded special consideration without acknowledging the true basis of its action. . . .

As the Court points out, . . . no previous decision has deemed the presence of just a wealth classification to be sufficient basis to call forth "rigorous judicial scrutiny" of allegedly discriminatory state action. Compare, *e.g.*, *Harper* v. *Virginia Board of Elections, supra*, with *e.g., James* v. *Valtierra*, 402 U.S. 137 (1971). That wealth classifications alone have not necessarily been considered to bear the same high degree of suspectness as have classifications based on, for instance, race or alienage may be explainable on a number of grounds. The "poor" may not be seen as politically powerless as certain discrete and insular minority groups. Personal poverty may entail much the same social stigma as historically attached to certain racial or ethnic groups. But personal poverty is not a permanent disability; its shackles may be escaped. Perhaps, most importantly, though, personal wealth may not necessarily share the general irrelevance as basis for legislative action that race or nationality is recognized to have. While the "poor" have frequently been a legally disadvantaged group, it cannot be ignored that social legislation must frequently take cognizance of the economic status of our citizens. Thus, we have generally gauged the invidiousness of wealth classifications with an awareness of the importance of the interests being affected and the relevance of personal wealth to those interests. See *Harper* v. *Virginia Board of Elections, supra.*

When evaluated with these considerations in mind, it seems to me that discrimination on the basis of group wealth in this case likewise calls for careful judicial scrutiny. . . .

> *Note and quaere: Gideon* (above) and *Argersinger,* (above), recognize a right to appointed counsel for indigents. *Griffin* v. *Illinois,* 351 U.S. 12 (1956), ruled that indigent defendants must be given trial transcripts and other papers necessary for appeal purposes. Are these poverty or fair-trial decisions?

ALIENAGE CLASSIFICATIONS

Foley v. *Connelie*
98 S. Ct. 1067 (1978)

Foley, an alien lawfully in the country and eligible for citizenship, could not become a state police officer because of a New York law excluding aliens from such positions. He challenged the measure on equal-protection grounds.

Mr. Chief Justice Burger delivered the opinion of the Court . . . .

The decisions of this Court with regard to the rights of aliens living in our society have reflected fine, and often difficult questions of values. As a Nation we exhibit extraordinary hospitality to those who come to our country, which is not surprising for we have often been described as "a nation of immigrants." Indeed, aliens lawfully residing in this society have many rights which are accorded to noncitizens by few other countries. Our cases generally reflect a close scrutiny of restraints imposed by States on aliens. But we have never suggested that such legislation is inherently invalid, nor have we held that all limitations on aliens are suspect. See *Sugarman* v. *Dougall,* 413 U.S. 634, 648 (1973). Rather, beginning with a case which involved the denial of welfare assistance essential to life itself, the Court has treated certain restrictions on aliens with "heightened judicial solicitude," *Graham* v. *Richardson,* 403 U.S. 365, 372 (1971), a treatment deemed necessary since aliens—pending their eligibility for citizenship—have no direct voice in the political processes. . . .

Following *Graham,* a series of decisions has resulted requiring state action to meet close scrutiny to exclude aliens as a class from educational benefits, . . . eligibility for a broad range of public employment, . . or the practice of licensed professions. . . . These exclusions struck at the noncitizens' ability to exist in the community, a position seemingly inconsistent with the congressional determination to admit the alien to permanent residence. See *Graham, supra,* 403 U.S. at 377–378; Barrett, Judicial Supervision of Legislative Classifications, 1976 *B.Y.U.L.Rev.* 89, 101 (1976).

It would be inappropriate, however, to require every statutory exclusion of aliens to clear the high hurdle of "strict scrutiny," because to do so would "obliterate all the distinctions between citizens and aliens, and thus depreciate the historic values of citizenship." . . . The act of becoming a citizen is more than a ritual with no content beyond the fanfare of ceremony. A new citizen has become a member of a Nation, part of a people distinct from others. . . . The individual, at that point, belongs to the polity and is entitled to participate in the processes of democratic decisionmaking. Accordingly, we have recognized "a State's historical power to exclude aliens from participation in its democratic political institutions," *Dougall, supra,* 413 U.S. at 648, as part of the sovereign's obligation "to preserve the basic conception of a political community." *Id.,* at 647.

The practical consequence of this theory is that "our scrutiny will not be so demanding where we deal with matters firmly within a State's constitutional prerogatives." *Dougall, supra,* at 648. The State need only justify its classification by a showing of some rational relationship between the interest sought to be protected and the limiting classification. This is not intended to denigrate the valuable contribution of aliens who benefit from our traditional hospitality. It is no more than recognition of the fact that a democratic society is ruled by its people. Thus, it is clear that a State may deny aliens the right to vote, or to run for elective office, for these lie at the heart of our political institutions. . . . Similar considerations support a legislative determination to exclude aliens from jury service. . . . Likewise, we have recognized that citizenship may be a relevant qualification for fulfilling those "important nonelective executive, legislative and judicial positions," held by "officers who participate directly in the formulation, execution, or review of broad public policy." . . . This is not because our society seeks to reserve the better jobs to its members. Rather, it is because this country entrusts many of its most important policy responsibilities to these officers, the discretionary exercise of which can often more immediately affect the lives of citizens than even the ballot of a voter or the choice of a legislator. In sum, then, it represents the choice, and right, of the people to be governed by their citizen peers. To effectuate this result, we must necessarily examine each position in question to determine whether it involves discretionary decisionmaking, or

execution of policy, which substantially affects members of the political community.

The essence of our holdings to date is that although we extend to aliens the right to education and public welfare, along with the ability to earn a livelihood and engage in licensed professions, the right to govern is reserved to citizens.

A discussion of the police function is essentially a description of one of the basic functions of government, especially in a complex modern society where police presence is pervasive. The police function fulfills a most fundamental obligation of government to its constituency. Police officers in the ranks do not formulate policy, *per se,* but they are clothed with authority to exercise an almost infinite variety of discretionary powers. . . .

Clearly the exercise of police authority calls for a very high degree of judgment and discretion, the abuse or misuse of which can have serious impact on individuals. . . . A policeman vested with the plenary discretionary powers we have described is not to be equated with a private person engaged in routine public employment or other "common occupations of the community" who exercises no broad power over people generally. Indeed, the rationale for the qualified immunity historically granted to the police rests on the difficult and delicate judgments these officers must often make. . . .

In short, it would be as anomalous to conclude that citizens may be subjected to the broad discretionary powers of noncitizen police officers as it would be to say that judicial officers and jurors with power to judge citizens can be aliens. It is not surprising, therefore, that most States expressly confine the employment of police officers to citizens, whom the State may reasonably presume to be more familiar with and sympathetic to American traditions. Police officers very clearly fall within the category of "important nonelective . . . officers who participate directly in the . . . *execution* . . . of broad public policy." *Dougall, supra,* 413 U.S. at 647 (emphasis added). In the enforcement and execution of the laws the police function is one where citizenship bears a rational relationship to the special demands of the particular position. A State may, therefore, consonant with the Constitution, confine the performance of this important public responsibility to citizens of the United States.

Mr. Justice Stewart, concurring.

The dissenting opinions convincingly demonstrate that it is difficult if not impossible to reconcile the Court's judgment in this case with the full sweep of the reasoning and authority of some of our past decisions. It is only because I have become increasingly doubtful about the validity of those decisions (in at least some of which I concurred) that I join the opinion of the Court in this case.

Mr. Justice Blackmun, concurring in the result.

Once again the Court is called upon to adjudicate the constitutionality of one of New York's many statutes that impose a requirement of citizenship for occupational activity. Although I have joined the Court in striking down citizenship requirements of this kind, . . . including, specifically, some imposed by the State of New York, . . . I have no difficulty in agreeing with the result the Court reaches here. . . .

Mr. Justice Marshall, with whom Mr. Justice Breenan and Mr. Justice Stevens joins, dissenting. . . .

Today the Court upholds a law excluding aliens from public employment as state troopers. It bases its decision largely on dictum from *Sugarman* v. *Dougall, supra,* to the effect that aliens may be barred from holding "state elective or important nonelective executive, legislative, and judicial positions," because persons in

these positions "participate directly in the formulation, execution, or review of broad public policy." 413 U.S., at 647. I do not agree with the Court that state troopers perform functions placing them within this "narrow . . . exception," *Nyquist* v. *Mauclet, supra,* 432 U.S., at 11, to our usual rule that discrimination against aliens is presumptively unconstitutional. Accordingly I dissent. . . .

In *Griffiths* we held that the State could not limit the practice of law to citizens, "despite a recognition of the vital public and political role of attorneys," *Nyquist* v. *Mauclet, supra,* 432 U.S., at 11. It is similarly not a denigration of the important public role of the state trooper—who, as the Court notes, *ante,* at 1071, operates "in the most sensitive areas of daily life,"—to find that his law enforcement responsibilities do not "make him a formulator of government policy." *In re Griffiths, supra,* 413 U.S., at 729. Since no other rational reason, let alone a compelling state interest, has been advanced in support of the statute here at issue, I would hold that the statute's exclusion of aliens from state trooper positions violates the Equal Protection Clause of the Fourteenth Amendment.

Mr. Justice Stevens, with whom Mr. Justice Brennan joins, dissenting. . . .

The Court's misapprehension of the role of the institutionalized police function in a democratic society obfuscates the true significance of the distinction between citizenship and alienage. The privilege of participating in the formulation of broad public policy—a privilege largely denied to the institutions exercising the police function in our society—is the essence of individual citizenship. It is this privilege which gives dramatic meaning to the naturalization ceremony. The transition from alienage to citizenship is a fundamental change in the status of a person. This change is qualitatively different from any incremental increase in economic benefits that may accrue to holders of citizenship papers. The new citizen's right to vote and to participate in the democratic decisionmaking process is the honorable prerogative which no alien has a constitutional right to enjoy.

In final analysis, therefore, our society is governed by its citizens. But it is a government of and for all persons subject to its jurisdiction, and the Constitution commands their equal treatment. Although a State may deny the alien the right to participate in the making of policy, it may not deny him equal access to employment opportunities without a good and relevant reason. *Sugarman* plainly teaches us that the burgeoning public employment market cannot be totally foreclosed to aliens. Since the police officer is not a policymaker in this country, the total exclusion of aliens from the police force must fall.

Even if the Court rejects this analysis, it should not uphold a statutory discrimination against aliens, as a class, without expressly identifying the group characteristic that justifies the discrimination. If the unarticulated characteristic is concern about possible disloyalty, it must equally disqualify aliens from the practice of law; yet the Court does not question the continuing vitality of its decision in *Griffiths*. Or if that characteristic is the fact that aliens do not participate in our democratic decisionmaking process, it is irrelevant to eligibility for this category of public service. If there is no group characteristic that explains the discrimination, one can only conclude that it is without any justification that has not already been rejected by the Court.

Because the Court's unique decision fails either to apply or to reject established rules of law, and for the reasons stated by Mr. Justice Marshall, I respectfully dissent.

Note: Ambach v. *Norwick,* 99 S. Ct. 1589 (1979), upheld a New York law prohibiting any alien from teaching in the public schools (a "governmental function") unless he or she "has manifested an intention to apply for citizenship."

10

Privacy and Race: The State-Action Problem

PRIVATE DISCRIMINATION AND THE FOURTEENTH AMENDMENT

Civil Rights Cases
109 U.S. 3 (1883)

These five cases tested the validity of the Civil Rights Act of 1875, which made it a crime for "any person" to deny anyone because of race "the full and equal enjoyment of the accommodations, advantages, facilities, and privileges of inns, public conveyances . . . theaters, and other places of public amusement." The measure had been adopted by Congress pursuant (so it was thought) to Section 5 of the Fourteenth Amendment. (Note carefully the "no state"—there is no "no person"— prohibitory language in this amendment.) These cases involve prosecutions of *private persons* for denying accommodations to blacks in hotels, theaters, and a railroad car.

Mr. Justice Bradley delivered the opinion of the Court. . . .

The first section of the Fourteenth Amendment,—which is the one relied on,— after declaring who shall be citizens of the United States, and of the several states, is prohibitory in its character, and prohibitory upon the states. . . . It is state action of a particular character that is prohibited. Individual invasion of individual rights is not the subject-matter of the amendment. It has a deeper and broader scope. It nullifies and makes void all State legislation, and State action of every kind, which impairs the privileges and immunities of citizens of the United States, or which injures them in life, liberty, or property without due process of law, or which denies to any of them the equal protection of the laws. It not only does this, but, in order that the national will, thus declared, may not be a mere *brutum fulmen*, the last section of the amendment invests Congress with

627

power to enforce it by appropriate legislation. To enforce what? To enforce the prohibition. To adopt appropriate legislation for correcting the effects of such prohibited State law and State acts, and thus to render them effectually null, void, and innocuous. This is the legislative power conferred upon congress, and this is the whole of it. It does not invest Congress with power to legislate upon subjects which are within the domain of state legislation; but to provide modes of relief against State legislation, or State action, of the kind referred to. It does not authorize Congress to create a code of municipal law for the regulation of private rights; but to provide modes of redress against the operation of State laws, and the action of State officers, executive or judicial, when these are subversive of the fundamental rights specified in the amendment. . . .

In this connection it is proper to state that civil rights, such as are guaranteed by the Constitution against State aggression, cannot be impaired by the wrongful acts of individuals, unsupported by State authority in the shape of laws, customs, or judicial or executive proceedings. The wrongful act of an individual, unsupported by any such authority, is simply a private wrong, or a crime of that individual; an invasion of the rights of the injured party, it is true, whether they affect his person, his property, or his reputation; but if not sanctioned in some way by the State, or not done under State authority, his rights remain in full force, and may presumably be vindicated by resort to the laws of the State for redress. An individual cannot deprive a man of his right to vote, to hold property, to buy and to sell, to sue in the courts, or to be a witness or a juror; he may, by force or fraud, interfere with the enjoyment of the right in a particular case; he may commit an assult against the person, or commit murder, or use ruffian violence at the polls, or slander the good name of a fellow-citizen; but unless protected in these wrongful acts by some shield of State law or State authority, he cannot destroy or injure the rights; he will only render himself amenable to satisfaction or punishment; and amenable therefor to the laws of the State where the wrongful acts are committed. . . .

Mr. Justice Harlan dissenting . . . .

Congress, has not, in these matters, entered the domain of State control and supervision. It does not, as I have said, assume to prescribe the general conditions and limitations under which inns, public conveyances, and places of public amusement, shall be conducted or managed. It simply declares, in effect, that since the nation has established universal freedom in this country, for all time, there shall be no discrimination, based merely upon race or color, in respect of the accommodations and advantages of public conveyances, inns, and places of public amusement.

I am of the opinion that such discrimination practised by corporations and individuals in the exercise of their public or quasi-public functions is a badge of servitude the imposition of which Congress may prevent under its power, by appropriate legislation, to enforce the Thirteenth Amendment; and, consequently, without reference to its enlarged power under the Fourteenth Amendment, the act of March 1, 1875, is not, in my judgment, repugnant to the Constitution. . . . The assumption that this amendment [the Fourteenth] consists wholly of prohibitions upon State laws and State proceedings in hostility to its provisions, is unauthorized by its language. The first clause of the first section—"All persons born or naturalized in the United States, and subject to the jurisdiction thereof, are citizens of the United States, and of the State wherein they reside"—is of a distinctly affirmative character. In its application to the colored race, previously liberated, it created and granted, as well citizenship of the United States, as citizenship of the State in which they respectively resided. It introduced all of that race, whose ancestors had been imported and sold as slaves, at once, into the political community known as the "People of the United

States." They became, instantly, citizens of the United States, *and* of their respective States. Further, they were brought, by this supreme act of the nation, within the direct operation of that provision of the Constitution which declares that "the citizens of each State shall be entitled to all privileges and immunities of citizens in the several States." Art. 4, § 2.

The citizenship thus acquired, by that race, in virtue of an affirmative grant from the nation, may be protected, not alone by the judicial branch of the government, but by congressional legislation of a primary direct character; this, because the power of Congress is not restricted to the enforcement of prohibitions upon State laws or State action. It is, in terms distinct and positive, to enforce "the *provisions* of *this article*" of amendment; not simply those of a prohibitive character, but the provisions—*all* of the provisions—affirmative and prohibitive, of the amendment. It is, therefore, a grave misconception to suppose that the fifth section of the amendment has reference exclusively to express prohibitions upon State laws or State action. If any right was created by that amendment, the grant of power, through appropriate legislation, to enforce its provisions, authorized Congress, by means of legislation, operating throughout the entire Union, to guard, secure, and protect that right. . . .

Burton v. *Wilmington Parking Authority*
365 U.S. 715 (1961)

Mr. Justice Clark delivered the opinion of the Court. . . .

. . . It is clear, as it always has been since the *Civil Rights Cases,* that "individual invasion of individual rights is not the subject matter of the amendment," and that private conduct abridging individual rights does no violence to the Equal Protection Clause unless to some significant extent the State in any of its manifestations has been found to have become involved in it.

Because the virtue of the right to equal protection of the laws could lie only in the breadth of its application, its constitutional assurance was reserved in terms whose imprecision was necessary if the right were to be enjoyed in the variety of individual-state relationships which the Amendment was designed to embrace. For the same reason, to fashion and apply a precise formula for recognition of state responsibility under the Equal Protection Clause is "an impossible task" which "this Court has never attempted." Only by sifting facts and weighing circumstances can the nonobvious involvement of the State in private conduct be attributed its true significance.

. . . [T]he Delaware Supreme Court seems to have placed controlling emphasis on its conclusion, as to the accuracy or which there is doubt, that only some 15% of the total cost of the facility was "advanced" from public funds; that the cost of the entire facility was allocated three-fifths to the space for commercial leasing and two-fifths to parking space; that anticipated revenue from parking was only some 30.5% of the total income, the balance of which was expected to be earned by the leasing; that the Authority had no original intent to place a restaurant in the building, it being only a happenstance resulting from the bidding; that Eagle expended considerable moneys on furnishings; that the restaurant's main and marked public entrance is on Ninth Street without any public entrance direct from the parking area; and that "the only connection Eagle has with the public facility . . . is the furnishing of the sum of $28,700 annually in the form of rent which is used by the Authority to defray a portion of the operating expense of an otherwise unprofitable enterprise." While these factual considerations are indeed validly accountable aspects of the enterprise upon which the State has embarked, we cannot say that they lead inescapably to the conclusion that state action is not present. Their persuasiveness is diminished when evaluated in the context of other factors which must be acknowledged.

The land and building were publicly owned. As an entity, the building was dedicated to "public uses" in performance of the Authority's "essential governmental functions." 22 Del. Code, c. 5, §§ 501, 514. The costs of land acquisition, construction, and maintenance are defrayed entirely from donations by the City of Wilmington, from loans and revenue bonds and from the proceeds of rentals and parking services out of which the loans and bonds were payable. Assuming that the distinction would be significant, the commercially leased areas were not surplus state property, but constituted a physically and financially integral and, indeed, indispensable part of the State's plan to operate its project as a self-sustaining unit. Upkeep and maintenance of the building, including necessary repairs, were responsibilities of the Authority and were payable out of public funds. It cannot be doubted that the peculiar relationship of the restaurant to the parking facility in which it is located confers on each an incidental variety of mutual benefits. Guests of the restaurant are afforded a convenient place to park their automobiles, even if they cannot enter the restaurant directly from the parking area. Similarly, its convenience for diners may well provide additional demand for the Authority's parking facilities. Should any improvements effected in the leasehold by Eagle become part of the realty, there is no possibility of increased taxes being passed on to it since the fee is held by a tax-exempt government agency. Neither can it be ignored, especially in view of Eagle's affirmative allegation that for it to serve Negroes would injure its business, that profits earned by discrimination not only contribute to, but are indispensable elements in the financial success of a governmental agency.

Addition of all these activities, obligations and responsibilities of the Authority, the benefits mutually conferred, together with the obvious fact that the restaurant is operated as an integral part of a public building devoted to a public parking service, indicates that degree of state participation and involvement in discrim-inatory action which it was the design of the Fourteenth Amendment to condemn. It is irony amounting to grave injustice that in one part of a single building, erected and maintained with public funds by an agency of the State to serve a public purpose, all persons have equal rights, while in another portion, also serving the public, a Negro is a second-class citizen, offensive because of his race, without rights and unentitled to service, but at the same time fully enjoys equal access to nearby restaurants in wholly privately owned buildings. As the Chancellor pointed out, in its lease with Eagle the Authority could have affirmatively required Eagle to discharge the responsibilities under the Fourteenth Amendment imposed upon the private enterprise as a consequence of State participation. But no State may effectively abdicate its responsibilities by either ignoring them or by merely failing to discharge them whatever the motive may be. It is of no consolation to an individual denied the equal protection of the laws that it was done in good faith. Certainly the conclusions drawn in similar cases by the various Courts of Appeals do not depend upon such a distinction. By its inaction, the Authority, and through it the State, has not only made itself a party to the refusal of service, but has elected to place its power, property and prestige behind the admitted discrimination. The State has so far insinuated itself into a position of interdependence with Eagle that it must be recognized as a joint participant in the challenged activity, which, on that account, cannot be considered to have been so "purely private" as to fall without the scope of the Fourteenth Amendment.

Because readily applicable formulae may not be fashioned, the conclusions drawn from the facts and circumstances of this record are by no means declared as universal truths on the basis of which every state leasing agreement is to be tested. Owing to the very "largeness" of government, a multitude of relationships might appear to some to fall within the Amendment's embrace, but that, it must be remembered, can be determined only in the framework of the peculiar facts or circumstances present. Therefore respondents' prophecy of nigh universal application of a constitutional precept so peculiarly dependent for its invocation upon appropriate facts fails to take into account "Differences in circumstances [which] beget appropriate differences in law." Specifically defining the limits of our inquiry, what we hold today is that when a State leases public property in the manner and for the purpose shown to have been the case here, the proscriptions of the Fourteenth Amendment must be complied with by the lessee as certainly as though they were binding covenants written into the agreement itself.

The judgment of the Supreme Court of Delaware is reversed. . . .

Mr. Justice Stewart, concurring.

I agree that the judgment must be reversed, but I reach that conclusion by a route much more direct that the one traveled by the Court. In upholding Eagle's right to deny service to the appellant solely because of his race, the Supreme Court of Delaware relied upon a statute of that State which permits the proprietor of a restaurant to refuse to serve "persons whose reception or entertainment by him would be offensive to the major part of his customers. . . ." There is no suggestion in the record that the appellant as an individual was such a person. The highest court of Delaware has thus construed this legislative enactment as authorizing discriminatory classification based exclusively on color. Such a law seems to me clearly violative of the Fourteenth Amendment. I think, therefore, . . . that the statute, as authoritatively construed . . . , is constitutionally invalid.

Mr. Justice Harlan, whom Mr. Justice Whittaker joins, dissenting.

The Court's opinion, by a process of first undiscriminatingly throwing together various factual bits and pieces and then undermining the resulting structure by an equally vague disclaimer, seems to me to leave completely at sea just what it is in this record that satisfies the requirement of "state action."

I find it unnecessary, however, to inquire into the matter at this stage, for it seems to me apparent that before passing on the far-reaching constitutional questions that may, or may not, be lurking in this judgment, the case should first be sent back to the state court for clarification as to the precise basis of its decision. . . .

If . . . the Delaware court construed this state statute "as authorizing discriminatory classification based exclusively on color," I would certainly agree, without more, that the enactment is offensive to the Fourteenth Amendment. It would then be quite unnecessary to reach the much broader questions dealt with in the Court's opinion. If, on the other hand, the state court meant no more than that under the statute, as at common law, Eagle was free to serve only those whom it pleased, then, and only then, would the question of "state action" be presented in full-blown form. . . .

Mr. Justice Frankfurter, dissenting. . . .

I certainly do not find the clarity that my brother Stewart finds . . . . If I were forced to construe that court's construction, I should find the balance of considerations leading to the opposite conclusion from his, namely, that it was merely declaratory of the common law and did not give state sanction to refusing service to a person merely because he is colored. The Court takes no position regarding the statutory meaning which divides my brothers Harlan and Stewart. If it [took Justice Stewart's view], it would undoubtedly take his easy road to decision . . . . Since the pronouncement of the Supreme Court of Delaware thus lends itself to three views, none of which is patently irrational, why is not my brother Harlan's suggestion for solving this conflict the most appropriate solution? . . .

Reitman v. *Mulkey*
387 U.S. 369 (1967)

Mr. Justice White delivered the opinion of the Court.

The question here is whether Art. I, § 26 of the California Constitution denies "to any person . . . the equal protection of the laws" within the meaning of the Fourteenth Amendment of the Constitution of the United States. Section 26 of Art. I, an initiated measure submitted to the people as Proposition 14 in a statewide ballot in 1964, provides in part as follows:

> "Neither the State nor any subdivision or agency thereof shall deny, limit or abridge, directly or indirectly, the right of any person, who is willing or desires to sell, lease or rent any part or all of his real property, to decline to sell, lease or rent such property to such person or persons as he, in his absolute discretion, chooses."

The real property covered by § 26 is limited to residential property and contains an exception for state-owned real estate. . . .

. . . [The California Supreme Court] held that Art. I, § 26, was invalid as denying the equal protection of the laws guaranteed by the Fourteenth Amendment. . . .

We affirm the judgment of the California Supreme Court. We first turn to the opinion of that court, which quite properly undertook to examine the constitutionality of § 26 in terms of its "immediate objective," its "ultimate impact" and its "historical context and the condition existing prior to its enactment." Judgments such as these we have frequently undertaken ourselves. But here the California Supreme Court has addressed itself to these matters and we should give careful consideration to its views because they concern the purpose, scope, and operative effect of a provision of the California Constitution.

First, the court considered whether § 26 was concerned at all with private discriminations in residential housing. This involved a review of past efforts by the California Legislature to regulate such discriminations. The Unruh Act, Civ. Code §§ 51–52, on which respondents based their cases, was passed in 1959. . . . Finally, in 1963, came the Rumford Fair Housing Act, Health & Saf. Code . . . prohibiting racial discrimination in the sale or rental of any private dwelling containing more than four units. That act was enforceable by the State Fair Employment Practice Commission.

It was against this background that Proposition 14 was enacted. Its immediate design and intent, the California court said, was "to overturn state laws that bore on the right of private sellers and lessors to discriminate," the Unruh and Rumford Acts, and "to forestall future state action that might circumscribe this right." . . .

Second, the court conceded that the State was permitted a neutral position with respect to private racial discriminations and that the State was not bound by the Federal Constitution to forbid them. But, because a significant state involvement in private discriminations could amount to unconstitutional state action, the court deemed it necessary to determine whether Proposition 14 invalidly involved the State in racial discriminations in the housing market. Its conclusion was that it did.

To reach this result, the state court examined certain prior decisions in this Court in which discriminatory state action was identified. Based on these cases, it concluded that a prohibited state involvement could be found "even where the state can be charged with only encouraging," rather than commanding discrimination. . . .

. . . Petitioners contend that the California court has misconstrued the Fourteenth Amendment since the repeal of any statute prohibiting racial discrimination, which is constitutionally permissible, may be said to "authorize" and "encourage" discrimination because it makes legally permissible that which was formerly proscribed. But as we understand the California court, it did not posit a constitutional violation on the mere repeal of the Unruh and Rumford Acts. It did not read either our cases or the Fourteenth Amendment as establishing an automatic constitutional barrier to the repeal of an existing law prohibiting racial discriminations in housing; nor did the court rule that a State may never put in statutory form an existing policy of neutrality with respect to private discriminations. What the court below did was first to reject the notion that the State was required to have a statute prohibiting racial discriminations in housing. Second, it held the purpose and intent of § 26 was to authorize private racial discriminations in the housing market, to repeal the Unruh and Rumford Acts and to create a constitutional right to discriminate on racial grounds in the sale and leasing of real property. Hence, the court dealt with § 26 as though it expressly authorized and constitutionalized the private right to discriminate. Third, the court assessed the ultimate impact of § 26 in the California environment and concluded that the section would encourage and significantly involve the State in private racial discrimination contrary to the Fourteenth Amendment.

The California court could very reasonably conclude that § 26 would and did have wider impact than a mere repeal of existing statutes. . . . Private discriminations in housing were now not only free from Rumford and Unruh but they also enjoyed a far different status than was true before the passage of those statutes. The right to discriminate, including the right to discriminate on racial grounds, was now embodied in the State's basic charter, immune from legislative, executive, or judicial regulation at any level of the state government. Those practicing racial discriminations need no longer rely solely on their personal choice. They could now invoke express constitutional authority, free from censure or interference of any kind from official sources. . . .

This Court has never attempted the "impossible task" of formulating an infallible test for

determining whether the State "in any of its manifestations" has become significantly involved in private discriminations. "Only by sifting the facts and weighing the circumstances" on a case-to-case basis can a "nonobvious involvement of the State in private conduct be attributed its true significance." Here the California court, armed as it was with the knowledge of the facts and circumstances concerning the passage and potential impact of § 26, and familiar with the milieu in which that provision would operate, has determined that the provision would involve the State in private racial discriminations to an unconstitutional degree. We accept this holding of the California court. . . .

. . . [No decision] squarely controls the case we now have before us. But [prior cases] do illustrate the range of situations in which discriminatory state action has been identified. They do exemplify the necessity for a court to assess the potential impact of official action in determining whether the State has significantly involved itself with invidious discriminations. Here we are dealing with a provision which does not just repeal an existing law forbidding private racial discriminations. Section 26 was intended to authorize, and does authorize, racial discrimination in the housing market. The right to discriminate is now one of the basic policies of the State. The California Supreme Court believes that the section will significantly encourage and involve the State in private discriminations. We have been presented with no persuasive considerations indicating that this judgment should be overturned. . . .

Justice Douglas, concurring.

While I join the opinion of the Court, I add a word to indicate the dimensions of our problem.

. . . We deal here with a problem in the realm of zoning, similar to the one we had in *Shelley* v. *Kraemer*. . . .

Those covenants are one device whereby a

neighborhood is kept "white" or "Caucasian" as the dominant interests desire. Proposition 14 in the setting of our modern housing problem is only another device of the same character.

Real estate brokers and mortgage lenders are largely dedicated to the maintenance of segregated communities. Realtors commonly believe it is unethical to sell or rent to a Negro in a predominantly or all-white neighborhood, and mortgage lenders throw their weight alongside segregated communities, rejecting applications by a member of a minority group who tries to break the white phalanx save and unless the neighborhood is in process of conversion into a mixed or a Negro community. . . .

The builders join in the same scheme. . . .

Proposition 14 is a form of sophisticated discrimination whereby the people of California harness the energies of private groups to do indirectly what they cannot under our decisions allow their government to do. . . .

Justice Harlan, whom Justice Black, Justice Clark, and Justice Stewart join, dissenting. . . .

The Court attempts to fit § 26 within the coverage of the Equal Protection Clause by characterizing it as in effect an affirmative call to residents of California to discriminate. The main difficulty with this viewpoint is that it depends upon a characterization of § 26 that cannot fairly be made. The provision is neutral on its face, and it is only by in effect asserting that this requirement of passive official neutrality is camouflage that the Court is able to reach its conclusion. In depicting the provision as tantamount to active state encouragement of discrimination the Court essentially relies on the fact that the California Supreme Court so concluded. It is said that the findings of the highest court of California as to the meaning and impact of the enactment are entitled to great weight. I agree, of course, that *findings of fact* by a state court should be given great weight, but this familiar proposition hardly aids the Court's holding in this case.

There is no disagreement whatever but that § 26 was meant to nullify California's fair-housing legislation and thus to remove from private residential property transactions the state-created impediment upon freedom of choice. There were no disputed issues of fact at all, and indeed the California Supreme Court noted at the outset of its opinion that "[i]n the trial court proceedings allegations of the complaint were not factually challenged, no evidence was introduced, and the only matter placed in issue was the legal sufficiency of the allegations." There was no finding, for example, that the defendants' actions were anything but the product of their own private choice. Indeed, since the alleged racial discrimination that forms the basis for the *Reitman* refusal to rent on racial grounds occurred in 1963, it is not possible to contend that § 26 in any way influenced this particular act. There were no findings as to the general effect of § 26. The Court declares that the California court "held the purpose and intent of § 26 was to authorize private racial discriminations in the housing market . . . ," *ante*, p. 1631, but there is no supporting fact in the record for this characterization. Moreover, the grounds which prompt legislators or state voters to repeal a law do not determine its constitutional validity. That question is decided by what the law does, not by what those who voted for it wanted it to do, and it must not be forgotten that the Fourteenth Amendment does not compel a State to put or keep any particular law about race on its books. The Amendment forbids only a State to pass or keep in effect laws discriminating on account of race. California has not done this.

A state enactment, particularly one that is simply permissive of private decision-making rather than coercive and one that has been adopted in this most democratic of processes, should not be struck down by the judiciary under the Equal Protection Clause without persuasive evidence of an invidious purpose or effect. The only "factual" matter relied on by the majority of the California Supreme Court was the context in which Proposition 14 was adopted, namely, that several strong antidiscrimination acts had been passed by the legislature and opposed by many of those who successfully led the movement for adoption of Proposition 14 by popular referendum. These circumstances, and these alone, the California court held, made § 26 unlawful under this Court's cases interpreting the Equal Protection Clause. This, of course, is nothing but a legal conclusion as to federal constitutional law, the California Supreme Court not having relied in any way upon the State Constitution. Accepting all the suppositions under which the state court acted, I cannot see that its conclusion is entitled to any special weight in the discharge of our own responsibilities. Put in another way, I cannot transform the California court's conclusion of law into a finding of fact that the State through the adoption of § 26 is actively promoting racial discrimination. It seems to me manifest that the state court decision rested entirely on what that court conceived to be the compulsion of the Fourteenth Amendment, not on any fact-finding by the state courts. . . .

. . . The core of the Court's opinion is that § 26 is offensive to the Fourteenth Amendment because it effectively *encourages* private discrimination. By focusing on "encouragement" the Court, I fear, is forging a slippery and unfortunate criterion by which to measure the constitutionality of a statute simply permissive in purpose and effect, and inoffensive on its face.

It is true that standards in this area have not been definitely formulated, and that acts of discrimination have been included within the compass of the Equal Protection Clause not merely when they were compelled by a state statute or other governmental pressures, but also when they were said to be "induced" or "authorized" by the State. Most of these cases, however, can be approached in terms of the impact and extent of affirmative state governmental activities, *e.g.*, the action of a sheriff, *Lombard* v. *Louisiana*, 337 U.S. 267; the official supervision over a park, *Evans* v. *Newton*, 382

U.S. 296; a joint venture with a lessee in a municipally owned building, *Burton* v. *Wilmington Parking Authority*. In situations such as these the focus has been on positive state cooperation or partnership in affirmatively promoted activities, an involvement that could have been avoided. Here, in contrast, we have only the straight-forward adoption of a neutral provision restoring to the sphere of free choice, left untouched by the Fourteenth Amendment, private behavior within a limited area of the racial problem. The denial of equal protection emerges only from the conclusion reached by the Court that the implementation of a new policy of governmental neutrality, embodied in a constitutional provision and replacing a former policy of antidiscrimination, has the effect of lending encouragement to those who wish to discriminate. In the context of the actual facts of the case, this conclusion appears to me to state only a truism: people who want to discriminate but were previously forbidden to do so by state law are now left free because the State has chosen to have no law on the subject at all. Obviously whenever there is a change in the law it will have resulted from the concerted activity of those who desire the change, and its enactment will allow those supporting the legislation to pursue their private goals.

A moment of thought will reveal the far-reaching possibilities of the Court's new doctrine, which I am sure the Court does not intend. Every act of private discrimination is either forbidden by state law or permitted by it. There can be little doubt that such permissiveness—whether by express constitutional or statutory provision, or implicit in the common law—to some extent "encourages" those who wish to discriminate to do so. Under this theory "state action" in the form of laws that do nothing more than passively permit private discrimination could be said to tinge *all* private discrimination with the taint of unconstitutional state encouragement.

This type of alleged state involvement, simply evincing a refusal to involve itself at all, is of course very different from that illustrated in such cases as *Lombard, Peterson, Evans* and *Burton,* where the Court found active involvement of state agencies and officials in specific acts of discrimination. It is also quite different from cases in which a state enactment could be said to have the obvious purpose of fostering discrimination. I believe the state action required to bring the Fourteenth Amendment into operation must be affirmative and purposeful, actively fostering discrimination. Only in such a case is ostensibly "private" action more properly labeled "official." I do not believe that the mere enactment of § 26, on the showing made here, falls within this class of cases.

. . . Opponents of state antidiscrimination statutes are now in a position to argue that such legislation should be defeated because, if enacted, it may be unrepealable. More fundamentally, the doctrine underlying this decision may hamper, if not preclude, attempts to deal with the delicate and troublesome problems of race relations through the legislative processes. . . .

Moose Lodge v. *Irvis*
407 U.S. 163 (1972)

Mr. Justice Rehnquist delivered the opinion of the Court.

Appellee Irvis, a Negro, was refused service by appellant Moose Lodge, a local branch of the national fraternal organization located in Harrisburg, Pennsylvania. Appellee then brought this action under 42 U.S.C. § 1983 for injunctive relief in the United States District Court for the Middle District of Pennsylvania. He claimed that because the Pennsylvania liquor board had issued appellant Moose Lodge a private club license that authorized the sale of alcoholic beverages on its premises, the refusal of service to him was "state action" for the purposes of the Equal Protection Clause of the Fourteenth Amendment. . . .

A three-judge district court, convened at appellee's request, upheld his contention on the merits, and entered a decree declaring invalid the liquor license issued to Moose Lodge "as long as it follows a policy of racial discrimination in its membership or operating policies or practices." . . .

Moose Lodge is a private club in the ordinary meaning of that term. It is a local chapter of a national fraternal organization having well defined requirements for membership. It conducts all of its activities in a building that is owned by it. It is not publicly funded. Only members and guests are permitted in any lodge of the order; one may become a guest only by invitation of a member or upon invitation of the house committee.

Appellee, while conceding the right of private clubs to choose members upon a discriminatory basis, asserts that the licensing of Moose Lodge to serve liquor by the Pennsylvania Liquor Control Board amounts to such state involvement with the club's activities as to make its discriminatory practices forbidden by the Equal Protection Clause of the Fourteenth Amendment. . . .

The Court has never held, of course, that discrimination by an otherwise private entity would be violative of the Equal Protection Clause if the private entity receives any sort of benefit or service at all from the State, or if it is subject to state regulation in any degree whatever. Since state-furnished services include such necessities of life as electricity, water, and police and fire protection, such a holding would utterly emasculate the distinction between private as distinguished from state conduct set forth in *The Civil Rights Cases,* and adhered to in subsequent decisions. Our holdings indicate that where the impetus for the discrimination is private, the State must have "significantly involved itself with invidious discriminations," in order for the discriminatory action to fall within the ambit of the constitutional prohibition.

. . . With one exception, which is discussed

infra, there is no suggestion in this record that the Pennsylvania statutes and regulations governing the sale of liquor are intended either overtly or covertly to encourage discrimination. . . .

Here there is nothing approaching the symbiotic relationship between lessor and lessee that was present in *Burton.* . . . Unlike *Burton,* the Moose Lodge building is located on land owned by it, not by any public authority. Far from apparently holding itself out as a place of public accommodation, Moose Lodge quite ostentatiously proclaims the fact that it is not open to the public at large. Nor is it located and operated in such surroundings that although private in name, it discharges a function or performs a service that would otherwise in all likelihood be performed by the State. In short, while Eagle was a public restaurant in a public building, Moose Lodge is a private social club in a private building.

With the exception hereafter noted, the Pennsylvania Liquor Control Board plays absolutely no part in establishing or enforcing the membership or guest policies of the club which it licenses to serve liquor. There is no suggestion in this record that the Pennsylvania Act, either as written or as applied, discriminates against minority groups either in their right to apply for club licenses themselves or in their right to purchase and be served liquor in places of public accommodation. The only effect that the state licensing of Moose Lodge to serve liquor can be said to have on the right of any other Pennsylvanian to buy or be served liquor on premises other than those of Moose Lodge is that for some purposes club licenses are counted in the maximum number of licenses which may be issued in a given municipality. Basically each municipality has a quota of one retail license for each 1,500 inhabitants. Licenses issued to hotels, municipal golf courses and airport restaurants are not counted in this quota, nor are club licenses until the maximum number of retail licenses is reached. Beyond that point, neither additional retail licenses

nor additional club licenses may be issued so long as the number of issued and outstanding retail licenses remains above the statutory maximum.

The District Court was at pains to point out in its opinion what it considered to be the "pervasive" nature of the regulation of private clubs by the Pennsylvania Liquor Control Board. As that court noted, an applicant for a club license must make such physical alterations in its premises as the board may require, must file a list of the names and addresses of its members and employees, and must keep extensive financial records. The board is granted the right to inspect the licensed premises at any time when patrons, guests or members are present.

However detailed this type of regulation may be in some particulars, it cannot be said to in any way to foster or encourage racial discrimination. Nor can it be said to make the State in any realistic sense a partner or even a joint venturer in the club's enterprise. The limited effect of the prohibition against obtaining additional club licenses when the maximum number of retail licenses allotted to a municipality has been issued, when considered together with the availability of liquor from hotel, restaurant, and retail licensees, falls far short of conferring upon club licensees a monopoly in the dispensing of liquor in any given municipality or in the State as a whole. We therefore hold that, with the exception hereafter noted, the operation of the regulatory scheme enforced by the Pennsylvania Liquor Control Board does not sufficiently implicate the State in the discriminatory guest policies of Moose Lodge so as to make the latter "state action" within the ambit of the Equal Protection Clause of the Fourteenth Amendment.

The District Court found that the regulations of the Liquor Control Board adopted pursuant to statute affirmatively require that "every club licensee shall adhere to all the provisions of its constitution and by-laws." Appellant argues that the purpose of this provision "is purely and simply and plainly the prevention of subterfuge," pointing out that the *bona fides* of a private club, as opposed to a place of public accommodation masquerading as a private club, is a matter with which the State Liquor Control Board may legitimately concern itself. Appellee concedes this to be the case, and expresses disagreement with the District Court on this point. There can be no doubt that the label "private club" can and has been used to evade both regulations of state and local liquor authorities, and statutes requiring places of public accommodation to serve all persons without regard to race, color, religion, or national origin. . . .

The effect of this particular regulation on Moose Lodge under the provisions of the constitution placed in the record in the court below would be to place state sanctions behind its discriminatory membership rules, but not behind its guest practices, which were not embodied in the constitution of the lodge. Had there been no change in the relevant circumstances since the making of the record in the District Court, our holding . . . that appellee has standing to challenge only the guest practices of Moose Lodge would have a bearing on our disposition of this issue. Appellee stated upon oral argument, though, and Moose Lodge conceded in its Brief that the bylaws of the Supreme Lodge have been altered since the lower court decision to make applicable to guests the same sort of racial restrictions as are presently applicable to members.

Even though the Liquor Control Board regulation in question is neutral in its terms, the result of its application in a case where the constitution and bylaws of a club required racial discrimination would be to invoke the sanctions of the State to enforce a concededly discriminatory private rule. . . . *Shelley* v. *Kraemer*, makes it clear that the application of state sanctions to enforce such a rule would violate the Fourteenth Amendment. Although the record before us is not as clear as one would like, appellant has not persuaded us that the District Court should have denied any and all relief.

Appellee was entitled to a decree enjoining

the enforcement of § 113.09 of the regulations promulgated by the Pennsylvania Liquor Control Board insofar as that regulation requires compliance by Moose Lodge with provisions of its constitution and by-laws containing racially discriminatory provisions. He was entitled to no more. The judgment of the District Court is reversed, and the cause remanded with instructions to enter a decree in conformity with this opinion.

Reversed and remanded.

Justice Douglas, with whom Justice Marshall joins, dissenting.

. . . [T]he fact that a private club gets some kind of permit from the State or municipality does not make it *ipso facto* a public enterprise or undertaking, any more than the grant to a householder of a permit to operate an incinerator puts the householder in the public domain. We must therefore examine whether there are special circumstances involved in the Pennsylvania scheme which differentiate the liquor license possessed by Moose Lodge from the incinerator permit.

Pennsylvania has a state store system of alcohol distribution. Reseale is permitted by hotels, restaurants, and private clubs which all must obtain licenses from the Liquor Control Board. . . . Once a license is issued the licensee must comply with many detailed requirements or risk suspension or revocation of the license. Among these requirements is Regulation No. 113.09 which says "Every club licensee shall adhere to all the provisions of its Constitution and By-laws." This regulation means, as applied to Moose Lodge, that it must adhere to the racially discriminatory provision of the Constitution of its Supreme Lodge. . . .

. . . The result, as I see it, is the same as though Pennsylvania had put into its liquor licenses a provision that the license may not be used to dispense liquor to Blacks, Browns, Yellows—or atheists or agnostics. Regulation No. 113.09 is thus an invidious form of state action.

Were this regulation the only infirmity in Pennsylvania's licensing scheme, I would perhaps agree with the majority that the appropriate relief would be a decree enjoining its enforcement. But there is another flaw in the scheme not so easily cured. Liquor licenses in Pennsylvania, unlike driver's licenses, or marriage licenses, are not freely available to those who meet racially neutral qualifications. There is a complex quota system, which the majority accurately describes. What the majority neglects to say is that the Harrisburg quota, where Moose Lodge No. 107 is located, has been full for many years. No more club licenses may be issued in that city.

This state-enforced scarcity of licenses restricts the ability of blacks to obtain liquor, for liquor is commercially available *only* at private clubs for a significant portion of each week. Access by blacks to places that serve liquor is further limited by the fact that the state quota is filled. A group desiring to form a nondiscriminatory club which would serve blacks must purchase a license held by an existing club, which can exact a monopoly price for the transfer. The availability of such a license is speculative at best, however, for, as Moose Lodge itself concedes, without a liquor license a fraternal organization would be hard-pressed to survive.

Thus, the State of Pennsylvania is putting the weight of its liquor license, concededly a valued and important adjunct to a private club, behind racial discrimination. . . .

Justice Brennan, with whom Justice Marshall joins, dissenting.

When Moose Lodge obtained its liquor license, the State of Pennsylvania became an active participant in the operation of the Lodge bar. Liquor licensing laws are only incidentally revenue measures; they are primarily pervasive regulatory schemes under which the State dictates and continually supervises virtually every detail of the operation of the licensee's business. Very few, if any, other licensed businesses experience such complete state involvement. . . .

Plainly, the State of Pennsylvania's liquor regulations intertwine the State with the operation of the Lodge bar in a "significant way [and] lend [the State's] authority to the sordid business of racial discrimination." . . .

Hudgens v. *NLRB*
See p. 456, above.

Jackson v. *Metropolitan Edison Co.*
419 U.S. 345 (1974)

Defendant, a state-authorized and privately owned public utility, cut off its electric service to plaintiff (for nonpayment of amounts due) allegedly without notice, a hearing, and an opportunity to pay whatever might be due on her account for past services. Plaintiff sought damages and injunctive relief under an act of Congress based on the Fourteenth Amendment.

Mr. Justice Rehnquist delivered the opinion of the Court. . . .

Here the action complained of was taken by a utility company which is privately owned and operated, but which in many particulars of its business is subject to extensive state regulation. The mere fact that a business is subject to state regulation does not by itself convert its action into that of the State for purposes of the Fourteenth Amendment. *Moose Lodge No. 107* v. *Irvis, supra,* at 176–177. Nor does the fact that the regulation is extensive and detailed, as in the case of most public utilities, do so. *Public Utilities Comm'n* v. *Pollak,* 343 U.S. 451, 462 (1952). It may well be that acts of a heavily regulated utility with at least something of a governmentally protected monopoly will more readily be found to be "state" acts than will the acts of an entity lacking these characteristics. But the inquiry must be whether there is a sufficiently close nexus between the State and the challenged action of the regulated entity so that the action of the latter may be fairly treated as that of the State itself. *Moose Lodge No. 107, supra,* 407 U.S. at 176. The true nature of the State's involvement may not be immediately obvious, and detailed inquiry may be required in order to determine whether the test is met. *Burton* v. *Wilmington Parking Authority, supra.*

Petitioner advances a series of contentions which, in her view, lead to the conclusion that this case should fall on the *Burton* side of the line drawn in the *Civil Rights Cases, supra,* rather than on the *Moose Lodge* side of that line. We find none of them persuasive.

Petitioner first argues that "state action" is present because of the monopoly status allegedly conferred upon Metropolitan by the State of Pennsylvania. As a factual matter, it may well be doubted that the State ever granted or guaranteed Metropolitan a monopoly. But assuming that it had, this fact is not determinative in considering whether Metropolitan's termination of service to petitioner was "state action" for purposes of the Fourteenth Amendment. In *Pollak, supra,* where the Court dealt with the activities of the District of Columbia Transit Company, a congressionally established monopoly, we expressed disclaimed reliance on the monopoly status of the transit authority. *Id.,* 343 U.S. at 462. Similarly, although certain monopoly aspects were presented in *Moose Lodge No. 107, supra,* we found that the lodge's action was not subject to the provisions of the Fourteenth Amendment. In each of those cases,

there was insufficient relationship between the challenged actions of the entities involved and their monopoly status. There is no indication of any greater connection here.

Petitioner next urges that state action is present because respondent provides an essential public service required to be supplied on a reasonably continuous basis by 66 Pa.Stat. § 1171, and hence performs a "public function." We have of course found state action present in the exercise by private entity of powers traditionally exclusively reserved to the State. See, e.g., *Nixon* v. *Condon,* 286 U.S. 73 (1931) (election); *Terry* v. *Adams,* 345 U.S. 461 (1953) (election); *Marsh* v. *Alabama,* 326 U.S. 501 (1946) (company town); *Evans* v. *Newton,* 382 U.S. 296 (1966) (municipal park). If we were dealing with the exercise by Metropolitan of some power delegated to it by the State which is traditionally associated with sovereignty, such as eminent domain, our case would be quite a different one. But while the Pennsylvania statute imposes an obligation to furnish service on regulated utilities, it imposes no such obligation on the State. The Pennsylvania courts have rejected the contention that the furnishing of utility services are either state functions or municipal duties. *Girard Life Insurance Co.* v. *City of Philadelphia,* 88 Pa. 393 (1879); *Bailey* v. *Philadelphia,* 184 Pa. 594, 39 A. 494 (1898).

Perhaps in recognition of the fact that the supplying of utility service is not traditionally the exclusive prerogative of the State, petitioner invites the expansion of the doctrine of this limited line of cases into a broad principle that all businesses "affected with the public interest" are state actors in all their actions.

We decline the invitation for reasons stated long ago in *Nebbia* v. *New York,* 291 U.S. 502 (1934), in the course of rejecting a substantive due process attack on state legislation: . . .

Doctors, optometrists, lawyers, Metropolitan, and *Nebbia's* upstate New York grocery selling a quart of milk are all in regulated businesses, providing arguably essential goods and services, "affected with a public interest." We do not believe that such a status converts their every action, absent more, into that of the State.

We also reject the notion that Metropolitan's termination is state action because the State "has specifically authorized and approved" the termination practice. In the instant case, Metropolitan filed with the Public Utilities Commission a general tariff—a provision of which states Metropolitan's right to terminate service for nonpayment. This provision has appeared in Metropolitan's previously filed tariffs for many years and has never been the subject of a hearing or other scrutiny by the Commission. Although the Commission did hold hearings on portions of Metropolitan's general tariff relating to a general rate increase, it never even considered the reinsertion of this provision in the newly filed general tariff. The provision became effective 60 days after filing when not disapproved by the Commission.

As a threshold matter, it is less than clear under state law that Metropolitan was even required to file this provision as part of its tariff or that the Commission would have had the power to disapprove it. The District Court observed that the sole connection of the Commission with this regulation was Metropolitan's simple notice filing with the Commission and the lack of any Commission action to prohibit it.

The case most heavily relied on by petitioner is *Public Utilities Comm'n* v. *Pollak, supra.* There the Court dealt with the contention that Capital Transit's installation of a piped music system on its buses violated the First Amendment rights of the bus riders. It is not entirely clear whether the Court alternatively held that Capital Transit's action was action of the "state" for First Amendment purposes, or whether it merely assumed *arguendo* that it was and went on to resolve the First Amendment question adversely to the bus riders. In either event, the nature of the state involvement there was quite different than it is here. The District of Columbia Public Utilities Commission, on its own motion, commenced an investigation of the effects of the piped music, and after a full hearing concluded not only that Capital Transit's practices were "not inconsistent with public convenience, comfort, and safety," 81 P.U.R.(N.S.) 122, 127 (1950), but that the practice "in fact through the creation of better will among passengers, . . . tends to improve the conditions under which the public rides." *Id.*, at 126. Here, on the other hand, there was no such *imprimatur* placed on the practice of Metropolitan about which petitioner complains. The nature of governmental regulation of private utilities is such that a utility may frequently be required by the state regulatory scheme to obtain approval for practices a business regulated in less detail would be free to institute without any approval from a regulatory body. Approval by a state utility commission of such a request from a regulated utility, where the Commission has not put its own weight on the side of the proposed practice by ordering it, does not transmute a practice initiated by the utility and approved by the Commission into "state action." At most, the Commission's failure to overturn this practice amounted to no more than a determination that a Pennsylvania utility was authorized to employ such a practice if it so desired. Respondent's exercise of the choice allowed by state law where the initiative comes from it and not from the State, does not make its action in doing so "state action" for purposes of the Fourteenth Amendment.

We also find absent in the instant case the symbiotic relationship presented in *Burton* v. *Wilmington Parking Authority*, 365 U.S. 715 (1961). . . .

Metropolitan is a privately owned corporation, and it does not lease its facilities from the State of Pennsylvania. It alone is responsible for the provision of power to its customers. In common with all corporations of the State it pays taxes to the State, and it is subject to a form of extensive regulation by the State in a way that most other business enterprises are not. But this was likewise true of the appellant club in *Moose Lodge No. 107* v. *Irvis.* . . .

All of petitioner's arguments taken together

show no more than that Metropolitan was a heavily regulated private utility, enjoying at least a partial monopoly in the providing of electrical service within its territory, and that it elected to terminate service to petitioner in a manner which the Pennsylvania Public Utilities Commission found permissible under state law. Under our decision this is not sufficient to connect the State of Pennsylvania with respondent's action so as to make the latter's conduct attributable to the State for purposes of the Fourteenth Amendment.

We conclude that the State of Pennsylvania is not sufficiently connected with respondent's action in terminating petitioner's service so as to make respondent's conduct in so doing attributable to the State for purposes of the Fourteenth Amendment. We therefore have no occasion to decide whether petitioner's claim to continued service was "property" for purposes of that Amendment, or whether "due process of law" would require a State taking similar action to accord petitioner the procedural rights for which she contends. . . .

Mr. Justice Douglas, dissenting.

I reach the opposite conclusion from that reached by the majority on the state action issue. . . .

Mr. Justice Brennan, dissenting.

I do not think that a controversy existed between petitioner and respondent entitling petitioner to be heard in this action. . . .

Mr. Justice Marshall, dissenting.

I agree with my Brother Brennan that this case is a very poor vehicle for resolving the difficult and important questions presented today. . . . Since the Court has disposed of the case by finding no state action, however, I think it appropriate to register my dissent on that point. . . .

The fact that the Metropolitan Edison Company supplies an essential public service that is in many communities supplied by the government weighs more heavily for me than for the majority. . . .

Private parties performing functions affecting the public interest can often make a persuasive claim to be free of the constitutional requirements applicable to governmental institutions because of the value of preserving a private sector in which the opportunity for individual choice is maximized. See *Evans* v. *Newton,* 382 U.S., at 298, Friendly, *The Dartmouth College Case and the Private-Public Penumbra* (1969). Maintaining the private status of parochial schools, cited by the majority, advances just this value. In the due process area, a similar value of diversity may often be furthered by allowing various private institutions the flexibility to select procedures that fit their particular needs. See *Wahba* v. *New York University,* 492 F.2d 96, 102 (C.A.2), cert. denied, 419 U.S. 874 (1974). But it is hard to imagine any such interests that are furthered by protecting public utility companies from meeting the constitutional standards that would apply if the companies were state-owned. The values of pluralism and diversity are simply not relevant when the private company is the only electric company in town. . . .

What is perhaps most troubling about the Court's opinion is that it would appear to apply to a broad range of claimed constitutional violations by the company. The Court has not adopted the notion, accepted elsewhere, that different standards should apply to state action analysis when different constitutional claims are presented. See *Adickes* v. *S. H. Kress & Co.,* 398 U.S. 144, 190–191 (1970) (Brennan, J., concurring and dissenting); *Grafton* v. *Brooklyn Law School,* 478 F.2d 1137, 1142 (C.A.2, 1973). Thus, the majority's analysis would seemingly apply as well to a company that refused to extend service to Negroes, welfare recipients, or any other group that the company preferred, for its own reasons, not to serve. I cannot believe that this

Court would hold that the State's involvement with the utility company was not sufficient to impose upon the company an obligation to meet the constitutional mandate of nondiscrimination. Yet nothing in the analysis of the majority opinion suggests otherwise. . . .

Quaere: Would ERA outlaw only *governmental* gender discrimination? Are its terms analogous to those of the Fourteenth Amendment with respect to *whose* discriminatory action is forbidden? Does any provision of the Constitution prohibit any conduct of any private person or persons?

Of course purely private discrimination may be outlawed by the states under their reserved (police) powers, and by Congress under, for example, its Commerce Clause power. As to the latter, see *Heart of Atlanta Motel* (Chapter 3, above). See also *Runyon,* below.

PRIVATE DISCRIMINATION AND THE THIRTEENTH AMENDMENT

Runyon v. *McCrary* (with two other cases)
427 U.S. 160 (1976)

In this case and its predecessor, *Jones* v. *Alfred H. Mayer Co.,* 392 U.S. 409 (1968), the Court circumvents the state-action requirement of the Fourteenth Amendment by relying on the Thirteenth Amendment and the "badges of slavery" approach used by Mr. Justice Harlan in his lone dissent in the *Civil Rights Cases,* above. If the resulting broad meaning of the Thirteenth Amendment (as in this case and in *Jones*) is correct, would there have been any need to adopt Sections 1 and 5 of the Fourteenth Amendment? Wasn't the Fourteenth Amendment adopted after the Black Code experience precisely because it was recognized that the Thirteenth Amendment deals only with *slavery* itself, not with mere "badges of slavery," that is, racial discrimination?

Mr. Justice Stewart delivered the opinion of the Court.

The principal issue presented by these consolidated cases is whether a federal law, namely 42 U.S.C. § 1981, prohibits private schools from excluding qualified children solely because they are Negroes. . . .

It is worth noting at the outset some of the questions that these cases do not present. They do not present any question of the right of a private social organization to limit its membership on racial or any other grounds. They do not present any question of the right of a private school to limit its student body to boys, to girls, or to adherents of a particular religious faith, since 42 U.S.C. § 1981 is in no way addressed to such categories of selectivity. They do not even present the application of § 1981 to private sectarian schools that practice *racial* exclusion on religious grounds. Rather, these cases present only two basic questions: whether § 1981 prohibits private, commercially operated, nonsectarian schools from denying admission to prospective students because they are Negroes, and, if so, whether that federal law is constitutional as so applied.

Applicability of § 1981. . . . In [*Jones* v. *Alfred*

H. Mayer Co.] the Court held that the portion of § 1 of the Civil Rights Act of 1866 presently codified as 42 U.S.C. § 1982 prohibits private racial discrimination in the sale or rental of real or personal property. Relying on the legislative history of § 1, from which both § 1981 and § 1982 derive, the Court concluded that Congress intended to prohibit "all racial discrimination, private and public, in the sale . . . of property," and that this prohibition was within Congress' power under § 2 of the Thirteenth Amendment . . . . As the Court indicated in Jones, that holding necessarily implied that the portion of § 1 of the 1866 Act presently codified as 42 U.S.C. § 1981 likewise reaches purely private acts of racial discrimination. . . . Just as in Jones a Negro's § 1 right to purchase property on equal terms with whites was violated when a private person refused to sell to the prospective purchaser solely because he was a Negro, so also a Negro's § 1 right to "make and enforce contracts" is violated if a private offeror refuses to extend to a Negro, solely because he is a Negro, the same opportunity to enter into contracts as he extends to white offerees. . . .

Constitutionality of § 1981 as Applied. The question remains whether § 1981, as applied, violates constitutionally protected rights of free association and privacy, or a parent's right to direct the education of his children.

1. *Freedom of Association.* In *NAACP* v. *Alabama,* and similar decisions, the Court has recognized a First Amendment right "to engage in association for the advancement of beliefs and ideas . . . ." From this principle it may be assumed that parents have a First Amendment right to send their children to educational institutions to promote the belief that racial segregation is desirable, and that the children have an equal right to attend such institutions. But it does not follow that the *practice* of excluding racial minorities from such institutions is also protected by the same principle. As the Court stated in *Norwood* v. *Harrison,* 413 U.S. 455, "the Constitution . . . places no value on discrimination," and while "[i]nvidious pri-

vate discrimination may be characterized as a form of exercising freedom of association protected by the First Amendment . . . it has never been accorded affirmative constitutional protections. . . ." In any event, as the Court of Appeals noted, "there is no showing that discontinuance of [the] discriminatory admission practices would inhibit in any way the teaching in these schools of any ideas or dogma."

2. *Parental Rights.* In *Meyer* v. *Nebraska,* 262 U.S. 390, the Court held that the liberty protected by the Due Process Clause of the Fourteenth Amendment includes the right "to acquire useful knowledge, to marry, establish a home and bring up children," and, concomitantly, the right to send one's children to a private school that offers specialized training—in that case, instruction in the German language. In *Pierce* v. *Society of Sisters,* 268 U.S. 510, the Court applied "the doctrine of *Meyer* v. *Nebraska*" to hold unconstitutional an Oregon law requiring the parent, guardian, or other person having custody of a child between eight and 16 years of age to send that child to public school on pain of criminal liability. *Wisconsin* v. *Yoder* and *Norwood* v. *Harrison* both stressed the "limited scope of Pierce," which simply "affirmed the right of private schools to exist and to operate. . . ."

It is clear that the present application of § 1981 infringes no parental right recognized in *Meyer, Pierce, Yoder,* or *Norwood.* No challenge is made to the petitioners' right to operate their private schools or the right of parents to send their children to a particular private school rather than a public school. Nor do these cases involve a challenge to the subject matter which is taught at any private school. Thus, the [schools] remain presumptively free to inculcate whatever values and standards they deem desirable. *Meyer* and its progeny entitle them to no more.

3. *The Right of Privacy.* The Court has held that in some situations the Constitution confers a right of privacy. While the application of § 1981 to the conduct at issue [does] not repre-

sent governmental intrusion into the privacy of the home or a similarly intimate setting, it does implicate parental interests. These interests are related to the procreative rights protected in *Roe* v. *Wade* and *Griswold* v. *Connecticut*. A person's decision whether to bear a child and a parent's decision concerning the manner in which his child is to be educated may fairly be characterized as exercises of familial rights and responsibilities. But it does not follow that because government is largely or even entirely precluded from regulating the childbearing decision, it is similarly restricted by the Constitution from regulating the implementation of parental decisions concerning a child's education.

The Court has repeatedly stressed that while parents have a constitutional right to send their children to private schools and a constitutional right to select private schools that offer specialized instruction, they have no constitutional right to provide their children with private school education unfettered by reasonable government regulation. See *Wisconsin* v. *Yoder*; *Pierce* v. *Society of Sisters*; *Meyer* v. *Nebraska*.

Section 1981, as applied to the conduct at issue here, constitutes an exercise of federal legislative power under § 2 of the Thirteenth Amendment fully consistent with *Meyer*, *Pierce*, and the cases that followed in their wake. The prohibition of racial discrimination that interferes with the making and enforcement of contracts for private educational services furthers goals closely analogous to those served by § 1981's elimination of racial discrimination in the making of private employment contracts and, more generally, by § 1982's guarantee that "a dollar in the hands of a Negro will purchase the same thing as a dollar in the hands of a white man." [*Jones*.] . . .

Mr. Justice Powell, concurring.

If the slate were clean I might well be inclined to agree with Mr. Justice White that § 1981 was not intended to restrict private contractual choices. Much of the review of the history and purpose of this statute set forth in his dissenting opinion is quite persuasive. It seems to me, however, that it comes too late.

The applicability of § 1981 to private contracts has been considered maturely and recently, and I do not feel free to disregard these precedents. Although [most] cases involved § 1982, rather than § 1981, I agree that their considered holdings with respect to the purpose and meaning of § 1982 necessarily apply to both statutes in view of their common derivation.

Although the range of consequences suggested by the dissenting opinion go far beyond what we hold today, I am concerned that our decision not be construed more broadly than would be justified. [O]ur holding that this restriction extends to certain actions by private individuals does not imply the intrusive investigation into the motives of every refusal to contract by a private citizen that is suggested by the dissent. As the Court of Appeals suggested, some contracts are so personal "as to have a discernible rule of exclusivity which is inoffensive to § 1981." [In] certain personal contractual relationships, [such] as those where the offeror selects those with whom he desires to bargain on an individualized basis, or where the contract is the foundation of a close association (such as, for example, that between an employer and a private tutor, babysitter, or housekeeper), there is reason to assume that, although the choice made by the offeror is selective, it reflects "a purpose of exclusiveness" other than the desire to bar members of the Negro race. Such a purpose, certainly in most cases, would invoke associational rights long respected.

The case presented on the record before us does not involve this type of personal contractual relationship. . . . The schools are operated strictly on a commercial basis, and one fairly could construe their open-end invitations as offers that matured into binding contracts when accepted by those who met the academic, financial, and other racially neutral specified conditions as to qualifications for entrance. There is no reason to assume that the schools had any special reason for exercising an option of personal choice among those who responded to their public offers. A small kindergarten or music class, operated on the basis of personal invitations extended to a limited number of preidentified students, for example, would present a far different case.

I do not suggest that a "bright line" can be drawn that easily separates the type of contract offer within the reach of § 1981 from the type without. The case before us is clearly on one side of the line, however defined, and the kindergarten and music school examples are clearly on the other side. Close questions undoubtedly will arise in the grey area that necessarily exists in between. But some of the applicable principles and considerations, for the most part identified by the Court's opinion, are clear: Section 1981, as interpreted by our prior decisions, does reach certain acts of racial discrimination that are "private" in the sense that they involve no *state* action. But choices, including those involved in entering into a contract, that are "private" in the sense that they are not part of a commercial relationship offered generally or widely, and that reflect the selectivity exercised by an individual entering into a personal relationship, certainly were never intended to be restricted by the Nineteenth Century Civil Rights Acts. The open offer to the public generally involved in the case before us is simply not a "private" contract in this sense. Accordingly, I join the opinion of the Court.

Mr. Justice Stevens, concurring.

. . . Jones has been decided and is now an important part of the fabric of our law. Although I recognize the force of Mr. Justice White's argument that the construction of § 1982 does not control § 1981, it would be most incongruous to give those two sections a fundamentally different construction. I am persuaded [that] we must either apply the rationale of *Jones* or overrule that decision.

There are two reasons which favor overruling. First, [my] conviction that *Jones* was wrongfully decided is firm. Second, it is extremely unlikely that reliance upon *Jones* has been so extensive that this Court is foreclosed from overruling it. There are, however, opposing arguments of greater force.

The first is the interest in stability and orderly development of the law. In this case, [that interest favors] adherence to, rather than departure from, precedent. For even if *Jones* did not accurately reflect the sentiments of the Reconstruction Congress, it surely accords with the prevailing sense of justice today.

The policy of the Nation as formulated by the Congress in recent years has moved constantly in the direction of eliminating racial segregation in all sectors of society. This Court has given a sympathetic and liberal construction to such legislation. For the Court now to overrule *Jones* would be a significant step backwards, with effects that would not have arisen from a correct decision in the first instance. Such a step would be so clearly contrary to my understanding of the mores of today that I think the Court is entirely correct in adhering to *Jones*.

Mr. Justice White, with whom Mr. Justice Rehnquist joins, dissenting.

We are urged here to extend the meaning and reach of 42 U.S.C. § 1981 so as to establish a general prohibition against a private individual or institution refusing to enter into a contract with another person because of that person's race. Section 1981 has been on the books since 1870 and to so hold for the first time would be contrary to the language of the section, to its legislative history and to the clear dictum of this Court in the *Civil Rights Cases,* almost contemporaneously with the passage of the statute, that the section reaches only discriminations imposed by state law. The majority's belated discovery of a congressional purpose which escaped this Court only a decade after the statute was passed and which escaped all other federal courts for almost 100 years is singularly unpersuasive. . . .

The legislative history of 42 U.S.C. § 1981 confirms that the statute means what it says and no more, i.e., that it outlaws any legal rule disabling any person from making or enforcing a contract, but does not prohibit private racially motivated refusals to contract. . . .

The majority's holding that 42 U.S.C. § 1981 prohibits all racially motivated contractual decisions . . . threatens to embark the judiciary on a treacherous course. Whether such conduct should be condoned or not, whites and blacks will undoubtedly choose to form a variety of associational relationships pursuant to contracts which exclude members of the other race. Social clubs, black and white, and associations designed to further the interests of blacks or whites are but two examples. Lawsuits by members of the other race attempting to gain admittance to such an association are not pleasant to contemplate. As the associational or contractual relationships become more private, the pressures to hold § 1981 inapplicable to them will increase. Imaginative judicial construction of the word "contract" is foreseeable; Thirteenth Amendment limitations on Congress' power to ban "badges and incidents of slavery" may be discovered; the doctrine of the right to association may be bent to cover a given situation. In any event, courts will be called upon to balance sensitive policy considerations against each other—which considerations have never been addressed by any Congress—all under the guise of "construing" a statute. This is a task appropriate for the legislature, not for the judiciary. . . .

Quaere: Suppose a white family frequently invites some of its white, but never any of its black, neighbors to its home for dinner. Suppose it buys groceries at a white-owned store, but never at a comparable, equally convenient black-owned store. Would such conduct come within the *Runyon* "badges of slavery" rule?

11

Freedom of Religion

SEPARATION OF CHURCH AND STATE: THE ESTABLISHMENT PROHIBITION

Governmental Aid for Religion

Everson v. *Board of Education*
330 U.S. 1 (1947)

Mr. Justice Black delivered the opinion of the Court.

A New Jersey statute authorizes its local school districts to make rules and contracts for the transportation of children to and from schools. The appellee, a township board of education, acting pursuant to this statute authorized reimbursement to parents of money expended by them for the bus transportation of their children on regular busses operated by the public transportation system. Part of this money was for the payment of transportation of some children in the community to Catholic parochial schools. These church schools give their students, in addition to secular education, regular religious instruction conforming to the religious tenets and modes of worship of the Catholic Faith. The superintendent of these schools is a Catholic priest.

The appellant, in his capacity as a district taxpayer, filed suit in a State court challenging the right of the Board to reimburse parents of parochial school students. . . . The New Jersey Court of Errors and Appeals [held] that neither the statute nor the resolution passed pursuant to it was in conflict with the State constitution or the provisions of the Federal Constitution in issue. . . .

The only contention here is that the State statute and the resolution, in so far as they authorized reimbursement to parents of children attending parochial schools, violate the Federal Constitution in these two respects, which to some extent, overlap. *First.* They authorize the State to take by taxation the private property of some and bestow it upon others, to be used for their own private purposes. This, it is alleged, violates the due process clause of the Fourteenth Amendment. *Second.* The statute and the resolution forced inhabitants to pay taxes to help support and maintain schools which are dedicated to, and which regularly teach, the Catholic Faith. This is alleged to be a use of state power to support church schools contrary to the prohibition of the First Amendment which the

Fourteenth Amendment made applicable to the states.

First. . . . It is much too late to argue that legislation intended to facilitate the opportunity of children to get a secular education serves no public purpose. *Cochran* v. *Louisiana State Board of Education,* 281 U.S. 370. . . . The same thing is no less true of legislation to reimburse needy parents, or all parents, for payment of the fares of their children so that they can ride in public busses to and from schools rather than run the risk of traffic and other hazards incident to walking or "hitchhiking." . . .

Second. The New Jersey statute is challenged as a "law respecting an establishment of religion." The First Amendment, as made applicable to the states by the Fourteenth, . . . commands that a state "shall make no law respecting an establishment of religion, or prohibiting the free exercise thereof." . . . Whether this New Jersey law is one respecting the "establishment of religion" requires an understanding of the meaning of that language, particularly with respect to the imposition of taxes. . . .

The "establishment of religion" clause of the First Amendment means at least this: Neither a state nor the Federal Government can set up a church. Neither can pass laws which aid one religion, aid all religions, or prefer one religion over another. Neither can force nor influence a person to go to or to remain away from church against his will or force him to profess a belief or disbelief in any religion. No person can be punished for entertaining or professing religious beliefs or disbeliefs, for church attendance or nonattendance. No tax in any amount, large or small, can be levied to support any religious activities or institutions, whatever they may be called, or whatever form they may adopt to teach or practice religion. Neither a state nor the Federal Government can, openly or secretly, participate in the affairs of any religious organizations or groups and vice versa. In the words of Jefferson, the clause against establishment of religion by law was intended to erect "a wall

of separation between Church and State." *Reynolds* v. *United States, supra,* 98 U.S. at page 164.

We must consider the New Jersey statute in accordance with the foregoing limitations imposed by the First Amendment. But we must not strike that State statute down if it is within the State's constitutional power even though it approaches the verge of that power. . . . New Jersey cannot consistently with the "establishment of religion" clause of the First Amendment contribute tax-raised funds to the support of an institution which teaches the tenets and faith of any church. On the other hand, other language of the amendment commands that New Jersey cannot hamper its citizens in the free exercise of their own religion. Consequently, it cannot exclude individual Catholics, Lutherans, Mohammedans, Baptists, Jews, Methodists, Non-believers, Presbyterians, or the members of any other faith, *because of their faith, or lack of it,* from receiving the benefits of public welfare legislation. While we do not mean to intimate that a state could not provide transportation only to children attending public schools, we must be careful, in protecting the citizens of New Jersey against State-established churches, to be sure that we do not inadvertently prohibit New Jersey from extending its general State law benefits to all its citizens without regard to their religious belief.

Measured by these standards, we cannot say that the First Amendment prohibits New Jersey from spending tax-raised funds to pay the bus fares of parochial school pupils as a part of a general program under which it pays the fares of pupils attending public and other schools. It is undoubtedly true that children are helped to get to church schools. There is even a possibility that some of the children might not be sent to the church schools if the parents were compelled to pay their children's bus fares out of their own pockets when transportation to a public school would have been paid for by the State. The same possibility exists where the state requires a local transit company to provide reduced fares to school children including those attending parochial schools, or where a municipally owned transportation system undertakes to carry all school children free of charge. Moreover, state-paid policemen, detailed to protect children going to and from church schools from the very real hazards of traffic, would serve much the same purpose and accomplish much the same result as state provisions intended to guarantee free transportation of a kind which the state deems to be best for the school children's welfare. And parents might refuse to risk their children to the serious danger of traffic accidents going to and from parochial schools, the approaches to which were not protected by policemen. Similarly, parents might be reluctant to permit their children to attend schools which the state had cut off from such general government services as ordinary police and fire protection, connections for sewage disposal, public highways and sidewalks. Of course, cutting off church schools from these services, so separate and so indisputably marked off from the religious function, would make it far more difficult for the schools to operate. But such is obviously not the purpose of the First Amendment. That Amendment requires the state to be a neutral in its relations with groups of religious believers and non-believers; it does not require the state to be their adversary. State power is no more to be used so as to handicap religions, than it is to favor them.

This Court has said that parents may, in the discharge of their duty under state compulsory education laws, send their children to a religious rather than a public school if the school meets the secular educational requirements which the state has power to impose. See *Pierce* v. *Society of Sisters,* 268 U.S. 510. It appears that these parochial schools meet New Jersey's requirements. The State contributes no money to the schools. It does not support them. Its legislation, as applied, does no more than provide a general program to help parents get their children, regardless of their religion, safely and expeditiously to and from accredited schools. . . .

The First Amendment has erected a wall between church and state. That wall must be kept high and impregnable. We could not approve the slightest breach. New Jersey has not breached it here.

Mr. Justice Jackson [and Mr. Justice Frankfurter], dissenting. . . .

The Court's opinion marshals every argument in favor of state aid and puts the case in its most favorable light, but much of its reasoning confirms my conclusions that there are no good grounds upon which to support the present legislation. In fact, the undertones of the opinion, advocating complete and uncompromising separation of Church from State, seem utterly discordant with its conclusion yielding support to their commingling in educational matters. The case which irresistibly comes to mind as the most fitting precedent is that of Julia who, according to Byron's reports, "whispering 'I will ne'er consent,'—consented." . . .

Mr. Justice Rutledge, with whom Mr. Justice Frankfurter, Mr. Justice Jackson and Mr. Justice Burton, agree, dissenting. . . .

Two great drives are constantly in motion to abridge, in the name of education, the complete division of religion and civil authority which our forefathers made. One is to introduce religious education and observances into the public schools. The other, to obtain public funds for the aid and support of various private religious schools. See Johnson, *The Legal Status of Church-State Relationships in the United States* (1934); Thayer, *Religion in Public Education* (1947); Note (1941) 50 *Yale L.J.* 917. In my opinion both avenues were closed by the Constitution. Neither should be opened by this Court. The matter is not one of quantity, to be measured by the amount of money expended. Now as in Madison's day it is one of principle, to keep separate the separate spheres as the First Amendment drew them; to prevent the first experiment upon our liberties; and to keep the question from becoming entangled in corrosive precedents. We should not be less strict to keep strong and untarnished the one side of the shield of religious freedom than we have been of the other.

> *Note:* Without Mr. Justice Douglas there would have been only four votes to uphold the challenged law in this case. In *Engel* v. *Vitale,* below, Mr. Justice Douglas found that his position in *Everson* was wrong.

Walz v. *Tax Commission*
397 U.S. 664 (1970)

New York gave a tax exemption for property used solely for "religious, educational, or charitable purposes." This was challenged as a violation of the Establishment Clause. The measure was upheld by an 8 to 1 vote. The crux of the Douglas dissent is mentioned in the majority opinion.

Mr. Chief Justice Burger delivered the opinion of the Court. . . .

The course of constitutional neutrality in this area cannot be an absolutely straight line; rigidity could well defeat the basic purpose of these provisions, which is to insure that no religion be sponsored or favored, none commanded, and none inhibited. The general principle deducible from the First Amendment and all that has been said by the Court is this: that we will not tolerate either governmentally established religion or governmental interference with religion. Short of those expressly proscribed governmental acts there is room for play in the joints productive of a benevolent neutrality which will permit religious exercise to exist without sponsorship and without interference. . . .

The legislative purpose of a property tax exemption is neither the advancement nor the inhibition of religion; it is neither sponsorship nor hostility. New York, in common with the other States, has determined that certain entities that exist in a harmonious relationship to the community at large, and that foster its "moral or mental improvement," should not be inhibited in their activities by property taxation or the hazard of loss of those properties for non-

payment of taxes. It has not singled out one particular church or religious group or even churches as such; rather, it has granted exemption to all houses of religious worship within a broad class of property owned by nonprofit, quasi-public corporations which include hospitals, libraries, playgrounds, scientific, professional, historical and patriotic groups. The State has an affirmative policy that considers these groups as beneficial and stabilizing influences in community life and finds this classification useful, desirable, and in the public interest. . . .

Determining that the legislative purpose of tax exemption is not aimed at establishing, sponsoring, or supporting religion does not end the inquiry, however. We must also be sure that the end result—the effect—is not an excessive government entanglement with religion. The test is inescapably one of degree. Either course, taxation of churches or exemption, occasions some degree of involvement with religion. Elimination of exemption would tend to expand the involvement of government by giving rise to tax valuation of church property, tax liens, tax foreclosures, and the direct confrontations and conflicts that follow in the train of those legal processes.

Granting tax exemptions to churches necessarily operates to afford an indirect economic benefit and also gives rise to some, but yet a lesser, involvement than taxing them. In analyzing either alternative the questions are whether the involvement is excessive, and whether it is a continuing one calling for official and continuing surveillance leading to an impermissible degree of entanglement. Obviously a direct money subsidy would be a relationship pregnant with involvement and, as with most governmental grant programs, could encompass sustained and detailed administrative relationships for enforcement of statutory or administrative standards, but that is not this case. The hazards of churches supporting government are hardly less in their potential than the hazards of governments supporting churches; each relationship carries some involvement rather than the desired insulation and separation. We cannot ignore the instances in history when church support of government led to the kind of involvement we seek to avoid.

The grant of a tax exemption is not sponsorship since the government does not transfer part of its revenue to churches but simply abstains from demanding that the church support the state. No one has ever suggested that tax exemption has converted libraries, art galleries, or hospitals into arms of the state or employees "on the public payroll." There is no genuine nexus between tax exemption and establishment of religion. . . .

It is obviously correct that no one acquires a vested or protected right in violation of the Constitution by long use, even when that span of time covers our entire national existence and indeed predates it. Yet an unbroken practice of according the exemption to churches, openly and by affirmative state action, not covertly or by state inaction, is not something to be lightly cast aside. . . .

Nothing in this national attitude toward religious tolerance and two centuries of uninterrupted freedom from taxation has given the remotest sign of leading to an established church or religion and on the contrary it has operated affirmatively to help guarantee the free exercise of all forms of religious beliefs. Thus, it is hardly useful to suggest that tax exemption is but the "foot in the door" or the "nose of the camel in the tent" leading to an established church. If tax exemption can be seen as this first step toward "establishment" of religion, as Mr. Justice Douglas fears, the second step has been long in coming. Any move which realistically "establishes" a church or tends to do so can be dealt with "while this Court sits." . . .

[Justices Brennan and Harlan concurred in separate opinions. Justice Douglas dissented.]

Roemer v. *Board of Public Works of Maryland* (excerpt)
426 U.S. 736 (1976)

The following excerpt from an opinion by Mr. Justice Blackmun provides a careful resumé of the Court's recent handling of the problem of government aid to religion:

A system of government that makes itself felt as pervasively as ours could hardly be expected never to cross paths with the church. In fact, our State and Federal Governments impose certain burdens upon, and impart certain benefits to, virtually all our activities, and religious activity is not an exception. The Court has enforced a scrupulous neutrality by the State, as among religions, and also as between religious and other activities,[1] but a hermetic separation of the two is an impossibility it has never required. It long has been established, for example, that the State may send a cleric, indeed even a clerical order,

---
[1] See, *e.g.*, Epperson v. Arkansas, 393 U.S. 97, 104 (1968); McCollum v. Board of Education, 333 U.S. 203, 209–212 (1948); Everson v. Board of Education, 330 U.S., at 15–16.

to perform a wholly secular task. In *Bradfield* v. *Roberts*, 175 U.S. 291 (1899), the Court upheld the extension of public aid to a corporation which, although composed entirely of members of a Roman Catholic sisterhood acting "under the auspices of said church," *id.*, at 297, was limited by its corporate charter to the secular purpose of operating a charitable hospital.

And religious institutions need not be quarantined from public benefits that are neutrally available to all. The Court has permitted the State to supply transportation for children to and from church-related as well as public schools. *Everson* v. *Board of Education*, 330 U.S. 1 (1947). It has done the same with respect to secular textbooks loaned by the State on equal terms to students attending both public and church-related elementary schools. *Board of Education* v. *Allen*, 392 U.S. 236 (1968). Since it had not been shown in *Allen* that the secular textbooks would be put to other than secular purposes, the Court concluded that, as in *Everson*, the State was merely "extending the benefits of state laws to all citizens." *Id.*, at 242. Just as *Bradfield* dispels any notion that a religious person can never be in the State's pay for a secular purpose,[2] *Everson* and *Allen* put to rest any argument that the State may never act in such a way that has the incidental effect of facilitating religious activity. The Court has not been blind to the fact that in aiding a religious institution to perform a secular task, the State frees the institution's resources to be put to sectarian ends.[3] If this were impermissible, however, a church could not be protected by the police and fire departments, or have its public sidewalk kept in repair. The Court never has held that religious activities must be discriminated against in this way.

Neutrality is what is required. The State must confine itself to secular objectives, and neither advance nor impede religious activity. Of course, that principle is more easily stated than applied. The Court has taken the view that a secular purpose and a facial neutrality may not be enough, if in fact the State is lending direct support to a religious activity. The State may not, for example, pay for what is actually a religious education, even though it purports to be paying for a secular one, and even though it makes its aid available to secular and religious institutions alike. The Court also has taken the view that the State's efforts to perform a secular task, and at the same time avoid aiding in the performance of a religious one, may not lead it into such an intimate relationship with religious authority that it appears either to be sponsoring or to be excessively interfering with that authority.[4] In *Lemon I*, as noted above, the Court distilled these concerns into a three-prong test, resting in part on prior case law, for the constitutionality of statutes affording state aid to church-related schools:

"First, the statute must have a secular legislative purpose; second, its principal or primary effect must be one that neither advances nor inhibits religion . . . ; finally, the statute must not foster 'an excessive government entanglement with religion.'" 403 U.S., at 612–613.

At issue in *Lemon I* were two state-aid plans, a Rhode Island program to grant a 15% supplement to the salaries of private, church-related school teachers teaching secular courses, and a

---

[2] It could scarcely be otherwise, or individuals would be discriminated against for their religion, and the Nation would have to abandon its accepted practice of allowing members of religious orders to serve in the Congress and in other public offices.

[3] See Hunt v. McNair, 413 U.S. 734, 743 (1973) ("the Court has not accepted the recurrent argument that all aid is forbidden because aid to one aspect of an institution frees it to spend its other resources on religious ends"). See also Committee for Public Education v. Nyquist, 413 U.S. 756, 775 (1973); Tilton v. Richardson, 403 U.S. 672, 679 (1971) (plurality opinion); Lemon v. Kurtzman, 403 U.S. 602, 664 (1971) (opinion of White, J.); Board of Education v. Allen, 392 U.S. 236, 244 (1968); Everson v. Board of Education, 330 U.S., at 17.

[4] The importance of avoiding persistent and potentially frictional contact between governmental and religious authorities is such that it has been held to justify the *extension*, rather than the withholding, of certain benefits to religious organizations. The Court upheld the exemption of such organizations from property taxation partly on this ground. Walz v. Tax Commission, 397 U.S. 664, 674–675 (1970).

Pennsylvania program to reimburse private church-related schools for the entire cost of secular courses also offered in public schools. Both failed the third part of the test, that of "excessive government entanglement." This part the Court held in turn required a consideration of three factors: (1) the character and purposes of the benefited institutions, (2) the nature of the aid provided, and (3) the resulting relationship between the State and the religious authority. *Id.*, at 615. As to the first of these, in reviewing the Rhode Island program, the Court found that the aided schools, elementary and secondary, were characterized by "substantial religious activity and purpose." *Id.*, at 616. They were located near parish churches. Religious instruction was considered "part of the total educational process." *Id.*, at 615. Religious symbols and religious activities abounded. Two-thirds of the teachers were nuns, and their operation of the schools was regarded as an " 'integral part of the religious mission of the Catholic Church.' " *Id.*, at 616. The schooling came at an impressionable age. The form of aid also cut against the programs. Unlike the textbooks in *Allen* and the bus transportation in *Everson*, the services of the state-supported teachers could not be counted on to be purely secular. They were bound to mix religious teachings with secular ones, not by conscious design, perhaps, but because the mixture was inevitable when teachers (themselves usually Catholics) were "employed by a religious organization, subject to the direction and discipline of religious authorities, and work[ed] in a system dedicated to rearing children in a particular faith." *Id.*, at 618. The State's efforts to supervise and control the teaching of religion in supposedly secular classes would therefore inevitably entangle it excessively in religious affairs. The Pennsylvania program similarly foundered.

The Court also pointed to another kind of church-state entanglement threatened by the Rhode Island and Pennsylvania programs, namely, their "divisive political potential." *Id.*, at 622. They represented "successive and very likely permanent annual appropriations that benefit relatively few religious groups." *Id.*, at 623. Political factions, supporting and opposing the programs, were bound to divide along religious lines. This was "one of the principal evils against which the First Amendment was intended to protect." *Id.*, at 622. It was stressed that the political divisiveness of the programs was "aggravated . . . by the need for continuing annual appropriations." *Id.*, at 623.[5]

In *Tilton* v. *Richardson*, 403 U.S. 672 (1971), a companion case to *Lemon I*, the Court reached the contrary result. The aid challenged in *Tilton* was in the form of federal grants for the construction of academic facilities at private colleges, some of them church related, with the restriction that the facilities not be used for any sectarian purpose.[6] Applying *Lemon I*'s three-part test, the Court found the purpose of the federal aid program there under consideration to be secular. Its primary effect was not the advancement of religion, for sectarian use of the facilities was prohibited. Enforcement of this prohibition was made possible by the fact that religion did not so permeate the defendant colleges that their religious and secular functions were inseparable. On the contrary, there was no evidence that religious activities took place in the funded facilities. Courses at the colleges were "taught according to the academic requirements intrinsic to the subject matter," and "an atmosphere of academic freedom rather than religious indoctrination" was maintained. 403 U.S., at 680–682 (plurality opinion).

Turning to the problem of excessive entanglement, the Court first stressed the character of

---

[5] The danger of political divisiveness had been noted by Members of the Court in previous cases. See Walz v. Tax Commission, 397 U.S., at 695 (opinion of Harlan, J.); Board of Education v. Allen, 392 U.S. at 249 (Harlan, J., concurring); Abington School Dist. v. Schempp, 374 U.S. 203, 307 (1963) (Goldberg, J., concurring).

[6] The restriction, as imposed, was to remain in effect for 20 years following construction. Since the Court could not approve the facilities' sectarian use even after a 20-year period, it excised that time limitation from the statute. 403 U.S., at 682–684 (plurality opinion).

the aided institutions. It pointed to several general differences between college and precollege education: College students are less susceptible to religious indoctrination; college courses tend to entail an internal discipline that inherently limits the opportunities for sectarian influence; and a high degree of academic freedom tends to prevail at the college level. It found no evidence that the colleges in *Tilton* varied from this pattern. Though controlled and largely populated by Roman Catholics, the colleges were not restricted to adherents of that faith. No religious services were required to be attended. Theology courses were mandatory, but they were taught in an academic fashion, and with threatment of beliefs other than Roman Catholicism. There were no attempts to proselytize among students, and principles of academic freedom prevailed. With colleges of this character, there was little risk that religion would seep into the teaching of secular subjects, and the state surveillance necessary to separate the two, therefore, was diminished. The Court next looked to the type of aid provided, and found it to be neutral or nonideological in nature. Like the textbooks and bus transportation in *Allen* and *Everson*, but unlike the teachers' services in *Lemon I*, physical facilities were capable of being restricted to secular purposes. Moreover, the construction grant was a one-shot affair, not involving annual audits and appropriations.

As for political divisiveness, no "continuing religious aggravation" over the program had been shown, and the Court reasoned that this might be because of the lack of continuity in the church-state relationship, the character and diversity of the colleges, and the fact that they served a dispersed student constituency rather than a local one. "[C]umulatively," all these considerations persuaded the Court that church-state entanglement was not excessive. 403 U.S., at 684–689.

In *Hunt* v. *McNair*, 413 U.S. 734 (1973), the challenged aid was also for the construction of secular college facilities, the state plan being one to finance the construction by revenue bonds issued through the medium of a state authority. In effect, the college serviced and repaid the bonds, but at the lower cost resulting from the tax-free status of the interest payments. The Court upheld the program on reasoning analogous to that in *Tilton*. In applying the second of the *Lemon I*'s three-part test, that concerning "primary effect," the following refinement was added:

> "Aid normally may be thought to have a primary effect of advancing religion when it flows to an institution in which religion is so pervasive that a substantial portion of its functions are subsumed in the religious mission or when it funds a specifically religious activity in an otherwise substantially secular setting." 413 U.S., at 743.

Although the college which *Hunt* concerned was subject to substantial control by its sponsoring Baptist Church, it was found to be similar to the colleges in *Tilton* and not "pervasively sectarian." As in *Tilton*, state aid went to secular facilities only, and thus not to any "specifically religious activity." 413 U.S., at 743–745.

Committee for Public Education v. *Nyquist*, 413 U.S. 756 (1973), followed in *Lemon I*'s wake much as *Hunt* followed in *Tilton*'s. The aid in *Nyquist* was to elementary and secondary schools which, the District Court found, generally conformed to a "profile" of a sectarian or substantially religious school.[7] The state aid took three forms: direct subsidies for the maintenance and repair of buildings; reimbursement of parents for a percentage of tuition paid; and certain tax benefits for parents. All three forms of aid were

---

[7] The elements of the "profile" were that the schools placed religious restrictions on admission and also faculty appointments; that they enforced obedience to religious dogma; that they required attendance at religious services and the study of particular religious doctrine; that they were an " 'integral part' " of the religious mission of the sponsoring church; that they had religious indoctrination as a " 'substantial purpose' "; and that they imposed religious restrictions on how and what the faculty could teach. 413 U.S., at 767–768.

found to have an impermissible primary effect. The maintenance and repair subsidies, being unrestricted, could be used for the upkeep of a chapel or classrooms used for religious instruction. The reimbursements and tax benefits to parents could likewise be used to support wholly religious activites.

In *Levitt* v. *Committee for Public Education*, 413 U.S. 472 (1973), the Court also invalidated a program for public aid to church-affiliated schools. The grants, which were to elementary and secondary schools in New York, were in the form of reimbursements for the schools' testing and recordkeeping expenses. The schools met the same sectarian profile as did those in *Nyquist*, at least in some cases. There was therefore "substantial risk" that the state-funded tests would be "drafted with an eye, unconsciously or otherwise, to inculcate students in the religious precepts of the sponsoring church." 413 U.S., at 480.

Last Term, in *Meek* v. *Pittenger*, 421 U.S. 349 (1975), the Court ruled yet again on a state-aid program for church-related elementary and secondary schools. On the authority of *Allen*, it upheld a Pennsylvania program for lending textbooks to private school students. It found, however, that *Lemon I* required the invalidation of two other forms of aid to the private schools. The first was the loan of instructional materials and equipment. Like the textbooks, these were secular and nonideological in nature. Unlike the textbooks, however, they were loaned directly to the schools. The schools, similar to those in *Lemon I,* were ones in which "the teaching process is, to a large extent, devoted to the inculcation of religious values and belief." 421 U.S., at 366. Aid flowing directly to such "religion-pervasive institutions," *ibid.*, had the primary effect of advancing religion. See *Hunt* v. *McNair, supra.* The other form of aid was the provision of "auxiliary" educational services: remedial instruction, counseling and testing, and speech and hearing therapy. These also were intended to be neutral and nonideological, and in fact were to be provided by public school

teachers. Still, there was danger that the teachers, in such a sectarian setting, would allow religion to seep into their instruction. To attempt to prevent this from happening would excessively entangle the State in church affairs. The Court referred again to the danger of political divisiveness, heightened, as it had been in *Lemon I* and *Nyquist,* by the necessity of annual legislative reconsideration of the aid appropriation. 421 U.S., at 372.

So the slate we write on is anything but clean. Instead, there is little room for further refinement of the principles governing public aid to church-affiliated private schools. Our purpose is not to unsettle those principles, so recently reaffirmed, see *Meek* v. *Pittenger, supra,* or to expand upon them substantially, but merely to insure that they are faithfully applied in this case.

Religious Activity outside the Church

Zorach v. *Clauson*
443 U.S. 306 (1952)

Mr. Justice Douglas delivered the opinion of the Court.

New York City has a program which permits its public schools to release students during the school day so that they may leave the school buildings and school grounds and go to religious centers for religious instruction or devotional exercises. A student is released on written request of his parents. Those not released stay in the classrooms. The churches make weekly reports to the schools, sending a list of children who have been released from public school but who have not reported for religious instruction.

This "released time" program involves neither religious instruction in public school classrooms nor the expenditure of public funds. All costs, including the application blanks, are paid by the religious organizations. The case is therefore unlike *McCollum* v. *Board of Education*, 333 U.S. 203, which involved a "released time" program from Illinois. In that case the classrooms were turned over to religious instructors. We accordingly held that the program violated the First Amendment which (by reason of the Fourteenth Amendment) prohibits the states from establishing religion or prohibiting its free exercise.

Appellants, who are taxpayers and residents of New York City and whose children attend its public schools, challenge the present law, contending it is in essence not different from the one involved in the *McCollum* case. Their argument, stated elaborately in various ways, reduces itself to this: the weight and influence of the school is put behind a program for religious instruction; public school teachers police it, keeping tab on students who are released; the classroom activities come to a halt while the students who are released for religious instruction are on leave; the school is a crutch on which the churches are leaning for support in their religious training; without the cooperation of the schools this "released time" program, like the one in the *McCollum* case, would be futile and ineffective. The New York Court of Appeals sustained the law against this claim of unconstitutionality.

The briefs and arguments are replete with data bearing on the merits of this type of "released time" program. . . . Those matters are of no concern here, since our problem reduces itself to whether New York by this system has either prohibited the "free exercise" of religion or has made a law "respecting an establishing of religion" within the meaning of the First Amendment.

It takes obtuse reasoning to inject any issue of the "free exercise" of religion into the present case. No one is forced to go to the religious classroom and no religious exercise or instruction is brought to the classrooms of the public schools. A student need not take religious instruction. He is left to his own desires as to the

manner or time of his religious devotions, if any.

There is a suggestion that the system involves the use of coercion to get public school students into religious classrooms. There is no evidence in the record before us that supports that conclusion. The present record indeed tells us that the school authorities are neutral in this regard and do no more than release students whose parents so request. If in fact coercion were used, if it were established that any one or more teachers were using their office to persuade or force students to take the religious instruction, a wholly different case would be presented. Hence we put aside that claim of coercion both as respects the "free exercise" of religion and "an establishment of religion" within the meaning of the First Amendment.

Moreover, apart from that claim of coercion, we do not see how New York by this type of "released time" program has made a law respecting an establishment of religion within the meaning of the First Amendment. . . . There cannot be the slightest doubt that the First Amendment reflects the philosophy that Church and State should be separated. And so far as interference with the "free exercise" of religion and an "establishment" of religion are concerned, the separation must be complete and unequivocal. The First Amendment within the scope of its coverage permits no exception; the prohibition is absolute. The First Amendment, however, does not say that in every and all respects there shall be a separation of Church and State. Rather, it studiously defines the manner, the specific ways, in which there shall be no concert or union or dependency one on the other. That is the common sense of the matter. Otherwise the state and religion would be aliens to each other—hostile, suspicious, and even unfriendly. Churches could not be required to pay even property taxes. Municipalities would not be permitted to render police or fire protection to religious groups. Policemen who helped parishioners into their places of worship would violate the Constitution.

Prayers in our legislative halls; the appeals to the Almighty in the messages of the Chief Executive; the proclamations making Thanksgiving Day a holiday; "so help me God" in our courtroom oath—these and all other references to the Almighty that run through our laws, our public rituals, our ceremonies would be flouting the First Amendment. A fastidious atheist or agnostic could even object to the supplication with which the Court opens each session: "God save the United States and this Honorable Court."

We would have to press the concept of separation of Church and State to these extremes to condemn the present law on constitutional grounds. The nullification of this law would have wide and profound effects. A Catholic student applies to his teacher for permission to leave the school during hours on a Holy Day of Obligation to attend a mass. A Jewish student asks his teacher for permission to be excused for Yom Kippur. A Protestant wants the afternoon off for a family baptismal ceremony. In each case the teacher requires parental consent in writing. In each case the teacher, in order to make sure the student is not a truant, goes further and requires a report from the priest, the rabbi, or the minister. The teacher in other words cooperates in a religious program to the extent of making it possible for her students to participate in it. Whether she does it occasionally for a few students, regularly for one, or pursuant to a systematized program designed to further the religious needs of all the students does not alter the character of the act.

We are a religious people whose institutions presuppose a Supreme Being. We guarantee the freedom to worship as one chooses. We make room for as wide a variety of beliefs and creeds as the spiritual needs of man deem necessary. We sponsor an attitude on the part of government that shows no partiality to any one group and that lets each flourish according to the zeal of its adherents and the appeal of its dogma. When the state encourages religious instruction or cooperates with religious authorities by adjusting the schedule of public events to sectarian needs, it follows the best of our traditions. For it then respects the religious nature of our people and accommodates the public service to their spiritual needs. To hold that it may not would be to find in the Constitution a requirement that the government show a callous indifference to religious groups. That would be preferring those who believe in no religion over those who do believe. Government may not finance religious groups nor undertake religious instruction nor blend secular and sectarian education nor use secular institutions to force one or some religion on any person. But we find no constitutional requirement which makes it necessary for government to be hostile to religion and to throw its weight against efforts to widen the effective scope of religious influence. The government must be neutral when it comes to competition between sects. It may not thrust any sect on any person. It may not make a religious observance compulsory. It may not coerce anyone to attend church, to observe a religious holiday, or to take religious instruction. But it can close its doors or suspend its operations as to those who want to repair to their religious sanctuary for worship or instruction. No more than that is undertaken here. . . .

In the *McCollum* case the classrooms were used for religious instruction and the force of the public school was used to promote that instruction. Here, as we have said, the public schools do no more than accommodate their schedules to a program of outside religious instruction. We follow the *McCollum* case. But we cannot expand it to cover the present released time program unless separation of Church and State means that public institutions can make no adjustments of their schedules to accommodate the religious needs of the people. We cannot read into the Bill of Rights such a philosophy of hostility to religion.

Mr. Justice Black, dissenting. . . .

In considering whether a state has entered this forbidden field the question is not whether it has entered too far but whether it has entered at all. New York is manipulating its compulsory education laws to help religious sects get pupils. This is not separation but combination of Church and State. . . .

Mr. Justice Frankfurter, dissenting.

By way of emphasizing my agreement with Mr. Justice Jackson's dissent, I add a few words. . . .

Of course a State may provide that the classes in its schools shall be dismissed, for any reason, or no reason, on fixed days, or for special occasions. The essence of this case is that the school system did not "close its doors" and did not "suspend its operations". . . .

The pith of the case is that formalized religious instruction is substituted for other school activity which those who do not participate in the released-time program are compelled to attend. The school system is very much in operation during this kind of released time. . . .

Mr. Justice Jackson, dissenting. . . .

A number of Justices just short of a majority of the majority that promulgates today's passionate dialectics joined in answering them in *McCollum* v. *Board of Education,* 333 U.S. 203. The distinction attempted between that case and this is trivial, almost to the point of cynicism, magnifying its nonessential details and disparaging compulsion which was the underlying reason for invalidity. A reading of the Court's opinion in that case along with its opinion in this case will show such difference of overtones and undertones as to make clear that the *McCollum* case has passed like a storm in a teacup. The wall which the Court was professing to erect between Church and State has become even more warped and twisted than I expected. Today's judgment will be more interesting to students of psychology and of the judicial processes than to students of constitutional law.

Engel v. *Vitale*
370 U.S. 421 (1962)

Mr. Justice Black delivered the opinion of the Court.

The respondent Board of Education of Union Free School District No. 9, New Hyde Park, New York, acting in its official capacity under state law, directed the School District's principal to cause the following prayer to be said aloud by each class in the presence of a teacher at the beginning of each school day:

"Almighty God, we acknowledge our dependence upon Thee, and we beg Thy blessings upon us, our parents, our teachers and our country."

This daily procedure was adopted on the recommendation of the State Board of Regents, a governmental agency. . . . These state officials composed the prayer which they recommended and published as a part of their "Statement on Moral and Spiritual Training in the Schools," . . .

[T]he parents of ten pupils brought this action in a New York State Court insisting that use of this official prayer in the public schools was contrary to the beliefs, religions, or religious practices of both themselves and their children. . . . The New York Court of Appeals, . . . sustained an order of the lower state courts which had upheld the power of New York to use the Regents' prayer as a part of the daily procedures of its public schools so long as the schools did not compel any pupil to join in the prayer over his or his parents' objection. . . .

The petitioners contend among other things that the state laws requiring or permitting use of the Regents' prayer must be struck down as a violation of the Establishment Clause. . . . We agree with that contention since we think that the constitutional prohibition against laws respecting an establishment of religion must at least mean that in this country it is no part of the business of government to compose official prayers for any group of the American people to recite as a part of a religious program carried on by government. . . .

There can be no doubt that New York's state prayer program officially establishes the religious beliefs embodied in the Regents' prayer. . . . Neither the fact that the prayer may be denominationally neutral, nor the fact that its observance on the part of the students is voluntary can serve to free it from the limitations of the Establishment Clause, as it might from the Free Exercise Clause, of the First Amendment, both of which are operative against the States by virtue of the Fourteenth Amendment. Although these two clauses may in certain instances overlap, they forbid two quite different kinds of governmental encroachment upon religious freedom. The Establishment Clause, unlike the Free Exercise Clause, does not depend upon any showing of direct governmental compulsion and is violated by the enactment of laws which establish an official religion whether those laws operate directly to coerce nonobserving individuals or not. This is not to say, of course, that laws officially prescribing a particular form of religious worship do not involve coercion of such individuals. When the power, prestige and financial support of government is placed behind a particular religious belief, the indirect coercive pressure upon religious minorities to conform to the prevailing officially approved religion is plain. But the purposes underlying the Establishment Clause go much further than that. Its first and most immediate purpose rested on the belief that a union of government and religion tends to destroy government and to degrade religion. . . . Another purpose of the Establishment Clause rested upon an awareness of the historical fact that governmentally established religions and religious persecutions go hand in hand. . . . It was in large part to get completely away from this sort of systematic religious persecution that the Founders brought into being our Nation, our Constitution, and our Bill of Rights with its prohibition against any governmental establishment of reli-

gion. The New York laws officially prescribing the Regents' prayer are inconsistent with both the purposes of the Establishment Clause and with the Establishment Clause itself.

Mr. Justice Frankfurter took no part in the decision of this case.

Mr. Justice White took no part in the consideration or decision of this case.

Mr. Justice Douglas, concurring.

. . . The point for decision is whether the Government can constitutionally finance a religious exercise. Our system at the federal and state levels is presently honeycombed with such financing. Nevertheless, I think it is an unconstitutional undertaking whatever form it takes.

First, a word as to what this case does not involve.

Plainly, our Bill of Rights would not permit a State or the Federal Government to adopt an official prayer and penalize anyone who would not utter it. This, however, is not that case, for there is no element of compulsion or coercion in New York's regulation requiring that public schools be opened each day with the . . . [prayer]. . . .

At the same time I cannot say that to authorize this prayer is to establish a religion in the strictly historic meaning of those words. A religion is not established in the usual sense merely by letting those who choose to do so say the prayer that the public school teacher leads. Yet once government finances a religious exercise it inserts a divisive influence into our communities. . . .

My problem today would be uncomplicated but for *Everson* v. *Board of Education*, 330 U.S. 1, 17, which allowed taxpayers' money to be used to pay "the bus fares of parochial school pupils as a part of a general program under which" the fares of pupils attending public and other schools were also paid. The *Everson* case seems in retrospect to be out of line with the First

Amendment. Its result is appealing, as it allows aid to be given to needy children. Yet by the same token, public funds could be used to satisfy other needs of children in parochial schools—lunches, books, and tuition being obvious examples. Mr. Justice Rutledge stated in dissent what I think is durable First Amendment philosophy. . . .

What New York does with this prayer is a break with that tradition. I therefore join the Court in reversing the judgment below.

Mr. Justice Stewart, dissenting. . . . .

With all respect, I think the Court has misapplied a great constitutional principle. I cannot see how an "official religion" is established by letting those who want to say a prayer say it. On the contrary, I think that to deny the wish of these school children to join in reciting this prayer is to deny them the opportunity of sharing in the spiritual heritage of our Nation. . . .

School District of Abington v. *Schemp* [No. 142]
Murray v. *Curlett* [No. 119]
374 U.S. 203 (1963)

Mr. Justice Clark delivered the opinion of the Court . . . .

Applying the Establishment Clause principles to the cases at bar we find that the States are requiring the selection and reading at the opening of the school day of verses from the Holy Bible and the recitation of the Lord's Prayer by the students in unison. These exercises are prescribed as part of the curricular activities of students who are required by law to attend school. They are held in the school buildings under the supervision and with the participation of teachers employed in those schools. None of these factors, other than compulsory school attendance, was present in the program upheld in *Zorach* v. *Clauson.* The trial court in No. 142 has found that such an opening exercise is a reli-

gious ceremony and was intended by the State to be so. We agree with the trial court's finding as to the religious character of the exercises. Given that finding the exercises and the law requiring them are in violation of the Establishment Clause.

There is no such specific finding as to the religious character of the exercises in No. 119, and the State contends (as does the State in No. 142) that the program is an effort to extend its benefits to all public school children without regard to their religious belief. Included within its secular purposes, it says, are the promotion of moral values, the contradiction to the materialistic trends of our times, the perpetuation of our institutions and the teaching of literature. The case came up on demurrer, of course, to a petition which alleged that the uniform practice under the rule had been to read from the King James version of the Bible and that the exercise was sectarian. The short answer, therefore, is that the religious character of the exercise was admitted by the State. But even if its purpose is not strictly religious, it is sought to be accomplished through readings, without comment, from the Bible. Surely the place of the Bible as an instrument of religion cannot be gainsaid, and the State's recognition of the pervading religious character of the ceremony is evident from the rule's specific permission of the alternative use of the Catholic Douay version as well as the recent amendment permitting nonattendance at the exercises. None of these factors is consistent with the contention that the Bible is here used either as an instrument for nonreligious moral inspiration or as a reference for the teaching of secular subjects.

The conclusion follows that in both cases the laws require religious exercises and such exercises are being conducted in direct violation of the rights of the appellees and petitioners. Nor are these required exercises mitigated by the fact that individual students may absent themselves upon parental request, for that fact furnishes no defense to a claim of unconstitutionality under the Establishment Clause. See *Engel* v.

662   Part II: Limitations on Governmental Power as a Shield for Freedom

Vitale. Further, it is no defense to urge that the religious practices here may be relatively minor encroachments on the First Amendment. The breach of neutrality that is today a trickling stream may all too soon become a raging torrent and, in the words of Madison, "it is proper to take alarm at the first experiment on our liberties." *Memorial and Remonstrance Against Religious Assessments.*

It is insisted that unless these religious exercises are permitted a "religion of secularism" is established in the schools. We agree of course that the State may not establish a "religion of secularism" in the sense of affirmatively opposing or showing hostility to religion, thus "preferring those who believe in no religion over those who do believe." We do not agree, however, that this decision in any sense has that effect. In addition, it might well be said that one's education is not complete without a study of comparative religion or the history of religion and its relationship to the advancement of civilization. It certainly may be said that the Bible is worthy of study for its literary and historic qualities. Nothing we have said here indicates that such study of the Bible or of religion, when presented objectively as part of a secular program of education, may not be effected consistent with the First Amendment. But the exercises here do not fall into those categories. They are religious exercises, required by the States in violation of the command of the First Amendment that the Government maintain strict neutrality, neither aiding nor opposing religion.

Finally, we cannot accept that the concept of neutrality, which does not permit a State to require a religious exercise even with the consent of the majority of those affected, collides with the majority's right to free exercise of religion. While the Free Exercise Clause clearly prohibits the use of station action to deny the rights of free exercise to *anyone*, it has never meant that a majority could use the machinery of the State to practice its beliefs. . . .

[Justices Douglas, Brennan, and Goldberg gave concurring opinions.]

Mr. Justice Stewart, dissenting. . . .

To be specific, it seems to me clear that certain types of exercises would present situations in which no possibility of coercion on the part of secular officials could be claimed to exist. Thus, if such exercises were held either before or after the official school day, or if the school schedule were such that participation were merely one among a number of desirable alternatives, it could hardly be contended that the exercises did anything more than to provide an opportunity for the voluntary expression of religious belief. On the other hand, a law which provided for religious exercises during the school day and which contained no excusal provision would obviously be unconstitutionally coercive upon those who did not wish to participate. And even under a law containing an excusal provision, if the exercises were held during the school day, and no equally desirable alternative were provided by the school authorities, the likelihood that children might be under at least some psychological compulsion to participate would be great. In a case such as the latter, however, I think we would err if we *assumed* such coercion in the absence of any evidence.

Viewed in this light, it seems to me clear that the records in both the cases before us are wholly inadequate to support an informed or responsible decision. . . . There is no evidence in either case as to whether there would exist any coercion of any kind upon a student who did not want to participate. No evidence at all was adduced in the *Murray* case, because it was decided upon a demurrer. . . . In the *Schempp* case the record shows no more than a subjective prophecy by a parent of what he thought would happen if a request were made to be excused from participation in the exercises under the amended statute. No such request was ever made, and there is no evidence whatever as to what might or would actually happen, nor of what administrative arrangements the school actually might or could make to free from pressure of any kind those who do not want to participate in the exercises. . . .

. . . It is conceivable that these school boards, or even all school boards, might eventually find it impossible to administer a system of religious exercises during school hours in such a way as to meet this constitutional standard—in such a way as completely to free from any kind of official coercion those who do not affirmatively want to participate. But I think we must not assume that school boards so lack the qualities of inventiveness and good will as to make impossible the achievement of that goal.

I would remand both cases for further hearing.

McGowan v. *Maryland*
366 U.S. 420 (1961)

Mr. Chief Justice Warren delivered the opinion of the Court.

The issues in this case concern the constitutional validity of Maryland criminal statutes, commonly known as Sunday Closing Laws or Sunday Blue Laws. These statutes, with exceptions to be noted hereafter, generally proscribe all labor, business and other commercial activities on Sunday. The questions presented are whether the classifications within the statutes bring about a denial of equal protection of the law, whether the laws are so vague as to fail to give reasonable notice of the forbidden conduct and therefore violate due process, and whether the statutes are laws respecting an establishment of religion or prohibiting the free exercise thereof.

Appellants are seven employees of a large discount department store located on a highway in Anne Arundel County, Maryland. They were indicted for the Sunday sale of a three-ring loose-leaf binder, a can of floor wax, a stapler and staples, and a toy submarine in violation of Md. Ann. Code, Art. 27, § 521. Generally, this section prohibited, throughout the State, the Sunday sale of all merchandise except the retail sale of tobacco products, confectioneries, milk,

bread, fruits, gasoline, oils, greases, drugs and medicines, and newspapers and periodicals. Recently amended, this section also now excepts from the general prohibition the retail sale in Anne Arundel County of all foodstuffs, automobile and boating accessories, flowers, toilet goods, hospital supplies and souvenirs. It now further provides that any retail establishment in Anne Arundel County which does not employ more than one person other than the owner may operate on Sunday. . . .

The final questions for decision are whether the Maryland Sunday Closing Laws conflict with the Federal Constitution's provisions for religious liberty. First, appellants contend here that the statutes applicable to Anne Arundel County violate the constitutional guarantee of freedom of religion in that the statutes' effect is to prohibit the free exercise of religion in contravention of the First Amendment, made applicable to the States by the Fourteenth Amendment. But appellants allege only economic injury to themselves; they do not allege any infringement of their own religious freedoms due to Sunday closing. In fact, the record is silent as to what appellants' religious beliefs are. Since the general rule is that "a litigant may only assert his own constitutional rights or immunities," *United States* v. *Raines,* 362 U.S. 17, 22, we hold that appellants have no standing to raise this contention. *Tileston* v. *Ullman,* 318 U.S. 44, 46. Furthermore, since appellants do not specifically allege that the statutes infringe upon the religious beliefs of the department store's present or prospective patrons, we have no occasion here to consider the standing question of *Pierce* v. *Society of Sisters,* 268 U.S. 510, 535–536. Those persons whose religious rights are allegedly impaired by the statutes are not without effective ways to assert these rights. Cf. *NAACP* v. *State of Alabama,* 357 U.S. 449, 459–460; *Barrows* v. *Jackson,* 346 U.S. 249, 257. Appellants present no weighty countervailing policies here to cause an exception to our general principles. See *United States* v. *Raines, supra.*

Secondly, appellants contend that the statutes violate the guarantee of separation of church and state in that the statutes are laws respecting an establishment of religion contrary to the First Amendment, made applicable to the states by the Fourteenth Amendment. If the purpose of the "establishment" clause was only to insure protection for the "free exercise" of religion, then what we have said above concerning appellant's standing to raise the "free exercise" contention would appear to be true here. However, the writings of Madison, who was the First Amendment's architect, demonstrate that the establishment of a religion was equally feared because of its tendencies to political tyranny and subversion of civil authority. Thus, in *Everson* v. *Board of Education, supra*, the Court permitted a district taxpayer to challenge, on "establishment" grounds, a state statute which authorized district boards of education to reimburse parents for fares paid for the transportation of their children to both public and Catholic schools. Appellants here concededly have suffered direct economic injury, allegedly due to the imposition on them of the tenets of the Christian religion. We find that, in these circumstances, these appellants have standing to complain that the statutes are laws respecting an establishment of religion.

The essence of appellant's "establishment" argument is that Sunday is the Sabbath day of the predominant Christian sects; that the purpose of the enforced stoppage of labor on that day is to facilitate and encourage church attendance; that the purpose of setting Sunday as a day of universal rest is to induce people with no religion or people with marginal religious beliefs to join the predominant Christian sects; that the purpose of the atmosphere of tranquility created by Sunday closing is to aid the conduct of church services and religious observance of the sacred day. In substantiating their "establishment" argument, appellants rely on the wording of the present Maryland statutes, on earlier versions of the current Sunday laws and on prior judicial characterizations of these laws by the Maryland Court of Appeals. Although only the constitutionality of § 521, the section

under which appellants have been convicted, is immediately before us in this litigation, inquiry into the history of Sunday Closing Laws in our country, in addition to an examination of the Maryland Sunday closing statutes in their entirety and of their history, is relevant to the decision of whether the Maryland Sunday law in question is one respecting an establishment of religion. There is no dispute that the original laws which dealt with Sunday labor were motivated by religious forces. But what we must decide is whether present Sunday legislation, having undergone extensive charges from the earliest forms, still retains its religious character. . . .

Throughout this century and longer, both the federal and state governments have oriented their activities very largely toward improvement of the health, safety, recreation and general well-being of our citizens. Numerous laws affecting public health, safety factors in industry, laws affecting hours and conditions of labor of women and children, week-end diversion at parks and beaches, and cultural activities of various kinds, now point the way toward the good life for all. Sunday Closing Laws, like those before us, have become part and parcel of this great governmental concern wholly apart from their original purposes or connotations. The present purpose and effect of most of them is to provide a uniform day of rest for all citizens; the fact that this day is Sunday, a day of particular significance for the dominant Christian sects, does not bar the State from achieving its secular goals. To say that the States cannot prescribe Sunday as a day of rest for these purposes solely because centuries ago such laws had their genesis in religion would give a constitutional interpretation of hostility to the public welfare rather than one of mere separation of church and State. . . .

The distinctions between the statutes in the case before us and the state action in *People of State of Illinois ex rel. McCollum* v. *Board of Education, supra*, the only case in this Court finding a violation of the "establishment" Clause, lend further substantiation to our conclusion. In *McCollum*, state action permitted religious instruction in public school buildings during school hours and required students not attending the religious instruction to remain in their classrooms during that time. The Court found that this system had the effect of coercing the children to attend religious classes; no such coercion to attend church services is present in the situation at bar. In *McCollum*, the only alternative available to the nonattending students was to remain in their classrooms; the alternatives open to nonlaboring persons in the instant case are far more diverse. In *McCollum*, there was direct cooperation between state officials and religious ministers; no such direct participation exists under the Maryland laws. In *McCollum*, tax supported buildings were used to aid religion; in the instant case, no tax monies are being used in aid of religion.

Finally, we should make clear that this case deals only with the constitutionality of § 521 of the Maryland statute before us. We do not hold that Sunday legislation may not be a violation of the "Establishment" Clause if it can be demonstrated that its purpose—evidenced either on the face of the legislation, in conjunction with its legislative history, or in its operative effect—is to use the State's coercive power to aid religion.

Accordingly, the decision is affirmed.

[*McGowan* was one of four Sunday Closing Law cases decided on the same day. *Braunfeld* v. *Brown*, 366 U.S. 599 (1961), and *Gallagher* v. *Crown Kosher Market*, 366 U.S. 617 (1961), raised, in addition to the establishment problem, a problem in free exercise, because they involved Orthodox Jewish merchants who would have to give up their Sabbath or suffer economic disadvantage by having to close their businesses two days each week. Overriding this objection, the Court observed that "To strike, without the most critical scrutiny, legislation which imposes only an indirect burden on the exercise of religion, i.e., legislation which does not make unlawful the religious practice itself, would radically restrict the operating latitude of the legislature."]

[Mr. Justice Frankfurter, joined by his brother Harlan, wrote an extensive concurring opinion covering all four cases. Mr. Justice Douglas's dissenting opinion which follows covers all four cases.]

Mr. Justice Douglas, dissenting.

The question is not whether one day out of seven can be imposed by a State as a day of rest. The question is not whether Sunday can by force of custom and habit be retained as a day of rest. The question is whether a State can impose criminal sanctions on those who, unlike the Christian majority that makes up our society, worship on a different day or do not share the religious scruples of the majority.

If the "free exercise" of religion were subject to reasonable regulations, as it is under some constitutions, or if all laws "respecting the establishment of religion" were not proscribed, I could understand how rational men, representing a predominantly Christian civilization, might think these Sunday laws did not unreasonably interfere with any one's free exercise of religion and took no step toward a burdensome establishment of any religion.

But that is not the premise from which we start, as there is agreement that the fact that a State, and not the Federal Government, has promulgated these Sunday laws does not change the scope of the power asserted. For the classic view is that the First Amendment should be applied to the States with the same firmness as it is enforced against the Federal Government. . . .

It seems to me plain that by these laws the States compel one, under sanction of law, to refrain from work or recreation on Sunday because of the majority's religious views about that day. The State by law makes Sunday a symbol of respect or adherence. Refraining from works or recreation in deference to the majority's religious feelings about Sunday is within every person's choice. By what authority can government compel it?

Cases are put where acts that are immoral by our standards but not by the standards of other religious groups are made criminal. That category of cases, until today, has been a very restricted one confined to polygamy (*Reynolds* v. *United States,* 98 U.S. 145,) and other extreme situations. . . .

The Court balances the need of the people for rest, recreation, late-sleeping, family visiting and the like against the command of the First Amendment that no one need bow to the religious beliefs of another. There is in this realm no room for balancing. I see no place for it in the constitutional scheme. A legislature of Christians can no more make minorities conform to their weekly regime than a legislature of Moslems, or a legislature of Hindus. The religious regime of every group must be respected— unless it crosses the line of criminal conduct. But no one can be forced to come to a halt before it, or refrain from doing things that would offend it. That is my reading of the Establishment Clause and the Free Exercise Clause. Any other reading imports, I fear, an element common in other societies but foreign to us. Thus Nigeria in Article 23 of her Constitution, after guaranteeing religious freedom, adds, "Nothing in this section shall invalidate any law that is reasonably justified in a democratic society in the interest of defence, public safety, public order, public morality, or public health." And see Article 25 of the Indian Constitution. That may be a desirable provision. But when the Court adds it to our First Amendment, as it does today, we make a sharp break with the American ideal of religious liberty as enshrined in the First Amendment.

The State can of course require one day of rest a week: one day when every shop or factory is closed. Quite a few States make that requirement. Then the "day of rest" becomes purely and simply a health measure. But the Sunday laws operate differently. They force minorities to obey the majority's religious feelings of what is due and proper for a Christian community; they provide a coercive spur to the "weaker brethren," to those who are indifferent to the claims of a Sabbath through apathy or scruple. Can there be any doubt that Christians, now aligned vigorously in favor of these laws, would be as strongly opposed, if they were prosecuted under a Moslem law that forbade them from engaging in secular activities on days that violated Moslem scruples?

There is an "establishment" of religion in the constitutional sense if any practice of any religious group has the sanction of law behind it. There is an interference with the "free exercise" of religion if what in conscience one can do or omit doing is required because of the religious scruples of the community. Hence I would declare each of those laws unconstitutional as applied to the complaining parties, whether or not they are members of a sect which observes as their Sabbath a day other than Sunday.

When these laws are applied to Orthodox Jews, as they are in No. 11 and No. 67, or to Sabbatarians their vice is accentuated. If the Sunday laws are constitutional, Kosher markets are on a five-day week. Thus those laws put an economic penalty on those who observe Saturday rather than Sunday as the Sabbath. For the economic pressures on these minorities, created by the fact that our communities are predominantly Sunday-minded, there is no recourse. When, however, the State uses its coercive powers—here the criminal law—to compel minorities to observe a second Sabbath, not their own, the State undertakes to aid and "prefer one religion over another"—contrary to the command of the Constitution. See *Everson* v. *Board of Education, supra,* 330 U.S. 15.

In large measure the history of the religious clause of the First Amendment was a struggle to be free of economic sanctions for adherence to one's religion. *Everson* v. *Board of Education, supra,* 330 U.S. 11–14. A small tax was imposed in Virginia for religious education. Jefferson and Madison led the fight against the tax, Madison writing his famous Memorial and Remonstrance against that law. *Id.*, 330 U.S. 12. As a result, the tax measure was defeated and instead Virginia's famous "Bill of Religious Liberty," written by Jefferson, was enacted. *Id.*, 330 U.S. 12. That Act provided:

> "That no man shall be compelled to frequent or support any religious worship, place, or ministry whatsoever, nor shall be enforced, restrained, molested, or burthened in his body or goods, nor shall otherwise suffer on account of his religious opinions or belief. . . ."

The reverse side of an "establishment" is a burden on the "free exercise" of religion. Receipts of funds from the state benefits the established church directly; laying an extra tax on nonmembers benefits the established church indirectly. Certainly the present Sunday laws place Orthodox Jews and Sabbatarians under extra burdens because of their religious opinions or beliefs. Requiring them to abstain from their trade or business on Sunday reduces their workweek to five days, unless they violate their religious scruples. This places them at a competitive disadvantage and penalizes them for adhering to their religious beliefs.

"The sanction imposed by the state for observing a day other than Sunday as holy time is certainly more serious economically than the imposition of a license tax for preaching," which we struck down in *Murdock* v. *Commonwealth of Pennsylvania*, 319 U.S. 105, and in *Follett* v. *Town of McCormick*, 321 U.S. 573. The special protection which Sunday laws give the dominant religious groups and the penalty they place on minorities whose holy day is Saturday constitute in my view state interference with the "free exercise" of religion.

[Justices Brennan and Stewart dissented in *Gallagher* and *Braunfeld*.]

Note: Epperson v. *Arkansas*, 393 U.S. 97 (1968), held invalid on establishment grounds a state law forbidding the teaching of the theory of biological evolution in the public schools: The First Amendment "forbids alike the preference of a religious doctrine or the prohibition of a theory which is deemed antagonistic to a particular [religious belief]." Here "fundamentalist sectarian conviction was and is the law's reason for existence." Justices Black and Stewart concurred solely on vagueness grounds. The former said he was not prepared to hold "that a person hired to teach schoolchildren takes with him into the classroom a constitutional right to teach sociological, economic, political, or religious subjects that the school's managers do not want discussed."

THE FREE EXERCISE OF RELIGION

Reynolds v. *United States* (excerpt)
98 U.S. 145 (1879)

. . . [T]here never has been a time in any State of the Union when polygamy has not been an offense against society, cognizable by the civil courts and punishable with more or less severity. In the face of all this evidence, it is impossible to believe that the constitutional guaranty of religion freedom was intended to prohibit legislation in respect to this most important feature of social life. Marriage, while from its very nature a sacred obligation, is, nevertheless, in most civilized nations, a civil contract, and usually regulated by law. Upon it society may be said to be built, and out of its fruits spring social relations and social obligations and duties, with which government is necessarily required to deal. . . . An exceptional colony of polygamists under an exceptional leadership may sometimes exist for a time without appearing to disturb the social condition of the people who surround it; but there cannot be a doubt that, unless restricted by some form of constitution, it is within the legitimate scope of the power of every civil government to determine whether polygamy or monogamy shall be the law of social life under its dominion.

In our opinion the statute immediately under consideration is within the legislative power of Congress. It is constitutional and valid as prescribing a rule of action for all those residing in the Territories, and in places over which the United States have exclusive control. This being so, the only question which remains is, whether those who make polygamy a part of their religion are excepted from the operation of the statute. If they are, then those who do not make polygamy a part of their religious belief may be found guilty and punished, while those who do must be acquitted and go free. This would be introducing a new element into criminal law. Laws are made for the government of actions, and while they cannot interfere with mere religious belief and opinions, they may with practices. Suppose one believed that human sacrifices were a necessary part of religious worship, would it be seriously contended that the civil government under which he lived could not interfere to prevent a sacrifice? Or if a wife religiously believed it was her duty to burn herself upon the funeral pile of her dead husband, would it be beyond the power of the civil government to prevent her carrying her belief into practice?

So here, as a law of the organization of society under the exclusive dominion of the United States, it is provided that plural marriages shall not be allowed. Can a man excuse his practices to the contrary because of his religious belief? To permit this would be to make the professed doctrines of religious belief superior to the law of the land, and in effect to permit every citizen to become a law unto himself. Government could exist only in name under such circumstances.

Cantwell v. Connecticut (excerpt)
310 U.S. 296 (1940)

Here the Court struck down a law requiring a permit prior to solicitation for religious purposes.

. . . The constitutional inhibition of legislation on the subject of religion has a double aspect. On the one hand, it forestalls compulsion by law of the acceptance of any creed or the practice of any form of worship. Freedom of conscience and freedom to adhere to such religious organization or form of worship as the individual may choose cannot be restricted by law. On the other hand, it safeguards the free exercise of the chosen form of religion. Thus the Amendment embraces two concepts,—freedom to believe and freedom to act. The first is absolute but, in the nature of things, the second cannot be. Conduct remains subject to regulation for the protection of society. The freedom to act must have appropriate definition to preserve the enforcement of that protection. In every case the power to regulate must be so exercised as not, in attaining a permissible end, unduly to infringe the protected freedom. No one would contest the proposition that a state may not, by statute, wholly deny the right to preach or to disseminate religious views. Plainly such a previous and absolute restraint would violate the terms of the guarantee. It is equally clear that a state may be general and non-discriminatory legislation regulate the times, the places, and the manner of soliciting upon its streets, and of holding meetings thereon; and may in other respects safeguard the peace, good order and comfort of the community, without unconstitutionally invading the liberties protected by the Fourteenth Amendment. The appellants are right in their insistence that the Act in question is not such a regulation. If a certificate is procured, solicitation is permitted without restraint but, in the absence of a certificate, solicitation is altogether prohibited.

Note: In accordance with the *Cantwell* distinction between religious beliefs and acts, Mormons have been penalized for practicing polygamy (*Reynolds*); conscientious pacifists for refusing peace-time military training in college (*Hamilton v. Regents of the University of California,* 293 U.S. 245 [1934]); parents (or guardians) for involving their children in violations of child-labor laws by distribution of religious literature (*Prince* v. *Massachusetts,* 321 U.S. 158 [1944]); and Sabbatarians (indirectly?) if they choose to observe their sabbath (*Braunfeld,* below).

Braunfeld v. *Brown*
366 U.S. 599 (1961)

Here Orthodox Jewish merchants argued that the state's Sunday-closing law would force them either to abandon their own Saturday Sabbath observance, or to suffer economic disadvantage by having to close their business operations two days a week, whereas their competitors need close only one day a week.

Mr. Chief Justice Warren delivered the opinion of the Court. . . .

. . . in Reynolds v. United States, this Court upheld the polygamy conviction of a member of the Mormon faith despite the fact that an accepted doctrine of his church then imposed upon its male members the *duty* to practice polygamy. And, in *Prince* v. *Commonwealth of Massachusetts,* 321 U.S. 158, this Court upheld a statute making it a crime for a girl under eighteen years of age to sell any newspapers, periodicals or merchandise in public places despite the fact that a child of the Jehovah's Witnesses faith believed that it was her religious *duty* to perform this work.

It is to be noted that, in the two cases just mentioned, the religious practices themselves conflicted with the public interest. In such cases, to make accommodation between the religious action and an exercise of state authority is a particularly delicate task, *id.,* 321 U.S. at

page 165, because resolution in favor of the State results in the choice to the individual of either abandoning his religious principle or facing criminal prosecution.

But, again, this is not the case before us because the statute at bar does not make unlawful any religious practices of appellants; the Sunday law simply regulates a secular activity and, as applied to appellants, operates so as to make the practice of their religious beliefs more expensive. Furthermore, the law's effect does not inconvenience all members of the Orthodox Jewish faith but only those who believe it necessary to work on Sunday. And even these are not faced with as serious a choice as forsaking their religious practices or subjecting themselves to criminal prosecution. Fully recognizing that the alternatives open to appellants and others similarly situated—retaining their present occupations and incurring economic disadvantage or engaging in some other commercial activity which does not call for either Saturday or Sunday labor—may well result in some financial sacrifice in order to observe their religious beliefs, still the option is wholly different than when the legislation attempts to make a religious practice itself unlawful.

To strike down, without the most critical scrutiny, legislation which imposes only an indirect burden on the exercise of religion, *i.e.*, legislation which does not make unlawful the religious practice itself, would radically restrict the operating latitude of the legislature. Statutes which tax income and limit the amount which may be deducted for religious contributions impose an indirect economic burden on the observance of the religion of the citizen whose religion requires him to donate a greater amount to his church; statutes which require the courts to be closed on Saturday and Sunday impose a similar indirect burden on the observance of the religion of the trial lawyer whose religion requires him to rest on a weekday. The list of legislation of this nature is nearly limitless.

[Appellants contended their religious practice would be protected while the secular purposes of the state were achieved if the legislation excepted from its Sunday closing ban those who, because of their religious convictions, observed a day of rest other than Sunday.]

A number of States provide such an exemption, and this may well be the wiser solution to the problem. But our concern is not with the wisdom of legislation but with its constitutional limitation. Thus, reason and experience teach that to permit the exemption might well undermine the State's goal of providing a day that, as best possible, eliminates the atmosphere of commercial noise and activity. Although not dispositive of the issue, enforcement problems would be more difficult since there would be two or more days to police rather than one and it would be more difficult to observe whether violations were occurring.

Additional problems might also be presented by a regulation of this sort. To allow only people who rest on a day other than Sunday to keep their businesses open on that day might well provide these people with an economic advantage over their competitors who must remain closed on that day; this might cause the Sunday-observers to complain that their religions are being discriminated against. With this competitive advantage existing, there could well be the temptation for some, in order to keep their businesses open on Sunday, to assert that they have religious convictions which compel them to close their businesses on what had formerly been their least profitable day. This might make necessary a state-conducted inquiry into the sincerity of the individual's religious beliefs, a practice which a State might believe would itself run afoul of the spirit of constitutionally protected religious guarantees. Finally, in order to keep the disruption of the day at a minimum, exempted employers would probably have to hire employees who themselves qualified for the exemption because of their own religious beliefs, a practice which a State might feel to be opposed to its general policy prohibiting religious discrimination in hiring. For all of these reasons, we cannot say that the Pennsylvania statute before us is invalid, either on its face or as applied.

[Mr. Justice Frankfurter gave an extensive concurring opinion in which Mr. Justice Harlan joined. Justices Brennan and Stewart dissented. Mr. Justice Douglas's dissenting opinion in *McGowan*, above, covers this case also.]

Sherbert v. *Verner*
374 U.S. 398 (1963)

Mr. Justice Brennan delivered the opinion of the Court.

Appellant, a member of the Seventh-day Adventist Church, was discharged by her South Carolina employer because she would not work on Saturday, the Sabbath Day of her faith. When she was unable to obtain other employment because from conscientious scruples she would not take Saturday work, she filed a claim for unemployment compensation benefits under the South Carolina Unemployment Compensation Act. That law provides that, to be eligible for benefits, a claimant must be "able to work and is available for work;" and, further, that a claimant is ineligible for benefits "[i]f . . . he has failed, without good cause . . . to accept available suitable work when offered him by the employment office or the employer . . . ." The appellee Employment Security Commission . . . found that appellant's restriction upon her availability for Saturday work brought her within the provision disqualifying for benefits insured workers who fail, without good cause, to accept "suitable work when offered . . . ." The State Supreme Court held . . . that appellant's ineligibility infringed no constitutional liberties . . . . We reverse the judgment . . . .

. . . [If] the decision of the South Carolina Supreme Court is to withstand appellant's constitutional challenge, it must be either because her disqualification as a beneficiary represents no infringement by the State of her constitutional rights of free exercise; or because any incidental burden on the free exercise of appellant's religion may be justified by a "compelling state interest in the regulation of a subject within the State's constitutional power to regulate . . . ." NAACP v. Button, 371 U.S. 415, 438. . .

We turn first to the question whether the disqualification for benefits imposes any burden on the free exercise of appellant's religion. We think it is clear that it does. In a sense the consequences of such a disqualification to religious principles and practices may be only an indirect result of welfare legislation within the State's general competence to enact; it is true that no criminal sanctions directly compel appellant to work a six-day week. But this is only the beginning, not the end of our inquiry. . . . Here not only is it apparent that appellant's declared ineligibility for benefits derives solely from the practice of her religion, but the pressure upon her to forego that practice is unmistakable. The ruling forces her to choose between following the precepts of her religion and forfeiting benefits, on the one hand, and abandoning one of the precepts of her religion in order to accept work, on the other hand. Governmental imposition of such a choice puts the same kind of burden upon the free exercise of religion as would a fine imposed against appellant for her Saturday worship. . . .

We must next consider whether some compelling state interest enforced in the eligibility provisions of the South Carolina statute justifies the substantial infringement of appellant's First Amendment right. It is basic that no showing merely of a rational relationship to some colorable state interest would suffice; in this highly sensitive constitutional area, "[o]nly the gravest abuses, endangering paramount interests, give occasion for permissible limitation," Thomas v. Collins, 323 U.S. 516, 530. No such abuse or danger has been advanced in the present case. The appellees suggest no more than a possibility that the filing of fraudulent claims by unscrupulous claimants feigning religious objections to Saturday work might not only dilute the unemployment compensation fund but also hinder the scheduling by employers of necessary Saturday work. But that possibility is not apposite here because no such objection appears to have been made before the South Carolina Supreme Court, and we are unwilling to assess the importance of an asserted state interest without the views of the state court. Nor, if the contention had been made below, would the record appear to sustain it; there is no proof whatever to warrant such fears of malingering or deceit as those which the respondents now advance. Even if consideration of such evidence is not foreclosed by the prohibition against judicial inquiry into the truth or falsity of religious beliefs, United States v. Ballard, 322 U.S. 78,—a question as to which we intimate no view since it is not before us—it is highly doubtful whether such evidence would be sufficient to warrant a substantial infringement of religious liberties. For even if the possibility of spurious claims did threaten to dilute the fund and disrupt the scheduling of work, it would plainly be incumbent upon the appellees to demonstrate that no alternative forms of regulation would combat such abuses without infringing First Amendment rights. . . .

In these respects, then, the state interest asserted in the present case is wholly dissimilar to the interests which were found to justify the less direct burden upon religious practices in *Braunfeld* v. *Brown*, *supra*. . . . [That statute was] saved by a countervailing factor which finds no equivalent in the instant case—a strong state interest in providing one uniform day of rest for all workers. That secular objective could be achieved, the Court found, only by declaring Sunday to be that day of rest. . . . In the present case no such justifications underlie the determination of the state court that appellant's religion makes her ineligible to receive benefits. . . .

In holding as we do, plainly we are not fostering the "establishment" of the Seventh-day Adventist religion in South Carolina, for the extension of unemployment benefits to Sabbatarians in common with Sunday worshippers reflects nothing more than the governmental obligation of neutrality in the face of religious differences, and does not represent that involvement of religious with secular institutions which it is the object of the Establishment Clause to forestall. . . . Nor do we, by our decision today, declare the existence of a constitutional right to unemployment benefits on the part of all persons whose religious convictions are the cause of their unemployment. This is not a case in which an employee's religious convictions serve to make him a nonproductive member of society. . . . Our holding today is only that South Carolina may not constitutionally apply the eligibility provisions so as to constrain a worker to abandon his religious convictions respecting the day of rest. . . .

Mr. Justice Douglas, concurring. . . .

This case is resolvable not in terms of what an individual can demand of government, but solely in terms of what government may not do to an individual in violation of his religious scruples. The fact that government cannot exact from me a surrender of one iota of my religious scruples does not, of course, mean that I can demand of government a sum of money, the better to exercise them. . . .

Those considerations, however, are not relevant here. If appellant is otherwise qualified for unemployment benefits, payments will be made to her not as a Seventh-day Adventist, but as an unemployed worker. Conceivably these payments will indirectly benefit her church, but no more so than does the salary of any public employee. Thus, this case does not involve the problems of direct or indirect state assistance to a religious organization—matters relevant to the Establishment Clause, not in issue here.

Mr. Justice Stewart, concurring.

Although fully agreeing with the result which the Court reaches in this case, I cannot join the Court's opinion. This case presents a double-barreled dilemma, which in all candor I think the Court's opinion has not succeeded in papering over. The dilemma ought to be resolved. . . .

I am convinced that no liberty is more essential to the continued vitality of the free society which our Constitution guarantees than is the religious liberty protected by the Free Exercise Clause . . . And I regret that on occasion, and specifically in *Braunfeld* v. *Brown*, *supra*, the Court has shown what has seemed to me a distressing insensitivity to the appropriate demands of this constitutional guarantee. By contrast I think that the Court's approach to the Establishment Clause has on occasion, and specifically in *Engel*, *Schempp* and *Murray*, been not only insensitive, but positively wooden, and that the Court has accorded to the Establishment Clause a meaning which neither the words, the history, nor the intention of the authors of that specific constitutional provision even remotely suggests.

But my views as to the correctness of the Court's decisions in these cases are beside the point here. The point is that the decisions are on the books. And the result is that there are many situations where legitimate claims under the Free Exercise Clause will run into head-on collision with the Court's insensitive and sterile construction of the Establishment Clause. The controversy now before us is clearly such a case.
. . .

South Carolina would deny unemployment benefits to a mother unavailable for work on Saturdays because she was unable to get a babysitter. Thus, we do not have before us a situation where a State provides unemployment compensation generally, and singles out for disqualification only those persons who are unavailable for work on religious grounds. This is not, in short, a scheme which operates so as to discriminate against religion as such. But the Court nevertheless holds that the State must prefer a religious over a secular ground for being unavailable for work . . . .

Yet in cases decided under the Establishment Clause the Court has decreed otherwise. It has decreed that government must blind itself to the differing religious beliefs and traditions of the people. With all respect, I think it is the Court's duty to face up to the dilemma posed by the conflict between the Free Exercise Clause of the Constitution and the Establishment Clause as interpreted by the Court. It is a duty, I submit, which we owe to the people, the States, and the Nation, and a duty which we owe to ourselves. For so long as the resounding but fallacious fundamentalist rhetoric of some of our Establishment Clause opinions remains on our books, to be disregarded at will as in the present case, or to be undiscriminatingly invoked as in the *Schempp* case . . . , so long will the possibility of consistent and perceptive decision

in this most difficult and delicate area of constitutional law be impeded and impaired. And so long, I fear, will the guarantee of true religious freedom in our pluralistic society be uncertain and insecure. . . .

My second difference with the Court's opinion is that I cannot agree that today's decision can stand consistently with *Braunfeld* v. *Brown*, *supra*. The Court says that there was a "less direct burden upon religious practices" in that case than in this. With all respect, I think the Court is mistaken, simply as a matter of fact.
. . .

. . . I think the *Braunfeld* case was wrongly decided and should be overruled, and accordingly I concur in the result reached by the Court in the case before us.

Mr. Justice Harlan, whom Mr. Justice White joins, dissenting. . . .

. . . What the Court is holding is that if the State chooses to condition unemployment compensation on the applicant's availability for work, it is constitutionally compelled to *carve out an exception*—and to provide benefits—for those whose unavailability is due to their religious convictions. Such a holding has particular significance in two respects.

First, despite the Court's protestations to the contrary, the decision necessarily overrules *Braunfeld* v. *Brown*. . . .

Second, the implications of the present decision are far more troublesome than its apparently narrow dimensions would indicate at first glance. The meaning of today's holding . . . is that the State . . . must *single out* for financial assistance those whose behavior is religiously motivated, even though it denies such assistance to others whose identical behavior . . . is not religiously motivated.

It has been suggested that such singling out of religious conduct for special treatment may violate the constitutional limitations on state action. See Kurland, Of Church and State and The

Supreme Court, 29 *U. of Chi. L. Rev.* 1. . . . My own view, however, is that at least under the circumstances of this case it would be a permissible accommodation of religion for the State, if it *chose* to do so, to create an exception to its eligibility requirements for persons like the appellant. The constitutional obligation of "neutrality" . . . is not so narrow a channel that the slightest deviation from an absolutely straight course leads to condemnation. . . .

For very much the same reasons, however, I cannot subscribe to the conclusion that the State is constitutionally *compelled* to carve out an exception to its general rule of eligibility in the present case. . . .

Quaere: In protecting "free exercise" in *Sherbert,* does the Court "establish" a particular religious group by giving it a special exemption from a general law that all others must obey? (Cf. *Braunfeld.*)

Wisconsin v. *Yoder*
406 U.S. 205 (1972)

Chief Justice Burger delivered the opinion of the Court. . . .

Respondents Jonas Yoder and Adin Yutzy are members of the Old Order Amish Religion, and respondent Wallace Miller is a member of the Conservative Amish Mennonite Church. They and their families are residents of Green County, Wisconsin. Wisconsin's compulsory school attendance law required them to cause their children to attend public or private school until reaching age 16 but the respondents declined to send their children, ages 14 and 15, to public school after completing the eighth grade. The children were not enrolled in any private school, or within any recognized exception to the compulsory attendance law, and they are conceded to be subject to the Wisconsin statute.

On complaint of the school district adminis-

trator for the public schools, respondents were charged, tried, and convicted of violating the compulsory attendance law in Green County Court and were fined the sum of $5 each. Respondents defended on the ground that the application of the compulsory attendance law violated their rights under the First and Fourteenth Amendments. The trial testimony showed that respondents believed, in accordance with the tenets of Old Order Amish communities generally, that their children's attendance at high school, public or private, was contrary to the Amish religion and way of life. They believed that by sending their children to high school, they would not only expose themselves to the danger of the censure of the church community, but, as found by the county court, endanger their own salvation and that of their children. The State stipulated that respondents' religious beliefs were sincere. . . .

There is no doubt as to the power of a State, having a high responsibility for education of its citizens, to impose reasonable regulations for the control and duration of basic education. See, *e.g., Pierce* v. *Society of Sisters,* 268 U.S. 510, 534 (1925). Providing public schools ranks at the very apex of the function of a State. Yet even this paramount responsibility was, in *Pierce,* made to yield to the right of parents to provide an equivalent education in a privately operated system. There the Court held that Oregon's statute compelling attendance in a public school from age eight to age 16 unreasonably interfered with the interest of parents in directing the rearing of their offspring including their education in church-operated schools. . . .

. . . [I]n order for Wisconsin to compel school attendance beyond the eighth grade against a claim that such attendance interferes with the practice of a legitimate religious belief, it must appear either that the State does not deny the free exercise of religious belief by its requirement, or that there is a state interest of sufficient magnitude to override the interest claiming protection under the Free Exercise Clause. . . .

. . . [T]he record in this case abundantly supports the claim that the traditional way of life of the Amish is not merely a matter of personal preference, but one of deep religious conviction, shared by an organized group, and intimately related to daily living. . . .

The impact of the compulsory attendance law on respondents' practice of the Amish religion is not only severe, but inescapable, for the Wisconsin law affirmatively compels them, under threat of criminal sanction, to perform acts undeniably at odds with fundamental tenets of their religious beliefs. Nor is the impact of the compulsory attendance law confined to grave interference with important Amish religious tenets from a subjective point of view. It carries with it precisely the kind of objective danger to the free exercise of religion which the First Amendment was designed to prevent. As the record shows, compulsory school attendance to age 16 for Amish children carries with it a very real threat of undermining the Amish community and religious practice as it exists today; they must either abandon belief and be assimilated into society at large, or be forced to migrate to some other and more tolerant region.

. . . The Court must not ignore the danger that an exception from a general obligation of citizenship on religious grounds may run afoul of the Establishment Clause, but that danger cannot be allowed to prevent any exception no matter how vital it may be to the protection of values promoted by the right of free exercise. . . .

The State advances two primary arguments in support of its system of compulsory education. It notes, as Thomas Jefferson pointed out early in our history, that some degree of education is necessary to prepare citizens to participate effectively and intelligently in our open political system if we are to preserve freedom and independence. Further, education prepares individuals to be self-reliant and self-sufficient participants in society. We accept these propositions. . . .

. . . Whatever their idiosyncrasies as seen by the majority, this record strongly shows that the Amish community has been a highly successful social unit within our society even if apart from the conventional "mainstream." Its members are productive and very law-abiding members of society; they reject public welfare in any of its usual modern forms. The Congress itself recognized their self-sufficiency by authorizing exemption of such groups as the Amish from the obligation to pay social security taxes. . . .

The State, however, supports its interest in providing an additional one or two years of compulsory high school education to Amish children because of the possibility that some such children will choose to leave the Amish community, and that if this occurs they will be ill-equipped for life. The State argues that if Amish children leave their church they should not be in the position of making their way in the world without the education available in the one or two additional years the State requires. However, on this record, that argument is highly speculative. There is no specific evidence of the loss of Amish adherents by attrition, nor is there any showing that upon leaving the Amish community Amish children, with their practical agricultural training and habits of industry and self-reliance would become burdens on society because of educational shortcomings. . . .

. . . The independence and successful social functioning of the Amish community for a period approaching almost three centuries and more than 200 years in this country is strong evidence that there is at best a speculative gain, in terms of meeting the duties of citizenship, from an additional one or two years of compulsory formal education. Against this background it would require a more particularized showing from the State on this point to justify the severe interference with religious freedom such additional compulsory attendance would entail. . . .

The requirement of compulsory schooling to age 16 must therefore be viewed as aimed not merely at providing educational opportunities for children, but as an alternative to the equally undesirable consequence of unhealthful child labor displacing adult workers, or, on the other hand, forced idleness. The two kinds of statutes—compulsory school attendance and child labor laws—tend to keep children of certain ages off the labor market and in school; this in turn provides opportunity to prepare for a livelihood of a higher order than that children could perform without education and protects their health in adolescence.

In these terms, Wisconsin's interest in compelling the school attendance of Amish children to age 16 emerges as somewhat less substantial than requiring such attendance for children generally. For, while agricultural employment is not totally outside the legitimate concerns of the child labor laws, employment of children under parental guidance and on the family farm from age 14 to age 16 is an ancient tradition which lies at the periphery of the objectives of such laws. . . .

Finally, the State . . . argues that a decision exempting Amish children from the State's requirement fails to recognize the substantive right of the Amish child to a secondary education, and fails to give due regard to the power of the State as *parens patriae* to extend the benefit of secondary education to children regardless of the wishes of their parents. . . .

Contrary to the suggestion of the dissenting opinion of Mr. Justice Douglas, our holding today in no degree depends on the assertion of the religious interest of the child as contrasted with that of the parents. It is the parents who are subject to prosecution here for failing to cause their children to attend school, and it is their right of free exercise, not that of their children, that must determine Wisconsin's power to impose criminal penalties on the parent. The dissent argues that a child who expresses a desire to attend public high school in conflict with the wishes of his parents should not be prevented from doing so. There is no reason for the Court to consider that point since it is not an issue in the case. The children are not parties to

this litigation. The State has at no point tried this case on the theory that respondents were preventing their children from attending school against their expressed desires, and indeed the record is to the contrary. . . .

. . . Our disposition of this case, however, in no way alters our recognition of the obvious fact that courts are not school boards or legislatures, and are ill-equipped to determine the "necessity" of discrete aspects of a State's program of compulsory education. This should suggest that courts must move with great circumspection in performing the sensitive and delicate task of weighing a State's legitimate social concern when faced with religious claims for exemption from generally applicable educational requirements. It cannot be over-emphasized that we are not dealing with a way of life and mode of education by a group claiming to have recently discovered some "progressive" or more enlightened process for rearing children for modern life. . . .

Justice Powell and Justice Rehnquist took no part in the consideration or decision of this case.

Justice Douglas, dissenting in part.

. . . The Court's analysis assumes that the only interests at stake in the case are those of the Amish parents on the one hand, and those of the State on the other. The difficulty with this approach is that, despite the Court's claim, the parents are seeking to vindicate not only their own free exercise claims, but also those of their high-school-age children.

. . . Where the child is mature enough to express potentially conflicting desires, it would be an invasion of the child's rights to permit such an imposition without canvassing his views. . . . As the child has no other effective forum, it is in this litigation that his rights should be considered. And if an Amish child desires to attend high school, and is mature enough to have that desire respected, the State may well be able to override the parents' religiously motivated objections. . . .

The Draft and the Conscientious Objector

The Supreme Court has never held that anyone is constitutionally exempt from conscription for military service by reason of religious or other conscientious scruple. Such exemptions have been granted only by act of Congress. The *Selective Draft Law Cases,* 245 U.S. 366 (1918), upheld conscription itself and found no free-exercise or establishment problem in exemption for conscientious objectors in World War I draft legislation. See also *Hamilton* v. *Regents of the University of California,* 293 U.S. 245 (1934), upholding, in the face of conscientious objection, compulsory peacetime military training for male college students. Are these old decisions compatible with *Yoder* and *Sherbert?*

For an interesting Court interpretation of draft exemptions granted by Congress with respect to conscientious objection, see *United States* v. *Seeger,* 380 U.S. 163 (1965):

. . . We have concluded that Congress, in using the expression "Supreme Being" rather than the designation "God," was merely clarifying the meaning of religious training and belief so as to embrace all religions and to exclude political, sociological, or philosophical views. We believe that under this construction, the test of belief "in a relation to a Supreme Being" is whether a given belief that is sincere and meaningful occupies a place in the life of its possessor parallel to that filled by the orthodox belief in God of one who clearly qualifies for the exemption. Where such beliefs have parallel positions in the lives of their respective holders we cannot say that one is "in a relation to a Supreme Being" and the other is not. We have concluded that the beliefs of the objectors in these cases meet these criteria.

The 1967 draft act restricted the conscientious objector exemption to those "conscientiously opposed to participation in war in any form." The Court found this to exclude those who objected not to war in general but only to "unjust" wars (in this instance, as the objectors saw it, the Vietnam war). *Gillette* v. *United States,* 401 U.S. 437 (1971); *Negre* v. *Larson,* 401 U.S. 437 (1971). The Court also found that congressional failure to exempt such *selective* objectors did not violate the Constitution. *Johnson* v. *Robinson,* 415 U.S. 361 (1974), following *Gillette,* found no free-exercise problem in a denial by Congress of veterans' educational benefits to alternate-service conscientious objectors. Only Mr. Justice Douglas dissented (as did he alone in *Gillette*), on *Sherbert-Yoder* grounds.

APPENDIX A
The Constitution of the United States

We the people of the United States, In Order to form a more perfect Union, establish Justice, insure domestic Tranquility, provide for the common defense, promote the general Welfare, and secure the Blessings of Liberty to ourselves and our Posterity, do ordain and establish this Constitution for the United States of America.

ARTICLE I

Section 1. All legislative Powers herein granted shall be vested in a Congress of the United States, which shall consist of a Senate and House of Representatives.

Section 2. The House of Representatives shall be composed of members chosen every second Year by the People of the several States, and the Electors in each State shall have the Qualifications requisite for Electors of the most numerous Branch of the State Legislature.

No Person shall be a representative who shall not have attained to the Age of twenty five Years, and been seven Years a Citizen of the United States, and who shall not, when elected, be an Inhabitant of that State in which he shall be chosen.

Representatives and direct Taxes shall be apportioned among the several States which may be included within this union, according to their respective Numbers, which shall be determined by adding to the whole Number of free Persons, including those bound to Service for a Term of Years, and excluding Indians not taxed, three fifths of all other Persons. The actual Enumeration shall be made within three Years after the first Meeting of the Congress of the United States, and within every subsequent Term of ten Years, in such Manner as they shall by Law direct. The Number of Representatives shall not exceed one for every thirty Thousand, but each State shall have at Least one Representative; and until such enumeration shall be made, the State of New Hampshire shall be entitled to chuse three, Massachusetts eight, Rhode-Island and Providence Plantations one, Connecticut five, New York six, New Jersey four, Pennsylvania eight, Delaware one, Maryland six, Virginia ten, North Carolina five, South Carolina five, and Georgia three.

When vacancies happen in the Representation from any State, the Executive Authority thereof shall issue Writs of Election to fill such Vacancies.

The House of Representatives shall chuse their speaker and other Officers; and shall have the sole Power of Impeachment.

Section 3. The Senate of the United States shall be composed of two Senators from each State, chosen by the Legislature thereof, for six Years; and each Senator shall have one Vote.

Immediately after they shall be assembled in

Consequence of the first Election, they shall be divided as equally as may be into three Classes. The Seats of the Senators of the first Class shall be vacated at the Expiration of the second Year, of the second Class at the Expiration of the fourth Year, and of the third Class at the Expiration of the sixth Year, so that one third may be chosen every second Year; and if Vacancies happen by Resignation, or otherwise, during the Recess of the Legislature of any State, the Executive thereof may make temporary Appointments until the next Meeting of the Legislature, which shall then fill such Vacancies.

No Person shall be a Senator who shall not have attained to the Age of thirty Years, and been nine Years a Citizen of the United States, and who shall not, when elected, be an Inhabitant of that State for which he shall be chosen.

The Vice President of the United States shall be President of the Senate, but shall have no Vote, unless they be equally divided.

The Senate shall chuse their other Officers, and also a President pro tempore, in the Absence of the Vice President, or when he shall exercise the Office of the President of the United States.

The Senate shall have the sole Power to try all Impeachments. When sitting for that Purpose, they shall be on Oath of Affirmation. When the President of the United States is tried, the Chief Justice shall preside: And no Person shall be convicted without the Concurrence of two thirds of the Members present.

Judgment in Cases of Impeachment shall not extend further than to removal from Office, and disqualification to hold and enjoy any Office of honor, Trust or Profit under the United States: but the Party convicted shall nevertheless be liable and subject to Indictment, Trial, Judgment and Punishment, according to law.

Section 4. The Times, Places and Manner of holding Elections for Senators and Representatives, shall be prescribed in each State by the Legislature thereof; but the Congress may at any time by Law make or alter such Regulations, except as to the Places of chusing Senators.

The Congress shall assemble at least once in every Year, and such Meeting shall be on the first Monday in December, unless they shall by Law appoint a different Day.

Section 5. Each House shall be the Judge of the Elections, Returns and Qualifications of its own Members, and a Majority of each shall constitute a Quorum to do Business; but a smaller Number may adjourn from day to day, and may be authorized to compel the Attendance of absent Members, in such Manner, and under such Penalties as each House may provide.

Each House may determine the Rules of its Proceedings, punish its Members for disorderly Behaviour, and, with the Concurrence of two thirds, expel a Member.

Each House shall keep a Journal of its Proceedings, and from time to time publish the same, excepting such Parts as may in their Judgment require Secrecy; and the Yeas and Nays of the Members of either House on any question shall, at the Desire of one fifth of those Present, be entered on the Journal.

Neither House, during the Session of Congress, shall, without the Consent of the other, adjourn for more than three days, nor to any other Place than that in which the two Houses shall be sitting.

Section 6. The Senators and Representatives shall receive a Compensation for their Services, to be ascertained by Law, and paid out of the Treasury of the United States. They shall in all Cases, except Treason, Felony and Breach of the Peace, be privileged from Arrest during their Attendance at the Session of their respective Houses, and in going to and returning from the same; and for any Speech or Debate in either House, they shall not be questioned in any other Place.

No Senator or Representative shall, during the Time for which he was elected, be appointed to any civil Office under the Authority of the United States, which shall have been created, or the Emoluments whereof shall have been encreased during such time; and no Person holding any Office under the United States, shall be a Member of either House during his Continuance in Office.

Section 7. All Bills for raising Revenue shall originate in the House of Representatives; but the Senate may propose or concur with Amendments as on other Bills.

Every Bill which shall have passed the House of Representatives and the Senate, shall, before it become a Law, be presented to the President of the United States; If he approve he shall sign it, but if not he shall return it, with his Objections to that House in which it shall have originated, who shall enter the Objections at large on their Journal, and proceed to reconsider it. If after such Reconsideration two thirds of that House shall agree to pass the Bill, it shall be sent, together with the Objections, to the other House, by which it shall likewise be reconsidered, and if approved by two thirds of that House, it shall become a Law. But in all such Cases the Votes of both Houses shall be determined by Yeas and Nays, and the Names of the Persons voting for and against the Bill shall be entered on the Journal of each House respectively. If any Bill shall not be returned by the President within ten Days (Sundays excepted) after it shall have been presented to him, the Same shall be a Law, in like Manner as if he had signed it, unless the Congress by their Adjournment prevent its Return, in which Case it shall not be a Law.

Every Order, Resolution, or Vote to which the Concurrence of the Senate and House of Representatives may be necessary (except on a question of Adjournment) shall be presented to the President of the United States; and before the Same shall take Effect, shall be approved by him, or being disapproved by him, shall be repassed by two thirds of the Senate and House of Representatives, according to the Rules and Limitations prescribed in the Case of a Bill.

Section 8. The Congress shall have Power To lay and collect Taxes, Duties, Imposts and Excises, to pay the Debts and provide for the common Defence and general Welfare of the United States; but all Duties, Imposts and Excises shall be uniform throughout the United States;

To borrow Money on the credit of the United States;

To regulate Commerce with foreign Nations, and among the several States, and with the Indian Tribes;

To establish an uniform Rule of Naturalization, and uniform Laws on the subject of Bankruptcies throughout the United States;

To coin Money, regulate the Value thereof, and of foreign Coin, and fix the Standard of Weights and Measures;

To provide for the Punishment of counterfeiting the Securities and current Coin of the United States;

To establish Post Offices and post Roads;

To promote the Progress of Science and useful Arts, by securing for limited Times to Authors and Inventors the exclusive Right to their respective Writings and Discoveries;

To constitute Tribunals inferior to the supreme Court;

To define and punish Piracies and Felonies committed on the high Seas, and Offences against the Law of Nations;

To declare War, grant Letters of Marque and Reprisal, and make Rules concerning Captures on Land and Water;

To raise and support Armies, but no Appropriation of Money to that Use shall be for a longer Term than two Years;

To provide and maintain a Navy;

To make Rules for the Government and Regulation of the land and naval Forces;

To provide for calling forth the Militia to execute the Laws of the Union, suppress Insurrections and repel Invasions;

To provide for organizing, arming, and disciplining, the Militia, and for governing such Part of them as may be employed in the Service of the United States, reserving to the States respectively, the Appointment of the Officers, and the Authority of training the Militia according to the discipline prescribed by Congress;

To exercise exclusive Legislation in all Cases whatsoever, over such District (not exceeding ten Miles square) as may, by Cession of particular States, and the Acceptance of Congress, become the Seat of the Government of the United States, and to exercise like Authority over all Places purchased by the Consent of the Legislature of the State in which the Same shall be for the Erection of Forts, Magazines, Arsenals, dock-Yards, and other needful Buildings;- And

To make all Laws which shall be necessary and proper for carrying into Execution the foregoing Powers, and all other Powers vested by this Constitution in the Government of the United States, or in any Department or Officer thereof.

Section 9. The Migration or Importation of such Persons as any of the States now existing shall think proper to admit, shall not be prohibited by the Congress prior to the Year one thousand eight hundred and eight, but a Tax or duty may be imposed on such Importation, not exceeding ten dollars for each Person.

The Privilege of the Writ of Habeas Corpus shall not be suspended, unless when in Cases of Rebellion or Invasion the public Safety may require it.

No Bill of Attainder or ex post facto Law shall be passed.

No Capitation, or other direct, Tax shall be laid, unless in Proportion to the Census or Enumeration herein before directed to be taken.

No Tax or Duty shall be laid on Articles exported from any State.

No Preference shall be given by any Regulation of Commerce or Revenue to the Ports of one State over those of another: nor shall Vessels bound to, or from, one State be obliged to enter, clear, or pay Duties in another.

No Money shall be drawn from the Treasury, but in Consequence of Appropriations made by Law; and a regular Statement and Account of the Receipts and Expenditures of all public Money shall be published from time to time.

No Title of Nobility shall be granted by the United States: And no Person holding any office of Profit or Trust under them, shall, without the Consent of the Congress, accept of any present, Emolument, Office, or Title, of any kind whatever, from any King, Prince, or foreign States.

Section 10. No State shall enter into any Treaty, Alliance, or Confederation; grant Letters of Marque and Treaty; Alliance, or Confederation; grant Letters of Marque and Reprisal; coin Money; emit Bills of Credit; make any Thing but gold and silver Coin a Tender in Payment of Debts; pass any Bill of Attainder, ex post facto Law, or Law impairing the Obligation of Contracts, or grant any Title of Nobility.

No State shall, without the Consent of the Congress, lay any Imposts or Duties on Imports or Exports, except what may be absolutely necessary for executing its inspection Laws: and the net Produce of all Duties and Imposts, laid by any State on Imports or Exports, shall be for the Use of the Treasury of the United States; and all such Laws shall be subject to Revision and Controul of the Congress.

No State shall, without the Consent of Congress, lay any Duty of Tonnage, keep Troops, or Ships of War in time of Peace, enter into any Agreement or Compact with another State, or with a foreign Power, or engage in War, unless actually invaded, or in such imminent Danger as will not admit of delay.

ARTICLE II

Section 1. The executive Power shall be vested in a President of the United States of America. He shall hold his Office during the Term of four Years, and, together with the Vice President, chosen for the same term, be elected, as follows

Each State shall appoint, in such Manner as the Legislature thereof may direct, a Number of Electors, equal to the whole Number of Senators and Representatives to which the State may be entitled in the

Congress: but no Senator or Representative, or Person holding an office of Trust or Profit under the United States, shall be appointed an Elector.

The Electors shall meet in their respective States, and vote by Ballot for two Persons, of whom one at least shall not be an Inhabitant of the same State with themselves. And they shall make a List of all the Persons voted for, and of the Number of Votes for each; which List they shall sign and certify, and transmit sealed to the Seat of the Government of the United States, directed to the President of the Senate. The President of the Senate shall, in the Presence of the Senate and House of Representatives, open all the Certificates, and the Votes shall then be counted. The Person having the greatest Number of Votes shall be the President, if such Number be a Majority of the whole Number of Electors appointed; and if there be more than one who have such Majority, and have an equal Number of Votes, then the House of Representatives shall immediately chuse by Ballot one of them for President: and if no Person have a Majority, then from the five highest on the List the said House shall in like Manner chuse the President. But in chusing the President, the Votes shall be taken by States, the Representation from each State having one Vote; A quorum for this Purpose shall consist of a Member or Members from two thirds of the States, and a Majority of all the States shall be necessary to a Choice. In every Case, after the Choice of the President, the Person having the greatest Number of Votes of the Electors shall be the Vice President. But if there should remain two or more who have equal Votes, the Senate shall chuse from them by Ballot the Vice President.

The Congress may determine the Time of chusing the Electors and the Day on which they shall give their Votes; which Day shall be the same throughout the United States.

No Person except a natural born Citizen, or a Citizen of the United States, at the time of the Adoption of this Constitution, shall be eligible to the Office of President; neither shall any Person be eligible to that Office who shall not have attained to the Age of thirty five Years, and been fourteen Years a Resident within the United States.

In Case of the Removal of the President from Office, or of his Death, Resignation, or Inability to discharge the Powers and Duties of the said Office, the Same shall devolve on the Vice President, and the Congress may by Law provide for the Case of Removal, Death, Resignation or Inability, both of

Preface

This book differs in several ways from other "political science" casebooks on constitutional law. It generally avoids editorial "explanations" of the leading cases. Too many students read them rather than the opinions—and too many others, instead of analyzing the opinions for themselves, accept the editor's analysis at face value. This defeats the purpose of a casebook: student exposure to the challenge of the primary source material with all its subtleties and cross currents. Indeed in my view the material is so rich and so subject to differing interpretations, that any editor's "explanations"—attempting to simplify—are bound to be misleading.

Another difficulty in editorial predigestion of the cases is that it may—innocently no doubt—taint the material with the editor's biases and possible misunderstandings. Thus the instructor becomes something of a captive in his own classroom. For with many students the printed word is apt to carry more weight than the oral. In sum, I have tried to present the raw material with minimal interference in other people's classrooms. I have, however, presented numerous quaeres—in the hope of stimulating scholarly thought and discussion. This entails some risk. Authors may slant questions of course—so too straightforward questions may seem slanted to a biased reader. The rewards of the socratic method, one hopes, will justify these risks. The ultimate safeguard is the good sense of our students.

Unlike some case collections this one presents not only majority, but concurring and dissenting opinions. This, of course, is crucial for minority views often clarify or delineate the scope of the majority position. They sometimes indicate what lies beyond the legal horizon.

Finally, I have not skimped quantitatively. Not all of the cases are apt to be covered in a one-semester course. Yet this surely is a bonus. It gives the instructor room for choice (and experimentation from semester to semester). Above all, it serves the needs of specially gifted students, those who crave more than the average class can handle. Surely we owe them something extra. Even instructors who offer two-semester courses may find at least some leeway for choice—and a bit extra for students who want it.

For those who are not acquainted with the recording of Supreme Court decisions a few words of guidance may be useful. Prior to 1875, the Court's work was published by "authorized" reporters, as follows: Dallas (Dall.) 1789–1800; Cranch (Cr.) 1801–1815; Wheaton (Wheat.) 1816–1827; Peters (Pet.) 1828–1842; Howard (How.) 1843–1860; Black (Bl.) 1861–1862; Wallace (Wall.) 1863–1874. The famous case of *Marbury* v. *Madison,* for example, is found in 1 Cr. 137 (1803). This reference, or citation, means that the case was decided in 1803 and is included in Vol. 1 of the Cranch reports at page 137. Since 1874 the work of the Supreme Court has been set out in the official *Supreme Court Reports* (U.S. Government Printing Office). In this series a case is cited, or referred to, by a volume number; the abbreviation, U.S.; a page number; and the date of the decision. Thus *Gitlow* v. *New York,* 268 U.S. 652 (1925), was decided in 1925 and will be found in vol. 268 of the *Supreme Court Reports* at page 652. The foregoing citation systems are used in this book. There are, however, two rival private reporting systems; namely, *The Supreme Court Reporter* (West Publishing Company) and *United States Supreme Court Reports, Lawyers Edition* (Lawyer's Cooperative Publishing Company). The former is identified by the abbreviation, S. Ct., the latter by the abbreviation, L. Ed. Volume and page numbers and decision dates are used with these identifying symbols just as they are used as indicated above with respect to the official *Supreme Court Reports.* Thus the *Gitlow* case will be found in 268 U.S. 652 (1925) and also in 45 S. Ct. 625 (1925) and 69 L.Ed. 1138 (1925). At the beginning of each volume of the two private reporter systems there is a conversion table which translates the official into the private citation and vice versa.

Cases referred to in the text without citation have been cited earlier, or are reproduced with citations following the text material in which they are mentioned. Footnotes have been eliminated from virtually all of the opinions represented herein. Those that remain have been renumbered.

I gratefully acknowledge help from Henry Abraham, Robert Dixon, David Fellman, Tinsley Yarbrough, and several anonymous "readers".

Above all I am indebted to Kelly McWhirter, who worked so hard and pleasantly on the manuscript.

December 1979   **Wallace Mendelson**

Summary of Contents

Table of Contents

Note: An asterisk preceding a case title indicates that the case has been listed earlier, and is being used again to make a
different point in a different context.

part
I

DIFFUSION OF GOVERNMENTAL POWER AS A SHIELD FOR FREEDOM

the President and Vice President, declaring what Officer shall then act as President, and such Officer shall act accordingly, until the Disability be removed, or a President shall be elected.

The President shall, at stated Times, receive for his Services a Compensation, which shall neither be encreased nor diminished during the Period for which he shall have been elected, and he shall not receive within that Period any other Emolument from the United States, or any of them.

Before he enter on the Execution of his Office, he shall take the following Oath or Affirmation:- "I do solemnly swear (or affirm) that I will faithfully execute the Office of President of the United States, and will to the best of my Ability, preserve, protect and defend the Constitution of the United States."

Section 2. The President shall be Commander in Chief of the Army and Navy of the United States, and of the Militia of the several States, when called into the actual Service of the United States; he may require the Opinion, in writing, of the principal Officer in each of the executive Departments, upon any Subject relating to the Duties of their respective Offices, and he shall have power to grant Reprieves and Pardons for Offences against the United States, except in Cases of Impeachment.

He shall have Power, by and with the Advice and Consent of the Senate, to make Treaties, provided two thirds of the Senators present concur; and he shall nominate, and by and with the Advice and Consent of the Senate, shall appoint Ambassadors, other public Ministers and Consuls, Judges of the supreme Court, and all other Officers of the United States, whose Appointments are not herein otherwise provided for, and which shall be established by Law; but the Congress may by Law vest the Appointment of such inferior Officers, as they think proper, in the President alone, in the Courts of Law, or in the Heads of Departments.

The President shall have Power to fill up all Vacancies that may happen during the Recess of the Senate, by granting Commissions which shall expire at the End of their next Session.

Section 3. He shall from time to time give to the Congress Information of the State of the Union, and recommend to their Consideration such Measures as he shall judge necessary and expedient; he may, on extraordinary Occasions, convene both Houses, or either of them, and in Case of Disagreement between them, with Respect to the Time of Adjournment, he may adjourn them to such Time as he shall

think proper; he shall receive Ambassadors and other public Ministers; he shall take Care that the Laws be faithfully executed, and shall Commission all of the officers of the United States.

Section 4. The President, Vice President and all civil Officers of the United States, shall be removed from Office on Impeachment for, and Conviction of, Treason, Bribery, or other High Crimes and Misdemeanors.

ARTICLE III

Section 1. The Judicial Power of the United States, shall be vested in one supreme Court, and in such inferior Courts as the Congress may from time to time ordain and establish. The Judges, both of the supreme and inferior Courts, shall hold their Offices during good Behaviour, and shall, at stated Times, receive for their Services, a Compensation, which shall not be diminished during their Continuance in Office.

Section 2. The judicial Power shall extend to all Cases, in Law and Equity, arising under this Constitution, the Laws of the United States, and Treaties made, or which shall be made, under their Authority;-to all Cases affecting Ambassadors, other public Ministers and Consuls;-to all Cases of admiralty and maritime Jurisdiction;-to Controversies to which the United States shall be a Party;-to Controversies between two or more States; between a State and Citizens of another State;-between Citizens of different States;-between Citizens of the same State claiming Lands under Grants of different States, and between a State, or the Citizens thereof, and foreign States, Citizens or Subjects.

In all Cases affecting Ambassadors, other public Ministers and Consuls, and those in which a State shall be Party, the supreme Court shall have original Jurisdiction. In all the other Cases before mentioned, the supreme Court shall have appellate Jurisdiction, both as to Law and Fact, with such Exceptions, and under such Regulations as the Congress shall make.

The Trial of all Crimes, except in Cases of Impeachment, shall be by Jury; and such Trial shall be held in the State where the said Crimes shall have been committed; but when not committed within any State, the Trial shall be at such Place or Places as the Congress may by Law have directed.

Section 3. Treason against the United States, shall consist only in levying War against them, or in adhering to their Enemies, giving them Aid and

Comfort. No Person shall be convicted of Treason unless on the Testimony of two Witnesses to the same overt Act, or on Confession in open Court.

The Congress shall have Power to declare the Punishment of Treason, but no Attainder of Treason shall work Corruption of Blood, or Forfeiture except during the Life of the Person attainted.

ARTICLE IV

Section 1. Full Faith and Credit shall be given in each State to the public Acts, Records, and judicial Proceedings of every other State. And the Congress may by general Laws prescribe the Manner in which such Acts, Records and Proceedings shall be proved, and the Effect thereof.

Section 2. The Citizens of each State shall be entitled to all Privileges and Immunities of Citizens in the several States.

A Person charged in any State with Treason, Felony, or other Crime, who shall flee from Justice, and be found in another State, shall on Demand of the executive Authority of the State from which he fled, be delivered up, to be removed to the State having Jurisdiction of the Crime.

No Person held to Service or Labour in one State, under the Laws thereof, escaping into another, shall, in Consequence of any Law or Regulation therein, be discharged from such Service or Labour, but shall be delivered up on Claim of the Party to whom such Service or Labour may be due.

Section 3. New States may be admitted by the Congress into this Union; but no new State shall be formed or erected within the Jurisdiction of any other State; nor any State be formed by the Junction of two or more States, or Parts of States, without the Consent of the Legislatures of the States concerned as well as of the Congress.

The Congress shall have Power to dispose of and make all needful Rules and Regulations respecting the Territory or other Property belonging to the United States; and nothing in this Constitution shall be so construed as to Prejudice any Claims of the United States, or of any particular State.

Section 4. The United States shall guarantee to every State in this Union a Republican Form of Government, and shall protect each of them against Invasion; and on Application of the Legislature, or of the Executive (when the Legislature cannot be convened) against domestic Violence.

ARTICLE V

The Congress, whenever two thirds of both Houses shall deem it necessary, shall propose Amendments to this Constitution, or, on the Application of the Legislatures of two thirds of the several States, shall call a Convention for proposing Amendments, which, in either Case, shall be valid to all Intents and Purposes, as Part of this Constitution, when ratified by the Legislatures of three fourths of the several States, or by Conventions in three fourths thereof, as the one or the other Mode of Ratification may be proposed by the Congress; Provided that no Amendment which may be made prior to the Year One thousand eight hundred and eight shall in any Manner affect the first and fourth Clauses in the Ninth Section of the first Article; and that no State, without its Consent, shall be deprived of its equal Suffrage in the Senate.

ARTICLE VI

All Debts contracted and Engagements entered into, before the Adoption of this Constitution, shall be as valid against the United States under this Constitution, as under the Confederation.

This Constitution, and the Laws of the United States which shall be made in Pursuance thereof; and all Treaties made, or which shall be made, under the Authority of the United States, shall be the supreme Law of the Land; and the Judges in every State shall be bound thereby, any Thing in the Constitution or Laws of any State to the Contrary notwithstanding.

The Senators and Representatives before mentioned, and the Members of the several State Legislatures, and all executive and judicial Officers, both of the United States and of the several States, shall be bound by Oath or Affirmation, to support this Constitution; but no religious Test shall ever be required as a Qualification to any Office or public Trust under the United States.

ARTICLE VII

The Ratification of the Conventions of nine States, shall be sufficient for the Establishment of this Constitution between the States so ratifying the Same.

Done in Convention by the Unanimous Consent

of the States present the Seventeenth Day of September in the Year of our Lord one thousand seven hundred and Eighty seven and of the Independence of the United States of America the Twelfth. In witness whereof We have hereunto subscribed our Names.

[The first 10 Amendments were ratified December 15, 1791, and form what is known as the Bill of Rights.]

AMENDMENT 1

Congress shall make no law respecting an establishment of religion, or prohibiting the free exercise thereof; or abridging the freedom of speech, or of the press; or the right of the people peaceably to assemble, and to petition the Government for a redress of grievances.

AMENDMENT 2

A well regulated Militia, being necessary to the security of a free State, the right of the people to keep and bear Arms, shall not be infringed.

AMENDMENT 3

No Soldier shall, in time of peace be quartered in any house, without the consent of the Owner, nor in time of war, but in a manner to be prescribed by law.

AMENDMENT 4

The right of the people to be secure in their persons, houses, papers, and effects, against unreasonable searches and seizures, shall not be violated, and no Warrants shall issue, but upon probable cause, supported by Oath or affirmation, and particularly describing the place to be searched and the persons or things to be seized.

AMENDMENT 5

No person shall be held to answer for a capital, or otherwise infamous crime, unless on a presentment or indictment of a Grand Jury, except in cases arising in the land or naval forces, or in the Militia, when in actual service in time of War or public danger; nor shall any person be subject for the same offence to be twice put in jeopardy of life or limb; nor shall be compelled in any criminal case to be a witness against himself, nor be deprived of life, liberty, or property, without due process of law; nor shall private property be taken for public use, without just compensation.

AMENDMENT 6

In all criminal prosecutions, the accused shall enjoy the right to a speedy and public trial, by an impartial jury of the State and district wherein the crime shall have been committed, which district shall have been previously ascertained by law, and to be informed of the nature and cause of the accusation; to be confronted with the witnesses against him; to have compulsory process for obtaining witnesses in his favor, and to have the Assistance of Counsel for his defence.

AMENDMENT 7

In Suits at common law, where the value in controversy shall exceed twenty dollars, the right of trial by jury shall be preserved, and no fact tried by a jury, shall be otherwise re-examined in any Court of the United States, than according to the rules of the common law.

AMENDMENT 8

Excessive bail shall not be required, nor excessive fines imposed, nor cruel and unusual punishments inflicted.

AMENDMENT 9

The enumeration in the Constitution, of certain rights, shall not be construed to deny or disparage others retained by the people.

AMENDMENT 10

The powers not delegated to the United States by the Constitution, nor prohibited by it to the States, are reserved to the States respectively, or to the people.

AMENDMENT 11
[Ratified February 7, 1795]

The Judicial power of the United States shall not be construed to extend to any suit in law or equity, commenced or prosecuted against one of the United States by Citizens of another State, or by Citizens or Subjects of any Foreign State.

AMENDMENT 12
[Ratified July 27, 1804]

The Electors shall meet in their respective states and vote by ballot for President and Vice-President, one of whom, at least, shall not be an inhabitant of the same state with themselves; they shall name in their ballots the person voted for as President, and in district ballots the person voted for as Vice-President, and they shall make distinct lists of all persons voted for as President, and of all persons voted for as Vice-President, and of the number of votes for each, which lists they shall sign and certify, and transmit sealed to the seat of the government of the United States, directed to the President of the Senate;-The President of the Senate shall, in the presence of the Senate and House of Representatives, open all the certificates and the votes shall then be counted;-The person having the greatest number of votes for President, shall be the President, if such number be a majority of the whole number of Electors appointed; and if no person have such majority, then from the persons having the highest numbers not exceeding three on the list of those voted for as President, the House of Representatives shall choose immediately, by ballot, the President. But in choosing the President, the votes shall be taken by states, the representation from each state having one vote; a quorum for this purpose shall consist of a member or members from two-thirds of the states, and a majority of all the states shall be necessary to a choice. And if the House of Representatives shall not choose a President whenever the right of choice shall devolve upon them, before the fourth day of March next following, then the Vice-President shall act as President, as in the case of the death or other constitutional disability of the President.-The person having the greatest number of votes as Vice-President, shall be the Vice-President, if such number be a majority of the whole number of Electors appointed, and if no person have a majority, then from the two highest numbers on the list, the Senate shall choose the Vice-President; a quorum for the purpose shall consist of two-thirds of the whole number of Senators, and a majority of the whole number shall be necessary to a choice. But no person constitutionally ineligible to the office of President shall be eligible to that of Vice-President of the United States.

AMENDMENT 13
[Ratified December 6, 1865]

Section 1. Neither slavery nor involuntary servitude, except as a punishment for crime whereof the party shall have been duly convicted, shall exist within the United States, or any place subject to their jurisdiction.

Section 2. Congress shall have the power to enforce this article by appropriate legislation.

AMENDMENT 14
[Ratified July 9, 1868]

Section 1. All persons born or naturalized in the United States, and subject to the jurisdiction thereof, are citizens of the United States and of the State wherein they reside. No State shall make or enforce any law which shall abridge the privileges or immunities of citizens of the United States; nor shall any State deprive any person of life, liberty, or property, without due process of law; nor deny to any person within its jurisdiction the equal protection of the laws.

Section 2. Representatives shall be appointed among the several States according to their respective numbers, counting the whole number of persons in each State, excluding Indians not taxed. But when the right to vote at any election for the choice of electors for President and Vice President of the United States, Representatives in Congress, the Executive and Judicial Officers of a State, or the members of the Legislature thereof, is denied to any of the male inhabitants of such State, being twenty-one years of age, and citizens of the United States, or in any way abridged, except for participation in rebellion, or other crime, the basis of representation therein shall be reduced in the proportion which the number of such male citizens shall bear to the whole number of male citizens twenty-one years of age in such State.

Section 3. No person shall be a Senator or Representative in Congress, or elector of President and

Vice President, or hold any office, civil or military, under the United States, or under any State, who, having previously taken an oath, as a member of Congress, or as an officer of the United States, or as a member of any State legislature, or as an executive or judicial officer of any State, to support the Constitution of the United States, shall have engaged in insurrection or rebellion against the same, or given aid or comfort to the enemies thereof. But Congress may by a vote of two-thirds of each House, remove such disability.

Section 4. The validity of the public debt of the United States, authorized by law, including debts incurred for payment of pensions and bounties for for services in suppressing insurrection or rebellion, shall not be questioned. But neither the United States nor any State shall assume or pay any debt or obligation incurred in aid of insurrection or rebellion against the United States, or any claim for the loss or emancipation of any slave; but all such debts, obligations and claims shall be held illegal and void.

Section 5. The Congress shall have power to enforce, by appropriate legislation, the provisions of this article.

AMENDMENT 15
[Ratified February 3, 1870]

Section 1. The right of citizens of the United States to vote shall not be denied or abridged by the United States or by any State on account of race, color, or previous condition of servitude.

Section 2. The Congress shall have power to enforce this article by appropriate legislation.

AMENDMENT 16
[Ratified February 3, 1913]

The Congress shall have power to lay and collect taxes on incomes, from whatever source derived, without apportionment among the several States, and without regard to any census or enumeration.

AMENDMENT 17
[Ratified April 8, 1913]

The Senate of the United States shall be composed of two Senators from each State, elected by the people thereof for six years; and each Senator shall have one vote. The electors in each State shall have the qualifications requisite for electors of the most numerous branch of the State legislatures.

When vacancies happen in the representation of any State in the Senate, the executive authority of such State shall issue writs of election to fill such vacancies: *Provided*, That the legislature of any State may empower the executive thereof to make temporary appointments until the people fill the vacancies by election as the legislature may direct.

This amendment shall not be so construed as to affect the election or term of any Senator chosen before it becomes valid as part of the Constitution.

AMENDMENT 18
[Ratified January 16, 1919]

Section 1. After one year from the ratification of this article the manufacture, sale, or transportation of intoxicating liquors within, the importation thereof into, or the exportation thereof from the United States and all territory subject to the jurisdiction thereof for beverage purposes is hereby prohibited.

Section 2. The Congress and the several States shall have concurrent power to enforce this article by appropriate legislation.

Section 3. This article shall be inoperative unless it shall have been ratified as an amendment to the Constitution by the legislatures of the several States, as provided in the Constitution, within seven years from the date of the submission hereof to the States by the Congress.

AMENDMENT 19
[Ratified August 18, 1920]

The right of citizens of the United States to vote shall not be denied or abridged by the United States or by any State on account of sex. Congress shall have the power to enforce this article by appropriate legislation.

AMENDMENT 20
[Ratified January 23, 1933]

Section 1. The terms of the President and Vice President shall end at noon on the 20th day of January, and the terms of Senators and Representatives at noon on the 3d day of January, of the years in which such terms would have ended if this article had not been ratified; and the terms of their successors shall then begin.

Section 2. The Congress shall assemble at least once in every year, and such meetings shall begin at noon on the 3d day of January, unless they shall by law appoint a different day.

Section 3. If, at the time fixed for the beginning of the term of the President, the President elect shall have died, the Vice President elect shall become President. If a President shall not have been chosen before the time fixed for the beginning of his term, or if the President elect shall have failed to qualify, then the Vice President elect shall act as President until a President shall have qualified; and the Congress may by law provide for the case wherein neither a President elect nor a Vice President elect shall have qualified, declaring who shall then act as President, or the manner in which one who is to act shall be selected, and such person shall act accordingly until a President or Vice President shall have qualified.

Section 4. The Congress may by law provide for the case of the death of any of the persons from whom the House of Representatives may choose a President whenever the right of choice shall have devolved upon them, and for the case of the death of any of the persons from whom the Senate may choose a Vice President whenever the right of choice shall have devolved upon them.

Section 5. Sections 1 and 2 shall take effect on the 15th day of October following the ratification of this article.

Section 6. This article shall be inoperative unless it shall have been ratified as an amendment to the Constitution by the legislatures of three-fourths of the several states within seven years from the date of its submission.

AMENDMENT 21
[Ratified December 5, 1933]

Section 1. The eighteenth article of amendment to the Constitution of the United States is hereby repealed.

Section 2. The transportation or importation into any State, Territory, or possession of the United States for delivery or use therein of intoxicating liquors, in violation of the laws thereof, is hereby prohibited.

Section 3. This article shall be inoperative unless it shall have been ratified as an amendment to the

Constitution by conventions in the several States, as provided in the Constitution, within seven years from the date of the submission hereof to the States by the Congress.

AMENDMENT 22
[Ratified February 27, 1951]

Section 1. No person shall be elected to the office of the President more than twice, and no person who has held the office of President, or acted as President, for more than two years of a term to which some other person was elected President shall be elected to the office of the President more than once. But this Article shall not apply to any person holding the office of President when this Article was proposed by the Congress, and shall not prevent any person who may be holding the office of President, or acting as President, during the term within which this Article becomes operative from holding the office of President or acting as President during the remainder of such term.

Section 2. This article shall be inoperative unless it shall have been ratified as an amendment to the Constitution by the legislatures of three-fourths of the several States within seven years from the date of its submission to the States by the Congress.

AMENDMENT 23
[Ratified March 29, 1961]

Section 1. The District constituting the seat of Government of the United States shall appoint in such manner as the Congress may direct:

A number of electors of President and Vice President equal to' the whole number of Senators and Representatives in Congress to which the District would be entitled if it were a state, but in no event more than the least populous State; they shall be in addition to those appointed by the States, but they shall be considered, for the purposes of the election of President and Vice President, to be electors appointed by a State; and they shall meet in the District and perform such duties as provided by the twelfth article of amendment.

Section 2. The Congress shall have power to enforce this article by appropriate legislation.

AMENDMENT 24
[Ratified January 23, 1964]

Section 1. The right of citizens of the United States to vote in any primary or other election for

President or Vice President, for electors for President or Vice President, or for Senator or Representative in Congress, shall not be denied or abridged by the United States or by any State by reason or failure to pay any poll tax or other tax.

Section 2. The Congress shall have power to enforce this article by appropriate legislation.

AMENDMENT 25
[Ratified February 10, 1967]

Section 1. In case of the removal of the President from office or of his death or resignation, the Vice President shall become President.

Section 2. Whenever there is a vacancy in the office of the Vice President, the President shall nominate a Vice President who shall take office upon confirmation by a majority vote of both Houses of Congress.

Section 3. Whenever the President transmits to the President pro tempore of the Senate and the Speaker of the House of Representatives his written declaration that he is unable to discharge the powers and duties of his office, and until he transmits to them a written declaration to the contrary, such powers and duties shall be discharged by the Vice President as Acting President.

Section 4. Whenever the Vice President and a majority of either the principal officers of the executive departments or of such other body as Congress may by law provide, transmit to the President pro tempore of the Senate and the Speaker of the House of Representatives their written declaration that the President is unable to discharge the powers and duties of his office, the Vice President shall immediately assume the powers and duties of the office as Acting President.

Thereafter, when the President transmits to the President pro tempore of the Senate and the Speaker of the House of Representatives his written declaration that no inability exists, he shall resume the powers and duties of his office unless the Vice President and a majority of either the principal officers of the executive department or of such other body as Congress may by law provide, transmit within four days to the President pro tempore of the Senate and the Speaker of the House of Representatives their written declaration that the President is unable to discharge the powers and duties of his office. Thereupon Congress shall decide the issue, assembling within forty-eight hours for that purpose if not in session. If the Congress, within twenty-one days after receipt of the latter written declaration, or, if Congress is not in session, within twenty-one days after Congress is required to assemble, determined by two-thirds vote of both Houses that the President is unable to discharge the powers and duties of his office, the Vice President shall continue to discharge the same as Acting President; otherwise, the President shall resume the powers and duties of his office.

AMENDMENT 26
[Ratified June 30, 1971]

Section 1. The right of citizens of the United States, who are eighteen years of age or older, to vote shall not be denied or abridged by the United States or by any State on account of age.

Section 2. The Congress shall have the power to enforce this article by appropriate legislation.

EQUAL RIGHTS FOR WOMEN
[Proposed March 22, 1972]

Section 1. Equality of rights under the law shall not be denied or abridged by the United States or by any State on account of sex.

Section 2. The Congress shall have power to enforce, by appropriate legislation, the provisions of this article.

Section 3. This amendment shall take effect two years after date of ratification.

DISTRICT OF COLUMBIA REPRESENTATION
[Proposed August 22, 1978]

Section 1. For purposes of representation in the Congress, election of the President and Vice President, and article V of this Constitution, the District constituting the seat of government of the United States shall be treated as though it were a State.

Section 2. The exercise of the rights and powers conferred under this article shall be by the people of the District constituting the seat of government, and as shall be provided by the Congress.

Section 3. The twenty-third article of amendment to the Constitution of the United States is hereby repealed.

Section 4. This article shall be inoperative, unless it shall have been ratified as an amendment to the Constitution by the legislatures of three-fourths of the several States within seven years from the date of its submission.

APPENDIX B
Justices of the Supreme Court

Justices of the Supreme Court of the United States, their terms of service, political affiliation (F., Federalist; R., Republican; D., Democrat; W., Whig; Ind., Independent), residence at time of appointment, and the Presidents who appointed them are listed here. The names of the Chief Justices are indicated by italics. The letter preceding the name of each Justice is used to identify the line of succession for each "seat" on the bench. Thus, "seat" A was held first by Chief Justice Jay, next by Chief Justice Rutledge, then by Chief Justice Ellsworth, and so on.

Appointed by
President Washington (1789–1797)
Federalist from Virginia

A. *John Jay* (1789–1795) F., N.Y.
B. John Rutledge (1789–1791) F., S.C.
C. William Cushing (1789–1810) F., Mass.
D. James Wilson (1789–1798) F., Pa.
E. John Blair (1789–1796) F., Va.
F. James Iredell (1790–1799) F., N.C.
B. Thomas Johnson (1791–1793) F., Md.
B. William Paterson (1793–1806) F., N.J.
A. *John Rutledge* (1795) F., S.C.
E. Samuel Chase (1796–1811) F., Md.
A. *Oliver Ellsworth* (1796–1800) F., Conn.

Appointed by
President Adams (1797–1801)
Federalist from Massachusetts

D. Bushrod Washington (1789–1829) F., Va.
F. Alfred Moore (1799–1804) F., N.C.
A. *John Marshall* (1801–1835) F., Va.

Appointed by
President Jefferson (1801–1809)
Republican from Virginia

F. William Johnson (1804–1834) R., S.C.
B. Brockholst Livingston (1806–1823) R., N.Y.
G. Thomas Todd (1807–1826) R., Ky.

Appointed by
President Madison (1809–1817)
Republican from Virginia

E. Gabriel Duval (1811–1835) R., Md.
C. Joseph Story (1811–1845) R., Mass.

Appointed by
President Monroe (1817–1825)
Republican from Virginia

B. Smith Thompson (1823–1843) R., N.Y.

Appointed by
President Adams (1825–1829)
Republican from Massachusetts

G. Robert Trimble (1826–1828) R., Ky.

Appointed by
President Jackson (1829–1837)
Democrat from Tennessee

G. John McLean (1829–1861) D. (later R.), Ohio
D. Henry Baldwin (1830–1844) D., Pa.
F. James M. Wayne (1835–1867) D., Ga.
A. *Roger B. Taney* (1836–1864) D., Md.
E. Philip P. Barbour (1836–1841) D., Va.

Appointed by
President Van Buren (1837–1841)
Democrat from New York

H. John Catron (1837–1865) D., Tenn.
I. John McKinley (1837–1852) D., Ky.
E. Peter V. Daniel (1841–1860) D., Va.

Appointed by
President Tyler (1841–1845)
Whig from Virginia

B. Samuel Nelson (1845–1872) D., N.Y.

Appointed by
President Polk (1845–1849)
Democrat from Tennessee

C. Levi Woodbury (1845–1851) D., N.H.
D. Robert C. Grier (1846–1870) D., Pa.

Appointed by
President Fillmore (1850–1853)
Whig from New York

C. Benjamin R. Curtis (1851–1857) W., Mass.

Appointed by
President Pierce (1853–1857)
Democrat from New Hampshire

I. John A. Campbell (1853–1861) D., Ala.

Appointed by
President Buchanan (1857–1861)
Democrat from Pennsylvania

C. Nathan Clifford (1858–1881) D., Me.

Appointed by
President Lincoln (1861–1865)
Republican from Illinois

G. Noah H. Swayne (1862–1881) R., Ohio
E. Samuel F. Miller (1862–1890) R., Iowa
I. David Davis (1862–1877) R., (Later D.), Ill.
J. Stephen J. Field (1863–1897) D., Cal.
A. *Salmon P. Chase* (1864–1873) R., Ohio

Appointed by
President Grant (1869–1877)
Republican from Illinois

D. William Strong (1870–1880) R., Pa.
F. Joseph P. Bradley (1870–1892) R., N.J.
B. Ward Hunt (1872–1882) R., N.Y.
A. *Morrison R. Waite* (1874–1888) R., Ohio

Appointed by
President Hayes (1877–1881)
Republican from Ohio

I. John Marshall Harlan (1877–1911) R., Ky.
D. William B. Woods (1880–1887) R., Ga.

Appointed by
President Garfield (Mar.–Sept. 1881)
Republican from Ohio

G. Stanley Matthews (1881–1889) R., Ohio

Appointed by
President Arthur (1881–1885)
Republican from New York

C. Horace Gray (1881–1902) R., Mass.
B. Samuel Blatchford (1882–1893) R., N.Y.

Appointed by
President Cleveland (1885–1889)
Democrat from New York

D. Lucius Q. C. Lamar (1888–1893) D., Miss.
A. *Melville W. Fuller* (1888–1910) D., Ill.

Appointed by
President Harrison (1889–1893)
Republican from Indiana

G. David J. Brewer (1889–1910) R., Kans.
E. Henry B. Brown (1890–1906) R., Mich.
F. George Shiras (1892–1903) R., Pa.
D. Howell E. Jackson (1893–1895) D., Tenn.

Appointed by
President Cleveland (1893–1897)
Democrat from New York

B. Edward D. White (1894–1910) D., La.
D. Rufus W. Peckham (1895–1909) D., N.Y.

Appointed by
President McKinley (1897–1901)
Republican from Ohio

J. Joseph McKenna (1898–1925) R., Cal.
or
H.

Appointed by
President Roosevelt (1901–1909)
Republican from New York

C. Oliver Wendell Holmes (1902–1932) R., Mass.
F. William R. Day (1903–1922) R., Ohio
E. William H. Moody (1906–1910) R., Mass.

Appointed by
President Taft (1909–1913)
Republican from Ohio

D. Horace H. Lurton (1909–1914) D., Tenn.
G. Charles E. Hughes (1910–1916) R., N.Y.
A. *Edward D. White* (1910–1921)
Promoted from associate justiceship
B. Willis Van Devanter (1910–1937) R., Wyo.
E. Joseph R. Lamar (1910–1916) D., Ga.
I. Mahlon Pitney (1912–1922) R., N.J.

Appointed by
President Wilson (1913–1921)
Democrat from New Jersey

D. James C. McReynolds (1914–1941) D., Tenn.
E. Louis D. Brandeis (1916–1939) D., Mass.
G. John H. Clarke (1916–1922) D., Ohio

Appointed by
President Harding (1921–1923)
Republican from Ohio

A. William H. Taft (1921–1930) R., Conn.
G. George Sutherland (1922–1938) R., Utah
F. Pierce Butler (1922–1939) D., Minn.
I. Edward T. Sanford (1923–1930) R., Tenn.

Appointed by
President Coolidge (1923–1929)
Republican from Massachusetts

H. Harlan F. Stone (1925–1941) R., N.Y.

Appointed by
President Hoover (1929–1933)
Republican from California

A. *Charles E. Hughes* (1930–1941) R., N.Y.
I. Owen J. Roberts (1932–1945) R., Pa.
C. Benjamin N. Cardozo (1932–1938) D., N.Y.

Appointed by
President Roosevelt (1933–1945)
Democrat from New York

B. Hugo L. Black (1937–1971) D., Ala.
G. Stanley F. Reed (1938–1957) D., Ky.

C. Felix Frankfurter (1939–1965) Ind., Mass.
E. William O. Douglas (1939–1975) D., Conn.
F. Frank Murphy (1940–1949) D., Mich.
D. James F. Byrnes (1941–1942) D., S.C.
A. *Harlan F. Stone* (1941–1946)
Promoted from associate justiceship
H. Robert H. Jackson (1941–1954) D., N.Y.
D. Wiley B. Rutledge (1943–1949) D., Iowa

Appointed by
President Truman (1945–1953)
Democrat from Missouri

I. Harold H. Burton (1945–1958) R., Ohio
A. *Fred M. Vinson* (1946–1953) D., Ky.
F. Tom C. Clark (1949–1967) D., Tex.
D. Sherman Minton (1949–1956) D., Ind.

Appointed by
President Eisenhower (1953–1961)
Republican from New York

A. *Earl Warren* (1953–1969) R., Cal.
H. John M. Harlan (1955–1971) R., N.Y.
D. William J. Brennan (1956–   ) D., N.J.
G. Charles E. Whittaker (1957–1962) R., Mo.
I. Potter Stewart (1958–   ) R., Ohio

Appointed by
President Kennedy (1961–1963)
Democrat from Massachusetts

C. Arthur J. Goldberg (1962–1965) D., Ill.
G. Byron R. White (1962–   ) D., Colo.

Appointed by
President Johnson (1963–1968)
Democrat from Texas

C. Abe Fortas (1965–1969), D., Tenn.
F. Thurgood Marshall (1967–   ), D., N.Y.

Appointed by
President Nixon (1969–1974)
Republican from California

A. *Warren Burger* (1969–   ), R., Va. and Minn.
C. Harry Blackmun (1970–   ), R., Minn.
B. Lewis Powell (1972–   ), D., Va.
H. William Rehnquist (1972–   ), R., Ariz.

Appointed by
President Ford (1974–1977)
Republican from Michigan

E. John P. Stevens (1975–   ), R., Ill.

Index of Cases

This book has been set VIP in 10 and 9 point Optima, leaded 2 points. Part and chapter titles are 18 point Palatino. The size of the type page is 37 ½ picas by 48 picas.